T0211643

Lecture Notes in Computer Science 12309

More information about this series at http://www.springer.com/series/7410

Liqun Chen · Ninghui Li ·
Kaitai Liang · Steve Schneider (Eds.)

Computer Security – ESORICS 2020

25th European Symposium
on Research in Computer Security, ESORICS 2020
Guildford, UK, September 14–18, 2020
Proceedings, Part II

 Springer

Editors
Liqun Chen [iD]
University of Surrey
Guildford, UK

Kaitai Liang [iD]
Delft University of Technology
Delft, The Netherlands

Ninghui Li
Purdue University
West Lafayette, IN, USA

Steve Schneider [iD]
University of Surrey
Guildford, UK

ISSN 0302-9743　　　　　　　ISSN 1611-3349　(electronic)
Lecture Notes in Computer Science
ISBN 978-3-030-59012-3　　　　ISBN 978-3-030-59013-0　(eBook)
https://doi.org/10.1007/978-3-030-59013-0

LNCS Sublibrary: SL4 – Security and Cryptology

This Springer imprint is published by the registered company Springer Nature Switzerland AG
The registered company address is: Gewerbestrasse 11, 6330 Cham, Switzerland

Liqun Chen · Ninghui Li ·
Kaitai Liang · Steve Schneider (Eds.)

Computer Security – ESORICS 2020

25th European Symposium
on Research in Computer Security, ESORICS 2020
Guildford, UK, September 14–18, 2020
Proceedings, Part II

 Springer

Editors
Liqun Chen 🅐
University of Surrey
Guildford, UK

Kaitai Liang 🅐
Delft University of Technology
Delft, The Netherlands

Ninghui Li
Purdue University
West Lafayette, IN, USA

Steve Schneider 🅐
University of Surrey
Guildford, UK

ISSN 0302-9743　　　　　ISSN 1611-3349　(electronic)
Lecture Notes in Computer Science
ISBN 978-3-030-59012-3　　　　ISBN 978-3-030-59013-0　(eBook)
https://doi.org/10.1007/978-3-030-59013-0

LNCS Sublibrary: SL4 – Security and Cryptology

This Springer imprint is published by the registered company Springer Nature Switzerland AG
The registered company address is: Gewerbestrasse 11, 6330 Cham, Switzerland

Preface

The two volume set, LNCS 12308 and 12309, contain the papers that were selected for presentation and publication at the 25th European Symposium on Research in Computer Security (ESORICS 2020) which was held together with affiliated workshops during the week September 14–18, 2020. Due to the global COVID-19 pandemic, the conference and workshops ran virtually, hosted by the University of Surrey, UK. The aim of ESORICS is to further research in computer security and privacy by establishing a European forum, bringing together researchers in these areas by promoting the exchange of ideas with system developers and by encouraging links with researchers in related fields.

In response to the call for papers, 366 papers were submitted to the conference. These papers were evaluated on the basis of their significance, novelty, and technical quality. Except for a very small number of papers, each paper was carefully evaluated by three to five referees and then discussed among the Program Committee. The papers were reviewed in a single-blind manner. Finally, 72 papers were selected for presentation at the conference, yielding an acceptance rate of 19.7%. We were also delighted to welcome invited talks from Aggelos Kiayias, Vadim Lyubashevsky, and Rebecca Wright.

Following the reviews two papers were selected for Best Paper Awards and they share the 1,000 EUR prize generously provided by Springer: "Pine: Enabling privacy-preserving deep packet inspection on TLS with rule-hiding and fast connection establishment" by Jianting Ning, Xinyi Huang, Geong Sen Poh, Shengmin Xu, Jason Loh, Jian Weng, and Robert H. Deng; and "Automatic generation of source lemmas in Tamarin: towards automatic proofs of security protocols" by Véronique Cortier, Stéphanie Delaune, and Jannik Dreier.

The Program Committee consisted of 127 members across 25 countries. There were submissions from a total of 1,201 authors across 42 countries, with 24 countries represented among the accepted papers.

ESORICS 2020 would not have been possible without the contributions of the many volunteers who freely gave their time and expertise. We would like to thank the members of the Program Committee and the external reviewers for their substantial work in evaluating the papers. We would also like to thank the organization/department chair, Helen Treharne, the workshop chair, Mark Manulis, and all of the workshop co-chairs, the poster chair, Ioana Boureanu, and the ESORICS Steering Committee. We are also grateful to Huawei and IBM Research – Haifa, Israel for their sponsorship that enabled us to support this online event. Finally, we would like to express our thanks to the authors who submitted papers to ESORICS 2020. They, more than anyone else, are what made this conference possible.

We hope that you will find the proceedings stimulating and a source of inspiration for future research.

September 2020

Liqun Chen
Ninghui Li
Kaitai Liang
Steve Schneider

Organization

General Chair

Steve Schneider   University of Surrey, UK

Program Chairs

Liqun Chen   University of Surrey, UK
Ninghui Li   Purdue University, USA

Steering Committee

Sokratis Katsikas (Chair)
Michael Backes
Joachim Biskup
Frederic Cuppens
Sabrina De Capitani di Vimercati
Dieter Gollmann
Mirek Kutylowski
Javier Lopez
Jean-Jacques Quisquater
Peter Y. A. Ryan
Pierangela Samarati
Einar Snekkenes
Michael Waidner

Program Committee

Yousra Aafer	University of Waterloo, Canada
Mitsuaki Akiyama	NTT, Japan
Cristina Alcaraz	UMA, Spain
Frederik Armknecht	Universität Mannheim, Germany
Vijay Atluri	Rutgers University, USA
Erman Ayday	Bilkent University, Turkey
Antonio Bianchi	Purdue University, USA
Marina Blanton	University at Buffalo, USA
Carlo Blundo	Università degli Studi di Salerno, Italy
Alvaro Cardenas	The University of Texas at Dallas, USA
Berkay Celik	Purdue University, USA
Aldar C-F. Chan	BIS Innovation Hub Centre, Hong Kong, China
Sze Yiu Chau	Purdue University, USA

Pawel Szalachowski	SUTD, Singapore
Qiang Tang	Luxembourg Institute of Science and Technology, Luxembourg
Qiang Tang	New Jersey Institute of Technology, USA
Juan Tapiador	Universidad Carlos III de Madrid, Spain
Dave Jing Tian	Purdue University, USA
Nils Ole Tippenhauer	CISPA, Germany
Helen Treharne	University of Surrey, UK
Aggeliki Tsohou	Ionian University, Greece
Luca Viganò	King's College London, UK
Michael Waidner	Fraunhofer, Germany
Cong Wang	City University of Hong Kong, Hong Kong, China
Lingyu Wang	Concordia University, Canada
Weihang Wang	SUNY University at Buffalo, USA
Edgar Weippl	SBA Research, Austria
Christos Xenakis	University of Piraeus, Greece
Yang Xiang	Swinburne University of Technology, Australia
Guomin Yang	University of Wollongong, Australia
Kang Yang	State Key Laboratory of Cryptology, China
Xun Yi	RMIT University, Australia
Yu Yu	Shanghai Jiao Tong University, China
Tsz Hon Yuen	The University of Hong Kong, Hong Kong, China
Fengwei Zhang	SUSTech, China
Kehuan Zhang	The Chinese University of Hong Kong, Hong Kong, China
Yang Zhang	CISPA Helmholtz Center for Information Security, Germany
Yuan Zhang	Fudan University, China
Zhenfeng Zhang	Chinese Academy of Sciences, China
Yunlei Zhao	Fudan University, China
Jianying Zhou	Singapore University of Technology and Design, Singapore
Sencun Zhu	Penn State University, USA

Workshop Chair

Mark Manulis	University of Surrey, UK

Poster Chair

Ioana Boureanu	University of Surrey, UK

Organization/Department Chair

Helen Treharne	University of Surrey, UK

Organizing Chair and Publicity Chair

Kaitai Liang   Delft University of Technology, The Netherlands

Additional Reviewers

Abbasi, Ali
Abu-Salma, Ruba
Ahlawat, Amit
Ahmed, Chuadhry Mujeeb
Ahmed, Shimaa
Alabdulatif, Abdulatif
Alhanahnah, Mohannad
Aliyu, Aliyu
Alrizah, Mshabab
Anceaume, Emmanuelle
Angelogianni, Anna
Anglés-Tafalla, Carles
Aparicio Navarro, Francisco Javier
Argyriou, Antonios
Asadujjaman, A. S. M.
Aschermann, Cornelius
Asghar, Muhammad Rizwan
Avizheh, Sepideh
Baccarini, Alessandro
Bacis, Enrico
Baek, Joonsang
Bai, Weihao
Bamiloshin, Michael
Barenghi, Alessandro
Barrère, Martín
Berger, Christian
Bhattacherjee, Sanjay
Blanco-Justicia, Alberto
Blazy, Olivier
Bolgouras, Vaios
Bountakas, Panagiotis
Brandt, Markus
Bursuc, Sergiu
Böhm, Fabian
Camacho, Philippe
Cardaioli, Matteo
Castelblanco, Alejandra
Castellanos, John Henry
Cecconello, Stefano

Chaidos, Pyrros
Chakra, Ranim
Chandrasekaran, Varun
Chen, Haixia
Chen, Long
Chen, Min
Chen, Zhao
Chen, Zhigang
Chengjun Lin
Ciampi, Michele
Cicala, Fabrizio
Costantino, Gianpiero
Cruz, Tiago
Cui, Shujie
Deng, Yi
Diamantopoulou, Vasiliki
Dietz, Marietheres
Divakaran, Dinil Mon
Dong, Naipeng
Dong, Shuaike
Dragan, Constantin Catalin
Du, Minxin
Dutta, Sabyasachi
Eichhammer, Philipp
Englbrecht, Ludwig
Etigowni, Sriharsha
Farao, Aristeidis
Faruq, Fatma
Fdhila, Walid
Feng, Hanwen
Feng, Qi
Fentham, Daniel
Ferreira Torres, Christof
Fila, Barbara
Fraser, Ashley
Fu, Hao
Galdi, Clemente
Gangwal, Ankit
Gao, Wei

Mercaldo, Francesco
Michailidou, Christina
Mitropoulos, Dimitris
Mohammadi, Farnaz
Mohammady, Meisam
Mohammed, Ameer
Moreira, Jose
Muñoz, Jose L.
Mykoniati, Maria
Nassirzadeh, Behkish
Newton, Christopher
Ng, Lucien K. L.
Ntantogian, Christoforos
Önen, Melek
Onete, Cristina
Oqaily, Alaa
Oswald, David
Papaioannou, Thanos
Parkinson, Simon
Paspatis, Ioannis
Patsakis, Constantinos
Pelosi, Gerardo
Pfeffer, Katharina
Pitropakis, Nikolaos
Poettering, Bertram
Poh, Geong Sen
Polato, Mirko
Poostindouz, Alireza
Puchta, Alexander
Putz, Benedikt
Pöhls, Henrich C.
Qiu, Tian
Radomirovic, Sasa
Rakotonirina, Itsaka
Rebollo Monedero, David
Rivera, Esteban
Rizomiliotis, Panagiotis
Román-García, Fernando
Sachidananda, Vinay
Salazar, Luis
Salem, Ahmed
Salman, Ammar
Sanders, Olivier
Scarsbrook, Joshua
Schindler, Philipp
Schlette, Daniel

Schmidt, Carsten
Scotti, Fabio
Shahandashti, Siamak
Shahraki, Ahmad Salehi
Sharifian, Setareh
Sharma, Vishal
Sheikhalishahi, Mina
Shen, Siyu
Shrishak, Kris
Simo, Hervais
Siniscalchi, Luisa
Slamanig, Daniel
Smith, Zach
Solano, Jesús
Song, Yongcheng
Song, Zirui
Soriente, Claudio
Soumelidou, Katerina
Spielvogel, Korbinian
Stifter, Nicholas
Sun, Menghan
Sun, Yiwei
Sun, Yuanyi
Tabiban, Azadeh
Tang, Di
Tang, Guofeng
Taubmann, Benjamin
Tengana, Lizzy
Tian, Yangguang
Trujillo, Rolando
Turrin, Federico
Veroni, Eleni
Vielberth, Manfred
Vollmer, Marcel
Wang, Jiafan
Wang, Qin
Wang, Tianhao
Wang, Wei
Wang, Wenhao
Wang, Yangde
Wang, Yi
Wang, Yuling
Wang, Ziyuan
Weitkämper, Charlotte
Wesemeyer, Stephan
Whitefield, Jorden

Wiyaja, Dimaz
Wong, Donald P. H.
Wong, Harry W. H.
Wong, Jin-Mann
Wu, Chen
Wu, Ge
Wu, Lei
Wuest, Karl
Xie, Guoyang
Xinlei, He
Xu, Fenghao
Xu, Jia
Xu, Jiayun
Xu, Ke
Xu, Shengmin
Xu, Yanhong
Xue, Minhui
Yamada, Shota
Yang, Bohan
Yang, Lin
Yang, Rupeng
Yang, S. J.
Yang, Wenjie
Yang, Xu

Yang, Xuechao
Yang, Zhichao
Yevseyeva, Iryna
Yi, Ping
Yin, Lingyuan
Ying, Jason
Yu, Zuoxia
Yuan, Lun-Pin
Yuan, Xingliang
Zhang, Bingsheng
Zhang, Fan
Zhang, Ke
Zhang, Mengyuan
Zhang, Yanjun
Zhang, Zhikun
Zhang, Zongyang
Zhao, Yongjun
Zhong, Zhiqiang
Zhou, Yutong
Zhu, Fei
Ziaur, Rahman
Zobernig, Lukas
Zuo, Cong

Keynotes

Decentralising Information and Communications Technology: Paradigm Shift or Cypherpunk Reverie?

Aggelos Kiayias

University of Edinburgh and IOHK, UK

Abstract. In the last decade, decentralisation emerged as a much anticipated development in the greater space of information and communications technology. Venerated by some and disparaged by others, blockchain technology became a familiar term, springing up in a wide array of expected and some times unexpected contexts. With the peak of the hype behind us, in this talk I look back, distilling what have we learned about the science and engineering of building secure and reliable systems, then I overview the present state of the art and finally I delve into the future, appraising this technology in its potential to impact the way we design and deploy information and communications technology services.

Lattices and Zero-Knowledge

Vadim Lyubashevsky

IBM Research - Zurich, Switzerland

Abstract. Building cryptography based on the presumed hardness of lattice problems over polynomial rings is one of the most promising approaches for achieving security against quantum attackers. One of the reasons for the popularity of lattice-based encryption and signatures in the ongoing NIST standardization process is that they are significantly faster than all other post-quantum, and even many classical, schemes. This talk will discuss the progress in constructions of more advanced lattice-based cryptographic primitives. In particular, I will describe recent work on zero-knowledge proofs which leads to the most efficient post-quantum constructions for certain statements.

Accountability in Computing

Rebecca N. Wright

Barnard College, New York, USA

Abstract. Accountability is used often in describing computer-security mechanisms that complement preventive security, but it lacks a precise, agreed-upon definition. We argue for the need for accountability in computing in a variety of settings, and categorize some of the many ways in which this term is used. We identify a temporal spectrum onto which we may place different notions of accountability to facilitate their comparison, including prevention, detection, evidence, judgment, and punishment. We formalize our view in a utility-theoretic way and then use this to reason about accountability in computing systems. We also survey mechanisms providing various senses of accountability as well as other approaches to reasoning about accountability-related properties.

This is joint work with Joan Feigenbaum and Aaron Jaggard.

Contents – Part II

Applied Cryptography III

Blockchain II

Contents – Part I

Network Security II

Privacy

Password and Policy

Formal Modelling

Automatic Generation of Sources Lemmas in TAMARIN: Towards Automatic Proofs of Security Protocols

Véronique Cortier[1], Stéphanie Delaune[2(✉)], and Jannik Dreier[1]

[1] Université de Lorraine, CNRS, Inria, LORIA, 54000 Nancy, France
[2] Univ Rennes, CNRS, IRISA, Rennes, France
stephanie.delaune@irisa.fr

Abstract. TAMARIN is a popular tool dedicated to the formal analysis of security protocols. One major strength of the tool is that it offers an interactive mode, allowing to go beyond what push-button tools can typically handle. TAMARIN is for example able to verify complex protocols such as TLS, 5G, or RFID protocols. However, one of its drawback is its lack of automation. For many simple protocols, the user often needs to help TAMARIN by writing specific lemmas, called "sources lemmas", which requires some knowledge of the internal behaviour of the tool.

In this paper, we propose a technique to *automatically* generate sources lemmas in TAMARIN. We prove formally that our lemmas indeed hold, for arbitrary protocols that make use of cryptographic primitives that can be modelled with a subterm convergent equational theory (modulo associativity and commutativity). We have implemented our approach within TAMARIN. Our experiments show that, in most examples of the literature, we are now able to generate suitable sources lemmas automatically, in replacement of the hand-written lemmas. As a direct application, many simple protocols can now be analysed fully automatically, while they previously required user interaction.

1 Introduction

Security protocols are notoriously subtle to design and analyse. Many different tools have been developed in order to detect flaws and prove security properties such as authentication, secrecy, or privacy. However, even a simple property like secrecy is undecidable in general [9]. Hence several tools focus on the analysis of a decidable fragment, e.g. by bounding the number of sessions (e.g. AVISPA [1], DeepSec [6]). But when considering wider classes of protocols, more general cryptographic primitives, and an unlimited number of sessions, one necessarily goes beyond the decidable fragment, possibly losing termination or even automation.

This work has been partially supported by the European Research Council (ERC) under the European Union's Horizon 2020 research and innovation program (grant agreement No 714955-POPSTAR and grant agreement No 645865-SPOOC), as well as from the French National Research Agency (ANR) under the project TECAP.

L. Chen et al. (Eds.): ESORICS 2020, LNCS 12309, pp. 3–22, 2020.
https://doi.org/10.1007/978-3-030-59013-0_1

One popular tool in that direction is ProVerif [4], a push-button tool that has been able to analyse hundred of protocols including e.g. TLS 1.3 [3], the ARINC823 avionic protocol [5], or the Neuchâtel voting protocol [7]. However, ProVerif may fail to prove some protocols because of some internal approximations. In that case, the user must either simplify the model or just give up.

Another approach has been developed in the tool TAMARIN [11]. One key feature of TAMARIN is that it provides an interactive mode: if the tool fails to automatically prove a property by itself, the user may help the tool, for example by writing intermediate lemmas, or by manually guiding the proof search. Thanks to this approach, TAMARIN supports many features that are typically out of reach of many tools (Diffie-Hellman, stateful protocols), and has been able to prove complex protocols such as 5G AKA [2] with exclusive or, group key agreement protocols [13], or Noise framework [10] with Diffie-Hellman keys.

However, the fact that TAMARIN is not fully automatic makes it more difficult to use, at least in the learning phase. In particular, TAMARIN fails to automatically prove some "simple" protocols of the literature such as the well-known Needham-Schroder protocol or the Denning-Sacco protocol. This is a barrier when teaching the tool for example at the university or in summer schools.

Automation in TAMARIN fails in particular if it encounters "partial deconstructions". To speed up the analysis, TAMARIN computes in advance, for each protocol and intruder fact, all possible origins (called *sources*) of these facts, which are then repeatedly used in later steps of the analysis. However, this pre-computation can stop in an incomplete stage if TAMARIN lacks sufficient information about the origins of some fact(s). In practice, as soon as TAMARIN encounters such a "partial deconstruction", it is unlikely that it will be able to prove any interesting property automatically. To solve the issue, the user needs to manually write a "sources lemma" to help TAMARIN. Unfortunately, this manual step has to be done for many protocols, even simple ones.

Our contribution. In this paper, we automate the generation of sources lemmas. The main idea is to provide a systematic analysis of the origins of a term in a protocol. Intuitively, either a term has been forged by the attacker, or it comes from an earlier step in the protocol. To avoid the exploration of too many cases, we base our analysis on "deepest protected" subterms. We prove that the sources lemmas that we generate are indeed true. Our result holds for any protocol provided that the cryptographic primitives can be expressed as a convergent subterm theory (modulo associativity and commutativity) with the finite variant property. This is the case of most standard cryptographic primitives such as symmetric and asymmetric encryptions, as well as signatures.

Interestingly, the correctness of TAMARIN does not rely on the fact that we are able to prove that our sources lemmas hold. TAMARIN will verify them anyway (as done with sources lemmas written by the user). This means that our technique can also be used even in cases where our theoretical justification does not apply. Our theoretical justification simply explains why TAMARIN has a good chance to work. We have implemented our technique in TAMARIN, as a new option `--auto-sources`. With this option, when partial deconstructions are detected, a sources lemma is generated automatically and added to the original model, so that the user can see it and possibly amend it, if needed. We have validated our approach with two kind of experiments.

- First, we consider simple protocols of the literature, used as benchmarks for most tools. We modelled a handful of them and ran TAMARIN. Our approach is able to solve all partial deconstructions. Actually, we found out that for these simple examples, this was the only reason they were not entirely automatic, hence thanks to our `--auto-sources` option, TAMARIN can now analyse all these examples automatically.
- We also wanted to evaluate how our technique behaves on more complex protocols and on protocols that have not been specified by ourselves. Hence we considered all the models provided within TAMARIN's distribution, and that contained "partial deconstructions". For a large majority of them, our technique successfully close all partial deconstructions and for about a half of them, TAMARIN is now even able to analyse the whole protocol automatically.

Unsurprisingly, complex protocols still require the existing manually written intermediate lemmas. However, our technique considerably improves the degree of automation of TAMARIN, yielding a better trade-off between what can be done automatically, and what needs to be done manually.

2 Overview

We illustrate our technique on a simple challenge-response protocol.

$$I \to R : \{\mathsf{req}, I, n\}_{\mathrm{pk}(R)}$$
$$R \to I : \{\mathsf{rep}, n\}_{\mathrm{pk}(I)}$$

The initiator sends a nonce n encrypted with the public key of the responder, and then waits for the corresponding answer, i.e. the nonce n encrypted with his own public key. The symbols req and rep are constants used to avoid confusion between the two types of messages: they indicate whether the ciphertext corresponds to a request or a reply. In TAMARIN the responder role is as follows:

```
rule Rule_R:
  [ In(aenc{'req', I, x}pk(ltkR)), !Ltk(R, ltkR), !Pk(I, pkI) ]
  --[]-> [ Out(aenc{'rep', x}pkI) ]
```

Intuitively, this rule can be read as follows: at the reception of a message of the form `aenc{'req', I, x}pk(ltkR)`, the agent R (with private key `ltkR`) sends the message `aenc{'rep', x}pkI` on the network to the agent I (with public key `pkI`). Note that there are other rules modelling the Initiator role, as well as the key generation. The latter rule creates the !LtK and !Pk facts used here to retrieve the agents' public and private keys.

This protocol rule models the behaviour of the responder role. It can be triggered arbitrary many times, possibly with different values for x. When loading this model in TAMARIN, it turns out that the proof attempt of e.g. a simple secrecy property of nonce n does not terminate due to partial deconstructions. In TAMARIN's interactive interface, they are identified by dashed green arrows as shown in Fig. 1. The green arrow symbolises a *deconstruction chain*. Deconstruction chains are used in TAMARIN's intruder reasoning to extract values from messages output by the protocol. In this example, TAMARIN tries to extract a fresh value from the message output by the rule Rule_R (at the top). TAMARIN has computed that if it can decrypt the output of the rule (rule d_0_adec) and then extract the second term (rule d_0_snd), it obtains the value x.7 (a renaming of the variable x given in the initial rule definition). However, here TAMARIN is unable to continue its deconstruction, as x.7 can potentially be any value: directly the desired fresh value, or a pair of values, or an encryption, or something completely different. As this deconstruction is incomplete, it is called a *partial deconstruction*.

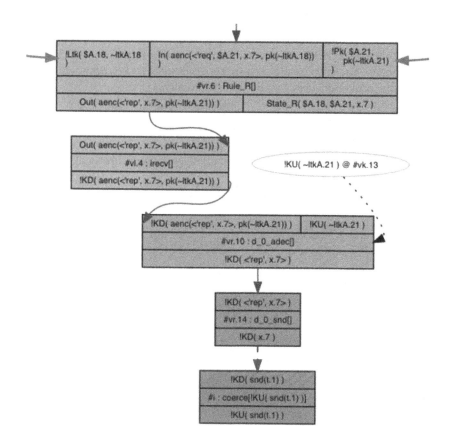

Fig. 1. Example of a partial deconstruction

In the above example, TAMARIN does not know anything about the contents of the variable x.7, hence, to ensure soundness, it is obliged to consider this case as a potential source for any value, which leads to an explosion of the number of cases, and often to non termination issues. This is the case here: the rule Rule_R producing the x.7 requires an input, which could itself be the result of (a different instantiation of) the same source, and so on.

To get rid of partial deconstructions, TAMARIN uses *source lemmas*. They are a special type of lemmas which are applied at the precomputation phase. More precisely, after computing the initial *raw sources* without any lemmas, TAMARIN computes the *refined sources* using the source lemmas to hopefully discard partial deconstructions. To ensure that the refined sources are correct, one further has to prove the source lemmas correct, using only the raw sources. This can be done either automatically by TAMARIN or manually in the interactive mode.

The idea behind a source lemma is to provide more information regarding the origin of the message mentioned in the partial deconstruction, i.e., the one corresponding to the variable identified by the dashed green arrow. Going back to our example and assuming that R(aenc{'req', I, x}pk(ltkR), x) (resp. I(aenc{'req', I, n}pkR)) is added as a label to the responder rule Rule_R (resp. initiator rule), a source lemma could be as follows:

```
lemma typing [sources]:
  "All x m #i. R(m,x)@#i ==> ( (Ex #j. I(m)@#j & #j < #i)
                             |(Ex #j. KU(x)@#j & #j < #i )) "
```

This lemma says that whenever the responder receives the value x inside a message m (at time point #i), either this message (actually a ciphertext) has been forged by the attacker who therefore knew x before, denoted KU(x), or it has been produced (for the first time) by another protocol rule, here the one denoted I(m). Indeed, a quick inspection of the protocol shows that here this is the only option to produce an output having the right format.

When generating the refined sources from the raw sources, TAMARIN applies the source lemmas. In this case, the source lemma above will allow it to learn that x is either a nonce (generated by the initiator role) or a message already known by the attacker. This solves the partial deconstruction as the previous source will be refined into two refined sources. The first one is the case where the intruder learns the nonce generated by the initiator, by passing the initiator's message to the responder, and then extracting the nonce like the variable x.7 above. However, TAMARIN now knows that x.7 is not any value, but the initiator's nonce. The second case will be discarded by TAMARIN since, if the intruder already knew x before, it is useless to extract it again.

3   TAMARIN Syntax and Semantics

We explain here the syntax and semantics of TAMARIN, as presented in [8,12], as necessary background for the remainder of the paper.

3.1   Term Algebra

Cryptographic messages are represented by a (sorted) term algebra. In TAMARIN, terms are all of sort *msg* and there are two incomparable subsorts *fr* and *pub* used to represent respectively fresh names (e.g. nonces or keys) and public names (e.g. agent names). We assume an infinite set $\mathcal{N}$ of names of each sort and an infinite set $\mathcal{V}$ of variables of each sort as well. A variable x of sort s is denoted $x : s$. The sort *msg* is often omitted, that is, the variable x typically denotes a variable of sort *msg*. Each cryptographic primitive is represented by a function symbol $f : s_1 \times \cdots \times s_n \to s$ that takes n arguments of sort resp. $s_1, \ldots, s_n$ and returns a term of sort s. We assume given a *signature* Σ, i.e. a set of function symbols with their arities. Then the set of terms is built from the application of symbols of Σ to names and variables and is denoted $T_\Sigma(\mathcal{N}, \mathcal{V})$. The set of variables occurring in a term t is denoted $vars(t)$. A term is *ground* if it contains no variable. A substitution θ is *grounding for* t if $t\theta$ is ground.

Example 1. The standard primitives are often expressed by the signature

$$\Sigma_{\mathsf{stand}} = \{\mathsf{enc}(\_, \_), \mathsf{dec}(\_, \_), \mathsf{encA}(\_, \_), \mathsf{decA}(\_, \_), \mathsf{pk}(\_), \langle \_, \_ \rangle, \mathsf{fst}(\_), \mathsf{snd}(\_)\}$$

where all functions are of sort $msg \times \cdots \times msg \to msg$. They model respectively symmetric encryption and decryption, asymmetric encryption and decryption, and concatenation and (left and right) projections.

The properties of the primitives are reflected through an equational theory E. In TAMARIN, user defined equational theories are given as a convergent rewrite system. TAMARIN additionally supports built-in theories such exclusive or [8] and a set of equations for Diffie-Hellman (DH) exponentiation [12]. The equality modulo associativity and commutativity (AC) is denoted $=_{AC}$ and the normal form of a term t, modulo AC, is denoted $t\downarrow$ (we consider any representative of the normal form of t). Two terms t_1 and t_2 are *unifiable* (modulo AC) if there exists a substitution θ such that $t_1\theta =_{AC} t_2\theta$. *Positions* of a term t are defined as usual considering AC operators as binary symbols. A *subterm* of t is a term t' such that $t' = t|_p$ for some position p.

TAMARIN assumes equational theories that have the finite variant property, that is where all the instances of a given term follow a finite number of different patterns. Formally, a convergent equational theory E has the *finite variant property* if for any term t, there exists a finite number of substitutions $\sigma_1, \ldots, \sigma_k$ such that, for any substitution θ, there is $1 \leq i \leq k$, there exists a substitution θ' such that $(t\theta)\downarrow =_{AC} t\sigma_i\theta'$. A particular class of rewriting systems is the class of *subterm* rewriting system. A rewriting system is said subterm if it is defined by a set of equations of the form $l \to r$ such that r is a subterm of l or a (public) constant. Many cryptographic primitives can be modelled by (convergent) subterm rewriting systems, such as signatures, symmetric and asymmetric encryption, pair, hash, etc. Our theoretical development only consider equational theories that can be defined by a subterm rewriting system, convergent modulo AC, that have the finite variant property. TAMARIN is not limited to subterm equational theories, and actually our approach can be applied in this general setting too relying on Tamarin to establish the correctness of the generated lemmas.

Example 2. Orienting from left to right the equations below yields a subterm convergent rewrite system that is usually used to model concatenation and asymmetric encryption. Here, there is no AC symbol.

$$\text{decA}(\text{encA}(x, \text{pk}(y)), y) = x \quad \text{fst}(\langle x, y \rangle) = x \quad \text{snd}(\langle x, y \rangle) = y$$

In what follows, we will consider sets and multisets. Given a multiset S, $set(S)$ denotes the set of its elements. The symbol $\subseteq$ denotes the set inclusion. We will write $S \subseteq S'$ even if S and S' are multisets, which is then interpreted as $set(S) \subseteq set(S')$. In contrast, $\subseteq^\sharp$ denotes the multiset inclusion. Similarly, $\cup^\sharp$ denotes the multiset union and $\backslash^\sharp$ the multiset difference.

3.2   Transition System

In TAMARIN, a protocol execution is modelled as a transition system where a state contains a multiset of facts, representing the current knowledge of the attacker and the current steps of the protocol, for each agent and each session. Formally, we assume a set of *fact symbols* $\mathcal{F}$ partitioned into *linear* and *persistent* fact symbols. A *fact* is an expression $\mathsf{F}(t_1, \ldots, t_n)$ where $\mathsf{F} \in \mathcal{F}$ and $t_1, \ldots, t_n \in T_\Sigma(\mathcal{N}, \mathcal{V})$. Given a multiset of facts F, *lfacts*(F) denotes the multiset of its linear facts while *pfacts*(F) denotes the multiset of its persistent facts.

Linear facts represent resources that are consumed. TAMARIN includes three pre-defined linear fact symbols: $\mathsf{Fr}(n)$ models the generation of a fresh name n, $\mathsf{Out}(m)$ represents a message m sent over the network by a participant, and $\mathsf{In}(m)$ denotes that the adversary has sent message m, that can then be received by an agent of the protocol. Persistent facts represent facts that remain forever and are not consumed by rules. TAMARIN includes the persistent fact symbol K that models the knowledge of the attacker, as well as $\mathsf{K}^\uparrow$ and $\mathsf{K}^\downarrow$ that allow to distinguish between the terms built by the attacker and those obtained from listening to the network or by decomposing learned messages. Then the protocol may use other user defined facts, that can be either linear or persistent.

The protocol execution is specified through labelled multiset rewriting rules $[l] \,\text{--}\!\!\mid a \mid\!\!\rightarrow [r]$ where l, a, r are multisets of facts. The multiset l denotes the *premises* of the rule that need to be present in the state in order for the rule to be executed; a denotes the *actions* of the rule (later used to specify properties), while r contains the *conclusions*, added to the state. There are three kinds of rules.

Fresh name generation (FRESH). This is the only rule that can produce facts of the form $\mathsf{Fr}(n)$. Moreover, to ensure freshness, a distinct name n is used for each application.

$$[] \,\text{--}\!\!\mid\, \mid\!\!\rightarrow [\mathsf{Fr}(x : fr)]$$

Message deduction rules (MD). They are pre-defined in TAMARIN and represents the attacker's actions.

$$[\mathsf{Out}(x)]\mathbin{\lrcorner}\mapsto[\mathsf{K}^{\downarrow}(x)] \quad \text{and} \quad [\mathsf{K}^{\uparrow}(x)]\mathbin{\lfloor}\mathsf{K}(x)\mapsto[\mathsf{In}(x)]$$

model the fact that the attacker can learn any message sent by the protocol and conversely, may send any message of her knowledge. Note that this is the only rule where the predicate K appears as an action of a rule. The rules

$$[]\mathbin{\lfloor}\mathsf{K}^{\uparrow}(x)\mapsto[\mathsf{K}^{\uparrow}(x:pub)] \quad \text{and} \quad [\mathsf{Fr}(x:fr)]\mathbin{\lfloor}\mathsf{K}^{\uparrow}(x)\mapsto[\mathsf{K}^{\uparrow}(x:fr)]$$

express respectively that the attacker can learn any public name and can create fresh name on his own. Finally, the attacker can extend his knowledge by applying function symbols. The intuitive rule is:

$$[\mathsf{K}(x_1),\ldots,\mathsf{K}(x_n)]\mathbin{\lrcorner}\mapsto[\mathsf{K}(\mathsf{f}(x_1,\ldots,x_n))] \quad \text{for any} \quad \mathsf{f} \in \Sigma$$

Actually, this rule is split into two cases in TAMARIN, depending on whether the attacker is building a term, or decomposing it. Formally, for any substitution θ (in normal form), we consider the rule

$$[\mathsf{K}^{\uparrow}(x_1\theta),\ldots,\mathsf{K}^{\uparrow}(x_n\theta)]\mathbin{\lfloor}\mathsf{K}^{\uparrow}(\mathsf{f}(x_1,\ldots,x_n)\theta)\mapsto[\mathsf{K}^{\uparrow}(\mathsf{f}(x_1,\ldots,x_n)\theta)]$$

when $\mathsf{f}(x_1,\ldots,x_n)\theta$ is in normal form. When the term $\mathsf{f}(x_1,\ldots,x_n)\theta$ reduces to a subterm of $x_{i_0}\theta$ for some i_0 (remember that we only consider subterm theories), then we consider

$$[\mathsf{K}^{\alpha_1}(x_1\theta),\ldots,\mathsf{K}^{\alpha_n}(x_n\theta)]\mathbin{\lfloor}\mathsf{K}^{\downarrow}(\mathsf{f}(x_1,\ldots,x_n)\theta\downarrow)\mapsto[\mathsf{K}^{\downarrow}(\mathsf{f}(x_1,\ldots,x_n)\theta\downarrow)]$$

where $\alpha_i =\uparrow$ for all $i \neq i_0$ and $\alpha_{i_0} =\downarrow$. Intuitively, the deduction rule is annotated with $\mathsf{K}^{\uparrow}$ when the attacker applies a "constructor" term such as an encryption and a pair. It can also be annotated with $\mathsf{K}^{\uparrow}$ when the attacker applies a deconstructor (for example, a decryption), if the term cannot be further reduced (for example, the decryption fails). Conversely, the deduction rule is annotated with $\mathsf{K}^{\downarrow}$ when the attacker decomposes a term. Finally, it is possible to switch from $\mathsf{K}^{\downarrow}$ to $\mathsf{K}^{\uparrow}$ thanks to the "coerce" rule:

$$[\mathsf{K}^{\downarrow}(m)]\mathbin{\lfloor}\mathsf{K}^{\uparrow}(m)\mapsto[\mathsf{K}^{\uparrow}(m)]$$

for any m in normal form that is not a pair.

Protocol rules. Then the protocol as well as additional attacker capabilities are specified through protocol rules, that are multiset rewriting rules that satisfy some conditions.

Definition 1. *A protocol rule is a multiset rewriting rule* $[l]\mathbin{\lfloor}a\mapsto[r]$ *such that*

1. *it does not contain fresh names and* Fr *does not occur in* r
2. K, $\mathsf{K}^{\uparrow}$, $\mathsf{K}^{\downarrow}$, *and* Out *do not occur in* l

3. K, $K^\uparrow$, $K^\downarrow$, In *do not occur in* r
4. $vars(r) \subseteq vars(l) \cup \{x \in \mathcal{V} \mid x : pub\}$.

The first condition guarantees in particular that fresh names are only produced thanks to the fresh name generation rule. The last three rules are easily met by any rule modelling a protocol step.

Example 3. Going back to our running example, the rule given in Sect. 2 is a protocol rule where Ltk and Pk are user-defined persistent facts used to model generation of long-term keys. Actually, our model contains the following rule:

$$[\mathsf{Fr}(xsk)] \mathbin{-[\,]\!\!\rightarrow} [!\mathsf{Ltk}(xid, xsk), !\mathsf{Pk}(xid, \mathrm{pk}(xsk)), \mathsf{Out}(\mathrm{pk}(xsk))]$$

where xsk is variable of sort fr, and xid is a variable of sort pub. This protocol rule represents the possibility to generate key pairs $(xsk, \mathrm{pk}(xsk))$ for any identity xid. The public part of the key is revealed to the attacker.

3.3 Execution Traces

A set of protocol rules P induces a transition relation $\rightarrow_P$ between states. Namely, we have $S \leadsto_P^{set(a\theta)} S'$ if there exists a rule $ru \in P \cup \mathsf{MD} \cup \{\mathsf{Fresh}\}$ and a grounding substitution θ for ru such that

- $lfacts(l\theta) \subseteq^\sharp S$, the linear facts of $l\theta$ should be present in S, with enough occurrences,
- $pfacts(l\theta) \subseteq S$,
- and $S' = (S \setminus^\# lfacts(l\theta)) \cup^\# r\theta$. The linear facts of $l\theta$ are removed and all the conclusion facts are added to the state.

Moreover, if the applied rule is the FRESH rule then $r\theta = \{\mathsf{Fr}(n)\}$ and n must be a new name not used earlier. The execution of a protocol is simply modelled by a sequence of transitions. A *trace* of a protocol is the sequence of actions that appear in the execution. Formally, we have that:

$$traces(P) = \{[A_1, \dots, A_n] \mid \emptyset \leadsto_P^{A_1} \cdots \leadsto_P^{A_n} S'\}.$$

Example 4. Continuing Example 3, the protocol rule modelling key generation can be used twice (or even more) to generate two key pairs for two different identities leading to the following trace:

$$\{\} \leadsto \{\mathsf{Fr}(ska)\} \leadsto F_a \cup \{\mathsf{Out}(\mathrm{pk}(ska))\}$$
$$\leadsto \{\mathsf{Fr}(skb)\} \leadsto F_a \cup F_b \cup \{\mathsf{Out}(\mathrm{pk}(ska)), \mathsf{Out}(\mathrm{pk}(skb))\}$$
$$\leadsto F_a \cup F_b \cup \{\mathsf{K}^\downarrow(\mathrm{pk}(ska)), \mathsf{Out}(\mathrm{pk}(skb))\}$$

where $F_a = \{!\mathsf{Ltk}(A, ska), !\mathsf{Pk}(A, \mathrm{pk}(ska))\}$, $F_b = \{!\mathsf{Ltk}(B, skb), !\mathsf{Pk}(B, \mathrm{pk}(skb))\}$. Here ska and skb are names of sort fr whereas A, B are public names of sort pub. This corresponds to the application of the FRESH rule followed by the protocol rule to obtain key material for the first agent A and then for a second agent B. The last rule corresponds to an application of an MD rule adding the public key of A to the knowledge of the attacker.

3.4   Properties

Security properties are expressed as properties on the traces of a protocol. TAMARIN offers a first order logic to specify properties. Formulas make use of variables of a novel sort *temp* to reason about when a fact occurs and to be able to express that some event occurs before another one. The full syntax and semantics of the logic is provided in [12]. We provide here only informally the semantics of atomic formulas:

- $F@i$, where i is of sort *temp*, refers to the fact F that occurs in the ith element of the trace;
- $i \doteq j$ expresses that the timepoints i and j are equal;
- $i \lessdot j$ expresses that timepoint i occurs before j;
- $t_1 \approx t_2$ says that t_1 and t_2 are equal (modulo the equational theory).

The first order logic is built from atomic formulas and closed by the boolean connectors $\lor$, $\land$, and $\neg$, as well as the quantificators $\exists$ and $\forall$.

A set of protocol rules P *satisfies* a formula ϕ, denoted $P \models \phi$ if, for any trace $tr \in traces(P)$, then tr satisfies ϕ.

Example 5. Continuing the running example, a typical lemma expressing nonce secrecy of the challenge is as follows:

```
lemma nonce_secrecy:
  "not(Ex A B s #i #j. (SecretI(A, B, s)@#i  &  K(s)@#j))"
```

This requires us to annotate the rule of the Initiator role with the action fact SecretI. Then intuitively this lemma expresses that there does not exit any trace such that SecretI(A,B,s) occurs at stage i (for some A, B, and s) and the attacker knows s at stage j. If we consider only the three protocol rules mentioned so far (initiator's rule, responder's rule, and key generation), then this security property is satisfied. However, as expected, the same lemma is not satisfied as soon as we model corruption, for example with the following rule.

```
rule Reveal_ltk: [!Ltk(xid, xsk)] --[RevLtk(xid)]-> [Out(xsk)]
```

TAMARIN also allows to express diff-equivalence, a refined notion of equivalence. This can be used for example to state that a protocol preserves unlinkability, anonymity, or other privacy properties such as ballot privacy. For example, the fact that Alice remains anonymous is often expressed as the property that $P(Alice) \sim P(Bob)$. This intuitively says that an adversary should not see the difference when Alice is playing protocol P or Bob is playing protocol P. The formal definition of diff-equivalence can be found in [12]. We do not need to provide it here as our automatically generated lemmas are simple trace properties and do not use diff-equivalence. Note however that our approach applies to protocols with diff-equivalence as well since our generated lemmas also helps TAMARIN to terminate in the case of diff-equivalence properties.

4   Automatically Generated Sources Lemmas

Whenever TAMARIN fails to complete a deconstruction, we aim at providing the tool with a sources lemma that resolves the partial deconstruction. We formalise here our approach and prove it to be correct.

4.1   Definitions

We introduce the notion of *protected* term, which is any term that is headed by a function symbol that is not a pair (because we know the adversary can always open such terms) nor an *AC* symbol (simply because our heuristic does not apply to case of failures due to an *AC* theory).

Definition 2. *A protected term t is a term whose head symbol is not $\langle \_, \_ \rangle$ nor an AC symbol. Given a term t and a variable x occurring in t, we say that t' is a* deepest protected subterm *w.r.t. x if t' is a protected subterm of t that contains x and such that one of the paths from the root of t' to x contains only pair symbols $\langle \_, \_ \rangle$ (except for head symbol at top level).*

Intuitively, if t' is a deepest protected subterm w.r.t. x, then the only way to obtain t' is either by extracting it directly from some output, or by building it, in which case x is already known to the attacker.

Example 6. Let $t = \mathsf{enc}(\langle x, \mathsf{enc}(\langle b, x \rangle, k_2) \rangle, k_1)$. There are two deepest protected subterms w.r.t. x, namely t itself and $t' = \mathsf{enc}(\langle b, x \rangle, k_2)$.

We denote by $St_{\mathsf{pair}}(u)$ the set of subterms of u that can be obtained from u simply by projecting. Formally, $St_{\mathsf{pair}}(u)$ is formally defined as

$$St_{\mathsf{pair}}(u) = \left\{ \begin{array}{ll} \{u\} \cup St_{\mathsf{pair}}(u_1) \cup St_{\mathsf{pair}}(u_2) & \text{if } u = \langle u_1, u_2 \rangle \\ \{u\} & \text{otherwise} \end{array} \right.$$

Normalised traces. In order to keep track of the origin of a protected subterm, we need to assume that the shape of a term is not modified by the application of the equational theory. Fortunately, since we assume an equational theory with the finite variant property, it is possible to compute in advance the shapes of all the terms obtained after normalisation. Given a set of protocol rules P, TAMARIN computes the variants $\mathsf{Variant}(P)$ of P such that, for any rule $ru \in P$, for any substitution θ, there is $ru' \in \mathsf{Variant}(P)$ and a substitution θ' such that $ru\theta =_E ru'\theta'$ and (ru', θ') is *normalised*, that is, for any fact $F(u')$ occurring in ru', we have that $(u'\theta')\!\downarrow =_{AC} u'\theta'$. Moreover, $ru' = (ru\sigma)\!\downarrow$ for some σ.

TAMARIN considers only traces that are *normalised*, i.e. executions of the form $\emptyset \leadsto_{\mathsf{Variant}(P)}^{A_1} S_1 \cdots \leadsto_{\mathsf{Variant}(P)}^{A_n} S_n$ and such that:

– the execution involves only rules $ru \in \mathsf{Variant}(P)$ and substitutions θ such that (ru, θ) is normalised;

– pairs are always decomposed before been used, that is, if $\mathsf{K}^\uparrow(u)$ appears in the left-hand-side of A_i then $\mathsf{K}^\uparrow(t) \in S_{i-1}$ for any $t \in St_{\mathsf{pair}}(u)$.[1]

We write $P \models_{\mathsf{norm}} \phi$ if for any normalised trace tr of P, tr satisfies ϕ. Then, given a formula ϕ that does not contain the fact $\mathsf{K}^\uparrow$ nor $\mathsf{K}^\downarrow$, we have $P \models \phi$ if, and only if, $P \models_{\mathsf{norm}} \phi$, which is what is actually checked by TAMARIN. This follows from the soundness of TAMARIN [12].

In some cases, computing the variants $\mathsf{Variant}(ru)$ of a protocol rule ru may introduce new variables on the right of the rule, and thus lead to rules that are not protocol rules (according to Definition 1).

Example 7. The rule $[\mathsf{In}(\mathsf{decA}(x, y))] \mathbin{-\!\![}\; \mathbin{]\!\!\rightarrow} [\mathsf{Out}(x)]$ is a protocol rule. However, one of its variant is $[\mathsf{In}(z)] \mathbin{-\!\![}\; \mathbin{]\!\!\rightarrow} [\mathsf{Out}(\mathsf{encA}(z, \mathsf{pk}(y)))]$ which is not a protocol rule according to Definition 1.

However, such cases correspond to badly defined protocols and TAMARIN typically raises a warning in this case. Hence, in what follows, we consider *well-formed protocol rules* P, that is such that $\mathsf{Variant}(P)$ is still a set of protocol rules. In practice, protocol rules representing a protocol are indeed well-formed.

4.2 Algorithm

Given a set P of protocol rules, TAMARIN first computes its variants $\mathsf{Variant}(P)$. It then precomputes sources as already explained. Whenever TAMARIN fails to complete a deconstruction, it returns the partial deconstruction. For the moment, assume that from there we can extract a rule $ru = [l] \mathbin{-\!\![}\; a \mathbin{]\!\!\rightarrow} [r]$ of $\mathsf{Variant}(P)$ and a variable x for which the deconstruction has failed (in practice there might be multiple composed rules, as explained below, but the approach is similar). It must be the case that x appears in some fact of l.

For each fact symbol F occurring in P, for each rule ru of $\mathsf{Variant}(P)$, and each (deepest) protected subterm t occurring in of ru, we assume new fact symbols $\mathsf{Left}_{F,ru,t}$ and $\mathsf{Right}_{F,ru,t}$ that will be used to further annotate the rules of $\mathsf{Variant}(P)$. These facts will appear only in the sources lemmas we generate.

The sources lemma $\mathsf{SourceLemma}(P, ru, x)$ associated to a failed deconstruction on variable x and rule ru for protocol P is defined by Algorithm 1. Intuitively, we first look for any occurrence of x in the premisses of ru, under a (deepest) protected term t_1 and we annotate the rule ru with $\mathsf{Left}_{F,ru,t_1}(t_1, x)$. Then we look for all facts in the conclusions of a rule ru' that may have produced t_1, that is that contain a term t_2 that can be unified with t_1 and we annotate ru' with $\mathsf{Right}_{F',ru',t_1}(t_2)$. Finally, we generate the formula that says that if we have $\mathsf{Left}_{F,ru,t_1}(y, x)$ at some step i, then either x is already known to the attacker, that is $\mathsf{K}(x)$ holds at an earlier step, or y has been obtained from the protocol, that is $\mathsf{Right}_{F',ru',t_1}(y)$ holds at some earlier step.

---

[1] This comes from the fact that, whenever the attacker learns a pair $\mathsf{K}^\downarrow(\langle m_1, m_2 \rangle)$, she cannot directly convert it in $\mathsf{K}^\uparrow(\langle m_1, m_2 \rangle)$ since the coerce rule does not apply to terms headed with a pair. Hence it is necessary to decompose it first (with $\mathsf{K}^\downarrow$ rules) and then reconstruct it (with $\mathsf{K}^\uparrow$ rules).

Algorithm 1. SourceLemma(P, ru, x)

Input: P, $ru = [l] \!-\!\!\lfloor a \rceil\!\!\mapsto\! [r]$, x

   for all t_1 deepest protected term w.r.t. x that is subterm of $F(v) \in l$ **do**

      % we annotate ru with the fact that x may provide from t_1

      $a := a \cup \{\mathsf{Left}_{F,ru,t_1}(t_1, x)\}$

      % then we identify from which facts t_1 may provide.

      for all rule $ru' = [l'] \!-\!\!\lfloor a' \rceil\!\!\mapsto\! [r'] \in P$ **do**

         if t_1 unifiable with t_2 modulo AC for some t_2 protected subterm in $F'(v') \in r'$

         then

            % we annotate ru' with the fact that t_2 may be used to produce x

            $a' := a' \cup \{\mathsf{Right}_{F',ru',t_1}(t_2)\}$

         end if

      end for

      Let ϕ the formula defined as follows

$$\forall y, x, i \; \mathsf{Left}_{F,ru,t_1}(y,x)@i \Longrightarrow \begin{array}{l} (\exists k \; \mathsf{Right}_{F',ru'_1,t_1}(y)@k \;\wedge\; k < i) \\ \vee \quad \cdots \\ \vee \; (\exists k \; \mathsf{Right}_{F',ru'_n,t_1}(y)@k \;\wedge\; k < i) \\ \vee \; (\exists k \; \mathsf{K}^{\uparrow}(x)@k \;\wedge\; k < i) \end{array}$$

      return ϕ

   end for

We can show that under our assumptions the generated sources lemmas always hold, which explains why TAMARIN is usually able to prove them.

Theorem 1. *Given a set of well-formed protocol rules P, a rule $ru \in$ Variant(P), a variable x occurring in ru, and ϕ returned by SourceLemma (Variant(P), ru, x), then ϕ is satisfied by Variant(P), that is Variant(P) $\models_{\mathsf{norm}} \phi$.*

4.3 Dealing with Composed Rules

Actually, during the precomputations, TAMARIN might compute the composition of several rules. For example, when a rule ru_1 depends on a rule ru_2 in the sense that ru_1 can only be executed if ru_2 has been executed previously, TAMARIN will return the composition of both, not only ru_1. This yields bigger steps and it allows TAMARIN to prove lemmas more quickly.

Thus, the sources computed by TAMARIN are actually composed variants of initial protocol rules. Formally, given two rules $ru_1 = [l_1] \!-\!\!\lfloor a_1 \rceil\!\!\mapsto\! [r_1]$ and $ru_2 = [l_2] \!-\!\!\lfloor a_2 \rceil\!\!\mapsto\! [r_2]$, we define the *composition* of ru_1 and ru_2 w.r.t. θ, denoted $ru_1 \circ_\theta ru_2$ as the rule $[l] \!-\!\!\lfloor a \rceil\!\!\mapsto\! [r]$ defined as follows:

$$l = l_1\theta \cup^{\#} (l_2\theta \setminus^{\#} r_1\theta), \quad a = a_1\theta \cup a_2\theta, \quad \text{and} \quad r = (r_1\theta \setminus^{\#} l_2\theta) \cup^{\#} r_2\theta.$$

We denote $ru_1 \circ_\theta ru_2 \circ_\theta \cdots \circ_\theta ru_k$ the rule ru obtained by iterating $k-1$ compositions: $ru = ((ru_1 \circ_\theta ru_2) \circ_\theta \cdots) \circ_\theta ru_k$. Since the rules do not share any variable, θ is just the union of substitutions θ_i where the domain of θ_i is the set of variables of ru_i. It is easy to check that compositions of protocol rules yield protocol rules. Not all compositions are computed by TAMARIN, but we do not need to characterise which compositions are considered exactly. We simply show that any sources lemma generated from a composed rule is also sound.

Algorithm 2. SourceLemmaComp(P, ru, x)

Input: $P, ru = ru_1 \circ_\theta ru_2 \circ_\theta \cdots \circ_\theta ru_k,\ x$

let l, a, r such that $ru = [l] \dashv\!\!\mid a \mid\!\rightarrow [r]$

for all position p such that there exists $F(v) \in l$ such that $v|_p = x$ do

for all i such that $F(v) = F(v_i\theta)$ with $F(v_i)$ in the premises of ru_i do

if p is a position of v_i then

call SourceLemma$(P, ru_i, v_i|_p)$

end if

end for

end for

Algorithm 2 describes how to generate a sources lemma from a composed rule. The idea is simply to identify, given a variable x, for which the partial deconstruction is incomplete, at which positions x appears in the composed rule ru. Then whenever the position exists in the some rule ru_i used for composition, we generate the sources lemmas based on this rule. Algorithm 2 is well defined only if whenever SourceLemma$(P, ru_i, v_i|_p)$ is called, then $v_i|_p$ is a variable. This follows from the fact that $v_i\theta|_p = x$ is a variable (with the notations of Algorithm 2).

Theorem 2. *Given a set of well-formed protocol rules P, a composed rule $ru = ru_1 \circ_\theta ru_2 \circ_\theta \cdots \circ_\theta ru_k$ with $ru_i \in$ Variant(P), a variable x occurring in ru, and ϕ returned by* SourceLemmaComp(Variant$(P), ru, x)$, *then* Variant$(P) \models_{\mathsf{norm}} \phi$.

5 Implementation and Experimental Evaluation

We have implemented our approach in TAMARIN version 1.6.0 [15]. The automatic generation of source lemmas is activated using the command line option `--auto-sources`. When TAMARIN is called with this option, it will first load the theory and run the pre-computations normally (in particular compute rule variants and sources). If TAMARIN is called using `--auto-sources`, and the theory does not contain a sources lemma but has partial deconstructions, our new algorithm is executed on the computed rule variants to generate a new sources lemma, which is then added to the theory, as well as the required rule annotations. In the interactive mode, the user can inspect the generated lemma and annotations, and prove lemmas as usual. He can also download the modified theory if he wants to export the lemma, or modify it. In the automatic mode, TAMARIN directly tries to prove the generated sources lemma. When showing the results, TAMARIN displays the sources lemma among the other lemmas, and whether it managed to prove it.

Heuristic. Our first experiments using Algorithm 2 showed that, for some examples, the generated lemmas, while true, caused TAMARIN to loop in the precomputations. This happened when the algorithm considered the case where a fact in the premises of a rule might have been produced by a fact in the conclusion of the same rule. Hence, we have implemented an additional check that ignores this case, should it arise. This means that the generated lemmas could potentially be false, however we did not observe this in practice. In particular, the examples that looped can now be proven correct. Note that this does not contradict our theorems, as our lemmas are not minimal - we consider potentially too many cases, so removing some (unnecessary) ones can still result in a correct lemma.

Evaluation. To evaluate the effectiveness of our approach, we selected several classical examples from the SPORE library of cryptographic protocols [14] and checked for standard properties such as secrecy of the exchanged key and mutual (injective and non-injective) authentication. Because of partial deconstructions, many of them were not entirely automatically verifiable in TAMARIN previously (except for extremely simple examples such as CCITT with only one message). The results are presented in Table 1, the TAMARIN models are available in the

Table 1. SPORE examples. "Partial Dec." indicates the number of partial deconstructions, "Resolved" indicates whether our auto-generated lemmas resolve them, and can be proven correct by TAMARIN. "Automatic" means that our auto-generated lemmas are then sufficient to directly prove or disprove the desired security properties.

Protocol Name	Partial Dec.	Resolved	Automatic	Time
Andrew Secure RPC	14	✓	✓	42.8s
Modified Andrew Secure RPC	21	✓	✓	134.3s
BAN Concrete Andrew Secure RPC	0	-	✓	10.6s
Lowe modified BAN Andrew Secure RPC	0	-	✓	29.8s
CCITT 1	0	-	✓	0.8s
CCITT 1c	0	-	✓	1.2s
CCITT 3	0	-	✓	186.1s
CCITT 3 BAN	0	-	✓	3.7s
Denning Sacco Secret Key	5	✓	✓	0.8s
Denning Sacco Secret Key - Lowe	6	✓	✓	2.7s
Needham Schroeder Secret Key	14	✓	✓	3.6s
Amended Needham Schroeder Secret Key	21	✓	✓	7.1s
Otway Rees	10	✓	✓	7.7s
SpliceAS	10	✓	✓	5.9s
SpliceAS 2	10	✓	✓	7.3s
SpliceAS 3	10	✓	✓	8.7s
Wide Mouthed Frog	5	✓	✓	0.6s
Wide Mouthed Frog Lowe	14	✓	✓	3.5s
WooLam Pi f	5	✓	✓	0.6s
Yahalom	15	✓	✓	3.1s
Yahalom - BAN	5	✓	✓	0.9s
Yahalom - Lowe	21	✓	✓	2.2s

directory `examples/features/auto-sources/spore` of the TAMARIN repository [15]. Our approach succeeded in all cases.

To see whether our approach works on more complicated examples, we
selected all files from the TAMARIN github repository [15] that contained lemmas
annotated with `sources`, and that were not marked as "experimental" or "work
in progress". It turned out that in some cases these examples did not actually
contain any partial deconstructions, and that these "sources" lemmas were actually used to prove other protocol invariants. As our approach is only meant to
handle partial deconstructions, we removed these examples from the set. Table 2
summarises our results on the remaining examples, the files can be found in the
directory `examples/features/auto-sources/tamarin-repo` of the TAMARIN
repository [15].

It turns out that our algorithm still succeeds in generating successful sources
lemmas in the majority of cases, in the sense that the sources lemma resolve
all the partial deconstructions and can be proved by TAMARIN. Our examples

Table 2. Examples from TAMARIN repository. [1] The sources lemma needs to be annotated with `reuse` for the following lemmas to be proven automatically. [2] The file
contains further intermediate lemmas annotated with reuse. [3] The generated lemma
removes all partial deconstructions, however TAMARIN does not terminate while trying
to prove its correctness automatically.

Name	Partial Dec.	Resolved	Automatic	Time (new)	Time (previous)
Feldhofer (Equivalence)	5	✓	✓	3.8s	3.5s
NSLPK3	12	✓	✓	1.8s	1.8s
NSLPK3 untagged	12	✓	x^1	-	-
NSPK3	12	✓	✓	2.4s	2.2s
JCS12 Typing Example	7	✓	x^2	0.3s	0.2s
Minimal Typing Example	6	✓	✓	0.1s	0.1s
Simple RFID Protocol	24	✓	x^2	0.7s	0.5s
StatVerif Security Device	12	✓	✓	0.3s	0.4s
Envelope Protocol	9	✓	x^2	25.7s	25.3s
TPM Exclusive Secrets	9	✓	x^2	1.8s	1.8s
NSL untagged (SAPIC)	18	✓	✓	4.3s	19.9s
StatVerif Left-Right (SAPIC)	18	✓	✓	28.8s	29.6s
TPM Envelope (Equivalence)	9	x^3	-	-	-
5G AKA	240	✗	-	-	-
Alethea	30	✗	-	-	-
PKCS11-templates	68	✗	-	-	-
NSLPK3XOR	24	✗	-	-	-
Chaum Offline Anonymity	128	✗	-	-	-
FOO Eligibility	70	✗	-	-	-
Okamoto Eligibility	66	✗	-	-	-

include protocols with equivalence properties and SAPIC-generated[2] theories. However, as the examples are more complex, even with a correct sources lemma, TAMARIN does not always succeed in proving all other lemmas fully automatically.

We also analysed the examples where our algorithm failed to generate a correct sources lemma. The reasons turned out to be a too complex equational theory (e.g., FOO and Okamoto, using blind signatures, or NSLPK3XOR and Chaum using XOR), or a complex protocol model where the partial deconstructions stem from the handling of state facts, which escapes our definition of protected subterms (5G AKA, Alethea, PKCS'11). We only encountered one example where the algorithm generated a lemma resolving the partial deconstructions, but TAMARIN was unable to (automatically) verify its correctness.

When our approach succeeds, the verification times are close to timings measured using the manual sources lemmas. All timings have been measured on a standard laptop (Core i7, 16 GB RAM, Ubuntu 18.04).

6   Conclusion

We have provided a technique that allows to automatically generate sources lemmas in TAMARIN, which otherwise had to be written by the user. In return, most simple protocols can now be analysed automatically with TAMARIN.

As future work, we plan to look for even more automation. First, in several cases where our sources lemmas solve the partial deconstructions but are not yet sufficient to prove the security properties specified by the user, we are actually close to full automation. What is missing is simply to indicate to TAMARIN that it should reuse one of the properties (e.g. secrecy of some long-term key) to prove another property (e.g. authentication). We plan to investigate how to automate these "re-use" annotations, without increasing the complexity of the tool.

Our result holds for subterm convergent theories (modulo AC) that have the variant property. However, our algorithm does not generate lemmas for terms headed with an AC symbol (for example exclusive or) as the resulting lemmas would be false in most cases. Hence, manual sources lemmas are still necessary. We plan to explore how to extend our result to tackle this case, which may require to write more complex sources lemmas, e.g. to account for all possible decompositions induced by the exclusive or operator.

Our algorithm also fails when the model uses state facts in such a way that the variables in question do not occur within protected subterms. By generalising the notion of protected subterms, we hope to also cover these cases.

Thanks to our sources lemma, the automation of TAMARIN has improved, in particular on simple protocols. It would be interesting to compare extensively the tools ProVerif and TAMARIN, in order to identify on which cases they are both automatic, and on which kind of protocols, one of the two tools is more likely to conclude automatically. This should also provide directions to improve the automation of both tools.

---

[2] SAPIC translates from applied pi models to TAMARIN theories.

A   Proofs of Theorems 1 and 2

Theorem 1. *Given a set of well-formed protocol rules* P, *a rule* $ru \in$ Variant(P), *a variable* x *occurring in* ru, *and* ϕ *returned by* SourceLemma (Variant$(P), ru, x$), *then* ϕ *is satisfied by* Variant(P), *that is* Variant$(P) \models_{\mathsf{norm}} \phi$.

Proof. Let P be a set of protocol rules, $ru \in$ Variant(P) and a variable x occurring in ru, let ϕ be a formula returned by SourceLemma(Variant$(P), ru, x$). The rule ru is of the form $[l] \dashv a \mapsto [r]$ and ϕ is of the form:

$$\forall y, x, i \; \mathsf{Left}_{F, ru, t_1}(y, x)@i \implies \begin{array}{l} (\exists k \; \mathsf{Right}_{F', ru'_1, t_1}(y)@k \; \wedge \; k < i) \\ \vee \\ \vee (\exists k \; \mathsf{Right}_{F', ru'_n, t_1}(y)@k \; \wedge \; k < i) \\ \vee (\exists k \; \mathsf{K}^{\uparrow}(x)@k \; \wedge \; k < i) \end{array}$$

for some t_1 deepest protected term w.r.t. x, subterm of $F(t) \in l$. By definition of a deepest protected subterm, $t_1|_p = x$ for some position p and there are only pairs along the path p (except at position ϵ).

Let tr be a normalised trace of Variant(P). Let us show that tr satisfies ϕ.

$$tr = \emptyset \rightsquigarrow^{A_1} S_1 \cdots \rightsquigarrow^{A_{n-1}} S_{n-1} \rightsquigarrow^{A_n} S_n$$

Let i be such that $\mathsf{Left}_{F, ru, t_1}(m, n) \in S_i$ for some terms m, n. Then the ith applied rule must the rule ru in Variant(P) mentioned above which has the form:

$$ru = \{[F(t)] \cup l'] \dashv \mathsf{Left}_{F, ru, t_1}(t_1, x) \cup a' \mapsto [r]$$

Moreover, there exists a substitution σ_i in normal form (the one used to instantiate ru) such that $m =_{AC} (t_1\sigma_i)\!\downarrow$ and $n =_{AC} x\sigma_i\!\downarrow$. Since the trace is normalised, $m =_{AC} t_1\sigma_i$ and $n =_{AC} x\sigma_i$. Let $u =_{AC} (t\sigma_i)\!\downarrow$. Again, we have $u =_{AC} t\sigma_i$. Since t_1 is a subterm of t and t_1 is not headed by an AC symbol, we have that m is a subterm of u (modulo AC). Moreover $F(u) \in S_{i-1}$ by definition of the application of a rule.

Let $j < i$ be the first occurrence of j such that m (modulo AC) is a subterm of a fact in S_j and consider the jth rule that has been applied.

– Either this rule is a rule ru'' in Variant(P) of the form

$$ru'' = [l''] \dashv a'' \mapsto [\{F'(w)\} \cup r'']$$

and there exists σ_j in normal form (the substitution used to instantiate ru'') such that m (modulo AC) is a subterm of $u' = (w\sigma_j)\!\downarrow$. Since the trace is normalised, $(w\sigma_j)\!\downarrow =_{AC} w\sigma_j$. Let p' be the position at which m occurs in $w\sigma_j$, i.e. such that $w\sigma_j|_{p'} =_{AC} m$.
  • Either p' is a path of w that does not end on a variable. Then $w|_{p'} = w'$ with w' a protected subterm of w.

  We have that $w'\sigma_j =_{AC} m =_{AC} t_1\sigma_i$ thus w' and t_1 are unifiable (modulo AC) thus we have annotated ru'', that is, $\mathsf{Right}_{F', ru'', t_1}(w') \in a''$, which concludes this case.

- Or p' is a path of w that ends on a variable or is not a path at all. Then there must exist a variable y in w such that m (modulo AC) is a subterm of $y\sigma_j$. Then y also appears in some premise fact $F''(w'')$, thanks to the definition of a protocol rule and the fact that the variant rules are still protocol rules. Therefore m (modulo AC) is a subterm of a fact in S_{j-1} (since $(w''\sigma_j){\downarrow} =_{AC} w''\sigma_j$), which contradicts the minimality of j.

– Or the rule is one of the MD rules. Since m is a protected term, the rule cannot be $[]\multimap K^\uparrow(x) \mapsto [K^\uparrow(x : pub)]$ nor $[Fr(x : fr)]\multimap K^\uparrow(x) \mapsto [K^\uparrow(x : fr)]$ since these two rules only generate names. By minimality of j, it cannot be the rule $[Out(x)]\multimap[]\mapsto[K^\downarrow(x)]$, nor $[K^\uparrow(x)]\multimap K(x) \mapsto [In(x)]$, nor the rule $[K^\downarrow(x)]\multimap K^\uparrow(x) \mapsto [K^\uparrow(x)]$ either. So it must be the deduction rule, either in the $K^\uparrow$ version or in the $K^\downarrow$ version.

  – Either it is the rule

  $$[K^\uparrow(x_1\theta), \ldots, K^\uparrow(x_n\theta)]\multimap K^\uparrow(f(x_1, \ldots, x_n)\theta) \mapsto [K^\uparrow(f(x_1, \ldots, x_n)\theta)]$$

  with $f(x_1, \ldots, x_n)\theta$ in normal form. We have $K^\uparrow(x_1\theta), \ldots, K^\uparrow(x_k\theta) \in S_{j-1}$. Then, by minimality of j, and since m is not headed with an AC symbol, we must have $m =_{AC} t_1\sigma_i =_{AC} f(x_1\theta, \ldots, x_k\theta)$, otherwise we would have that m is subterm of some $x_i\theta$ hence subterm of S_{j-1} or m is a constant, which cannot be the case since m is a protected subterm. Remember that $x\sigma_i$ is a subterm at position $p = i_0.p'$ (for some i_0) of t_1 such that there are only pairs along p', that is, $x\sigma_i \in St_{pair}(x_{i_0}\theta)$. Since the trace is normalised (i.e. pairs are decomposed before being used), we get that $K^\uparrow(x\sigma_i) \in S_{j-1}$, that is $K^\uparrow(n) \in S_{j-1}$. Now, by inspection of the rules, we notice that the only way to obtain $K^\uparrow(t)$ in a state is through a rule annotated by $K^\uparrow(t)$, hence we can conclude that $K^\uparrow(n)$ appears in one of the actions of an earlier rule.

  – Or the rule

  $$[K^{\alpha_1}(x_1\theta), \ldots, K^{\alpha_n}(x_n\theta)]\multimap K^\downarrow(f(x_1, \ldots, x_n)\theta{\downarrow}) \mapsto [K^\downarrow(f(x_1, \ldots, x_n)\theta{\downarrow})]$$

  has been applied, with $f(x_1, \ldots, x_k)\theta$ that can be reduced at top level. Since the equational theory is a subterm theory, it must be the case that $m = (f(x_1, \ldots, x_k)\theta) {\downarrow}$ is a subterm of one of the $x_i\sigma$, hence m is a subterm of a fact of S_{j-1}, which contradicts the minimality of j. □

Theorem 2. *Given a set of well-formed protocol rules P, a composed rule $ru = ru_1 \circ_\theta ru_2 \circ_\theta \cdots \circ_\theta ru_k$ with $ru_i \in \mathsf{Variant}(P)$, a variable x occurring in ru, and ϕ returned by $\mathsf{SourceLemmaComp}(\mathsf{Variant}(P), ru, x)$, then $\mathsf{Variant}(P) \models_{\mathsf{norm}} \phi$.*

Proof. The correctness of Algorithm 2 is a direct consequence of Theorem 1. Indeed, let ϕ be a formula returned by $\mathsf{SourceLemmaComp}(\mathsf{Variant}(P), ru, x)$. Then ϕ is actually a formula returned by $\mathsf{SourceLemma}(\mathsf{Variant}(P), ru_i, v_i|_p)$ for some $ru_i \in \mathsf{Variant}(P)$ and some variable $v_i|_p$ of ru_i. Applying Theorem 1, we have that $\mathsf{Variant}(P) \models_{\mathsf{norm}} \phi$, hence the conclusion. □

References

1. Armando, A., et al.: The AVISPA tool for the automated validation of internet security protocols and applications. In: Etessami, K., Rajamani, S.K. (eds.) CAV 2005. LNCS, vol. 3576, pp. 281–285. Springer, Heidelberg (2005). https://doi.org/10.1007/11513988_27
2. Basin, D., Dreier, J., Hirschi, L., Radomirovic, S., Sasse, R., Stettler, V.: A formal analysis of 5G authentication. In: 25th ACM Conference on Computer and Communications Security (CCS 2018) (2018)
3. Bhargavan, K., Blanchet, B., Kobeissi, N.: Verified models and reference implementations for the TLS 1.3 standard candidate. In: IEEE Symposium on Security and Privacy (S&P 2017), San Jose, CA, pp. 483–503 (2017)
4. Blanchet, B.: An efficient cryptographic protocol verifier based on prolog rules. In: 14th IEEE Computer Security Foundations Workshop (CSFW 2014), Cape Breton, Nova Scotia, Canada, June 2001, pp. 82–96. IEEE Computer Society (2001)
5. Blanchet, B.: Symbolic and computational mechanized verification of the ARINC823 avionic protocols. In: 30th IEEE Computer Security Foundations Symposium (CSF 2017), Santa Barbara, CA, USA, pp. 68–82 (2017)
6. Cheval, V., Kremer, S., Rakotonirina, I.: DEEPSEC: deciding equivalence properties in security protocols - theory and practice. In: Proceedings of the 39th IEEE Symposium on Security and Privacy (S&P 2018), pp. 525–542. IEEE Computer Society Press, May 2018
7. Cortier, V., Galindo, D., Turuani, M.: A formal analysis of the Neuchâtel e-voting protocol. In: 3rd IEEE European Symposium on Security and Privacy (EuroSP 2018), London, UK, pp. 430–442, April 2018
8. Dreier, J., Hirschi, L., Radomirovic, S., Sasse, R.: Automated unbounded verification of stateful cryptographic protocols with exclusive OR. In: CSF 2018, pp. 359–373 (2018)
9. Durgin, N., Lincoln, P., Mitchell, J., Scedrov, A.: Undecidability of bounded security protocols. In: Workshop on Formal Methods and Security Protocols, Trento, Italia (1999)
10. Girol, G., Hirschi, L., Sasse, R., Jackson, D., Cremers, C., Basin, D.: A spectral analysis of noise: a comprehensive, automated, formal analysis of Diffie-Hellman protocols. In: USENIX Security (2020)
11. Meier, S., Schmidt, B., Cremers, C., Basin, D.: The TAMARIN prover for the symbolic analysis of security protocols. In: Sharygina, N., Veith, H. (eds.) CAV 2013. LNCS, vol. 8044, pp. 696–701. Springer, Heidelberg (2013). https://doi.org/10.1007/978-3-642-39799-8_48
12. Schmidt, B., Meier, S., Cremers, C.J.F., Basin, D.A.: Automated analysis of Diffie-Hellman protocols and advanced security properties. In: CSF 2012, pp. 78–94 (2012)
13. Schmidt, B., Sasse, R., Cremers, C., Basin, D.: Automated verification of group key agreement protocols. In: IEEE Symposium on Security and Privacy (S&P 2014) (2014)
14. Security protocols open repository. http://www.lsv.fr/Software/spore/. Accessed 24 Apr 2020
15. Main source code repository of the tamarin prover for security protocol verification. https://github.com/tamarin-prover/tamarin-prover. Accessed 06 Dec 2019

When Is a Test Not a Proof?

Eleanor McMurtry[1], Olivier Pereira[2], and Vanessa Teague[3(✉)]

[1] University of Melbourne, Melbourne, Australia
emcmurtry@student.unimelb.edu.au
[2] Université catholique de Louvain, ICTEAM, Louvain-la-Neuve, Belgium
olivier.pereira@uclouvain.be
[3] Thinking Cybersecurity Pty. Ltd. and the Australian National University,
Canberra, Australia
vanessa@thinkingcybersecurity.com

Abstract. A common primitive in election and auction protocols is a *plaintext equivalence test* (PET) in which two ciphertexts are tested for equality of their plaintexts, and a verifiable proof of the test's outcome is provided. The most commonly-cited PETs require at least one honest party, but many applications claim *universal verifiability*, at odds with this requirement. If a *test* that relies on at least one honest participant is mistakenly used in a place where a *universally verifiable proof* is needed, then a collusion by all participants can insert a forged proof of equality into the tallying transcript. We show this breaks universal verifiability for the JCJ/Civitas scheme among others, because the only PETs they reference are not universally verifiable. We then demonstrate how to fix the problem.

1 Introduction

We consider the distinction between *universal verifiability* and *distributed trust*, in particular for Plaintext Equivalence Tests (PETs). Commonly-cited PETs such as [17] and [19] require at least one honest participant. Although this is clear enough in the original papers, numerous uses of PETs assume universal verifiability, which requires that a convincing proof of an untrue fact cannot be fabricated even if all the authorities collude. Many e-voting and verifiable auction protocols use a Plaintext Equivalence *Test* (PET, with distributed trust) as if it were a Plaintext Equivalence *Proof* (PEP), when it is not. They require their PET to have universal verifiability, but reference only PETs that do not have this property. Specifically, in Jakobsson and Juels [17] a collusion of all authorities can forge a "proof" that two encrypted values are equal when they are not. If in a real implementation this PET was used instead of a PEP, the consequence would completely undermine universal verifiability for:

- the JCJ e-voting scheme [18] and its implementation, Civitas [8];
- a linear-time modification to JCJ [23];
- the Pretty Good Democracy scheme [21];
- the Caveat Coercitor scheme [12];

© Springer Nature Switzerland AG 2020
L. Chen et al. (Eds.): ESORICS 2020, LNCS 12309, pp. 23–41, 2020.
https://doi.org/10.1007/978-3-030-59013-0_2

- the Selections scheme [7];
- the Cobra scheme [11]; and
- several verifiable auction schemes [2,6,20]

In each case, the forged PEP enables a collusion among all tallying authorities to exclude valid votes or include invalid votes while passing verification, thus breaking universal verifiability. We stress that this is not a fault in the PET of [17], but in the misalignment between the properties it provides and the properties it is assumed to have when used in the above schemes.

We show further that this problem combines with an existing issue in the Civitas implementation of the Fiat-Shamir transform to disastrous effect, allowing colluding authorities to also forge a proof that two encrypted values are *not* equal when in fact they are.

1.1   Addressing the Problem

PETs with distributed trust, including [17], are generally easy to transform into a universally-verifiable Plaintext Equality Proof (PEP). We demonstrate how a faked positive test can be detected in [17] with an additional check in the verification procedure, and that there is a negligible soundness error, *i.e.* probability of a false positive.

1.2   Our Contribution

We examine each protocol in turn, explaining the implications of using a PET that can be forged when all tallying authorities collude. We then explain how to patch the verification algorithm in the Jakobsson-Juels PET so that its transcript does allow universal verifiability. We also explore the implications of weak Fiat-Shamir transforms in one protocol, and explain how this can be fixed.

Mathematical details are provided in the following section. An examination of each affected scheme is in Sect. 4. The correction of the PET verification algorithm and a proof of universal verifiability are in Sect. 5.

2   The Jakobsson-Juels PET

We demonstrate that if all the trustees of a secret key collude, they can produce a valid plaintext equivalence proof for two ciphertexts that are not encryptions of the same value. We begin by reviewing the details of a PET from the widely-referenced Jakobsson-Juels paper [17], and explain why it does not form a PEP.

2.1   Plaintext Equivalence Test

Let $(\mathbb{G}, g, p, q, y)$ be the parameters for ElGamal encryption, with g a generator for the group $\mathbb{G}$, and $q = \langle g \rangle$, *i.e.* $a^q = 1 \bmod p$ for all $a \neq 0$ where p and q are large prime numbers. The public key is $y = g^x$ for secret key x. Consider two

ElGamal ciphertexts $(a_1, b_1) = (g^{r_1}, m_1 y^{r_1})$ and $(a_2, b_2) = (g^{r_2}, m_2 y^{r_2})$ where $m_1 \neq m_2$.

For ease of exposition, suppose there are two trustees T_1 and T_2 who collude (but it works just as well for more trustees). Each trustee has its own share x_i ($i = 1, 2$) of the secret key, corresponding to its own public key $y_i = g^{x_i}$, arranged so that $x_1 + x_2 = x \bmod q$ and hence $y_1 y_2 = y \bmod p$.

They will produce a false proof that $m_1 = m_2 \bmod q$. We (publicly) set

$$C = (a_1/a_2, b_1/b_2) = \left(g^{r_1 - r_2}, (m_1/m_2)y^{r_1 - r_2}\right)$$

The main idea of the PET is that the two trustees will each raise (each element of) C to a random power, prove in zero knowledge that they indeed used the same power on all the elements of C, multiply all their exponentiated values together, then decrypt the result, using another Zero Knowledge Proof to prove they decrypted correctly. Call the trustees' random exponents ρ_1 (for T_1) and ρ_2 (for T_2). If ρ_1 and ρ_2 are chosen randomly, and if the decrypted value $(m_1/m_2)^{\rho_1 + \rho_2} = 1$, then with high probability[1] $m_1/m_2 = 1$. So as long as at least one trustee is honest, the proof is both sound and privacy-preserving. A detailed example is shown in Fig. 1.

Exponential ElGamal. A common variant of ElGamal, called *exponential ElGamal*, encrypts a message m by first computing g^m and then encrypting this value as usual in order to create additively-homomorphic ciphertexts. We will work with this variant when discussing protocols that use it.

2.2   Why the PET Is Not a Proof

The PET described above does not form a plaintext equivalence *proof*. If the trustees collude and set $\rho_1 = -\rho_2 \bmod q$ (easy to do in a setting like ElGamal where q is public), then they turn C into an encryption of 1 because $(m_1/m_2)^q = 1$ even when $m_1 \neq m_2$. In fact, they turn C into the trivial ciphertext $(1, 1)$, which looks unusual to a human eye but is a perfectly valid ElGamal encryption of 1. Hence the colluding trustees, even if they decrypt honestly, can produce a false proof that $m_1 = m_2$.

Adding a simple check for the trivial ciphertext $(1, 1)$ solves the problem and produces a universally verifiable Proof of Plaintext Equality (PEP). We prove this in Sect. 5.

However, the PEP is strongly dependent on the soundness of its ZKPs. If these are not properly implemented, the PEP is not sound.

3   Flaws in a Practical Implementation of the PEP

One particularly influential implementation of the PEP and zero knowledge proofs discussed above[2] is Civitas [8]. In the following section we discuss how

---

[1] The test may fail if by pure bad luck, $\rho_1 = -\rho_2 \bmod q$. This happens only with the negligible probability $1/q$, where q is large.

[2] Indeed, one of the *only* implementations we were able to find.

weaknesses in Civitas' implementations further undermine its PEPs, even if we ensure the PEP does not produce the trivial ciphertext.

3.1 Use of Zero Knowledge Proofs (ZKPs)

A practical implementation of the Jakobsson-Juels PET outlined above depends on two zero knowledge proofs. **First**, when trustee T_i takes $C = (a_1/a_2, b_1/b_2)$ and produces a randomised output $((a_1/a_2)^{\rho_i}, (b_1/b_2)^{\rho_i})$, an observer has no way to guarantee that T_i did indeed raise both elements to the same power. To this end, a zero knowledge proof must be used to prove the equality of two discrete logarithms. Set $d = a_1/a_2, d_i = d^{\rho_i}$ and $e = b_1/b_2, e_i = e^{\rho_i}$; then we must prove

$$\mathsf{dlog}_d d_i = \mathsf{dlog}_e e_i$$

Second, the trustees (collectively) need to prove that they faithfully decrypted the resulting ciphertext $(a, b) = (\prod_i d_i, \prod_i e_i)$. They do this by publishing $a_i = a^{x_i}$ and a proof that

$$\mathsf{dlog}_g y_i = \mathsf{dlog}_a a_i$$

guaranteeing that a really was raised to the power of the secret key to form a_i.

We will use $\mathsf{EqDlogs}(a, b, x, y)$ to mean a proof that $\mathsf{dlog}_a x = \mathsf{dlog}_b y$.

3.2 Making Equivalent Ciphertexts Look Different

The plaintext equivalence test (used as a proof) from the Civitas technical report [8] is reproduced as Fig. 1 below.

B.3 Main protocols

PROTOCOL: Plaintext Equivalence Test (PET)

Due to:	Jakobsson and Juels [51]
Principals:	Tabulation tellers TT_i
Public input:	$c_j = \mathsf{Enc}(m_j; K_{TT}) = (a_j, b_j)$ for $j \in \{1, 2\}$
Private input (TT_i):	Private key share x_i
	Let $R = (d, e) = (a_1/a_2, b_1/b_2)$
Output:	If $m_1 = m_2$ then 1 else 0

1. TT_i: $z_i \leftarrow \mathbb{Z}_q^*$; $(d_i, e_i) = (d^{z_i}, e^{z_i})$

2. TT_i: Publish $\mathsf{Commit}(d_i, e_i)$

3. TT_i: Barrier: wait until all commitments are available

4. TT_i: Publish (d_i, e_i) and proof $\mathsf{EqDlogs}(d, e, d_i, e_i)$

5. TT_i: Verify all commitments and proofs

6. Let $c' = (\prod_i d_i, \prod_i e_i)$

7. All TT: Compute $m' = \mathsf{DistDec}(c')$ using private key shares

8. If $m' = 1$ then output 1 else output 0

Fig. 1. PET protocol specification from the Civitas technical report

We demonstrate that trustees can produce a valid proof that two plaintexts encrypt different values, even though they are encryptions of the same value. Here, we proceed in a single trustee setting, but this can be trivially extended to the multiple trustee setting.

We take advantage of a weaknesses in the way the Fiat-Shamir transform is implemented as part of the decryption proof in the Civitas documentation (Step 7 of Fig. 1). The proof is specified as follows, for an ElGamal public key (g, y) where $y = g^x$, a ciphertext (a, b), and a decryption factor d that is supposed to be equal to a^x:

- Select a random $r \in \mathbb{Z}_q$ and compute the commitment $(r_0, r_1) = (g^r, a^r)$
- Compute the challenge $e = H(y, d, r_0, r_1)$
- Compute the response $f = r + ex$

The proof is considered to be valid if the following two equations are satisfied:

$$g^f = r_0 y^e \qquad a^f = r_1 d^e$$

and if e can be recomputed correctly. This is supposed to form a proof

$$\mathsf{EqDlogs}(g, a, y, d)$$

Note that the ciphertext's elements a and b have not been included in the hash, so a malicious prover can choose them after computing the challenge. Here is a strategy that a malicious trustee could use to produce a ciphertext that is an encryption of 1 and prove that it is an encryption of something else.

- Select random $r, s, t \in \mathbb{Z}_q$ and set $(r_0, r_1) = (g^r, g^s)$ and $d = g^t$
- Compute the challenge $e = H(y, d, r_0, r_1)$
- Compute the response $f = r + ex$
- Compute $a = g^{(s+et)/f}$

This is enough to make a proof that passes verification, and will prove that d is a valid decryption factor for a with respect to the public key (g, y), even though it is not the case (with overwhelming probability): d is just picked as a random group element. At this stage, we still have the freedom to choose any b we like in order to complete our ciphertext. In particular, we can set $b = y^{(s+et)/f}$, which guarantees that (a, b) is an encryption of 1. Thus we can produce a valid proof that (a, b) decrypts to b/d for arbitrary d, even though it is actually an encryption of 1.

In order to use this to devise a fake PEP, the cheating prover needs to know the randomness used to generate the ciphertexts. Take two ciphertexts (a_1, b_1) and (a_2, b_2) that we know are encryptions of the same plaintext and for which we know the randomness; say, $a_1 = g^{r_1}$ and $a_2 = g^{r_2}$ for some r_1, r_2. We will take their quotient and raise it to a "random" power $\rho = \rho_1 + \rho_2$ as per the PET:

$$(a, b) = \left(\left(\frac{a_1}{a_2} \right)^\rho, \left(\frac{b_1}{b_2} \right)^\rho \right)$$

However, we will cheat to ensure that

$$\rho = \frac{s + et}{f} \frac{1}{r_1 - r_2}$$

We are left with $a = g^{(s+et)/f}$ as per our cheated proof. Because we may freely choose d, we can now produce a valid proof that this decrypts to some value other than 1, and thus a valid proof that the ciphertexts encrypt different plaintexts.

This will not only look perfectly fine, but it will also be infeasible to distinguish these ciphertexts and proofs from those expected in the system, unless we know x of course. This prevents the easy resolution discussed in Sect. 1.1.

In summary, a cheating prover, given two arbitrary equivalent ciphertexts, can forge a proof that they are different. This requires knowing the randomness used to generate the ciphertexts.

3.3   Making Encryptions of Different Messages Look Equivalent

The same issue can be exploited to produce proofs that two ciphertexts encrypting different messages actually encrypt the same message in a way that is undetectable to a public observer. This time, we will exploit the use of the weak Fiat-Shamir transform in the EqDlogs proof in the plaintext equivalence test (Step 4 of Fig. 1). Again, for simplicity, we focus on the setting where we have a single trustee, which is malicious. This trustee can proceed as follows:

-   Select a random encryption of 1 as $c' = (d_1, e_1) = (g^t, y^t)$
-   Produce an EqDlogs proof as follows:
    1. Select random $r, s \in \mathbb{Z}_q$ and set $(r_0, r_1) = (g^r, y^s)$
    2. Compute the challenge $e_p = H(d_1, e_1, r_0, r_1)$
    3. Pick a random response $f \in \mathbb{Z}_q$
    4. Set $R = (d, e) = (g^{(r+te_p)/f}, y^{(s+te_p)/f})$
    and observe that (e_p, f) makes an EqDlogs(d, e, d_1, e_1) proof that passes verification despite the fact that $\log_d(d_1) \neq \log_e(e_1)$ with overwhelming probability.
-   Complete the fake PEP by picking any pair of ciphertexts c_1, c_2 whose quotient is R, and producing a decryption proof for c' in a perfectly honest way.

Since c' is indeed an encryption of 1, the test will conclude that c_1 and c_2 are encryptions of the same plaintext, despite the fact that they encrypt different plaintexts with overwhelming probability. Below are two practical ways to exploit this.

If we are given one ciphertext with unknown randomness c_1 (say on a web bulletin board), we can construct a second ciphertext $c_2 = Rc_1$ so that $c_1/c_2 = R$, where we may freely choose R as above. Colluding tellers could exploit this by adding an extra ballot to the mix, and producing a PEP that falsely claims the targeted vote was cast with a duplicate credential. Note that this would require knowledge of some valid credential. This can be done by a colluding majority of authorities, where a PEP is meant to reveal the cheat, but of course we have broken the PEP [23].

If we know the randomness for both c_1 and c_2 (say z_1 and z_2) encrypting g^{m_1} and g^{m_2} (Civitas uses exponential ElGamal here) so that $c_1 = (g^{z_1}, g^{m_1}g^{xz_1})$ and $c_2 = (g^{z_2}, g^{m_2}g^{xz_2})$, we

1. choose t and set $\rho = \rho_1 + \rho_2 = \frac{r+te_p}{f(z_1-z_2)}$
2. choose f and set $w = \frac{f}{x}\frac{m_1}{m_2}$ (so that $f = wx\frac{m_2}{m_1}$)
3. choose r and set $s = r + w$

Now when we produce the re-randomised quotient $R = (c_1/c_2)^\rho$, we need to satisfy

$$R = \left(g^{\rho(z_1-z_2)}, g^{m_1/m_2}g^{x\rho(z_1-z_2)}\right)$$

We must satisfy $\rho(z_1 - z_2) = (r+te_p)/f$ and $m_1/m_2+x\rho(z_1-z_2) = x(s+te_p)/f$ as per Step 4 of the cheated proof above. The former is satisfied by definition of ρ. For the latter:

$$\frac{m_1}{m_2} + x\rho(z_1 - z_2) = \frac{m_1}{m_2} + x\frac{r+te_p}{wx\frac{m_2}{m_1}} \qquad \text{(Eqn 1)}$$

$$= \frac{m_1}{m_2}\left(1 + \frac{r+te_p}{w}\right)$$

$$= \frac{m_1}{m_2}\frac{r+w+te_p}{w}$$

$$= \frac{m_1}{m_2}(s+te_p)\frac{x}{f}\frac{m_2}{m_1} \qquad \text{(Eqns 2, 3)}$$

$$= x(s+te_p)/f$$

Colluding tellers could exploit this in the same way as the previous attack, but without needing to add an extra ballot to the mix.

3.4   Summary and Implications of These Vulnerabilities

If every party performing the PET colludes, they can

– produce a false proof that any two ciphertexts are equivalent, without needing to know the randomness used to generate them.

This problem can be prevented by adding a check for the trivial ciphertext to the verification algorithm.

Using the Fiat-Shamir weakness, they can additionally

– produce a false proof that two equivalent ciphertexts are different, if they know the randomness used to generate them (Sect. 3.2)
– produce a false proof that two ciphertexts are equivalent (Sect. 3.3), if
  • they know the randomness used to generate them, or
  • they can generate one of them (in which case there is no need to know the randomness of the other).

These further attacks will produce plausible non-trivial ciphertexts.

4   Why this Undermines Universal Verifiability in JCJ/Civitas and Other Protocols

Universal verifiability (UV) means that any observer can confirm an election's tally matches its cast votes; in particular, any voter could perform this verification [9]. See [1,3,22] for early work on this concept.

If the verification specification does not consider the case where all trustees of the PEP collude to produce a false outcome, then only the trustees can verify the plaintext equivalence proof — since they know whether they colluded. Therefore, missing this step results in a scheme whose tallying phase is not universally verifiable.

4.1   JCJ/Civitas

We investigate whether Civitas [8], an implementation of a well-known voting protocol we refer to as JCJ [18], correctly performs the check for a trivial ciphertext in its PEPs. The key idea behind the JCJ protocol is to assign each voter an encrypted credential. To provide coercion resistance, a voter can provide the coercer with an invalid credential, and the coercer cannot tell that the credential is not valid. Voters submit their encrypted votes and encrypted credentials, together with proofs of plaintext knowledge, to a bulletin board. To tally votes, the tabulation tellers:

1. check the proofs of plaintext knowledge for submitted votes,
2. identify (using a PEP) and exclude any votes with duplicate credentials,
3. perform a cryptographic mix on the encrypted votes,
4. identify (using a PEP) and exclude any votes cast with a credential that does not match any on the list of valid credentials, and
5. decrypt the resulting list of valid votes (but not the corresponding credentials).

We can immediately see that a flawed PEP could be abused by the tabulation tellers to cheat in the election.

In its technical report [8], Civitas explicitly claims universal verifiability regardless of whether the tellers collude on page 10: "Trust Assumption 6. There exists at least one honest tabulation teller. If all the tellers were corrupted, then the adversary could trivially violate coercion resistance by decrypting credentials and votes. This assumption is not needed for verifiability, even if all the tellers collude or are corrupted—the proofs posted by tellers during tabulation will reveal any attempt to cheat". Its verification specification, page 43 of the technical report reproduced as Fig. 1 here, does not mention checking for a $(1,1)$ ciphertext which is necessary for this property.

How did this happen? The JCJ paper has a proof of universal verifiability of the overall voting protocol that is not exactly wrong, but leaves a trap for the unwary implementer. It says of their PETs that "we model the ideal properties of the primitive as an oracle [...] with the property of public verifiability",[3] citing the Jakobsson-Juels paper [17]. However, the protocol in that paper does not have the UV property, and does not claim it, proving instead that it is sound under the assumption that at least one participant is honest. (It also does not explicitly mention that even with this assumption, the protocol has a negligible but non-zero soundness error).

JCJ also cites [19], which in its Sect. 4.4 describes another PET, also with the explicit assumption that fewer than a threshold of trustees are compromised; however, this paper correctly points out that the protocol has a negligible but non-zero soundness error. So if JCJ were implemented using a PEP with universal verifiability, then (we believe) the overall protocol would also be UV, but since its only cited example is a PET that is not UV, a natural implementation risks failing UV—as indeed the Civitas implementation does.

The incorrect PEP together with the Civitas scheme's weak Fiat-Shamir transform allows various attacks that undermine universal verifiability for JCJ, such as:

- falsely proving that two different credentials are duplicates, hence excluding them at Step 2,
- falsely proving that a valid credential is different from everything on the list of valid credentials, hence excluding it at Step 4,
- falsely proving that an invalid credential is equivalent to something on the list of valid credentials, hence including it at Step 4.

4.2 A Linear-Time Enhancement to JCJ

In [23], an enhancement to the JCJ protocol is proposed whereby tallying can be done in linear time instead of a worst-case quadratic time. They "assume the application of publicly verifiable group threshold mechanisms whenever registering or tallying authorities perform joint computations", which could be taken to mean that our attack is outside their threat model; however this seems at odds with the notion of universal verifiability, and the majority of their discussion of security properties relies on that of JCJ. So the protocol is not broken as such, but does lay a similar trap for the unsuspecting reader: they are referred to JCJ, which claims UV but refers the reader to Mix & Match.

4.3 Introduction to Cryptography Textbook

The textbook *Introduction to Cryptography: Principles and Applications* (3rd edition) [10] discusses distributed plaintext equivalence tests in Sect. 4.7, basing their discussion on JCJ (and referencing Mix & Match). They unfortunately make the same oversight, commenting that "the test may give a wrong result only if $z = \sum_{i=1}^{n} z_i = [0]$" and that "this happens only with the negligible probability $1/q$", not accounting for the case where every party colludes. When

---

[3] Public verifiability is a synonym for UV.

discussing *privacy* of the distributed PEP, they explain "the privacy of $\mathcal{P}k$-encrypted ciphertexts and the threshold decryption are guaranteed if at least t of the n parties are honest and no coalition of t parties behaves dishonestly", but do not discuss the implications of dishonest parties on the *integrity* of the proof.

4.4 Pretty Good Democracy

Pretty Good Democracy [15,21] also uses Plaintext Equivalence Tests in a critical part of the tallying process, claiming that Counted-as-Cast and Tallied Correctly "can be verified from the Bulletin Board using standard techniques, which do not require trusting any of the authorities". But it refers only to the PETs of [17], which do require trusting at least one authority to be honest. A collusion of all tallying authorities could fake a match with a correct vote code, thus tricking a voter into thinking that the vote had been properly received when in fact an invalid vote had been substituted.

4.5 Selections

The Selections protocol [7] falls victim to a similar trap. It focuses on over-the-shoulder coercion-resistance, meaning that an adversary who is present during vote casting cannot coerce the voter. To achieve this, the paper mentions that the voter must trust at least one "registrar". However, it

1. explicitly claims end-to-end verifiability;
2. mentions the protocol can work with distributed registrars; and
3. clarifies its trust assumption by saying the trusted registrar must not collude with a coercer, but *may still misbehave in any other regard.*

In particular, the trustees that perform the tallying are not required to be honest, and the security assumptions for them are left unclear—they may or may not be the same entities as the registrars.

The tallying protocol (Algorithm 3 in the paper) uses a plaintext equality test among tallying trustees, and explicitly refers the reader to Mix & Match despite the lack of universal verifiability.

4.6 Cobra

The Cobra protocol [11] has the same problem as Selections because it is based on it, claiming to have universally verifiable proofs yet referring the reader to Juels and Jakobsson for a plaintext equality test.

4.7 Caveat Coercitor

Caveat Coercitor [12] aims to provide a new property called *coercion evidence* by giving voters an opportunity to signal that they have been coerced. A voter can cancel their vote (assuming it has been cast in a way that did not represent their true wishes) by simply re-voting with the same credential but a different vote. This nullifies the vote and is interpreted as evidence of coercion. The talliers produce a tally showing which votes were cast with repeated credentials, for which they use PEPs. Those that are duplicates are not included in the final count. The exact protocol is similar to JCJ, except that when a credential is used twice to cast the same vote it is included (once). The talliers:

1. check the proofs of plaintext knowledge for submitted votes;
2. identify (using a PET) any votes with duplicate credentials:
   (a) identify (using a PET) whether all the corresponding votes are equal, in which case one is included;
   (b) or, if there are at least two different votes cast with the same credential, exclude them all.
3. perform a cryptographic mix on the encrypted votes;
4. identify (using a PET) and exclude any votes cast with a credential that does not match any from the list of valid credentials; and
5. decrypt the resulting list of valid votes (but not the corresponding credentials).

The idea is that coerced voters give up their vote, but that "unforgeable evidence about the degree of coercion that took place is included in the election output". If the talliers can fake apparently-equal PEPs for credentials or votes that are actually different, there are a number of ways they can cheat.

- In Step 2 they can take two unique credentials and fake a proof that they are equal, thus nullifying one of them (if the votes are equal) or both (if the votes are different).
- In Step 2a they can take two different votes cast with the same credential and fake a proof that the votes are equal, thus getting one of them included when both should be excluded. This is particularly important because this is exactly the case that Caveat Coercitor is designed to flag as coercion and exclude—instead, a faked PEP allows it to be treated as a repeat-casting of the same vote, so a vote is accepted and no coercion is flagged.
- Like JCJ/Civitas, in Step 4 Caveat Coercitor uses PEPs to test whether a vote's credential is equal to one of those on the list of valid credentials, so just as in JCJ/Civitas, a faked PEP for equality again allows corrupt authorities to stuff the ballot by pretending that an invalid credential is valid.

It is not entirely clear whether the possibility for all talliers to collude and fake PEPs is included in the trust model of Caveat Coercitor. The paper refers to the PETs as proofs, (petproof), and does not give an explicit construction, but cites the distributed-trust-based test of [17].

On p. 371 (Sec B) it says "We assume that one mix server in M, one tallier in T and the voting machines are honest". The talliers correspond to the authorities for the PET, so if they are assuming that at least one tallier is honest then our attack is not within the security model. However, the paper in several places claims universal/public verifiability, such as "The talliers will execute an algorithm whose output can be used by any external observer to determine the amount of coercion", (p. 371) and "Observers can perform universal and eligibility verification, because the computations of algorithm 3 are publicly verifiable", (p. 375). The crucial Lemma is Lemma 4, which considers whether the set of accepted votes corresponds correctly to the set of those that were cast with a unique credential or a repeated credential for the same vote. The proof (in the Appendix) simply treats the PETs as perfect and does not mention the honest tallier. The paper concludes by saying that "A major feature of the system is that the degree of coercion that actually took place is publicly verifiable". The assumptions and claims are thus somewhat ambiguous and inconsistent.

In summary, the degree of coercion is not universally verifiable because without at least one trustworthy tallier, evidence of coercion can be hidden.

4.8   Universally Verifiable Auctions

Several cryptographic auction protocols also use the PET from [17] while claiming universal verifiability, and therefore are are vulnerable to the same attack. In a verifiable auction there are n players who place a secret bid, and engage in an interaction to determine which was the highest bid (and who placed it) with convincing evidence that this was done correctly. There are two distinct settings: one where this evidence is enough for *each player* to be sure of the result, and one where it is enough for *any public observer* to verify the result.

For example, the scheme of Abe et al. [2] is claimed to be UV but uses the Mix & Match PET, so it cannot have this property. The protocol of Bradford et al. [6] also claims UV, citing Mix & Match for its PET as well as [16], an almost-identical PET (which is also not UV). Most notably, Quaglia et al. [20] present a method for converting a verifiable election protocol into a verifiable auction protocol; they use Helios as a case study, in which a plaintext equivalence proof is used to construct a universally verifiable auction from mixnet tallying. However, they once again cite Mix & Match as their PET, so fail to achieve UV.

5   Correcting the Problems to Achieve UV

5.1   The Fiat-Shamir Transform

When using the Fiat-Shamir transform to convert an interactive zero knowledge proof to a non-interactive equivalent, it is crucial that one includes the full statement to be proved in the hash [4]. Focusing on Civitas, for the decryption proof it uses $H(y, d, g^r, a^r)$ when it should also include a, b, b^r. For the equality of discrete logs it uses $H(v, w, a, b)$ (where $a = f^z$ and $b = h^z$ for a random factor z) when it should also include f, h. Note that these inclusions break the attacks outlined above.

5.2 The Correct Plaintext Equivalence Proof

It is easy to fix the weakness in the distributed PET by simply checking that the ciphertext is not $(1, 1)$. However, this check is not present in either the original Mix & Match paper by Jakobsson & Juels (which does not claim UV), nor JCJ (which assumes UV and points to Mix & Match), nor the Civitas verification code (for which the TR claims UV). We outline the setting of the Civitas PET (a direct implementation of the Mix & Match PET) below.

Let $x_i \leftarrow \mathbb{Z}_q^*$ be the private key shares and $y_i = g^{x_i} \bmod p$ be the public key shares such that

$$Y = \prod_i y_i \bmod p = \prod_i g^{x_i} \bmod p = g^{\sum_i x_i \bmod q} \bmod p$$

is the public key. We assume $\mathsf{EqDlogs}(d, e, x, y)$ is an existentially sound[4] noninteractive zero knowledge proof that $\mathsf{dlog}_d x = \mathsf{dlog}_e y$. We stress that $\mathsf{EqDlogs}$ as presented in [8] is **not** existentially sound due to the issue in its implementation of the Fiat-Shamir transform. However, [4,5] give an argument that a correctly implemented transform including all inputs to the protocol in the hash function results in an existentially sound version.

We are given as public input ciphertexts

$$c_j = (a_j, b_j) = (g^{r_j} \bmod p, g^{m_j} Y^{r_j} \bmod p) \text{ for } j \in \{1, 2\}$$

The goal is to prove in a universally-verifiable manner whether $m_1 = m_2 \bmod q$.

Let $(d, e) = (a_1/a_2, b_1/b_2)$. Each teller TT_i is supposed to randomly choose $z_i \in \mathbb{Z}_q^*$, calculate their share $(d_i, e_i) = (d^{z_i}, e^{z_i})$, and publish a commitment $\mathsf{Commit}(d_i, e_i)$.[5] A distributed decryption is then performed on c', where each TT_i publishes their share $a_i' = a'^{x_i} \bmod p$ and a proof $\mathsf{EqDlogs}(g, a', y_i, a_i')$, guaranteeing they faithfully calculated a_i' from a private key share x_i.

Under the assumption that the Fiat-Shamir weakness is addressed (see [4] for details on this), we present a proof that the PET in Civitas is universally verifiable when a check for trivial ciphertexts are added, following the approach of [5] (sections 19–20). The corrected protocol is shown in Protocol 1, in which $\mathcal{P}$ is the prover (playing the role of all tellers simultaneously since we allow the possibility of collusion) and $\mathcal{V}$ is the public verifier. We will construct the protocol to allow both proofs of both equality and inequality; this will make the argument a little more complex, but much more general.

Protocol 1. PlaintextEquivalenceProof
Setup: public ElGamal parameters $(\mathbb{G}, p, q, g)$; public key shares y_i for $i \in [n]$ (where n is the number of tellers). Corresponding private key shares x_i for $i \in [n]$.

---

[4] Also called *adaptively sound* in other literature.
[5] The commitment is elided from Protocol 1, as it is not relevant in the case that every teller colludes.

1. $\mathcal{P}$ *sends ciphertexts* $c_j = (a_j, b_j)$ *for* $j \in \{1, 2\}$ *to* $\mathcal{V}$.
2. $\mathcal{P}, \mathcal{V}$ *calculate* $d = a_1/a_2, e = b_1/b_2$.
3. $\mathcal{P}$ *sends* $(d_i, e_i),$ EqDlogs(d, e, d_i, e_i) *to* $\mathcal{V}$.
4. $\mathcal{P}, \mathcal{V}$ *calculate* $c' = (a', b') = (\prod_i d_i, \prod_i e_i)$.
5. $\mathcal{P}$ *sends* $a_i',$ EqDlogs(g, a', y_i, a_i') *to* $\mathcal{V}$ *with a bit* IsEq *corresponding to whether the proof is of equality (*IsEq $= 1$*) or inequality (*IsEq $= 0$*).*
6. $\mathcal{V}$ *calculates*

$$M = \frac{b'}{\prod_i a_i'} \bmod p$$

7. $\mathcal{V}$ *verifies the* EqDlogs *ZKPs (as will be made precise below with* Check$_{EqD}$*)*
8. *If* IsEq $= 1, \mathcal{V}$ *outputs* $\begin{cases} \text{accept} & \text{if } M = 1, \text{ the ZKPs pass verification, and } c' \neq (1, 1) \\ \text{reject} & \text{otherwise} \end{cases}$

   If IsEq $= 0, \mathcal{V}$ *outputs* $\begin{cases} \text{accept} & \text{if } M \neq 1 \text{ and the ZKPs pass verification} \\ \text{reject} & \text{otherwise} \end{cases}$

We show that the combination of ZKP facts and equations checked directly by $\mathcal{V}$ implies that the two plaintexts are equal (mod q).

Lemma 1. *In the setting of Protocol 1,* $m_1 = m_2 \bmod q$ *if and only if* $M = 1$, $c' \neq (1, 1)$, dlog$_d d_i =$ dlog$_e e_i$, *and* dlog$_g y_i =$ dlog$_{a'} a_i'$ *for all* $i \in [n]$.

Proof. With the setup done, an observer may compute (explicitly labelling modulo operations):

$$c' = (a', b') = \left(\prod_i d^{z_i}, \prod_i e^{z_i} \right) = (d^{z \bmod q}, e^{z \bmod q}) \text{ where } z = \sum_i z_i$$

$$= \left(\left(\frac{a_1}{a_2} \right)^{z \bmod q}, \left(\frac{b_1}{b_2} \right)^{z \bmod q} \right)$$

$$= \left(\left(\frac{g^{r_1}}{g^{r_2}} \right)^{z \bmod q} \bmod p, \left(\frac{g^{m_1} y^{r_1}}{g^{m_2} y^{r_2}} \right)^{z \bmod q} \bmod p \right)$$

as well as

$$A' = \prod_i a_i' = \prod_i \left(\frac{g^{r_1}}{g^{r_2}} \right)^{z x_i \bmod q} \pmod{p}$$

$$= \left(\frac{g^{r_1}}{g^{r_2}} \right)^{z \sum_i x_i \bmod q} = \left(\frac{Y^{r_1}}{Y^{r_2}} \right)^{z \bmod q} \pmod{p}$$

and thereby recover

$$M = \frac{b'}{A'} = \frac{\left(\frac{g^{m_1}}{g^{m_2}} \frac{Y^{r_1}}{Y^{r_2}} \right)^{z \bmod q}}{\left(\frac{Y^{r_1}}{Y^{r_2}} \right)^{z \bmod q}} = \left(\frac{g^{m_1}}{g^{m_2}} \right)^{z \bmod q} \pmod{p}$$

$$= 1 \text{ if and only if } \frac{g^{m_1}}{g^{m_2}} = 1 \bmod p \text{ or } z = 0 \bmod q$$

In particular, note that if $z = 0 \bmod q$, $c' = (1,1)$ which trivially decrypts to 1 regardless of whether $m_1 = m_2$.

5.3 Security Proof for the Corrected PEP

We follow [5] for formalising the security requirements on the ZKPs, as well as the plaintext equivalence proof system itself. The general idea is to decide what a "proof" should mean mathematically: a statement whose truth can be checked by a public observer. We will argue that any efficient adversary should have only a negligible probability of forging a proof for a false statement.

Definition 1. Non-interactive proof system
*Let $\mathcal{R} \subseteq \mathcal{X} \times \mathcal{Y}$ be an effective relation, where if $(x,y) \in \mathcal{R}$, y is a statement and x is a witness for the statement. A **non-interactive proof system** for $\mathcal{R}$ is a pair of algorithms (Gen, Check) where*

1. *Gen is an efficient probabilistic algorithm that is invoked as $\pi \leftarrow_{\mathcal{R}} \mathsf{Gen}(x,y)$, where $(x,y) \in \mathcal{R}$, and π belongs to some proof space $\mathcal{PS}$;*
2. *Check is an efficient deterministic algorithm that is invoked as $\mathsf{Check}(y, \pi)$, where $y \in \mathcal{Y}$ and $\pi \in \mathcal{PS}$; the output of Check is either accept or reject. If $\mathsf{Check}(y, \pi) = \mathsf{accept}$, we say π is a valid proof for y.*

We will assume that EqDlogs is corrected to satisfy this requirement. Given public input f, h, v, w we would like to prove that we know x such that $v = f^x$ and $w = h^x$. After choosing a random z, the statement (for prime p, q) is $(p, q, f, h, v, w, a = f^z \bmod p, b = h^z \bmod p)$ with witness x. We will publish $c = H(f, h, v, w, a, b)$ and $r = z + cx \bmod q$. We then have algorithms

- Gen_{EqD} which maps $(x, p, q, f, h, v, w, a, b)$ to $\pi = (c, r)$
- $\mathsf{Check}_{EqC}(p, q, f, h, v, w, a, b, \pi)$ which outputs accept if and only if $f^r = av^c \bmod p$ and $h^r = bw^c \bmod p$ (otherwise, it outputs reject)

From here we will use $\mathsf{EqDlogs}(f, h, v, w)$ less formally to mean "the proof output by $\mathsf{Gen}_{EqD}(x, p, q, f, h, v, w, a, b)$" where context makes x, p, q clear.

PlaintextEquivalenceProof also satisfies this definition: given ciphertexts $c_1 = (a_1, b_1)$, $c_2 = (a_2, b_2)$, ElGamal parameters $(\mathbb{G}, p, q, g)$, and public key shares y_i, the statement is

$$(\mathbb{G}, p, q, g, c_1, c_2, \{y_i\}_{i \in [n]}, \mathsf{IsEq})$$

with witnesses $\{x_i\}_{i \in [n]}$. The algorithms are:

- Gen_{PEP} which maps $(\{x_i\}_{i \in [n]}, \mathbb{G}, p, q, g, c_1, c_2, \{y_i\}_{i \in [n]}, \mathsf{IsEq})$ to

$$\pi = \{(d_i, e_i, a'_i, \mathsf{EqDlogs}(d, e, d_i, e_i), \mathsf{EqDlogs}(g, a', y_i, a'_i))\}_{i \in [n]}$$

- $\mathsf{Check}_{PEP}(\mathbb{G}, p, q, g, c_1, c_2, \{y_i\}_{i \in [n]}, \mathsf{IsEq}, \pi)$ which is as per Steps 2, 4, 6, 7, 8 of Protocol 1, with additional checks on the ElGamal parameters:
  1. Check that $(\prod_i d_i \bmod p, \prod_i e_i \bmod p) \neq (1,1)$.

2. Check that $d = a_1/a_2$ and $e = b_1/b_2$ in $\mathsf{EqDlogs}(d, e, d_i, e_i)$, and that it is a valid proof.
3. Check that g has order q in $\mathbb{G}$, that $a' = \prod_i d_i$ in $\mathsf{EqDlogs}(g, a', y_i, a_i')$, and that it is a valid proof.
4. If $\mathsf{IsEq} = 1$, output $\begin{cases} \text{accept} & \text{if the above checks succeed and } \prod_i \frac{e_i}{a_i'} = 1 \bmod p \\ \text{reject} & \text{otherwise} \end{cases}$

   If $\mathsf{IsEq} = 0$, output $\begin{cases} \text{accept} & \text{if the above checks succeed and } \prod_i \frac{e_i}{a_i'} \neq 1 \bmod p \\ \text{reject} & \text{otherwise} \end{cases}$

The requirement we will use for universal verifiability is that of *existential soundness*:[6] the adversary who produces our proof should not be able to falsify a proof even if they freely choose all of the parameters, given a verifier who holds only public knowledge [5, Definition 20.2]. If we can achieve this, then we satisfy universal verifiability.

Definition 2. *Existential soundness*
*Let $\Phi = (\mathsf{Gen}, \mathsf{Check})$ be a non-interactive proof system for $\mathcal{R} \subseteq \mathcal{X} \times \mathcal{Y}$ with proof space $\mathcal{PS}$. To attack Φ, an adversary $\mathcal{A}$ outputs a statement $y \in \mathcal{Y}$ and a proof $\pi \in \mathcal{PS}$. We say that the adversary wins the game if $\mathsf{Check}(y, \pi) = \mathsf{accept}$ but there is no witness x such that $(x, y) \in \mathcal{R}$. We define $\mathcal{A}$'s advantage with respect to Φ, denoted $\mathsf{niESadv}[\mathcal{A}, \Phi]$, as the probability that $\mathcal{A}$ wins the game. Φ is **existentially sound** if for all efficient adversaries $\mathcal{A}$, $\mathsf{niESadv}[\mathcal{A}, \Phi]$ is negligible.*

Theorem 1. *Assume $\mathsf{EqDlogs}$ is an existentially sound non-interactive proof system. For all efficient adversaries $\mathcal{A}$ with security parameter k, suppose that for some negligible $\varepsilon(k)$, we have: $\mathsf{niESadv}[\mathcal{A}, \mathsf{EqDlogs}] < \varepsilon(k)$. Then $\mathsf{PlaintextEquivalenceProof}$ is existentially sound.*

Proof. Consider an efficient adversary $\mathcal{A}$ with security parameter k for whom

$$\mathsf{niESadv}[\mathcal{A}, \mathsf{PlaintextEquivalenceProof}] = P(k)$$

Suppose $\mathcal{A}$ outputs a proof π for the false statement $(\mathbb{G}, p, q, g, c_1, c_2, \mathsf{IsEq})$.

Case 1: $\mathsf{IsEq} = 1$. Then if $\mathsf{Check}_{PEP}(\mathbb{G}, p, q, g, c_1, c_2, \mathsf{IsEq}, \pi)$ outputs accept, by definition $m_1 \neq m_2 \bmod q$ and $\frac{g^{m_1}}{g^{m_2}} = 1 \bmod p$.

Case 2: $\mathsf{IsEq} = 0$. Then if $\mathsf{Check}_{PEP}(\mathbb{G}, p, q, g, c_1, c_2, \mathsf{IsEq}, \pi)$ outputs accept, by definition $m_1 = m_2 \bmod q$ and $\frac{g^{m_1}}{g^{m_2}} \neq 1 \bmod p$.

In either case $c' \neq (1, 1)$, and $\mathsf{EqDlogs}(d, e, d_i, e_i)$, $\mathsf{EqDlogs}(g, a', y_i, a_i')$ are valid proofs. We checked that $\langle g \rangle = q$, so Lemma 1 implies (at least) one of the following two statements is false for some $i \in [n]$:

(i) $\mathsf{dlog}_d d_i = \mathsf{dlog}_e e_i$
(ii) $\mathsf{dlog}_g y_i = \mathsf{dlog}_{a'} a_i'$

---

[6] Also called *adaptive soundness*.

So $\mathcal{A}$ must have cheated in at least one instance of EqDlogs. We can now construct an adversary $\mathcal{B}$ (with security parameter k) to defeat EqDlogs. $\mathcal{B}$ runs $\mathcal{A}$ to obtain two proofs $\mathsf{EqDlogs}(d, e, d_i, e_i)$, $\mathsf{EqDlogs}(g, a', y_i, a_i')$. At least one is valid; we do not know which one, so $\mathcal{B}$ tosses a coin. On heads, $\mathcal{B}$ chooses $\mathsf{EqDlogs}(d, e, d_i, e_i)$, and on tails it chooses $\mathsf{EqDlogs}(g, a', y_i, a_i')$. $\mathcal{B}$ then outputs the chosen statement and proof. In this way, $\mathcal{B}$ wins with probability at least $P(k)/2$.

Therefore given that an efficient adversary attacking EqDlogs has advantage at most ε, an efficient adversary attacking PlaintextEquivalenceProof has advantage at most 2ε. $\qquad\square$

6 Discussion and Conclusion

We have found a subtle misalignment of assumptions in a very influential paper (624 citations): they require a PET to have universal verifiability, but reference only PETs that do not have this property. As with many cryptographic protocols, this small unmet assumption completely undermines one of the protocol's primary security goals, in this case universal verifiability. This oversight affects a large number of follow-on protocols in exactly the same way, hence undermining their universal verifiability too. Furthermore, the issue is not unique to the electronic voting domain, but also appears in verifiable auction schemes. To our knowledge, other work has not noticed this important subtlety.

Although our most detailed analysis describes errors in the Civitas implementation, this is primarily because Civitas is the only one of the affected papers to provide a detailed technical report and code, rather than because the other projects understood the subtle assumption better. Comments in other papers suggest that, if the authors had implemented their designs, they would likely have made the same confusion between PETs with PEPs. This is further demonstrated by their reference to the PET of [17], which lacks the crucial property. Fortunately, the mistake is easily rectifiable—but if the Fiat-Shamir transform is used improperly by a protocol, a related attack opens up to catastrophically undermine any plaintext equivalence proofs used.

The discovery has significant parallels with Bernhard et al.'s discovery of errors in the implementation of the Fiat-Shamir heuristic that undermined soundness in the context of Helios [4], and again in the SwissPost-Scytl sVote scheme [13,14]. This suggests that errors of this nature are not unique to the schemes discussed in this paper, but may be indicative of a more systemic problem in the misalignment of assumptions between separate work.

Acknowledgements. The research carried out by O. Pereira was partially supported by the F.N.R.S. PDR SeVoTe.

References

1. Abe, M.: Universally verifiable mix-net with verification work independent of the number of mix-servers. In: Nyberg, K. (ed.) EUROCRYPT 1998. LNCS, vol. 1403, pp. 437–447. Springer, Heidelberg (1998). https://doi.org/10.1007/BFb0054144

2. Abe, M., Suzuki, K.: M+ 1-st price auction using homomorphic encryption. In: Naccache, D., Paillier, P. (eds.) PKC 2002. LNCS, vol. 2274, pp. 115–124. Springer, Heidelberg (2002). https://doi.org/10.1007/3-540-45664-3_8
3. Benaloh, J.: Verifiable secret-ballot elections (1988)
4. Bernhard, D., Pereira, O., Warinschi, B.: How not to prove yourself: pitfalls of the Fiat-Shamir heuristic and applications to helios. In: Wang, X., Sako, K. (eds.) ASIACRYPT 2012. LNCS, vol. 7658, pp. 626–643. Springer, Heidelberg (2012). https://doi.org/10.1007/978-3-642-34961-4_38
5. Boneh, D., Shoup, V.: A graduate course in applied cryptography. Draft 0.5 (2020)
6. Bradford, P.G., Park, S., Rothkopf, M.H., Park, H.: Protocol completion incentive problems in cryptographic vickrey auctions. Electron. Commer. Res. **8**(1–2), 57–77 (2008)
7. Clark, J., Hengartner, U.: Selections: internet voting with over-the-shoulder coercion-resistance. In: Danezis, G. (ed.) FC 2011. LNCS, vol. 7035, pp. 47–61. Springer, Heidelberg (2012). https://doi.org/10.1007/978-3-642-27576-0_4
8. Clarkson, M.R., Chong, S., Myers, A.C.: Civitas: Toward a secure voting system. In: 2008 IEEE Symposium on Security and Privacy (SP 2008), pp. 354–368. IEEE (2008)
9. Cortier, V., Galindo, D., Küsters, R., Mueller, J., Truderung, T.: SoK: verifiability notions for e-voting protocols. In: 2016 IEEE Symposium on Security and Privacy (SP), pp. 779–798. IEEE (2016)
10. Delfs, H., Knebl, H.: Introduction to Cryptography, vol. 3. Springer, Heidelberg (2015). https://doi.org/10.1007/978-3-662-47974-2
11. Essex, A., Clark, J., Hengartner, U.: Cobra: toward concurrent ballot authorization for internet voting. EVT/WOTE **12** (2012)
12. Grewal, G.S., Ryan, M.D., Bursuc, S., Ryan, P.Y.: Caveat coercitor: coercion-evidence in electronic voting. In: 2013 IEEE Symposium on Security and Privacy, pp. 367–381. IEEE (2013)
13. Haenni, R.: Swiss Post Public Intrusion Test: Undetectable attack against vote integrity and secrecy, March 2019. https://e-voting.bfh.ch/app/download/7833162361/PIT2.pdf?t=1552395691
14. Haines, T., Lewis, S.J., Pereira, O., Teague, V.: How not to prove your election outcome. In: 2020 IEEE Symposium on Security and Privacy (SP), pp. 784–800 (2019)
15. Heather, J., Ryan, P.Y.A., Teague, V.: Pretty good democracy for more expressive voting schemes. In: Gritzalis, D., Preneel, B., Theoharidou, M. (eds.) ESORICS 2010. LNCS, vol. 6345, pp. 405–423. Springer, Heidelberg (2010). https://doi.org/10.1007/978-3-642-15497-3_25
16. Hevia, A., Kiwi, M.: Electronic jury voting protocols. Theoret. Comput. Sci. **321**(1), 73–94 (2004)
17. Jakobsson, M., Juels, A.: Mix and match: secure function evaluation via ciphertexts. In: Okamoto, T. (ed.) ASIACRYPT 2000. LNCS, vol. 1976, pp. 162–177. Springer, Heidelberg (2000). https://doi.org/10.1007/3-540-44448-3_13
18. Juels, A., Catalano, D., Jakobsson, M.: Coercion-resistant electronic elections. In: Chaum, D., et al. (eds.) Towards Trustworthy Elections. LNCS, vol. 6000, pp. 37–63. Springer, Heidelberg (2010). https://doi.org/10.1007/978-3-642-12980-3_2
19. MacKenzie, P., Shrimpton, T., Jakobsson, M.: Threshold password-authenticated key exchange. In: Yung, M. (ed.) CRYPTO 2002. LNCS, vol. 2442, pp. 385–400. Springer, Heidelberg (2002). https://doi.org/10.1007/3-540-45708-9_25
20. Quaglia, E.A., Smyth, B.: Secret, verifiable auctions from elections. Theoret. Comput. Sci. **730**, 44–92 (2018)

21. Ryan, P.Y.A., Teague, V.: Pretty good democracy. In: Christianson, B., Malcolm, J.A., Matyáš, V., Roe, M. (eds.) Security Protocols 2009. LNCS, vol. 7028, pp. 111–130. Springer, Heidelberg (2013). https://doi.org/10.1007/978-3-642-36213-2_15

22. Sako, K., Kilian, J.: Receipt-free mix-type voting scheme. In: Guillou, L.C., Quisquater, J.-J. (eds.) EUROCRYPT 1995. LNCS, vol. 921, pp. 393–403. Springer, Heidelberg (1995). https://doi.org/10.1007/3-540-49264-X_32

23. Spycher, O., Koenig, R., Haenni, R., Schläpfer, M.: A new approach towards coercion-resistant remote E-voting in linear time. In: Danezis, G. (ed.) FC 2011. LNCS, vol. 7035, pp. 182–189. Springer, Heidelberg (2012). https://doi.org/10.1007/978-3-642-27576-0_15

Hardware Fingerprinting for the ARINC 429 Avionic Bus

Nimrod Gilboa-Markevich and Avishai Wool[✉]

School of Electrical Engineering, Tel Aviv University, 69978 Ramat Aviv, Israel
gmnimrod@gmail.com, yash@eng.tau.ac.il

Abstract. ARINC 429 is the most common data bus in use today in civil avionics. Despite this, the protocol lacks any form of source authentication. A technician with physical access to the bus is able to replace a transmitter by a rogue device, and receivers will accept its malicious data as they have no method of verifying the authenticity of messages.

Updating the protocol would close off security loopholes in new aircrafts but would require thousands of airplanes to be modified. An interim solution is required. We propose a hardware fingerprinting method for the ARINC 429 data bus, and analyze its performance in a sender authentication setting. Our approach relies on the observation that changes in hardware, such as replacing a transmitter or a receiver with a rogue one, modify the electric signal of the transmission.

In this paper we explore the feasibility of designing an intrusion detection system based on hardware fingerprinting. Our analysis includes both a theoretical Markov-chain model and an extensive empirical evaluation. For this purpose, we collected a data corpus of ARINC 429 data traces, which may be of independent interest since, to the best of our knowledge, no public corpus is available.

In our experiments, we show that it is feasible for an intrusion detection system to achieve a near-zero false alarms per second, while detecting a rogue transmitter in under 50 ms, and detecting a rogue receiver in under 3 s. This would allow a rogue component installed by a malicious technician to be detected during the pre-flight checks, well before the aircraft takes off. This is made possible due to the fact that we rely on the analog properties, and not on the digital content of the transmissions. Thus we are able to detect a hardware switch as soon as it occurs, even if the data that is being transmitted is completely normal.

1 Introduction

1.1 Background

ARINC 429 [1] is a prominent standard for wired intra-vehicle communication in civil aviation released in 1977. Most active and retired airplanes contain ARINC buses [14], connecting the many digital systems that are necessary for the operation of an aircraft: sensors, radars, engines, cockpit controls and more.

© Springer Nature Switzerland AG 2020
L. Chen et al. (Eds.): ESORICS 2020, LNCS 12309, pp. 42–62, 2020.
https://doi.org/10.1007/978-3-030-59013-0_3

Safety and reliability are key objectives in avionics [14]. Security on the other hand, as we understand it today, was not a primary concern. ARINC 429 was designed without any security features, such as encryption or source authentication, that are perceived today as essential to secure communication. Over the last 10 years, systems of the same vintage have been attacked (cf. [9,20,22]). A recent study [28] has found that attacks on wireless safety-related avionics systems have the potential of disrupting ongoing flights. In contrast to advancements in cybersecurity, there were no major revisions of the ARINC 429 standard since 1980 [29]. There is a successor to ARINC 429 - AFDX. However, it is likely that ARINC 429 will continue to serve for many years in older aircrafts and alongside the new protocol in newer aircrafts [14].

A major concern is that ARINC 429 has no mechanism for source authentication. One way to add authentication without an industry-wide update of the protocol is to implement it at a higher layer of the protocol stack. Unfortunately, in ARINC 429 there are only 19 data bits in a message. This is typically insufficient for a secure implementation of message code authentication (MAC).

Another solution is to employ an intrusion detection system (IDS) to retrofit security into the existing protocol. We propose an IDS that relies on hardware fingerprints, i.e, on characteristics of the electrical signal, in order to identify changes in bus topology and connected hardware.

1.2   Related Work

To the best of our knowledge, this is the first academic research to suggest hardware fingerprinting in ARINC 429. However, hardware fingerprinting was explored previously in a number of different domains: Ethernet [15,19,30]; wireless radio [5,12,31]; smartphone accelerometers, gyroscopes, microphones and cameras [10,11].

One domain in particular interests us: controller area network (CAN bus) [27], the most commonly used standard for in-vehicle communication in the automotive industry. ARINC 429 and CAN bus have a lot in common: Both protocols were formulated more than 30 years ago, and both were not designed for security but rather for safety, and as a consequence lack source authentication.

In recent years a number of successful cyber-attacks were demonstrated on cars [22], motivating researchers to search for new ways to hinder attacks. A number of papers demonstrate the use of hardware fingerprints for detecting changes in hardware: [6,8,18,24].

CAN bus and ARINC 429 use different line protocols and have different attack models, therefore methods presented in the above papers cannot be directly applied to our problem without change. They can, however, serve as a starting point for ARINC 429 hardware fingerprinting.

1.3   Contributions

We propose the use of hardware fingerprinting in order to imbue ARINC 429 buses with source authentication capabilities. Applying the method only requires the attachment of a standard-compliant monitoring unit to the bus. This method does not require hardware or software updates to existing systems and is compliant with the current version of the ARINC standard.

We describe the adversary models that our method is effective at protecting against. We then design a preliminary intrusion detection system with hardware fingerprinting capabilities, and evaluate its performance in these attack scenarios.

We explore the ability to distinguish between devices by using the hardware fingerprints of individual transmitted words. We find that it is possible to distinguish between transmitters and receivers by their electric signal, with low error rates. This observation applies both to devices from different vendors and to devices from the same vendor and model, which are supposedly identical.

We explore the effect of receivers and transmission lines on performance. We see that adding a receiver does not yield a significant change in the signal. However, switching a receiver by another receiver, when combined with a change to the transmission line, is detectable by our method.

We compare different feature sets under different adversarial models. Somewhat surprisingly, we find that using the raw samples, without extracting any features, yields the best outcome when detecting a transmitter switch. In case of a receiver switch, we find that features derived from a polynomial fit outperform the other feature sets.

In order to drive the false-alarms-per-second rate to zero, we suggest to augment the per-word anomaly detection by a "suspicion counter" that increases with each word flagged as an anomaly, and decreases with every normal word. We first analyze the suspicion counter using a Markov-chain model, and then evaluate the performance of the combined system using the empirical data. In this experimental work, our intrusion detection system achieves near-zero false alarms per second, while detecting a rogue transmitter in under 50 ms, and detecting a rogue receiver in under 3 s. In other words, an intrusion detection system could potentially be used to detect attacks during the pre-flight checks, well before the aircraft takes off.

2   Preliminaries

2.1   The ARINC 429 Standard

ARINC Specification 429 [1] or "Mark 33 Digital Transfer System (DITS)", is a standard of the avionics industry. It defines a protocol for the communication between avionics system elements over a local area network. First published in 1977 by Aeronautical Radio, Inc., it has since become one of the most widely used data bus protocols in civil aircrafts [23]. The protocol encompasses different layers: from the physical requirements, through the electronic characteristics of the signal, data format and ending with a file transfer technique.

In ARINC 429 the communicating entities are called line-replaceable units (LRU). Data is transmitted over a single twisted and shielded pair of wires. The cable shield is grounded on both ends. The lines are denoted Line A and Line B.

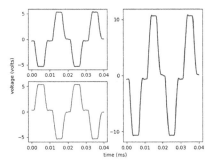

Fig. 1. ARINC 429 bus showing the voltage difference between twisted pair for bits 0101. Counter-clockwise starting from the top left: Line A, Line B, the differential signal

Differential signaling is used, meaning that the signal is the voltage difference from Line A to Line B, rather than the difference from one wire to ground. Bipolar return-to-zero (BRTZ) modulation is used as a line protocol. BRTZ is a tri-level state modulation: we refer to the three voltage levels as "HI", "LO" and "NULL". A binary 1 is encoded as a positive voltage pulse "HI", and a binary 0 is encoded as a negative voltage pulse "LO". In between transmissions, the voltage drops to 0 V, "NULL". Every "HI" and every "LO" are preceded and are followed by a "NULL", even if repeating bit values are transmitted consecutively. The differential output voltage from line A to line B is 10 V ± 1 in "HI" mode, 0 ± 0.5 in "NULL" mode and −10 V ± 1 in "LO" mode. Figure 1 shows a recording of a transmission on an ARINC 429 data bus.

Data is transmitted in words that are 32-bit long. The bits are transmitted in the following order, from first to last: 8, 7, ..., 2, 1, 9, 10, ..., 32. This order is a legacy from older systems. In this paper, words are interpreted as though an MSB-first transmission order is in place.

Data on the ARINC 429 bus is transmitted unidirectionally from a single transmitter LRU to up to 20 receiver LRUs. Only one transmitter LRU is allowed on the bus - a separate bus is required for each transmitter. Since there is only one transmitter on each bus, there is no sender ID field in ARINC messages.

The protocol allows a choice of one of two bit rates: Slow, at 12.0 to 14.5 Kbits/sec, and fast, at 100 Kbits/sec. The bit rate on a bus is fixed and maintained within %1. The signal is self-clocking.

2.2   The Adversary Model

Our method is designed to guard against "technician attacks". This type of attack involves an adversary that has brief physical access to the system. Such an adversary is able to replace LRUs or add new ones to the bus.

The adversary may have prior knowledge of the hardware and of the topology of the attacked system. The reverse is not true: As defenders, we have no prior knowledge of what the adversary's hardware might be. However, we do assume that the adversary will use commercial off-the-shelf hardware.

We only consider attacks, where the adversary changes the hardware that is connected to the bus, as other types of attack do not affect the signal. We distinguish between several types of attacks.

A Rogue Transmitter. In this type of attack an adversary replaces a legitimate transmitter LRU by a rogue one. During an initial latent phase of the attack, the new device imitates the behavior of the original transmitter, transmitting data exactly as requested, in order to remain hidden. Later, the rogue transmitter LRU sends out messages which are meant to disrupt the work of the system.

A Rogue Receiver. In this type of attack the adversary replaces a legitimate receiver LRU by a rogue one, or adds a rogue receiver LRU without detaching another LRU. By doing this the adversary gains access to the transmitted data, which might be otherwise inaccessible, and may use this data to cause harm through another attack channel.

Adding a Transmitter or Converting a Receiver to a Transmitter. An attack wherein the adversary adds another transmitter LRU to the bus, without detaching the legitimate transmitter, is actually not possible to perform on the ARINC bus. The ARINC 429 bus is designed to allow exactly one transmitter LRU. Connecting two transmitters to the same bus irreparably violates the electrical properties of the system. Therefore, an adversary cannot simply add a transmitter (built from off-the-shelf components) to the bus. An adversary may possibly construct special hardware that would allow the bus to function with two or more transmitters, but the fact remains that standard commercial components would not suffice.

Furthermore, it is not possible to turn a receiver LRU into a transmitter LRU by hijacking its software, since the LRU's wiring does not permit it.

3   The Data Set

To the best of our knowledge, there is no publicly available data set that contains high rate voltage samples of ARINC 429 protocol. We gathered our own data set, with the kind assistance of *Astronautics C.A. LTD.* [3]. We sampled two types of transmitters:

1. An M4K429RTx test equipment from *Excalibur Systems* [13]. The Excalibur equipment hosts two transmitters which we label E_1 and E_2.
2. ADK-3220 Evaluation boards, manufactured by *Holt Integrated Circuits INC.* [17]. The board contains a HI-3220PQ ARINC 429 Protocol IC connected to 8 HI-8597PSIFF line drivers chips. We use 4 of the transmitters and 2 different boards. We label the transmitters H_{xy}, where x is the board number, 1 or 2, and y is the transmitter number from 0 to 3.

Fig. 2. The Holt evaluation board and the fabricated connector board

The transmitters were connected to one or more of the following receivers:

1. An EDCU, a proprietary device manufactured by *Astronautics C.A. LTD.* [2]. The device has 2 receivers which we label P_1 and P_2.
2. The ADK-3220 Evaluation boards also host 16 integrated line receivers. We use 2 of the ports with the 2 boards. We label the receivers the same way as the transmitters with H_{xy} (x is the board number, y is the receiver number).

Using a Keysight DSO9254A scope, all signals were sampled at 50 Msa/s at a scope bandwidth of 25 MHz. The probes are 500 MHz, 10 MΩ, 11 pF. Each line was sampled individually. We further downsampled digitally by a factor of 10 to a rate of 5 MSa/s using a 30 point FIR filter with a Hamming window.

The transmitters and the receivers were connected through a custom board that exposes the wires, which we fabricated for this purpose (Fig. 2).

All the devices transmitted the same data at a bit rate of 100 Kbits/sec. 6 values of words were transmitted. Interpreting the words with MSB-first transmission order, the values are: 0x00000000, 0xFFFFFFFF, 0x55555555, 0xAAAAAAAA, 0x5A5A5A5A, 0xA5A5A5A5. Note that these words include all the possible segment types. By transmitting the same data on all devices we ensure that the IDS cannot unintentionally use the message content to make its decisions.

In addition to the recordings from different transmitter-receiver pairs, we recorded E_1 and E_2 transmitting to P_1 and P_2 respectfully, with different Holt devices attached as additional receivers.

Table 1 shows the different combinations of transmitter-receiver in our data set, and the number of words recorded for each combination.

4   The Hardware Fingerprinting Approach

The fingerprinting IDS we propose has to be attached to the bus it is guarding. During a training period it samples the bus and learns the transmitter LRU's

Table 1. Distribution of recorded words in the data set

Row #	Transmitter	Receiver	#Words
1	E_1	P_1	4920
2	E_1	P_1 & H_{10}	4920
3	E_1	P_1 & H_{12}	4920
4	E_1	P_1 & H_{20}	4920
5	E_1	P_1 & H_{22}	4920
6	H_{10}	P_1	4920
7	H_{11}	P_1	4920
8	H_{12}	P_1	4920
9	H_{13}	P_1	4920
10	H_{20}	P_1	4920
11	H_{21}	P_1	4920
12	H_{22}	P_1	4920
13	H_{23}	P_1	4920
14	E_2	P_2	4920
15	E_2	P_2 & H_{10}	4920
16	E_2	P_2 & H_{12}	4920
17	E_2	P_2 & H_{20}	4920
18	E_2	P_2 & H_{22}	4920
19	H_{10}	P_2	4920
20	H_{11}	P_2	4920
21	H_{12}	P_2	4920
22	H_{13}	P_2	4920
23	H_{20}	P_2	4920
24	H_{21}	P_2	4920
25	H_{22}	P_2	4920
26	H_{23}	P_2	4920

characteristics. We assume that during this time only legitimate devices are present on the bus. We further assume that access to the IDS is restricted; only authorized personnel are able to trigger the training mechanism. This restriction is in place in order to prevent an adversary from retraining the IDS after switching the guarded transmitter by the rogue one. Usually, before takeoff, the aircraft systems are checked for basic integrity. During the pre-flight operations changes to the bus can be detected, even if the transmitter LRU is sending normal data. This makes it possible to handle the attack before takeoff, as opposed to mid-flight.

4.1   IDS Overview

We will next describe our proposed method of anomaly detection. We divide the algorithm into several stages. This section provides an overview of these steps. In the subsequent sections selected stages are explained in greater detail as needed.

1. [**Acquisition**] We sample both lines of the bus at a sampling rate that is 50 times higher than the bit rate. We used a sample rate of 5 MSa/s. The differential signal is obtained by subtracting the samples of line B from the samples of line A.
2. [**Segmentation**] Each word is split into 127 segments of 10 different types, based on voltage levels. The purpose of the segmentation is to eliminate the effect of the transmitted data, i.e., the content of the word, on the final decision of the anomaly detector. See Sect. 5 for details.
3. [**Feature Extraction**] We extract multiple features from each segment. See Sect. 6 for details.
4. [**Anomaly Detection per Segment**] The features from each segment are fed into a trained anomaly detector. Each *segment* is marked as either "normal" or "anomaly".
5. [**Voting**] A word is flagged as an "anomaly", if the number of "normal" segments it contains does not exceed T_{votes}, a calibrated threshold.
6. [**Suspicion Counter**] We keep a counter of anomalous words. The counter is increased by 1 when a word is marked as an "anomaly", and decreased by 1 to a minimum of 0 when a word is marked as "normal". Once the counter reaches a threshold of $T_{suspicion}$ an alarm is raised.

4.2   Anomaly Detection per Segment

Our basic building block uses per-segment anomaly detection. As we shall see there are 10 types of segments, as detailed in Table 2. A segment's characteristics depend on its type. Therefore, we opted to train a different anomaly detector for each type of segment.

There are numerous outlier and anomaly detection algorithms available in the literature. An extensive review of various algorithms is presented in [26]. For the anomaly detection task, we chose to work with the Local Outlier Factor (LOF) [4]. LOF was shown to work better than other algorithms for the task of network intrusion detection [21]. This fact, together with the available scikit-learn [25] Python implementation, made it an appealing choice. Comparing different anomaly detection algorithms is beyond the scope of this paper.

LOF is a density-based outlier detection algorithm. According to the LOF algorithm, an outlier is defined as a data point (feature vector), whose local density is greater than the average of local densities of its neighbors by a large enough margin. A local density of a data point is the inverse of the average distance of the point from its neighbors.

There are several hyper-parameters for the LOF algorithm. In all cases we used the default parameters provided by the implementation. For the number of neighbors examined when calculating the LOF the default is 20. We used the Euclidean metric for the distance measure. The threshold on the local outlier factor that defines an anomaly is automatically set so that 10% of the samples in the *training set* are outliers.

We constructed one detector per each type of segment. Each segment is fed individually into its appropriate LOF anomaly detector. The LOF outputs its determination regarding the source of the segment, either "normal" or "anomaly".

4.3 Voting

We gather the decisions made by the different LOF detectors for all segments of the same word. The number of segments that have been identified as normal is subjected to a voting threshold T_{votes}. If it does not exceed T_{votes}, the word is flagged as an "anomaly", otherwise, it is flagged as "normal".

4.4 Suspicion Counter

According to our adversary model, an attacker tampers with the system only once. Therefore, we expect the true label of all words in the incoming stream to be identical—either all the words originate from the original system, or all the words originate from a compromised system. We utilize this attack model to reduce the probability of making an error. Taking note from [18] we incorporate an anomaly counter, which we name the suspicion counter.

The suspicion counter is a counter that is updated on the arrival of a new word. The initial value of the counter is 0. When a word is declared as an "anomaly", the counter is increased by 1, and when a word is declared as "normal", the counter is decreased by 1, to a minimum of 0. Once the counter reaches a calibrated threshold of $T_{suspicion}$ an alarm is raised.

5 Signal Segmentation

Our method aims to rely solely on the physical characteristics of the hardware, and aims to be completely agnostic to the transmitted data. In order to achieve this goal, we divide each word into sub-bit non-overlapping segments.

In a BRTZ line protocol, each bit comprises of 4 distinct segments. For example, a '1' bit starts with a transition up from "NULL" to "HI", then a plateau on "HI", then a transition down from "HI" back to "NULL", and finally a "NULL" plateau. Furthermore, we observed 4 different variants of "NULL", depending on the current and on the next bit. E.g., a "NULL" between two '1' bits tends to be "smile"-shaped, while a "NULL" between two '0' bits has a "frown" shape. All in all, we identified 10 different segment types, see Table 2.

Thus, we split every 32-bit word into 127 segments. Note that there are only 127 segments, not 128, because the last bit is followed by a long "NULL" that

Table 2. Voltage thresholds per segment type

Segment	Starting threshold	Ending threshold
LO	falls below $-V_{h_1}$	rises above $-V_{h_2}$
HI	rises above V_{h_1}	falls below V_{h_2}
NULL, HI to HI	falls below V_{l_1}	rises above V_{l_2}
NULL, HI to LO	falls below V_{l_1}	falls below $-V_{l_2}$
NULL, LO to LO	rises above $-V_{l_1}$	falls below $-V_{l_2}$
NULL, LO to HI	rises above $-V_{l_1}$	rises above V_{l_2}
Up from LO	rises above $-V_{h_2}$	rises above $-V_{l_1}$
Up from NULL	rises above V_{l_2}	rises above V_{h_1}
Down from HI	falls below V_{h_2}	falls below V_{l_1}
Down from NULL	falls below $-V_{l_2}$	falls below $-V_{h_1}$

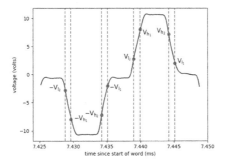

Fig. 3. A segmentation example of the bits 01. The trace exhibits all 4 up/down transitions, the "HI" and "LO" plateaus, and 3 of the 4 possible "NULL" segment types

lasts until the next word and has a unique shape. We do not associate this segment with any word.

The segmentation is performed in the following manner. A segment starts where the voltage level of the signal rises above/falls below a certain threshold, and ends where it falls below/rises above another threshold. 4 different thresholds are employed in order to produce a stabling hysteresis effect. We denote them as follows, and use them and their negative to define segment boundaries: $V_{l_1} = 2.0\,\text{V}$, $V_{l_2} = 2.8\,\text{V}$, $V_{h_1} = 8.0\,\text{V}$, $V_{h_2} = 7.2\,\text{V}$.

Table 2 shows the voltage levels used for each segment type. Figure 3 shows an example of word segmentation.

6   Feature Sets

In our work we compare the performance of the feature sets described below.

Raw Time-Domain Samples. This feature set consists of the raw vector of sequential voltage samples. The only operation we perform after segmentation is truncating the segments to a common length, since the LOF algorithm expects all data points to be vectors of the same dimension. The length varies depending on the segment type, as shown in Table 4. At the sample rate we use (recall Sect. 4.1) the number of samples per segment is quite low - between 4–24. This makes the Raw feature set a practical choice.

Generic Time-Domain Feature Set. As discussed in Sect. 1.2, in recent years a number of papers suggested using extracted features to perform hardware fingerprinting [7,8,11,18]. They all utilized time-domain features such as mean, standard deviation, skewness etc., with good results.

We use the features that were presented in [18] as our Generic set. Six of the eight features in this feature set are used in all four cited papers. The features we used are listed in Table 3.

In addition to time-domain features, the cited papers also employ frequency-domain features. We do not use frequency-domain features in this paper. We argue that the non-periodic nature of the signals, that are the result of our segmentation method, does not benefit from frequency analysis.

Polynomial Feature Set. The features in this set are calculated by performing a least squares polynomial fit and taking each coefficient as a separate feature, plus the residual as an additional feature.

In order to avoid overfitting, we fit each type of segment with a polynomial function of an appropriate degree. For the four transitions ("Up from LO", "Up from NULL", "Down from HI", "Down from NULL") we use a degree of 2. For "NULL, HI to HI" and "NULL, LO to LO" we use a degree of 6, on account of these segments being even functions. For the remaining segments we use a

Table 3. Generic feature set

Feature	Description
Mean	$\mu = \frac{1}{N}\sum_{i=1}^{N} x(i)$
Standard deviation	$\sigma = \sqrt{\frac{1}{N}\sum_{i=1}^{N}(x(i) - \mu)^2}$
Variance	$\sigma^2 = \frac{1}{N}\sum_{i=1}^{N}(x(i) - \mu)^2$
Skewness	$skew = \frac{1}{N}\sum_{i=1}^{N}(\frac{x(i)-\mu}{\sigma})^3$
Kurtosis	$kurt = \frac{1}{N}\sum_{i=1}^{N}(\frac{x(i)-\mu}{\sigma})^4$
Root mean square	$rms = \sqrt{\frac{1}{N}\sum_{i=1}^{N} x(i)^2}$
Maximum	$max = max(x(i))_{i=1...N}$
Energy	$en = \frac{1}{N}\sum_{i=1}^{N} x(i)^2$

Table 4. Number of features per segment type

Segment	Segment length	Raw	Generic	Polynomial	Hand-crafted
LO	20−24	20	8	7	10
HI	20−23	20	8	7	10
NULL, HI to HI	17−22	17	8	7	2
NULL, HI to LO	17−21	17	8	8	0
NULL, LO to LO	17−22	17	8	7	2
NULL, LO to HI	17−21	17	8	8	0
Up from LO	4−6	4	8	3	2
Up from NULL	4−6	4	8	3	2
Down from HI	4−5	4	8	3	2
Down from NULL	4−5	4	8	3	2

degree of 7 for similar reasons. Note that the number of features is always one more than the degree due to the residual.

Hand-Crafted Feature Set. In this feature set there are different features for each segment type. We observed that the "HI" segments contain an overshoot followed by ripples. We denote by $(t_1, v_1), (t_2, v_2), (t_3, v_3)$ the time and voltage level at the first local maxima (the overshoot), then the first local minima that follows and then the first local maxima that follows. Time is measured from the beginning of the segment. The features we take are the above 6 values, in addition to the differences in time and voltage of the second and third points from the first point: $t_2 - t_1, v_2 - v_1, t_3 - t_1, v_3 - v_1$. The features in the "LO" segments are a mirror image of the features in the "HI" segment.

For "NULL, HI to HI" and "NULL, LO to LO" we only take the time and voltage levels at the overshoot (t_1, v_1): not all segments of these types in the data set have ripples.

The 4 transition segments are linear-like. For them we extract 2 features. The first is the mean of the first derivative. This quantifies the slope. The second is the mean of differences of the segment from a line that passes between the segment's endpoints. This feature quantifies the segment's deviation from a straight line.

The segments "NULL, LO to HI" and "NULL, HI to LO" do not participate: not all segments of these types in the data set contain an overshoot.

7 Detection Based on a Single Word

7.1 Methodology

We evaluated the performance of our algorithm with an extensive series of experiments spanning over 125,000 recorded words from 12 transmitters. In each experiment we selected one transmitter LRU as a guarded device. Its measurements are labeled as normal, indicating the legitimate state where the adversary has not yet tampered with the system. In each experiment we selected a group of other devices as rogue devices. Their measurements are labeled as anomalies, representing the state of the system after it was changed by an adversary. In all cases we used a train-test split of 60%–40% of the measurements labeled as normal. Anomaly-labeled measurements are not present in the training set.

For the purpose of comparing the different feature sets, we set $T_{suspicion} = 1$. We then run our algorithm and calculate the false alarm and misdetection rates (FAR & MDR respectively) as functions of T_{votes}. Next, we find the equal error rate (EER), the rate at which the FAR equals the MDR. The EER is the metric we use for comparing different hyper-parameters.

In our graphs we convert the EER to "false alarms per second" (FA/Sec) under normal operation (system unaltered by an adversary). This gives a more concrete meaning to the numbers. The FA/Sec is calculated by multiplying the EER by the message rate, and is the inverse of mean time between failures. Note that each word occupies 36 bits, because the protocol mandates a minimum inter-word gap of at least 4 bit times. Thus the FA/Sec metric is defined as:

$$FA/Sec = \frac{1}{MTBF} = EER \cdot \frac{100^{Kbits/sec}}{36bits}$$

Note that since the FA/Sec is linear in the EER, we can discuss the graphs as though they display the EER when giving a qualitative analysis.

7.2   Identifying a Rogue Transmitter

In this series of experiments we simulate an attack, where the adversary switches the guarded transmitter LRU by a rogue transmitter LRU. In each experiment we designate one of the transmitters as the legitimate device to be guarded. In addition, we choose one receiver, either P_1 or P_2. We train our IDS to identify samples from the chosen Tx-Rx pair as normal.

We then test the trained IDS. We simulate a rogue transmitter LRU by using measurements of other transmitters connected to the chosen receiver as anomalies. We remind the reader that during each measurement, only one transmitter is connected to the bus.

Only the Holt devices were used to simulate rogue transmitters, regardless of whether the guarded transmitter is an Excalibur (E_1 or E_2) or a Holt (H_{10}, ..., H_{13}, H_{20}, ..., H_{23}).

For example, if we choose E_1 as the guarded transmitter and P_1 as the receiver, words from row 1 in Table 1 are labeled as normal and used in the training stage and in the testing stage. Words from rows 6–13 are labeled as anomalies and used in the testing stage.

We repeat this process for all possible values of T_{votes} (0–127) while keeping $T_{suspicion} = 1$. For each value of T_{votes} we indicate the MDR and the FAR. From these values we obtain the EER and the FA/sec.

We repeat this process for four feature sets with all pairs of guarded transmitter and receiver. We end up with 18 experiments per feature set.

The results are presented as a box plot in Fig. 4. The x axis splits the results according to the used feature set. The y axis shows the false alarms per second:

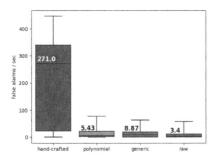

Fig. 4. Comparing the feature sets for identifying a rogue transmitter.

0 is the perfect score. The horizontal line in the middle of the box and the number written next to it indicate the median. The bottom and top boundaries of the box indicate the 1st and 3rd quartiles respectively. The horizontal lines outside of the box (the whiskers) indicate the minimum and maximum values.

The figure shows that intruder detection yields the best results in term of EER when we use the Raw feature set. Both the median and the spread of the values are low. The EER values for the Generic and Polynomial feature sets are slightly more spread out, and the median is greater. The Hand-Crafted feature set is clearly inferior.

The Generic, Raw and Polynomial feature sets have comparable performance, with Raw being slightly better with a median EER value of 0.12% compared to 0.32% and 0.19% for the Generic and Polynomial feature sets. Since there is no significant reduction in memory costs from using the Generic feature set (recall Table 4), we conclude that in our case it is best to use the raw voltage samples, since in the trade-off between memory/runtime and performance, with the Generic set we spend significant effort to extract the features, and obtain no gain in comparison to the raw signal.

We point out that there is a correlation between the number of features in the set and the performance of the feature set. The feature sets with reduced performance, namely the Hand-Crafted and Polynomial sets, have significantly fewer features for some segments - as few as 2 - and the Hand-Crafted sets totally ignores two segment types. The more features there are in the set, the more expressive the model is. Perhaps the two feature sets would perform better if they included additional features.

Interestingly, for all feature sets there are experiments which reached a perfect EER value of 0. The guarded transmitters in these perfect experiments are E_1, E_2 and H_{10}. Why do we achieve these results for E_1 and E_2? We point out that we only use the Holt boards to simulate rogue devices. This means that in experiments where E_1 and E_2 are used as guarded devices, the IDS is tasked with differentiating between a guarded device and rogue devices that are manufactured by different vendors. We expect devices from different models to have different characteristics. However, we achieve EER = 0 for the Holt device H_{10}

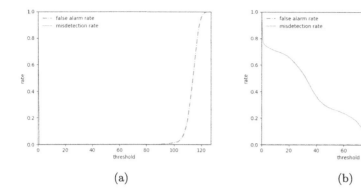

Fig. 5. FAR and MDR as a function of the threshold for different (a) E_1 as a guarded device and (b) H_{21} as a guarded device

as a guarded device as well - indicating that even for the same manufacturer there are significant differences in the hardware fingerprint of individual devices.

We demonstrate this point by examining two selected experiments. We plot the MDR and the FAR vs. the threshold value using E_1 (Fig. 5a) and of H_{21} (Fig. 5b) as guarded devices. Both are connected to P_1 and in both figures the Raw feature set is used. Note that again, in these graphs, lower is better.

Figures 5a and 5b show that the two cases pose different levels of challenge for the IDS. In case of the E_1 transmitter (Fig. 5a), the MDR and the FAR curves do not intersect. In fact, the MDR overlaps the left-side boundary of the figure. There is a wide range of thresholds, for which an error rate of 0 can be achieved simultaneously for both rates. This makes E_1 easily distinguishable from Holt transmitters. In contrast, in the case of the H_{21} transmitter (Fig. 5b) there is only a narrow range of thresholds for which both error rates are small, and the EER is greater than 0, making the tuning of the threshold important.

Another thing to observe is that in both Figs. 5a and 5b the FAR curve is roughly the same, while the MDR curve spreads to higher thresholds in Fig. 5b. Note that the FAR is only calculated from samples of the guarded transmitter, and that the MDR is only calculated from samples of the rogue transmitters. The task of labeling a word from a guarded device as normal is not affected by the type of the guarded device. However, the success of labeling rogue transmitters as anomalies heavily depends on the uniqueness of the guarded device.

Our experimental results regarding the identification of a rogue receiver switch, and identification of an addition of a rogue receiver, have been omitted due to space constraints. The results can be found in our full technical report [16].

8 Modeling the Suspicion Counter

In this section we analyze the effect of the suspicion counter on the overall false alarm rate, using a Markov-chain approach. Let the probability that a word is

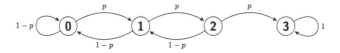

Fig. 6. Suspicion counter example for $T_{suspicion} = 3$

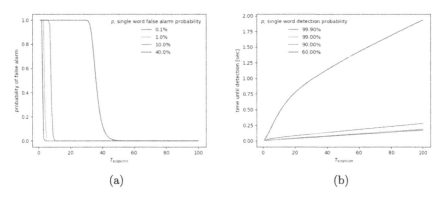

(a)   (b)

Fig. 7. (a) Probability for a false alarm during a 10-h flight (b) Time until the probability of a true detection exceeds 99.999%

detected as anomalous be denoted by p, and assume that the events of detecting a word as anomalous are i.i.d. Then we can describe the value of the counter after word i arrives as a Markov random process. Figure 6 shows, for example, the Markov process that corresponds to $T_{suspicion} = 3$.

A transition to the right indicates that a word was detected as an anomaly, and a transition to the left indicates that a word was detected as normal. The counter cannot be decreased below the initial value of 0. The state for $i = T_{suspicion}$ is a final state indicating that an alarm is raised.

Figure 7a shows the probability of a false alarm occurring during a 10-h flight as a function of $T_{suspicion}$ for different values of p. We assume an average transmission rate of 610 words per second, which is about 20% of the maximal available bandwidth. This is the rate used in our data set. We can see that for every value of p, if $T_{suspicion}$ is high enough, the false alarm rate probability drops to 0. The lower p is, the minimal $T_{suspicion}$ that is required is lower. Interestingly, even for a very high single-word false alarm probability of 40%, at a $T_{suspicion}$ value of just 50 the probability of a false alarm drops to 0.

Figure 7b show the time it takes for the probability for a positive (anomaly) detection to reach 99.999%. Here all the transmitted words are assumed to originate from a rogue system, therefore we set $p > 0.5$. A low detection time means that the system is quick at detecting the adversary. The figure shows that the time until detection rises as $T_{suspicion}$ rises. The rise is quicker for low values of p. Even so, with a very poor detection probability of $p = 0.6$ and $T_{suspicion} = 100$, (which is much more than the threshold required to bring the false alarm rate to near 0), the time until detection reaches only 2 s. So, we can see from the

Markov model that using a suspicion counter drastically reduces the false alarm rate, while slowing down the detection only mildly.

9   Performance of the Complete Method

The results we attained in Sect. 7 are encouraging: we can successfully fingerprint a transmitter based on a single word. However, the FA/Sec metric of around 5 alarms per second is still too high for a realistic system. To reduce the FA/Sec rate to near-zero, we use the suspicion counter we analyzed in Sect. 8, and raise an alarm only when the counter exceeds $T_{suspicion}$. In this section we empirically evaluate the behavior of the complete system as a function of the threshold. We do not discuss how to identify an additional receiver, since we could not identify it with sufficient certainty in Sect. 7.

In our full technical report [16] we showed that different feature sets are suited for detecting different adversary models; the Raw feature set for detecting a rogue transmitter, and the Polynomial feature set for detecting a rogue receiver. We now continue our evaluation with these two feature sets.

We wish to examine the FAR as a function of the counter threshold. For each transmitter-receiver pair in our data set we repeat the following procedure. First, we train an anomaly detector on words recorded with the selected pair. Then we test the detector 1000 times on words recorded with the same pair. Each time we use the same 1968 words after cyclically shifting them by a random integer in order to start the counter at a different point in time. We compute the FAR by dividing the number of times an anomaly was detected by the total number of measurements. Overall there are such 18000 measurements (9 transmitters × 2 receivers × 1000 repetitions). We repeat this procedure with different values of $T_{suspicion}$, once for each feature set. We use $T_{votes} = 100$ in all experiments. Experiments in Sect. 7 show that this is a reasonable choice that balances the FAR and the MDR for detection based on single words. The train-test split is 60%–40%. Figure 8a shows the results.

As predicted by the Markov analysis, the false alarm rate drops dramatically as $T_{suspicion}$ increases. For $T_{suspicion}$ greater than 16, there were no false alarms: the empirical results and the Markov analysis are in agreement, and the empirical Fig. 8a is similar to the theoretical Fig. 7a. In both the false alarm probability starts at 1, is stable for low values of $T_{suspicion}$, drops quickly and finally decays to 0.

For observing the trade-off of using an anomaly counter, measuring the MDR rate is inefficient, since given sufficient time an anomaly will eventually be detected. Instead of measuring the MDR, we measure the *time* it takes for our detector to raise an alarm. The procedure is similar to the procedure of measuring the FAR. Instead of testing the trained detector on words recorded with the same transmitter-receiver pair as the one on which it was trained, we test it on words from other pairs, according to the adversary model that is being simulated, as explained in Sect. 7.1. The Raw feature set is used for measuring a rogue transmitter detection, and the polynomial feature set is used when detecting a rogue receiver. We count the number of words it takes for the detector to

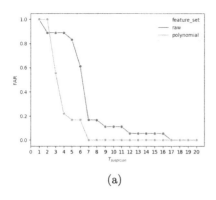 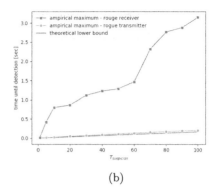

(a)   (b)

Fig. 8. (a) FAR as a function of $T_{suspicion}$ (b) Maximal length of time for detecting an attack. $T_{votes} = 100$

raise an alarm. Overall, for a rogue transmitter there are 144000 measurements (9 guarded transmitters × 8 rogue transmitters × 2 receivers × 1000 repetitions) and for a rogue receiver there are 8000 (8 transmitters × 1 guarded receiver × 1 rogue receiver × 1000 repetitions) for each value of $T_{suspicion}$.

Figure 8b shows the maximal (worst case) time we measured for detecting a rogue transmitter over all combinations of guarded and attacking transmitters. Figure 8b shows the same for detecting a rogue receiver. The blue line indicates a lower bound—the time it takes to transmit $T_{suspicion}$ messages. In our test set the average transmission rate is 610 words per second, which is about 20% of the maximal available bandwidth.

The figures show that the suspicion counter reduces false alarms at the expense of only mildly delaying the detection of an attack. We find the trade-off worthwhile. Even when $T_{suspicion} = 20$ and there are no false alarms, a rogue transmitter is detected in under 50 ms, which greatly reduces the adversaries ability to mount a successful attack, and a rogue receiver is detected in several seconds, which is still good.

In both cases, the maximal observed detection time rises faster than lower bound. For rogue transmitter detection, the maximal time is of the same order of magnitude of as the lower bound, while for the case of rogue receiver detection, the maximal time is an order of magnitude higher. The gap is explained by the difference in misdetection rates for single words, measured in Sect. 7. The difference between the slopes is predicted by the Markov analysis. Figure 7b shows that as the misdetection rate of a single word increases, so does the rate at which the detection time rises.

10   Conclusions

We presented a hardware fingerprinting method for the ARINC 429 bus. The method can be used to retrofit source authentication into existing avionic systems with low effort, since it does not require modifications to existing components.

We showed that our method is especially effective for identifying a technician attack, in which an adversary replaces a legitimate LRU with a rogue one. We demonstrated that even transmitter LRUs of the same make and model are different enough for them to generate distinguishable signals. All the more so when dealing with devices from different vendors. We found that skipping the feature extraction stage and using the raw signal achieves the best result.

In our full technical report [16] we showed that the method can also detect a switched receiver and that the Polynomial feature set, which was conceived for the purpose of this paper, achieves the best performance among the feature sets we examined for this task.

We showed that by augmenting the per-word anomaly detection by a "suspicion counter", we can drastically reduce the false-alarm rate. Using both a Markov-chain analysis and an extensive empirical evaluation, we showed that an intrusion detection system based on hardware fingerprinting could potentially be used to detect hardware changes during pre-flight checks, well before the aircraft takes off. In our experiments, a preliminary intrusion detection system achieves near-zero false alarms per second, while detecting a rogue transmitter in under 50 ms, and detecting a rogue receiver in under 3 s.

Further research is required in order to evaluate the sensitivity of the hardware fingerprints to external changes such as fluctuations in temperature or supply voltage levels, and to evaluate its stability over time.

ARINC 429 lacks essential security features. It is a safety liability that is present today in almost every civil aircraft. Our hardware fingerprinting method could help close the gap between ARINC 429 and modern security requirements.

Acknowledgments. This work was supported in part by a grant from the Interdisciplinary Cyber Research Center at Tel Aviv University. The authors would like to thank Astronautics C.A. LTD. for sharing their equipment and expert knowledge.

References

1. Aeronautical Radio INC.: Mark 33 digital information transfer system (DITS), May 2004. http://www.bosch-semiconductors.de/media/ubk. ARINC specification 429 part 1–17
2. Astronautics C.A. LTD: Astronautics EDCU Brochure (2019). http://www.astronautics.co.il/sites/default/files/edcu.pdf
3. Astronautics C.A. LTD: home page (2019). http://www.astronautics.com
4. Breunig, M.M., Kriegel, H.P., Ng, R.T., Sander, J.: LOF: identifying density-based local outliers. In: ACM SIGMOD Record, vol. 29, pp. 93–104. ACM (2000)
5. Brik, V., Banerjee, S., Gruteser, M., Oh, S.: Wireless device identification with radiometric signatures. In: Proceedings of the 14th ACM International Conference on Mobile Computing and Networking, pp. 116–127. ACM (2008)
6. Cho, K.T., Shin, K.G.: Viden: attacker identification on in-vehicle networks. In: Proceedings of the 2017 ACM SIGSAC Conference on Computer and Communications Security, pp. 1109–1123. ACM (2017)
7. Choi, W., Jo, H.J., Woo, S., Chun, J.Y., Park, J., Lee, D.H.: Identifying ECUs using inimitable characteristics of signals in controller area networks. IEEE Trans. Veh. Technol. **67**(6), 4757–4770 (2018)

8. Choi, W., Joo, K., Jo, H.J., Park, M.C., Lee, D.H.: VoltageIDS: low-level communication characteristics for automotive intrusion detection system. IEEE Trans. Inf. Forensics Secur. **13**(8), 2114–2129 (2018)
9. Costin, A., Francillon, A.: Ghost in the air (traffic): on insecurity of ADS-B protocol and practical attacks on ADS-B devices. Black Hat USA, pp. 1–12 (2012)
10. Das, A., Borisov, N., Caesar, M.: Tracking mobile web users through motion sensors: attacks and defenses. In: NDSS (2016)
11. Dey, S., Roy, N., Xu, W., Choudhury, R.R., Nelakuditi, S.: AccelPrint: imperfections of accelerometers make smartphones trackable. In: NDSS (2014)
12. Ellis, K., Serinken, N.: Characteristics of radio transmitter fingerprints. Radio Sci. **36**(4), 585–597 (2001)
13. Excalibur Systems: M4K429RTx test and simulation module (2019). https://www.mil-1553.com/m4k429rtx
14. Fuchs, C.M., et al.: The evolution of avionics networks from ARINC 429 to AFDX. Innov. Internet Technol. Mob. Commun. (IITM) Aerosp. Netw. (AN) **65**, 1551–3203 (2012)
15. Gerdes, R.M., Mina, M., Russell, S.F., Daniels, T.E.: Physical-layer identification of wired ethernet devices. IEEE Trans. Inf. Forensics Secur. **7**(4), 1339–1353 (2012)
16. Gilboa-Markevich, N., Wool, A.: Hardware fingerprinting for the ARINC 429 avionic bus. Technical report arXiv:2003.12456 [cs.CR] (2020). http://arxiv.org/abs/2003.12456
17. Holt Integrated Circuits INC.: ADK-3200: HI-3200 avionics data management engine evaluation board (2011). http://www.holtic.com/product/p/pb/15-adk-3200-hi-3200-avionics-data-management-engine-evaluation-board.aspx
18. Kneib, M., Huth, C.: Scission: signal characteristic-based sender identification and intrusion detection in automotive networks. In: Proceedings of the 2018 ACM SIGSAC Conference on Computer and Communications Security, pp. 787–800. ACM (2018)
19. Kohno, T., Broido, A., Claffy, K.C.: Remote physical device fingerprinting. IEEE Trans. Dependable Secure Comput. **2**(2), 93–108 (2005)
20. Langner, R.: Stuxnet: dissecting a cyberwarfare weapon. IEEE Secur. Priv. **9**(3), 49–51 (2011)
21. Lazarevic, A., Ertoz, L., Kumar, V., Ozgur, A., Srivastava, J.: A comparative study of anomaly detection schemes in network intrusion detection. In: Proceedings of the 2003 SIAM International Conference on Data Mining, pp. 25–36. SIAM (2003)
22. Miller, C., Valasek, C.: Remote exploitation of an unaltered passenger vehicle. Black Hat USA 2015, p. 91 (2015)
23. Moir, I., Seabridge, A., Jukes, M.: Data bus networks (chapter 3). In: Civil Avionics Systems, pp. 79–118. Wiley, Chichester (2013)
24. Murvay, P.S., Groza, B.: Source identification using signal characteristics in controller area networks. IEEE Signal Process. Lett. **21**(4), 395–399 (2014)
25. Pedregosa, F., et al.: Scikit-learn: machine learning in Python. J. Mach. Learn. Res. **12**, 2825–2830 (2011)
26. Pimentel, M.A., Clifton, D.A., Clifton, L., Tarassenko, L.: A review of novelty detection. Sig. Process. **99**, 215–249 (2014)
27. Robert Bosch GmbH: CAN specification, v2.0 (1991)
28. Smith, M., Strohmeier, M., Harman, J., Lenders, V., Martinovic, I.: A view from the Cockpit: exploring pilot reactions to attacks on avionic systems. In: Network and Distributed Systems Security (NDSS) Symposium. Internet Society, San Diego (2020)

29. Spitzer, C.R.: ARINC specification 429 mark 33 digital information transfer system (chapter 2). In: Avionics: Elements, Software and Functions. The Electrical Engineering Handbook Series. CRC Press, Boca Raton (2007)
30. Uluagac, A.S., Radhakrishnan, S.V., Corbett, C., Baca, A., Beyah, R.: A passive technique for fingerprinting wireless devices with wired-side observations. In: 2013 IEEE Conference on Communications and Network Security (CNS), pp. 305–313. IEEE (2013)
31. Xu, Q., Zheng, R., Saad, W., Han, Z.: Device fingerprinting in wireless networks: challenges and opportunities. IEEE Commun. Surv. Tutorials **18**(1), 94–104 (2015)

Applied Cryptography I

Semantic Definition of Anonymity in Identity-Based Encryption and Its Relation to Indistinguishability-Based Definition

Goichiro Hanaoka[1], Misaki Komatsu[2], Kazuma Ohara[1], Yusuke Sakai[1], and Shota Yamada[1(✉)]

[1] National Institute of Advanced Industrial Science and Technology (AIST), 2-4-7 Aomi, Koto-ku, Tokyo 135-0064, Japan
{hanaoka-goichiro,ohara.kazuma,yusuke.sakai,yamada-shota}@aist.go.jp
[2] Toshiba Corporation Corporate Research & Development Center, 1 Komukai-Toshiba-cho, Saiwai-ku Kawasaki-shi, Kanagawa 212-8582, Japan
misaki1.komatsu@toshiba.co.jp

Abstract. In this paper we point out an overlooked subtlety in providing proper security definitions of anonymous identity-based encryption (anonymous IBE) and its applications such as searchable encryption. Namely, we find that until now there is no discussion whether the widely used indistinguishability-based notion of anonymity for IBE implies simulation-based definition of anonymity, which directly captures the intuition that recipients' IDs are not leaked from ciphertexts. We compensate this undesirable situation by providing a simulation-based notion, which requires that a ciphertext can be simulated without knowing the associated ID, by specializing the anonymity notion defined for more generalized notion of attribute-based encryption in previous work to the setting of IBE and then proving that this definition is equivalent to the conventional indistinguishability-based definition. We note that while the final result is something one would expect, our proof is not completely trivial. In particular, previous proofs that show the equivalence between semantic security and indistinguishability-based one in the setting where the security of payload is the main concern do not work immediately in our setting due to the difference between the semantics of identities and messages and the existence of the key extraction oracles.

Keywords: Identity-based encryption · Anonymity · Semantic security

1 Introduction

We identify an overlooked issue in the security definitions of the anonymous identity-based encryption (anonymous IBE) and application thereof such as searchable encryption. In particular, we point out that there are no arguments

L. Chen et al. (Eds.): ESORICS 2020, LNCS 12309, pp. 65–85, 2020.
https://doi.org/10.1007/978-3-030-59013-0_4

on the relation between commonly accepted indistinguishability definition for anonymity and simulation-based one, where the latter directly captures the intuition that recipients' IDs are not leaked from ciphertexts. In this paper, we fill this gap and for the first time demonstrate that the widely accepted indistinguishability-based definition implies a simulation-based definition.

1.1   Background

Searchable Encryption. Searchable encryption is today one of the active research trends in cryptography. Searchable encryption allows to search a piece of information over an encrypted data, while keeping the data content and the query secret even from the server holding the encrypted data.

With the rapid development of information technology, such as cloud computing, the guarantee of user privacy (without compromising usability as much as possible) has become an important issue for service providers. Therefore, searchable encryption has attracted a lot of attention as a method to realize encrypted databases (EDB). Since CryptDB [37] demonstrated the practicality of its approach, a number of EDBs have been proposed [2,42]. The fact that there are many commercial EDB among them (such as Microsoft SQL Server [34], Google Encrypted Big Query [25], SAP SEEED [26]) shows the demand for EDBs. In recent days, startups [3,18,41] also developed products and services based on searchable encryption.

In academia, searchable encryption is still actively being studied from functional aspects such as range queries [29] and conjunctive queries [23,35], efficiency aspects such as trade-off between storage size and search efficiency [4,5,15,19,20], and security aspects such as verifiability [32,44].

Relation to Anonymous IBE. It is widely believed that these searchable encryption schemes are proven secure under some appropriate security definitions. In particular, (public-key) searchable encryption can be constructed from anonymous identity-based encryption (anonymous IBE), and thus such searchable encryption schemes is believed to be secure if the underlying anonymous IBE is secure. Furthermore, it is worth noting that an anonymous IBE scheme can be constructed from a public-key searchable encryption scheme [9], these two cryptographic primitives are in fact equivalent.

Overlooked Issue in the Security Definitions. However, there seems to be an overlooked subtlety in the theoretical efforts to construct secure searchable encryption schemes. Concretely, a number of public key encryption with key word search (PEKS) schemes are mostly based on indistinguishability (IND)-based security [1,9,12] and there has been no discussion on the notion for semantic security (SS), whereas the security for symmetric searchable encryption (SSE), which is a symmetric-key variant of PEKS, are proven SS-based definition. In many cases, SS-based and IND-based definitions achieve same level of security, however, it is also known that IND and SS are not equivalent in some cases [11].

Therefore, there is a room for consideration on the difference between the security on PEKS and SSE, and discussion for the SS-based security on PEKS would help to properly understand the security of these schemes. As mentioned above, one of the most basic construction of PEKS is based on anonymous IBE, and the confidentiality of keywords in PEKS corresponds to the anonymity of the identity in the IBE. The anonymity of IBE has also been proposed so far with only the IND-based definition, and the SS-based is not known. That is, it would be worth considering about SS-based definition for anonymity in IBE, as a first step for considering SS-based security in PEKS.

Remind that Goldwasser and Micali introduced the IND-CPA definition (indistinguishability against chosen-plaintext attacks) [24] as an easy-to-deal-with alternative of semantic security [24]. Semantic security is meant to directly capture our intuition that the adversary learns nothing on the plaintext from a ciphertext, which is expressed in terms of a simulation-based definition. However, this definition is complex and not easy to deal with. Contrary to this, IND-CPA is less intuitive and does not directly capture the idea of not leaking any partial information of the encrypted message, but is simple and easy to deal with. Goldwasser and Micali proved that these definitions are equivalent. Therefore, by only proving a public-key encryption scheme is secure under the IND-CPA definition we can confirm that the scheme satisfies more intuitive notion of semantic security.

Their approach is generalized to formalize the security of various cryptographic primitives. In general, we consider that the simulation-based security notion as a preferable goal for cryptographic primitives to achieve compared to IND-based notion. This is because the former seems to be more intuitive and is usually at least as strong as the latter. If we can prove that both security notions are in fact equivalent, we can use IND-based definition as a handy alternative for the simulation-based security. However, it is possible for (appropriately defined) IND-based and simulation-based definitions not to be equivalent, which is evidenced by some separation results between IND-based and simulation-based definitions in various cryptographic primitives and notions, such as functional encryption [11], security against selective-opening attacks [8], and non-malleability [36].

1.2 Our Contribution

In this paper, we provide a simulation-based definition of anonymity for IBE and study the relationship between this simulation-based definition and the conventional IND-based definition of anonymity. In more details, we define the simulation-based definition of anonymity of IBE by specializing Wee's definition of anonymity for attribute-based encryption [28] to the setting of IBE. Then, we investigate the two directions of implications, namely, *(i) whether the simulation-based definition implies the IND-based definition*, and *(ii) whether the IND-based definition implies the simulation-based definition*. These establish the equivalence between the two notions.

While the result is something one would expect, we emphasize that our proof for the latter direction (ii) is not straightforward. In particular, previous proofs [6,24] that show the equivalence between semantic security and IND-based one in the setting where the security of payload is the main concern do not work immediately in our setting due to the difference between the semantics of identities and messages and the existence of the key extraction oracles. In more details, in our setting, we have to come up with a reduction that abides by the restriction on key extraction queries, which is not present in the payload hiding settings. The crux of the proof boils down to showing that the adversary is unable to make a key query for certain identity with more than negligible probability. In order to prove this, we introduce several game hops and crucially use the IND-based security of the IBE. We refer to Sect. 4 for details.

This result for the first time shows that the IND-based anonymity definition implies the simulation-based anonymity definition. This implies that the existing IBE schemes secure under the IND-based anonymity definition indeed do not leak recipients' IDs. In addition, this fact not only guarantees the security of the IBE schemes proven secure under the IND-based definition, does it allow us to keep using the easy-to-use IND-based definition as we did.

However, the fact that our proof is not trivial suggests that the equivalence between indistinguishability-based definition and simulation-based one is not necessarily always true. Indeed, the difference between the two security notions has been identified for the case of functional encryption and selective opening security (Please refer to the next subsection for more discussion). Our conclusion is that it would be risky to prove the secrecy of information in an IND-based style for some primitive and use it as if it also satisfied simulation-based security without a careful consideration.

1.3   Related Work

The idea of IBE is due to Shamir [39], and first practical solutions were proposed by Sakai et al. [38], Boneh et al. [10], Cocks [17] independently. In particular, Boneh et al. have provided a definition of plaintext secrecy in the IBE, which has been standardly used until today. The definition by Boneh et al. was based on IND, and thus SS-based security was not strictly discussed at first, but Attrapadung et al. [6] later showed the equivalence of both definitions. Later, Izabachene et al. [30] discussed various definitions of plaintext secrecy and their relations. Abdalla et al. [1] defined the anonymity of IBE based on IND (namely, Ano-LOR), and many follow-up works adopted the IND-based definition of anonymity or variants thereof [7,13,14,22,27,31,33,43]. However, since the introduction of the IND-based definition of anonymity, there has been little in-depth study on the definition on anonymity, and in particular, the concrete formulation of the definition based on SS and its relation to the IND-based definition were not well understood. Notably Boneh et al. [11] indicates that security definitions based on IND and SS may not be equivalent in functional encryption, which is a superordinate concept of IBE.

2   Preliminaries

In this section, we first denote notations used in this work. Then we give syntax and correctness of Identity-Based Key Encapsulation Mechanism (IB-KEM). After that, we present two security notions for IB-KEM, namely, IND-ID-CPA and Ano-LOR.

Notations. For set Y, $y \leftarrow Y$ denotes that y is uniformly chosen from Y. If Y is a function or algorithm, it denotes that Y outputs y. By PPT, we denote a probabilistic polynomial-time algorithm. For PPT algorithm A, $A^{\mathcal{O}}$ denotes that A has access to the oracle $\mathcal{O}$. $\perp$ is a symbol that means failure of decryption. Throughout, we use 1^k as the security parameter. A function $\varepsilon(k)$ is negligible if for any $c > 0$ there exists an $k_c > 0$ such that, for all $k > k_c$ we have: $\varepsilon(k) < k^{-c}$.

2.1   Identity-Based Key Encapsulation Mechanism

Here, we define Identity-Based Key Encapsulation Mechanism (IB-KEM). While the main focus of this paper is on the security definition of anonymous IBE, using IB-KEM instead will simplify the discussion. We can convert IB-KEM to IBE by using appropriate secret key encryption.

Syntax. An IB-KEM scheme Σ is a tuple (S, K, E, D) of PPT algorithms, where $\mathcal{ID}$ is a identity space and $\mathcal{K}$ is a symmetric-key space.

$S(1^k)$: The setup algorithm gets as input the security parameter 1^k. It outputs the public parameter prm, and the master secret key msk. We assume prm is implicitly provided as input to all algorithms.

$K(msk, id)$: The key generation algorithm gets as input the msk, and $id \in \mathcal{ID}$. It outputs a user secret key usk_{id}.

$E(prm, id)$: The encryption algorithm gets as input prm, and $id \in \mathcal{ID}$. It outputs a ciphertext ct and a symmetric-key $kem \in \mathcal{K}$.

$D(ct, usk_{id})$: The decryption algorithm gets as input ct, and usk_{id}. It outputs kem or $\perp$.

Correctness. IB-KEM is said to have correctness if we consider probabilities for $(prm, msk) \leftarrow S(1^k)$, $usk_{id} \leftarrow K(msk, id)$ and $(ct, kem) \leftarrow E(prm, id)$, then $\Pr[kem = D(ct, usk_{id})] = 1$ holds.

2.2   Security Definitions for IB-KEM

We denote two security definitions for IB-KEM, namely, IND-ID-CPA and Ano-LOR.

Here, we define IND-ID-CPA security and Ano-LOR for IB-KEM. IND-ID-CPA security is an indistinguishability based security notion that stipulates that an encrypted message is hidden. On the other hand, SS-ID-CPA is more natural security notion that captures the intuition that any information of the message is not leaked to the adversary. It is known that these two notions are equivalent [6]. The definition of IND-ID-CPA security in this paper is based on [6], where we adapted their definition to the IB-KEM setting. The definition of Ano-LOR is indistinguishability-based definition that is widely used in the literature.

IND-ID-CPA. Let $\Sigma = (S, K, E, D)$ be an IB-KEM scheme and $A = (A_1, A_2)$ be a PPT adversary. We consider the following experiments IND-ID-CPA-b for $b \in \{0, 1\}$.

$$\underline{\mathbf{Exp}_{\Sigma,A}^{\text{IND-ID-CPA-}b}(k)}$$

$$(prm, msk) \leftarrow S(1^k);$$

$$(id^*, s) \leftarrow A_1^{K(msk, \cdot)}(prm);$$

$$(ct, kem) \leftarrow E(id^*, prm);$$

$$kem_0 = kem; \; kem_1 \leftarrow \mathcal{K};$$

$$b' \leftarrow A_2^{K^{\{id^*\}}(msk, \cdot)}(ct, kem_b, s);$$

In the above, key generation oracle $K(msk, \cdot)$ gets as input the msk and arbitrary $id \in \mathcal{ID}$, and outputs a user secret key usk_{id} associated with id. A_1 cannot use the id^* that is queried to $K(msk, \cdot)$ as the target ID. If A_2 queries id^* to $K^{\{id^*\}}(msk, \cdot)$, $K^{\{id^*\}}(msk, \cdot)$ outputs $\perp$. We define the advantage $\mathbf{Adv}_{\Sigma,A}^{\text{IND-ID-CPA}}(k)$ as follows;

$$\mathbf{Adv}_{\Sigma,A}^{\text{IND-ID-CPA}}(k)$$
$$:= |\Pr[\; \mathbf{Exp}_{\Sigma,A}^{\text{IND-ID-CPA-0}}(k) \to 1\;] - \Pr[\; \mathbf{Exp}_{\Sigma,A}^{\text{IND-ID-CPA-1}}(k) \to 1\;]|.$$

Definition 1 (IND-ID-CPA). *We say that IB-KEM scheme $\Sigma = (S, K, E, D)$ is IND-ID-CPA secure if $\mathbf{Adv}_{\Sigma,A}^{\text{IND-ID-CPA}}(k)$ is negligible for any PPT adversary $A = (A_1, A_2)$.*

Ano-LOR. Let $\Sigma = (S, K, E, D)$ be an IB-KEM scheme and $B = (B_1, B_2)$ be a PPT adversary. We consider the following experiments Ano-LOR-b for $b \in \{0, 1\}$

$$\underline{\mathbf{Exp}_{\Sigma,B}^{\text{LOR-}b}(k)}$$

$$(prm, msk) \leftarrow S(1^k);$$

$$(id_0, id_1, s) \leftarrow B_1^{K(msk, \cdot)}(prm);$$

$$(ct, kem) \leftarrow E(id_b, prm);$$

$$b' \leftarrow B_2^{K^{\{id_0, id_1\}}(msk, \cdot)}(ct, kem, s);$$

In the above, key generation oracle $K(msk, \cdot)$ gets as input the msk, and arbitrary $id \in \mathcal{ID}$. It outputs a user secret key usk_{id} associated with id. B_1 cannot use the already queried ID to $K(msk, \cdot)$ as the target ID (id_0, id_1). If B_2

queries id_0 or id_1 to $K^{\{id_0,id_1\}}(msk, \cdot)$, $K^{\{id_0,id_1\}}(msk, \cdot)$ outputs $\perp$. We define the advantage $\mathbf{Adv}_{\Sigma,B}^{\mathrm{LOR}}(k)$ as follows;

$$\mathbf{Adv}_{\Sigma,B}^{\mathrm{LOR}}(k) := |\Pr[\mathbf{Exp}_{\Sigma,B}^{\mathrm{LOR}\text{-}0}(k) \to 1] - \Pr[\mathbf{Exp}_{\Sigma,B}^{\mathrm{LOR}\text{-}1}(k) \to 1].|.$$

Definition 2 (Ano-LOR). *We say that IBE scheme $\Sigma = (S, K, E, D)$ is Ano-LOR secure if $\mathbf{Adv}_{\Sigma,B}^{\mathrm{LOR}}(k)$ is negligible for any PPT adversary $B = (B_1, B_2)$.*

Discussion of Ano-LOR. Ano-LOR already captures certain kind of security, but we do not know whether it captures more natural semantic security notion of anonymity because Ano-LOR is defined based on the notion of indistinguishability.

To make the point clearer, let us recall the relationship between the security notion of public key encryption (PKE), which is simpler than IBE. To capture the intuition that the adversary cannot learn any information about encrypted message, Goldwasser and Micali [24] introduced the notion of semantic security (SS). In addition, they also defined simpler, but less intuitive notion of indistinguishability (IND). As shown by them, these definitions are in fact equivalent. Thanks to their result, we can use the simpler IND security notion when we give a security proof for a PKE scheme.

3   Simulation-Based Definition of Anonymity

In this section, we provide our definition of anonymity for IB-KEM named Ano-SS. Our definition captures a natural notion of security that the adversary cannot get any information on ID associated with a ciphertext. To validate our definition, we prove that our security notion implies Ano-LOR.

3.1   Defining Ano-SS for IB-KEM

Here, we address semantic security style definition of the anonymity for IB-KEM that we call Ano-SS in the following. A natural starting point for doing so would be adapt the definition of semantic security by Goldwasser and Micali [24] to our setting. Since their security notion has been successfully extended to other primitives including IBE and the equivalence to indistinguishability security notions have been shown [6], this seems to be a promising approach. However, as we explain in Appendix A, it turned out that it is not straightforward to define the notion based on their approach. The difficulty stems from the fact that while most of the previous work defining semantic security including [6] focuses on the data privacy of IBE, we focus on the anonymity and asymmetry between message and identity prohibits us from naturally extending the security notion to our setting. We refer to Appendix A for more details. Alternatively, we provide our semantic security notion of anonymity for IB-KEM by specializing the definition by Wee [28] that is defined for more general notion of attribute-based encryption to the setting of IB-KEM.

Definition. In the following, we provide the special case of Wee's definition for anonymity [28] where we only consider IB-KEM instead of ABE. We call our definition Ano-SS. Let $\Sigma = (S, K, E, D)$ be an IB-KEM scheme and $C = (C_1, C_2)$ be a PPT adversary. We also let $\Sigma^* = (S^*, K^*, E^*)$ be a simulator, which possibly depends on the adversary. We consider the following two experiments $\mathbf{Exp}_{\Sigma,C}^{\text{SS-REAL}}(k)$ and $\mathbf{Exp}_{\Sigma,\Sigma^*,C}^{\text{SS-IDEAL}}(k)$.

$$\underline{\mathbf{Exp}_{\Sigma,C}^{\text{SS-REAL}}(k)}$$
$$(prm, msk) \leftarrow S(1^k);$$
$$(id^*, s) \leftarrow C_1^{K(msk,\cdot)}(prm);$$
$$(ct, kem) \leftarrow E(prm, id^*);$$
$$v \leftarrow C_2^{K^{\{id^*\}}(msk,\cdot)}(ct, kem, s);$$

$$\underline{\mathbf{Exp}_{\Sigma,\Sigma^*,C}^{\text{SS-IDEAL}}(k)}$$
$$(prm, msk) \leftarrow S^*(1^k);$$
$$(id^*, s) \leftarrow C_1^{K^*(msk,\cdot)}(prm);$$
$$ct \leftarrow E^*(msk); \; kem' \leftarrow \mathcal{K};$$
$$v \leftarrow C_2^{K^*(msk,\cdot)}(ct, kem', s);$$

In the above, $\mathcal{K}$ is a symmetric-key space. Key generation oracle $K(msk, \cdot)$ and simulator $K^*(msk, \cdot)$ get as input the msk and arbitrary $id \in \mathcal{ID}$, and output user secret key usk_{id} associated with id. C_1 cannot use id^* that is queried to KeyGen oracle as the target ID. If C_2 queries id^* to $K^{\{id^*\}}(msk,\cdot)$, $K^{\{id^*\}}(msk, \cdot)$ outputs $\bot$. At the end of the game, C_2 outputs a bit $v = \{0, 1\}$. We define the advantage $\mathbf{Adv}_{\Sigma,\Sigma^*,A}^{\text{Ano-SS}}(k)$ as follows

$$\mathbf{Adv}_{\Sigma,\Sigma^*,C}^{\text{SS}}(k) := \left| \Pr\left[\mathbf{Exp}_{\Sigma,C}^{\text{SS-REAL}}(k) \rightarrow 1 \right] - \Pr\left[\mathbf{Exp}_{\Sigma,\Sigma^*,C}^{\text{SS-IDEAL}}(k) \rightarrow 1 \right] \right|$$

Definition 3 (Ano-SS). *We say that IB-KEM scheme $\Sigma = (S, K, E, D)$ is Ano-SS secure if for any PPT adversary $C = (C_1, C_2)$ there exists a PPT simulator $\Sigma^* = (S^*, K^*, E^*)$ such that $\mathbf{Adv}_{\Sigma,\Sigma^*,C}^{\text{Ano-SS}}(k)$ is negligible.*

In the above, C tries to guess whether it is in SS-REAL or SS-IDEAL from the information it obtains during the game. In SS-REAL, C gets (ct, kem) that is generated with respect to the challenge identity id^* chosen by C. In SS-IDEAL, C gets (ct, kem'), which is generated by the simulator E^* that does not see id^* at all. If C cannot distinguish SS-REAL from SS-IDEAL, it indicates that the information of id^* is not leaked to C.

3.2   Proof that Ano-SS Implies Ano-LOR

In this section we show that any Ano-SS secure IB-KEM is also Ano-LOR secure. The theorem and the proof is as follows.

Theorem 1. *If an IB-KEM scheme $\Sigma = (S, K, E, D)$ is Ano-SS secure, Σ is Ano-LOR secure.*

Proof. We will prove that if Σ is not Ano-LOR secure, then Σ is not Ano-SS secure. That is, we construct PPT adversary against Ano-SS security using PPT adversary against Ano-LOR security.

$$B_1^{\mathcal{O}}(prm): \qquad\qquad\qquad \left| \quad B_2^{\mathcal{O}^{\{id_b\}}}(ct, kem, s): \right.$$
$$\quad (id_0, id_1, s) \leftarrow A_1^{K(msk, \cdot)}(prm) \quad \left| \quad b' \leftarrow A_2^{K^{\{id_0, id_1\}}(msk, \cdot)}(ct, kem, s) \right.$$
$$\quad b \leftarrow \{0, 1\} \qquad\qquad\qquad \left| \quad \text{If} \right.$$
$$\quad \text{output } (id_b, s) \qquad\qquad \left| \quad v := b' \right.$$
$$\qquad\qquad\qquad\qquad\qquad\quad \left| \quad \text{output } v \right.$$

Fig. 1. The construction of Ano-SS adversary $B = (B_1, B_2)$ using Ano-LOR adversary $A = (A_1, A_2)$.

$$\mathbf{Exp}_{\Sigma, B}^{\text{SS-REAL}} \qquad\qquad\qquad \left| \quad \mathbf{Exp}_{\Sigma, \Sigma^*, B}^{\text{SS-IDEAL}} \right.$$

$$\overline{(msk, prm) \leftarrow S(1^k)} \qquad\qquad \left| \quad \overline{(msk, prm) \leftarrow S^*(1^k)} \right.$$
$$\quad (id_b, s) \leftarrow B_1^{K(msk, \cdot)}(prm) \quad \left| \quad (id_b, s) \leftarrow B_1^{K^*(msk, \cdot)}(prm) \right.$$
$$\quad (ct, kem) \leftarrow E(id_b, prm) \quad \left| \quad (ct, kem) \leftarrow E^*(msk) \right.$$
$$\qquad\qquad\qquad\qquad\qquad\quad \left| \quad kem' \leftarrow \mathcal{K} \right.$$
$$\quad v \leftarrow B_2^{K^{\{id_b\}}(msk, \cdot)}(ct, kem, s) \quad \left| \quad v \leftarrow B_2^{K^*\{id_b\}(msk, \cdot)}(ct, kem', s) \right.$$

Fig. 2. Adversary $B = (B_1, B_2)$ in the Ano-SS game.

Let $A = (A_1, A_2)$ be an arbitrary PPT adversary against the Ano-LOR security of Σ. The construction of PPT adversary $B = (B_1, B_2)$ against Ano-SS security using A is shown in Fig. 1.

In Fig. 1, $\mathcal{O}$ is key generation oracle, that takes msk and arbitrary $id' \in \mathcal{ID}$ as input and outputs $usk_{id'}$ associated with id'. When A queries id', B queries id' to $\mathcal{O}$ and return $usk_{id'}$ to A. In Fig. 2, we provide the description of the Ano-SS game with B.

Here, we discuss that if B is in the real game, B perfectly simulates the Ano-LOR game for A. First, we observe that any key query made by A is answered by B, who queries the same identity to $K(msk, \cdot)$ to obtain the secret key and passes it to A. Furthermore, B can answer any secret key query made by A because A is prohibited from making secret key query for id_0 or id_1 whereas B is prohibited the query only for id_b. Thus we have

$$\Pr[\mathbf{Exp}_{\Sigma, B}^{\text{SS-REAL}}(k) \to 1] = \Pr[b = b' | \mathbf{Exp}_{\Sigma, A}^{\text{LOR-}b}(k) \to b'].$$

Next, we will discuss the view of A in case B is in the ideal game. In this case, b is information theoretically hidden from A because (ct, kem) is generated by E^* that does not take id^* as input. Since b' is independent from b, we have

$$\Pr[\mathbf{Exp}_{\Sigma, \Sigma^*, B}^{\text{SS-IDEAL}}(k) \to 1] = \frac{1}{2}.$$

Finally, we have that

$$\mathbf{Adv}^{\mathrm{SS}}_{\Sigma,\Sigma^*,B}(k) = |\Pr[\mathbf{Exp}^{\mathrm{SS\text{-}REAL}}_{\Sigma,B}(k) \to 1] - \Pr[\mathbf{Exp}^{\mathrm{SS\text{-}IDEAL}}_{\Sigma,\Sigma^*,B}(k) \to 1]|$$
$$= |\Pr[b = b'|\mathbf{Exp}^{\mathrm{LOR}-b}_{\Sigma,A}(k) \to b'] - \frac{1}{2}|$$
$$= \mathbf{Adv}^{\mathrm{LOR}}_{\Sigma,A}(k).$$

Since A is the Ano-LOR adversary, $\mathbf{Adv}^{\mathrm{LOR}}_{\Sigma,A}(k)$ is a non-negligible. Hence, $\mathbf{Adv}^{\mathrm{SS}}_{\Sigma,\Sigma^*,B}(k)$ is also a non-negligible function.

From the above, it is true that if there is an Ano-LOR adversary A, then there is also an Ano-SS adversary B. Accordingly, if Σ is Ano-SS secure, then Σ is Ano-LOR secure.   □

$$
\begin{array}{l|l}
S^*(1^k): & E^*(msk): \\
\quad (prm, msk) \leftarrow S(1^k) & \quad id_1 \leftarrow \mathcal{ID} \\
\quad \text{output } (prm, msk) & \quad (ct, kem) \leftarrow E(id_1, prm) \\
\cline{1-1} & \quad \text{output } ct \\
K^*(msk, id): & \\
\quad usk \leftarrow K(msk, id) & \\
\quad \text{output } usk & \\
\end{array}
$$

Fig. 3. The construction of Σ^*.

4   Equivalence Between Ano-LOR and Ano-SS

In this section, we show that any Ano-LOR secure IB-KEM is also Ano-SS secure. Since we proved the other direction of the implication in Theorem 1, this implies that these two security notions are in fact equivalent.

As mentioned in the introduction, the security proof will be done by standard techniques with one exception. We elaborate on this in the following. In the security proof, we let the simulator generate a ciphertext for random identity. We then gradually change the game from the real game where the adversary is given a ciphertext corresponding to the identity chosen by itself to the ideal game where the ciphertext is chosen by the simulator. If our focus was on payload hiding, this change would be straightforward. However, our focus is on anonymity and this means that we have to come up with a reduction that abides by the restriction on key extraction queries, which is a challenge that is not present in the payload hiding settings. In particular, in order to invoke Ano-LOR security to prove indistinguishability between the real and ideal games, we have to make sure that the underlying Ano-SS adversary does not make a key extraction query for the random identity chosen by the simulator more than negligible probability, even if it is given the ciphertext corresponding to that identity. This step cannot be done without computational assumption since the challenge ciphertext carries the information of the associated identity in information theoretic sense. Instead of information theoretic argument, we prove this by the additional invocation of Ano-LOR security.

The theorem and the proof is as follows. The proof will be done by considering sequence of games. While the changes from Game 0 to Game 3 are standard, the change from Game 3 to Game 4 requires more complicated argument reflecting the difficulty we outlined above.

Theorem 2. *If an IB-KEM scheme $\Sigma = (S, K, E, D)$ is Ano-LOR secure and IND-ID-CPA secure, then Σ is Ano-SS secure.*

Proof. Let $A = (A_1, A_2)$ be an arbitrary probabilistic polynomial-time adversary against the Ano-SS security of Σ. We construct a simulator $\Sigma^* = (S^*, E^*, K^*)$ satisfying $\mathbf{Adv}^{\mathrm{SS}}_{\Sigma, \Sigma^*, A}(k) \leq \varepsilon(k)$. The construction of Σ^* is shown in Fig. 3. The proof proceeds with a sequence of games. The description of the games is shown

Game 0:
$$(prm, msk) \leftarrow S(1^k)$$
$$(id_0, s) \leftarrow A_1^{K(msk,\cdot)}(prm)$$

$$(ct, kem) \leftarrow E(prm, id_0)$$

$$v \leftarrow A_2^{K^{\{id_0\}}(msk,\cdot)}(ct, kem, s)$$

Game 1:
$$(prm, msk) \leftarrow S(1^k)$$
$$(id_0, s) \leftarrow A_1^{K(msk,\cdot)}(prm)$$
$$id_1 \leftarrow \mathcal{ID}$$
$$(ct, kem) \leftarrow E(prm, id_0)$$

$$v \leftarrow A_2^{K^{\{id_0, id_1\}}}(ct, kem, s)$$

Game 2:
$$(prm, msk) \leftarrow S(1^k)$$
$$(id_0, s) \leftarrow A_1^{K(msk,\cdot)}(prm)$$
$$id_1 \leftarrow \mathcal{ID}$$
$$(ct, kem) \leftarrow E(prm, id_1)$$

$$v \leftarrow A_2^{K^{\{id_0, id_1\}}(msk,\cdot)}(ct, kem, s)$$

Game 3:
$$(prm, msk) \leftarrow S(1^k)$$
$$(id_0, s) \leftarrow A_1^{K(msk,\cdot)}(prm)$$
$$id_1 \leftarrow \mathcal{ID}$$
$$(ct, kem) \leftarrow E(prm, id_1)$$
$$kem' \leftarrow \mathcal{K}$$
$$v \leftarrow A_2^{K^{\{id_0, id_1\}}(msk,\cdot)}(ct, kem', s)$$

Game 4:
$$(prm, msk) \leftarrow S^*(1^k)$$
$$(id_0, s) \leftarrow A_1^{K(msk,\cdot)}(prm)$$

$$ct \leftarrow E^*(msk)$$
$$kem' \leftarrow \mathcal{K}$$
$$v \leftarrow A_2^{K^{\{id_0\}}(msk,\cdot)}(ct, kem', s)$$

Fig. 4. The sequence of games for the proof of the Ano-SS security.

in Fig. 4. In the description of the games, by $K^S(msk, \cdot)$ we denote the oracle that returns $K(msk, id)$ to the query id if $id \notin S$ and returns $\perp$ if $id \in S$.

In the following, let G_i be the event that the output v of the adversary A_2 is equal to 1. Since Game 0 is identical to the SS-REAL game, it holds that $\Pr[G_0] = \Pr[\mathbf{Exp}_{\Sigma, A}^{\text{SS-REAL}}(k) \to 1]$. Similarly, Game 4 is identical to the SS-IDEAL game, it also holds that $\Pr[G_4] = \Pr[\mathbf{Exp}_{\Sigma, \Sigma^*, A}^{\text{SS-IDEAL}}(k) \to 1]$. Due to the triangle inequality, it holds that $|\Pr[\mathbf{Exp}_{\Sigma, A}^{\text{SS-REAL}}(k) \to 1] - \Pr[\mathbf{Exp}_{\Sigma, \Sigma^*, A}^{\text{SS-IDEAL}}(k) \to 1]| \leq \sum_{i=0}^{3} |\Pr[G_i] - \Pr[G_{i+1}]|$.

We bound these terms by proving the following propositions. Let q be an upper bound on the number of the queries that A_1 and A_2 issue in total.

Proposition 1. *It holds that $|\Pr[G_0] - \Pr[G_1]| \leq q/|\mathcal{ID}|$.*

Proof (of Proposition 1). The games differ only when A_2 issues id_1 as a query to the oracle. Since the choice of id_1 is completely hidden from A_2 and is chosen uniformly random over $\mathcal{ID}$, the probability that A_2 issues id_1 as an oracle query is at most that $q/|\mathcal{ID}|$. Hence due to the difference lemma [40], the proposition follows.

$B_1(prm)$:
$\quad (id_0, s) \leftarrow A_1^{K(msk, \cdot)}(prm)$
$\quad id_1 \leftarrow \mathcal{ID}$
$\quad$ output (id_0, id_1, s)

$B_2(ct, kem, s)$:
$\quad v \leftarrow C^{K^{\{id_0, id_1\}}(msk, \cdot)}(ct, kem, s)$
$\quad$ output $b' \leftarrow v$

Fig. 5. The adversary $B = (B_1, B_2)$ for proving Proposition 2.

$B_1'(prm)$:
$\quad (id_0, s) \leftarrow A_1^{K(msk, \cdot)}(prm)$
$\quad id_1 \leftarrow \mathcal{ID}$
$\quad$ output (id_1, s)

$B_2'(ct, kem, s)$:
$\quad v \leftarrow C^{K^{\{id_0, id_1\}}(msk, \cdot)}(ct, kem, s)$
$\quad$ output $b' \leftarrow v$

Fig. 6. The adversary $B' = (B_1', B_2')$ for proving Proposition 3.

Proposition 2. *There exists an adversary $B = (B_1, B_2)$ attacking the Ano-LOR security of Σ whose advantage satisfies $|\Pr[G_1] - \Pr[G_2]| = \mathbf{Adv}_{\Sigma, B}^{\text{Ano-LOR}}(k)$.*

Proof (of Proposition 2). We construct an adversary $B = (B_1, B_2)$ as in Fig. 5. The adversary B_2 is prohibited from obtaining a user secret key for id_0 and id_1, however, it is able to simulate the oracle for A_2, since for the oracle queries

id_0 or id_1 form A_2, it is sufficient to return $\perp$ to properly simulate the oracle $K^{\{id_0,id_1\}}(msk,\cdot)$. For the other oracle queries from A_2, it is sufficient to forward the queries to B_2's own oracle. Furthermore, if ct is an encapsulation with identity id_0, B perfectly simulates Game 1. Similarly, if ct is an encapsulation with identify id_1, B perfectly simulates Game 2. Therefore, it holds that

$$|\Pr[G_1] - \Pr[G_2]|$$
$$= |\Pr[\mathbf{Exp}_{\Sigma,B}^{\text{LOR-0}}(k) \to 1] - \Pr[\mathbf{Exp}_{\Sigma,B}^{\text{LOR-1}}(k) \to 1]|$$
$$= \mathbf{Adv}_{\Sigma,B}^{\text{LOR}}(k),$$

which proves the proposition.

Proposition 3. *There exists an adversary* $B' = (B_1', B_2')$ *attacking the IND-ID-CPA security of* Σ *whose advantage satisfies* $|\Pr[G_2] - \Pr[G_3]| = \mathbf{Adv}_{\Sigma,B'}^{\text{IND-ID-CPA}}(k)$.

Proof (of Proposition 3). We construct an adversary $B' = (B_1', B_2')$ as in Fig. 6. Similarly to the proof of Proposition 2, the adversary B_2' is not allowed to obtain a user secret key for id_1. This does not cause B_2''s failure in simulating the oracle for A_2, because for A_2' query id_1 it is sufficient to responds with $\perp$. In addition, if kem is the real session key encapsulated in ct, B' perfectly simulates Game 2. Similarly, if kem is the random session key, B' perfectly simulates Game 3. Thus we have that

$$|\Pr[G_2] - \Pr[G_3]|$$
$$= |\Pr[\mathbf{Exp}_{\Sigma,B'}^{\text{IND-ID-CPA-0}}(k) \to 1] - \Pr[\mathbf{Exp}_{\Sigma,B'}^{\text{IND-ID-CPA-1}}(k) \to 1]|$$
$$= \mathbf{Adv}_{\Sigma,B'}^{\text{IND-ID-CPA}}(k),$$

which proves the proposition.

Game 3-1:
$$(prm, msk) \leftarrow S(1^k)$$
$$(id_0, s) \leftarrow A_1^{K(msk,\cdot)}(prm)$$
$$id_1 \leftarrow \mathcal{ID}$$
$$id_2 \leftarrow \mathcal{ID}$$
$$(ct, kem) \leftarrow E(prm, id_1)$$
$$kem' \leftarrow \mathcal{K}$$
$$v \leftarrow A_2^{K^{\{id_0,id_1,id_2\}}(prm,\cdot)}(ct, kem', s)$$

Game 3-2:
$$(prm, msk) \leftarrow S(1^k)$$
$$(id_0, s) \leftarrow A_1^{K(msk,\cdot)}(prm)$$
$$id_1 \leftarrow \mathcal{ID}$$
$$id_2 \leftarrow \mathcal{ID}$$
$$(ct, kem) \leftarrow E(prm, id_2)$$
$$kem' \leftarrow \mathcal{K}$$
$$v \leftarrow A_2^{K^{\{id_0,id_1,id_2\}}(prm,\cdot)}(ct, kem', s)$$

Fig. 7. The subsidiary games for proving Proposition 4.

$B_1''(prm)$:
$\quad (id_0, s) \leftarrow A_1^{K(msk, \cdot)}(prm)$
$\quad id_1 \leftarrow \mathcal{ID}$
$\quad id_2 \leftarrow \mathcal{ID}$
$\quad$ output (id_1, id_2, s)

$B_2''(ct, kem, s)$:
$\quad kem' \leftarrow \mathcal{K}$
$\quad v \leftarrow A_2^{K^{\{id_0, id_1, id_2\}}(msk, \cdot)}(ct, kem', s)$
$\quad$ if id_1 is queried by A_2 then
$\quad\quad b' \leftarrow 1$
$\quad$ else
$\quad\quad b' \leftarrow 0$
$\quad$ output b'

Fig. 8. The adversary $B'' = (B_1'', B_2'')$ for proving Lemma 2.

Proposition 4. *There exists adversary* $\mathcal{B}'' = (B_1'', B_2'')$ *attacking the Ano-LOR security of* Σ *whose advantage satisfies* $|\mathrm{Pr}[G_3] - \mathrm{Pr}[G_4]| \leq 2q/|\mathcal{ID}| + \mathbf{Adv}_{\Sigma, B''}^{\mathrm{LOR}}(k)$.

Proof (of Proposition 4). Game 3 and 4 differ only when A_2 issues the oracle query id_1. Let us denote by F this event. Due to the difference lemma [40], we have that $|\mathrm{Pr}[G_3] - \mathrm{Pr}[G_4]| \leq \mathrm{Pr}[F]$. To bound the probability $\mathrm{Pr}[F]$, we introduce the following subsidiary sequence of games (Fig. 7). Let $F_{3\text{-}i}$ be the event that A_2 queries id_1 in Game 3-i. From the triangle inequality, we have that $\mathrm{Pr}[F] \leq |\mathrm{Pr}[F_3] - \mathrm{Pr}[F_{3\text{-}1}]| + |\mathrm{Pr}[F_{3\text{-}1}] - \mathrm{Pr}[F_{3\text{-}2}]| + \mathrm{Pr}[F_{3\text{-}2}]$. We bound these three terms in the following lemmas.

Lemma 1. *It holds that* $|\mathrm{Pr}[F_3] - \mathrm{Pr}[F_{3\text{-}1}]| \leq q/|\mathcal{ID}|$.

Proof (of Lemma 1). The games differ only when $\mathcal{A}_2$ issues the oracle query id_2. Since id_2 is completely hidden from A_2 and is chosen uniformly random over $\mathcal{ID}$, the probability that A_2 issues id_2 as an oracle query is at most $q/|\mathcal{ID}|$. Then, from the difference lemma [40], the lemma holds.

Lemma 2. *There exists an adversary* $B'' = (B_1'', B_2'')$ *attacking the IND-ID-CPA security of* Σ *whose advantage satisfies* $|\mathrm{Pr}[F_{3\text{-}1}] - \mathrm{Pr}[F_{3\text{-}2}]| = \mathbf{Adv}_{\Sigma, B''}^{\mathrm{IND\text{-}ID\text{-}CPA}}(k)$.

Proof (of Lemma 2). We construct an adversary $B'' = (B_1'', B_2'')$ as in Fig. 8. The adversary B_2'' is not allowed to obtain a user secret key for id_1 and id_2. However, this does not cause B_2'''s failure of the simulation of the oracle $K^{\{id_0, id_1, id_2\}}(msk, \cdot)$, because for the oracle query id_1 and id_2 it is sufficient to respond with $\bot$. Moreover, if ct is an encapsulation with identity id_1, B'' perfectly simulates Game 3-1, and if ct is an encapsulation with identity id_2, B'' perfectly simulates Game 3-2. Furthermore, both in Game 3-1 and 3-2, if and only if A_2 queries id_1, namely, if and only if the event $F_{3\text{-}1}$ or $F_{3\text{-}2}$ occur, B_2'' outputs 1. Therefore, it holds that

$$|\mathrm{Pr}[F_{3\text{-}1}] - \mathrm{Pr}[F_{3\text{-}1}]|$$
$$= |\mathrm{Pr}[\mathbf{Exp}_{\Sigma, B''}^{\mathrm{LOR\text{-}0}}(k) \rightarrow 1] - \mathrm{Pr}[\mathbf{Exp}_{\Sigma, B''}^{\mathrm{LOR\text{-}1}}(k) \rightarrow 1]|$$
$$= \mathbf{Adv}_{\Sigma, B''}^{\mathrm{LOR}}(k),$$

which proves the lemma.

Lemma 3. *It holds that* $\Pr[F_{3\text{-}2}] \leq q/|\mathcal{ID}|$.

Proof (of Lemma 3). In Game 3-2, id_1 is completely hidden from A_2 and is chosen uniformly random over $\mathcal{ID}$. Thus the probability that A_2 issues the oracle query id_1 is at most $q/|\mathcal{ID}|$.

Lemmas 1, 2, and 3 show that $\Pr[F] \leq |\Pr[F_3] - \Pr[F_{3\text{-}1}]| + |\Pr[F_{3\text{-}1}] - \Pr[F_{3\text{-}2}]| + \Pr[F_{3\text{-}2}] \leq q/|\mathcal{ID}| + \mathbf{Adv}^{\mathrm{LOR}}_{\Sigma,B''}(k) + q/|\mathcal{ID}|$, which concludes the proof of the proposition.

Finally, combining all the propositions, we have that

$$\mathbf{Adv}^{\mathrm{SS}}_{\Sigma,\Sigma^*,A}(k) = |\Pr[\mathbf{Exp}^{\mathrm{SS\text{-}REAL}}(k) \to 1] - \Pr[\mathbf{Exp}^{\mathrm{SS\text{-}IDEAL}}(k) \to 1]|$$
$$\leq \frac{q}{|\mathcal{ID}|} + \mathbf{Adv}^{\mathrm{LOR}}_{\Sigma,B}(k) + \mathbf{Adv}^{\mathrm{IND\text{-}ID\text{-}CPA}}_{\Sigma,B'}(k) + \frac{2q}{|\mathcal{ID}|} + \mathbf{Adv}^{\mathrm{LOR}}_{\Sigma,B''}(k).$$

Since q is a polynomial of the security parameter k, and $|\mathcal{ID}|$ is exponential in k, then $q/|\mathcal{ID}|$ is negligible in k. Therefore, if Σ is Ano-LOR secure and IND-ID-CPA secure, then Σ is Ano-SS secure.

5 Discussion

In this section we discuss some theoretical and practical implications drawn from our results.

Equivalence of Simulation-Based and IND-Based Definitions. Firstly and obviously, our results claim that the IND-based definition is equivalent to the simulation-based definition for anonymity of IBE. This equivalence brings the following two desirable effects to the community. The first is that all the existing Ano-LOR secure IBE schemes are now automatically Ano-SS secure. Therefore, their anonymity becomes more reliable and theoretically well-founded all at once. The second is that if we want to design a new Ano-SS secure IBE scheme, it is sufficient to prove that a scheme is Ano-LOR secure. We notice that it eases the cost of providing a security proof, since the IND-based notion of Ano-LOR is easier to deal with than the simulation-based notion of Ano-SS. Nevertheless, our results ensure that a scheme which is proven Ano-LOR secure is also Ano-SS secure without any additional proofs.

Clarification of the Relation Between the Intuition and the Definition. Secondly, our results clarify the relationship between our intuition of anonymity and the security that is captured by Ano-LOR. As mentioned in the introduction, our Ano-SS notion captures the intuition that the recipient's ID is not leaked from a ciphertext more directly. In contrast to this, the Ano-LOR notion is designed analogously to the IND-CPA notion, which in turn results in an easier-to-deal-with but less intuitive notion. Filling this subtle gap between the two security notions, which has not been investigated more than 15 years, would improve our understanding on the security notions of IBE.

Potential Nontriviality in Proving Equivalence. Finally, our security proof suggests that we may encounter a situation where the IND-based notion is *not* equivalent to simulation-based notion depending on a cryptographic primitive in question. This is because in our security proof that Ano-LOR implies Ano-SS, there are several non-trivialities. For this nontriviality, we could not straightforwardly apply Goldwasser-Micali's technique [24] of proving the equivalence of an IND-based notion and a simulation-based notion.

This suggests that for more sophisticated primitives, there is possibility of not holding the equivalence between an IND-based secrecy notion and an simulation based one. Such a situation has already occurred in the context of functional encryption, where their IND-based and simulation-based notions are in fact *not* equivalent [11]. In addition, for selective-opening security of public-key encryption, the simulation-based security and the IND-based security do not imply each other [8]. For non-malleability of public-key encryption, there are variations of simulation-based definitions and IND-based definitions, and the relationships between them are quite complicated depending on whether the adversary has access to decryption oracle [36].

We conjecture that if the behavior of oracles and restriction on the adversary's queries become more and more complicated, it becomes more and more plausible to be unable to apply classical techniques to prove the equivalence between a simulation-based definition and an IND-based definition. We remark that the root of the non-triviality of our proof was the existence of *the key generation oracle*, which can be seen as an oracle with very basic type of functionality and it still brought an involved situation to the security game. Thus, it is important to study the equivalence between IND-based and simulation-based security notions for various cryptographic primitives, otherwise we may overlook a subtlety in the (in)equivalence between security notions of the different natures.

Other Studies that Rely on a Variant of Anonymity. As one possible application of our research, we mention that there are other studies on the security against key generation center (KGC) in IBE [16,21], which is a variant of the work on anonymity in IBE.

Chow [16] and Emura et al. [21] discuss the ciphertext anonymity against KGC to tackle the problem on the key escrow problem in IBE. If we try to discuss this idea formally, we need a security definition in which the ciphertext is anonymous, even if the master key is given to the malicious adversary. They discussed this problem based on IND-based ciphertext anonymity introduced by Chow [16].

As we have discussed in this paper, it would be desirable here as well if the relationship between IND-based security and SIM-based security are clarified so that we can better understand what the definition actually means.

Although our definition does not provide a definition capturing the situation that master key is given to adversary, we believe that our results are useful as first step in providing such a definition.

Acknowledgement. We would like to thank the reviewers of ESORICS 2020 and Sherman S. M. Chow for precious comments. A part of this work was supported by JSPS KAKENHI Grant Number 18K18055, JSPS KAKENHI Grant Number 19H01109, and JST CREST Grant Number JPMJCR19F6.

A   Attempt to Define Anonymity Based on Goldwasser and Micali's Approach

Definition Based on Goldwasser-Micali [24]. Here, we briefly recall the notion of semantic security (SS) defined by Goldwasser and Micali [24]. We say that a PKE scheme satisfies SS if there exists a simulator that can simulate view for an adversary that is indistinguishable from that of the real world where the adversary chooses a message and is given a ciphertext that encrypts it and the simulator is not provided any information of the message. In this section, we attempt to define SS for anonymity of IB-KEM following their approach [24] and observe that there seems no straightforward way to do so.

Let $\Sigma = (S, K, E, D)$ be an IB-KEM scheme, and $C = (C_1, C_2)$ be a PPT adversary. We also let $\mathcal{S} = (\mathcal{S}_1, \mathcal{S}_2)$ be a simulator. We formulate Ano-SS as follows: if the game SS-REAL ($\mathbf{Exp}_{\Sigma,C}^{\text{SS-REAL}}(k)$) where the adversary receives the ciphertext and guesses the information of the identity and the game SS-IDEAL ($\mathbf{Exp}_{\Sigma,\mathcal{S}}^{\text{SS-IDEAL}}(k)$) where the simulator $\mathcal{S}$ generates a simulated ciphertext without receiving the identity, is indistinguishable, then the IB-KEM scheme is said to satisfy Ano-SS.

$$
\begin{aligned}
&\underline{\mathbf{Exp}_{\Sigma,C}^{\text{SS-REAL}}(k)} \\
&(prm, msk) \leftarrow S(1^k); \\
&((P, F), s) \leftarrow C_1^{K(msk, \cdot)}(prm); \\
&id^* \leftarrow P(\mathcal{ID}) \\
&(ct, kem) \leftarrow E(prm, id^*); \\
&v \leftarrow C_2^{K(msk, \cdot)}(ct, kem, s); \\
&\beta := 1 \leftrightarrow v = F(id^*)
\end{aligned}
\qquad
\begin{aligned}
&\underline{\mathbf{Exp}_{\Sigma,\mathcal{S}}^{\text{SS-IDEAL}}(k)} \\
&(prm, msk) \leftarrow S(1^k); \\
&((P, F), s) \leftarrow \mathcal{S}_1(prm); \\
&id^* \leftarrow P(\mathcal{ID}) \\
& \\
&v \leftarrow \mathcal{S}_2(s); \\
&\beta := 1 \leftrightarrow v = F(id^*)
\end{aligned}
$$

In the above, P and F are PPT algorithms. P samples id^* from the ID space $\mathcal{ID}$, and F outputs partial information of the input. Key generation oracle $K(msk, \cdot)$ in $\mathbf{Exp}_{\Sigma,C}^{\text{SS-REAL}}(k)$ gets as input msk and arbitrary $id \in \mathcal{ID}$, and outputs a user secret key usk_{id} associated with id. C_1 cannot use the challenge identity id^* that is queried to $K^{\{id^*\}}(msk, \cdot)$ as the target ID. We define $\mathbf{Adv}_{\Sigma,C,\mathcal{S}}^{\text{SS}}(k)$, the advantage of the Ano-SS adversary as follows

$$
\mathbf{Adv}_{\Sigma,C,\mathcal{S}}^{\text{SS}}(k) := |\Pr[\mathbf{Exp}_{\Sigma,C}^{\text{SS-REAL}}(k) \to 1] - \Pr[\mathbf{Exp}_{\Sigma,\mathcal{S}}^{\text{SS-IDEAL}}(k) \to 1]|.
$$

Definition 4. *We say that IB-KEM scheme $\Sigma = (S, K, E, D)$ is* Ano-SS *secure if for any PPT adversary $C = (C_1, C_2)$ there exists PPT simulator $\mathcal{S}$ such that* $\mathbf{Adv}_{\Sigma,C,\mathcal{S}}^{\text{Ano-SS}}(k)$ *is negligible.*

Discussion on Definition 4. As we discuss here, Definition 4 is an incomplete security definition since there is an adversary that trivially breaks the security. For example, let us assume that $K(msk, \cdot)$ returns the user secret key usk_{id^*} associated with id^* when id^* is queried to the key generation oracle. In this case, the adversary can decrypt (ct, kem) encrypted with respect to the target ID id^* using usk_{id^*} and the adversary can identify the target ID by seeing if the decryption result matches with kem. We then discuss whether the adversary can indeed get a secret key for id^* from the oracle, since this is a sufficient condition for the above attack to succeed. Recall that id^* is sampled from the ID space $\mathcal{ID}$ by the polynomial time algorithm P. If the total number of IDs that P can output is at most a polynomial size, C is in fact able to find id^* by brute force attack in polynomial time. For this reason, in order to make Definition 4 an achievable security definition, it is necessary to add some constraint on the adversary's behavior. However, with such a constraint, we do not know whether the security notion is still meaningful. For example, we can consider following constraints. However, all of them have problems as we explain below.

Prohibit queries on key generation oracle

As mentioned above, one of the trivial attacks is to query id^* on key generation oracle. If the user secret key usk_{id^*} is given to the adversary, it can learn the information of the target identity from it. To prevent this kind of attack, let us restrict the adversary so that it cannot make a key query for id^*. More concretely, let us consider an alternative security definition where key generation oracle $K(msk, \cdot)$ sends $\perp$ back to the adversary C_2 when it queries id^* to key generation oracle $K(msk, \cdot)$ in the SS-REAL environment. However, the adversary can learn the information of id^* from the fact that the user secret key query is prohibited for this particular identity.

Changing the sampling P settings

In the above discussion, it was assumed that the total number of ID that P will output is of polynomial size, and thus the above attack was possible. A natural approach to prevent the attack is to restrict the adversary C to output P such that the number of ID that P can output is exponential. In this case, it seems that there is no trivial attack on the security. However, this restriction is less general because we pose a strict restriction on the sampler chosen by the adversary and thus significantly narrow the class of adversaries we capture. Since the meaning of the definition is unclear, we do not take this approach either.

As we discussed above, we do not know of any natural restrictions on the adversary that makes the security notion natural and meaningful. Therefore, we do not adopt the approach by [24] for defining semantic security style notion of anonymity.

References

1. Abdalla, M., et al.: Searchable encryption revisited: consistency properties, relation to anonymous IBE, and extensions. In: Shoup, V. (ed.) CRYPTO 2005. LNCS, vol. 3621, pp. 205–222. Springer, Heidelberg (2005). https://doi.org/10.1007/11535218_13
2. Arasu, A., Eguro, K., Kaushik, R., Kossmann, D., Ramamurthy, R., Venkatesan, R.: A secure coprocessor for database applications. In: 23rd International Conference on Field programmable Logic and Applications (FPL 2013), Porto, Portugal, 2–4 September 2013, pp. 1–8. IEEE (2013)
3. Aroki Systems: End to End Encryption for Active Data. https://www.aroki.com
4. Asharov, G., Naor, M., Segev, G., Shahaf, I.: Searchable symmetric encryption: optimal locality in linear space via two-dimensional balanced allocations. In: Wichs, D., Mansour, Y. (eds.) STOC 2016, pp. 1101–1114. ACM (2016)
5. Asharov, G., Segev, G., Shahaf, I.: Tight tradeoffs in searchable symmetric encryption. In: Shacham, H., Boldyreva, A. (eds.) CRYPTO 2018. LNCS, vol. 10991, pp. 407–436. Springer, Cham (2018). https://doi.org/10.1007/978-3-319-96884-1_14
6. Attrapadung, N., et al.: Relations among notions of security for identity based encryption schemes. In: Correa, J.R., Hevia, A., Kiwi, M. (eds.) LATIN 2006. LNCS, vol. 3887, pp. 130–141. Springer, Heidelberg (2006). https://doi.org/10.1007/11682462_16
7. Blazy, O., Brouilhet, L., Phan, D.H.: Anonymous identity based encryption with traceable identities. In: ARES 2019, pp. 13:1–13:10 (2019)
8. Böhl, F., Hofheinz, D., Kraschewski, D.: On definitions of selective opening security. In: Fischlin, M., Buchmann, J., Manulis, M. (eds.) PKC 2012. LNCS, vol. 7293, pp. 522–539. Springer, Heidelberg (2012). https://doi.org/10.1007/978-3-642-30057-8_31
9. Boneh, D., Di Crescenzo, G., Ostrovsky, R., Persiano, G.: Public key encryption with keyword search. In: Cachin, C., Camenisch, J.L. (eds.) EUROCRYPT 2004. LNCS, vol. 3027, pp. 506–522. Springer, Heidelberg (2004). https://doi.org/10.1007/978-3-540-24676-3_30
10. Boneh, D., Franklin, M.: Identity-based encryption from the Weil pairing. In: Kilian, J. (ed.) CRYPTO 2001. LNCS, vol. 2139, pp. 213–229. Springer, Heidelberg (2001). https://doi.org/10.1007/3-540-44647-8_13
11. Boneh, D., Sahai, A., Waters, B.: Functional encryption: definitions and challenges. In: Ishai, Y. (ed.) TCC 2011. LNCS, vol. 6597, pp. 253–273. Springer, Heidelberg (2011). https://doi.org/10.1007/978-3-642-19571-6_16
12. Boneh, D., Waters, B.: Conjunctive, subset, and range queries on encrypted data. In: Vadhan, S.P. (ed.) TCC 2007. LNCS, vol. 4392, pp. 535–554. Springer, Heidelberg (2007). https://doi.org/10.1007/978-3-540-70936-7_29
13. Boyen, X., Waters, B.: Anonymous hierarchical identity-based encryption (without random oracles). In: Dwork, C. (ed.) CRYPTO 2006. LNCS, vol. 4117, pp. 290–307. Springer, Heidelberg (2006). https://doi.org/10.1007/11818175_17
14. Camenisch, J., Kohlweiss, M., Rial, A., Sheedy, C.: Blind and anonymous identity-based encryption and authorised private searches on public key encrypted data. In: Jarecki, S., Tsudik, G. (eds.) PKC 2009. LNCS, vol. 5443, pp. 196–214. Springer, Heidelberg (2009). https://doi.org/10.1007/978-3-642-00468-1_12
15. Cash, D., Tessaro, S.: The locality of searchable symmetric encryption. In: Nguyen, P.Q., Oswald, E. (eds.) EUROCRYPT 2014. LNCS, vol. 8441, pp. 351–368. Springer, Heidelberg (2014). https://doi.org/10.1007/978-3-642-55220-5_20

16. Chow, S.S.M.: Removing Escrow from identity-based encryption. In: Jarecki, S., Tsudik, G. (eds.) PKC 2009. LNCS, vol. 5443, pp. 256–276. Springer, Heidelberg (2009). https://doi.org/10.1007/978-3-642-00468-1_15

17. Cocks, C.: An identity based encryption scheme based on quadratic residues. In: Honary, B. (ed.) Cryptography and Coding 2001. LNCS, vol. 2260, pp. 360–363. Springer, Heidelberg (2001). https://doi.org/10.1007/3-540-45325-3_32

18. Crypteron: Crypteron introduces secure, searchable encryption. https://crypteron. com/blog/practical-searchable-encryption-and-security

19. Demertzis, I., Papadopoulos, D., Papamanthou, C.: Searchable encryption with optimal locality: achieving sublogarithmic read efficiency. In: Shacham, H., Boldyreva, A. (eds.) CRYPTO 2018. LNCS, vol. 10991, pp. 371–406. Springer, Cham (2018). https://doi.org/10.1007/978-3-319-96884-1_13

20. Demertzis, I., Papamanthou, C.: Fast searchable encryption with tunable locality. In: Salihoglu, S., Zhou, W., Chirkova, R., Yang, J., Suciu, D. (eds.) Proceedings of the 2017 ACM International Conference on Management of Data, SIGMOD Conference 2017, Chicago, IL, USA, 14–19 May 2017, pp. 1053–1067. ACM (2017)

21. Emura, K., Katsumata, S., Watanabe, Y.: Identity-based encryption with security against the KGC: a formal model and its instantiation from lattices. In: Sako, K., Schneider, S., Ryan, P.Y.A. (eds.) ESORICS 2019. LNCS, vol. 11736, pp. 113–133. Springer, Cham (2019). https://doi.org/10.1007/978-3-030-29962-0_6

22. Fan, C., Tseng, Y.: Anonymous multi-receiver identity-based authenticated encryption with CCA security. Symmetry 7(4), 1856–1881 (2015)

23. Gajek, S.: Dynamic symmetric searchable encryption from constrained functional encryption. In: Sako, K. (ed.) CT-RSA 2016. LNCS, vol. 9610, pp. 75–89. Springer, Cham (2016). https://doi.org/10.1007/978-3-319-29485-8_5

24. Goldwasser, S., Micali, S.: Probabilistic encryption. J. Comput. Syst. Sci. 28(2), 270–299 (1984)

25. Google: Encrypted BigQuery client. https://github.com/google/encrypted-bigquery-client

26. Grofig, P., et al.: Experiences and observations on the industrial implementation of a system to search over outsourced encrypted data. In: Katzenbeisser, S., Lotz, V., Weippl, E.R. (eds.) Sicherheit 2014: Sicherheit, Schutz und Zuverlässigkeit, Beiträge der 7. Jahrestagung des Fachbereichs Sicherheit der Gesellschaft für Informatik e.V. (GI), 19–21 März 2014, Wien, Österreich. LNI, vol. P-228, pp. 115–125. GI (2014). http://subs.emis.de/LNI/Proceedings/Proceedings228/article7.html

27. He, K., Weng, J., Liu, J., Liu, J.K., Liu, W., Deng, R.H.: Anonymous identity-based broadcast encryption with chosen-ciphertext security. In: AsiaCCS 2016, pp. 247–255 (2016)

28. Wee, H.: Attribute-hiding predicate encryption in bilinear groups, revisited. In: Kalai, Y., Reyzin, L. (eds.) TCC 2017. LNCS, vol. 10677, pp. 206–233. Springer, Cham (2017). https://doi.org/10.1007/978-3-319-70500-2_8

29. Ishai, Y., Kushilevitz, E., Lu, S., Ostrovsky, R.: Private large-scale databases with distributed searchable symmetric encryption. In: Sako, K. (ed.) CT-RSA 2016. LNCS, vol. 9610, pp. 90–107. Springer, Cham (2016). https://doi.org/10.1007/978-3-319-29485-8_6

30. Izabachène, M., Pointcheval, D.: New anonymity notions for identity-based encryption. In: SCN 2008, pp. 375–391 (2008)

31. Katz, J., Sahai, A., Waters, B.: Predicate encryption supporting disjunctions, polynomial equations, and inner products. In: Smart, N. (ed.) EUROCRYPT 2008. LNCS, vol. 4965, pp. 146–162. Springer, Heidelberg (2008). https://doi.org/10.1007/978-3-540-78967-3_9

32. Kurosawa, K., Ohtaki, Y.: How to update documents *verifiably* in searchable symmetric encryption. In: Abdalla, M., Nita-Rotaru, C., Dahab, R. (eds.) CANS 2013. LNCS, vol. 8257, pp. 309–328. Springer, Cham (2013). https://doi.org/10.1007/978-3-319-02937-5_17

33. Ma, X., Wang, X., Lin, D.: Anonymous identity-based encryption with identity recovery. In: Susilo, W., Yang, G. (eds.) ACISP 2018. LNCS, vol. 10946, pp. 360–375. Springer, Cham (2018). https://doi.org/10.1007/978-3-319-93638-3_21

34. Microsoft SQL Server: Always Encrypted Database Engine. https://goo.gl/51LwQ9

35. Park, D.J., Kim, K., Lee, P.J.: Public key encryption with conjunctive field keyword search. In: Lim, C.H., Yung, M. (eds.) WISA 2004. LNCS, vol. 3325, pp. 73–86. Springer, Heidelberg (2005). https://doi.org/10.1007/978-3-540-31815-6_7

36. Pass, R., Shelat, A., Vaikuntanathan, V.: Relations among notions of nonmalleability for encryption. In: Kurosawa, K. (ed.) ASIACRYPT 2007. LNCS, vol. 4833, pp. 519–535. Springer, Heidelberg (2007). https://doi.org/10.1007/978-3-540-76900-2_32

37. Popa, R.A., Redfield, C.M.S., Zeldovich, N., Balakrishnan, H.: CryptDB: processing queries on an encrypted database. Commun. ACM **55**(9), 103–111 (2012)

38. Sakai, R., Ohgishi, K., Kasahara, M.: Cryptosystems based on pairings. In: Proceedings of Symposium on Cryptography and Information Security, Japan (2000)

39. Shamir, A.: Identity-based cryptosystems and signature schemes. In: Blakley, G.R., Chaum, D. (eds.) CRYPTO 1984. LNCS, vol. 196, pp. 47–53. Springer, Heidelberg (1985). https://doi.org/10.1007/3-540-39568-7_5

40. Shoup, V.: Sequences of games: a tool for taming complexity in security proofs. IACR Cryptology ePrint Archive 2004, p. 332 (2004). http://eprint.iacr.org/2004/332

41. StrongSalt: Introducing the First Privacy API. https://www.strongsalt.com

42. Tu, S., Kaashoek, M.F., Madden, S., Zeldovich, N.: Processing analytical queries over encrypted data. PVLDB **6**(5), 289–300 (2013). http://www.vldb.org/pvldb/vol6/p289-tu.pdf

43. Xu, P., Li, J., Wang, W., Jin, H.: Anonymous identity-based broadcast encryption with constant decryption complexity and strong security. In: AsiaCCS 2016, pp. 223–233 (2016)

44. Yoneyama, K., Kimura, S.: Verifiable and forward secure dynamic searchable symmetric encryption with storage efficiency. In: Qing, S., Mitchell, C., Chen, L., Liu, D. (eds.) ICICS 2017. LNCS, vol. 10631, pp. 489–501. Springer, Cham (2018). https://doi.org/10.1007/978-3-319-89500-0_42

SHECS-PIR: Somewhat Homomorphic Encryption-Based Compact and Scalable Private Information Retrieval

Jeongeun Park[1] and Mehdi Tibouchi[2(✉)]

[1] Department of Mathematics, Ewha Womans University, Seoul, Republic of Korea
jungeun7430@ewhain.net
[2] NTT Corporation, Tokyo, Japan
mehdi.tibouchi.br@hco.ntt.co.jp

Abstract. A Private Information Retrieval (PIR) protocol allows a client to retrieve arbitrary elements from a database stored in a server without revealing to the server any information about the requested element. PIR is an important building block of many privacy-preserving protocols, and its efficient implementation is therefore of prime importance. Several concrete, practical PIR protocols have been proposed and implemented so far, particularly based on very low-depth somewhat homomorphic encryption. The main drawback of these protocols, however, is their large communication cost, especially in terms of the server's reply, which grows like $O(d\sqrt[d]{n})$ for an n-element database, where d is a parameter typically chosen as 2 or 3.

In this paper, we describe an efficient PIR protocol called SHECS-PIR, based on deeper circuits and GSW-style homomorphic encryption. SHECS-PIR reduces the communication cost down to $O(\log n)$ removing all other factors apart from database size while maintaining a high level of efficiency. In fact, for large databases, we achieve faster server processing time in addition to more compact queries.

Keywords: PIR · Privacy-preserving technique · Homomorphic encryption · TFHE

1 Introduction

Retrieving data even from a public database can be a privacy-sensitive operation, which may reveal unwanted information about the client to the database operator: this could be the case for example for databases of patents, stock quotes, medical conditions, compromised passwords and more. As a result, clients may request that the content of their queries be protected from the database server. This can be achieved using *private information retrieval* (PIR) protocols, as introduced by Chor et al. [16].

J. Park—This work was partially carried out while the first author was a research intern at NTT Corporation, Japan.

ⓒ Springer Nature Switzerland AG 2020
L. Chen et al. (Eds.): ESORICS 2020, LNCS 12309, pp. 86–106, 2020.
https://doi.org/10.1007/978-3-030-59013-0_5

In PIR, the database is modeled as an array of elements[1], and clients are allowed to retrieve those elements by querying their indices in the array. The required security property is that those queries remain hidden from the database operator(s). A consequence of that property is that, in order to answer a query, the server has to process the entire database, making the protocol computationally heavy on the server side.

We can ask the security to hold either in a statistical sense or in a computational sense: this corresponds to two classes of protocols, called information-theoretic PIR (IT-PIR) on the one hand [7,16,19,20,25], and computational PIR (cPIR) on the other [1,5,8,10,18,21,23,27,28,30,33]. IT-PIR offers unconditional security guarantees, and is usually more computationally efficient, since it usually involves simple bit operations on the database. However, any non-trivial IT-PIR requires multiple non-colluding servers (as Chor et al. [16] proved that the trivial protocol in which clients are sent the entire database is communication optimal in the single-server setting), which is often not achievable in practical scenarios. On the other hand, cPIR can achieve sublinear communication with a single server, but is typically more computationally expensive as it usually involves cryptographic operations based on public-key primitives to be carried out on each element of the database (and its security guarantees rely on some hardness assumption).

Standard PIR schemes do not normally offer any guarantee regarding the privacy of the server, in the sense that a client may learn information about elements of the database other than just the requested one. A PIR protocol which ensures that a client only learns the desired element and no more is called a symmetric PIR, and can be seen as a single-server, multi-client variant of oblivious transfer.

The focus of this paper is (single-server) cPIR based on somewhat homomorphic encryption.

1.1   Achieving Efficient cPIR

Recent constructions of cPIR all rely on broadly similar approaches based on homomorphic encryption. Since homomorphic encryption makes it possible to compute on encrypted data, it is a natural fit for PIR.

In fact, cPIR can be achieved with asymptotically essentially optimal efficiency (both in terms of communication and computation) using *fully* homomorphic encryption (FHE): the client sends as its query an encryption of its desired index using the FHE scheme, and the server homomorphically applies to this ciphertext the function mapping an index to the corresponding database element and sends the result back to the client. For an n-element database, this protocol has an optimal query size of $O(\log n)$, an optimal server computation complexity of $O(n)$ (since the function can be represented as a circuit of size

---

[1] This basic building block enabling private queries to a contiguous array can then be combined with techniques like cuckoo hashing to achieve private queries to more advanced data structures like key-value stores.

$O(n))$ and the reply size is again optimal, linear in the size of a database entry. Unfortunately, those nice asymptotic formulas tend to hide impractically large constants corresponding to the considerable overhead of FHE, in terms of ciphertext expansion and in computation cost, due to the expensive *bootstrapping* step required to homomorphically evaluate large circuits.

Protocols suggested so far for practical cPIR have therefore been substantially more complicated than this simple description, so as to circumvent the large overhead of FHE and rely instead on more efficient *somewhat* homomorphic encryption schemes (SHE), that only support the homomorphic evaluation of circuits of limited depth. For instance, one of the first practical cPIR protocol, XPIR [1] is based on the BV somewhat homomorphic encryption scheme [9]. Several subsequent works [5,23] then considered other SHE primitives to achieve better efficiency in terms of communication or computation cost.

The basic underlying technique in those works can be described as follows: if we represent the database as an n-dimensional vector, and the query for the i-th database element as the vector of size n with all zeroes and a 1 in the i-th component, the desired element is simply the inner product between those two vectors. If the query vector is encrypted componentwise using an (at least) additively homomorphic scheme, the inner product can easily be evaluated in encrypted form and returned to the client. An obvious difficulty, however, is that the query itself consists of n ciphertexts, and hence communication is no longer sublinear. This can be solved using a technique due to J.P. Stern [33] in which the database is structured as a d-dimensional hypercube. With this structure, $d\sqrt[d]{n}$ ciphertexts are needed as query vectors rather than n. Computing the reply then involves the homomorphic evaluation of an arithmetic circuit of depth d instead of just a linear function: this is the basic structure of XPIR.

SealPIR improves upon XPIR in terms of query size at the cost of additional work on the server side. Instead of sending d query vectors of length $\sqrt[d]{n}$, the client sends d ciphertexts containing the information on the desired index, and the server expands those ciphertexts into ciphertext vectors in a homomorphic way. Further optimizations of this technique have recently been proposed in [3], in order to further reduce communication at the cost of increased computation and noise on the server side.

1.2   Our Contribution

The main observation of this work is that the basic FHE approach to cPIR described at the beginning of the previous section can in fact be instantiated in practice, *without bootstrapping*, and achieve the same level of efficiency as state-of-the-art schemes like SealPIR or even better, and with lower communication cost overall.

To do so, we rely on the TFHE homomorphic encryption scheme [12–14], which is an efficient implementation of the GSW [24] approach to homomorphic encryption. With respect to suitably structured circuits, GSW enjoys a slow (additive rather than multiplicative) noise growth, and can therefore evaluate relatively deep circuits without bootstrapping. This is in particular the case for the circuits representing a large lookup table, which is exactly what we want to evaluate in PIR. This lookup table circuit consists of a binary tree of depth $O(\log n)$ of multiplexer gates (CMUX gates in TFHE; see Fig. 1), and can be evaluated homomorphically without bootstrapping using the basic TFHE parameters even for very large database sizes.

We also use suitable key-switching techniques in order to efficiently implement the query expansion, whereby the packed query of the client, containing all the bits of the index in a single ciphertext, is decomposed bitwise into several ciphertexts to be fed into the CMUX tree. Since there are fewer resulting ciphertexts than in SealPIR ($O(\log n)$ compared to $O(d\sqrt[d]{n})$), this step is also more efficient in an asymptotic sense, although the implied constant in the big-O is actually larger in our case.

The resulting scheme, which we call SHECS-PIR (Somewhat Homomorphic[2] Encryption-based Compact and Scalable PIR), is competitive with SealPIR in terms of computation cost, and achieves better communication cost (particularly for the server's reply, where we are essentially optimal). In addition, SHECS-PIR scales better to larger databases: thanks to slower noise growth, no increase in parameters is needed until a much larger database size than SealPIR. In addition, our query ciphertext can contain multiple indices up to the point not exceeding the dimension of plaintext degree without increasing query size. Therefore, SHECS-PIR can be combined with all the efficient (cheap computation cost) multi-query PIR techniques using probabilistic batch codes [5] or just batch codes [26,32] for better performance on server's computation time with much lower network cost increase and query generation time.

1.3 A Note on Communication Cost

We mentioned earlier that the FHE approach to cPIR achieves *essentially* optimal complexity since the query size is $O(\log n)$ and the answer size is linear in the size of database entries. The caveat implied by "essentially" here is that, while that bound certainly holds if size is measured in terms of numbers of ciphertexts, there can be some additional overhead due to the *ciphertext expansion factor*, namely the ratio F between the size of ciphertexts and plaintexts in the underlying homomorphic encryption scheme. In fact, that expansion factor is an even larger contributor to communication cost in schemes like XPIR, since answer size incurs an overhead of F^{d-1}, which can be large when d grows (i.e. for larger database sizes).

One can mention recent efforts to reduce this expansion factor F down to a constant close to 1, e.g. in [23], which proposes novel techniques to achieve an asymptotically close to optimal communication complexity even when ciphertext

---

[2] We stress that SHECS-PIR uses *somewhat* homomorphic (or arguably "leveled fully homomorphic") encryption in the sense that it does not rely on bootstrapping. This is despite the fact that the underlying homomorphic encryption TFHE is bootstrappable, and hence an FHE scheme. Not using bootstrapping is simply better for efficiency.

expansion is taken into account. Those efforts, however, are largely orthogonal to the line of work in which this paper fits: while they do obtain better communication rate in an asymptotic sense, they have a substantial fixed cost. For instance, query size in [23] is around 200 MB for typical parameters, so the scheme only offers an attractive communication rate when database entries themselves have sizes in the hundreds of megabytes, and server computation time is accordingly large. This can be relevant in specific settings, but for more common cPIR use cases where database entries have sizes in kilobytes or less, it is not very practical.

Regarding the underlying encryption scheme of SHECS-PIR itself, it satisfies $F \approx 4$ for the security level and the large database sizes we consider, so the corresponding overhead is small (and communication cost is effectively smaller than the state of the art for this range of parameters). In an asymptotic sense, F would increase very slightly with both database size (in order to accommodate noise growth) and security level (to ensure the hardness of the underlying lattice problem), but the scaling is an iterated logarithm, so practically speaking, F can be considered a constant.

Along similar lines as [23], a previous paper due to Kiayias et al. [27] achieves cPIR with optimal communication rate for databases with large entries, in the sense that the total size of communication asymptotically approaches the size of the unencrypted database entry alone. Moreover, it does so by relying on leveled homomorphic encryption, and thus does not require bootstrapping, similarly to the present work. While this is an important feasibility result, it again has limited practicality, however, due to the heavy computational cost of the underlying encryption scheme, as the authors themselves underscore. Moreover, as in [23], there are substantial fixed communication costs that limit the applicability of the scheme to only databases with very large entries (the authors consider the retrieval of movie files of several gigabytes), which is again a different setting as the one we focus on.

Another recent work discussing various approaches to reducing communication costs for PIR in a range of parameters more in line with the focus of this work is Ali et al.'s paper [3]. It presents a number of ways to optimize concrete cPIR schemes for lower communication, a number of which are largely independent of this work, and in fact compatible (e.g., modulus switching in queries). It does however introduce a new cPIR scheme called MulPIR, which is slower than SealPIR but more compact. We do not include a detailed comparison with MulPIR, due to the lack of a readily available implementation; however, since it has larger query size than SealPIR and since replies consist of multiple ciphertexts, it should be less efficient than SHECS-PIR in terms of both communication (by comparison of query and answer sizes) and computation (because we perform similarly to SealPIR or better).

2   Basic Tools (Homomorphic Encryption Scheme)

2.1   Homomorphic Encryption

Our PIR protocol is constructed by a somewhat homomorphic encryption scheme which allows limited number of operations on ciphertexts. Homomorphic Encryption (HE) allows a computation on encrypted data, where PIR scenario wants to do. We give properties of our base homomorphic encryption scheme first and concrete algorithms next. Homomorpic encryption scheme consists of four algorithms (KeyGen, Enc, Dec, Eval). It is an encryption scheme having additional Eval algorithm to evaluate arbitrary function on ciphertexts. Our protocol uses the full power of homomorphic encryption (multiplication, addition on ciphertexts) to evaluate a homomorphic mux gate (data selector).

- Homomorphic mux gate: Given two encrypted data d_0, d_1 and an encryption of $b \in \{0, 1\}$, say C, it outputs d_0 if $C = \mathsf{Enc}(0)$, otherwise d_1.

It is easy to construct homomorphic mux gate using standard FHE schemes. However, the most concern is the efficiency in terms of error growth and computational time for a practical use. The less noise overhead after any operation of an FHE scheme, the more operations are possible with it, i.e. the deeper circuit can be constructed from it. The ciphertext of all existing FHE schemes contains a noise component in it. The noise grows with homomorphic operation with regard to Euclidean norm. GSW-style homomorphic encryption [24] which keeps noise overhead additive after homomorphic multiplication has deeper depth by utilizing asymmetric noise propagation. Furthermore, its multiplication is natural i.e. just multiplication over ciphertexts avoiding other additional algorithms (relinearization, key switching, modulus switching e.t.c). To obtain a ciphertext (usually a vector) encrypting multiplication of plaintexts using homomorphic operation in other non-GSW style FHE schemes, tensor product of ciphertexts vectors are done at first. The product of vectors causes size of vector quadratic so that extra algorithms such as relinearization are required to reduce the size as original ciphertext. TFHE [14] adapts GSW encryption over Torus, but makes multiplication faster preserving GSW property using its algebraic fact. From this reason, we can eventually implement an efficient PIR protocol so we introduce this TFHE scheme below. We implemented our protocol based on TFHE library [15].

2.2   TLWE and TRLWE

Notation: We denote λ as the security parameter. We define vectors and matrices in lowercase bold and uppercase bold, respectively. Dot product of two vectors $\mathbf{v}, \mathbf{w}$ is denoted by $<\mathbf{v}, \mathbf{w}>$. For a vector $\mathbf{x}$, $\mathbf{x}_i$ denotes the i-th component scalar. We denote that $\mathbb{B}$ as the set $\{0, 1\}$ and $\mathbb{T}$ as the real torus $\mathbb{R}/\mathbb{Z}$, the set of real number modulo 1. We denote $\mathbb{Z}_N[X]$ and $\mathbb{T}_N[X]$ by $\mathbb{Z}[X]/(X^N + 1)$ and $\mathbb{R}[X]/(X^N + 1) \bmod 1$, respectively. $\mathbb{B}_N[X]$ denotes the polynomials in $\mathbb{Z}_N[X]$

with binary coefficients. The norm notation $\| \cdot \|$ denotes infinity norm. $\log(\cdot)$ is binary logarithm. We use the same notation as [14] for better understanding.

The TFHE scheme [14] is working entirely on real torus $\mathbb{T}$ and $\mathbb{T}_N[X]$ based on TLWE problem and TRLWE problem which are torus variant of LWE problem and RLWE problem respectively, where N is a power of two. It is easy to see that $(\mathbb{T}, +, \cdot)$(resp. $(\mathbb{T}_N[X], +, \cdot)$) is $\mathbb{Z}$(resp. $\mathbb{Z}_N[X]$) module.

A TLWE (resp. TRLWE) sample is defined as $(\mathbf{a}, b) \in \mathbb{T}^{kn+1}$ (resp. $\mathbb{T}_N[X]^{k+1}$) for any $k > 0$, where $\mathbf{a}$ is chosen uniformly over $\mathbb{T}^{kn}$(resp. $\mathbb{T}_N^k$) and $b = <\mathbf{a}, \mathbf{s}>+e$. The vector $\mathbf{s}$ is a secret key which is chosen uniformly from $\mathbb{B}^{kn}$(resp. $\mathbb{B}_N[X]^k$) and the error e is chosen from Gaussian distribution with standard deviation $\delta \in \mathbb{R} > 0$. Furthermore, we follow the definition of trivial sample in [14]. as having $\mathbf{a} = \mathbf{0}$ and noiseless sample as having the standard deviation $\delta = 0$. Throughout this paper, we set $k = 1$ and $n = N$. Here, we denote the message space to $\mathcal{M} \subseteq \mathbb{T}$. A TLWE ciphertext of $\mu \in \mathcal{M}$ is constructed by adding a trivial TLWE message sample $(0, \mu)$ to a non-trivial TLWE sample. Therefore, the TLWE ciphertext of μ, say $\mathfrak{c}$, which we will interpret as a TLWE sample (of μ) is $(\mathbf{a}, b) \in \mathbb{T}^{k+1}$, where $b = <\mathbf{a}, \mathbf{s}> + e + \mu$. To decrypt it correctly, we use a linear function $\varphi_\mathbf{s}$ called *phase*, which results in $\varphi_\mathbf{s}(\mathfrak{c}) = b - <\mathbf{a}, \mathbf{s}> = \mu + e$ and we round it to the nearest element in $\mathcal{M}$. For a TRLWE encryption, it follows the same way over $\mathbb{T}_N$ but a message μ is a polynomial of degree N with coefficients $\in \mathcal{M}$.

2.3   TRGSW and CMUX Gate

As we can see, TLWE and TRLWE samples have additive homomorphic property. In order to support multiplication, the authors of [14] define TGSW ciphertext which supports external product with TLWE ciphertext to get a TLWE sample encrypting multiplication of messages. It is possible to be extended to polynomials. In this paper, since we only use TGSW samples in ring mode, we use the notation TRGSW which is working with TRLWE and also give the definition of a TRGSW sample only.

For any positive integer $B_g \geq 2, \ell, k$, a TRGSW sample is a matrix $\mathbf{C} = \mathbf{Z} + \mu \cdot \mathbf{H} \in \mathbb{T}_N[X]^{(k+1)\ell \times (k+1)}$, where each row of $\mathbf{Z}$ is a TRLWE sample of zero and $\mathbf{H}$ is a gadget matrix which is defined by $\mathbf{H} = \mathbf{I}_{k+1} \otimes \mathbf{g} \in \mathbb{T}_N[X]^{(k+1)\ell \times (k+1)}$, where $\mathbf{g} = (1/B_g, \dots, 1/B_g^\ell)$.

The message μ is in $\mathbb{Z}_N[X]$. In this paper, we restrict the message space of TRGSW to $\{0, 1\}$ and set $k = 1$ as we mentioned above. We denote TLWE(μ), TRLWE(μ), and TRGSW(μ) as a ciphertext of each proper message μ of TLWE, TRLWE, and TRGSW, respectively. An external product between a TRGSW sample and a TRLWE sample, denoted as $\boxdot$, is defined as $\mathbf{A} \boxdot \mathbf{b} = \mathbf{H}^{-1}(\mathbf{b}) \cdot \mathbf{A}$, where $\mathbf{A}$ is a TRGSW sample of μ_A, $\mathbf{b}$ is a TRLWE sample of μ_b and $\mathbf{H}^{-1}(\cdot)$ is the gadget decomposition function $Dec_{\mathbf{H}, \beta, \epsilon}$ of [14] with different notation.

This external product outputs a TRLWE sample of $\mu_A \cdot \mu_b$. With the homomorphic operations, we can construct a small circuit which is called CMUX gate. It outputs one of two TRLWE samples depending on a message of TRGSW sample without decrypting it. To be concrete, $\mathsf{CMUX}(C, \mathbf{d}_0, \mathbf{d}_1) = C \boxdot (\mathbf{d}_1 - \mathbf{d}_0) + \mathbf{d}_0$, where $C = \mathsf{TRGSW}(\mu_C)$, $\mathbf{d}_0 = \mathsf{TRLWE}(\mu_{d_0})$, and $\mathbf{d}_1 = \mathsf{TRLWE}(\mu_{d_1})$. Since we restricted the message space of TRGSW to $\{0,1\}$, if $\mu_C = 0$, CMUX gate outputs $\mathsf{TRLWE}(\mu_{d_0})$ otherwise, $\mathsf{TRLWE}(\mu_{d_1})$ is the output. We refer to [14] for more detail.

2.4   Basic Algorithms for TFHE

We introduce basic algorithms $\mathsf{SampleExtract}$ and PrivKS, which we use in our PIR protocol. $\mathsf{SampleExtract}$ converts TRLWE samples of polynomial with message coefficient under a key K (denoted as $\mathsf{TRLWE}_K(\sum_{i=0}^{N-1} \mu_i X^i)$) into $\mathsf{TLWE}(\mu_i)$ under a key $\mathfrak{K}$ (denoted as $\mathsf{TLWE}_{\mathfrak{K}}(\mu_i)$), where $\mu_i \in \mathbb{T}$ for $\forall i \in [0, N-1]$. It is possible because we can extract a coefficient of a polynomial (viewed as slots) as a scalar with algebraic operation and it works on the FHE ciphertext. This algorithm does not add any noise.

There is an algorithm called the Private Functional Key Switching (PrivKS) which allows to switch the message space from $\mathbb{T}$ to $\mathbb{T}_N[X]$. In other words, it can convert a TLWE sample under a key $\mathfrak{K}$ into a TRLWE sample under a key K. We use this algorithm for unpacking query step. This function takes a key switching key $\mathsf{KS}_{i,j(f)} \in \mathsf{TRLWE}_K(f_u(\frac{\mathfrak{K}_i}{2^j}))$ and a $\mathsf{TLWE}_{\mathfrak{K}}(\mu)$ on input and outputs $\mathsf{TRLWE}_K(f_u(\mu))$. One can use the function f_u mapping from $\mathbb{T}^p$ to $\mathbb{T}_N[X]$ with p TLWE samples, however, $p = 1$ is enough for our protocol. Furthermore, we use two kinds of function f_u where u indicates the position where the input is added in a TRLWE sample. In detail, $\mathsf{TRLWE}_K(f_0(x)) = (a + x, b)$, $\mathsf{TRLWE}_K(f_1(x)) = (a, b + x)$, where $(a, b) \in \mathsf{TRLWE}_K(0)$, $x \in \mathbb{T}_N[X]$.

3   Overall Description

A PIR protocol consists of three basic procedure: query generation, response encoding(main computation), and response decoding [31]. Our PIR protocol requires a somewhat homomorphic encryption (SHE) scheme consists of four algorithms ($\mathsf{KeyGen}, \mathsf{Enc}, \mathsf{Dec}, \mathsf{Eval}$). Unlike other basic cPIR protocols based on SHE, we use full power of homomorphic encryption i.e., multiplication over ciphertexts. Basically, multiplication is the most tricky step as we mention in Sect. 2, since it is usually followed by additional steps such as relinearization, modulus switching, key switching etc., furthermore, large noise growth is another trouble. However, GSW-style schemes support simple multiplication (with no other additional steps) and additive noise growth. So one of GSW-style scheme, TFHE, is adequate for instantiating our protocol. We introduce our protocol below.

3.1   Our PIR Protocol

Query Generation. A client chooses an index i to retrieve the ith item out of n data from server's DB and encrypts each bit of the index as $\log n$ ciphertexts. Then it sends to a server. Therefore, the query complexity is $O(\log n)$.

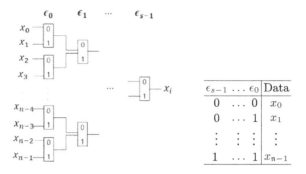

Fig. 1. The Cmux binary decision tree (left figure) and Look Up Table (right table): the database with $\mathfrak{n}$ elements ($\mathfrak{n} = 2^s$). The figure represents how a server computes the desired i-th item from whole database. x_j stands for each data elements $\forall j \in [0, \mathfrak{n} - 1]$ and each ϵ_d is an binary element of the index $i = \sum_{d=0}^{s-1} \epsilon_d 2^d$, $\forall d \in [0, s - 1]$.

Response Encoding. As a preprocessing, server saves a database as the look up table (See Fig. 1). The server runs $n - 1$ times MUX gate (a homomorphic mux gate) where it selects one of the input elements to output the encrypted i-th data. In our case, a MUX gate takes two data elements and one query ciphertext which encrypts a bit of the index. Depending on a query ciphertext, it obliviously selects one of two data inputs. After running MUX gates $n/2$ times (let's say it is the first level), all the outputs are ciphertexts so that the server does not know which items are chosen. It is possible thanks to homomorphic encryption. The server does the second level with the next query ciphertext and previous outputs running $n/4$ times MUX gates. Finally, after $\log n$ levels, it gives the output to the server. The total number of MUX gates for a server to evaluate is $n - 1$, then the server's computational complexity is $O(n)$. This process is done via a look up table and binary decision tree (see Fig. 1).

Response Decoding. The client decrypts the ciphertext given by the server with his secret key. Unlike the previous efficient protocols (XPIR [1], SealPIR [5]), the complexity of PIR response does not depend on the expansion factor of cryptosystem, $F = |\text{ciphertext size}|/|\text{plaintext size}|$, in our approach. Note that constructing a look up table (LUT) is inefficient with traditional schemes like BV [9] or FV [22] in XPIR and SealPIR respectively, due to their structure with high noise level for every multiplication and large parameter. However, TFHE is suitable to construct our protocol with concrete parameters due to its nature. We give the concrete protocol, SHECS-PIR, from TFHE.

3.2 Concrete PIR Protocol (SHECS-PIR) from TFHE

We assume that a server has $\mathfrak{n} = 2^s$ data with β bit size (for convention, we set $\mathfrak{n}$ is a power of 2) and a client wants to retrieve the i-th data from server's database for $i \in [0, \mathfrak{n}-1]$. Before sending a query, each client registers its own key switching input set $\mathsf{KS}^{f_u} = \{\mathsf{KS}_{a,b}^{(f_u)}\}_{a \in [N+1], b \in [t]}$ which is a set of TRLWE ciphertexts of a secret key bits to a server as a setup process, for $u \in [0, 1]$. This seems quite necessary for every somewhat homomorphic encryption schemes as SealPIR also requires cryptographic material for substitution operation (key switching) from each client as a setup. However, It is sent only once by each client and the server uses it for the computation, every time a client who registered those. In fact, a server sets the database as a Look Up Table (LUT). It contains a list of indices from 0 to n-1 with binary representation in the left column and corresponding data represented as TRLWE message polynomial of degree at most N in the right column, where each coefficient is in $\mathbb{T}$ (see Fig. 1). Moreover, server can pack the database as much as possible by storing bit length of plaintext modulus $(\log p)$ of the data element into a coefficient of message polynomial. Then, the database size can be decreased to $m = \mathfrak{n}/P_d$, where $P_d = \frac{N \log p}{\beta}$.

Query Generation:

(1) Choose an index $i \in [\mathfrak{n}]$ and represent $i = \sum_{j=0}^{j=s-1} \epsilon_j 2^j$ for $\epsilon_j \in \{0, 1\}$.
(2) A client encrypts each bit ϵ_j as a TRGSW ciphertext. $\rightarrow \log \mathfrak{n}$ TRGSW ciphertexts as a query.
(3) Send them to a server.

Response Encoding: The server starts the main computation with its $\mathfrak{n}$ database. The server converts data element (as Fig. 1) into as a trivial TRLWE sample, $(0, D_j)$, where $D_j \in \mathbb{T}[X]/(X^N + 1)$ for $j \in [0, \mathfrak{n} - 1]$. He makes a binary tree with these data and runs CMUX gates $\mathfrak{n} - 1$ times via the binary CMUX tree to evaluate one TRLWE sample which contains the desired data. Note that one CMUX gate contains 2ℓ times ring multiplication.

Response Decoding: After receiving the answer from the server, the client can get the i-th data by decrypting the answer with the TRLWE secret key. In this case, the client only gets one ciphertext which is a TRLWE sample.

4 Implementation Details

4.1 Reducing Communication Cost

Packing and Unpacking Query. It is possible to compress query size as a ciphertext encrypting all the bits of the index i. In other words, a client packs all the bits of the index in a plaintext polynomial batching each bit into a coefficient then encrypt it. To unpack a query to $\log \mathfrak{n}(= s)$ ciphertexts encrypting each bit, we let the server do additional work which is called query unpacking step. Then the number of ciphertext for query is reduced to $\lceil \log \mathfrak{n}/N \rceil$ from $\log \mathfrak{n}$. As soon as a server gets a query ciphertext from a client, he unpacks the query as $\log \mathfrak{n}$ ciphertexts of each binary element of i. For example, let $i = 3, \mathfrak{n} = 16$ then the binary representation of 3 is 0011. A client gives an output of Enc(0011) to the server and he unpacks it to outputs of Enc(0), Enc(0), Enc(1), and Enc(1), where Enc is an encryption algorithm. If there exists an algorithm extracting (unbatching) one bit obliviously, a server runs it $\log n$ times, hence this step has $O(\log n)$ computational complexity.

We show how to construct all the procedure with TFHE. Due to TRGSW sample's structure, client needs ℓ number of ciphertexts to pack query. Client gives TRLWE samples as a query then server unpacks it to TRGSW samples. A query consists of ℓTRLWE ciphertexts under the key K having $\log n$ binary elements of i. It is unpacked as $\ell \times \log n$ TLWE samples under the key $\mathcal{K}$ then converted to $\log n$ TRGSW samples under the key K.

[Query Generation]

(1) Choose an index $i \in [n]$ and represent $i = \sum_{j=0}^{j=s-1} \epsilon_j 2^j$ for $\epsilon_j \in \{0, 1\}$.
(2) Set ℓ message polynomials as $\sum_{j=0}^{j=s-1} \frac{\epsilon_j}{B_g} X^j, \ldots \sum_{j=0}^{j=s-1} \frac{\epsilon_j}{B_g^\ell} X^j$ for a positive integer $B_g > 2$.
(3) A client encrypts these polynomials as ℓ TRLWE samples.
   $\rightarrow$ $\mathsf{TRLWE}_K(\sum_{j=0}^{j=s-1} \frac{\epsilon_j}{B_g} X^j), \ldots, \mathsf{TRLWE}_K(\sum_{j=0}^{j=s-1} \frac{\epsilon_j}{B_g^\ell} X^j)$, where K is a TRLWE secret key of the client and $\epsilon_j \in \{0, 1\}$ for $j \in [0, s-1]$.
(4) Send them to the server.

So a query consists of $\ell \lceil \frac{\log n}{N} \rceil$TRLWE ciphertexts in SHECS-PIR. Since $\log n$ is much smaller than N, in general, just ℓ ciphertexts are required.

[Query Unpacking: Converting ℓ TRLWE samples to $\log n$ TRGSW samples.]

(1) Run $\mathsf{SampleExtract}(\mathsf{TRLWE}_K(\sum_{j=0}^{j=s-1} \frac{\epsilon_j}{B_g^w} X^j)) \rightarrow \{\mathsf{TLWE}_\mathcal{K}(\frac{\epsilon_j}{B_g^w})\}_{j \in [0,s-1], w \in [1,\ell]}$
   for $w \in [1, \ell]$
(2) For $j \in [0, s-1]$, $u \in [0, 1]$ and $w \in [1, \ell]$, run $\mathsf{PrivKS}(\mathsf{KS}^{f_u}, \mathsf{TLWE}_\mathcal{K}(\frac{\epsilon_j}{B_g^w})) \rightarrow$
   $\{\mathsf{TRGSW}_K(\epsilon_j)\}_{j \in [0,s-1]}$.

In total, server runs $\mathsf{SampleExtract}$ $\ell \log n$ times and PrivKS $2\ell \log n$ times. Essentially, $\mathsf{SampleExtract}$ is free since it just extracts coefficients from a polynomial, but PrivKS has a large constant (at most Nt) times ciphertext addition itself, where N is the dimension of ciphertext polynomial and t is a parameter of PrivKS. Usually $N = 1024$ or $N = 2048$, $t = 12$. To optimize query size, the client can concatenate all the $\ell \log n$ bits in one polynomial then only one ciphertext a query but the server's unpacking time is twice as a trade off.

Using Random Oracle. TFHE is basically a symmetric key encryption scheme so that a client can give just seed of uniformly random part of a TRLWE sample using random oracle. Then the server generates the exact value using the same oracle. Roughly, the query size is reduced by half since the seed size is $\{0, 1\}^\lambda$. In general, LWE based symmetric key encryption scheme can use random oracle to reduce the communication cost.

Table 1. Communication and computation complexity, n = database size

	Query	Answer	First-Step	Main
XPIR	$O(d\sqrt[d]{n})$	$O(F^{d-1})$	N/A	$\Omega(n + F\sqrt{n})$
SealPIR($d=2$)	$O(d\lceil\sqrt[d]{n}/N\rceil)$	$O(F^{d-1})$	$O(d\sqrt[d]{n})$	$\Omega(n + F\sqrt{n})$
SHECS-PIR w query unpacking	$O(\lceil\log n/N\rceil)$	$O(1)$	$O(\log n)$	$O(\ell n)$
SHECS-PIR w/o query unpacking	$O(\log n)$	$O(1)$	N/A	$O(\ell n)$

Table 2. Communication cost of SHECS-PIR and SealPIR for the same n, N, and β.

	With First-step		Without First-step	
	SHECS-PIR	SealPIR($d=2$)	SHECS-PIR	SealPIR($d=2$)
Query[ctxt]	$\ell\lceil\frac{\log n}{N}\rceil$	$d\lceil\frac{\sqrt{n}}{N}\rceil$	$\log n$	$d\sqrt{n}$
Answer[ctxt]	1	$\lceil\frac{2\log q}{\log p}\rceil$	1	$\lceil\frac{2\log q}{\log p}\rceil$

Modulus Switching for Answer Ciphertext. In order to reduce the answer size, a naive approach is modulus switching. Other homomorphic encryption primitives [9,22] use this technique either to reduce the noise contained in a ciphertext or to reduce the size of a ciphertext. We can easily employ it since both the ciphertext modulus and plaintext modulus can be set as a power of 2.

4.2   Comparison with Other Protocols

Communication and Computation Cost: We give a complexity comparison among previous works below in Table 1 (First-step is query unpacking in SHECS-PIR and query expansion in SealPIR). The complexity of main computation is expressed in polynomial multiplication unit so that SHECS-PIR has other factor ℓ since one CMUX gate consists of 2ℓ polynomial multiplication. The server does $2\ell(n - 1)$ polynomial multiplication finally. This is because the schemes TFHE and FV work over different algebraic structure. The elements over the torus $\mathbb{T}_N[X]$ is rescaled by a factor 2^{64} to be mapped to 64 bit integers for implementation. Then we can view the ciphertext modulus as $q = 2^{64}$ and plaintext modulus as $p(<q)$. However, FV (or BGV) works over $\mathbb{Z}_q[X]/(X^N + 1)$ (q is a prime s.t. $q = 1 \mod 2N$) so that they can use NTT operation while TFHE uses FFT operation for ring multiplication. Furthermore, FFT can be more scaled than NTT in general. Therefore, the actual cost comparison does not seem proper. In SealPIR and XPIR's main computation, server does $2(n + F\sqrt{n})$ ring multiplication when $d = 2$. Roughly, SHECS-PIR's server seems to work twice since we set $\ell = 2$. However, the actual cost is similar because the FFT operation in TFHE library [15] is more scaled than NTT used in SealPIR library [29].

SealPIR can also use some our optimization technique such as random oracle (when it uses symmetric key version) and modulus switching, hence, we can have similar ciphertext size in both protocols. Therefore, how many ciphertexts are needed for query and answer is important for communication cost. Although SHECS-PIR doesn't run query unpacking, we can see that the query size becomes smaller than the size of SealPIR with query expansion at some point since our query size complexity is $O(\log \mathfrak{n})$. Table 2 shows the exact number of ciphertexts of a query and an answer in SHECS-PIR and SealPIR. A query which is a TRLWE ciphertext can represent 2^N indices and usually $N \geq 1024$ so that we can say that the query size actually does not increase for realistic size of database. For $\mathfrak{n} = 2^{32}$, $N = 2048$, one ciphertext (=16 kB) is required for SHECS-PIR with query unpacking while 64 ciphertexts (=2048 kB) are needed for SealPIR with query expansion and database dimension $d = 2$ (so the database is a $2^{16} \times 2^{16}$ matrix). This is because SealPIR represents an index using $2^{16}/2048(= \lceil \sqrt{\mathfrak{n}}/N \rceil) = 32$ for each database dimension. This size is as same as SHECS-PIR's just giving all $\log \mathfrak{n}(= 32)$ TRGSW ciphertexts (=2048 kB) in SHECS-PIR without query unpacking so that the server's running time would be much smaller also. In fact, the query unpacking would be faster than expansion if $\sqrt{\mathfrak{n}}$ is much larger than $N \log \mathfrak{n}$. For noise issue, SealPIR may increase N and decrease p, while we do not need to do. Moreover, the answer size does not increase since it does not depend on the expansion factor F. Therefore, we can achieve better performance on both total communication cost and server's computation for large database.

Noise Growth: Somewhat homomorphic encryption supports limited number of operation over ciphertexts, hence, the deeper depth a scheme has, the larger database its application can support without bootstrapping. Since bootstrapping takes relatively long time and require other material (quite large size) as an input, it is important not to use it as much as possible. Multiplication over ciphertexts, in general, incurs large noise growth. In fact, noise growth is depending on the size of plaintext in FV so that SealPIR keeps downsizing the plaintext modulus to achieve more depth. But it causes the factor F large, hence, it has an influence on server's answer size and main computation time as well. However, TFHE has larger depth since it has additive noise growth for both addition and multiplication and also the noise growth of it does not depend on plaintext modulus.

We show heuristic noise bound after server's computation of SealPIR and SHECS-PIR then how much noise has left until decryption will fail using noise budget defined in [11]. First, we can redefine TFHE ciphertext with rescaled version for integer representation of implementation ($q = 2^{64}$).

Definition 1 (Rescaled TFHE for implementation). *Let* $\mathbf{ct} = (c_0, c_1)$, *where* $c_i \in \mathbb{Z}_q[X]/(X^N + 1), i \in \{0, 1\}$ *be an* TRLWE *cipertext encrypting a message* $m \in \mathbb{Z}_p[X]/(X^N + 1)$. *Its scaled inherent noise* v *is the polynomial with the smallest infinity norm such that,*

$$\frac{p}{q}\mathbf{ct}(s) = \frac{p}{q}(c_0 + c_1 s) = m + v + ap,$$

where a *is a polynomial with integer coefficient.*

Table 3. TFHE error growth ($N = 2048, p = 2^{12}, q = 2^{64}$, the number of trial $= 10000$)

	Fresh Ciphertext	Addition	Multiplication
mean(bit)	11	12	42
standard deviation	0.12	0	0.12

Lemma 1. *A* TRLWE *ciphertext* **ct** *encrypting a message* m *can be correctly decrypted if the scaled inherent noise* v *satisfies*

$$\|v\| < \frac{1}{2}$$

Noise budget for rescaled TFHE is actually as same as FV's [11], where q is ciphertext modulus and p is plaintext modulus and v is the invariant noise contained in a ciphertext. In TFHE, p divides q since the two are both powers of 2 so that it causes less noise than the case $p \nmid q$ of SealPIR. The noise budget of both schemes is $-\log 2v$ A ciphertext is decryptable only when the noise budget of it is positive (>0). Now we can observe that how fast the noise budget contained in the reply ciphertext reaches to 0 in parameter database size $\mathfrak{n}$.

SealPIR(**based on FV**) **error growth.** Let v_{in} be the initial error, which is an error of a query essentially, and v_s be the error contained in a ciphertext which is generated after server's computation. We set $\|v_{out}\| = \|(\lfloor \frac{p}{q} v_s \rceil) \bmod p\|$, where $\|v_s\| \leq N p^2 \mathfrak{n} \sqrt{\mathfrak{n}}(\|v_{in}\| + B)$ [5], where N is the dimension of plaintext, p is plaintext modulus, $\mathfrak{n}$ is the number of database, and B is a constant error generated from query expansion step. We assume the database dimension $d = 2$. Since the noise budget of this result ciphertext is $-\log \|2v_{out}\|$, it decreases with $O(\log \mathfrak{n})$ complexity.

SHECS-PIR(**based on TFHE**) **error growth.** Let v_{in} and v_{out} be the same notation defined above. Then we observe the final error based on TFHE noise analysis [14]. It satisfies $\|v_{out}\| \leq \log \mathfrak{n}((k + 1)\ell N \beta(\|v_{in}\| + (N + 1)2^{-(t+1)} + t(N + 1)\|v_{ks}\|)$, where N is the dimension of plaintext, p is plaintext modulus, $\mathfrak{n}$ is the number of database, ℓ, t, β are constant of TRGSW sample and v_{ks} is key switching error (encryption of secret key). Then the noise budget of this result ciphertext decreases with $O(\log \log \mathfrak{n})$ complexity. Table 3 shows how much TFHE noise is added after addition and multiplication to the original fresh ciphertext having noise 11 bits (for 120 bits of security). All the operation is done over fresh ciphertext (non-evaluated) with the same noise distribution. Since query unpacking step which consists of addition does not add much error, we focus on multiplication error growth. According to our noise estimation above, we can see that $\log \log \mathfrak{n} + 42$ bits are the final error contained in server's reply. To decrypt it correctly (the noise budget > 0), $\log \log \mathfrak{n}$ should be smaller than 9. which means, $\mathfrak{n} < 2^{512}$. As a result, we are able to run large enough database without changing parameter using only somewhat homomorphic encryption functionalities. We can expect that the noise budget of the reply ciphertext would still remain positive with large enough data while SealPIR may not be able to support.

4.3 Security

The security of our cPIR scheme follows directly from the IND-CPA (i.e., semantic) security of the underlying homomorphic encryption scheme TFHE [14]. Indeed, the query consists of TFHE ciphertexts, and semantic security ensures that the server cannot learn any information about the underlying plaintexts, which encode the queried database index. Therefore, SHECS-PIR is a secure cPIR protocol.

The assumptions for security are slightly different in the version of the protocol with query compression and the version without: this is because in the latter one, the key material sent to the server consists of just the evaluation key, allowing the semantic security of TFHE to be proved under plain Ring-LWE). On the other hand, in the former case, the server is also provided with key-switching material, encrypting key-dependent information; the security proof for TFHE then relies on an additional circular security assumption, as is always the case for FHE schemes. This discrepancy, however, is not believed to have any impact on concrete security, since no attack is known on circular security.

As usual for lattice-based cryptographic schemes, we can estimate concrete security by evaluating the cost of the best possible attack against the proposed parameters (which in our case are selected as $N = 2048$, $q = 2^{64}$, and $\alpha = 6.957 \cdot 10^{-17}$ for the error magnitude, corresponding to our error distribution with standard deviation 2^{-55}). Albrecht et al.'s LWE estimator [2] shows that the best attack is then the primal uSVP attack [4,6], which yields 121 bits of security. As a comparison, SealPIR achieves 115 bits of security with their choice of parameters ($N = 2048$, $q = 2^{60} - 2^{18} + 1$, and $\alpha = 8/q$).

5 Experimental Result

Implementation Setup. All experiments are performed on a single core of a server with Xeon Platinum 8160 @ 2.10 10 GHz CPUs. In the concrete protocol SHECS-PIR, we set $k = 1$, then TRLWE sample consists of two polynomials, $(a, b) \in \mathbb{T}_N[X]^2$, where a is chosen uniformly. For TRGSW sample, we set $\ell = 2$, $B_g = 2^{15}$.

Communication and Computation Cost. Table 4 shows the actual cost using each library (SHECS-PIR based on TFHE [15] and SealPIR [29]). We stress that those numbers corresponds to the case when only one database element is stored in a given plaintext. It is possible to pack multiple database elements per plaintext in order to support larger databases.

We set $N = 2048$ and ciphertext modulus $q \approx 2^{60}$ for both protocols. Since the FFT multiplication in TFHE library performs better than SEAL's NTT, our main computation time is similar to SealPIR. However, the First step (query

Table 4. Computation cost of SHECS-PIR and SealPIR for the same n, $q \approx 2^{60}$, $N = 2048$.

DB size n	SHECS-PIR			SealPIR ($d = 2$)		
	2^{16}	2^{18}	2^{20}	2^{16}	2^{18}	2^{20}
Query[kB]	32	32	32	32	32	32
Answer[kB]	32	32	32	320	320	320
Server preprocessing[ms]	0	0	0	5733	23101	92944
First-step[ms]	4507	5073	5846	187	422	840
Main[ms]	2282	9024	35902	1935	7025	26833
NB	8	7	7	7	6	5
NB (w/o unpack)	8	7	7	N/A		

expansion, consisting of mainly polynomial additions) of SHECS-PIR is more expensive than SealPIR's for the database sizes considered in the table. It scales slower with database size, however (logarithmically rather than in the square root), so becomes negligible for larger databases.

Both protocols are based on "symmetric key" homomorphic encryption, so that they use the random oracle model to reduce the query size by half. We observe how much signal is left after the noise increase in homomorphic operations. NB represents the "noise budget" after server's computation in the table, namely the number of bits of plaintext recoverable above the noise in each of the N coefficients of the plaintext. For example, for $n = 2^{16}$ in SHECS-PIR, each coefficient of the reply can store up to 8 bits of information, for a total bandwidth of $8N = 16384$ bits of information (2048 bytes) per plaintext: this means that if database entries are $\beta = 288$ bytes long, we can store 7 of them per plaintext, and hence support database of size $\approx 2^{19}$ in that case). NB(w/o unpack) denotes the noise budget after server's computation without query unpacking step. As we can see that, query unpacking has very small error growth so that it has little impact on the noise budget. The noise growth in SHECS-PIR is in $\log \log n$ compared to SealPIR's $\log n$, so the noise budget is higher in SHECS-PIR, and we can support very large databases before this budget is reduced significantly. In SealPIR on the other hand, parameters have to be increased somehow to support large databases; there is a complicated set of trade-offs between the data element size β, the plaintext modulus p, the polynomial degree N and the array size n, with an increase in one resulting in a decrease on another, making parameter selection somewhat tricky. Comparatively, SHECS-PIR is relatively free of trade-offs as n increases.

For the computation time of the database in the applicable range, the server processing time (main computation) scales very close to linearly with n (the database size) and it is similar to SealPIR. We have a small overhead over SealPIR due to the choice of avoiding any database preprocessing, more precisely, storing database elements as NTT/FFT form in advance. Note that a plaintext is a

Table 5. Comparison between SHECS-PIR and SealPIR for large $\mathfrak{n}$, $q \approx 2^{60}$, $N = 2048$.

DB size $\mathfrak{n}$		2^{22}	2^{24}	2^{25}	2^{26}	2^{27}
SHECS-PIR	Compressed-Query[#]	2	2	2	2	2
	Query[#]	2×22	2×24	2×25	2×26	2×27
	Answer[#]	1	1	1	1	1
SealPIR ($d = 3$)	Compressed-Query[#]	3	3	3	3	3
	Answer[#]	100	100	100	100	100
SHECS-PIR	First-step[s]	15	16	17	18	18
	Main[s]	143	574	1167	2327	4645
	NB	7	6	6	6	6
SealPIR ($d = 3$)	Server preprocessing[s]	291	1192	*[out of memory]*		
	Server time[s]	132	489			

polynomial of 12 bit coefficients, while ciphertext consists of 64 bit coefficient. As a result, we have almost no storage overhead for the database in memory, compared to an overhead of more than 5 ($=64/12$) in SealPIR. This lets us support very large databases up to 2^{27} (corresponding to 2^{30} entries of 384 KB each, 384 GB of data in total), while the same could not be achieved with SealPIR on commodity hardware (See Table 5). In addition, for large databases, SealPIR makes it necessary to increase d, which results in a larger response size. Specifically, SealPIR simply fails if d is set to 2 for $\mathfrak{n} \geq 2^{22}$, so we have to set d to at least 3, and get a response consists of a hundred ciphertexts or more; due to memory constraints, we could run it only up to $\mathfrak{n} = 2^{24}$, with larger instances too big to fit in memory our relatively high-end server.

The communication cost (query and answer size) is expressed in the number of ciphertexts. Compressed-Query[#] denotes an optimization of query size (query unpacking in SHECS-PIR, query expansion in SealPIR). We can see that our total communication cost *even without query unpacking* is actually lower than SealPIR with query expansion for large database sizes, due to the much larger response size in SealPIR. Nevertheless, query unpacking becomes relatively negligible for large database sizes, so it would seem natural to use it as well and enjoy our close to optimal communication complexity.

The server computation time may seem large, but it is almost completely embarrassingly parallel, so on our 48-core server the total server computation time can be brought down to less than 100 s for $\mathfrak{n} = 2^{27}$, say, by using multi-threading.

A   Optimization Options of Reducing Communication Cost

We explain modulus switching technique which is widely used in several homomorphic encryption schemes as one of optimization options. It changes the ciphertext space to lower space by switching modulus, hence it makes answer size smaller in PIR protocol. Another factor which has an effect on communication cost is ciphertext polynomial degree. In fact, it directly affects not only the size of query and answer but also computation time.

As stated in Sect. 5, there is a complicated relation on multiple factors of both computation and communication cost. One change of the factors results in small or big trade-offs in many cPIR protocols. There are several reasons to increase the polynomial degree such as controlling error growth, handling larger database e.t.c. However, we show that we can keep ciphertext polynomial size lower dealing with larger database and having no noise problem.

A.1   Modulus Switching

We just set a new ciphertext modulus $\bar{p}$ such that $p < \bar{p} < q$. Then modulus switching takes original TRLWE ciphertext $\mathsf{ct} = (c_0, c_1)$ gives a new TRLWE ciphertext $\bar{\mathsf{ct}} = (\bar{c}_0, \bar{c}_1)$, where $\left[\lceil \bar{c}_0 = \frac{\bar{p}}{q} c_0 \rfloor\right]$ mod $\bar{p}$, $\left[\lceil \bar{c}_1 = \frac{\bar{p}}{q} c_1 \rfloor\right]$ mod $\bar{p}$. This is almost free in implementation since it just shifts all the coefficients. Furthermore, it causes fairly small noise growth comparing to FV ciphertext [17] since all the modulus $p, \bar{p}, q$ are power of 2. As a result, we can reduce the communication cost without increasing the server's computation cost.

A.2   Smaller Polynomial Degree

As a ciphertext of query in SHECS-PIR has just bit length information which is usually much smaller than polynomial degree N, there is no need to keep the polynomial degree large. It may hardly happen that $\log \mathfrak{n} > N$, hence, we could keep the same modulus q and N. Larger N may contain large data element size in one ciphertext but decreases the efficiency of protocol having more computation and noise. Therefore, SHECS-PIR has a benefit on maintaining smaller query size not increasing other factors (no trade-offs), while more ciphertexts are required for a query in SealPIR as $\mathfrak{n}$ increases.

B   Multi-query PIR

Our protocol with packed query naturally supports multi-query scenario where the same client wants to retrieve multiple elements from the same server or multiple indices are asked to a server for one answer. For the former, we can obtain single query size cost even for realistic large enough number of database and the answer size is linear on the number of indices. For the latter, the communication cost is as same as single query version. The reason is that we only use $\log \mathfrak{n}$ coefficients of polynomial to generate the single query ciphertext for fixed the number of data $\mathfrak{n}$ and the degree N. Then it is possible to have at most $\lfloor N/\log \mathfrak{n} \rfloor$ indices in one polynomial as a multi query without increasing query size. It just maintains the communication cost of single query.

There are some multi query protocols to improve CPU costs. SHECS-PIR gives a benefit on communication cost if it is applied to any computationally efficient technique (batch codes [26,32], probabilistic batch codes [5]) of multi query PIR protocol. Comparing to the previous work in [5], SealPIR requires each query ciphertext to be expanded to each dimension's query vector by expand algorithm for an index. Therefore, a query ciphertext cannot contain more information apart from the desired index using their way. It implies that a client has to encrypts b times which outputs b ciphertexts to request b items from a server's DB. However, unpacking query step in our protocol is only dependent on coefficient of polynomial. For example, to retrieve 64 items out of 2^{20}, SealPIR requires more than 64 query ciphertexts (using probabilistic batch codes, they require $b(= 1.5 \times 64)$ query). But our approach requires only one query ciphertext having b indices for fixed $N = 2048, \mathfrak{n} = 2^{20}$ having the same efficient computational cost. Furthermore, for the server's reply, only one ciphertext per query is given by server with SHECS-PIR, while F^{d-1} ciphertexts are required per query to answer for a server in SealPIR and usually $F \geq 4, d \geq 2$.

References

1. Aguilar Melchor, C., Barrier, J., Fousse, L., Killijian, M.O.: XPIR: private information retrieval for everyone. PoPETs **2016**(2), 155–174 (2016)
2. Albrecht, M.R., Player, R., Scott, S.: On the concrete hardness of learning with errors. J. Math. Cryptol. **9**(3), 169–203 (2015). http://www.degruyter.com/view/j/jmc.2015.9.issue-3/jmc-2015-0016/jmc-2015-0016.xml
3. Ali, A., et al.: Communication-computation trade-offs in PIR. Cryptology ePrint Archive, Report 2019/1483 (2019). https://eprint.iacr.org/2019/1483
4. Alkim, E., Ducas, L., Pöppelmann, T., Schwabe, P.: Post-quantum key exchange - a new hope. In: Holz, T., Savage, S. (eds.) USENIX Security 2016, pp. 327–343. USENIX Association, August 2016
5. Angel, S., Chen, H., Laine, K., Setty, S.T.V.: PIR with compressed queries and amortized query processing. In: 2018 IEEE Symposium on Security and Privacy, pp. 962–979. IEEE Computer Society Press, May 2018
6. Bai, S., Galbraith, S.D.: Lattice decoding attacks on binary LWE. In: Susilo, W., Mu, Y. (eds.) ACISP 2014. LNCS, vol. 8544, pp. 322–337. Springer, Cham (2014). https://doi.org/10.1007/978-3-319-08344-5_21
7. Beimel, A., Ishai, Y., Kushilevitz, E., Raymond, J.F.: Breaking the $O(n^{1/(2k-1)})$ barrier for information-theoretic private information retrieval. In: 43rd FOCS, pp. 261–270. IEEE Computer Society Press, November 2002
8. Brakerski, Z., Vaikuntanathan, V.: Efficient fully homomorphic encryption from (standard) LWE. In: Ostrovsky, R. (ed.) 52nd FOCS, pp. 97–106. IEEE Computer Society Press, October 2011
9. Brakerski, Z., Vaikuntanathan, V.: Fully homomorphic encryption from ring-LWE and security for key dependent messages. In: Rogaway, P. (ed.) CRYPTO 2011. LNCS, vol. 6841, pp. 505–524. Springer, Heidelberg (2011). https://doi.org/10.1007/978-3-642-22792-9_29
10. Cachin, C., Micali, S., Stadler, M.: Computationally private information retrieval with polylogarithmic communication. In: Stern, J. (ed.) EUROCRYPT 1999. LNCS, vol. 1592, pp. 402–414. Springer, Heidelberg (1999). https://doi.org/10.1007/3-540-48910-X_28

11. Chen, H., Laine, K., Player, R.: Simple encrypted arithmetic library - SEAL v2.2. Technical report (2017)
12. Chillotti, I., Gama, N., Georgieva, M., Izabachène, M.: Faster fully homomorphic encryption: bootstrapping in less than 0.1 seconds. In: Cheon, J.H., Takagi, T. (eds.) ASIACRYPT 2016. LNCS, vol. 10031, pp. 3–33. Springer, Heidelberg (2016). https://doi.org/10.1007/978-3-662-53887-6_1
13. Chillotti, I., Gama, N., Georgieva, M., Izabachène, M.: Faster packed homomorphic operations and efficient circuit bootstrapping for TFHE. In: Takagi, T., Peyrin, T. (eds.) ASIACRYPT 2017. LNCS, vol. 10624, pp. 377–408. Springer, Cham (2017). https://doi.org/10.1007/978-3-319-70694-8_14
14. Chillotti, I., Gama, N., Georgieva, M., Izabachène, M.: TFHE: fast fully homomorphic encryption over the torus. J. Cryptol. $33(1)$, 34–91 (2020)
15. Chillotti, I., Gama, N., Georgieva, M., Izabachène, M.: TFHE: Fast fully homomorphic encryption library, August 2016. https://tfhe.github.io/tfhe/
16. Chor, B., Goldreich, O., Kushilevitz, E., Sudan, M.: Private information retrieval. In: 36th FOCS, pp. 41–50. IEEE Computer Society Press, October 1995
17. Costache, A., Laine, K., Player, R.: Homomorphic noise growth in practice: comparing BGV and FV. Cryptology ePrint Archive, Report 2019/493 (2019). https://eprint.iacr.org/2019/493
18. Dams, D., Lataille, J., Sanchez, R., Wade, J.: WIDESEAS: a lattice-based PIR scheme implemented in EncryptedQuery. Cryptology ePrint Archive, Report 2019/855 (2019). https://eprint.iacr.org/2019/855
19. Demmler, D., Herzberg, A., Schneider, T.: Raid-PIR: practical multi-server PIR. In: Proceedings of the 6th Edition of the ACM Workshop on Cloud Computing Security, CCSW 2014, pp. 45–56. ACM, New York (2014)
20. Devet, C., Goldberg, I., Heninger, N.: Optimally robust private information retrieval. In: Kohno, T. (ed.) USENIX Security 2012, pp. 269–283. USENIX Association, August 2012
21. Dong, C., Chen, L.: A fast single server private information retrieval protocol with low communication cost. In: Kutyłowski, M., Vaidya, J. (eds.) ESORICS 2014. LNCS, vol. 8712, pp. 380–399. Springer, Cham (2014). https://doi.org/10.1007/978-3-319-11203-9_22
22. Fan, J., Vercauteren, F.: Somewhat practical fully homomorphic encryption. Cryptology ePrint Archive, Report 2012/144 (2012). http://eprint.iacr.org/2012/144
23. Gentry, C., Halevi, S.: Compressible FHE with applications to PIR. In: Hofheinz, D., Rosen, A. (eds.) TCC 2019. LNCS, vol. 11892, pp. 438–464. Springer, Cham (2019). https://doi.org/10.1007/978-3-030-36033-7_17
24. Gentry, C., Sahai, A., Waters, B.: Homomorphic encryption from learning with errors: conceptually-simpler, asymptotically-faster, attribute-based. In: Canetti, R., Garay, J.A. (eds.) CRYPTO 2013. LNCS, vol. 8042, pp. 75–92. Springer, Heidelberg (2013). https://doi.org/10.1007/978-3-642-40041-4_5
25. Goldberg, I.: Improving the robustness of private information retrieval. In: 2007 IEEE Symposium on Security and Privacy, pp. 131–148. IEEE Computer Society Press, May 2007
26. Ishai, Y., Kushilevitz, E., Ostrovsky, R., Sahai, A.: Batch codes and their applications. In: Babai, L. (ed.) 36th ACM STOC, pp. 262–271. ACM Press, June 2004
27. Kiayias, A., Leonardos, N., Lipmaa, H., Pavlyk, K., Tang, Q.: Optimal rate private information retrieval from homomorphic encryption. PoPETs $2015(2)$, 222–243 (2015)

28. Kushilevitz, E., Ostrovsky, R.: Replication is NOT needed: SINGLE database, computationally-private information retrieval. In: 38th FOCS, pp. 364–373. IEEE Computer Society Press, October 1997

29. Laine, K., et al.: SealPIR: a computational PIR library that achieves low communication costs and high performance. https://github.com/microsoft/SealPIR

30. Lipmaa, H., Pavlyk, K.: A simpler rate-optimal CPIR protocol. In: Kiayias, A. (ed.) FC 2017. LNCS, vol. 10322, pp. 621–638. Springer, Cham (2017). https://doi.org/10.1007/978-3-319-70972-7_35

31. Olumofin, F.G., Goldberg, I.: Revisiting the computational practicality of private information retrieval. In: Danezis, G. (ed.) FC 2011. LNCS, vol. 7035, pp. 158–172. Springer, Heidelberg (2012). https://doi.org/10.1007/978-3-642-27576-0_13

32. Paterson, M.B., Stinson, D.R., Wei, R.: Combinatorial batch codes. Adv. Math. Commun. **3**(1), 13–27 (2009)

33. Stern, J.P.: A new efficient all-or-nothing disclosure of secrets protocol. In: Ohta, K., Pei, D. (eds.) ASIACRYPT' 1998. LNCS, vol. 1514, pp. 357–371. Springer, Heidelberg (1998)

Puncturable Encryption: A Generic Construction from Delegatable Fully Key-Homomorphic Encryption

Willy Susilo[1,3(✉)], Dung Hoang Duong[1,3(✉)], Huy Quoc Le[1,2(✉)],
and Josef Pieprzyk[2,3(✉)]

[1] Institute of Cybersecurity and Cryptology,
School of Computing and Information Technology, University of Wollongong,
Northfields Avenue, Wollongong, NSW 2522, Australia
{wsusilo,hduong}@uow.edu.au, qhl576@uowmail.edu.au
[2] CSIRO Data61, Sydney, NSW, Australia
Josef.Pieprzyk@data61.csiro.au
[3] Institute of Computer Science, Polish Academy of Sciences, Warsaw, Poland

Abstract. Puncturable encryption (PE), proposed by Green and Miers at IEEE S&P 2015, is a kind of public key encryption that allows recipients to revoke individual messages by repeatedly updating decryption keys without communicating with senders. PE is an essential tool for constructing many interesting applications, such as asynchronous messaging systems, forward-secret zero round-trip time protocols, public-key watermarking schemes and forward-secret proxy re-encryptions. This paper revisits PEs from the observation that the puncturing property can be implemented as efficiently computable functions. From this view, we propose a generic PE construction from the fully key-homomorphic encryption, augmented with a key delegation mechanism (DFKHE) from Boneh et al. at Eurocrypt 2014. We show that our PE construction enjoys the selective security under chosen plaintext attacks (that can be converted into the adaptive security with some efficiency loss) from that of DFKHE in the standard model. Basing on the framework, we obtain the first post-quantum secure PE instantiation that is based on the learning with errors problem, selective secure under chosen plaintext attacks (CPA) in the standard model. We also discuss about the ability of modification our framework to support the unbounded number of ciphertext tags inspired from the work of Brakerski and Vaikuntanathan at CRYPTO 2016.

Keywords: Puncturable encryption · Attribute-based encryption · Learning with errors · Arithmetic circuits · Fully key-homomorphic encryption · Key delegation

1 Introduction

Puncturable encryption (PE), proposed by Green and Miers [18] in 2015, is a kind of public key encryption, which can also be seen as a tag-based encryption

© Springer Nature Switzerland AG 2020
L. Chen et al. (Eds.): ESORICS 2020, LNCS 12309, pp. 107–127, 2020.
https://doi.org/10.1007/978-3-030-59013-0_6

(TBE), where both encryption and decryption are controlled by tags. Similarly to TBE, a plaintext in PE is encrypted together with tags, which are called *ciphertext tags*. In addition, the puncturing property of PE allows to produce new punctured secret keys associated some *punctures* (or *punctured tags*). Although the new keys (*puncture keys*) differ from the old ones, they still allow recipients to decrypt old ciphertexts as long as chosen *punctured tags* are different from tags embedded in the ciphertext. The puncturing property is very useful when the current decryption key is compromised. In a such situation, a recipient merely needs to update his key using the puncturing mechanism. PE is also useful when there is a need to revoke decryption capability from many users in order to protect some sensitive information (e.g., a time period or user identities). In this case, the puncturing mechanism is called for time periods or user identities.

Also, PE can provide forward security in a fine-grained level. Forward security, formulated in [19] in the context of key-exchange protocols, is a desired security property that helps to reduce a security risk caused by key exposure attacks. In particular, forward secure encryption (FSE) guarantees confidentiality of old messages, when the current secret key has been compromised. Compared to PE, FSE provides a limited support for revocation of decryption capability. For instance, it is difficult for FSE to control decryption capability for any individual ciphertext (or all ciphertexts) produced during a certain time period, which, in contrast, can be easily done with PE.

Due to the aforementioned advantages, PE has become more and more popular and has been used in many important applications in such as asynchronous messaging transport systems [18], forward-secure zero round–trip time (0-RTT) key-exchange protocols [15,20], public-key watermarking schemes [12] and forward-secure proxy re-encryptions [16].

Related Works. Green and Miers [18] propose the notion of PE and also present a specific ABE-based PE instantiation. The instantiation is based on the decisional bilinear Diffie-Hellman assumption (DBDH) in bilinear groups and is proven to be CPA secure in the random oracle model (ROM). Following the work [18], many other constructions have been proposed such as [10,12,15,20,26] (see Table 1 for a summary). For instance, Günther et al. [20] have provided a generic PE construction from *any* selectively secure hierarchical identity-based key encapsulation (HIBEKEM) combined with an *any* one time signature (OTS). In fact, the authors of [20] claim that their framework can be instantiated as the first post-quantum PE. Also, in the work [20], the authors present the first PE-based forward-secret zero round-trip time protocol with full forward secrecy. However, they instantiate PE that is secure in the standard model (SDM) by combining a (DDH)-based HIBE with a OTS based on discrete logarithm. The construction supports a predetermined number of ciphertext tags as well as a limited number of punctures. Derler et al. [15] introduce the notion of Bloom filter encryption (BFE), which can be converted to PE. They show how to instantiate BFE using identity-based encryption (IBE) with a specific construction that assumes intractability of the bilinear computational Diffie-Hellman (BCDH) problem. Later, Derler et al. [14] extend the result of

[15] and give a generic BFE construction from identity-based broadcast encryption (IBBE). The instantiation in [14] is based on a generalization of the Diffie-Hellman exponent (GDDHE) assumption in parings. However, the construction based on BFE suffers from *non-negligible correctness error*. This excludes it from applications that require negligible correctness error, as discussed in [26]. Most recently, Sun et al. [26] have introduced a new concept, which they call key-homomorphic identity-based revocable key encapsulation mechanism (KH-IRKEM) with extended correctness, from which they obtain a modular design of PE with *negligible correctness errors*. In particular, they describe four modular and compact instantiations of PE, which are secure in SDM. However, all of them are based on hard problems in pairings, namely q-decision bilinear Diffie-Hellman exponent problem (q–DBDHE), the decision bilinear Diffie-Hellman problem (DBDH), the q-decisional multi-exponent bilinear Diffie-Hellman (q-MEBDH) problem and the decisional linear problem (DLIN). We emphasize that all existing instantiations mentioned above are insecure against quantum adversaries. Some other works like [10,12] based PE on the notion of indistinguishability obfuscation, which is still impractical. The reader is referred to [26] for a state-of-the-art discussion.

To the best of our knowledge, there has been no specific lattice-based PE instantiation, which simultaneously enjoys negligible correctness error as well as post-quantum security in the standard model.

Our Contribution. We first give a *generic* construction of PE from *delegatable fully key-homomorphic encryption* (DFKHE) framework. The framework is a generalisation of fully key-homomorphic encryption (FKHE) [5] by adding a key delegation mechanism. The framework is closely related to the functional encryption [7].

We also present an explicit PE construction based on lattices. Our design is obtained from LWE-based DFKHE that we build using FKHE for the learning with errors (LWE) setting [5]. This is combined with the key delegation ability supplied by the lattice trapdoor techniques [1,11,17]. Our lattice FE construction has the following characteristics:

- It supports a predetermined number of ciphertext tags per ciphertext. The ciphertext size is short and depends linearly on the number of ciphertext tags, which is fixed in advance. However, we note that following the work of Brakerski and Vaikuntanathan [8], our construction might be extended to obtain a variant that supports unbounded number of ciphertext tags (see Sect. 5 for a detailed discussion),
- It works for a predetermined number of punctures. The size of decryption keys (i.e., puncture keys) increases quadratically with the number of punctured tags,
- It offers selective CPA security in the standard model (that can be converted into full CPA security using the complexity leveraging technique as discussed in [4,5,9,21]). This is due to CPA security of LWE-based underlying DFKHE (following the security proof for the generic framework).
- It enjoys post-quantum security and negligible correctness errors.

Table 1 compares our work with the results obtained by other authors. At first sight, the FE framework based on key homomorphic revocable identity-based (KH-IRKEM) [26] looks similar to ours. However, both frameworks are different. While key-homomorphism used by us means the capacity of transforming (as claimed in [5, Subsection 1.1]) "*an encryption under key* $\mathbf{x}$ *into an encryption under key* $f(\mathbf{x})$", key-homomorphism defined in [26, Definition 8] reflects the ability of preserving the algebraic structure of (mathematical) groups.

Overview and Techniques. We start with a high-level description of fully-key homomorphism encryption (FHKE), which was proposed by Boneh et al. [5]. Afterwards, we introduce what we call the *delegetable fully-key homomorphism encryption (DFHKE)*. At high-level description, FKHE possesses a mechanism that allows to convert a ciphertext $ct_{\mathbf{x}}$ (associated with a public variable $\mathbf{x}$) into the evaluated one ct_f for the same plaintext (associated with the pair (y, f)), where f is an efficiently computable function and $f(\mathbf{x}) = y$. In other words, FKHE requires a special key-homomorphic evaluation algorithm, called Eval, such that $ct_f \leftarrow \mathsf{Eval}(f, ct_{\mathbf{x}})$. In order to successfully decrypt an evaluated ciphertext, the decryptor needs to evaluate the initial secret sk to get sk_f. An extra algorithm, called KHom, is needed to do this, i.e. $sk_f \leftarrow \mathsf{KHom}(sk, (y, f))$. A drawback of FKHE is that it supports only a single function f.

Actually, we would like to perform key-homomorphic evaluation for many functions $\{f_1, \cdots, f_k\}$ that belong to a family $\mathcal{F}$. To meet the requirement and obtain DFKHE, we generalise FKHE by endowing it with two algorithms ExtEval and KDel. The first algorithm transforms $(ct_{\mathbf{x}}, \mathbf{x})$ into $(ct_{f_1,\cdots,f_k}, (y, f_1, \cdots f_k))$, where $f_1(\mathbf{x}) = \cdots = f_k(\mathbf{x}) = y$. This is written as $ct_{f_1,\cdots,f_k} \leftarrow \mathsf{ExtEval}(f_1, \cdots, f_k, ct_{\mathbf{x}})$. The second algorithm allows to delegate the secret key step by step for the next function or $sk_{f_1,\cdots,f_k} \leftarrow \mathsf{KDel}(sk_{f_1,\cdots,f_{k-1}}, (y, f_k))$.

Our generic PE framework is inspired by a simple but subtle observation that puncturing property requires equality of ciphertext tags and punctures. This can be provided by functions that can be efficiently computed by arithmetic circuits. We call such functions *equality test functions*. Note that for PE, ciphertext tags play the role of variables $\mathbf{x}$'s and equality test functions act as functions f's defined in FKHE. For FE, one more puncture added defines one extra equality test function, which needs a delegation mechanism to take the function into account. We note that the requirement can be easily met using the same idea as the key delegation mentioned above. In order to be able to employ the idea of DFKHE for $(y_0, \mathcal{F})$ to PE, we define an efficiently computable family $\mathcal{F}$ of equality test functions $f_{t^*}(\mathbf{t})$ allowing us to compare the puncture t^* with ciphertext tags $\mathbf{t} = (t_1, \cdots, t_d)$ under the definition that $f_{t^*}(\mathbf{t}) = y_0$ iff $t^* \neq t_j \forall j \in [d]$, for some fixed value y_0.

For concrete DHKHE and PE constructions, we employ the LWE-based FKHE proposed in [5]. In this system, the ciphertext is $ct = (\mathbf{c}_{\mathsf{in}}, \mathbf{c}_1, \cdots, \mathbf{c}_d, \mathbf{c}_{\mathsf{out}})$, where $\mathbf{c}_i = (t_i \mathbf{G} + \mathbf{B}_i)^T \mathbf{s} + \mathbf{e}_i$ for $i \in [d]$. Here the gadget matrix $\mathbf{G}$ is a special one, whose associated trapdoor $\mathbf{T}_{\mathbf{G}}$ (i.e., a short basis for the q-ary lattice

Table 1. Comparison of some existing PE constructions in the literature with ours. Note that, here all works are being considered in the CPA security setting. The notation "$< \infty$" means "bounded" or "predetermined", while "∞" means "unlimited" or "arbitrary". The column entitled "Post-quantum" says whether the specific construction in each framework is post-quantum secure or not regardless its generic framework. The last column mentions to supporting the negligible correctness error. **ROM***: For the BFE-based FE basing on the IBBE instantiation of Derler et al. [14], we note that, the IBBE instantiation can be modified to remove ROM, as claimed by Delerablée in [13, Subsection 3.2]

Literature	From	Assumption	Security model	#Tags	#Punctures	Post-quantum	Negl. Corr. Error
Green [18]	ABE	DBDH	ROM	$<\infty$	∞	×	✓
Günther [20]	Any HIBE + any OTS	DDH (HIBE) + DLP (OTS)	SDM	$<\infty$	$<\infty$	×	✓
Derler [14]	BFE (IBBE)	GDDHE	**ROM***	1	$<\infty$	×	×
Derler [15]	BFE (IBE)	BCDH	ROM	1	$<\infty$	×	×
Sun [26]	KH-IRKEM	q–DBDHE	SDM	$<\infty$	∞	×	✓
		DBDH		$<\infty$	∞	×	
		q–MEBDH		∞	∞	×	
		DLIN		$<\infty$	∞	×	
This work	DFKHE	DLWE	SDM	$<\infty$	$< \infty$	✓	✓

$\Lambda_q^{\perp}(\mathbf{G}))$ is publicly known (see [22] for details). Also, there exist three evaluation algorithms named $\mathsf{Eval}_{\mathsf{pk}}$, $\mathsf{Eval}_{\mathsf{ct}}$ and $\mathsf{Eval}_{\mathsf{sim}}$ [5], which help us to homomorphically evaluate a circuit (function) for a ciphertext ct. More specifically, from $\mathbf{c}_i := [t_i\mathbf{G} + \mathbf{B}_i]^T\mathbf{s} + \mathbf{e}_i$, where $\|\mathbf{e}_i\| < \delta$ for all $i \in [d]$, and a function $f : (\mathbb{Z}_q)^d \to \mathbb{Z}_q$, we get $\mathbf{c}_f = [f(t_1, \cdots, t_d)\mathbf{G} + \mathbf{B}_f]^T\mathbf{s} + \mathbf{e}_f, \|\mathbf{e}_f\| < \Delta$, where $\mathbf{B}_f \leftarrow \mathsf{Eval}_{\mathsf{pk}}(f, (\mathbf{B}_i)_{i=1}^d)$, $\mathbf{c}_f \leftarrow \mathsf{Eval}_{\mathsf{ct}}(f, ((t_i, \mathbf{B}_i, \mathbf{c}_i))_{i=1}^d)$, and $\Delta < \delta \cdot \beta$ for some β sufficiently small. The algorithm $\mathsf{ExtEval}$ mentioned above can be implemented calling many times $\mathsf{Eval}_{\mathsf{pk}}, \mathsf{Eval}_{\mathsf{ct}}$, each time for each function. Meanwhile, $\mathsf{Eval}_{\mathsf{sim}}$ is only useful in the simulation for the security proof. In the LWE-based DFKHE construction, secret keys are trapdoors for q-ary lattices of form $\Lambda_q^{\perp}([\mathbf{A}|\mathbf{B}_{f_1}| \cdots |\mathbf{B}_{f_k}])$. For the key delegation KDel, we can utilize the trapdoor techniques [1,11,17] . For the LWE-based PE instantiation, we employ the equality test function with $y_0 := 0 \pmod q$. Namely, for a puncture t^* and a list of ciphertext tags $t_1, \cdots, t_d$ we define $f_{t^*}(t_1, \cdots, t_d) := eq_{t^*}(t_1) + \cdots + eq_{t^*}(t_d)$, where $eq_{t^*} : \mathbb{Z}_q \to \mathbb{Z}_q$ satisfying that $\forall t \in \mathbb{Z}_q$, $eq_{t^*}(t) = 1 \pmod q$ iff $t = t^*$, otherwise $eq_{t^*}(t) = 0 \pmod q$. Such functions has also been employed in [6] to construct a privately puncturable pseudorandom function. It follows from generic construction that our PE instantiation is selective CPA-secure.

Efficiency. Table 2 summarizes the asymptotic bit-size of public key, secret key, punctured key and ciphertext. We can see that the public key size is a linear function in the number of ciphertext tags (i.e., d). The (initial) secret key size is independent of both d and η (the number of punctures). The punctured key (decryption key) size is a quadratic function of η. Lastly, the ciphertext size is a linear function of d.

On Unbounded Ciphertext Tags. We believe that our framework can be extended to support unbounded number of ciphertext tags by exploiting the interesting technique of [8]. The key idea of [8] is to use homomorphic evaluation of a family pseudorandom functions. This helps to stretch a predetermined parameter (e.g., the length of a seed) to an arbitrary number of ciphertext tags. The predetermined parameter will be used to generate other public parameters (e.g., public matrices). More details is given in Sect. 5.

Table 2. Keys and ciphertext's size of our LWE-based PE as functions in number of ciphertext tags d and number of punctures η.

Public key size	$O((d+1) \cdot n^2 \log^2 q)$
Secret key size	$O(n^2 \log^2 q \cdot \log(n \log q))$
Punctured key size	$(\eta + 1) \cdot n \log q \cdot (O(\log(\beta_{\mathcal{F}}) + \eta \cdot \log(n \log q)))$
Ciphertext size	$O((d+2) \cdot n \log^2 q))$

2 Preliminaries

2.1 Framework of Puncturable Encryption

Syntax of Puncturable Encryption. For a security parameter λ, let $d = d(\lambda)$, $\mathcal{M} = \mathcal{M}(\lambda)$ and $\mathcal{T} = \mathcal{T}(\lambda)$ be maximum number of tags per ciphertext, the space of plaintexts and the set of valid tags, respectively. Puncturable encryption (PE) is a collection of the following four algorithms KeyGen, Encrypt, Puncture and Decrypt:

- $(pk, sk_0) \leftarrow \mathsf{KeyGen}(1^\lambda, d)$: For a security parameter λ and the maximum number d of tags per ciphertext, the probabilistic polynomial time (PPT) algorithm KeyGen outputs a public key pk and an initial secret key sk_0.
- $ct \leftarrow \mathsf{Encrypt}(pk, \mu, \{t_1, \cdots, t_d\})$: For a public key pk, a message μ, and a list of tags $t_1, \cdots, t_d$, the PPT algorithm Encrypt returns a ciphertext ct.
- $sk_i \leftarrow \mathsf{Puncture}(pk, sk_{i-1}, t_i^*)$: For any $i > 1$, on input pk, sk_{i-1} and a tag t_i^*, the PPT algorithm Puncture outputs a punctured key sk_i that decrypts any ciphertexts, except for the ciphertext encrypted under any list of tags containing t_i^*.
- $\mu/\bot \leftarrow \mathsf{Decrypt}(pk, sk_i, (ct, \{t_1, \cdots, t_d\}))$: For input pk, a ciphertext ct, a secret key sk_i, and a list of tags $\{t_1, \cdots, t_d\}$, the deterministic polynomial time (DPT) algorithm Decrypt outputs either a message μ if the decryption succeeds or $\bot$ if it fails.

Correctness. The correctness requirement for PE is as follows:
For all $\lambda, d, \eta \geq 0$, $t_1^*, \cdots, t_\eta^*, t_1, \cdots, t_d \in \mathcal{T}$, $(pk, sk_0) \leftarrow \mathsf{KeyGen}(1^\lambda, d)$, $sk_i \leftarrow \mathsf{Punc}(pk, sk_{i-1}, t_i^*), \forall i \in [\eta]$, $ct = \mathsf{Encrypt}(pk, \mu, \{t_1, \cdots, t_d\})$, we have

- If $\{t_1^*, \cdots, t_\eta^*\} \cap \{t_1, \cdots, t_d\} = \emptyset$, then $\forall i \in \{0, \cdots, \eta\}$,

$$\Pr[\mathsf{Decrypt}(pk, sk_i, (ct, \{t_1, \cdots, t_d\})) = \mu] \geq 1 - \mathsf{negl}(\lambda).$$

- If there exist $j \in [d]$ and $k \in [\eta]$ such that $t_k^* = t_j$, then $\forall i \in \{k, \cdots, \eta\}$,

$$\Pr[\mathsf{Decrypt}(pk, sk_i, (ct, \{t_1, \cdots, t_d\})) = \mu] \leq \mathsf{negl}(\lambda).$$

Definition 1 (Selective Security of PE). *PE is IND-sPUN-ATK if the advantage of any PPT adversary $\mathcal{A}$ in the game* $\mathsf{IND\text{-}sPUN\text{-}ATK}_{\mathsf{PE}}^{\mathsf{sel}, \mathcal{A}}$ *is negligible, where $ATK \in \{CPA, CCA\}$. Formally,*

$$\mathsf{Adv}_{\mathsf{PE}}^{\mathsf{IND\text{-}sPUN\text{-}ATK}}(\mathcal{A}) = |\Pr[b' = b] - \frac{1}{2}| \leq \mathsf{negl}(\lambda).$$

The game $\mathsf{IND\text{-}sPUN\text{-}ATK}_{\mathsf{PE}}^{\mathsf{sel}, \mathcal{A}}$ proceeds as follows.

1. **Initialize.** The adversary announces the target tags $\{\widehat{t_1}, \cdots, \widehat{t_d}\}$.
2. **Setup.** The challenger initializes a set punctured tags $\mathcal{T}^* \leftarrow \emptyset$, a counter $i \leftarrow 0$ that counts the current number of punctured tags in $\mathcal{T}^*$ and a set of corrupted tags $\mathcal{C}^* \leftarrow \emptyset$ containing all punctured tags at the time of the first corruption query. Then, it runs $(pk, sk_0) \leftarrow \mathsf{KeyGen}(1^\lambda, d)$. Finally, it gives pk to the adversary.
3. **Query 1.**
    - Once the adversary makes a puncture key query $\mathsf{PQ}(t^*)$, the challenger updates $i \leftarrow i + 1$, returns $sk_i \leftarrow \mathsf{Punc}(pk, sk_{i-1}, t^*)$ and adds t^* to $\mathcal{T}^*$.
    - The first time the adversary makes a corruption query $\mathsf{CQ}()$, the challenger returns $\perp$ if it finds out that $\{\widehat{t_1}, \cdots, \widehat{t_d}\} \cap \mathcal{T}^* = \emptyset$. Otherwise, the challenger returns the most recent punctured key sk_η, then sets $\mathcal{C}^*$ as the most recent $\mathcal{T}^*$ (i.e., $\mathcal{C}^* \leftarrow \mathcal{T}^* = \{t_1^*, \cdots, t_\eta^*\}$). All subsequent puncture key queries and corruption queries are answered with $\perp$.
    - If $ATK = CCA$: Once the adversary makes a decryption query $\mathsf{DQ}(ct, \{t_1, \cdots, t_d\})$, the challenger runs $\mathsf{Decrypt}(pk, sk_\eta, (ct, \{t_1, \cdots, t_d\}))$ using the most recent punctured key sk_η and returns its output.
    If $ATK = CPA$: the challenger returns $\perp$.
4. **Challenge.** The adversary submits two messages μ_0, μ_1. The challenger rejects the challenge if it finds out that $\{\widehat{t_1}, \cdots, \widehat{t_d}\} \cap \mathcal{C}^* = \emptyset$[1]. Otherwise, the challenger chooses $b \xleftarrow{\$} \{0, 1\}$ and returns $\widehat{ct} \leftarrow \mathsf{Encrypt}(pk, \mu_b, \{\widehat{t_1}, \cdots, \widehat{t_d}\})$.

---

[1] Note that, after making some queries that are different from the target tags, the adversary may skip making corruption query but goes directly to the challenge phase and trivially wins the game. This rejection prevents the adversary from such a trivial win. It also force the adversary to make the corruption query before challenging.

5. **Query 2.** The same as Query 1 with the restriction that for $DQ(ct, \{t_1, \cdots, t_d\})$, the challenger returns $\perp$ if $(ct, \{t_1, \cdots, t_d\}) = (\widehat{ct}, \{\widehat{t_1}, \cdots, \widehat{t_d}\})$.
6. **Guess.** The adversary outputs $b' \in \{0, 1\}$. It wins if $b' = b$.

The full security for PE is defined in the same way, except that the adversary can choose target tags at Challenge phase, after getting the public key and after Query 1 phase. In this case, the challenger does not need to check the condition $\{\widehat{t_1}, \cdots, \widehat{t_d}\} \cap \mathcal{T}^* = \emptyset$ in the first corruption query $CQ()$ of the adversary in Query 1 phase.

2.2 Background on Lattices

A lattice is the set $\mathcal{L} = \mathcal{L}(\mathbf{B}) := \{\sum_{i=1}^{m} \mathbf{b}_i x_i : x_i \in \mathbb{Z} \ \forall i \in [m]\} \subseteq \mathbb{Z}^m$ generated by a basis $\mathbf{B} = [\mathbf{b}_1 | \cdots | \mathbf{b}_m] \in \mathbb{Z}^{n \times m}$. We are interested in the following lattices: $\Lambda_q^{\perp}(\mathbf{A}) := \{\mathbf{e} \in \mathbb{Z}^m \mid \mathbf{A}\mathbf{e} = 0 \pmod{q}\}$, $\Lambda_q^{\mathbf{u}}(\mathbf{A}) := \{\mathbf{e} \in \mathbb{Z}^m | \mathbf{A}\mathbf{e} = \mathbf{u} \pmod{q}\}$, $\Lambda_q^{\mathbf{U}}(\mathbf{A}) := \{\mathbf{R} \in \mathbb{Z}^{m \times k} | \mathbf{A}\mathbf{R} = \mathbf{U} \pmod{q}\}$, where $\mathbf{A} \xleftarrow{\$} \mathbb{Z}^{n \times m}$, $\mathbf{u} \in \mathbb{Z}_q^n$ and $\mathbf{U} \in \mathbb{Z}_q^{n \times k}$.

For a vector $\mathbf{s} = (s_1, \cdots, s_n)$, $\|\mathbf{s}\| := \sqrt{s_1^2 + \cdots + s_n^2}$, $\|\mathbf{s}\|_{\infty} := \max_{i \in [n]} |s_i|$. For a matrix $\mathbf{S} = [\mathbf{s}_1 \cdots \mathbf{s}_k]$ and any vector $\mathbf{x} = (x_1, \cdots, x_k)$, we define $\|\mathbf{S}\| := \max_{i \in [k]} \|\mathbf{s}_i\|$, the GS norm of $\mathbf{S}$ is $\|\widetilde{\mathbf{S}}\|$, the sup norm is $\|\mathbf{S}\|_{sup} = \sup_{\mathbf{x}} \frac{\|\mathbf{S}\mathbf{x}\|}{\|\mathbf{x}\|}$. This yields for all $\mathbf{x}$ that $\|\mathbf{S}\mathbf{x}\| \leq \|\mathbf{S}\|_{sup} \cdot \|\mathbf{x}\|$. We call a basis $\mathbf{S}$ of some lattice *short* if $\|\widetilde{\mathbf{S}}\|$ is short.

Gaussian Distributions. Assume $m \geq 1$, $\mathbf{v} \in \mathbb{R}^m$, $\sigma > 0$, and $\mathbf{x} \in \mathbb{R}^m$. We define the function $\rho_{\sigma, \mathbf{v}}(\mathbf{x}) = \exp(-\pi \|\mathbf{x} - \mathbf{v}\|^2 / \sigma^2)$.

Definition 2 (Discrete Gaussians). *Suppose that $\mathcal{L} \subseteq \mathbb{Z}^m$ is a lattice, and $\mathbf{v} \in \mathbb{R}^m$ and $\sigma > 0$. The discrete Gaussian distribution over $\mathcal{L}$ with center $\mathbf{v}$ and parameter σ is defined by $\mathcal{D}_{\mathcal{L}, \sigma, \mathbf{v}}(\mathbf{x}) = \frac{\rho_{\sigma, \mathbf{v}}(\mathbf{x})}{\rho_{\sigma, \mathbf{v}}(\mathcal{L})}$ for $\mathbf{x} \in \mathcal{L}$, where $\rho_{\sigma, \mathbf{v}}(\mathcal{L}) := \sum_{\mathbf{x} \in \mathcal{L}} \rho_{\sigma, \mathbf{v}}(\mathbf{x})$.*

Lemma 1 ([23, Lemma 4.4]). *Let $q > 2$ and let $\mathbf{A}, \mathbf{B}$ be a matrix in $\mathbb{Z}_q^{n \times m}$ with $m > n$. Let $\mathbf{T_A}$ be a basis for $\Lambda_q^{\perp}(\mathbf{A})$. Then, for $\sigma \geq \|\widetilde{\mathbf{T_A}}\| \cdot \omega(\sqrt{\log n})$, $\Pr[\mathbf{x} \leftarrow \mathcal{D}_{\Lambda_q^{\perp}(\mathbf{A}), \sigma} : \|\mathbf{x}\| > \sigma\sqrt{m}] \leq \mathsf{negl}(n)$.*

Learning with Errors. The security for our construction relies on the decision variant of the learning with errors (DLWE) problem defined below.

Definition 3 (DLWE, [25]). *Suppose that n be a positive integer, q is prime, and χ is a distribution over $\mathbb{Z}_q$. The (n, m, q, χ)-DLWE problem requires to distinguish $(\mathbf{A}, \mathbf{A}^T \mathbf{s} + \mathbf{e})$ from $(\mathbf{A}, \mathbf{c})$, where $\mathbf{A} \xleftarrow{\$} \mathbb{Z}_q^{n \times m}$, $\mathbf{s} \xleftarrow{\$} \mathbb{Z}_q^n$, $\mathbf{e} \leftarrow \chi^m$, $\mathbf{c} \xleftarrow{\$} \mathbb{Z}_q^m$.*

Let χ be a χ_0-bounded noise distribution, i.e., its support belongs to $[-\chi_0, \chi_0]$. The hardness of DLWE is measured by q/χ_0, which is always greater than 1 as χ_0 is chosen such that $\chi_0 < q$. Specifically, the smaller q/χ_0 is, the harder DLWE is. (See [5, Subsection 2.2] and [8, Section 3] for further discussions.)

Lemma 2 ([8, Corollary 3.2]). *For all $\epsilon > 0$, there exist functions $q = q(n) \leq 2^n$, $m = \Theta(n \log q) = \mathsf{poly}(n)$, $\chi = \chi(n)$ such that χ is a χ_0-bounded for some $\chi_0 = \chi_0(n)$, $q/\chi_0 \geq 2^{n^\epsilon}$ and such that $DLWE_{n,m,q,\chi}$ is at least as hard as the classical hardness of $GapSVP_\gamma$ and the quantum hardness of $SIVP_\gamma$ for $\gamma = 2^{\Omega(n^\epsilon)}$.*

Leftover Hash Lemma. The following variant of the so-called leftover hash lemma will be used in this work to support our arguments.

Lemma 3 ([1, Lemma 13]). *Let m, n, q be such that $m > (n + 1) \log_2 q + \omega(\log n)$ and that $q > 2$ is prime. Let $\mathbf{A}$ and $\mathbf{B}$ are uniformly chosen from $\mathbb{Z}_q^{n \times m}$ and $\mathbb{Z}_q^{n \times k}$, respectively. Then for any uniformly chosen matrix $\mathbf{S}$ from $\{-1, 1\}^{m \times k}$ (mod q) and for all vectors $\mathbf{e} \in \mathbb{Z}_q^m$,*

$$(\mathbf{A}, \mathbf{AS}, \mathbf{S}^T \mathbf{e}) \overset{s}{\approx} (\mathbf{A}, \mathbf{B}, \mathbf{S}^T \mathbf{e}).$$

We conclude this section with some standard results regarding trapdoor mechanism often used in lattice-based cryptography.

Lattice Trapdoor Mechanism. In our context, a (lattice) trapdoor is a short basis $\mathbf{T_A}$ for the q-ary lattice $\Lambda_q^\perp(\mathbf{A})$, i.e., $\mathbf{A} \cdot \mathbf{T_A} = 0$ (mod q) (see [17]). We call $\mathbf{T_A}$ the associated trapdoor for $\Lambda_q^\perp(\mathbf{A})$ or even for $\mathbf{A}$.

Lemma 4. *Let $n, m, q > 0$ and q be prime.*

1. *$(\mathbf{A}, \mathbf{T_A}) \leftarrow \mathsf{TrapGen}(n, m, q)$ ([3,22]): This is a PPT algorithm that outputs a pair $(\mathbf{A}, \mathbf{T_A}) \in \mathbb{Z}_q^{n \times m} \times \mathbb{Z}_q^{m \times m}$, where $\mathbf{T_A}$ is a trapdoor for $\Lambda_q^\perp(\mathbf{A})$ such that $\mathbf{A}$ is negligibly close to uniform and $\|\widetilde{\mathbf{T_A}}\| = O(\sqrt{n \log q})$. The algorithm works if $m = \Theta(n \log q)$.*
2. *$\mathbf{T_D} \leftarrow \mathsf{ExtBasisRight}(\mathbf{D} := [\mathbf{A}|\mathbf{AS} + \mathbf{B}], \mathbf{T_B})$ ([1]): This is a DPT algorithm that, for the input $(\mathbf{D}, \mathbf{T_B})$, outputs a trapdoor $\mathbf{T_D}$ for $\Lambda_q^\perp(\mathbf{D})$ such that $\|\widetilde{\mathbf{T_D}}\| \leq \|\widetilde{\mathbf{T_B}}\|(1 + \|\mathbf{S}\|_{sup})$, where $\mathbf{A}, \mathbf{B} \in \mathbb{Z}_q^{n \times m}$.*
3. *$\mathbf{T_E} \leftarrow \mathsf{ExtBasisLeft}(\mathbf{E} := [\mathbf{A}|\mathbf{B}], \mathbf{T_A})$ ([11]): This is a DPT algorithm that for $\mathbf{E}$ of the form $\mathbf{E} := [\mathbf{A}|\mathbf{B}]$ and a trapdoor $\mathbf{T_A}$ for $\Lambda_q^\perp(\mathbf{A})$, outputs a trapdoor $\mathbf{T_E}$ for $\Lambda_q^\perp(\mathbf{E})$ such that $\|\widetilde{\mathbf{T_E}}\| = \|\widetilde{\mathbf{T_A}}\|$, where $\mathbf{A}, \mathbf{B} \in \mathbb{Z}_q^{n \times m}$.*
4. *$\mathbf{R} \leftarrow \mathsf{SampleD}(\mathbf{A}, \mathbf{T_A}, \mathbf{U}, \sigma)$ ([17]): This is a PPT algorithm that takes a matrix $\mathbf{A} \in \mathbb{Z}_q^{n \times m}$, its associated trapdoor $\mathbf{T_A} \in \mathbb{Z}^{m \times m}$, a matrix $\mathbf{U} \in \mathbb{Z}_q^{n \times k}$ and a real number $\sigma > 0$ and returns a short matrix $\mathbf{R} \in \mathbb{Z}_q^{m \times k}$ chosen randomly according to a distribution that is statistically close to $\mathcal{D}_{\Lambda_q^U(\mathbf{A}), \sigma}$. The algorithm works if $\sigma = \|\widetilde{\mathbf{T_A}}\| \cdot \omega(\sqrt{\log m})$. Furthermore, $\|\boldsymbol{R}^T\|_{sup} \leq \sigma\sqrt{mk}$, $\|\boldsymbol{R}\|_{sup} \leq \sigma\sqrt{mk}$ (see also in [5, Lemma 2.5]).*

5. $\mathbf{T'_A} \leftarrow \mathsf{RandBasis}(\mathbf{A}, \mathbf{T_A}, \sigma)$ *([11]): This is a PPT algorithm that takes a matrix $\mathbf{A} \in \mathbb{Z}_q^{n \times m}$, its associated trapdoor $\mathbf{T_A} \in \mathbb{Z}^{m \times m}$, and a real number $\sigma > 0$ and returns a new basis $\mathbf{T'_A}$ for $\Lambda_q^\perp(\mathbf{A})$ chosen randomly according to a distribution that is statistically close to $(\mathcal{D}_{\Lambda_q^\perp(\mathbf{A}), \sigma})^m$, and $\|\widetilde{\mathbf{T'_A}}\| \leq \sigma\sqrt{m}$. The algorithm works if $\sigma = \|\widetilde{\mathbf{T_A}}\| \cdot \omega(\sqrt{\log m})$.*

3   Generic PE Construction from DFKHE

3.1   Delegatable Fully Key-Homomorphic Encryption

Delegatable fully key-homomorphic encryption (DFKHE) can be viewed as a generalised notion of the so-called fully key-homomorphic encryption (FKHE) [5] augmented with a key delegation mechanism [5]. DFHKP together with the key delegation mechanism allows one to do the same but with more functions, i.e., $(y, f_1, \cdots, f_k)$, and the condition for successful decryption is that $f_1(\mathbf{x}) = \cdots = f_k(\mathbf{x}) = y$.

Definition 4 (DFKHE). *Let $\lambda, d = d(\lambda) \in \mathbb{N}$ be two positive integers and let $\mathcal{T} = \mathcal{T}(\lambda)$ and $\mathcal{Y} = \mathcal{Y}(\lambda)$ be two finite sets. Define $\mathcal{F} = \mathcal{F}(\lambda) = \{f | f : \mathcal{T}^d \to \mathcal{Y}\}$ to be a family of efficiently computable functions. $(\lambda, d, \mathcal{T}, \mathcal{Y}, \mathcal{F})$–DFKHE is a tuple consisting of algorithms as follows.*

$(\mathsf{dfkhe}.pk, \mathsf{dfkhe}.sk) \leftarrow \mathsf{DFKHE.KGen}(1^\lambda, \mathcal{F})$: *This PPT algorithm takes as input a security parameter λ and outputs a public key $\mathsf{dfkhe}.pk$ and a secret key $\mathsf{dfkhe}.sk$.*

$\mathsf{dfkhe}.sk_{y,f} \leftarrow \mathsf{DFKHE.KHom}(\mathsf{dfkhe}.sk, (y, f))$: *This PPT algorithm takes as input the secret key $\mathsf{dfkhe}.sk$ and a pair $(y, f) \in \mathcal{Y} \times \mathcal{F}$ and returns a secret homomorphic key $sk_{y,f}$.*

$\mathsf{dfkhe}.sk_{y,f_1,\cdots,f_{k+1}} \leftarrow \mathsf{DFKHE.KDel}(\mathsf{dfkhe}.pk, \mathsf{dfkhe}.sk_{y,f_1,\cdots,f_k}, (y, f_{k+1}))$: *This PPT algorithm takes as input the public key $\mathsf{dfkhe}.pk$, a function $f_{k+1} \in \mathcal{F}$ and the secret key $\mathsf{dfkhe}.sk_{y,f_1,\cdots,f_k}$ and returns the delegated secret key $\mathsf{dfkhe}.sk_{y,f_1,\cdots,f_{k+1}}$. Further, the key $\mathsf{dfkhe}.sk_{y,f_1,\cdots,f_k}$ is produced either by $\mathsf{DFKHE.KHom}$ if $k = 1$, or iteratively by $\mathsf{DFKHE.KDel}$ if $k > 1$.*

$(\mathsf{dfkhe}.ct, \mathbf{t}) \leftarrow \mathsf{DFKHE.Enc}(\mathsf{dfkhe}.pk, \mu, \mathbf{t})$: *This PPT algorithm takes as input the public key $\mathsf{dfkhe}.pk$, a plaintext μ and a variable $\mathbf{t} \in \mathcal{T}^d$ and returns a ciphertext $\mathsf{dfkhe}.ct$– an encryption of μ under the variable $\mathbf{t}$.*

$\mathsf{dfkhe}.ct_{f_1,\cdots,f_k} \leftarrow \mathsf{DFKHE.ExtEval}(f_1, \cdots, f_k, (\mathsf{dfkhe}.ct, \mathbf{t}))$: *The DPT algorithm takes as input a ciphertext $\mathsf{dfkhe}.ct$ and the associated variable $\mathbf{t} \in \mathcal{T}^d$ and returns an evaluated ciphertext $\mathsf{dfkhe}.ct_{f_1,\cdots,f_k}$. If $f_1(\mathbf{t}) = \cdots = f_k(\mathbf{t}) = y$, then we say that $\mathsf{dfkhe}.ct_{f_1,\cdots,f_k}$ is an encryption of μ using the public key $(y, f_1, \cdots, f_k)$.*

$\mu/\perp \leftarrow \mathsf{DFKHE.Dec}(\mathsf{dfkhe}.sk_{y,f_1,\cdots,f_k}, (\mathsf{dfkhe}.ct, \mathbf{t}))$: *The DPT algorithm takes as input a delegated secret key $\mathsf{dfkhe}.sk_{y,f_1,\cdots,f_k}$ and a ciphertext $\mathsf{dfkhe}.ct$ associated with $\mathbf{t} \in \mathcal{T}^d$ and recovers a plaintext μ. It succeeds if $f_i(\mathbf{t}) = y$ for all $i \in [k]$. Otherwise, it fails and returns $\perp$. To recover μ, the algorithm first* *calls* DFKHE.ExtEval$(f_1, \cdots, f_k, (\mathsf{dfkhe}.ct, \mathbf{t}))$ *and gets* dfkhe.$ct_{f_1, \cdots, f_k}$. *Next it uses* dfkhe.$sk_{y, f_1, \cdots, f_k}$ *and opens* dfkhe.$ct_{f_1, \cdots, f_k}$.

Obviously, DFKHE from Definition 4 is identical to FKHE [5] if $k = 1$.

Correctness. For all $\mu \in \mathcal{M}$, all $k \in \mathbb{N}$, all $f_1, \cdots, f_k \in \mathcal{F}$ and $\mathbf{t} \in \mathcal{T}^d$, $y \in \mathcal{Y}$, over the randomness of $(\mathsf{dfkhe}.pk, \mathsf{dfkhe}.sk) \leftarrow$ FKHE.KGen$(1^\lambda, \mathcal{F})$, $(\mathsf{dfkhe}.ct, \mathbf{t}) \leftarrow$ FKHE.Enc$(\mathsf{dfkhe}.pk, \mu, \mathbf{t})$, dfkhe.$sk_{y, f_1} \leftarrow$ FKHE.KHom$(\mathsf{dfkhe}.sk, (y, f_1))$ and dfkhe.$sk_{y, f_1, \cdots, f_i} \leftarrow$ FKHE.KDel$(\mathsf{dfkhe}.sk_{y, f_1, \cdots, f_{i-1}}, (y, f_i))$, dfkhe.$ct_{f_1, \cdots, f_k} \leftarrow$ DFKHE.ExtEval $(f_1, \cdots, f_k, (\mathsf{dfkhe}.ct, \mathbf{t}))$ for all $i \in \{2, \cdots, k\}$, then

- $\Pr[\mathsf{FKHE.Dec}(\mathsf{dfkhe}.sk, (\mathsf{dfkhe}.ct, \mathbf{t})) = \mu] \geq 1 - negl(\lambda)$,
- if $y = f_1(\mathbf{t}) = \cdots = f_k(\mathbf{t})$, then

$$\Pr[\mathsf{FKHE.Dec}(\mathsf{dfkhe}.sk, (\mathsf{dfkhe}.ct_{f_1, \cdots, f_k}, \mathbf{t})) = \mu] \geq 1 - negl(\lambda),$$
$$\Pr[\mathsf{FKHE.Dec}(\mathsf{dfkhe}.sk_{y, f_1, \cdots, f_i}, (\mathsf{dfkhe}.ct, \mathbf{t})) = \mu] \geq 1 - negl(\lambda), \forall i \in [k],$$

- For any $i \in [k]$, if $y \neq f_i(\mathbf{t})$,

$$\Pr[\mathsf{FKHE.Dec}(\mathsf{dfkhe}.sk_{y, f_1, \cdots, f_j}, (\mathsf{dfkhe}.ct, \mathbf{t})) = \mu] \leq negl(\lambda), \forall j \in \{i, k\}.$$

Security. Security of DFKHE is similar to that of FKHE from [5] with an extra evaluation that includes the key delegation mechanisms.

Definition 5 (Selectively-secure CPA of DFKHE). *DFKHE is IND-sVAR-CPA if for any polynomial time adversary $\mathcal{B}$ in the game* IND-sVAR-CPA$_{\mathsf{DFKHE}}^{\mathsf{sel}, \mathcal{B}}$, *the adversary advantage* Adv$_{\mathsf{DFKHE}}^{\mathsf{IND\text{-}sVAR\text{-}CPA}}(\mathcal{B}) = |\Pr[b' = b] - \frac{1}{2}| \leq negl(\lambda)$.

The IND-sVAR-CPA$_{\mathsf{DFKHE}}^{\mathsf{sel}, \mathcal{B}}$ game is as follows.

1. **Initialize.** On the security parameter λ and λ–dependent tuple $(d, (\mathcal{T}, \mathcal{Y}, \mathcal{F}))$, $\mathcal{B}$ releases the target variable $\widehat{\mathbf{t}} = (\widehat{t_1}, \cdots, \widehat{t_d}) \in \mathcal{T}^d$.
2. **Setup.** The challenger runs $(\mathsf{dfkhe}.pk, \mathsf{dfkhe}.sk) \leftarrow$ DFKHE.KGen$(1^\lambda, \mathcal{F})$. Then, it gives dfkhe.pk to $\mathcal{B}$.
3. **Query.** $\mathcal{B}$ adaptively makes delegated key queries DKQ$(y, (f_1, \cdots, f_k))$ to get the corresponding delegated secret keys. Specifically, $\mathcal{B}$ is allowed to access the oracle $KG(\mathsf{dfkhe}.sk, \widehat{\mathbf{t}}, y, (f_1, \cdots, f_k))$, which takes as input dfkhe.sk, $\widehat{\mathbf{t}}$, a list of functions $f_1, \cdots, f_k \in \mathcal{F}$ and $y \in \mathcal{Y}$ and returns either $\perp$ if all $f_j(\widehat{\mathbf{t}}) = y$, or the delegated secret key dfkhe.$sk_{y, f_1, \cdots, f_k}$, otherwise. The delegated secret key dfkhe.$sk_{y, f_1, \cdots, f_k}$ is computed calling dfkhe.$sk_{y, f_1} :=$ DFKHE.KHom$(\mathsf{dfkhe}.sk, (y, f_1))$ and dfkhe.$sk_{y, f_1, \cdots, f_i} \leftarrow$ DFKHE.KDel $(\mathsf{dfkhe}.pk, \mathsf{dfkhe}.sk_{y, f_1, \cdots, f_{i-1}}, (y, f_i))$ for all $i \in \{2, \cdots, k\}$.
4. **Challenge.** The adversary submits two messages μ_0, μ_1 (with $\widehat{\mathbf{t}}$). The challenger in turn chooses $b \xleftarrow{\$} \{0, 1\}$ and returns the output $(\mathsf{dfkhe}.\widehat{ct}, \widehat{\mathbf{t}})$ of DFKHE.Enc$(\mathsf{dfkhe}.pk, \mu_b, \widehat{\mathbf{t}})$.
5. **Guess.** The adversary outputs $b' \in \{0, 1\}$. It wins if $b' = b$.

3.2 Generic PE Construction from DFKHE

The main idea behind our construction is an observation that ciphertext tags can be treated as variables $\mathbf{t} = (t_1, \cdots, t_d) \in \mathcal{T}^d$. The puncturing property, which is related to the "equality", suggests us to construct a family $\mathcal{F}$ of equality test functions, allowing to compare each pair of ciphertext tags and punctures. Using this idea, we then can have a PE construction from DFKHE.

Let $\lambda, d = d(\lambda) \in \mathbb{N}$ be two positive integers. Let $\mathcal{T} = \mathcal{T}(\lambda)$ be a finite set (that henceforth called the *tag space*) and $\mathcal{Y} = \mathcal{Y}(\lambda)$ be also a finite set. In addition, let $y_0 \in \mathcal{Y}$ be a some fixed special element. Define a family of all equality test functions indicated by $\mathcal{T}$,

$$\mathcal{F} = \mathcal{F}(\lambda) := \left\{ f_{t^*} | t^* \in \mathcal{T}, \forall \mathbf{t} = (t_1, \cdots, t_d), f_{t^*} : \mathcal{T}^d \to \mathcal{Y} \right\}, \tag{1}$$

where $f_{t^*}(\mathbf{t}) := y_0$ if $t^* \neq t_i, \forall i \in [d]$, $f_{t^*}(\mathbf{t}) := y_{t^*,\mathbf{t}} \in \mathcal{Y} \setminus \{y_0\}$. Here, $y_{t^*,\mathbf{t}}$ means depending on the value of t^* and $\mathbf{t}$. Now, let $\Pi = (\mathsf{DFKHE.KGen}, \mathsf{DFKHE.KHom}, \mathsf{DFKHE.Enc}, \mathsf{DFKHE.ExtEval}, \mathsf{DFKHE.KDel}, \mathsf{DFKHE.Dec})$ be $(\lambda, d, \mathcal{T}, \mathcal{Y}, \mathcal{F})$–DFKHE. Using Π, we can construct a PE system $\Psi = (\mathsf{PE.key}, \mathsf{PE.enc}, \mathsf{PE.pun}, \mathsf{PE.dec})$ of which both tags and punctures reside in $\mathcal{T}$. The description of Ψ is below:

Parameters: Set λ as a security parameter, and $d = d(\lambda)$ as the maximum number of tags per ciphertext.

$(\mathsf{pe}.pk, \mathsf{pe}.sk_0) \leftarrow \mathsf{PE.key}(1^\lambda, d)$: For input λ and d, run $(\mathsf{dfkhe}.pk, \mathsf{dfkhe}.sk) \leftarrow \mathsf{DFKHE.KGen}(1^\lambda, \mathcal{F})$, and return $\mathsf{pe}.pk := \mathsf{dfkhe}.pk$, and $\mathsf{pe}.sk_0 := \mathsf{dfkhe}.sk$.

$\mathsf{pe}.ct \leftarrow \mathsf{PE.enc}(\mathsf{pe}.pk, \mu, \mathbf{t} = (t_1, \cdots, t_d))$: For a public key $\mathsf{pe}.pk$, a message μ, and ciphertext tags $\mathbf{t} = (t_1, \cdots, t_d)$, return $\mathsf{pe}.ct \leftarrow \mathsf{DFKHE.Enc}(\mathsf{pe}.pk, \mu, \mathbf{t})$.

$\mathsf{pe}.sk_i \leftarrow \mathsf{PE.pun}(\mathsf{pe}.pk, \mathsf{pe}.sk_{i-1}, t_i^*)$: For input $\mathsf{pe}.pk$, $\mathsf{pe}.sk_{i-1}$ and a punctured tag t_i^*,

- If $i = 1$: run $\mathsf{dfkhe}.sk_{y_0, f_{t_1^*}} \leftarrow \mathsf{DFKHE.KHom}(\mathsf{pe}.sk_0, (y_0, f_{t_1^*}))$ and output $\mathsf{pe}.sk_1 := \mathsf{dfkhe}.sk_{y_0, f_{t_1^*}}$.
- If $i \geq 2$: compute $\mathsf{pe}.sk_i \leftarrow \mathsf{DFKHE.KDel}(\mathsf{dfkhe}.pk, \mathsf{pe}.sk_{i-1}, (y_0, f_{t_i^*}))$.
- Finally, output $\mathsf{pe}.sk_i$.

$\mu/\perp \leftarrow \mathsf{PE.dec}(\mathsf{pe}.pk, (\mathsf{pe}.sk_i, (t_1^*, \cdots, t_i^*)), (\mathsf{pe}.ct, \mathbf{t}))$: For input the public key $\mathsf{pe}.pk$, a puncture key $\mathsf{pe}.sk_i$ together with punctures $(t_1^*, \cdots, t_i^*)$, a ciphertext $\mathsf{pe}.ct$ and its associated tags $\mathbf{t} = (t_1, \cdots, t_d)$, the algorithm first checks whether or not $f_{t_1^*}(\mathbf{t}) = \cdots = f_{t_i^*}(\mathbf{t}) = y_0$. If not, the algorithm returns $\perp$. Otherwise, it returns the output of $\mathsf{DFKHE.Dec}(\mathsf{pe}.sk_i, \mathsf{pe}.ct)$.

Correctness. Remark that, over the choice of $(\lambda, d, \eta, (t_1^*, \cdots, t_\eta^*), (t_1, \cdots, t_d)$, $\eta \geq 0$, $t_1^*, \cdots, t_\eta^* \in \mathcal{T}$, $t_1, \cdots, t_d \in \mathcal{T} \setminus \{t_1^*, \cdots, t_\eta^*\}$, we have $f_{t_j^*}(\mathbf{t}) = y_0$ for all $j \in [\eta]$. Then, it is clear that, the induced PE Ψ is correct if and only if the DFKHE Π is correct.

Theorem 1. *PE Ψ is selectively-secure CPA assuming that the underlying DFKHE Π is selectively-CPA secure.*

Proof. See the full version [27] for the details.

4 DFKHE and FE Construction from Lattices

At first, in Subsect. 4.1 below, we will review the key-homomorphic mechanism, which is an important ingredient for our lattice-based construction.

4.1 Key-Homomorphic Mechanism for Arithmetic Circuits

Let $n, q > 0$, $k := \lceil \log q \rceil$ and $m := n \cdot k$. We exploit the gadget matrix $\mathbf{G}$ and its associated trapdoor $\mathbf{T_G}$. According to [22, Section 4], the matrix $\mathbf{G} := \mathbf{I}_n \otimes \mathbf{g}^T \in \mathbb{Z}_q^{n \times m}$, where $\mathbf{g}^T = [1 \ 2 \ 4 \ \cdots \ 2^{k-1}]$. The associated trapdoor $\mathbf{T_G} \in \mathbb{Z}^{m \times m}$ is publicly known and $\|\widetilde{\mathbf{T_G}}\| \leq \sqrt{5}$ (see [22, Theorem 4.1]).

Key-Homomorphic Mechanism. We recap some basic facts useful for construction of evaluation algorithms for the family of polynomial depth and unbounded fan-in arithmetic circuits (see [5, Section 4] for details). Let $\mathbf{G} \in \mathbb{Z}_q^{n \times m}$ be the gadget matrix given above. For $x \in \mathbb{Z}_q$, $\mathbf{B} \in \mathbb{Z}_q^{n \times m}$, $\mathbf{s} \in \mathbb{Z}_q^n$ and $\delta > 0$, define the following set $E_{\mathbf{s},\delta}(x, \mathbf{B}) := \{(x\mathbf{G} + \mathbf{B})^T\mathbf{s} + \mathbf{e}, \text{ where } \|\mathbf{e}\| < \delta\}$. More details can be found in [5].

Lemma 5 ([5, Section 4]). *Let n, $q = q(n)$, $m = \Theta(n \log q)$ be positive integers, $\mathbf{x} = (x_1, \cdots, x_d) \in \mathbb{Z}_q^d$, $\mathbf{x}^* = (x_1^*, \cdots, x_d^*) \in \mathbb{Z}_q^d$, $\mathbf{B}_i \in \mathbb{Z}_q^{n \times m}$, $\mathbf{c}_i \in E_{\mathbf{s},\delta}(x_i, \mathbf{B}_i)$ for some $\mathbf{s} \in \mathbb{Z}_q^n$ and $\delta > 0$, $\mathbf{S}_i \in \mathbb{Z}_q^{m \times m}$ for all $i \in [d]$. Also, let $\beta_{\mathcal{F}} = \beta_{\mathcal{F}}(n) : \mathbb{Z} \to \mathbb{Z}$ be a positive integer-valued function, and $\mathcal{F} = \{f : (\mathbb{Z}_q)^d \to \mathbb{Z}_q\}$ be a family of functions, in which each function can be computed by some circuit of a family of depth τ, polynomial-size arithmetic circuits $(C_\lambda)_{\lambda \in \mathbb{N}}$. Then there exist DPT algorithms $\mathsf{Eval}_{\mathsf{pk}}$, $\mathsf{Eval}_{\mathsf{ct}}$, $\mathsf{Eval}_{\mathsf{sim}}$ associated with $\beta_{\mathcal{F}}$ and $\mathcal{F}$ such that the following properties hold.*

1. *If $\mathbf{B}_f \leftarrow \mathsf{Eval}_{\mathsf{pk}}(f \in \mathcal{F}, (\mathbf{B}_i)_{i=1}^d)$, then $\mathbf{B}_f \in \mathbb{Z}_q^{n \times m}$.*
2. *Let $\mathbf{c}_f \leftarrow \mathsf{Eval}_{\mathsf{ct}}(f \in \mathcal{F}, ((x_i, \mathbf{B}_i, \mathbf{c}_i))_{i=1}^d)$, then $\mathbf{c}_f \in E_{\mathbf{s},\Delta}(f(\mathbf{x}), \mathbf{B}_f)$, where $\mathbf{B}_f \leftarrow \mathsf{Eval}_{\mathsf{pk}}(f, (\mathbf{B}_i)_{i=1}^d)$ and $\Delta < \delta \cdot \beta_{\mathcal{F}}$.*
3. *The output $\mathbf{S}_f \leftarrow \mathsf{Eval}_{\mathsf{sim}}(f \in \mathcal{F}, ((x_i^*, \mathbf{S}_i))_{i=1}^d, \mathbf{A})$ satisfies the relation $\mathbf{AS}_f - f(\mathbf{x}^*)\mathbf{G} = \mathbf{B}_f$ and $\|\mathbf{S}_f\|_{sup} < \beta_{\mathcal{F}}$ with overwhelming probability, where $\mathbf{B}_f \leftarrow \mathsf{Eval}_{\mathsf{pk}}(f, (\mathbf{AS}_i - x_i^*\mathbf{G})_{i=1}^d)$. In particular, if $\mathbf{S}_1, \cdots, \mathbf{S}_d \xleftarrow{\$} \{-1, 1\}^{m \times m}$, then $\|\mathbf{S}_f\|_{sup} < \beta_{\mathcal{F}}$ with all but negligible probability for all $f \in \mathcal{F}$.*

In general, for a family $\mathcal{F}$ of functions represented by polynomial-size and unbounded fan-in circuits of depth τ, the function $\beta_{\mathcal{F}}$ is given by the following lemma.

Lemma 6 ([5, Lemma 5.3]). *Let n, $q = q(n)$, $m = \Theta(n \log q)$ be positive integers. Let C_λ be a family of polynomial-size arithmetic circuits of depth τ and $\mathcal{F} = \{f : (\mathbb{Z}_q)^d \to \mathbb{Z}_q\}$ be the set of functions f that can be computed by some circuit $C \in C_\lambda$ as stated in Lemma 5. Also, suppose that all (but possibly one) of the input values to the multiplication gates are bounded by $p < q$. Then, $\beta_{\mathcal{F}} = (\frac{p^d-1}{p-1} \cdot m)^\tau \cdot 20\sqrt{m} = O((p^{d-1}m)^\tau \sqrt{m})$.*

Definition 6 (FKHE enabling functions). *The tuple* $(\mathsf{Eval}_{\mathsf{pk}}, \mathsf{Eval}_{\mathsf{ct}}, \mathsf{Eval}_{\mathsf{sim}})$ *together with the family* $\mathcal{F}$ *and the function* $\beta_{\mathcal{F}} = \beta_{\mathcal{F}}(n)$ *in the Lemma 5 is called* $\beta_{\mathcal{F}}$-*FKHE enabling for the family* $\mathcal{F}$.

4.2 LWE-Based DFKHE Construction

Our LWE-based DFKHE construction Π is adapted from LWE–based FKHE and the key delegation mechanism, both of which proposed in [5]. Roughly speaking, the key delegation mechanism in the lattice setting is triggered using the algorithms ExtBasisLeft and ExtBasisRight and RandBasis in Lemma 4. Formally, LWE-based DFKHE Π consists of the following algorithms:

Parameters: Let $\lambda \in \mathbb{N}$ be a security parameter. Set $n = n(\lambda)$, $q = q(\lambda)$ and $d = d(\lambda)$ to be fixed such that $d < q$. Let $\eta \in \mathbb{N}$ be the maximum number of variables that can be delegated and $\sigma_1, \cdots, \sigma_\eta$ be Gaussian parameters. Also, we choose a constant $\epsilon \in (0, 1)$, which is mentioned in Lemma 2. The constant is used to determine the tradeoff between the security level and the efficiency of the system. Let $\mathcal{F} := \{f | f : (\mathbb{Z}_q)^d \to \mathbb{Z}_q\}$ be a family of efficiently computable functions over $\mathbb{Z}_q$ that can be computed by some circuit of a family of depth τ, polynomial-size arithmetic circuits $(C_\lambda)_{\lambda \in \mathbb{N}}$. Take the algorithms $(\mathsf{Eval}_{\mathsf{pk}}, \mathsf{Eval}_{\mathsf{ct}}, \mathsf{Eval}_{\mathsf{sim}})$ together with a function $\beta_{\mathcal{F}} = \beta_{\mathcal{F}}(n)$ to be $\beta_{\mathcal{F}}$–FKHE enabling for $\mathcal{F}$.

DFKHE.KGen($1^\lambda, \mathcal{F}$): For the input pair (a security parameter $\lambda \in \mathbb{N}$ and a family $\mathcal{F})^2$, do the following:

1. Choose $m = \Theta(n \log q)$. The plaintext space is $\mathcal{M} := \{0, 1\}^m$, $\mathcal{T} := \mathbb{Z}_q$. Additionally, let χ be a χ_0–bounded noise distribution (i.e, its support belongs to $[-\chi_0, \chi_0]$) for which the $(n, 2m, q, \chi)$–DLWE is hard.

2. Generate $(\mathbf{A}, \mathbf{T_A}) \leftarrow \mathsf{TrapGen}(n, m, q)$, sample $\mathbf{U}, \mathbf{B}_1, \cdots, \mathbf{B}_d \xleftarrow{\$} \mathbb{Z}_q^{n \times m}$.

3. Output the public key $pk = \{\mathbf{A}, \mathbf{B}_1, \cdots \mathbf{B}_d, \mathbf{U}\}$ and the initial secret key $sk = \{\mathbf{T_A}\}$.

DFKHE.KHom($sk, (y, f_1)$): For the input pair (the initial secret key sk and a pair $(y, f_1) \in \mathbb{Z}_q \times \mathcal{F}$) do the following:

1. $\mathbf{B}_{f_1} \leftarrow \mathsf{Eval}_{\mathsf{pk}}(f_1, (\mathbf{B}_k)_{k=1}^d)$, $\mathbf{E}_{y,f_1} \leftarrow \mathsf{ExtBasisLeft}([\mathbf{A} | y\mathbf{G} + \mathbf{B}_{f_1}], \mathbf{T_A})$.

2. $\mathbf{T}_{y,f_1} \leftarrow \mathsf{RandBasis}([\mathbf{A} | y\mathbf{G} + \mathbf{B}_{f_1}], \mathbf{E}_{y,f_1}, \sigma_1)$, output the secret key $sk_{y,f_1} = \{\mathbf{T}_{y,f_1}\}$. Here, we set $\sigma_1 = \omega(\beta_{\mathcal{F}} \cdot \sqrt{\log(2m)})$ for the security proof to work.

DFKHE.KDel($sk_{y,f_1,\cdots,f_{\eta-1}}, (y, f_\eta)$): For the input pair (the delegated secret key $sk_{y,f_1,\cdots,f_{\eta-1}}$ and a pair $(y, f_\eta) \in \mathbb{Z}_q \times \mathcal{F}$) do the following:

1. $\mathbf{B}_{f_\eta} \leftarrow \mathsf{Eval}_{\mathsf{pk}}(f_\eta, (\mathbf{B}_k)_{k=1}^d)$.

2. $\mathbf{E}_{y,f_1,\cdots,f_\eta} \leftarrow \mathsf{ExtBasisLeft}([\mathbf{A} | y\mathbf{G} + \mathbf{B}_{f_1} | \cdots | y\mathbf{G} + \mathbf{B}_{f_{\eta-1}} | y\mathbf{G} + \mathbf{B}_{f_\eta}], \mathbf{T}_{y,f_1,\cdots,f_{\eta-1}})$.

3. $\mathbf{T}_{y,f_1,\cdots,f_\eta} \leftarrow$
$\mathsf{RandBasis}([\mathbf{A} | y\mathbf{G} + \mathbf{B}_{f_1} | \cdots | y\mathbf{G} + \mathbf{B}_{f_{\eta-1}} | y\mathbf{G} + \mathbf{B}_{f_\eta}], \mathbf{E}_{y,f_1,\cdots,f_\eta}, \sigma_\eta)$.

---

[2] Here, d also appears implicitly as an input.

4. Output the secret key $sk_{y,f_1,\cdots,f_\eta} = \{\mathbf{T}_{y,f_1,\cdots,f_\eta}\}$.
   We set $\sigma_\eta = \sigma_1 \cdot (\sqrt{m}\log m)^{\eta-1}$ and discuss on setting parameters in details later.

DFKHE.Enc($\mu, pk, \mathbf{t}$): For the input consiting of (a message $\mu = (\mu_1,\cdots,\mu_m) \in \mathcal{M}$, the public key pk and ciphertext tags $\mathbf{t} = (t_1,\cdots,t_d) \in \mathcal{T}^d$), perform the following steps:

1. Sample $\mathbf{s} \xleftarrow{\$} \mathbb{Z}_q^n$, $\mathbf{e}_{\text{out}}, \mathbf{e}_{\text{in}} \leftarrow \chi^m$, and $\mathbf{S}_1,\cdots,\mathbf{S}_d \xleftarrow{\$} \{-1,1\}^{m\times m}$.
2. Compute $\mathbf{e} \leftarrow (\mathbf{I}_m|\mathbf{S}_1|\cdots|\mathbf{S}_d)^T \mathbf{e}_{\text{in}} = (\mathbf{e}_{\text{in}}^T, \mathbf{e}_1^T, \cdots, \mathbf{e}_d^T)^T$.
3. Form $\mathbf{H} \leftarrow [\mathbf{A}|t_1\mathbf{G} + \mathbf{B}_1|\cdots|t_d\mathbf{G} + \mathbf{B}_d]$ and compute $\mathbf{c} = \mathbf{H}^T\mathbf{s} + \mathbf{e} \in \mathbb{Z}_q^{(d+1)m}$,
   $\mathbf{c} = [\mathbf{c}_{\text{in}}|\mathbf{c}_1|\cdots|\mathbf{c}_d]$, where $\mathbf{c}_{\text{in}} = \mathbf{A}^T\mathbf{s} + \mathbf{e}_{\text{in}}$ and $\mathbf{c}_i = (t_i\mathbf{G} + \mathbf{B}_i)^T\mathbf{s} + \mathbf{e}_i$ for $i \in [d]$.
4. Compute $\mathbf{c}_{\text{out}} \leftarrow \mathbf{U}^T\mathbf{s} + \mathbf{e}_{\text{out}} + \mu\lceil\frac{q}{2}\rceil$.
5. Output the ciphertext $(ct_{\mathbf{t}} = (\mathbf{c}_{\text{in}}, \mathbf{c}_1, \cdots, \mathbf{c}_d, \mathbf{c}_{\text{out}}), \mathbf{t})$.

DFKHE.ExtEval($f_1,\cdots,f_\eta, ct_{\mathbf{t}}$): For the input (a ciphertext $ct_{\mathbf{t}} = (\mathbf{c}_{\text{in}}, \mathbf{c}_1, \cdots, \mathbf{c}_d, \mathbf{c}_{\text{out}})$ and its associated tags $\mathbf{t} = (t_1,\cdots,t_d)$, and a list of functions $f_1,\cdots,f_\eta \in \mathcal{F}$), execute the following steps:

1. Evaluate $\mathbf{c}_{f_j} \leftarrow \text{Eval}_{\text{ct}}(f_j, ((t_k, \mathbf{B}_k, \mathbf{c}_k))_{k=1}^d)$ for $j \in [\eta]$.
2. Output the evaluated ciphertext $\mathbf{c}_{f_1,\cdots,f_\eta} := (\mathbf{c}_{f_1}, \cdots, \mathbf{c}_{f_\eta})$.

DFKHE.Dec($ct_{\mathbf{t}}, sk_{y,f_1,\cdots,f_\eta}$): For the input (a ciphertext $ct_{\mathbf{t}} = (\mathbf{c}_{\text{in}}, \mathbf{c}_1, \cdots, \mathbf{c}_d, \mathbf{c}_{\text{out}})$, the associated tags $\mathbf{t} = (t_1,\cdots,t_d)$, and a delegated secret key $sk_{y,f_1,\cdots,f_\eta}$, execute the following steps:

1. If $\exists j \in [\eta]$ s.t. $f_j(\mathbf{t}) \neq y$, then output $\bot$. Otherwise, go to Step 2.
2. Sample $\mathbf{R} \leftarrow \text{SampleD}([\mathbf{A}|y\mathbf{G} + \mathbf{B}_{f_1}|\cdots|y\mathbf{G} + \mathbf{B}_{f_\eta}], \mathbf{T}_{y,f_1,\cdots,f_\eta}, \mathbf{U}, \sigma_\eta)$.
3. Evaluate $(\mathbf{c}_{f_1}, \cdots, \mathbf{c}_{f_\eta}) \leftarrow \text{DFKHE.ExtEval}(f_1,\cdots,f_\eta, ct_{\mathbf{t}})$.
4. Compute $\bar{\mu} := (\bar{\mu}_1,\cdots,\bar{\mu}_m) \leftarrow \mathbf{c}_{\text{out}} - \mathbf{R}^T(\mathbf{c}_{\text{in}}|\mathbf{c}_{f_1}|\cdots|\mathbf{c}_{f_\eta})$.
5. For $\ell \in [m]$, if $|\bar{\mu}_\ell| < q/4$ then output $\mu_\ell = 0$; otherwise, output $\mu_\ell = 1$.

In the following, we will demonstrate the correctness and the security of the LWE-based DFKHE Π.

Theorem 2 (Correctness of Π). *The proposed DFKHE Π is correct if the condition*

$$(\eta + 1)^2 \cdot \sqrt{m} \cdot \omega((\sqrt{m}\log m)^\eta) \cdot \beta_{\mathcal{F}}^2 + 2 < \frac{1}{4}(q/\chi_0) \qquad (2)$$

holds, assuming that $f_j(\mathbf{t}) = y$ for all $j \in [\eta]$.

Proof. See the full version [27] for the detail.

Theorem 3 (IND-sVAR-CPA of Π). *Assuming the hardness of $(n, 2m, q, \chi)$–DLWE, the proposed DFKHE Π is IND-sVAR-CPA.*

Proof. See the full version [27] for the details.

Setting Parameters. In order to choose parameters, we should take the following into consideration:

- For the hardness of DLWE, by Theorem 2, we choose ϵ, n, q, χ, where χ is a χ_0-bounded distribution, such that $q/\chi_0 \geq 2^{n^\epsilon}$. We also note that, the hardness of DLWE via the traditional worst-case reduction (e.g., Lemma 2) does not help us much in proposing concrete parameters for lattice-based cryptosystems. Instead, a more conservative methodology that has been usually used in the literature is the so-called "core-SVP hardness"; see [2, Subsection 5.2.1] for a detailed reference.
- Setting Gaussian parameters:
  1. *First approach:* Without caring the security proof, for trapdoor algorithms to work, we can set $\sigma_1 = \|\widetilde{\mathbf{T}_A}\| \cdot \omega(\sqrt{\log(2m)})$, with $\|\widetilde{\mathbf{T}_A}\| = O(\sqrt{n \log m})$ by Item 1 of Lemma 4. Note that, in DFKHE.KHom we have $\|\widetilde{\mathbf{T}_{y,f_1}}\| < \sigma_1 \cdot \sqrt{2m}$ by Item 5 of Lemma 4. Then, $\sigma_2 = \|\widetilde{\mathbf{T}_{y,f_1}}\| \cdot \omega(\sqrt{\log(3m)}) = \sigma_1 \cdot \omega(\sqrt{m \log m})$. Similarly, we can set $\sigma_k = \sigma_1 \cdot (\sqrt{m \log m})^{k-1}$ for all $k \in [\eta]$.
  2. *Second approach:* For the security proof to work, we choose $\sigma_k = \omega(\beta_{\mathcal{F}} \cdot \sqrt{\log m})$ for all $k \in [\eta]$ (see the full version [27] for the details).
  3. Compared with σ_k of the first approach, σ_k's of the second approach are essentially smaller. Therefore, in order for both trapdoor algorithms and the security to work, we should set $\sigma_1 = \omega(\beta_{\mathcal{F}} \cdot \sqrt{\log m})$ and choose $\beta_{\mathcal{F}} > \|\widetilde{\mathbf{T}_A}\| = \sqrt{n \log m}$ and then follow the first approach in setting Gaussian parameters. Recall that, $\beta_{\mathcal{F}} = (\frac{p^d - 1}{p - 1} \cdot m)^\tau \cdot 20\sqrt{m} = O((p^{d-1}m)^\tau \sqrt{m})$ by Lemma 6.
- For the correctness: We need Condition (2) to hold, i.e., $(\eta + 1)^2 \cdot \sqrt{m} \cdot \omega((\sqrt{m \log m})^\eta) \cdot \beta_{\mathcal{F}}^2 + 2 < \frac{1}{4}(q/\chi_0)$.

Sizes of Keys and Ciphertext. Recall that, throughout this work, we set $m = \Theta(n \log q)$. The public key corresponding d variables consists of $d+1$ matrices of dimension $n \times m$ over $\mathbb{Z}_q$. Then the public key size is $O((d+1) \cdot n^2 \log^2 q)$. The initial secret key is the short trapdoor matrix $\mathbf{T}_A$ of dimension $m \times m$ generated by TrapGen such that $\|\mathbf{T}_A\| \leq O(\sqrt{n \log q})$, then size is $O(n^2 \log^2 q \cdot \log(n \log q))$. The secret key after delegating η functions is the trapdoor matrix $\mathbf{T}_{y,f_1,\cdots,f_\eta}$ of dimension $(\eta + 1)m \times (\eta + 1)m$ and $\|\mathbf{T}_{y,f_1,\cdots,f_\eta}\| < \sigma_\eta \cdot \sqrt{(\eta + 1)m} = \beta_{\mathcal{F}} \cdot \omega((\sqrt{m \log m})^\eta)$ with overwhelming probability by Lemma 1. Therefore its size is $(\eta + 1) \cdot n \log q \cdot (O(\log(\beta_{\mathcal{F}}) + \eta \cdot \log(n \log q)))$. The ciphertext is a tuple of $(d + 2)$ vectors of in $\mathbb{Z}_q^m$ hence its size is $O((d + 2) \cdot n \log^2 q)$.

4.3   LWE-Based PE Construction from DFKHE

We define the family of equality functions $\mathcal{F} := \{f_{t^*} : \mathbb{Z}_q^d \to \mathbb{Z}_q | t^* \in \mathbb{Z}_q\}$, where $f_{t^*}(\mathbf{t}) := eq_{t^*}(t_1) + \cdots + eq_{t^*}(t_d)$, $\mathbf{t} = (t_1, \cdots, t_d)$, $eq_{t^*} : \mathbb{Z}_q \to \mathbb{Z}_q$, satisfying that $\forall t \in \mathbb{Z}_q$, $eq_{t^*}(t) = 1 \pmod{q}$ iff $t = t^*$, otherwise $eq_{t^*}(t) = 0 \pmod{q}$. Then $f_{t^*}(\mathbf{t}) = 0 \pmod{q}$ iff $eq_{t^*}(t_i) = 0 \pmod{q}$ if $d < q$, for all $i \in [d]$. By applying the generic framework in Sect. 3 to DFKHE demonstrated in Subsect. 4.2 and modifying the resulting PE, we come up with the LWE-based PE construction $\Psi = \{\mathsf{PE.key}, \mathsf{PE.enc}, \mathsf{PE.pun}, \mathsf{PE.dec}\}$ presented below:

<u>PE.key(1^λ)</u>: For the input security parameter λ, do the following:

1. Choose $n = n(\lambda)$, $q = q(\lambda)$ prime, and the maximum number of tags $d = d(\lambda)$ per a ciphertext such that $d < q$.
2. Choose $m = \Theta(n \log q)$. The plaintext space is $\mathcal{M} := \{0,1\}^m$, $\mathcal{T} := \mathbb{Z}_q$. Additionally, let χ be a χ_0–bounded noise distribution (i.e, its support belongs to $[-\chi_0, \chi_0]$ for which the $(n, 2m, q, \chi)$–DLWE is hard. Set $\sigma = \omega(\beta_\mathcal{F} \cdot \sqrt{\log m})$.
3. Sample $(\mathbf{A}, \mathbf{T_A}) \leftarrow \mathsf{TrapGen}(n, m, q)$, $\mathbf{U}, \mathbf{B}_1, \cdots, \mathbf{B}_d \xleftarrow{\$} \mathbb{Z}_q^{n \times m}$.
4. Output $pk = \{\mathbf{A}, \mathbf{B}_1, \cdots \mathbf{B}_d, \mathbf{U}\}$ and $sk_0 = \{\mathbf{T_A}\}$.

<u>PE.enc$(\mu, pk, \{t_1, \cdots, t_d\})$</u>: For the input consiting of (a message μ, the public key pk and ciphertext tags $(t_1, \cdots, t_d) \in \mathcal{T}^d$), perform the following steps:

1. Sample $\mathbf{s} \xleftarrow{\$} \mathbb{Z}_q^n$, $\mathbf{e}_{\mathsf{out}}, \mathbf{e}_{\mathsf{in}} \leftarrow \chi^m$, $\mathbf{S}_1, \cdots, \mathbf{S}_d \xleftarrow{\$} \{-1, 1\}^{m \times m}$.
2. Compute $\mathbf{e} \leftarrow (\mathbf{I}_m|\mathbf{S}_1|\cdots|\mathbf{S}_d)^T \mathbf{e}_{\mathsf{in}} = (\mathbf{e}_{\mathsf{in}}^T, \mathbf{e}_1^T, \cdots, \mathbf{e}_d^T)^T$.
3. Form $\mathbf{H} \leftarrow [\mathbf{A}|t_1\mathbf{G} + \mathbf{B}_1|\cdots|t_d\mathbf{G} + \mathbf{B}_d]$ and compute $\mathbf{c} = \mathbf{H}^T\mathbf{s} + \mathbf{e} \in \mathbb{Z}_q^{(d+1)m}$,
   $\mathbf{c} = [\mathbf{c}_{\mathsf{in}}|\mathbf{c}_1|\cdots|\mathbf{c}_d]$, where $\mathbf{c}_{\mathsf{in}} = \mathbf{A}^T\mathbf{s} + \mathbf{e}_{\mathsf{in}}$ and $\mathbf{c}_i = (t_i\mathbf{G} + \mathbf{B}_i)^T\mathbf{s} + \mathbf{e}_i$ for $i \in [d]$.
4. Compute $\mathbf{c}_{\mathsf{out}} \leftarrow \mathbf{U}^T\mathbf{s} + \mathbf{e}_{\mathsf{out}} + \mu\lceil\frac{q}{2}\rceil$, output $(ct = (\mathbf{c}_{\mathsf{in}}, \mathbf{c}_1, \cdots, \mathbf{c}_d, \mathbf{c}_{\mathsf{out}}), (t_1, \cdots, t_d))$.

<u>PE.pun$(sk_{\eta-1}, t_\eta^*)$</u>: For the input (a puncture key $sk_{\eta-1}$ and a punctured tag $t_\eta^* \in \mathcal{T}$), do:

1. Evaluate $\mathbf{B}_{eq_\eta} \leftarrow \mathsf{Eval}_{\mathsf{pk}}(f_{t_\eta^*}, (\mathbf{B}_k)_{k=1}^d)$.
2. Compute $\mathbf{E}_{eq_\eta} \leftarrow \mathsf{ExtBasisLeft}([\mathbf{A}|\mathbf{B}_{eq_1}|\cdots|\mathbf{B}_{eq_{\eta-1}}|\mathbf{B}_{eq_\eta}], \mathbf{T}_{eq_{\eta-1}})$.
3. $\mathbf{T}_{eq_\eta} \leftarrow \mathsf{RandBasis}([\mathbf{A}|\mathbf{B}_{eq_1}|\cdots|\mathbf{B}_{eq_{\eta-1}}|\mathbf{B}_{eq_\eta}], \mathbf{E}_{eq_\eta}, \sigma_\eta)$.
4. Output $sk_\eta := (\mathbf{T}_{eq_\eta}, (t_1^*, \cdots, t_\eta^*), (\mathbf{B}_{eq_1}, \cdots, \mathbf{B}_{eq_\eta}))$.

<u>PE.dec$(ct, \mathbf{t}, (sk_\eta, \{t_1^*, \cdots, t_\eta^*\}))$</u>:   For   the   input   (a   ciphertext $ct = (\mathbf{c}_{\mathsf{in}}, \mathbf{c}_1, \cdots, \mathbf{c}_d, \mathbf{c}_{\mathsf{out}})$, the associated tags $\mathbf{t} = (t_1, \cdots, t_d)$, a puncture key sk_η and the associated punctured tags $\{t_1^*, \cdots, t_\eta^*\} \subset \mathcal{T}$), execute the following steps:

1. If there exists $j \in [\eta]$ such that $f_{t_j^*}(\mathbf{t}) \neq 0$, then output $\perp$. Otherwise, go to Step 2.
2. Parse $sk_\eta := (\mathbf{T}_{eq_\eta}, (t_1^*, \cdots, t_\eta^*), (\mathbf{B}_{eq_1}, \cdots, \mathbf{B}_{eq_\eta}))$.
3. Sample $\mathbf{R} \leftarrow \mathsf{SampleD}([\mathbf{A}|\mathbf{B}_{eq_1}|\cdots|\mathbf{B}_{eq_\eta}], \mathbf{T}_{eq_\eta}, \mathbf{U}, \sigma_\eta)$.
4. Evaluate $\mathbf{c}_{eq_j} \leftarrow \mathsf{Eval}_{\mathsf{ct}}(f_{t_j^*}, ((t_k, \mathbf{B}_k, \mathbf{c}_k))_{k=1}^d)$, for $j \in [\eta]$.
5. Compute $\bar{\mu} = (\bar{\mu}_1, \cdots, \bar{\mu}_m) \leftarrow \mathbf{c}_{\mathsf{out}} - \mathbf{R}^T(\mathbf{c}_{\mathsf{in}}|\mathbf{c}_{eq_1}|\cdots|\mathbf{c}_{eq_\eta})$.
6. For $\ell \in [m]$, if $|\bar{\mu}_\ell| < q/4$ then output $\mu_\ell = 0$; otherwise, output $\mu_\ell = 1$.

We remark that all analysis done for the LWE-based DFKHE in Subsect. 4.2 can perfectly applied to our LWE-based PE. Therefore, we do not mention the analysis again in this section. For completeness, we only state two main theorems as below.

Theorem 4 (Correctness of Ψ). *The proposed* PE Ψ *is correct if* $(\eta + 1)^2 \cdot m^{1+\frac{\eta}{2}} \cdot \omega((\sqrt{\log m})^{\eta+1}) \cdot \beta_{\mathcal{F}}^2 + 2 < \frac{1}{4}(q/\chi_0)$, *assuming that* $t_j^* \neq t_k$ *for all* $(j, k) \in [\eta] \times [d]$.

Theorem 5 (IND-sPUN-CPA). *The proposed PE Ψ scheme is IND-sPUN-CPA thanks to the IND-sVAR-CPA of the underlying DFKHE Π.*

5   Discussion on Unbounded Number of Ciphertext Tags

The idea of [8] might help us to extend the LWE-based DFKHE construction from Subsect. 4.2 (resp., PE from Subsect. 4.3) to a variant that supports arbitrary number of variables (resp., ciphertext tags). We call this variant *unDFKHE*. Although, the original idea of [8] is applied to ABE with attributes belonging to $\{0, 1\}$ using the XOR operation, we believe that it might be adapted to work well with our DFKHE with variables and punctures over $\mathbb{Z}_q$ using the addition modulo q (denoted $\oplus_q$.

In unDFKHE, the maximum number of ciphertext tags d is not fixed in advance. Then, in the key generation algorithm, we cannot generate $\mathbf{B}_1, \cdots, \mathbf{B}_d$ and give them to the public. In order to solve this issue, we utilize a family of pseudorandom functions PRF = (PRF.Gen, PRF.Eval), where PRF.Gen(1^λ) takes as input a security parameter λ and outputs a seed $\mathbf{s} \in \mathbb{Z}_q^\ell$ of length $\ell = \ell(\lambda)$ (which depends on λ) and PRF.Eval$(\mathbf{s}, \mathbf{x})$ takes as input a seed $\mathbf{s} \in \mathbb{Z}_q^\ell$ and a variable $\mathbf{x} \in \mathbb{Z}_q^*$ of *arbitrary length* and returns an element in $\mathbb{Z}_q$. The family of pseudorandom functions helps us to stretch a variable of fixed length ℓ to one of arbitrary length d as follows. In unDFKHE.KGen, for a variable $\mathbf{t}$ of length $d = |\mathbf{t}|$, instead of $\mathbf{B}_1, \cdots, \mathbf{B}_d$, we generate $\overline{\mathbf{B}}_1, \cdots, \overline{\mathbf{B}}_\ell$ and use them to produce $\mathbf{B}_1, \cdots, \mathbf{B}_d$ later. This can be done by running Eval$_{\mathsf{pk}}$(PRF.Eval$(\cdot, i)$, $(\overline{\mathbf{B}}_k)_{k=1}^\ell$), for $i \in [d]$, where PRF.Eval$(\cdot, i)$ acts as a function that can be evaluated by Eval$_{\mathsf{pk}}$. Accordingly, any function $f \in \mathcal{F}$ will also be transformed to f_Δ defined by $f_\Delta(\mathbf{t}) := f(\mathbf{t} \oplus_q \Delta_{\leq d})$ before joining to any computation later on. Here $\Delta_i := $ PRF.Eval$(\mathbf{s}, i)$ for $i \in [d]$, $\Delta_{\leq d} = (\Delta_1, \cdots, \Delta_d)$. Also remark that, $f_\Delta(\mathbf{t} \oplus_q (q_{\leq d} - \Delta_{\leq d})) = f(\mathbf{t})$, where $q_{\leq d} = (q, \cdots, q) \in \mathbb{Z}^d$. Therefore, in unDFKHE.KHom, $\mathbf{B}_f \leftarrow$ Eval$_{\mathsf{pk}}(f_\Delta, (\mathbf{B}_k)_{k=1}^d)$.

Actually, there are a lot of work left to be done. Due to space limitation, we leave details of this section for the future work.

6   Conclusion and Future Works

In this paper, we show puncturable encryption can be constructed from the so-called delegatable fully key-homomorphic encryption. From the framework, we instantiate our puncturable encryption construction using LWE. Our puncturable encryption enjoys the selective indistinguishability under chosen plaintext attacks, which can be converted into adaptive indistinguishability under chosen ciphertext attacks using well-known standard techniques. For future works, there are few investigation directions worth pursuing such as design of: (i) puncturable lattice-based ABE as in [24], (ii) efficient puncturable forward-secure encryption schemes as proposed in [18] or (iii) puncturable encryption schemes, whose puncture key size is constant or puncturable ecnryption schemes support unlimited number of punctures.

Acknowledgment. We all thank Sherman S.M. Chow and anonymous reviewers for their insightful comments which improve the content and presentation of this work a lot. This work is partially supported by the Australian Research Council Linkage Project LP190100984. Huy Quoc Le has been sponsored by a CSIRO Data61 PhD Scholarship and CSIRO Data61 Top-up Scholarship. Josef Pieprzyk has been supported by the Australian ARC grant DP180102199 and Polish NCN grant 2018/31/B/ST6/03003.

References

1. Agrawal, S., Boneh, D., Boyen, X.: Efficient lattice (H)IBE in the standard model. In: Gilbert, H. (ed.) EUROCRYPT 2010. LNCS, vol. 6110, pp. 553–572. Springer, Heidelberg (2010). https://doi.org/10.1007/978-3-642-13190-5_28

2. Alkim, E., Bos, J.W., Ducas, L., et al.: FrodoKEM: learning with errors key encapsulation (algorithm specifications and supporting documentation, version 25 March, 2020) (2020). https://frodokem.org/. Accessed 08 July 2020

3. Alwen, J., Peikert, C.: Generating shorter bases for hard random lattices. In: Proceedings of the 26th International Symposium on Theoretical Aspects of Computer Science, STACS 2009, 26–28 February 2009, Freiburg, Germany, pp. 75–86 (2009). https://doi.org/10.4230/LIPIcs.STACS.2009.1832

4. Boneh, D., Boyen, X.: Efficient selective-ID secure identity based encryption without random oracles. J. Cryptogr. **24**(4), 659–693 (2011)

5. Boneh, D., et al.: Fully key-homomorphic encryption, arithmetic circuit ABE and compact garbled circuits. In: Nguyen, P.Q., Oswald, E. (eds.) EUROCRYPT 2014. LNCS, vol. 8441, pp. 533–556. Springer, Heidelberg (2014). https://doi.org/10.1007/978-3-642-55220-5_30

6. Boneh, D., Kim, S., Montgomery, H.: Private puncturable PRFs from standard lattice assumptions. In: Coron, J.-S., Nielsen, J.B. (eds.) EUROCRYPT 2017. LNCS, vol. 10210, pp. 415–445. Springer, Cham (2017). https://doi.org/10.1007/978-3-319-56620-7_15

7. Boneh, D., Sahai, A., Waters, B.: Functional encryption: definitions and challenges. In: Ishai, Y. (ed.) TCC 2011. LNCS, vol. 6597, pp. 253–273. Springer, Heidelberg (2011). https://doi.org/10.1007/978-3-642-19571-6_16

8. Brakerski, Z., Vaikuntanathan, V.: Circuit-ABE from LWE: unbounded attributes and semi-adaptive security. In: Robshaw, M., Katz, J. (eds.) CRYPTO 2016. LNCS, vol. 9816, pp. 363–384. Springer, Heidelberg (2016). https://doi.org/10.1007/978-3-662-53015-3_13

9. Canetti, R., Halevi, S., Katz, J.: Chosen-ciphertext security from identity-based encryption. In: Cachin, C., Camenisch, J.L. (eds.) EUROCRYPT 2004. LNCS, vol. 3027, pp. 207–222. Springer, Heidelberg (2004). https://doi.org/10.1007/978-3-540-24676-3_13

10. Canetti, R., Raghuraman, S., Richelson, S., Vaikuntanathan, V.: Chosen-ciphertext secure fully homomorphic encryption. In: Fehr, S. (ed.) PKC 2017. LNCS, vol. 10175, pp. 213–240. Springer, Heidelberg (2017). https://doi.org/10.1007/978-3-662-54388-7_8

11. Cash, D., Hofheinz, D., Kiltz, E., Peikert, C.: Bonsai trees, or how to delegate a lattice basis. In: Gilbert, H. (ed.) EUROCRYPT 2010. LNCS, vol. 6110, pp. 523–552. Springer, Heidelberg (2010). https://doi.org/10.1007/978-3-642-13190-5_27

12. Cohen, A., Holmgren, J., Nishimaki, R., Vaikuntanathan, V., Wichs, D.: Watermarking cryptographic capabilities. In: Wichs, D., Mansour, Y. (eds.) STOC 2016: Proceedings of the Forty-Eighth Annual ACM Symposium on Theory of Computing, Cambridge, MA, USA, pp. 1115–1127 (2016). https://doi.org/10.1145/2897518.2897651

13. Delerablée, C.: Identity-based broadcast encryption with constant size ciphertexts and private keys. In: Kurosawa, K. (ed.) ASIACRYPT 2007. LNCS, vol. 4833, pp. 200–215. Springer, Heidelberg (2007). https://doi.org/10.1007/978-3-540-76900-2_12

14. Derler, D., Gellert, K., Jager, T., Slamanig, D., Striecks, C.: Bloom filter encryption and applications to efficient forward-secret 0-RTT key exchange. Cryptology ePrint Archive, Report 2018/199 (2018). https://eprint.iacr.org/2018/199

15. Derler, D., Jager, T., Slamanig, D., Striecks, C.: Bloom filter encryption and applications to efficient forward-secret 0-RTT Key exchange. In: Nielsen, J.B., Rijmen, V. (eds.) EUROCRYPT 2018. LNCS, vol. 10822, pp. 425–455. Springer, Cham (2018). https://doi.org/10.1007/978-3-319-78372-7_14

16. Derler, D., Krenn, S., Lorünser, T., Ramacher, S., Slamanig, D., Striecks, C.: Revisiting proxy re-encryption: forward secrecy, improved security, and applications. In: Abdalla, M., Dahab, R. (eds.) PKC 2018. LNCS, vol. 10769, pp. 219–250. Springer, Cham (2018). https://doi.org/10.1007/978-3-319-76578-5_8

17. Gentry, C., Peikert, C., Vaikuntanathan, V.: Trapdoors for hard lattices and new cryptographic constructions. Cryptology ePrint Archive, Report 2007/432 (2008). https://eprint.iacr.org/2007/432

18. Green, M.D., Miers, I.: Forward secure asynchronous messaging from puncturable encryption. In: 2015 IEEE Symposium on Security and Privacy, pp. 305–320, May 2015. https://doi.org/10.1109/SP.2015.26

19. Günther, C.G.: An identity-based key-exchange protocol. In: Quisquater, J.-J., Vandewalle, J. (eds.) EUROCRYPT 1989. LNCS, vol. 434, pp. 29–37. Springer, Heidelberg (1990). https://doi.org/10.1007/3-540-46885-4_5

20. Günther, F., Hale, B., Jager, T., Lauer, S.: 0-RTT key exchange with full forward secrecy. In: Coron, J.-S., Nielsen, J.B. (eds.) EUROCRYPT 2017. LNCS, vol. 10212, pp. 519–548. Springer, Cham (2017). https://doi.org/10.1007/978-3-319-56617-7_18

21. Kiltz, E.: Chosen-ciphertext security from tag-based encryption. In: Halevi, S., Rabin, T. (eds.) TCC 2006. LNCS, vol. 3876, pp. 581–600. Springer, Heidelberg (2006). https://doi.org/10.1007/11681878_30

22. Micciancio, D., Peikert, C.: Trapdoors for lattices: simpler, tighter, faster, smaller. In: Pointcheval, D., Johansson, T. (eds.) EUROCRYPT 2012. LNCS, vol. 7237, pp. 700–718. Springer, Heidelberg (2012). https://doi.org/10.1007/978-3-642-29011-4_41

23. Micciancio, D., Regev, O.: Worst-case to average-case reductions based on Gaussian measures. In: Proceedings of the 45th Symposium on Foundations of Computer Science (FOCS 2004), 17–19 October 2004, Rome, Italy, pp. 372–381 (2004). https://doi.org/10.1109/FOCS.2004.72

24. Phuong, T.V.X., Ning, R., Xin, C., Wu, H.: Puncturable attribute-based encryption for secure data delivery in internet of things. In: IEEE INFOCOM 2018 - IEEE Conference on Computer Communications, pp. 1511–1519, April 2018. https://doi.org/10.1109/INFOCOM.2018.8485909

25. Regev, O.: On lattices, learning with errors, random linear codes, and cryptography. In: Proceedings of the 37th Annual ACM Symposium on Theory of Computing, Baltimore, MD, USA, 22–24 May 2005, pp. 84–93 (2005). https://doi.org/10.1145/1060590.1060603

26. Sun, S.-F., Sakzad, A., Steinfeld, R., Liu, J.K., Gu, D.: Public-key puncturable encryption: modular and compact constructions. In: Kiayias, A., Kohlweiss, M., Wallden, P., Zikas, V. (eds.) PKC 2020, Part I. LNCS, vol. 12110, pp. 309–338. Springer, Cham (2020). https://doi.org/10.1007/978-3-030-45374-9_11

27. Susilo, W., Duong, D.H., Le, Q.H., Pieprzyk, J.: Puncturable encryption: a generic construction from delegatable fully key-homomorphic encryption (full version). https://arxiv.org/abs/2007.06353 (2020)

Analyzing Attacks

Linear Attack on Round-Reduced DES Using Deep Learning

Botao Hou[1,2], Yongqiang Li[1,2], Haoyue Zhao[1], and Bin Wu[1,2(✉)]

[1] State Key Laboratory of Information Security,
Institute of Information Engineering, CAS, Beijing, China
{houbotao,liyongqiang,wubin}@iie.ac.cn, zhaohaoyue1@gmail.com
[2] School of Cyber Security, University of Chinese Academy of Sciences,
Beijing, China

Abstract. Linear attack is a powerful known-plaintext cryptanalysis method on block ciphers, which has been successfully applied in DES, KATAN, SPECK and other ciphers. In this paper, we use deep learning networks to achieve linear attack on DES with plain-cipher pairs. Comparing with traditional linear attack algorithm, our work requires less knowledge about complex cryptanalysis as neural network can work well by data-driven. Thus, this paper has three main contributions. First, a new linear attack architecture based on deep residual network was proposed to train discriminative neural networks with auto-generated plain-cipher pair data. The results indicate that trained neural networks can effectively learn algorithmic representations of the XOR distributions of given linear expression on DES. Second, several novel neural network-based algorithms were designed to efficiently enforce key recovery on round-reduced DES using trained networks with moderate full and partial bits of linear expression as inputs. Third, as far as we know, it is the first time that neural networks are used to achieve known-plaintext attack on complex block ciphers.

Keywords: Linear attack · Deep learning · DES

1 Introduction

Linear cryptanalysis is one of the most powerful analysis techniques used in modern block ciphers. It can achieve key recovery attacks utilizing non-zero correlation with bits of plain-cipher text and key, which is expressed in a linear approximate equation. The first linear cryptanalysis [2] was presented to break Data Encryption Standard (DES) successfully in 1994. Since DES [1] was published in 1977, its security has been focused by all over the world. In that paper, Matsui provided some linear equations on round-reduced DES and proposed a key recovery algorithm for known-plaintext attack in 8-round and even only-plaintext attack in 8 rounds. And Matsui [3] proposed an improved version for linear cryptanalysis and its application to the full 16-round DES. Later, Hermelin et al. [4] improved linear cryptanalysis into multiple approximations

© Springer Nature Switzerland AG 2020
L. Chen et al. (Eds.): ESORICS 2020, LNCS 12309, pp. 131–145, 2020.
https://doi.org/10.1007/978-3-030-59013-0_7

and achieved a faster attack. Obviously, all of those traditional linear crypt-analysis works need amounts of mathematical knowledge and manual theory deduction.

Recently, some works have been explored to combine deep learning and applicable statistical cryptanalytic techniques [10,12]. At first, Abadi and Andersen [5] trained two neural networks which allow them to communicate using given key without advanced cipher design, and another adversarial network was trained to prove that it cannot recover information without the key. However, their work did not explain what net construction is in cryptography. Soon, Coutinho et al. [11] improved simple adversarial network above with chosen-plaintext attack and obtained a unbreakable One-Time Pad algorithm in unsupervised condition which explored the effect of adversarial network in security. And then, some works tried to achieve cracking directly by simulating ciphers [13]. An unsupervised CycleGAN neural network [8], named CipherGAN, was used to crack Shift and Vigenere ciphers. Their work showed that neural network can learn detail relationship about encrypt and decrypt processes, but it was limited to fixed key. Comparing with traditional encrypt algorithms, modern block cryptographical algorithms are more complex so that previous methods can't work well, and some works began to apply some mature cryptanalysis methods to improve availability of attacking using machine learning [14]. Recently, some works [9] explored the possibility of applying machine learning on side channel attack of Advance Encryption Standard (AES), but generally side channel is considered not to be cryptanalysis in the sense we discussed. And Gohr [6] tried to apply deep learning on Speck, a lightweight block encryption algorithm. They constructed a network to more accurately learn the distribution of output difference with a fixed input difference. However, they didn't give attacks on more complex ciphers.

1.1   Our Contribution

First of all, we devise and train neural networks and expect that we can achieve efficient key recovery on DES using trained network models. Those network models should obtain the ability of distinguishing different distributions by observing given linear expression on round-reduced DES. Considering two different key recovery methods, one bit key recovery and multiple bits key recovery, we train corresponding network models in different ways.

For one bit key recovery on round-reduced DES, we propose a new neural network attack framework that can successfully distinguish two different binomial distributions. Those distributions perform two different situations of n-round linear approximation expression. Using the trained network models, we established corresponding one bit key recovery algorithm and achieved successful key recovering on 3, 4 and 5 rounds DES. In order to know the availability of our models, we calculate the expected efficiency for round-reduced DES that use Bayesian model. Experimental results indicate that the performance of our models is very closed to theoretical value.

In multiple bits key recovery, another neural network model is proposed to train as a discriminator for distributions produced by real and random effective key bits. And this model is used in proposed multiple bits key recovery algorithm. We tested the performance of this algorithm on 4 rounds DES and obtained effective key rank.

1.2 Paper Organization

The rest of the paper is organized as follows. In Sect. 2, we present a brief description of the cryptographic modules employed in our linear cryptanalysis. In Sect. 3, we introduce our detail scheme of neural networks. The result of neural discriminators and corresponding key recovery attacks are in Sect. 4. Section 5 is the conclusion about our scheme in short.

2 Preliminaries

Before introducing our architecture, we briefly review some cryptographic building modules deployed in linear cryptanalysis method on DES and two classical key recovery attack algorithms.

2.1 DES

DES is a iterative cryptographic algorithm with Feistel structure, which has a profound impact on the design of later ciphers. DES uses 56 bits key to protect message with block divided into 64 bits. Omitting the initial permutation IP and the final permutation IP^{-1} in full DES, we call input and output of round iterations as plain text block P and cipher text block C. Each block will be divided into two 32 bits blocks (L, R), which will be encrypted by total 16 rounds. More details can be seen in [1].

For rth round, the output L_r and R_r are computed as follows.

$$\begin{aligned} L_r &= R_{r-1} \\ R_r &= L_{r-1} \oplus F(R_{r-1}, K_r) \end{aligned} \tag{1}$$

Where F(.) is the non-linear function called F function, it contains four operations which include extension operation E of R_r, bitwise XOR operation between subkey and extended R_r, S-box operation S and final permutation operation. F function is briefly expressed as:

$$F(R_{r-1}, K_r) = S(E(R_{r-1}) \oplus K_r) \tag{2}$$

2.2 Linear Attack

Linear Approximate Equation. Linear attack has been widely used to break block cipher algorithms. Indeed, given plain text P, master key K and corresponding cipher text C, linear approximate equation L try to describe the linear relationship of bits in serval fixed locations like:

$$\alpha \cdot P \oplus \beta \cdot C = \gamma \cdot K \tag{3}$$

Algorithm 1. ONE BIT KEY RECOVERY ALGORITHM

Input:

L_n, $n-$round linear approximate equation

Pr_{L_n}, the probability of L_n

$Pair$, plain-cipher text pairs generated by key K

Output: output result

1: $N_{pc} \leftarrow$ the number of $Pair$
2: $N_L \leftarrow 0$
3: **for** $pair$ in $Pair$ **do**
4:      $L^l \leftarrow$ compare the left side of L_n
5:      **if** $L^l == 0$ **then**
6:          $N_L += 1$
7: **if** $N_L > N_{pc}/2$ **then**
8:      **if** $Pr_L > 1/2$ **then**
9:          **return** $L^r = 0$
10:     **else**
11:         **return** $L^r = 1$
12: **else**
13:     **if** $Pr_L > 1/2$ **then**
14:         **return** $L^r = 1$
15:     **else**
16:         **return** $L^r = 0$

Where α, β and γ are the bit location masks and $\alpha \cdot P$ is the bitwise addition for bits in locations marked by α in P. There we name the value of left side in L as L^l and the right side as L^r. Generally, equation L holds with the probability Pr_L of $1/2$. But if there is an obvious deviation with $1/2$ and Pr_L, we call this expression L as a well linear approximate equation. The bigger this deviation is, the quicker this expression could be distinguished from other expressions. Moreover, key recovery mentioned in follows is relative with Pr_L closely.

Key Recovery Attack. There are two different linear attack algorithms divided by number of key bits can be recovered. First one is one bit key recovery attack, relying on a well linear expression. Multiple bits key recovery is another, it generally depend on the linear equation which expended by $(n\text{-}1)$-round expression. Both of those attacks can work well in DES, and many effective linear expressions can be found [2].

One Bit Key Recovery. Given linear approximate equation L like Function 3, we can judge whether L^r is 0 or 1 with probability Pr_L. If we have N_{pc} plain-cipher text pairs generated by fixed key, we count the number N_L of those pairs that satisfy $L^l = 0$. If N_L has obvious difference with $N_{pc}/2$, we can judge this one bit key L^r depending on the symbol of difference with high success rate. The detailed recovery process is showed in Algorithm 1.

Algorithm 2. MULTIPLE BITS CANDIDATE KEY RANK ALGORITHM

Input:
L_n, $n-$round linear approximate equation
$Pair$, Plain-cipher text pairs generated by key K
Output: output $Rank_{key}$

1: $N_t \leftarrow$ the number of effective text bits in left L_n
2: $T_t \leftarrow \{0\}_{2^{N_t}}$
3: **for** $pair$ in $Pair$ **do**
4:    $e \leftarrow$ bits extracted from $pair$ following L_n
5:    $T_t[e]+ = 1$
6: $N_k \leftarrow$ the number of effective key bits in left L_n
7: $T_k \leftarrow \{0\}_{2^{N_k}}$
8: **for** k in len(T_k) **do**
9:    **for** t in len(T_t) **do**
10:       $L^l \leftarrow$ compare the left side of L_n
11:       **if** $L^l == 0$ **then**
12:          $T_k[k]+ = t$
13: $N_{pc} \leftarrow$ the number of $Pair$
14: **for** k in $len(T_k)$ **do**
15:    $T_k[k] = T_k[k] - N_{pc}$
16: $Rank_{key} \leftarrow$ sort T_k by descending value order
17: **return** $Rank_{key}$

Multiple Bits Key Recovery. Generally, if we attack n rounds DES, we have to obtain a $(n$-$1)$-round linear approximate equation L_{n-i} with Pr_L. Considering the effect of F function in first round and nth round, n-round expression L_n is described as:

$$\alpha \cdot P \oplus \beta \cdot C \oplus \mu \cdot F_1(P, K_1) \oplus \nu \cdot F_n(C, K_n) = \gamma \cdot K \qquad (4)$$

Since L_n is expanded from L_{n-i}, Pr_{L_n} should be almost same with $Pr_{L_{n-i}}$, which makes us knowing the distribution of L_n^l. Obviously, this value is totally determined by some bits of plain-cipher text and key, and we call those bits as effective text bits and effective key bits respectively. Based on known Pr_L, we can recover those effective key bits as follows.

First, we list all possible effective key bits as key candidates. Considering that the probability Pr_{L_n} would almost equal to $Pr_{L_{n-i}}$ when K_1 and K_n are correctly guessed, this leads us to use maximum likelihood method in regard to those key candidates.

There we get N_{pc} plain-cipher text pairs generated with fixed key K. For each key candidate, compute L_n^l and add counter with 1 when it equals to 0. Sort all key candidates by the difference between counter and $N_{pc}/2$ as key rank. Generally, correct key bits will be in higher rank. The candidate key rank processing is showed in Algorithm 2.

3   Network Architectures

Our goal is to develop a learnable, end-to-end model for linear attack, and it should obtain statistical cryptanalytic characteristics. Thus, we proposed a new neural network architecture as a deep learning discriminator to distinguish different distributions. The diagram for our network is shown in Fig. 1.

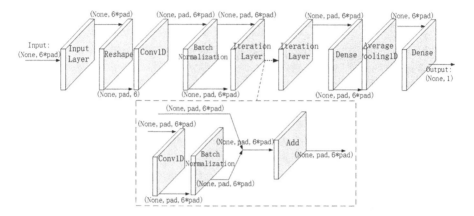

Fig. 1. Model overview. An universal neural network architecture used in our experiments

Those networks comprise three main components: input layer, iteration layer and predict layer. The iteration layer is built by classical residual neural network [7]. This network has been successfully applied in many domains. It consists of some residual blocks which add input layer to output layer and produce new output, the output will been sent to next block. The most important advantage of residual networks is that it can effectively avoid gradient dispersion when the number of layer increases.

The input layer receives training data with fixed length and applies reshape layer into the data. We expect that our network should simulate XOR operation better and form some intermediate representation. For this reason, we transpose and apply convolution into input data so that we can expend the effect of each bit. After batch normalization layer, data will be sent into iteration layer. Each iteration layer has same structure with a convolution and normalization following. What' more, a skip connection is applied to add input layer and output layer and this operation may allow next layer can mix bits in block more like bitwise addition. Iteration layer will repeat 5 or 10 rounds in our experiments, and then the predict layer will be following. The predict layer provides a fully connect operation in order to combines all bits and a single linear layer to produce one bit predicted result.

In our key recovery experiments, this neural network will be fed with bit sequences and is expected to distinguish those input into two different distributions. For each sequence, it consists of 6 units and each unit will be padded with

Algorithm 3. ONE BIT DEEP LEARNING NETWORK KEY RECOVERY ALGORITHM

Input:

L_n, n−round linear approximate equation

Net_{L_n}, neural net discriminator trained by L_n

$Pair$, Plain-cipher text pairs generated by fixed key K

Output: output

1: $N_{pc} \leftarrow$ the number of $Pair$
2: $G \leftarrow Net_{L_n}(Pair)$
3: **if** $sum(G) > N_{pc}/2$ **then**
4:     **return** right of $L_n = 1$
5: **else**
6:     **return** right of $L_n = 0$

---

0 to fixed length, which is determined by max length of each mark in L_n. Generally, this length is not longer than 8 and we will pad the sequence to $6 \times 8 = 48$. Input layer changes the size of this sequence into 8×48, and it will be trained in this size till predict layer. Pooling operation condenses it into 48×1 and output it with 1 bit by dense layer.

In each epoch, we will check networks by validation data, and we save and update the best model according to its accuracy.

4   Attack Architecture

In this section, we will introduce two new linear attack architectures: one bit key recovery and multiple bits key recovery. We apply them in round-reduced DES, and both of them can distinguish different distributions well using deep learning net and realize expected key recovery.

4.1   One Bit Key Recovery

Given n-round linear approximation expression L_n as Function 3, and we know that it will hold with certain probability Pr_{L_n} in previous. There, we don't need to know exact value about Pr_{L_n} and more details, and we can also obtain one bit key information $\gamma \cdot K$. For this, we propose one bit key recovery algorithm showed in Algorithm 3 to recover mentioned bit using deep learning networks.

Train and Recover. Supposed that Pr_{L_n} is the probability linear expression L_n holds, if we ask that L_n^r is fixed to 0, the distribution of L_n^r will be almost binomial distribution which means 0 will appear with the probability equaling to Pr_{L_n}. While the binomial distribution will be inverse if L_n^r is fixed to 1. Thus, we mark those different distributions with corresponding labels and expect trained networks can effectively distinguish them by inputting some bit sequences.

In order to obtain those network models, we generate training and validation by several phases as follows:

1. Generate plain texts P and master keys K ordering uniformly distribution.
2. Encrypt P with K by $n-$round DES cipher and obtain cipher texts C.
3. Extract $P - C$ pairs into bits sequence EX_{pc} and K into EX_k depending on linear equation L_n.
4. Pad EX_{pc} with 0 into X following the order of $(\alpha \cdot P || \beta \cdot C)$.
5. Set label Y relying on XOR value distribution of each EX_k.

After generating enough data, neural network discriminator Net_{L_n} will be trained to predict right label Y. Obviously, if Net_{L_n} is train well, its correct output will help us directly to recover corresponding one bit key information. Thus, we apply trained network into Algorithm 3 to recover this key bit.

Recovery phase need N_{pc} plain-cipher pairs generated by fixed key K. Repetitively run Phase 3–4 above and we can obtain extracted text sequences of those pairs. Those text sequences are feed into Net_{L_n} and output their prediction. Considering with the accuracy of Net_{L_n}, the success rate of Algorithm 3 rely on N_{pc} and performance of algorithm will be shown in following experiments.

Goal Model. After training mentioned above, we indeed obtain a deep learning discriminator. This discriminator would first learn the simulation of XOR operation, and then obtain the ability that distinguish the difference with different binomial distribution performance.

Our deep learning model didn't know any information about those distributions and even didn't know XOR operation before training, all they obtaining is input seems like random bit sequences. Obviously, if we can obtain those distribution information about linear expression L, we can estimate the best result of those networks using Bayesian rule.

As Pr_L is the possibility of linear approximation expression L holding and discriminator B_L with Bayesian model obtains distribution features of L^l fully, if L^l of a bit sequence is 1, the accuracy of B_L correctly judging that this sequence belongs into $L^r = 1$ is shown following Function 5.

$$P(\gamma \cdot K = 1|1) = \frac{P(1|\gamma \cdot K = 1)P(\gamma \cdot K = 1)}{P(1|\gamma \cdot K = 1)P(\gamma \cdot K = 1) + P(1|\gamma \cdot K = 0)P(\gamma \cdot K = 0)} \tag{5}$$

Supposing that K is generated following uniform distribution, accuracy of B_L will be equal to Pr_L.

This Bayesian model will be our goal model of deep learning network. We replace network discriminator Net_L with this Bayesian discriminator B_L in Algorithm 3 and can get one bit key recovery. After reducing, we find that the relationship between success rate of one bit key recovery and number of plain-cipher pairs required is same with Lemma 2 in [2]. Thus, we can measure key recovery effect which uses deep learning networks with this lemma.

Experiment. All of our experiments are run in a uniform environment, models are trained on a workstation with NVIDIA GeForce GTX 1080Ti and Intel(R) E5-2609 1.7 GHz CPU.

$$P_H[7, 18, 24, 29] \oplus P_L[15] \oplus C_H[7, 18, 24, 29] \oplus C_L[15] = K_1[22] \oplus K_3[22] \quad (6)$$

$$P_H[7, 18, 24, 29] \oplus P_L[15] \oplus C_H[15] \oplus C_L[7, 18, 24, 27, 28, 29, 30, 31]$$
$$= K_1[22] \oplus K_3[22] \oplus K_4[42, 43, 45, 46] \quad (7)$$

$$P_H[15] \oplus P_L[7, 18, 24, 27, 28, 29, 30, 31] \oplus C_H[15] \oplus C_L[7, 18, 24, 27, 28, 29, 30, 31]$$
$$= K_1[42, 43, 45, 46] \oplus K_2[22] \oplus K_4[22] \oplus K_5[42, 43, 45, 46] \quad (8)$$

First, we tested the performance of one bit key recovery algorithm on L_3 which can be seen in Function 6. Model was trained for 200 epochs using the Adam optimizer [15] with a batch size of 1000 against MSE loss with $L2-$regularization. And there were 10^5 train data and 10^4 validation data used. Figure 2a shows the learn history of Net_{L_3}. The accuracy on validation data is 67.23% which is very closed to theoretical goal model which is 70%, same with Pr_{L_3}.

To be clear, our neural network knows nothing about XOR operation and detailed data distribution, but it can still perform well almost like goal model which knows all about knowledge. All of those show that the presented approach equips excellent learning capability of describing XOR distributions. What's more, we found that the increase of train data can significant improve the accuracy, and the network with 10^5 data is improved with 0.43% than 10^4 data.

Apply those models to recover key information and we found that the success rate of neural network models is only lower than theoretical Bayesian model slightly. The number of plain-cipher text pairs required in key recovery in different success rate based on those discriminators are shown in Fig. 2b. For each result, we run key recovery process for 2000 times to obtain moderate observations. We can see that our neural network can complete key recovery given small plain-cipher text set, and Net_{L_3} trained by 10^5 training data even performs better than theoretical success rate. Thus, those network model showed their capacity to distinguish different distributions.

Table 1. results of different models on corresponding linear expression L_n. Meanwhile, we show the average number of plain-cipher text pairs that can achieve key recovery success rate, each of them are test in 2000 times

Index	Network	Train data	Epoch	Depth	Accuracy	Number of $P-C$ pairs for success rate			
						85%	90%	95%	99%
1	B_3	–	–	–	0.7	6	10	17	32
2	Net_{L_3}	10^4	10^3	5	0.668	14	18	32	64
3	Net_{L_3}	10^5	5×10^3	5	0.6723	10	18	25	32
4	B_4	–	–	–	0.561	67	112	190	358
5	Net_{L_4}	10^6	5×10^4	5	0.5375	115	200	332	633
6	B_5	–	–	–	0.519	2770	4617	7849	14774
7	Net_{L_5}	10^6	5×10^4	10	0.5128	5130	8631	–	–

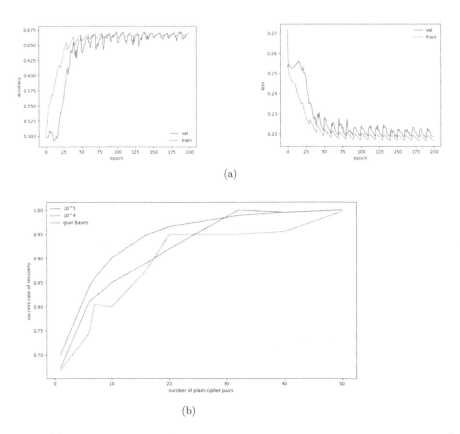

(a)

(b)

Fig. 2. (a) shows accuracy and loss of Net_3 in total train process data size of 10^5 respectively. Both valuation data and training data perform synchronously and indicate that network work well without over fitting. (b) shows key recovery performance of Bayesian model and our models. All of them will almost recover key information with success rate more than 99% when increase the number of plain-cipher pairs into 64. With same pair number, the success rate of neural network models only lower than theory Bayesian model slightly. And increasing the number of train data, neural networks will work better.

Excepted 3-round one bit key recovery, we also ran 4 and 5-round key recovery based on linear expression in Function 7 and Function 8. Comparing with L_3, the binomial distribution probability like Pr_{L_5} even decreases from 70% into 51.9% [2]. Obviously, the difficulty of distinguishing those two different distributions increases a lot. Table 1 shows the accuracy and key recovery of best models. There, B_n is the discriminator of goal model using Bayes mentioned above. And we can find that almost all of them can recover required one bit key with limited plain-cipher text pairs number. For neural discriminators Net_{L_5}, though it does not achieve success rate more than 95% with less than 20000 pairs plain-cipher text, it still performs its ability recovering key bit with success rate of even 90%.

Algorithm 4. MULTIPLE BITS DEEP LEARNING NETWORK CANDIDATE KEY RANK ALGORITHM

Input:
L'_n, n−round linear approximate equation
$Net_{L'_n}$, neural net discriminator trained by L'_n
$Pair$, Plain-cipher text pairs generated by key K
Output: output $Rank_{key}$
1: $N_k \leftarrow$ the number of effective subkey bits in left L'_n
2: $T_k \leftarrow \{0\}^{2^{N_k}}$
3: **for** key in $len(T_k)$ **do**
4:     $Ex \leftarrow$ bit sequences extracted from $(Pair, key)$ following L'_n
5:     $G_k \leftarrow Net_{L'_n}(Ex)$
6:     $T_k[key] = sum(G_{key})/len(G_{key})$
7: $Rank_k \leftarrow$ sort T_k by descending value order
8: **return** $Rank_k$

4.2 Multiple Bits Key Recovery

Like Function 4, we can apply $(n$-1$)$-round linear approximation expression L_{n-1} to consecutive F-functions from the first round to the $(n$-1$)$th round or from the second round to the nth round of n rounds DES, and obtain n-round linear equation L'_n with some bits in F-functions. Because K_n is added in expression, we can try all possible effective bits in K_n and test whether the value of left L'_n satisfies the similar distribution like L_{n-i}, so that recover those effective bits. Thus, we propose new multiple bits key candidate recovery algorithm showed in Algorithm 4 to recover multiple bits using deep learning networks.

Train and Recover. Similar with one bit key recovery algorithm, we also utilize the ability of deep learning networks that can distinguish different distributions. Of course, we have to consider the interference produced by right side of Function 4. In order to simplify our models, we suppose that the value of $\gamma \cdot K$ is 0 which may be happened with the probability of $1/2$. Then for once right guess of key, the distribution of L''_n will still be almost binomial distribution which 0 will appear in the probability equal to $Pr_{L'_n}$, and we call it real distribution. While the distribution for one wrong guess of key will be uniform, and we name it random distribution. Those difference is what our networks should distinguish. If given bit sequences generated by correct fixed key, neural network discriminator $Net_{L'_n}$ should output label of real distribution as 1 with a big probability, otherwise, it should be random distribution as 0.

Also, we give the generation phases of training and validation data.

1. Generate plain texts P and label Y ordering uniformly distribution, and Num_P is the number of those P.
2. Generate master key K ordering uniformly distribution, and filtrate out Num_PK that satisfy $\gamma \cdot K = 0$.

3. Encrypted P with K by $n-$round DES cipher and obtain cipher text C.
4. Extract $P - C$ pairs into bits sequence EX_{pc} and K into EX_k with linear equation L'_n.
5. For each label Y, do.
   – if $Y = 1$, Pad EX_{pc} with 0 into X following the order of $(\alpha \cdot P \| \beta \cdot C \| \mu \cdot F_1 \| \nu \cdot F_n)$.
   – if $Y = 0$, Pad EX_{pc} with 0 into X following the order of $(\alpha \cdot P \| \beta \cdot C \| Rand \| Rand)$, which $Rand$ is generated ordering uniformly distribution.

As we know, $F_1(P_L, K_1)$ and $F_n(C_L, K_n)$ are determined by effective text bits and effective key bits. Because the number of effective key bits are few enough, we can research those bit keys exhaustively and call those keys as key candidate. For each possible key candidate, we test this key candidate with some plain-cipher text pairs and input corresponding bit sequences extracted following L'_n into network model $Net_{L'n}$. We count those output as the score which support that this key candidate is the right bits of master key required. Sort those key candidates with corresponding score in descending order and we call those as key rank. A well discriminator should have the ability ranking real right subkey higher.

Once we get a key rank, we can run an exhaustive key search for remaining several bits key. In each trying, we will choose a candidate bit key from key rank by order. Obviously, the higher the rank of right subkey is, the quicker whole key recovery will complete.

Goal Model. Also, our neural network discriminator $Net_{L'}$ need distinguish two binomial distributions. However, different with distributions in one bit key recovery, these binomial distributions should be with $p_{real} = Pr_{L'}$ and $p_{ran} = \frac{1}{2}$. Use Function 5 and we can obtain the theory accuracy of $B_{L'}$ with Bayesian model.

Experiment. We run our network models on the number of 10^5 training data and 10^4 validation data. And we tested the performance of multiple bits key recovery on L'_4 showed in Function 9 extended from L_3. Thus $Pr_{L'_4}$ will almost equal to Pr_{L_3} if effective key bits in K_4 is right.

$$P_H[15] \oplus P_L[7, 18, 24, 29] \oplus C_H[7, 18, 24, 29] \oplus C_L[15] \oplus F_1(P_L, K_1)[15]$$
$$= K_2[22] \oplus K_4[22] \quad (9)$$

We trained this neural network about $4-$round with 200 epochs and each epoch is run in size of 5000. As no unit in L'_4 is more than 4 bits, we set *padding* as 5. And we contain 6×5 bits sequence, where the sixth unit is F_4 and it don't appear in Function 9, we will pad it into $\{0\}_5$. Real and random data determined by random label Y were sent to 5-depth residual network. And those two different distributions were separated with accuracy of 56.77%, while the accuracy of theoretical Bayesian model should be 58.3%.

Analysis the effective text and key bits in Function 9, we can easily ensure that the effective key bits effecting left side of L_4' are $\{K_1[42], K_1[43], K_1[44], K_1[45], K_1[46], K_1[47]\}$, all of them are related to S-box S_1. Those 6 bits subkey are what we aim to recover. We list all possibility of 6 bits may take and get key candidate table with size of $2^6 = 64$.

Table 2. Multiple bits key recovery on 4-round DES. We list the average key rank on different number of plain-cipher pairs. They are measured through 200 rounds in replicated test.

Network	Train data	depth	Accuracy	Average key rank in number of P-C pairs			
				32	64	128	256
$Net_{L_4'}$	10^5	5	0.5677	13	9	3	2

We set a random master key K which holds $\gamma \cdot K = 1$ asked by trained neural network $Net_{L_4'}$ above, and we obtained plain-cipher pairs $Pair$ with number of N_{pc} encrypted by K. Then we extract each pair following L_4' and obtain bit sequence $(\alpha \cdot P || \beta \cdot C)$. Up to now, we have no information about F_1 in L_4'. For each key candidate K_{can}, we compute $\mu \cdot F_1(P_L, K_{can})$ and insert $\mu \cdot F_1$ into sequence. Record the prediction $Net_{L_4'}$ and get score of K_{can}.

Count all score of key candidate K_{can}, the rank of those key candidates with score is key rank. Research the rank of correct effective key bits, and we can test the performance of $Net_{L_4'}$ is showed in Table 2. As key ranks using $Net_{L_4'}$ are no lower than $2^5 = 32$ in those small number of plain-cipher pairs, all of those indicate that our neural network models can distinguish different distribution in multiple bits key recovery and are pretty effective for key ranking.

5   Conclusion

In this paper, we used deep learning network achieving linear attack in round-reduced DES. We proposed the network structure to distinguish different performance of linear expressions. Our experiments indicated that those deep learning networks have the capacity of learning complex static characteristics like XOR and distinguishing different distributions. In order to make networks perform better, we also designed two linear attack algorithms which apply network in one bit and multiple bits key recovery. These end-to-end architectures need almost few knowledge about distribution of linear expressions and performs well in our experiments. And the representations of our results are also useful for cryptanalysis on other more complex block ciphers.

For further work, we will continue to test the performance using deep learning networks to research linear approximations with limited advanced knowledge.

What's more, we found a problem effecting performance of net when we trained our network. Limited by number N_t of plain-cipher text bits, there are only 2^{N_t} text sequences in train text. However, training data is usually larger than this value and make some same input may have different label, and this may make network puzzled. The same situation also happened in [8], and we will explore those further more.

Acknowledgments. The authors appreciate the anonymous reviewers valuable comments, which improved the paper greatly. This work was supported by National Nature Science Foundation of China under Grants No. 61941116, No. 61772517 and No. U1936119, and National Key R&D Program of China under Grant No. 2019QY(Y)0602.

References

1. National Burean of Standards: Data Encryption Standard. U.S. Department of Commercc, Federal Information Processing Standards 46 (1977)
2. Matsui, M.: Linear cryptanalysis method for DES cipher. In: Helleseth, T. (ed.) EUROCRYPT 1993. LNCS, vol. 765, pp. 386–397. Springer, Heidelberg (1994). https://doi.org/10.1007/3-540-48285-7_33
3. Matsui, M.: The first experimental cryptanalysis of the data encryption standard. In: Desmedt, Y.G. (ed.) CRYPTO 1994. LNCS, vol. 839, pp. 1–11. Springer, Heidelberg (1994). https://doi.org/10.1007/3-540-48658-5_1
4. Hermelin, M., Nyberg, K.: Linear cryptanalysis using multiple linear approximations. IACR Cryptology ePrint Archive (2011)
5. Abadi, M., Andersen,D.G.: Learning to protect communications with adversarial neural cryptography. arXiv Cryptography and Security (2017)
6. Gohr, A.: Improving attacks on round-reduced Speck32/64 using deep learning. In: Boldyreva, A., Micciancio, D. (eds.) CRYPTO 2019. LNCS, vol. 11693, pp. 150–179. Springer, Cham (2019). https://doi.org/10.1007/978-3-030-26951-7_6
7. He, K., et al.: Deep residual learning for image recognition. In: Computer Vision and Pattern Recognition, pp. 770–778 (2016)
8. Gomez, A.N., et al.: Unsupervised cipher cracking using discrete GANs. arXiv: Learning (2018)
9. Gohr, A., Jacob, S., Schindler, W.: CHES 2018 side channel contest CTF - solution of the AES challenges. IACR Cryptology ePrint Archive (2019)
10. Lytvyn, V., Peleshchak, I., Peleshchak, R., Vysotska, V.: Information encryption based on the synthesis of a neural network and AES algorithm. In: 3rd International Conference on Advanced Information and Communications Technologies, pp. 447–450 (2019)
11. Coutinho, M., et al.: Learning perfectly secure cryptography to protect communications with adversarial neural cryptography. Sensors **18**(5), 1306 (2018)
12. Preishuber, M., et al.: Depreciating motivation and empirical security analysis of chaos-based image and video encryption. IEEE Trans. Inf. Forensics Secur. **13**(9), 2137–2150 (2018)
13. Greydanus, S.: Learning the enigma with recurrent neural networks. arXiv Neural and Evolutionary Computing (2017)

14. Paterson, K.G., Poettering, B., Schuldt, J.C.N.: Big bias hunting in amazonia: large-scale computation and exploitation of rc4 biases (invited paper). In: Sarkar, P., Iwata, T. (eds.) ASIACRYPT 2014. LNCS, vol. 8873, pp. 398–419. Springer, Heidelberg (2014). https://doi.org/10.1007/978-3-662-45611-8_21
15. Kingma, D.P., Ba, J.: Adam: a method for stochastic optimization. In: International Conference on Learning Representations (2015)

Detection by Attack: Detecting Adversarial Samples by Undercover Attack

Qifei Zhou[1], Rong Zhang[1], Bo Wu[2], Weiping Li[1(✉)], and Tong Mo[1]

[1] Peking University, Haidian District, Beijing, China
{qifeizhou,rzhangpku}@pku.edu.cn, {wpli,motong}@ss.pku.edu.cn
[2] MIT-IBM Watson AI Lab, Cambridge, MA, USA
bo.wu@ibm.com

Abstract. The safety of artificial intelligence systems has aroused great concern due to the vulnerability of deep neural networks. Studies show that malicious modifications to the inputs of a network classifier, can fool the classifier and lead to wrong predictions. These modified inputs are called adversarial samples. In order to resolve this challenge, this paper proposes a novel and effective framework called *Detection by Attack* (DBA) to detect adversarial samples by *Undercover Attack*. DBA works by converting the difficult adversarial detection problem into a simpler attack problem, which is inspired by the espionage technique. It appears to be attacking the system, but it is actually defending the system. Reviewing the literature shows that this paper is the first attempt to introduce a detection method that can effectively detect adversarial samples in both images and texts. Experimental results show that the DBA scheme yields state-of-the-art detection performances in both detector-unaware (95.66% detection accuracy on average) and detector-aware (2.10% attack success rate) scenarios. Furthermore, DBA is robust to the perturbation size and confidence of adversarial samples. The code is available at https://github.com/Mrzhouqifei/DBA.

Keywords: Artificial intelligence · Deep neural network · Detection by attack · Undercover attack · Adversarial sample

1 Introduction

Deep neural networks (DNNs) are vulnerable to adversarial samples [10,12,21]. Studies show that imperceptible perturbations to the inputs of a classifier can lead to incorrect predictions. This issue is more challenging in safety-critical applications such as autonomous driving and face payment. The first line in Fig. 1 illustrates how an adversarial sample makes neural network-based systems vulnerable. Human beings recognize each of the two images as a vehicle no-pass

---

Q. Zhou and R. Zhang—contribute equally to this paper.

© Springer Nature Switzerland AG 2020
L. Chen et al. (Eds.): ESORICS 2020, LNCS 12309, pp. 146–164, 2020.
https://doi.org/10.1007/978-3-030-59013-0_8

sign. The image x_o on the left is an ordinary image of the vehicle no-pass sign. However, the image on the right $x_o + \Delta x$ is crafted by adding tiny perturbations Δx to the original x_o that forces a particular DNN to classify it as a tree. Researchers have shown that these transformations are effective in the physical world [17]. More specifically, considering the vulnerability of DNNs, someone with ulterior motives can make autonomous-driving cars behave dangerously by designing this adversarial road sign.

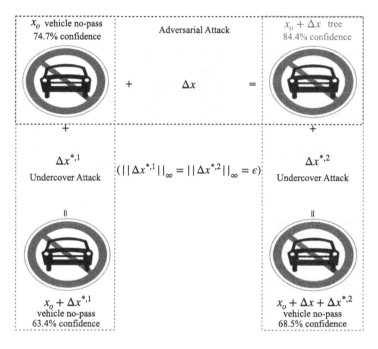

Fig. 1. The normal and adversarial images of the vehicle no-pass sign. After applied *Undercover Attack*, the predicted class of the adversarial sample $x_o + \Delta x$ has changed ("tree" → "vehicle no-pass"), while the normal sample x_o has not.

Considering the challenges in existing network schemes, this paper aims to detect adversarial samples from normal ones. A review of the literature shows that most previous studies have focused on analyzing the difference in dimensional distribution between normal and adversarial samples [8,13,19,20,28]. However, our method works by exploiting the vulnerability asymmetry between adversarial and normal samples, which indicates that adversarial samples are more vulnerable than normal ones. Therefore, if we attack an adversarial sample and a normal sample with the same ∞-norm perturbation ($||\Delta x^*||_\infty = \epsilon$), the disturbance brought to the prediction of the adversarial sample is higher than that of the normal sample. As shown in the two vertical columns in Fig. 1, after applied *Undercover Attack*, the predicted class of the adversarial sample $x_o + \Delta x$ has changed, while the normal sample x_o has not.

Detection by Attack (DBA) is designed to detect adversarial samples by leveraging the vulnerability asymmetry. In this paper, DBA focuses on applying *Undercover Attack* to distinguish whether the sample is adversarial. Although the features may be completely different in language tasks due to the finite set of words, DBA is also applicable. It is sufficient to attack the word embeddings, and we do not have to find the corresponding real words. The main contributions of this paper are summarized as follows:

1. A new direction is proposed to detect adversarial samples by converting the difficult detection problem into a simpler attack problem. Future research can protect the system by designing superb attack methods.
2. This paper reveals that the adversarial samples are more vulnerable than normal ones when they are attacked for the second time. DBA works by leveraging the vulnerability asymmetry and is robust to the perturbation size and confidence of adversarial samples.
3. It is demonstrated that DBA can be effectively applied to images and texts. Moreover, it does not rely on the knowledge of the attack mechanism, and performs well in both detector-unaware and detector-aware scenarios.

2   Background and Related Work

2.1   Adversarial Attack

The main goal of the attacker is to craft a sample that looks like a normal one. It may be modifying a few pixels in the input image, or changing a few words in the input text. These minor changes in the input can lead to a wrong prediction by the target model, while it remains correctly classified by human eyes. A significant number of adversarial attacks satisfying this goal have been proposed in recent years. Therefore, it is possible to select a wide range of well-known attacks in this paper, including the L_∞-bounded fast gradient sign method (FGSM) [10] and basic iterative method (BIM) [17], the L_0-bounded jacobian-based saliency map attack (JSMA) [22], and the L_2-bounded Carlini and Wagner attack (CW$_2$) [4] and Boundary Attack [3]. As for texts, the method proposed by Papernot et al. [23] is adopted in our paper, and it is named as Replace Attack.

2.2   Adversarial Defense

Defense on Images. The existence of adversarial samples has aroused great concern in academia. Researchers have tried to explain adversarial samples and proposed different schemes to defend against them effectively. Zheng et al. [30] proposed the boundary differential privacy (ϵ-BDP) as a solution to protect the system by obfuscating the prediction responses near the decision boundary. Moreover, some other direct defense techniques, including image compression or filtering [7,28], defensive distillation [24], and many defenses summarized as the gradient masking [21] have been proposed so far. However, most of these defenses can be totally or partially evaded by stronger attacks [1]. Due to the challenge of direct defense, many recent studies have turned to the detection of adversarial samples. Feinman et al. [8] claimed that the kernel density (KD) and Bayesian uncertainty (BU) of adversarial samples are different from the normal ones. Furthermore, the randomized methods have been employed in several studies [19,28] by introducing noise to smoothen the features. However, most detectors fail in the white box case, where the attacker is aware of the detector [5,15].

Defense on Texts. Since text data has discrete nature in the scenario of natural language processing (NLP), existing attack and defense methods cannot be directly applied to texts [29]. Rosenberg et al. [25] proposed the use of adversarial training, adversarial signatures, RNN ensemble, and defense SeqGAN to increase the robustness of the text classifier against adversarial samples. They showed that the adversarial training obtains the best defensive performance.

3 Detection by Attack

In this section, it is intended to introduce the DBA scheme to distinguish adversarial samples from normal ones. It is worth noting that since most defensive methods can be easily evaded by specifically designed attacks, the defense is much more difficult than attack. Therefore, the DBA scheme is proposed to solve the difficult defense problem by converting it into a simpler attack problem. The training process of the framework consists of two steps, as the following:

1. Injecting adversarial samples to train the classification model.
2. Training a simple multi-layer perceptron (MLP) classifier to judge whether the sample is adversarial.

Step 1 and step 2 correspond to Sect. 3.1 and Sect. 3.2, respectively. It should be noted that only the pipeline in step 2 is required in adversarial detection.

3.1 Adversarial Training with L_∞-bounded FGSM

The adversarial training with L_∞-bounded attack can significantly improve the performance of DBA. The adversarial sample $x_o + \Delta x$ injected into the classification model is generated through FGSM:

$$x_o + \Delta x = x_o + \epsilon \text{sign}(\nabla_{x_o} J(\theta, x_o, y_{\text{true}})) \tag{1}$$

where x_o, ϵ, θ, and y_{true} denote the corresponding original (normal) sample used to craft the adversarial sample, the parameter that determines the perturbation size in the gradient direction, the parameters of the model, and the correct label of x_o, respectively. The adversarial training objective can be described as:

$$\arg\min_\theta \sum_{(x_o,y)} \mathcal{L}(x_o, y; \theta) + \alpha \cdot \mathcal{L}(x_o + \Delta x, y, \epsilon; \theta) \tag{2}$$

where $\mathcal{L}$ and α denote the loss function for the task (e.g. cross-entropy), and the positive scalar which controls the intensity of adversarial training, respectively. Generally speaking, as α increases, the accuracy of adversarial samples will increase, while the accuracy of normal samples will decrease.

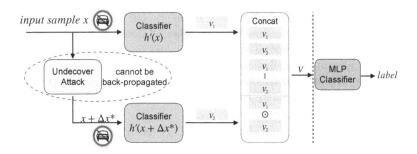

Fig. 2. The detection pipeline of DBA. It is only required to train the MLP to detect adversarial samples, and the classifier $h'(\cdot)$ should not be fine-tuned. Because the process of obtaining $x + \Delta x^*$ is an independent *Undercover Attack* that cannot be back-propagated.

3.2   Detecting via DBA

Figure 2 illustrates the detection pipeline of DBA. For an input x (x may be normal or adversarial), $x + \Delta x^*$ is initially obtained via *Undercover Attack* as follows:

$$x + \Delta x^* = x + \epsilon \operatorname{sign}(\nabla_x J(\theta, x, y_{\mathbf{pred}})) \tag{3}$$

Remark. The perturbation size ϵ is the same as that in adversarial training, and the reason is given in Corollary 2. The difference between FGSM and *Undercover Attack* is y, where y_{true} is replaced with $y_{\mathbf{pred}}$. It is worth noting that $y_{\mathbf{pred}}$ is the predicted class produced by the classifier $h(x)$ rather than the true class of the input x. This change is conducted for two reasons. Firstly, it is impossible to access the true class in the real world. Secondly, the primary purpose of DBA is to measure the vulnerability of the sample. In our framework, such vulnerability originates from the disturbance between the current hidden vector V_1 and the attacked hidden vector V_2. The form is as follows:

$$h(x) = \operatorname{Linear}\left(h'(x)\right), V_1 = h'(x), V_2 = h'(x + \Delta x^*) \tag{4}$$

$$V = [V_1; V_2; V_1 - V_2; V_1 \odot V_2] \tag{5}$$

where $h(\cdot) \in \mathbb{R}^k$ (k classes) and $h'(\cdot)$ denote the target classifier and the set of all layers except the last Linear layer in the classifier, respectively. Moreover, V_1 and V_2 are the corresponding hidden vectors of x and $x + \Delta x^*$, respectively. Then, the vector V in Eq. 5 is obtained to capture more information between V_1 and V_2 by referring to ESIM [6], and a simple MLP is trained to classify the input x as adversarial or normal:

$$label = \operatorname{MLP}(V), label = \begin{cases} +1, & \text{``adversarial''} \\ -1, & \text{``normal''} \end{cases} \tag{6}$$

3.3 Why DBA is Effective?

DBA works by leveraging the vulnerability asymmetry between adversarial and normal samples. After attacking a normal input x_1 and an adversarial input x_2 with the same ∞-norm perturbation ($||\Delta x_1^*||_\infty = ||\Delta x_2^*||_\infty = \epsilon$), the probability of $Q(x_1) \neq Q(x_1 + \Delta x_1^*)$ is lower than that of $Q(x_2) \neq Q(x_2 + \Delta x_2^*)$.

$$P(x)_j = \frac{\exp h(x)_j}{\sum_{i=1}^k \exp h(x)_i}, \quad Q(x) = \arg\max_j P(x)_j \tag{7}$$

Linearly Separable. The vulnerability asymmetry is investigated through the theorem analysis. Therefore, the case where normal samples and adversarial samples are linearly separable is initially considered.

$$f(x) = \langle w, x \rangle + b, \ label = \mathrm{sign} f(x) \tag{8}$$

The hyperplane $f(x) = 0$ is defined, which aims to separate adversarial samples ($label = +1$) from normal samples ($label = -1$). x_o denotes the corresponding original (normal) sample used to craft x if x is an adversarial input:

$$\mathrm{sign}\, f(x) = +1 \Rightarrow x = x_o + \Delta x, \delta < ||\Delta x||_\infty < \xi \tag{9}$$

where δ and ξ are the safe boundary and the maximum value of the adversarial perturbation, respectively. It is assumed that as long as δ is small enough, no adversarial sample could be found within the δ-norm ball of x_o. *Undercover Attack* aims at adding Δx^* to x and making $\mathrm{sign}\, f(x + \Delta x^*) \neq \mathrm{sign}\, f(x)$:

$$\text{if } x = x_o, \text{ then } \mathrm{sign}\, f(x + \Delta x^*) = \begin{cases} -1, & \text{if } ||\Delta x^*||_\infty < \delta \\ \mp 1, & \text{if } ||\Delta x^*||_\infty > \delta \end{cases} \tag{10}$$

$$\text{if } x = x_o + \Delta x, \text{ then } \mathrm{sign}\, f(x + \Delta x^*) = \pm 1$$

Theorem 1. *It is assumed that normal and adversarial samples each account for 50% in overall samples, and they are uniformly distributed in their corresponding regions. Moreover, r is the minimum detection accuracy of normal and adversarial samples. Considering the perturbation of Undercover Attack subject to $||\Delta x^*||_\infty \leq \delta$, then the following equation is obtained:*

$$\frac{1}{2} + \frac{\delta}{2\xi} < r < 1, \ r \in (\frac{1}{2}, 1) \tag{11}$$

Proof. For a normal input $x = x_o$, $x_o + \Delta x^*$ is obtained after applying *Undercover Attack*. Figure 3(a) illustrates that, since $||\Delta x^*||_\infty < \delta$, $x_o + \Delta x^{*,1}$ could be obtained instead of $x_o + \Delta x^{*,2}$, which means $\mathrm{sign}\, f(x_o) = \mathrm{sign}\, f(x_o + \Delta x^*) = -1$.
    For an adversarial input $x = x_o + \Delta x$, $x_o + \Delta x + \Delta x^*$ is obtained after applying *Undercover Attack*. The attacker aims at making $\mathrm{sign}\, f(x + \Delta x^*) \neq \mathrm{sign}\, f(x)$,

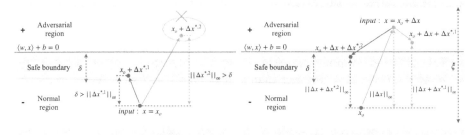

(a) Normal input sample   (b) Adversarial input sample

Fig. 3. *Undercover Attack* on normal and adversarial samples in the linearly separable case. With the constrains in Theorem 1, $x_o + \Delta x^{*,1}$ could be obtained instead of $x_o + \Delta x^{*,2}$ in (a), while both $x_o + \Delta x + \Delta x^{*,1}$ and $x_o + \Delta x + \Delta x^{*,2}$ could be obtained in (b). Therefore, input x satisfying sign $f(x + \Delta x^*) = $ sign $f(x)$ is regarded as "normal", and x satisfying sign $f(x + \Delta x^*) \neq $ sign $f(x)$ is regarded as "adversarial".

which means it will work in the direction to move x closer to the hyperplane or out of the adversarial region. This results in the following equation:

$$||\Delta x + \Delta x^*||_\infty < ||\Delta x||_\infty < \xi \tag{12}$$

Therefore, as shown in Fig. 3(b), both $x_o + \Delta x + \Delta x^{*,1}$ and $x_o + \Delta x + \Delta x^{*,2}$ could be obtained:

$$\text{sign } f(x_o + \Delta x + \Delta x^*) = \begin{cases} -1, & \text{if } ||\Delta x + \Delta x^*||_\infty \in (0, \delta) \\ \mp 1, & \text{if } ||\Delta x + \Delta x^*||_\infty \in (\delta, \xi) \end{cases} \tag{13}$$

After applying *Undercover Attack*, all the normal samples (50% of all) satisfy sign $f(x + \Delta x^*) = $ sign $f(x) = -1$. Based on the assumption of uniform distribution, at most $\frac{\xi - \delta}{\xi}$ adversarial samples satisfy sign $f(x + \Delta x^*) = $ sign $f(x) = +1$, and at least $\frac{\delta}{\xi}$ adversarial samples satisfy sign $f(x + \Delta x^*) \neq $ sign $f(x)$. We regard inputs satisfying sign $f(x + \Delta x^*) = $ sign $f(x)$ as normal samples, and inputs satisfying sign $f(x + \Delta x^*) \neq $ sign $f(x)$ as adversarial samples. Then Eq. 11 in Theorem 1 is proved. Moreover, the vector V in DBA contains more information than sign $f(\cdot)$, so it is reasonable to consider r as the minimum detection accuracy.

Corollary 1. *Suppose that the maximum value of the adversarial perturbation ξ approaches δ. Then, the minimum detection accuracy r will approach 1.*

$$\lim_{\xi \to \delta} r = \lim_{\xi \to \delta} \frac{1}{2} + \frac{1}{2} \cdot \frac{\delta}{\xi} = 1 \tag{14}$$

Corollary 1 indicates that if the perturbations of adversarial samples are smaller, the vulnerability asymmetry between normal and adversarial inputs will become more prominent. Moreover, since the strong attacks work by perturbing minimal pixels Δx, DBA becomes more effective when facing adversarial samples generated by stronger attack methods (e.g. CW_2).

Corollary 2. *Suppose that the training objective in Eq. 2 reaches the global opti-mum. Then, the following equation is obtained:*

$$\frac{1}{2} + \frac{1}{2} \cdot \frac{\epsilon}{\xi} < r < 1, \ r \in (\frac{1}{2}, 1) \tag{15}$$

Proof. If the training objective in Eq. 2 reaches the global optimum, then no adversarial sample could be found within the ϵ-norm ball of x_o:

$$\text{sign } f(x_o + \Delta x^*) = \text{sign } f(x_o) = -1, \ ||\Delta x^*||_\infty = \epsilon \le \delta \tag{16}$$

$$\frac{1}{2} + \frac{1}{2} \cdot \frac{\epsilon}{\xi} \le \frac{1}{2} + \frac{1}{2} \cdot \frac{\delta}{\xi} < r < 1, \ r \in (\frac{1}{2}, 1) \tag{17}$$

Corollary 2 demonstrates the necessity of ensuring ϵ in adversarial training is the same as that in *Undercover Attack*. If no adversarial sample could be found within the ϵ-norm ball of x_o, then $\epsilon \to \delta$ and the minimum detection accuracy r can be determined by ϵ. Theoretically, DBA performs better with larger ϵ. However, an excessive ϵ will decrease the accuracy of the original classifier on normal samples.

Non-linearly Separable. For the general setting, if the normal and adversarial samples are separable in some feature space Φ, the hyperplane can be written as:

$$f(x) = \langle w, \Phi(x) \rangle + b \tag{18}$$

Therefore, it is straightforward to lift the analysis of Theorem 1 to this setting.

Limitations. Although DBA can work well in ideal conditions, there are two limitations in practical applications. On the one hand, when the samples are non-linearly separable, such analysis requires inputs to be initially transformed into a more complex feature space Φ. However, such a feature space is not easy to find, so we do not perform the transformation in this paper. On the other hand, *Undercover Attack* in our paper can guarantee Eq. 12 in binary classification, while it may fail in multi-class classification.

Nevertheless, we observe empirically through experiments that DBA is still effective even with the two limitations. Firstly, the experiments in Sect. 4.1 shows that *Undercover Attack* can capture the vulnerability asymmetry well in practical applications. Secondly, another possible reason is that the vector V in DBA can capture more information than sign $f(\cdot)$, and the theoretical proof is an interesting topic for future research.

4   Experiments

In order to inspect the effectiveness of DBA, results are presented according to the detectability of adversarial samples on some well-known datasets, including

MNIST and CIFAR10 on images, and IMDB and QQP on texts. Normal and adversarial samples each account for 50% in the training and test sets. The test sets consist of 4,500 MNIST digits, 4,500 CIFAR10 images, 1,000 IMDB sequences, and 1,000 QQP sequence pairs. Moreover, in the detector-unaware scenario, four attack techniques (FGSM, BIM, JSMA, and CW_2) are employed on images, and Replace Attack is employed on texts. Additionally, Boundary Attack is employed in the detector-aware scenario. It should be noted that all the test samples and the latter five attack techniques (BIM, JSMA, CW_2, Replace Attack, and Boundary Attack) are not involved in the design phase of DBA.

Classifier Setup. The models used in the above classification tasks are briefly described as follows:

- **MNIST.** A 5-layer convolutional network is utilized, which achieves 99.2% accuracy. The ϵ in adversarial training and *Undercover Attack* is set to 0.1.
- **CIFAR10.** The 18-layer PreActResNet [14] is used as the classifier, which reports 95.49% accuracy. The ϵ is set to 4/255.
- **Large movie review dataset (IMDB).** This dataset[1] contains movie reviews along with their associated binary sentiment polarity labels. It serves as a benchmark for the sentiment classification. The bidirectional LSTM is utilized, which achieves 89.24% accuracy. Prior to being fed into the network, the maximum length of the sentence is set to 500, and sentences exceeding this length will be truncated. Moreover, the ϵ is set to 0.001.
- **Quora question pairs (QQP).** This dataset[2] consists of question pairs, and each of them is annotated with a binary value indicating whether the two questions are duplicate or not. It serves as a benchmark for paraphrase identification. ESIM [6] is utilized, which achieves 86.0% accuracy. Moreover, the ϵ is set to 0.001.

It should be noted that DBA achieves competitive performance with α in Eq. 2 ranges from 0.5 to 1.0, and it is set to 0.8 in the adversarial training of the following experiments.

Evaluation Metrics. In order to evaluate the effectiveness of DBA, the recall, precision, F1 score, and accuracy are adopted to quantify the detection performance.

$$Recall = \frac{TP}{TP + FN}, Precision = \frac{TP}{TP + FP} \tag{19}$$

$$F1 = \frac{2 \cdot Recall \cdot Presion}{Recall + Precision}, Accuracy = \frac{TP + TN}{TP + TN + FP + FN} \tag{20}$$

where TP, TN, FN, and FP denote the number of correctly detected adversarial samples (true positive), the number of correctly detected normal samples

---

[1] https://www.kaggle.com/iarunava/imdb-movie-reviews-dataset.
[2] https://data.quora.com/First-Quora-Dataset-Release-Question-Pairs.

(true negative), the number of adversarial samples that are detected as normal ones (false negative), and the number of normal samples that are detected as adversarial ones (false positive), respectively.

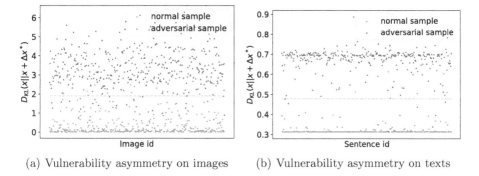

(a) Vulnerability asymmetry on images   (b) Vulnerability asymmetry on texts

Fig. 4. The distribution of D_{KL} on images and texts. MNIST and IMDB are selected as example datasets, and the results on other datasets of images/texts are similar. The blue dots and red triangles represent normal and adversarial samples, respectively. (Color figure online)

4.1 Vulnerability Asymmetry Analysis

In this section, we will experimentally study the vulnerability asymmetry between adversarial and normal samples when facing *Undercover Attack*. The Kullback–Leibler divergence [27] $D_{KL}(x \| x + \Delta x^*)$ is adopted to measure the disturbances brought to the softmax prediction $P(x)$:

$$D_{KL}(x \| x + \Delta x^*) = \sum_{i=1}^{k} P(x)_i \log \left(\frac{P(x)_i}{P(x + \Delta x^*)_i} \right) \tag{21}$$

where k is the class number of the classification task. Figure 4 shows the distribution of D_{KL} for normal and adversarial samples. It is observed that the D_{KL} of adversarial samples are significantly larger than that of normal samples on both images and texts.

4.2 Detecting in Detector-Unaware Scenario

Detecting FGSM Samples. Goodfellow et al. [10] hypothesized that adversarial samples could be found using only a linear approximation of the target model. They introduced the fast gradient sign method to craft adversarial samples efficiently.

$$x_o + \Delta x = x_o + \epsilon \text{sign}(\nabla_{x_o} J(\theta, x_o, y_{\text{true}})) \tag{22}$$

Table 1. Detection results of DBA. #F denotes the number of inputs that cannot be perturbed to adversarial ones. The **bold line** is used to compare with other detectors in Sect. 4.4.

Dataset	Attack	#F	TP	FN	FP	TN	Recall	Precision	F1	Accuracy
MNIST	FGSM ($\epsilon = 0.10$)	3730	764	6	34	736	99.22%	95.74%	97.45%	97.40%
	FGSM ($\epsilon = 0.15$)	2510	1955	35	75	1915	98.24%	96.31%	97.26%	97.24%
	FGSM ($\epsilon = 0.20$)	1420	3029	51	322	2758	98.34%	90.39%	94.20%	93.94%
	BIM ($\epsilon = 0.10$)	3463	1029	8	26	1011	99.23%	97.54%	98.37%	98.36%
	BIM ($\epsilon = 0.15$)	1416	3066	18	158	2926	99.42%	95.10%	97.21%	97.15%
	BIM ($\epsilon = 0.20$)	304	4154	42	383	3813	99.00%	91.56%	95.13%	94.94%
	JSMA ($\gamma = 0.1$)	467	524	9	20	513	98.31%	96.32%	97.31%	97.28%
	JSMA ($\gamma = 0.2$)	340	654	6	17	643	99.09%	97.47%	98.27%	98.26%
	JSMA ($\gamma = 0.3$)	286	703	11	21	693	98.46%	97.10%	97.77%	97.76%
	CW$_2$ (k = 0.0)	**0**	**993**	**7**	**2**	**998**	**99.30%**	**99.80%**	**99.55%**	**99.55%**
	CW$_2$ ($k = 1.0$)	0	991	9	5	995	99.10%	99.50%	99.30%	99.30%
	CW$_2$ ($k = 2.0$)	0	984	16	8	992	98.40%	99.19%	98.80%	98.80%
CIFAR10	FGSM ($\epsilon = 4/255$)	3862	624	14	43	595	97.81%	93.55%	95.63%	95.53%
	FGSM ($\epsilon = 6/255$)	3222	1267	11	103	1175	99.14%	92.48%	95.69%	95.54%
	FGSM ($\epsilon = 8/255$)	2563	1918	19	148	1789	99.02%	92.84%	95.83%	95.69%
	BIM ($\epsilon = 4/255$)	1733	2720	47	234	2533	98.30%	92.08%	95.09%	94.92%
	BIM ($\epsilon = 6/255$)	936	3464	100	384	3180	97.19%	90.02%	93.47%	93.21%
	BIM ($\epsilon = 8/255$)	391	3921	188	772	3337	95.42%	83.55%	89.09%	88.32%
	JSMA ($\gamma = 0.1$)	368	630	2	9	623	99.68%	98.59%	99.13%	99.13%
	JSMA ($\gamma = 0.2$)	340	658	2	13	647	99.70%	98.06%	98.87%	98.86%
	JSMA ($\gamma = 0.3$)	327	666	7	18	655	98.96%	97.37%	98.16%	98.14%
	CW$_2$ ($k = 0.0$)	0	997	3	8	992	99.70%	99.20%	99.45%	99.45%
	CW$_2$ ($k = 1.0$)	0	997	3	9	991	99.70%	99.11%	99.40%	99.40%
	CW$_2$ ($k = 2.0$)	0	991	9	19	981	99.10%	98.12%	98.61%	98.60%
IMDB	Replace ($w = 4$)	668	325	7	6	326	97.89%	98.19%	98.04%	98.04%
	Replace ($w = 8$)	431	563	6	16	553	98.95%	97.24%	98.08%	98.07%
	Replace ($w = 16$)	205	791	4	29	766	99.50%	96.46%	97.96%	97.92%
QQP	Replace ($w = 4$)	668	324	8	11	321	97.59%	96.72%	97.15%	97.14%
	Replace ($w = 8$)	431	562	7	26	543	98.77%	95.58%	97.15%	97.10%
	Replace ($w = 16$)	205	787	8	42	753	98.99%	94.93%	96.92%	96.86%
Total/Average		30286	41051	663	2961	38753	98.41%	93.27%	95.77%	95.66%

The FGSM works by linearizing the loss function in the L_∞ neighborhood of the original image x_o. Specifically, ϵ is an important and adjustable parameter. The larger the ϵ is, the more adversarial samples can be successfully crafted. However, an excessive ϵ is likely to introduce noticeable perturbation and be easily spotted by a human. In order to evaluate the capability of DBA for detecting adversarial samples with different perturbation sizes, the adversarial samples are crafted with some acceptable ϵ values. It is set from 0.1 to 0.2 for MNIST and 4/255 to 8/255 for CIFAR10. Table 1 shows that DBA achieves an average detection accuracy of 96.19% on MNIST and 95.59% on CIFAR10.

Detecting BIM Samples. Kurakin et al. [17] applied the FGSM multiple times with a small perturbation size β, called the basic iterative method. This method can be mathematically expressed as follows:

$$\text{iter} = \min(255\epsilon + 4, 1.25 \cdot 255\epsilon), \quad x_o + \Delta x_n := x_n^{\text{adv}} \tag{23}$$

$$x_0^{\text{adv}} = x_o, \quad x_n^{\text{adv}} = \text{Clip}_{x_o, \epsilon}\{x_{n-1}^{\text{adv}} + \beta \text{sign}(\nabla_x J(\theta, x_{n-1}^{\text{adv}}, y_{\text{true}}))\} \tag{24}$$

In addition to ϵ, iter is another hyperparameter that influences the attack performance. Generally speaking, the larger the iter is, the more adversarial samples can be successfully crafted. The iter used in Table 1 is introduced in Eq. 23, as [17] suggested. Moreover, $\text{Clip}_{x_o, \epsilon}(\cdot)$ performs per-pixel clipping of the original image x_o. Subsequently, x_n^{adv} will be in the L_∞ ϵ-neighborhood of the original image. The setting of ϵ is the same as that in FGSM, and the average detection accuracy of DBA is 96.82% on MNIST and 92.15% on CIFAR10. They are lower than the accuracies in FGSM due to the iterative characteristic.

Detecting JSMA Samples. The above methods (FGSM and BIM) modify each pixel within small ϵ-ball perturbation. However, Papernot et al. [22] introduced the Jacobian-based saliency map attack, which works by modifying a limited number of input pixels with relatively large perturbations. The JSMA iteratively perturbs pixels that have high saliency scores S:

$$S(x, t)[i] = \begin{cases} 0, & \text{if } \frac{\partial F_t(x)}{\partial x_i} < 0 \text{ or } \Sigma_{j \neq t} \frac{\partial F_j(x)}{\partial x_i} > 0 \\ (\frac{\partial F_t(x)}{\partial x_i})|\Sigma_{j \neq t} \frac{\partial F_j(x)}{\partial x_i}|, & \text{otherwise} \end{cases} \tag{25}$$

In order to achieve a target class t, $F_t(x)$ must increase, while the probabilities of all other classes $\Sigma_{j \neq t} \frac{\partial F_j(x)}{\partial x_i}$ should decrease. The maximum number of iterations is defined as follows:

$$\text{max\_iter} = \frac{size \cdot size \cdot \gamma}{2 \cdot 100} \tag{26}$$

where $size$ and γ refer to the image size and the maximum distortion of the image, respectively. Moreover, JSMA is more expensive than other attack techniques. Therefore, the last $1,000$ MNIST digits and CIFAR10 images are selected in our experiments. The average detection accuracy with γ from 0.1 to 0.3 is 97.77% on MNIST and 98.71% on CIFAR10. It amounts that DBA is still effective when faced with the L_0-bounded attack.

Detecting CW$_2$ Samples. Carlini et al. [4] introduced an optimized attack framework that passed a range of defenses. They designed a loss function with smaller values on adversarial samples and higher values on normal samples, which resulted in three kinds of attacks, including an L_∞ attack, an L_0 attack, and an L_2 attack. Specifically, they achieved the strongest L_2 attack, which is considered in this paper with the following loss function:

$$\text{minimize } ||\Delta x||_2^2 + c \cdot g(x_o + \Delta x) \tag{27}$$

where $g(\cdot)$ depends on the best objective function found in the previous stages:

$$g(x) = \max\{\max\{Z(x)_i : i \neq t\} - Z(x)_t, -k\} \tag{28}$$

where k is a parameter to control the misclassification confidence. Adversarial samples can be crafted with high confidence by increasing k. In our experiments, k is set from 0.0 to 2.0.

Among the four attack techniques in the detector-unaware scenario, CW_2 is the strongest one. It is an optimization-based algorithm, which can seek out as small as possible perturbations. The #F column of Table 1 demonstrates that CW_2 can craft adversarial samples with 100% success rates. Similar to JSMA, CW_2 is computationally expensive. Therefore, the last 1,000 samples (as [19] do) of MNIST and CIFAR10 are selected. Table 1 shows that our method yields excellent detection performance with an average accuracy of 99.22% on MNIST and 99.15% on CIFAR10. It demonstrates that the detection ability of DBA for stronger attacks is better than weaker attacks, which is consistent with the previous intuition in Corollary 1.

Detecting Replace Attack Samples. Adversarial texts are usually generated by adding, deleting, or replacing words in the sentences. Papernot et al. [23] showed that the above algorithms for crafting adversarial samples misclassified by feed-forward neural networks could be applied to recurrent neural networks. However, due to the finite set of words, these methods cannot be applied to texts directly. Since a real word corresponding to the modified word embedding may not be found, the word embedding cannot be modified casually. Therefore, they followed a heuristic procedure to solve the problem. They iteratively found a word z in the dictionary that the sign of the difference between the embedding of z and the original word is closest to $\text{sign}(J_f(x)[i, f(x)])$. In our experiments, the replacement dictionary of Replace Attack consists of 50 most common words. w is the hyperparameter that controls the number of replaced words, which is set to 4, 8, and 16 in our experiments. The two-step training processes are the same as those on images. DBA can achieve an average detection accuracy of 98.01% on IMDB and 97.03% on QQP.

Detecting Without Adversarial Training. In Corollary 2, the importance of adversarial training is emphasized, and it is investigated through experiments in this part. Table 2 shows the detection results of DBA without adversarial training. In comparison with Table 1, it is observed that the classifiers are more robust to attacks after adversarial training (the numbers in column #F of Table 2 are smaller than that of Table 1). Moreover, the evaluation metrics (recall, precision, F1 score, and accuracy) are all improved by adversarial training.

4.3   Detecting in Detector-Aware Scenario

Finally, DBA is evaluated in a setting where the attacker is fully aware of the detector. DBA is different from the detectors in [5] because the parameters of the latter detectors can be optimized by the attacker. However, DBA involves an independent *Undercover Attack* to produce the hidden vector V, and the behavior of *Undercover Attack* cannot be changed or optimized. One possible

Table 2. Detection results of DBA without adversarial training.

Dataset	Attack	#F	TP	FN	FP	TN	Recall	Precision	F1	Accuracy
MNIST	FGSM ($\epsilon = 0.10$)	3092	1309	99	194	1214	92.97%	87.09%	89.93%	89.60%
	BIM ($\epsilon = 0.10$)	2433	1943	124	247	1820	94.00%	88.72%	91.28%	91.03%
	JSMA ($\gamma = 0.1$)	421	525	54	103	476	90.67%	83.60%	86.99%	86.44%
	CW$_2$ ($k = 0.0$)	0	981	19	10	990	98.10%	98.99%	98.54%	98.55%
CIFAR10	FGSM ($\epsilon = 4/255$)	2135	1820	545	436	1929	76.96%	80.67%	78.77%	79.26%
	BIM ($\epsilon = 4/255$)	286	3169	1045	1251	2963	75.20%	71.70%	73.41%	72.76%
	JSMA ($\gamma = 0.1$)	285	578	137	27	688	80.84%	95.54%	87.58%	88.53%
	CW$_2$ ($k = 0.0$)	0	836	164	18	982	83.60%	97.89%	90.18%	90.90%
IMDB	Replace ($w = 4$)	561	429	10	27	412	97.72%	94.08%	95.87%	95.79%
QQP	Replace ($w = 4$)	561	421	18	42	397	95.90%	90.93%	93.35%	93.17%
Total/Average		9774	12011	2215	2355	11871	84.43%	83.61%	84.02%	83.94%

way to bypass DBA is to generate new adversarial samples iteratively. After generating a new adversarial sample, it will be tested on DBA to judge whether it can fool DBA. If not, we will continue to craft new adversarial samples until we find a sample that can bypass DBA or reach the iteration limit.

The decision-based Boundary Attack [3] is a powerful attack that can meet our requirements. The algorithm is initialized from a point that is already adversarial, then performs a random walk along the boundary between the adversarial and non-adversarial region. Therefore, it stays in the adversarial region, and the distance towards the target image decreases. In the n-th step, the perturbation η^n is drawn from a maximum entropy distribution, subject to the following constraint:

$$x_o + \Delta x_n := x_n^{adv}, \ ||x_o - x_{n-1}^{adv}||_2^2 - ||x_o - x_{n-1}^{adv} - \eta^n||_2^2 = \lambda \cdot ||x_o - x_{n-1}^{adv}||_2^2 \quad (29)$$

However, it cannot be adopted to texts. Therefore, it is only tested on MNIST and CIFAR10. The results turn out that the success rate of Boundary Attack drops from 100% to 2.1% on MNIST and from 100% to 1.9% on CIFAR10 after incorporating DBA. In other words, if the attacker wants to bypass DBA, then it cannot find an adversarial sample in most cases (Table 3).

4.4   DBA vs. Other Detectors

In this paper, we follow the methodology of Liang et al. [19], and leverage their result to compare our method with related ones in the detector-unaware and detector-aware scenarios. We adopt the same configurations as [5, 19], i.e., using the default k value (0.0) to generate CW$_2$ samples. The detection results of our method are presented in Table 1 (**bold line**). DBA can achieve a high recall rate of 99.30% and a low false positive rate of 0.20%. In the detector-aware scenario, DBA can remarkably downgrade the attack success rate from 67.37% to 2.10%. Compared with the existing methods, we can conclude that our method outperforms them in both the detector-unaware and detector-aware scenarios.

Table 3. DBA vs. other detectors. A higher detection recall is better in the detector-unaware scenario, while a lower attack success rate is better in the detector-aware scenario.

Method	Detector-unaware	Detector-aware
	Detection recall	Attack success rate
Network Uncertainty [8]	75.00%	98.00%
3 × 3 Filter [18]	80.00%	100%
KDE [8]	–	100%
PCA [16]	–	100%
Dimensionality Reduction [2]	97.00%	100%
Adversarial Training [9]	98.00%	100%
Adversarial Retraining [11]	98.50%	100%
Adaptive Noise Reduction [19]	98.89%	67.37%
Defense-GAN [26]	98.90%	45.00%
DBA	**99.30%**	**2.10%**

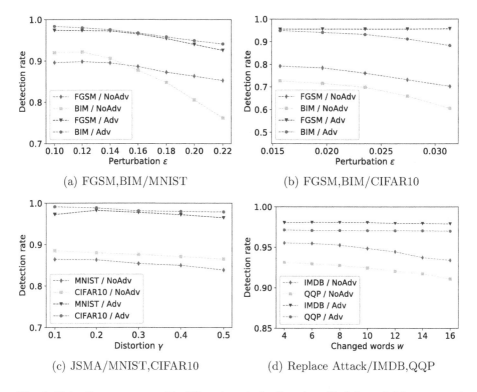

(a) FGSM,BIM/MNIST

(b) FGSM,BIM/CIFAR10

(c) JSMA/MNIST,CIFAR10

(d) Replace Attack/IMDB,QQP

Fig. 5. Detection accuracy with different perturbation sizes. NoAdv and Adv represent "without adversarial training" and "with adversarial training", respectively.

4.5   Impact of Perturbation Size and Confidence

Theorem 1 indicates that the detection accuracy increases with smaller adversarial perturbation. Since the four attacks (FGSM, BIM, JSMA, and Replace Attack) can control the perturbation size easily by adjusting their hyperparameters, the impact of perturbation size based on the four attacks is investigated in Fig. 5. The results show that as the perturbation size increases, the detection accuracy decreases. In particular, FGSM and BIM are L_∞-bounded attacks, which directly impact the ∞-norm perturbation as we adopted in DBA. Therefore, DBA is more sensitive to the perturbation ϵ of FGSM and BIM. However, DBA is more robust to the increase of perturbation size with the cooperation of adversarial training.

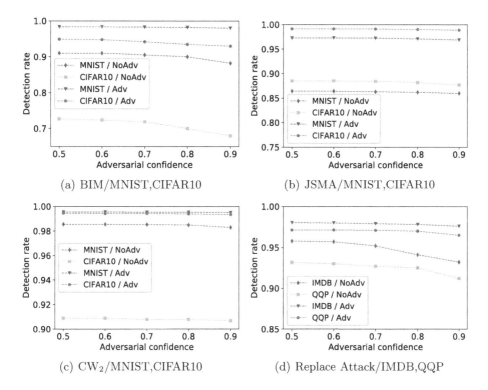

Fig. 6. Detection accuracy with different confidences. NoAdv and Adv represent "without adversarial training" and "with adversarial training", respectively.

Another essential issue is whether DBA works well on high-confidence adversarial samples. The impact of confidence is investigated on BIM, JSMA, CW_2, and Replace Attack by increasing the number of iterations until the confidence of the target adversarial class subject to:

$$P(x + \Delta x)_{target} > confidence, \ confidence \in [0.5, 1) \qquad (30)$$

Figure 6 shows that DBA is more robust to adversarial confidence than perturbation size. Especially for CW_2, the detection accuracy is always at a high level. The results prove that the core factor that affects the performance of DBA is the perturbation size (especially ∞-norm perturbation) rather than confidence.

5   Conclusion

This paper points a new direction for detecting adversarial samples by converging the detection problem into an attack problem. We propose an effective method DBA to detect adversarial samples crafted by various attacks on both images and texts. Furthermore, the reasons why DBA is effective are analyzed through the theorem and corollaries. Compared with the existing detection methods, DBA performs better in both the detector-unaware and detector-aware scenarios.

If someone wants to bypass DBA, it is required to generate a sample that can fool the model and be robust to *Undercover Attack*. However, it is difficult to make an adversarial sample robust to *Undercover Attack*. Since an adversarial sample is generated from a normal x_o, it is inherently vulnerable. At least one attack method is to roll back to the original x_o, which is a successful attack for the adversarial sample.

In future work, we will mainly conduct research from two aspects. On the one hand, we will try to overcome the two limitations introduced in Sect. 3.3. On the other hand, it is planned to improve the performance of DBA by adopting other attack forms, such as L_0 and L_2 attacks.

Acknowledgements. This work is supported by the the the National Key Research and Development Program of China (2017YFC0803609, 2017YFB1400401 and 2016YFB0801104).

References

1. Athalye, A., Carlini, N., Wagner, D.A.: Obfuscated gradients give a false sense of security: circumventing defenses to adversarial examples. In: International Conference on Machine Learning, pp. 274–283 (2018)
2. Bhagoji, A.N., Cullina, D., Mittal, P.: Dimensionality reduction as a defense against evasion attacks on machine learning classifiers. arXiv preprint arXiv:1704.02654 (2017)
3. Brendel, W., Rauber, J., Bethge, M.: Decision-based adversarial attacks: reliable attacks against black-box machine learning models. arXiv preprint arXiv:1712.04248 (2017)
4. Carlini, N., Wagner, D.: Towards evaluating the robustness of neural networks (2016)
5. Carlini, N., Wagner, D.A.: Adversarial examples are not easily detected: bypassing ten detection methods. arXiv Learning, pp. 3–14 (2017)
6. Chen, Q., Zhu, X., Ling, Z.H., Wei, S., Jiang, H., Inkpen, D.: Enhanced lstm for natural language inference. In: Proceedings of the 55th Annual Meeting of the Association for Computational Linguistics (Volume 1: Long Papers), pp. 1657–1668 (2017)

7. Das, N., et al.: Keeping the bad guys out: Protecting and vaccinating deep learning with jpeg compression. arXiv Computer Vision and Pattern Recognition (2017)

8. Feinman, R., Curtin, R.R., Shintre, S., Gardner, A.B.: Detecting adversarial samples from artifacts. arXiv Machine Learning (2017)

9. Gong, Z., Wang, W., Ku, W.S.: Adversarial and clean data are not twins. arXiv preprint arXiv:1704.04960 (2017)

10. Goodfellow, I.J., Shlens, J., Szegedy, C.: Explaining and harnessing adversarial examples. Comput. Sci. (2014)

11. Grosse, K., Manoharan, P., Papernot, N., Backes, M., McDaniel, P.: On the (statistical) detection of adversarial examples. arXiv preprint arXiv:1702.06280 (2017)

12. Guo, C., Gardner, J.R., You, Y., Wilson, A.G., Weinberger, K.Q.: Simple black-box adversarial attacks. arXiv preprint arXiv:1905.07121 (2019)

13. Guo, F., et al.: Detecting adversarial examples via prediction difference for deep neural networks. Inf. Sci. **501**, 182–192 (2019)

14. He, K., Zhang, X., Ren, S., Sun, J.: Identity mappings in deep residual networks. In: Leibe, B., Matas, J., Sebe, N., Welling, M. (eds.) ECCV 2016. LNCS, vol. 9908, pp. 630–645. Springer, Cham (2016). https://doi.org/10.1007/978-3-319-46493-0_38

15. He, W., Wei, J., Chen, X., Carlini, N., Song, D.: Adversarial example defenses: ensembles of weak defenses are not strong (2017)

16. Hendrycks, D., Gimpel, K.: Early methods for detecting adversarial images. arXiv preprint arXiv:1608.00530 (2016)

17. Kurakin, A., Goodfellow, I., Bengio, S.: Adversarial examples in the physical world (2016)

18. Li, X., Li, F.: Adversarial examples detection in deep networks with convolutional filter statistics. In: Proceedings of the IEEE International Conference on Computer Vision, pp. 5764–5772 (2017)

19. Liang, B., Li, H., Su, M., Li, X., Shi, W., Wang, X.: Detecting adversarial image examples in deep neural networks with adaptive noise reduction. IEEE Trans. Dependable Secure Comput. (2018)

20. Ma, X., et al.: Characterizing adversarial subspaces using local intrinsic dimensionality. In: International Conference on Learning Representations (2018)

21. Papernot, N., Mcdaniel, P., Goodfellow, I.: Transferability in machine learning: from phenomena to black-box attacks using adversarial samples (2016)

22. Papernot, N., Mcdaniel, P.D., Jha, S., Fredrikson, M., Celik, Z.B., Swami, A.: The limitations of deep learning in adversarial settings. In: IEEE European Symposium on Security and Privacy, pp. 372–387 (2016)

23. Papernot, N., Mcdaniel, P.D., Swami, A., Harang, R.E.: Crafting adversarial input sequences for recurrent neural networks. In: Military Communications Conference, pp. 49–54 (2016)

24. Papernot, N., Mcdaniel, P.D., Wu, X., Jha, S., Swami, A.: Distillation as a defense to adversarial perturbations against deep neural networks. In: IEEE Symposium on Security and Privacy, pp. 582–597 (2016)

25. Rosenberg, I., Shabtai, A., Elovici, Y., Rokach, L.: Defense methods against adversarial examples for recurrent neural networks (2019)

26. Samangouei, P., Kabkab, M., Chellappa, R.: Defense-GAN: protecting classifiers against adversarial attacks using generative models. In: International Conference on Learning Representations (2018)

27. Van Erven, T., Harremos, P.: Rényi divergence and kullback-leibler divergence. IEEE Trans. Inf. Theory **60**(7), 3797–3820 (2014)

28. Xu, W., Evans, D., Qi, Y.: Feature squeezing: detecting adversarial examples in deep neural networks. In: Network and Distributed System Security Symposium (2018)
29. Zhang, W.E., Sheng, Q.Z., Alhazmi, A., Li, C.: Adversarial attacks on deep learning models in natural language processing: a survey (2019)
30. Zheng, H., Ye, Q., Hu, H., Fang, C., Shi, J.: BDPL: a boundary differentially private layer against machine learning model extraction attacks. In: Sako, K., Schneider, S., Ryan, P.Y.A. (eds.) ESORICS 2019. LNCS, vol. 11735, pp. 66–83. Springer, Cham (2019). https://doi.org/10.1007/978-3-030-29959-0_4

Big Enough to Care Not Enough to Scare! Crawling to Attack Recommender Systems

Fabio Aiolli[1], Mauro Conti[1], Stjepan Picek[2], and Mirko Polato[1(✉)]

[1] Department of Mathematics, University of Padova, Padua, Italy
{aiolli,conti,mpolato}@math.unipd.it
[2] Delft University of Technology, Delft, The Netherlands
s.picek@tudelft.nl

Abstract. Online recommendation services, such as e-commerce sites, rely on a vast amount of knowledge about users/items that represent an invaluable resource. Part of this acquired knowledge is public and can be accessed by anyone through the Internet. Unfortunately, that same knowledge can be used by competitors or malicious users. A large body of research proposes methods to attack recommender systems, but most of these works assume that the attacker knows or can easily access the rating matrix. In practice, this information is not directly accessible, but can only be gathered via crawling.

Considering such real-life limitations, in this paper, we assess the impact of different crawling approaches when attacking a recommendation service. From the crawled information, we mount different shilling attacks. We determine the value of the collected knowledge through the reconstruction of the user/item neighborhood. Our results show that while crawling can indeed bring knowledge to the attacker (up to 65% of neighborhood reconstruction), this will not be enough to mount a successful shilling attack in practice.

Keywords: Recommender systems · Security · Crawling · Shilling attack · Collaborative filtering

1 Introduction

With the advent of the Internet, many companies base large parts of their business on the knowledge they gather online and over a long period. This is particularly evident on platforms where users generate almost all the content. Let us take, for example, e-commerce sites like amazon.com. Products are added by users who want to sell them, while buyers' profiles are created by those users who buy on the web site. Every type of interaction between users and the e-commerce web pages can potentially be monitored and stored to perform analysis for the marketing or for improving the provided service. Recommendation

© Springer Nature Switzerland AG 2020
L. Chen et al. (Eds.): ESORICS 2020, LNCS 12309, pp. 165–184, 2020.
https://doi.org/10.1007/978-3-030-59013-0_9

engines, mostly known as Recommender Systems (RSs), are one of these services offered by companies to help users in finding what they want/like [10,13,25,30].

Most of the state-of-the-art recommendation algorithms are based on the concept that similar users tend to be interested in similar products (in the rest of this paper, we will use the terms item and product interchangeably), for some notion of similarity. The computation of this similarity often relies on the history of the purchases/rates (interactions in general) of the users with items. This approach is known as collaborative filtering (CF). To get reliable similarities, and knowledge in general, collecting as much information about the past users' behavior is crucial. Famous and successful companies (e.g.., Amazon [25], Pinterest [13], or Netflix [10]) base their recommendation on information about the users-items interaction collected through the years among millions of users.

The collected knowledge about users is a valuable resource for the companies and must be kept safe. However, giving the nature of such e-services, part of this knowledge is public and can be accessed by anyone who has an Internet connection. For instance, ratings and reviews of a product, the user profile, and his/her reviews' history, and product details are usually public. Additionally, other forms of aggregated information may be publicly available, such as the total number of reviews or an item's average rating. Even though public information is only a fraction of the whole amount of knowledge owned by the service provider, competitors can leverage it to improve their services. Potentially, a competitor can design a way to collect as much public information as possible at almost zero cost, and then use such "stolen" knowledge. In an ideal case, this scenario could represent a substantial competitive advantage.

In this paper, we investigate the feasibility of such an attack. Specifically, we design a straightforward and almost cost-free attack pipeline analyzing in what conditions it can be potentially successful and to which extent. We focus our analysis on the computation of the similarity between users/items as a measure of success. The employed similarities, namely Pearson's correlation and cosine similarity, are standard indices used in RSs [21,32]. Our research particularly stresses the data collection phase, which is often overlooked or given for granted by most of the literature about attacks on RSs [8,26], i.e., they assume knowing the full user-item rating matrix.

Since their early days, recommender systems have been put to the test by various types of attacks. Among all the proposed attacks against RSs, the profile injection attack (also known as the shilling attack) is undoubtedly the most discussed one. As the name suggests, the profile injection attack seeks to mislead the RS by injecting well crafted fake users into the system. The type of damage provoked by fake user profiles depends on the attacker's goal. There are three common goals: (i) increase the popularity of some targeted items (push attack); (ii) decrease the popularity of some targeted items (nuke attack); (iii) deterioration of the performance of the system. Previous works have shown that the more the knowledge used by the attacker, the higher the rate of success [4].

In this paper, we aim to (partially) fill the gap between the ideal threat and the feasibility of an attack on a recommendation service. To this end, we examine different crawling strategies to assess the most efficient ones in gathering information. We also propose a crawling strategy, dubbed backlink$_{++}$, which showed to be highly effective. Additionally, we study how these strategies behave concerning a specific intent: performing a shilling attack. We test different standard profile injection attacks in which the fake users are crafted based on the crawled information. We analyze the strength of the attacks and whether the fake users are easy to detect by standard defense measures. In our research, we assume an attacker with no information about the target system except the ones that can be retrieved publicly. This assumption aims at putting the attacker in a realistic scenario where there is a need to collect such information systematically and in an automated way. Crawling is the most generic way to collect information from the web systematically, and it is applicable almost in any context. The experimental results show that the crawling process can allow competitors to gather valuable information, e.g., partially reconstructing the user/item neighborhood, while it is usually not enough to mount an effective shilling attack using standard strategies.

Summarizing, we try to answer the following questions:

- Which crawling algorithm should be preferred to maximize the amount of collected information?
- Which crawling algorithm should be preferred for gathering valuable knowledge for a competitor?
- In practice, is the collected information enough to attack a Recommender Systems with standard approaches successfully?

The rest of the paper is structured as follows. Section 2 presents the notation we use, crawling approaches, and the datasets we investigate. Section 3 describes the related work underlining the main differences with our analysis. Section 4 describes the methodology and assumptions used in our analysis. Section 5 shows the results of our experiments, along with a thorough discussion. Finally, Sect. 6 wraps up the main results of the paper with some insights about possible future research paths.

2   Background

In this section, we summarize the notation (Sect. 2.1), background knowledge on crawling (Sect. 2.2), and datasets (Sect. 2.3) used throughout the paper.

2.1   Notation

We refer to the set of users of an RS with $\mathcal{U}$, where $|\mathcal{U}| = n$. Similarly, the set of items is denoted by $\mathcal{I}$, such that $|\mathcal{I}| = m$. The set of ratings is denoted by $\mathcal{R} \equiv \{(u, i, r) \mid u \in \mathcal{U} \wedge i \in \mathcal{I}, u \text{ rated } i \text{ with rating } r\}$. We add a subscription to both user and item sets to indicate, respectively, the set of items rated by a user u ($\mathcal{I}_u$), and the set of users who rated the item i ($\mathcal{U}_i$). Moreover, we refer to the rating matrix with $\mathbf{R} \in \mathbb{R}^{n \times m}$ such that $\mathbf{r}_{ui}$ is the rating given by u to i.

Finally, with $G(\mathcal{U}, \mathcal{I}, \mathcal{R})$, we indicate the weighted bipartite graph representing the rating matrix. Nodes are users and items, while the edges (between users and items) are weighted by the rating. When clear from the context, we simply use the letter G.

2.2   Crawling a Recommendation-Based Website

When discussing recommendation (online) services, we refer to those services that, based on information about users, items, and their interactions, provide a personalized recommendation to the users. As mentioned above, users, items, and interactions information are usually (partially) public. A malicious user can potentially automatically collect (for example, via a crawling bot) such information to design an attack against the recommender. However, online services are aware of such possibilities, and their websites are often "secure" against automatic crawling. The most gentle countermeasure that they can use is responding with a control web page to check whether the requests come from a human or a machine. These control pages usually contain a captcha-based query [33]. Other, more severe countermeasures are temporary IP blacklisting, or in the extreme case, an indefinite ban of the IP address. The attacker can try to circumvent such defenses by using VPN, proxy, TOR[1], and so on, but modern online services are nowadays equipped to fight against such strategies. For these reasons, crawling an entire (large) website can be expensive or even infeasible. Thus, an attacker has to rely on incomplete information collected through a crawling process. This limited crawling process must be as effective as possible, minimizing the number of requests (and in general the crawling cost), while maximizing the amount of collected knowledge. This optimization problem can be cast into a well-known computational problem, i.e., an Online graph exploration problem. The online graph exploration problem (OGEP) considers visiting all graph nodes and coming back to the starting node with the minimum total traverse cost. The main issue in this problem is that only the already visited sub-graph is known, hence only "local" decisions can be made. It is worth noticing that in the OGEP, there are constraints that do not apply to the problem at hand. While crawling an RS's website, we are not obliged to follow a path, i.e., we can jump from a node (web page) to another even if they are not directly linked. Moreover, we do not have to go back to the starting node. We can further assume that each item (e.g.., web page) contains links to all the users who rated it and vice-versa. So, the graph at hand is an undirected (bipartite) graph.

In the most general case, this problem has already been studied by researchers in the context of search engines [7]. Even though the final aim is different, the optimization problem is the same. As the problem is an unconstrained TSP with incomplete information (i.e., partial knowledge of the graph), it is safe to state that it is NP-hard. However, there are heuristic-based algorithms that allow us to crawl the graph efficiently. In particular, Cho et al. proposed the following crawling strategies [7]:

---

[1] https://www.torproject.org/.

– **random**: the algorithm randomly chooses its next node from the known (but unseen) set of nodes;
– **random$_=$**: this strategy is similar to the random but, it first flips a coin to decide whether to pick a user's node or an item's node and then picks uniformly from the selected set of known but unseen nodes. This strategy aims at avoiding biases towards the most numerous set between users and items;
– **breadth-first**: the algorithm chooses its next node according to the First In First Out (FIFO) policy, i.e., when a new node is visited its neighbors are added to the queue (without a specific order);
– **backlink**: the algorithm chooses the (unvisited) node with the highest in-degree according to the known graph. In the case of the undirected graph, in-degree and out-degree are the same;
– **pagerank**: the algorithm chooses the (unvisited) node with the highest pagerank score according to the known graph.

2.3 Datasets

In our experiments, to emulate a real e-service (e.g.., e-commerce) recommendation-based website, we use four small- to large-scale datasets commonly used as benchmark in the RSs community [30] (details are summarized in Table 1). In particular:

Movielens this dataset contains users (5-stars) ratings collected from a movie recommendation service designed by the GroupLens Research. In our experiments, we used three different versions of the dataset with an increasing number of ratings, users, and items, namely `ml100k`, `ml1m`, and `ml20m`.
Netflix this is the user-movie (5-stars) ratings data from the Netflix Prize[2]. The main difference with the `Movielens` datasets is its sparsity, that is five times the most sparse `Movielens` dataset (i.e., `ml20m`).

Table 1. Datasets information: number of users, number of items, number of interactions (i.e., ratings), average number of ratings per user, and number of ratings per item.

Dataset	$|\mathcal{U}|$	$|\mathcal{I}|$	$|\mathcal{R}|$	Avg. u deg.	Avg. i deg.
ml100k	943	1 639	99 955	165.6 ± 192.7	270.9 ± 384.4
ml1m	6 040	3 691	1 000 192	105.9 ± 100.7	60.9 ± 80.8
ml20m	138 493	26 164	19 999 645	209.2 ± 230.2	764.4 ± 3 117.8
Netflix	480 188	17 770	100 462 736	144.4 ± 302.2	5 653.5 ± 16 909.2

---

[2] http://www.netflixprize.com/.

3   Related Works

In this section, we discuss the related work regarding the web crawling and the shilling attack.

3.1   Crawling

A Web crawler, also known as spider/spiderbot, is an Internet bot that systematically browses the World Wide Web. Crawling the web is almost as old as the World Wide Web itself [3,6,7,22]. Search engines have been the first technology to rely on such methods to index the web. Since then, many efforts have been devoted to increasing the crawling procedure's efficiency and effectiveness [1,11,23]. Focused web crawling [5] is one of the main strategies to improve the crawling quality in specific contexts. Focused web crawling is a procedure that collects Web pages that satisfy some specific property, by prioritizing the so-called crawl frontier. The crawl frontier is the set (more specifically, a queue) of known but not visited web pages. However, it is not always easy or feasible to define properties that can help focus the crawling. Since we focus on the graph's mere structural properties, the most promising property is the pagerank [27] of a page. Unfortunately, the pagerank value computed on a partially known graph is not so accurate [17,18]. As we will see, using pagerank is empirically as good as using simple heuristics based on the in/out-degree of the web page.

3.2   Shilling Attack

The shilling attack (a.k.a. profile injection attack) is the most popular attack against recommender systems [15,28,31]. As mentioned in Sect. 1, a profile injection attack consists in injecting well crafted fake users into the system. The goal of the attacker is usually of the following: (i) increase the popularity of some targeted items (push attack); (ii) decrease the popularity of some targeted items (nuke attack); (iii) deterioration of the performance of the system. For simplicity, in this paper, we focus on the push attack, but we argue that all the final considerations apply to the other goals. Besides the standard shilling attacks, there are also attacks designed for specific kinds of recommendation engines, such as [14] for memory-based models, [12] for graph-based models, and [24] for factorization-based models. Unfortunately, the details behind a recommendation engine are usually unknown, which cripples the applicability of the approaches mentioned above. More recent and sophisticated attacks, like [8] and [26], assume knowing the whole rating matrix, which is, in most of the cases, not realistic. For these reasons, to generalize, we will consider standard shilling attacks as testbeds. Details about the considered attacks are reported in Sect. 4.3.

The literature also offers studies about the effectiveness of shilling attacks under different constraints or scenarios. Burke et al. made an analysis related to the one proposed in this paper [4]. In their study, the attacker has limited knowledge about a target user. Our results confirm some of the drawn conclusions in this paper. Still, our analysis is broader and with a different goal. Moreover, we also cover a new attack scenario, which includes a potential competitor. In [19], a cost-benefit analysis about a shilling attack is performed. However, the only conclusion the authors draw is that the higher the number of available items in the catalog, the higher the attack cost. Also, in this case, some of our conclusions support their results. Finally, Deldjoo et al. studied the effectiveness of the attack on different groups of users (more/less active) [9]. They had quite different results on the two tested datasets, namely Movielens and Yelp. Nevertheless, they found that BPR-MF [29] seems to be more resistant than the other tested recommendation approaches.

4 Methodology

We will consider two main attack scenarios that can threaten an RS. These two attacks are independent of each other, but both rely on the information gathered through a starting crawling phase (Sect. 4.2). The two considered type of attacks are:

Shilling attack (Sect. 4.3) the standard profile injection attack. The attacker crafts the fake profiles exclusively using the crawled information;

Neighborhood reconstruction (Sect. 4.4) the attacker aims at collecting valuable information about the system. We assess the informative content of the crawled data by reconstructing the neighborhood of a target node. The higher the overlap w.r.t. the actual neighborhood (computed with the complete knowledge of the graph), the more effective the crawling process.

4.1 Threat Model

We assume the following attacker's capabilities:

- The attacker can access only the public information of the target service. The data collection is performed using a crawling procedure, as described in Sect. 2.2.
- The crawling strategies leverage only information about the user-item rating graph.
- The information of a user (item) is gathered when the corresponding page is requested (i.e., visited). The visit also allows us to know the linked/rated items (users), but not their details.
- The attacker targets a particular node in the graph (either user or item), which is also its starting node for the crawling.

4.2 Crawling

In addition to the techniques described in Sect. 2, we propose a variation of the *backlink* strategy. In our variation, the known degree for a node is the actual degree in the full graph. We denote this strategy **backlink$_{++}$**. This strategy aims to take advantage of the additional information about the graph structure (i.e., the actual out-degree) provided by the targeted web site. Even though it might be impractical in the general case, there are e-service websites where one can access the (public) degree information without visiting the page corresponding to the node. For example, in booking.com search page, the number of reviews (i.e., the out-degree of the item node) is reported before visiting the item page.

Figure 1 shows an example of the application of all the strategies mentioned in Sect. 2, including backlink$_{++}$, on a small bipartite graph. The crawling strategies are applied to crawl the entire graph. Note that the algorithms stop when all the graph is known, but it is not required to visit every single node. It is enough to discover the structure (and possibly weights) of the graph without visiting all of them for our purposes.

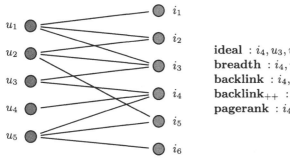

ideal : i_4, u_3, u_5, i_3, u_1 (5)
breadth : $i_4, u_3, u_4, u_5, i_3, i_5, i_6, u_1$ (8)
backlink : $i_4, u_3, i_3, u_4, u_1, i_1, u_5$ (7)
backlink$_{++}$: $i_4, u_5, i_5, u_2, i_3, u_1$ (6)
pagerank : $i_4, u_3, i_3, u_4, u_1, i_1, u_5$ (7)

Fig. 1. Example of exploration strategies on a bipartite (recommendation) graph. All the explorations start from the target node i_4. Inside the parenthesis ($\cdot$) is reported the number of node visited by the strategy. Note that in the graph, we omitted the weight of the edges.

The crawling phase for collecting the rating information is performed starting from a target node (either a user or an item). Figure 1 shows an example of crawling starting from the item i_4. For our purposes, the starting node is also the target one that is used for the reconstruction of its neighborhood (discussed in Sect. 4.4) or to make a push shilling attack (discussed in Sect. 4.3). Algorithm 1 provides the pseudo-code of a general crawling procedure.

In our simulation, a node in the (unknown) user-item ratings graph (excluding the starting node) passes through three states (depicted in Fig. 2):

Unknown. The node exists in the whole graph but is currently unknown.
Discovered. The node has been discovered through another just visited node that is linked to it. Discovered but not visited nodes can be considered in the frontier of the graph exploration.
Visited. The node has been visited, allowing the discovery of (potentially) new nodes. The visiting of a node simulates the request of its web page.

Algorithm 1: Crawling procedure.

Input: $G(U, I, E)$: user-item rating bipartite graph; p: percentage of node to visit, $p \in [0, 1]$; x: target node (user/item)
Output: G': explored sub-graph ($G' \subseteq G$)

1 $n \leftarrow |U| + |I|$
2 $U_{G'}, I_{G'}, \mathcal{E} \leftarrow \emptyset, \emptyset, \emptyset$
3 add node x to either $I_{G'}$ or $U_{G'}$ on the basis of its type
4 $Q \leftarrow [x]$
5 **while** $|Q| > 0$ *and* $|U_{G'}| + |I_{G'}| < pn$ **do**
6 $\quad$ $x \leftarrow pop(Q)$
7 $\quad$ update $I_{G'}$ or $U_{G'}$ on the basis of the type of x
8 $\quad$ update Q with $\{y | (x, y) \in E\}$
9 $\quad$ update $\mathcal{E}$ with $\{e \in E | e = (x, y) \in E\}$
10 $\quad$ sort Q according to the ordering policy of the algorithm
11 **end**
12 $G'(U_{G'}, I_{G'}, \mathcal{E})$
13 **return** G'

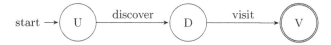

Fig. 2. Possible states of a node (with the exception of the starting node) during the crawling procedure. U = unknown, D = discovered, and V = visited.

4.3 Shilling Attack on Recommender Systems

For performing a profile injection attack, there is a need for establishing how fake profiles are defined. The number of fake profiles injected into the targeted system is usually called **attack size**, while **filler size** refers to the number of ratings each attack profile has to assign. An effective attack size highly depends on how well the system has been developed. A reasonable amount of fake profiles is 1–15%; otherwise, the associated cost of creating such additional profiles could be prohibitive. In a standard shilling attack [31], a malicious profile can be defined by four disjoint set of items, i.e., $(\mathcal{I}_T, \mathcal{I}_S, \mathcal{I}_F, \mathcal{I}_\emptyset)$ such that $\mathcal{I} \equiv \mathcal{I}_T \cup \mathcal{I}_S \cup \mathcal{I}_F \cup \mathcal{I}_\emptyset$:

Target item(s) the set of target items, $\mathcal{I}_T$, along with a rating function γ, which assigns a rating based on the goal of the attack (e.g.., in a push attack the maximum rating value);

Selected items set of items $\mathcal{I}_S$ useful to support the attack. Often items in $\mathcal{I}_S$ are related (e.g.., bought together) to items in $\mathcal{I}_T$. In most of the standard Sybil attack, $\mathcal{I}_S$ is the empty set;

Filler items set of items, $\mathcal{I}_F$, used to "camouflage" the fake profile to make it less detectable. Usually, ratings are randomly selected;

Unrated items all the remaining set of items for which the fake profile does not give any rating $\mathcal{I}_\emptyset \equiv \mathcal{I} \setminus (\mathcal{I}_T \cup \mathcal{I}_S \cup \mathcal{I}_F)$.

We test four shilling attacks in our analysis: random attack, average attack, Random Bandwagon attack, and Average Bandwagon attack [15,28]. The way user profiles are crafted in these attacks is summarized in Table 2.

4.4   Neighborhood Reconstruction

In competitive scenarios, collecting as much data as possible cannot be the most efficient strategy, i.e., it may be more useful to collect less but more informative data. To this end, we assess the quality of the collected knowledge by comparing how close are the most similar users/items computed with the crawled data w.r.t. the ones computed with the whole dataset. This comparison is based on the fact that the most popular recommendation engines are neighborhood-based [21,30, 32]. Hence, if the neighborhood reconstruction is accurate enough, we can affirm that the collected knowledge has a competitive value.

Similarity Measures. For computing the neighborhood of a node, we need a similarity function. We employed two of the most widely used similarity measures in the recommender system community [30]: Pearson's correlation and cosine similarity. The mathematical definition of these measures is reported in the following. In our experiments, to avoid biases, similarities have been computed only between users/items with support greater or equal than 5, that is, given $u, v \in \mathcal{U}$, $|\mathcal{I}_{uv}| \geq 5$, and, similarly, given $i, j \in \mathcal{I}$, $|\mathcal{U}_{ij}| \geq 5$, where $\mathcal{I}_{uv} \equiv \mathcal{I}_u \cap \mathcal{I}_v$, and $\mathcal{U}_{ij} \equiv \mathcal{U}_i \cap \mathcal{U}_j$.

Pearson's correlation:
  – user-based

$$\text{pearson}\,(\mathbf{r}_u, \mathbf{r}_v) = \frac{\sum_{i \in \mathcal{I}_{uv}} (r_{ui} - \bar{r}_u)(r_{vi} - \bar{r}_v)}{\sqrt{\sum_{i \in \mathcal{I}_{uv}} (r_{ui} - \bar{r}_u)^2 \sum_{i \in \mathcal{I}_{uv}} (r_{vi} - \bar{r}_v)^2}};$$

  – item-based

$$\text{pearson}\,(\mathbf{r}_i, \mathbf{r}_j) = \frac{\sum_{u \in \mathcal{U}_{ij}} (r_{ui} - \bar{r}_i)(r_{uj} - \bar{r}_j)}{\sqrt{\sum_{u \in \mathcal{U}_{ij}} (r_{ui} - \bar{r}_i)^2 \sum_{u \in \mathcal{U}_{ij}} (r_{uj} - \bar{r}_j)^2}};$$

where $\bar{r}_{(\cdot)}$ is the average ratings of the user/item.
Cosine similarity: user-based (left) and item-based (right)

$$\cos\,(\mathbf{r}_u, \mathbf{r}_v) = \frac{\sum_{i \in \mathcal{I}_{uv}} r_{ui} \cdot r_{vi}}{\sqrt{\sum_{i \in \mathcal{I}_u} r_{ui}^2 \sum_{j \in \mathcal{I}_v} r_{vj}^2}}, \cos\,(\mathbf{r}_i, \mathbf{r}_j) = \frac{\sum_{u \in \mathcal{U}_{ij}} r_{ui} \cdot r_{uj}}{\sqrt{\sum_{u \in \mathcal{U}_i} r_{ui}^2 \sum_{u \in \mathcal{U}_j} r_{uj}^2}}.$$

The neighborhood reconstruction evaluation procedure is summarized in Algorithm 2. Given the crawled data (by a crawling strategy), the similarity matrix is computed and compared with the similarity matrix computed on the whole dataset. The evaluation is performed in terms of the overlap size between the k most similar users/items computed with the crawled data and the whole dataset. The higher the overlap size, the higher the value of the crawled information.

Table 2. Summary of the diverse attack models. Note that the filler size (f) and the selection size (s) are attack parameters. $\bar{r}_\mathcal{I}$ and $\bar{r}_i$ respectively indicate the average rating over all items, and the average rating of i over all users. $s_\mathcal{I}$ and s_i are the corresponding standard deviations. pop stands for popular items, and $\text{sam}(X, n)$ is a random sampling function over X of dimension n. Items in the set $\mathcal{I}_\emptyset$ are associated to a missing rating (i.e., *null*).

			Ratings		
Attack	$\mathcal{I}_S$	$\mathcal{I}_F$	S	F	T
Random	$\emptyset$	$\text{sam}(\mathcal{I} \setminus \mathcal{I}_T, f)$	–	$\mathcal{N}(\bar{r}_\mathcal{I}, s_\mathcal{I})$	r_{max}
Average	$\emptyset$	$\text{sam}(\mathcal{I} \setminus \mathcal{I}_T, f)$	–	$\mathcal{N}(\bar{r}_i, s_i)$	r_{max}
Bandwagon rand.	$\text{sam}(pop, s)$	$\text{sam}(\mathcal{I} \setminus \mathcal{I}_T, f)$	r_{max}	$\mathcal{N}(\bar{r}_\mathcal{I}, s_\mathcal{I})$	r_{max}
Bandwagon avg.	$\text{sam}(pop, s)$	$\text{sam}(\mathcal{I} \setminus \mathcal{I}_T, f)$	r_{max}	$\mathcal{N}(\bar{r}_i, s_i)$	r_{max}

Algorithm 2: Neighborhood Reconstruction Evaluation

Input: **R**: rating matrix; *crawler*: crawling algorithm, p: percentage of node to visit, $p \in [0, 1]$; *sim*: similarity measure, x: target node (user/item)
Output: overlap percentage $\forall k \in \{10, 20, 50, 100, 200\}$

1 construct G, the user-rating bipartite graph, from **R**
   /* extracts the sub-graph of G using the algorithm *crawler* starting
     from node x visiting 100p% nodes of G */
2 $G' \leftarrow crawler(G, p, x)$
   /* computes the similarity, according to *sim* between x and all the
     other nodes, of the same type, in the graph.   */
3 $S_G \leftarrow \text{argsort } sim(x, G)$
4 $S_{G'} \leftarrow \text{argsort } sim(x, G')$
5 $\mathbf{O} \leftarrow []$
6 **for** $k \in \{10, 20, 50, 100, 200\}$ **do**
7 | $S_k \leftarrow set(S_G[: k])$
8 | $S'_k \leftarrow set(S'_G[: k])$
9 | $O_k \leftarrow \frac{|S_k \cap S'_k|}{k}$
10 **end**
11 **return O**

---

5   Experiments and Results

We conduct experiments for each of the phases described in the previous sections. First, we compare the crawling strategies in terms of coverage of a recommendation graph. Then, starting from the crawled information (Sect. 5.1):

- we assess whether standard shilling attacks are as effective as they were built upon the full data (Sect. 5.2);
- we measure the informative value of the crawled data by reconstructing the neighborhood of a target node. If the reconstruction is sufficiently good, then

the collected data has collaborative value, and it can be leveraged by competitors (Sect. 5.3).

5.1   Crawling and Recommendation Graph Coverage

The first set of performed experiments compares the crawling algorithm's effectiveness in terms of graph (edge) coverage fixing the number of the visited node. Experiments have been performed for the data sets described in Table 1, and in particular, we fix a maximum number of nodes defined in terms of percentage w.r.t. the whole graph. Results are reported in Fig. 3. We do not report the pagerank algorithm since it is computationally prohibitive, and in practice, it achieves performance comparable with the ones of the backlink algorithm.

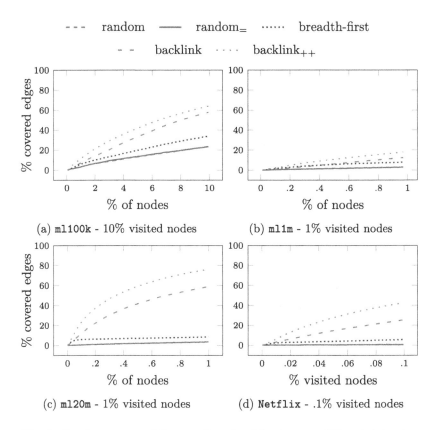

Fig. 3. Graph coverage of the crawling algorithms across different datasets.

Unsurprisingly, in all the cases, the worst-performing algorithm is random, while the best ones are backlink and backlink$_{++}$. It is also worth mentioning the poor coverage of the breadth-first algorithm, which is not much higher than the random algorithm. This is due to its ordering policy, which is not informed. It simply visits the first node in the frontier queue; hence the prioritization is not better than choosing a completely random node. However, the way the graph is explored is highly different from the other strategies, and we expect very different performance in the successive experiments. It is also worth noticing that the percentage of node visited is not a direct indicator of how much the crawling procedure can cover the graph. An evident example is the difference between ml-1m and ml-20m where for both, 1% of the nodes has been visited. The core difference, in this case, is the connectivity of the graph (see Table 1). Even though ml-20m is more sparse than ml-1m, its connectivity is higher (on average) but with a higher variance. This means that it contains many *hub nodes* [16,20] that allows covering in a single visit many edges explaining the huge difference in the resulting coverage.

5.2   Shilling Attack Using Crawled Information

With this experiment, we want to assess whether a shilling attack is influenced by the amount and type of information that the attacker possesses. In particular, we test whether crafting malicious user profiles using crawled data harms standard shilling attacks' effectiveness. We chose a popular k-nearest neighbour [30] recommender system ($k = 40$) as the target recommendation engine. Each attack is a push attack performed over a target item selected from the most popular items' second quintile. The size of the attacks has been set to 5% of the entire data set. Additionally, the filler percentage has been set to 5%. The experiment has been performed on the ml-1m dataset. The crawling algorithm stopped after visiting 0.5% of the graph that corresponds to roughly 50 nodes. We argue that the visited percentage would be much lower in a real setting and with limited resources. The performance of the attacks has been measured in terms of *prediction shift*, i.e., how the average rating of the target item changes before and after the attack, and *hit@n* in which, given a rank R and an item i, hit@n$(R,i) = 1$ iff i is in the first n positions of R, 0 otherwise. The results of the experiment are reported in Fig. 4.

It is evident from the figure that in terms of hit@10, having the full knowledge of the rating matrix increases the attack's effectiveness. The only exception is the Bandwagon average attack in which all methods achieve an hit@10 around 10/15%. However, on average, it is clear that crafting user profiles on crawled information is less harmful to the targeted system.

We also check whether the crafted profiles are also easier to be detected using standard statistical detection mechanisms [2,34], such as RDMA, WDA, WMDA, FMTD, and MeanVar. We discovered that all the crafted profiles are detected by each of the detection methods in all cases. This further supports the previous results underlining that performing a shilling attack on crawled data can hardly be successful.

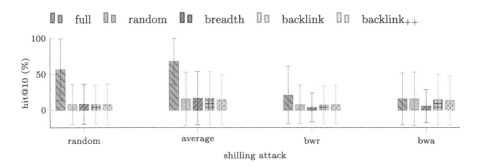

Fig. 4. Comparison of different (push) shilling attacks based on data crawled using different algorithms (and the full dataset) on ml-1m. Reported results are in Hit@10% over all users that do not rated the target item. Target item has been randomly selected from the 2nd quintile of the most popular items. On average, the prediction shift has been +0.6 for all methods. On the x axis, *bwr* means Bandwagon Random, and *bwa* means Bandwagon Average.

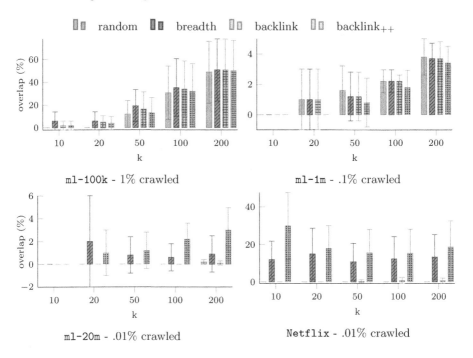

Fig. 5. Neighborhood reconstruction using user-based Pearson's correlation. The results are the average ($\pm$ standard deviation) over five randomly selected users. k on the x-axis is the dimension of the considered neighborhood.

5.3 Neighborhood Reconstruction

In this section, we discuss the achieved results reconstructing the neighborhood. These experiments have been performed following the procedure described in Sect. 4.4. Figure 5 shows the overlap percentage of the neighborhood reconstruction using a user-based similarity based on Pearson's correlation.

The first observation regards the random crawling strategy that does not allow almost any kind of neighborhood reconstruction. This is intuitively reasonable since this strategy does not consider any properties of the nodes/graph to prioritize the nodes. On average, backlink$_{++}$ is the most successful strategy, but, as we already mentioned, it is not always applicable. However, even though its coverage performance is not as good, breadth-first can achieve comparable results w.r.t. backlink$_{++}$. It is also worth to notice the backlink drop in performance on the bigger datasets, namely ml-20m and Netflix. We argue that this is due to the poor approximation quality of the degree of the nodes, i.e., the degree in the full graph (this is also supported by the higher gap in coverage w.r.t. backlink$_{++}$, see Fig. 3) but it is surely something that needs further investigation.

Figure 6 depicts the overlap percentage of the neighborhood reconstruction using a item-based similarity based on cosine similarity. Note that we used

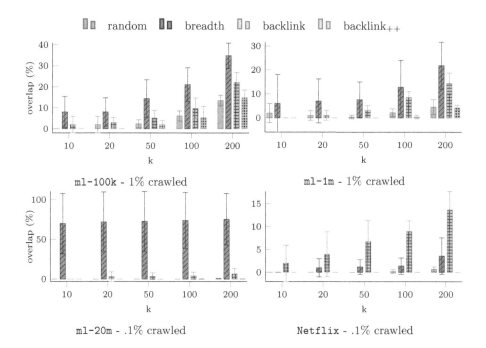

Fig. 6. Neighborhood reconstruction using item-based cosine similarity. The results are the average ($\pm$ standard deviation) over five randomly selected average popular items. k on the x-axis is the dimension of the considered neighborhood.

a higher crawling percentage than the user-based case in `ml-1m`, `ml-20m`, and `Netflix`.

The need to increase the crawling percentage underlines the fact that it is harder to reconstruct an item's neighborhood. This can be due to a longer tail in the long tail distribution. However, it is further confirmed that breadth-first works pretty well, with the only exception for `Netflix`. Strangely, here backlink seems to be the best performing strategy. It can be noticed that, on average, the reconstruction over the cosine similarity is easier than with Pearson's correlation. This can be seen more clearly when comparing these plots with the ones in the Appendix (Figs. 7 and 8). We only reported user-based with Pearson's correlation and item-based with cosine similarity due to the page limit. In general, we can state that it is possible for a competitor to collect useful knowledge crawling a target e-service. The extent highly depends on the size of the target site and available resources to perform the crawling. It empirically seems that a standard breadth-first strategy does the job nicely, but when possible using more information to prioritize the crawling frontier (e.g.., $backlink_{++}$) can improve the results.

6   Conclusions and Future Work

In this paper, we discussed and assessed whether attacking an online RS can be successful in a practical scenario where the attacker must collect useful data in the first place. We can draw some conclusions about the vulnerability of online recommendation services:

- When applicable, the $backlink_{++}$ (our proposal) ensures good coverage of the recommendation graph. In general, it is advisable to prioritize the crawling frontier using as much information as possible. When no information is available, the backlink strategy is a good choice.
- The breadth-first strategy has shown pretty consistent results thanks to the way the nodes are visited. Breadth-first ensures that the closest nodes to the target are visited first when starting from the target node itself. This is a good prioritization strategy when it comes to collect competitive knowledge about the target item.
- In general, they are not enough. However, the Average Bandwagon attack has shown to be less sensitive to the amount/quality of the collected information (similar conclusion as in [4]). Unfortunately, all the tested attacks are easy to detect and hence not effective in practice.

In future work, we aim to expand this analysis to other types of attacks and perform a real attack on a running online recommendation service. Moreover, it will be worth investigating new crawling policies that also use the content information about the items rather than the graph's mere structural information.

Acknowledgments. This work was supported by the European Commission under the Horizon 2020 Programme (H2020), as part of the LOCARD project (Grant Agreement no. 832735).

A   Neighborhood Reconstruction: User-Based with Cosine Similarity

In Fig. 7, we depict the results for all four considered datasets for the neighborhood reconstruction when using user-based cosine similarity.

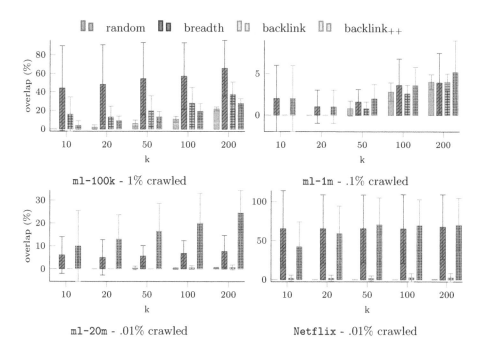

Fig. 7. Neighborhood reconstruction using user-based cosine similarity. The results are the average ($\pm$ standard deviation) over five randomly selected users. k on the x-axis is the dimension of the considered neighborhood.

B   Neighborhood Reconstruction: Item-Based with Pearson's Correlation

Finally, in Fig. 8, we depict the results for the neighborhood reconstruction when using an item-based Pearson correlation.

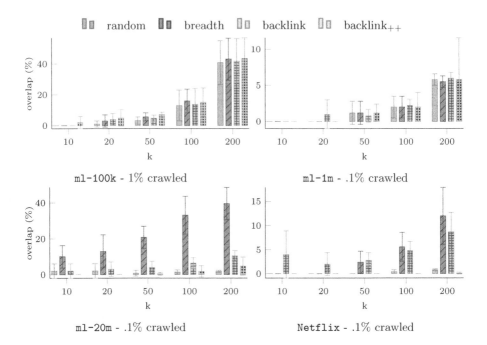

Fig. 8. Neighborhood reconstruction using item-based Pearson's correlation. The results are the average (± standard deviation) over five randomly selected average popular items. k on the x-axis is the dimension of the considered neighborhood.

References

1. Baeza-Yates, R., Castillo, C., Marin, M., Rodriguez, A.: Crawling a country: better strategies than breadth-first for web page ordering. In: Special Interest Tracks and Posters of the 14th International Conference on World Wide Web, WWW 2005, New York, NY, USA, pp. 864–872. Association for Computing Machinery (2005). https://doi.org/10.1145/1062745.1062768
2. Bhebe, W., Kogeda, O.P.: Shilling attack detection in collaborative recommender systems using a meta learning strategy. In: 2015 International Conference on Emerging Trends in Networks and Computer Communications, pp. 56–61 (2015)
3. Brin, S., Page, L.: The anatomy of a large-scale hypertextual web search engine. In: Proceedings of the Seventh International Conference on World Wide Web, WWW 2007, pp. 107–117. Elsevier, NLD (1998)
4. Burke, R., Mobasher, B., Bhaumik, R.: Limited knowledge shilling attacks in collaborative filtering systems. In: Proceedings of the 3rd IJCAI Workshop in Intelligent Techniques for Personalization (2005)
5. Chakrabarti, S.: Focused Web Crawling, pp. 1147–1155. Springer, Boston (2009). https://doi.org/10.1007/978-0-387-39940-9_165
6. Chakrabarti, S., Dom, B., Raghavan, P., Rajagopalan, S., Gibson, D., Kleinberg, J.: Automatic resource compilation by analyzing hyperlink structure and associated text. In: Proceedings of the Seventh International Conference on World Wide Web 2007, WWW 2007, pp. 65–74. Elsevier, NLD (1998)

7. Cho, J., Garcia-Molina, H., Page, L.: Efficient crawling through URL ordering. Comput. Netw. ISDN Syst. **30**(1), 161–172 (1998). https://doi.org/10.1016/S0169-7552(98)00108-1. http://www.sciencedirect.com/science/article/pii/S0169755298001081. Proceedings of the Seventh International World Wide Web Conference

8. Christakopoulou, K., Banerjee, A.: Adversarial attacks on an oblivious recommender. In: Proceedings of the 13th ACM Conference on Recommender Systems, RecSys 2019, pp. 322–330. ACM (2019). https://doi.org/10.1145/3298689.3347031. http://doi.acm.org/10.1145/3298689.3347031

9. Deldjoo, Y., Di Noia, T., Merra, F.A.: Assessing the impact of a user-item collaborative attack on class of users. In: In Proceedings of the 13th ACM RecSys Workshop on Impact of Recommender Systems (ImpactRS@RecSys 2019) (2019). http://sisinflab.poliba.it/publications/2019/DDM19

10. Eksombatchai, C., et al.: Pixie: a system for recommending 3+ billion items to 200+ million users in real-time. In: Proceedings of the 2018 World Wide Web Conference, WWW 2018, pp. 1775–1784. WWW Conferences Steering Committee, Republic and Canton of Geneva, CHE (2018). https://doi.org/10.1145/3178876.3186183

11. Ester, M., Kriegel, H.P., Schubert, M.: Accurate and efficient crawling for relevant websites. In: Proceedings of the Thirtieth International Conference on Very Large Data Bases - Volume 30, VLDB 2004, pp. 396–407. VLDB Endowment (2004)

12. Fang, M., Yang, G., Gong, N.Z., Liu, J.: Poisoning attacks to graph-based recommender systems. In: Proceedings of the 34th Annual Computer Security Applications Conference, ACSAC 2018, New York, NY, USA, pp. 381–392. Association for Computing Machinery (2018). https://doi.org/10.1145/3274694.3274706

13. Gomez-Uribe, C., Hunt, N.: The netflix recommender system: algorithms, business value, and innovation. ACM Trans. Manage. Inf. Syst. **6**(4) (2016). https://doi.org/10.1145/2843948

14. Gunes, I., Bilge, A., Polat, H.: Shilling attacks against memory-based privacy-preserving recommendation algorithms. TIIS **7**, 1272–1290 (2013)

15. Gunes, I., Kaleli, C., Bilge, A., Polat, H.: Shilling attacks against recommender systems: a comprehensive survey. Artif. Intell. Rev. **42**(4), 767–799 (2012). https://doi.org/10.1007/s10462-012-9364-9

16. Hara, K., Suzuki, I., Kobayashi, K., Fukumizu, K.: Reducing hubness: a cause of vulnerability in recommender systems. In: Proceedings of the 38th International ACM SIGIR Conference on Research and Development in Information Retrieval, SIGIR 2015, New York, NY, USA, pp. 815–818. Association for Computing Machinery (2015). https://doi.org/10.1145/2766462.2767823

17. Holzmann, H., Anand, A., Khosla, M.: Delusive PageRank in incomplete graphs. In: Aiello, L.M., Cherifi, C., Cherifi, H., Lambiotte, R., Lió, P., Rocha, L.M. (eds.) COMPLEX NETWORKS 2018. SCI, vol. 812, pp. 104–117. Springer, Cham (2019). https://doi.org/10.1007/978-3-030-05411-3_9

18. Holzmann, H., Anand, A., Khosla, M.: Estimating PageRank deviations in crawled graphs. Appl. Netw. Sci. **4**, 86–107 (2019)

19. Hurley, N.J., O'Mahony, M.P., Silvestre, G.C.M.: Attacking recommender systems: a cost-benefit analysis. IEEE Intell. Syst. **22**(3), 64–68 (2007)

20. Knees, P., Schnitzer, D., Flexer, A.: Improving neighborhood-based collaborative filtering by reducing hubness. In: Proceedings of International Conference on Multimedia Retrieval, ICMR 2014, New York, NY, USA, pp. 161–168. Association for Computing Machinery (2014). https://doi.org/10.1145/2578726.2578747

21. Koren, Y., Bell, R.: Advances in Collaborative Filtering, pp. 145–186. Springer, Boston (2011). https://doi.org/10.1007/978-0-387-85820-3_5
22. Koster, M.: Robots in the web: threat or treat? ConneXions **9**(4), 8–18 (1995)
23. Lawankar, A., Mangrulkar, N.: A review on techniques for optimizing web crawler results. In: 2016 World Conference on Futuristic Trends in Research and Innovation for Social Welfare (Startup Conclave), pp. 1–4 (2016)
24. Li, B., Wang, Y., Singh, A., Vorobeychik, Y.: Data poisoning attacks on factorization-based collaborative filtering. In: Proceedings of the 30th International Conference on Neural Information Processing Systems, NIPS 2016, pp. 1893–1901 (2016). http://dl.acm.org/citation.cfm?id=3157096.3157308
25. Linden, G., Smith, B., York, J.: Amazon.com recommendations: item-to-item collaborative filtering. IEEE Internet Comput. **7**(1), 76–80 (2003)
26. Muñoz-González, L., Pfitzner, B., Russo, M., Carnerero-Cano, J., Lupu, E.C.: Poisoning attacks with generative adversarial nets. ArXiv abs/1906.07773 (2019)
27. Page, L., Brin, S., Motwani, R., Winograd, T.: The PageRank citation ranking: bringing order to the web. In: WWW 1999 (1999)
28. Patel, K., Thakkar, A., Shah, C., Makvana, K.: A state of art survey on shilling attack in collaborative filtering based recommendation system. In: Satapathy, S.C.C., Das, S. (eds.) Proceedings of First International Conference on Information and Communication Technology for Intelligent Systems: Volume 1. SIST, vol. 50, pp. 377–385. Springer, Cham (2016). https://doi.org/10.1007/978-3-319-30933-0_38
29. Rendle, S., Freudenthaler, C., Gantner, Z., Schmidt-Thieme, L.: BPR: Bayesian personalized ranking from implicit feedback. In: Proceedings of the Twenty-Fifth Conference on Uncertainty in Artificial Intelligence, UAI 2009, Arlington, Virginia, USA, pp. 452–461. AUAI Press (2009)
30. Ricci, F., Rokach, L., Shapira, B.: Recommender Systems Handbook. Springer, Boston (2011). https://doi.org/10.1007/978-0-387-85820-3_25
31. Si, M., Li, Q.: Shilling attacks against collaborative recommender systems: a review. Artif. Intell. Rev. **53**(1), 291–319 (2018). https://doi.org/10.1007/s10462-018-9655-x
32. Su, X., Khoshgoftaar, T.M.: A survey of collaborative filtering techniques. Adv. Artif. Intell. **2009** (2009). https://doi.org/10.1155/2009/421425
33. Zhang, Y., Gao, H., Pei, G., Luo, S., Chang, G., Cheng, N.: A survey of research on captcha designing and breaking techniques. In: 2019 18th IEEE International Conference On Trust, Security and Privacy in Computing and Communications/13th IEEE International Conference on Big Data Science and Engineering (TrustCom/BigDataSE), pp. 75–84 (2019)
34. Zhou, W., et al.: Shilling attacks detection in recommender systems based on target item analysis. PLoS ONE **10**(7), 1–26 (2015). https://doi.org/10.1371/journal.pone.0130968

Active Re-identification Attacks on Periodically Released Dynamic Social Graphs

Xihui Chen, Ema Këpuska, Sjouke Mauw, and Yunior Ramírez-Cruz[⊠]

SnT, DCS, University of Luxembourg, 6, av. de la Fonte, 4364 Esch-sur-Alzette, Luxembourg
{xihui.chen,sjouke.mauw,yunior.ramirez}@uni.lu,
kepuskaema@gmail.com

Abstract. Active re-identification attacks pose a serious threat to privacy-preserving social graph publication. Active attackers create fake accounts to enforce structural patterns that can be used to re-identify legitimate users on published anonymised graphs, even without additional background knowledge. So far, this type of attacks has only been studied in the scenario where the inherently dynamic social graph is published once. In this paper, we present the first active re-identification attack in the more realistic scenario where a dynamic social graph is periodically published. Our new attack leverages tempo-structural patterns, created by a dynamic set of sybil nodes, for strengthening the adversary. We evaluate our new attack through a comprehensive set of experiments on real-life and synthetic dynamic social graphs. We show that our new attack substantially outperforms the most effective static active attack in the literature by increasing success probability by at least two times and efficiency by at least 11 times. Moreover, we show that, unlike the static attack, our new attack remains at the same level of efficiency as the publication process advances. Additionally, we conduct a study on the factors that may thwart our new attack, which can help design dynamic graph anonymisation methods displaying a better balance between privacy and utility.

Keywords: Dynamic social graphs · Privacy-preserving publication · Re-identification attacks · Active adversaries

1 Introduction

Social graphs are a valuable source of data for conducting societal studies, market analyses, and other forms of complex data analysis. Analysts profit from social graph data for conducting their studies, whereas data owners find additional business and public service opportunities in making these data available to third parties. However, releasing social network data raises serious privacy concerns, due to the sensitive nature of the information contained in social graphs. Thus, the data needs to be properly sanitised before publication. It has been shown that *pseudonymisation*, i.e. removing users' identities and personally identifying information from the data, is insufficient for protecting sensitive information, as most users can be unambiguously *re-identified* in the pseudonymised graph by means of simple structural patterns [2,10,15]. User re-identification subsequently allows a malicious agent, or *adversary*, to infer relations

© Springer Nature Switzerland AG 2020
L. Chen et al. (Eds.): ESORICS 2020, LNCS 12309, pp. 185–205, 2020.
https://doi.org/10.1007/978-3-030-59013-0_10

between users, group affiliations, etc. A method allowing an adversary to re-identify (a subset of) the users in a sanitised social graph is called a *re-identification attack*. Numerous anonymisation methods have been proposed for publishing social graphs that effectively resist re-identification attacks, e.g. [3,10,12,13,20,22,26,27]. These methods depend on an adversary model, which encodes assumptions about the adversary capabilities. There are two classes of adversaries in social graph publication. On the one hand, *passive* adversaries exploit publicly available information obtainable from online resources, public records, etc., without interacting with the social network before publication. On the other hand, *active* adversaries interact with the network before the sanitised dataset is released. Active adversaries operate by inserting fake accounts in the network, commonly called *sybil nodes*, and creating connection patterns between these fake accounts and a set of legitimate users, the *victims*. After the publication of the sanitised graph, the attacker uses these unique patterns for re-identifying the victims. Active adversaries have been shown to be a serious threat to social graph publication [2,14], as they remain plausible even if no public background knowledge is available.

Social networks are inherently dynamic. Moreover, analysts require datasets containing dynamic social graphs for conducting tasks such as community evolution analysis [4], link prediction [11] and link persistence analysis [17]. Despite the need for sanitised dynamic social graphs, studies on graph anonymisation have overwhelmingly focused on the scenario where a social graph is released only once. The rather small number of studies on dynamic social graph publication have addressed passive adversary models only. Thus, the manners in which active adversaries can profit from a dynamic publication scenario remain unknown. In this paper, we remedy this situation by formulating active re-identification attacks in the scenario of dynamic social graphs. We consider a scenario where snapshots of the underlying dynamic graph are *periodically* taken, sanitised, and published. We model active adversaries whose knowledge consists in *tempo-structural* patterns, instead of exclusively structural patterns as those used by the original (static) active adversaries. Moreover, in our model the adversary knowledge is incremental and evolves along the publication process. The new dynamic active attack is more effective than the alternative of executing independent static attacks on different snapshots. Furthermore, it is also considerably more efficient than the previous attacks, because it profits from temporal patterns to accelerate several of its components.

Our Contributions. The main contributions of this paper are listed in what follows:

- We formulate, for the first time, active re-identification attacks in the scenario of periodically released dynamic social graphs. We describe an instance of the new attack strategy based on tempo-structural patterns for re-identification.
- We conduct a comprehensive set of experiments on real-life and synthetic dynamic social graphs, which demonstrate that the dynamic active attack is at least two times more effective than the alternative of repeatedly executing the strongest active attack reported in the literature for the static scenario [14].
- Our experiments also show that, as the number of snapshots grows, the dynamic active attack runs at least 11 times faster than the static active attack from [14].

– We analyse the factors that affect the effectiveness of our new attack. The conclusions of this study serve as a starting point for the development of anonymisation methods for the periodical publication scenario.

2   Related Work

Re-identification attacks are a relevant threat for privacy-preserving social graph publication methods that preserve a mapping between the real users and a set of pseudonymised nodes in the sanitised release, e.g. [3, 10, 12, 13, 20, 22, 26, 27]. Depending on the manner in which the attacker obtains the knowledge used for re-identification, these attacks can be divided into two classes: passive and active attacks. *Passive* adversaries collect publicly available knowledge, such as public profiles in other social networks, and searches the sanitised graph for vertices with an exact or similar profile. For example, Narayanan and Shmatikov [15] used information from Flickr to re-identify users in a pseudonymised subgraph of Twitter. Subsequently, a considerable number of passive attacks have been proposed, e.g. [6, 7, 15, 16, 18, 23]. On the other hand, *active* adversaries interact with the real network before publication, and force the existence of the structural patterns that allow for re-identification after release. The earliest examples of active attacks are the *walk-based attack* and the *cut-based attack*, introduced by Backstrom *et al.* in [2]. Both attacks insert sybil nodes in the network, and create connection patterns between the sybil nodes that allow their efficient retrieval in the pseudonymised graph. In both attacks, the connection patterns between sybil nodes and victims are used as unique fingerprints allowing re-identification once the sybil subgraph is retrieved. Due to the low resilience of the walk-based and cut-based attacks, a robust active attack was introduced by Mauw *et al.* in [14]. The robust active attack introduces noise-tolerant sybil subgraph retrieval and fingerprint mapping, at the cost of larger computational complexity. The attack proposed in this paper preserves the noise resiliency of the robust active attack, but puts a larger emphasis on temporal consistency constraints for reducing the search space. As a result, for every re-identification attempt, our attack is comparable to the original walk-based attack in terms of efficiency, and to the robust active attack in terms of resilience against modifications in the graph.

Notice that, by itself, the use of connection fingerprints as adversary knowledge does not make an attack active. The key feature of an active attack is the fact that the adversary interacts with the network to enforce the existence of such fingerprints. For example, Zou *et al.* [27] describe an attack that uses the distances of the victims to a set of hubs as fingerprints. This is a passive attack, since hubs exist in the network without intervention of the attacker.

The attacks discussed so far assume a single release scenario. A smaller number of works have discussed re-identification in a dynamic scenario. Some works assume an adversary who can exploit the availability of multiple snapshots, although they only give a coarse overview of the increased adversary capabilities, without giving details on attack strategies. Examples of these works are [21], which models a passive adversary that knows the evolution of the degrees of all vertices; and [27], which models another passive adversary that knows the evolution of a subgraph in the vicinity of the victims. An example of a full dynamic de-anonymization method is given in [5]. Although they do not model an active adversary, the fact that the method relies on the existence of a seed graph makes it potentially extensible with an active first stage for seed re-identification, as done for example in [19]. Our attack differs from the methods above in the fact that it uses an evolving set of sybil nodes that dynamically interact with the network and adapt to its evolution.

3   A Dynamic Active Attack on Periodical Graph Publication

In this section we describe the scenario where the owner of a social network periodically publishes sanitised snapshots of the underlying dynamic social graph, accounting for the presence of active adversaries. We describe this scenario in the form of an attacker-defender game between the data owner and the active adversary. We first introduce the basic notation and terminology, and give an overview of the entire process. Then, we introduce the notions of temporal consistency, which are the backbone of the new attack strategy. Finally, we give a detailed description of the publication process, along with an instantiation of the attack strategy, which exploits tempo-structural patterns and temporal consistency for dynamic re-identification.

3.1   Notation and Terminology

We represent a dynamic social graph as a sequence $\mathcal{G} = (G_1, G_2, \ldots, G_i, \ldots)$, where each G_i is a static graph called the i-th *snapshot* of $\mathcal{G}$. Each snapshot of $\mathcal{G}$ has the form $G_i = (V_i, E_i)$, where V_i is the set of vertices (also called *nodes* indistinctly throughout the paper) and $E_i \subseteq V_i \times V_i$ is the set of edges. We will use the notations V_G and E_G for the vertex and edge sets of a graph G. In this paper, we assume that graphs are simple and undirected. The *neighbourhood* of a vertex v in a graph G is the set $N_G(v) = \{w \in V \mid (v, w) \in E\}$, and its *degree* is $\delta_G(v) = |N_G(v)|$. For the sake of simplicity, in the previous notations we drop the subscript when it is clear from the context and simply write $N(v)$, $\delta(v)$, etc. For a subset of nodes $S \subseteq V_G$, we use $\langle S \rangle_G$ to represent the subgraph of G *induced* by S, i.e. $\langle S \rangle_G = (S, E_G \cap (S \times S))$. Similarly, the subgraph of G *weakly induced* by S is defined as $\langle S \rangle_G^w = (S \cup N_G(S), E_G \cap (S \times (S \cup N_G(S))))$. For every graph G and every $S \subseteq V_G$, $\langle S \rangle_G$ is a subset of $\langle S \rangle_G^w$, as $\langle S \rangle_G^w$ additionally contains the neighbourhood of S and every edge between elements of S and their neighbours. Also notice that $\langle S \rangle_G^w$ does not contain the edges linking pairs of elements of $N_G(S)$. An *isomorphism* between two graphs $G = (V, E)$ and $G' = (V', E')$ is a bijective function $\varphi \colon V \to V'$ such that $\forall_{v,w \in V} \ (v, w) \in E \iff (\varphi(v), \varphi(w)) \in E'$. Additionally, we denote by $\varphi(S)$ the restriction of φ to a vertex subset $S \subseteq V$, that is $\varphi(S) = \{\varphi(v) \mid v \in S\}$.

3.2   Overview

Figure 1 depicts the process of periodical graph publication in the presence of an active adversary. We model this process as a game between two players, the *data owner* and the *adversary*. The data owner selects a set of time-stamps $T = \{t_1, t_2, \ldots, t_i, \ldots\}$, $t_1 < t_2 < \ldots < t_i < \ldots$, and incrementally publishes the sequence $\mathcal{G}^\star = (G_{t_1}^\star, G_{t_2}^\star,$

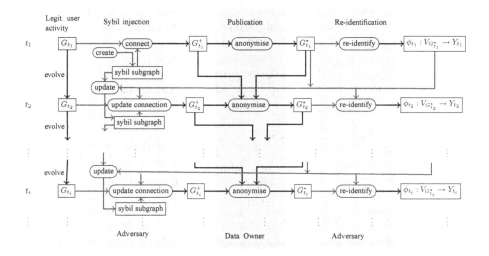

Fig. 1. Overview of periodical graph publication in the presence of active adversaries.

$\ldots, G_{t_i}^{\star}, \ldots$) of sanitised snapshots of the underlying dynamic social graph. The adversary's goal is to re-identify, in a subset $T' \subseteq T$ of the releases, a (possibly evolving) set of legitimate users referred to as the *victims*. To achieve this goal, the active adversary injects an (also evolving) set of fake accounts, commonly called *sybils*, in the graph. The sybil accounts create connections among themselves, and with the victims. The connection patterns between each victim and some of the sybil nodes is used as a unique *fingerprint* for that victim. The likely unique patterns built by the adversary will enable her to effectively and efficiently re-identify the victims in the sanitised snapshots. At every re-identification attempt, the adversary first re-identifies the set of sybil nodes, and then uses the fingerprints to re-identify the victims.

The data owner and the adversary have different partial views of the dynamic social graph. On the one hand, the data owner knows the entire set of users, both legitimate users and sybil accounts, but she cannot distinguish them. The data owner also knows all relations. On the other hand, the adversary knows the identity of her victims and the structure of the subgraph weakly induced by the set of sybil nodes, but she does not know the structure of the rest of the network. In this paper we conduct the analysis from the perspective of an external observer who can view all of the information. We will use the sequence $\mathcal{G}^+ = (G_{t_1}^+, G_{t_2}^+, \ldots, G_{t_i}^+, \ldots)$ to denote the view of the network according to the data owner, i.e. the real network containing the nodes representing all users, both legitimate and malicious. Further we use $\mathcal{G} = (G_{t_1}, G_{t_2}, \ldots, G_{t_i}, \ldots)$ to represent the view of the unattacked network, that is the view of the dynamic subgraph induced in $\mathcal{G}^+$ by the nodes representing legitimate users.

In the original formulation of active attacks, a single snapshot of the graph is released, so all actions executed by the sybil nodes are assumed to occur before the publication. This is not the case in the scenario of a periodically released dynamic social graph. Here, the adversary has the opportunity to schedule actions in such a way that the subgraph induced by the sybil nodes evolves, as well as the set of fingerprints. In turn, that allows her to use temporal patterns in addition to structural patterns for re-identification. Additionally, the adversary can target different sets of victims along the publication process and adapt the induced tempo-structural patterns to the evolution of the graph and the additional knowledge acquired in each re-identification attempt. In the new scenario, the actions performed by the adversary and the data owner alternate as follows before, during and after each time-stamp $t_i \in T$.

Before t_i, the adversary may remain inactive, or she can modify the set of sybil nodes, as well as the set of sybil-to-sybil and sybil-to-victim edges. The result of these actions is the graph $G_{t_i}^+ = (V_{t_i} \cup S_{t_i}, E_{t_i} \cup E_{t_i}^+)$, where V_{t_i} is the current set of legitimate users, S_{t_i} is the current set of sybil nodes, $Y_{t_i} \subseteq V_{t_i}$ is the current set of victims, $E_{t_i} = E_{G_{t_i}} \subseteq V_{t_i} \times V_{t_i}$ is the set of connections between legitimate users, and $E_{t_i}^+ \subseteq (S_{t_i} \times S_{t_i}) \cup (S_{t_i} \times Y_{t_i})$ is the set of connections created by the sybil accounts. The subgraph $\langle S_{t_i} \rangle_{G_{t_i}^+}^w$, weakly induced in $G_{t_i}^+$ by the set of sybil nodes, is the *sybil subgraph*. We refer to the set of modifications of the sybil subgraph executed before the adversary has conducted any re-identification attempt as *sybil subgraph creation*. If the adversary has conducted a re-identification attempt on earlier snapshots, we refer to the modifications of the sybil subgraph as *sybil subgraph update*.

During t_i, the data owner applies an anonymisation method to $G_{t_i}^+$ to obtain the sanitised version $G_{t_i}^\star$, which is then released. The anonymisation must preserve the consistency of the pseudonyms. That is, every user must be labelled with the same pseudonym throughout the sequence of snapshots where it appears. Consistent annotation is of paramount importance for a number of analysis tasks such as community evolution analysis [4], link prediction [11], link persistence analysis [17], among others, that require to track users along the sequence of releases. The data owner anonymises every snapshot exactly once.

After t_i, the adversary adds $G_{t_i}^\star$ to her knowledge. At this point, she can remain inactive, or execute a re-identification attempt on $G_{t_i}^\star$. The result of a re-identification attempt is a mapping $\phi_{t_i} : V_{G_{t_i}^\star} \to Y_{t_i}$ determining the pseudonyms assigned to the victims by the anonymisation method. The adversary can additionally modify the results of a re-identification attempt executed on some of the preceding releases.

3.3   Temporal Consistency Constraints

As we discussed in Sect. 3.2, the data owner must assign the same time-persistent pseudonym to each user throughout the subsequence of snapshots where it appears. Since the adversary receives all sanitised snapshots, she is able to determine when a pseudonym was used for the first time, whether it is still in use, and in case it is not, when it was used for the last time. In our attack, the adversary exploits this information in all stages of the re-identification process. For example, consider the following situation. The set of sybil nodes at time-step t_6 is $S_{t_6} = \{s_1, s_2, s_3, s_4\}$. The adversary inserted s_1 and s_2 in the interval preceding the publication of $G_{t_2}^\star$. Additionally, she inserted s_3 before the publication of $G_{t_3}^\star$ and s_4 before the publication of $G_{t_5}^\star$. After the release of $G_{t_6}^\star$, during the sybil subgraph retrieval phase of the first re-identification attempt, the adversary needs to determine whether a set $X \subseteq V_{G_{t_6}^\star}$, say

$X = \{v_1, v_2, v_3, v_4\}$, is a valid candidate. Looking at the first snapshot where each of these pseudonyms was used, the adversary observes that v_1 and v_3 were first used in $G^\star_{t_2}$, so they are feasible matches for s_1 and s_2, in some order. Likewise, v_2 was first used in $G^\star_{t_5}$, so it is a feasible match for s_4. However, she observes that v_4 was first used in $G^\star_{t_4}$, unlike any element of S_{t_6}. From this observation, the adversary infers that X is not a valid candidate, regardless of how structurally similar $\langle X \rangle^w_{G_{t_6}}$ and $\langle S_{t_6} \rangle^w_{G^+_{t_6}}$ are.

We now formalise the different types of constraints used in our attack. To that end, we introduce some new notation. The function $\alpha^+ \colon \cup_{t_i \in T} V_{G^+_{t_i}} \to T$ yields, for every vertex $v \in \cup_{t_i \in T} V_{G^+_{t_i}}$, the order of the first snapshot where v exists, that is $\alpha^+(v) = \min\{\{t_i \in T \mid v \in V_{G^+_{t_i}}\}\}$. Analogously, the function $\alpha^\star \colon \cup_{t_i \in T} V_{G^\star_{t_i}} \to T$ yields the order of the first snapshot where each pseudonym is used, that is $\alpha^\star(x) = t_i \iff \exists_{v \in V_{G^+_{t_i}}} \alpha^+(v) = t_i \wedge \varphi_{t_i}(v) = x$. Clearly, the adversary knows the values of the function $\alpha^\star$ for all pseudonyms used by the data owner. Additionally, she knows the values of α^+ for all of her sybil nodes. These functions allow us to define the notion of *first-use-as-sybil* consistency, which is used by the sybil subgraph retrieval method.

Definition 1. *Let $X \subseteq V_{G^\star_{t_i}}$ be a set of pseudonyms such that $|X| = |S_{t_i}|$ and let $\phi \colon S_{t_i} \to V_{G^\star_{t_i}}$ be a mapping from the set of real sybil nodes to the elements of X. We say that X and S_{t_i} satisfy* first-use-as-sybil *consistency according to ϕ, denoted as $X \simeq_\phi S_{t_i}$, if and only if $\forall_{s \in S_{t_i}} \alpha^+(s) = \alpha^\star(\phi(s))$.*

Note that *first-use-as-sybil* consistency depends on the order in which the elements of the candidate set are mapped to the real sybil nodes, which is a requirement of the sybil subgraph retrieval method. We define an analogous notion of first use consistency for victims. In this case, the adversary may or may not know the value of α^+. In our attack, we assume that she does not, and introduce an additional function to represent the temporal information the adversary must necessarily have about victims. The function $\beta^+ \colon \cup_{t_i \in T} Y_{t_i} \to T$ yields, for every $v \in \cup_{t_i \in T} Y_{t_i}$, the order of the snapshot where v was targeted for the first time, that is $\beta^+(v) = \min\{\{t_i \in T \mid v \in Y_{t_i}\}\}$. The new function allows us to define the notion of *first-time-targeted* consistency, which is used in the fingerprint matching method.

Definition 2. *Let $v \in V_{G^\star_{t_i}}$ be a victim candidate and let $y \in Y_{t_i}$ be a real victim. We say that v and y satisfy* first-time-targeted *consistency, denoted as $v \simeq y$, if and only if $\alpha^\star(v) \leq \beta^+(y)$.*

This temporal consistency notion encodes the rationale that the adversary can ignore during fingerprint matching those pseudonyms that the data owner used for the first time after the corresponding victim had been targeted. Next, we define the notion of *sybil-removal-count* consistency, which is used by the re-identification refinement method to encode the rationale that a sybil set candidate X, for which no temporal inconsistencies were found during the t_i-th snapshot, can be removed from $\mathcal{X}_{t_i}$ when the t_{i+1}-th snapshot is released, if the number of sybil nodes removed by the adversary in the interval between these snapshots does not match the number of elements of X that cease to exist in $G^\star_{t_{i+1}}$.

Definition 3. *We say that a set of pseudonyms* $X \subseteq V_{G_{t_i}^*}$ *satisfies* sybil-removal-count consistency *with respect to the pair* $(S_{t_i}, S_{t_{i+1}})$, *which we denote as* $X \simeq (S_{t_i}, S_{t_{i+1}})$, *if and only if* $|X \setminus V_{G_{t_{i+1}}^*}| = |S_{t_i} \setminus S_{t_{i+1}}|$.

In certain social networks, the adversary can detect when one victim leaves the network, e.g. by detecting that all connections to the victim from her sybil nodes are simultaneously lost. From this, the adversary infers that the victim's pseudonym will not be present in the next release of the graph. This rationale can be used to further refine the re-identification of victims in previously released snapshots, by discarding those mappings where the pseudonyms continue to be present in the snapshots released after the corresponding victims terminate their membership of the network. To encode this rationale, the function $\gamma^+ \colon \cup_{t_i \in T} V_{G_{t_i}^+} \to T$ yields the order of the last snapshot where a node is present in the social network. Note that the adversary is certain about $\gamma^+(s)$ for every sybil node s. Analogously, the function $\gamma^\star \colon \cup_{t_i \in T} V_{G_{t_i}^*} \to T$ yields the order of the last snapshot where a pseudonym appears. By comparing the vertex sets of two consecutive snapshots, the adversary can learn $\gamma^\star(v)$ for any pseudonym v.

Definition 4. *Let* $v \in V_{G_{t_i}^*}$ *be a victim candidate and let* $y \in Y_{t_i}$ *be a real victim. We say that* v *and* y *satisfy* last-time-targeted *consistency, denoted as* $v \simeq_\ell y$, *if and only if* $\gamma^\star(v) = \gamma^+(y)$.

In what follows, we discuss how the temporal consistency constraints introduced in Definitions 1 to 4 are used in our new dynamic re-identification attack.

3.4   Stages of the Attacker-Defender Game

We now discuss the actions performed by the data owner and the adversary at every time-stamp t_i. We first discuss sybil subgraph creation and update, then graph publication, and finally re-identification.

Sybil Subgraph Creation. The adversary can build the initial sybil subgraph along several releases. This allows the creation of tempo-structural patterns incorporating information about the first snapshot where each sybil node appears, to facilitate the sybil subgraph retrieval stage during re-identification. As in all active attacks, the patterns created must ensure that, with high probability, $\langle S_{t_i} \rangle_{G_{t_i}^+}^w$ is unique. We denote by $F_{t_i}(y)$ the fingerprint of a victim $y \in Y_{t_i}$ in terms of S_{t_i}. Throughout this paper we consider that $F_{t_i}(y)$ is uniquely determined by the neighbourhood of y in S_{t_i}, that is $F_{t_i}(y) = S_{t_i} \cap N_{G_y^+}$. We denote by $\mathcal{F}_{t_i}$ the set of fingerprints of all victims in $G_{t_i}^+$.

Sybil Subgraph Update. In this step, the adversary can modify the set of sybil nodes, by adding new sybil nodes or replacing existing ones. The adversary can also modify the inter-sybil connections and the fingerprints. Sybil subgraph update is executed after at least one re-identification attempt has been conducted, so the adversary can use information from this attempt, such as the level of uncertainty in the re-identification, to decide the changes to introduce in the sybil subgraph. Finally, if the number of fingerprints that can be constructed using the new set of sybil nodes is larger than the previous number of targeted victims, that is $2^{|S_{t_i}|} - 1 > |Y_{t_{i-1}}|$, the adversary can additionally target new victims, either new users that joined the network in the last inter-release interval, or previously enrolled users that had not been targeted so far. In the latter case, even if these victims had not been targeted before, the consistency of the labelling in the sequence of sanitised snapshots entails that a re-identification in the t_i-th snapshot can be traced back to the previous ones. Additional details on the implementation of sybil subgraph creation and update in the instantiation of the dynamic active attack presented in this paper can be found in Appendix A.

Graph Publication. At time step t_i, the data owner anonymises $G_{t_i}^+$ and publishes the sanitised version $G_{t_i}^\star$. We formally view anonymisation as a two-step process. The first step is *pseudonymisation*, which consists in building an isomorphism $\varphi_{t_i} : V_{G_{t_i}^+} \rightarrow V_{t_i}'^\star$, with $V_{t_i}'^\star \cap V_{G_{t_i}^+} = \emptyset$, that replaces every real identity in $G_{t_i}^+$ for a pseudonym. The pseudonymised graph is denoted as $\varphi_{t_i} G_{t_i}^+$. If $i = 1$, all pseudonyms are freshly generated. In the remaining cases, the pseudonyms for previously existing vertices are kept, and fresh pseudonyms are assigned to new vertices. The second step of the anonymisation process consists in applying a *perturbation* method $\Phi_{t_i} : \varphi_{t_i} G_{t_i}^+ \rightarrow (V_{t_i}^\star, V_{t_i}^\star \times V_{t_i}^\star)$ to the pseudonymised graph. Perturbation consists in editing the vertex and/or edge sets of the pseudonymised graph. Finally, the data owner releases the graph $G_{t_i}^\star$ obtained as the result of applying pseudonymisation on $G_{t_i}^+$ and perturbation on $\varphi_{t_i} G_{t_i}^+$.

First Re-identification Attempt. The first re-identification attempt is composed of two steps, *sybil subgraph retrieval* and *fingerprint matching*. Sybil subgraph retrieval consists in the following substeps:

1. Find in $G_{t_i}^\star$ a set $\mathcal{X}_{t_i} = \{X_1, X_2, \ldots, X_p\}$, $X_j \subseteq V_{G_{t_i}^\star}$, of candidate sybil sets. For every $X \in \mathcal{X}_{t_i}$, the graph $\langle X \rangle_{G_{t_i}^\star}^w$ is a candidate sybil subgraph. In the instantiation of the dynamic active attack presented in this paper, we apply two filtering criteria:
   (i) Every element X of $\mathcal{X}_{t_i}$ must satisfy $\Delta(\langle X \rangle_{G_{t_i}^\star}^w, \langle S_{t_i} \rangle_{G_{t_i}^+}^w) \leq \theta_{t_i}$, where Δ is the structural dissimilarity function defined in [14] and θ_{t_i} is a tolerance threshold. The value of θ_{t_i} may be fixed (as in [14]), or it may be increased as new snapshots are released in order to adapt to the accumulation of modifications in successive instances of the graph publication step.
   (ii) Every element of $\mathcal{X}_{t_i}$ must satisfy the *first-use-as-sybil* consistency constraint with respect to $\langle S_{t_1} \rangle_{G_{t_1}^+}^w, \langle S_{t_2} \rangle_{G_{t_2}^+}^w, \ldots, \langle S_{t_{i-1}} \rangle_{G_{t_{i-1}}^+}^w$.
2. If $\mathcal{X}_{t_i} = \emptyset$, the attack fails. Otherwise, proceed to fingerprint matching (step 2).

For its part, fingerprint matching consists in the following substeps:

1. Select one element $X \in \mathcal{X}_{t_i}$ with probability $\frac{1}{|\mathcal{X}_{t_i}|}$.
2. Using X and $\mathcal{F}_{t_i}$, find a set of candidate mappings $\mathcal{Y}_X = \{\phi_1, \phi_2, \ldots, \phi_q\}$, where every ϕ_j ($1 \leq j \leq q$) has the form $\phi_j : V_{G_{t_i}^\star} \setminus S_{t_i} \rightarrow Y_{t_i}$. Every element of $\mathcal{Y}_{X_{t_i}}$ represents a possible re-identification of the victims in $G_{t_i}^\star$. In the instantiation of the dynamic active attack presented in this paper, $\mathcal{Y}_{X_{t_i}}$ is composed of the elements simultaneously satisfying two criteria:

(i) Maximise the noise-tolerant fingerprint similarity function defined in [14], provided that the similarity is above a threshold η.

(ii) Satisfy the *first-time-targeted* and *last-time-targeted* consistency constraints with respect to $\mathcal{F}_{t_1}, \mathcal{F}_{t_2}, \ldots, \mathcal{F}_{t_{i-1}}$.

3. If $\mathcal{Y}_{\mathcal{X}'_{t_i}} = \emptyset$, the attack fails. Otherwise, select one element of $\mathcal{Y}_{\mathcal{X}'_{t_i}}$ and give it as the result of the re-identification. As in the previous steps, every specific attack defines how the selection is made.

The combination of structural similarity and temporal consistency in steps 1.a and 2.b considerably speed-up the overall re-identification process, and increase its effectiveness, as will be empirically demonstrated in Sect. 4. Additional details on the implementation of steps 1.a and 2.b are given in Appendix B.

Re-identification Refinement. As we discussed above, the first re-identification attempt on $G^{\star}_{t_i}$ can be executed immediately after the snapshot is published. Then, after the publication of $G^{\star}_{t_j}$, $j > i$, the re-identification refinement step allows the adversary to improve her certainty on the previous re-identification, by filtering out elements of $\mathcal{X}_{t_i}$ that fail to satisfy the *sybil-removal-count* consistency constraint with respect to $\langle S_{t_i} \rangle^w_{G^+_{t_i}}$ and $\langle S_{t_j} \rangle^w_{G^+_{t_j}}$, and then repeating the fingerprint matching step, excluding the candidate nodes that do not comply with the *first-time-targeted* or the *last-time-targeted* consistency constraints.

4 Experiments

In this section, we empirically evaluate our new dynamic active attack. Our evaluation has three goals. First, we show that our dynamic attack outperforms the alternative of repeatedly executing Mauw *et al.*'s static robust active attack [14] in terms of both effectiveness and efficiency. Secondly, we determine the factors that affect the performance of our new attack, and evaluate their impact. From this analysis, we derive a number of recommendations allowing data owners to balance privacy preservation and utility in random perturbation methods for periodical social graph publication. Due to the scarcity of real-life temporally labelled social graphs, and the complete non-existence of datasets of this type where the phenomenon of users abandoning the social network is observed, we conducted these experiments on synthetic dynamic social graphs. To that end, we developed a flexible synthesiser which generates synthetic dynamic graphs with several parameter settings. Finally, we replicate the second experiment on two real-life datasets, to show that some of the findings obtained on synthetic data remain valid in practical scenarios. For simplicity, throughout this section we use the acronym D-AA for our new dynamic attack and S-RAA for the static robust active attack.

4.1 Experimental Setting

We implemented an evaluation tool based on the attacker-defender game described in Sect. 3. A dynamic social graph simulator loads a real-life dataset, or uses the synthesiser, to generate the sequence $\mathcal{G} = (G_{t_1}, G_{t_2}, \ldots, G_{t_i}, \ldots)$ containing only legitimate users. Each snapshot is then processed by a second module that simulates sybil sub-graph creation or update. The output, which is the data owner's view of the social graph, is processed by a graph perturbation module, where we implement a simple perturbation method based on cumulative noise addition. Finally, a fourth module simulates the re-identification on the perturbed graph and computes the success probability of the attack. Sybil subgraph creation and update, as well as re-identification, have been discussed in Sect. 3.4 (with extensive details given in Appendixes A and B, respectively). We describe in what follows the implementation of the remaining modules.

Dynamic Social Graph Simulator. Our simulator allows us to conduct experiments on temporally annotated real-life datasets, as well as synthetic datasets. In the first case, the simulator extracts the graph snapshots from each dataset using a specific handler. The simulator is parameterised with a sequence of time-stamps indicating when each snapshot should be taken. A snapshot is built by taking all vertices and edges created at a moment earlier or identical to the corresponding time-stamp and still not eliminated.

In the second case, our simulator synthesises a sequence of snapshots according to the Barabási-Albert (BA) generative graph model [1]. We use BA because it preserves the properties of real social graphs, namely power-law degree distribution, shrinking diameter, and preferential attachment. The BA model has two parameters: the number of nodes n_0 of a (small) seed graph, and the initial degree M_e ($M_e \leq n_0$) of every newly added node. The initial seed graph can be any graph. In our case we use a complete graph K_{n_0}. Every time a new node v is added to the current version G of the BA graph, M_e edges are added between v and randomly selected vertices in V_G. The probability of selecting a vertex $w \in V_G$ for creating the new edge (v, w) is $\frac{\delta_G(w)}{\sum_{x \in V_G} \delta_G(x)}$, as prescribed by preferential attachment. We simulate the phenomenon of users abandoning the social network by removing z randomly selected nodes before creating a new snapshot. The value of z is randomly selected in the interval $[0, z^*]$, where z^* is 10% of the current number of nodes. The synthesiser takes four parameters as input: the parameter n_0 of the BA model, the parameter M_e of the BA model, the number n_v of vertices of the first snapshot, and the growth rate r_Δ, which is defined as the proportion of new edges with respect to the previous number. The parameters n_v and r_Δ determine when snapshots are taken. The first snapshot is taken when the number of vertices of the graph generated by the BA model reaches n_v, and every other snapshot is taken when the ratio between the number of new edges and that of the previous snapshot reaches r_Δ.

Graph Perturbation via Cumulative Noise Addition. To the best of our knowledge, all existing anonymisation methods against active attacks based on formal privacy properties [12, 13] assume a single release scenario, and are thus insufficient for handling multiple releases. Proposing formal privacy properties that take into account the specificities of the multiple release scenario is part of the future work. In our experiments, we adapted the other known family of perturbation methods, random noise addition, to the multiple release scenario. To account for the incrementality of the publication process, the noise is added in a cumulative manner. That is, when releasing $G_{t_i}^\star$, the noise incrementally added on $G_{t_1}^\star, G_{t_2}^\star, \ldots, G_{t_{i-1}}^\star$ is re-applied on the pseudonymised graph $\varphi_{t_i} G_{t_i}^+$ to obtain an intermediate noisy graph $\tilde{G}_{t_i}^\star$, and then fresh noise is added on $\tilde{G}_{t_i}^\star$ to obtain the graph $G_{t_i}^\star$ that is released. In re-applying the old noise, all noisy edges incident in a vertex $v \in V_{G^\star_{t_{i-1}}} \setminus V_{\varphi_{t_i} G^+_{t_i}}$, removed after the release of $G^\star_{t_{i-1}}$, are forgotten. The fresh noise addition consists in randomly flipping a number of edges of $\tilde{G}^\star_{t_i}$. For every flip, a pair $(v, w) \in V_{\tilde{G}^\star_{t_i}} \times V_{\tilde{G}^\star_{t_i}}$ is uniformly selected and, if $(v, w) \in E_{\tilde{G}^\star_{t_i}}$, the edge is removed, otherwise it is added. The cumulative noise addition method has one parameter: the amount of fresh noise to add in each snapshot, called *noise ratio* and denoted Ω_{noise}. It is computed with respect to $|E_{\tilde{G}^\star_{t_i}}|$, the number of edges of the pseudonymised graph after restoring the accumulated noise.

Success Probability. As in previous works on active attacks for the single release scenario [12–14], we evaluate the adversary's success in terms of the probability that she correctly re-identifies all victims, which in our scenario is computed by the following formula for the t_i-th snapshot:

$$Pr^{(t_i)}_{succ} = \begin{cases} \frac{\sum_{X \in \mathcal{X}_{t_i}} p^{(t_i)}_X}{|\mathcal{X}_{t_i}|} & \text{if } \mathcal{X}_{t_i} \neq \emptyset \\ 0 & \text{otherwise} \end{cases}, \text{ with } p^{(t_i)}_X = \begin{cases} \frac{1}{|\mathcal{Y}_X|} & \text{if } \exists_{\phi \in \mathcal{Y}_X} \phi^{-1} = \varphi_{t_i}|_{Y_{t_i}} \\ 0 & \text{otherwise} \end{cases}$$

and, as discussed in Sect. 3.4, φ_{t_i} is the isomorphism applied on $G^+_{t_i}$ to obtain the pseudonymised graph $\varphi_{t_i} G^+_{t_i}$. For every snapshot $G^\star_{t_i}$, we compute success probability after the re-identification refinement is executed.

4.2 Results and Discussion

We begin our discussion with the comparison of D-AA and S-RAA. Then, we proceed to study the factors that affect the effectiveness of our attack, and characterise their influence. Finally, we illustrate the effectiveness of our attack in practice using the real-life datasets Petster [9] and BitcoinOTC [8]. For the first two sets of results, we use synthetic dynamic graphs generated by our synthesiser. Table 1 summarises the different configurations used for the generation. For each parameter combination, we generated 100 synthetic dynamic graphs, and the results shown are the averages over each subcollection. Every synthetic dynamic graph is grown up to the 20-th snaphsot. In all cases, the number of new victims targeted in each new release is randomly chosen in the interval $[1, 5]$.

Table 1. Parameter combinations for the graph synthesiser.

	n_0	M_e	n_v	r_Δ	$\Omega_{noise}(\%)$
Comparison of D-AA and S-RAA	30	5	200, 400, 800	5%	0.5
Detailed analysis of our D-AA attack	30	5, 10	8000, 10000, 15000	5%	0.5, 1.0, 1.5, 2.0

As can be observed in the table, we used considerable smaller graphs for comparing D-AA and S-RAA than the ones used for the detailed analysis of the factors influencing the effectiveness of our new attack. The reason for this difference lies in the considerably poorer performance, in terms of execution time, of the static attack. Since these limits only apply to the static attack, the detailed analysis of our dynamic attack is performed on considerably larger graphs. For example, for $M_e = 5$ and $n_v = 15000$, the graphs generated at the 20-th snapshots have around 80000 nodes.

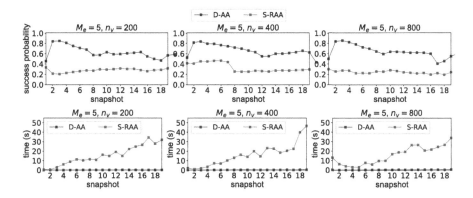

Fig. 2. Comparison of S-RAA and D-AA in terms of effectiveness (top) and efficiency (bottom).

Comparing D-AA and S-RAA. The goal of this comparison is to show that our dynamic active attack outperforms the repeated execution of the original attack in both effectiveness and efficiency. We use three parameter settings for the dynamic graph synthesiser. We fix $M_e = 5$ and set the initial number of vertices n_v at 200, 400 and 800. In all our experiments, sybil subgraph creation spans the first and second snapshots, and the re-identification is executed for the first time on the second snapshot. Both attacks are executed independently. That is, for every run we create two identical copies of each synthetic graph to ensure that both attacks are compared in the same scenario, yet the actions performed by D-AA have no impact on S-RAA, and *vice versa*. S-RAA is allowed to create a fresh sybil subgraph for every snapshot and to increase its number of sybils if D-AA increases hers. In D-AA, we use the variable tolerance threshold $\theta_{t_i} = \min\{1500, 16 + 250 \times (i - 2)^2\}$ for the i-th snapshot. Since S-RAA becomes prohibitively slow with arbitrarily large values of θ, we run it with the fixed tolerance threshold $\theta = 16$, for which the attack runs in reasonable time for the largest graphs used in this comparison. These settings guarantee that, to the largest possible extent, D-AA is compared to the most effective feasible instantiation of S-RAA.

In Fig. 2 (top) we show the success probabilities of the two attacks on graphs with different initial sizes. From these results, we can see that, as we had intuitively foreseen, D-AA significantly outperforms S-RAA in terms of success probability. Except for a few cases, D-AA outperforms S-RAA by at least a factor of 2 and by up to 4 in some cases. Moreover, the average success probability of our attack remains above 0.5 in almost all cases, whereas that of S-RAA never reaches this value. Figure 2 (bottom) shows the average run times of S-RAA and D-AA in different scenarios. We can see that D-AA runs in almost constant time on all snapshots, whereas S-RAA becomes considerably slower as the graphs grow. In fact, D-AA runs at least 11 times faster than

S-RAA in all cases, especially in late snapshots, where it runs up to 350 times faster in some cases. This clearly shows that the use of temporal information in dynamic social graphs helps D-AA to effectively avoid the computation overhead. Indeed, as the released snapshots become larger, the number of equally similar matches (in terms of structure alone) grows considerably, which dramatically increases the search space for S-RAA. In this scenario, temporal consistency constraints allow D-AA to discard most of the false positives and thus skip large areas of the search space.

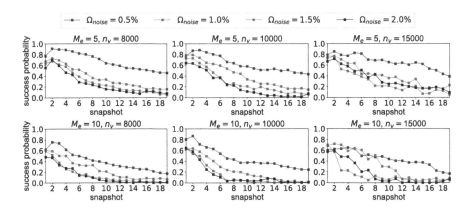

Fig. 3. Factors influencing success probability of D-AA.

Factors Influencing our Attack. This analysis aims to serve as a guide for customising the settings of privacy-preserving publication methods for dynamic social graphs, in particular for determining the amount of perturbation needed to balance the privacy requirements and the utility of published graphs. We evaluate the impact of three factors on the effectiveness of D-AA on dynamic graphs: the size of graphs, the speed of growth between releases, and the amount of added noise. To that end, we analyse three parameters which determine these factors in our simulator: n_v, M_e, and Ω_{noise}. The number n_v of vertices in the initial snapshots determines the scale of the released graphs, while the parameter M_e of the BA model controls the number of new nodes and edges added before the next release. Finally, Ω_{noise} determines the amount of added noise.

Figure 3 shows the success probability of our attack when different noise ratios are applied on dynamic graphs with different initial sizes and growth speeds. Our first observation is that the success probability decreases when more noise is applied. This is a natural behaviour, as more perturbation makes it more difficult for the attacker to find the correct sybil subgraph, either because it has been excessively perturbed to be found as a candidate, or because edge perturbation makes other subgraphs appear more similar to the original sybil subgraph. When $M_e = 5$ and the noise ratio is set to 0.5%, success probability always remains above 0.5. For this value of M_e, even with Ω_{noise} at 2.0%, the attack still displays success probability above 0.5 in the first three snapshots. Our second observation is that increases in noise ratio do not translate into proportionally large decreases in success probability. Indeed, the largest drop in success probability occurs when we increase Ω_{noise} from 0.5 to 1.0. This suggests that arbitrarily increasing the amount of perturbation may not necessarily guarantee a better privacy protection, but just damage the utility of the released graphs. Our third observation is that success probability values show a weak dependence on the initial size of the graphs, with other parameters fixed. Finally, we observe that success probability decreases faster, and is around 10% lower, snapshot-by-snapshot, when dynamic graphs grow faster (in this case, when M_e grows). Summing up, we observe that re-identification risk decreases when more perturbation is applied, or when the graphs grow faster, whereas the initial size of the graphs has a relatively small impact on the attacker's success probability.

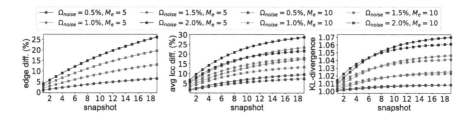

Fig. 4. Factors influencing the utility of released graphs.

We evaluate the utility of released graphs (Fig. 4) in terms of three measures: the percentage of edge editions, the variation of the average local clustering coefficient, and the Kullback-Leibler divergence of degree distributions. As all three measures present very similar patterns for different values of n_v, we only show the results for $n_v = 15000$. We have two major observations. First, as expected, the values of all three measures increase as the noise accumulates, indicating that the utility of released graphs deteriorates. Even with Ω_{noise} set to just 1.0%, at the 10-th snapshot we can have up to 10% of edges flipped and changes in edge density around 15%. Second, when the dynamic graph grows faster, the impact of noise becomes smaller, as a larger number of legitimate edges offsets the impact of noisy edges. Combining these results on utility with the finding that larger growth speed results in smaller success probability for the attacker, we can enunciate the following global recommendation for the design of publication strategies and anonymisation methods for dynamic social graphs: the data owner should publish dynamic social graphs that grow fast among releases, as they feature the best balance between re-identification risk and utility.

Results on Real-Life Dynamic Social Graphs. We use two publicly available datasets to validate to what extent the results reported on synthetic data remain valid in a more realistic domain. The first one was collected from Petster, a website for pet owners to communicate [9]. The Petster dataset is an undirected graph whose vertices represent pet owners, and are labelled by their joining date. The graph contains 1898 vertices and 16750 edges. We take a snapshot every six months. The second dataset was collected from the platform BitcoinOTC, where users can trade with bitcoins. This platform allows members to rate others. In the resulting social graph, nodes represent members and an edge between two nodes indicates that one of them rated the other. Every edge is tagged with the date of the first rating between the corresponding pair of users. The joining date of a member is set as the date when his first rating is posted. The graph contains 5881 nodes and 21455 edges. We take the first snapshot at the 9th month, and every other snapshot every 3 months, totalling 20 snapshots. Both datasets are incremental, that is nodes are added but never removed.

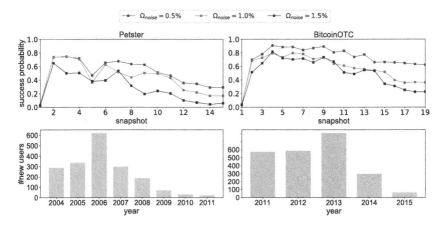

Fig. 5. Evaluation on real-life datasets.

We present in Fig. 5 (top) the success probabilities of our D-AA attack on the two datasets when the noise ratio is set to 0.5%, 1.0% and 1.5%. Compared to the success probabilities discussed above on synthetic graphs, the curves have different shapes and more fluctuations. This is because, instead of a fixed growth speed (determined by r_Δ and M_e in our synthesiser), real-life graphs grow at different speeds in different periods, as shown in Fig. 5 (bottom). For example, consider the evolution of Petster. After the first few years of steady growth, it gradually lost its popularity, especially in the last three years, where few new users joined. By cross-checking the attack's behaviour on Petster with the network's evolution, we can see that the success probability changes with the amount of growth before the corresponding release. It first increases steadily, due to the steady growth of the graph, until the fifth snapshot, which shows an abrupt growth in the number of new vertices, along with a drop of success probability. Then, when the growth slows down, the success probability also recovers; and when the growth stops (from the 12-th snapshot), it starts increasing again, even though the noise continues to accumulate. These observations validate our finding on synthetic graphs that the speed of growth among releases is the dominating factor that affects the success probability of our dynamic attack.

5 Conclusions

We have presented the first dynamic active re-identification attack on periodically released social graphs. Unlike preceding attacks, our new attack exploits the inherent dynamic nature of social networks by leveraging tempo-structural patterns, enforced by a dynamic set of sybil nodes. Compared to the best static active attack, our new attack significantly improves success probability, by at least two times, and efficiency, by at least 11 times. Moreover, unlike the static attack, our new attack remains at the same level of efficiency as the publication process advances. Through comprehensive experiments on synthetic data, we determined the factors that influence the success probability of our new attack against a data owner using cumulative noise addition for graph perturbation, namely the speed of growth and the amount of noise injected. These findings can subsequently be used to develop dynamic graph anonymisation methods that better balance privacy protection and the utility of the released graphs. Additionally, we evaluated our attack on two real-life datasets, which allowed us to ascertain that these findings obtained on synthetic data remain valid in practical scenarios.

Acknowledgements. This work received funding from Luxembourg's Fonds National de la Recherche (FNR), via grant C17/IS/11685812 (PrivDA).

A   Implementation Details of Sybil Subgraph Creation and Update

Sybil Subgraph Creation. Let $G_{t_i}^\star$ be the first snapshot where the adversary conducts a re-identification attempt. Sybil subgraph creation is executed during the entire time window preceding t_i. The adversary initially inserts a small number of sybil nodes, no more than $\left\lfloor \log_2 \left(|V_{G_{t_i}^+}| \right) \right\rfloor$. This makes the sybil subgraph very unlikely to be detected by sybil defences [2, 13, 14, 24, 25], while allowing to create unique fingerprints for a reasonably large number of potential initial victims. Spreading sybil injection over several snapshots helps create temporal patterns that reduce the search space during sybil subgraph retrieval. Inter-sybil edges are created in a manner that has been shown in [2] to make the sybil subgraph unique with high probability. First, an arbitrary (but fixed) order is established among the sybil nodes. In our case, we simply take the order in which the sybils are created. Let $s_1 \prec s_2 \prec \ldots \prec s_{|S_{t_i}|}$ represent the order established among the sybils. Then, the edges (s_1, s_2), (s_2, s_3), $\ldots$, $(s_{|S_{t_i}|-1}, s_{|S_{t_i}|})$ are added to force the existence of the path $s_1 s_2 \ldots s_{|S_{t_i}|}$. Additionally, every other edge (s_j, s_k), $|j - k| \geq 2$, is added with probability 0.5. The initial fingerprints of the elements of Y_{t_i} are randomly generated (yet enforcing that all fingerprints are unique) by connecting each victim to each sybil node with probability 0.5.

Sybil Subgraph Update. Let $G_{t_{i-1}}^\star$ and $G_{t_i}^\star$ be two consecutive releases occurring after the first snapshot where the adversary conducted a re-identification attempt ($G_{t_{i-1}}^\star$ itself may have been this snapshot). In the interval between $G_{t_{i-1}}^\star$ and $G_{t_i}^\star$, the adversary updates the sybil subgraph by adding and/or removing sybil nodes and inter-sybil edges, updating the fingerprints of (a subset of) the victims, and possibly targeting new victims. We describe each of these modifications in detail in what follows.

Adding and Replacing Sybil Nodes. In our attack, the adversary is conservative regarding the number of sybil nodes, balancing the capacity to target more victims with the need to keep the likelihood of being detected by sybil defences sufficiently low. Thus, the number of sybil nodes is increased as the number of nodes in the graph grows, but keeping $|S_{t_i}| \leq \left\lfloor \log_2 \left(|V_{G_{t_{i-1}}^\star}| \right) \right\rfloor$. Additionally, the attacker may select a small random number of existing sybil nodes and replace them for fresh sybil nodes.

Let $S_{t_{i-1}} = \{s_1, s_2, \ldots, s_{|S_{t_{i-1}}|}\}$ be the set of sybil nodes present in $G_{t_{i-1}}^+$, and let $s_1 \prec s_2 \prec \ldots \prec s_{|S_{t_{i-1}}|}$ be the order established among them. We first consider the case of sybil node addition. Let $S' = \{s_1', s_2', \ldots, s_q'\}$ be the set of new sybil nodes that will be added to $G_{t_i}^+$, and let $s_1' \prec s_2' \prec \ldots \prec s_q'$ be the order established on them. The path $s_1 s_2 \ldots s_{|S_{t_{i-1}}|}$ is extended into $s_1 s_2 \ldots s_{|S_{t_{i-1}}|} s_1' s_2' \ldots s_q'$ by adding to $G_{t_i}^+$ the edges $(s_{|S_{t_{i-1}}|}, s_1'), (s_1', s_2'), \ldots, (s_{q-1}', s_q')$. Additionally, the adversary adds to $G_{t_i}^+$ every node (x, y), $x \in S'$, $y \in (S_{t_{i-1}} \cup S') \setminus N_{G_{t_i}^+}(x)$, with probability 0.5. In order to replace a sybil node $s_j \in S_{t_{i-1}}$ for a new sybil node s ($s \notin S'$), the adversary adds to $G_{t_i}^+$ the edges (s_{j-1}, s) and (s, s_{j+1}), where s_{j-1} and s_{j+1} are the sybil nodes immediately preceding and succeeding s_j according to $\prec$. The order $\prec$ is updated accordingly to make $s_1 \prec s_2 \prec \ldots \prec s_{j-1} \prec s \prec s_{j+1} \prec \ldots \prec s_{|S_{i-1}|}$. These modifications ensure that the path $s_1 s_2 \ldots s_{|S_{t_{i-1}}|}$ guaranteed to exist in $G_{t_{i-1}}^+$ is replaced in $G_{t_i}^+$ for $s_1 s_2 \ldots s_{j-1} s s_{j+1} \ldots s_{|S_{i-1}|}$. Additionally, the new sybil node s is connected to every other sybil node with probability 0.5. In our attack, every sybil node removal is part of a replacement, so the number of sybil nodes never decreases.

Updating Fingerprints of Existing Victims. After replacing a sybil node $s \in S_{t_{i-1}}$ for a new sybil node $s' \in S_{t_i} \setminus S_{t_{i-1}}$, the adversary adds to $G_{t_i}^+$ the edge (s', y) for every $y \in Y_{t_{i-1}} \cap N_{G_{t_{i-1}}^+}(s)$, to guarantee that the replacement of s for s' does not render any pair of fingerprints identical in $G_{t_i}^+$. Additionally, if new sybil nodes were added, the fingerprints of all previously targeted victims in $Y_{t_{i-1}}$ are modified by creating edges linking them to a subset of the new sybil nodes. For each new sybil node $s \in S_{t_i} \setminus S_{t_{i-1}}$ and every victim $y \in Y_{t_{i-1}}$, the edge (s, y) is added with probability 0.5. Finally, if the adversary has conducted a re-identification attempt on $G_{t_{i-1}}^\star$, she makes additional changes in the set $\mathcal{F}_{t_i}$ of fingerprints in $G_{t_i}^+$ based on the outcomes of the re-identification. To that end, she selects a subset $Y_{t_{i-1}}'$ of victims whose fingerprints were the least useful during the re-identification attempt, in the sense that they were the most likely to lead to a larger number of equally likely options after fingerprint mapping. The adversary modifies the fingerprint of every $y \in Y_{t_{i-1}}'$ by randomly flipping one edge of the form (y, s), $s \in S_{t_{i-1}}$, checking that the new fingerprint does not coincide with a previously existing fingerprint. The set $Y_{t_{i-1}}'$ is obtained as follows. For every victim $y_j \in Y_{t_{i-1}}$ and every vertex v mapped to y_j according to some $X \in \mathcal{X}_{t_{i-1}}$ and the corresponding $\mathcal{Y}_X$, let $p_j(v)$ be the probability that v has been mapped to y_j in the previous re-identification attempt according to some sybil subgraph candidate and some of the resulting fingerprint matchings. We make $Y'_{t_{i-1}} = \arg\max_{y_j \in Y_{t_{i-1}}} \{H(p_j)\}$, where $H(p_j)$ is the entropy of the distribution p_j.

B   Implementation Details of Dynamic Re-identification

Sybil Subgraph Retrieval. The sybil subgraph retrieval method is a breadth-first search procedure, which shares the rationale of analogous methods devised for active attacks on static graphs [2,14], but differs from them in the use of temporal consistency constraints for pruning the search space. To establish the order in which the search space is traversed, our method relies on the existence of an arbitrary (but fixed) total order $\prec$ among the set of sybil nodes, which is enforced by the sybil subgraph creation method and maintained by the sybil subgraph update method.

Let $s_1 \prec s_2 \prec \ldots \prec s_{|S_{t_i}|}$ be the order established on the elements of S_{t_i}. The search procedure first builds a set of cardinality-1 partial candidates $\mathcal{X}_{t_i,1} = \{\{v_{j_1}\} \mid v_{j_1} \in V_{G^\star_{t_i}}\}$. Then, it obtains the pruned set of candidates $\mathcal{X}'_{t_i,1}$ by removing from $\mathcal{X}_{t_i,1}$ all elements $\{v_{j_1}\}$ such that $\alpha^\star(v_{j_1}) \neq \alpha^+(s_1)$, or $\left|\delta_{G^\star_{t_i}}(v_{j_1}) - \delta_{G^+_{t_i}}(s_1)\right| > \theta$. The first condition verifies that the *first-use-as-sybil* consistency property $\{v_{j_1}\} \simeq_\phi \{s_1\}$ holds, with $\phi = \{(s_1, v_{j_1})\}$. The second condition excludes from the search tree all candidates X such that $\Delta(\langle X \rangle^w_{G^\star_{t_i}}, \langle S_{t_i} \rangle^w_{G^+_{t_i}}) > \theta$, where Δ is a structural dissimilarity function, defined in [14], and θ is a tolerance threshold. Then, for every $\ell \leq |S_{t_i}|$, the method builds the set of partial candidates

$$\mathcal{X}_{t_i,\ell} = \{\{v_{j_1}, \ldots, v_{j_\ell}\} \mid \{v_{j_1} \ldots, v_{j_{\ell-1}}\} \in \mathcal{X}_{t_i,\ell-1}, v_{j_\ell} \in V_{G^\star_{t_i}} \setminus \{v_{j_1}, \ldots, v_{j_{\ell-1}}\}\}$$

and obtains the pruned candidate set $\mathcal{X}'_{t_i,\ell}$ by removing from $\mathcal{X}_{t_i,\ell}$ all elements $\{v_{j_1}, \ldots, v_{j_\ell}\}$ such that $\{v_{j_1}, \ldots, v_{j_\ell}\} \not\simeq_\phi \{s_1, \ldots, s_\ell\}$, with $\phi = \{(s_1, v_{j_1}), \ldots, (s_\ell, v_{j_\ell})\}$, and $\Delta(\langle\{v_{j_1}, \ldots, v_{j_\ell}\}\rangle^w_{G^\star_{t_i}}, \langle\{s_1, \ldots, s_\ell\}\rangle^w_{G^+_{t_i}}) > \theta$. Finally, the method gives as output the pruned set of cardinality-$|S_{t_i}|$ candidates, that is $\mathcal{X}_{t_i} = \mathcal{X}'_{t_i,|S_{t_i}|}$. Summing up, our method outputs the set of temporally consistent vertex subsets whose weakly induced subgraphs in $G^\star_{t_i}$ are structurally similar to that of the original set of sybil nodes in $G^+_{t_i}$.

Fingerprint Matching. The fingerprint matching step is conducted for a sybil subset candidate $X = \{v_{j_1}, v_{j_2}, \ldots v_{j_{|S_{t_i}|}}\}$ randomly selected from $\mathcal{X}_{t_i}$, with probability $\frac{1}{|\mathcal{X}_{t_i}|}$. Let $v_{j_1} \prec v_{j_2} \prec \ldots \prec v_{j_{|S_{t_i}|}}$ be the order established on the elements of X by the sybil subgraph retrieval method. Our fingerprint matching method is a depth-first search procedure, which gives as output a set $\mathcal{Y}_X = \{\phi_1, \phi_2, \ldots, \phi_q\}$, where every $\phi \in \mathcal{Y}_X$ has the form $\phi : Y_{t_i} \to N_{G^\star_{t_i}}(X)$. Every element of $\mathcal{Y}_X$ maximises the pairwise similarities between the original fingerprints of the victims and the fingerprints, with respect to X, of the corresponding pseudonymised vertices. The method first finds all equally best matches between the (real) fingerprint F_j of a victim $y_j \in Y_{t_i}$ and that of a temporally consistent vertex $u \in N_{G^\star_{t_i}}(X)$ with respect to X, that is $F^\star_u = N_{G^\star_{t_i}}(u) \cap X$. Then, for every such match, it recursively applies the search procedure to match the remaining real victims to other temporally consistent candidate victims. For every victim y_j and every candidate match u, the similarity function $\text{sim}(F_u^\star, F_j)$ integrates the verification of the temporal consistency and the structural fingerprint, and is computed as

$$\text{sim}(F_u^\star, F_j) = \begin{cases} \text{sim}_c(F_u^\star, F_j) & \text{if } u \simeq y_j \text{ and } \text{sim}_c(F_u^\star, F_j) \geq \eta \\ 0 & \text{otherwise.} \end{cases}$$

where η is a tolerance threshold allowing to ignore insufficiently similar matches and the function $\text{sim}_c(F_u^\star, F_j)$ is defined as $\text{sim}_c(F_u^\star, F_j) = \sum_{k=1}^{|S_{t_i}|} \mu_k(F_u^\star, F_j)$ with

$$\mu_k(F_u^\star, F_j) = \begin{cases} 1 & \text{if } v_{j_k} \in F_u^\star \text{ and } s_k \in F_j \\ 0 & \text{otherwise.} \end{cases}$$

References

1. Albert, R., Barabási, A.L.: Statistical mechanics of complex networks. Rev. Modern Phys. **74**, 47–97 (2002)
2. Backstrom, L., Dwork, C., Kleinberg, J.M.: Wherefore art thou r3579x?: anonymized social networks, hidden patterns, and structural steganography. Commun. ACM **54**(12), 133–141 (2011)
3. Casas-Roma, J., Herrera-Joancomartí, J., Torra, V.: k-degree anonymity and edge selection: improving data utility in large networks. Knowl. Inf. Syst. **50**(2), 447–474 (2017)
4. Dakiche, N., Tayeb, F.B., Slimani, Y., Benatchba, K.: Tracking community evolution in social networks: a survey. Inf. Process. Manag. **56**(3), 1084–1102 (2019)
5. Ding, X., Zhang, L., Wan, Z., Gu, M.: De-anonymizing dynamic social networks. In: Proceedings of GLOBECOM 2011, pp. 1–6 (2011)
6. Ji, S., Li, W., Srivatsa, M., Beyah, R.: Structural data de-anonymization: quantification, practice, and implications. In: Proceedings of CCS 2014, pp. 1040–1053 (2014)
7. Korula, N., Lattanzi, S.: An efficient reconciliation algorithm for social networks. Proc. VLDB Endow. **7**(5), 377–388 (2014)
8. Kumar, S., Spezzano, F., Subrahmanian, V.S., Faloutsos, C.: Edge weight prediction in weighted signed networks. In: Proceedings of ICDM 2016, pp. 221–230 (2016)
9. Kunegis, J.: KONECT: the Koblenz network collection. In: Proceedings of WWW 2013, pp. 1343–1350 (2013)
10. Liu, K., Terzi, E.: Towards identity anonymization on graphs. In: Proceedings of SIGMOD 2008, pp. 93–106 (2008)
11. Martínez, V., Berzal, F., Cubero, J.C.: A survey of link prediction in complex networks. ACM Comput. Surv. **49**(4), 69 (2017)
12. Mauw, S., Ramírez-Cruz, Y., Trujillo-Rasua, R.: Anonymising social graphs in the presence of active attackers. Trans. Data Privacy **11**(2), 169–198 (2018)
13. Mauw, S., Ramírez-Cruz, Y., Trujillo-Rasua, R.: Conditional adjacency anonymity in social graphs under active attacks. Knowl. Inf. Syst. **61**(1), 485–511 (2018). https://doi.org/10.1007/s10115-018-1283-x
14. Mauw, S., Ramírez-Cruz, Y., Trujillo-Rasua, R.: Robust active attacks on social graphs. Data Mining Knowl. Discov. **33**(5), 1357–1392 (2019). https://doi.org/10.1007/s10618-019-00631-5
15. Narayanan, A., Shmatikov, V.: De-anonymizing social networks. In: Proceedings of S&P 2009, pp. 173–187 (2009)

16. Nilizadeh, S., Kapadia, A., Ahn, Y.: Community-enhanced de-anonymization of online social networks. In: Proceedings of CCS 2014, pp. 537–548 (2014)
17. Papadopoulos, F., Kleineberg, K.K.: Link persistence and conditional distances in multiplex networks. Phys. Rev. E **99**(1), 012322 (2019)
18. Pedarsani, P., Figueiredo, D.R., Grossglauser, M.: A Bayesian method for matching two similar graphs without seeds. In: Proceedings of the 51st Annual Allerton Conference on Communication, Control, and Computing, pp. 1598–1607 (2013)
19. Peng, W., Li, F., Zou, X., Wu, J.: A two-stage deanonymization attack against anonymized social networks. IEEE Trans. Comput. **63**(2), 290–303 (2014)
20. Rousseau, F., Casas-Roma, J., Vazirgiannis, M.: Community-preserving anonymization of graphs. Knowl. Inf. Syst. **54**(2), 315–343 (2017). https://doi.org/10.1007/s10115-017-1064-y
21. Tai, C.H., Tseng, P.J., Philip, S.Y., Chen, M.S.: Identities anonymization in dynamic social networks. In: Proceedings of ICDM 2011, pp. 1224–1229 (2011)
22. Wu, W., Xiao, Y., Wang, W., He, Z., Wang, Z.: K-symmetry model for identity anonymization in social networks. In: Proceedings of the 13th International Conference on Extending Database Technology, pp. 111–122 (2010)
23. Yartseva, L., Grossglauser, M.: On the performance of percolation graph matching. In: Proceedings of COSN 2013, pp. 119–130 (2013)
24. Yu, H., Gibbons, P.B., Kaminsky, M., Xiao, F.: Sybillimit: a near-optimal social network defense against sybil attacks. In: Procs. of S&P 2008. pp. 3–17 (2008)
25. Yu, H., Kaminsky, M., Gibbons, P.B., Flaxman, A.: SybilQuard: defending against sybil attacks via social networks. In: Proceedings of SIGCOMM 2006, pp. 267–278 (2006)
26. Zhou, B., Pei, J.: Preserving privacy in social networks against neighborhood attacks. In: Proceedings of ICDE 2008, pp. 506–515 (2008)
27. Zou, L., Chen, L., Özsu, M.T.: K-automorphism: a general framework for privacy preserving network publication. Proc. VLDB Endow. **2**(1), 946–957 (2009)

System Security II

Fooling Primality Tests on Smartcards

Vladimir Sedlacek[1,2(✉)], Jan Jancar[1], and Petr Svenda[1]

[1] Masaryk University, Brno, Czechia
[2] Ca' Foscari University of Venice, Venice, Italy
{vlada.sedlacek,j08ny}@mail.muni.cz, svenda@fi.muni.cz

Abstract. We analyse whether the smartcards of the JavaCard platform correctly validate primality of domain parameters. The work is inspired by Albrecht et al. [1], where the authors analysed many open-source libraries and constructed pseudoprimes fooling the primality testing functions. However, in the case of smartcards, often there is no way to invoke the primality test directly, so we trigger it by replacing (EC)DSA and (EC)DH prime domain parameters by adversarial composites. Such a replacement results in vulnerability to Pohlig-Hellman [30] style attacks, leading to private key recovery.

Out of nine smartcards (produced by five major manufacturers) we tested (See https://crocs.fi.muni.cz/papers/primality_esorics20 for more information), all but one have no primality test in parameter validation. As the JavaCard platform provides no public primality testing API, the problem cannot be fixed by an extra parameter check, making it difficult to mitigate in already deployed smartcards.

Keywords: Pseudoprimes · Primality testing · JavaCard · (EC)DSA · (EC)DH

1 Introduction

Many public key cryptosystems crucially rely on prime numbers for their security. Yet for performance reasons (especially on constrained devices such as smartcards), most widely used primality tests, such as the Miller-Rabin (MR) test [23,32], are only probabilistic [1,9]. Thus there exist *pseudoprimes*, i.e., composite numbers passing these tests. When implemented correctly, probabilistic tests still provide a sufficient assurance of primality. However, carefully crafted pseudoprimes [4] can fool an implementation that is not utilizing enough randomness [1]. In (EC)DH and (EC)DSA, this can lead to private key recovery, using Pohlig-Hellman [30] style attacks.

JavaCard [29] is a popular platform for building systems based on programmable smart cards. It offers a Java-like environment on which multiple applications, *applets*, can be installed. Thanks to Javacard's rich cryptographic API (supporting (EC)DSA, (EC)DH and much more [33]), these applets include electronic passports and IDs, EMV applets for credit-cards, key managers, cryptocurrency wallets or applets for two-factor authentication. While the API is

© Springer Nature Switzerland AG 2020
L. Chen et al. (Eds.): ESORICS 2020, LNCS 12309, pp. 209–229, 2020.
https://doi.org/10.1007/978-3-030-59013-0_11

defined by an open standard, the implementation of the platform itself is almost always proprietary, with manufacturers releasing very little information about the code used in a particular family of cards. This black-box nature makes the public assessment of implementation security more difficult, but nevertheless, security problems have been discovered in the past [25].

In this paper, we test the robustness of present primality tests in JavaCards by replacing (EC)DSA and (EC)DH prime parameters with MR pseudoprimes and other composites. In contrast to [1], we do not have access to the code inside the smartcard and are not able to call a primality testing function on its own. Instead, we resort to performing standard operations (such as signature generation) using modified parameters (which still need to have specific properties), and observe any deviations from the expected behaviour. This is further complicated by the fact that the smartcards do not act deterministically, do not have debugging functionality, and are prone to many errors.

The main contributions of this paper are:

- We open the topic of fooling primality tests on black-box devices and propose a method for a systematic review of primality tests (and the relevant domain parameter validation) in black-box devices that use (EC)DSA/(EC)DH.
- We develop new ways in which parameters can be replaced with pseudoprimes in (EC)DH and (EC)DSA, along with practical attacks against these parameters. In particular, the attack against composite p in ECDSA is new to the best of our knowledge.
- We examine the implementation security of ECDH and ECDSA in nine smartcards from five major manufacturers, showing that all cards but one are vulnerable due to insufficient primality testing of domain parameters. Issues found were responsibly disclosed to affected vendors.
- We systematically survey the relevant attacker scenarios and types of attacks with possible real-world impact and propose defence mechanisms.

We review the previous work on attacking primality tests in Sect. 2. Section 3 analyses the attack scenarios and briefly presents possible attacks. The methodology for testing the cards is given in Sect. 4, along with a basic explanation of the used domain parameters. Readers interested only in practical security should feel free to skip this section, while still grasping most of the contents of Sect. 5 that analyses the testing results, and Sect. 7 that follows up with a discussion of proposed defences. Section 6 provides technical details about the full parameter generation and possible attacks and Sect. 8 concludes our paper. Finally, the appendices contain an overview of the MR test (Appendix 1), the pseudoprime construction (Appendix 2), datasets of generated domain parameters (Appendix 2.1) and example implementations of concrete attacks (Appendix 3).

2   Previous Work

The idea of breaking a cryptographic protocol by fooling primality tests was first mentioned in [9]. In [1], the authors analysed primality tests in open-source libraries, and fooled many of them with carefully crafted pseudoprimes. Their construction (extending the one in [4] and briefly described in Appendix 2) relies on the assumption that the implementation of the MR test uses only a small number of bases that are either fixed or chosen from a relatively small set. This was indeed the case for many libraries.

Note that all the inspected libraries had a dedicated function for primality testing whose source code was accessible. In contrast, the situation for black-box devices where the code is not known, and the primality test (if present) cannot be separated from the rest of the program, has not been studied before to the best of our knowledge.

Furthermore, somewhat practical examples of attacks against various (EC)DH implementations with insufficient primality tests, including the case when pseudoprimes are included in elliptic curve domain parameters, were described in [16].

3   Attack Scenarios

As in [1], we assume a setting where the attacker can control or affect the cryptosystem domain parameters used by the applet – so that primes can be replaced by composites – and wants to break the confidentiality of (EC)DH or unforgeability in (EC)DSA. We also assume that the attacker knows the factorization of the injected parameters, as he most likely crafted them himself.

However, with the exception of primality testing, we still expect that all of parameter validation is implemented properly (with the exception of a cofactor check of an elliptic curve, as the cards lack the performance to do it).

In our scenario an *applet* developed by an *applet developer* uses the functions of the JavaCard API on a card supplied by a *manufacturer* to perform some cryptographic operations while allowing untrusted parameters provided by the attacker to be used.

3.1   Rationale for the Attack Scenarios

To explain the rationale behind such a scenario, we consider the specifics of the JavaCard environment as well as existing cryptographic protocols and standards. Note that physical access (as is commonly relevant for the smartcard usage domain) is often not required.

A JavaCard applet developer might use untrusted domain parameters, because:

- The API functions that set parameter values, like ECPrivateKey. setFieldFP(), place no limitation (except bit-sizes) on the parameters, which are provided as sequences of bytes and are interpreted as unsigned integers.
- The API documentation contains no security notice that the set parameters should be trusted or a warning of what are the consequences of setting domain parameters that are untrusted or otherwise invalid [29].

– The API contains no functionality for direct primality testing or domain
parameter validation for (EC)DSA or (EC)DH and no way to implement
it efficiently. Thus the developer might (understandably) assume that the
validation is performed implicitly.

Multiple protocols allow to transmit the domain parameters and thus force
a party to either authenticate or validate them:

– TLS, up to version 1.2 [8] and prior to RFC8422 [26], allowed explicit (EC)DH
parameters to be sent from the server to the client, although authenticated
by the server public key.
– The certificate format specified in the X.509 standard allows public keys to
hold full domain parameters for (EC)DH or (EC)DSA [31]. Using this format in a JavaCard applet (e.g., for interoperability reasons) might lead to
untrusted parameters being used.
– The ICAO document 9303 [18] specifying the security requirements for
machine-readable travel documents allows transmitting the (EC)DH domain
parameters in the Chip Authentication and PACE protocols. The specification warns that insecure domain parameters will cause leaks of secret data
and that parameters should not be used unless explicitly known to be secure
(without further elaboration). As the card transmits the parameters to the
reader, it is the one responsible for the validation.

All relevant (EC)DH and (EC)DSA standards specify procedures for validating the domain parameters and allow the use of untrusted domain parameters
provided the validation succeeds. For (EC)DSA, two standards specify the validation requirements:

– FIPS 186-4 [14] refers to the NIST Special publication 800-89 [27] that in turn
requires the primes used in the domain parameters to be accompanied by a
seed and verifies they were generated using the specified verifiably random
method.
– ANSI X9.62 [2] requires a primality test of the prime domain parameters,
using the MR test with the number of rounds equal or larger than 50, using
random bases. The IEEE P1363 [19] standard for (EC)DH has exactly the
same requirement.

The strong requirements for primality testing and domain parameter validation in the above standards might lead the applet developer to believe that
an appropriate validation is performed by the card and that the use of given
parameters is secure. As the detailed implementation guidance is not provided by
JavaCard specifications and recommendations from standards like IEEE P1363
and x9.62 are not explicitly mentioned, the platform vendor is left with decision
what level of checks to implement.

We also consider another scenario where primality testing and domain parameter validation make a significant difference in security. TLS is an open system
where communicating parties are likely to be realised by different software vendors. In the case of closed systems like dedicated network line encryption boxes,

the same entity configures both communicating endpoints, which may be based on the commodity cards. A *platform integrator* (not the same as the card *manufacturer*) supplies the software responsible for setting the domain parameters on both ends. These two endpoints are designed to communicate with each other and to establish a secure channel using (EC)DH (and potentially (EC)DSA for authentication). Without robust primality testing and domain parameter validation on the card, the domain parameters supplied to cards at both ends can contain pseudoprimes or composites and be weak to a passive eavesdropping attacker. These parameters can even be authenticated by the *platform integrator*, yet without proper validation and primality testing, the card will accept them. The *platform integrator* could then also claim some plausible deniability, by blaming the weak parameters on a bug in the customised curve generation codebase or arguing the pseudoprime in the parameters passed their primality tests. A similar case happened in the Juniper Dual EC incident [11], where the exploitable weakness was a result of a series of small coding errors, seemingly unintentional.

One example of a vulnerability, where attacker-controlled domain parameters were used, was the Microsoft CryptoAPI ECDSA verification vulnerability (CVE-2020-0601) [28]. It was due to a faulty certificate verification mechanism, which matched certificates provided to the trusted ones by comparing the public key. This allowed an attacker to supply a certificate with modified domain parameters, which would be trusted.

Even when not directly using untrusted parameters, the adversarial setting makes sense when we account for the physical nature of cards and, thus, for fault injection attacks. These could be mounted to manipulate any trusted parameters [7,34] that the applet will use (e.g., in (EC)DH).

3.2   Attacks Overview

We focus on attacks theoretically applicable to all implementations accepting composite parameters, instead of those stemming from specific behaviour of any one implementation. We present four different attacks, based on the cryptosystem and the injected parameter. In all four cases, it is possible to efficiently recover the private key for suitable injected parameters. The details will be given in Sect. 6.

When the group order n is composite in ECDSA/ECDH or DSA/DH, it is well known that the discrete logarithm problem (DLP) in the group can be decomposed into DLPs in its quotient groups of prime-power order, which are much easier [30]. Thus for sufficiently smooth injected group orders, the discrete logarithm can be computed.

A similar decomposition and DLP difficulty reduction occurs when injecting a composite in place of the prime defining the full multiplicative group in DH/DSA [12].

We use yet another decomposition when injecting a composite in place of the prime defining the finite field for ECDSA/ECDH. As far as we know, this is a new result.

4   Methodology for Assessing Primality Tests

In this section, we describe the method we used to analyse primality testing in cards of the JavaCard platform. Throughout the remaining text, the term *pseudoprime* will always mean a composite number that passes the MR test with respect to several small bases (the first t primes in our case).

In [1], the library functions for testing primality are ready to be called directly, and the source code can be analysed to see for what purpose and with what parameters they are invoked. In contrast, we cannot even be sure if such functions exist in the closed-source implementation of the JavaCard platform. Hence we need to guess where they could be likely present and invoked (e.g., during domain parameter validation or key generation) and what parts of the algorithm could behave problematically if a prime input was replaced with a composite one. Also, unlike in [1], we only have a very limited amount of pseudoprime bit lengths to choose from.

JavaCard specifies five main cryptographic algorithms involving prime numbers or domain parameters: RSA, DSA, ECDSA, DH and ECDH (though not all cards support all of them). We analysed all the relevant functions from the JavaCard specification and found no way to invoke primality testing in the RSA API with user-provided inputs. Also, the primes used there constitute the private key, and a scenario with them being replaced with pseudoprimes does not trigger a primality test. As a result, only the methods of the (EC)DH and (EC)DSA algorithms are applicable. Additionally, we restricted the testing focus on the ECDSA and ECDH algorithms only, as none of the tested cards support DH and only one supports DSA. However, we still analyse the theoretical aspects of using DSA/DH parameters.

The practical analysis of primality testing consists of three steps:

1. Constructing pseudoprimes and other composites (Sect. 4.2 and Sect. 4.3).
2. Generating (EC)DSA and (EC)DH parameters with primes replaced with the numbers crafted in the previous step (Sect. 6).
3. Triggering the card's primality test with the modified parameters as input, e.g., key generation, signing, verification in case of (EC)DSA or key agreement in case of (EC)DH. (The rest of this section.)

In the last step, for any operation we perform on the card, the card only returns a response (output or error value) and the duration of the computation, which is often insufficient to understand exactly what happened due to implementations being closed-source. By the behaviour of the card under test, we mean such a response to our calls of API functions. To gain more information, we could also observe the card's power consumption or EM emissions during computation, but we do not consider these here. We use three types of basic operations in sequence to observe the behaviour:

3a) *Parameter setting.* Individual (EC)DSA or (EC)DH parameters are set on a Key object as byte arrays, interpreted as unsigned integers.

3b) *Key generation.* After setting all parameters, a `Keypair` can be generated. Note that the JavaCard does not differentiate between an ECDSA and ECDH keypair. In our tests, we skip this operation if it fails and continue with a manually generated private key, to also test the scenario where a keypair to be used is imported to the card.

3c) *Signing and verification* or *Key agreement.* After a `Keypair` object is successfully generated, it can be used to initialise a `Signature` or a `KeyAgreement` object and perform the operation. We supplied random data for signing and performed the key agreement between two keypairs generated on the card if possible. If the key generation failed, we instead substituted the private key and performed key agreement between it and the generator point on the curve.

To perform these operations, we developed and released our `ECTester` tool [21], which accesses the public JavaCard API and is generic to all cards.

4.1   Domain Parameters

In this section, we examine the requirements on domain parameters used in (EC)DSA and (EC)DH, specifically primality requirements and show what requirements need to be fulfilled while replacing a prime with a composite. Since the parameters and the corresponding implementation checks for the finite field case and for the elliptic curve case differ significantly, we study them separately.

The DSA/DH Case. In DSA/DH, there are three domain parameters [14]:

- p is the prime defining the multiplicative group $\mathbb{Z}_p^*$ in which we compute,
- g is an element of $\mathbb{Z}_p^*$,
- q is the order of g in $\mathbb{Z}_p^*$.

Note that the above already implies $g^q \equiv 1 \pmod{p}$, $q \mid p - 1$ and $g \neq 1$ (unless $q = 1$) and we can expect that these conditions could be checked by the implementation.

The supported sizes include $\{(1024, 160), (2048, 224), (2048, 256)\}$ bits for p, q respectively. Classically, q is required to be prime, as the running time of the Pohlig-Hellman algorithm [30] depends on the size of the largest factor of q. Also, the random nonce k, which is generated during signing, needs to be invertible mod q. Thus for testing, we could replace either p or q with a pseudoprime. However, this replacement is non-trivial, as the conditions above are quite easy to satisfy when computing p and g from q, but somewhat hard if given p, as one needs to factor $p - 1$ and hope it has a prime factor q of the correct size. We discuss this in Sect. 4.7.

In DH on the JavaCard platform, the domain parameters are the same as in DSA, but the q parameter is optional [29]. This means that either no checks related to q are performed, or that p is assumed to be a safe-prime, i.e. $p = 2q+1$. We do not consider the case when the safe prime condition is assumed in the remainder of this paper and instead refer the reader to [16]. Similarly, we do not consider the case where there are no checks related to q present, as it is straightforward to subvert the parameters in such a system (for example, q can be very small).

Note that we did not test actual DSA/DH parameter sets, as mentioned earlier in Sect. 4, due to lack of support in the tested cards.

The ECDSA/ECDH Case. This case is a little more complicated. The JavaCard API supports curves in the short Weierstrass form either over prime fields $\mathbb{F}_p$ or binary fields $\mathbb{F}_{2^m}$. We do not work with the binary field case, as most cards at our disposal do not support it. The prime field case then requires the inputs p, a, b, G_x, G_y, n, h, where:

- p is the prime defining the field $\mathbb{F}_p$ over which we will work,
- a, b are the coefficients of the elliptic curve E in short Weierstrass form over $\mathbb{F}_p$,
- G_x, G_y are the affine coordinates of the generator point $G \in E(\mathbb{F}_p)$,
- n is the order of G,
- h is the cofactor, equal to the order of $E(\mathbb{F}_p)$ divided by n.

As for supported sizes, p should have either $160, 192, 224, 256, 384, 512$ or 521 bits. Computing the group order or n is prohibitively expensive for the card, so it is reasonable to assume that only the condition $[n]G = \infty$ will be checked, possibly together with the size of n (by Hasse's theorem, $n \cdot h$ should be roughly the same size as p). Again, for ECDSA/ECDH, n should be prime for the same reasons as q in DSA/DH. Thus for testing, we could replace either p or n with a pseudoprime and tested (the case of pseudoprime n was discussed in [16]). For the replacement, we need to either construct an elliptic curve with a prescribed number of points (we used our tool ecgen [20] that supports the complex multiplication method [10]) when n is replaced, or to construct an "elliptic curve" over $\mathbb{Z}_p$ (with composite p) and correctly compute its order.

For each card and each bit-size in $\{160, 192, 224, 256, 384, 512, 521\}$, we test the card's behaviour for ECDSA and ECDH with parameter sets described in Table 2. The rest of this section shows how we generated p and n, while Sect. 6 explains how we constructed the malicious parameters from them. The full parameters used for testing in this paper are included in Appendix 2.1.

4.2 Generating Pseudoprimes

As we are considering only the MR primality test, we use a slightly tweaked version of Arnault's method with three pseudoprime factors, described in Appendix 2. We construct numbers that are pseudoprime to t smallest primes taken as bases, assuming the resource constrained smartcard will choose its bases from a set of small primes. The only limitation is that the bit-size of the pseudoprime must be one of the supported ones, as discussed in Sect. 4. To achieve this, we must try many combinations of t, k_2, k_3 to arrive precisely at the supported bit-sizes, while also trying to maximise t (Table 1). For each bit-size, the pseudoprime generation process took at most a few minutes on an ordinary laptop (using the precomputed values of t, k_2 and k_3).

4.3   Generating Special Composites

To systematically compare the card behaviour, we also used random composites with controlled numbers of factors or varying levels of smoothness, to get finer granularity. In this way, we can detect if the primality test is present at all (though possibly faulty).

Composites with a Given Number of Factors. To generate a composite number of a given bit-size with a given number of factors, we use a greedy approach. In each step, we generate a random prime number of size b/r, where b is the number of remaining bits, and r is the number of remaining factors to be generated.

Table 1. Parameters for constructing pseudoprimes by tweaked Arnault's method [1,3].

bit-size	t	k_2	k_3
160	11	73	101
192	13	61	101
224	14	197	257
256	16	233	101
384	23	137	157
512	30	137	157
521	30	137	157
1024	52	241	281

Composites with a Given Smoothness Level. For the smooth case, we employ a similar greedy algorithm that randomly chooses prime factors up to the smoothness bound and retries until a number with the right bit-size is constructed.

4.4   Generating Complete Domain Parameters

In this section, we explain how to generate complete parameters for ECDSA/ECDH and DSA/DH, based on the pseudoprime and other composite inputs generated in Sect. 4.2 and Sect. 4.3. In the ECDSA/ECDH case, these are exactly the parameters we used for testing the cards.

The challenge in embedding composites into the domain parameters lies in the fact that the card might check many properties of the parameters, while the only thing we are currently interested in is the compositeness of some of them. Thus the parameters should be as close to correct parameters as possible. The properties of the parameters that the card might verify are listed in the standards specifying domain parameter validation algorithms [2,19] and we listed them in Sect. 4.1. For each scenario, we also list the corresponding attack.

4.5   ECDSA/ECDH: Prime p, Composite n

The approach, in this case, is almost the same as the one described in [16]. We use the complex multiplication method (described in [10], realised by our tool ecgen

218   V. Sedlacek et al.

[20]), which is able to construct a curve over a prime field in short Weierstrass form with a given number of points. We need to take into account that the structure of $E(\mathbb{F}_p)$ is either cyclic or a product of two cyclic groups. This poses an issue because the JavaCard platform limits the size of the cofactor to an unsigned short integer, so just 16 bits. In the curves generated by two points, often the cofactor does not fit into 16 bits, even if we pick a large subgroup. Thankfully, the cards do not perform validation of the cofactor, as it is an optional input, so we just pick the generator with the largest order and set the cofactor to 1. Given the composite n, generating a suitable 256-bit curve took just a few minutes on an ordinary laptop.

One of the forms of composite n we tried to generate was that of an appropriately sized primorial (i.e., the product of all the primes up to some bound). However, the complex multiplication method, as implemented in the ecgen tool, was unable to generate them, even after a significant time spent on the task (e.g., a week on a single curve). The method searches for the curves by enumerating values of their complex multiplication discriminant, starting from 1, until a suitable curve and prime field is found. This points to an absence of prime field curves with primorial order and a small complex multiplication discriminant, which is an interesting observation.

4.6 ECDSA/ECDH: Composite p, Arbitrary n

Here we assume for simplicity that p is square-free and has no small factors (up to some bound, we chose 50). We want to find a curve whose order has no small divisors; otherwise, the card might reject the curve for a wrong reason, as we have observed before.

For each prime factor p_i of p, we iterate over all possible curves over $\mathbb{Z}_{p_i}$ until we find one whose order is prime (this will minimise the number of prime factors of the resulting curve over $\mathbb{Z}_p$). We also prefer if the order of the curve is never repeated for different p_i's, but this is easily satisfied in practice. When such a curve is found for each p_i, we create the desired curve modulo p just by using the CRT on the Weierstrass coefficients a, b of the individual curves. Since p has no small prime divisors, we can expect the same to be true for the order of the final curve as well, thanks to the construction, as the resulting order is the product of the individual orders.

To obtain a generator point of the resulting curve, we simply pick a generator point of each curve, and we use the CRT again on their coordinates. Since each curve over $\mathbb{Z}_{p_i}$ was cyclic and their orders were distinct, the final curve is cyclic as well, so we can set the cofactor to be 1. This whole process takes just seconds for the 3- and 10-factor 256-bit composites used in this paper.

4.7 DSA/DH: Prime p, Composite q

This is the easiest scenario, as it almost completely follows the way ordinary DSA parameters are generated. We first pick a composite or pseudoprime q, then choose random properly sized integers k until $p = kq + 1$ becomes a prime.

Then we repeatedly pick a random $r \in \mathbb{Z}_p^*$ until we get a generator of $\mathbb{Z}_p^*$ and compute $g = r^{(p-1)/q}$. In this way, we ensure that g has order q modulo p. This generation process is very fast, and takes just seconds to generate 1024-bit parameters.

4.8   DSA/DH: Composite p, Prime q

This case is more problematic to construct than the above one. First, let us assume that p is a Carmichael number (as is the case for the pseudoprimes we are constructing (Appendix 2). We assume that either of the conditions

$$q \mid p - 1, \quad g^q \equiv 1 \pmod{p} \quad \text{and } g \neq 1$$

could be checked, so we will want to satisfy all of them.

These conditions imply that $g^q \equiv 1 \pmod{p_i}$ for all prime factors p_i of p, hence $g^{\gcd(q,p_i-1)} \equiv 1 \pmod{p_i}$. Since q is a prime and $g \neq 1 \pmod{p_i}$ for some i (otherwise $g = 1$), this implies $q \mid p_i - 1$ for some i.

Thus we need $p - 1$ to have a prime factor q of a size corresponding to the size of p (e.g., if p has 1024 bits, then we need q to have 160 bits). Given a specially constructed p, this means factoring $p - 1$ and hoping for a factor of the correct size. This is exactly what we did for generating the DSA parameters, even though it was only practical for the 1024-bit parameters, given that factoring larger than 1024-bit random integers and hoping for a factor of a correct bit-size is computationally hard for our computation cluster. Finding an appropriate 1024-bit pseudoprime p such that $p - 1$ has a 160-bit factor took a few days on an equivalent of an ordinary laptop.

Once we have p and q, we can again loop through random r from $\mathbb{Z}_p^*$ and compute g as $g = r^{(p-1)/q}$ until $g \neq 1$. This will imply that $g \not\equiv 1 \pmod{p_i}$ for at least one i, so that the primality of q together with the congruence $g^q \equiv r^{p-1} \equiv 1 \pmod{p}$ (as p is a Carmichael number) will imply that the order of g modulo p_i is q, hence $q \mid p_i - 1$.

Note that it is possible that no such g exists, even if p is a pseudoprime - for example for the Carmichael number $p = 7 \cdot 19 \cdot 67$ and $q = 5$, we have that $q \mid p - 1$, but $q \nmid p_i - 1$ for any i, so there is no element of order q modulo p. However, it can be empirically seen that is unlikely to happen when p and q are large enough.

It seems hard to adapt this strategy of generating parameters for a fixed composite non-Carmichael p (which instead has a given number of factors or is smooth). One would have to simultaneously force $q \mid p - 1$ and $q \mid p_i - 1$ for some prime factor p_i of p, which is equivalent to $q \mid \gcd(p - 1, p_i - 1)$. But unlike in the Carmichael case (where $\gcd(p - 1, p_i - 1) = p_i - 1$), heuristics show that we cannot expect $\gcd(p - 1, p_i - 1)$ to have a large prime factor for most composite p, let alone a factor of an exactly given size. Thus we do not consider this case further, but we stress that its significance is mostly limited to testing of black-box devices. A motivated attacker would use pseudoprime (or just Carmichael) p, as it has a much better chance to bypass potential primality tests, while making the generation of the other parameters easier.

5   Practical Results

The analysis was performed on cards with ECC support that we were able to obtain in small quantities and covers most major vendors (except for Gemalto and Idemia). The cards were fabricated in the period between 2012 and 2018. Note that due to lengthily and costly certification processes, the pace of software changes in the smartcard environment is significantly slower than for standard software development. As a result, the products by the same vendor tend to reuse the same existing codebase (as visible from results for the NXP cards), and our findings are likely valid for the newer product versions as well. The results are summarized in Tables 2a and 2b.

The main result of our testing is that most manufacturers, apart from *Athena* and *Infineon*, seem to lack primality tests of the p and n parameters for ECDSA and ECDH. This follows from the same observed card behaviour for the tests with pseudoprime parameters (Sect. 4.2) as for the tests with general composite parameters (Sect. 4.3). Missing primality testing invites Pohlig-Hellman style attacks mentioned in Sect. 3. Due to the non-deterministic nature of ECDSA key and nonce generation, we had to run the tests many times to get representative results. The different bit-sizes of the curves used, ranging from 160 bits to 521, do not impact the results in an unexpected way.

We may have passed the primality test using a pseudoprime curve order in the case of the *Infineon CJTOP 80k* card, as the key generation and ECDSA signing and verification worked in a few rare cases, even though the card rejected the parameters most of the time. We observed this in roughly 3 out of 1000 tries on a 192-bit pseudoprime order curve. Our hypothesis is that the implementation is choosing small MR bases, which occasionally lie in the set of liars for our provided pseudoprime.

We were not able to pass the primality test present on the *Athena IDProtect* card, perhaps because it uses random MR bases or some other primality test.

We also observed that cards occasionally went mute and did not respond to the command, often upon invoking key generation. This behaviour is outside of the PCSC specification[1] and results in a PCSC error being raised by the reader's driver. It could also mean that the cards perform some kind of a self-test during the operation and stop responding as a security measure if the test fails. The presence of such self-tests is well documented in cards. In ECDSA, this error might stem from the card generating a nonce k that is non-invertible modulo n, which the system might not expect.

In the ECDSA case, several cards occasionally produced invalid signatures. This is possibly due to the modular inversion algorithm assuming a prime modulus. We did not investigate this matter further, but these invalid signatures might leak information about the private key or the used nonce, which might be abused by a lattice attack.

---

[1] The PCSC specification specifies the general communication protocol between the card and the reader device.

Table 2. Results of domain parameters validation using on-card primality testing by nine different cards from five major manufacturers. Multiple values separated with a slash indicate that multiple results are present with decreasing occurrence from left to right. *IL (see below) happens on verification, key generation and signing works.

Card		p			n			
	prime	pseudo	3f	pseudo	3f	10f	11s odd	11s even
Athena IDProtect	OK	IL	IL	IL	IL	IL	CYC	EXC
G&D SmartCafe 6.0	OK	OK	OK	OK	OK	OK	CYC	EXC
G&D SmartCafe 7.0	OK	OK/MUT	OK/MUT	OK	OK	OK	MUT	EXC
Infineon CJTOP 80k	OK	IL	IL	IL/OK	IL	IL	EXC	EXC
NXP JCOP v2.4.1	OK	OK/VRF	OK/VRF	OK	OK	OK	IL	IL
NXP JCOP CJ2A081	OK	OK	OK	OK	OK	OK	IL	IL
NXP JCOP v2.4.2 J2E145G	OK	OK/VRF	OK/VRF	OK	OK	OK	IL	IL
NXP JCOP J3H145	OK	OK/MUT	OK/VRF/MUT	OK	OK	OK	EXC	EXC
TaiSYS SIMoME VAULT	OK	OK/MUT	IL/MUT*	OK	OK	OK	EXC	EXC

(a) ECDSA results.

Card		p			n			
	prime	pseudo	3f	pseudo	3f	10f	11s odd	11s even
Athena IDProtect	OK	IL	IL	IL	IL	IL	CYC	EXC
G&D SmartCafe 6.0	OK	MUT	MUT	MUT	MUT	MUT	CYC	EXC
G&D SmartCafe 7.0	OK	OK	OK	OK	OK	OK	MUT	EXC
Infineon CJTOP 80k	OK	IL	IL	IL	IL	IL	EXC	EXC
NXP JCOP v2.4.1	OK	OK	OK	OK	OK	OK	IL	IL
NXP JCOP CJ2A081	OK	OK	OK	OK	OK	OK	IL	IL
NXP JCOP v2.4.2 J2E145G	OK	OK	OK	OK	OK	OK	IL	IL
NXP JCOP J3H145	OK	OK/MUT	OK/MUT	OK	OK	OK	EXC	EXC
TaiSYS SIMoME VAULT	OK	OK	OK	OK	OK	OK	EXC	EXC

(b) ECDH results.

Result types

OK	Operation without error
IL	ILLEGAL_VALUE exception
VRF	Failed to verify signature
EXC	Unexpected exception
CYC	Card cycles indefinitely
MUT	Card does not respond

Parameter names

prime	standard parameters
pseudo p	pseudoprime p
3f p	3-factor composite p
pseudo n	pseudoprime n
3f n	3-factor composite n
10f n	10-factor composite n
11s odd n	11-smooth odd n
11s even n	11-smooth even n

☐ Green background signifies tests with the expected result, i.e. the card correctly computed with the parameters or the card correctly rejected them.

☐ Yellow background marks tests where the card exhibits unexpected behaviour, but are not vulnerabilities, and are not exploitable by the attacks from Section 3.

☐ Red background marks tests where the card accepted parameters it should have rejected, and is thus vulnerable to attacks from Section 3.

The behaviour of the cards also differs for smooth n and for 10-factor n. We think this is due to some unknown checks failing when such a smooth order is given, not due to a primality test. Furthermore, two cards (*Athena IDProtect, G&D SmartCafe 6.0*) cycle indefinitely on key generation on a curve with smooth odd order, we do not have any explanation for this behaviour.

Algorithms used during the operations, such as the modular multiplicative inverse or the modular square root, may be implemented to rely on the modulus being prime. Thus we were surprised to see the cards mostly working for composite p.

6   The Attacks in Detail

In this section, we discuss the attack details in each of the four scenarios we consider.

6.1   Attack on ECDSA/ECDH with Prime p and Composite n

Using the classical Pohlig-Hellman algorithm [30], the DLP asymptotically becomes only as hard as the DLP in a subgroup of order l, where l is the largest prime factor of the group order n. There it can be solved by the Pollard ρ algorithm, which costs roughly $\sqrt{\frac{\pi}{4} l} \approx 0.886 \sqrt{l}$ point additions [5]. Thus for example, when using a 256-bit curve and n has three factors of roughly the same size, the total computation cost of the DLP is approximately $3 \times 0.886 \times \sqrt{2^{86}} \approx 2^{44}$, which is already practical (and can be much cheaper for a larger number of factors). Compare this with a case of using the Pollard ρ algorithm to solve DLP on a standard 256-bit curve, where one gets the cost of $0.886 \times \sqrt{2^{256}} \approx 2^{128}$. An example of this attack is given in Appendix 3.

6.2   Attack on ECDSA/ECDH with Composite p, and Arbitrary n

When a composite p is a product of distinct primes $p_1, \ldots, p_e$ in ECDSA or ECDH, we are working with an "elliptic curve" over $\mathbb{Z}_p$ (see [37] for a proper definition and basic properties), whose group can be thought of as a direct sum of groups of the same elliptic curve regarded over $\mathbb{Z}_{p_i}$, i.e., $E(\mathbb{Z}_p) \cong \bigoplus_{i=1}^{e} E(\mathbb{Z}_{p_i})$. The isomorphism is essentially realised by the CRT applied to point coordinates. Thus the DLP on $E(\mathbb{Z}_p)$ again asymptotically becomes only as hard as the hardest DLP on some $E(\mathbb{Z}_{p_i})$ (since after solving the DLP in all individual groups, we can use the CRT to obtain the desired discrete logarithm). Since the order of $E(\mathbb{Z}_{p_i})$ is roughly p_i, the situation is very similar to the one for composite n in ECDSA/ECDH. An example of this attack is given in Appendix 3.

6.3   The Attack on DSA/DH with Prime p and Composite q

The Pohlig-Hellman algorithm is applicable in an exact analogy to the composite n case in ECDSA/ECDH. Note that the sub-exponential index calculus algorithm could also be used to solve the individual DLPs, but we expect it to perform worse than Pollard ρ (whose cost is asymptotically the same as for ECDSA/ECDH), as it cannot efficiently use the extra information about the factorisation of q.

6.4   The Attack on DSA/DH with Composite p and Prime q

In this case, we know the value g^x modulo p, where $0 < x < q$ and $q \mid p_i - 1$ for some prime factor p_i of p (this follows from the construction described in Sect. 4.8). Thus we also know the value g^x modulo p_i and finding x modulo p_i gives us x directly, since $x < q \leq p_i - 1$. Therefore it is sufficient to solve the DLP modulo p_i. Note that Pollard ρ does not have an advantage compared with the case with a real prime p, as the group order is still q. On the other hand, the complexity of an index calculus algorithm only depends on p_i, which can be much lower than p. Hence the security level will be lower than it should be and might lead to a private key recovery for small enough p_i. The practicality of this approach is demonstrated in Appendix 3.

7   Proposed Defences

Without a robust primality test, a card cannot properly validate domain parameters. As the public JavaCard API lacks primality testing functionality, we cannot expect the developers to perform the validation either. Thus applications that allow the setting of custom domain parameters may result in a vulnerable applet.

Furthermore, the absence of primality testing functionality hinders the development of more complex cryptographic applications. For example, the vulnerability in the RSA key generation presented in the ROCA attack [25] could have been mitigated by applets generating the primes for their RSA keypairs themselves, thus avoiding full firmware fixes of the affected devices (which are often impossible in the case of cards). The lack of solid number-theoretic functionality in the JavaCard API prevented this though.

Fortunately, most of the protocols and implementations use standard named curves such as NIST P-256 or Curve25519. This seems to limit the current real-world impact of the aforementioned absence of primality testing in domain parameter validation.

We analysed an extensive list of open-source implementations of JavaCard applets [13] and found none that would use unauthenticated domain parameters in (EC)DSA or (EC)DH. Most used a fixed standard curve, with a few using domain parameters supplied in a command, but those were either authenticated or it was apparent from the context that they were provided by a trusted party, for example during the setup of the applet. However, one should keep in mind the possibilities of an untrusted setup described in Sect. 3, as well as the possibility of fault injection attacks. We also note that open-source JavaCard development comprises only a very small part of deployed JavaCards and that most applets are closed-source.

The recent trends in cryptography head towards misuse-resistance, the property of protocols and APIs that makes it hard for the developers to use and implement them incorrectly. Protocols and cryptosystems should allow simple implementations, as those are more likely to be correct and secure. Furthermore, the simple and fast implementation should always be a secure one. Examples of this include the nonce-misuse resistant authenticated encryption modes such as the SIV [17] or libraries with a very simple API such as libsodium or NaCl [6]. With this direction in mind, the missing domain parameter validation steers the developers to misuse the API and undermine the security of their applets.

We thus propose several changes to the JavaCard specification:

- Require full domain parameter validation, for example as specified in ANSI X9.62 [2] and IEEE P1363 [19], which includes primality tests of prime parameters.
- Add API that supports using a set of named curves and allow manufacturers to only support this API. Consider perhaps deprecating or discouraging explicit domain parameter setting.
- Add a primality test to the public API.

Validating elliptic curve domain parameters consists of more than primality testing and general sanity checks on the parameters. It contains tests on certain algebraic properties of the curves that might make the DLP easier (e.g., by allowing transfers into weaker groups). Luckily, these are all specified in the aforementioned standards.

The modification of JavaCard API to accept only named curves instead of the full specification of curve parameters limits flexibility for the future inclusion of new curves as it might not be possible to update the list after card deployment. On the other hand, strict usage of only named curves prevents attacks similar to the recent attack on the Microsoft CryptoAPI library (CVE-2020-0601) [28], which cannot be prevented only by domain parameter validation.

The Miller-Rabin with random bases or Baillie-PSW primality tests should allow a robust and reasonably efficient (even on limited smartcard chips) implementation of primality testing. For an example of a performant and misuse-resistant primality test, see Massimo and Paterson [22].

8   Summary

We have explored the robustness of primality testing in domain parameter validation by smartcards of the JavaCard platform. Due to unavailability of primality testing functionality in the public JavaCard API, we tried to trigger the tests indirectly by using specially crafted composite domain parameters for ECDSA and ECDH operations.

We analysed nine different smartcards from five major manufacturers and found that all but one failed to properly verify the primality of the provided ECDSA and ECDH domain parameters, not even requiring pseudoprimes to fool them, just composites. This results in a vulnerability to Pohlig-Hellman [30] style attacks, allowing the extraction of the private key. Our approach is generic to all black-box devices performing ECDSA and ECDH and the tooling can be reused.

Furthermore, the vulnerability is not easily mitigated for the already deployed smartcards. The code responsible for the domain parameter validation is often stored in a read-only memory without the possibility for an update. In addition, the on-card verification of the provided domain parameters by the developer cannot be efficiently performed due to a lack of a primality testing functionality in the public JavaCard API.

Acknowledgements. The authors would like to thank K.G. Paterson, M. Sys, V. Matyas and anonymous reviewers for their helpful comments. J. Jancar was supported by the grant MUNI/C/1701/2018, V. Sedlacek by the Czech Science Foundation project GA20-03426S. Some of the tools used and P. Svenda were supported by the CyberSec4Europe Competence Network. Computational resources were supplied by the project e-INFRA LM2018140.

Appendix

1   The Miller-Rabin Primality Test

The MR test [23,32] was one of the first practical primality tests and to this day remains very popular because of its simplicity and efficiency. In particular, we believe that if a low-resource device such as a smartcard (shortened as *card* for the rest of text) uses a primality test, MR is the most probable choice (perhaps followed by the Lucas test, which does not seem to be that widespread, and a Ballie-PSW test, which is a combination of these two), as most other tests are too resource-heavy.

However, the MR test cannot be used to prove that a number is prime; only compositeness can be proven. It relies on the fact that there exist no nontrivial roots of unity modulo a prime. More precisely, let n be the number we want to test for primality and let $n - 1 = 2^s d$, where d is odd. If n is prime, Fermat's Little Theorem implies that for any $1 \leq a < n$, we have either $a^d \equiv 1 \pmod{n}$ or $a^{2^i d} \equiv -1 \pmod{n}$ for some $0 \leq i < s$. By taking the contrapositive, if there is some $1 \leq a < n$ such that none of these congruences hold, then n is composite (and a is called a *witness of compositeness* for n). However, if at least one of the congruences holds, then we say that n is *pseudoprime with respect to base a* (or that a is a *non-witness of compositeness* for n, or also a *liar* for n). There is the Monier-Rabin bound [24] for the number $S(n)$ of such bases (that are less than n): $S(n) \leq \frac{\varphi(n)}{4}$, where φ is the Euler totient function.

Since $\varphi(n) \approx n$ for large n, we get a practical upper bound for the number of inputs that pass the test for a given a. Thus if we repeat the test t times for random a's, the probability of fooling the MR test will be at most $(\frac{1}{4})^t$.

The fact that the a's were picked randomly is crucial for the guarantees above. If the bases are fixed and known in advance (as in [1]), it is possible to construct a pseudoprime (see Appendix 2), i.e., a number that passes the test with respect to these bases.

2   Constructing Pseudoprimes

We will briefly describe how to generate pseudoprimes having 3 prime factors with respect to given distinct prime bases $a_1, \ldots, a_t$ according to [1] and [3], where more details can be found. The whole method can be summarised as follows:

1. Choose t odd prime bases $a_1 < \cdots < a_t$ (we always choose the first t smallest primes) and let $A := \{a_1, \ldots, a_t\}$.
2. Let $k_1 = 1$ and choose distinct coprime $k_2, k_3 \in \mathbb{Z}$, $k_2, k_3 > a_t$ (see Table 1).
3. For each $a \in A$, compute the set S_a of primes p reduced modulo $4a$ s.t. $\left(\frac{a}{p}\right) = -1$. This can be done constructively by looping over values $x \in \{1, 2, \ldots, 4a - 1\}$ and adding x to S_a iff $\left(\frac{x}{a}\right)(-1)^{(x-1)(a-1)/4} = -1$ (using quadratic reciprocity).
4. For each $a \in A$, compute the intersection $R_a := \bigcap_{j=1}^{3} k_j^{-1}(S_a + k_j - 1)$, where $k_j^{-1}(S_a + k_j - 1)$ denotes the set $\{k_j^{-1}(s + k_j - 1) \mod 4a \mid s \in S_a\}$ for each $a \in A$. If any are empty, go back to step 2.
5. For each $a \in A$, randomly pick an element $r_a \in R_a$.
6. Using the Chinese Remainder Theorem, find p_1 such that $$p_1 \equiv k_3^{-1} \,(\mathrm{mod}\ k_2), p_1 \equiv k_2^{-1} \,(\mathrm{mod}\ k_3) \text{ and } p_1 \equiv r_a \,(\mathrm{mod}\ 4a) \text{ for all } a \in A.$$
7. Compute $p_2 = k_2(p_1-1)+1$ and $p_3 = k_3(p_1-1)+1$. If all p_1, p_2, p_3 are primes, then $p_1 p_2 p_3$ is pseudoprime with respect to all bases $a \in A$. Otherwise, go back to step 4 (or even 2 or 1 after a certain amount of time has passed).

If we take $a_1 = 2$ and enforce the condition $p_1 \equiv 3 \pmod 8$ (by slightly tweaking some steps above), the constructed pseudoprimes will meet the Monier-Rabin bound (maximizing the probability of passing the test for a random base choice) and will also pass the MR test for any composite base with no prime divisors greater than a_t [1].

Recall that Carmichael numbers are composite n that divide $a^{n-1} - 1$ for all $a \in \mathbb{Z}$ coprime to n. Equivalently, a composite integer n is a Carmichael number if and only if n is square-free, and $p - 1 \mid n - 1$ for all prime divisors p of n [24]. The pseudoprimes generated in this way are automatically Carmichael numbers [1] and we are using this fact in Sect. 4.8.

2.1   Generated Domain Parameters

The generated domain parameters and scripts used to generate them and produce our results are available at https://crocs.fi.muni.cz/papers/primality_esorics20.

3   Examples of Attacks

3.1   ECDSA/ECDH: Composite n

This case uses the 10-factor n parameters as specified in Appendix 2.1. Such a smooth order of the curve allows for a direct application of the Pohlig-Hellman algorithm for computing discrete logarithms to obtain the private key.

The SAGE [36] code (embedded) recovered the private key on a 256-bit curve in just about 7 s on an ordinary laptop. Computing such a discrete logarithm on a standard 256-bit curve is currently computationally infeasible.

3.2   ECDSA/ECDH: Composite p

This case uses the 10-factor p parameters as specified in Appendix 2.1. Such a curve with composite p can be decomposed into ten much smaller curves modulo the prime divisors of p. On these curves, it is trivial to compute the discrete logarithm of the public key. The resulting discrete logarithm (and the private key) is then recovered via the CRT.

The SAGE code (embedded) recovered the private key on a 256-bit curve in about 9 s on an ordinary laptop.

3.3   DSA/DH: Composite q

In case of composite q in DSA/DH, the Pohlig-Hellman algorithm for computing discrete logarithms applies again. The SAGE code (embedded) computed the private key of a public key using the 1024 bit DSA/DH parameters given in Appendix 2.1 in 35 min on one Intel Xeon X7560 @ 2.26 GHz processor.

3.4   DSA/DH: Composite p

We have used the CADO-NFS [35] implementation of the Number Field Sieve, to demonstrate the ease of computing the discrete logarithm of a public key using the 1024 bit DSA/DH parameters given in Appendix 2.1. We computed the discrete logarithm in the order q subgroup of $\mathbb{Z}_{p_1}^*$ as it defined the smallest group of only 336 bits.

The computation took 70 min to recover the private key on three Intel Xeon X7560 @ 2.26 GHz processors (24 cores total), with total CPU time of 22 h. Furthermore, this computation is generic for all public keys using the given domain parameters. The per-key computation is trivial and takes a few minutes at most.

Only one computation of the discrete logarithm on prime 1024 bit DSA/DH parameters is publicly known [15]. It used the fact that the prime was trapdoored and ran much faster than random parameters. Even then, it took two months on a large computation cluster, with a total CPU time of 385 CPU years.

References

1. Albrecht, M.R., Massimo, J., Paterson, K.G., Somorovsky, J.: Prime and prejudice: primality testing under adversarial conditions. In: Proceedings of the 2018 ACM SIGSAC Conference on Computer and Communications Security, pp. 281–298. ACM, New York (2018). https://doi.org/10.1145/3243734.3243787
2. American National Standard X9.62-1998, Public key cryptography for the financial services industry: the elliptic curve digital signature algorithm (ECDSA). Preliminary draft, Accredited Standards Committee X9 (1998)
3. Arnault, F.: Constructing Carmichael numbers which are strong pseudoprimes to several bases. J. Symb. Comput. **20**(2), 151–161 (1995). https://doi.org/10.1006/jsco
4. Arnault, F.: Rabin-Miller primality test: composite numbers which pass it. Math. Comput. **64**(209), 355–361 (1995). https://doi.org/10.1090/S0025-5718-1995-1260124-2
5. Bernstein, D.J., Lange, T.: SafeCurves: choosing safe curves for elliptic-curve cryptography (2017). https://safecurves.cr.yp.to/
6. Bernstein, D.J., Lange, T., Schwabe, P.: The security impact of a new cryptographic library. In: Hevia, A., Neven, G. (eds.) LATINCRYPT 2012. LNCS, vol. 7533, pp. 159–176. Springer, Heidelberg (2012). https://doi.org/10.1007/978-3-642-33481-8_9
7. Biehl, I., Meyer, B., Müller, V.: Differential fault attacks on elliptic curve cryptosystems. In: Bellare, M. (ed.) CRYPTO 2000. LNCS, vol. 1880, pp. 131–146. Springer, Heidelberg (2000). https://doi.org/10.1007/3-540-44598-6_8
8. Blake-Wilson, S., Bolyard, N., Gupta, V., Hawk, C., Moeller, B.: Elliptic Curve Cryptography (ECC) Cipher Suites for Transport Layer Security (TLS). RFC 4492, pp. 1–35. RFC Editor (2006)
9. Bleichenbacher, D.: Breaking a cryptographic protocol with pseudoprimes. In: Vaudenay, S. (ed.) PKC 2005. LNCS, vol. 3386, pp. 9–15. Springer, Heidelberg (2005). https://doi.org/10.1007/978-3-540-30580-4_2
10. Bröker, R.: Constructing elliptic curves of prescribed order. Thomas Stieltjes Institute for Mathematics (2006)
11. Checkoway, S., et al.: A systematic analysis of the juniper dual EC incident. In: Proceedings of the 2016 ACM SIGSAC Conference on Computer and Communications Security, Vienna, Austria, 24–28 October 2016, pp. 468–479 (2016). https://doi.org/10.1145/2976749.2978395
12. Dorey, K., Chang-Fong, N., Essex, A.: Indiscreet Logs: Persistent Diffie-Hellman Backdoors in TLS (2016). https://eprint.iacr.org/2016/999
13. EnigmaBridge: Curated list of JavaCard applications (2019). https://github.com/EnigmaBridge/javacard-curated-list. Accessed 17 Mar 2020
14. Federal Information Processing Standards Publication 186-4 Digital Signature Standard (DSS). Standard, National Institute for Standards and Technology (2013)
15. Fried, J., Gaudry, P., Heninger, N., Thomé, E.: A kilobit hidden SNFS discrete logarithm computation. In: Coron, J.-S., Nielsen, J.B. (eds.) EUROCRYPT 2017. LNCS, vol. 10210, pp. 202–231. Springer, Cham (2017). https://doi.org/10.1007/978-3-319-56620-7_8
16. Galbraith, S.D., Massimo, J., Paterson, K.G.: Safety in numbers: on the need for robust Diffie-Hellman parameter validation. In: Lin, D., Sako, K. (eds.) PKC 2019. LNCS, vol. 11443, pp. 379–407. Springer, Cham (2019). https://doi.org/10.1007/978-3-030-17259-6_13

17. Harkins, D.: Synthetic Initialization Vector (SIV) Authenticated Encryption Using the Advanced Encryption Standard (AES). RFC 5297, pp. 1–26. RFC Editor (2008)
18. Doc 9303 - Machine Readable Travel Documents. Document, International Civil Aviation Organization (2015)
19. IEEE Standard - Specifications for Public-Key Cryptography. Standard, IEEE Std 1363-2000 Working Group (2000)
20. Jancar, J.: ecgen (2019). https://github.com/J08nY/ecgen
21. Jancar, J., Svenda, P.: ECTester (2019). https://crocs-muni.github.io/ECTester/
22. Massimo, J., Paterson, K.G.: A Performant, Misuse-Resistant API for Primality Testing (2020). https://eprint.iacr.org/2020/065
23. Miller, G.L.: Riemann's hypothesis and tests for primality. In: Proceedings of the Seventh Annual ACM Symposium on Theory of Computing, STOC 1975, Albuquerque, New Mexico, USA, pp. 234–239. ACM (1975). https://doi.org/10.1145/800116.803773
24. Monier, L.: Evaluation and comparison of two efficient probabilistic primality testing algorithms. Theor. Comput. Sci. **12**(1), 97–108 (1980). https://doi.org/10.1016/0304-3975(80)90007-9
25. Nemec, M., Sys, M., Svenda, P., Klinec, D., Matyas, V.: The return of coppersmith's attack: practical factorization of widely used RSA moduli. In: 24th ACM Conference on Computer and Communications Security (CCS 2017), pp. 1631–1648. ACM, New York (2017). https://doi.org/10.1145/3133956.3133969
26. Nir, Y., Josefsson, S., Pegourie-Gonnard, M.: Elliptic Curve Cryptography (ECC) Cipher Suites for Transport Layer Security (TLS) Versions 1.2 and Earlier. RFC 8422, pp. 1–34. RFC Editor (2018)
27. Special Publication 800-89: Recommendation for Obtaining Assurances for Digital Signature Applications. Standard, National Institute for Standards and Technology (2006)
28. NSA: Windows CryptoAPI Spoofing Vulnerability (CVE-2020-0601) (2020). https://nvd.nist.gov/vuln/detail/CVE-2020-0601. Accessed 17 Mar 2020
29. Oracle: Java Card API 3.0.5, Classic Edition (2019). https://docs.oracle.com/javacard/3.0.5/api/index.html. Accessed 17 Mar 2020
30. Pohlig, S., Hellman, M.: An improved algorithm for computing logarithms over GF(p) and its cryptographic significance. IEEE Trans. Inf. Theory **24**(1), 106–110 (1978). https://doi.org/10.1109/TIT.1978.1055817
31. Polk, T., Housley, R., Bassham, L.: Algorithms and Identifiers for the Internet X.509 Public Key Infrastructure Certificate and Certificate Revocation List (CRL) Profile. RFC 3279, pp. 1–27. RFC Editor (2002)
32. Rabin, M.O.: Probabilistic algorithm for testing primality. J. Number Theory **12**, 128–138 (1980). https://doi.org/10.1016/0022-314X(80)90084-0
33. Svenda, P.: JCAlgTest: detailed analysis of cryptographic smart cards running with Java- Card platform (2019). https://www.fi.muni.cz/xsvenda/jcalgtest/. Accessed 17 Mar 2020
34. Takahashi, A., Tibouchi, M.: Degenerate Fault Attacks on Elliptic Curve Parameters in OpenSSL (2019). https://eprint.iacr.org/2019/400
35. The CADO-NFS Development Team: CADO-NFS, An Implementation of the Number Field Sieve Algorithm. Release 2.3.0. (2017). http://cado-nfs.gforge.inria.fr
36. The Sage Developers: SageMath, the Sage Mathematics Software System (Version 8.9) (2019). https://www.sagemath.org
37. Washington, L.C.: Elliptic Curves: Number Theory and Cryptography, 2nd edn. Chapman & Hall/CRC, Boca Raton (2008)

An Optimizing Protocol Transformation for Constructor Finite Variant Theories in Maude-NPA

Damián Aparicio-Sánchez[1], Santiago Escobar[1(✉)], Raúl Gutiérrez[2], and Julia Sapiña[1]

[1] VRAIN, Universitat Politècnica de València, Valencia, Spain
{daapsnc,sescobar,jsapina}@upv.es
[2] Universidad Politécnica de Madrid, Madrid, Spain
r.gutierrez@upm.es

Abstract. Maude-NPA is an analysis tool for cryptographic security protocols that takes into account the algebraic properties of the cryptosystem. Maude-NPA can reason about a wide range of cryptographic properties. However, some algebraic properties, and protocols using them, have been beyond Maude-NPA capabilities, either because the cryptographic properties cannot be expressed using its equational unification features or because the state space is unmanageable. In this paper, we provide a protocol transformation that can *safely* get rid of cryptographic properties under some conditions. The time and space difference between verifying the protocol with all the crypto properties and verifying the protocol with a minimal set of the crypto properties is remarkable. We also provide, for the first time, an encoding of the theory of bilinear pairing into Maude-NPA that goes beyond the encoding of bilinear pairing available in the Tamarin tool.

Keywords: Crypto protocol analysis · Diffie-Hellman · Exponentiation · Bilinear pairing · Protocol transformation

1 Introduction

Maude-NPA [13] is an analysis tool for cryptographic security protocols that takes into account the algebraic properties of the cryptosystem. Sometimes algebraic properties can uncover weaknesses of cryptosystems and, in other cases, they are part of the protocol security assumptions. Maude-NPA uses an approach similar to its predecessor, the NRL Protocol Analyzer (NPA) [23], i.e., it is based on unification and performs backwards search from an attack state pattern to

Partially supported by the EU (FEDER) and the Spanish MCIU under grant RTI2018-094403-B-C32, by the Spanish Generalitat Valenciana under grant PROMETEO/2019/098, and by the US Air Force Office of Scientific Research under award number FA9550-17-1-0286. Julia Sapiña has been supported by the Generalitat Valenciana APOSTD/2019/127 grant.

determine whether or not it is reachable. However, unlike the original NPA, it has a theoretical basis on *rewriting logic* [12] and *narrowing* [7], and while NPA could only be used to reason about equational theories involving a fixed set of rewrite rules, Maude-NPA can be used to reason about a wide range of cryptographic properties [1,13], including cancellation of encryption and decryption, Diffie-Hellman exponentiation [11], exclusive-or [29], and some approximations of homomorphic encryption [14,33].

However, some algebraic properties and protocols using them have been beyond Maude-NPA capabilities, either because the cryptographic properties cannot be expressed using its equational unification features or because the state space is unmanageable. We provide a protocol transformation that can substantially reduce the search space, i.e., given some cryptographic properties, expressed using the equational unification features of Maude-NPA, and a protocol, we are able to transform the protocol in such a way that some cryptographic properties are no longer necessary, and thus can be safely removed. The time and space difference between verifying the protocol with all the crypto properties and verifying the protocol with a minimal set of the crypto properties is remarkable. We also provide, for the first time, an encoding of the theory of bilinear pairing into Maude-NPA that goes beyond the encoding of bilinear pairing available in Tamarin [2], the only crypto tool with such an equational theory.

Our protocol transformation relies on a program transformation from [27] for rewrite theories in Maude that we have improved by relaxing some of its applicability conditions. Such program transformation relies on *constructor term variants* [26], which is an extension of *term variants* [8,16]. Nowadays, several crypto analysis tools rely on the variant-based equational unification capabilities of Maude, such as Maude-NPA but also Tamarin [10] and AKISS [5]. These tools may be benefited from our protocol transformation and, furthermore, from our encoding of the theory of bilinear pairing. Our contributions may even be useful for other tools with more limited crypto properties such as ProVerif [6], Scyther [9] or Scyther-proof [24].

The main contributions of this work are: (i) we provide a non-trivial protocol transformation based on [27]; (ii) since the protocols of Sect. 5 do not satisfy the conditions of [27], we provide a more powerful protocol transformation that we implemented, made available online, and pays off in practice; (iii) we provide an encoding of bilinear pairing that can handle all the protocols of Sect. 5 that Tamarin cannot handle; (iv) we implemented the algorithm of [31] for the computation of constructor variants [26] from scratch; and (v) there was no implementation of the program transformation of [27] and we implemented it.

After some preliminaries on Sect. 2, we present how Maude-NPA works in Sect. 3. We introduce our protocol transformation in Sect. 4. Section 5 presents several increasingly complex case studies: Diffie-Hellman protocol in Sect. 5.1, STR protocol in Sect. 5.2, Joux protocol in Sect. 5.3, and TAK protocols in Sect. 5.4. Our experiments are presented in Sect. 6 and we conclude in Sect. 7.

2   Preliminaries

We follow the classical notation and terminology for term rewriting [32], and for rewriting logic and order-sorted notions [25]. We assume an order-sorted signature Σ with a poset of sorts $(\mathsf{S}, \leq)$. We also assume an S-sorted family $\mathcal{X} = \{\mathcal{X}_{\mathsf{s}}\}_{\mathsf{s} \in \mathsf{S}}$ of disjoint variable sets with each $\mathcal{X}_{\mathsf{s}}$ countably infinite. $\mathcal{T}_{\Sigma}(\mathcal{X})_{\mathsf{s}}$ is the set of terms of sort s, and $\mathcal{T}_{\Sigma, \mathsf{s}}$ is the set of ground terms of sort s. We write $\mathcal{T}_{\Sigma}(\mathcal{X})$ and $\mathcal{T}_{\Sigma}$ for the corresponding order-sorted term algebras. For a term t, $Var(t)$ denotes the set of variables in t. Throughout this paper, Σ is assumed to be *preregular*, so each term t has a least sort, denoted $ls(t)$.

A *substitution* $\sigma \in \mathcal{S}ubst(\Sigma, \mathcal{X})$ is a sorted mapping from a finite subset of $\mathcal{X}$ to $\mathcal{T}_{\Sigma}(\mathcal{X})$. Substitutions are written as $\sigma = \{X_1 \mapsto t_1, \ldots, X_n \mapsto t_n\}$, where the domain of σ is $Dom(\sigma) = \{X_1, \ldots, X_n\}$ and the set of variables introduced by terms $t_1, \ldots, t_n$ is written $Ran(\sigma)$. The identity substitution is denoted *id*. Substitutions are homomorphically extended to $\mathcal{T}_{\Sigma}(\mathcal{X})$. The application of a substitution σ to a term t is denoted by $t\sigma$ or $\sigma(t)$. The restriction of σ to a set of variables V is $\sigma|_V$. Composition of two substitutions σ and σ' is written $\sigma\sigma'$.

A Σ-*equation* is an unoriented pair $t = t'$, where $t, t' \in \mathcal{T}_{\Sigma}(\mathcal{X})_{\mathsf{s}}$ for some sort $\mathsf{s} \in \mathsf{S}$. Given Σ and a set E of Σ-equations, order-sorted equational logic induces a congruence relation $=_E$ on terms $t, t' \in \mathcal{T}_{\Sigma}(\mathcal{X})$. The E-equivalence class of a term t is denoted by $[t]_E$ and $\mathcal{T}_{\Sigma/E}(\mathcal{X})$ and $\mathcal{T}_{\Sigma/E}$ denote the corresponding order-sorted term algebras modulo E. Throughout this paper we assume that $\mathcal{T}_{\Sigma, \mathsf{s}} \neq \emptyset$ for every sort s, because this affords a simpler deduction system. An *equational theory* (Σ, E) is a pair with Σ an order-sorted signature and E a set of Σ-equations.

An E-*unifier* for a Σ-equation $t = t'$ is a substitution σ such that $t\sigma =_E t'\sigma$. A set of substitutions $CSU_E(t = t')$ is said to be a *complete* set of unifiers for the equality $t = t'$ modulo E iff: (i) each $\sigma \in CSU_E(t = t')$ is an E-unifier of $t = t'$; (ii) for any E-unifier ρ of $t = t'$ there is $\sigma \in CSU_E(t = t')$ and τ s.t. $\sigma\tau =_E \rho$; (iii) for all $\sigma \in CSU_E(t = t')$, $Dom(\sigma) \subseteq (Var(t) \cup Var(t'))$. An E-unification algorithm is *complete* if for any equation $t = t'$ it generates a complete set of E-unifiers. A unification algorithm is said to be *finitary* and complete if it always terminates after generating a finite and complete set of solutions.

A *rewrite rule* is an oriented pair $l \rightarrow r$, where $l \notin \mathcal{X}$ and $l, r \in \mathcal{T}_{\Sigma}(\mathcal{X})_{\mathsf{s}}$ for some sort $\mathsf{s} \in \mathsf{S}$. An *(unconditional) order-sorted rewrite theory* is a triple (Σ, E, R) with Σ an order-sorted signature, E a set of Σ-equations, and R a set of rewrite rules. The relation $\rightarrow_{R,E}$ on $\mathcal{T}_{\Sigma}(\mathcal{X})$ is defined as: $t \rightarrow_{p,R,E} t'$ (or just $t \rightarrow_{R,E} t'$) iff there exist $p \in Pos_{\Sigma}(t)$, a rule $l \rightarrow r$ in R, and a substitution σ such that $t|_p =_E l\sigma$ and $t' = t[r\sigma]_p$. The transitive (resp. transitive and reflexive) closure of $\rightarrow_{R,E}$ is denoted by $\rightarrow^+_{R,E}$ (resp. $\rightarrow^*_{R,E}$). A term t is (R, E)-irreducible if there is no t' s.t. $t \rightarrow_{R,E} t'$. The R, E-*narrowing* relation on $\mathcal{T}_{\Sigma}(\mathcal{X})$ is defined as $t \rightsquigarrow_{p,\sigma,R,E} t'$ ($\rightsquigarrow_{\sigma}$ if R, E are understood, and $\rightsquigarrow$ if σ is also understood) if there is a non-variable position $p \in Pos_{\Sigma}(t)$, a rule $l \rightarrow r \in R$ standardized apart (i.e., contains no variable previously met during any previous computation) and a unifier $\sigma \in CSU_E(t|_p = l)$, such that $t' = (t[r]_p)\sigma$. The transitive (resp. transitive and reflexive) closure of $\rightsquigarrow$ is denoted by $\rightsquigarrow^+$ (resp. $\rightsquigarrow^*$).

3   The Maude-NPA

Given a protocol $\mathcal{P}$ to be specified, protocol states are modeled as elements of an initial algebra $T_{\Sigma_\mathcal{P}/\mathcal{E}_\mathcal{P}}$, i.e., each state is an equivalence class $[t]_{\mathcal{E}_\mathcal{P}} \in T_{\Sigma_\mathcal{P}/\mathcal{E}_\mathcal{P}}$ where $\Sigma_\mathcal{P}$ is the set of symbols defining the protocol $\mathcal{P}$, and $\mathcal{E}_\mathcal{P}$ specifies the *algebraic properties* of the cryptographic functions $\Sigma_\mathcal{P}$. The cryptographic properties $\mathcal{E}_\mathcal{P}$ may vary depending on different protocols.

The signature $\Sigma_\mathcal{P}$ incorporates some predefined symbols for protocol infrastructure. A state is a term of the form $\{S_1 \ \& \ \cdots \ \& \ S_n \ \& \ \{IK\}\}$ where $\&$ is an associative-commutative union operator with identity symbol $\emptyset$.

The *intruder knowledge IK* of a state $\{S_1 \ \& \ \cdots \ \& \ S_n \ \& \ \{IK\}\}$ is defined as a set of facts using the comma as an associative-commutative union operator with identity element $\emptyset$. There are two kinds of intruder facts: *positive* knowledge facts (the intruder knows m, i.e., $m \in \mathcal{I}$), and *negative* knowledge facts (the intruder *does not yet know m* but *will know it in a future state*, i.e., $m \notin \mathcal{I}$), where m is a message expression.

Each S_i of a state $\{S_1 \ \& \ \cdots \ \& \ S_n \ \& \ \{IK\}\}$ is called a strand and specifies the sequence of messages sent and received by a principal executing the protocol. *Strands* [17] are represented as a sequence of messages $[msg_1^\pm, msg_2^\pm, msg_3^\pm, \ldots, msg_{k-1}^\pm, msg_k^\pm]$ with $msg_i^\pm$ either msg_i^- (also written $-msg_i$) representing an input message, or msg_i^+ (also written $+msg_i$) representing an output message. Note that each msg_i is a term of a special sort Msg; this sort is extended by the user to allow any user-definable protocol syntax. Variables of a special sort Fresh are used to represent pseudo-random values (nonces) and Maude-NPA ensures that two distinct fresh variables will never be merged. Strands are extended with all the fresh variables created by that strand, i.e., $:: f_1, \ldots, f_k :: [msg_1^\pm, msg_2^\pm, \ldots, msg_k^\pm]$. Section 5 includes several examples of honest and Dolev-Yao strands.

Strands are used to represent both the actions of honest principals (with a strand specified for each protocol role) and the actions of an intruder (with a strand for each action an intruder is able to perform on messages). In Maude-NPA strands evolve over time; the symbol | is used to divide past and future. That is, given a strand $[\ msg_1^\pm, \ \ldots, \ msg_i^\pm \mid msg_{i+1}^\pm, \ \ldots, \ msg_k^\pm \ ]$, messages $msg_1^\pm, \ldots, msg_i^\pm$ are the *past messages*, and messages $msg_{i+1}^\pm, \ldots, msg_k^\pm$ are the *future messages* ($msg_{i+1}^\pm$ is the immediate future message). A strand $[msg_1^\pm, \ldots, msg_k^\pm]$ is shorthand for $[nil \mid msg_1^\pm, \ldots, msg_k^\pm, nil]$. An *initial state* is a state where the bar is at the beginning for all strands in the state, and the intruder knowledge has no fact of the form $m \in \mathcal{I}$. A *final state* is a state where the bar is at the end for all strands in the state and there is no intruder fact of the form $m \notin \mathcal{I}$.

Since the number of states $T_{\Sigma_\mathcal{P}/\mathcal{E}_\mathcal{P}}$ is in general infinite, rather than exploring concrete protocol states $[t]_{\mathcal{E}_\mathcal{P}} \in T_{\Sigma_\mathcal{P}/\mathcal{E}_\mathcal{P}}$ Maude-NPA explores *state patterns* $[t(x_1, \ldots, x_n)]_{\mathcal{E}_\mathcal{P}} \in T_{\Sigma_\mathcal{P}/\mathcal{E}_\mathcal{P}}(\mathcal{X})$ on the free $(\Sigma_\mathcal{P}, \mathcal{E}_\mathcal{P})$-algebra over a set of variables $\mathcal{X}$. In this way, a state pattern $[t(x_1, \ldots, x_n)]_{\mathcal{E}_\mathcal{P}}$ represents not a single concrete state but a possibly infinite set of such states, namely all the *instances* of the pattern $[t(x_1, \ldots, x_n)]_{\mathcal{E}_\mathcal{P}}$ where the variables $x_1, \ldots, x_n$ have been instantiated by concrete ground terms.

The semantics of Maude-NPA is expressed in terms of a Maude rewrite theory, including *rewrite rules* that describe how a protocol moves from one state to another via the intruder's interaction with it [13]. One uses Maude-NPA to find an attack by specifying an insecure state pattern called an *attack pattern*. Maude-NPA attempts to find a path from an initial state to the attack pattern via *backwards narrowing* (using the narrowing capabilities of Maude [7] but with the reversed orientation of the rewrite rules). That is, a sequence from an initial state to an attack state is searched *in reverse* as a *backwards path* from an attack state pattern to an initial state. Maude-NPA attempts to find paths until it can no longer form any backwards narrowing steps, at which point it terminates. If at that point it has not found an initial state, the attack pattern is judged *unreachable*; providing a proof of security rather than finding attacks. However, note that Maude-NPA places *no bound on the number of sessions*, so reachability is undecidable in general. Maude-NPA does not achieve termination by any data abstraction, e.g. a bounded number of nonces. Instead, the tool makes use of a number of sound and complete state space reduction techniques that help to identify unreachable and redundant states [15], and thus make termination more likely.

4   Protocol Transformation

Maude-NPA relies on equational unification to perform each backwards narrowing step. Some cryptographic properties often involve the development of dedicated algorithms (see [4]). Maude-NPA provides built-in support for theories involving symbols with any combination of associativity (A), commutativity (C), and identity (U) axioms. Furthermore, by relying on the variant-based equational unification [7,16], Maude-NPA allows users to augment the basic set of equational axioms supported with rewrite rules such as cancellation of encryption and decryption, Diffie-Hellman exponentiation [11], exclusive-or [29], and some approximations of homomorphic encryption [14,33].

4.1   Finite Variant Theories

An equational theory $(\Sigma, \mathcal{E})$ is often decomposed into a disjoint union $\mathcal{E} = E \uplus B$, where B is a set of algebraic axioms (which are implicitly expressed in Maude as operator attributes `assoc`, `comm`, and `id:` keywords) and E consists of variant equations that are implicitly oriented from left to right as a set $\vec{E}$ of rewrite rules (and operationally used as simplification rules modulo B).

Definition 1 (Decomposition [16]). *Let $(\Sigma, \mathcal{E})$ be an order-sorted equational theory. We call $(\Sigma, B, \vec{E})$ a decomposition of $(\Sigma, \mathcal{E})$ if $\mathcal{E} = E \uplus B$ and $(\Sigma, B, \vec{E})$ is an order-sorted rewrite theory satisfying the following properties:*

1. *B is regular, i.e., for each $t = t'$ in B, we have $Var(t) = Var(t')$, and linear, i.e., for each $t = t'$ in B, each variable occurs only once in t and in t'.*

2. B is sort-preserving, i.e., for each $t = t'$ in B and substitution σ, we have $t\sigma \in T_{\Sigma}(\mathcal{X})_s$ iff $t'\sigma \in T_{\Sigma}(\mathcal{X})_s$. Furthermore, for each equation $t = t'$ in B, all variables in $Var(t)$ and $Var(t')$ have a common top sort.
3. B has a finitary and complete unification algorithm.
4. The rewrite rules in $\vec{E}$ are convergent, i.e., confluent, terminating, and coherent modulo B, and sort-decreasing.

In a decomposition, for each term $t \in T_{\Sigma}(\mathcal{X})$, there is a unique (up to B-equivalence) $(\vec{E}, B)$-irreducible term that can be obtained by rewriting t to its *normal* form, which is denoted by $t\downarrow_{\vec{E},B}$. We often abuse notation and say that $(\Sigma, B, \vec{E})$ is a decomposition of an order-sorted equational theory $(\Sigma, \mathcal{E})$ even if $\mathcal{E} \neq E \uplus B$ but E is instead the explicitly extended B-coherent completion of a set E' such that $\mathcal{E} = E' \uplus B$ (see [16]).

Example 1. The property associated to Diffie-Hellman exponentiation is described using the following equational theory in Maude, including an auxiliary associative-commutative symbol $*$ for exponents so that $(z^x)^y = (z^y)^x = z^{x*y}$.

```
fmod DH-FVP is
  sorts Exp Nonce NeNonceSet Gen .
  subsort Nonce < NeNonceSet . subsort Gen < Exp .
  op exp : Exp NeNonceSet -> Exp .
  op _*_ : NeNonceSet NeNonceSet -> NeNonceSet [assoc comm] .
  var X : Exp . vars Y Z : NeNonceSet .
  eq exp(exp(X,Y),Z) = exp(X,Y * Z) [variant] .
endfm
```

Note that X admits any exponentiation and Y and Z are restricted to non-empty multisets of nonces. For an arbitrary term g of sort Gen and three arbitrary terms n_A, n_B, n_C of sort Nonce, $t = exp(exp(exp(g, n_A), n_B), n_C)$ is simplified into $t\downarrow_{\vec{E},B} = exp(g, n_A * n_B * n_C)$.

In order to provide a finitary and complete unification algorithm for a decomposition $(\Sigma, B, \vec{E})$, the *folding variant narrowing* strategy is defined in [16]. Intuitively, an $(\vec{E}, B)$-*variant* of a term t is the $(\vec{E}, B)$-irreducible form of an *instance* $t\sigma$ of t. That is, the variants of t are all of the possible $(\vec{E}, B)$-irreducible terms to which instances of t evaluate.

Definition 2 (Term Variant [8,16]**).** *Given a term t and a decomposition $(\Sigma, B, \vec{E})$, we say that (t', θ) is a variant of t if $t' =_B (t\theta)\downarrow_{\vec{E},B}$, where $Dom(\theta) \subseteq Var(t)$ and $Ran(\theta) \cap Var(t) = \emptyset$.*

Example 2. Following Example 1, the set of variants for the term $exp(X,Y)$ is infinite, since we have $(exp(X',Y*Y'), \{X \mapsto exp(X',Y')\})$, $(exp(X'',Y*Y'*Y''), \{X \mapsto exp(exp(X'',Y''),Y')\})$, ...

It is possible to compute a complete and finite set of variants for some equational theories.

Definition 3 (Complete set of Variants [16]**).** *Given a decomposition* $(\Sigma, B, \vec{E})$ *and a term* t, *we write* $[\![t]\!]_{\vec{E},B}$ *for a* complete *set of variants of* t, *i.e., for any variant* (t_2, θ_2) *of* t, *there is a variant* $(t_1, \theta_1) \in [\![t]\!]_{\vec{E},B}$ *such that* $(t_1, \theta_1) \leq_{\vec{E},B} (t_2, \theta_2)$, *where* $(t_1, \theta_1) \leq_{\vec{E},B} (t_2, \theta_2)$ *iff there is a substitution* ρ *such that* $(\theta_1 \rho)|_{Var(t)} =_B (\theta_2 \downarrow_{\vec{E},B})|_{Var(t)}$ *and* $t_1 \rho =_B t_2$. *An equational theory has the* finite variant property *(FVP) (also called* finite variant theory*) iff for all* $t \in \mathcal{T}_\Sigma(\mathcal{X})$, $[\![t]\!]_{\vec{E},B}$ *is a finite set.*

Example 3. Following Example 2, there exists a complete and finite set of variants for the term $exp(X,Y)$: the variant $(exp(X,Y), id)$ and the variant $(exp(X', Y * Y'), \{X \mapsto exp(X', Y')\})$. Any other variant includes a substitution not in irreducible form.

4.2   Constructor Finite Variant Theories

Quite often, the signature Σ of a decomposition $(\Sigma, B, \vec{E})$, on which $\mathcal{T}_{\Sigma/B}$ is defined, has a natural subsignature of *constructor* symbols Ω. The elements of the *canonical algebra* $C_{\Sigma/\vec{E},B} = \{[t\downarrow_{\vec{E},B}]_B \mid t \in \mathcal{T}_\Sigma\}$, i.e., the B-equivalence classes computed by $\vec{E}, B$-simplification, are Ω-terms, whereas the other symbols are viewed as functions which are simplified into constructor symbols.

Proverif [6] already incorporated this distinction between what they called *destructor and constructor symbols* time ago in contrast to other crypto tools such as AKISS [5], Maude-NPA [1], OFMC [28], Scyther [9], Scyther-proof [24], and Tamarin [2]. In the rest of the paper, we exploit this distinction in Maude-NPA without altering the tool.

A decomposition $(\Sigma, B, \vec{E})$ *protects* a *constructor decomposition* $(\Omega, B_\Omega, \vec{E}_\Omega)$ iff $\Omega \subseteq \Sigma$, $B_\Omega \subseteq B$, and $\vec{E}_\Omega \subseteq \vec{E}$, and for all $t, t' \in \mathcal{T}_\Omega(\mathcal{X})$ we have: (i) $t =_{B_\Omega} t' \iff t =_B t'$, (ii) $t = t\downarrow_{\vec{E}_\Omega, B_\Omega} \iff t = t\downarrow_{\vec{E},B}$, and (iii) $C_{\Omega/\vec{E}_\Omega, B_\Omega} = C_{\Sigma/\vec{E},B}|_\Omega$. A constructor decomposition $(\Omega, B_\Omega, \emptyset)$ is called *free*. A decomposition $(\Sigma, B, \vec{E})$ is called *sufficiently complete* with respect to a free constructor decomposition $(\Omega, B_\Omega, \emptyset)$ iff for each $t \in \mathcal{T}_\Sigma$ we have: (i) $t\downarrow_{\vec{E},B} \in \mathcal{T}_\Omega$, and (ii) if $u \in \mathcal{T}_\Omega$ and $u =_B v$, then $v \in \mathcal{T}_\Omega$. This ensures that if any element in an equivalent class is a constructor term, all the other elements are also constructor.

Example 4. We can extend the equational theory of Example 1 to protect a constructor subsignature[1] by overloading symbol `exp` to use the former[2] sorts Exp and Gen.

---

[1] Operator declarations labeled `ctor`, their associated sorts, and no equation.

[2] This equational theory, as well as all the ones in Sect. 5, should be parametric on sorts Gen, GenP and Nonce but we omit such more general-purpose definitions for simplicity (see [7] for details on parametric equational theories).

```
fmod DH-CFVP is
  sorts Exp Nonce NeNonceSet Gen .
  subsort Nonce < NeNonceSet .
  op exp : Gen NeNonceSet -> Exp [ctor] .
  op exp : Exp NeNonceSet -> Exp .
  op _*_ : NeNonceSet NeNonceSet -> NeNonceSet [assoc comm ctor] .
  var X : Gen . vars Y Z : NeNonceSet .
  eq exp(exp(X,Y),Z) = exp(X,Y * Z) [variant] .
endfm
```

For an arbitrary term g of sort Gen and three arbitrary terms n_A, n_B, n_C of sort Nonce, $t = exp(exp(exp(g, n_A), n_B), n_C)$ is simplified into the constructor term $t\downarrow_{\vec{E},B} = exp(g, n_A * n_B * n_C)$.

The notion of a constructor variant, rather than a variant, is defined in [26].

Definition 4 (Constructor Variant [26]). *Given a decomposition $(\Sigma, B, \vec{E})$ protecting a constructor decomposition $(\Omega, B_\Omega, \vec{E}_\Omega)$ and a Σ-term t, we say that a variant (t', θ) of t is a* constructor variant *if $t' \in \mathcal{T}_\Omega(\mathcal{X})$.*

Example 5. Following Example 4, the set of constructor variants for the term $exp(X, Y)$ is infinite, as in Example 2, since we have $(exp(X', Y * Y'), \{X \mapsto exp(X', Y')\})$, $(exp(X'', Y * Y' * Y''), \{X \mapsto exp(exp(X'', Y''), Y')\})$, ...

Definition 5 (Complete set of Constructor Variants [26]). *Given a decomposition $(\Sigma, B, \vec{E})$ protecting a constructor decomposition $(\Omega, B_\Omega, \vec{E}_\Omega)$ and a Σ-term t, we write $[\![t]\!]^\Omega_{\vec{E},B}$ for a* complete *set of constructor variants of t, i.e., for any constructor variant (t_2, θ_2) of t, there is a constructor variant $(t_1, \theta_1) \in [\![t]\!]^\Omega_{\vec{E},B}$ such that $(t_1, \theta_1) \leq_{\vec{E},B} (t_2, \theta_2)$. A decomposition $(\Sigma, B, \vec{E})$ has* the constructor finite variant property *(CFVP) (or it is called a* constructor finite variant theory*) iff for all $t \in \mathcal{T}_\Sigma(\mathcal{X})$, $[\![t]\!]^\Omega_{\vec{E},B}$ is a finite set.*

Example 6. Following Example 5, there exists a finite and complete set of constructor variants for the term $exp(X, Y)$ where X is of sort Exp, since we have $(exp(XG, Y * Y'), \{X \mapsto exp(XG, Y')\})$ where XG is a new variable of sort Gen instead of sort Exp.

An algorithm for computing $[\![t]\!]^\Omega_{\vec{E},B}$ is provided in [31] for equational theories that are FVP. This algorithm assumes an extra condition called *preregular below*, i.e., a term cannot have a constructor typing above a non-constructor typing.

Definition 6 (Preregular below [26]). *Given a decomposition $(\Sigma, B, \vec{E})$ protecting a constructor decomposition $(\Omega, B_\Omega, \vec{E}_\Omega)$, the (preregular) order-sorted signature $(\Sigma, <)$ is called* preregular below *iff $\forall t \in \mathcal{T}_\Sigma(\mathcal{X})$, $ls_\Omega(t) = ls_\Sigma(t)$.*

Example 7. Consider the following equational theory

```
fmod DH-NoPreregularBelow is
  sorts Nonce NeNonceSet GenSub Gen ExpSub Exp .
  subsort GenSub < Gen . subsort ExpSub < Exp .
  subsort Nonce < NeNonceSet .
  op gSub : -> GenSub [ctor] .
  op g : -> Gen [ctor] .
  op exp : GenSub NeNonceSet -> ExpSub .
  op exp : Gen NeNonceSet -> Exp [ctor] .
  op exp : Exp NeNonceSet -> Exp .
endfm
```

The signature is not preregular below since, given an arbitrary term n_A of sort Nonce, the least sort of the term $exp(gSub, n_A)$ is ExpSub in the original signature but Exp in the constructor subsignature.

The set of constructor variants of the form $[\![\langle l, r \rangle]\!]_{\vec{E},B}^{\Omega}$, where l and r are, respectively, the lefthand and righthand sides of a rewrite rule in a rewrite theory, play a crucial role in the following theory transformation $\mathcal{R} \mapsto \mathcal{R}_{l,r}^{\Omega}$ from [27].

Definition 7 ($\mathcal{R} \mapsto \mathcal{R}_{l,r}^{\Omega}$ [27]). *Given a rewrite theory $(\Sigma, B \uplus E, R)$ such that $(\Sigma, B, \vec{E})$ is CFVP and preregular below, the rewrite theory $(\Sigma, B \uplus E, R_{l,r}^{\Omega})$ is defined as $R_{l,r}^{\Omega} = \{l' \to r' \mid l \to r \in R \wedge (\langle l', r' \rangle, \sigma) \in [\![\langle l, r \rangle]\!]_{\vec{E},B}^{\Omega}\}$.*

Section 5 shows how several protocols are transformed using a protocol transformation that relies on this program transformation.

Example 8. Any expression of the form $exp(X, Y)$, where X is of sort Exp and Y is of sort NeNonceSet, occurring in any lefthand or righthand side of a rule in a rewrite theory will be replaced by the constructor variant shown in Example 6.

Theorem 1 ([27, Theo. 7]). *Given a rewrite theory $(\Sigma, B \uplus E, R)$ such that $(\Sigma, B, \vec{E})$ is a decomposition protecting a free constructor decomposition $(\Omega, B_\Omega, \emptyset)$, it is CFVP, it is sufficiently complete with respect to $(\Omega, B_\Omega, \emptyset)$, and Σ is preregular below, then the rewrite theory $(\Sigma, B_\Omega, R_{l,r}^{\Omega})$ is ground semantically equivalent to $(\Sigma, B \uplus E, R)$.*

The equational theory for Diffie-Hellman of Example 4 is sufficiently complete w.r.t. its constructor subsignature, since any ground term rooted by symbol exp is either already using the constructor typing or can be simplified into the constructor typing of exp. However, some other theories of interest are not.

Example 9. Consider the cancellation of encryption and decryption.

```
fmod DE is
  sorts Msg Key .
  op enc : Key Msg -> Msg [ctor] .
  op dec : Key Msg -> Msg .
  var K : Key . vars X : Msg .
  eq dec(K,enc(K,X)) = X [variant] .
endfm
```

Given arbitrary keys k_1, k_2 and an arbitrary term a, the term $dec(k_1, enc(k_2, a))$ cannot be reduced.

Terms that cannot be simplified into a constructor term are understood as an erroneous expression and discarded. This is the behaviour of *destructor symbols* in Proverif [6], i.e., functions that may fail. In the rest of the paper, we relax the condition on sufficiently completeness of Theorem 1 and follow the spirit of Proverif's approach[3]: a NF rewrite theory below ensures that erroneous expressions cannot occur in the righthand sides of rewrite rules or in equations, preventing any function to capture that any of its arguments fails. Typical security protocols do however not satisfy the conditions of [27], and in particular all protocols studied in Sect. 5 did not.

Definition 8 (NF Rewrite Theory). *Given a rewrite theory* $(\Sigma, B \uplus E, R)$ *such that* $(\Sigma, B, \vec{E})$ *is a decomposition protecting a free constructor decomposition* $(\Omega, B_\Omega, \emptyset)$, *erroneous terms are defined as* $\mathcal{E}rr_\perp = \{t \in \mathcal{T}_\Sigma(\mathcal{X}) \mid \nexists \sigma : (t\sigma) \downarrow_{\vec{E},B} \in \mathcal{T}_\Omega(\mathcal{X})\}$ *whereas possibly erroneous terms are defined as* $\mathcal{E}rr_\top = \{t \in \mathcal{T}_\Sigma(\mathcal{X}) \mid \exists \sigma : (t\sigma) \downarrow_{\vec{E},B} \notin \mathcal{T}_\Omega(\mathcal{X})\}$. *We say the rewrite theory is NF if, for each* $l = r \in E$, $l, r \notin \mathcal{E}rr_\perp$ *and, for each* $l \to r \in R$, $r|_p \in \mathcal{E}rr_\top \implies \exists q : l|_q =_B r|_p$.

Theorem 2. *Given a NF rewrite theory* $(\Sigma, B \uplus E, R)$ *such that* $(\Sigma, B, \vec{E})$ *is a decomposition protecting a free constructor decomposition* $(\Omega, B_\Omega, \emptyset)$ *and it is CFVP, then any term reachable from a constructor term is also constructor.*

Proof. By induction on the length of the narrowing sequence $t_0 \leadsto^n t_n$. If $n = 0$, then $t_n = t_0$ and t_0 is constructor. If $n > 0$, then $t_0 \leadsto_\sigma t_1 \leadsto^{n-1} t_n$ s.t. $\sigma \in CSU_{E \uplus B}(t_0|_p = l)$ and $t_1 = (t_0[r]_p)\sigma$. Since t_0 is a constructor term, there is no equation applicable to t_0, i.e., $(t_0|_p)\sigma =_B (l\sigma) \downarrow_{\vec{E},B}$. Since t_0 is a constructor term, the bindings in $\sigma|_{Var(t_0)}$ contain only constructor terms. Since erroneous expressions do not appear in the equations E, $\sigma|_{Var(l)}$ contains also constructor terms. Since r does not contain any extra possible erroneous expression, t_1 is constructor. The conclusion follows by the induction hypothesis. $\qquad \square$

Corollary 1. *Given a NF rewrite theory* $(\Sigma, B \uplus E, R)$ *such that* $(\Sigma, B, \vec{E})$ *is a decomposition protecting a free constructor decomposition* $(\Omega, B_\Omega, \emptyset)$, *it is CFVP, and* Σ *is preregular below, then the rewrite theory* $(\Sigma, B_\Omega, R_{l,r}^\Omega)$ *is ground semantically equivalent to* $(\Sigma, B \uplus E, R)$.

We have implemented both the algorithm for computing $[\![t]\!]_{\vec{E},B}^\Omega$ provided in [31] for equational theories that are FVP and the rewrite theory transformation $\mathcal{R} \mapsto \mathcal{R}_{l,r}^\Omega$ from [27]. As far as we know, there was no implementation available of the rewrite theory transformation $\mathcal{R} \mapsto \mathcal{R}_{l,r}^\Omega$ of [27]. We have used $[\![t]\!]_{\vec{E},B}^\Omega$ and $\mathcal{R} \mapsto \mathcal{R}_{l,r}^\Omega$ to create a *protocol* transformation available online at http://safe-tools.dsic.upv.es/cvtool. This web page accepts a protocol specification, using the

---

[3] A detailed comparison is outside the scope of this paper.

Maude-NPA syntax, and returns the transformed version, including strands and attack patterns. The proof of soundness and completeness of the protocol transformation is omitted but relies on Theorem 1 and Corollary 1. Informally speaking, Maude-NPA internally transforms a protocol specification into a rewrite theory (see Sect. 3). This transformed rewrite theory is then transformed using the program transformation $\mathcal{R} \mapsto \mathcal{R}^{\Omega}_{l,r}$. And, finally, this resulting rewrite theory is mapped back into a protocol specification. Note that the web page assumes that the conditions of Corollary 1 are satisfied without enforcing them. All the protocols presented in the next section need the relaxed conditions of application of Corollary 1 to safely apply the protocol transformation. These relaxed conditions allow us to deal with more complex protocol specifications efficiently.

$$A \longrightarrow B : g^{N_a}$$
$$B \longrightarrow A : g^{N_b}$$
$$B \longrightarrow C : g^{((g^{N_b})^{N_a})}$$
$$C \longrightarrow A, B : g^{N_c}$$

$$A \longrightarrow B : g^{N_a}$$
$$B \longrightarrow A : g^{N_b}$$

$$K_A = (g^{N_b})^{N_a}$$
$$K_B = (g^{N_a})^{N_b}$$
$$K_{AB} = g^{N_a * N_b}$$

Fig. 1. DH

$$K_A = (g^{N_c})^{(g^{((g^{N_b})^{N_a})})}$$
$$K_B = (g^{N_c})^{(g^{((g^{N_a})^{N_b})})}$$
$$K_C = (g^{((g^{N_b})^{N_a})})^{N_c}$$
$$K_{ABC} = g^{g^{N_a * N_b} * N_c}$$

Fig. 2. STR

$$A \longrightarrow B, C : aP$$
$$B \longrightarrow A, C : bP$$
$$C \longrightarrow A, B : cP$$

$$K_A = \hat{e}(bP, cP)^a$$
$$K_B = \hat{e}(aP, cP)^b$$
$$K_C = \hat{e}(aP, bP)^c$$
$$K_{ABC} = \hat{e}(P, P)^{a*b*c}$$

Fig. 3. Joux

$$A \longrightarrow B, C : aP; \{xP\}_A$$
$$B \longrightarrow A, C : bP; \{yP\}_B$$
$$C \longrightarrow A, B : cP; \{zP\}_C$$

$$K_A = h(\hat{e}(bP, cP)^a; \hat{e}(yP, zP)^x)$$
$$K_B = h(\hat{e}(aP, cP)^b; \hat{e}(xP, zP)^y)$$
$$K_C = h(\hat{e}(aP, bP)^c; \hat{e}(xP, yP)^z)$$
$$K_{ABC} = h(\hat{e}(P, P)^{a*b*c}; \hat{e}(P, P)^{x*y*z})$$

Fig. 4. TAK1

$$K_A = \hat{e}(bP, zP)^a \cdot \hat{e}(yP, cP)^a \cdot \hat{e}(bP, cP)^x$$
$$K_B = \hat{e}(aP, zP)^b \cdot \hat{e}(xP, cP)^b \cdot \hat{e}(aP, cP)^y$$
$$K_C = \hat{e}(aP, yP)^c \cdot \hat{e}(xP, bP)^c \cdot \hat{e}(aP, bP)^z$$
$$K_{ABC} = \hat{e}(P, P)^{a*y*c} \cdot \hat{e}(P, P)^{x*b*c} \cdot \hat{e}(P, P)^{a*b*z}$$

Fig. 5. TAK2

$$K_A = \hat{e}(yP, cP)^x \cdot \hat{e}(bP, zP)^x \cdot \hat{e}(yP, zP)^a$$
$$K_B = \hat{e}(aP, zP)^y \cdot \hat{e}(xP, cP)^y \cdot \hat{e}(xP, zP)^b$$
$$K_C = \hat{e}(aP, yP)^z \cdot \hat{e}(xP, bP)^z \cdot \hat{e}(xP, yP)^c$$
$$K_{ABC} = \hat{e}(P, P)^{x*y*c} \cdot \hat{e}(P, P)^{x*b*z} \cdot \hat{e}(P, P)^{a*y*z}$$

Fig. 6. TAK3

$$K_A = \hat{e}(bP + h(bP; yP)yP, cP + h(cP; zP)zP)^{a+(h(aP;xP)*x)}$$
$$K_B = \hat{e}(aP + h(aP; xP)xP, cP + h(cP; zP)zP)^{b+(h(bP;yP)*y)}$$
$$K_C = \hat{e}(aP + h(bP; yP)yP, bP + h(bP; yP)yP)^{a+(h(cP;cP)*c)}$$
$$K_{ABC} = \hat{e}(P, P)^{(a+(h(aP;xP)*x))*(b+(h(bP;yP)*y))*(c+(h(cP;zP)*z))}$$

Fig. 7. TAK4

5   Case Studies

This section presents several increasingly complex case studies: Diffie-Hellman protocol in Sect. 5.1, STR protocol in Sect. 5.2, Joux protocol in Sect. 5.3, and TAK protocols in Sect. 5.4. The Joux and TAK protocols use bilinear pairing but TAK4 requires properties beyond the encoding of bilinear pairings available in Tamarin, the only crypto tool with such an equational theory.

5.1   The Diffie-Hellman Protocol

In this section, we describe the analysis performed on the Diffie-Hellman (DH) protocol. This protocol was already analysed using Maude-NPA in [11]. DH uses exponentiation to share a secret between two parties. The description of the protocol using an Alice & Bob notation is given in Fig. 1.

Alice and Bob agree on a common generator g. Alice sends the generator g raised to the power of a new nonce generated by her. Bob sends the generator g raised to the power of a new nonce generated by him. Both Alice and Bob take the received nonce and raised it to the power of their own respective nonce. The cryptographic property here allows $(g^{N_A})^{N_B} = (g^{N_B})^{N_A} = g^{N_A*N_B}$. This cryptographic property is represented using the equational theory of Example 4.

The informal description of Fig. 1 is specified using strands as follows. We represent an exponentiation x^y as $exp(x, y)$. We represent a nonce N_A as $n(A, f)$ where f is a Fresh variable. We have added the identifiers of the participants in the message exchange for clarity. And we have appended a final encryption of some random secret using the generated key to make explicit the different keys used by the honest participants before and after the transformation.

$$(\textbf{Alice}) :: f_a, f :: [+(A; B; exp(g, n(A, f_a))), -(B; A; X),$$
$$+ (enc(exp(X, n(A, f_a)), sec(A, f)))]$$
$$(\textbf{Bob}) :: f_b :: [-(A; B; Y), +(B; A; exp(g, n(B, f_b))),$$
$$- (enc(exp(Y, n(B, f_b)), Sr))]$$

After applying the protocol transformation, we obtain

$$(\textbf{Alice}) :: f_a, f :: [+(A; B; exp(g, n(A, f_a))), -(B; A; exp(G, N)),$$
$$+ (enc(exp(G, n(A, f_a) * N), sec(A, f)))]$$
$$(\textbf{Bob}) :: f_b :: [-(A; B; exp(G, N)), +(B; A; exp(g, n(B, f_b))),$$
$$- (enc(exp(G, N * n(B, f_b)), Sr))]$$

As explained in Example 6, the expression $exp(X{:}Exp, n(A, f_a))$ has only one constructor variant using substitution $X{:}Exp \mapsto exp(G{:}Gen, N{:}NeNonceSet)$. Similarly for $exp(Y{:}Exp, n(B, f_b))$. The duplication of symbols in one defined and one constructor, the coincidence that each defined symbol has only one equation, and the use of associativity and commutativity, makes each strand of the protocols of this paper is replaced by just one strand. This may not always be the case and a strand may be replaced by several new strands (see [27, Example 7]). The Dolev-Yao capabilities for exponentiation are as follows.

$$(\textbf{DY\_exp\_ctor})[-(G{:}Gen), -(N{:}NeNonceSet), +(exp(G{:}Gen, N{:}NeNonceSet)]$$
$$(\textbf{DY\_exp\_func})[-(E{:}Exp), -(N{:}NeNonceSet), +(exp(E{:}Exp, N{:}NeNonceSet)]$$

The second one is transformed as follows

$$(\textbf{DY\_exp\_cvar})[-(exp(G{:}Gen, X{:}NeNonceSet)), -(N{:}NeNonceSet),$$
$$+ (exp(G{:}Gen, X{:}NeNonceSet * N{:}NeNonceSet))]$$

5.2   The STR Protocol

One extension of the Diffie-Hellman protocol is to consider that every time a new member is joined the exchange key is repeated, allowing for an unbounded number of participants a priori. We consider the tree-party group key agreement protocol STR from [20], where STR is a short name for **Skinny TR**ee. The description of the protocol using an informal Alice & Bob notation is given in Fig. 2. The only difference between the cryptographic properties of STR and DH is that we can have an exponentiation as an exponent, where DH could not. Therefore, the only difference to the equational theory of Example 4 is "**subsort Nonce Exp < NeNonceSet**". The equational theory still satisfies all the conditions of Corollary 1. The informal description of Fig. 2 is specified using strands as follows, we remove the identifiers of the participants for simplicity.

$(\textbf{Alice}) :: f_a, f :: [+(exp(g, n(A, f_a))), -(XB), -(XC),$
$\qquad\qquad + (enc(exp(XC, exp(XB, n(A, f_a))), sec(A, f)))]$
$\quad (\textbf{Bob}) :: f_b :: [-(XA), +(exp(g, n(B, f_b))), +(exp(g, exp(XA, n(B, f_b)))),$
$\qquad\qquad - (XC), -(enc(exp(XC, exp(XA, n(B, f_b))), Sr))]$
$\quad (\textbf{Carol}) :: f_c :: [-(XAB), +(exp(g, n(C, f_c))), -(enc(exp(XAB, n(C, f_c)), Sr))]$

After applying the protocol transformation, we obtain

$$(\textbf{Alice}) :: f_a, f :: [+(exp(g, n(A, f_a))), -(exp(G1, NB)), -(exp(G2, NC)),$$
$$+ (enc(exp(G2, exp(G1, n(A, f_a) * NB) * NC), sec(A, f))))]$$
$$(\textbf{Bob}) :: f_b :: [-(exp(G, NA)), +(exp(g, n(B, f_b))),$$
$$+ (exp(g, exp(G, n(B, f_b) * NA))), -(exp(G, NC)),$$
$$- (enc(exp(G, exp(G, n(B, f_b) * NA) * NC), Sr))]$$
$$(\textbf{Carol}) :: f_c :: [-(exp(G, NAB)), +(exp(g, n(C, f_c))),$$
$$- (enc(exp(G, NAB * n(C, f_c)), Sr))]$$

5.3   The Joux Protocol

When you want to keep the spirit of the Diffie-Hellman protocol, where no extra sharing is necessary apart of the initial broadcast information, an interesting alternative for three participants is the Joux protocol [19], which relies on bilinear pairing. The description of the protocol using an informal Alice & Bob notation is given in Fig. 3.

Pairing-based cryptography makes use of a pairing function $\hat{e} : G_1 \times G_2 \rightarrow G_T$ of two cryptographic groups G_1 and G_2 into a third group G_T. Typically, $G_1 = G_2$ and it will be a subgroup of the group of points on an elliptic curve over a finite field, and G_T will be a subgroup of the multiplicative group of a related finite field and the map $\hat{e}$ will be derived from either the Weil or Tate pairing on the elliptic curve. When $G = G_1 = G_2$, the pairing is called *symmetric* and the pairing function $\hat{e}$ is commutative, i.e., if the participants agree on a generator $g \in G$, for any P, Q in G there exist integers i, j s.t. $P = g^i$, $Q = g^j$, $\hat{e}(P, Q) = \hat{e}(g^i, g^j) = \hat{e}(g, g)^{i*j} = \hat{e}(g^j, g^i) = \hat{e}(Q, P)$. In Fig. 3, we follow the syntax of [19] and use letter P as the agreed generator. We write aP instead of P^a for P added to itself a times, also called scalar multiplication of P by a. Note that we write [a]P in the equational theory below for clarification. The bilinear pairing is specified as follows.

```
fmod BP-CFVP is
  sorts Nonce NeNonceSet Gen GenP Exp ExpP .
  subsort Nonce < NeNonceSet .
  op exp : Gen NeNonceSet -> Exp [ctor] .
  op exp : Exp NeNonceSet -> Exp .
  op _*_ : NeNonceSet NeNonceSet -> NeNonceSet [assoc comm ctor] .
  op p : -> GenP [ctor] .
  op em : GenP GenP -> Gen [ctor comm] .
  op em : ExpP ExpP -> Exp [comm] .
  op [_]_ : NeNonceSet GenP -> ExpP [ctor] .
  op [_]_ : NeNonceSet ExpP -> ExpP .
  var X : Gen . vars Y Z : NeNonceSet . vars P Q : GenP .
  eq exp(exp(X,Y),Z) = exp(X,Y * Z) [variant] .
  eq [Z]([Y]P) = [Z * Y]P [variant] .
  eq em([Y]P, [Z]Q) = exp(em(P,Q),Y * Z) [variant] .
endfm
```

We adapted the built-in theory of bilinear pairing of Tamarin [2,30] to satisfy[4] the conditions of Corollary 1. The informal description of Fig. 3 is specified using strands as follows.

$$(\textbf{Alice}) :: f_a, f :: [+([n(A, f_a)]p), -(XB), -(XC),$$
$$+ (enc(exp(em(XB, XC), n(A, f_a)), sec(A, f)))]$$
$$(\textbf{Bob}) :: f_b :: [-(XA), +([n(B, f_b)]p), -(XC),$$
$$- (enc(exp(em(XA, XC), n(B, f_b)), Sr)]$$
$$(\textbf{Carol}) :: f_c :: [-(XA), -(XB), +([n(C, f_c)]p),$$
$$- (enc(exp(em(XA, XB), n(C, f_c)), Sr)]$$

After applying the protocol transformation, we obtain

$$(\textbf{Alice}) :: f_a, f :: [+([n(A, f_a)]p), -([NB]PB), -([NC]PC),$$
$$+ (enc(exp(em(PB, PC), n(A, f_a) * NB * NC), sec(A, f)))]$$
$$(\textbf{Bob}) :: f_b :: [-([NA]PA), +([n(B, f_b)]p), -([NC]PC),$$
$$+ (enc(exp(em(PA, PC), n(B, f_b) * NA * NC), Sr)]$$
$$(\textbf{Carol}) :: f_c :: [-([NA]PA), -([NB]PB), +([n(C, f_c)]p),$$
$$+ (enc(exp(em(PA, PB), n(C, f_c) * NA * NB), Sr)]$$

5.4   The TAK Group Protocols

The Tripartite Authenticated Key group protocols [3] is a set of authenticated key agreement protocols that still require only one round of communication. It is an improvement of the Joux protocol. The four versions of TAK share the same exchanged message but the computation key is different for each version. The description of the TAK protocol using an informal Alice & Bob notation is given in Fig. 4. However, the four different ways of computing the keys are given in Figs. 4, 5, 6, and 7. These four protocols use the bilinear pairing cryptographic properties explained in Sect. 5.3 plus a hash function h and the following additive property (and its symmetric version, since $\hat{e}$ is commutative)

$$\hat{e}(Q, W + Z) = \hat{e}(Q, W) \cdot \hat{e}(Q, Z) \tag{1}$$

where $+$ is the additive symbol for the group G and $\cdot$ is the additive symbol for the group G_T given $\hat{e} : G \times G \to G_T$. These properties are specified[5] as follows.

---

[4] Confluence is proved by the absence of critical pairs between the lefthand sides of the three equations. Termination and FVP are proved by strongly right-irreducibility [16], i.e., righthand sides do not unify with any lefthand side. CFVP is proved because it is preregular below.

[5] The additive property (1) is not supported by the bilinear pairing of Tamarin [2,30].

```
fmod BPAdd-CFVP is
  sorts Nonce NeNonceSet Gen GenP Exp ExpP ExpT .
  subsort Nonce < NeNonceSet . subsort Exp < ExpT .
  op exp : Gen NeNonceSet -> Exp [ctor] .
  op exp : Exp NeNonceSet -> Exp .
  op _*_ : NeNonceSet NeNonceSet -> NeNonceSet [ctor assoc comm] .
  op p : -> GenP [ctor] .
  op em : GenP GenP -> Gen [ctor comm] .
  op em : ExpP ExpP -> Exp [comm] .
  op [_]_ : NeNonceSet GenP -> ExpP [ctor] .
  op [_]_ : NeNonceSet ExpP -> ExpP .
  op _+_ : NeNonceSet NeNonceSet -> NeNonceSet [ctor assoc comm] .
  op _+_ : ExpP ExpP -> ExpP .
  op _·_ : ExpT ExpT -> ExpT [ctor assoc comm] .
  var X : Gen . vars Y Z : NeNonceSet . vars P Q : GenP .
  eq exp(exp(X,Y),Z) = exp(X,Y * Z) [variant] .
  eq [Z]([Y]P) = [Z * Y]P [variant] .
  eq em([Y]P, [Z]Q) = exp(em(P,Q),Y * Z) [variant] .
  eq ([Y]P) + ([Z]P) = [Y + Z]P [variant] .
endfm
```

Note that Property 1 does not appear explicitly in the equational theory above
and it is transformed as follows. The addition symbol $+$ is split into two versions,
one of them being an associative-commutative constructor and the other one
being a defined symbol. A new equation relating these two versions of $+$ is added.
And symbol $\cdot$ is simply represented as an associative-commutative constructor.
The last, new equation denotes a homomorphic addition and it is easily handled
by variant-based unification because it is defined on disconnected sorts ExpP and
NeNonceSet (see [33] for approximations of homomorphism following the same
idea). For example, the key generated by Alice in TAK4

$$K_A = exp(em([b]p + [h([b]p; [y]p) * y]p, [c]p + [h([c]p; [z]p) * z]p),$$
$$a + (h([a]p; [x]p) * x))$$

is transformed into the common key

$$K_{ABC} = exp(em(p, p),(a + (h([a]p; [x]p) * x))*$$
$$(b + (h([b]p; [y]p) * y)) * (c + (h([c]p; [z]p) * z)))$$

by applying the last equation two times, followed by the third and the first
equations (we underline the replaced subterm)

$$exp(em([b]p + [h([b]p; [y]p) * y]p, [c]p + [h([c]p; [z]p) * z]p),$$
$$a + (h([a]p; [x]p) * x)) =$$
$$exp(em([b + (h([b]p; [y]p) * y)]p, [c + (h([c]p; [z]p) * z)]p),$$
$$a + (h([a]p; [x]p) * x))) =$$
$$\underline{exp(exp(em(p, p), a + (h([a]p; [x]p) * x),}$$
$$\underline{(b + h([b]p; [y]p) * y) * (c + h([c]p; [z]p) * z)) =}$$
$$exp(em(p, p), (a + (h([a]p; [x]p) * x)) *$$
$$(b + (h([b]p; [y]p) * y)) * (c + (h([c]p; [z]p) * z)))$$

If the non-constructor version of $+$ becomes associative-commutative, then the theory is not FVP. This equational theory works for all the TAK protocols even if it is not the most general possible; it is left for future work whether Property 1 can be encoded directly. This equational theory satisfies the conditions of Corollary 1. The original and transformed versions of TAK1, TAK2, and TAK3 are omitted but are available online. The informal description of the TAK4 protocol given in Fig. 7 is specified using strands as follows.

$(\textbf{Alice}) :: f_a, f_x, f :: [+([n(A, f_a)]p), +([n(A, f_x)]p), -(BP), -(YP), -(CP), -(ZP),$
$\quad + (enc(exp(\hat{e}(BP + [h(BP; YP)]YP, CP + [h(CP; ZP)]ZP),$
$\quad\quad f_a + h([n(A, f_a)]p; [n(A, f_x)]p * f_x)), sec(A, f)))]$

$(\textbf{Bob}) :: f_b, f_y :: [-(AP), -(XP), +([n(B, f_b)]p), +([n(B, f_y)]p), -(CP), -(ZP),$
$\quad - (enc(exp(\hat{e}(AP + [h(AP; XP)]XP, CP + [h(CP; ZP)]ZP),$
$\quad\quad f_b + h([n(B, f_b)]p; [n(B, f_y)]p * f_y)), Sr))]$

$(\textbf{Carol}) :: f_c, f_z :: [-(AP), -(XP), -(BP), -(YP), +([n(C, f_c)]p), +([n(C, f_z)]p),$
$\quad - (enc(exp(\hat{e}(AP + [h(AP; XP)]XP, BP + [h(BP; YP)]YP),$
$\quad\quad f_c + h([n(C, f_c)]p; [n(C, f_c)]p * f_c)), Sr))]$

After applying the protocol transformation, we obtain

$(\textbf{Alice}) :: f_a, f_x, f :: [+([n(A, f_a)]p), +([n(A, f_x)]p),$
$\quad -([NB]PB), -([NY]PB), -([NC]PC), -([NZ]PC),$
$\quad +(enc(exp(\hat{e}(PB, PC), (NB + (h([NB]PB; [NY]PB) * NY))$
$\quad\quad * (NC + (h([NC]PC; [NZ]PC) * NZ))$
$\quad\quad * (f_a + h([n(A, f_a)]p; [n(A, f_x)]p * f_x))), sec(A, f)))]$

$(\textbf{Bob}) :: f_b, f_y :: [- ([NA]PA), -([NX]PA), +([n(B, f_b)]p), +([n(B, f_b)]p),$
$\quad - ([NC]PC), -([NZ]PC),$
$\quad - (enc(exp(\hat{e}(PA, PC), (NA + (h([NA]PA; [NX]PA) * NX))$
$\quad\quad * (NC + (h([NC]PC; [NZ]PC) * NZ))$
$\quad\quad * (f_b + h([n(B, f_b)]p; [n(B, f_y)]p * f_y))), Sr))]$

$$(\textbf{Carol}) :: f_c, f_z :: [\, - ([NA]PA), -([NX]PA), -([NB]PB), -([NB]PB),$$
$$+ ([n(C, f_c)]p), +([n(C, f_c)]p),$$
$$- (enc(exp(\hat{e}(PA, PB), (NA + (h([NA]PA; [NX]PA) * NX))$$
$$* (NB + (h([NB]PB; [NY]PB) * NY))$$
$$* (f_c + h([n(C, f_c)]p; [n(C, f_z)]p * f_z))), Sr))]$$

6   Experiments

We have evaluated all the protocols of Sect. 5, both before and after the transformation. For DH, STR and Joux, we consider two general attack patterns, one for authentication and another for secrecy of the session key. For TAKs we consider only a secrecy attack pattern. Both properties of DH are insecure, authentication of STR is insecure but secrecy is secure [20], both properties of Joux are insecure [19], and TAK1, TAK2, TAK3, and TAK4 are secure [3].

In Table 1, we report both the number of states and the generation time of the search space associated to each attack pattern. The transformation itself is almost immediate, since the equational theories in these examples are not so complex. The time and space difference is shown in columns *States (%)* and *Speedup*. These columns demonstrate that the difference between verifying the protocol with all the crypto properties and verifying the protocol with a minimal set of the crypto properties is remarkable in three different aspects. First, for the STR protocol, the transformed protocol produces only 46.80% of the total number of states of the untransformed version. Second, for the TAK3 protocol, the execution time of the transformed protocol is three times faster than the untransformed version. Third, for the Joux protocol, even if the analysis of the transformed protocol produces more states than the analysis of the untransformed protocol, the execution time is three times faster.

Table 1. Experimental results for the transformed protocols.

Protocol	Property	Before transformation		After transformation		States (%)	Speedup
		States	Time (ms)	States	Time (ms)		
DH	auth	137	308,066	111	132,756	81.02	2.32
	secrecy	138	322,731	104	142,015	75.36	2.27
STR	auth	34	43,144	31	16,010	91.18	2.69
	secrecy	250	1,016,469	117	408,960	46.80	2.49
Joux	auth	38	85,579	37	30,012	97.37	2.85
	secrecy	55	247,712	58	78,384	105.45	3.16
TAK1	secrecy	25	259,619	20	126,998	80.00	2.04
TAK2	secrecy	67	365,797	46	152,842	68.66	2.39
TAK3	secrecy	117	670,775	67	216,350	57.26	3.10
TAK4	secrecy	57	371,770	48	181,850	84.21	2.04

All the experiments were conducted on a PC with a 3.3 GHz Intel Xeon E5-1660 and 64 GB RAM. We used Maude v3.0 [7] and Maude-NPA v3.1.4 [1]. The protocol specifications of both before and after the transformation and the output of each analysis are available at http://safe-tools.dsic.upv.es/cvtool.

7   Conclusions

Our first contribution is a protocol transformation that can safely get rid of cryptographic properties under some mild conditions. We have demonstrated with experiments that the time and space difference between verifying the protocol with all the crypto properties and verifying the protocol with a minimal set of the crypto properties is remarkable (an average speedup of 2.54). A similar idea is presented in [22] for XOR and in [21] for DH. These works are however not comparable to ours, since they are not protocol transformations but classes of protocols were the analysis using Proverif is sound. In [18], protocol transformations are studied. However the goal it not to optimize the verification, but to ensure that a transformed protocol satisfies some security goals, when the source protocol did, focusing on incremental protocol construction. Our second contribution is an encoding of the theory of bilinear pairing into Maude-NPA. This encoding goes beyond the encoding of bilinear pairing available in the Tamarin tool, the only crypto tool with such an equational theory. Since Tamarin [10] and AKISS [5] use term variants, they could be adapted to use both our protocol transformation and our encoding of the theory of bilinear pairing. They may even be useful for other crypto tools with more limited crypto properties such as ProVerif [6], OFMC [28], Scyther [9] or Scyther-proof [24]. Specially, since Proverif [6] already incorporated the notion of destructors and constructors time ago. As future work, we plan to study how the protocol transformation applies to other families of protocols and crypto properties such as homomorphisms [33].

References

1. Maude-NPA manual v3.1. http://maude.cs.illinois.edu/w/index.php/Maude_Tools:_Maude-NPA
2. The Tamarin-Prover Manual, 4 June 2019. https://tamarin-prover.github.io/manual/tex/tamarin-manual.pdf
3. Al-Riyami, S.S., Paterson, K.G.: Tripartite authenticated key agreement protocols from pairings. In: Paterson, K.G. (ed.) Cryptography and Coding 2003. LNCS, vol. 2898, pp. 332–359. Springer, Heidelberg (2003). https://doi.org/10.1007/978-3-540-40974-8_27
4. Baader, F., Snyder, W.: Unification theory. In: Robinson, J.A., Voronkov, A. (eds.) Handbook of Automated Reasoning, vol. 1, pp. 447–533. Elsevier Science (2001)
5. Baelde, D., Delaune, S., Gazeau, I., Kremer, S.: Symbolic verification of privacy-type properties for security protocols with XOR. In: 30th IEEE Computer Security Foundations Symposium, CSF 2017, pp. 234–248. IEEE Computer Society (2017)
6. Blanchet, B.: Modeling and verifying security protocols with the applied pi calculus and ProVerif. Found. Trends Privacy Secur. 1(1–2), 1–135 (2016)

7. Clavel, M., et al.: Maude manual (version 3.0). Technical report, SRI International, Computer Science Laboratory (2020). http://maude.cs.uiuc.edu
8. Comon-Lundh, H., Delaune, S.: The finite variant property: how to get rid of some algebraic properties. In: Giesl, J. (ed.) RTA 2005. LNCS, vol. 3467, pp. 294–307. Springer, Heidelberg (2005). https://doi.org/10.1007/978-3-540-32033-3_22
9. Cremers, C.J.F.: The scyther tool: verification, falsification, and analysis of security protocols. In: Gupta, A., Malik, S. (eds.) CAV 2008. LNCS, vol. 5123, pp. 414–418. Springer, Heidelberg (2008). https://doi.org/10.1007/978-3-540-70545-1_38
10. Dreier, J., Duménil, C., Kremer, S., Sasse, R.: Beyond subterm-convergent equational theories in automated verification of stateful protocols. In: Maffei, M., Ryan, M. (eds.) POST 2017. LNCS, vol. 10204, pp. 117–140. Springer, Heidelberg (2017). https://doi.org/10.1007/978-3-662-54455-6_6
11. Escobar, S., Hendrix, J., Meadows, C., Meseguer, J.: Diffie-Hellman cryptographic reasoning in the Maude-NRL protocol analyzer. In: Proceedings of 2nd International Workshop on Security and Rewriting Techniques (SecReT 2007) (2007)
12. Escobar, S., Meadows, C., Meseguer, J.: A rewriting-based inference system for the NRL protocol analyzer and its meta-logical properties. Theor. Comput. Sci. **367**(1–2), 162–202 (2006)
13. Escobar, S., Meadows, C., Meseguer, J.: Maude-NPA: cryptographic protocol analysis modulo equational properties. In: Aldini, A., Barthe, G., Gorrieri, R. (eds.) FOSAD 2007-2009. LNCS, vol. 5705, pp. 1–50. Springer, Heidelberg (2009). https://doi.org/10.1007/978-3-642-03829-7_1
14. Escobar, S., et al.: Protocol analysis in Maude-NPA using unification modulo homomorphic encryption. In: Proceedings of PPDP 2011, pp. 65–76. ACM (2011)
15. Escobar, S., Meadows, C.A., Meseguer, J., Santiago, S.: State space reduction in the Maude-NRL protocol analyzer. Inf. Comput. **238**, 157–186 (2014)
16. Escobar, S., Sasse, R., Meseguer, J.: Folding variant narrowing and optimal variant termination. J. Log. Algebr. Program. **81**(7–8), 898–928 (2012)
17. Fabrega, F.J.T., Herzog, J.C., Guttman, J.D.: Strand spaces: why is a security protocol correct? In: Proceedings of IEEE Symposium on Security and Privacy, pp. 160–171 (1998)
18. Guttman, J.D.: Security goals and protocol transformations. In: Mödersheim, S., Palamidessi, C. (eds.) TOSCA 2011. LNCS, vol. 6993, pp. 130–147. Springer, Heidelberg (2012). https://doi.org/10.1007/978-3-642-27375-9_8
19. Joux, A.: A one round protocol for tripartite Diffie-Hellman. In: Bosma, W. (ed.) ANTS 2000. LNCS, vol. 1838, pp. 385–393. Springer, Heidelberg (2000). https://doi.org/10.1007/10722028_23
20. Kim, Y., Perrig, A., Tsudik, G.: Communication-efficient group key agreement. In: Dupuy, M., Paradinas, P. (eds.) SEC 2001. IIFIP, vol. 65, pp. 229–244. Springer, Boston, MA (2002). https://doi.org/10.1007/0-306-46998-7_16
21. Küsters, R., Truderung, T.: Using ProVerif to analyze protocols with Diffie-Hellman exponentiation. In: IEEE Computer Security Foundations, pp. 157–171 (2009)
22. Küsters, R., Truderung, T.: Reducing protocol analysis with XOR to the XOR-free case in the horn theory based approach. J. Autom. Reason. **46**(3–4), 325–352 (2011)
23. Meadows, C.: The NRL protocol analyzer: an overview. J. Logic Program. **26**(2), 113–131 (1996)
24. Meier, S., Cremers, C., Basin, D.: Strong invariants for the efficient construction of machine-checked protocol security proofs. In: 2010 23rd IEEE Computer Security Foundations Symposium, pp. 231–245 (2010)

25. Meseguer, J.: Conditional rewriting logic as a united model of concurrency. Theoret. Comput. Sci. **96**(1), 73–155 (1992)
26. Meseguer, J.: Variant-based satisfiability in initial algebras. Sci. Comput. Program. **154**, 3–41 (2018)
27. Meseguer, J.: Generalized rewrite theories, coherence completion, and symbolic methods. J. Log. Algebr. Meth. Program. **110**, 100483 (2020)
28. Mödersheim, S., Viganò, L.: The open-source fixed-point model checker for symbolic analysis of security protocols. In: Aldini, A., Barthe, G., Gorrieri, R. (eds.) FOSAD 2007-2009. LNCS, vol. 5705, pp. 166–194. Springer, Heidelberg (2009). https://doi.org/10.1007/978-3-642-03829-7_6
29. Sasse, R., Escobar, S., Meadows, C., Meseguer, J.: Protocol analysis modulo combination of theories: a case study in Maude-NPA. In: Cuellar, J., Lopez, J., Barthe, G., Pretschner, A. (eds.) STM 2010. LNCS, vol. 6710, pp. 163–178. Springer, Heidelberg (2011). https://doi.org/10.1007/978-3-642-22444-7_11
30. Schmidt, B., Sasse, R., Cremers, C., Basin, D.A.: Automated verification of group key agreement protocols. In: 2014 IEEE Symposium on Security and Privacy, SP 2014, pp. 179–194. IEEE Computer Society (2014)
31. Skeirik, S., Meseguer, J.: Metalevel algorithms for variant satisfiability. J. Log. Algebraic Methods Program. **96**, 81–110 (2018)
32. TeReSe: Term Rewriting Systems. Cambridge University Press, Cambridge (2003)
33. Yang, F., Escobar, S., Meadows, C.A., Meseguer, J., Narendran, P.: Theories of homomorphic encryption, unification, and the finite variant property. In: Proceedings of PPDP 2014, pp. 123–133. ACM (2014)

On the Privacy Risks of Compromised Trigger-Action Platforms

Yu-Hsi Chiang[1]([✉]), Hsu-Chun Hsiao[1][ID], Chia-Mu Yu[2][ID],
and Tiffany Hyun-Jin Kim[3]

[1] National Taiwan University, Taipei, Taiwan
r06922023@csie.ntu.edu.tw
[2] National Chiao Tung University, Hsinchu, Taiwan
[3] HRL Laboratories LLC, Malibu, CA, USA

Abstract. Trigger-action platforms empower users to interconnect various physical devices and online services with custom automation. While providing convenience, their centralized design raises privacy concerns for end users. Unlike prior work that consider privacy leakage to action services, we consider privacy leakage to compromised platforms. After investigating potential privacy exposure to a popular trigger-action platform, IFTTT, we identified three types of leakages: *event data, trigger event presence, and device possession*. We also found that 91% of the top 500 triggers on IFTTT potentially leak sensitive information to the platform, and 25% leak implicitly. To achieve the paradoxical goal of hiding the event data and presence while asking the platform to trigger corresponding actions when an event occurs, we propose Obfuscated Trigger-Action Platform (OTAP) and Anonymous Trigger-Action Platform (ATAP). ATAP additionally provides *device set confidentiality* at the cost of minor platform modification. Our schemes can preserve user privacy without sacrificing convenience, and are incrementally deployable in various use cases. Our work addresses a crucial missing piece in securing the trigger-action ecosystem, and can be integrated with solutions that ensure integrity against untrusted platforms or solutions that address untrusted vendor services and users.

1 Introduction

Fueled by the growing demand for home automation, *trigger-action platforms* (e.g.., IFTTT [7], Zapier [11], and Microsoft Power Automate [1]) are gaining popularity among smart home users. Such cloud-based platforms empower users to connect heterogeneous devices from different vendors and write automation rules, which often take the form of "If a certain *trigger* occurs, then do a certain *action*."[1] In addition to home devices, these platforms are also integrated with many online services such as Google, Amazon, and Instagram. Due to their ease of use and the variety of supported services, these platforms have attracted millions of users running billions of rules per month [8].

---

[1] For example, "If I am approaching home, turn on the air conditioner.".

© Springer Nature Switzerland AG 2020
L. Chen et al. (Eds.): ESORICS 2020, LNCS 12309, pp. 251–271, 2020.
https://doi.org/10.1007/978-3-030-59013-0_13

The convenience comes at the cost of privacy. Because trigger-action platforms are authorized to collect and manipulate data from various services, some of which may contain sensitive information including users' location, purchase history, private social media posts or photos, privacy concerns are raised if the platforms are untrusted or hacked. Moreover, cloud-based centralized architecture makes these platforms an attractive target for attackers, as demonstrated by recent incidents targeting the cloud services of famous companies, including Equifax [9], Yahoo [3,4] and Target [2]. Therefore, unlike prior work [13,14,23,28] which focused on the privacy leakage to action services or rule authors through improperly configured rules, we consider the case of compromised platforms. We also note that a compromised trigger-action platform is more dangerous than any single compromised vendor (e.g., Samsung, Google, etc.) due to the amount of aggregated information.

To better understand the privacy risks of a compromised trigger-action platform, we first conduct a case study on one popular trigger-action platform, IFTTT. Instead of categorizing triggers by the functionality of their associated services [13], we categorize by the types of information they may leak, and identified three types of leakage: *event data, trigger event presence, or device possession*. Among the most popular 500 triggers, we found that 91% potentially send sensitive data to IFTTT, and 25% may leak sensitive information implicitly by the presence of their triggers. For example, a hearing-aid device leaks health conditions, and a surfing sports application leaks a user's personal interest. Categorizing potentially-leaking information types revealed that IFTTT can build a profile of a user who installs a sufficient number of rules.

To enhance the privacy of the trigger-action ecosystem in a practical manner, we investigate the problem of preventing an untrusted platform from learning users' private information (via either *received data, trigger event presence, or device possession*), while simultaneously keeping the benefits of a cloud-based solution. The goal seems paradoxical, as we would like to maintain both of the trigger data and trigger event presence secrecy, while asking the platform to trigger corresponding actions when an event occurs. Existing solutions based on encryption or fine-grained access control such as DTAP [20] fail to achieve this goal, as they can only hide the data but not the presence of triggers, and simply limiting access to sensitive information could affect the platforms functionality. In this work, we demonstrate that it is possible to build such schemes using *obfuscation* and *anonymization* techniques, and propose (1) Obfuscated Trigger-Action Platform (OTAP) and (2) Anonymous Trigger-Action Platform (ATAP). In short, OTAP hides real triggers by also sending fake triggers to confuse the platform, and ATAP preserves users' privacy by breaking the links between a user and his/her data. According to our empirical evaluation using realistic configurations, our schemes can balance the trade-offs between security and utility under different assumptions and requirements. For example, our schemes add at most 25 ms to rule execution time and can achieve the same throughput as existing solutions with at most 8× computation resources.

To summarize, this work makes the following contributions:

- We conducted an empirical study on potential privacy exposures to trigger-action platforms. We categorized the types of leaked information and the ways they are leaked.
- We designed and implemented two privacy-preserving trigger-action platform solutions, OTAP and ATAP, based on trigger *obfuscation* and *anonymization*. OTAP hides information about data and trigger event presence. ATAP additionally hides information about device/account possession.
- Through security analysis and empirical experiments, we show that our proposed schemes can be deployed in various practical scenarios.

2   Problem Definition

Our core goals are to (1) identify the privacy risks of trigger-action platforms and information leakage types, and (2) alleviate the exposed privacy risks in a practical manner. We provide formal privacy framework and proofs in Appendix A.

2.1   Threat Model

We consider an untrusted trigger-action platform that can be compromised and violate end-users' confidentiality. An adversary can collect users' information through the following three sources:

Data & parameter: The raw data of trigger and action parameters and trigger event data.

Trigger event presence: The occurrence of trigger events. For example, the occurrence of trigger-event "leave home" allows an attacker to infer if the user is at home.[2]

Device/account possession: Status of users' ownership of devices or online accounts. For example, if one connects a hearing aid (e.g.., Oticon [6]), an attacker may infer that the user has hearing issues.

We do not consider action presence in our threat model since no information is sent back from the action service to the platform when an action is fired. Thus, there is no way for the platform to verify whether an action is indeed executed. We also assume that the platform will not collude with partner services and there are secured channels (e.g., HTTPS) between different parties.

Since we only focus on confidentiality in this work, the following attacks are considered out of our scope.

- Breaking action integrity, including replaying old triggers or triggering unauthorized actions, which can be mitigated with existing solution [20].
- Denial-of-service, which has low incentives from platforms' perspectives as DoS attacks will drive users away and hurt the platform's reputations.
- Leaking sensitive information to partner services.

---

[2] Turn off WiFi on your Android when you leave home to save power [10].

2.2 Desired Properties

In respect to Sect. 2.1, we define the following three types of confidentiality that a privacy-preserving trigger-action platform should preserve.

Table 1. Example of a trigger-action rule

Rule	If saying a specific phrase to Google Home, then set the Hue light brightness
Trigger	Say a phrase with a number
Trigger params	phrase: set hue brightness to #
Action	Set brightness
Action params	brightness: *number_spoken*
Event data	number_spoken: 50 triggered_at: 2020/01/01 12:00

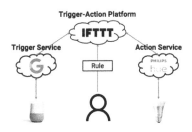

Fig. 1. Example of a trigger-action ecosystem

Data & Parameters Confidentiality. The platform should not learn the trigger and action parameters and the event data.

Trigger Event Presence Confidentiality. The trigger-action platform should not be capable of infering when or whether a trigger event occurs.

Device Set Confidentiality. The trigger-action platform should not learn what devices or service accounts a user possesses.

For practicality, the following should also be taken into account.

Minimal Information Exposure. Every entity in the system should not learn additional information compared to what it knows from the original scheme (i.e., IFTTT). Otherwise, a solution simply delegates the job of the platform (i.e., rule storage and execution) to partner services, which does not protect users' privacy. In the existing IFTTT ecosystem, the trigger and action services know the trigger and action-related information, respectively, while the platform knows both of the information and the rules. Though the attacker we considered in this work is the platform, we would also want to ensure that the proposed solutions do not leak additional information to either of the trigger or action service so that the privacy risks are not shifted or raised.

Performance. The system should be able to handle thousands of concurrent triggers per second, the rule execution should be fast enough, and the delay between the trigger and action being done should be reasonable (e.g.., 15 min of maximum delay in IFTTT as of 2020).

3 Case Study: Privacy-Risks of IFTTT

To understand the security risks of a compromised trigger-action platform, we inspect the trigger specifications of 500 most popular triggers on IFTTT, and investigate the types of information that IFTTT can learn and the sources of leakage. Datasets are available [12].

3.1   Background: IFTTT & Trigger-Action Platforms

A trigger-action platform is a cloud service that allows end-users to connect different IoT devices and online services based on conditional *rules*. The rules are in the form of "IF a certain trigger happens, THEN do a certain action," such as "IF saying a specific phrase to Google Home, THEN set the Hue light brightness," or "IF someone posts a new photo on Instagram, THEN upload it to my Google Drive." As shown in Table 1, triggers and actions are provided by certain third-party partner *services* such as Phillips Hue, Instagram, or Google, and they are customized by the trigger and action parameters, respectively.

A rule will be triggered when there is an *event* that satisfies the condition described by its trigger and trigger parameters. *Event data* represents the data associated with the event, and the event data can be used as part of action parameters. Some platforms also allow users to write a piece of code (called *filter code*), which filters and transforms the event data.

Figure 1 illustrates a typical ecosystem of trigger-action platforms [27]: upon executing a rule, the trigger-action platform receives the data from the trigger service, transforms them into the parameters of the action, and calls the API of the action service. The platform usually does not connect to devices directly, but through cloud services provided by their vendors for ease of management. Partner services communicate to their devices using proprietary protocols, and use the platform's web-based protocols to fire triggers or receive action requests.

3.2   Methodology

Dataset. We obtained the list of event-data fields (known as ingredients in IFTTT) of each trigger using IFTTT's undocumented GraphQL API [12]. We queried in March 2019, and retrieved all of the 524 services and 2,396 triggers. We identified the 500 most popular triggers based on a popularity rank derived from a public dataset collected in May 2017 [27]. Their dataset includes about 280,000 rules of IFTTT, and contains the number of installed users for each rule. We assessed the popularity of each trigger by summing up the number of installed users having that trigger.

Approach. We assigned several labels to each trigger to indicate what types of information may be leaked and how the leakage would occur. To indicate the possibility of containing private information, we assigned a score from 1 to 3: Scores of 1, 2, or 3 indicate that the data does not contain, possibly contains, or absolutely contains private information, respectively. For example, a "photo uploaded" trigger may leak private information depending on the content of the photo and hence we assigned the score of 2; an "arrive at" trigger definitely leaks a user's location and hence we assigned 3.

3.3   Results

Types of Leaked Information. As shown in Table 2, we identified 12 categories of leaked information, and labeled triggers for each category. Note that a

Table 2. Categories of leaked information

Basic information	Name, age, email address, phone number, physical address, occupation, etc.
Location	Current location, location history
Finance	Bank account balance, transaction logs, purchase history, etc.
Health status	Weight, BMI, blood pressure, heart rate, etc.
Social	Contacts, membership status of organizations, etc.
Communication	Call records, SMS, voicemail, email, social media posts, etc.
Lifestyle/Activities	Data or logs that show user's activities. e.g., the time the user wakes up, turns on the TV or goes to work, etc.
Activities summary	The summary of user's activities. e.g., total working hours, distance of driving, etc.
Interest	Videos liked or watched, interested news topics, followed stocks, etc.
Physical sensor	Temperature of a room, indoor CO_2 level, etc.
Others (Personal)	Information not publicly available and not fit in any of the above categories
Public	Publicly available information. e.g., weather forecasts, Public posts, etc.

Table 3. Sources of leakage ($n = 500$)

Sources of leakage	# of triggers	%
Event data	456	91%
Trigger event presence	127	25%
Device/account possession	2	0.4%

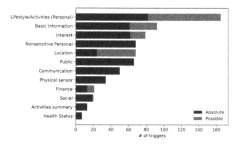

Fig. 2. # of triggers for each category

trigger may be assigned to more than one category. This list captures the most common types, but is not exhaustive.

Among these triggers, 91% leak at least one type of private information (i.e., not labeled as public). As shown in Fig. 2, lifestyle/activities category is a broad category into which most of the state change events fall, and hence is most likely to be leaked, while health status is least likely.

Sources of Leakage. We labeled the sources of leakage of each trigger event based on our definitions in Sect. 2.1. We found that a trigger may leak information through multiple sources, and triggers that leak information by trigger event presence or device/account possession will always leak information by data too.

Table 3 shows the number of triggers subject to each of the three leakage sources. We count the number of triggers assigned a score 2 or 3. We found the most of the information is leaked through event data. Even if event data were to be hidden from IFTTT, 25% of triggers still leak information by their presence.

4 Proposed Solutions

We propose OTAP and ATAP that achieve different sets of security goals as outlined in the previous section. Table 4 provides a preview of comparisons of the different schemes. Besides IFTTT, we also compare our schemes with a Pairwise Connection approach, in which trigger and action services connect to each other directly without communicating with the platform.

Pairwise Connection achieves the security goals, since no information is given to the platform. However, Pairwise Connection breaks *minimal information exposure*, as a trigger service can gain the information of what other device a user owns if it connects to the action service. Also, removing the platform from the system makes the maintenance more difficult. Without a trigger-action platform, a service must notify all other services when it changes its API, but with a trigger-action platform, the service only needs to notify the platform.

Table 4. Comparison of Schemes. Properties 4–6 are compared against the baseline. The Pairwise Connection approach has no platform, and thus trivially achieves Properties 1–3 and 5 (*).

Property/Scheme	IFTTT (baseline)	Pairwise connection	OTAP	ATAP
1. Data & Parameters Confidentiality	No	Yes*	Yes	Yes
2. Trigger Event Presence Confidentiality	No	Yes*	Yes	Yes
3. Device Set Confidentiality	No	Yes*	No	Yes
4. Minimal Information Exposure	-	No	Yes	Yes
5. No Platform Modification Required	-	Yes*	Yes	No
6. No Service Modification Required	-	No	No	No
7. Ease of Maintenance	Easy	Hard	Easy	Easy

Core Techniques. In both OTAP and ATAP, encryption is employed to provide *data & parameters confidentiality*. One challenge is that, due to the requirement of *minimal information exposure*, the trigger and action services should not connect to each other directly, thus making key establishment a non-trivial task.

Another challenge is to provide *trigger event presence confidentiality*. Indeed, it sounds paradoxical to hide triggers from the platform while asking the platform to execute certain rules when a trigger is fired. To that end, we propose two techniques: *trigger obfuscation* and *trigger anonymization*.

For trigger obfuscation, we can notify the platform when some trigger occurs, along with fake triggers when there is no actual event. In this way, the platform cannot be sure whether there is a real event happening when receiving triggers.

On the other hand, the idea of trigger anonymization is different. We still allow the trigger-action platform to learn when a trigger occurs, but make it impossible to associate the trigger with a certain user. The advantage of this technique is that, in our system, we already have trigger and action services which can act as proxies or "mixes" naturally, and thus it is unnecessary to add other parties for anonymization.

For the rest of this paper, we assume that user U wants to setup a rule r, the associated trigger and action services are T and A, respectively, and the trigger-action platform is denoted by P.

4.1 Obfuscated Trigger-Action Platform (OTAP)

OTAP is based on trigger *obfuscation* and is designed to protect both *data & parameters confidentiality* and *trigger event presence confidentiality* without platform modification. The protocol flow of OTAP is the same as the existing IFTTT flow except that encryption is used to provide *data & parameters confidentiality*. In addition, to obfuscate the trigger-action platform, the trigger service periodically sends out a trigger event, either real or fake, every τ seconds, where τ refers to *trigger period* and the time points are called *trigger points*. Note that τ is configurable by the user and will be part of the trigger parameters. A symmetric encryption is used and the encryption function is denoted by $\mathsf{Enc}(k, m)$, where k is the encryption key and m is the message to be encrypted. We also introduce two types of encryption keys:

- **User-Service Keys**: For each user U and service S, there is a shared key k_{US}, which will be used for encrypting trigger and action parameters.
- **Rule-Specific Keys**: For each rule r, there is a key k_r shared by the corresponding trigger and action services, and is used for encrypting event data.

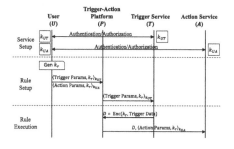

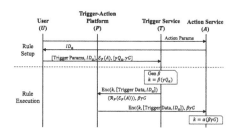

Fig. 3. OTAP protocol   **Fig. 4.** ATAP protocol

We now present the phases of the protocol, as shown in Fig. 3. From the user's perspectives, note that the key managements and encryption/decryption can be done by installing a local app or a browser plugin to ease the burden.

Phase 1: Service Setup. Besides the authentication and authorization flows in the original scheme, in OTAP, the user's client (e.g.., local app or browser plugin) establishes the shared keys k_{UT} and k_{UA} with T and A during this phase.

Phase 2: Rule Setup. Before uploading the rule to the platform, the rule-specific key k_r must be obtained. As highlighted earlier, the trigger and action services should not be directly connected. Thus, OTAP relies on the user's client to do this job since the user can connect with both parties. After generating k_r, the key will be uploaded by the user client to the platform as part of the rule along with the trigger and action parameters. If there are multiple actions in a single rule, then all of the involved action services will share the same key.

To ensure security and *parameter confidentiality*, the parameters must be encrypted, Therefore, the actual messages received by the platform will be $\langle \text{Trigger Params}, k_r \rangle_{k_{UT}}$ and $\langle \text{Action Params}, k_r \rangle_{k_{UA}}$, where

$$\langle m, k_r \rangle_k = [\mathsf{Enc}(k, m), \mathsf{Enc}(k, k_r), \mathsf{HMAC}(k, \mathsf{Enc}(k, m) \| \mathsf{Enc}(k, k_r))].$$

The first two terms are the parameters and k_r encrypted by the user-service key, and the last term is a Message Authentication Code providing integrity check.

Phase 3: Rule Execution. The trigger service is able to decrypt the trigger parameters and rule-specific key k_r using k_{UT}. At each trigger point, T sends to the platform a trigger event, with event data encrypted by k_r. The platform then forwards the encrypted data, encrypted action parameters, and the key to the action service. Upon receiving these, the action service first decrypts using k_{UA} to obtain the action parameters and k_r. Finally, with k_r, the action service decrypts event data and perform the action.

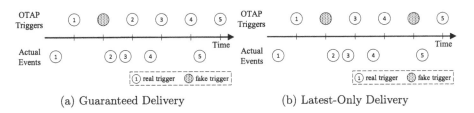

(a) Guaranteed Delivery   (b) Latest-Only Delivery

Fig. 5. Illustration of two delivery strategies

Note that the size of the encrypted event data can still leak sensitive information. However, we observed that the trigger fields of the same type are in fixed size in most cases. For example, the temperature is always an integer with the size of one block after encryption. If such a side-channel attack is a concern, the trigger service can pad the trigger field to its maximum allowed size.

To summarize, in OTAP, the information learned by the trigger and action services is the same as the existing solution. The platform knows the rules (i.e., which trigger and action are related), but not trigger and action data as they are encrypted. Trigger presence is also hidden by having fake triggers. The delay, whether deterministic or not, does not expose information about the real triggered events, as real triggers are indistinguishable from fake ones in OTAP.

Obfuscated Trigger and Delivery Strategies. Thus far, we have claimed that a fake event may be sent out at some trigger points. However, we have not discussed how to decide when to send out a fake trigger and how to cancel a false action when a fake trigger is sent. The latter issue can be caused because the platform is unaware of the truthfulness of the trigger and fires an action even if the incoming trigger is fake. To address this issue, we add an additional Boolean field is_real to the event data so that the action service can safely discard the message when it is set to be $false$. Since the flag resides in the event data, which is encrypted, the platform is unable to infer its value.

As for the former issue, we propose two main strategies called $guaranteed$ $delivery$ and $latest$-$only$ $delivery$ to decide which trigger is to be sent at each trigger point, as illustrated in Fig. 5. The guaranteed delivery strategy ensures that every real trigger event is sent out. Specifically, the trigger service will queue all the trigger events and send out the oldest unreported event at trigger points. However, the delay (the time between when an event occurs and is fired) may increase quickly if the trigger period is not short enough.

In contrast, the latest-only delivery strategy keeps only the latest trigger that is not yet fired. Hence, if many trigger events occur between two consecutive trigger points, only the latest one would be sent out. This strategy effectively shortens the delay, but may lead to event loss (e.g., event 2 in Fig. 5b).

How to choose the best trigger period and delivering strategy depends on the type of trigger and the rule, and can be adjusted dynamically to adapt the scenario of use. For example, for the rule "If the motion sensor detects I'm in the room, then turn on the light," one might want to have a short trigger period so that the action can be fired near real-time.

As for the delivery strategies, the guaranteed delivery is probably a better option for rules like "Log the time I enter and leave the office and home," as one would simply like all the events to be logged and might care less about delays. For the rule "If the temperature changes, adjust the thermostat," one may choose the latest-only delivery strategy as only the most recent temperature is the relevant information.

Finally, one may also wonder that if it is possible to use a randomized trigger period instead of a constant τ. Indeed, using a randomized trigger period will not weaken the security as long as the distribution of the trigger period is independent of actual trigger events. However, as shown in Appendix B, among all trigger period distributions of the same mean value, the constant trigger period will minimize the average delay. Note that the selection of trigger period and strategy will only affect the utility but not security.

To integrate OTAP with the existing IFTTT ecosystem, the user clients (i.e., app or browser plugin) and partner services need to implement the encryption and decryption functionalities, while no $platform$ $modification$ is required. The existing IFTTT basically sends the user-provided parameters to the partner services and forwards the data from the trigger service to the action service. In OTAP, the only difference is that the parameters and data are now encrypted and an additional parameter is added (i.e., the rule-specific key). Since the platform can operate without knowing the actual content of parameters and data, there is no need to change the platform's implementation.

4.2 Anonymous Trigger-Action Platform (ATAP)

ATAP achieves all three security goals at the cost of trigger-action platform modification. The scheme preserves trigger event presence confidentiality based on the idea of anonymization. The trigger service will drop user information before sending out a trigger to the trigger-action platform.

However, with this approach, we can no longer rely on the trigger-action platform to execute the rule. This is because if the platform were to know which rule to execute, it can distinguish between triggers of different users, contradicting our goal. Therefore, we have to store the rules on trigger and action services and use the platform only for forwarding, which also achieves our intention to preserve *device set confidentiality*. Although most of the functionality of the platform are discarded, we achieve *minimal information exposure* and easier system maintenance by keeping the platform, which the Pairwise Connection approach of removing the platform fails to do so. Also, as the approach is based on anonymization, its security is bounded by the number of users of the system.

Before diving into the protocol, we first introduce some cryptographic-related notations and techniques that will be used. We use a symmetric encryption function denoted by $\mathsf{Enc}(k, m)$, where k is the key and m is the plaintext to be encrypted. We use $\mathcal{E}_S(m)$ to represent the ciphertext of m encrypted by S's public key under ElGamal. Finally, an elliptic curve $\mathcal{G}$ is also used in ATAP with G being its base point.

To preserve data confidentiality, we need to encrypt the event data and a shared key must be established between the trigger and the action services. OTAP accomplishes this requirement by having the user's client generate the key and distribute it to both services. However, ATAP requires different approach because the triggers are anonymized. Specifically, the action service cannot determine which key to use for decryption upon receiving the event data. Public key exchange protocols, such as ECDH, would break *minimal information exposure*, since the trigger and action service can identify their counterparts by matching the public key. Therefore, the public key needs to be randomized. The modified ECDH protocol is described as follows.

Suppose that the ECDH public key of A is Q_A and the associated private key is α (i.e., $Q_A = \alpha G$). The protocol consists of three steps:

1. Client U selects a random scalar γ and sends γQ_A, γG to trigger service T.
2. T selects another random scalar β and sends $\beta \gamma G$ to action service A.
3. T and A can both compute the shared key $k = \beta(\gamma Q_A) = \alpha(\beta \gamma G)$.

Figure 4 shows the protocol of ATAP. Note that there is no service setup phase since the user no longer needs to register on the trigger-action platform.

Phase 1: Rule Registration. When setting up a new rule, the client starts by registering the action with A and receives an action ID ID_a. Then the client registers the trigger with T. The information given to T falls into three groups.

1. Trigger params and ID_a: Information needed for trigger-action.
2. $\mathcal{E}_P(A)$: The name of the action service encrypted by P's public key, such that the platform knows where the event data should be forwarded to.
3. γQ_A and γG: Used for ECDH key exchange, as described previously.

Phase 2: Rule Execution. When a trigger event occurs, the trigger service simply fires the event to the platform. The event data and ID_a will be encrypted by the shared key k. Similar to OTAP, the event data can be padded to prevent leaking sensitive information through data sizes, if necessary. The service name is re-randomized through $\mathcal{R}_P(\mathcal{E}_P(A)) = \mathcal{E}_P(A) + \mathcal{E}_P(0)$ exploiting the homomorphic property of ElGamal. The key exchange message $\beta\gamma G$ is also sent out. Upon receiving the messages, the platform obtains the service name A by decrypting $\mathcal{R}_P(\mathcal{E}_P(A))$, and forwards the rest of the messages to A. The action service computes the shared key k and decrypts the event data and action ID ID_a. With ID_a, the action service can find the corresponding action parameters and fire the action.

Re-randomization is needed for $\mathcal{E}_P(A)$ since $\mathcal{E}_P(A)$ is fixed for a given rule. Without re-randomization, some information can be used to fingerprint the user—the platform can learn that two different triggers are from the same user. Re-randomization is required to limit the attack impact: even if the attacker can break trigger presence confidentiality of one trigger, he/she cannot easily break trigger presence confidentiality of other triggers by linking them together.

To sum up, in ATAP, the trigger and action services know only the information of trigger and action, respectively. The platform knows nothing but some triggers of a service occurred and some actions of a service were fired.

4.3 Security Analysis

We provide security proof sketc.hes here and detailed analysis in Appendix A.

Assume the use of IND-CPA symmetric encryption scheme $\mathsf{Enc}(\cdot)$ (e.g., AES-CBC) and IND-CPA asymmetric encryption scheme $\mathcal{E}(\cdot)$ (e.g., ElGamal encryption). For OTAP, since all transmitted messages are encrypted by $\mathsf{Enc}(\cdot)$, data & parameter confidentiality is satisfied. By the definition of IND-CPA, an adversary cannot distinguish between pairs of ciphertexts even with the knowledge of plaintexts, and hence an adversary cannot distinguish between real and fake trigger events. Hence, OTAP preserves trigger event presence confidentiality.

For ATAP, all transmitted messages are encrypted by either $\mathsf{Enc}(\cdot)$ or $\mathcal{E}(\cdot)$, and thus data & parameters confidentiality is satisfied. In addition, since IND-CPA leads to randomized encryption, this implies that the adversary in ATAP is unable to link between different triggers, achieving trigger event presence confidentiality. Device set confidentiality is also achieved, as no further information is provided to the platform.

5 Performance Evaluation

To evaluate the performance of our proposed schemes, we implemented prototypes of our systems and a skeleton version of IFTTT as our baseline (referred to as the plain scheme). We ran several experiments to measure the end-to-end latency and the throughput of our systems, as described in Sects. 5.1 and 5.2.

Experiments Settings. We implemented all the partner services and trigger-action platforms as web servers using Node.js, and used MongoDB as the backend database. We used 128-bits AES-GCM for symmetric encryption and curve P-256 for elliptic curve algorithms. Inspired by Fernandes et al. [20], we use the rule "IF new item added to TODO list contains the word 'cat', THEN send an SMS of this item." This contains all the essential elements of a typical rule: a trigger parameter that indicates the trigger condition, and using event data as action parameters.

We hosted each service on separate Google Compute Engine g1-small instances. Each instance was configured with 1 Intel Xeon vCPU @ 2.2 GHz, 1.7 GB memory, and 10 GB SSD storage in Ubuntu 18.04.

5.1 Latency

We compare end-to-end latency of the privacy-preserving versions with the plain version. The latency increment mainly derived from (1) computational overhead of the cryptographic operations, and (2) the delay caused by sending triggers periodically, only for OTAP.

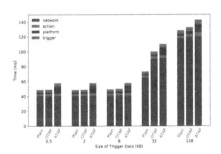

Fig. 6. Latency breakdown

Table 5. Goodput of different schemes

Scheme	Avg. (req/sec)
Plain	411.78
OTAP ($\tau = 17$, guaranteed)	52.46
OTAP ($\tau = 1796$, latest-only)	162.64
ATAP	69.54
ATAP (w/o re-randomization)	360.27

Computational Overhead. We measured the time spent at different services and the network overheads. The end-to-end latencies are largely affected by the size of the event data, as they need to be encrypted and decrypted by the trigger and the action services, respectively. Therefore, we varied their size from 0.5 KB to 128 KB, and the experiment result is shown in Fig. 6.

A gap exists between the network overheads of the plain scheme and OTAP (ATAP) when the trigger size is 32 KB, which is caused by TCP congestion control. With encryption, transferred data is slightly bigger than the congestion window size, requiring an additional round-trip for OTAP and ATAP. Despite network overhead, the results show that OTAP adds at most 5 ms latency while ATAP adds at most 25 ms. Both are small compared to network overheads or other delays, given that there are no real-time requirements in these systems.

Triggering Delay. For OTAP, we conducted an empirical study on how the trigger period affects the delay between the time a trigger occurs and the time it is sent out. We used the CASAS hh104 dataset [17], which contains sensor data that was collected in the home of a volunteer adult for about two years. We selected the MA022 motion sensor events as triggers, which are the most frequent events in this dataset. Appendix C describes the event distribution.

We ran the experiment for both delivery strategies, and the result is in Fig. 7a. For guaranteed delivery, the delay grows quickly as the trigger period increased; in this case, if we still want to guarantee real-time triggering, then the trigger period should be set around the bursty rate of the trigger (2 s in this example). For latest-only delivery, in contrast, the delay remains low as the trigger period increases; the delay is around one-third of the trigger period. However, there is a trade-off between the delay time and trigger event loss. For reference, we show the resulting event loss rate of different trigger periods in Fig. 7b.

5.2   Goodput

Besides the end-to-end delay of a single rule execution, we also examine the number of rules our schemes can handle, which affects the delay. We define the goodput to be the maximum number of *real* rules being executed per second. The rule we used in this experiment is the same as in Sect. 5.1 with size being 0.5 KB, and we used ApacheBench [5] to conduct the experiment by sending 10,000 trigger activations with up to 400 concurrent connections. The results are presented in Table 5. We set the concurrency level to 400 by estimating the maximum concurrent execution of the current IFTTT. According to their website [8], around 1 billion rules are executed per month, which means, on average, approximately 385 rules are executed per second.

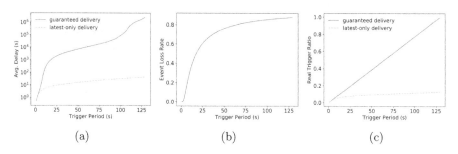

Fig. 7. Trigger period vs. (a) Delay, (b) Event loss rate, (c) Real trigger ratio

For OTAP, the goodput depends heavily on the delivery strategy and the trigger period τ. A longer trigger period will not only increase the goodput but also increase the latency, as shown in Figs. 7a and 7c. In the experiment, we choose the maximum τ such that the average trigger delay is less than 15 min. Choosing a "best" trigger period to balance the trade-offs depends on the distribution of the trigger and other system requirements. We leave the parameter selection as future work.

For ATAP, the goodput (which is the same as the throughput in this case) dropped drastically by about 80%. We found that one of the performance bottlenecks is the re-randomization of action service ID on the trigger service. However, the action service ID is fixed for each rule and is not event-dependent, which indicates that the re-randomization does not need to be performed for each trigger and can be generated beforehand. Without re-randomization, our test results show that the goodput only decreases by 12.5%.

6 Discussion

Incentive of Adoption. Similar to anonymous communication, which cannot achieve strong anonymity, low bandwidth, low delay simultaneously as proved in [18], our solution does not aim at providing all of them. Instead, by presenting various modes and configurable parameters, our system allows users to best fit their requirements. For example, for delay-critical applications in trigger-action platform, the user can decide whether to activate our schemes for strong anonymity at the cost of performance.

From the perspective of trigger-action platforms and partner services, we acknowledge that adopting our schemes may increase their operating costs. With the increased interest in the pay-for-privacy model [19], business incentives may exist to offer privacy-enhanced trigger-action system for additional revenues.

Deployability. Though several changes are required to adopt our scheme, we will explain how the transition to our schemes can be made easier with the help of a proxy. In our schemes, the core functions of the partner services remain the same. Therefore, the adoption of our schemes could be done by having a proxy that sits in between the service and the platform and transforms the requests and responses. Since all partner services follow the same API specification, the proxy can be written once by the platform and distributed to all partner services. It should be published in an open-source manner and run by each partner service on its own, so that the proxy can be trusted.

For OTAP, as discussed in Sect. 4.1, the existing trigger-action platform can be reused, though all the data and parameters sent to the trigger-action platform must be encrypted by the user clients and partner services.

Compared to OTAP, ATAP requires modifying the platform, and a reimplementation is inevitable. However, since its function is simpler compared to the existing one, it is likely that it would not require excessive development effort.

As for the user-side, the key managements and encryption/decryption can be done by installing a local app or a browser plugin to ease the burden.

7   Related Work

Researchers have worked on the security and privacy issues in the trigger-action ecosystem. We first review the related work on the platforms, and review other parts of the ecosystem, including automation rules, and IFTTT.

Untrusted Trigger-Action Platform. Xu et al. [30] studied privacy leakage in smart homes to the trigger-action services and the mitigation. They proposed "Filter-and-Fuzz (F&F)" that filters out events unneeded by IFTTT and fuzzes the event data and their frequencies. This fuzzing component is somewhat similar to our OTAP scheme, as it randomizes the values of event data and sometimes sends fake triggers. However, their usage scenario is limited to Boolean or numerical event data fields and they only consider the cases where the trigger and action services are the same.

Fernandes et al. [20] studied the security of IFTTT's OAuth-based authentication protocols, and they found that 75% of the tokens are over-privileged and can be exploited by the attackers to control users' devices when the platform is compromised. They proposed a decentralized trigger-action platform framework (DTAP), which allows the use of fine-grained transfer tokens (XToken). The trigger-action platform stores only rule-specific tokens while the XToken is stored in the newly-introduced trusted-client, which is controlled by the user. Although DTAP does not provide data confidentiality and privacy, DTAP can be combined with our solution to enhance the system privacy and integrity.

Security and Privacy Concerns of Automation Rules. Bastys et al. [13,14] examined IFTTT applets that contain *filter code*, and found that such applets are susceptible to URL-based attacks, which can exfiltrate private information to a third-party when the applet is created by a malicious maker. A malicious applet could also lead to integrity and availability violations. Authors proposed FlowIT that can monitor and prevent malicious apps from being executed.

Surbatovich et al. [28] analyzed 19,323 IFTTT rules based on information-flow techniques. They defined a four point lattice that checks whether the information flows from a trusted source to an untrusted sink using static analysis. A series of work utilized dynamic analysis techniques such as model checking or symbolic execution to detect and fix insecure interactions between rules or to synthesize secure trigger-action programs [15,23–25,29,31].

IFTTT Ecosystem. Mi et al. [27] conducted an empirical study on IFTTT to understand its ecosystem and the performance of rule executions. They leveraged the self-implemented IFTTT server to profile the interaction among different entities. Their work provides a deeper understanding of the architecture and the execution path of a rule, which inspired our design.

8   Conclusion

Emerging trigger-action platforms empower users to conveniently combine various online services and physical devices for customized automation. However, their centralized design allows these platforms to collect personal information from multiple services, which raises privacy concerns. This work conducted the first empirical study on potential privacy exposures to trigger-action platforms, and presents two practical mitigations that enhance privacy without sacrificing the convenience promised by these platforms. In our empirical study of the 500 most popular IFTTT triggers, we found that the platform is capable of obtaining a variety of sensitive information, and 91% of the popular triggers are susceptible to privacy leakage. To mitigate the problem, we designed and implemented two privacy-preserving trigger-action platform systems, OTAP and ATAP. Trigger *obfuscation* and trigger *anonymization* techniques can hide trigger presence, so that the platform (1) sees real and fake triggers that are indistinguishable, or (2) cannot determine which user is related to a given trigger. We believe that our work provides an immediate remedy to enhance today's trigger-action platforms, and an interesting future direction is utilizing a clean-slate approach that ensures security and privacy by design.

Acknowledgments. This research was supported by the Ministry of Science and Technology of Taiwan under grants MOST 109-2636-E-002-021 and MOST 109-2636-E-005-002.

A   Formal Security Analysis

Privacy Framework. We adopt the ideal/real-world paradigm to analyze the privacy of our schemes, which is standard in MPC literature [16,21,22]. Conceptually, there are two worlds, one is ideal and the other is real, both evaluating the functionality $\mathcal{F}_{tap}$, the trigger-action platform protocol. The "ideal-world" has a trusted party $\mathcal{T}$ carrying out all the computations. All other parties send their input to $\mathcal{T}$ and receive their prescribed output through a secure channel. In "real-world", no such party exists and all parties perform the computation themselves. To show that a real-world protocol is secure, we need to show that for every possible real-world adversary $\mathcal{A}$, there exists an ideal-world simulator $\mathcal{S}$ such that when controlling same parties as $\mathcal{A}$, the outputs of the protocols in ideal-world and real-world are computationally indistinguishable. This implies that every attack that can be done by $\mathcal{A}$ in real-world can be done by $\mathcal{S}$ in the ideal-world. Since the simulator learns nothing but the input/output of the corrupted parties, the real-world adversary $\mathcal{A}$ can only learn the same information.

Adopting this framework, the security of a privacy-preserving trigger-action system can be defined as follows.

Definition 1. *A trigger-action protocol Π that computes $\mathcal{F}_{tap}$ is secure if given any adversarial trigger-action platform $\mathcal{A}$, there exists a simulator $\mathcal{S}$ such that* $\text{IDEAL}_{\mathcal{F}_{tap},\mathcal{S}} \approx \text{REAL}_{\Pi,\mathcal{A}}$ *are computationally indistinguishable, where* $\text{IDEAL}_{\mathcal{F}_{tap},\mathcal{S}}$ *is the joint output of simulator $\mathcal{S}$ in the ideal-world, while* $\text{REAL}_{\Pi,\mathcal{A}}$ *is the output of adversary $\mathcal{A}$ in the real-world.*

Theorem 1. *Let Π be the protocol of OTAP and assume $\mathsf{Enc}(\cdot)$ is an IND-CPA encryption scheme. Given any adversarial trigger-action platform P, there exists* *a probabilistic simulator $\mathcal{S}$ which takes as inputs the rules sets $\boldsymbol{r}_1, \cdots, \boldsymbol{r}_M$ and the trigger periods $\boldsymbol{\tau}$ satisfies Definition 1.*

Proof. Let $I = \{(u, d_t) \in \boldsymbol{r}_i \mid i = 1, \ldots, M\}$ be the set of users and trigger parameters of rules, and $\tau_{(u,d_t)}$ be the associated trigger period for each $(u, d_t) \in I$. The simulator $\mathcal{S}$ will interact with the adversary $\mathcal{A}$ internally, and can be constructed as follows. For each $(u, d_t) \in I$, $\mathcal{S}$ passes (u, d_t, c) to $\mathcal{A}$ as input as if it was sent by the triggering service T at each corresponding trigger point (i.e., $\tau_{(u,d_t)}, 2 \cdot \tau_{(u,d_t)}, \ldots$) and outputs whatever $\mathcal{A}$ outputs, where c is randomly sampled from the ciphertext space of $\mathsf{Enc}(\cdot)$.

Now we show that the output of $\mathcal{S}$ is computationally indistinguishable from the output of $\mathcal{A}$ in real-world. In the real-world, the service T sends out $(u, d_t, \mathsf{Enc}(k, \delta))$ to $\mathcal{A}$ periodically for every $(u, d_t) \in I$, where δ is the event data. Based on the CPA secure assumption of Enc, we know that (u, d_t, c) and $(u, d_t, \mathsf{Enc}(k, \delta))$ are computationally indistinguishable. Thus, the outputs of $\mathcal{S} = \mathcal{A}(u, d_t, c)$ and $\mathcal{A}(u, d_t, \mathsf{Enc}(k, \delta))$ must also be computationally indistinguishable, which completes the proof.

Since the simulator is given only the rules sets $\boldsymbol{r}_i$ of every user i and the trigger periods, it is clear that the platform learns nothing about the trigger events, and thus preserved *trigger presence confidentiality* and *trigger data confidentiality*. However, *device set confidentiality* is broken, as the devices owned by a user can be inferred from the rules they are using.

Theorem 2. *Let Π be the protocol of ATAP, and $\mathcal{G}$ be the elliptic curve used in Π, whose base point being G and order being q. Assume that use of IND-CPA encryption schemes $\mathsf{Enc}(\cdot)$ and $\mathcal{E}(\cdot)$, then given any adversarial trigger-action platform $\mathcal{A}$, there exists a probabilistic simulator $\mathcal{S}$ satisfies Definition 1, while $\mathcal{S}$ takes as input a list $\boldsymbol{E}$ that contains the 3-tuples of events occurrence time, trigger service name, and action service name.*

Proof. The simulator $\mathcal{S}$ will interact with the adversary $\mathcal{A}$ internally, and can be constructed as follows. For each $(t, T, A) \in \boldsymbol{E}$, the simulator $\mathcal{S}$ passes $(\mathcal{E}_P(A), c, \gamma'G)$ to $\mathcal{A}$ as if it was sent by the trigger service T, where c is randomly picked up from the ciphertext space of Enc and γ is randomly chosen from $\{1, \ldots, q-1\}$. Then $\mathcal{S}$ simply outputs whatever $\mathcal{A}$ outputs.

Now we show that the output of $\mathcal{S}$ is computationally indistinguishable from the output of $\mathcal{A}$ in real-world. It is suffices to show that $(\mathcal{E}_P(A), c, \gamma'G)$ and $(\mathcal{E}_P(A), \mathsf{Enc}(k, \delta), \beta\gamma G)$ are computationally indistinguishable, following from the CPA security of underlying encryption schemes and the decisional Diffie-Hellman (DDH) assumption.

From the above proof we know that the platform learns nothing but the time of each event. However, since the platform will not know the name of the event and the associated user, the *trigger presence confidentiality* is still preserved. *Trigger data confidentiality* and *device set confidentiality* are also achieved, as no further information is provided to the platform.

B   Triggering Delay Analysis

This subsection will show that the average delay for OTAP with the guaranteed delivery strategy is minimized when using a constant trigger period.

Consider a general case where the trigger period is not a constant but follows a distribution $\mathcal{I}$ with $E[\mathcal{I}] = \tau$. In the following, we focus on a particular trigger event and its corresponding service. We assume that the arrival of events is a Poisson process with a rate of λ. We model the trigger service of OTAP as a M/G/1 queueing system, where the customers (events) are served only at the trigger points and the service time is zero.

When an event arrives, it first needs to wait a short period of time before the queue starts serving new events, denoted as $\mathcal{R}$. Then the event needs to wait for all the events in the queue to be served before it is sent out. The duration is the sum of $\mathcal{N}_Q$ trigger periods, where $\mathcal{N}_Q$ denotes the size of the queue when the event arrives. As a result, we can derive the average delay of an event: $E[\mathcal{D}] = E[\mathcal{R}] + E[\mathcal{N}_Q] \cdot E[\mathcal{I}]$. By Little's Law [26], we have $E[\mathcal{N}_Q] = \lambda E[\mathcal{D}]$, and from queueing theory, we know that $E[\mathcal{R}] = \frac{\lambda}{2} E[\mathcal{I}^2]$, which implies

$$E[\mathcal{D}] = \frac{E[\mathcal{R}]}{1 - \lambda E[\mathcal{I}]} = \frac{\lambda E[\mathcal{I}^2]}{2(1 - \lambda\tau)} = \frac{\lambda(\mathrm{Var}[\mathcal{I}] + (E[\mathcal{I}])^2)}{2(1 - \lambda\tau)} = \frac{\lambda(\mathrm{Var}[\mathcal{I}] + \tau^2)}{2(1 - \lambda\tau)}$$

The result shows that the average delay is minimized when the trigger period is constant, since the minimum of $\mathrm{Var}[\mathcal{I}]$ $(= 0)$ happens when $\mathcal{I}$ is constant.

C   Trigger Distribution

Figure 8a shows the distribution of the intervals between consecutive triggers and Fig. 8b shows the number of trigger events in each hour from the first 720 h of the CASAS hh104 dataset [17]. The occurrence of events is not uniformly distributed. Since the sensor only monitors motions within a specific area, a series of bursty triggers occurs when the user is present in that area, and no trigger occurs when the user is elsewhere.

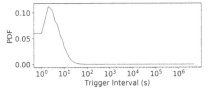
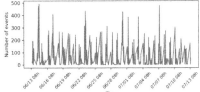

(a) Distribution of Inter-trigger Intervals

(b) Number of Triggers in Each Hour

Fig. 8. Trigger distribution in the CASAS hh104 dataset

D   Supporting Filter Code

As mentioned in Sect. 3.1, some trigger-action platforms allow users to write code to run during rule execution. Our schemes are capable of supporting a filter code by letting the action services store and run such codes. However, it might not be ideal to put this workload on action services instead of the trigger-action platform. Therefore, we propose two potential solutions to support this feature and leave them as future work.

The first direction is to replace the current encryption scheme with Homomorphic Encryption (HE), which allows computation over ciphertext without knowing the underlying plaintext. However, a challenge is achieving acceptable performance as HE schemes are computationally expensive.

Another possible solution is to build the trigger-action platform on trusted hardware. Intel Software Guard Extension (SGX), for example, provides an isolated execution environment called an enclave whose contents are protected, and only processes running inside the enclave are allowed access. Since the protection is at the hardware level, a malicious OS cannot read those data. SGX also provides another mechanism called remote attestation, which allows the client to attest that the code running on the remote machine is indeed the expected one. Thus, an SGX-based solution would support the trigger-action platform to handle sensitive data inside an enclave and partner services to attest that the platform is indeed running the privacy-preserving version at each interaction. However, the resources inside an enclave are limited and hence, a challenge becomes designing an algorithm that can use memory effectively.

References

1. Microsoft Flow. https://flow.microsoft.com
2. Target Expects $148 Million Loss from Data Breach (2014). https://time.com/3086359/target-data-breach-loss/
3. Yahoo Says Hackers Stole Data on 500 Million Users in 2014 (2016). https://www.nytimes.com/2016/09/23/technology/yahoo-hackers.html
4. Yahoo Triples Estimate of Breached Accounts to 3 Billion (2017). https://www.wsj.com/articles/yahoo-triples-estimate-of-breached-accounts-to-3-billion-1507062804
5. ApacheBench (2019). https://httpd.apache.org/docs/2.4/programs/ab.html
6. Do more with Oticon - IFTTT (2019). https://ifttt.com/oticon
7. IFTTT (2019). https://ifttt.com
8. IFTTT Platform (2019). https://platform.ifttt.com/lp/learn_more
9. The Equifax Data Breach (2019). https://www.ftc.gov/equifax-data-breach
10. Turn off WiFi on your Android when you leave home to save power (2019). https://ifttt.com/applets/302237p
11. Zapier (2019). https://zapier.com
12. (2020). https://github.com/csienslab/tap-privacy
13. Bastys, I., Balliu, M., Sabelfeld, A.: If this then what?: controlling flows in IoT apps. In: ACM CCS (2018)

14. Bastys, I., Piessens, F., Sabelfeld, A.: Tracking information flow via delayed output. In: Gruschka, N. (ed.) NordSec 2018. LNCS, vol. 11252, pp. 19–37. Springer, Cham (2018). https://doi.org/10.1007/978-3-030-03638-6_2
15. Bu, L., et al.: Systematically ensuring the confidence of real-time home automation IoT systems. ACM Trans. Cyber-Phys. Syst. **2**(3), 1–23 (2018)
16. Canetti, R.: Security and composition of multiparty cryptographic protocols. J. CRYPTOLOGY **13**(1), 143–202 (2000)
17. Cook, D.J., Crandall, A.S., Thomas, B.L., Krishnan, N.C.: CASAS: a smart home in a box. Computer **46**(7), 62–69 (2012)
18. Das, D., Meiser, S., Mohammadi, E., Kate, A.: Anonymity trilemma: strong anonymity, low bandwidth overhead, low latency-choose two. In: IEEE Symposium on Security and Privacy (S&P) (2018)
19. Elvy, S.A.: Paying for privacy and the personal data economy. Columbia Law Rev. **117**, 1369 (2017)
20. Fernandes, E., Rahmati, A., Jung, J., Prakash, A., Rahmati, A.: Decentralized action integrity for trigger-action IoT platforms. In: NDSS (2018)
21. Goldreich, O.: Foundations of Cryptography: Volume 2, Basic Applications. Cambridge University Press, Cambridge (2009)
22. Goldreich, O., Micali, S., Wigderson, A.: How to play any mental game. In: ACM Symposium on Theory of Computing (1987)
23. Hsu, K.H., Chiang, Y.H., Hsiao, H.C.: SafeChain: securing trigger-action programming from attack chains. IEEE Trans. Inf. Forensics Secur. **14**(10), 2607–2622 (2019)
24. Liang, C.J.M., et al.: Systematically debugging IoT control system correctness for building automation. In: ACM BuildSys (2016)
25. Liang, C.J.M., et al.: Sift: building an internet of safe things. In: IEEE/ACM IPSN (2015)
26. Little, J.D.: A proof for the queuing formula: L = λW. Oper. Res. **9**(3), 383–387 (1961)
27. Mi, X., Qian, F., Zhang, Y., Wang, X.: An empirical characterization of IFTTT: ecosystem, usage, and performance. In: ACM IMC (2017)
28. Surbatovich, M., Aljuraidan, J., Bauer, L., Das, A., Jia, L.: Some recipes can do more than spoil your appetite: analyzing the security and privacy risks of IFTTT recipes. In: International Conference on World Wide Web (2017)
29. Wang, Q., Datta, P., Yang, W., Liu, S., Bates, A., Gunter, C.A.: Charting the attack surface of trigger-action IoT platforms. In: ACM CCS (2019)
30. Xu, R., Zeng, Q., Zhu, L., Chi, H., Du, X., Guizani, M.: Privacy leakage in smart homes and its mitigation: IFTTT as a case study. IEEE Access **7**, 63457–63471 (2019)
31. Zhang, L., He, W., Martinez, J., Brackenbury, N., Lu, S., Ur, B.: AutoTap: synthesizing and repairing trigger-action programs using LTL properties. In: IEEE/ACM ICSE (2019)

Plenty of Phish in the Sea: Analyzing Potential Pre-attack Surfaces

Tobias Urban[1,3](✉)[iD], Matteo Große-Kampmann[1,2,3], Dennis Tatang[3],
Thorsten Holz[3], and Norbert Pohlmann[1]

[1] Institute for Internet-Security, Westphalian University of Applied Sciences,
Gelsenkirchen, Germany
urban@internet-sicherheit.de
[2] Aware7 GmbH, Gelsenkirchen, Germany
[3] Ruhr-Universität Bochum, Bochum, Germany

Abstract. *Advanced Persistent Threats* (APTs) are one of the main challenges in modern computer security. They are planned and performed by well-funded, highly-trained and often state-based actors. The first step of such an attack is the reconnaissance of the target. In this phase, the adversary tries to gather as much intelligence on the victim as possible to prepare further actions. An essential part of this initial data collection phase is the identification of possible gateways to intrude the target.

In this paper, we aim to analyze the data that threat actors can use to plan their attacks. To do so, we analyze in a first step 93 APT reports and find that most (80%) of them begin by sending phishing emails to their victims. Based on this analysis, we measure the extent of data openly available of 30 entities to understand if and how much data they leak that can potentially be used by an adversary to craft sophisticated spear phishing emails. We then use this data to quantify how many employees are potential targets for such attacks. We show that 83% of the analyzed entities leak several attributes of uses, which can all be used to craft sophisticated phishing emails.

Keywords: Advanced persistent threats · Phishing · OSINT · Reconnaissance · MITRE · Cyber kill chain · Measurement study

1 Introduction

Today, *advanced persistent threats* (APTs) represent one of the most dangerous types of attacks, as a malicious actor focuses a tremendous amount of resources into an attack on a selected target. Often such attacks utilize social engineering methods—especially *spear phishing*—to initially infect the system in the target's network (e.g., via an email attachment) [19]. For an attacker, one of the first steps is to collect as much information as possible on the target to plan their further steps (e.g., used technologies or intelligence on employees to craft spear-phishing emails) [22]. This data collection mostly happens unnoticed since the adversaries often rely on *open-source intelligence* (OSINT) data, which can be accessed by

© Springer Nature Switzerland AG 2020
L. Chen et al. (Eds.): ESORICS 2020, LNCS 12309, pp. 272–291, 2020.
https://doi.org/10.1007/978-3-030-59013-0_14

anyone. The collection of such data cannot be measured, or at least the crawling cannot be distinguished from benign traffic.

In this paper, we aim to understand and measure which publicly available data malicious actors can potentially utilize to plan and conduct their attacks with a strong emphasis on data an adversary can use to design sophisticated phishing campaigns. To the best of our knowledge, all previous work exclusively aims to detect attacks while they happen, to investigate them after the adversaries performed the attack, or to compare different APT campaigns (e.g., [4,10,11,16,21,25]). We aim to illuminate the data publicly available to adversaries during their *initial reconnaissance phase* by analyzing a diverse set of organizations ($n = 30$). In a first step, we analyze 93 APT reports with a strong focus on the different approaches how actors get access to a company's network and which techniques they use to do so. We show that an overwhelming majority of 80% use targeted phishing emails to lure users to unknowingly infect their system (e.g., clicking on a malicious email attachment). Based on this finding, we crawled nearly 5 million websites, analyzed more than 250,000 documents, and over 18,000 social media profiles regarding data that can be used to create personalized phishing emails. We then quantify the magnitude of publicly available data companies (unknowingly) leak and show that 90% of them leak data that adversaries can use for the desired task. Furthermore, we show that, on average, 71% of the employees we identified leaked several attributes that can be used for phishing attacks as we found several work-related information on them that an adversary can use in a targeted phishing campaign (e.g., supervisors, the focus of work, or the used software).

In summary, we make the following key contributions:

1. We analyze real-world APT campaigns and identify the most common tactics adversaries use during an attack and map these tactics and techniques onto the *MITRE PRE-ATT&CK* framework.
2. We measure the magnitude of data that companies (unknowingly) expose that can be used by adversaries to craft spear phishing emails. To this end, we crawl several publicly available data sources (e.g., social networks and openly available information on data leaks) and the company's infrastructure.
3. We analyze how many employees of a company leak enough attributes to write highly sophisticated phishing mails. We find that over 83% of all analyzed companies provide rich target for spear phishing attacks.

2   Background

Before describing our approach to determine the Internet-facing attack surface of a company, we provide background information necessary to follow our method.

2.1   Advanced Persistent Threats

Advanced Persistent Threats (APTs) are attacks executed by sophisticated and well-resourced, often state-sponsored, groups. In contrast to other adversaries, the actions of these groups are often politically motivated, but they also aim to achieve an economic gain from their efforts. They target every business sector and design their attacks in a way that remains undetected for a very long time, in contrast to e.g., ransomware attacks. While common adversaries often choose their target by chance, APT threat actors typically target a specific company or business sector and invest a lot of time and energy until they eventually successfully obtain access. To enable such attacks, these groups utilize traditional attack vectors like social engineering (e.g., spear phishing), but also sometimes collect information by physically infiltrating the target companies (e.g., dumpster diving).

Spear Phishing. In computer security, *phishing* describes the act when an adversary impersonates a trusted entity (e.g., a popular brand or bank) with the intent to trick users into exposing personal data (e.g., credit card numbers or credentials) or spreading malware via malicious attachments or links [27]. While these attempts commonly target tens of thousands of users, spear phishing targets a limited group of people (e.g., few people within a company or one research group at a university) or sometimes only a single person (e.g., the head of a department). As these phishing campaigns target specific individuals, adversaries can craft emails in a way that they perfectly suit the audience (e.g., by personal salutations in emails) and are often successful [3]. Adversaries persistently exploit phishing and spear-phishing because exploiting humans is often easier compared to bypassing technical security measures [8].

Cyber Kill Chain. The term *cyber kill chain*, coined by *Lockheed Martin* [22], is referring to the military term "kill chain", and both terms describe the structure of an attack. However, the cyber kill chain is often used defensively in incidence response or digital forensics to model the attack performed by an adversary [32]. The chain maps each attack to seven phases that can be grouped into two sections, based on the stage of the attack. First, the attacker profiles the target (1: "Reconnaissance"), then she builds the malware used to infiltrate the target (2: "Weaponize"), which is then transferred to the target (3: "Delivery"). Afterwards, the attacker triggers the payload (4: "Exploitation"), and installs a backdoor and establishes a persistent bridgehead into the target's network (5: "Installation"). Finally, she builds a C&C infrastructure to communicate with the infected hosts (6: "Command and Control") and performs the malicious actions of desire (7: "Act on Objective"). Phases one, two, and sometimes three are referred to as the *pre-attack stage*, while the remaining stages are referred to as *attack stage*. In this work, we only focus on the pre-attack phase and specifically on the *reconnaissance* phase.

2.2   MITRE Framework

The *MITRE* cooperation created and still maintains the *PRE-ATT&CK* [31] and *ATT&CK* ("Adversarial Tactics, Techniques, and Common Knowledge") [30] frameworks. The platform collects and systematizes techniques and tactics of real-world adversaries which were obtained from several attacks with the goal that companies can learn from those attacks and improve their security concepts. All collected events are organized in different categories based on their appearance in the cyber kill chain [32]. The framework assigns a unique four-digit identifier to each category and technique so that it can be referenced easier (e.g., T1189 in TA0001).

The *PRE-ATT&CK* framework is designed to focus on the stages that usually occur before the attack is performed. For example, this includes choosing a victim, collecting data on the victim, or setting up the infrastructure needed to perform the attack (e.g., implementing the needed malware or setting up the C&C infrastructure). While the *ATT&CK* framework often contains very technical and specific information, the *PRE-ATT&CK* framework is often more general as it is by nature not as easy to determine which actions the actor performed. For example, if an adversary used a specific type of malware, one can analyze it and draw conclusions based on the sample. However, one cannot undoubtedly determine why a specific employee was phished based on technical data. Appendix A provides an overview of the pre-attack techniques and tactics of the framework that are relevant for our work.

3 Advance Persistent Threat Analysis

In this section, we provide the results of an analysis of 93 real-world APT reports we studied. More specifically, we perform a technical mapping of these reports onto the *MITRE PRE-ATT&CK* framework.

3.1 APT Report Analysis

As noted above, the *cyber kill chain* describes the multiple stages of an attack. To the best of our knowledge, no systematic research went into the analysis of the early steps of this process in which adversaries collect data on their victims to plan and initiate their campaigns. To close this gap and to gain further insights into the methods adversaries use, we manually analyze 93 openly available reports and technical blogs on APT campaigns with a strong emphasis on these steps (i.e., the *reconnaissance* phase). We use these reports as security companies, in contrast to academic researchers, often have unique insights into these APTs, especially in terms of incident response. In total, 40 different companies provide the reports of the APTs (e.g., *Symantec*, *Kaspersky Lab* or *Palo Alto Networks*).

Overall, the analysis of the APT reports in our dataset attributed them to 66 different malicious actors. In 32 cases, the report does neither identify nor disclose the actor. We argue that this broad distribution of actors allows us to draw a more generalizable conclusion on the methods used by them. According to the analyzed reports, the attacks in our dataset happened between 2011 and 2020. Figure 1a provides a detailed overview of the number of analyzed APTs each year. Two reports do not report on the year in which the APT happened.

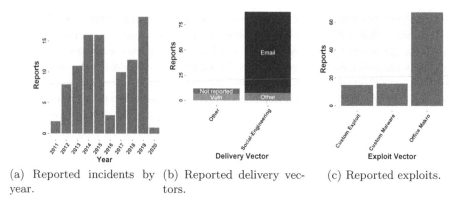

(a) Reported incidents by year. (b) Reported delivery vectors. (c) Reported exploits.

Fig. 1. Overview of the analyzed APT reports.

Nearly all reports lack information about the reconnaissance phase (91%). This knowledge gap probably roots in the fact that this cannot easily be analyzed, especially from an incident response point of view. However, in 41% of the cases, the target group (e.g., business sector or company type) could be identified. In rare cases where data on the reconnaissance phase is present, the actor used data publicly available ("Open-Source Intelligence" or OSINT) to identify promising targets for further steps. Reportedly, an overwhelming majority (88%) of all APTs used social engineering techniques to deploy their attack tools (e.g., malware) in companies' infrastructure. Furthermore, email seems to be the most popular way to get in touch with the victim (80%). Other means of communication with victims include social media (3%), phishing websites (4%), or SMS (1%). In the cases where the malicious actor did not rely on social engineering, the attackers abused vulnerabilities collected from public data on the companies infrastructure (4%), data collected from other services (3%) or the reports only hold vague or inconclusive data on the delivery phase (e.g., "*banks in Russia*"). Figure 1b provides an overview of the reported delivery vectors. In the exploitation phase, the actors mostly used *Microsoft Office* documents that contained malicious macros (69%). In the remaining cases, the adversaries either used case-specific malware or exploits they tailored for a product the company uses, as shown in Fig. 1c.

In summary, there is a lack of knowledge of how attackers collect the data on their victims. However, in the early stages of an attack, social engineering is the most common attack vector. Most malicious actors use email (e.g., spear phishing) as a primary channel to get in touch with their targets. In these emails, they utilized office documents that contain malicious macros to infect the user's system. While the analysis of the APT campaigns yielded the most common ways of how adversaries try to infiltrate companies, it is unclear which data they used to perform these attacks, or how and where they acquired it.

3.2   MITRE PRE-ATT&CK Analysis

The *MITRE PRE-ATT&CK* framework consists of 15 groups that describe different stages of the pre-attack phase [31]. In this work, we focus on data that can be publicly accessed by an adversary that provides her insights on the target company, the used infrastructure, and employees of the company. As previously described, an adversary can use this data to perform sophisticated social engineering attacks, like spear phishing.

We analyzed the framework to test which of the listed tactics can be analyzed using publicly measurable data using only non-offensive collection methods, which we used as a basis to design our measurement. Adversaries probably also use offensive tools (e.g., vulnerability scanners or buying information leaks online) to collect information, but due to ethical considerations, we renounce to use such tactics. Three computer security experts with a strong background in online measurements or threat intelligence (i.e., the first three authors of this paper) analyzed the framework. The experts were instructed to analyze all techniques and tactics in the framework and assessed whether they are publicly measurable using only non-offensive collection methods. The final inter-rater agreement whether a technique is measurable in our setting or not shows substantial agreement (Fleiss' Kappa: $\kappa = 0.73$; agreement $> 90\%$). In the rare cases of discrepancies, the option that got the majority was selected to resolve such matters.

The results show that one cannot measure several techniques using data that is publicly available. As a result, we only consider four of the 15 groups (i.e., *Technical Information Gathering, People Information Gathering, Organizational Information Gathering*, and *Technical Weakness Identification*) in our analysis (see Table A in Appendix A). The remaining groups are not measurable without internal insights of the adversary. For example, an analyst could measure the *Target Selection* or *Adversary OPSEC* phase if she infiltrates the adversary's internal infrastructure and monitors all events. We consider this to be out-of-scope as (1) we want to identify protection mechanisms for companies, and only highly specialized experts can perform such infiltration and (2) such penetration is likely in a legal gray (if not black) area. The techniques that we exclude are often either (1) described too general in the framework (e.g., "Conduct active scanning"), (2) out-of-scope because we refrain from using offensive technologies (e.g., "Conduct social engineering"), or (3) can be done reliably in an automated fashion (e.g., "Identify supply chains").

Summary. The analysis of the APT campaigns revealed that social engineering enables most of them, commonly conducted via spear-phishing emails. However, the reports could only rarely reconstruct which data attackers used to write the emails. The MITRE PRE-ATT&CK lists several techniques adversaries can use to collect such data. However, several of these described techniques are very broad, cannot be measured straightforwardly, and are sometimes not under the control of the company. Therefore, the question arises to what extend companies (unknowingly) expose such data.

4   Measuring Data Collection Opportunities

Based on the analysis of the framework presented in the previous section, we developed tools to collect the data types that a malicious actor can use to craft sophisticated spear-phishing emails as they are the most prevalent intrusion vector. We used two different crawling approaches to collect data for each company: (1) Analyzing sources directly maintained by the companies (e.g., websites) and (2) information present on third-party websites but that the company directly or indirectly provides (e.g., job postings or social media profiles).

4.1   Data Description

In our analysis, we perform an in-depth analysis of 30 entities (27 companies, two government agencies, and one non-profit organization). For the sake of simplicity, we use the term *company* for these 30 entities in the following. To choose these companies, we used a list of large, international companies and chose 27 from this list, with an emphasis on banking and e-payment companies. We focused on one sector as the described malicious actors tend to attack financial institutions or large organizations. However, the chosen companies are active in a variety of industry sectors and are of different sizes regarding revenue and number of employees. On average, the revenue of the analyzed companies is 60 billion USD (min: 27 million USD; max: 790 billion USD), and they employ 55,484 people (min: 49; max: 375,000). We took these numbers from the official figures the companies provided for 2018. Ten of the companies are active in the "banking" or "digital payment" sector (37%), while the others are distributed over eleven sectors (e.g., "Food" or "Aeronautics").

For ethical reasons, we refrain from naming any of the companies and will use pseudonyms for all companies in the remainder of this work (i.e., *Comp. #X*). In our measurements, we used no legal or ethical questionable tools and only accessed data that is publicly available. More specifically, we use in this study three different types of data sources to measure the pre-attack surface of a company: (1) data the company (unknowingly) provides, (2) data publicly available through social media sites, and (3) data leaked in known data breaches. An extended ethical discussion is presented in Sect. 7.

4.2   Data Collection

As previously mentioned, we rely for our analysis on "Open Source Intelligence" (OSINT) data, i.e., data sources that are publicly available. In the following, we describe the used data sources in more detail.

Company Controlled Entities. To crawl each companies' infrastructure, we built a crawler that we initialize with 1 to n domains owned by a company (*seed domains*). If possible, we read the TLS certificate present on these domains and try to identify further domains that can be protected by this certificate (i.e., *Subject Alternative Name* (SAN) and multi-domain SSL certificates). Furthermore, we perform a DNS enumeration to discover further domains and infrastructure operated by the company. After identifying the "landing pages" of all domains associated with a company, we visit each page and recursively all first-party links occurring on each website to a certain depth ($n = 6$). Hence, we try to visit every single webpage publicly linked by a company. Using this approach, we miss resources that are only available if the user has a specific link to the resource.

Analyzing Metadata. Most popular file types offer proprietary options to store additional information regarding the file ("metadata"). Such metadata, for example, includes authors of the document, the software used to create the document (e.g., `pdfTeX-1.40.17`), email addresses of the author, or its title. From an adversary's point of view, this information may provide specific insights into the victim. For example, the authors of a document, in combination with its title/content, can be used to craft specific phishing emails for a single or small group of users. With a given type of software, the adversary might also be able to attach a file that exploits a specific bug in that software to infect the user's system. We only used email addresses whose domain part's effective top-level domain (eTLD) +1 fit the eTLD+1 of the seed domain(s) we analyzed. For example, if our crawler scanned `foo.com` and extracted the email address `smith@bar.com` in one file, we dropped the file. Aside from metadata analysis, we identified emails by analyzing the content of websites and documents. For our study, we download all files that we find during the crawling process and extract the metadata. Overall, we analyze 36 different file types. These files includes `.pdf` files, office documents (e.g., `*.docx` or `*.odt`), and various image types (e.g., `*.png` or `*.jpeg`). If a document contains an author or other personally identifiable information (e.g., email addresses or names), we map them to other properties (e.g., used software). More specifically, we create relations between users, the software they use, and possible topics on which they work. For example, if we identified a *Microsoft Office v1.0* document written by two authors (*Alice* and *Bob*) with the title *World Peace—Status Quo and Outlook*, we can conclude that both worked on "World Peace" using Microsoft Office.

Company Infrastructure. We mainly focus on the vulnerability of companies towards social engineering attacks, especially spear phishing. Thus, we describe our measurements regarding parts of the companies infrastructure that might be abused by an adversary for this specific kind of attack. Adversaries might use so-called *homoglyph domains* (e.g., changing 'l' to 1) to trick employees into visiting them with the belief to navigate on the secure infrastructure of the company (but an adversary, of course, controls this infrastructure). We perform a simple *cybersquatting* detection by creating a list—based on the seed domains—of URLs that "look" similar to humans by applying techniques like homoglyphs, simple permutations, or by using different eTLDs. Afterward, we test if any of these URLs exist and try to assess who registered them. We use `whois` requests and data from SSL certificates to identify the registering organization.

Furthermore, we aim to identify isolated components in a company's infrastructure that is not connected to any other entity of the company's infrastructure. Examples for connections between the components are hyperlinks or shared IP addresses. Such isolated components could be legacy systems running without the direct knowledge of the responsible administrators, might be used as test systems, or in case of domains, might be run by an adversary in preparation of an attack. For all domains registered by a company (excluding homoglyph domains), we tested if the websites use trustworthy SSL certificates (e.g., not expired ones). If companies use certificates that are not trustworthy, adversaries might be able to intercept or eavesdrop the connection, which allows them to collect sensitive data. Finally, we check whether companies register domains with names similar to their original domain. Domain parking can be used to register domains up front before a service is run on the domain. Furthermore, a service provider can use this practice to avoid "domain drop catching". Domain drop catching is a (malicious) practice to registers a domain right after it expired and then to use it for different purposes [18, 26]. As users usually do not know when and if domains expire, they will still visit the domain and might be exposed to malicious content.

Social Media. Employment-oriented social media platforms, like *LinkedIn*, are commonly used by millions of people [20]. As these platforms are supposed to maintain business relationships, they can also be abused by adversaries to collect intelligence on a company [1]. This data might provide several details about the internal workings of a company, and its employees and their careers, contacts, or supervisors. Furthermore, companies do not have real control over which data is shared and posted on such platforms, and adversaries might use these sites to get in touch with the employees, undetected by any security mechanism of the company.

In this work, we use data obtained from various sources (e.g., different APIs). Some of these APIs are deprecated as of July 2020 but were still available when we collected our dataset. One example was the *LinkedIn* API that allowed to crawl user data based on an email address (i.e., *https://www.linkedin.com/sales/gmail/profile/viewByEmail/mailaddress*). The malicious actor could use this endpoint to determine whether an identified email address had a corresponding profile. To mimic the potential workflow of an adversary, we utilized search engines to perform site-specific searches (e.g., *site:linkedin.com <COMPANY-NAME>*). To further enrich our dataset, we utilized publicly available tools that automate the crawling process of social media sites (e.g., *CrossLinked* [24]).

Data Leaks. Finally, adversaries may utilize data from previous data breaches to prepare their attack. In this work, we use the *Have I Been Pwned* API [15] to test if a company ever leaked data that can be used in another attack on that company. The API exposes data leaks from over 400 websites and over 110.000

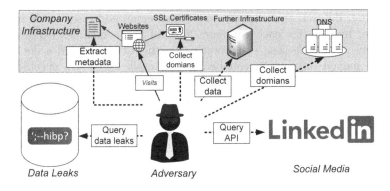

Fig. 2. Overview of our data collection approach.

"pastes". In this case, pastes are indications of data leaks in which the adversaries provides examples of the acquired data to prove that she actually got access to sensitive information. The API does not directly provide any of the breached data but returns categories of data that the leak contained. For example, if one provides an email address, the API will return data types that were leaked along with the address in different data breaches (e.g., `foo@bar.com`) results in `dates of birth`, `employers`, and `job titles`). Figure 2 provides an overview of the three types of data sources we analyzed.

4.3   Identified Data

Data Crawled from Companies' Infrastructure. In total, we scanned 30 entities and identified 492 domains (eTLD+1 and suffix) operated by them. Furthermore, we identified 18,873 employees, of which 8,994 appeared in data leaks, or they provided valuable data in public social media profiles.

Metadata Analysis. During the measurement, we visited 4,912,938 distinct web-pages and extracted metadata from 271,124 documents. Table 1a provides an overview of the identified data types identified based on the metadata of files we found on the crawled webpages. The `min`, `max`, and `mean` value describe how many instances were obtained for each company (e.g., we identified the names of 634 employees of a company). Ninety percent of the analyzed companies leak the names of their employees. Overall, we identified 22,361 email addresses, of which 6,335 were exclusively exposed via metadata (intentionally or unintentionally). As we extracted them from metadata, this might also provide insights to the adversary on which projects they work on (e.g., based on the file's content). Aside from names, the email address is essential as actors can use them to get in touch with potential victims. Almost three-quarters of all companies in our dataset leaked an employee's email address.

Furthermore, once the malicious actor understands the structure of a company's email addresses (e.g., `lastname@foo.com`), she can presumably make educated guesses on the local parts of further addresses if she knows the employees' names. In our dataset, the amount of identified email addresses would increase, on average, by 52% for each company. 81% of the companies exposed third parties they work with (i.e., collaborating partners that created a document). The three named data types can be used to craft user/team specific spear-phishing campaigns. For example, an adversary could impersonate a partner the employee worked with. Aside from personal data, the metadata of a file might expose intelligence on the inner workings of a company. In our dataset, 90% of the companies leaked the software they used to create a document, and almost two-thirds leaked data paths they use in the company to store documents (e.g., Z:\Project_X\Results). An attacker can use this information when preparing for the attack (e.g., zero-day exploits for the used software).

Company Domains. Table 1b presents potential information on the infrastructure that an actor can collect and later use for an attack. Furthermore, it provides hints that adversaries already actively make use of homoglyph domains. The most troubling finding of this measurement is that for 18 (60%) of the analyzed companies, an adversary actively abuse a homoglyph domain, at the time of our crawl. Note that we only counted domains for which we find a substantial string similarity of more than 95%, and therefore, our results can be seen as a lower bound. For one company, we found twelve active domains of this type (avg: 4.5). The presence of such domains indicates that adversaries are likely already actively trying to misguide users or employees of such services (e.g., password phishing). However, we also observed that some companies are aware of this endangerment and acquire some of these domains and "park" them for brand protection purposes as a kind of proactive defense.

Often websites or other services are connected by various mechanisms (e.g., hyperlinks or services that share the same IP address). In our dataset, half of the companies operate services that have no connection to others. These domains might pose a problem if the companies no longer maintain them and, therefore, could be less protected (e.g., legacy interfaces). On the other hand, these services might not pose a problem at all because the companies are fully aware of them. We found that eight entities (26%) operated domains that use an invalid or outdated certificate. An adversary might abuse these by intercepting the TLS encryption to such domains to collect more data on users or employees, whoever primarily uses these services. All of these companies operated at least one isolated domain (avg: 5) that uses an expired or otherwise untrusted certificate, which reinforces the assumption that the companies no longer maintain them.

Data Available in Data Leaks and in Social Media Profiles. In addition to the analysis of the companies' infrastructure and data they expose via metadata, we analyzed if the business accounts of employees (e.g., email addresses) occur in publicly known data breaches (see Sect. 4.2). For each company in our dataset, we found data on at least three of the identified employees (max: 1,102). In absolute numbers, 11 companies (46%) leaked data of less than 30 employees, and only four (12%) did not leak data on any employee that we identified.

Table 1. Overview of the data extracted from the company's own infrastructure.

(a) Overview of the identified information. The min and mean values exclude companies that did not provide the type of data.

Data type	aff. comp.	min	max	mean
Names	90 %	7	634	227
Mail addresses	71 %	1	96	19
Third Parties	81 %	1	53	15
Software	90 %	5	205	71
Path	65 %	1	30	7

(b) Overview of the identified infrastructure information.

Type	min	max	mean
Homoglyph Domains	1	12	4.5
Parked Domains	5	379	41.6
Isolated Domains	7	89	27.3
Untrusted Certificates	1	20	5.9

In relative numbers, two-thirds (20) of the analyzed companies leaked data of more than one-third of the identified employees (max: 88%). We found no statistical significance between the amount of identified emails and the amount of leaked data (ANOVA-Test p-value ≈ 0.03). Hence, companies that expose more emails are not automatically likely to be present in more data leaks. As this might seem to be counter-intuitive, it hints that some companies have policies in place to reduce the potential of such data leaks (e.g., awareness campaigns). Overall, the analyzed data leaks include 65 different data categories. The categories range from personal data (e.g., *credit status information, government issued IDs*, or *device usage tracking data*) over data directly tied to the employee's professional live (e.g., *job titles, employers*, or *occupations*) to other data an adversary could use to plan an attack (e.g., *instant messenger identities* or *password hints*). The category of a data leak shows a statistical correlation with the number of instances that this data is leaked (ANOVA-Test p-value < 0.0001). Hence, some data types leak more often than others.

Figure 3 shows the type of leaked data for each company. The heatmap highlights the ratio of identified leaks with the email addresses that we could identify. The figure only lists the top 15 categories, which account for 89% of all leaking instances. It shows that some companies leak excessively more data than others (ANOVA-Test p-value < 0.0001) but that there is no dominating data type that is leaked. In our dataset, the top leaked types are passwords (10%), phone numbers (8%), and geolocations (7%), excluding the name and email addresses of the users that the adversary needs to identify an employee. The biggest challenge with data actors collect from data leaks is that companies have virtually no measure to delete it. Furthermore, in none of the cases, it was the company itself that leaked the data but other platforms on which the employees registered to use the service, using their business email address. Hence, one solution could be to raise awareness with employees only to use the work email if necessary and to provide as little information as possible when using the respective services.

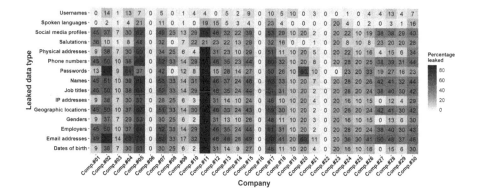

Fig. 3. Overview of the data extracted from other data sources.

Summary. In this section, we demonstrated that companies excessively leak data that provides insights into their inner workings or on the employees of the companies. However, it is not clear whether an adversary can meaningfully combine this data to plan further steps link designing successful phishing campaigns.

5   Assessing Potential Phishing Targets

Based on the insights of our study, we now introduce a metric to asses the likeliness that an employee serves as a good spear phishing target. The presence of data that we identify in this work does not necessarily pose a security problem per se. Each data point on its own is properly not problematic if obtained by an adversary, but taken together, they reveal intelligence that can be used, for example, to craft personalized phishing emails. Therefore, it is important to analyze and interpret the collected data.

5.1   Identifying Potential Phishing Targets

We now numerically analyze whether users are promising targets for spear phishing attacks from an adversary's point of view. In this work, we only analyze technical aspects and not the personal experience of each person, which is out-of-scope of this work but an essential aspect if someone falls for a phishing attempt [17]. Previous work that analyzed the effectiveness of spear phishing found that sources that impersonate an individual from the victim's company (e.g., from the human resources department) are quite effective [3,12]. The work shows that 34%–60% of all participants clicked on a link in such email. Therefore, we assume that if we could identify other persons working in the company and especially if they are working together (e.g., co-worker, supervisor, or team member), a phishing attempt might be more effective. Furthermore, if the adversary knows the software used by the victim, she can craft and append an exploit specifically for the used software to the email, which increases the chances of

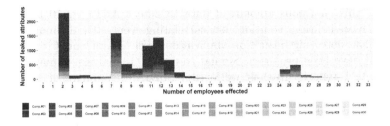

Fig. 4. Number of leaked attributes for each user in our dataset.

a successful compromise. Thus, we also consider the used technology of each employee as an essential aspect.

5.2 Spear Phishing Targets in the Wild

Figure 4 shows the number of attributes leaked for each employee in our dataset. Most employees only leak two categories of information (i.e., their name and email address), which we use to identify users of a company. For those individuals, it is not possible to craft targeted phishing mails (at least using our data). However, we identified 5,910 (62%) employees that leak between seven and 15 attributes. Those employees are employed at 25 different companies (83%). 878 (9%) employees leak between 24 and 28 attributes and are employed at 18 companies (60%). From both employee groups, an adversary can potentially pick several attributes and craft highly specific spear phishing mails. Only four (13%) companies in our dataset do not leak any additional data on their employees, aside the name and email address). For all of these companies, we identified relatively few employees. One reason for this is that most of these companies are active in business fields with no (public) customer interaction (e.g., investment banking). The results show that almost all companies in our dataset provide a considerable pre-attack surface to motivated attackers. In absolute numbers, companies that leaked more data also provide more targets for an attacker (ANOVA-Test p-value ≈ 0.001). However, taking the relation between the amount of identified emails and leaked data into account (similar to Fig. 3), we did not find a correlation. Hence, leaking more data does not necessarily mean that the adversary can identify more spear phishing targets. Our results show that the OSINT data sources that we utilized provide a rich data source from which threat actors can profit.

6 Related Work

Previously research on effective APT detection or prevention mostly focused on detecting them at and/or after the "Delivery" phase in the cyber kill chain [32]. APT detection is highly complicated as information from many sources (e.g., human behavior, intrusion detection systems, or system logs) have to be combined to make an informed decision. Machine learning approaches were studied to process this enormous amount of data to detect APTs [2,10,16,21]. Furthermore, more heuristic solutions like correlating events [25], defining detection rule sets [33], detecting misuse on application level [23], or annotating security events [11] have been proposed. Similar to our APT analysis, Lemay et al. [19] analyzed APT reports. In their work, they provide a summary of 40 analyzed APT reports. A large number of different works focus on the technical detection of spear-phishing emails, content analysis of phishing websites, and the detection of such websites based on their URLs (e.g., [13,14]). Furthermore, various studies analyzed human aspects to understand why spear-phishing attacks are successful (e.g., [3,12]). Finally, several papers systematize the extensive research that was conducted in this area (e.g., [5–7]). Our work differs from these approaches as we solely focus on the very first steps adversaries take when they plan their malicious actions, the *reconnaissance* phase. To the best of our knowledge, we are the first ones to show the variety and magnitude of information companies (unknowingly) provide that can be abused by adversaries to perform spear-phishing attacks. Furthermore, we do not aim to understand the effectiveness of specific phishing campaigns, but provide insights on how companies expose data.

7   Ethical Consideration

For this study, we gathered and analyzed sensitive information on companies and employees, thus individual persons. Our research institution does not require approval for this type of study, nor does it provide an Institutional Review Board (IRB). Nevertheless, we took strict ethical considerations into account. Additionally, we followed the research community's standard guidelines to protect those whose data was collected and the infrastructure of the services we use. A recent court ruling, according to the Electronic Frontier Foundation, found that "*automated scraping of publicly available data is unlikely to violate the Computer Fraud and Abuse Act (CFAA)*" [9]. As a general rule, the collection of personal information requires user consent; however, there are exceptions for cases where this is not practical. In our case, publicly available sources are the basis of the collection of information. By nature of our analysis, we cannot preempt to process personal data. We also want to highlight that none of our collections tools use any questionable tools to identify systems or persons. We do not perform any kind of penetration testing to collect data and send all requests at a courteous rate. The gathered data was collected for scientific purposes only, and we only disclosed it to the involved companies. To protect the collected personal data, we took additional safety measures: We encrypt the raw files for storage and delete unused samples and data.

8   Discussion and Conclusion

Our approach comes with limitations that need further clarification. The most decisive one, from a researchers' perspective, is that there exists no ground truth for our collected data. Hence, it implies that we do not know if adversaries profit from the data sources that we utilize to plan their actions or if all companies are unaware of the leakage of such data. However, the analyzed APT reports and several other sources (e.g., [22,28,29]) indicate that adversaries make excessive use of OSINT data, and even if companies are aware of the leakage of data, it might still be used by the adversaries. There is very little raw data available on incidents especially how the attackers infiltrated their victims. Furthermore, to build a ground truth for our research, one would need to impersonate the malicious actor while she plans her attack, which is ethically not tenable. With a company's consent, we could perform an awareness phishing campaign using the identified data. However, previous work already performed similar studies and demonstrated that they are often successful (see Sect. 6). With our work, we do not aim to determine the exact data used by adversaries in each attack, which is probably impossible in an automated fashion, but we demonstrate the sheer scale of data leaked by companies. Our results highlight that all analyzed companies provide a large attack surface to adversaries that is not monitored or protected by state-of-the-art security solutions. Furthermore, this data leakage is not always under the control of the companies, nor is it always possible to revert the leakage. Therefore, there is no clear path how to circumvent this type of leakage or straightforward countermeasure. It is quite hard to successfully prevent attacks on third party providers or reduce attack surfaces and therefore to apply countermeasures. One way to decrease the potential damage by these data leaks is to raise awareness with employees that this kind of data is regularly abused by adversaries and that the principle of "data economy" should be followed. Actionable tools to counter misuse of our analyzed data sources can be to wipe the metadata from all uploaded files, to continually monitor data leaks if they include passwords or other personal data of employees, or to increase awareness in a way that empowers employees not to provide too much work-related information on social media platforms.

Acknowledgment. This work was partially supported by the Ministry of Culture and Science of North Rhine-Westphalia (MKW grant 005-1703-0021 "MEwM"), the federal Ministry of Research and Education (BMBF grant 16KIS1016 "AWARE7"), and the Deutsche Forschungsgemeinschaft (DFG, German Research Foundation) under Germany's Excellence Strategy – EXC-2092 CASA – 390781972. We would like to thank Sweepatic NV—a cybersecurity company which maps, monitors and manages attack surfaces—for their support and access to their technology.

A   Analyzed MITRE PRE-ATT&CK Techniques

Table A lists the groups analyzed in this work. For each group, the techniques and tactics are shown and we indicate whether we analyzed it (*"Meas."*), if we collected the needed information on third-party websites (*"3rd"* or from first-party resources (*"1st)"*, and how we collected them (*"How obtained"*). If we did not collect data on a technique, the column "How obtained" provides a brief explanation why.

Technique	Meas.	1st	3rd	How obtained
Technical Information Gathering (TA0015)				
Acquire OSINT data sets and information	✗	—	—	Too general
Conduct active scanning	✗	—	—	Too general
Conduct passive scanning	✗	—	—	out of scope
Conduct social engineering	✗	—	—	out of scope
Determine 3rd party infrastructure services	✓	✓	✓	Shodan and IP addresses
Determine domain and IP address space	✓	✓	✓	log addresses during crawls
Determine external network trust dependencies	✓	✓	✗	log 3rd party usage
Determine firmware version	✓	✓	✓	during crawl & metadata
Discover target logon/email address format	✓	✓	✗	extract from metadata
Enumerate client configurations	✓	✓	✗	during crawl & metadata
Enumerate externally facing entities	✓	✓	✗	during crawl & metadata
Identify job postings and needs/gaps	✓	✗	✗	No API present
Identify security defensive capabilities	✗	—	—	out of scope
Identify supply chains	✗	—	—	very hard automatically
Identify technology usage patterns	✓	✓	✗	logged during crawls
Identify web defensive services	✓	✓	✗	analyzing 3rd party usage
Map network topology	✓	✓	✓	based on identified data
Mine technical blogs/forums	✗	✗	✗	out of scope
Obtain domain/IP registration information	✓	✓	✓	whois queries
Spearphishing for Information	✗	—	—	out of scope
People Information Gathering (TA0016)				
Acquire OSINT data sets and information	✗	—	—	Too general
Aggregate individual's digital footprint	✗	—	—	very hard automatically
Conduct social engineering	✗	—	—	out of scope
Identify business relationships	✗	—	—	out of scope
Identify groups/roles	✓	✗	✓	Based on social media data
Identify job postings and needs/gaps	✓	✗	✓	No API present
Identify people of interest	✓	✗	✗	based on collected data
Identify personnel with an authority/privilege	✓	✗	✗	based on collected data
Identify sensitive personnel information	✗	—	—	out of scope
Identify supply chains	✗	—	—	out of scope
Mine social media	✓	✗	✓	APIs of platforms
Organizational Information Gathering (TA0017)				
Acquire OSINT data sets and information	✗	—	—	Too general
Conduct social engineering	✗	—	—	out of scope
Determine 3rd party infrastructure services	✓	✓	✗	extracted during crawl
Determine centralization of IT management	✗	—	—	very hard automatically
Determine physical locations	✓	✓	✗	extracted during crawl
Dumpster dive	✗	—	—	out of scope
Identify business processes/tempo	✗	—	—	out of scope
Identify business relationships	✗	—	—	social media data
Identify job postings and needs/gaps	✓	✗	✓	No API present
Identify supply chains	✗	—	—	out of scope
Obtain templates/branding materials	✓	✓	✗	extracted during crawl

Concluded

References

1. Balduzzi, M., Platzer, C., Holz, T., Kirda, E., Balzarotti, D., Kruegel, C.: Abusing social networks for automated user profiling. In: Jha, S., Sommer, R., Kreibich, C. (eds.) RAID 2010. LNCS, vol. 6307, pp. 422–441. Springer, Heidelberg (2010). https://doi.org/10.1007/978-3-642-15512-3_22
2. Barre, M., Gehani, A., Yegneswaran, V.: Mining data provenance to detect advanced persistent threats. In: Proceedings of the 11th International Workshop on Theory and Practice of Provenance, TaPP 2019. USENIX Association, Berkeley (2019)
3. Caputo, D., Pfleeger, S., Freeman, J., Johnson, M.: Going spear phishing: exploring embedded training and awareness. IEEE Secur. Privacy **12**(1), 28–38 (2014). https://doi.org/10.1109/MSP.2013.106
4. Chen, P., Desmet, L., Huygens, C.: A study on advanced persistent threats. In: De Decker, B., Zúquete, A. (eds.) CMS 2014. LNCS, vol. 8735, pp. 63–72. Springer, Heidelberg (2014). https://doi.org/10.1007/978-3-662-44885-4_5
5. Chiew, K., Yong, K., Tan, C.: A survey of phishing attacks: their types, vectors and technical approaches. Expert Syst. Appl. **106**, 1–20 (2018). https://doi.org/10.1016/j.eswa.2018.03.050
6. Das, A., Baki, S., El Aassal, A., Verma, R., Dunbar, A.: SoK: a comprehensive reexamination of phishing research from the security perspective. IEEE Commun. Surv. Tutor. (2019). https://doi.org/10.1109/COMST.2019.2957750
7. Dou, Z., Khalil, I., Khreishah, A., Al-Fuqaha, A., Guizani, M.: SoK: a systematic review of software-based web phishing detection. IEEE Commun. Surv. Tutor. **19**(4), 2797–2819 (2017). https://doi.org/10.1109/COMST.2017.2752087
8. Ferreira, A., Vieira-Marques, P.: Phishing through time: a ten year story based on abstracts. In: Proceedings of the 4th International Conference on Information Systems Security and Privacy, ICISSP 2018, pp. 225–232. INSTICC, SciTePress, Setúbal, Portugal (2018). https://doi.org/10.5220/0006552602250232
9. Fischer, C., Crocker, A.: Victory! Ruling in hiQ v. Linkedin Protects Scraping of Public Data. https://www.eff.org/deeplinks/2019/09/victory-ruling-hiq-v-linkedin-protects-scraping-public-data
10. Ghafir, I., et al.: Detection of advanced persistent threat using machine-learning correlation analysis. Future Gener. Comput. Syst. **89**, 349–359 (2018). https://doi.org/10.1016/j.future.2018.06.055
11. Gianvecchio, S., Burkhalter, C., Lan, H., Sillers, A., Smith, K.: Closing the gap with APTs through semantic clusters and automated cybergames. In: Chen, S., Choo, K.-K.R., Fu, X., Lou, W., Mohaisen, A. (eds.) SecureComm 2019. LNICST, vol. 304, pp. 235–254. Springer, Cham (2019). https://doi.org/10.1007/978-3-030-37228-6_12
12. Halevi, T., Memon, N., Nov, O.: Spear-phishing in the wild: a real-world study of personality, phishing self-efficacy and vulnerability to spear-phishing attacks. SSRN Electron. J. (2015). https://doi.org/10.2139/ssrn.2544742
13. Han, Y., Shen, Y.: Accurate spear phishing campaign attribution and early detection. In: Proceedings of the 31st ACM Symposium on Applied Computing, SAC 2016, pp. 2079–2086. ACM Press, New York (2016). https://doi.org/10.1145/2851613.2851801
14. Ho, G., Sharma, A., Javed, M., Paxson, V., Wagner, D.: Detecting credential spearphishing in enterprise settings. In: Proceedings of the 26th USENIX Security Symposium, USENIX Sec 2017, pp. 469–485. USENIX Association, Berkeley (2017)

15. Hunt, T.: Have I Been Pwned: API v3 (2020). https://haveibeenpwned.com/API/v3. Accessed 15 Apr 2020
16. Kumar, G.R., Mangathayaru, N., Narsimha, G., Cheruvu, A.: Feature clustering for anomaly detection using improved fuzzy membership function. In: Proceedings of the 4th International Conference on Engineering & MIS, ICEMIS 2018. ACM Press, New York (2018). https://doi.org/10.1145/3234698.3234733
17. Kumaraguru, P., Rhee, Y., Acquisti, A., Cranor, L.F., Hong, J., Nunge, E.: Protecting people from phishing: the design and evaluation of an embedded training email system. In: Proceedings of the 25thACM SIGCHI Conference on Human Factors in Computing Systems, CHI 2007, pp. 905–914. ACM Press, New York (2007). https://doi.org/10.1145/1240624.1240760
18. Lauinger, T., Chaabane, A., Buyukkayhan, A.S., Onarlioglu, K., Robertson, W.: Game of registrars: an empirical analysis of post-expiration domain name takeovers. In: USENIX Security Symposium (2017)
19. Lemay, A., Calvet, J., Menet, F., Fernandez, J.M.: Survey of publicly available reports on advanced persistent threat actors. Comput. Secur. **72**, 26–59 (2018). https://doi.org/10.1016/j.cose.2017.08.005
20. LinkedIn Corporation: Statistics (2020). https://news.linkedin.com/about-us#statistics. Accessed 15 Apr 2020
21. Liu, F., Wen, Y., Zhang, D., Jiang, X., Xing, X., Meng, D.: Log2vec: a heterogeneous graph embedding based approach for detecting cyber threats within enterprise. In: Proceedings of the 26th ACM Conference on Computer and Communications Security, CCS 2019, pp. 1777–1794. ACM Press, New York (2019). https://doi.org/10.1145/3319535.3363224
22. Lockheed Martin Corporation: Gaining the Advantage-Applying Cyber Kill Chain Methodology to Network Defense (2014). https://www.lockheedmartin.com/content/dam/lockheed-martin/rms/documents/cyber/Gaining_the_Advantage_Cyber_Kill_Chain.pdf. Accessed 15 Apr 2020
23. Milajerdi, S.M., Eshete, B., Gjomemo, R., Venkatakrishnan, V.N.: ProPatrol: attack investigation via extracted high-level tasks. In: Ganapathy, V., Jaeger, T., Shyamasundar, R.K. (eds.) ICISS 2018. LNCS, vol. 11281, pp. 107–126. Springer, Cham (2018). https://doi.org/10.1007/978-3-030-05171-6_6
24. m8r0wn: CrossLinked (2020). https://github.com/m8r0wn/CrossLinked. Accessed 20 Apr 2020
25. Milajerdi, S., Gjomemo, R., Eshete, B., Sekar, R., Venkatakrishnan, V.: HOLMES: real-time APT detection through correlation of suspicious information flows. In: Proceedings of the IEEE Symposium on Security and Privacy, S&P 2019, pp. 1137–1152. IEEE Computer Society, Washington (2019). https://doi.org/10.1109/SP.2019.00026
26. Miramirkhani, N., Barron, T., Ferdman, M., Nikiforakis, N.: Panning for gold.com: understanding the dynamics of domain dropcatching. In: International Conference on World Wide Web (2018)
27. Parsons, K., McCormac, A., Pattinson, M., Butavicius, M., Jerram, C.: The design of phishing studies: the design of phishing studies: challenges for researchers. Comput. Secur. **52**, 194–206 (2015). https://doi.org/10.1016/j.cose.2015.02.008
28. Paterson, A., Chappell, J.: The Impact of Open Source Intelligence on Cybersecurity, pp. 44–62. Palgrave Macmillan UK, London (2014). https://doi.org/10.1057/9781137353320_4
29. RSA Research: Reconnaissance–A Walkthrough of the "APT" Intelligence Gathering Process (2015). http://www.kerneronsec.com/2015/10/a-walkthrough-of-apt-intelligence.html. Accessed 15 Apr 2020

30. The MITRE Corporation: MITRE ATT&CK matrix for enterprise (2019). https://attack.mitre.org/matrices/enterprise/. Accessed 15 Apr 2020

31. The MITRE Corporation: MITRE PRE-ATT&CK Matrix (2019). https://attack.mitre.org/matrices/enterprise/. Accessed 15 Apr 2020

32. Yadav, T., Rao, A.M.: Technical aspects of cyber kill chain. In: Abawajy, J.H., Mukherjea, S., Thampi, S.M., Ruiz-Martínez, A. (eds.) SSCC 2015. CCIS, vol. 536, pp. 438–452. Springer, Cham (2015). https://doi.org/10.1007/978-3-319-22915-7_40

33. Yu, H., Li, A., Jiang, R.: Needle in a haystack: attack detection from large-scale system audit. In: Proceedings of the 19th International Conference on Communication Technology, ICCT 2019, pp. 1418–1426 (2019). https://doi.org/10.1109/ICCT46805.2019.8947201

Post-quantum Cryptography

Towards Post-Quantum Security for Cyber-Physical Systems: Integrating PQC into Industrial M2M Communication

Sebastian Paul[(✉)] and Patrik Scheible

Corporate Sector Research and Advance Engineering, Robert Bosch GmbH,
Renningen, 70465 Stuttgart, Germany
sebastian.paul2@de.bosch.com

Abstract. The threat of a cryptographically relevant quantum computer contributes to an increasing interest in the field of post-quantum cryptography (PQC). Compared to existing research efforts regarding the integration of PQC into the Transport Layer Security (TLS) protocol, industrial communication protocols have so far been neglected. Since industrial cyber-physical systems (CPS) are typically deployed for decades, protection against such long-term threats is needed. In this work, we propose two novel solutions for the integration of post-quantum (PQ) primitives (digital signatures and key establishment) into the industrial protocol Open Platform Communications Unified Architecture (OPC UA): a hybrid solution combining conventional cryptography with PQC and a solution solely based on PQC. Both approaches provide mutual authentication between client and server and are realized with certificates fully compliant to the X.509 standard. Moreover, we implement the two solutions and measure and evaluate their performance across three different security levels. All selected algorithms (Kyber, Dilithium, and Falcon) are candidates for standardization by the National Institute of Standards and Technology (NIST). We show that Falcon is a suitable option—especially—when using floating-point hardware provided by our ARM-based evaluation platform. Our proposed hybrid solution provides PQ security for early adopters but comes with additional performance and communication requirements. Our solution solely based on PQC shows superior performance across all evaluated security levels in terms of handshake duration compared to conventional OPC UA but comes at the cost of increased sizes for handshake messages.

Keywords: Cyber-Physical systems · Post-quantum cryptography · X.509 certificates · Authentication · Key establishment · OPC UA

1 Introduction

Google's recent shot at quantum supremacy attracted much public attention, but the road to a stable and large-scale quantum computer is still long and

© Springer Nature Switzerland AG 2020
L. Chen et al. (Eds.): ESORICS 2020, LNCS 12309, pp. 295–316, 2020.
https://doi.org/10.1007/978-3-030-59013-0_15

uncertain [5]. Once one is built, however, it will be able to solve mathematical problems previously thought to be intractable. As a consequence, public key primitives that have become the "security backbone" of our digital society will be broken. This threat can be mitigated by deploying new cryptographic primitives that withstand attacks from both quantum and traditional computers, i. e. post-quantum cryptography. NIST addressed this issue by starting a PQC standardization process in 2016, which is currently in its second round.[1] Eventually, NIST will standardize quantum-resistant encapsulation mechanisms (KEMs) and digital signature algorithms (DSAs).

A migration to new primitives requires various forms of cryptographic agility, which typically is not present in existing systems [31,40]. Therefore, research how to securely and effectively integrate PQC into protocols and applications is required. Furthermore, it is essential to plan for the cryptographic transition, especially for devices with long life spans and high security requirements. Several governmental institutes have proposed to use hybrid modes for this cryptographic transition [9,17]. In such a hybrid mode at least two cryptographic primitives are applied simultaneously. On the one hand, a hybrid approach implies various advantages: 1) As long as one of the involved schemes remains unbroken the "entire" security property holds. Therefore, early adopters can benefit from additional security against quantum adversaries but don't have to fully rely on relatively new primitives; 2) Being compliant to industrial or governmental standards that have not been updated yet to include PQC; 3) Provide backward compatibility to legacy devices. On the other hand, hybrid modes negatively affect performance and increase the required communication bandwidth as well as memory footprint.

One domain where components have long life spans and many industrial (or even governmental) regulations are in place are industrial control systems (ICS). In recent years, ICS have shifted away from isolated networks and serial communication towards highly connected networks and TCP/IP-based communication, ultimately, providing access to the Internet. In fact, modern industrial communication has shifted away from proprietary protocols towards standardized machine-to-machine (M2M) protocols such as OPC UA [34,42,50]. Taking into consideration that CPS deployed today could still be in use when a cryptographically relevant quantum computer is available, a migration plan towards PQC is highly recommended. Such a migration plan is even more critical regarding confidentiality, because any communication passively recorded today can be retroactively decrypted once sufficiently powerful quantum computers become available. The fact that attacks related to industrial espionage play a major role in ICS further emphasizes the need for long-term confidentiality of transmitted data [49]. Although authentication can not be broken retroactively, we consider a preliminary investigation beneficial. As components of ICS are seldom updated during their long lifetime, they should support PQ DSAs rather sooner than later. As a consequence, we address the integration of PQC (KEM and DSA)

---

[1] As of June 2020, the second round is in its final stage; NIST plans to either conduct a third round or to directly announce a final selection of algorithms.

into the widespread industrial communication protocol OPC UA in this work. Previous research efforts largely focused on the integration of PQC into common Internet protocols, mainly, concentrating on PQ key exchange. To the best of our knowledge, this is the first work that evaluates the integration of PQC into an industrial protocol.

Contribution. In this work, we integrate quantum-resistant means of key establishment and authentication into OPC UA's security handshake, thereby demonstrating that industrial CPS are capable of handling the increased cost of PQC. The main contributions of our work are summarized as follows:

→ We investigate all lattice-based schemes of NIST's second round standardization process with regards to a security-size trade-off and conduct a standalone performance analysis of promising candidates on our evaluation platform.
→ We propose two novel integrations of PQC into OPC UA's security handshake: *Hybrid OPC UA* and *PQ OPC UA*. The first makes use of hybrid constructions for key exchange, digital signatures, and X.509 certificates. The latter is solely based on PQ schemes including PQ X.509 certificates. Both solutions do not alter the existing structure of the security handshake, and our hybrid approach provides backward compatibility to legacy devices. Besides that, we present a novel way for verifying hybrid X.509 certificates using the cryptographic library mbedTLS.
→ We implement and evaluate the two solutions on our ARM-based evaluation platform and provide detailed performance measurements for three different NIST security levels. By combining post-quantum key exchange and post-quantum digital signatures we evaluate the total impact of PQC on OPC UA.
→ Finally, we show that our *PQ* solution outperforms conventional OPC UA in terms of handshake duration at all evaluated security levels. In addition, in four of our six instantiations we make use of Falcon's highly efficient floating-point implementation, which—to the best of our knowledge—has previously not been examined in integration studies.

Outline. In Sect. 2, we introduce the reader to OPC UA and its security mechanisms, and we provide preliminaries on PQC. Section 3 highlights related work. In Sect. 4, we describe our two integrations of PQC into OPC UA. The performance measurements of our two proposed solutions are presented in Sect. 5. Section 6 concludes our paper.

2 Preliminary Background

2.1 OPC UA in Industrial Communication

OPC UA has been specified by the (IEC) in the standard series 62541. Furthermore, OPC UA is widely considered a de facto standard for future industrial applications. Because of its service-oriented architecture, OPC UA offers a standardized interface to exchange data between industrial applications independent from manufacturer of automation technology. Recently, it has also been adopted by popular cloud services demonstrating its increasing popularity [7,33]. OPC UA offers two modes for the transfer of information: a client-server mode and a relatively new publish-subscribe mode [34]. In this work, we focus on the client-server mode, since it is widely deployed in current automation systems and fully supported by open-source implementations.

OPC UA provides mutual authentication based on X.509 certificates and it ensures integrity and confidentiality of communication. The bottom layer of OPC UA's security architecture handles the transmission and reception of information. A secure channel is created within the communication layer and is crucial for meeting the aforementioned security objectives. The exchange of information is realized within sessions, which are logical connections between clients and servers. The following description of OPC UA's certificate-based authenticated key exchange is based on the relevant parts of its official specification [35,36]. After a transport connection has been established between client and server, the client requests *EndpointDescriptions*, which later allow him to access services or information offered by the server. In addition, an *EndpointDescription* contains information required for the security handshake: server certificate, message security mode, and security policy. The server certificate contains the authenticated public key of the server, which the client verifies before initiating the security handshake. OPC UA offers different message security modes for established sessions: *None*, *SignOnly*, and *SignAndEncrypt*. The set of cryptographic mechanisms used during the handshake phase and in subsequent sessions are specified using *SecurityPolicy Profiles*. For example, the security policy *Basic256Sha256* uses RSA2048 to encrypt/decrypt (RSA-OAEP) and sign/verify messages (RSA-PKCS1.5) during the security handshake; symmetric keying material is derived using the hash function SHA256 in a (PRF); within sessions, AES256 in Cipher Block Chaining mode is used for encryption, and a (HMAC) based on SHA256 is used for signatures. In contrast to TLS, OPC UA so far only offers a security handshake that relies on RSA.[2] In essence, it is based on encrypting random client and server nonces that are used to derive session keys.

The following characteristics of the security handshake are specified in the *SecureChannel Service Set*. First, the client sends an *OpenSecureChannel Request (OSC Req.)* to the server. This request contains a cryptographically secure random number (*client nonce*), a client certificate (including certificate chain), and a requested lifetime for the secure channel. The request message is encrypted using the authenticated public key of the server and signed using the secret key of the client. In case the verification of the client certificate succeeds, decryption and signature verification take place. Afterwards, the server generates a cryptographic random number (*server nonce*). In order to derive the required

---

[2] It should be noted that the OPC Foundation plans to standardize a security policy that supports Diffie-Hellman (DH) key exchange based on (ECC) in the near future [37].

session keys, both nonces serve as inputs to a PRF. Two sets of symmetric keys are derived this way: one is associated with the server and the other is associated with the client. The message body of the *OpenSecureChannel Response (OSC Rsp.)* contains a server nonce and a revised lifetime, the server certificate is placed in the security header of the response message. Secure channels are identified by security tokens, which expire after a specified lifetime. The revised lifetime tells the client when to renew the secure channel. The response message itself is encrypted using the client's authenticated public key and signed using the server's private key. After decryption and signature verification, the client derives the keying material from its own nonce and the received server nonce by applying the same PRF as the server. Finally, client and server end up with an identical set of cryptographic keys completing OPC UA's security handshake. The security properties of this handshake have been formally analyzed and the entire security architecture has been investigated in previous works [16,43].

2.2   Post-quantum Cryptography

Once a cryptographically relevant quantum computer becomes available, current public key primitives based on the mathematical problem of integer factorization (RSA) and (elliptic curve) discrete logarithm (DH and ECDH) will be broken because of Shor's quantum algorithm [45]. The last decade has seen an increased interest from academia and industry in finding novel cryptosystems that can withstand attacks from quantum computers. In essence, one needs to find a NP-hard problem that is not solvable in polynomial-time by quantum and classical computers.

PQ schemes can be grouped into five families: code-based, lattice-based, hash-based, multivariate, and supersingular EC isogeny cryptography. Out of the five families lattice-based cryptography has arguably attracted the most attention in research: 12 of the remaining 26 schemes in NIST's standardization process are based on lattice problems. Besides that, lattice schemes offer efficient implementations, reasonably sized public keys and ciphertexts, as well as strong security properties [32]. Consequently, we focus on lattice-based cryptography in this work.

A lattice consists of a set of points in a n-dimensional space with a periodic structure. By using n-linearly independent vectors any point in this structure can be reproduced. The security of lattice-based cryptographic primitives are based on NP-hard problems of high-dimensional lattices, such as the shortest vector problem (SVP). All lattice schemes submitted to NIST's standardization process rely on variants of the (LWE) problem, learning with rounding (LWR) problem, or NTRU. These problems can be related to aforementioned NP-hard lattice problems via reductions. We investigate the following lattice-based KEMs for potential integration into OPC UA: CRYSTALS-Kyber [6], FrodoKEM [2], LAC [51], NewHope [1], NTRU [20], NTRU-Prime [10], Round5 [8], Saber [22], and ThreeBears [27]. In addition, we investigate the following lattice-based signature schemes: CRYSTALS-Dilithium [24], Falcon [25], and qTESLA [11]. Table 2 and Table 3 in Appendix A list all lattice-based schemes considered in this work including characteristics of their parameter sets.

NIST defined five security levels corresponding to different security strengths in bits for its PQC standardization process. We focus on level 1, 3, and 5 in this work. NIST security level 1 corresponds to 128 bit (classical) security, whereas level 3 and 5 correspond to 192 bit and 256 bit security respectively. KEMs consist of a triple of algorithms: key generation, encapsulation, and decapsulation. Key generation is a probabilistic algorithm that generates a public and private key pair. The probabilistic encapsulation requires a public key as input and generates a shared secret and the corresponding ciphertext. Input to the decapsulation algorithm is a ciphertext and a private key, it either returns a shared secret or an error. Many lattice-based schemes show a small (cryptographically negligible) failure probability during the decapsulation step, in such cases a shared secret can not be derived. Typically, KEMs offer either indistinguishability under cho- sen plaintext attack (IND-CPA) or indistinguishability under chosen ciphertext attack (IND-CCA). IND-CPA offers security against passive adversaries, i. e. no information is learned by observing ciphertexts being transmitted. IND-CCA offers a stronger notion of security and provides security in presence of active adversaries. For the integration into OPC UA we rely on an ephemeral key exchange scheme. Any KEM can be easily transformed into an ephemeral key exchange as follows. An initiator generates a public and private key pair and sends its ephemeral public key to a receiving entity. The receiving entity generates a random secret, encrypts it using the received ephemeral public key (encapsulation), and sends the resulting ciphertext back to the initiator. Ultimately, the initiator decrypts the received ciphertext using its ephemeral private key (decapsulation) giving both parties a shared random secret.

Similar to KEMs, signature schemes consist of a triple of algorithms: key generation, signature generation, and signature verification. Key generation returns a public and private key pair. Signature generation takes a private key and a given message to produce a signature. The deterministic signature verification algorithm takes a public key, a message, and a signature and either rejects or accepts the signature. The standard security notion for DSAs is existential unforgeability under chosen message attack (EUF-CMA). NIST required all submitted signature schemes to reach this notion. For specific details of the schemes, we refer the reader to the corresponding specifications.

3   Related Work

There have been a lot of research efforts integrating PQC into widespread Internet protocols such as TLS, SSH (Secure Shell), and IKEv2 (Internet Key Exchange version 2). Since OPC UA's security handshake is loosely inspired by TLS's handshake protocol, we focus on previous works in this area. In general, existing integration studies can be grouped into the following three categories: standardization efforts, implementation works, and experimental studies. Two active Internet Engineering Task Force (IETF) Internet-Drafts exist that describe the integration of hybrid key exchange into TLS 1.2 [19] and TLS 1.3 [48]. Many experimental studies have been conducted under real network conditions [15,30,46] or under lab conditions [21,39]. In aforementioned studies, the authors typically make use of already existing open source implementations of PQC. For example, Open Quantum Safe provides prototypical integrations of PQ schemes into the the popular library OpenSSL [47]. Other works exist where PQC has been either integrated into embedded libraries [18] or has been optimized for specific platforms [29]. Our implementations of PQ schemes are mainly based on PQClean[3], which provides portable implementations for an easy integration into other codebases. When investigating authentication, another difficulty must be dealt with: a long-term public key is involved, which is typically stored and distributed via certificates. Previous works proposed hybrid certificates for the post-quantum transition where extension fields are used to bind an additional public key to an entity using an additional PQ signature scheme [12,14]. In addition, the impact of hybrid and PQ certificates on various Internet protocols has been investigated [28,46].

Since it enables confidentiality against future quantum adversaries, hybrid key exchange has so far attracted the most attention. If authentication and key exchange are considered, they are typically evaluated separately, hence not showing the entire impact of PQC on protocols. Hybrid authentication has been addressed, but it was evaluated separately from key exchange and no performance measurements were conducted [21]. The authors of [18] investigated the combined impact of PQ key exchange and authentication on TLS for embedded devices, but only considered one set of PQ primitives at one security level.

4 Integration of PQC into OPC UA

4.1 Hybrid OPC UA

In hybrid modes, different options for combining cryptographic material exist. We use the XOR-then-MAC combiner from [13] regarding confidentiality of data, which is provably secure against fully quantum adversaries. Besides the integration of a hybrid key exchange scheme, we need to convey two long-term public keys and two digital signatures for authenticity and integrity. For reasons of backward compatibility, we work with X.509 certificates that consist of two non-critical extensions as proposed in [12]. The first contains the public key of the additional PQ signature scheme, the second holds the signature over the certified data. Messages are signed independently from each other using two different signature schemes. The security properties of this concatenation combiner have been investigated in [14]. While the merits of a hybrid key exchange are obvious, there is a slightly weaker need for hybrid authentication and hybrid digital signatures. However, applications will have to support conventional and PQ schemes in order to be backward compatible with applications, which have not been

---

[3] https://github.com/PQClean/PQClean.

upgraded yet. Therefore, we also consider hybrid signatures and authentication in this work to fully understand its impact on OPC UA.

The integration of hybrid modes into the security handshake of OPC UA requires modifications to the *SecureChannel Service Set*. We define a new security policy *Hybrid{1,3,5}_Basic256*, which the server suggests to the client within the *GetEndpoints Response*. In our approach, this response contains the hybrid X.509 certificate (including the certificate chain). First, the client verifies the entire certificate chain assuming a hybrid root certificate has been preinstalled. In addition to a random client nonce, the ephemeral key generation function of a PQ KEM needs to be called (pk_{PQ}, sk_{PQ}). The hybrid *OSC Req.* is initialized using the client nonce, pk_{PQ}, and the security settings obtained from the *GetEndpoints Response*. The additional public key is positioned within the security header, which also includes the hybrid client certificate. Before the request is sent to the server in form of an OPC UA message, it is signed using the aforementioned hybrid signature scheme: A hash is computed over the entire message that is then signed conventionally and by a PQ signature scheme. According to the specification of OPC UA, the sequence header, the message body containing the client nonce, and the message footer containing RSA-padding fields and signatures are encrypted. We avoid expensive RSA encryption/decryption by placing the additional values of our hybrid solution (pk_{PQ} and PQ signature) outside the encrypted message parts.

Once the server receives the request message, it verifies the hybrid client certificate (including the certificate chain). After the certificate verification, the conventionally encrypted message parts are decrypted and the two signatures are verified. As in conventional OPC UA, the server then creates his server nonce. For our proposed hybrid mode, the encapsulation function of the respective PQ KEM is called using the received public key pk_{PQ} as input. This generates a ciphertext ct_{pq} and a shared secret ss_{pq}. In order to maintain the original structure of OPC UA's security handshake, we expand the shared secret using a PRF to obtain additional nonce values. Further calls to PRFs generate two types of keying material: a conventional set and a post-quantum set. In a subsequent step, the two sets are combined using XOR. To complete the XOR-then-MAC combiner, we compute a MAC over the ciphertext ct_{pq} and the original server and client nonce using the generated server's symmetric signing key. The ciphertext and MAC are placed in the security header. We keep the server nonce inside the body of the response message alongside the revised lifetime of the secure channel. The response message is signed using the aforementioned concatenation combiner. After signing the message, the sequence header, the message body, and message footer are encrypted. Again, this avoids expensive encryption of additional, potentially large values (ct_{pq}, MAC, and PQ signature).

The client receives the response message, conventionally decrypts it, and verifies the included hybrid signature. Utilizing the received PQ ciphertext ct_{pq} and the client's own PQ secret key sk_{pq}, the corresponding decapsulation function of the respective KEM is called, which outputs the shared secret ss_{pq}. As in processing the *OSC Req.*, this shared secret is expanded to create additional nonce values. Having obtained all required nonces, we generate two types of keying material (conventional and PQ) and combine them using XOR. We verify the received MAC by using the computed symmetric signing key completing our hybrid security handshake.

4.2 Post-quantum OPC UA

Once PQ schemes have been standardized, they will be adopted in protocols and will be considered state-of-the-art. Consequently, hybrid modes will not be required any longer. For our *PQ OPC UA* solution, we keep the structure of the original security handshake but replace conventional asymmetric primitives with PQ key encapsulation and digital signature schemes.

We introduce a new security policy *PQ{1,3,5}*, which is sent to the client in *GetEndpoints Response*. The conveyed server certificate contains a single PQ public key and is signed with a PQ signature scheme. The client verifies the server certificate including the certificate chain. Again, we assume the PQ root certificate has been preinstalled on both client and server. The generation of the *OSC Req.* is the same as in our hybrid mode. First, a random client nonce is created and then the ephemeral key pair of a PQ KEM (pk_{PQ}, sk_{PQ}). Since we base the key exchange of our PQ solution solely on a PQ KEM, we do not require secrecy of the random client and server nonce. As a consequence, sequence header, message body, and message footer of the *OSC Req.* and *OSC Rsp.* are sent unencrypted. The resulting *OSC Req.* is signed using the client's private PQ signing key, the certificate containing the corresponding PQ public key is part of the request message sent to the server.

The server verifies the PQ client certificate (including the certificate chain) and the signature of the *OSC Req.* using the client's authenticated public key. After the verification step, the encapsulation function of the KEM is invoked resulting in a ciphertext (ct_{PQ}) and shared secret (ss_{PQ}). Besides that, we generate a random server nonce. The shared secret and both random nonces serve as input to a PRF. We consider the output of the PRF our *master secret*. Subsequently, we use the *master secret* as input to another PRF to obtain symmetric keying material. By keeping the random nonces from the conventional security handshake and by using them as input to the first PRF we ensure that both parties contribute to the *master secret*. The *OSC Rsp.* contains the generated ciphertext, the server certificate, the server nonce, and the revised lifetime of the secure channel. The response message is signed using the server's private PQ signing key and the signature is appended.

Once the client receives the *OSC Rsp.*, the signature is verified using the server's authenticated public key. Then, the client calls the decapsulation function of the PQ KEM resulting in the shared secret (ss_{PQ}). Again, this shared secret serves as input to a PRF alongside the client and server nonce. The output is fed to another PRF to compute the final keying material. Server and client derive the same keying material, which is used in subsequent communication sessions. This completes OPC UA's handshake solely based on PQ schemes: Client and server are mutually authenticated via PQ certificates and signatures. Keying material is derived using a key exchange scheme based on a PQ KEM.

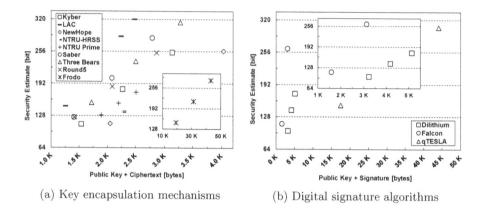

(a) Key encapsulation mechanisms   (b) Digital signature algorithms

Fig. 1. Security-size trade-off for lattice-based quantum-resistant schemes.

4.3   Selection of Quantum-Resistant Primitives

In principle, our generic approach allows us to integrate any KEM and DSA. Our criteria for the selection of quantum-resistant schemes are as follows. We require lattice-based algorithms that offer a balanced trade-off in terms of estimated security, public key + ciphertext/signature size, and performance, since the time to establish a secure channel should not substantially increase. In addition, we only consider algorithms that are part of NIST's ongoing PQC standardization process (Round 2). Consequently, their official specification should offer various parameter sets that cover different security levels; KEMs should provide IND-CCA. Integration into OPC UA needs to be possible without any modifications to cryptographic algorithms, since we do not want to invalidate any of their security claims.

Security-Size Trade-Off. First, we study the trade-off in terms of security and size of all remaining lattice-based Round 2 submissions. The size metric is important to allow for an easy integration into existing protocols. In our case, the size metric for KEMs consists of the public key and ciphertext size, since both need to be transmitted in our proposed solutions. Regarding DSAs, we use public key and signature size as metric. Both are transmitted via certificates to other nodes during the handshake. Considering the security metric, we use security strength estimations provided in the specification of each submission. These figures are based on the estimated cost of the best known attacks against the underlying lattice-problem, typically core-SVP hardness is evaluated.

Figure 1 shows the trade-off for estimated security and size for lattice-based schemes remaining in NIST's PQC process. Note that for submissions containing multiple schemes or multiple parameter sets we only consider one scheme or one set of parameters. In case of NTRU, we consider the recommended KEM parameter set NTRU-HRSS; for NTRU Prime, we only consider the parameter sets of Streamlined NTRU Prime. For Round 5, which specifies a total of 21 parameter sets, we only consider their specified IND-CCA secure KEM with ring parameter set and no error correction, i. e. R5ND_CCA_0d_KEM.

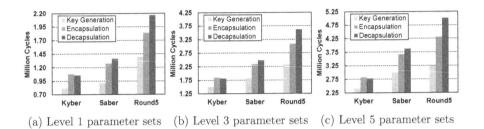

(a) Level 1 parameter sets   (b) Level 3 parameter sets   (c) Level 5 parameter sets

Fig. 2. Average performance of selected key encapsulation mechanisms.

Our evaluation shows that parameter sets for Kyber (Kyber512, Kyber768, and Kyber1024), Round 5 (R5ND_1CCA_0d, R5ND_3CCA_0d, and R5ND_5CCA_0d), and Saber (LightSaber, Saber, and FireSaber) offer a very good trade-off in terms of public key + ciphertext size and estimated security strength. Consequently, we select these three schemes for a further performance evaluation. From the trade-off in Fig. 1a, LAC seems like another promising candidate. However, attacks on LAC that allow to fully recover the secret key have been discovered decreasing our trust in this scheme [23,26]. We do not select other schemes for further evaluation, as their parameter sets imply an imbalanced security-size trade-off (NTRU-HRSS, NewHope, and Frodo), they have not attracted much attention in previous experimental studies (Three Bears and NTRU Prime), or known attacks significantly reduce their security estimations (LAC).

The security-size trade-off for digital signature schemes is shown in Fig. 1b. After an update to its Round 2 specification, qTESLA only provides provably-secure parameter sets that come with very large sizes for signatures and public keys. Ultimately, we select the remaining two signature algorithms—Falcon and Dilithium—for a further performance evaluation. Both seem to be promising signature algorithms, since public key and signature are reasonably sized and they provide parameter sets for different security strengths (level 1: Falcon512 and Dilithium2, level 3: Dilithium4, level 5: Falcon1024).

Preliminary Performance Evaluation. We continue with an evaluation of the standalone performance of the selected algorithms on our target platform—Raspberry Pi 3 Model B (see Sect. 5.2 for detailed description). In order to obtain cycle-accurate measurements, we added a kernel extension that enables access to the CPU cycle count register [3]. Our goal is to select parameter sets for three security levels with a balanced trade-off in terms of security, size, and performance. Our implementations of Kyber and Saber are based on code from PQClean. Round 5 has not been integrated there; consequently, we work with code from the official Round 5 submission[4]. Figure 2 shows the average cycle counts of 100 executions of the selected KEMs. Across all security levels Kyber shows the best performance. Considering all processing steps of KEMs, Kyber is significantly faster than Round 5 (in average 3.6×10^6 cycles at each security level) and also faster than Saber (in average 1.5×10^6 cycles at each security level). In comparison, the standalone performance of an ECDH key exchange based on SECP256R1, which corresponds to security level 1, takes 6.9×10^7 cycles on our evaluation platform, whereas Kyber512 only takes 2.9×10^6 cycles. Kyber has also been part of several previous studies resulting in similar assessment of its performance [18,39]. Consequently, we select the three parameter sets of Kyber for instantiating our solutions.

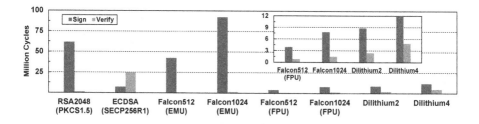

Fig. 3. Average performance of selected digital signature algorithms.

Having analyzed KEMs, we turn to the two selected signature schemes. Exploiting Falcon's floating-point arithmetic requires an underlying hardware floating-point unit (FPU) to support double-precision floating-point as defined by the IEEE 754 standard [41]. For devices without hardware FPU an implementation exists that emulates floating-point precision (Falcon-EMU). The ARMv8 instruction set of the Raspberry Pi 3 fulfills the aforementioned requirement, which allows us to evaluate both implementations, i.e. Falcon-FPU and Falcon-EMU [4]. Our implementation of Dilithium is based on code from PQClean, for the implementation of Falcon we make use of reference code from the official website[5]. Figure 3 shows the average cycle counts of signature generation and verification of the selected DSAs in comparison with ECDSA and RSA over 100 executions. Please note, we do not report performance measurements of key generation, since generation of new signing keys is typically required only rarely. Enabling floating-point operations by using Falcon-FPU increases signature generation in average 11.4 times compared to Falcon-EMU. Furthermore, Falcon's highest

---

[4] https://github.com/round5/code/tree/master/configurable.
[5] https://falcon-sign.info.

security parameter set is even 1.9×10^6 cycles faster than Dilithium's level 1 configuration in case floating-point operations are enabled. All parameter sets of Dilithium and Falcon-FPU outperform the conventional ECDSA SECP256R1, which corresponds to security level 1. The total runtime (signature generation plus verification) of SECP256R1 corresponds to 3.2×10^7 cycles on our evaluation platform. In comparison, Falcon512-FPU only takes 4.7×10^6 cycles and Dilithium2 1.1×10^7 cycles. Since Falcon provides very efficient sizes for signatures and public key and since our evaluation platform is able to use Falcon's floating-point arithmetic, we select it for instantiating our proposed solutions. However, Falcon does not offer a parameter set covering security level 3, thus for the instantiation regarding that security strength we work with Dilithium4. Besides that, we are not aware of any works that have shown fundamental weaknesses in either Falcon or Dilithium, and both have been part of previous experimental studies [39,46].

In accordance with our initial requirements, we instantiate our two proposed solutions with the following algorithms: We use Kyber512 and Falcon512-FPU regarding NIST security level 1, for security level 3 we use Kyber768 and Dilithium4, and for level 5 we work with Kyber1024 and Falcon1024-FPU.

5   Experimental Results and Evaluation

5.1   Implementation Notes

We rely on an open-source OPC UA stack—open62541 [38]—to implement our two solutions. Integration of hybrid key exchange, hybrid authentication, and hybrid signatures requires significant changes to the codebase of open62541. To allow for backward compatibility with non-hybrid aware nodes we implement a new security policy *Hybrid{1,3,5}_Basic256*. We add the respective parts of the hybrid key exchange based on KEM to the client and server code. The key derivation function is adapted to generate two sets of keying material and to combine these two sets using XOR. Alongside this combiner construction, the MAC creation and verification is added as part of the hybrid key exchange. The handling of hybrid authentication based on certificates is integrated and hybrid signature creation and verification is added to the source code. The quantum-resistant signature is appended to the message buffer (not encrypted), while the additional PQ public key and ciphertext of the respective KEM and MAC-value are added to the security header. Our PQ solution requires fewer modifications and uses the new security policy *PQ{1,3,5}*. The KEM-based key exchange is integrated in client and server code. In addition, the generation and verification of PQ signatures and the verification of PQ certificates is implemented. The handling of request and response message needs to be adapted accordingly.

Available tools for generating hybrid certificates either make use of combiners that are not fully backward compatible [47] or implement only a small subset of PQ schemes [12]. Because of these limitations, we implement a new software package capable of creating hybrid and PQ certificates. Our software is capable of creating the X.509 certificate structure from scratch and can freely modify the desired fields. In our case, we rely on two non-critical extensions for storing the additional public key and signature. Open62541 uses the cryptographic library mbedTLS for all security relevant functions including the verification of certificates. Therefore, the certificate chain and the trusted root certificates are passed to the verification function provided by mbedTLS. We are able to use this function without modifications, since our generated hybrid certificates are fully compliant to the X.509 standard. The verification function of mbedTLS allows to provide an optional callback function as parameter that is called after each certificate in the chain was verified. We use this callback mechanism to verify the additional PQ signature inside the custom extension of our hybrid certificates. It should be noted that verification of PQ certificates takes place outside mbedTLS, since we did not integrate our selected PQ schemes into this cryptographic library. Instead, we rely on its mechanism to parse encoded certificates, which required minor changes to mbedTLS because of unique algorithm identifiers used in our PQ X.509 certificates.

Table 1. Message and certificate sizes for both solutions (in bytes).

Solution		OSC Req.		OSC Rsp.		Cert. Chain	
		Single Cert.	Attch. CA Cert.	Single Cert.	Attch. CA Cert.	Single Cert.	Attch. CA Cert.
Conventional (RSA2048)		1,597	2,373	1,601	2,377	908	1,750
Hybrid	1 (Kyber512 + Falcon512 + RSA2048)	4,698	7,147	4,670	7,119	2,515	4,964
	3 (Kyber768 + Dilithium4 + RSA2048)	11,945	17,929	11,885	17,869	6,050	12,034
	5 (Kyber1024 + Falcon1024 + RSA2048)	7,770	11,755	7,806	11,791	4,051	8,036
PQ	1 (Kyber512 + Falcon512)	3,618	5,472	3,593	5,447	1,924	3,778
	3 (Kyber768 + Dilithium4)	10,211	15,598	10,154	15,541	5,457	10,844
	5 (Kyber1024 + Falcon1024)	6,562	9,952	6,601	9,991	3,460	6,850

5.2   Measurement Setup

Our setup resembles a typical use case for OPC UA within an industrial network: Two CPS (e.g.. control unit and gateway) wish to exchange data which requires the establishment of a secure channel. We select the Raspberry Pi 3 Model B as our evaluation platform. It features a 1.2 GHz quad-core CPU (ARM Cortex-A53), 1024 MB RAM, and requires a SD-card to store operating system and software. As affordable single-board computer, Raspberry Pis have become very popular prototyping platforms even for industrial use cases [44]. The two Raspberry Pis are connected to the same network via their 100 Mbit Ethernet interfaces, one is instantiated as OPC UA client and the other as OPC UA server. For our timing measurements we rely on the same kernel extensions introduced in *Preliminary Performance Evaluation* (see Sect. 4.3). Since our measurements also include network round-trip time and overhead of the network stack, we report the time elapsed until completion of the OPC UA handshake in milliseconds. Therefore, we convert the cycle counts obtained from the two Raspberry Pis to milliseconds.

Besides handshake completion time, we report the performance of OPC UA's security handshake in terms of message and certificate size. Our baseline measurement considers a conventional OPC UA security handshake using security policy *Basic256Sha256*. Both solutions are evaluated at three NIST security levels (see Sect. 4.3). This leads to a total of six different test cases: *Hybrid-{1,3,5}* and *PQ-{1,3,5}*. In addition, we evaluate each test case in two different scenarios regarding included certificates. In the first scenario, only a single device certificate (Single Cert.) is conveyed. The second scenario assumes that OPC UA client and server are part of a larger industrial network containing an intermediate (CA). In this case, the certificate chain contains the device and one attached intermediate CA certificate (Attch. CA Cert.). For each of the above test cases and the two scenarios, we record the establishment of 100 secure channels and state average values.

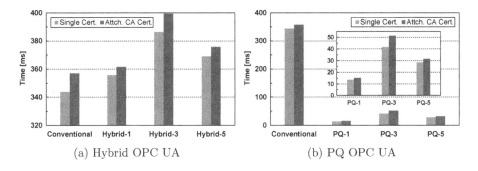

(a) Hybrid OPC UA   (b) PQ OPC UA

Fig. 4. Comparison of average handshake duration at different security levels.

5.3   Results and Evaluation

Hybrid OPC UA. Table 1 shows the impact of our hybrid security handshake on the size of the *OSC Req.* and *OSC Rsp.* message at different security levels. Besides that, certificate sizes for both scenarios are reported. As expected, because of the hybrid mode the message sizes increase at all levels. The highest increment compared to conventional OPC UA can be observed at security level 3: In case an additional CA certificate is attached, the size of the *OSC Req.* and *OSC Rsp.* message increases in average 7.5 times. Considering certificate sizes, the smallest increase with a factor of 2.8 is observed in certificates containing an additional Falcon512 public key and signature.

Figure 4a shows the results of the conducted performance measurements. As expected, the duration of the handshake increases at all security levels. However, the most time during the handshake is spent conventionally decrypting and signing the request and response message. In case a single hybrid certificate is conveyed, the fastest observed hybrid handshake adds only 11.9 ms to the total duration (Hybrid-1), while the slowest leads to an overhead of 42.6 ms (Hybrid-3). The extra time spent verifying an attached intermediate CA certificate is clearly visible in Fig. 4a and correlates to the reported verification times in Fig. 3. Since our implementation of Falcon makes use of floating-point operations, the overhead in Hybrid-1 and Hybrid-5 remains very small. Because both nodes are connected via fast network interfaces, the larger message sizes have only little impact on the total duration of the handshake. For example, sending the response and request message in Hybrid-3 (Attch. CA Cert.) takes 0.4 ms in total.

PQ OPC UA. Table 1 also shows the message and certificate sizes for our solution solely based on PQC. Similar to our hybrid solution, we observe that message sizes as well as certificate sizes increase at all security levels due to the larger public keys and signatures of the integrated PQ schemes. Besides that, instantiations using Falcon show a significantly lower overhead.

The results of our performance measurements (see Fig. 4b), however, show a significant improvement compared to OPC UA's conventional security handshake. Across all security levels our PQ solution is in average 11.5 times faster than conventional OPC UA. The fact that we omit all cryptographic operations based on RSA from OPC UA's conventional security handshake substantially increases its performance. With a handshake duration of just 28.6 ms, PQ-5 (Single Cert.) is even faster than PQ-3 with 41.8 ms. As the signature generation and verification times of Falcon and Dilithium are generally slower than Kyber's KEM functions, client and server spend most of the time during the handshake performing operations of the respective DSA. For example, deriving symmetric keying material requires 3.5 ms compared to 10.2 ms spent on the creation and verification of signatures in PQ-1. Similar to our hybrid approach, message sizes have only little impact on the overall duration of the security handshake.

Both our solutions demonstrate that Falcon is preferable over Dilithium in case both communicating nodes are capable of using its efficient floating-point arithmetic. Our Hybrid-5 and PQ-5 solution even leads to significantly less overhead—in terms of handshake duration and size—than Hybrid-3 and PQ-3. Since message sizes do not negatively impact the performance of the security handshake as much as slower algorithms do, we recommend to use Dilithium2 in case security level 1 is required and floating-point support can not be assumed.

6   Conclusion

In this work, we proposed two novel solutions for the integration of PQC into the security handshake of the industrial M2M protocol OPC UA. Our first solution considers hybrid key exchange, hybrid authentication, and hybrid signatures, while the second is solely based on quantum-resistant primitives. Compared to other works, this approach allowed us to investigate the total impact of PQC.

After the description of our two solutions, we selected three algorithms based on an investigation of all lattice-based schemes submitted to NIST's PQC standardization process. Subsequently, we instantiated our two solutions at three different NIST security levels using the respective parameter sets of Kyber{512,768,1024} for key establishment and Falcon{512,1024}-FPU or Dilithium4 for digital signatures. In our performance measurements, we compared the handshake duration of both solutions to that of conventional OPC UA for different security levels and certificate scenarios. Our hybrid integration leads to acceptable overhead in terms of latency and message sizes, while our PQ solution significantly outperforms conventional OPC UA at all security levels in terms of handshake duration. OPC UA provides mutual authentication based on X.509 certificates. Our hybrid solution works with hybrid certificates using non-critical extension fields to achieve backward compatibility with non-hybrid aware clients and servers. Furthermore, our described verification of hybrid certificates using mbedTLS applies to use cases outside the industrial domain. Ultimately, our two solutions provide comprehensive insights into the feasibility of integrating PQC into OPC UA and demonstrate that PQC is practical for ICS. Falcon and Dilithium are efficient options for PQ signature schemes; in case floating-point support is available, Falcon provides faster performance at smaller public key and signature size. In our two solutions, Kyber showed very efficient performance throughout all evaluated security levels. As future work, we will continue to investigate our two solutions, especially with regards to time-sensitive industrial applications and a formal security analysis of our proposed integrations including a detailed threat model. In addition, we plan to evaluate our proposed solutions in industrial networks under realistic conditions.

Acknowledgment. The work presented in this paper has been partly funded by the German Federal Ministry of Education and Research (BMBF) under the project "FLOQI" (ID 16KIS1074).

A   Algorithm Overview

Table 2. Conventional and PQ KEMs evaluated in this work.

KEM	NIST category	Intractable problem	Classical security	PQ security	sk (bytes)	pk (bytes)	ct (bytes)	Failure rate
Frodo640	1	LWE	144 bit	103 bit	19888	9616	9720	2^{-139}
Kyber512		Module LWE	111 bit	100 bit	1632	800	736	2^{-178}
LAC-128		Ring LWE	147 bit	133 bit	512	544	712	2^{-116}
LightSaber		Modules LWR	125 bit	114 bit	1568	672	736	2^{-120}
NewHope512		Ring LWE	112 bit	101 bit	1888	928	1120	2^{-213}
NTRU-HRSS		NTRU	136 bit	123 bit	1450	1138	1138	–
R5ND-1CCA-0d		General LWR	125 bit	115 bit	16	676	740	2^{-157}
SECP256R1		EC Discrete Log.	128 bit	–	32	65	65	–
SNTRUP653		NTRU	129 bit	117 bit	1518	994	897	–
BabyBear	2	Module LWE	154 bit	140 bit	40	804	917	2^{-156}
Frodo976	3	LWE	209 bit	150 bit	31296	15632	15744	2^{-200}
Kyber768		Module LWE	181 bit	164 bit	2400	1184	1088	2^{-164}
LAC-192		Ring LWE	286 bit	259 bit	1024	1056	1188	2^{-143}
R5ND-3CCA-0d		General LWR	186 bit	174 bit	16	983	1103	2^{-154}
Saber		Module LWR	203 bit	185 bit	2304	992	1088	2^{-136}
SNTRUP761		NTRU	153 bit	139 bit	1763	1158	1039	–
MamaBear	4	Module LWE	235 bit	213 bit	40	1194	1307	2^{-206}
FireSaber	5	Module LWR	283 bit	257 bit	3040	1312	1472	2^{-165}
Frodo1344		LWE	274 bit	196 bit	43088	21520	21632	2^{-253}
Kyber1024		Module LWE	254 bit	230 bit	3168	1568	1568	2^{-174}
LAC-256		Ring LWE	320 bit	290 bit	1024	1056	1424	2^{-122}
NewHope1024		Ring LWE	257 bit	233 bit	3680	1824	2208	2^{-216}
PapaBear		Module LWE	314 bit	280 bit	40	1584	1697	2^{-256}
R5ND-5CCA-0d		General LWR	253 bit	238 bit	16	1349	1509	2^{-145}
SNTRUP857		NTRU	175 bit	159 bit	1999	1322	1184	–

Table 3. Conventional and PQ DSAs evaluated in this work.

DSA	NIST category	Intractable problem	Classical security	PQ security	sk (byte)	pk(byte)	Signature (byte)
RSA2048	<1	Integer factorization	112 bit	–	256	259	256
Dilithium2	1	Module LWE	100 bit	91 bit	2800	1184	2044
Falcon512		NTRU	114 bit	103 bit	1281	897	690
qTESLAp-I		RingLWE	151 bit	140 bit	5184	14880	2592
SECP256R1		EC Discrete Logarithm	128 bit	–	32	65	73
Dilithium3	2	Module LWE	141 bit	128 bit	3504	1472	2701
Dilithium4	3	Module LWE	174 bit	158 bit	3856	1760	3366
qTESLAp-III		Ring LWE	305 bit	279 bit	12352	38432	5664
Falcon1024	5	NTRU	263 bit	230 bit	2305	1793	1330

References

1. Alkim, E., Avanzi, R., Bos, J.W., Ducas, L., de la Piedra, A., et al.: NewHope. NIST Post-Quantum Cryptography Standardization: Round 2 (2019)
2. Alkim, E., Bos, J.W., Ducas, L., Longa, P., Mironov, I., et al.: FrodoKEM. NIST Post-Quantum Cryptography Standardization: Round 2 (2019)
3. Arcus, M.: Using the Cycle Counter Registers on the Raspberry Pi 3 (2018). https://matthewarcus.wordpress.com/2018/01/27/using-the-cycle-counter-registers-on-the-raspberry-pi-3/
4. Arm Limited: Arm Architecture Reference Manual: Armv8 (2020). https://static.docs.arm.com/ddi0487/fb/DDI0487F_b_armv8_arm.pdf, ID040120
5. Arute, F., Arya, K., Babbush, R., Bacon, D., Bardin, J.C., et al.: Quantum supremacy using a programmable superconducting processor. Nature **574**, 505–510 (2019). https://doi.org/10.1038/s41586-019-1666-5
6. Avanzi, R., Bos, J.W., Ducas, L., Kiltz, E., Lepoint, T., et al.: CRYSTALS-Kyber. NIST Post-Quantum Cryptography Standardization: Round 2 (2019)
7. AWS Blog: Converting industrial protocols with AWS IoT Greengrass (2019). https://aws.amazon.com/de/blogs/iot/converting-industrial-protocols-with-aws-iot-greengrass/
8. Baan, H., Bhattacharya, S., Fluhrer, S., Garcia-Morchon, O., Laarhoven, T., et al.: Round5. NIST Post-Quantum Cryptography Standardization: Round 2 (2019)
9. Barker, E., Chen, L., Davis, R.: Recommendation for Key-Derivation Methods in Key-Establishment Schemes. Special Publication 800–56C Revision 2. NIST (2020). https://doi.org/10.6028/NIST.SP.800-56Cr2-draft
10. Bernstein, D.J., Chuengsatiansup, C., Lange, T., van Vredendaal, C.: NTRU Prime. NIST Post-Quantum Cryptography Standardization: Round 2 (2019)
11. Bindel, N., Akleylek, S., Alkim, E., Bareto, P.S.L.M., Buchmann, J., et al.: qTESLA. NIST Post-Quantum Cryptography Standardization: Round 2 (2019)

12. Bindel, N., Braun, J., Gladiator, L., Stckert, T., Wirth, J.: X.509-compliant hybrid certificates for the post-quantum transition. J. Open Source Softw. **4**, 1606 (2019). https://doi.org/10.21105/joss.01606

13. Bindel, N., Brendel, J., Fischlin, M., Goncalves, B., Stebila, D.: Hybrid key encapsulation mechanisms and authenticated key exchange. In: Ding, J., Steinwandt, R. (eds.) PQCrypto 2019. LNCS, vol. 11505, pp. 206–226. Springer, Cham (2019). https://doi.org/10.1007/978-3-030-25510-7_12

14. Bindel, N., Herath, U., McKague, M., Stebila, D.: Transitioning to a quantum-resistant public key infrastructure. In: Lange, T., Takagi, T. (eds.) PQCrypto 2017. LNCS, vol. 10346, pp. 384–405. Springer, Cham (2017). https://doi.org/10.1007/978-3-319-59879-6_22

15. Braithwaite, M.: Experimenting with Post-Quantum Cryptography (2016). https://security.googleblog.com/2016/07/experimenting-with-post-quantum.html

16. BSI: OPC UA Security Analysis (2017). https://www.bsi.bund.de/SharedDocs/Downloads/EN/BSI/Publications/Studies/OPCUA/OPCUA.html

17. BSI: Migration zu Post-Quanten-Kryptografie. Handlungsempfehlungen des BSI (2020). https://www.bsi.bund.de/SharedDocs/Downloads/DE/BSI/Krypto/Post-Quanten-Kryptografie. (available only in German)

18. Brstinghaus-Steinbach, K., Krauß, C., Niederhagen, R., Schneider, M.: Post-Quantum TLS on Embedded Systems. Cryptology ePrint Archive, Report 2020/308 (2020). https://eprint.iacr.org/2020/308

19. Campagna, M., Crockett, E.: Hybrid Post-Quantum Key Encapsulation Methods (PQ KEM) for Transport Layer Security 1.2 (TLS). Internet-Draft (work in progress) (2019). https://datatracker.ietf.org/doc/html/draft-campagna-tls-bike-sike-hybrid-01

20. Chen, C., Danba, O., Hoffstein, J., Hlsing, A., Rijneveld, J., et al.: NTRU. NIST Post-Quantum Cryptography Standardization: Round 2 (2019)

21. Crockett, E., Paquin, C., Stebila, D.: Prototyping post-quantum and hybrid key exchange and authentication in TLS and SSH. Cryptology ePrint Archive, Report 2019/858, 1–24 (2019). https://eprint.iacr.org/2019/858

22. D'Anvers, J.P., Karmakar, A., Roy, S.S., Vercauteren, F.: SABER: Mod-LWR based KEM. NIST Post-Quantum Cryptography Standardization: Round 2 (2019)

23. D'Anvers, J.P., Tiepelt, M., Vercauteren, F., Verbauwhede, I.: Timing attacks on error correcting codes in post-quantum schemes. In: Proceedings of ACM Workshop on Theory of Implementation Security Workshop - TIS 2019, pp. 2–9. ACM Press (2019). https://doi.org/10.1145/3338467.3358948

24. Ducas, L., Kiltz, E., Lepoint, T., Lyubashevsky, V., Schwabe, P., et al.: CRYSTALS-Dilithium. NIST Post-Quantum Cryptography Standardization: Round 2 (2019)

25. Fouque, P.A., Hoffstein, J., Kirchner, P., Lyubashevsky, V., Pornin, T., et al.: Falcon: Fast-Fourier Lattice-based Compact Signatures over NTRU. NIST Post-Quantum Cryptography Standardization: Round 2 (2019)

26. Guo, Q., Johansson, T., Yang, J.: A novel CCA attack using decryption errors against LAC. In: Galbraith, S.D., Moriai, S. (eds.) ASIACRYPT 2019. LNCS, vol. 11921, pp. 82–111. Springer, Cham (2019). https://doi.org/10.1007/978-3-030-34578-5_4

27. Hamburg, M.: ThreeBears. NIST Post-Quantum Cryptography Standardization: Round 2 (2019)

28. Kampanakis, P., Panburana, P., Daw, E., van Geest, D.: The Viability of Post-Quantum X.509 Certificates. Cryptology ePrint Archive, Report 2018/063, 1–18 (2018). https://eprint.iacr.org/2018/063

29. Kannwischer, M.J., Rijneveld, J., Schwabe, P., Stoffelen, K.: pqm4: Testing and Benchmarking NIST PQC on ARM Cortex-M4. Cryptology ePrint Archive, Report 844, 1–22 (2019). https://eprint.iacr.org/2019/844
30. Kwiatkowski, K., Valenta, L.: The TLS Post-Quantum Experiment (2019). https://blog.cloudflare.com/the-tls-post-quantum-experiment/
31. McGrew, D.: Cryptographic agility in the real world. In: Cryptographic Agility and Interoperability: Proceedings of a Workshop, pp. 34–38. National Academies Press (2016). https://doi.org/10.17226/24636
32. Micciancio, D., Regev, O.: Lattice-based cryptography. In: Bernstein, D.J., Buchmann, J., Dahmen, E. (eds.) Post-Quantum Cryptography, pp. 146–191. Springer, Heidelberg (2008). https://doi.org/10.1007/978-3-540-88702-7_5
33. Microsoft Azure: What is Connected Factory IoT solution accelerator? (2019). https://docs.microsoft.com/en-gb/azure/iot-accelerators/iot-accelerators-connected-factory-features
34. OPC Foundation: OPC UA Specification. Part 1 - Overview and Concepts Release 1.04 (2017)
35. OPC Foundation: OPC UA Specification. Part 4 - Services Release 1.04 (2017)
36. OPC Foundation: OPC UA Specification. Part 6 - Mappings Release 1.04 (2017)
37. OPC Foundation: OPC UA Roadmap (2020). https://opcfoundation.org/about/opc-technologies/opc-ua/opcua-roadmap/
38. Palm, F., Gruner, S., Pfrommer, J., Graube, M., Urbas, L.: Open source as enabler for OPC UA in industrial automation. In: 2015 IEEE 20th Conference on Emerging Technologies & Factory Automation (ETFA), pp. 1–6. IEEE (2015). https://doi.org/10.1109/ETFA.2015.7301562
39. Paquin, C., Stebila, D., Tamvada, G.: Benchmarking Post-Quantum Cryptography in TLS. Cryptology ePrint Archive, Report 2019/1447 (2019)
40. Paul, S., Niethammer, M.: On the importance of cryptographic agility for industrial automation. at - Automatisierungstechnik **67**, 402–416 (2019). https://doi.org/10.1515/auto-2019-0019
41. Pornin, T.: PQClean - Falcon implementations (integer-only code, constant-time) (2019). https://github.com/PQClean/PQClean/pull/210#issuecomment-513827611
42. Profanter, S., Tekat, A., Dorofeev, K., Rickert, M., Knoll, A.: OPC UA versus ROS, DDS, and MQTT: performance evaluation of industry 4.0 protocols. In: 2019 IEEE International Conference on Industrial Technology (ICIT), pp. 955–962 (2019). https://doi.org/10.1109/ICIT.2019.8755050
43. Puys, M., Potet, M.-L., Lafourcade, P.: Formal analysis of security properties on the OPC-UA SCADA protocol. In: Skavhaug, A., Guiochet, J., Bitsch, F. (eds.) SAFECOMP 2016. LNCS, vol. 9922, pp. 67–75. Springer, Cham (2016). https://doi.org/10.1007/978-3-319-45477-1_6
44. Sfera Labs: Strato Pi: Industrial Raspberry Pi (2020). https://www.sferalabs.cc/strato-pi/
45. Shor, P.W.: Polynomial-time algorithms for prime factorization and discrete logarithms on a quantum computer. SIAM J. Comput. **26**, 1484–1509 (1997). https://doi.org/10.1137/S0097539795293172
46. Sikeridis, D., Kampanakis, P., Devetsikiotis, M.: Post-quantum authentication in TLS 1.3. In: NDSS Symposium 2020 (2020). https://doi.org/10.14722/ndss.2020.24203
47. Stebila, D., Mosca, M.: Post-quantum key exchange for the internet and the open quantum safe project. In: Avanzi, R., Heys, H. (eds.) SAC 2016. LNCS, vol. 10532, pp. 14–37. Springer, Cham (2017). https://doi.org/10.1007/978-3-319-69453-5_2

48. Steblia, D., Fluhrer, S., Gueron, S.: Hybrid key exchange in TLS 1.3. Internet-Draft (work in progress) (2020). https://datatracker.ietf.org/doc/html/draft-ietf-tls-hybrid-design-00

49. Verizon: Data Breach Investigations Report (2020). https://enterprise.verizon.com/resources/reports/2020/2020-data-breach-investigations-report.pdf

50. Wollschlaeger, M., Sauter, T., Jasperneite, J.: The future of industrial communication. IEEE Ind. Electron. Mag. **11**, 17–27 (2017). https://doi.org/10.1109/MIE.2017.2649104

51. Xianhui, L., Yamin, L., Dingding, J., Haiyang, X., Jingnan, H., et al.: LAC. NIST Post-Quantum Cryptography Standardization: Round 2, pp. 1–28 (2019)

CSH: A Post-quantum Secret Handshake Scheme from Coding Theory

Zhuoran Zhang[1,2], Fangguo Zhang[1,2(✉)], and Haibo Tian[1,2]

[1] School of Data and Computer Science, Sun Yat-sen University,
Guangzhou 510006, China
`isszhfg@mail.sysu.edu.cn`
[2] Guangdong Province Key Laboratory of Information Security Technology,
Guangzhou 510006, China

Abstract. In secret handshake schemes, the members in the same organization can anonymously authenticate each other and commonly negotiate a secret key for communication. Since its proposing in 2003, secret handshake schemes become an important privacy protection cryptographic technique on internet applications. In this paper, a secret handshake scheme based on coding theory (we call CSH) is presented. This is the first code-based secret handshake scheme. CSH is constructed by combining the CFS signature system and Stern's identification system, thus the security of CSH relies on the syndrome decoding problem just like the two above systems. Moreover, as far as we know, CSH is the first scheme to use a generic construction of Fiat-Shamir paradigm in secret handshake schemes. This may lead to a more generic framework construction.

Keywords: Secret handshaking · Code-based cryptography · Post quantum cryptography · Privacy-preserving

1 Introduction

With the rapid development of information techniques, the Internet plays a more and more important role in people's life. On the one hand, we can shop, chat, and do many other daily routines online conveniently. On the other hand, the collecting of personal privacy becomes an easy task too. Given the pervasiveness and public nature of today's Internet, communication privacy is becoming a grave concern. Imagining that Alice is an FBI agent, and she is assigned to a criminal gang to connect with another agent Bob. For her own safety, Alice does not want to reveal her FBI credentials unless Bob is a genuine FBI agent. And vice versa for Bob. They not only need to find each other on the open channel, but also need to make sure their identities will not be recognized by other organizations or spies. In order to solve this problem, the notion of *Secret Handshake* has been proposed by Balfanz *et al.* [2] in 2003. They also introduced

© Springer Nature Switzerland AG 2020
L. Chen et al. (Eds.): ESORICS 2020, LNCS 12309, pp. 317–335, 2020.
https://doi.org/10.1007/978-3-030-59013-0_16

the first secret handshake scheme based on pairing, which can be viewed as a variant of Sakai *et al.*'s non-interactive key agreement scheme [22].

A secret handshake scheme usually contains a group authority (GA), a user initiator, and a user responder. Such privacy-preserving authentication means that one user will reveal his/her affiliation to the other user only if they both belong to the same organization. Thus if the participants are coming from different organizations, nothing about their identity and their affiliation will be leaked. Because of its wide application, the secret handshake scheme has become a hotspot since its proposing. Many different forms of secret handshake authentication schemes are proposed based on different cryptography primitives, which further improve the theoretical basis of secret handshake protocol, and promote the application of secret handshake protocol.

In 2004, Castelluccia *et al.* [6] constructed an efficient secret handshake scheme through the use of so-called CA-oblivious encryption. One year later, Zhou *et al.* [31] introduced an oblivious signature based envelope (OSBE) scheme to build secret handshake schemes. Both of them build their security over the computational Diffie-Hellman (CDH) assumption. Specifically, the former combines ElGamal encryption and Schnorr signature, and the latter is a compound of ElGamal encryption and DSA signature. Under the RSA assumption, Vergnaud [26] constructed some secret handshake schemes but fails to provide affiliation-hiding. In 2008, Stanislaw *et al.* [15] proposed an improved scheme based on RSA assumption called affiliation-hiding authenticated key exchange protocol. Xu and Yung [30] presented a secret handshake scheme based on PKI-like infrastructures. Their scheme is the first one which achieves weaker unlinkability with reusable credential, instead of one-time credential. From then on, lots of researches went into the so-called unlinkable secret handshake schemes, such as [13,14]. In order to meet the needs of more application scenarios, secret handshake schemes which can satisfy more requirements such as [28,29] were proposed.

However, the security of nearly all the above secret handshake schemes is based on the hardness of factoring or the presumed intractability of the discrete logarithm problem. With the discovery of Shor Algorithm [23] and the rapid development of quantum computers, the above problems together with many other problems that are thought to be difficult to solve by current electronic computers, may become not hard anymore. Thus, the conception of post-quantum cryptosystems raises public concern. Up to now, the code-based cryptography, lattice-based cryptography, multivariate cryptography, and hash-based cryptography are most commonly known types of post-quantum cryptography. Although many encryption and signature systems have been proposed to resist quantum computing attacks, there is no post-quantum secret handshake scheme as far as we know.

Among the post-quantum cryptosystems, code-based cryptosystems own many advantages. The code-based cryptosystems not only have effective encryption and decryption algorithms, but also rely their security on the NP-hard problems. The first code-based public-key encryption system was proposed in 1978 by McEliece [20]. It has already resisted more than 40 years of cryptanalysis since its invention. In 1986, Niederreiter [21] presented a variant of the McEliece encryption system. This variant inspired the first construction of code-based digital signature system in 2001, which is known as CFS signature [7] now. In 1993, Stern [24] presented an identification system from coding, and this scheme can be transformed into a signature system by Fiat-Shamir paradigm [10]. With the help of CFS signature system and Stern's identification system, we are going to construct a secret handshake scheme based on coding theory, which may be the first post-quantum secret handshake scheme.

Our Contributions: We propose the first post-quantum secret handshake scheme CSH from code-based cryptographic primitives. We use the CFS signature system in the AddMember step. Then we transform Stern's identification system by Fiat-Shamir paradigm into a signature system and use it in the Handshake step. The security of the CSH scheme relies on the syndrome decoding problem, which is known as an NP-hard problem. Our scheme is not only the first code-based post-quantum secret handshake scheme, but also the first one constructed from a signature transformed by generic Fiat-Shamir paradigm.

Organization: The remainder of this paper is organized as follows. In Sect. 2, we recall some preliminaries on coding theory and code-based cryptosystems. In Sect. 3, the definition and security properties of secret handshake scheme are reviewed. In Sect. 4, CSH is presented together with its security analysis, and then the performance and applications are showed. Sect. 5 concludes the paper.

2 Preliminaries

In this section, we present the notions of coding theory that are prerequisite for the following sections as well as basic knowledge about code-based cryptography.

2.1 Linear Codes

We now recall some basic definitions for linear codes.

An $[n, k]_q$ linear error-correcting code $\mathcal{C}$ is a linear subspace of a vector space $\mathbb{F}_q^n$, where $\mathbb{F}_q$ denotes the finite field of q elements, and k denotes the dimension of the subspace. The generator matrix G for a linear code is a $k \times n$ matrix with rank k which defines a linear mapping from $\mathbb{F}_q^k$ (called the message space) to $\mathbb{F}_q^n$. Namely, the code $\mathcal{C}$ is

$$\mathcal{C} = \mathcal{C}(\mathsf{G}) = \{\boldsymbol{x}\mathsf{G} \mid \boldsymbol{x} \in \mathbb{F}_q^k\}.$$

If $\mathcal{C}$ is the kernel of a matrix $\mathsf{H} \in \mathbb{F}_q^{(n-k) \times k}$, we call H a parity check matrix of $\mathcal{C}$, i.e.

$$\mathcal{C} = \mathcal{C}^\perp(\mathsf{H}) = Ker(\mathsf{H}) = \{\boldsymbol{y} \in \mathbb{F}_q^n \mid \mathsf{H}\boldsymbol{y} = \boldsymbol{0}\}.$$

We call a vector in $\mathcal{C}$ a codeword.

Given a codeword $\boldsymbol{c} = (c_1, c_2, \ldots, c_n) \in \mathbb{F}_q^n$, its Hamming weight $\mathsf{wt}(\boldsymbol{c})$ is defined to be the number of non-zero coordinates, i.e. $\mathsf{wt}(\boldsymbol{c}) = |\{i \mid c_i \neq 0, 1 \leq i \leq n\}|$. The distance of two codewords $\boldsymbol{c}_1, \boldsymbol{c}_2$, denoted by $d(\boldsymbol{c}_1, \boldsymbol{c}_2)$ counts the number of coordinates in which they differ. The minimum distance $d(\mathcal{C})$ of code $\mathcal{C}$ is the minimal value of the distance between any two different codewords. By the linearity of $\mathcal{C}$, we know that $d(\mathcal{C})$ is determined by the minimum Hamming weight among all non-zero codewords in $\mathcal{C}$, i.e.

$$d(\mathcal{C}) = \min\{\text{wt}(\boldsymbol{c}) \mid \boldsymbol{c} \in \mathcal{C} \setminus \{\boldsymbol{0}\}\}.$$

If $\boldsymbol{c}$ is a codeword and $\boldsymbol{c} + \boldsymbol{e}$ is the received word, then we call $\boldsymbol{e}$ the error vector and $\{i|e_i \neq 0\}$ the set of error positions, $\text{wt}(\boldsymbol{e})$ is the number of errors of the received word. If $\boldsymbol{r} = \boldsymbol{c} + \boldsymbol{e}$ is the received word and the distance from $\boldsymbol{r}$ to the code $\mathcal{C}$ is t', then there exists a codeword $\boldsymbol{c}'$ and an error vector $\boldsymbol{e}'$ such that $\boldsymbol{r} = \boldsymbol{c}' + \boldsymbol{e}'$ and $\text{wt}(\boldsymbol{e}') = t'$. If the number of errors is at most $(d-1)/2$, then it is sure that $\boldsymbol{c} = \boldsymbol{c}'$ and $\boldsymbol{e} = \boldsymbol{e}'$. In other words, the nearest codeword to $\boldsymbol{r}$ is unique when $\boldsymbol{r}$ has distance at most $(d-1)/2$ to $\mathcal{C}$.

There are many hard problems in coding theory, one of the well-known problems is general decoding problem. Syndrome decoding (SD) problem is a dual variant of general decoding problem, both of them have been proved to be NP-hard for general linear codes in [4]. Nowadays, most of the code-based cryptosystems are constructed on SD problem or its variant such as rank-SD problem. An instance of computation SD problem is as follows:

Instance 1. *Given an $(n-k) \times n$ parity check matrix H of code $\mathcal{C}$ over $\mathbb{F}_q$, a syndrome $\boldsymbol{s} \in \mathbb{F}_q^{n-k}$, the Computation SD Problem $CSD(n, k, w)$ asks for a vector $\boldsymbol{x} \in \mathbb{F}_q$, whose weight $\text{wt}(\boldsymbol{x}) = w$, such that $\mathsf{H}\boldsymbol{x} = \boldsymbol{s}$.*

An SD distribution is defined as follows: For positive integers, n, k, and w, the $SD(n, k, w)$ distribution chooses $\mathsf{H} \leftarrow_\$ \mathbb{F}_q^{(n-k) \times n}$ and $\boldsymbol{x} \leftarrow_\$ \mathbb{F}_q^n$ such that $\text{wt}(\boldsymbol{x}) = w$, and outputs $(\mathsf{H}, \boldsymbol{s} = \mathsf{H}\boldsymbol{x}^T)$. An instance of Decision SD problem is as follows:

Instance 2. *Given an matrix $\mathsf{H} \in \mathbb{F}_q^{(n-k) \times n}$ and a vector $\boldsymbol{y} \in \mathbb{F}_q^{n-k}$, the Decision SD Problem $DSD(n, k, w)$ asks to decide with non-negligible advantage whether $(\mathsf{H}, \boldsymbol{y})$ comes from the $SD(n, k, w)$ distribution or the uniform distribution over $\mathbb{F}_q^{(n-k) \times n} \times \mathbb{F}_q^{n-k}$.*

2.2   Goppa Codes and CFS Digital Signature System

A Goppa code $\Gamma(L, g)$ is defined by a support $L = \{\alpha_1, \alpha_2, \ldots, \alpha_n\}$ where $\alpha_i \in \mathbb{F}_{q^m}$ and a Goppa polynomial $g(x) \in \mathbb{F}_{q^m}[x]$ with degree $\deg(g) = t$ such that $g(\alpha_i) \neq 0$ for all i. The codewords $\boldsymbol{c} = (c_1, \ldots, c_n)$ in $\mathbb{F}_{q^m}^n$ is defined by

$$\sum_{i=1}^n \frac{c_i}{x - \alpha_i} = 0 \quad \mod g(x).$$

All the codewords form a linear code $\Gamma_{q^m}(L, g)$ of length n and dimension $n - t$ over $\mathbb{F}_{q^m}$. The Goppa code $\Gamma_q(L, g)$ with support L and Goppa polynomial g is the restriction of $\Gamma_{q^m}(L, g)$ to the field $\mathbb{F}_q$. As a subfield subcode of $\Gamma_{q^m}(L, g)$, the code $\Gamma_q(L,g)$ has dimension $k \geq n - mt$. Assuming $\Gamma_q(L,g)$ has dimension exactly $n - mt$, then a parity check matrix for $\Gamma_q(L,g)$ is given by

$$
\begin{aligned}
\mathsf{H} &= \begin{pmatrix}
g(\alpha_1)^{-1} & g(\alpha_2)^{-1} & \cdots & g(\alpha_n)^{-1} \\
\alpha_1 g(\alpha_1)^{-1} & \alpha_2 g(\alpha_2)^{-1} & \cdots & \alpha_n g(\alpha_n)^{-1} \\
\vdots & \vdots & \ddots & \vdots \\
\alpha_1^{t-1} g(\alpha_1)^{-1} & \alpha_2^{t-1} g(\alpha_2)^{-1} & \cdots & \alpha_n^{t-1} g(\alpha_n)^{-1}
\end{pmatrix} \\
&= \begin{pmatrix}
1 & 1 & \cdots & 1 \\
\alpha_1 & \alpha_2 & \cdots & \alpha_n \\
\vdots & \vdots & \ddots & \vdots \\
\alpha_1^{t-1} & \alpha_2^{t-1} & \cdots & \alpha_n^{t-1}
\end{pmatrix} \cdot \mathsf{diag}(g(\alpha_1)^{-1}, g(\alpha_2)^{-1}, \cdots, g(\alpha_n)^{-1})
\end{aligned}
$$

By written $\alpha_i^j g(\alpha_i)^{-1} \in \mathbb{F}_{q^m}$ into the sequence of coefficients $[a_0, \ldots, a_{m-1}]^T$ in the ground field $\mathbb{F}_q$, we can write the parity check matrix H into field $\mathbb{F}_q$ with size $mt \times n$.

CFS digital signature system [7] is the most widely known code-based signature system, its security relies on the SD problem. The original CFS signature system was introduced by Courtois et al. in 2001, and it uses a high rate Goppa code. Although it is attacked by a distinguisher that can distinguish a high rate Goppa code and random code [9], the CFS system is still thought to be safe under suitable parameters. The main idea of the CFS signature is to hide a Goppa code matrix with parameters $[2^m, 2^m - mt, 2t+1]$ correcting up to t errors. A CFS signature on a message m is generated by hashing m to a syndrome and then trying to decode it. However, for a t-error correcting Goppa code of length $n = 2^m$, only about $1/t!$ of the syndromes are decodable. Thus, a counter is appended to m, and the signer updates the counter until the hash value is decodable. The signature consists of both the error pattern with weight t and the counter value. There are also many variants of CFS signature system, such as modified-CFS [8], parallel-CFS [11] and so on. The modified-CFS scheme is very similar to the original CFS scheme, the only difference is to change the counter into a random value which will result in a formal security proof. In our CSH scheme, the modified-CFS is used, and we summarize it in Fig. 1. The parallel-CFS scheme achieves a higher security level with the sacrifice of computational cost, which is not necessary for our construction.

The security of modified-CFS signature is analysed in [8]. The modified-CFS signature system is existentially unforgeable under adaptively chosen message attack in the random oracle model, under the assumptions that Goppa parameterized bounded decoding (GPBD) problem and the Goppa code distinguishing problem is hard. GPBD problem is a variant of SD problem, with parameters $n = q^m, k = n - mt$ and $w = t$. Since there are no efficient algorithms to solve this problem, the assumption that GPBD problem is hard remains valid. Faugere et al. [9] points out that it is possible to efficiently distinguish a CFS public key (a binary Goppa parity check matrix) from a random matrix of the same size. However, this does not lead to any efficient key recovery attack up to now.

CFS.KeyGen(λ):	**CFS.Sign(m, sk):**
$H \in \mathbb{F}_q^{(n-k) \times n}$ is a parity check matrix of Goppa code $\mathcal{C}$ with error correcting capability t. C.SDecode is a syndrome decoding algorithm for $\mathcal{C}$. P is an $n \times n$ random permutation matrix. $M \in \mathbb{F}_q^{(n-k) \times (n-k)}$ is a matrix such that MHP is systematic. $H^{pub} \leftarrow$ MHP. $\mathcal{H}: \{0,1\}^* \to \mathbb{F}_q^{n-k}$ is a secure hash function. Output: $$param = \langle q, n, k, t, \mathcal{H} \rangle, pk = H^{pub},$$ $$sk = \langle M, P, C.SDecode \rangle.$$	do $\quad i \leftarrow_\$ \{1, 2, \ldots, q^{n-k}\}$ $\quad e = $ C.SDecode($M^{-1}\mathcal{H}(m\|i)$) until such e is found Output: $\sigma = (i, eP)$ **CFS.Verify(m, σ, pk):** compute $s = H^{pub}(eP)^T$ if $s = \mathcal{H}(m\|i)$ and wt(eP) $\leq t$ then output TRUE otherwise output FALSE.

Fig. 1. Modified-CFS signature system [8]

In practice, the best-known techniques for forging a signature are based on generic decoding of linear codes, which is equal to solving the CSD problem.

2.3   Stern Identification System

Stern proposed a code-based zero-knowledge system [24,25] whose security also relies on the SD problem. This system is a 3-pass prover-verifier protocol with cheating probability equal to 2/3. The prover $\mathcal{P}$ can make a zero-knowledge proof to the verifier $\mathcal{V}$ on that he knows a secret vector x solving an CSD(H, s, w) problem. The original version in [24] is thought to be inefficient, and thus many other code-based identification systems are proposed [5,12]. But Stern's system

Public data: $(H, \mathcal{H}, s, w)$ where $H \in \mathbb{F}_q^{(n-k) \times n}$ is a parity check of code $\mathcal{C}$ with error correcting capability w, and $\mathcal{H}$ is a collision-resistance hash function. s is a syndrome of code $\mathcal{C}$.	2. $\mathcal{P}$ sends $\quad cmt = (cmt(1), cmt(2), cmt(3))$ to $\mathcal{V}$.
$\mathcal{P}$ proves knowledge of $x \in \mathbb{F}_q^n$ such that $s = Hx$ and wt(x) $= w$ to $\mathcal{V}$ as follows:	3. $\mathcal{V}$ sends $ch \leftarrow \{0, 1, 2\}$.
1. $\mathcal{P}$ computes commitments by randomly choose a permutation π and a vector $y \in \mathbb{F}_q^n$: $cmt(1) = \mathcal{H}(\pi\|Hy), cmt(2) = \mathcal{H}(\pi(y)),$ $cmt(3) = \mathcal{H}(\pi(x+y)).$	4. if $ch = 0$, $\mathcal{P}$ sends $rsp = \langle \pi, y \rangle$, if $ch = 1$, $\mathcal{P}$ sends $rsp = \langle \pi, x+y \rangle$, if $ch = 2$, $\mathcal{P}$ sends $rsp = \langle \pi(x), \pi(y) \rangle$. 5. if $ch = 0$, $\mathcal{V}$ checks $cmt(1), cmt(2)$, if $ch = 1$, $\mathcal{V}$ checks $cmt(1), cmt(3)$, if $ch = 2$, $\mathcal{V}$ checks $cmt(2), cmt(3)$.

Fig. 2. Stern identification system [25]

is still the most widely recognized secure code-based identification system. We summarize Stern's system in Fig. 2.

Stern's protocol can be transformed into a signature system by Fiat-Shamir paradigm [10]. The main idea is changing the random challenge ch from the verifier into a value generated by a random oracle $\mathcal{H}_O$, which can be simulated by a hash function. Indeed, to sign a message m, the signer (who knows the secret) produces a valid transcript (cmt, ch, rsp) of the interactive protocol where $ch = \mathcal{H}_O(cmt, m)$. In our following construction, we need that each rsp has the same length no matter what the value of ch is. Since π has length $n \log n$ and the vector has length $n \log q$, we can achieve this property by adding a random string to the shorter one.

3   Model and Security Properties

In this section, the model and security definitions for secret handshakes are reviewed. Secret handshake scheme (denoted by SHS) operates in an environment which consists of a set of groups managed by a set of group authorities, and a set of users $U_1, \ldots, U_n$ registered into some groups. Based on the definitions in [2], our scheme consists of the following probabilistic polynomial-time algorithms:

- **SHS.Setup**: The Setup algorithm selects a security parameter λ to generate the public parameters *params* common to all subsequently generated groups.
- **SHS.CreateGroup**: CreateGroup can be viewed as a key generation algorithm executed by Group Authority (GA) to establish a group G. It takes *params* as input, and outputs group public key and secret key $(\mathsf{gpk}_G, \mathsf{gsk}_G)$.
- **SHS.AddMember**: AddMember is a two-party protocol run by user and GA, which adds a user to become a legitimate member of the group. After verifying the users' real identity (ID), GA outputs the user's group credential $cred_{ID}$ using GA's group keys $(\mathsf{gpk}_G, \mathsf{gsk}_G)$.
- **SHS.Handshake**: Handshake is a two-party authenticate protocol executed by a pair of anonymous users (U, V), where (U, V) are possible members belong to different groups. Generally, the handshake protocol is asymmetric. The protocol takes the anonymous users' secrets and some other public information as the input, and output "1" or "0" for each party. If U and V belong to the same group, the output is "1" and a session key K will be produced which can be used for subsequent secure communication between the two members.
- **SHS.TraceMember**: TraceMember is a polynomial time algorithm that is executed by GA. The algorithm outputs the identity of the user U while a transcript of secret handshake between one user U and the other user is submitted.
- **SHS.RemoveMember**: RemoveMember is a polynomial time algorithm that is authorized by GA. It takes its current Credential Revocation List $(\mathcal{CRL})$ and U's revocation tokens as inputs, whilst outputs an up-to-date $\mathcal{CRL}$ that includes new revocation records.

Now we recall some basic security definitions of SHS in brief. The formal definitions can be referred to the literature [2] for details. In general, a secret handshake scheme must satisfy the following security requirements:

1. **Completeness**: It means that the SHS protocol always outputs "1" when the interactive participants belong to the same group.
2. **Impersonator resistance**: This property means that an adversary who attempts to impersonate a legitimate member of one group can only succeed with a negligible probability. Namely, it is computationally infeasible without the knowledge of some secret key associated with the group key to successfully execute the protocol SHS with a member of this group. Formally, the property is defined in the following game $Game_{IR}$ between an adversary $\mathcal{A}$ and a challenger $\mathcal{B}$:
   - **Init**: The adversary $\mathcal{A}$ first sets chosen as (G^*, i^*). Then $\mathcal{B}$ simulates Setup, CreateGroup, and AddMember, and sends group public keys and up-to-date $\mathcal{CRL}$ to $\mathcal{A}$.
   - **Queries**: $\mathcal{A}$ can make the following queries, where the responses will be simulated by $\mathcal{B}$.
     - **Corruption Queries**: The corruption list Cor is initialized as $\emptyset$. The adversary $\mathcal{A}$ can query CreateGroup and AddMember for the secret information of some groups and members, except for (G^*, i^*). $\mathcal{B}$ will respond to the simulated information and update the corruption list Cor.
     - **Handshake Queries**: The adversary $\mathcal{A}$ can make queries on the Handshake protocol with the group members. The transcripts of the queried members can be generated by $\mathcal{B}$. During a handshake, $\mathcal{A}$ can query the hash functions used in the Handshake protocol. In particular, $\mathcal{A}$ can request non-interactive proof of knowledge on a random message for any member at the current interval.
   - **Challenge**: The challenger $\mathcal{B}$ acts as the group member i^* of G^* and executes handshake protocol with the adversary $\mathcal{A}$. $\mathcal{A}$ attempts to convince $\mathcal{B}$ that $\mathcal{A}$ is a legitimated member of the group G^*.
   - **Output**: If the adversary $\mathcal{A}$ on behalf of a member in the group G^* succeeds in executing Handshake with $\mathcal{B}$, the output of the game is "1". Otherwise, the output is "0". Note that it is required that $\mathcal{A}$ never queried any secret information with respect to the member i^* of the group G^*, i.e., $i^* \cap Cor = \emptyset$.

   Let $Adv_{\mathcal{A}}^{IR} = \Pr[Game^{IR} = 1]$, we say that SHS satisfies the impersonator resistance if the function $Adv_{\mathcal{A}}^{IR}$ is negligible for any polynomially-bounded adversary.
3. **Detector resistance**: This property means that an adversary will only succeed with a negligible probability when he activates an SHS with an honest user in order to identify his affiliation. Namely, it is computationally infeasible to determine whether a user's U is associated with the group public key gpk. Formally, the property is defined in the following game $Game_{DR}$ between an adversary $\mathcal{A}$ and a challenger $\mathcal{B}$:

- **Init**: The adversary $\mathcal{A}$ first sets chosen as (i_0, G_0, i_1, G_1). Then $\mathcal{B}$ simulates Setup, CreateGroup, and AddMember, and sends group public keys together with revocation lists of all groups to $\mathcal{A}$.
- **Queries**: $\mathcal{A}$ can make the following queries, where the responses will be simulated by $\mathcal{B}$.
  - **Corruption Queries**: The corruption list Cor is initialized as $\emptyset$. The adversary $\mathcal{A}$ can query CreateGroup and AddMember for the secret information of some groups and members, except for (i_0, G_0, i_1, G_1). Thus, $\mathcal{B}$ will respond to the simulated information and update the corruption list Cor.
  - **Handshake Queries**: The adversary $\mathcal{A}$ can make queries on the Handshake protocol with the group members. The transcripts of the queried members can be generated by $\mathcal{B}$. During a handshake, $\mathcal{A}$ can query the hash functions used in the Handshake protocol. In particular, $\mathcal{A}$ can request non-interactive proof of knowledge on a random message for any member at the current interval.
- **Challenge**: The challenger $\mathcal{B}$ selects a random bit $\phi \leftarrow \{0, 1\}$. And then $\mathcal{B}$ acts as the member i_ϕ in the group G_ϕ and executes handshake protocol with the adversary $\mathcal{A}$. $\mathcal{A}$ attempts to distinguish which group $\mathcal{B}$ belongs to.
- **Output**: The adversary $\mathcal{A}$ outputs ϕ' as its guess of ϕ.

Let $Adv_{\mathcal{A}}^{DR} = |\Pr[\text{Game}^{DR}(\phi = 0) = 1] - \Pr[\text{Game}^{DR}(\phi = 1) = 1]|$, we say that SHS satisfies the detector resistance if the function $Adv_{\mathcal{A}}^{DR}$ is negligible for any polynomially bounded adversary.

4. **Unlinkability**: This property means that no adversary can successfully associate two executions of SHS protocol involving the same honest user with a non-negligible probability.

4 Secret Handshake from Coding Theory

In this section, a code-based secret handshake scheme CSH will be described. First, we will present the construction of the CSH scheme. Second, the security and performance are analysed in the following subsections respectively. At last, we will give a short look at its applications.

4.1 The CSH Scheme

In the construction of our scheme, we use the techniques from CFS digital signature system and Stern's identification system. Since secret handshakes are private mutual authentications, the identification system with public verification can not be directly used to construct a secret handshake scheme. Therefore, we borrow the idea from the construction of secret handshake schemes from message recovery signatures. In the beginning, we transform Stern's identification system into a Fiat-Shamir type signature with 3 parts (cmt, ch, rsp). Instead of signing a message $\boldsymbol{m}$ by setting $ch = \mathcal{H}_O(cmt\|\boldsymbol{m})$, we make the signature by setting $ch = \mathcal{H}_O(ID\|\mathsf{gpk})$ where ID is the participant's pseudonym and gpk is the group public key, and do not send it to the receiver. Hence the ch can only be recovered with a proper group public key. Moreover, we abandon the cmt part when sending the signatures. Thus, although the receiver can not directly verify whether the signature is valid, some knowledge (we denote by CK) about the commitments cmt can be recovered through ch and rsp. Consequently, the receiver and signer will share the same CK if they are in the same group.

The CSH scheme is designed as follows.

- CSH.Setup: Given a security parameter λ, generates the global parameters $\mathsf{param} = (q, n, k, t, \kappa)$. Choosing secure hash functions $\mathcal{H}_1 : \{0,1\}^* \rightarrow \mathbb{F}^{n-k}$, $\mathcal{H}_2 : \{0,1\}^* \rightarrow \{0,1,2\}^\kappa$, $\{0,1\}^* \leftarrow \{0,1\}^\lambda \rightarrow \{0,1\}^\lambda$ and $\{0,1\}^* \leftarrow \{0,1\}^\lambda \rightarrow \{0,1\}^\lambda$.
- CSH.CreatGroup: The group author GA takes param as input to create a group G. GA runs CFS.KeyGen to get the group key pair $(\mathsf{gpk}_G, \mathsf{gsk}_G) = (\mathsf{H}, \Phi)$, where H is a party check matrix for a $[n, k, t]_q$ Goppa code, Φ is its syndrome decoding algorithm embedded the matrix M, P as described in Fig. 1.
- CSH.AddMember: When a user U wants to join to the group G, he chooses ID_u as his pseudonym. Then GA runs CFS.Sign(ID_u, gsk_G) and outputs a signature $cred_u = (e_u, c_u)$ as user U's credentials, i.e. $\mathsf{H}e_u^T = \mathcal{H}_1(ID_u\|c_u)$. GA sends $cred_u$ to the user and adds $(U, ID_u, cred_u)$ to the group member list $\mathcal{L}$.
- CSH.Handshake: Suppose the member U from group G_1 with credential $cred_u$, and another member V from group G_2 with $cred_v$, engage in handshake protocol.
  - $U \rightarrow V$: (ID_u, c_u, σ_u)
    1. U makes a signature by Stern's system with public data $(\mathsf{H}_{G1}, \mathcal{H}_4, \mathcal{H}_1(ID_u\|c_u), t)$ and secret value e_u:

    $$\Pi_u = (cmt_u^1, \ldots, cmt_u^\kappa; ch_u^1, \ldots, ch_u^\kappa; rsp_u^1, \ldots, rsp_u^\kappa)$$

    where $(ch_u^1, \ldots, ch_u^\kappa) = \mathcal{H}_2(ID_u\|\mathsf{gpk}_{G1})$.
    2. U sets $\sigma_u = (rsp_u^1, \ldots, rsp_u^\kappa)$.
    3. Denotes the checked value corresponds to ch_u^i and rsp_u^i as CK_u^i, and $CK_u = (CK_u^1, \ldots, CK_u^\kappa)$. Namely, V sets

    $$CK_u^i = \begin{cases} \langle cmt_u^i(1), cmt_u^i(2) \rangle, \ ch_u^i = 0 \\ \langle cmt_u^i(1), cmt_u^i(3) \rangle, \ ch_u^i = 1 \\ \langle cmt_u^i(2), cmt_u^i(3) \rangle, \ ch_u^i = 2 \end{cases}$$

    where

    $$\begin{cases} cmt_u^i(1) = \mathcal{H}_4(\pi_u^i\|\mathsf{H}_{G1}r_u^i) \\ cmt_u^i(2) = \mathcal{H}_4(\pi_u^i(r_u^i)) \\ cmt_u^i(3) = \mathcal{H}_4(\pi_u^i(e_u + r_u^i)) \end{cases}$$

    and π_u^i is a random permutation, $r_u^i \in \mathbb{F}_q^n$ is a random vector as described in Fig. 2.

- $V \rightarrow U$: $(ID_v, c_v, \sigma_v, RSP_v)$
  1. V checks $\mathcal{CRL}_{G2}$. If ID_u is in $\mathcal{CRL}_{G2}$, outputs "0" and abort. Otherwise continues.
  2. V computes $(ch_u'^1, \ldots, ch_u'^\kappa) = \mathcal{H}_2(ID_u \| \mathsf{gpk}_{G2})$.
  3. V computes $CK_u' = (CK_u'^1, \ldots, CK_u'^\kappa)$ for $i \in [1, \ldots, \kappa]$ by checking the rsp_u^i with correspond $ch_u'^i$. Namely, V departs rsp_u^i as

  $$rsp_u^i = \begin{cases} \langle \pi_u'^i, \boldsymbol{x}_u^i \rangle, & ch_u'^i = 0 \\ \langle \pi_u'^i, \boldsymbol{y}_u^i \rangle, & ch_u'^i = 1 \\ \langle \pi_u'^i(\boldsymbol{e}_u), \pi_u'^i(\boldsymbol{x}_u^i) \rangle, & ch_u'^i = 2 \end{cases}$$

  and then calculates

  $$CK_u'^i = \begin{cases} \langle \mathcal{H}_4(\pi_u'^i \| \mathsf{H}_{G2}\boldsymbol{x}_u^i), \mathcal{H}_4(\pi_u'^i(\boldsymbol{x}_u^i)) \rangle, & ch_u'^i = 0 \\ \langle \mathcal{H}_4(\pi_u'^i \| (\mathsf{H}_{G2}\boldsymbol{y}_u^i - \mathcal{H}_1(ID_u \| c_u)), \mathcal{H}_4(\pi_u'^i(\boldsymbol{y}_u^i)) \rangle, & ch_u'^i = 1 \\ \langle \mathcal{H}_4(\pi_u'^i(\boldsymbol{x}_u^i)), \mathcal{H}_4(\pi_u'^i(\boldsymbol{e}_u) + \pi_u'^i(\boldsymbol{x}_u^i)) \rangle, & ch_u'^i = 2 \end{cases}$$

  4. V makes a signature by Stern's system with public data $(\mathsf{H}_{G2}, \mathcal{H}_4, \mathcal{H}_1(ID_v \| c_v), t)$ and secret value $\boldsymbol{e}_v$:

  $$\Pi_v = (cmt_v^1, \ldots, cmt_v^\kappa; ch_v^1, \ldots, ch_v^\kappa; rsp_v^1, \ldots, rsp_v^\kappa)$$

  where $(ch_v^1, \ldots, ch_v^\kappa) = \mathcal{H}_2(ID_v \| \mathsf{gpk}_{G2})$.
  5. V sets $\sigma_v = (rsp_v^1, \ldots, rsp_v^\kappa)$.
  6. Denote the checked value corresponds to ch_v^i and rsp_v^i as CK_v^i, and $CK_v = (CK_v^1, \ldots, CK_v^\kappa)$. Namely, v sets

  $$CK_v^i = \begin{cases} \langle cmt_v^i(1), cmt_v^i(2) \rangle, & ch_v^i = 0 \\ \langle cmt_v^i(1), cmt_v^i(3) \rangle, & ch_v^i = 1 \\ \langle cmt_v^i(2), cmt_v^i(3) \rangle, & ch_v^i = 2 \end{cases}$$

  where

  $$\begin{cases} cmt_v^i(1) = \mathcal{H}_4(\pi_v^i \| \mathsf{H}_{G2}\boldsymbol{r}_v^i) \\ cmt_v^i(2) = \mathcal{H}_4(\pi_v^i(\boldsymbol{r}_v^i)) \\ cmt_v^i(3) = \mathcal{H}_4(\pi_v^i(\boldsymbol{e}_v + \boldsymbol{r}_v^i)) \end{cases}$$

  and π_v^i is a random permutation, $\boldsymbol{r}_v^i \in \mathbb{F}_q^n$ is a random vector.
  7. $RSP_v = \mathcal{H}_3(CK_u', CK_v, 0)$.
- $U \rightarrow V$: RSP_u
  1. U checks $\mathcal{CRL}_{G1}$. If ID_v is in $\mathcal{CRL}_{G1}$, outputs "0" and abort. Otherwise continues.
  2. U computes $(ch_v'^1, \ldots, ch_v'^\kappa) = \mathcal{H}_2(ID_v \| \mathsf{gpk}_{G1})$.

3. U computes $CK'_v = (CK'^1_v, \ldots, CK'^\kappa_v)$ for $i \in [1, \ldots, \kappa]$ by check the rsp^i_v with respective to ch'^i_v. Namely, U departs rsp^i_v as

$$rsp^i_v = \begin{cases} \langle \pi'^i_v, \boldsymbol{x}^i_v \rangle, & ch'^i_v = 0 \\ \langle \pi'^i_v, \boldsymbol{y}^i_v \rangle, & ch'^i_v = 1 \\ \langle \pi'^i_v(\boldsymbol{e}_v), \pi'^i_v(\boldsymbol{x}^i_v) \rangle, & ch'^i_v = 2 \end{cases}$$

and then calculates

$$CK'^i_v = \begin{cases} \langle \mathcal{H}_4(\pi'^i_v || \mathsf{H}_{G1}\boldsymbol{x}^i_v), \mathcal{H}_4(\pi'^i_v(\boldsymbol{y}^i_v)) \rangle, & ch'^i_v = 0 \\ \langle \mathcal{H}_4(\pi'^i_v || (\mathsf{H}_{G1}\boldsymbol{y}^i_v - \mathcal{H}_1(ID_v || c_v)), \mathcal{H}_4(\pi'^i_v(\boldsymbol{y}^i_v)) \rangle, & ch'^i_v = 1 \\ \langle \mathcal{H}_4(\pi'^i_v(\boldsymbol{x}^i_v)), \mathcal{H}_4(\pi'^i_v(\boldsymbol{e}_v) + \pi'^i_v(\boldsymbol{x}^i_v)) \rangle, & ch'^i_v = 2 \end{cases}$$

4. If $\mathcal{H}_3(CK_u, CK'_v, 0) = RSP_v$, U outputs "1".
   Then U sets $RSP_u = \mathcal{H}_3(CK_u, CK'_v, 1)$ and computes the session key as $K = \mathcal{H}_3(CK_u) \oplus \mathcal{H}_3(CK'_v)$.
5. Otherwise U outputs "0" and sets $RSP_u = \mathcal{H}_3(r)$ where r is a random number.
   - V checks whether $\mathcal{H}_3(CK'_u, CK_v, 1) = RSP_v$. If true, V outputs "1" and computes the session key $K = \mathcal{H}_3(CK'_u) \oplus \mathcal{H}_3(CK_v)$. Otherwise V output "0".

- CSH.TraceMember: When a dispute happens, the trace authority of GA will retrieve the handshaking transcript of U and V. GA can easily obtain the pseudonyms ID_u and ID_v from a transcript of a secret handshake instance. Through looking up in the lists of pseudonyms corresponding to the genuine identities, GA can identify which users have executed the malicious secret handshakes.
- CSH.RemoveMember: GA maintains and updates the information of a $\mathcal{CRL}$ after tracing a malicious group member. To remove a user U from the group, the GA looks up and removes the user's UserSecret $(ID_u, cred_u)$. Then the GA adds $(ID_u, cred_u)$ to the $\mathcal{CRL}$, and distributes warning notice to every other group member via an authenticated anonymous channel, which alerts not to execute any handshake performed by a user using any pseudonym in the $\mathcal{CRL}$.

Completeness: The completeness of CSH scheme relies on both participants can successfully recover the CK part by their group knowledge. When the responder V gets (ID_u, σ_u), he knows that the user U wants to prove he has a credential associated with ID_u given by the GA, and σ_u is the response part of the proof. Now take a look at the step of recovering CK_u. Suppose that U and V come from the same group with group public key H, and they are both honest participants. Then U's signature $\Pi_u = (cmt^i_u; ch^i_u; rsp^i_u)$ from Stern's system is a valid one, which means the verification of each (ch^i_u, rsp^i_u) will meet the corresponding commitment, i.e. for $ch^i_u = 0, 1, 2$ and rsp^i_u, the verifier can calculate $\langle cmt'^i_u(1), cmt'^i_u(2) \rangle, \langle cmt'^i_u(2), cmt'^i_u(3) \rangle$ and $\langle cmt'^i_u(1), cmt'^i_u(3) \rangle$ which exactly equal to the original commitment value. Since U and V are in the same group, V can recover the correct challenge part ch_u, and then calculates a correct CK_u. Thus U and V will share the same CK_u, and vice versa for CK_v. A session key $K = \mathcal{H}_3(CK_u) \oplus \mathcal{H}_3(CK_v)$ is also agreed for the following two-party communications.

4.2   Security Analysis

Now we provide the security results on CSH with respect to the impersonator resistance, detector resistance, and unlikability described in Sect. 3.

Theorem 1. *If there exists an adversary $\mathcal{A}$ can break the Impersonator Resistance of CSH with non-negligible probability, then there exists an algorithm $\mathcal{B}$ can solve the Decision SD problem with non-negligible probability.*

Proof. Suppose there exists an adversary $\mathcal{A}$ who can break the impersonator resistance property against some honest member U in group G^* identified by ID^*, then we can build an algorithm $\mathcal{B}$ to solve a Decision SD problem. When given a $\mathrm{DSD}(n, k, w)$ problem with a parity check matrix H^* and a vector s^*, $\mathcal{B}$ builds a sequence of games as follows:

– $Game^0$: This is the real impersonator resistance challenge game. In such a challenge, the adversary $\mathcal{A}$ has access to oracles

$$\{\mathcal{O}_{CG}, \mathcal{O}_{AM}, \mathcal{O}_{SH}, \mathcal{O}_{H1}, \mathcal{O}_{H2}, \mathcal{O}_{H3}, \mathcal{O}_{H4}\}$$

which execute CSH.CreateGroup, CSH.AddMember, CSH.Handshake and hash function $\mathcal{H}_1, \mathcal{H}_2, \mathcal{H}_3, \mathcal{H}_4$ respectively. $\mathcal{A}$ takes the public parameters as input, and outputs a triple (G^*, ID^*). $\mathcal{A}$ succeeds if ID^* belongs to G^*, G^* remains uncorrupt during $\mathcal{A}$'s execution, all corrupt users from G^* are excluded from G^* and if in the protocol CSH.Handshake between $\mathcal{A}$ and ID^*, the member ID^* returns "1". In each game $Game^i$ ($i \in [0, \dots, 3]$), we denote by IpR_i this event. Without loss of generality, we can suppose that any time $\mathcal{A}$ makes a query involving a pseudonym ID to one of the oracles $\mathcal{O}_{CG}, \mathcal{O}_{AM}, \mathcal{O}_{SH}$, and $\mathcal{A}$ has previously queried ID to the random oracle $\mathcal{O}_{H1}$. In particular, we suppose that $\mathcal{A}$ has queried ID^* and ID_A (the pseudonym used by $\mathcal{A}$ in the final execution of CSH.Handshake) to the random oracle $\mathcal{O}_{H1}$. By definition, we have $\Pr[\mathrm{IpR}_0] = Succ_{\mathcal{A}} = \epsilon$.
– $Game^1$: $\mathcal{B}$ randomly choose $i \leftarrow [1, \dots, q_{CG}]$ where q_{CG} is the maximum number for $\mathcal{A}$ to query $\mathcal{O}_{CG}$. Then in the i-th query, $\mathcal{B}$ simulates the oracle $\mathcal{O}_{CG}$, sets the public key as H^*, and public parameters (n, k, w). $\mathcal{B}$ aborts if the group G^* was not obtained at the i-th query to the oracle $\mathcal{O}_{CG}$. Hence we have $\Pr[\mathrm{IpR}_1] = \Pr[\mathrm{IpR}_0]/q_{CG}$.
– $Game^2$: $\mathcal{B}$ simulates the oracles $\mathcal{O}_{H1}$ and $\mathcal{O}_{AM}$ in CSH.AddMember in the following way:
  For a group G, let $\Lambda(ID)$ be a list stores the random number r such that $\mathcal{H}_1(ID||r)$ be a decodable syndrome. This list has been settled when the ID

occurs in the query in the first time by randomly choose r. Let Λ_G be a list stores (e, r) where $\mathsf{H}_G e = \mathcal{H}_1(ID\|r), \mathrm{wt}(e) = w$, i.e. the weight of e can be any possible value. Let Λ_H be a list stores s indexed by (ID, r). Namely, $\Lambda_G(ID) = (e, r)$ and $\Lambda_H(ID, r) = \mathcal{H}_1(ID\|r) = s$.

Then for each query (ID, r), $\mathcal{B}$ checks whether (ID, r) is in Λ_H or Λ_G. If not, $\mathcal{B}$ checks whether $\Lambda(ID) = r$. If so, $\mathcal{B}$ randomly choose e where $\mathrm{wt}(e) = t$, and calculates $s = \mathsf{H}_G e$. Meanwhile $\mathcal{B}$ adds (e, r) corresponds to ID into Λ_G, and adds s corresponds to (ID, r) into Λ_H. Else $\mathcal{B}$ randomly choose e, and adds $s = \mathsf{H} e$ corresponds to (ID, r) into Λ_H.

$\mathcal{B}$ outputs s in Λ_H corresponds to the query of (ID, r) to $\mathcal{O}_H$, and outputs (e, r) in Λ_G corresponds to the query of ID to $\mathcal{O}_{AM}$.

Specifically, in the query to $\mathcal{O}_{H1}(G_i)$, $\mathcal{B}$ randomly choose $j \leftarrow [1, \ldots, q_{H1}]$ where q_{H1} is the maximum number for $\mathcal{A}$ to query $\mathcal{O}_{H1}$. Then in the j-th query, $\mathcal{B}$ simulates the oracle $\mathcal{O}_{H1}$ by setting the hash value as s^*. $\mathcal{B}$ discards execution if ID_A was not the j-th query to the oracle $\mathcal{O}_{H1}$. Hence we have $\Pr[\mathrm{IpR}_2] = \Pr[\mathrm{IpR}_1]/q_{H1}$.

- *Game*^{3}: Finally, $\mathcal{B}$ simulates the CSH.Handshake protocols for members with pseudonyms say ID_u and ID_v. $\mathcal{B}$ can perfectly simulate the $\mathcal{O}_{SH}$ by querying other hash oracles. Therefore, we have $\Pr[\mathrm{IpR}_3] = \Pr[\mathrm{IpR}_2]$.

To summarize, when the *Game*^{3} terminates, $\mathcal{A}$ outputs (G^*, ID^*) such that G^*'s public key is H^* and $\mathcal{O}_{H1}(ID_A\|r_A) = s^*$. Then $\mathcal{A}$ interacts with the algorithm $\mathcal{B}$ emulating the member with pseudonym ID^* to execute the protocol CSH.Handshake.

- If the protocol is successful, $\mathcal{B}$ retrieves in its transcript and calculates CK'_A by ID_A and σ_A. In Stern's system, when $ch = 1$, the verifier will calculate $\mathsf{H} y$ by the knowledge of $x + y$ and public parameters, i.e. $\mathsf{H} y = \mathsf{H}(x + y) - \mathsf{H} x = \mathsf{H}(x + y) - s$. Hence there must exist e_A with $\mathrm{wt}(e_A) = t$ such that $\mathsf{H}^* e_A = \mathsf{H}^*(e_A + y) - \mathsf{H}^* e_A = \mathsf{H}^*(e_A + y) - s^*$, i.e. $\mathsf{H}^* e_A = s^*$. Therefore $\mathcal{B}$ outputs SD.
- Else $\mathcal{B}$ outputs $b \leftarrow_\$ \{SD, Uniform\}$.

As a result, the advantage for $\mathcal{B}$ to win a $\mathrm{DSD}(n, k, w)$ problem is $Adv_\mathcal{B} = Succ_\mathcal{A}/(q_{H1}q_{CG})$, which means that if the advantage for adversary $\mathcal{A}$ to break the impersonance resistance of CSH is non-negligible, then the algorithm $\mathcal{B}$ can solve the $\mathrm{DSD}(n, k, w)$ problem with non-negligible probability.

Theorem 2. *If there exists an adversary $\mathcal{A}$ can break the Detector Resistance of* CSH *with non-negligible probability, then there exists an algorithm $\mathcal{B}$ can solve the Decision SD problem with non-negligible probability.*

Proof. Suppose there exists an adversary $\mathcal{A}$ who can break the detector resistance property by distinguishing honest member U_0 in group G_0 identified by ID_0 and another honest member U_1 in group G_1 identified by ID_1, then we can build an algorithm $\mathcal{B}$ to solve a $\mathrm{DSD}(n, k, w)$ problem. In fact, using different group public key, a participant in the handshake protocol will recover different ch and CK when he receives (ID, c, σ). And he can not know whether the information he recovered is right or wrong until a RSP is received. More precisely, if there exists an adversary $\mathcal{A}$ who can break the detector resistance property against some honest member U in a group G identified by ID_u and group public key $\mathsf{gpk} = \mathsf{H}_G$, then $\mathcal{A}$ can verify the Stern's signature made by U. However, since U did not send any message about U's challenge ch_u and commitment cmt_u to $\mathcal{A}$, the only way for $\mathcal{A}$ to verify U's identity is to recover the correct ch'_u and CK'_u. Furthermore, the correctness of CK'_u can only be checked from the RSP_u by verifying $RSP_u = \mathcal{H}_3(CK'_u, CK_v, b)$ where $b = 0$ if $\mathcal{A}$ is the initiator and $b = 1$ otherwise. This means $\mathcal{A}$ has to make sure U will recover the correct CK_A by ID_A and σ_A. In Stern's system, when $ch = 1$, the verifier will calculate $\mathsf{H}y$ by the knowledge of $x + y$ and public parameters, i.e. $\mathsf{H}y = \mathsf{H}(x + y) - \mathsf{H}x = \mathsf{H}(x + y) - s$. In CSH, the above equation turns into $\mathsf{H}_G y = \mathsf{H}_G(e_A + y) - \mathsf{H}_G e_A = \mathsf{H}_G(e_A + y) - \mathcal{H}_G(ID_A \| c_A)$, where (e_A, c_A) is a valid credential from GA, i.e. $\mathsf{H}_G e_A = \mathcal{H}_1(ID_A \| c_A)$. Thus, $\mathcal{A}$ has to break the impersonate resistance of CSH. By Theorem 1, this theorem holds.

The **unlinkability** of CSH is ensured by one-time pseudonyms. Namely, CSH specify that a user obtains a list of pseudonyms for one-time use. The members in a group G will ask for a new credential for each secret handshake, and the used credential will be added to $\mathcal{CRL}$. This allows handshakes to be unlinkable.

4.3   Performance

In this subsection, we will analyse the performance of CSH from communication cost and computation cost. CSH is a code-based secret handshake scheme constructed by combining the CFS signature system and Stern's identification system. The main attacks on CFS system are information set decoding (ISD) attack and generalized birthday algorithm (GBA) attack. Up to now, the most effective ISD algorithms in binary field [3, 18, 19] take about $O(2^{n/20})$ in decoding. For GBA [27], the complexity of this attack against CFS with a counter is given by $L \log(L)$ with $L = \min\left(\dfrac{2^{mt}}{\binom{n}{t-\lfloor t/3 \rfloor}}, \sqrt{\dfrac{2^{mt}}{\binom{n}{\lfloor t/3 \rfloor}}}\right)$. The Goppa code distinguishing attack [9] only affects high rate Goppa codes. However, this result did not give rise to any attack on the scheme which then remains usable. In fact, in practice and despite the aforesaid distinguisher, the best attacks to the CFS problem are still generic and treat the public parity check matrix in CFS scheme as a random one. We choose parameters to reach the security level of 80 bits as $(q, m, t, \kappa) = (2, 19, 11, 137)$.

- **Communication Cost**: In CSH.AddMember, the user sends his ID to GA and GA returns $cred = (e, c)$ to the user. Since the group identifies their member by CFS signature system, w.l.g we can suppose the number of total members will not larger than $\binom{n}{t}$ where $n = 2^m$ is the length of underlying codes and t is its error correcting capability. And thus the length of ID is shorter than $\log(\binom{n}{t}) \leq 2^m - 1$. The credential has length $n + (n - k) = 2^m + mt < 64.1$ KB. The communication cost in this step is $2 \cdot 2^m - 1 + mt < 128.1$

KB. CSH.HandShake is a 3-round protocol, each member needs transmit 4 elements (ID, c, σ, RSP) to the other. ID is a string with length $2^m - 1$. c is a random counter with length mt. σ is the response part in a Stern's signature system, each single rsp in σ has length $n + n \log n$. In order to make the cheating probability under 2^{-80}, the interactive protocol should be executed 137 times, i.e. $\kappa = 137$. Hence the length of σ is $137 \cdot (n + n \log n) = 137(m + 1) \cdot 2^m$ bits and is about 171.2 MB. The length of RSP is 160 bits. Thus, the total communication cost in CSH.Handshake for each participant is $(2^m - 1) + mt + 137(m + 1) \cdot 2^m + 160$ bits ≈ 171.3 MB.

- **Computational Cost**: In CSH.AddMember, GA should calculate the credential for users by making CFS signatures. The CFS signature system cannot find a preimage for any syndrome $\mathcal{H}(ID)$, it does it only with probability $1/t!$, this fact is managed through the randomly choice of c which appended to ID, and then decode $\mathcal{H}(ID||c)$, i.e. modified-CFS system is used. Thus, on average, a credential (e, c) correspond to ID given by the CFS public matrix H is found with a small failure probability. If we choose Berlekamp-Massey algorithm [17] with complexity $O(n^2)$ as the syndrome decoding algorithm, the total computational complexity for making one CFS signature is about $2^{O(t)}O(n^2)$. The number of syndromes 2^{mt}, for a $[2^m, 2^m - mt, 2t + 1]$ Goppa code, gives an upper bound on the number of valid credentials. Considering each user needs a new credential to ensure the unlinkability of CSH, the CSH scheme can support valid group members to execute 2^{mt-1} successful secret handshake protocols. The above parameters take 13.1 MB for GA's public key. In CSH.Handshake, the main cost is the sign and verify algorithm in Stern's signature system. Here the public matrix H is GA's public key with size $mt \times n$, and the secret vector is e which is a part of user's credential with length n and weight t. The main computation cost here is the multiplication of one vector and a matrix in $O(n^2)$ and three hash computation. Thus the computational cost of CSH.Handshake is considered to be very small.

4.4   Application

For sensitive applications with strong privacy protection requirements, 2-party anonymous authentication that can hide the knowledge of organizations is needed. In a nutshell, secret handshake is such a technology proposed to solve this kind of 2-party anonymous authentication problem. With the help of secret handshake protocol, we can not only realize the secret transmission of data, but also avoid the leakage of important information such as organization.

With the arrival of the 5G era, the data transmission speed is faster and faster. It only takes a few seconds to download a high-definition film. In this context, the communication cost of secret handshake protocol is no longer the key factor restricting its application. The handshake protocol, which can be executed quickly, will play an increasingly important role. Since the AddMember step has finished before a handshake is requested, we can mainly consider the cost of the Handshake step in actual use. Thus, CSH.Handshake is such a protocol with high communication costs but small computational cost.

Nowadays, while people enjoy the convenience brought by the Internet and big data, how to protect personal privacy becomes a thorny problem. Thus, other than serves for state affairs with high confidentiality, secret handshake schemes play a more and more important role in people's daily life. Secret handshake schemes can be applied in the e-commerce field, e-medical system and information technique services, such as the communication and transmission of confidential documents between company partners, the sharing of patient's diagnosis data among different departments in hospitals, and so on. The secret handshake schemes have also become one of the important password authentication technologies to protect the privacy of users in Internet services. In the communication between companies, the group management center can be built with the help of trusted cloud server, and the anonymous authentication handshake scheme or group secret handshake scheme can be used to realize the authentication communication according to the needs. Another specific application of secret handshake protocol is defence against copyright infringement of videos that need a high-speed transmission. For example, HDMI is an interface standard of HDTV, which can provide high-definition lossless transmission of digital video or audio signals. By using anonymous two-way secret handshake schemes, the video providers can prevent illegal infringement interface from matching their HDMI. Considering the fast speed of executing CSH.Handshake, our scheme CSH may play a significant role in similar applications.

Li *et al.* [16] applied the secret handshake protocol [2] to the anonymous routing protocol and shows that it outperforms its predecessors in all the aspects of anonymity, security, and efficiency. With the continuous development of network application requirements, the secret handshake protocol can be applied in a more complex environment. For example, as mentioned by Ateniese *et al.* in [1], the secret handshake protocols can allow dynamic matching of attributes associated with the role in a treshold way. This can further extend to the designated role-based secret handshake protocol. The application of secret handshake can also be extended to protocols with dynamic matching, which plays an important role in the social network applications and vehicular ad-hoc network applications.

5   Conclusion

This paper aims to propose a new secret handshake scheme from coding theory. We combined the modified CFS signature system and Stern's identification system to construct CSH. Hence more efficient variants of CFS system and Stern's system will lead to a more efficient secret handshake scheme. For achieving simple traceability and unlinkability, our construction still uses one-time pseudonyms and achieves basic security requirements while GA is a trusted authority. Thus how to build post-quantum secret handshake schemes with stronger anonymity is still an open problem. As far as we know, this is the first time to use a Fiat-Shamir type signature in constructing secret handshake schemes. Since Fiat-Shamir paradigm is a generic transformation, we are considering whether this means that secret handshake protocols can be built based on any zero-knowledge proof system, which may lead to a more generic framework to construct secret handshake schemes. For future work, it is also interesting to build secret handshakes from other post-quantum cryptographic primitives, such as lattice based cryptosystems and supersingular isogeny based cryptosystems.

Acknowledgements. This work is supported by the National Key R& D Program of China (2017YFB0802500) and the National Natural Science Foundation of China (No. 61672550, No. 61972429) and Guangdong Major Project of Basic and Applied Basic Research (2019B030302008).

References

1. Ateniese, G., Kirsch, J., Blanton, M.: Secret handshakes with dynamic and fuzzy matching. In: Network and Distributed System Security Symposium, NDSS 2007, pp. 783–788. The Internet Society (2007)
2. Balfanz, D., Durfee, G., Shankar, N., Smetters, D., Staddon, J., Wong, H.: Secret handshakes from pairing-based key agreements. In: IEEE Symposium on Security and Privacy 2003, pp. 180–196. IEEE (2003)
3. Becker, A., Joux, A., May, A., Meurer, A.: Decoding random binary linear codes in $2^{n/20}$: how $1 + 1 = 0$ improves information set decoding. In: Pointcheval, D., Johansson, T. (eds.) EUROCRYPT 2012. LNCS, vol. 7237, pp. 520–536. Springer, Heidelberg (2012). https://doi.org/10.1007/978-3-642-29011-4_31
4. Berlekamp, E., McEliece, R., van Tilborg, H.: On the inherent intractability of certain coding problems. IEEE Trans. Inf. Theory **24**(3), 384–386 (1978)
5. Cayrel, P.-L., Véron, P., El Yousfi Alaoui, S.M.: A zero-knowledge identification scheme based on the q-ary syndrome decoding problem. In: Biryukov, A., Gong, G., Stinson, D.R. (eds.) SAC 2010. LNCS, vol. 6544, pp. 171–186. Springer, Heidelberg (2011). https://doi.org/10.1007/978-3-642-19574-7_12
6. Castelluccia, C., Jarecki, S., Tsudik, G.: Secret handshakes from CA-oblivious encryption. In: Lee, P.J. (ed.) ASIACRYPT 2004. LNCS, vol. 3329, pp. 293–307. Springer, Heidelberg (2004). https://doi.org/10.1007/978-3-540-30539-2_21
7. Courtois, N.T., Finiasz, M., Sendrier, N.: How to achieve a McEliece-based digital signature scheme. In: Boyd, C. (ed.) ASIACRYPT 2001. LNCS, vol. 2248, pp. 157–174. Springer, Heidelberg (2001). https://doi.org/10.1007/3-540-45682-1_10
8. Dallot, L.: Towards a concrete security proof of Courtois, Finiasz and Sendrier signature scheme. In: Lucks, S., Sadeghi, A.-R., Wolf, C. (eds.) WEWoRC 2007. LNCS, vol. 4945, pp. 65–77. Springer, Heidelberg (2008). https://doi.org/10.1007/978-3-540-88353-1_6
9. Faugère, J., Gauthier-Umaña, V., Otmani, A., Perret, L., Tillich, J.: A distinguisher for high-rate McEliece cryptosystems. IEEE Trans. Inf. Theory **59**(10), 6830–6844 (2013)
10. Fiat, A., Shamir, A.: How to prove yourself: practical solutions to identification and signature problems. In: Odlyzko, A.M. (ed.) CRYPTO 1986. LNCS, vol. 263, pp. 186–194. Springer, Heidelberg (1987). https://doi.org/10.1007/3-540-47721-7_12
11. Finiasz, M.: Parallel-CFS. In: Biryukov, A., Gong, G., Stinson, D.R. (eds.) SAC 2010. LNCS, vol. 6544, pp. 159–170. Springer, Heidelberg (2011). https://doi.org/10.1007/978-3-642-19574-7_11
12. Gaborit, P., Girault, M.: Lightweight code-based identification and signature. In: ISIT 2007, pp. 191–195. IEEE (2007)

13. Gu, J., Xue, Z.: An improved efficient secret handshakes scheme with unlinkability. IEEE Commun. Lett. **15**(2), 259–261 (2011)
14. Huang, H., Cao, Z.: A novel and efficient unlinkable secret handshake scheme. IEEE Commun. Lett. **13**(5), 363–365 (2009)
15. Jarecki, S., Kim, J., Tsudik, G.: Beyond secret handshakes: affiliation-hiding authenticated key exchange. In: Malkin, T. (ed.) CT-RSA 2008. LNCS, vol. 4964, pp. 352–369. Springer, Heidelberg (2008). https://doi.org/10.1007/978-3-540-79263-5_23
16. Li, S., Ephremides, A.: Anonymous routing: a cross-layer coupling between application and network layer. In: 2006 40th Annual Conference on Information Sciences and Systems, pp. 783–788. IEEE (2006)
17. Massey, J.: Shift-register synthesis and BCH decoding. IEEE Trans. Inf. Theory **15**(1), 122–127 (1969)
18. May, A., Meurer, A., Thomae, E.: Decoding random linear codes in $\tilde{O}(2^{0.054n})$. In: Lee, D.H., Wang, X. (eds.) ASIACRYPT 2011. LNCS, vol. 7073, pp. 107–124. Springer, Heidelberg (2011). https://doi.org/10.1007/978-3-642-25385-0_6
19. May, A., Ozerov, I.: On computing nearest neighbors with applications to decoding of binary linear codes. In: Oswald, E., Fischlin, M. (eds.) EUROCRYPT 2015. LNCS, vol. 9056, pp. 203–228. Springer, Heidelberg (2015). https://doi.org/10.1007/978-3-662-46800-5_9
20. Mceliece, R.J.: A public-key cryptosystem based on algebraic coding theory. DSN Progress report 42-44, pp. 114–116 (1978)
21. Niederreiter, H.: Knapsack-type cryptosystems and algebraic coding theory. Prob. Control Inf. Theory **15**(2), 159–166 (1986)
22. Sakai, R., Ohgishi, K., Kasahara, M.: Cryptosystems based on pairings. In: Symposium on Cryptography and Information Security, SCIS 2000 (2000)
23. Shor, P.: Algorithms for quantum computation: discrete logarithms and factoring. In: FOCS 1994, pp. 124–134. IEEE (1994)
24. Stern, J.: A new identification scheme based on syndrome decoding. In: Stinson, D.R. (ed.) CRYPTO 1993. LNCS, vol. 773, pp. 13–21. Springer, Heidelberg (1994). https://doi.org/10.1007/3-540-48329-2_2
25. Stern, J.: A new paradigm for public key identification. IEEE Trans. Inf. Theory **42**(6), 1757–1768 (1996)
26. Vergnaud, D.: RSA-based secret handshakes. In: Ytrehus, Ø. (ed.) WCC 2005. LNCS, vol. 3969, pp. 252–274. Springer, Heidelberg (2006). https://doi.org/10.1007/11779360_21
27. Wagner, D.: A generalized birthday problem. In: Yung, M. (ed.) CRYPTO 2002. LNCS, vol. 2442, pp. 288–304. Springer, Heidelberg (2002). https://doi.org/10.1007/3-540-45708-9_19
28. Wen, Y., Zhang, F.: Delegatable secret handshake scheme. J. Syst. Softw. **84**(12), 2284–2292 (2011)
29. Wen, Y., Zhang, F., Xu, L.: Secret handshakes from ID-based message recovery signature: a new generic approach. Comput. Electr. Eng. **38**(1), 96–104 (2012)
30. Xu, S., Yung, M.: K-anonymous secret handshakes with reusable credentials. In: CCS 2004, pp. 158–167. ACM (2004)
31. Zhou, L., Susilo, W., Mu, Y.: Three-round secret handshakes based on ElGamal and DSA. In: Chen, K., Deng, R., Lai, X., Zhou, J. (eds.) ISPEC 2006. LNCS, vol. 3903, pp. 332–342. Springer, Heidelberg (2006). https://doi.org/10.1007/11689522_31

A Verifiable and Practical Lattice-Based Decryption Mix Net with External Auditing

Xavier Boyen[1], Thomas Haines[2], and Johannes Müller[3]([✉])

[1] Queensland University of Technology, Brisbane, Australia
[2] Norwegian University of Science and Technology, Trondheim, Norway
[3] SnT, University of Luxembourg, Luxembourg City, Luxembourg
johannes.mueller@uni.lu

Abstract. Mix nets are often used to provide privacy in modern security protocols, through shuffling. Some of the most important applications, such as secure electronic voting, require mix nets that are *verifiable*. In the literature, numerous techniques have been proposed to make mix nets verifiable. Some of them have also been employed for securing real political elections.

With the looming possibility of quantum computers and their threat to cryptosystems based on classical hardness assumptions, there is significant pressure to migrate mix nets to post-quantum alternatives. At present, no verifiable and practical post-quantum mix net with external auditing is available as a drop-in replacement of existing constructions. In this paper, we give the first such construction.

We propose a verifiable decryption mix net which solely employs practical lattice-based primitives. We formally prove that our mix net provides a high level of verifiability, and even accountability which guarantees that misbehaving mix servers can also be identified. Verification is executed by a (temporarily trusted) public auditor whose role can easily be distributed. To demonstrate practicality for real-world systems, we provide detailed performance benchmarks on our stand-alone implementation based only on the most conservative lattice hardness assumptions.

Keywords: Lattice-based · Verifiability · Accountability · Mix net · e-voting

1 Introduction

Mix nets are indispensable building blocks of many secure e-voting systems. Essentially, a mix net consists of a sequence of mix servers which take as input the encrypted messages provided by the senders (e.g., the voters' ballots), secretely shuffle them, and eventually output the permutated plain messages (e.g., votes). Unless all mix servers are corrupted, the mixing breaks the individual connections between the senders and their revealed messages in the output. In the context of e-voting, this property guarantees vote privacy.

© Springer Nature Switzerland AG 2020
L. Chen et al. (Eds.): ESORICS 2020, LNCS 12309, pp. 336–356, 2020.
https://doi.org/10.1007/978-3-030-59013-0_17

However, for *secure* e-voting, it is also important to ensure that the voters' intent be reflected correctly in the election result, even if the mix servers are corrupted and actively try to tamper with the votes. Therefore, the employed mix net must be *verifiable* to guarantee that manipulating the senders' input, and generally incorrect mixing, can be detected. Moreover, in order to deter parties from misbehaving in the first place, *accountability* is often also desirable. This stronger form of verifiability provides identification of misbehaving parties and adjudication of possible disputes. In the literature, numerous mix nets [1,2, 4,10,11,14,15,17,19–21,23,27,28,31–33,35–37] have been proposed that aim to achieve verifiability and, in some cases, accountability. Some of them have also been used for securing real political elections (see, e.g., [12,34]).

With more and more powerful quantum computers on the horizon (see, e.g., [3]), it is important to protect mix nets even when actively targeted by quantum attackers, either contemporary or future. Due to the stark possibility that future quantum attackers could retrospectively break vote privacy, there is significant pressure to employ verifiable post-quantum mix nets *already today.*

Unfortunately, to the best of our knowledge, only a single verifiable mix net scheme [23], named sElect, has been proposed so far that could employ *practical* post-quantum, e.g., lattice-based, cryptosystems. The unique characteristic of sElect, in contrast to all other known verifiable mix nets, is to avoid (zero-knowledge) proofs of correct decryption, for which, at present, there exist no practical solutions whose security can be reduced to hardness assumptions over lattices (see Sect. 2 for more details). Alas, although sElect is provably secure, its security relies on the assumption that the senders/voters themselves verify the correctness of the final outcome. While this assumption is reasonable for some election scenarios, it cannot be justified in general; in particular, recourse and adjudication in case of voter-detected fraud is problematic.

Therefore, it is still an open problem to construct a practical and provably secure mix net with external auditing that can defend against quantum attacks.

Our Contributions. In this paper, we present the first highly efficient and practically realizable lattice-based decryption mix net that provides a high level of verifiability and even accountability. Verification is completely executed by a (temporarily trusted) public auditor whose role can easily be distributed. This structure is the same as the one of the prominent randomized partial checking (RPC) technique [20] which was, for instance, used for elections in the Australian state of Victoria [12].

To be more precise, our mix net employs a generalized version of the *trip wire technique* that was, in a specific variant, originally employed in the mix net by Khazaei et al. [21] as a subroutine. At a high level, in this technique, the input to the mix net consists of the real input messages plus a number of trip wire messages which to a mix server are indistinguishable from the real ones. Now, if a mix server wants to manipulate the outcome, it faces the risk of "touching" at least one trip wire, in which case the mix server would be caught cheating. In contrast to the specific variant in the mix net by Khazaei et al. [21], where each *mix server* can only inject a *single* trip wire in order to be able to guarantee correctness of the verification (which furthermore requires a proof of correct decryption), we depart from this as follows. First, we do not assume that the mix servers themselves inject the trip wires to "verify each other", but place that responsibility on a number of public auditors. Just one of these auditors needs to be trusted, and in fact only temporarily, because each auditor opens its inner state once mixing has finished—which incidentally greatly simplifies adjudication in case of dispute, and could not be done to the mixers themselves. Second, each auditor does not inject just a single but many trip wires, so that the probability of being caught cheating can be made very high even for manipulating just a few messages. Trip wires are cost effective, and since we further use only the most basic and black-box cryptographic primitives (namely, public-key encryption and digital signatures), the resulting mix net can be run with extremely efficient (lattice-based) primitives that more than compensate for the trip wires' overhead compared to ZKP-based approaches.

Altogether, our contributions are as follows:

1. We first discuss the unique constraints that come into play when building mix nets with quantum resistance, and related works (Sect. 2).
2. We describe how to extend an arbitrary *plain* (i.e., unverifiable, proof-less) decryption mix net (Sect. 3) with our general version of the trip wire technique (Sect. 4).
3. We precisely characterize how a decryption mix net with trip wires provides a high level of verifiability and even accountability (Sect. 5). A formal proof is provided in our technical report [7].
4. We instantiate the generic trip wire decryption mix net using *practical* lattice-based cryptography from conservative hardness assumptions (plain LWE). We have created a self-contained optimized implementation of the lattice construction, and provide detailed benchmarks that demonstrate its practicality for real-world elections at a high level of security (Sect. 6).
5. We candidly discuss the general properties, benefits and drawbacks of trip wire mix nets (Sect. 7) and conclude in Sect. 8.

2   Feasibility of Post-quantum Secure Mixing

Existing mix nets can be divided into two classes: decryption mix nets and re-encryption mix nets. In this section, we describe the main ideas of these two different approaches, and explain why the re-encryption approach is currently impractical for defending against quantum attackers.

In a *decryption mix net*, originally proposed by Chaum [8], an IND-CCA2 secure public-key encryption scheme is employed. Each mix server holds a public/secret key pair. Each sender iteratively encrypts its input message under the mix servers' public keys in reverse order, forming a multi-layered *onion*. Mixing starts with the first mix server, which "peels off" the outermost encryption layer, shuffles the result, forwards it to the second mix server, and so on. Eventually, all encryption layers have been removed and the plain input messages are published in the resulting random order.

In a *re-encryption mix net*, originally proposed by Park et al. [29], an IND-CPA secure public-key encryption scheme with re-encryption is employed. There is one public key whose secret key shares are distributed among a number of trustees. Each sender encrypts its input message under this public key. Mixing starts with the first mix server which re-encrypts its input ciphertexts, shuffles the result, forwards it to the second mix server, and so on. Eventually, all re-encrypted input ciphertexts are published in random order. Depending on the application, the output ciphertexts are either decrypted by the trustees or not.

In their plain unverifiable modes, re-encryption mix nets are more lightweight than decryption mix nets because input messages are not encrypted iteratively but only once under a single public key. However, when *verifiability in the presence of quantum attackers* is required, the trade-offs get more complicated. In general, there are two different approaches for making re-encryption mix nets verifiable, namely, by using randomized partial checking (RPC) [20] or by a proof of correct shuffle [1,2,4,10,11,14,15,17,19,27,28,32,33,36]. On the positive side, RPC could potentially be used for making a lattice-based re-encryption mix net verifiable, for instance using one of three recently proposed lattice-based proofs of correct shuffle [10,11,32], although it is unclear whether or not these are practical. On the negative side, both proof-based approaches merely guarantee that the output *ciphertexts* are in fact shuffled re-encryptions of the input ciphertexts. In order to be useful for our motivating application, i.e., secure e-voting, we also have to *decrypt* the output ciphertexts verifiably. Unfortunately, to the best of our knowledge, no *practical* zero-knowledge proofs of correct decryption for lattice-based encryption have been proposed so far, whose security can itself be reduced to lattice-based hardness assumptions. Even with recent developments on sublinear arguments from lattices [5], ZK proofs tend to be, and will likely remain, much heavier and more cumbersome than simple primitives such as public-key encryption based on comparable assumptions.

As the main purpose of our mix nets would be for quantum-secure e-voting where integrity, performance and simplicity of implementation are paramount, our best bet is to devise a lattice-based *decryption* mix net that provides external auditability using only the simplest fastest primitives as building blocks.

3   Plain Decryption Mix Net

In this section, we first recall the main idea of a plain unverifiable decryption mix net [8] and then precisely describe its protocol. In Sect. 4, we describe the generic trip wire technique to endow a plain decryption mix net with correctness verification (and external/third-party adjudication) of its outcome.

3.1   Idea

At a high level, a decryption mix net works as follows. It consists of a number of mix servers $M_1, \ldots, M_{n_{MS}}$ each of which holds a public/private (encryption/decryption) key pair (pk_k, sk_k). Each sender iteratively encrypts its plain input message m under the public keys $pk_1, \ldots, pk_{n_{MS}}$ of the mix servers in reverse order, and submits the resulting "nested" ciphertext c to the first mix server M_1. The first mix server uses its secret key sk_1 to "peel off" the outermost encryption layer of all input ciphertexts, then shuffles the decrypted messages, and forwards the permutated list to the second mix server M_2. The second mix server uses its secret key sk_2 to "peel off" the second encryption layer, then shuffles the result, and so on. Eventually, the last mix server $M_{n_{MS}}$ outputs all the plain messages initially chosen by the senders in random order.

3.2   Protocol

We now precisely describe the protocol of a plain decryption mix net.

Protocol Participants. A plain decryption mix net protocol is run among *senders*, $S_1, \ldots, S_{n_S}$, and *mix servers*, $M_1, \ldots, M_{n_{MS}}$, using a public, append-only *bulletin board* B.

Channels. For each sender S_i, we assume that there is an authenticated channel from S_i to the bulletin board B. These channels ensure that only eligible senders are able to submit their inputs.[1]

Cryptographic Primitives. We use the following cryptographic primitives:

- An IND-CCA2-secure public-key encryption scheme $\mathcal{E}$.[2]
- An EUF-CMA-secure signature scheme $\mathcal{S}$.

Protocol Overview. A protocol run consists of the following consecutive phases. In the *setup* phase, parameters are generated. In the *submission* phase, the senders generate and submit their input. In the *mixing* phase, the mix servers collaboratively mix the input.

We now describe each of the protocol phases in more detail.

Setup Phase. Each mix server M_k runs the key generation algorithm of the digital signature scheme $\mathcal{S}$ to generate its public/private (verification/signing) keys. The verification keys are published on the bulletin board B.

Each mix server M_k runs the key generation algorithm KeyGen of the public-key encryption scheme $\mathcal{E}$ to generate its public/private (encryption/decryption) key pair (pk_k, sk_k), and posts its public key pk_k on the bulletin board B.

Submission Phase. Each sender S_i iteratively encrypts its secret input m_i under the mix servers' public keys in reverse order, i.e., starting with the public key

---

[1] By assuming such authenticated channels, we abstract away from the exact method the senders use to authenticate to the bulletin board; in practice, several methods can be used, such as one-time codes, passwords, or external authentication services.

[2] We also require that $\mathcal{E}$, for every public-key and any two plaintexts of the same length, always yields ciphertexts of the same length. This seems to be satisfied by all practical schemes in existence, unless implemented with entropic compression.

$pk_{n_{MS}}$ of the last mix server $M_{n_{MS}}$ to the public key pk_1 of the first mix server M_1:

$$c_i = \mathsf{Enc}(pk_1, (\dots, \mathsf{Enc}(pk_{n_{MS}}, m_i))).$$

Mixing Phase. The list of ciphertexts $C_0 \leftarrow (c_i)_{i=1}^{ns}$ posted by the senders on the bulletin board B is the input to the mixing phase. Starting with the first mix server M_1, each mix server M_k takes C_{k-1} as input and performs the following tasks:

1. M_k decrypts all ciphertexts in C_{k-1} under its private key sk_k:

$$\forall i \in \{1, \dots, n_S\} \colon C_k'[i] \leftarrow \mathsf{Dec}(sk_k, C_{k-1}[i])$$

2. M_k chooses a permutation π_k over $\{1, \dots, n_S\}$ uniformly at random, and sets

$$\forall i \in \{1, \dots, n_S\} \colon C_k[\pi_k(i)] \leftarrow C_k'[i].$$

3. M_k posts C_k on the bulletin board B.

The output $C_{n_{MS}}$ of the last mix server $M_{n_{MS}}$ is the output of the mixing phase. It equals $(m_{\pi(i)})_{i=1}^{ns}$, where $\pi = \pi_{n_{MS}} \circ \dots \circ \pi_1$ is the overall permutation of the mix net.

4   Trip Wire Technique

We describe how to extend a plain decryption mix net (Sect. 3) with trip wires. We will show in Sect. 5 that the resulting mix net provides a high level of verifiability and accountability in the presence of fully malicious mix servers (Fig. 1).

4.1   Idea

At a high level, the trip wire technique works as follows. The plain decryption mix net is extended with a number of auditors $AD_1, \dots, AD_{n_{AD}}$ each of which executes the submission program of the senders n_{tw} times. For this purpose, AD_j chooses dummy input messages (e.g., 0^l) and encrypts them in layers as a normal user would. The resulting ciphertexts are called AD_j's *trip wires*. Furthermore, AD_j stores the random coins that it has used to generate its n_{tw} trip wires.

Now, the plain decryption mix net (with only "main mixing" servers for now) is run with this extended set of inputs. Once mixing has finished, each auditor AD_j reveals its inner states, including its trip wires' random coins. With this, the traces of AD_j's trip wires through the mix net can publicly be verified. If a mix server M_k did manipulate one of these dummy traces, this can be detected, and furthermore M_k can be held accountable through its digital signature (more on this later).

AD_1 AD_2 AD_3 M_1 M_2 M_3 $AD_{1,2,3}$

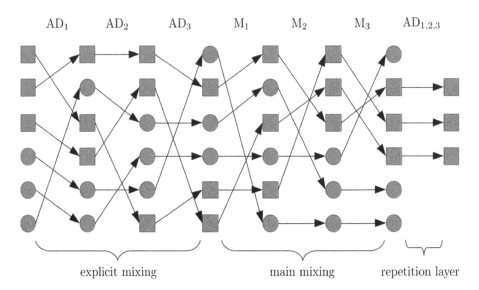

explicit mixing   main mixing   repetition layer

Fig. 1. Exemplified run of a decryption mix net with trip wires, where $n_{AD} = 3$, $n_{MS} = 3$, $n_S = 3$, and $n_{tw} = 1$. Rectangles and circles symbolize senders' and auditors' message traces, respectively.

Even though this high-level description gives some intuition on the "integrity challenge" underlying the trip wires, verifiability is obviously not yet guaranteed:

1. At the start of the mix, it is clear which input ciphertexts belong to the senders and which ones to the auditors. Hence, if the first mix server M_1 is malicious, then the adversary can completely manipulate the outcome of the mix net without being detected.
2. In general, we cannot assume that the auditors are able to simulate the senders' message distribution. Therefore, realistically, the auditors' and the senders' plaintext distributions are distinguishable. Now, recall that the last mix server $M_{n_{MS}}$ knows the final plaintext output before it publishes it. Hence, if $M_{n_{MS}}$ is malicious, then the adversary can undetectably manipulate the outcome of the mix net.

We propose the following additional mechanisms to address the above problems:

1. Prior to the main mixing, the input ciphertexts are "pre-mixed" using the same kind of plain decryption mix net, but now run by the auditors. This phase is called *explicit mixing* (see below for the reason). Unless all auditors are corrupted, it is no longer possible, for the original *main mixing* servers, to distinguish between the senders' ciphertexts and the auditors' trip wires.
2. An additional layer of encryption (whose private key is secret-shared among the auditors) is added directly to the plain input messages. This is called the *repetition layer*. Unless all auditors are corrupted, the last mix server gets to know only the still encrypted output.

Since secrecy of the explicit mixing and of the repetition layer is required only during main mixing, these two phases can be verified explicitly once the main mixing has finished. For this purpose, each auditor is supposed to reveal its explicit-mixing secret key as well as its secret key share of the repetition encryption layer after the final mix server has published its output.

4.2 Protocol

In this section, we precisely describe how to extend a plain decryption mix net (Sect. 3) with the trip wire technique.

To preserve readibility, we make the following implicit assumptions:

– Whenever a party (mix server or auditor) holding a verification/signing key pair publishes information, it signs this data with its secret signing key.
– Whenever a mix server or an auditor deviates from its honest program in an obvious way (e.g., refuses to participate, or publishes an invalid secret key), then the protocol aborts immediately and the misbehaving party is held accountable.
– In order to protect against replay attacks which may affect message privacy of senders (see, e.g., [9]), ciphertext deduplication is always in effect, where only the first instance of a multiply occurring ciphertext is retained.

Protocol Participants. The set of protocol participants is extended by a number of *auditors* $\mathsf{AD}_1, \ldots, \mathsf{AD}_{n_{\mathsf{AD}}}$.

Cryptographic Primitives. We additionally use an IND-CCA2-secure $(n_{\mathsf{AD}}, n_{\mathsf{AD}})$-threshold public-key encryption scheme $\mathcal{E}_{\mathsf{d}}$.[3]

Setup Phase. The following additional steps are executed.

Each auditor AD_j runs the key generation algorithm of the digital signature scheme $\mathcal{S}$ to generate its public/private (verification/signing) keys. The verification keys are published on the bulletin board B.

Each auditor AD_j runs the key generation algorithm KeyGen of the public-key encryption scheme $\mathcal{E}$ to generate a public/private key pair $(\mathsf{pk}_j^{\mathsf{expl}}, \mathsf{sk}_j^{\mathsf{expl}})$, and posts the public key $\mathsf{pk}_j^{\mathsf{expl}}$ on the bulletin board B.

Each auditor AD_j runs the key share generation algorithm KeyShareGen of the distributed public-key encryption scheme $\mathcal{E}_{\mathsf{d}}$ to generate a public/private key share pair $(\mathsf{pk}_j^{\mathsf{rep}}, \mathsf{sk}_j^{\mathsf{rep}})$, and posts the public key share $\mathsf{pk}_j^{\mathsf{rep}}$ on the bulletin board B. From those, using the deterministic algorithm PublicKeyGen, everyone can then compute the joint public key $\mathsf{pk}^{\mathsf{rep}}$.

Altogether, the public parameters consist of the public keys $\mathsf{pk}_1^{\mathsf{expl}}, \ldots, \mathsf{pk}_{n_{\mathsf{AD}}}^{\mathsf{expl}}$ for the explicit decryption mix net, the public keys $\mathsf{pk}_1, \ldots, \mathsf{pk}_{n_{\mathsf{MS}}}$ for the main decryption mix net, and the joint public key $\mathsf{pk}^{\mathsf{rep}}$ for the repetition encryption layer.

---

[3] Note that to jointly decrypt a ciphertext in $\mathcal{E}_{\mathsf{d}}$, all secret key shares are required.

Submission Phase (Senders). Each sender S_i first encrypts its message m_i under the auditors' joint public key pk^{rep}:

$$c_i^{rep} = Enc(pk^{rep}, m_i).$$

After that, S_i encrypts c_i^{rep} under the mix servers' public keys $pk_1, \ldots, pk_{n_{MS}}$ of the main decryption mix net in reverse order:

$$c_i^{main} = Enc(pk_1, (\ldots, Enc(pk_{n_{MS}}, c_i^{rep}))).$$

Afterwards, S_i encrypts c_i^{main} under the auditors' public keys $pk_1^{expl}, \ldots, pk_{n_{AD}}^{expl}$ of the explicit decryption mix net in reverse order:

$$c_i^{expl} = Enc(pk_1^{expl}, (\ldots, Enc(pk_{n_{AD}}^{expl}, c_i^{main}))).$$

The resulting ciphertext $c_i \leftarrow c_i^{expl}$ is S_i's input to the mix net.

Submission Phase (Auditors). Each auditor AD_j executes n_{tw} times the senders' submission steps described above, every time with (dummy) input message $m = 0^l$ (where l is the bit size of a sender's message). We denote AD_j's *trip wire* ciphertexts by $(c_{n_S+(j-1)\cdot n_{tw}+l})_{l=1}^{n_{tw}}$. Furthermore, AD_j stores the random coins that were used to generate its trip wire ciphertexts.

Mixing Phase. The input to the mixing phase is $(c_i)_{i \in I^{expl}}$ which consists of (a subset of)[4] the n_S ciphertexts submitted by the senders and the $n_{AD} \cdot n_{tw}$ ciphertexts submitted by the auditors. Then, the overall mixing phase consists of two consecutive parts:

1. *Explicit mixing:* The auditors use their secret decryption keys $sk_1^{expl}, \ldots, sk_{n_{AD}}^{expl}$ to run the plain decryption mix net (Sect. 3) with input $(c_i)_{i \in I^{expl}}$. The output of this mix net is $(\tilde{c}_i^{main})_{i \in I^{main}}$, where $I^{main} \subseteq I^{expl}$.

2. *Main mixing:* The mix servers use their secret decryption keys $sk_1, \ldots, sk_{n_{MS}}$ to run the plain decryption mix net (Sect. 3) with input $(\tilde{c}_i^{main})_{i \in I^{main}}$. The output of this mix net is $(\tilde{c}_i^{rep})_{i \in I^{rep}}$, where $I^{rep} \subseteq I^{main}$.

Auditing Phase. Each auditor AD_j publishes its secret key sk_j^{expl} associated to the explicit decryption mix net. With this, everyone can verify that the explicit mixing was executed correctly. If verification fails, a misbehaving auditor is identified through its signature and the whole protocol stops.

After that, each auditor AD_j publishes the random coins that it used to create its trip wires. With this, everyone can verify the integrity of trip wires' traces through the main decryption mix net. If verification fails, a misbehaving mix server is identified and the whole protocol stops.

Final Decryption Phase. Each auditor AD_j publishes its secret key share sk_j^{rep} on the bulletin board B. Then, for each ciphertext $\tilde{c}_i^{rep}$ ($i \in I^{rep}$), the decryption key share is publicly computed: $dec_{j,i}^{rep} \leftarrow DecShare(sk_j^{rep}, \tilde{c}_i^{rep})$. After that, the

---

[4] Recall that ciphertext duplicates or invalid ciphertexts are continuously removed.

decryption shares are combined to decrypt $\tilde{c}_i^{\mathsf{rep}}$: $\tilde{m}_i \leftarrow \mathsf{Dec}(\mathsf{dec}_{1,i}^{\mathsf{rep}}, \ldots, \mathsf{dec}_{n_{\mathsf{AD}},i}^{\mathsf{rep}})$. Alternatively, and more efficiently if the threshold encryption scheme supports it (it normally would), the joint secret key $\mathsf{sk}^{\mathsf{rep}}$ iz explicitly reconstituted from the published secret key shares $(\mathsf{sk}_j^{\mathsf{rep}})_{j \in [n_{\mathsf{AD}}]}$ and from there using $\mathsf{sk}^{\mathsf{rep}}$ each ciphertext $\tilde{c}_i^{\mathsf{rep}}$ is directly decrypted into $\tilde{m}_i$.

The list of decrypted messages $(\tilde{m}_i)_{i \in I^{\mathsf{rep}}}$ is the final outcome of the mix net.

5 Verifiability

In this section, we analyze verifiability of the decryption mix net with trip wires in the generic verifiability framework by Küsters, Truderung, and Vogt [25]. We briefly recall a specific instance of their general framework (Sect. 5.2) that was previously applied to analyze a number of further mix nets [18,23,24,26] and that we now apply to the decryption mix net with trip wires (Sect. 5.3).

5.1 Notation

The decryption mix net extended with the trip wire technique can be modeled in a straightforward way as a protocol $P_{\mathsf{DMN}}^{\mathsf{tw}}(n_{\mathsf{S}}, n_{\mathsf{S}}^{\mathsf{hon}}, n_{\mathsf{MS}}, n_{\mathsf{AD}}, n_{\mathsf{tw}})$, described next. The protocol participants consist of n_{S} senders (in total), $n_{\mathsf{S}}^{\mathsf{hon}}$ honest senders, n_{MS} mix servers, n_{AD} auditors, a scheduler SC, and a public append-only bulletin board B. The scheduler SC plays the role of the mix net authority and schedules all other agents in a run according to the protocol phases. We assume that SC and the bulletin board B are honest, i.e., they are never corrupted. While SC is merely a virtual entity, in reality, B should be implemented in a distributed way (see, e.g., [13,22]). The parameter n_{tw} denotes the number of trip wires per auditor.

5.2 Verifiability Definition

Intuitively, a mix net is verifiable if an incorrect final outcome is not accepted. More precisely, an outcome of the mix net should be rejected if it does not correspond to the actual input as provided by the senders. However, such a naïve definition of verifiability would be too strong for most reasonably verifiable mix nets. Instead, the intuitive definition is judiciously adjusted as follows:

1. Completeness is relaxed such that an incorrect outcome may falsely be accepted with some (small) probability $\delta \in [0, 1]$. This parameter is called the *verifiability tolerance* of the mix net.
2. Many verifiable mix nets (besides the ones equipped with a proof of correct shuffle) do not aim to ensure that *all* input messages are reflected correctly in the final outcome but *almost of them*. Therefore, we allow for manipulating a small number of k input messages. (Typically, the verifiability tolerance $\delta = \delta_k$ decreases when k increases.)

3. Since corrupted senders may not (necessarily) complain in case their messages were dropped or manipulated by a colluding mix net authority (e.g., mix server), it is often sufficient to guarantee the integrity of the final result only w.r.t. the honest input messages (as long as no input message stuffing by dishonest senders occurs.)

These refinements lead to the following expressive, widely applicable and currently accepted definition of verifiability. Due to space limitations, we state it informally, and refer to [25] for the complete formal definition.

Definition 1 (Verifiability (informal)). *A mix net protocol P provides (δ, k)-verifiability if and only if an outcome of the mix net is accepted with probability at most δ in case more than k honest input messages were manipulated (or any dishonest messages were inserted).*

5.3   Verifiability Result

We are now able to precisely state the verifiability level offered by the decryption mix net with trip wires according to Definition 1. The level depends on the number of honest senders n_S^{hon} and the number of dummy messages per auditor n_{tw}, as described in Sect. 5.1.

Assumptions. We prove the verifiability result under the following assumptions:

(V1) The public-key encryption scheme $\mathcal{E}$ is IND-CCA2-secure.
(V2) The (n_{AD}, n_{AD})-threshold public-key encryption scheme $\mathcal{E}_d$ is IND-CCA2-secure.
(V3) The signature scheme $\mathcal{S}$ is EUF-CMA-secure.
(V4) The scheduler SC, the bulletin board B, and at least one auditor are honest.
(V5) For all honest senders and auditors, the length of the message plaintext has the same size in each run of the protocol (given a security parameter).
(V6) For $\mathcal{E}$ and $\mathcal{E}_d$, we require that for any two plaintexts of the same length, their encryption always yields ciphertexts of the same length.

Our Result. Intuitively, the following theorem states that the probability that, in a run of the trip wire decryption mix net, more than k honest sender inputs have been manipulated, but the final result of this run is nevertheless accepted, is bounded by a function $\delta_k(n_S^{hon}, n_{tw})$ which we can quantify.

Theorem 1 (Verifiability). *Under the assumptions (V1) to (V6) stated above, the decryption mix net protocol with trip wires $P_{DMN}^{tw}(n_S, n_S^{hon}, n_{MS}, n_{AD}, n_{tw})$ is $(\delta_k(n_S^{hon}, n_{tw}), k)$-verifiable, where*

$$\delta_k(n_S^{hon}, n_{tw}) = \frac{\binom{n_S^{hon}}{k+1}}{\binom{n_S^{hon}+n_{tw}}{k+1}}.$$

The main reasoning behind this theorem is as follows. Since the explicit mixing and the shared decryption of the repetition layer are perfectly verifiable, an adversary can only manipulate honest senders' messages in the main mix net without being detected. However, due to the IND-CCA2-security of the underlying public-key encryption schemes, the adversary has to do this manipulation "blindly" as the $n_S^{hon} + n_{tw}$ ciphertexts related to the honest input parties (one ciphertext for each of the n_S^{hon} honest senders plus n_{tw} ciphertexts by the honest auditor) are indistinguishable. Now, if an adversary wants to manipulate $k + 1$ honest inputs, the probability that he is not caught cheating is captured by the following urn experiment. An urn contains n_S^{hon} white and n_{tw} black balls, representing honest messages and trip wires respectively. Upon picking $k + 1$ balls from this urn without replacement, the probability that none of the removed balls was black (i.e., no trip wire was touched) is exactly $\binom{n_S^{hon}}{k+1} / \binom{n_S^{hon}+n_{tw}}{k+1}$.

Importantly, for all k, the verifiability tolerance $\delta_k(n_S^{hon}, n_{tw})$ is bounded by $(n_S^{hon}/(n_S^{hon} + n_{tw}))^{k+1}$ which converges exponentially fast to 0 in the number of manipulated honest inputs k. For example, if we choose $n_{tw} = n_S$, then the adversary's risk is more than 90% for manipulating more than 4 honest messages, and even more than 99% for manipulating more than 7 honest messages.

Theorem 1 follows immediately from the even stronger result of *accountability* which we state and formally prove in our technical report [7]. Precisely, we show that a decryption mix net with trip wires even provides *individual accountability*. This security property not only guarantees that the correctness of the mix net outcome can be verified and adjudicated externally, but also that misbehaving parties can be identified and held accountable. Since Küsters et al. [25] proved that accountability is a stronger form of verifiability, the formal proof of our accountability result [7] implies the verifiability result (Theorem 1) stated above.

6   Implementation

In terms of efficiency, the core component of the verifiable mix net protocol is the (post-quantum) IND-CCA2-secure public-key encryption scheme: this component must be fast and robust enough to process thousands, possibly millions, of untrusted encrypted ballots, and do so safely and efficiently. Decryption performance is of particular importance since each mix server will be decrypting (one layer of) the entire set of encrypted ballots, while encryption is naturally done piecemeal in a distributed way by the individual voters. Encryption performance will start to matter (for the auditors) if the number of trip wires is large, or (for the voters) if there are many mix servers hence encryption layers.

6.1   Design

We implement essentially the textbook Regev scheme (technically its dual), which is provably secure under the now-classic LWE hardness assumption [30]. Our implementation attempts to remain faithful to the theoretical scheme, but rearranges it to optimize its computation. We merely summarize the salient points in Appendix A, while referring the reader to standard texts or surveys on lattice-based cryptography for background. We also elaborate on our implementation rationale in our technical report [7], in particular on why we refrained from choosing one of the current NIST proposals.

6.2   Technical Details

The concrete IND-CCA2-secure scheme we implement is a hybrid consisting of a lattice-based CCA2-secure KEM, combined with an AES256-based DEM with MAC. The KEM closely follows the original Regev cryptosystem [30]. For efficiency, much of the secret data is obtained from privately or randomly seeded AES256-based PRNG, and likewise much of the public key is generated on the fly from a publicly seeded AES128-based PRNG. The data is aligned and ordered so as to maximize performance of decryption over that of encryption. Standard techniques are used to provide chosen-ciphertext security for each of the KEM and the DEM, albeit only *implicitly* in the sense of [6], causing malformed ciphertexts to decrypt indistinguishably randomly rather than be explicitly rejected.

Our implementation targets the 240-bit security level, and accordingly uses 240-bit or wider data paths everywhere including the KEM-crypted symmetric session key and the DEM redundancy. As stated, we erred on the side of overshooting our target, and used lattices of dimension $n = 1024$, modulus $q = 2^{16}$ and sampler-mandated LWE discrete Gaussian noise $\sigma \approx 2$, providing sufficient headroom to reliably encode 5-bit payload per 16-bit ciphertext component. These parameters are conservative but not normative, and were selected mainly for the purpose of conducting a realistic performance evaluation.

As stated in the theoretical part of the paper, the final decryption (in the repetition layer) does not need to operate as a true threshold scheme, as long as the private key can be reconstructed from the revealed private-key shares. Regev key generation supports this, by linearity of the public key in the private key. We can thus reuse the same implementation for the final layer, by letting each auditor create its own private-key share and publish the corresponding share of the public key. The "dependent part" of the public key is reconstituted as the modular sum of the public shares. The "independent part" of the public key, namely the large public matrix "A", does not need to be shared and continues to be pseudorandomly expanded from a public random seed that the auditors will have agreed on. The private-key shares eventually revealed by the auditors can be verified for correctness based on the corresponding public-key shares, before the final decryption of the repetition layer takes place.

Our implementation is completely independent and does not borrow any code from anywhere, other than a few lines for the canonical usage of AESNI.

6.3   Local-Scale Performance

Our test platform is a 2019 Dell XPS 13 Intel i7-8565U CPU, fully mitigated in microcode and OS (Linux) against all known speculative execution/loading attacks, and running a single core 4.1 GHz measured clock frequency. At the

240-bit target security level, using 1024-dimension lattices, the performance of our IND-CCA2 subsystem (assuming 240-bit canary and 16-bit payload for the DEM plaintext) is as follows:

- Public-key size: 93 kB
- Ciphertext overhead incl. canary: 2.3 kB
- Key generation time: 36 μs (0.036 s)
- Encryption time: 201 μs (0.000201 s)
- Decryption time: 133 μs (0.000133 s)

For the verifiable mix net application, except when the number of ballots is extremely small, the processing time for each mix layer will be almost entirely dominated by the time it takes to decrypt the incoming ballots. As one would expect, the total decryption time for one layer of the mix net using a single core scales almost perfectly linearly with the number of ballots (see Sect. 6.4), and we measure (on the same hardware as above):

- 7500 ballots in 1.02 s, or
- 1 million ballots in 132.22 s.

In practice, the decryption running time for a large number of independent ciphertexts can be divided almost exactly by the number of available CPU cores.

6.4   Whole-System Performance

The random permutation of the ballots in each layer of the mix net does not add any appreciable time to the mixing, as long as it can be assumed that the entire set fits in random-access memory (normally a reasonable assumption). Likewise, while lattice-based signatures are generally much more expensive than lattice-based encryption, the overhead of issueing a single signature on the published mix does not make any difference with a large number of ballots.

Therefore, when considering the performance of the entire mix net, the two principal factors are the sequential nature of the encryption and decryption operations (by the voter and the mix servers respectively), and the growth of the multi-layer encrypted ballot with the number of layers. Clearly, the first consideration introduces a linear factor in the total mixing time, since each mix server must finish its mixing task on the entire set of ballots before certifying the result and passing the baton to the next mix server.

The ciphertext growth is also linear in the number of layers (or equivalently, mix servers). In our implementation at 240-bit security level, each layer adds an overhead of 2.3 kB (consisting of 2.1 kB of KEM data plus 0.2 kB of redundancy, to be added to the size of the plaintext, which in every layer except the first one is the total size of the previous layer's ciphertext). In theory, this makes the total mixing time quadratic in the number n of mix servers as $n \to \infty$. In practice, however, the hybrid encryption and decryption running times are dominated by the public-key KEM component, the processing of which at each layer is independent of the size of the DEM hence the number of layers.

Our experiments (Table 1) show the evolution of encryption and decryption running time of one layer of the "onion" or encrypted ballot, in function of the number of layers of encryption beneath it (level 0 indicates direct encryption of the plaintext vote, while level 1,000,000 is clearly impractical and provided only to show asymptotic behavior).

Table 1. Encryption/decryption times and ciphertext size in function of layer height.

# layers	ctx size (kB)	Encrypt time	Decrypt time
0	2,144	201 us	133 us
1	4,256	201 us	134 us
10	23,264	209 us	141 us
30	65,504	214 us	154 us
100	213,344	254 us	194 us
300	635,744	368 us	308 us
1,000	2,114,144	792 us	753 us
1,000,000	2,112,002,144	0.641 s	0.607 s

In practice, each layer corresponds to a different mixing server, so the total number of layers will likely remain small (less or much less than 100). Nevertheless, the experiments show that encryption and decryption times remain essentially constant (per layer) far beyond the range of practical applications, and that it is the size of the encrypted onions, rather than the time to encrypt or decrypt them, that is likely to be a limiting factor. The asymptotic linearity of encryption and decryption times (for each layer) only starts to show at very high numbers of layers. We also note that only the total number of layers and the total number of ciphertexts will matter, in terms of performance. How these are partitioned between explicit and main mixers, as well as between actual and trip wire ballots, has no significant impact on running time.

On the voter's size, encrypting a complete onion even for an exceedingly large 1000-layer mixnet would still require less than one second on most modern commodity consumer hardware.

7   Discussion

In this section, we discuss the main properties of the decryption mix net with trip wires.

Verifiability and Accountability. We have formally proven that, even if all mix servers are malicious, an adversary's risk of being caught cheating is high.

More precisely, our accountability result implies that, if an adversary wants to manipulate more than k honest inputs, then (at least) one misbehaving mix server is identified with probability at least $1 - (n_{\mathsf{S}}^{\mathsf{hon}}/(n_{\mathsf{S}}^{\mathsf{hon}} + n_{\mathsf{tw}}))^{k+1}$, where

$n_{\mathsf{S}}^{\mathsf{hon}}$ is the given number of honest senders and n_{tw} is the given number of trip wires per auditor. In particular, an adversary knows upfront that its risk of being caught cheating converges exponentially fast against 1 in the number of manipulated messages k.

Moreover, recall that during the main mixing, both the explicit mixing and the repetition layer are still locked. Hence, even if the race between two candidates A and B was very close, an adversary trying to manipulate the election outcome in favor of A by swapping just a few votes from B to A, has to do this "blindly". In particular, the adversary may accidentally swap a message from A to A. Hence, an adversary's chance of successfully manipulating the outcome is significantly reduced, independently of whether the adversary is caught cheating or not.

Altogether, for applications like secure e-voting where misbehaving parties have to face severe financial or legal penalties, an adversary knows a priori that manipulating the mix net outcome would be completely unreasonable.

External Auditing. At a high level, the verification procedure of the trip wire mix net can be regarded as an "integrity experiment" that is run between an adversary (controlling all mix servers) and an external auditor who challenges the adversary by "injecting" trip wires. If the adversary is able to manipulate (a significant number of) honest inputs without touching one of the trip wires, then the adversary wins. Our verifiability/accountability result (see above) provides an upper bound for an adversary's advantage in this experiment.

Obviously, the external auditor needs to be trusted for the integrity experiment but this trust assumption is mitigated by two means. First, the auditor's role can easily be distributed among several auditors, only one of which needs to be trusted. Second, the auditor opens its complete inner states once the integrity challenge has finished so that the correctness of its internal computation can publicly be verified.

Privacy. The original purpose of employing a mix net is to break the individual links between the senders and their plain input messages. This property is called *(message) privacy.* Assuming one honest mix server and one honest auditor, the trip wire mix net guarantees privacy. A formal proof of this statement can be based on a sequence of games similar to the one of our accountability proof.

Post-quantum Practicality. We experimentally benchmarked our verifiable mix net scheme using an optimized post-quantum IND-CCA2-secure hybrid encryption scheme, consisting of a lattice-based CCA2-secure KEM, combined with an AES256-based DEM/MAC. The benchmarks on our prototype demonstrate that our verifiable mix net with trip wires is highly practical, even for large-scale elections run entirely on commodity hardware.

Example: Practical PQ-secure e-voting. We now demonstrate how to put all these pieces together. For this purpose, we consider two different kinds of elections, one with few and one with many voters. Clearly, for an election with few voters, manipulating just a single message can have a major impact on the election result with significant probability, whereas this is much less likely for an election with many voters. In what follows, we exemplify how the decryption mix net with trip wires can be set up to take this aspect into account.

Assume we have one election with 100 and one with 100,000 voters. We choose $n_{tw} = 100,000$ for both elections. (For the sake of simplicity, we assume that all voters are honest, i.e., $n_S = n_S^{hon}$.) From the verifiability theorem, it follows that the risk of being caught cheating is $\geq 99\%$ both in the election with 100 voters for manipulating $k \geq 1$ votes, and in the election with 100,000 voters for manipulating $k \geq 7$ votes. Therefore, in both cases, an adversary knows upfront that tampering *significantly* with the election result is extremely risky.

At the same time, our benchmarks demonstrate that increasing n_{tw}, and hence tightening the verifiability tolerance, is practically negligible for applications like secure e-voting where the tallying phase is typically not too time-critical.

8   Conclusion

We have presented the first practical and verifiable lattice-based decryption mix net with external auditing which can be dropped into existing e-voting schemes. Our mix net is fully implemented and supports arbitrarily many authorities.

Acknowledgements. All authors acknowledge support from the Luxembourg National Research Fund (FNR) and the Research Council of Norway for the joint INTER project SURCVS (Number 11747298). Xavier Boyen thanks the Australian Research Council for support as Future Fellow under ARC grant FT140101145.

A   Optimizations

As mentioned in Sect. 6, our implementation attempts to remain faithful to Regev's theoretical scheme [30], but rearranges it to optimize its computation. In what follows, we summarize the salient points.

Our first optimization, which does deviate from the theoretical scheme, is, rather than to publish the encryption key as a truly random matrix, we publish a random seed from which the key is pseudo-randomly generated it using AES. This is a trick used by several NIST submissions, including the "front runners" still in play, but we have the opportunity to do it much faster without function calls as explained in our technical report [7].

We also mentioned the use of a strictly data-independent integer Gaussian sampler for generating the secret LWE noise. Using the Central Limit Theorem, we build a novel circuit-based sampler, which, when paired with hardware-accelerated AES, is able to produce i.i.d. integer samples of zero mean and small fixed variance (e.g., $\sigma \approx 2$) with provable 64-bit or 128-bit accuracy, suitable as LWE noise, in a few clock cycles.[5] For comparison, we note that FrodoKEM

---

[5] Sampling accuracy is here meant in the sense of KL divergence to a true integer Gaussian; clearly the output itself is just a small integer that fits in a few bits.

which also implements plain-LWE Regev encryption, samples from a cumulative probability table of about 20-bit effective accuracy, and goes to lengths to show that this is okay. Our equally fast sampler is far more accurate, and closely matches the theoretical Regev scheme which requires high accuracy. It is also data-independent (unlike table lookups whose access patterns could lead to certain cache-based side-channel leakage). The main downside of our sampler is that it is highly inflexible and specifically suited for that particular usage.[6]

Another extension to the textbook Regev scheme that we make, is the addition of an "all-or-nothing" transform such as [16] to obtain chosen-ciphertext security, as is standard practice. Unlike [16], though, our all-or-nothing transform does not cause invalid ciphertexts to be *rejected*, but only *scrambled* (or randomized), as proposed in [6]. We do this to ensure that there truly is no data-dependent test anywhere in the crypto code. We still get true CCA2 security, and we can recover the classic explicit rejection behavior simply by adding and testing a known string such as 0^λ to the plaintext, i.e., outside of the crypto code, to act as a "canary".

Other that those differences, the mathematical functions computed by our implementation are functionally very similar to the NIST submission FrodoKEM, which both implement the Regev scheme. This allows us to borrow from its extensive security analyses and use similar lattice dimension parameters to target similar security levels. In particular, we were pleasantly surprised that the FrodoKEM designers *chose* a Gaussian noise variance parameter close to that which was *forced* on us by our optimized but inflexible sampler circuit design—making their analysis a good match for our implementation. Nevertheless, to err on the side of caution, we collected lattice hardness estimates from multiple sources and, seeing that they loosely agreed with the FrodoKEM recommendations, we still rounded up the main lattice dimension to the higher power of 2. Minor optimizations included selecting the modulus $q = 2^{16}$ "`sizeof(short)`" for its ability to give us vectorized (SIMD) modular reductions for free.[7]

We reiterate that our optimizations mostly affect not *what* we compute but *how* we compute it. Unbound from the NIST rules, our code is not only faster, but also safer, not in a cryptographic sense but against side-channel attacks. None of our code borrows from the NIST contest; we merely frame this discussion in relation with NIST to preempt any preconception than official standardization would necessarily produce an optimal outcome.

---

[6] Describing and analyzing the sampler is very much out of the scope of this paper, but it is one example of a very impactful optimization we could make that does not involve *what* we compute, only *how* we do it.

[7] FrodoKEM had nearly the same idea, but for reasons unclear chose $q = 2^{15}$ not 2^{16}, perhaps because they could not use x86_64 vectorization intrinsics.

References

1. Adida, B., Wikström, D.: How to shuffle in public. In: Vadhan, S.P. (ed.) TCC 2007. LNCS, vol. 4392, pp. 555–574. Springer, Heidelberg (2007). https://doi.org/10.1007/978-3-540-70936-7_30

2. Adida, B., Wikström, D.: Offline/online mixing. In: Arge, L., Cachin, C., Jurdziński, T., Tarlecki, A. (eds.) ICALP 2007. LNCS, vol. 4596, pp. 484–495. Springer, Heidelberg (2007). https://doi.org/10.1007/978-3-540-73420-8_43

3. Arute, F., et al.: Quantum supremacy using a programmable superconducting processor. Nature **574**(7779), 505–510 (2019)

4. Bayer, S., Groth, J.: Efficient zero-knowledge argument for correctness of a shuffle. In: Pointcheval, D., Johansson, T. (eds.) EUROCRYPT 2012. LNCS, vol. 7237, pp. 263–280. Springer, Heidelberg (2012). https://doi.org/10.1007/978-3-642-29011-4_17

5. Baum, C., Bootle, J., Cerulli, A., del Pino, R., Groth, J., Lyubashevsky, V.: Sublinear lattice-based zero-knowledge arguments for arithmetic circuits. In: Shacham, H., Boldyreva, A. (eds.) CRYPTO 2018. LNCS, vol. 10992, pp. 669–699. Springer, Cham (2018). https://doi.org/10.1007/978-3-319-96881-0_23

6. Boyen, X.: Miniature CCA2 PK encryption: tight security without redundancy. In: Kurosawa, K. (ed.) ASIACRYPT 2007. LNCS, vol. 4833, pp. 485–501. Springer, Heidelberg (2007). https://doi.org/10.1007/978-3-540-76900-2_30

7. Boyen, X., Haines, T., Mueller, J.: A verifiable and practical lattice-based decryption mix net with external auditing. IACR Cryptology ePrint Archive, 2020:115 (2020)

8. Chaum, D.: Untraceable electronic mail, return addresses, and digital pseudonyms. Commun. ACM **24**(2), 84–88 (1981)

9. Cortier, V., Smyth, B.: Attacking and fixing helios: an analysis of ballot secrecy. In: IEEE CSF 2011, pp. 297–311 (2011)

10. Costa, N., Martínez, R., Morillo, P.: Proof of a shuffle for lattice-based cryptography. In: Lipmaa, H., Mitrokotsa, A., Matulevičius, R. (eds.) NordSec 2017. LNCS, vol. 10674, pp. 280–296. Springer, Cham (2017). https://doi.org/10.1007/978-3-319-70290-2_17

11. Costa, N., Martínez, R., Morillo, P.: Lattice-based proof of a shuffle. IACR Cryptology ePrint Archive, 2019:357 (2019)

12. Culnane, C., Ryan, P.Y.A., Schneider, S.A., Teague, V.: vVote: a verifiable voting system. ACM Trans. Inf. Syst. Secur. **18**(1), 3:1–3:30 (2015)

13. Culnane, C., Schneider, S.A.: A peered bulletin board for robust use in verifiable voting systems. In: IEEE CSF 2014, pp. 169–183 (2014)

14. Fauzi, P., Lipmaa, H., Siim, J., Zając, M.: An efficient pairing-based shuffle argument. In: Takagi, T., Peyrin, T. (eds.) ASIACRYPT 2017. LNCS, vol. 10625, pp. 97–127. Springer, Cham (2017). https://doi.org/10.1007/978-3-319-70697-9_4

15. Fauzi, P., Lipmaa, H., Zając, M.: A shuffle argument secure in the generic model. In: Cheon, J.H., Takagi, T. (eds.) ASIACRYPT 2016. LNCS, vol. 10032, pp. 841–872. Springer, Heidelberg (2016). https://doi.org/10.1007/978-3-662-53890-6_28

16. Fujisaki, E., Okamoto, T.: Secure integration of asymmetric and symmetric encryption schemes. J. Cryptol. **26**(1), 80–101 (2011). https://doi.org/10.1007/s00145-011-9114-1

17. Furukawa, J., Sako, K.: An efficient scheme for proving a shuffle. In: Kilian, J. (ed.) CRYPTO 2001. LNCS, vol. 2139, pp. 368–387. Springer, Heidelberg (2001). https://doi.org/10.1007/3-540-44647-8_22

18. Haines, T., Müller, J.: SoK: techniques for verifiable mix nets. In: IEEE CSF 2020 (2020, to appear)
19. Hébant, C., Phan, D.H., Pointcheval, D.: Linearly-homomorphic signatures and scalable mix-nets. IACR Cryptology ePrint Archive, 2019:547 (2019)
20. Jakobsson, M., Juels, A., Rivest, R.L.: Making mix nets robust for electronic voting by randomized partial checking. In: USENIX Security Symposium 2002, pp. 339–353 (2002)
21. Khazaei, S., Moran, T., Wikström, D.: A mix-net from any CCA2 secure cryptosystem. In: Wang, X., Sako, K. (eds.) ASIACRYPT 2012. LNCS, vol. 7658, pp. 607–625. Springer, Heidelberg (2012). https://doi.org/10.1007/978-3-642-34961-4_37
22. Kiayias, A., Kuldmaa, A., Lipmaa, H., Siim, J., Zacharias, T.: On the security properties of e-voting bulletin boards. In: Catalano, D., De Prisco, R. (eds.) SCN 2018. LNCS, vol. 11035, pp. 505–523. Springer, Cham (2018). https://doi.org/10.1007/978-3-319-98113-0_27
23. Küsters, R., Müller, J., Scapin, E., Truderung, T.: sElect: a lightweight verifiable remote voting system. In: IEEE CSF 2016, pp. 341–354 (2016)
24. Küsters, R., Truderung, T.: Security analysis of re-encryption RPC mix nets. In: IEEE EuroS&P 2016, pp. 227–242 (2016)
25. Küsters, R., Truderung, T., Vogt, A.: Accountability: definition and relationship to verifiability. In: ACM CCS 2010, pp. 526–535 (2010)
26. Küsters, R., Truderung, T., Vogt, A.: Formal analysis of chaumian mix nets with randomized partial checking. In: IEEE SP 2014, pp. 343–358 (2014)
27. Lipmaa, H., Zhang, B.: A more efficient computationally sound non-interactive zero-knowledge shuffle argument. In: Visconti, I., De Prisco, R. (eds.) SCN 2012. LNCS, vol. 7485, pp. 477–502. Springer, Heidelberg (2012). https://doi.org/10.1007/978-3-642-32928-9_27
28. Neff, C.A.: A verifiable secret shuffle and its application to e-voting. In: ACM CCS 2001, pp. 116–125. ACM (2001)
29. Park, C., Itoh, K., Kurosawa, K.: Efficient anonymous channel and all/nothing election scheme. In: Helleseth, T. (ed.) EUROCRYPT 1993. LNCS, vol. 765, pp. 248–259. Springer, Heidelberg (1994). https://doi.org/10.1007/3-540-48285-7_21
30. Regev, O.: On lattices, learning with errors, random linear codes, and cryptography. In: Proceedings of the 37th Annual ACM Symposium on Theory of Computing, 2005, pp. 84–93 (2005)
31. Schneier, B.: Applied Cryptography - Protocols, Algorithms, and Source Codein C, 2nd edn. Wiley, Hoboken (1996)
32. Strand, M.: A verifiable shuffle for the GSW cryptosystem. In: Zohar, A., Eyal, I., Teague, V., Clark, J., Bracciali, A., Pintore, F., Sala, M. (eds.) FC 2018. LNCS, vol. 10958, pp. 165–180. Springer, Heidelberg (2019). https://doi.org/10.1007/978-3-662-58820-8_12
33. Terelius, B., Wikström, D.: Proofs of restricted shuffles. In: Bernstein, D.J., Lange, T. (eds.) AFRICACRYPT 2010. LNCS, vol. 6055, pp. 100–113. Springer, Heidelberg (2010). https://doi.org/10.1007/978-3-642-12678-9_7
34. Verificatum Mix Net (VMN). https://www.verificatum.org/html/product_vmn.html
35. Wikström, D.: A sender verifiable mix-net and a new proof of a shuffle. In: Roy, B. (ed.) ASIACRYPT 2005. LNCS, vol. 3788, pp. 273–292. Springer, Heidelberg (2005). https://doi.org/10.1007/11593447_15

36. Wikström, D.: A commitment-consistent proof of a shuffle. In: Boyd, C., González Nieto, J. (eds.) ACISP 2009. LNCS, vol. 5594, pp. 407–421. Springer, Heidelberg (2009). https://doi.org/10.1007/978-3-642-02620-1_28

37. Wikström, D., Groth, J.: An adaptively secure mix-net without erasures. In: Bugliesi, M., Preneel, B., Sassone, V., Wegener, I. (eds.) ICALP 2006. LNCS, vol. 4052, pp. 276–287. Springer, Heidelberg (2006). https://doi.org/10.1007/11787006_24

A Lattice-Based Key-Insulated and Privacy-Preserving Signature Scheme with Publicly Derived Public Key

Wenling Liu[1,2], Zhen Liu[1(✉)], Khoa Nguyen[3], Guomin Yang[4], and Yu Yu[1,2(✉)]

[1] Shanghai Jiao Tong University, Shanghai, China
{lingeros,liuzhen,yyuu}@sjtu.edu.cn
[2] Shanghai Qi Zhi Institute, Shanghai, China
[3] Nanyang Technological University, Singapore, Singapore
khoantt@ntu.edu.sg
[4] University of Wollongong, Wollongong, Australia
gyang@uow.edu.au

Abstract. As a widely used privacy-preserving technique for cryptocurrencies, Stealth Address constitutes a key component of Ring Confidential Transaction (RingCT) protocol and it was adopted by Monero, one of the most popular privacy-centric cryptocurrencies. Recently, Liu et al. [EuroS&P 2019] pointed out a flaw in the current widely used stealth address algorithm that once a derived secret key is compromised, the damage will spread to the corresponding master secret key, and all the derived secret keys thereof. To address this issue, Liu et al. introduced Key-Insulated and Privacy-Preserving Signature Scheme with Publicly Derived Public Key (PDPKS scheme), which captures the functionality, security, and privacy requirements of stealth address in cryptocurrencies. They further proposed a paring-based PDPKS construction and thus provided a provably secure stealth address algorithm. However, while other privacy-preserving cryptographic tools for RingCT, such as ring signature, commitment, and range proof, have successfully found counterparts on lattices, the development of lattice-based stealth address scheme lags behind and hinders the development of quantum-resistant privacy-centric cryptocurrencies following the RingCT approach.

In this paper, we propose the first lattice-based PDPKS scheme and prove its security in the random oracle model. The scheme provides

Z. Liu—Supported by the National Natural Science Foundation of China (No. 61672339) and the National Cryptography Development Fund (No. MMJJ20170111).

K. Nguyen—Supported by the Gopalakrishnan - NTU Presidential Postdoctoral Fellowship 2018.

G. Yang—Supported by the Australian Research Council Discovery Project DP200100144.

Y. Yu—Supported by the The National Key Research and Development Program of China (Grant No. 2018YFA0704701), National Natural Science Foundation of China (Grant Nos. 61872236 and 61971192), the National Cryptography Development Fund (Grant No. MMJJ20170209), and the Major Program of Guangdong Basic and Applied Research (Grant No. 2019B030302008).

L. Chen et al. (Eds.): ESORICS 2020, LNCS 12309, pp. 357–377, 2020.
https://doi.org/10.1007/978-3-030-59013-0_18

(potentially) quantum security not only for the stealth address algorithm but also for the deterministic wallet. Prior to this, the existing deterministic wallet algorithms, which have been widely adopted by most Bitcoin-like cryptocurrencies due to its easy backup/recovery and trustless audits, are not quantum resistant.

Keywords: Lattice-based · Signature · Privacy preservation · Stealth address

1   Introduction

The past decade has witnessed the rapid development of cryptocurrencies since the invention of the Bitcoin [20]. Bitcoin had been regarded as an innovative payment network with high anonymity, and its emergence brings the prosperity of blockchain technology and cryptocurrency. However, as shown by [17,26], Bitcoin is not truly "anonymous" but only "pseudonymous". In Bitcoin-like cryptocurrency systems, digital signature schemes are used to authorize and authenticate transactions. Each coin is assigned a public key and a value, where the public key specifies the ownership of the coin. When a user wants to spend a coin (pk_{in}, v) and transfer the value to another owner with public key pk_{out}, he issues a transaction tx that takes in (say, consumes) the coin (pk_{in}, v) and outputs (say, generates) a new coin (pk_{out}, v), and associate the transaction with a signature σ which is valid with respect to the transaction (as the signed message) and the spent coin's public key pk_{in}. Bitcoin achieves only pseudonym since information including the sender, the receiver, and the amount of the transactions are public and accessible to all participants.

Note that privacy preservation is one of the top desired features for cryptocurrencies, since the privacy weakness in Bitcoin was identified [17,26], enhancing user's privacy in cryptocurrencies has attracted much attention from community [6,13,19,27]. Among the proposed privacy-preserving technologies, ***Stealth Address*** [28,29], provides a simple yet efficient way to enhance privacy by hiding the receiver of transactions. Roughly speaking, stealth address is a key-derivation mechanism. In a cryptocurrency system with the stealth address, each user publishes his long-term master public key MPK, and if a payer, say Alice, wants to transfer funds to a payee, say Bob, she can generate a *fresh* derived public key dpk from Bob's master public key MPK_B and use dpk to specify the receiver of the transaction, without any interaction with Bob. On the other side, to spend the coin on such a dpk, Bob can generate a corresponding derived secret key dsk use his long term master secret key MSK_B, and then generate a signature that can be verified using dpk only. In such a mechanism, the receiver's master public key (referred to as 'address' in cryptocurrency) never appears in the transactions or on the blockchain, and neither the derived public key or the signature leaks any information about the master public key. Due to its simplicity and convenience (i.e., each coin is assigned a *fresh* derived public key, and no interaction between the payer and payee) and privacy-preserving virtues, stealth address has been widely adopted by many cryptocurrencies. Particularly, stealth address is a core component of RingCT protocol for Monero [21], which is one of the most popular privacy-centric cryptocurrencies and ranks the 14th in all cryptocurrencies in terms of market capitalization [9].

Recently, Liu et al. [16] have pointed out the current widely used stealth address algorithms [28,29] suffers a security flaw in designs. In particular, once a derived secret key was compromised, the damage would spread to the corresponding master secret key, and all the derived secret keys thereof. To address this problem, Liu et al. [16] introduced and formalized the concept of Signature Scheme with Publicly Derived Public key (PDPKS), capturing the functionality, security, and privacy requirements that steal address should satisfy when applied in cryptocurrencies in practice. Liu et al. also proposed a pairing-based construction, with provable security and privacy based on the discrete logarithm assumption. It is worth mentioning that, as shown by Liu et al. [16], a PDPKS scheme does not only implies a secure stealth address algorithm, but also implies a secure deterministic wallet [31] algorithm, supporting the promising applications such as easy backup and recovery, trustless audits, treasurers allocating funds to departments.

On the other side, due to the advance of quantum computing technologies, quantum-resistant cryptography, especial lattice-based cryptography has been attracting much attention and making significant progress. Cryptocurrency is also developing towards post-quantum cryptocurrencies. However, to the best of our knowledge, as so far, quantum-resistant stealth address algorithm satisfying the functionality, security, and privacy requirements captured by Liu et al.'s work [16] has not been proposed yet. This lags behind other privacy-preserving cryptographic primitives for cryptocurrencies. In particular, in the RingCT approach for building privacy-centric cryptocurrencies, linkable ring signature, stealth address, and commitment with range proof are used to hide the transaction's sender, receiver, and amount, respectively. While lattice-based linkable ring signature schemes [15,30] and lattice-based commitment with range proof schemes [10,32] have been proposed, the lack of lattice-based stealth address schemes is hindering the development of quantum-resistant privacy-centric cryptocurrencies following the RingCT approach.

1.1   Our Results

In this paper, we propose a lattice-based PDPKS construction, and prove the security and privacy in the random oracle model, based on the hardness of the Learning With Errors (LWE) problem [25]. As our construction satisfies the definitions and models on functionality, security, and privacy by Liu et al. [16], our lattice-based PDPKS construction provides potential quantum-resistance for both the stealth address algorithm and the deterministic wallet scheme.

As for many LWE-based cryptographic constructions with advanced features, the public key and signature sizes of our construction are still too large for practical use. We do not want to oversell our results, but take this as a stepping-stone towards the goal of practical and quantum-resistant stealth address, as this is the first concrete instantiation of PDPKS scheme that has the potential to be resistant against quantum computers.

To enable the signature scheme with publicly derived public key, where the compromising of a derived secret key will not impact other secret keys, we resort to the techniques of lattice basis delegation [1,2,8]. We noticed that the delegation algorithm by Agrawa et al. [1] has the property that the delegated lattice conceals the original one. Note that when PDPKS is applied in cryptocurrency, to achieve that no attackers can learn the master public key from the derived public key and corresponding signatures, we have to make sure that only the payee who owns the corresponding master secret key can know the secret information that was used by the payer to create a derived public key. To achieve this, we resort to the key-private public key encryption introduced by Bellare et al. [5]. Due to the adversary's adaptively querying of derived public keys in the privacy game, an adaptive key-indistinguishable PKE scheme is needed in our scheme. However, to the best of our knowledge, no explicit construction of quantum-resistant key-indistinguishable PKE has been proposed prior to us. To construct such PKE scheme, We start the passive key-indistinguishable Regev's LWE-based PKE scheme and prove the Fujisaki-Okamoto transformation [11] transforms a passively key-indistinguishable PKE scheme to an adaptively key-indistinguishable one.

1.2 Related Work

Liu et al. [15] proposed a lattice-based linkable ring signature scheme with stealth address, but the security model does not consider the case that derived secret keys are generated and compromised, while all the signatures are generated using the master secret key. The setting increases the risk of the master key being compromised and cannot support the applications of deterministic wallet, such as treasurers allocating funds to departments.

2   Preliminary

In this section, we review the definition of PDPKS by Liu et al. [16] and some lattice-based background as well as the definition of PKE with key-privacy [5].

2.1   Definition of Publicly Derived Public Key Scheme

Syntax. A PDPKS scheme consists of the following polynomial-time algorithms:

- Setup(1^λ) → PP. On input the security parameter 1^λ, the algorithm outputs the public parameter PP.
- MasterKeyGen(PP) → (mpk, msk). On input the public parameter PP, the algorithm outputs a master public-secret key pair (mpk, msk).
- DpkDerive(PP, mpk) → dpk. On input the public parameter PP and a master public key mpk, the algorithm outputs a derived public key dpk. We say such a dpk is linked to mpk.

- DpkCheck(PP, mpk, msk, dpk) → 1/0. On input the public parameter PP, a master key pair (mpk, msk), and a derived public key dpk, the algorithm outputs a bit $b \in \{0, 1\}$, with $b = 1$ meaning that dpk is linked to mpk and $b = 0$ otherwise.
- DskDerive(PP, mpk, msk, dpk) → dsk. On input the public parameter PP, a master key pair (mpk, msk), and a derived public key dpk that is linked to mpk, the algorithm outputs a derived secret key dsk corresponding to dpk.
- Sign(PP, dpk, μ, dsk) → s. On input the public parameter PP, a derived public key dpk, a message μ, and a derived secret key dsk corresponding to dpk, the algorithm outputs a signature s.
- Verify(PP, dpk, μ, s) → 1/0. On input the public parameter PP, a derived public key dpk, a message μ, and a signature s, the algorithm outputs a bit $b \in \{0, 1\}$, with $b = 1$ meaning valid and $b = 0$ meaning invalid.

For a cryptocurrency system with PDPKS scheme, it runs the PP ← Setup(1^λ) and publish PP to all participants. Each participant can run the (mpk, msk) ← MasterKeyGen(PP) to obtain his long-term master key pair and publish mpk. When a payer, say Alice, wants to pay the payee, say Bob, Alice runs dpk ← DpkDerive(PP, mpk_B) where mpk_B is Bob's master public key, and assigns dpk to the output coin. For Bob, when a new coin appears in the system, he runs b ← DpkCheck(PP, mpk_B, msk_B, dpk) where msk_B is his master secret key and dpk is the coin's (derived) public key, Bob puts such a coin into his wallet only if $b = 1$. To spend such a coin, Bob runs dsk ← DpkCheck(PP, mpk_B, msk_B, dpk) to obtain the derived secret key dsk corresponding to dpk, then he runs the sign algorithm Sign to sign a transaction spending the coin. For a transaction that consumes a coin with (derived) public key dpk, anyone can run the Verify algorithm to check whether the associated signature is valid, only using the dpk, without needing the corresponding master public key.

Correctness. The scheme must satisfy the following correctness properties: for any PP ← Setup(1^λ), (mpk, msk) ← MasterKeyGen(PP), dpk ← DpkDerive(PP, mpk), dsk ← DskDerive(PP, mpk, msk, dpk), and any message μ, it holds that

$$\Pr[\text{DpkCheck}(PP, mpk, msk, dpk) = 1] = 1 - \text{negl}(n), \text{ and}$$
$$\Pr[\text{Verify}(PP, dpk, \mu, \text{Sign}(PP, dpk, \mu, dsk)) = 1] = 1 - \text{negl}(n).$$

Security. We define the existentially unforgeable (EUF) security of PDPKS scheme below:

Definition 1. *We say a PDPKS scheme is existentially unforgeably (EUF) secure, if all probabilistic polynomial time (PPT) adversaries $\mathcal{A}$ win the following game* Game$_{\text{euf}}$ *with negligible probabilities.*

- **Setup.** PP $\leftarrow$ Setup(1^λ) *and* $(mpk, msk) \leftarrow$ MasterKeyGen(PP) *are run.* PP *and mpk are given to* $\mathcal{A}$. *An empty set* $L_{dpk} = \emptyset$ *is initialized.*[1]
- **Probing Phase.** $\mathcal{A}$ *can adaptively query the following oracles:*
  - *Derived Public Key Check Oracle* ODpkCheck($\cdot$):
    On input a derived public key dpk, this oracle returns $c \leftarrow$ DpkCheck(PP, mpk, msk, dpk) *to* $\mathcal{A}$. *If* $c = 1$, *set* $L_{dpk} = L_{dpk} \cup \{dpk\}$.
  - *Derived Secret Key Corruption Oracle* ODskCorrupt($\cdot$):
    On input a derived public key dpk $\in L_{dpk}$, *this oracle returns* $dsk \leftarrow$ DskDerive(PP, mpk, msk, dpk) *to* $\mathcal{A}$.
  - *Signing Oracle* OSign($\cdot, \cdot$): *On input a derived public key dpk* $\in L_{dpk}$ *and a message* μ, *this oracle returns* $\sigma \leftarrow$ Sign(PP, dpk, μ, dsk) *to* $\mathcal{A}$, *where* $dsk \leftarrow$ DskDerive(PP, mpk, msk, dpk).
- **Output Phase.** $\mathcal{A}$ *outputs a derived public key* $dpk^* \in L_{dpk}$, *a message* μ^*, *and a signature* σ^*.

$\mathcal{A}$ *succeeds if* Verify(PP, dpk^*, μ^*, s^*) $= 1$ *under the* **restrictions** *that (1)* ODskCorrupt(dpk^*) *is never queried, and (2)* OSign(dpk^*, μ^*) *is never queried.*

Privacy. The definition captures the fact that derived public keys and corresponding signatures do not leak the corresponding master public key.

Definition 2. *A PDPKS scheme is master public key unlinkable (MPK-UNL), if for all PPT adversaries* $\mathcal{A}$, *the advantage of* $\mathcal{A}$ *in the following game* Game$_{\mathsf{mpkunl}}$, *denoted by* $Adv_{\mathcal{A}}^{mpkunl}$, *is negligible.*

- **Setup.** PP $\leftarrow$ Setup(λ) *is run and* PP *is given to* $\mathcal{A}$.
  $(mpk_0, msk_0) \leftarrow$ MasterKeyGen(PP) *and* $(mpk_1, msk_1) \leftarrow$ MasterKeyGen(PP) *are run, and* mpk_0, mpk_1 *are given to* $\mathcal{A}$. *Two empty sets* $L_{dpk,0} = L_{dpk,1} = \emptyset$ *are initialized.*[2]
- **Challenge Phase.** *A random bit* $b \leftarrow \{0, 1\}$ *is chosen.*
  $dpk^* \leftarrow$ DpkDerive(PP, mpk_b) *is given to* $\mathcal{A}$.
- **Probing Phase.** $\mathcal{A}$ *can adaptively query the following oracles:*
  - *Derived Public Key Check Oracle* ODpkCheck($\cdot, \cdot$):
    On input a derived public key dpk $\neq dpk^*$ *and an index* $i \in \{0, 1\}$, *this oracle returns* $c \leftarrow$ DpkCheck(PP, mpk_i, msk_i, dpk) *to* $\mathcal{A}$. *If* $c = 1$, *set* $L_{dpk,i} = L_{dpk,i} \cup \{dpk\}$.
  - *Derived Secret Key Corruption Oracle* ODskCorrupt($\cdot$):
    On input a derived public key dpk $\in L_{dpk,0} \cup L_{dpk,1}$, *this oracle returns* $dsk \leftarrow$ DskDerive(PP, mpk_i, msk_i, dpk) *to* $\mathcal{A}$, *with* $i = 0$ *if* $dpk \in L_{dpk,0}$, *and* $i = 1$ *if* $dpk \in L_{dpk,1}$.

---

[1] This set serves only to describing the game easier. It stores the derived public keys that have been checked and accepted as being linked to the target master public key, where are all known to the adversary.

[2] The two sets are defined only for describing the game easier. $L_{dpk,i}(i = 0, 1)$ stores the derived public keys that have been checked and accepted as being linked to the target master public key mpk_i. The two sets are known to the adversary.

- *Signing Oracle* $\mathsf{OSign}(\cdot,\cdot)$: *On input a derived public key* $dpk \in L_{dpk,0} \cup L_{dpk,1} \cup \{dpk^*\}$ *and a message* μ, *this oracle returns* $\sigma \leftarrow \mathsf{Sign}(PP, dpk, \mu, dsk)$ *to* $\mathcal{A}$, *where* $dsk \leftarrow \mathsf{DskDerive}(PP, mpk_i, msk_i, dpk)$, *with* $i = 0$ *if* $dpk \in L_{dpk,0}$, $i = 1$ *if* $dpk \in L_{dpk,1}$, *and* $i = b$ *if* $dpk = dpk^*$.
- **Guess**. $\mathcal{A}$ *outputs a bit* $b' \in \{0,1\}$ *as its guess to* b.

2.2   Lattice Backgrounds

Notations. We denote matrices by bold capitals, e.g., $\mathbf{A}$, and column vectors by bold small letters e.g., $\mathbf{x}$. For a matrix $\mathbf{A}$, denote its transpose by $\mathbf{A}^T$. For two matrices, $\mathbf{A}$ and $\mathbf{B}$, we denote their concatenation by $[\mathbf{A}|\mathbf{B}]$. We denote the inner product of two vectors $\mathbf{a}, \mathbf{b}$ by $\langle \mathbf{a}, \mathbf{b} \rangle = \mathbf{a}^T \mathbf{b}$. For an ordered vector set $\mathbf{T} = \{\mathbf{t}_1, \cdots, \mathbf{t}_m\}$, we denote its Gram-Schmidt orthogonalization by $\tilde{\mathbf{T}} = \{\tilde{\mathbf{t}}_1, \cdots, \tilde{\mathbf{t}}_m\}$; we also denote the matrix $[\mathbf{t}_1 | \cdots | \mathbf{t}_m]$ by $\mathbf{T}$. We denote the identity matrix of order m by $\mathbf{I}_m$ and omits m without ambiguity. We denote the ℓ_2 norm of a vector $\mathbf{x}$ by $\|\mathbf{x}\|$ and define $\|\mathbf{T}\| := \max \|\mathbf{t}_i\|$. For a matrix $\mathbf{R} \in \mathbb{Z}_q^{m \times m}$, define the parameter $s_{\mathbf{R}} = \sup_{\mathbf{x} \in \mathbb{R}^m \setminus \{\mathbf{0}\}} \frac{\|\mathbf{R}\mathbf{x}\|}{\|\mathbf{x}\|}$.

For a randomized algorithm or a distribution $\mathcal{A}$, we denote its once execution (or sampling) output x by $x \leftarrow \mathcal{A}$. Let S be a finite set, we abuse the notion to denote the uniform distribution over S by S. We say a function $\epsilon : \mathbb{R}_+ \to \mathbb{R}_+$ is negligible if for any polynomial p, it holds that $\epsilon(n) < 1/p(n)$ for sufficient large n. We denote an arbitrary negligible function by $\mathrm{negl}(n)$. We say a function $g : \mathbb{R}_+ \to [0,1]$ is overwhelming if $g(n) = 1 - \mathrm{negl}(n)$. For $x \in \mathbb{R}$, we define $\lfloor x \rceil = \lfloor x + \frac{1}{2} \rfloor$. For an integer $m \in \mathbb{Z}_+$, we denote $\{1, 2, \cdots, m\}$ by $[m]$.

We denote m-dimensional lattice generated by a basis $\mathbf{T}$ by $\mathcal{L}(\mathbf{T})$. Denote integer lattice $\{\mathbf{z} \in \mathbb{Z}^m : \mathbf{A}\mathbf{z} = \mathbf{0} \mod q\}$ by $\Lambda_q^\perp(\mathbf{A})$ and omits q without ambiguity. Denote the discrete Gaussian distribution on lattice Λ, with Gaussian parameter s and center $\mathbf{c}$ by $D_{\Lambda,s,\mathbf{c}}$.

For Gaussian Distribution we have the following Lemma 1 and Lemma 2, where Lemma 2 is obtained by combining the smoothing lemma [18] and "the new bound of smoothing parameter" in [12].

Lemma 1 ([18]). *Let* $q \geq 2$ *and* $\mathbf{A} \in \mathbb{Z}_q^{n \times m}$. *Let* $\mathbf{T}$ *be a basis of* $\Lambda^\perp(\mathbf{A})$, $s \geq \|\tilde{\mathbf{T}}\| \cdot \omega(\sqrt{\log m})$. *Then for any* $\mathbf{c} \in \mathbb{Z}_q^m$,

$$\Pr_{\mathbf{x} \leftarrow D_{\Lambda^\perp(\mathbf{A}),s,\mathbf{c}}} [\|\mathbf{x} - \mathbf{c}\| > s\sqrt{m}] = \mathrm{negl}(n).$$

Lemma 2 ([12,18]). *For any* m-*dimensional lattice* Λ, *define*

$$\tilde{bl}(\Lambda) = \min_{\mathbf{T}:\Lambda=\mathcal{L}(\mathbf{T})} \|\tilde{\mathbf{T}}\|.$$

Let $\mathbf{A} \in \mathbb{Z}_q^{n \times m}$ *be a matrix whose columns generate* $\mathbb{Z}_q^n$, $s \geq \tilde{bl}(\Lambda^\perp(\mathbf{A})) \cdot \omega(\sqrt{\log m})$ *be a real number. Then for a* $\mathbf{x} \leftarrow D_{\mathbb{Z}^m,s}$, *the distribution of* $\mathbf{u} = \mathbf{A}\mathbf{x} \mod q$ *is statistically close to the uniform distribution over* $\mathbb{Z}_q^n$.

Assumptions. The security and privacy of our PDPKS construction will be based on the following Short Integer Solution (**SIS**) assumption and **LWE** assumption.

Definition 3 (SIS Assumption) ([3,12,18,22]). *Let q, β, m be functions of n. Define $\mathsf{SIS}_{n,q,\beta,m}$ problem as: Given a matrix $\mathbf{A} \leftarrow \mathbb{Z}_q^{n \times m}$, find a non-zero integer vector $\mathbf{z} \in \mathbb{Z}^m$ s.t. $\mathbf{Az} = \mathbf{0} \mod q$ and $\|\mathbf{z}\| \leq \beta$.*
    For $m, \beta = \mathrm{poly}(n)$, $q \geq \beta \cdot \tilde{O}(\sqrt{n})$, no (quantum) algorithm can solve $\mathsf{SIS}_{n,q,\beta,m}$ problem in polynomial time.

Definition 4 (LWE Assumption) ([22,25]). *Let m, q be functions of n, $q > 2$, χ be a distribution on $\mathbb{Z}_q$ called the error distribution, defines the LWE distribution $A_{\mathbf{s},\chi}$ as: Choose a vector $\mathbf{a} \leftarrow \mathbb{Z}_q^n$ and an error $e \leftarrow \chi$, output $(\mathbf{a}, \langle \mathbf{a}, \mathbf{s} \rangle + e)$. Defines the Search-$\mathsf{LWE}_{n,q,\chi,m}$ problem as: fix an $\mathbf{s} \leftarrow \mathbb{Z}_q^n$, given at most m samples from $A_{\mathbf{s},\chi}$, work out $\mathbf{s}$. Define the Decision-$\mathsf{LWE}_{n,q,\chi,m}$ problem as: For a uniformly chosen $\mathbf{s} \leftarrow \mathbb{Z}_q^n$, given the oracle to be (1) $A_{\mathbf{s},\chi}$ or (2) the uniform distribution over $\mathbb{Z}_q^{n+1}$, decide which is the case with at most m oracle calls.*
    For parameters $m = \mathrm{poly}(n)$, $q \leq 2^{\mathrm{poly}(n)}$, $r = 2\sqrt{n}$ and χ be the (discrete) Gaussian distribution with Gaussian parameter r, no (quantum) algorithm can solve the (Search/Decision)-$\mathsf{LWE}_{n,q,\chi,m}$ problem in polynomial time.

Lemma 3 ([24]). *With such parameters in SIS assumption and LWE assumption, SIS assumption implies LWE assumption for $\beta \leq q/r$.*

Algorithms on Lattices. Our construction will use the following SamplePre and TrapGen algorithms.

Lemma 4 (SamplePre Algorithm [12]). *There exists a PPT algorithm SamplePre that, on input a matrix $\mathbf{A} \in \mathbb{Z}_q^{n \times m}$, a basis $\mathbf{T} \in \mathbb{Z}_q^{m \times m}$ of $\Lambda = \Lambda^{\perp}(\mathbf{A})$, a Gaussian parameter $s \geq \|\tilde{\mathbf{T}}\| \cdot \omega(\sqrt{\log m})$ and a vector $\mathbf{u} \in \mathbb{Z}_q^n$, outputs a vector $\mathbf{x}$ such that $\mathbf{Ax} = \mathbf{u} \mod q$ and the distribution of $\mathbf{x}$ is statistically close to the distribution of $\mathbf{x}' \leftarrow D_{\mathbb{Z}^m,s}$ conditioned on $\mathbf{Ax}' = \mathbf{u} \mod q$. The short basis $\mathbf{T}$ is called the trapdoor of $\mathbf{A}$.*

Lemma 5 (TrapGen Algorithm, [4,7]). *For fixed constant $\delta > 0$, there is a PPT algorithm TrapGen that, on input n (in unary), an odd prime $q = \mathrm{poly}(n)$, and $m \geq (5 + 3\delta)n \log q$, outputs a statistically $(m \cdot q^{-\delta_0 n/2})$-close to uniform matrix $\mathbf{A} \in \mathbb{Z}_q^{n \times m}$ and a basis $\mathbf{T}$ of $\Lambda^{\perp}(\mathbf{A})$ such that with overwhelming probability $\|\tilde{\mathbf{T}}\| \leq O(\sqrt{n \log q})$.*

Note that we can set $\delta = 1/3$, then we have $m \geq 6n \log q$ and output matrix $\mathbf{A}$ by the above TrapGen algorithm distributes statistically $(6n \cdot q^{-n/6} \log q)$-close to the uniform distribution over $\mathbb{Z}_q^{n \times m}$. In addition, the following Lemma 6 shows that the output matrix $\mathbf{A}$ by the above TrapGen algorithm generates $\mathbb{Z}_q^n$ with overwhelming probability.

Lemma 6 ([12]). *Let $m \geq 2n \log q$, then for all but q^{-n} fractions of $\mathbf{A} \in \mathbb{Z}_q^{n \times m}$, the columns of $\mathbf{A}$ generate $\mathbb{Z}_q^n$.*

Trapdoor Delegation Algorithms. On the basis/trapdoor delegation, we have the following Lemma 7, 8, and 9.

Lemma 7 ([1,7]). *There exists a PPT algorithm* DeleRight' *that, on input a matrix* $\mathbf{A} \in \mathbb{Z}_q^{n \times m}$, *a matrix* $\mathbf{B} \in \mathbb{Z}_q^{n \times m}$ *whose columns generate* $\mathbb{Z}_q^n$, *a trapdoor* $\mathbf{T_B}$ *of* $\mathbf{B}$ *s.t.* $\|\tilde{\mathbf{T}}_{\mathbf{B}}\| \leq L$, *and a matrix* $\mathbf{R} \in \mathbb{Z}_q^{m \times m}$, *outputs a trapdoor* $\mathbf{T}_{\mathbf{F}}'$ *for* $\mathbf{F} = [\mathbf{A}|\mathbf{AR} + \mathbf{B}]$ *s.t.* $\|\tilde{\mathbf{T}}_{\mathbf{F}}'\| \leq L \cdot (s_{\mathbf{R}} + 1)$.

Lemma 8 ([8]). *There exists a PPT algorithm* DeleLeft' *that, on input a matrix* $\mathbf{A} \in \mathbb{Z}_q^{n \times m}$ *whose columns generate* $\mathbb{Z}_q^n$, *a matrix* $\mathbf{C} \in \mathbb{Z}_q^{n \times m}$, *and a trapdoor* $\mathbf{T_A}$, *outputs a trapdoor* $\mathbf{T}_{\mathbf{F}}'$ *for* $\mathbf{F} = [\mathbf{A}|\mathbf{C}]$ *s.t.* $\|\tilde{\mathbf{T}}_{\mathbf{F}}'\| = \|\tilde{\mathbf{T}}_{\mathbf{A}}\|$.

Lemma 9 ([8]). *There exists a PPT algorithm* RandBasis *that, on input a basis* $\mathbf{T}'$ *of an* m-*dimensional integer lattice* Λ *s.t.* $\|\tilde{\mathbf{T}}'\| < L$, *a real number* $s \geq \|\tilde{\mathbf{T}}'\| \cdot \omega(\sqrt{\log m})$, *outputs a basis* $\mathbf{T}$ *of* Λ *s.t.* $\|\tilde{\mathbf{T}}\| \leq s\sqrt{m}$. *Moreover, for any two basis* $\mathbf{T}_1, \mathbf{T}_2$ *of* Λ, *let* $s \geq \max\{\|\tilde{\mathbf{T}}_1\|, \|\tilde{\mathbf{T}}_2\|\} \cdot \omega(\sqrt{\log m})$, *then the outputs of* RandBasis$(\mathbf{T}_1, s)$ *and* RandBasis$(\mathbf{T}_2, s)$ *are statistically close.*

With the parameter $\mathbf{A} \leftarrow \mathbb{Z}_q^{n \times m}$, $\mathbf{R} \leftarrow \{-1, 1\}^{m \times m}$ as chosen in [1], applying the above Lemma 7, 8, and 9, we have the following DeleRight and DeleLeft algorithms as shown by Theorem 1 and Theorem 2 respectively. Our PDPKS construction will be based on the DeleRight algorithm, while the proofs will be based on the DeleLeft algorithm.

Theorem 1 (DeleRight **Algorithm**). *Let* $q > 2$ *be a prime, fix some* $s_R = O(\sqrt{m})$. *There exists a PPT algorithm* DeleRight *that, on input a matrix* $\mathbf{A} \leftarrow \mathbb{Z}_q^{n \times m}$, *a matrix* $\mathbf{B} \in \mathbb{Z}_q^{n \times m}$ *whose columns generate* $\mathbb{Z}_q^n$, *a trapdoor* $\mathbf{T_B}$ *of* $\mathbf{B}$ *s.t.* $\|\tilde{\mathbf{T}}_{\mathbf{B}}\| \leq L$, *and a matrix* $\mathbf{R} \leftarrow \{-1, 1\}^{m \times m}$, *a real number* $s \geq L \cdot s_R \cdot \omega(\sqrt{\log m})$, *outputs a trapdoor* $\mathbf{T}_{\mathbf{F}}$ *for* $\mathbf{F} = [\mathbf{A}|\mathbf{AR} + \mathbf{B}]$ *such that* $\mathbf{F}$ *distributes statistical close to the uniform distribution over* $\mathbb{Z}_q^{n \times 2m}$ *and* $\|\tilde{\mathbf{T}}_{\mathbf{F}}\| \leq s \cdot \sqrt{2m}$.

Moreover, for any two trapdoors $\mathbf{T}_1, \mathbf{T}_2$ *of* $\mathbf{B}$ *s.t.* $\|\tilde{\mathbf{T}}_1\| \leq L$ *and* $\|\tilde{\mathbf{T}}_2\| \leq L$, *the distribution of* DeleRight$(\mathbf{A}, \mathbf{B}, \mathbf{T}_1, \mathbf{R}, s)$ *and* DeleRight$(\mathbf{A}, \mathbf{B}, \mathbf{T}_2, \mathbf{R}, s)$ *are statistically close.*

Theorem 2 (DeleLeft **Algorithm**). *Let* $q > 2$ *be a prime. There exists a PPT algorithm* DeleLeft *that, on input a matrix* $\mathbf{A} \in \mathbb{Z}_q^{n \times m}$ *s.t. columns of* $\mathbf{A}$ *generate* $\mathbb{Z}_q^n$, *a trapdoor* $\mathbf{T_A}$ *of* $\mathbf{A}$ *s.t.* $\|\tilde{\mathbf{T}}_{\mathbf{A}}\| \leq L$, *a matrix* $\mathbf{C} \in \mathbb{Z}_q^{n \times m}$ *and a real number* $s \geq L \cdot \omega(\sqrt{\log m})$, *outputs a trapdoor* $\mathbf{T}_{\mathbf{F}}$ *for* $\mathbf{F} = [\mathbf{A}|\mathbf{C}]$ *s.t.* $\|\tilde{\mathbf{T}}_{\mathbf{F}}\| \leq L \cdot \sqrt{2m} \cdot \omega(\sqrt{\log m})$.

Moreover, for $\mathbf{A} \leftarrow \mathbb{Z}_q^{n \times m}$ *and* $\mathbf{R} \leftarrow \{-1, 1\}^{m \times m}$, *let* $\mathbf{C} = \mathbf{AR} + \mathbf{B}$ *for some* $\mathbf{B} \in \mathbb{Z}_q^{n \times m}$, s_R *be such parameter in Theorem 1, if columns of* $\mathbf{B}$ *generate* $\mathbb{Z}_q^n$ *and* $\mathbf{T_B}$ *be a trapdoor of* $\mathbf{B}$ *s.t.* $\|\tilde{\mathbf{T}}_{\mathbf{B}}\| \leq L$, *then the outputs of* DeleLeft$(\mathbf{A}, \mathbf{T_A}, \mathbf{C}, L \cdot s_R \cdot \omega(\sqrt{\log m}))$ *and* DeleRight$(\mathbf{A}, \mathbf{B}, \mathbf{T_B}, \mathbf{R}, L \cdot s_R \cdot \omega(\sqrt{\log m}))$ *are statistically close.*

2.3 Key-Privacy in Public Key Encryption

Our construction is based on public key encryption (PKE) with **key-privacy**, which was introduced by Bellare et al. [5]. In particular, key-privacy requires that an adversary in possession of a ciphertext is not able to tell which specific public key, out of a set of known public keys.

Syntax. A public-key encryption scheme is a tuple of four PPT algorithms (Setup, KeyGen, Enc, Dec):

- Setup(1^λ) → GP. On input a security parameter 1^λ, the algorithm outputs the common global public parameters GP, that all users in the system will share, including the security parameter, the message space $\mathcal{M}$, the ciphertext space $\mathcal{C}$, etc.
- KeyGen(GP) → (pk, sk). On input GP, the algorithm outputs a public-secret key pair (pk, sk).
- Enc(GP, pk, μ) → $c \in \mathcal{C}$: On input GP, a public key pk and a plaintext $\mu \in \mathcal{M}$, the algorithm outputs a ciphertext $c \in \mathcal{C}$.
- Dec(GP, c, pk, sk) → $\mu' / \perp$. On input GP, a secret key sk and a ciphertext $c \in \mathcal{C}$, the algorithm outputs the a plaintext $\mu' \in \mathcal{M}$ or $\perp$.

Correctness and Security. The correctness, CPA-Security, and CCA2-security are identical to that of conventional PKE, and we omit the details here.

Key-Privacy. The key-privacy is captured by the following "indistinguishable of keys under adaptive chosen-ciphertext attack" (IK-CCA) property [5]:

Definition 5 (IK-CCA). *A PKE scheme is IK-CCA secure if for any PPT adversary $\mathcal{A}$, the advantage in the following IK-CCA game* Game$_{\mathsf{ikcca}}$*, denoted by* $Adv_\mathcal{A}^{ikcca}$*, is negligible.*

1. **Setup.** GP ← Setup(1^λ) *is computed and given to $\mathcal{A}$.*
   (pk_0, sk_0) ← KeyGen(GP) *and* (pk_1, sk_1) ← KeyGen(GP) *are run, and pk_1 and pk_2 are sent to adversary $\mathcal{A}$.*
2. **Probing Phase 1.** *$\mathcal{A}$ can adaptively query the decryption oracle* ODec($\cdot, \cdot$)*: On input a ciphertext $c \in \mathcal{C}$ and an index $i \in \{0, 1\}$, this oracle returns μ ← Dec(GP, c, pk_i, sk_i) to $\mathcal{A}$.*
3. **Challenge Phase.** *$\mathcal{A}$ chooses a challenge plaintext $\mu^* \in \mathcal{M}$. A uniform coin $b \leftarrow \{0, 1\}$ is tossed. $c^* \leftarrow$ Enc(GP, pk_b, μ^*) is given to $\mathcal{A}$.*
4. **Probing Phase 2.** *$\mathcal{A}$ can adaptively query the decryption oracle* ODec($\cdot, \cdot$)*, but cannot make query on $(c^*, 0)$ or $(c^*, 1)$.*
5. **Output Phase.** *$\mathcal{A}$ outputs a bit $b' \in \{0, 1\}$ as its guess to b.*

3 Our Lattice-Based PDPKS Construction

• Setup(1^λ) → PP. The algorithm takes λ (in unary) as input. Let n be a polynomial of λ, $q > 2$ be a prime, and $m \geq 6n \log q$. Fix some $\omega_1 = \omega(\sqrt{\log m})$

and $\omega_2 = \omega(\sqrt{\log 2m})$, let $s_R = O(\sqrt{m})$, $\sigma_B = L \cdot s_R \cdot \omega_1$ and $\sigma_F = \sigma_B \cdot \sqrt{2m} \cdot \omega_2$ for some $L \geq O(\sqrt{n \log q})$.

Let $\Pi_{\mathsf{pke}} = (\mathsf{Setup}, \mathsf{KeyGen}, \mathsf{Enc}, \mathsf{Dec})$ be a lattice-based CCA2 secure and IK-CCA secure PKE scheme. The algorithm runs $\mathsf{GP} \leftarrow \Pi_{\mathsf{pke}}.\mathsf{Setup}(1^\lambda)$. Let $\mathcal{M}_{\mathsf{pke}}$ and $\mathcal{C}_{\mathsf{pke}}$ be the message space and ciphertext space in GP respectively. Let k be polynomials of λ, and let $G_1 : \mathcal{M}_{\mathsf{pke}} \times \mathcal{C}_{\mathsf{pke}} \to \mathbb{Z}_q^{n \times m}$, $G_2 : \mathcal{M}_{\mathsf{pke}} \times \mathcal{C}_{\mathsf{pke}} \to \{-1,1\}^{m \times m}$, and $H : \{0,1\}^* \times \{0,1\}^k \to \mathbb{Z}_q^n$ be functions that will be modeled as random oracles in the proofs. The algorithm produces as output the public parameter $\mathsf{PP} = (1^\lambda, n, m, q, s_R, \sigma_B, \sigma_F, k, \mathsf{GP}, (G_1, G_2, H), \Pi_{\mathsf{pke}})$.

- MasterKeyGen(PP) $\to$ (mpk, msk). On input PP, the algorithm runs $(\mathbf{B}, \mathbf{T_B}) \leftarrow \mathsf{TrapGen}(1^n)$ to generate a random $\mathbf{B}$ and its trapdoor $\mathbf{T_B}$. It runs $(epk, esk) \leftarrow \Pi_{\mathsf{pke}}.\mathsf{KeyGen}(\mathsf{GP})$ to generate a PKE public-secret key pair. It outputs the master public key and master secret key as $mpk = (\mathbf{B}, epk)$, $msk = (\mathbf{T_B}, esk)$.

- DpkDerive(PP, mpk) $\to dpk$. On input PP, a master public key $mpk = (\mathbf{B}, epk)$, the algorithm samples $t \leftarrow \mathcal{M}_{\mathsf{pke}}$ and computes $\tau \leftarrow \Pi_{\mathsf{pke}}.\mathsf{Enc}(\mathsf{GP}, epk, t)$, $\mathbf{A} = G_1(t, \tau)$ and $\mathbf{R} = G_2(t, \tau)$. It then sets $\mathbf{F} = [\mathbf{A} | \mathbf{AR} + \mathbf{B}]$ and outputs the derived public key $dpk = (\mathbf{F}, \tau)$.

- DpkCheck($\mathsf{PP}, mpk, msk, dpk$): On input PP, a master key pair ($mpk = (\mathbf{B}, epk)$, $msk = (\mathbf{T_B}, esk)$), and a derived public key $dpk = (\mathbf{F} = [\mathbf{A} | \mathbf{C}], \tau)$, the algorithm computes $t \leftarrow \Pi_{\mathsf{pke}}.\mathsf{Dec}(\mathsf{GP}, \tau, epk, esk)$ and $\mathbf{A}' = G_1(t, \tau)$, $\mathbf{R}' = G_2(t, \tau)$. It outputs 0 if $\mathbf{A}' \neq \mathbf{A}$ or $\mathbf{C} \neq \mathbf{A}'\mathbf{R}' + \mathbf{B}$. Otherwise, it outputs 1.

- DskDerive($\mathsf{PP}, mpk, msk, dpk$) $\to dsk$. On input PP, a master key pair ($mpk = (\mathbf{B}, epk)$, $msk = (\mathbf{T_B}, esk)$), and a derived public key $dpk = (\mathbf{F} = [\mathbf{A} | \mathbf{C}], \tau)$, the algorithm computes $t \leftarrow \Pi_{\mathsf{pke}}.\mathsf{Dec}(\mathsf{GP}, \tau, epk, esk)$, $\mathbf{A}' = G_1(t, \tau)$ and $\mathbf{R}' = G_2(t, \tau)$. It outputs $\bot$ if $\mathbf{A}' \neq \mathbf{A}$ or $\mathbf{C} \neq \mathbf{A}'\mathbf{R}' + \mathbf{B}$. Otherwise (i.e., $\mathbf{A}' = \mathbf{A}$ and $\mathbf{C} = \mathbf{AR}' + \mathbf{B}$), it runs $\mathbf{T_F} \leftarrow \mathsf{DeleRight}(\mathbf{A}, \mathbf{B}, \mathbf{T_B}, \mathbf{R}', \sigma_B)$ to sample a trapdoor $\mathbf{T_F}$ for $\mathbf{F}$, then outputs the derived secret key $dsk = \mathbf{T_F}$ for dpk.

- Sign($\mathsf{PP}, dpk, \mu, dsk$) $\to s$. On input PP, a derived public key $dpk = (\mathbf{F}, \tau)$, a message $\mu \in \{0,1\}^*$, and the derived secret key $dsk = \mathbf{T_F}$ corresponding to dpk, the algorithm samples a random string $r \leftarrow \{0,1\}^k$ and computes $\mathbf{u} = H(\mu, r)$. It runs $\mathbf{z} \leftarrow \mathsf{SamplePre}(\mathbf{F}, \mathbf{T_F}, \mathbf{u}, \sigma_F)$, and outputs $s = (\mathbf{z}, r)$ as a signature for μ.

- Verify(PP, dpk, μ, s) $\to 1/0$. On input PP, a derived public key $dpk = (\mathbf{F}, \tau)$, a message μ, and a signature $s = (\mathbf{z}, r)$, the algorithm outputs 1 (accepts) if $\|\mathbf{z}\| \leq \sqrt{2m} \cdot \sigma_F$ and $\mathbf{Fz} = H(\mu, r) \mod q$, otherwise, it outputs 0 (rejects).

3.1 Correctness

Correctness of DpkCheck(). Due to the correctness of Π_{pke}, for a derived public key $dpk = (\mathbf{F} = [\mathbf{A} | \mathbf{C}], \tau)$, the t under τ can be recovered correctly with overwhelming probability. This implies that the recovered $\mathbf{A}' = G_1(t, \tau)$ and $\mathbf{R}' = G_2(t, \tau)$ will pass the checks $\mathbf{A}' = \mathbf{A}$ and $\mathbf{C} = \mathbf{AR}' + \mathbf{B}$.

Correctness of Verify(). For $(\mathbf{B}, \mathbf{T_B}) \leftarrow \mathsf{TrapGen}(1^n)$, recall Lemma 5 and Lemma 6, we have that $\|\tilde{\mathbf{T}}_{\mathbf{B}}\| \leq L$, the distribution of $\mathbf{B}$ is statistically close to the uniform distribution over $\mathbb{Z}_q^{n \times m}$, and the columns of $\mathbf{B}$ generate $\mathbb{Z}_q^n$ with overwhelming probability. Thus, for the $\mathbf{B}$, $\mathbf{A}$, and $\mathbf{R}$ in the construction, the distribution of $\mathbf{F}$ is statistically close to the uniform distribution over $\mathbb{Z}_q^{n \times 2m}$. And this implies that the columns of $\mathbf{F}$ generate $\mathbb{Z}_q^n$ with overwhelming probability. For $dsk \leftarrow \mathsf{DskDerive}(\mathsf{PP}, mpk, msk, dpk)$, due to Theorem 1, we have that $dsk = \mathbf{T_F}$ is a basis of $\Lambda^\perp(\mathbf{F})$ and $\|\tilde{\mathbf{T}}_{\mathbf{F}}\| \leq \sigma_B \cdot \sqrt{2m}$. For $s \leftarrow \mathsf{Sign}(\mathsf{PP}, dpk, \mu, dsk)$ where $s = (\mathbf{z}, r)$, due to Lemma 4, we have that the distribution of $\mathbf{z}$ is statistically close to $\mathbf{z}'$ s.t. $\mathbf{z}' \leftarrow D_{\mathbb{Z}^{2m}, \sigma_F}$ conditioned on $\mathbf{F}\mathbf{z}' = \mathbf{u} = H(\mu, r) \mod q$. This implies that with overwhelming probability, $\mathbf{z}$ satisfies $\|\mathbf{z}\| \leq \sigma_F \cdot \sqrt{2m}$, i.e., the Verify algorithm accepts such (μ, s) as valid (message, signature) pair with overwhelming probability.

3.2   Proof of Security

Theorem 3. *If the* $\mathsf{SIS}_{n,q,2\beta,2m}$ *assumption holds with* $\beta = \sqrt{2m} \cdot \sigma_F$, *then the PDPKS scheme is secure in the random oracle model.*

Proof. Let $\mathcal{F}$ be a forger of the PDPKS scheme that wins the game $\mathsf{Game}_{\mathsf{euf}}$ (w.r.t. Definition 1) with non-negligible probability $\epsilon(n)$. We construct an SIS solver $\mathcal{S}$ that invokes $\mathcal{F}$ as a subroutine and solves the $\mathsf{SIS}_{n,q,2\beta,2m}$ problem with non-negligible probability.

Setup. $\mathcal{S}$ is given an instance of SIS problem $\mathsf{SIS}_{n,q,2\beta,2m}$ with $\beta = \sqrt{2m} \cdot \sigma_F$, i.e., $\mathbf{F} = [\mathbf{A}|\mathbf{C}] \in \mathbb{Z}_q^{n \times 2m}$, where $\mathbf{A}, \mathbf{C} \in \mathbb{Z}_q^{n \times m}$. $\mathcal{S}$ samples $\mathbf{z} \leftarrow D_{\mathbb{Z}_q^{2m}, \sigma_F}$ and computes $\mathbf{u} = \mathbf{F}\mathbf{z} \mod q$.

$\mathcal{S}$ setups $\mathsf{PP} \leftarrow \mathsf{Setup}(1^\lambda)$ as in the construction and gives PP to $\mathcal{F}$, We assume WLOG that $\mathcal{F}$ queries G_1, G_2 and H for at most Q_1, Q_2 and Q_H times respectively and set $Q_G = \max\{Q_1, Q_2\}$. $\mathcal{S}$ chooses $k \leftarrow [Q_G]$ and $\ell \leftarrow [Q_H]$. $\mathcal{S}$ initializes empty lists L_1, L_2, L_H to record the oracle query-results of G_1, G_2, and H respectively.

$\mathcal{S}$ samples $\mathbf{R} \leftarrow \{-1, 1\}^{m \times m}$ and runs $(epk, esk) \leftarrow \Pi_{\mathsf{pke}}.\mathsf{KeyGen}(\mathsf{GP})$. $\mathcal{S}$ then sets $\mathbf{B} = \mathbf{C} - \mathbf{A}\mathbf{R}$, $mpk = (\mathbf{B}, epk)$ and gives mpk to $\mathcal{F}$. Note that $\mathbf{B}$ distributes statistically close to that in the real game. $\mathcal{S}$ initializes an empty list $\hat{L}_{dpk}$ to record the derived public keys linked to mpk and corresponding information.

Probing Phase. $\mathcal{F}$ can adaptively query the following oracles:
- For the j-th distinct query to G_1 on (t_j, τ_j): If $j \neq k$, $\mathcal{S}$ runs $(\mathbf{A}_j, \mathbf{T}_{\mathbf{A}_j}) \leftarrow \mathsf{TrapGen}(1^{\lambda_1})$, samples $\mathbf{R}_j \leftarrow \{-1, 1\}^{m \times m}$, stores $(t_j, \tau_j, \mathbf{A}_j, \mathbf{T}_{\mathbf{A}_j})$ and $(t_j, \tau_j, \mathbf{R}_j)$ into L_1 and L_2 respectively, and replies with $\mathbf{A}_j$. If $j = k$, $\mathcal{S}$ stores $(t_j, \tau_j, \mathbf{A}, \top)$ and $(t_j, \tau_j, \mathbf{R})$ into L_1 and L_2 respectively, and replies with $\mathbf{A}$.
- For a query to G_2 on any (t, τ): If $(t, \tau, \mathbf{R}')$ exists in L_2 with some $\mathbf{R}'$, $\mathcal{S}$ replies with $\mathbf{R}'$, otherwise $\mathcal{S}$ makes a query to G_1 on (t, τ), which triggers a new $(t, \tau, \mathbf{R}')$ to be put into L_2, then replies with the corresponding $\mathbf{R}'$.

- For j-th distinct query to H on (μ_j, r_j): If $j \neq \ell$, $\mathcal{S}$ chooses $\mathbf{z}_j \leftarrow D_{\mathbb{Z}^{2m}, \sigma_F}$, sets $\mathbf{u}_j = \mathbf{F}\mathbf{z}_j \bmod q$, stores $(\mu_j, r_j, \mathbf{u}_j, \mathbf{z}_j)$ into L_H, and replies with $\mathbf{u}_j$. If $j = \ell$, $\mathcal{S}$ stores $(\mu_j, r_j, \mathbf{u}, \mathbf{z})$ into L_H, and replies with $\mathbf{u}$.
- For a query to $\mathsf{ODpkCheck}(\cdot)$ on $dpk' = (\mathbf{F}' = [\mathbf{A}'|\mathbf{C}'], \tau')$: $\mathcal{S}$ runs $t' \leftarrow \Pi_{\mathsf{pke}}.\mathsf{Dec}(\mathsf{GP}, \tau', epk, esk)$, and makes query to G_1 and G_2 on (t', τ') respectively. Let $\mathbf{A}'' = G_1(t', \tau')$, $\mathbf{R}'' = G_2(t', \tau')$. If $\mathbf{A}' = \mathbf{A}''$ and $\mathbf{C}' = \mathbf{A}''\mathbf{R}'' + \mathbf{B}$, $\mathcal{S}$ replies with 1 and sets $\hat{L}_{dpk} = \hat{L}_{dpk} \cup \{(dpk, \mathbf{A}'', \mathbf{R}'')\}$, otherwise replies with 0.
- For a query to $\mathsf{ODskCorrupt}(\cdot)$ on $dpk' = (\mathbf{F}' = [\mathbf{A}'|\mathbf{C}'], \tau') \in L_{dpk}$: $\mathcal{S}$ finds $dpk' \in \hat{L}_{dpk}$, let $(\mathbf{A}', \mathbf{R}')$ be the corresponding matrices. We have that there is a tuple $(t', \tau', \mathbf{A}', \mathbf{T}_\mathbf{A}') \in L_1$ and a tuple $(t', \tau', \mathbf{R}') \in L_2$, where $t' = \Pi_{\mathsf{pke}}.\mathsf{Dec}(\mathsf{GP}, \tau', epk, esk)$. If $\mathbf{A}' = \mathbf{A}$, note that $\mathbf{T}_\mathbf{A}' = \top$, $\mathcal{S}$ aborts the game. Otherwise, $\mathcal{S}$ computes $\mathbf{T}_{\mathbf{F}'} \leftarrow \mathsf{DeleLeft}(\mathbf{A}', \mathbf{A}'\mathbf{R}' + \mathbf{B}, \mathbf{T}_\mathbf{A}', \sigma_B)$ and replies with $\mathbf{T}_{\mathbf{F}'}$.
- For a query to $\mathsf{OSign}(\cdot, \cdot)$ on $(dpk' = (\mathbf{F}', \tau'), \mu')$ such that $dpk' \in L_{dpk}$: If $\mathbf{F}' = \mathbf{F}$, $\mathcal{S}$ samples $r' \leftarrow \{0,1\}^k$ and makes a query to H on (μ', r'). With $(\mu', r', \mathbf{u}', \mathbf{z}')$ in L_H, $\mathcal{S}$ replies with $s' = (\mathbf{z}', r')$. If $\mathbf{F}' \neq \mathbf{F}$, $\mathcal{S}$ runs $t' \leftarrow \Pi_{\mathsf{pke}}.\mathsf{Dec}(\mathsf{GP}, \tau', epk, esk)$. Let $(t', \tau', \mathbf{A}', \mathbf{T}_\mathbf{A}') \in L_1$ be the tuple corresponding to (t', τ'), $\mathcal{S}$ computes $\mathbf{T}_{\mathbf{F}'} \leftarrow \mathsf{DeleLeft}(\mathbf{A}', \mathbf{A}'\mathbf{R}' + \mathbf{B}, \mathbf{T}_\mathbf{A}', \sigma_B)$ and sets $dsk' = \mathbf{T}_{\mathbf{F}'}$, then replies with $s' \leftarrow \mathsf{Sign}(\mathsf{PP}, dsk', dpk', \mu')$.

Output Phase. $\mathcal{F}$ outputs a forge $(dpk^*, \mu^*, s^* = (\mathbf{z}^*, r^*))$. $\mathcal{S}$ outputs $\mathbf{z}^* - \mathbf{z}$ as its solution to the SIS problem.

Analysis. Before analyzing the reduction, we prove the following claims.

Claim 1. G_2 *is perfectly simulated, and the responses of* G_1, H *are statistically close to such in the real game.*

Proof. Due to Lemma 5, the output of G_1 simulated by $\mathcal{S}$ is statistical close to uniform. Recall that by Lemma 2 the output of H simulated by $\mathcal{S}$ is statistically close to uniform.

Claim 2. *The replies of* $\mathsf{ODpkCheck}(\cdot)$ *simulated by* $\mathcal{S}$ *is statistical close to those in the real game.*

Proof. The only difference between the $\mathsf{ODpkCheck}(\cdot)$ simulated by $\mathcal{S}$ and such in the real game is that whether the simulated or the real G_1, G_2 are used. Due to Claim 1, the claim holds.

Claim 3. *With negligible probability,* $\mathcal{F}$ *adds some* $dpk' = (\mathbf{F}' = [\mathbf{A}|\mathbf{C}'], \tau')$ *for* $\mathbf{C}' \neq \mathbf{C}$ *to* L_{dpk}.

Proof. If $dpk' = (\mathbf{F}' = [\mathbf{A}|\mathbf{C}'], \tau')$ is added to L_{dpk}, then $\tau' \neq \tau$. Since $\mathbf{F}'$ is determined by τ', but distributes uniform before making queries to G_1, G_2 on (t', τ') where $t' = \mathsf{Dec}(\mathsf{GP}, \tau', epk, esk)$, this happens with negligible probability due to the limited query times.

Claim 4. $\mathcal{F}$ *produces a forgery with regards to* $\mathbf{A}$ *with probability* $\epsilon(n)/Q_G -$ $\mathsf{negl}(n)$.

Proof. To facilitate the analysis, suppose that there is an imaginary computational unbounded $\mathcal{S}'$ that behaves identical to $\mathcal{S}$ except when $\mathcal{F}$ queries ODskCorrupt on $(\mathbf{F}, \tau)$, where $\mathcal{F}$ is the SIS instance to solve and τ is arbitrary. Upon such a query, $\mathcal{S}'$ computes a trapdoor $\mathbf{T_A}$ of $\mathbf{A}$ s.t. $\|\tilde{\mathbf{T}}_\mathbf{A}\| \leq L$ and replies with the trapdoor delegated from $\mathbf{T_A}$. Then $\mathcal{S}'$ never aborts. In the game simulated by $\mathcal{S}'$, the view of $\mathcal{F}$ is statistically close to such in the real game. Since $\mathcal{F}$ outputs a forge in the real game with probability larger than $\epsilon(n)$, $\mathcal{F}$ outputs a forge with probability $\epsilon(n) - \mathrm{negl}(n)$ in the game simulated by $\mathcal{S}'$. If $\mathcal{F}$ output a forge, there exists some keys in L_{dpk} that hasn't been queried to ODskCorrupt. Due to the uniformity of $\mathbf{A}$, any such key has probability at least $1/Q_G$ regards to $\mathcal{A}$. Then with probability larger than $\epsilon(n)/Q_G - \mathrm{negl}(n)$, $\mathcal{F}$ does not query ODskCorrupt with keys regard to $\mathbf{A}$. Since before $\mathcal{S}$ abort, the view of $\mathcal{F}$ in the game simulated by $\mathcal{S}$ is identical to such in the game simulated by $\mathcal{S}'$, then with probability $\epsilon(n)/Q_G - \mathrm{negl}(n)$, $\mathcal{F}$ produces a forgery with regards to $\mathbf{A}$.

With probability larger than $\epsilon(n)/Q_G - \mathrm{negl}(n)$, $\mathcal{F}$ produces a forgery with regards to $\mathbf{A}$, also under this case, the probability that the forgery happens on $\mathbf{u}$ is $1/Q_H$, so the total probability is $\epsilon(n)/(Q_G \cdot Q_H) - \mathrm{negl}(n)$. If $\mathcal{F}$ produces a forgery with regards to $\mathbf{A}$, $\mathcal{S}$ will not abort. Since the view of $\mathcal{F}$ in the game simulated by $\mathcal{S}$ is statistically close to such in the real game, then if $\mathcal{S}$ does not abort, $\mathcal{F}$ outputs a valid forge $s^* = (\mathbf{z}^*, r^*)$ for some message with probability $\epsilon(n) - \mathrm{negl}(n)$. If $\mathcal{F}$ outputs a valid forge $(\mathbf{z}^*, r)$, then $\|\mathbf{z}^*\| < \sigma_F \cdot \sqrt{2m}$ with overwhelming probability. If such $\mathbf{z}$ is forged with $\mathbf{F}$, then $\mathbf{Fz}^* = \mathbf{u} \mod q$. Due to min-entropy of Gaussian distribution shown in [12,23], $\mathbf{z}$ has min-entropy at least $O(m)$, $\mathbf{z} \neq \mathbf{z}^*$ with overwhelming probability. With all the above events happen, $\|\mathbf{z} - \mathbf{z}^*\| \leq 2\sigma_F \cdot \sqrt{2m}$, $\mathbf{z} - \mathbf{z}^*$ is a solution to the SIS problem.

In conclusion, $\mathcal{S}$ outputs a valid solution $\mathbf{z} - \mathbf{z}^*$ of the given SIS instance will probability large than $\epsilon(n)^2/(Q_H \cdot Q_G^2) - \mathrm{negl}(n)$, which is non-negligible.

3.3   Proof of Privacy

Theorem 4. *If the CCA2-security and IK-CCA security of Π_{pke} holds, the PDPKS scheme is MPK-UNL privacy-preserving in random oracle model.*

Proof. Suppose there exists a PPT adversary $\mathcal{A}$ that breaks the privacy of the PDPKS scheme with non-negligible probability $\epsilon(n)$, we construct a PPT adversary $\mathcal{B}$ that breaks the IK-CCA security of Π_{pke} with non-negligible probability.

Setup. $\mathcal{B}$ is given the global public parameter GP of Π_{pke}, and two public keys epk_0, epk_1. $\mathcal{B}$ simulates the MPK-UNL game for $\mathcal{A}$ as follows: $\mathcal{B}$ sets $n, m, q, s_R, \sigma_B, \sigma_F, k, G_1, G_2, H$ as in the construction, and gives $\mathsf{PP} = (1^\lambda, n, m, q, s_R, \sigma_B, \sigma_F, k, \mathsf{GP}, (G_1, G_2, H), \Pi_{\mathsf{pke}})$ to $\mathcal{A}$. $\mathcal{B}$ runs $(\mathbf{B}_0, \mathbf{T}_0) \leftarrow \mathsf{TrapGen}(1^n)$ and $(\mathbf{B}_1, \mathbf{T}_1) \leftarrow \mathsf{TrapGen}(1^n)$, and gives $mpk_0 = (\mathbf{B}_0, epk_0)$ and $mpk_1 = (\mathbf{B}_1, epk_1)$ to $\mathcal{A}$.

$\mathcal{B}$ initializes empty lists L_1, L_2, L_H to record the oracle query-results of G_1, G_2, and H respectively. $\mathcal{B}$ initializes two empty lists $\hat{L}_{dpk,i}(i = 0, 1)$ to record the derived public keys linked to mpk_i and the corresponding information. $\mathcal{B}$ samples $t^* \leftarrow \mathcal{M}_{\mathsf{pke}}$ and submits t^* to his challenge in the IK-CCA game, and obtains a challenge ciphertext $\tau^* \leftarrow \Pi_{\mathsf{pke}}.\mathsf{Enc}(\mathsf{GP}, epk_b, t^*)$. $\mathcal{B}$ simulates dpk^* by running $(\mathbf{A}^*, \mathbf{T}_{\mathbf{A}^*}) \leftarrow \mathsf{TrapGen}(1^n)$, sampling $\mathbf{C}^* \leftarrow \mathbb{Z}_q^{n \times m}$ and then setting the challenge derived public key as $dpk^* = (\mathbf{F}^* = [\mathbf{A}^* | \mathbf{C}^*], \tau^*)$ and sending dpk^* to $\mathcal{A}$.

Probing Phase. $\mathcal{B}$ then answers $\mathcal{A}$'s oracle queries as follows:
- For the j-th distinct query to G_1 on (t_j, τ_j), if $t_j = t^*$, $\mathcal{B}$ aborts the game; otherwise, $\mathcal{B}$ samples $\mathbf{A}_j \leftarrow \mathbb{Z}_q^{n \times m}$ and stores $(t_j, \tau_j, \mathbf{A}_j)$ into L_1, then replies with $\mathbf{A}_j$.
- For the j-th distinct query to G_2 on (t_j, τ_j), if $t_j = t^*$, $\mathcal{B}$ aborts the game; otherwise, $\mathcal{B}$ samples $\mathbf{R}_j \leftarrow \{-1, 1\}^{m \times m}$ and stores $(t_j, \tau_j, \mathbf{R}_j)$ into L_2, then replies with $\mathbf{R}_j$.
- For the j-th distinct query to H on (μ_j, r_j), $\mathcal{B}$ samples $\mathbf{u}_j \leftarrow \mathbb{Z}_q^n$ and stores $(\mu_j, r_j, \mathbf{u}_j)$ into L_H, then replies with $\mathbf{u}_j$.
- For a query to $\mathsf{ODpkCheck}(\cdot, \cdot)$ on (dpk, i) where $i \in \{0, 1\}$ and $dpk = (\mathbf{F}, \tau) \neq dpk^*$: If $\tau \neq \tau^*$, $\mathcal{B}$ make a query to $\mathsf{ODec}(\cdot, \cdot)$ on (τ, i) and obtain a $t \in \mathcal{M}_{pke}$. Then $\mathcal{B}$ make a query to G_1 on (t, τ) and a query to G_2 on (t, τ), and sets $\mathbf{A} = G_1(t, \tau), \mathbf{R} = G_2(t, \tau)$. If $\mathbf{F} = [\mathbf{A} | \mathbf{A}\mathbf{R} + \mathbf{B}_i]$, $\mathcal{B}$ sets $\hat{L}_{dpk,i} = \hat{L}_{dpk,i} \cup \{(dpk, \mathbf{A}, \mathbf{R})\}$ and replies with 1, otherwise replies with 0. If $(\tau = \tau^*) \wedge (\mathbf{F} \neq \mathbf{F}^*)$, $\mathcal{B}$ returns 0.
- For a query to $\mathsf{ODskCorrupt}(\cdot)$ on $dpk = (\mathbf{F}, \tau) \in L_{dpk,i}$ s.t. $i \in \{0, 1\}$: as $dpk \in L_{dpk,i}$, $\mathcal{B}$ can find the corresponding $(\mathbf{A}, \mathbf{R})$ from $\hat{L}_{dpk,i}$ such that $\mathbf{F} = [\mathbf{A} | \mathbf{A}\mathbf{R} + \mathbf{B}_i]$, then $\mathcal{B}$ computes $\mathbf{T}_{\mathbf{F}} \leftarrow \mathsf{DeleRight}(\mathbf{A}, \mathbf{B}_i, \mathbf{T}_i, \mathbf{R}, \sigma_B)$ and replies with $dsk = \mathbf{T}_{\mathbf{F}}$.
- For a query to $\mathsf{OSign}(\cdot, \cdot)$ on a $dpk = (\mathbf{F}, \tau) \in L_{dpk,0} \cup L_{dpk,1} \cup \{dpk^*\}$ and a message μ: If $dpk \in L_{dpk,i}$ for $i \in \{0, 1\}$, $\mathcal{B}$ can find the corresponding $(\mathbf{A}, \mathbf{R})$ from $\hat{L}_{dpk,i}$ such that $\mathbf{F} = [\mathbf{A} | \mathbf{A}\mathbf{R} + \mathbf{B}_i]$, then $\mathcal{B}$ computes $\mathbf{T}_{\mathbf{F}} \leftarrow \mathsf{DeleRight}(\mathbf{A}, \mathbf{B}_i, \mathbf{T}_i, \mathbf{R}, \sigma_B)$, and runs $s \leftarrow \mathsf{Sign}(\mathsf{PP}, dpk, \mu, dsk = \mathbf{T}_{\mathbf{F}})$ and replies with s. If $dpk = dpk^*$, $\mathcal{B}$ computes $\mathbf{T}_{\mathbf{F}^*} \leftarrow \mathsf{DeleLeft}(\mathbf{A}^*, \mathbf{T}_{\mathbf{A}^*}, \mathbf{C}^*, \sigma_B)$, samples $r \leftarrow \{0, 1\}^k$, and computes $\mathbf{u} = H(\mu, r)$. Then $\mathcal{B}$ runs $\mathbf{z} \leftarrow \mathsf{SamplePre}(\mathbf{F}^*, \mathbf{T}_{\mathbf{F}^*}, \sigma_F)$ and outputs $s = (\mathbf{z}, r)$ as the signature.

Output Phase. $\mathcal{B}$ outputs whatever $\mathcal{A}$ outputs.

Analysis. We prove the following claims.

Claim 5. *If $\mathcal{A}$ does not query G_1, G_2 on t^*, the simulated $\mathbf{F}^*$ is statistical indistinguishable to the original MPK-UNL game.*

Proof. If $\mathcal{A}$ does not query G_1, G_2 on t^*, then $\mathbf{R}^* = G_2(t^*, \tau^*)$ is undefined and uniformly distributed, which means $\mathbf{F}^* = [\mathbf{A}^* | \mathbf{A}^*\mathbf{R}^* + \mathbf{B}_b^*]$ is statistically indistinguishable from $\mathbf{F}^* = [\mathbf{A}^* | \mathbf{C}^*]$ (Theorem 1).

Claim 6. *If $\mathcal{A}$ does not query G_1, G_2 on t^*, the simulation of $\mathsf{DpkCheck}$, $\mathsf{DskDerive}$ and OSign queries is statistically close to that in the real game.*

Proof. The only difference between the simulation and the real game is caused by the use of $\mathsf{DeleLeft}$ and $\mathsf{DeleRight}$, which produces statistically close results.

Claim 7. *$\mathcal{A}$ queries G_1, G_2 on t^* with negligible probability if Π_{PKE} is IND-CCA2 secure and $\mathcal{M}_{pke}$ has super-polynomial size.*

Proof. If $\mathcal{A}$ queries G_1 or G_2 on t^* with non-negligible probability, then we can construct $\mathcal{B}'$ to break the CCA2 security of Π_{PKE} with non-negligible probability.

$\mathcal{B}'$ is given a public key epk. $\mathcal{B}'$ then picks two random messages t_0^*, t_1^* from $\mathcal{M}_{pke}$ and obtains a challenge ciphertext $\tau^* \leftarrow \Pi_{\mathsf{pke}}.\mathsf{Enc}(\mathsf{GP}, epk, t_{b'}^*)$ where b' is chosen by the IND-CCA2 challenger. $\mathcal{B}'$ sets up the game for $\mathcal{A}$ as follows: $\mathcal{B}'$ tosses a coin b and sets $epk_b = epk$ and randomly generates (epk_{1-b}, esk_{1-b}). $\mathcal{B}'$ simulates $\mathbf{F}^*$ as $\mathcal{B}$ does and then gives epk_0, epk_1 and $dpk^* = (\mathbf{F}^*, \tau^*)$ to $\mathcal{A}$. $\mathcal{B}'$ answers all the queries as $\mathcal{B}$ does except that $\mathcal{B}'$ simulates all the queries related to epk_{1-b} honestly using esk_{1-b}. If in the game, $\mathcal{A}$ queries G_1 or G_2 on t_c^* for $c \in \{0,1\}$, then $\mathcal{B}'$ outputs c as his guess for b' in the IND-CCA2 game, otherwise, $\mathcal{B}'$ outputs a random bit. Since $\mathcal{M}_{pke}$ has super-polynomial size and $t_{1-b'}^*$ is never used in the simulation for $\mathcal{A}$, the chance that $\mathcal{A}$ outputs $t_{1-b'}^*$ in a query to G_1 or G_2 is negligible. On the other hand, by the assumption, $t_{b'}^*$ will appear in a query to G_1 or G_2 with a non-negligible probability, hence $\mathcal{B}'$ can win the IND-CCA2 game with a negligible probability.

If $\mathcal{A}$ does not query G_1 or G_2 on t^*, then $\mathcal{B}$ does not abort and the simulation is statistical close to the real game. If $\mathcal{A}$ can guess b correctly in the $\mathsf{Game}_{\mathsf{mpkunl}}$ with non-negligible advantage, $\mathcal{B}$ can break the IK-CCA security of Π_{pke} with non-negligible advantage.

3.4   Parameter Choosing

We fix the parameter $n = \lambda$. The other parameters can be instantiated in various ways. For a typical choice, we fix $k = n$ and $\epsilon > 0$ to some constant, choose $m = n^{1+\epsilon}$ and set $L = \sqrt{m}$. We fix $\omega_1 = \omega_2 = \omega(\sqrt{\log m})$ and set $\sigma_F = O(m^{3/2}) \cdot \omega(\sqrt{\log m})^2$. To ensure the security of our SIS problem, we set $\beta = \sqrt{2m} \cdot \sigma_F = O(m^2) \cdot \omega(\sqrt{\log m})^2$. According to the SIS assumption, we set $q = \tilde{O}(m^{5/2}) \cdot \omega(\sqrt{\log m})^2$.

3.5   Lattice-Based Key-Private Public Key Encryption

In this section, we construct a (quantumly) CCA2-secure and IK-CCA secure PKE based on the hardness of LWE. We states the theorem here and leave the construction of such PKE scheme and the proof to Appendix A.

Theorem 5. *Let $q > 2$ be a prime, m be some polynomial of n, χ be an efficiently sampleable distribution over $\mathbb{Z}_q$. Assume that the $\mathsf{LWE}_{n,q,\chi,m}$ problem is hard, there exists PKE scheme π that is IND-CCA2 secure and IK-CCA secure.*

4   Conclusion

Unlike other cryptographic components for RingCT (e.g., ring signature, commitment, and range proof) for which lattice-based constructions are known, we did not know any lattice based stealth address schemes, which hinders the development and deployment of quantum-resistant RingCT-based privacy-centric cryptocurrencies. In this paper, we fill this gap by proposing the first lattice-based PDPKS scheme and proving its security in the random oracle model. Our construction offers (potentially) quantum security not only for the stealth address algorithm but also for the deterministic wallet algorithm. Previously, deterministic wallet algorithms, despite their popularity in Bitcoin-like cryptocurrencies, were not quantum resistant.

A Construct Quantumly CCA2-Secure PKE Scheme with CCA2 with IK-CCA Security

The IK-CPA Privacy of PKE Schemes. The definition of IK-CPA privacy of PKE schemes follows [5].

Definition 6. *A PKE scheme is Key-Indistinguishable in Chosen-Plaintext-Attack (IK-CPA) secure if for any PPT adversary $\mathcal{A}$, the advantage in the following CCA-key-distinguish game $\mathsf{Game}_{\mathsf{ikcpa}}$, denoted by $Adv_{\mathcal{A}}^{ikcca}$, is negligible.*

1. **Setup.** GP $\leftarrow$ Setup(1^{λ}), (pk_0, sk_0) $\leftarrow$ KeyGen(GP), (pk_1, sk_1) $\leftarrow$ KeyGen(GP) *are run.* GP, pk_0, pk_1 *are sent to the adversary $\mathcal{A}$.*
2. **Challenge Phase.** $\mathcal{A}$ *choose a challenger ciphertext $\mu^* \in \mathcal{M}$. A uniform coin $b \leftarrow \{0, 1\}$ is tossed.* $c^* \leftarrow$ Enc(GP, pk_b, μ^*) *is given to $\mathcal{A}$.*
3. **Output Phase.** $\mathcal{A}$ *outputs a bit $b' \in \{0, 1\}$ as its guess to b and wins if $b' = b$.*

Let n, q, m, χ be the parameters in Theorem 5. Regev's PKE scheme [25] LWEPKE = (Setup, KeyGen, Enc, Dec) is a tuple of PPT algorithms.

- LWEPKE.Setup(1^{λ}): The algorithm computes $n = \text{poly}(n)$, $m = \text{poly}(n)$, fixes the error distribution χ according to n and outputs GP = $(1^n, q, \chi, m)$.
- LWEPKE.KeyGen(GP): The algorithm samples $\mathbf{s} \leftarrow \mathbb{Z}_q^n$, $\mathbf{A} \leftarrow \mathbb{Z}_q^{n \times m}$, and $\mathbf{e} \leftarrow \chi^m$. It then computes $\mathbf{b} = \mathbf{A}^T \mathbf{s} + \mathbf{e}$ and outputs secret key $sk = \mathbf{s}$ and public key $pk = (\mathbf{A}^T, \mathbf{b})$.
- LWEPKE.Enc(GP, $pk = (\mathbf{A}^T, \mathbf{b}), \mu \in \{0, 1\}$): The algorithm samples $\mathbf{r} \leftarrow \{0, 1\}^m$, computes and outputs $c = (\mathbf{a}^T = \mathbf{r}^T \mathbf{A}^T, b = \mathbf{r}^T \mathbf{b} + \lfloor \frac{q}{2} \rceil)$ as ciphertext.
- LWEPKE.Dec(GP, $c = (\mathbf{a}^T, b), pk, sk = \mathbf{s}$): The algorithm decrypts 0 if $b - \langle \mathbf{a}, \mathbf{s} \rangle$ is closer to 0 than to $\frac{q}{2}$. Otherwise decrypts to 1.

Lemma 10. LWEPKE *is IK-CPA private.*

Proof. We define the following games for a hybrid argument:

- Game_0: This is the original kd-cpa game of LWEPKE for $\mathcal{A}$.
- Game_1: $\mathbf{A}_0 \leftarrow \mathbb{Z}_q^{n \times m}$ and $\mathbf{b}_0 \leftarrow \mathbb{Z}_q^m$ are sampled. Based on Game_0, $(\mathbf{A}_0^T, \mathbf{b}_0)$ is sent to $\mathcal{A}$ instead of pk_0. The rest of the game remains unchanged.

– Game$_2$: $\mathbf{A}_1 \leftarrow \mathbb{Z}_q^{n \times m}$ and $\mathbf{b}_1 \leftarrow \mathbb{Z}_q^m$ are sampled. Based on Game$_1$, $(\mathbf{A}_1^T, \mathbf{b}_1)$ is sent to $\mathcal{A}$ instead of pk_1. The rest of the game remains unchanged.

Due to the LWE assumption, the views of $\mathcal{A}$ in Game$_0$ and Game$_1$ are computational indistinguishable, as are the views of $\mathcal{A}$ in Game$_1$ and Game$_2$. The rest of the proof can be done by showing that any PPT adversary $\mathcal{A}$ achieves only negligible advantage in Game$_2$ by using left-over hash lemma [14].

From IK-CPA to IK-CCA. We introduce Fujisaki-Okamoto transformation that transforms a CPA-secure PKE scheme to a CCA2-secure one [11] and prove it transforms a IK-CPA private PKE scheme to a IK-CCA private PKE scheme.

Let λ be the security parameter and n, N, ℓ be polynomials of λ. Let PKE = (Setup, KeyGen, Enc, Dec) be a PKE scheme with message space $\{0,1\}^n$. Denote the process "under global parameter GP, encrypts plaintext μ under public key pk with randomness r" by Enc(GP, pk, μ; r). Assume the algorithm Enc takes at most ℓ random bits and let $G : \{0,1\}^n \rightarrow \{0,1\}^N$, $H : \{0,1\}^{N+n} \rightarrow \{0,1\}^\ell$, be random oracles. The PKE2 = (Setup2, KeyGen2, Enc2, Dec2) scheme is defined as:

– PKE2.Setup2(1^λ): The algorithm runs GP $\leftarrow$ PKE.Setup(1^λ) and sets $\ell =$ poly(λ), $N =$ poly(λ). Let fix G, H and outputs GP2 = (GP, ℓ, N, G, H).
– KeyGen2(GP2): The algorithm runs $(pk', sk') \leftarrow$ KeyGen(GP). It outputs $pk = pk'$ as public key, outputs $sk = sk'$ as secret key.
– Enc2(GP2, pk, μ): For a public key $pk = pk'$ and a plaintext $\mu \in \{0,1\}^N$, the algorithm chooses $\sigma \leftarrow \{0,1\}^n$. It computes $w = G(\sigma) \oplus \mu$, $d \leftarrow$ PKE.Enc(GP, pk', σ; $H(\mu, \sigma)$) and outputs $c = (d, w)$ as ciphertext.
– Dec2(GP2, c, pk, sk): For a public key $pk = pk'$, a secret key $sk = sk'$ and a ciphertext $c = (d, w)$, the algorithm computes $\sigma \leftarrow$ Dec(GP2, sk', d) and $\mu = G(\sigma) \oplus w$. It outputs μ if $d =$ Enc(GP, pk', σ; $H(\mu, \sigma)$), otherwise it outputs $\bot$.

Theorem 6. *Let* PKE *be a PKE scheme with CPA-security and IK-CPA privacy,* PKE2 *is IK-CCA private.*

Proof. We prove by reduction. Let $\mathcal{A}$ be any PPT algorithm that breaks the IK-CCA private of PKE2, we construct a PPT algorithm $\mathcal{B}$ with $\mathcal{A}$ as a subroutine breaks the IK-CPA privacy of PKE.

On receiving the challenge keys GP, pk_0', pk_1' s.t $(pk_0', sk_0') \leftarrow$ PKE.KeyGen(GP) and $(pk_1', sk_1') \leftarrow$ PKE.KeyGen(GP), $\mathcal{B}$ computes and sends GP2, $pk_0 = pk_0'$, $pk_1 = pk_1'$ to $\mathcal{A}$. In the Game$_{ikcca}$ of $\mathcal{A}$ for PKE2, the decryption oracles of $\mathcal{A}$ are ODec2($\cdot, \cdot$), which equal to Dec2(GP2, $\cdot$, pk_i, sk_i) respectively. A query to ODec2($\cdot, \cdot$) on $c_j = (d_j, w_j)$ defines values $\sigma_j =$ PKE.Dec(GP, k_i, d_j), $\mu_j = G(\sigma_j) \oplus w_j$, where $i \in \{0,1\}$. We define the following events:
•inv$_j$: For j-th query to ODec2($\cdot, \cdot$) on $(i, c_j = (d_j, w_j))$, it replies $\bot$.
•gue$_j$: Before the j-th query to ODec2($\cdot, \cdot$) on $(i, c_j = (d_j, w_j))$, $G(\sigma_j)$ and $H(\mu_j, \sigma_j)$ are not queried, where $\sigma_j =$ Dec(GP, d_j, pk_j', sk_i') and $\mu_j = w_j \oplus G(\sigma_j)$.

•$\exp_j$: Defined to be the event $\mathbf{gue}_j \wedge \overline{\mathbf{inv}_j}$.

•$\exp$: Any of $\exp_j$ happen in the whole kd-cca game.

We prove that $\exp$ occurs with negligible probability. Assume that $\exp_j$ occurs, then c_j decrypts to μ_j. Without querying on $G(\sigma_j)$, $w_j = G(\sigma_j) \oplus \mu_j$ is uniformly random to $\mathcal{A}$. In order to achieve $\overline{\mathbf{inv}_j}$, $\mathcal{A}$ has to guess w_j right, but this happens with negligible probability. If $\mathcal{A}$ has queried $G(\sigma_j)$, then it hasn't queried $H(\mu_j, \sigma_j)$. The randomness $H(\mu_j, \sigma_j)$ in the encryption process $\mathsf{PKE.Enc}(\mathsf{GP}, pk_i, \mu_j)$ is uniformly random. Then $\mathcal{A}$ has to compute $d_j = \mathsf{Enc}(\mathsf{GP}, pk_i', \mu_j; H(\mu_j, \sigma_j))$ right with a uniformly random string $r_j \leftarrow \{0,1\}^\ell$ instead of $H(\mu_j, \sigma_j)$. This happens with negligible property, otherwise in the cpa game, one could try to encrypts the challenge plaintext to ciphertext with uniform randomness to break the CPA-security of PKE. The union bound of $\exp_j$ shows $\exp$ happens with negligible probability. Therefore, it holds that

$$\Pr[\mathcal{A} \text{ wins}] = \Pr[\mathcal{A} \text{ wins} \wedge \overline{\exp}] + \Pr[\mathcal{A} \text{ wins} \wedge \exp] \leq \Pr[\mathcal{A} \text{ wins} \wedge \overline{\exp}] + \Pr[\exp]$$
$$= \Pr[\mathcal{A} \text{ wins} \wedge \overline{\exp}] + \mathrm{negl}(n)$$

Assume $\mathsf{Adv}^{ikcca}_{\mathcal{A},\mathsf{PKE2}} = |\Pr[\mathcal{A} \text{ wins}] - \frac{1}{2}|$ is non-negligible, then $|\Pr[\mathcal{A} \text{ wins} \wedge \overline{\exp}] - \frac{1}{2}|$ is non-negligible. $\mathcal{B}$ is committed to win its kd-cpa game when $[\mathcal{A} \text{ wins} \wedge \overline{\exp}]$ happens. $\mathcal{B}$ simulates the oracles G, H by uniformly sampling and recording to list L_G, L_H, similar to the strategy of G_1, G_2 in the proof of Theorem 4. When $\mathcal{B}$ receives the challenge plaintext $\mu^* \in \{0,1\}^N$ from $\mathcal{A}$, it samples a $\sigma^* \leftarrow \{0,1\}^n$ as its challenge plaintext. On receiving challenge ciphertext $d^* = \mathsf{PKE.Enc}(\mathsf{GP}, pk_b', \sigma^*; r^*)$ for some $r^* \leftarrow \{0,1\}^\ell$, $\mathcal{B}$ sends $c^* = (d^*, w^*)$ to $\mathcal{A}$ as challenge ciphertext, where $w^* = G(\sigma^*) \oplus \mu^*$. For $\mathcal{A}$'s j-th query to $\mathsf{ODec2}(\cdot, \cdot)$ on $c_j = (d_j, w_j)$, $\mathcal{B}$ scans the whole L_G, L_H. If $\mathcal{B}$ finds some $(\sigma_j, G(\sigma_j)) \in L_G$ and $(\mu_j, \sigma_j, H(\mu_j, \sigma_j)) \in L_H$ s.t. $G(\sigma_j) \oplus \mu_j = w_j$ and $d_j = \mathsf{PKE.Enc}(\mathsf{GP}, pk_i, \mu_j, H(\mu_j, \sigma_j))$, it replies with μ_j, otherwise replies $\perp$.

When $\mathcal{A}$ outputs its guess b' to b, $\mathcal{B}$ outputs b'. Conditioned on that $\overline{\exp}$ occurs, $\mathcal{B}$ can answer all the decryption queries, and the view of $\mathcal{A}$ in the reduction is identical to that in the real game. Therefore, we have $\Pr[\mathcal{B} \text{ wins}] \geq \Pr[\mathcal{A} \text{ wins} \wedge \overline{\exp}] - \mathrm{negl}(n)$. Then $\mathsf{Adv}^{ikcpa}_{\mathcal{B},\mathsf{PKE}} = |\Pr[\mathcal{B} \text{ wins}] - \frac{1}{2}| = |\Pr[\mathcal{A} \text{ wins} \wedge \overline{\exp}] - \frac{1}{2}| - \mathrm{negl}(n)$, which is non-negligible if $\mathsf{Adv}^{ikcca}_{\mathcal{A},\mathsf{PKE}}$ is non-negligible.

References

1. Agrawal, S., Boneh, D., Boyen, X.: Efficient lattice (H)IBE in the standard model. In: Gilbert, H. (ed.) EUROCRYPT 2010. LNCS, vol. 6110, pp. 553–572. Springer, Heidelberg (2010). https://doi.org/10.1007/978-3-642-13190-5_28

2. Agrawal, S., Boneh, D., Boyen, X.: Lattice basis delegation in fixed dimension and shorter-ciphertext hierarchical IBE. In: Rabin, T. (ed.) CRYPTO 2010. LNCS, vol. 6223, pp. 98–115. Springer, Heidelberg (2010). https://doi.org/10.1007/978-3-642-14623-7_6

3. Ajtai, M.: Generating hard instances of lattice problems (extended abstract). In: 28th ACM STOC, pp. 99–108 (1996)

4. Alwen, J., Peikert, C.: Generating shorter bases for hard random lattices. In: STACS 2009, pp. 75–86. LIPIcs (2009)
5. Bellare, M., Boldyreva, A., Desai, A., Pointcheval, D.: Key-privacy in public-key encryption. In: Boyd, C. (ed.) ASIACRYPT 2001. LNCS, vol. 2248, pp. 566–582. Springer, Heidelberg (2001). https://doi.org/10.1007/3-540-45682-1_33
6. Ben-Sasson, E., et al.: Zerocash: decentralized anonymous payments from bitcoin. In: 2014 IEEE Symposium on Security and Privacy, pp. 459–474 (2014)
7. Boyen, X.: Lattice mixing and vanishing trapdoors: a framework for fully secure short signatures and more. In: Nguyen, P.Q., Pointcheval, D. (eds.) PKC 2010. LNCS, vol. 6056, pp. 499–517. Springer, Heidelberg (2010). https://doi.org/10.1007/978-3-642-13013-7_29
8. Cash, D., Hofheinz, D., Kiltz, E., Peikert, C.: Bonsai trees, or how to delegate a lattice basis. In: Gilbert, H. (ed.) EUROCRYPT 2010. LNCS, vol. 6110, pp. 523–552. Springer, Heidelberg (2010). https://doi.org/10.1007/978-3-642-13190-5_27
9. CoinMarketCap: Top 100 cryptocurrencies by market capitalization. https://coinmarketcap.com. Accessed 12 Feb 2020
10. Esgin, M.F., Steinfeld, R., Liu, J.K., Liu, D.: Lattice-based zero-knowledge proofs: new techniques for shorter and faster constructions and applications. In: Boldyreva, A., Micciancio, D. (eds.) CRYPTO 2019. LNCS, vol. 11692, pp. 115–146. Springer, Cham (2019). https://doi.org/10.1007/978-3-030-26948-7_5
11. Fujisaki, E., Okamoto, T.: Secure integration of asymmetric and symmetric encryption schemes. In: Wiener, M. (ed.) CRYPTO 1999. LNCS, vol. 1666, pp. 537–554. Springer, Heidelberg (1999). https://doi.org/10.1007/3-540-48405-1_34
12. Gentry, C., Peikert, C., Vaikuntanathan, V.: Trapdoors for hard lattices and new cryptographic constructions. In: 40th ACM STOC, pp. 197–206 (2008)
13. Heilman, E., Alshenibr, L., Baldimtsi, F., Scafuro, A., Goldberg, S.: TumbleBit: an untrusted bitcoin-compatible anonymous payment hub. In: NDSS 2017 (2017)
14. Impagliazzo, R., Levin, L.A., Luby, M.: Pseudo-random generation from one-way functions (extended abstracts). In: 21st ACM STOC, pp. 12–24 (1989)
15. Liu, Z., Nguyen, K., Yang, G., Wang, H., Wong, D.S.: A lattice-based linkable ring signature supporting stealth addresses. In: Sako, K., Schneider, S., Ryan, P.Y.A. (eds.) ESORICS 2019. LNCS, vol. 11735, pp. 726–746. Springer, Cham (2019). https://doi.org/10.1007/978-3-030-29959-0_35
16. Liu, Z., Yang, G., Wong, D.S., Nguyen, K., Wang, H.: Key-insulated and privacy-preserving signature scheme with publicly derived public key. In: IEEE EuroS&P 2019, pp. 215–230 (2019)
17. Meiklejohn, S., et al.: A fistful of bitcoins: characterizing payments among men with no names. Commun. ACM 59(4), 86–93 (2016)
18. Micciancio, D., Regev, O.: Worst-case to average-case reductions based on Gaussian measures. In: 45th FOCS, pp. 372–381 (2004)
19. Miers, I., Garman, C., Green, M., Rubin, A.D.: Zerocoin: anonymous distributed E-cash from Bitcoin. In: 2013 IEEE Symposium on Security and Privacy, pp. 397–411 (2013)
20. Nakamoto, S.: Bitcoin: a peer-to-peer electronic cash system (2009). http://www.bitcoin.org/bitcoin.pdf
21. Noether, S., Mackenzie, A.: Ring confidential transactions. Ledger 1, 1–18 (2016)
22. Peikert, C.: A decade of lattice cryptography. Cryptology ePrint Archive, Report 2015/939 (2015). http://eprint.iacr.org/2015/939
23. Peikert, C., Rosen, A.: Efficient collision-resistant hashing from worst-case assumptions on cyclic lattices. In: Halevi, S., Rabin, T. (eds.) TCC 2006. LNCS, vol. 3876, pp. 145–166. Springer, Heidelberg (2006). https://doi.org/10.1007/11681878_8

24. Peikert, C., Shiehian, S.: Noninteractive zero knowledge for NP from (plain) learning with errors. In: Boldyreva, A., Micciancio, D. (eds.) CRYPTO 2019. LNCS, vol. 11692, pp. 89–114. Springer, Cham (2019). https://doi.org/10.1007/978-3-030-26948-7_4

25. Regev, O.: On lattices, learning with errors, random linear codes, and cryptography. In: 37th ACM STOC, pp. 84–93 (2005)

26. Ron, D., Shamir, A.: Quantitative analysis of the full bitcoin transaction graph. In: Sadeghi, A.-R. (ed.) FC 2013. LNCS, vol. 7859, pp. 6–24. Springer, Heidelberg (2013). https://doi.org/10.1007/978-3-642-39884-1_2

27. Ruffing, T., Moreno-Sanchez, P., Kate, A.: CoinShuffle: practical decentralized coin mixing for bitcoin. In: Kutyłowski, M., Vaidya, J. (eds.) ESORICS 2014. LNCS, vol. 8713, pp. 345–364. Springer, Cham (2014). https://doi.org/10.1007/978-3-319-11212-1_20

28. van Saberhagen, N.: Cryptonote v 2.0 (2013). https://cryptonote.org/whitepaper.pdf

29. Todd, P.: Stealth addresses. https://lists.linuxfoundation.org/pipermail/bitcoin-dev/2014-January/004020.html

30. Torres, W.A.A., et al.: Post-quantum one-time linkable ring signature and application to ring confidential transactions in blockchain (lattice RingCT v1.0). In: ACISP 2018, pp. 558–576 (2018)

31. Wuille, P.: Bip32: hierarchical deterministic wallets, February 2012. https://github.com/bitcoin/bips/blob/master/bip-0032.mediawiki

32. Yang, R., Au, M.H., Zhang, Z., Xu, Q., Yu, Z., Whyte, W.: Efficient lattice-based zero-knowledge arguments with standard soundness: construction and applications. In: Boldyreva, A., Micciancio, D. (eds.) CRYPTO 2019. LNCS, vol. 11692, pp. 147–175. Springer, Cham (2019). https://doi.org/10.1007/978-3-030-26948-7_6

Post-Quantum Adaptor Signatures and Payment Channel Networks

Muhammed F. Esgin[1,2(✉)], Oğuzhan Ersoy[3], and Zekeriya Erkin[3]

[1] Faculty of Information Technology, Monash University, Melbourne, Australia
muhammed.esgin@monash.edu
[2] Data61, CSIRO, Melbourne, Australia
[3] Cyber Security Group,
Delft University of Technology, Delft, Netherlands
{o.ersoy,z.erkin}@tudelft.nl

Abstract. Adaptor signatures, also known as *scriptless scripts*, have recently become an important tool in addressing the scalability and interoperability issues of blockchain applications such as cryptocurrencies. An adaptor signature extends a digital signature in a way that a complete signature reveals a secret based on a cryptographic condition. It brings about various advantages such as (i) low on-chain cost, (ii) improved fungibility of transactions, and (iii) advanced functionality beyond the limitation of the blockchain's scripting language.

In this work, we introduce the *first post-quantum* adaptor signature, named LAS. Our construction relies on the standard lattice assumptions, namely Module-SIS and Module-LWE. There are certain challenges specific to the lattice setting, arising mainly from the so-called *knowledge gap* in lattice-based proof systems, that makes the realization of an adaptor signature and its applications difficult. We show how to overcome these technical difficulties without introducing additional on-chain costs. Our evaluation demonstrates that LAS is essentially as efficient as an ordinary lattice-based signature in terms of both communication and computation. We further show how to achieve *post-quantum* atomic swaps and payment channel networks using LAS.

Keywords: Post-quantum · Blockchain · Lattice · Adaptor signature · Scriptless script · Payment channel network.

1 Introduction

Blockchains are decentralized platforms run by miners, where each transaction on the blockchain can be seen as an application formed of some script(s). The scripting language of a blockchain defines potential functionalities that can be implemented on blockchain. Bitcoin, for example, consists of very few scripts, which restricts its use mainly into coin transactions. Ethereum, on the other hand, has a Turing-complete scripting language that enables users to run more advanced and complicated applications.

© Springer Nature Switzerland AG 2020
L. Chen et al. (Eds.): ESORICS 2020, LNCS 12309, pp. 378–397, 2020.
https://doi.org/10.1007/978-3-030-59013-0_19

A user who wants to deploy and execute a transaction needs to pay a fee to the miners. The fee is determined by the storage and computational costs of running each script of the transaction. Thus, it is beneficial to handle some operations off-chain to reduce the on-chain fee paid to the miners. In this manner, Poelstra introduced the notion of *scriptless scripts* [25], which is later named as *adaptor signatures* [3,15].

Adaptor signatures can be seen as an extension over a digital signature, where first a "pre-signature" is generated and its completion to a (full) signature reveals a secret based on a cryptographic condition. The conditions are defined over a hard relation such as the discrete log problem, and the complete signature reveals a witness matching with the statement embedded into the pre-signature. The verification of the signature is done in the same way as the original signature scheme. Thus, while the miners verify only the signature, parties involved in the signature generation can embed an additional condition.

The main advantages of adaptor signatures can be summarized as follows: (i) A significant reduction in on-chain costs, (ii) improved fungibility of transactions, and (iii) ability to incorporate complex conditions, which may otherwise be impossible to execute due to the limitation of the blockchain's scripting language. More specifically, if the condition is published on-chain separately, then it would incur additional storage and verification costs. At the same time, since the condition is embedded inside a signature, for the outsiders and miners the signature with a condition is indistinguishable from a regular one. This fungibility property is especially useful to hide payment channel network transactions among any other transactions [21]. Moreover, adaptor signatures enhance the functionality of blockchains with a limited scripting language. Since the condition embedded within the signature is not verified by miners, it is not limited by the blockchain's scripting language. These advantages have been utilized in payment channel networks [3,21], atomic swaps [24], and discrete log contracts [8].

None of these works, however, provide security against powerful quantum computers as they rely on discrete-log-related assumptions. As evident, e.g., from NIST's efforts for standardization of *post-quantum* (i.e., quantum-resistant) algorithms [22], there is a major need for designing quantum-secure alternatives of currently deployed schemes. In fact, in the blockchain community, there are already significant efforts and considerations towards migrating to post-quantum cryptography. For example, Ethereum 2.0 Serenity upgrade [5] is planned to have an option for a post-quantum signature, Zcash developers plan to update their protocol with post-quantum alternatives when they are mature enough [31], and Hcash is building a post-quantum privacy-preserving blockchain [17].

Lattice-based cryptography, studied extensively in the last decades, is a promising candidate for post-quantum security. For example, Dilithium [9], which is based on standard lattice assumptions, is among the 2nd round signature candidates in NIST's post-quantum standardization process. Beyond basic cryptographic schemes such as encryption and signature, lattice-based cryptography also supports advanced schemes such as zero-knowledge proofs (ZKP), which play a crucial role in blockchain applications. For example, advanced ZKPs have recently been studied in [12,13] and there are even recent efforts in constructing blockchain-specific applications based on lattice assumptions [14,30].

Our contributions. In this work, we introduce the *first post-quantum* adaptor signature, LAS, in support of the efforts towards migration to post-quantum cryptography. Our construction relies on standard lattice assumptions, namely Module-LWE and Module-SIS, and is essentially as efficient as an ordinary lattice-based signature scheme based on the same assumptions. In particular, the signature scheme underlying LAS is a simplified version of Dilithium [9].

We further show how to realize post-quantum payment channel networks and atomic swaps using LAS. Our results show that these applications can be realized in the post-quantum setting without incurring an additional on-chain cost. The on-chain cost is effectively the cost of an ordinary lattice-based signature.

The main technical difficulties in constructing lattice-based adaptor signatures, as well as atomic swaps and payment channel networks, stem from the following two related facts. First, hard-to-find pre-images of lattice-based one-way functions, and in general user's secret keys, are required to have *small* coefficients in comparison to the system modulus q. In this case, a common technique used to hide user's secrets is rejection sampling, which is applied depending on the secret. As a result, in the setting of a payment channel network where a multi-party interaction is required with each user having his/her own secret, the realization of a secure construction demands a more careful analysis.

Secondly, *efficient* lattice-based zero-knowledge proofs underlying the (ordinary) signature scheme we employ have an inherent *knowledge (soundness) gap* (see, for example, [12,19,20]). That is, a witness extracted from a protocol interaction satisfies an *extended* relation R' whereas an honest user's secret satisfies a *stronger* relation R such that $R \subseteq R'$. Therefore, we need to adjust the security model carefully and also show that the extended guarantees are still meaningful and sufficient for practical applications. To this end, we extend the formal model of adaptor signatures introduced recently in [3], and show how to overcome the technical difficulties in our applications.

Organization of the paper. In Sect. 2, we present our security assumptions, lattice-based signatures and the rejection sampling technique as well as our extended formal definition for adaptor signatures. We introduce LAS, our adaptor signature, in Sect. 3, where the security and performance analyses and the effect of the knowledge gap are also given. We discuss the application of LAS to atomic swaps and payment channel networks in Sect. 4.

2   Preliminaries

We define $\mathcal{R}_q = \mathbb{Z}_q[X]/(X^d + 1)$ to be a cyclotomic ring of power-of-2 degree d for an odd modulus q. We denote by $\mathbb{S}_c$ the set of polynomials in $\mathcal{R}_q$ whose maximum absolute coefficient is at most $c \in \mathbb{Z}^+$. Similarly, $\mathcal{R} = \mathbb{Z}[X]/(X^d + 1)$.

We denote by $\boldsymbol{I}_n$ the n-dimensional identity matrix. Vectors and matrices over $\mathcal{R}$ are denoted by lower-case and capital bold letters such $\boldsymbol{a}$ and $\boldsymbol{A}$, respectively. For a polynomial $f = f_0 + f_1 X + \cdots + f_{d-1}X^{d-1} \in \mathcal{R}$, we define the norms in the typical way: $\|f\| = \sqrt{\sum_{i=0}^{d-1} f_i^2}$, $\|f\|_\infty = \max_i |f_i|$ and $\|f\|_1 = \sum_{i=0}^{d-1} |f_i|$.

For a vector $v = (v_0, \ldots, v_{s-1}) \in \mathcal{R}^s$ of polynomials with $s \geq 1$, we further define $\|v\| = \sqrt{\sum_{i=0}^{s-1} \|v_i\|^2}$, $\|v\|_1 = \sum_{i=0}^{s-1} \|v_i\|_1$, $\|v\|_\infty = \max_i \|v_i\|_\infty$.

2.1 Security Assumptions: Module-SIS and Module-LWE

The security assumptions on which our constructions rely are the two well-known lattice problems, namely Module-SIS (M-SIS) and Module-LWE (M-LWE) [18]. They are generalizations of SIS [2] and LWE [28] problems, respectively. These problems are widely believed to resist attacks against powerful quantum adversaries. As in [9,12,13], we define below M-SIS in "Hermite normal form", which is as hard as M-SIS with a completely random matrix A.

Definition 1 (M-SIS$_{n,m,q,\beta_{\mathrm{SIS}}}$). *Let $A' \xleftarrow{\$} \mathcal{R}_q^{n \times (m-n)}$ and $A = [\,I_n \,\|\, A'\,]$. Given A, M-SIS problem with parameters $m > n > 0$ and $0 < \beta_{\mathrm{SIS}} < q$ asks to find a short non-zero $v \in \mathcal{R}_q^m$ such that $Av = 0$ over $\mathcal{R}_q$ and $\|v\| \leq \beta_{\mathrm{SIS}}$.*

We use a standard variant of M-LWE where both the error and secret coefficients are sampled uniformly from $\{-1, 0, 1\}$. This variant is commonly used in many recent proposals such as [12–14].

Definition 2 (M-LWE$_{\ell,m,q}$). *M-LWE problem with parameters $\ell, m > 0$ asks to distinguish between the following two cases: 1) $(A, b) \xleftarrow{\$} \mathcal{R}_q^{m \times \ell} \times \mathcal{R}_q^m$, and 2) $(A, As + e)$ for $A \xleftarrow{\$} \mathcal{R}_q^{m \times \ell}$, a secret vector $s \xleftarrow{\$} \mathbb{S}_1^\ell$ and an error vector $e \xleftarrow{\$} \mathbb{S}_1^m$.*

It is well-known that if the error and the secret coefficients are sampled from $\mathbb{S}_\gamma$ for $\gamma > 1$, then M-LWE problem gets harder. Therefore, M-LWE$_{\ell,m,q}$ hardness assumption implies that $t = As + e$ is (computationally) indistinguishable from a uniformly random element of $\mathcal{R}_q^m$ when $s \xleftarrow{\$} \mathbb{S}_\gamma^\ell$ and $e \xleftarrow{\$} \mathbb{S}_\gamma^m$ for any $\gamma \geq 1$.

2.2 Lattice-Based Signature and Rejection Sampling

The (ordinary) signature part of our construction can be seen as a simplified version of Dilithium [9], which is a 2nd round signature candidate in NIST's post-quantum standardization process. This signature scheme itself is based on Lyubashevsky's signatures [19,20]. In our construction, we do not employ the optimizations in Dilithium in order to simplify the presentation.

To make sure that the signature does not leak information about the secret key, we employ the rejection sampling technique from [19] as also done in Dilithium. The idea for this works as follows. Let $s \in \mathcal{R}_q^k$ be a secret-dependant vector with $\|s\|_\infty \leq p \in \mathbb{Z}^+$. In order to tie the security to M-SIS, we require the masked vector $z = y + s$ to be short relative to q. Therefore, y cannot be sampled uniformly at random from $\mathcal{R}_q^k$. Instead, we sample $y \xleftarrow{\$} \mathbb{S}_\gamma^k$ for $\gamma \approx kd \cdot p$. Then, we restart signing (i.e., reject $z = y + s$) if $\|z\|_\infty > \gamma - p$. It is easy to see that conditioned on z being accepted, the distribution of z is identical to the uniform distribution on $\mathbb{S}_{\gamma-p}^k$. That is, the distribution of z is forced to be uniform in a box, and thus is (perfectly) simulatable using public information.

2.3 Adaptor Signatures

In [3], an adaptor signature $\Pi_{R,\Sigma}$ is defined with respect to a hard relation R and a signature scheme $\Sigma = (\mathsf{KeyGen}, \mathsf{Sign}, \mathsf{Verify})$. A relation R with a language $L_R := \{Y \mid \exists y : (Y, y) \in R\}$ is said to be hard [6] if: (i) there exists a probabilistic polynomial time (PPT) generator $\mathsf{Gen}(1^n)$ that outputs $(Y, y) \in R$, (ii) for every PPT algorithm $\mathcal{A}$, given $Y \in L_R$, the probability of $\mathcal{A}$ outputting y is negligible. A signature scheme Σ is defined by three algorithms: (i) KeyGen generates a public-secret key pair $(\mathsf{pk}, \mathsf{sk})$, (ii) Sign produces a signature σ using the key $(\mathsf{pk}, \mathsf{sk})$ and message M, (iii) Verify verifies the correctness of a signature σ on a message M using a public key pk. Our underlying signature, Dilithium [9], is $\mathtt{SUF\text{-}CMA}$ (Strong existential unforgeability under chosen message attacks) secure.

In the lattice setting, we need to define two relations R, R' with $R \subseteq R'$. Here, R constitutes the relation for the statement-witness pairs output by Gen (i.e., those used by honest users) whereas R' is an *extended* relation that defines the relation for *extracted* witnesses. The reason for this extension is detailed in Section 3, and stems from the *knowledge/soundness gap* inherent in *efficient* lattice-based zero-knowledge proofs (see, e.g., the soundness definition in [13, Section 2.3]). We denote an adaptor signature scheme in this setting by $\Pi_{R,R',\Sigma}$, which extends the definition given in [3], and elaborate further below the reason why this extension is necessary.

Definition 3 (Adaptor Signature Scheme). *An adaptor signature scheme* $\Pi_{R,R',\Sigma}$ *consists of four algorithms* $(\mathsf{PreSign}, \mathsf{PreVerify}, \mathsf{Adapt}, \mathsf{Ext})$ *defined below.*

$\mathsf{PreSign}((\mathsf{pk}, \mathsf{sk}), Y, M)$: *on input a key pair* $(\mathsf{pk}, \mathsf{sk})$, *a statement* $Y \in L_R$ *and a message* $M \in \{0, 1\}^*$, *outputs a pre-signature* $\hat{\sigma}$.
$\mathsf{PreVerify}(Y, \mathsf{pk}, \hat{\sigma}, M)$: *on input a statement* $Y \in L_R$, *a pre-signature* $\hat{\sigma}$, *a public key* pk *and a message* $M \in \{0, 1\}^*$, *outputs a bit* b.
$\mathsf{Adapt}((Y, y), \mathsf{pk}, \hat{\sigma}, M)$: *on input a statement-witness pair* $(\hat{\sigma}, y)$, *a public key* pk, *a pre-signature* $\hat{\sigma}$ *and a message* $M \in \{0, 1\}^*$, *outputs a signature* σ.
$\mathsf{Ext}(Y, \sigma, \hat{\sigma})$: *on input a statement* $Y \in L_R$, *a signature* σ *and a pre-signature* $\hat{\sigma}$, *outputs a witness* y *such that* $(Y, y) \in R'$, *or* $\bot$.

Note that an adaptor signature $\Pi_{R,R',\Sigma}$ also inherits KeyGen, Sign and Verify algorithms from the signature scheme Σ. The authors in [3] define the security properties for an adaptor signature: aEUF-CMA security, pre-signature adaptability and witness extractability. In addition, they extend the standard correctness definition of signature algorithms with pre-signature correctness, which states that an honestly generated pre-signature of a statement $Y \in L_R$ passes $\mathsf{PreVerify}$ and can be completed into a signature where the witness y can be extracted. We extend further the formal definitions of the security properties in [3], where $R = R'$ yields the setting in [3].

Definition 4 (aEUF-CMA security). *An adaptor signature scheme* $\Pi_{R,R',\Sigma}$ *is aEUF-CMA secure if for every* PPT *adversary* $\mathcal{A}$ *there exists a negligible function* $\mathsf{negl}(\lambda)$ *such that* $\Pr[\mathsf{aSignForge}_{\mathcal{A},\Pi_{R,R',\Sigma}}(\lambda) = 1] \leq \mathsf{negl}(\lambda)$, *where the experiment* $\mathsf{aSignForge}_{\mathcal{A},\Pi_{R,R',\Sigma}}$ *is defined as follows:*

$\mathsf{aSignForge}_{\mathcal{A},\Pi_{R,R',\Sigma}}(\lambda)$	$\mathcal{O}_\mathsf{S}(M)$
1 : $\quad \mathcal{Q} := \emptyset$	1 : $\quad \sigma \leftarrow \mathsf{Sign}((\mathsf{pk},\mathsf{sk}), M)$
2 : $\quad (\mathsf{pk},\mathsf{sk}) \leftarrow \mathsf{KeyGen}(1^\lambda)$	2 : $\quad \mathcal{Q} := \mathcal{Q} \cup \{M\}$
3 : $\quad M^* \leftarrow \mathcal{A}^{\mathcal{O}_\mathsf{S}(\cdot), \mathcal{O}_\mathsf{pS}(\cdot,\cdot)}(\mathsf{pk})$	3 : $\quad \mathbf{return}\ \sigma$
4 : $\quad (Y, y) \leftarrow \mathsf{Gen}(1^\lambda)$	$\mathcal{O}_\mathsf{pS}(M, Y)$
5 : $\quad \hat{\sigma} \leftarrow \mathsf{PreSign}((\mathsf{pk},\mathsf{sk}), Y, M^*)$	1 : $\quad \hat{\sigma} \leftarrow \mathsf{PreSign}((\mathsf{pk},\mathsf{sk}), Y, M)$
6 : $\quad \sigma \leftarrow \mathcal{A}^{\mathcal{O}_\mathsf{S}(\cdot), \mathcal{O}_\mathsf{pS}(\cdot,\cdot)}(\hat{\sigma}, Y)$	2 : $\quad \mathcal{Q} := \mathcal{Q} \cup \{M\}$
7 : $\quad \mathbf{return}\ (M^* \notin \mathcal{Q} \wedge \mathsf{Verify}(\mathsf{pk}, \sigma, M^*))$	3 : $\quad \mathbf{return}\ \hat{\sigma}$

Definition 5 (Weak pre-signature adaptability). *An adaptor signature scheme $\Pi_{R,R',\Sigma}$ is* weak pre-signature adaptable *if for any message $M \in \{0,1\}^*$, any statement/witness pair $(Y, y) \in R$, any key pair $(\mathsf{pk},\mathsf{sk}) \leftarrow \mathsf{KeyGen}(1^\lambda)$ and any pre-signature $\hat{\sigma} \leftarrow \{0,1\}^*$ with $\mathsf{PreVerify}(Y, \mathsf{pk}, \hat{\sigma}, M) = 1$, we have $\Pr[\mathsf{Verify}(\mathsf{pk}, \mathsf{Adapt}((Y, y), \mathsf{pk}, \hat{\sigma}, M), M) = 1] = 1$.*

We call our pre-signature adaptability definition *weak* because only statement-witness pairs satisfying R are guaranteed to be adaptable, and not those satisfying R'. This is similar to the *knowledge gap* of the ZKP underlying Dilithium, where the soundness only guarantees extraction of a witness from an *extended* relation. Therefore, pre-signature adaptability does not guarantee, for example, that an *extracted* witness can be used to adapt a pre-signature successfully (see Remark 1). This issue becomes effective in the applications of our adaptor signature, and we show how to overcome it in Section 4. Note that still the pre-signature $\hat{\sigma}$ in the above definition can be adversarially generated as in [3].

Definition 6 (Witness extractability). *An adaptor signature scheme $\Pi_{R,R',\Sigma}$ is* witness extractable *if for every PPT adversary $\mathcal{A}$, there exists a negligible function $\mathsf{negl}(\lambda)$ such that the following holds: $\Pr[\mathsf{aWitExt}_{\mathcal{A},\Pi_{R,R',\Sigma}}(\lambda) = 1] \leq \mathsf{negl}(\lambda)$, where the experiment $\mathsf{aWitExt}_{\mathcal{A},\Pi_{R,R',\Sigma}}$ is defined as follows*

$\mathsf{aWitExt}_{\mathcal{A},\Pi_{R,R',\Sigma}}(\lambda)$	$\mathcal{O}_\mathsf{S}(M)$
1 : $\quad \mathcal{Q} := \emptyset$	1 : $\quad \sigma \leftarrow \mathsf{Sign}((\mathsf{pk},\mathsf{sk}), M)$
2 : $\quad (\mathsf{pk},\mathsf{sk}) \leftarrow \mathsf{KeyGen}(1^\lambda)$	2 : $\quad \mathcal{Q} := \mathcal{Q} \cup \{M\}$
3 : $\quad (M^*, Y) \leftarrow \mathcal{A}^{\mathcal{O}_\mathsf{S}(\cdot), \mathcal{O}_\mathsf{pS}(\cdot,\cdot)}(\mathsf{pk})$	3 : $\quad \mathbf{return}\ \sigma$
4 : $\quad \hat{\sigma} \leftarrow \mathsf{PreSign}((\mathsf{pk},\mathsf{sk}), Y, M^*)$	$\mathcal{O}_\mathsf{pS}(M, Y)$
5 : $\quad \sigma \leftarrow \mathcal{A}^{\mathcal{O}_\mathsf{S}(\cdot), \mathcal{O}_\mathsf{pS}(\cdot,\cdot)}(\hat{\sigma})$	1 : $\quad \hat{\sigma} \leftarrow \mathsf{PreSign}((\mathsf{pk},\mathsf{sk}), Y, M)$
6 : $\quad y' := \mathsf{Ext}(Y, \sigma, \hat{\sigma})$	2 : $\quad \mathcal{Q} := \mathcal{Q} \cup \{M\}$
7 : $\quad \mathbf{return}\ (M^* \notin \mathcal{Q} \wedge (Y, y') \notin R'$	3 : $\quad \mathbf{return}\ \hat{\sigma}$
8 : $\quad \wedge\ \mathsf{Verify}(\mathsf{pk}, \sigma, M^*))$	

Note that, in the above witness extractability definition, the adversary's winning condition is restricted to the extracted witness not being in R'.

Since $R \subseteq R'$, $(Y, y') \notin R'$ implies that $(Y, y') \notin R$. Therefore, it is sufficient to ensure that R' is a hard relation, which itself implies that R is also a hard relation. As a result, in our security assumptions, we make sure that R' is a hard relation.

3   LAS: An Efficient Adaptor Signature from Lattices

In this section, we describe our lattice-based adaptor signature, LAS. Let $A = [\,I_n \,\|\, A'\,] \in R_q^{n \times (n+\ell)}$ for $A' \xleftarrow{\$} R_q^{n \times \ell}$ and $H : \{0,1\}^* \to C$ be a hash function (modelled as a random oracle). We assume that the public parameters $pp = (A, H)$ are publicly available and can be used by any algorithm. In practice, A' can be generated from a small seed using an extendable output function (modelled as a random oracle) as done in Dilithium [9]. The function $f_A(x) = Ax$ over R_q is Ajtai's hash function [2] defined over module lattices where the matrix A is in Hermite normal form (HNF). It is clear that the function is additively homomorphic, and Ajtai [2] showed that it is one-way in the setting of SIS. In our case, the security is based on M-SIS (in HNF). Collision-resistance is also clear as a collision (x, x') yields an immediate M-SIS solution: $A(x-x') = 0$.

In Table 1, we first summarize the identifiers used for LAS, where the hard relations R, R' are given by $\mathfrak{R}_A, \mathfrak{R}'_A$ with $\mathfrak{R}_A \subseteq \mathfrak{R}'_A$. The statement-witness generation Gen for $\mathfrak{R}_A$ runs exactly as KeyGen. It is easy to see that if M-SIS$_{n,n+\ell+1,q,\beta}$ for $\beta = 2\gamma d(n + \ell)$ is hard, then $\mathfrak{R}_A$ and $\mathfrak{R}'_A$ are hard relations. This is because if one can find r such that $(t, r) \in \mathfrak{R}'_A$ for a random t, then

$$[\,A \,\|\, t\,] \cdot \begin{pmatrix} r \\ -1 \end{pmatrix} = 0. \text{ Hence, } \begin{pmatrix} r \\ -1 \end{pmatrix} \text{ is a solution to M-SIS}_{n,n+\ell+1,q,\beta} \text{ for } \beta = $$

$2\gamma d(n + \ell)$ since $\|r\| \leq \beta$.

Table 1. Identifiers for LAS.

Notation	Explanation	Value
d	a power-of-2 ring dimension	256
R_q	cyclotomic ring of degree d: $R_q = \mathbb{Z}_q[X]/(X^d + 1)$	$\log q \approx 24$
$\mathbb{S}_c$	the set of polynomials $f \in R_q$ with $\|f\|_\infty \leq c$ for $c \in \mathbb{Z}^+$	
n	M-SIS rank	4
ℓ	M-LWE rank	4
C	the challenge set and range of H: $\{c \in R : \|c\|_1 = \kappa \wedge \|c\|_\infty = 1\}$	$\kappa = 60$
γ	maximum absolute coefficient of a masking randomness	$\kappa d(n + \ell)$
$(Y, y) \in \mathfrak{R}_A$	the base relation with $[\,I_n \,\|\, A'\,] = A \in R_q^{n \times (n+\ell)}$: $(Y, y) = (t, r) \in \mathfrak{R}_A$ if $t = Ar$ and $\|r\|_\infty \leq 1$	
$(Y, y) \in \mathfrak{R}'_A$	the extended relation with $[\,I_n \,\|\, A'\,] = A \in R_q^{n \times (n+\ell)}$: $(Y, y) = (t, r) \in \mathfrak{R}_A$ if $t = Ar$ and $\|r\|_\infty \leq 2(\gamma - \kappa)$	$\gamma > \kappa$

Algorithm 1. Lattice-Based Signature

1: **procedure** KeyGen(): ▷ same as Gen
2:     $r \stackrel{\$}{\leftarrow} \mathbb{S}_1^{n+\ell}$
3:     $t = Ar$
4:     **return** (pk, sk) = (t, r)
5: **end procedure**

6: **procedure** Sign((pk, sk), M):
7:     $y \stackrel{\$}{\leftarrow} \mathbb{S}_\gamma^{n+\ell}$
8:     $w = Ay$
9:     $c = \mathsf{H}(\mathsf{pk}, w, M)$
10:     $z = y + cr$ where $r := \mathsf{sk}$

11:     **if** $\|z\|_\infty > \gamma - \kappa$, **then** Restart
12:     **return** $\sigma = (c, z)$
13: **end procedure**

14: **procedure** Verify(pk, σ, M):
15:     Parse $(c, z) := \sigma$
16:     **if** $\|z\|_\infty > \gamma - \kappa$, **then return** 0
17:     $w' = Az - ct$ where $t := \mathsf{pk}$
18:     **if** $c \neq \mathsf{H}(\mathsf{pk}, w', M)$, **then return** 0
19:     **return** 1
20: **end procedure**

We present the ordinary signature procedures in Algorithm 1, and then the procedures for the adaptor signature in Algorithm 2. The idea for the signature is similar to the Schnorr signature [29] with the main difference being the use of rejection sampling at Step 11. This is the so-called "Fiat-Shamir with Aborts" technique [19, 20].

In the adaptor signature part in Algorithm 2, PreSign and PreVerify operate very similar to Sign and Verify, respectively. The main issue is that the signer may not know (at the time of running PreSign) the witness y to the statement Y, and yet for many applications in practice (such as payment channel networks), one would want to make sure that having access only to the signature (but not the pre-signature) does not reveal any information on the witness y.

To this end, we need to modify the rejection sampling step. Even though the signer does not know the witness y, he does know how it is supposed to be generated in an honest run. Therefore, he knows that the maximum absolute coefficient of any honestly-generated witness is at most 1 (recall that Gen runs exactly as KeyGen). Since we have $z = y + cr + r'$ for $r' := y$ in an honestly-generated full signature, we know that the secret-dependant part $cr + r'$ has infinity norm at most $\kappa + 1$. Therefore, the signer artificially performs a stronger rejection sampling step in PreSign, where $\|\hat{z}\|_\infty \leq \gamma - \kappa - 1$ is required. This ensures that even when the witness is added to the response in Adapt, the response z still satisfies the rejection sampling condition in Sign, and thus remains publicly simulatable, i.e., no secret information including the witness is revealed.

In fact, there are further reasons for this important modification. One is in regards to adaptability. If the rejection sampling in PreSign is done exactly as in Sign, then verification of an adapted pre-signature (i.e., output of Adapt) via Verify may not succeed as the infinity norm condition may be violated due to the addition of $r' := y$. Another reason comes from the security analysis. In order to be able to simulate the outputs of both Sign and PreSign, this change to rejection sampling plays a crucial role.

Algorithm 2. LAS: Lattice-Based Adaptor Signature

1: **procedure** PreSign$((\mathsf{pk}, \mathsf{sk}), Y, M)$:
2:   $\boldsymbol{y} \xleftarrow{\$} \mathbb{S}_\gamma^{n+\ell}$
3:   $\boldsymbol{w} = \boldsymbol{A}\boldsymbol{y}$
4:   $c = \mathsf{H}(\mathsf{pk}, \boldsymbol{w} + \boldsymbol{t}', M)$ for $\boldsymbol{t}' := Y$
5:   $\hat{\boldsymbol{z}} = \boldsymbol{y} + c\boldsymbol{r}$ where $\boldsymbol{r} := \mathsf{sk}$
6:   **if** $\|\hat{\boldsymbol{z}}\|_\infty > \gamma - \kappa - 1$, **then** Restart
7:   **return** $\hat{\sigma} = (c, \hat{\boldsymbol{z}})$
8: **end procedure**

9: **procedure** PreVerify$(Y, \mathsf{pk}, \hat{\sigma}, M)$:
10:   Parse $(c, \hat{\boldsymbol{z}}) := \hat{\sigma}$ and $\boldsymbol{t}' := Y$
11:   **if** $\|\hat{\boldsymbol{z}}\|_\infty > \gamma - \kappa - 1$ **then**
12:     **return** 0
13:   **end if**
14:   $\boldsymbol{w}' = \boldsymbol{A}\hat{\boldsymbol{z}} - c\boldsymbol{t}$ where $\boldsymbol{t} := \mathsf{pk}$
15:   **if** $c \neq \mathsf{H}(\mathsf{pk}, \boldsymbol{w}' + \boldsymbol{t}', M)$ **then**
16:     **return** 0
17:   **end if**
18:     **return** 1
19: **end procedure**

20: **procedure** Adapt$((Y, y), \mathsf{pk}, \hat{\sigma}, M)$:
21:   **if** PreVerify$(Y, \mathsf{pk}, \hat{\sigma}, M) = 0$ **then**
22:     **return** $\perp$
23:   **end if**
24:   Parse $(c, \hat{\boldsymbol{z}}) := \hat{\sigma}$ and $\boldsymbol{r}' := y$
25:   **return** $\sigma = (c, \hat{\boldsymbol{z}} + \boldsymbol{r}')$
26: **end procedure**

27: **procedure** Ext$(Y, \sigma, \hat{\sigma})$:
28:   Parse $(c, \boldsymbol{z}) := \sigma$ and $(\hat{c}, \hat{\boldsymbol{z}}) := \hat{\sigma}$
29:   Parse $\boldsymbol{t}' := Y$
30:   $\boldsymbol{s} = \boldsymbol{z} - \hat{\boldsymbol{z}}$
31:   **if** $\boldsymbol{t}' \neq \boldsymbol{A}\boldsymbol{s}$, **then return** $\perp$
32:   **return** $\boldsymbol{s}$
33: **end procedure**

Let us summarize the following two facts as we will make use of them repeatedly in the security proofs.

Fact 1. *We can see that $\|c\boldsymbol{r}\|_\infty \leq \kappa$ since $\|c\|_1 \leq \kappa$ and $\|\boldsymbol{r}\|_\infty \leq 1$. Therefore, both $\hat{\boldsymbol{z}}$ in PreSign and $\boldsymbol{z}$ in Sign can be simulated publicly as they follow uniform distributions on $\mathbb{S}_{\gamma-\kappa-1}^{n+\ell}$ and $\mathbb{S}_{\gamma-\kappa}^{n+\ell}$, respectively, due to the rejection sampling.*

Fact 2. *Assuming the hardness of M-LWE$_{\ell,n,q}$, the result of $\boldsymbol{A}\boldsymbol{x}$ is (computationally) indistinguishable from a uniformly random element in $\mathcal{R}_q^n$ whenever $\boldsymbol{x} \xleftarrow{\$} \mathbb{S}_c^{n+\ell}$ for some $c \geq 1$. We can see this by realizing that $\boldsymbol{A}\boldsymbol{x} = [\boldsymbol{I}_n \| \boldsymbol{A}'] \cdot \begin{pmatrix} \boldsymbol{x}_0 \\ \boldsymbol{x}_1 \end{pmatrix} = \boldsymbol{x}_0 + \boldsymbol{A}'\boldsymbol{x}_1$. This is an M-LWE instance with the secret vector $\boldsymbol{x}_1 \in \mathbb{S}_c^\ell$ and the error vector $\boldsymbol{x}_0 \in \mathbb{S}_c^n$.*

Note that there is a *knowledge gap* between a witness used by an honest user and a witness extracted by Ext for a statement Y. In particular, an honest user's witness $y = \boldsymbol{r}$ satisfies $\|\boldsymbol{r}\|_\infty \leq 1$ (i.e., $(Y, y) \in \mathfrak{R}_A$), whereas an extracted witness $y' = \boldsymbol{r}'$ is only guaranteed to satisfy $\|\boldsymbol{r}'\|_\infty \leq 2(\gamma - \kappa)$ (i.e., $(Y, y') \in \mathfrak{R}_A'$). Such a knowledge gap is inherent in the existing *efficient* lattice-based zero-knowledge proofs such as the one underlying Dilithium. However, we emphasize that this knowledge gap does not raise a security concern as our hardness assumptions require that finding even a witness as big as an extracted witness is still hard, which itself implies that finding an honest user's witness is also hard. In the next section, we study the security aspects more rigorously.

3.1   Security Analysis

Pre-signature correctness follows via a straightforward investigation. In the following sequence of lemmas, we prove the security properties.

Lemma 1 (Weak pre-signature adaptability). LAS *satisfies weak pre-signature adaptability with respect to the relation* $\mathfrak{R}_A$ *given in Table 1.*

Proof. Let $\hat{\sigma} = (c, \hat{z})$ be a valid pre-signature with $\mathsf{PreVerify}(Y, \mathsf{pk}, \hat{\sigma}, M) = 1$ and $y = r' \in \mathbb{S}_1^{n+\ell}$ be a witness corresponding to Y. Note that $\|\hat{z}\|_\infty \leq \gamma - \kappa - 1$ since $\hat{\sigma}$ is valid. Then, $\mathsf{Adapt}((Y, y), \mathsf{pk}, \hat{\sigma}, M) = (c, \hat{z} + r') =: (c, z) = \sigma$. Now, we have

$$\|z\|_\infty = \|\hat{z} + r'\|_\infty \leq \|\hat{z}\|_\infty + \|r'\|_\infty = (\gamma - \kappa - 1) + 1 = \gamma - \kappa. \tag{1}$$

We further have

$$\mathsf{H}(\mathsf{pk}, \boldsymbol{A}z - ct, M) = \mathsf{H}(\mathsf{pk}, \boldsymbol{A}(\hat{z} + r') - ct, M) = \mathsf{H}(\mathsf{pk}, \boldsymbol{A}\hat{z} - ct + \boldsymbol{A}r', M)$$
$$= \mathsf{H}(\mathsf{pk}, \boldsymbol{A}\hat{z} - ct + t', M) = c. \tag{2}$$

From (1) and (2), it follows that σ is valid, i.e., $\mathsf{Verify}(\mathsf{pk}, \sigma, M) = 1$. □

Remark 1. Observe in the proof of Lemma 1 that we crucially rely on the fact that for a witness $y = r'$ in $\mathfrak{R}_A$, we have $\|r'\|_\infty \leq 1$. An *extracted* witness s does not necessarily obey this rule as the relation $\mathfrak{R}'_A$ only requires $\|s\|_\infty \leq 2(\gamma - \kappa)$. Therefore, extra care needs to be taken when dealing with the cases where an extracted witness is used to adapt a pre-signature.

Lemma 2 (Witness extractability). *If* M-LWE$_{\ell,n,q}$ *and* M-SIS$_{n,n+\ell+1,q,\beta}$ *for* $\beta = 2\gamma\sqrt{d(n + \ell)}$ *are hard, then* LAS *is witness extractable in the random oracle model.*

Proof. Here, we only investigate the case that the signature output by the adversary shares the same challenge with the pre-signature. The other case (where the two challenges are distinct) can be proven exactly as in **Case 2** of the proof of Lemma 3 because how Y is generated is irrelevant for that case.

For a given pair of public key and statement $(\mathsf{pk}, Y) = (t, t')$ and a message M, let $\hat{\sigma} = (c, \hat{z})$ and $\sigma = (c, z)$ be a valid pre-signature and a valid signature, respectively. Then, from the corresponding verification algorithms (i.e., Verify and $\mathsf{PreVerify}$), we have $\mathsf{H}(\mathsf{pk}, \boldsymbol{A}z - ct, M) = \mathsf{H}(\mathsf{pk}, \boldsymbol{A}\hat{z} - ct + t', M)$. Since H is modelled as a random oracle, this holds only when $\boldsymbol{A}z - ct = \boldsymbol{A}\hat{z} - ct + t'$, which implies that $\boldsymbol{A}z - \boldsymbol{A}\hat{z} = \boldsymbol{A}(z - \hat{z}) = t'$. It is easy to see that $\|z - \hat{z}\|_\infty \leq 2(\gamma - \kappa)$. Therefore, for the output $s = z - \hat{z}$ of $\mathsf{Ext}(Y, \sigma, \hat{\sigma})$, we have $(t', s) \in \mathfrak{R}'_A$. Note also that s is non-zero since t' is non-zero except for a negligible probability. □

Lemma 3 (Unforgeability). *If* M-SIS$_{n,n+\ell+1,q,\beta}$ *for* $\beta = 2\gamma\sqrt{d(n + \ell)}$ *and* M-LWE$_{\ell,n,q}$ *are hard, then* LAS *is* aEUF-CMA *secure in the random oracle model.*

Proof. First, from the assumptions in the statement, we know that

1. both $\mathfrak{R}_A$ and $\mathfrak{R}'_A$ are hard relations,
2. any public key output by KeyGen and any statement output by Gen is indistinguishable from a uniformly random element in $\mathcal{R}_q^n$ due to Fact 2.

Let $\mathcal{F}$ be a PPT adversary who wins the aEUF-CMA security game with non-negligible probability. We will build an adversary $\mathcal{S}$ that solves M-SIS$_{n,n+\ell+1,q,\beta}$. Let $\beta = 2\gamma\sqrt{d(n+\ell)}$ and $\boldsymbol{B} = [\,\boldsymbol{I}_n \,\|\, \boldsymbol{A}' \,\|\, \boldsymbol{a}\,] \in \mathcal{R}_q^{n \times (n+\ell+1)}$ for $\boldsymbol{A}' \xleftarrow{\$} \mathcal{R}_q^{n \times \ell}$ and $\boldsymbol{a} \xleftarrow{\$} \mathcal{R}_q^n$. Assume that $\mathcal{S}$ wants to solve M-SIS w.r.t. $\boldsymbol{B}$. Let $\boldsymbol{A}$ denote $[\,\boldsymbol{I}_n \,\|\, \boldsymbol{A}'\,]$.

Setup. $\mathcal{S}$ sets $\boldsymbol{A}$ together with some hash function H as the public parameters. It is clear that $\boldsymbol{A}$ has the correct distribution. Then, it sets $\mathsf{pk} = \boldsymbol{t} = \boldsymbol{B}\boldsymbol{r}$ where $\boldsymbol{r} = \begin{pmatrix} \boldsymbol{r}' \\ 1 \end{pmatrix}$ for $\boldsymbol{r}' \xleftarrow{\$} \mathbb{S}_1^{n+\ell}$. $\mathcal{S}$ sends pk to $\mathcal{F}$. By M-LWE$_{\ell,n,q}$, pk is indistinguishable from a public key output by KeyGen since $\boldsymbol{B}\boldsymbol{r} = \boldsymbol{A}\boldsymbol{r}' + \boldsymbol{a}$ looks uniformly random as $\boldsymbol{A}\boldsymbol{r}'$ does. Note also that $\boldsymbol{t} = \mathsf{pk}$ is non-zero with overwhelming probability.

Oracle simulation. For $\mathcal{O}_\mathsf{S}(M)$, $\mathcal{S}$ picks $\boldsymbol{z} \xleftarrow{\$} \mathbb{S}_{\gamma-\kappa}^{n+\ell}$ and $c \xleftarrow{\$} \mathcal{C}$, and programs the random oracle such that $c = \mathsf{H}(\mathsf{pk}, \boldsymbol{A}\boldsymbol{z} - c\boldsymbol{t}, M)$. If the input of H has been queried before, $\mathcal{S}$ aborts. Otherwise, $\mathcal{S}$ returns $\sigma = (c, \boldsymbol{z})$. The simulated output is indistinguishable from a real one due to Fact 1.

For $\mathcal{O}_\mathsf{pS}(M, Y)$, the simulator picks $\hat{\boldsymbol{z}} \xleftarrow{\$} \mathbb{S}_{\gamma-\kappa-1}^{n+\ell}$ and $c \xleftarrow{\$} \mathcal{C}$, and programs the random oracle such that $c = \mathsf{H}(\mathsf{pk}, \boldsymbol{A}\hat{\boldsymbol{z}} - c\boldsymbol{t} + \boldsymbol{t}', M)$ for $\boldsymbol{t}' := Y$. If the input of H has been queried before, $\mathcal{S}$ aborts. Otherwise, the simulator returns $\hat{\sigma} = (c, \hat{\boldsymbol{z}})$. The simulated output is indistinguishable from a real one due to Fact 1.

In both cases, the probability of an abort is negligible as $\mathcal{F}$ can make at most polynomially many queries to H.

Forgery. $\mathcal{F}$ returns the target message M^* to $\mathcal{S}$. $\mathcal{S}$ sets $Y = -\boldsymbol{a}$ and computes a pre-signature $\hat{\sigma}^* = (c^*, \hat{\boldsymbol{z}}^*)$ using the simulation method above. $\mathcal{S}$ sends $(Y, \hat{\sigma}^*)$ to $\mathcal{F}$. Again, note that Y is indistinguishable from a real output by Gen, and $\hat{\sigma}^*$ is indistinguishable from a real output of PreSign. Finally, $\mathcal{F}$ returns a forged signature $\sigma = (c, \boldsymbol{z})$ on M^*.

Case 1 $(c^* = c)$: If this is the case, then as shown in the proof of Lemma 2, $\mathcal{S}$ can extract a witness to $\mathfrak{R}'_A$. That is, $\mathcal{S}$ gets $(Y, y) \in \mathfrak{R}'_A$ with $\boldsymbol{s}' := y$, which implies that $\boldsymbol{A}\boldsymbol{s}' = -\boldsymbol{a}$ (since $Y = -\boldsymbol{a}$) and $\|\boldsymbol{s}'\|_\infty \leq 2(\gamma-\kappa)$. This is equivalent to $\boldsymbol{B}\boldsymbol{s} = \boldsymbol{0}$ for $\boldsymbol{s} = \begin{pmatrix} \boldsymbol{s}' \\ 1 \end{pmatrix}$. Note that $\|\boldsymbol{s}\| \leq \beta$. Hence, $\mathcal{S}$ finds a solution to M-SIS$_{n,n+\ell+1,q,\beta}$.

Case 2 $(c^* \neq c)$: In this case, we know that the forged signature's challenge comes from a random oracle query output (with overwhelming probability). Therefore, we can use a standard rewinding argument as in [26], where $\mathcal{S}$ rewinds $\mathcal{F}$ to get another forgery $\sigma' = (c', \boldsymbol{z}')$ such that $c' \neq c$ and $\mathsf{H}(\mathsf{pk}, \boldsymbol{A}\boldsymbol{z}' - c'\boldsymbol{t}, M^*) = \mathsf{H}(\mathsf{pk}, \boldsymbol{A}\boldsymbol{z} - c\boldsymbol{t}, M^*)$. Therefore, we have

$$\boldsymbol{A}\boldsymbol{z}' - c'\boldsymbol{t} = \boldsymbol{A}\boldsymbol{z} - c\boldsymbol{t} \iff \boldsymbol{A}(\boldsymbol{z}' - \boldsymbol{z}) = (c' - c)\boldsymbol{t}. \tag{3}$$

Since $c' \neq c$, we have $z' - z \neq 0$. The above equation (3) can be equivalently written as

$$B \begin{pmatrix} z' - z \\ 0 \end{pmatrix} = (c' - c)t. \tag{4}$$

Now recalling that $t = Br$, we also have

$$(c' - c)t = B \cdot (c' - c)r. \tag{5}$$

Subtracting (3) from (5), we get

$$B \left[(c' - c)r - \begin{pmatrix} z' - z \\ 0 \end{pmatrix} \right] = 0. \tag{6}$$

Recalling that the last coordinate of r is 1, i.e., non-zero, the above gives a non-trivial solution to M-SIS$_{n,n+\ell+1,q,\beta}$. Here note that $\|z' - z\| \leq 2(\gamma - \kappa)\sqrt{d(n+\ell)} < \beta$ and $\|(c' - c)r\| \leq 2\kappa\sqrt{d(n+\ell+1)}$. Since $\gamma \gg \kappa$, the total norm of the M-SIS solution remains below $\beta = 2\gamma\sqrt{d(n+\ell)}$. $\qquad\square$

3.2 Parameter Setting and Performance Analysis

First, we set $\gamma = \kappa d(n + \ell)$ so that the average number of restarts in Sign and PreSign is about $e < 3$. Then, we set $d = 256$ and $\kappa = 60$, which ensures that the challenge set $\mathcal{C}$ has more than 2^{256} elements. Finally, in order to meet the M-SIS$_{n,n+\ell+1,q,\beta}$ and M-LWE$_{\ell,n,q}$ security requirements for $\beta = 2\gamma\sqrt{d(n+\ell)}$, we set $n = \ell = 4$ and $q \approx 2^{24}$. Only the size of the modulus q is important, and therefore the concrete value can be chosen to allow fast computation such as Number Theoretic Transformation (NTT).

In estimating the practical security of M-SIS and M-LWE, we follow the methodology outlined in [10, Section 3.2.4] and measure the practical hardness in terms of "root Hermite factor" δ. This parameter setting yields $\delta < 1.0045$ for both M-SIS and M-LWE. $\delta \approx 1.0045$ has been used in recent works, e.g., [12–14] for targeting 128-bit post-quantum security. From here, we can compute the concrete signature length as

$$|\sigma| = d(n + \ell) \log(2\gamma)/8 + 32 \text{ bytes} \approx 3210 \text{ bytes}. \tag{7}$$

This length is slightly larger than the size of Dilithium (2701 bytes) [9] with recommended parameters. The main reason is because we do not employ the optimizations for ease of presentation.

In terms of the computational efficiency, the operations performed in LAS are almost identical to those in Dilithium. Thus, hundreds of signing (and even more verification) can be done per second on a standard PC as shown in [9, Table 2].

4   Applications

In this section, we present two blockchain applications of our adaptor signature, namely atomic swaps and payment channel networks. To match with the existing adaptor signature applications, we assume an Unspent Transaction Output (UTXO)-based blockchain like Bitcoin where the signature algorithm is replaced with a lattice-based signature scheme given in Algorithm 1 . In the UTXO model, coins are kept in addresses where each address consists of the amount and the spending condition. The spending condition is defined by the scripting language and the most common ones are signature and hash preimage verifications, and timing conditions. For our applications, we also assume that the underlying blockchain supports these scripts.

4.1   Atomic Swaps

An atomic swap can be defined between two users u_1 and u_2 who want to exchange two different cryptocurrencies c_1 and c_2. The crucial point of the exchange is ensuring fairness, i.e., either both parties receive their expected output or none do. In [23], an atomic swap protocol is presented with the following steps.

Setup. First, u_1 shares a hash value $h_1 := H(r_1)$ of a secret r_1 to u_2. Then, u_1 creates a transaction on the coins c_1 such that it can be spendable by u_2 only if the preimage of h_1 is presented. Similarly, u_2 also creates a transaction on the coins c_2 with the same preimage condition for u_1. Here, both transactions have timeouts t_i such that, once t_i elapses, u_i can redeem c_i if the counterparty does not continue to the exchange. Also, the timelock, t_2, on u_2's transaction is shorter (i.e., $t_2 < t_1$) to ensure that u_2 would have enough time to react. First, u_1 publishes her transaction on-chain, then u_2 does the same.

Swap. Once both transactions are on-chain, u_1 can obtain c_2 by revealing r_1, which yields to u_2 obtaining c_1. Note that this protocol requires both scripting languages of the cryptocurrencies to have preimage conditioned scripts. Later on, in [24], the scriptless version of the protocol is presented where the hash condition is embedded into the signature algorithm.

Let us explain how to achieve atomic swaps using LAS, which requires careful analysis because of the aforementioned knowledge gap. In the scenario below, an *extracted* witness, which satisfies an *extended* relation (i.e., $\mathfrak{R}'_A$, but not necessarily $\mathfrak{R}_A$), will constitute the opening condition to receive coins.

Let (pk_i, sk_i) be the public-secret key pair for user u_i for $i = 1, 2$. First, u_1 generates a statement-witness pair $(Y, y) = (t, r) \in \mathfrak{R}_A$ as in Section 3, and sends Y to u_2 along with a proof π of knowledge of a witness r such that $t = Ar$ and $\|r\|_\infty \leq 1$. Such a proof can be realized using the recent Esgin-Nguyen-Seiler proof system [11]. Then, u_1 also creates a pre-signature $\hat{\sigma}_1 \leftarrow \text{PreSign}((pk_1, sk_1), Y, tx_1)$ for tx_1 spending the coins c_1 to u_2. After verifying the proof π, u_2 similarly creates a pre-signature $\hat{\sigma}_2 \leftarrow \text{PreSign}((pk_2, sk_2), Y, tx_2)$ for tx_2 spending the coins c_2 to u_1. Then, the two pre-signatures are exchanged between the parties. Now u_1 adapts the pre-signature

$\hat{\sigma}_2$ as $\sigma_2 \leftarrow \mathsf{Adapt}((Y, y), \mathsf{pk}_2, \hat{\sigma}_2, \mathsf{tx}_2)$, and aborts if $\sigma_2 = \bot$. Otherwise, he publishes the full signature σ_2 on the second cryptocurrency's blockchain in order to receive the coins c_2. Then, seeing σ_2, u_2 runs $y' = s \leftarrow \mathsf{Ext}(Y, \sigma_2, \hat{\sigma}_2)$ and $\sigma_1 \leftarrow \mathsf{Adapt}((Y, y'), \mathsf{pk}_1, \hat{\sigma}_1, \mathsf{tx}_1)$. If any of them returns $\bot$, u_2 aborts. Otherwise, u_2 publishes σ_1 on the first cryptocurrency's blockchain to receive the coins c_1. This interaction is depicted in Figure 1.

Let us now analyze whether u_1 receives c_2 if and only if u_2 receives c_1. If u_1 does not receive c_2, i.e., u_1 aborts, then u_2 clearly cannot receive c_1 due to the aEUF-CMA security of LAS as u_2 only has the pre-signature $\hat{\sigma}_1$ and the statement Y (without a witness to Y). On the other hand, if u_1 does receive c_2, this means that σ_2 is valid signature published on a blockchain, i.e., accessible by u_2. Therefore, by the witness extractability of LAS, u_2 can extract a witness s to $Y = t$ such that $t = As$. Recall that u_1 proved knowledge of a witness r to $Y = t$ such that $\|r\|_\infty \leq 1$. By the hardness of M-SIS, it must be the case that $s = r$ as otherwise $A(s - r) = 0$ gives a solution to M-SIS$_{n, n+l, q, \beta}$ for $\beta = 2\gamma\sqrt{d(n+\ell)}$. As a result, we have that $\|s\|_\infty = \|r\|_\infty \leq 1$. Therefore, $s \in \mathfrak{R}_A$ and the pre-signature adaptability works, and hence the signature σ_1 adapted by u_2 passes the verification. Note that without the proof of knowledge π,

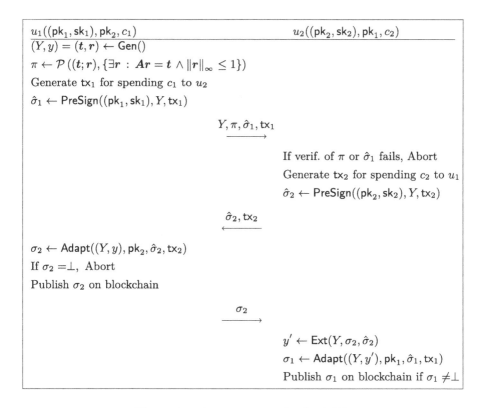

Fig. 1. Atomic swap protocol using LAS.

we cannot guarantee that the extracted witness s will satisfy $\|s\|_\infty \leq 1$, and hence pre-signature adaptability would not have been guaranteed without π. In other words, π is essential to make sure that u_2 receives the coins c_1.

We also note that even though a lattice-based proof of knowledge, π, is relatively costly in terms of communication in practice (but very efficient in computation), this proof is only exchanged between the parties, and not published on blockchain. Therefore, it does not incur additional on-chain storage costs.

4.2   Payment Channel Networks

Payment channel networks (PCNs) [7,16,21,27] are one of the promising solutions to the scalability issues of blockchains. More specifically, many blockchains have poor transaction throughput compared to alternatives like credit card networks because of their consensus mechanisms, where every party (miner) approves and stores every transaction. PCNs improve the throughput by moving some transactions off-chain while relying on the security of the blockchain. In a PCN, two parties can lock coins into a channel where they can make instant and arbitrarily many transactions between each other so long as they have enough balances. One of the most popular PCNs built on Bitcoin is the Lightning network [27]. The overall structure of our post-quantum PCN resembles the Lightning network.

A payment channel consists of three steps: create, update, and close. In the creation phase, parties deposit some coins into the channel and create a funding transaction that spends the input addresses into a single output of the channel. The funding transaction is published on the blockchain and afterward, all of the updates are done off-chain until the closing part. The output condition of funding is spendable only if both parties sign it, which ensures an agreement by both parties. The condition can be implemented by a two-party multi-signature.

In realizing a two-party multi-signature, a straightforward option is to simply combine two individual signatures. Alternatively, there is a lattice-based multi-signature in [4], which can be used in the two-party setting. The underlying signature uses the same "Fiat-Shamir with Aborts" technique, and as stated in [4], the multi-signature can be realized over module lattices as in our work.

When parties want to send/receive coins in the channel, they make off-chain transactions and update the channel balances. In each update, parties create new commit transactions that spend the output of the funding transaction into the two new addresses of the parties with their corresponding balances. Also, parties revoke the previous commits by sharing the signing keys with each other. The revocation can be seen as a punishment mechanism to prevent a malicious party from publishing an old commitment. Once parties are done with the channel, they can close it and obtain their coins by publishing the latest commitment on-chain. A payment channel creation, update, and closing can be done in the same manner as the Lightning network. Now, we investigate how to achieve *multi-hop* payments with our adaptor signature scheme.

A *network* of channels allows parties to make multi-hop payments. More specifically, parties, who do not have a direct channel, can route a payment using the channels of some intermediary nodes. In these multi-hop payments, it is crucial to synchronize each channel on the route so that either all of them update accordingly or no one does. The Lightning network achieves this by using HTLC (hash-time lock contract). However, in [21], the authors presented privacy concerns as well as the *wormhole attack* for the HTLC mechanism. In this manner, we adopt the AMHL (anonymous multi-hop lock) technique [21] for the multi-hop payments. Also, it is stated that AMHLs are sufficient to construct a payment channel network [21, Theorem 4]. In a scenario where sender S (or I_0) wants to send payment through the intermediary nodes $I_1, \ldots, I_{k-1}$ to the receiver R (or I_k), AMHL-based multi-hop payment works as follows (for simplicity, we omit the fees given to the intermediary nodes).

Setup. S chooses random strings $\ell_0, \ell_1, \ldots, \ell_{k-1}$, and computes $y_j := \sum_{i=0}^{j} \ell_i$ and $Y_j := G(y_j)$ for $j = 0, \ldots, k-1$ where G is an additively homomorphic one-way function. Then, S shares (Y_{j-1}, Y_j, ℓ_j) with each intermediary I_j for $i = 1, \ldots, k-1$ and (Y_{k-1}, y_{k-1}) with R. Each intermediary party I_j validates the correctness of values by using the homomorphism, i.e., checking that $G(\ell_j) \oplus Y_{j-1} = G(y_j) = Y_j$, where $\oplus$ denotes the operation in the range of G.

Payment. S makes a conditional payment to I_1 requiring preimage of Y_0, while each intermediary party I_j, for $j = 1, \ldots, k-1$, makes a payment of the same amount to I_{j+1} with a condition on preimage of Y_j after they receive a similar payment from I_{j-1}. Once all conditional payments are placed, S reveals the preimage y_{k-1} to $R = I_k$ showing that she can redeem the payment. This creates a chain reaction as follows. When an intermediary party I_j receives y_j from I_{j+1}, he can compute $y_{j-1} = y_j - \ell_j$ and redeem the payment by revealing y_{j-1} to I_{j-1}. The procedure is completed once all the channels are updated accordingly.

We can realize AMHL in the post-quantum setting using LAS, but again a special care is required due to the knowledge gap and the use of rejection sampling. First of all, we assume that the length of the PCN is at most $K \ll q$ (i.e., $k \le K \ll q$) and update the norm check at Steps 6 and 11 in Algorithm 2 by $\|\hat{z}\|_\infty > \gamma - \kappa - K$. Now, S samples $r_j \xleftarrow{\$} \mathbb{S}_1^{n+\ell}$, and computes $s_j = \sum_{i=0}^{j} r_i$ and $t_j = As_j$ for $j = 0, \ldots, k-1$. Observe that we have $\|s_j\|_\infty \le k \le K$ for all $j = 0, \ldots, k-1$. Then, S treats $Y_j = t_j$, $y_j = s_j$ and $\ell_j = r_j$ for $j = 0, \ldots, k-1$. The additively homomorphic function is $f_A(x) = Ax$ (over $\mathcal{R}_q$) mentioned in Section 3. Then, the Setup phase of AMHL described above is run. Additionally, for each $j = 0, \ldots, k-2$, S sends I_{j+1} a NIZK proof π_{j+1} that she knows a witness $y_j = s_j$ to $Y_j = t_j$ such that

$$\|s_j\|_\infty \le K. \tag{8}$$

After this setup, payment phase begins. Let $(\mathsf{pk}_j, \mathsf{sk}_j)$ be I_j's public-secret key pair used in his channel with I_{j+1}, and tx_j be the transaction transferring the relevant coins from I_j to I_{j+1}. S creates a pre-signature $\hat{\sigma}_0 \leftarrow \mathsf{PreSign}((\mathsf{pk}_0, \mathsf{sk}_0), Y_0, \mathsf{tx}_0)$ and sends it to I_1. Then, for $j = 1, \ldots, k-1$, each user I_j creates a pre-signature $\hat{\sigma}_j \leftarrow \mathsf{PreSign}((\mathsf{pk}_j, \mathsf{sk}_j), Y_j, \mathsf{tx}_j)$ after receiving the pre-signature $\hat{\sigma}_{j-1}$ from I_{j-1}. Once all pre-signatures are generated and transferred, S reveals y_{k-1}

$S(\mathsf{pk}_0, \mathsf{sk}_0)$ $\qquad\qquad\qquad$ **[SETUP]** $\qquad$ $I_j(\mathsf{pk}_j, \mathsf{sk}_j)$ $\qquad$ $j = 1, \ldots, k$

---

for $j = 0, \ldots, k-1$

$$s_j = \sum_{i=0}^{j} r_i \text{ for } r_j \stackrel{\$}{\leftarrow} \mathbb{S}_1^{n+\ell}$$

$t_j = A s_j$

$Y_j := t_j,\ y_j := s_j,\ \ell_j := r_j$

for $j = 0, \ldots, k-2$

$\mathsf{st}_j = \{\exists s : A s = t_j \wedge \|s\|_\infty \leq K\}$

$\pi_{j+1} \leftarrow \mathcal{P}((t_j; s_j), \mathsf{st}_j)$

$T_{j+1} := (Y_j, \ell_{j+1}, \pi_{j+1})$

$T_k := (Y_{k-1}, y_{k-1})$ $\qquad\qquad \xrightarrow{\quad T_j \quad}$

$\qquad\qquad\qquad\qquad\qquad\qquad$ **if** $j \neq k$ **then**

$\qquad\qquad\qquad\qquad\qquad\qquad$ $T_j =: (Y_{j-1}, \ell_j, \pi_j) =: (t_{j-1}, r_j, \pi_j)$

$\qquad\qquad\qquad\qquad\qquad\qquad$ **if** $\mathcal{V}(t_{j-1}, \mathsf{st}_{j-1}, \pi_j) = 0$, Abort

$\qquad\qquad\qquad\qquad\qquad\qquad$ $Y_j' := t_j' = A r_j + t_{j-1}$

$\qquad\qquad\qquad\qquad\qquad\qquad$ $Z_j := (Y_j', Y_{j-1}, \ell_j)$

$\qquad\qquad\qquad\qquad\qquad\qquad$ **[PAYMENT]**

$I_j((\mathsf{pk}_j, \mathsf{sk}_j), \mathsf{pk}_{j-1}, Z_j)$ $\qquad\qquad\qquad$ $I_{j+1}((\mathsf{pk}_{j+1}, \mathsf{sk}_{j+1}), \mathsf{pk}_j, Z_{j+1})$

Parse $Z_j = (Y_j', Y_{j-1}, \ell_j)$

Obtain $\hat{\sigma}_{j-1}$ from I_{j-1}

Generate tx_j, spending coins to I_{j+1}

$\hat{\sigma}_j \leftarrow \mathsf{PreSign}((\mathsf{pk}_j, \mathsf{sk}_j), Y_j', \mathsf{tx}_j)$ $\qquad \xrightarrow{\quad \hat{\sigma}_j \quad}$

$\qquad\qquad\qquad\qquad\qquad\qquad$ Parse $Z_{j+1} = (Y_{j+1}', Y_j, \ell_{j+1})$

$\qquad\qquad\qquad\qquad\qquad\qquad$ Obtain σ_{j+1} from I_{j+2}

$\qquad\qquad\qquad\qquad\qquad\qquad$ $y_{j+1}' \leftarrow \mathsf{Ext}(Y_{j+1}', \sigma_{j+1}, \hat{\sigma}_{j+1})$

$\qquad\qquad\qquad\qquad\qquad\qquad$ // Note $\hat{\sigma}_{j+1}$ is created by I_{j+1}

$\qquad\qquad\qquad\qquad\qquad\qquad$ $y_j'' = y_{j+1}' - \ell_{j+1}$

$\qquad\qquad\qquad\qquad\qquad\qquad$ $\sigma_j \leftarrow \mathsf{Adapt}((Y_j, y_j''), \mathsf{pk}_j, \hat{\sigma}_j, \mathsf{tx}_j)$

$\qquad\qquad\qquad\qquad \xleftarrow{\quad \sigma_j \quad}$

$y_j' \leftarrow \mathsf{Ext}(Y_j', \sigma_j, \hat{\sigma}_j)$

$y_{j-1}'' = y_j' - \ell_j$

$\sigma_{j-1} \leftarrow \mathsf{Adapt}((Y_{j-1}, y_{j-1}''), \mathsf{pk}_{j-1}, \hat{\sigma}_{j-1}, \mathsf{tx}_{j-1})$

Fig. 2. Anonymous multi-hop payments using LAS. We assume that (i) T_j's are transmitted confidentially, (ii) pre-signature transmission from I_j to I_{j+1} happens only if that from I_{j-1} to I_j already happened, and (iii) signature transmission from I_{j+1} to I_j happens only if that from I_{j+2} to I_{j+1} already happened.

to R, which allows R to adapt the pre-signature $\hat{\sigma}_{k-1}$ to σ_{k-1} in order to receive the relevant coins from I_{k-1}. R sends σ_{k-1} to I_{k-1}. From here, I_{k-1} extracts a witness y'_{k-1} to Y_{k-1}. Then, she computes $y''_{k-2} = y'_{k-1} - \ell_{k-1}$ and uses it to complete the pre-signature $\hat{\sigma}_{k-2}$. Continuing this way, completion of a pre-signature by I_j enables I_{j-1} to obtain a witness to Y_{j-1} and then compute a witness to Y_{j-2} using ℓ_j. The process ends with S receiving σ_0. This anonymous multi-hop payment procedure is depicted in Figure 2.

Let us analyze the details now. First of all, each party I_j has a proof that S knows a witness $y_{j-1} = s_{j-1}$ to Y_{j-1} satisfying (8). Due to the M-SIS hardness as before, no party I_j can obtain another witness to Y_{j-1}, but y_{j-1} generated by S. Therefore, each party I_j is ensured that the witness he extracts will have infinity norm at most K. As a result, each party I_j will be able to adapt the pre-signature $\hat{\sigma}_{j-1}$ successfully and claim his coins thanks to the aforementioned change to Steps 6 and 11 in Algorithm 2.

We emphasize again the importance of the proof π_j's that guarantee pre-signature adaptability. These proofs are only communicated off-chain and thus do not incur any additional on-chain cost, and can be realized using the techniques in [11]. Moreover, the change to Steps 6 and 11 in Algorithm 2 is also important as, in this setting, even honestly-generated witnesses have potentially absolute coefficients greater than 1, but still at most K. Note that this change does not affect the security assumptions as still the original conditions (and even stronger ones) in Algorithms 1 and 2 hold. The only effect is that PreSign may have more restarts, but for most practical settings of, say, $K \leq 50$ (i.e., the length of the PCN is at most 50), the effect will be minimal. In practice, for example, in Lightning Network, the route search algorithm typically stops after $K = 20$ [1].

5 Conclusion

In this work, we constructed the first post-quantum adaptor signature based on standard lattice assumptions. We also showed that our construction, LAS, leads to efficient atomic swaps and payment channel networks in the post-quantum world. In particular, our applications do not incur additional costs on the blockchain, other than the cost of an ordinary lattice-based signature.

References

1. Basis of lightning technology, available at: https://github.com/lightningnetwork/lightning-rfc/blob/master/00-introduction.md
2. Ajtai, M.: Generating hard instances of lattice problems (extended abstract). In: STOC. pp. 99–108. ACM (1996)
3. Aumayr, L., Ersoy, O., Erwig, A., Faust, S., Hostakova, K., Maffei, M., Moreno-Sanchez, P., Riahi, S.: Generalized bitcoin-compatible channels. Cryptology ePrint Archive, Report 2020/476 (2020), https://eprint.iacr.org/2020/476
4. El Bansarkhani, R., Sturm, J.: An efficient lattice-based multisignature scheme with applications to bitcoins. In: Foresti, S., Persiano, G. (eds.) CANS 2016. LNCS, vol. 10052, pp. 140–155. Springer, Cham (2016). https://doi.org/10.1007/978-3-319-48965-0_9

5. Buterin, V.: Understanding serenity, part i: Abstraction (2015), https://blog. ethereum.org/2015/12/24/understanding-serenity-part-i-abstraction/, Accessed on 20 April 2020

6. Damgård, I.: On Σ-protocols. Lecture Notes, University of Aarhus, Department for Computer Science (2002), https://www.cs.au.dk/~ivan/Sigma.pdf

7. Decker, C., Wattenhofer, R.: A fast and scalable payment network with bitcoin duplex micropayment channels. In: Pelc, A., Schwarzmann, A.A. (eds.) SSS 2015. LNCS, vol. 9212, pp. 3–18. Springer, Cham (2015). https://doi.org/10.1007/978-3-319-21741-3_1

8. Dryja, T.: Discreet log contracts, https://adiabat.github.io/dlc.pdf

9. Ducas, L., Lepoint, T., Lyubashevsky, V., Schwabe, P., Seiler, G., Stehlé, D.: Crystals-Dilithium: Digital signatures from module lattices. In: CHES. vol. 2018–1 (2018), https://eprint.iacr.org/2017/633.pdf

10. Esgin, M.F.: Practice-Oriented Techniques in Lattice-Based Cryptography. Ph.D. thesis, Monash University (5 2020). https://doi.org/10.26180/5eb8f525b3562, https://bridges.monash.edu/articles/Practice-Oriented_Techniques_in_Lattice-Based_Cryptography/12279728

11. Esgin, M.F., Nguyen, N.K., Seiler, G.: Practical exact proofs from lattices: New techniques to exploit fully-splitting rings. Cryptology ePrint Archive, Report 2020/518 (2020), https://eprint.iacr.org/2020/518

12. Esgin, M.F., Steinfeld, R., Liu, J.K., Liu, D.: Lattice-based zero-knowledge proofs: new techniques for shorter and faster constructions and applications. In: Boldyreva, A., Micciancio, D. (eds.) CRYPTO 2019. LNCS, vol. 11692, pp. 115–146. Springer, Cham (2019). https://doi.org/10.1007/978-3-030-26948-7_5

13. Esgin, M.F., Steinfeld, R., Sakzad, A., Liu, J.K., Liu, D.: Short lattice-based one-out-of-many proofs and applications to ring signatures. In: Deng, R.H., Gauthier-Umaña, V., Ochoa, M., Yung, M. (eds.) ACNS 2019. LNCS, vol. 11464, pp. 67–88. Springer, Cham (2019). https://doi.org/10.1007/978-3-030-21568-2_4

14. Esgin, M.F., Zhao, R.K., Steinfeld, R., Liu, J.K., Liu, D.: MatRiCT: Efficient, scalable and post-quantum blockchain confidential transactions protocol. In: Proceedings of the 2019 ACM SIGSAC Conference on Computer and Communications Security. pp. 567–584. CCS '19, ACM (2019). https://doi.org/10.1145/3319535. 3354200, (Full version at https://eprint.iacr.org/2019/1287)

15. Fournier, L.: One-time verifiably encrypted signatures a.k.a. adaptor signatures (2019), https://github.com/LLFourn/one-time-VES/blob/master/main.pdf

16. Gudgeon, L., Moreno-Sanchez, P., Roos, S., McCorry, P., Gervais, A.: Sok: off the chain transactions. IACR Cryptol. ePrint Arch. **2019**, 360 (2019)

17. Hcash: Hcash features, https://h.cash/#section4, Accessed on 20 April 2020

18. Langlois, A., Stehlé, D.: Worst-case to average-case reductions for module lattices. Design Code Cryptogr. **75**(3), 565–599 (2014). https://doi.org/10.1007/s10623-014-9938-4

19. Lyubashevsky, V.: Fiat-shamir with aborts: applications to lattice and factoring-based signatures. In: Matsui, M. (ed.) ASIACRYPT 2009. LNCS, vol. 5912, pp. 598–616. Springer, Heidelberg (2009). https://doi.org/10.1007/978-3-642-10366-7_35

20. Lyubashevsky, V.: Lattice signatures without trapdoors. In: Pointcheval, D., Johansson, T. (eds.) EUROCRYPT 2012. LNCS, vol. 7237, pp. 738–755. Springer, Heidelberg (2012). https://doi.org/10.1007/978-3-642-29011-4_43

21. Malavolta, G., Moreno-Sanchez, P., Schneidewind, C., Kate, A., Maffei, M.: Anonymous multi-hop locks for blockchain scalability and interoperability. In: 26th Annual Network and Distributed System Security Symposium, NDSS 2019, San Diego, California, USA, February 24–27, 2019 (2019), https://www.ndss-symposium.org/ndss-paper/anonymous-multi-hop-locks-for-blockchain-scalability-and-interoperability/
22. NIST: Post-quantum cryptography - call for proposals (2017), https://csrc.nist.gov/Projects/Post-Quantum-Cryptography/Post-Quantum-Cryptography-Standardization/Call-for-Proposals, Accessed on 20 April 2020
23. Nolan, T.: Alt chains and atomic transfers, https://bitcointalk.org/index.php?topic=193281.msg2224949#msg2224949
24. Poelstra, A.: Adaptor signatures and atomic swaps from scriptless scripts, https://github.com/ElementsProject/scriptless-scripts/blob/master/md/atomic-swap.md
25. Poelstra, A.: Scriptless scripts. Presentation Slides, https://lists.launchpad.net/mimblewimble/msg00086.html
26. Pointcheval, D., Stern, J.: Security arguments for digital signatures and blind signatures. J. Cryptol. **13**(3), 361–396 (2000)
27. Poon, J., Dryja, T.: The Bitcoin Lightning Network: Scalable Off-Chain Instant Payments (2016), draft version 0.5.9.2, available at https://lightning.network/lightning-network-paper.pdf
28. Regev, O.: On lattices, learning with errors, random linear codes, and cryptography. J. ACM **56**(6), 1–40 (2009)
29. Schnorr, C.P.: Efficient Identification and Signatures for Smart Cards. In: Brassard, G. (ed.) CRYPTO 1989. LNCS, vol. 435, pp. 239–252. Springer, New York (1990). https://doi.org/10.1007/0-387-34805-0_22
30. Alberto Torres, W., Kuchta, V., Steinfeld, R., Sakzad, A., Liu, J.K., Cheng, J.: Lattice RingCT V2.0 with multiple input and multiple output wallets. In: Jang-Jaccard, J., Guo, F. (eds.) ACISP 2019. LNCS, vol. 11547, pp. 156–175. Springer, Cham (2019). https://doi.org/10.1007/978-3-030-21548-4_9
31. Zcash: Frequently asked questions, https://z.cash/support/faq/#quantum-computers, Accessed on 20 April 2020

Security Analysis

Linear-Complexity Private Function Evaluation is Practical

Marco Holz[1]([✉]), Ágnes Kiss[1], Deevashwer Rathee[2], and Thomas Schneider[1]

[1] ENCRYPTO, Technische Universität Darmstadt, Darmstadt, Germany
{holz,kiss,schneider}@encrypto.cs.tu-darmstadt.de
[2] Department of Computer Science, IIT (BHU) Varanasi, Varanasi, India
deevashwer.student.cse15@iitbhu.ac.in

Abstract. Private function evaluation (PFE) allows to obliviously evaluate a private function on private inputs. PFE has several applications such as privacy-preserving credit checking and user-specific insurance tariffs. Recently, PFE protocols based on universal circuits (UCs), that have an inevitable superlinear overhead, have been investigated thoroughly. Specialized public key-based protocols with linear complexity were believed to be less efficient than UC-based approaches.

In this paper, we take another look at the linear-complexity PFE protocol by Katz and Malka (ASIACRYPT'11): We propose several optimizations and split the protocol in different phases that depend on the function and inputs respectively. We show that HE-based PFE is practical when instantiated with state-of-the-art ECC and RLWE-based homomorphic encryption. Our most efficient implementation outperforms the most recent UC-based PFE implementation of Alhassan et al. (JoC'20) in communication for all circuit sizes and in computation starting from circuits of a few thousand gates already.

Keywords: Private function evaluation · Homomorphic encryption · Secure computation

1 Introduction

While computations on a local machine can be secured against malicious eavesdropping, computations that are performed collaboratively on two or more devices typically rely on the trustworthiness of remote systems. This poses a risk to the sensitive data supplied by the participants. Privacy-preserving protocols aim to mitigate these risks by protecting the data using cryptographic approaches such that there is no need for a trusted remote party anymore.

Secure two-party computation (STPC) or secure function evaluation (SFE) protocols allow two parties to jointly compute a function on private data without learning the other party's inputs. Private function evaluation (PFE) extends this setting by also hiding the evaluated function from one of the parties: P_1 inputs a private function f, typically represented by a circuit $\mathcal{C}_f$, and P_2 inputs private data x and learns only $f(x)$ but no additional information on f (except its size).

© Springer Nature Switzerland AG 2020
L. Chen et al. (Eds.): ESORICS 2020, LNCS 12309, pp. 401–420, 2020.
https://doi.org/10.1007/978-3-030-59013-0_20

PFE has diverse applications that require to keep the participants' inputs private and hide the operations applied to these inputs from one of the participants. We describe a few example applications. In a *privacy-preserving intrusion detection system (IDS)* [Nik+14], a server holds a set of zero-day signatures (including regular expressions matching the payload) and is able to check whether sensitive data uploaded to the IDS matches those signatures such that the server learns nothing about the data and the client learns nothing about the signatures. Using PFE, *attribute-based access control* can be enhanced to protect both sensitive credentials and sensitive policies [FAL06]. PFE can be used for *privacy-preserving credit worthiness checking* [FAZ05], disclosing neither the customer's private financial data nor the private criteria of the loaner. In *privacy-preserving car insurance rate calculation* [Gün+19] the privacy-critical customer data, as well as the tariff calculation details remain private.

The most common approach for PFE is to reduce it to classical SFE by securely evaluating a public universal circuit (UC) [Val76, KS08a, KS16, LMS16, GKS17, Alh+20, Zha+19, Liu+20]. This series of works on optimizations and implementations of UCs has shown that UC-based PFE can be practical, but UCs introduce an inevitable logarithmic overhead [Val76]. Katz and Malka [KM11] propose a linear-complexity PFE scheme based on homomorphic encryption (HE) and Yao's garbled circuit protocol. They expect their scheme to be "easier to implement and more efficient (for larger circuits) than approaches relying on universal circuits". However, their scheme has not been implemented yet.

Our Contributions. Our paper takes another look at the linear-complexity PFE protocol by Katz and Malka [KM11]. We split the protocol into several phases so that parts of the protocol can be precomputed knowing, e.g., only the size of the private function or the private function itself. For instance, for a privacy-preserving IDS it is reasonable to precompute any function-dependent part so that the online phase where the client provides its input is fast. We optimize, instantiate, and implement their scheme using three state-of-the-art homomorphic encryption (HE) schemes: Elliptic curve (EC) ElGamal [Elg85], the Brakerski/Fan-Vercauteren (BFV) scheme [FV12], and the cryptosystem by Damgård/Jurik/Nielsen (DJN) [DJN10]. We implement our protocols using the ABY framework [DSZ15] and thereby provide the first implementation of a linear-complexity PFE scheme. Our experiments show that HE-based PFE outperforms today's most efficient UC-based PFE implementation [Alh+20] on the same platform already starting from circuits with only a few thousand gates.

2   Related Work

In this paper, we focus on PFE protocols that provide security against semi-honest adversaries. These can be categorized as follows:

UC-Based PFE. A universal circuit (UC) is a circuit that can be programmed to evaluate any Boolean circuit up to size n by specifying a set of program bits as its input. In recent years, a lot of research was put into optimizing and implementing UC-based PFE, which reduces the task of PFE to standard SFE that relies mostly on symmetric cryptography where the function is the publicly known UC. Valiant [Val76] proposed two recursive UCs with sizes $\sim 5n \log_2 n$ and $\sim 4.75n \log_2 n$ in the size of the simulated circuit n, which are optimal up to a constant factor because any UC must have size at least $\Omega(n \log n)$. Zhao et al. [Zha+19] present a UC with size $\sim 4.5n \log_2 n$. A hybrid UC with size $\sim 4.5n \log_2 n$, combining optimizations from [KS16, GKS17, Zha+19] was implemented in [Alh+20]. The most recent UC from [Liu+20] has size $\sim 3n \log_2 n$. These constructions have reached lower bounds for the most common ways UCs are constructed [Zha+19, Liu+20], so no significant improvements are expected.

OT-Based PFE. Mohassel and Sadeghian introduce an oblivious transfer (OT)-based approach based on the oblivious evaluation of a switching network of size $\Theta(n \log n)$ that hides the topology of the Boolean circuit [MS13]. Bingöl at al. [Bin+18] adapt the half gates optimization [ZRE15] to the OT-based approach of [MS13] and reduce the number of OTs by half. As shown in [Alh+20], the communication of both [MS13] and [Bin+18] is worse than that of UC-based PFE. PFE schemes based on both UCs and switching networks have an inevitable logarithmic overhead.

TEE-Based PFE. Felsen et al. [Fel+19] propose private function evaluation with a different trust assumption and implement PFE using Intel SGX as trusted execution environment (TEE), by evaluating a UC within the SGX enclave.

HE-Based PFE. The protocol by Katz and Malka [KM11] has linear complexity $\mathcal{O}(n)$, but its concrete practicality has not yet been explored. The authors use homomorphic encryption to hide the topology of the circuit $\mathcal{C}_f$ from the party that obliviously garbles the circuit (cf. Sect. 4.1). Mohassel and Sadeghian [MS13] include a linear-complexity protocol in their generic framework for PFE. They optimize the baseline protocol of [KM11], but their protocol is not more efficient than the improved protocol of [KM11] which we use. Mohassel et al. [MSS14] extend the protocol from [KM11, MS13] to security against malicious adversaries using zero-knowledge proofs while maintaining linear complexity. Biçer et al. present a reusable linear-complexity PFE scheme [Biç+18] based on the protocol of [KM11] which is efficient if the same private function f is evaluated multiple times. Their protocol in the first execution has slightly lower total communication, but around a factor four higher online computation than [KM11] (cf. [Biç+18, Table 1]). Later runs of the protocol with the same function are more efficient both in communication and computation than [KM11]. We leave investigating the concrete efficiency of the protocol of [Biç+18] for applications where the same function can be reused as future work.

In our paper, we resurrect the neglected line of research on linear-complexity HE-based PFE protocols and show that the protocol of [KM11] is practical.

3   Preliminaries

In this section, we describe preliminaries to our work from the fields of secure function evaluation (SFE) in Sect. 3.1 and private function evaluation (PFE) in Sect. 3.2, and recapitulate the homomorphic encryption (HE) schemes we use in Sect. 3.3.

3.1   Circuit-Based Secure Function Evaluation

We focus on security against semi-honest (passive) adversaries where all parties are assumed to follow the protocol. This allows for highly efficient protocols and is a starting point for constructing protocols with stronger security guarantees.

In the past, several SFE protocols have been proposed that rely on a circuit representation of the function f which is known to both parties, e.g., Yao's garbled circuit (GC) protocol [Yao82, Yao86, LP09] and the GMW protocol [GMW87]. In Yao's protocol, party P_1, *the garbler*, prepares an encrypted version of the circuit in the form of garbled tables, which are then sent to P_2. The other party P_2, *the evaluator*, evaluates the *garbled circuit* after receiving the keys corresponding to his input wires using oblivious transfers.[1] Oblivious transfer (OT) allows the receiver P_2 to retrieve one of two messages obliviously from the sender P_1 without the receiver learning the other message or the sender learning which message was retrieved. Though OTs require expensive public-key cryptography [IR89], OT extension [Ish+03, Ash+13] allows to perform a large number of OTs more efficiently by extending a few *base OTs* and obtain many oblivious transfers using only symmetric cryptographic operations. Recent optimizations to Yao's GC protocol include *point-and-permute* [BMR90], *free-XOR* [KS08b], *fixed-key AES garbling* [Bel+13], and *half gates* [ZRE15].

3.2   Private Function Evaluation

Private function evaluation (PFE) extends SFE to the case where only one party P_1 inputs a private function f represented by circuit $\mathcal{C}_f$. The protocol must guarantee that P_2 on private input x learns the output $f(x)$ but no other information about the function f whereas P_1 learns nothing.[2] Generally, PFE protocols reveal the size of the circuit $\mathcal{C}_f$ to the participants. If needed, the actual number of gates and wires can be hidden by adding dummy gates and dummy input/output wires to the circuit. One notable characteristic of PFE protocols is that P_1 typically must not be able to learn the output of the function f. The reason for this is that an adversarial party P_1 could reveal the inputs of party P_2 by defining f to leak information about x, e.g., $f(x) = x$.

---

[1] Even though the gates are encrypted and thus the gates' types can easily be hidden from P_2, P_2 must know the *topology* of the circuit for evaluating the garbled circuit.

[2] This can be extended to the case were P_1 also holds an input value in addition to the circuit $\mathcal{C}_f$. Our 2-party PFE implementation supports input values for both parties.

3.3   Homomorphic Encryption

Homomorphic encryption (HE) schemes allow for computations on encrypted data, i.e., operations performed on the ciphertexts are reflected in the output of decryption as if they were applied directly on the plaintexts.

The protocol of Katz and Malka [KM11] is based on additively homomorphic encryption, i.e., a HE scheme that supports only homomorphic addition. The authors of [KM11] suggest to instantiate their protocol with Paillier [Pai99] or ElGamal [Elg85] HE and mention that their protocol can be improved by using elliptic-curve cryptography (ECC). Since then, several significant improvements on additively HE were published that we consider in our implementation:

DJN. The DJN cryptosystem [DJN10], a generalization of Paillier's scheme [Pai99], has since then been optimized using CRT-based decryption [HMS12]. Our implementation is based on *libpaillier*[3] and uses this optimization.

EC ElGamal. EC ElGamal encryption offers exceptionally small ciphertexts, practical computation and an additive homomorphism over the underlying elliptic curve group. The use of elliptic curves over finite fields as a basis for a cryptosystem was suggested independently from each other by both Koblitz [Kob87] and Miller [Mil86]. In our implementation, we use the *RELIC Toolkit* [AG09] for ECC.

BFV. Significant improvements have been made in the area of RLWE-based HE [Reg05,LPR10,Bra12,FV12]. The RLWE-based BFV scheme [FV12,Lai17] is implemented in the Microsoft SEAL library [Sea19], which is among the fastest HE libraries available today. We present a high level overview of the BFV scheme restricted to only the part of its functionality which is relevant for our application. For additional details, see [Lai17]. We note that our discussion also applies to other popular Ring-LWE-based HE schemes such as BGV [BGV12].

The BFV scheme operates on polynomial rings of the form $R = \mathbb{Z}[x]/(x^n+1)$, where the *polynomial modulus degree* n is a power of 2. For a *plaintext modulus* t, the plaintext space is defined as $R_t = R/tR = \mathbb{Z}_t[x]/(x^n + 1)$, which consists of polynomials of degree $n - 1$ with coefficients in $\mathbb{Z}_t$. Similarly, the ciphertext space is defined as $(R_q)^2$, where q is called the *coefficient modulus* and $R_q = R/qR$. The encryption function Enc is probabilistic, takes a public key pk and a message $m \in R_t$ as inputs, and outputs a ciphertext $c \in (R_q)^2$. The ciphertext output by Enc has a noise component associated with it which is necessary for maintaining security. The decryption function Dec takes the secret key sk and a ciphertext $c \in (R_q)^2$ as inputs, and outputs a message $m \in R_t$. Decryption $m = \mathsf{Dec}(sk, \mathsf{Enc}(pk, m))$ works if the ciphertext noise is below a certain threshold defined by the scheme parameters. For ease of exposition, we omit the keys from the invocation of the encryption and decryption functions, and assume a single key-pair throughout the paper, which makes the functions compatible.

Enc is a homomorphic map from $(R_t, +)$ to $((R_q)^2, +)$, which provides the scheme with its additive homomorphic properties. Given ciphertexts

---

[3] http://hms.isi.jhu.edu/acsc/libpaillier/

$c_1 = \mathsf{Enc}(m_1)$ and $c_2 = \mathsf{Enc}(m_2)$, we have $\mathsf{Dec}(c_1 + c_2) = \mathsf{Dec}(c_1) + \mathsf{Dec}(c_2)$. The noise component grows as we perform homomorphic operations on the ciphertext until it reaches a threshold, beyond which decryption is not possible and the ciphertext is rendered useless. This is not a problem since addition does not grow the noise by much. The scheme described so far only provides IND-CPA security against parties other than the key owner. To hide the operations applied to the ciphertext from the key owner, which may include some private inputs from other parties, and only reveal the result of decryption, the ciphertext needs to be flooded with extra noise (cf. [Lai17], § 9.4). This requires larger parameters to accommodate the extra noise, and has been taken into account in our parameter selection.

4 Linear-Complexity Private Function Evaluation

In this section, we recapitulate the private function evaluation (PFE) protocol of Katz and Malka [KM11] in Sect. 4.1, introduce further improvements in Sect. 4.2, and propose efficient instantiations using EC ElGamal in Sect. 4.3 and the BFV homomorphic encryption scheme in Sect. 4.4.

4.1 The [KM11] Protocol

The PFE protocol proposed by Katz and Malka [KM11] combines homomorphic encryption (HE) with Yao's garbled circuit (GC) protocol to hide the topology of the circuit $\mathcal{C}_f$ in addition to the parties' inputs. They give a baseline protocol and a roughly twice as efficient improved protocol. We describe the improved protocol shown in Fig. 1 and refer to the original paper for the baseline version.

The Boolean circuit to be evaluated privately has g gates, u inputs and o outputs and has size $N = u + g$. The circuit is assumed to be built of only two-input NAND gates so that their functionality does not need to be hidden. There exist established highly optimized hardware synthesis tools that optimize for a small number of NAND gates when translating the function to a circuit. Moreover, it is assumed that *"the output wires of the circuit do not connect to any other gates"* [KM11] which is achieved by adding at most o gates to the circuit. [KM11] define the wiring among the gates as follows: Incoming wires are the inputs of the g gates. Outgoing wires are the output wires of the g gates and the u input wires of the circuit. Each incoming wire must be connected to exactly one outgoing wire, but an outgoing wire may be connected to more incoming wires, enabling gates with arbitrary fan-out. In contrast, UC-based PFE requires the fan-out to be at most two which requires additional copy-gates [Val76] that increase the circuit size.

Party P_2 inputs private data x of length $|x| = u$ and acts as the *circuit garbler* from Yao's protocol. P_1 inputs the private circuit $\mathcal{C}_f$ of g gates and acts as the *circuit evaluator*. Since P_2 must remain unaware of the circuit wiring, P_2 cannot directly garble the gates. Instead, P_1 creates a so-called encrypted garbled gate encGG_i for each gate i of the circuit and P_2 decrypts these to learn the keys required to create the garbled tables as in Yao's protocol (cf. Sect. 3.1 and [LP09]). By creating the encrypted garbled gates under HE, P_1 obliviously connects two *outgoing wires* to each gate of the circuit (the wire keys for the outgoing wires are provided by P_2 beforehand). Thereby, the circuit topology remains hidden from P_2.

Four Phases of PFE Protocols. We split the protocol of [KM11] and UC-based PFE into four phases: 1) a *precomputation* phase which is run only once, 2) a *setup$_N$* phase dependent on the size N of the function, 3) a *setup$_f$* phase dependent on the function f, and 4) an *online$_x$* phase dependent on the input x.

P_1 (inputs private circuit $\mathcal{C}_f$)	P_2 (inputs private data $x \in \{0,1\}^u$)
1) precomputation phase	
$\xleftarrow{\quad \text{pk} \quad}$	$(\text{pk}, \text{sk}) \leftarrow_\$ \text{KGen}(1^n)$
	$r \leftarrow_\$ \{0,1\}^\kappa$
2) setup$_N$ phase	
$\forall i \in \{1, \dots, g\}:$	$\forall i \in \{1, \dots, N\}:$
$b_i, b_i' \leftarrow_\$ \{0,1\}^\kappa$, compute	$(s_i^0) \leftarrow_\$ \{0,1\}^\kappa$
$\text{Enc}_{pk}(b_i), \text{Enc}_{pk}(b_i')$	$\forall i \in \{1, \dots, N-o\}:$
$\xleftarrow{\text{Enc}_{pk}(s_1^0), \dots, \text{Enc}_{pk}(s_{N-o}^0)}$	compute $\text{Enc}_{pk}(s_i^0)$
3) setup$_f$ phase	
$\forall i \in \{1, \dots, g\}:$ *gate i has*	
left input j, right input k	
$v_{iL} = \text{Enc}_{pk}(s_j^0 + b_i)$	
$v_{iR} = \text{Enc}_{pk}(s_k^0 + b_i')$	
$encGG_i = (v_{iL}, v_{iR})$ $\xrightarrow{encGG_1, \dots, encGG_g}$	$\forall i \in \{1, \dots, g\}:$
	gate i has output wire $u+i$
	$L_i^0 = \text{Dec}(v_{iL}), L_i^1 = L_i^0 + r$
	$R_i^0 = \text{Dec}(v_{iR}), R_i^1 = R_i^0 + r$
$\xleftarrow{\quad GT_1, \dots, GT_g \quad}$	$GT_i = \text{encYao}(L_i^0, L_i^1, R_i^0, R_i^1,$
	$i, s_{u+i}^0, s_{u+i}^1)$
4) online$_x$ phase	
$\forall i \in \{1, \dots, g\}:$ $\xleftarrow{\quad s_1^{x_1}, \dots, s_u^{x_u} \quad}$	
$L_i = s_j + b_i, R_i = s_k + b_i'$	
$s_{u+i} = \text{decYao}(L_i, R_i, i, GT_i)$ $\xrightarrow{s_{N-o+1}, \dots, s_N}$	*compare $s_{N-o+1}, \dots, s_N$ to*
	$(s_{N-o+1}^0, s_{N-o+1}^1), \dots, (s_N^0, s_N^1)$
	to determine output $f(x)$

Fig. 1. The [KM11] protocol. The circuit $\mathcal{C}_f$ has u input wires, o output wires, g gates, and size $N = u + g$. The symmetric security parameter is $\kappa = 128$.

In most applications, e.g., when a server provides a service with a pre-defined function (such as privacy-preserving IDS, cf. Sect. 1), the *precomputation* and both *setup* phases can be precomputed before the client provides its input, allowing for a very fast *online$_x$* phase. In other applications, the function may not be known beforehand, in which case the *precomputation* and *setup$_N$* phases can be precomputed, and the *setup$_f$* and *online$_x$* phases are run online.

1) precomputation phase. We first determine all operations that have to be done once, independently of the protocol run: For [KM11], this includes generating and sending the public key of the HE scheme, and for UC-based PFE, the construction of the UC itself. We do not include this phase in our performance evaluation in Sect. 5.

2) setup$_N$ phase. This phase precomputes all operations that depend only on the size N of the circuit. In [KM11], P_2 creates two wire keys representing the bit values 0 and 1 for each of the $N = g + u$ outgoing wires. The wire keys of all $g + u$ outgoing wires except the o output wires of the circuit are essential to define the mapping representing the topology of the circuit. We denote the wire key corresponding to the bit value $b \in \{0, 1\}$ on outgoing wire $i \in \{1, \ldots, N\}$ by s_i^b. The security of the protocol depends on the indistinguishability of the two keys. P_2 chooses the wire key s_i^0 at random and, similar to the *free-XOR* technique [KS08b], defines a global random shift r of the same size as the wire keys. P_2 then sets $s_i^1 = s_i^0 + r$ for $i \in \{1, \ldots, N\}$ and sends the homomorphically encrypted wire keys $\mathsf{Enc}(s_1^0)$, ..., $\mathsf{Enc}(s_{N-o}^0)$ to P_1. As a preparation for the *setup$_f$* phase, P_1 already creates and encrypts two random blinding values, b_i and b_i', for each gate G_i. This phase has complexity $\mathcal{O}(N)$.

In the UC-based PFE protocols, the UC is garbled and sent to the evaluator, which has complexity $\Theta(N \log N)$.

3) setup$_f$ phase. This depends on the specific function f. In [KM11], party P_1 creates the encrypted garbled gates. In order to hide the wiring of the circuit from P_2, each wire key is blinded. If outgoing wires j and k are connected to the incoming wires of gate G_i, P_1 constructs the encrypted garbled gate encGG_i by making use of the additively homomorphic property of Enc as

$$\mathsf{encGG}_i = \left(\mathsf{Enc}(s_j^0 + b_i), \mathsf{Enc}(s_k^0 + b_i') \right). \tag{1}$$

P_1 then sends $\mathsf{encGG}_1, \ldots, \mathsf{encGG}_g$ to P_2. P_2 is now able to create the garbled tables and thereby acts as the *circuit garbler* from Yao's protocol. For each gate G_i, P_2 decrypts the corresponding encrypted garbled gate and retrieves the blinded wire keys for the left and the right incoming wire of the gate:

$$L_i^0 = \mathsf{Dec}(\mathsf{Enc}(s_j^0 + b_i)), \quad R_i^0 = \mathsf{Dec}(\mathsf{Enc}(s_k^0 + b_i')). \tag{2}$$

P_2 is now able to obtain the blinded wire keys $s_j^1 + b_i$ and $s_k^1 + b_i'$ by defining $L_i^1 = L_i^0 + r$ and $R_i^1 = R_i^0 + r$. Note that the blinded wire keys L_i^0, L_i^1 and R_i^0, R_i^1 are independent of the keys assigned to the outgoing wires of gates j and k. This hides the circuit topology from P_2 while still enabling P_2 to create the garbled

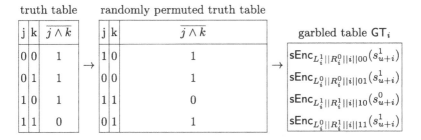

Fig. 2. encYao: creation of a garbled table [LP09]

tables. The garbled table GT_i is generated using function encYao, instantiated as shown in Fig. 2 [LP09]: The truth table of the NAND gate is randomly permuted and then for each combination of the left (L_i^0, L_i^1) and right (R_i^0, R_i^1) input key these keys are used to symmetrically encrypt the output key s_{u+i}^0 or s_{u+i}^1 using function sEnc which is instantiated using AES-128 (cf. Sect. 5.1 for details). We emphasize that the gates' output keys are pre-determined and the protocol of [KM11] applies additively homomorphic operations on input keys. Therefore, we cannot use GC optimizations like point-and-permute [BMR90], garbled row reduction [NPS99, Pin+09], or half-gates [ZRE15]. Instead, we have to use the classical GC from [LP09] with four entries per garbled table (GT), so each GT has size $4 \cdot (|s_{u+i}| + \sigma)$ bits, where $\sigma = 40$ is the statistical security parameter. Finally, P_2 sends $GT_1, \ldots, GT_g$ to P_1. This phase has complexity $\mathcal{O}(N)$.

In the UC-based PFE protocols, the wire keys specifying the values of the UC's programming bits are sent which yields $\Theta(N \log N)$ communication.

4) online$_x$ phase. In this final phase, the private data x is input by P_2. In [KM11], the wire keys $s_1^{x_1}, \ldots, s_u^{x_u}$ of the circuit input wires corresponding to P_2's input bits $x_1, \ldots, x_u$ are sent to P_1.[4] P_1 can now evaluate the garbled tables and determine the wire keys of the output wires as follows: To evaluate gate i, P_1 has to reconstruct the keys used to encrypt one entry of the garbled table. Starting with the first gate in topological order, P_1 uses for gate G_i with left input j and right input k the keys $s_j \in \{s_j^0, s_j^1\}$ and $s_k \in \{s_k^0, s_k^1\}$ and the blinding values b_i, b_i' from the *setup$_N$* phase to calculate $L_i = s_j + b_i$ and $R_i = s_k + b_i'$. P_1 now decrypts the garbled table GT_i to learn the wire key $s_{u+i} = \text{decYao}(L_i, R_i, i, GT_i)$ as in Yao's garbled circuit protocol and continues with the next gate in topological order. Once all gates have been evaluated, P_1 has obtained the wire keys $s_{N-o+1}, \ldots, s_N$ of the output wires. These can be mapped to plaintext outputs as in Yao's protocol. However, as mentioned in Sect. 3.2, the function holder P_1 should not learn the output of f, so the output is determined by party P_2. This phase has complexity $\mathcal{O}(N)$.

---

[4] The protocol can naturally be extended to the setting where also P_1 has private input data y. Either y is encoded in the private function f [PSS09], or the keys corresponding to the bits of y are obliviously sent to P_1 using oblivious transfer [Ish+03, LP09, Ash+13] as describe in [KM11].

In the UC-based PFE protocols, the wire keys corresponding to the private input x are sent, the garbled UC is evaluated, which requires $\Theta(N \log N)$ computation, and the output bits of the UC are decoded.

4.2 Optimizations of the [KM11] Protocol

In this section, we describe our optimizations to the protocol of [KM11].

Precomputation of All Homomorphic Encryptions. As described in Sect. 4.1, all homomorphic encryptions can be precomputed in the $setup_N$ phase where only the size N is known but neither $\mathcal{C}_f$ nor x. Since encryption is a relatively expensive operation, this drastically reduces the protocol runtime (see Sect. 5.2).

The wire keys are sampled randomly so depend neither on the inputs nor on the circuit $\mathcal{C}_f$, and are encrypted using the HE public key generated by P_2.

P_2 can sample and homomorphically encrypt the *encrypted wire keys* $\mathsf{Enc}(s_i^0)$, where $1 \leq i \leq N$. Similarly, P_1 can sample and encrypt the blinding values b_i, b_i', where $1 \leq i \leq g$, using P_1's public key. Here, it is necessary to exchange the public key of the HE scheme first. We argue that this is feasible in practice by P_2 publishing the public key beforehand.

Pipelining. The creation and evaluation of the garbled circuit (GC) is done in topological order which makes this process eligible for pipelining. When transmitting the garbled gates directly after creation, they can be ungarbled by the evaluator while subsequent gates are still being garbled by the garbler. This GC pipelining was proposed and implemented in [Hen+10, Hua+11].

In addition to the GC pipelining, we also implemented pipelining of the creation and evaluation of the encrypted garbled gates. The process of retrieving the wire keys from the encrypted garbled gates can then seamlessly be combined with the pipelined creation and evaluation of the GC. Since decryption of the encrypted garbled gates is the most expensive operations in the $setup_f$ phase, this significantly speeds up the protocol and reduces the time spent solely on network communication. In our experiments, we saw that pipelining improves the runtime in the $setup_f$ phase by about 25%.

Parallelization. The [KM11] protocol is very suitable for parallelization. We provide a fully parallelized implementation of 1) the creation of the encrypted wire keys by P_2 and the encrypted blinding values by P_1 in the $setup_N$ phase, 2) the creation of the encrypted garbled gates by P_1 in the $setup_f$ phase, 3) the decryption of the encrypted garbled gates and the creation of the garbled tables by P_2 in the $setup_f$ phase. Only the evaluation of the garbled tables by P_1 depends on the wire keys obtained from previous garbled tables and therefore cannot be fully parallelized.

4.3 Instantiating [KM11] with EC ElGamal

Katz and Malka suggest to use ElGamal encryption to instantiate their protocol [KM11], and briefly mention the possibility of using elliptic curve cryptography (ECC) in their protocol. In the following, we denote integers by lowercase letters and points on the elliptic curve by capital letters. The equivalent of choosing a random element of the residue field as the private key in standard ElGamal encryption is choosing a random integer a from the Galois field $GF(p)$ as the private key in the elliptic curve version. The public key A is then computed as $A = a * P$ where P is the base point of the elliptic curve.

In standard additively homomorphic lifted EC ElGamal, a message $m \in GF(p)$ is mapped to a curve point M as $M = m * P$. The reverse mapping used during decryption then requires solving the discrete logarithm of M which requires that m is from a small domain whereas we need to operate on $\kappa = 128$ bit keys. Instead, we observe that the only requirement for the choice of the wire keys and the blinding values in the [KM11] protocol is indistinguishability, so we can simply define curve points M as our plaintext values for wire keys and blinding values. Then, we perform plaintext additions using the ECC arithmetic on the elliptic curve when P_1 needs to apply the blinding value to a plaintext wire key in order to determine the values L_i and R_i. These points are then mapped to keys for AES using a KDF (cf. Sect. 5.1).

Analogous to standard ElGamal, we define encryption of a message M with a public key $A = a * P$ as follows:

$$\mathsf{Enc}(M) = (K, C) = (k * P, k * A + M). \tag{3}$$

Decryption of the ciphertext (K, C) can now be done as follows:

$$\mathsf{Dec}(K, C) = C - a * K = k * A + M - a * k * P = k * a * P + M - a * k * P = M. \tag{4}$$

EC ElGamal is additively homomorphic in the underlying elliptic curve group. We define the homomorphic addition of two ciphertexts as

$$\mathsf{Enc}(M_1) \oplus \mathsf{Enc}(M_2) = (K_1, C_1) \oplus (K_2, C_2) = (K_1 + K_2, C_1 + C_2). \tag{5}$$

This satisfies the additively homomorphic property over the EC group:

$$
\begin{aligned}
\mathsf{Dec}(\mathsf{Enc}(M_1) \oplus \mathsf{Enc}(M_2)) &= \mathsf{Dec}((k_1 * P, k_1 * A + M_1) \oplus (k_2 * P, k_2 * A + M_2)) \\
&= \mathsf{Dec}((k_1 * P + k_2 * P, k_1 * A + M_1 + k_2 * A + M_2)) \\
&= \mathsf{Dec}((k_1 + k_2) * P, (k_1 + k_2) * A + M_1 + M_2)) \\
&= (k_1 + k_2) * A + M_1 + M_2 - a * (k_1 + k_2) * P = M_1 + M_2.
\end{aligned} \tag{6}
$$

Semantic security naturally follows from that of ElGamal based in the DDH assumption in the EC group.

4.4   Instantiating [KM11] with BFV Homomorphic Encryption

Since the linear-complexity protocol of [KM11] was proposed in 2011, significant progress has been made in the area of Ring-LWE (RLWE) based homomorphic encryption. Thus, we revise the protocol of [KM11] with an HE instantiation based on these efficient Ring-LWE HE schemes. We specifically use the BFV scheme (cf. Sect. 3.3) as implemented in Microsoft's SEAL library [Sea19]. We take the plaintext modulus as $t = 2$, which results in the smallest possible polynomial modulus degree and thus ciphertext size in our scenario. The coefficient modulus q is chosen as a product of primes $q_1 = 12289$ and $q_2 = 1099510054913$. q_1 is the smallest prime that is large enough to allow homomorphic blinding of the key values and satisfies $q_1 \equiv 1 \mod 2n$, where n is *polynomial modulus degree* (cf. [Sea19] for details). For function privacy, which is necessary to prevent P_2 from learning the permutation of the keys employed by P_1, we flood the ciphertext with noise (cf. [Lai17, §9.4]) that is 40-bits larger than the noise of the output ciphertext, ensuring a statistical security of 40-bits against P_2. Thus, we require an additional 40-bits (in the form of q_2) in the coefficient modulus to contain the extra noise. Consequently, we choose $p = 2048$ as the polynomial modulus degree, which is the smallest n that maintains computational security of 128-bits for a q of 54-bits (cf. [Lai17], Table 3).

Encoding of the Wire Keys. When choosing a plaintext modulus of $t = 2$, each bit of the plaintext value is encoded as one coefficient of the polynomial. Assume we have a wire key v with a binary representation of $v = v_{127}||v_{126}||\ldots||v_0$, we define our plaintext polynomial as $v_{127}x^{127} + \ldots + v_1 x + v_0$. Since homomorphic addition is done coefficient-wise in the BFV scheme and we use $t = 2$, addition becomes equivalent to a *homomorphic XOR operation*.

Due to the requirement that each wire key has to be utilized separately when creating the encrypted garbled gates, Chinese Remainder Theorem (CRT) batching, as provided by SEAL, becomes inefficient for our use case. Using batching, one can pack n integers modulo t into one plaintext polynomial and apply SIMD (Single Instruction, Multiple Data) operations on those values. However, this would require a much larger value for t. A multiplication operation (by a one-hot encoded vector), that is needed to extract one wire key from the ciphertext containing n wire keys, is less efficient than encrypting and decrypting a smaller ciphertext on its own. We therefore decided against CRT batching.

Efficient Packing of the Ciphertexts. The encoding of the wire keys uses exactly 128 coefficients of the BFV ciphertext. Since the degree of the polynomial modulus (`poly_modulus_degree`) is set to 2048, we only use $\frac{1}{16}$ of the coefficients of each ciphertext. Even though we decided not to use CRT batching, utilizing the unused coefficients for packing additional 15 wire keys in a ciphertext seems desirable in order to reduce the communication of the protocol by a factor of 16.

Unfortunately, without access to the secret key, it is not possible for P_1 to homomorphically extract a subset of coefficients of the underlying plaintext, and thus a wire key. Therefore, multiple wire keys can only be packed in a response to P_2 holding the secret key.

Traditionally, each of the encrypted garbled gates consists of two ciphertexts, holding the blinded wire keys for the two incoming wires of that gate. First, we describe a way to combine the encrypted wire keys, $\mathsf{Enc}(s_j)$ and $\mathsf{Enc}(s_k)$, into one ciphertext $\mathsf{Enc}(s_j||s_k)$. Since in the plaintexts the wire keys of length 128-bits are followed by 15×128 coefficients set to zero, we can use these coefficients to encode further wire keys. We achieve this by applying a "homomorphic (right) bit shift" of 128-bits (respectively coefficients) to one of the wire keys (by multiplying a ciphertext by the plaintext constant 2^{128}) and adding both wire keys afterwards.

These wire keys still have to be blinded to form the encrypted garbled gate encGG_i, which can now be achieved by only one homomorphic addition. Therefore, we concatenate the blinding values b_i and b'_i and homomorphically add them to $\mathsf{Enc}(s_j\|s_k)$ to receive the encrypted garbled gate $\mathsf{encGG}_i = \mathsf{Enc}(s_j\|s_k) + \mathsf{Enc}(b_i\|b'_i) = \mathsf{Enc}((s_j + b_i)\|(s_k + b'_i))$. Since P_2 is in charge of telling the wire keys apart, "unpacking" is simply done by decrypting the ciphertext and assigning 128-bits to both wire keys.

Analogously, we can pack additional encrypted garbled gates into the same ciphertext and thereby use all 2048 coefficients to pack 8 encrypted garbled gates. This can be done efficiently using Horner's method as described in [KSS13]. Blinding of the wire keys can now be applied by concatenating 16 blinding values and add them to the ciphertext in a single homomorphic addition.

Compared to not using this packing technique, we require the same number of homomorphic additions (15 additions to pack the 16 wire keys + 1 addition for the combined blinding value instead of one addition of a blinding value per wire key) and 15 multiplications by 2^{256}, but we also eliminated 15 decryptions since P_2 only receives one ciphertext instead of 16. Since for our instantiation of the BFV protocol decryption is more expensive than homomorphic scalar multiplication, this also improves computation.

Wire Key Generation Using Seed Expansion. The wire keys are encrypted by the private key owner P_2 and can be homomorphically encrypted using the *secret* key to have smaller noise and smaller ciphertext size. When encrypting with the secret key, half of the ciphertext coefficients are chosen uniformly at random from R_q. Using a pseudo-random function, one can sample these coefficients by expanding a seed sent to P_1 instead. This nearly halves the ciphertext size of the encrypted wire keys and significantly improves communication which is the major bottleneck of the scheme.[5]

5   Evaluation

In this section, we describe our implementation of the different instantiations of the [KM11] protocol and point out bottlenecks and advantages. We experimentally compare our implementations with the best existing UC-based PFE implementation of [Alh+20]. We also give estimates on the efficiency of the recent UC improvements of [Liu+20] that results in 33% smaller UCs and hence would improve UC-based PFE of [Alh+20] by around 33% in both runtime and communication (cf. dashed lines in Fig. 4 and 3). The results of our performance tests show that HE-based linear-complexity PFE supersedes UC-based PFE in runtime starting from a few thousand gates already and in communication for all

---

[5] Since January 2020 (version 3.4.0) the SEAL library [Sea19] supports seed expansion and encryption with the secret key. Our implementation uses this optimization.

circuit sizes. Hence, linear-complexity PFE is a viable alternative for improving the performance of private function evaluation.

5.1   Implementation

We implemented our optimized and fully parallelized version of the [KM11] protocol described in Sect. 4 using the ABY SFE framework [DSZ15]. Our implementation is available as open-source at https://encrypto.de/code/linearPFE. This is the first implementation of a linear-complexity PFE protocol. We provide a fair comparison with today's most efficient UC-based PFE implementation of [Alh+20] with complexity $\Theta(N \log N)$ which is based on the same STPC framework ABY.

We instantiate sEnc as $\mathsf{sEnc}_{k'}(m) = (AES_{k'}(0)\|AES_{k'}(1)\| \ldots \| AES_{k'}(\lceil (|m| + \sigma)/128 \rceil - 1)) \oplus (m\|0^{\sigma})$, where AES is AES-128 and $\sigma = 40$ is the statistical security parameter. The arbitrary-length key k is mapped to a 128-bit key $k' = \mathrm{KDF}(k)$ where the KDF is instantiated with $PBKDF2$.

We instantiate the DJN cryptosystem with modulus size of 3072 bits.

In our EC ElGamal-based implementation we use the eBATS B-251 binary elliptic curve. RELIC encodes each point on the elliptic curve in 33 bytes.

SEAL serializes ciphertexts as 64-bit values using a compression function. For our specific choice of parameters, this compression did not achieve ideal results. For all ciphertexts except the encrypted wire keys where a seed is used to reduce their size, we implemented our own serialization where we eliminate unnecessary zeroes and thereby reduce the ciphertext size compared to the SEAL encoding.

5.2   Experimental Evaluation

We use two identical machines with a physical connection of 10 Gbit/s bandwidth and a round-trip time of 1 ms. We refer to this as the LAN setting and also simulated a WAN setting with 100 Mbit/s bandwidth and a round-trip time of 100 ms. Each machine is equipped with an Intel Core i9-7960X CPU (32 Cores, 2.8 GHz) and 128 GB RAM. All measurements are averaged over 10 executions. Because in all PFE protocols the costs for the input x is substantially lower than for the gates, we fix the number of input bits to $u = |x| = 64$. The exact performance measures used to plot the figures are given in the full version [Hol+20].

Communication. In Fig. 3, we depict the communication of the PFE protocols. The EC ElGamal instantiation clearly outperforms all other implementations, including UC-based PFE [Alh+20] and thereby offers the best PFE scheme in terms of communication known so far. Its communication is lower than UC-based PFE of [Alh+20] by a factor of $\sim 11\times$ for circuit size $N = 10^6$.

We observe that the communication complexity of DJN-based PFE is on par with UC-based approaches. Due to its large ciphertext size, BFV-based encryption has the worst communication of our instantiations but it is only a factor of about $1.8\times$ higher for $N = 10^6$ than that of UC-based PFE [Alh+20]. Its communication is significantly reduced by the seed expansion technique to

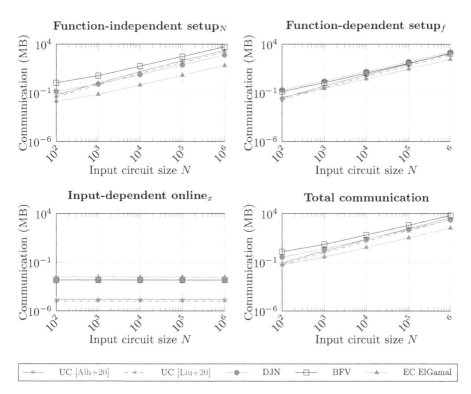

Fig. 3. Communication of PFE protocols (in MB).

reduce the size of the encrypted wire keys in the BFV scheme (cf. Sect. 3.3). In the $online_x$ phase, the communication of all protocols only depends on the size of the input x and is nearly negligible (only a few KB).

Runtime. In Fig. 4, we depict the runtime of our implementation compared to the most recent UC-based PFE implementation of [Alh+20].

ECC-based PFE is our fastest implementation: Compared to the state-of-the-art UC-based PFE implementation of [Alh+20], the total runtime for $N = 10^6$ gates is faster by a factor $\sim 3.3\times$ in LAN and $\sim 7.0\times$ in WAN.

BFV-based PFE offers promising total runtimes even though it is *less* efficient than ECC-based PFE of [Alh+20] by a factor of $\sim 1.4\times$ in LAN and $\sim 1.8\times$ in WAN for $N = 10^6$. The larger factor in the WAN setting results from its larger communication overhead compared to ECC-based PFE. These findings underline that though computational complexity is still relevant, communication complexity becomes the bottleneck for these PFE protocols. Therefore, the computational advances of BFV cannot compensate its larger ciphertext sizes any more. Still, our implementation instantiated with the BFV scheme beats [Alh+20] for circuits of about $N \geq 250000$ gates when function- and input-independent precomputations from the $setup_N$ phase are excluded cf. full version [Hol+20]).

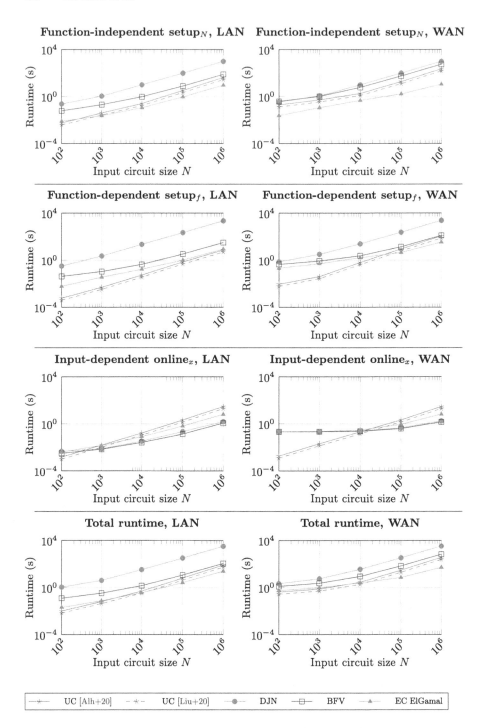

Fig. 4. Runtime of PFE protocols (in seconds).

DJN-based PFE has impractical computational overhead, i.e., about 53 minutes of runtime for $N = 10^6$ gates in LAN (compared to 24 s of the ECC-based instantiation), even with the optimizations described in Sect. 3.3. Its runtime in WAN is similar to WAN as it is dominated by computation.

Per-phase Comparison. In the $setup_N$ phase, computation and communication are independent of the function f and input x and only depend on the (maximum) size of f. This yields significant large precomputation capabilities of HE-based PFE, especially for our BFV-based instantiation.

In the $setup_f$ phase, the logarithmic overhead of UC-based PFE of [Alh+20] has a large performance impact. In contrast, HE-based protocols scale linearly and outperform UC-based PFE for $N \geq 10^6$ in LAN and $N \geq 250000$ in WAN.

In the $online_x$ phase, HE-based PFE outperforms UC-based PFE of [Alh+20] for about $N \geq 1000$ gates in LAN and $N \geq 10000$ gates in WAN. Here, the computation is dominated by GC evaluation. The logarithmic overhead of the UC size compared to the actual circuit leads to a noticeable performance drawback. Since our ECC-based implementation uses points on the elliptic curve as wire keys (encoded as 264 bit values), the GC is larger by a factor of about two compared to the BFV- and DJN-based instantiations where wire keys have size 128 bits. This impacts GC evaluation runtime and BFV-based PFE becomes the fastest instantiation in the $online_x$ phase.

When excluding precomputation of the $setup_N$ phase from the total runtime, BFV-based PFE outperforms UC-based PFE of [Alh+20] for about $N \geq 250000$ in LAN and WAN, and ECC-based PFE outperforms [Alh+20] for about $N \geq 10000$ in LAN and about $N \geq 25000$ in WAN (cf. full version [Hol+20]).

Summary. In this paper, we optimize and implement the linear-complexity PFE protocol of [KM11]. Our elliptic curve ElGamal-based implementation outperforms the state-of-the-art UC-based PFE implementation of [Alh+20] not only in communication, but also in total runtime: For private circuits of size $N = 10^6$, our implementation is ~3.3× faster in a LAN and ~7.0× faster in a WAN setting and scales with $\mathcal{O}(N)$ instead of $\Theta(N \log N)$.

Acknowledgement. This project received funding from the European Research Council (ERC) under the European Union's Horizon 2020 research and innovation program (grant agreement No. 850990 PSOTI). It was co-funded by the Deutsche Forschungsgemeinschaft (DFG) – SFB 1119 CROSSING/236615297 and GRK 2050 Privacy & Trust/251805230, and by BMBF and HMWK within ATHENE.

References

[AG09] Aranha, D.F., Gouvêa, C.: RELIC cryptographic toolkit (2009). https://github.com/relic-toolkit

[Alh+20] Alhassan, M.Y., Günther, D., Kiss, Á., Schneider, T.: Efficient and scalable universal circuits. J. Cryptol. **33**(3), 1216–1271 (2020). https://doi.org/10.1007/s00145-020-09346-z

[Ash+13] Asharov, G., Lindell, Y., Schneider, T., Zohner M.: More efficient oblivious transfer and extensions for faster secure computation. In: CCS 2013, pp. 535–548. ACM (2013)

[Bel+13] Bellare, M., Hoang, V.T., Keelveedhi, S., Rogaway, P.: Efficient garbling from a fixed-key blockcipher. In: S&P 2013, pp. 478–492. IEEE (2013)

[BGV12] Brakerski, Z., Gentry, C., Vaikuntanathan, V.: (Leveled) fully homomorphic encryption without bootstrapping. In: Innovations in Theoretical Computer Science (ITCS 2012), pp. 309–325. ACM (2012)

[Biç+18] Biçer, O., Bingöl, M.A., Kiraz, M.S., Levi, A.: Highly efficient and reusable private function evaluation with linear complexity. Cryptology ePrint Archive, Report 2018/515 (2018). https://ia.cr/2018/515

[Bin+18] Bingöl, M.A., Biçer, O., Kiraz, M.S., Levi, A.: An efficient 2-party private function evaluation protocol based on half gates. Comput. J. $62(4)$, 598–613 (2018)

[BMR90] Beaver, D., Micali, S., Rogaway, P.: The round complexity of secure protocols. In: STOC 1990, pp. 503–513. ACM (1990)

[Bra12] Brakerski, Z.: Fully homomorphic encryption without modulus switching from classical GapSVP. In: Safavi-Naini, R., Canetti, R. (eds.) CRYPTO 2012. LNCS, vol. 7417, pp. 868–886. Springer, Heidelberg (2012). https://doi.org/10.1007/978-3-642-32009-5_50

[DJN10] Damgård, I., Jurik, M., Nielsen, J.B.: A generalization of Paillier's public-key system with applications to electronic voting. Int. J. Inf. Secur. $9(6)$, 371–385 (2010). https://doi.org/10.1007/s10207-010-0119-9

[DSZ15] Demmler, D., Schneider, T., Zohner, M.: ABY - a framework for efficient mixed-protocol secure two-party computation. In: NDSS 2015. The Internet Society (2015)

[Elg85] ElGamal, T.: A public key cryptosystem and a signature scheme based on discrete logarithms. Trans. Inf. Theory $31(4)$, 469–472 (1985)

[FAL06] Frikken, K.B., Atallah, M.J., Li, J.: Attribute-based access control with hidden policies and hidden credentials. IEEE Trans. Comput. $55(10)$, 1259–1270 (2006)

[FAZ05] Frikken, K.B., Atallah, M.J., Zhang, C.: Privacy-preserving credit checking. In: ACM Conference on Electronic Commerce (EC 2005), pp. 147–154. ACM (2005)

[Fel+19] Felsen, S., Kiss, Á., Schneider, T., Weinert, C.: Secure and private function evaluation with Intel SGX. In: CCSW 2019, pp. 165–181. ACM (2019)

[FV12] Fan, J., Vercauteren, F.: Somewhat practical fully homomorphic encryption. Cryptology ePrint Archive, Report 2012/144 (2012). https://ia.cr.org/2012/144

[GKS17] Günther, D., Kiss, Á., Schneider, T.: More efficient universal circuit constructions. In: Takagi, T., Peyrin, T. (eds.) ASIACRYPT 2017. LNCS, vol. 10625, pp. 443–470. Springer, Cham (2017). https://doi.org/10.1007/978-3-319-70697-9_16

[GMW87] Goldreich, O., Micali, S., Wigderson, A.: How to play ANY mental game. In: STOC 1987, pp. 218–229. ACM (1987)

[Gün+19] Günther, D., Kiss, Á., Scheidel, L., Schneider, T.: Framework for semi-private function evaluation with application to secure insurance rate calculation. CCS 2019 Posters/Demos (2019)

[Hen+10] Henecka, W., Kögl, S., Sadeghi, A.-R., Schneider, T., Wehrenberg, I.: TASTY: tool for automating secure two-party computations. In: CCS 2010, pp. 451–462. ACM (2010)

[HMS12] Hu, Y., Martin, W.J., Sunar, B.: Enhanced flexibility for homomorphic encryption schemes via CRT. In: ACNS 2012 (Industrial Track) (2012)

[Hol+20] Holz, M., Kiss, Á., Rathee, D., Schneider, T.: Linear-complexity private function evaluation is practical (full version). Cryptology ePrint Archive, Report 2020/853 (2020). https://ia.cr/2020/853

[Hua+11] Huang, Y., Evans, D., Katz, J., Malka, L.: Faster secure two-party computation using garbled circuits. In: USENIX Security 2011. USENIX (2011)

[IR89] Impagliazzo, R., Rudich, S.: Limits on the provable consequences of one-way permutations. In: STOC 1989, pp. 44–61. ACM (1989)

[Ish+03] Ishai, Y., Kilian, J., Nissim, K., Petrank, E.: Extending oblivious transfers efficiently. In: Boneh, D. (ed.) CRYPTO 2003. LNCS, vol. 2729, pp. 145–161. Springer, Heidelberg (2003). https://doi.org/10.1007/978-3-540-45146-4_9

[KM11] Katz, J., Malka, L.: Constant-round private function evaluation with linear complexity. In: Lee, D.H., Wang, X. (eds.) ASIACRYPT 2011. LNCS, vol. 7073, pp. 556–571. Springer, Heidelberg (2011). https://doi.org/10.1007/978-3-642-25385-0_30

[Kob87] Koblitz, N.: Elliptic curve cryptosystems. Math. Comput. **48**(177), 203–209 (1987)

[KS08a] Kolesnikov, V., Schneider, T.: A practical universal circuit construction and secure evaluation of private functions. In: Tsudik, G. (ed.) FC 2008. LNCS, vol. 5143, pp. 83–97. Springer, Heidelberg (2008). https://doi.org/10.1007/978-3-540-85230-8_7

[KS08b] Kolesnikov, V., Schneider, T.: Improved garbled circuit: free XOR gates and applications. In: Aceto, L., Damgård, I., Goldberg, L.A., Halldórsson, M.M., Ingólfsdóttir, A., Walukiewicz, I. (eds.) ICALP 2008. LNCS, vol. 5126, pp. 486–498. Springer, Heidelberg (2008). https://doi.org/10.1007/978-3-540-70583-3_40

[KS16] Kiss, Á., Schneider, T.: Valiant's universal circuit is practical. In: Fischlin, M., Coron, J.-S. (eds.) EUROCRYPT 2016. LNCS, vol. 9665, pp. 699–728. Springer, Heidelberg (2016). https://doi.org/10.1007/978-3-662-49890-3_27

[KSS13] Kolesnikov, V., Sadeghi, A.-R., Schneider, T.: A systematic approach to practically efficient general two-party secure function evaluation protocols and their modular design. J. Comput. Secur. **21**(2), 283–315 (2013)

[Lai17] Laine, K.: Simple encrypted arithmetic library 2.3.1. Microsoft Research (2017). https://www.microsoft.com/en-us/research/uploads/prod/2017/11/sealmanual-2-3-1.pdf

[Liu+20] Liu, H., Yu, Y., Zhao, S., Zhang, J., Liu, W.: Pushing the limits of Valiant's universal circuits: simpler, tighter and more compact. Cryptology ePrint Archive, Report 2020/161 (2020). https://ia.cr/2020/161

[LMS16] Lipmaa, H., Mohassel, P., Sadeghian, S.S.: Valiant's universal circuit: improvements, implementation, and applications. Cryptology ePrint Archive, Report 2016/17 (2016). https://ia.cr/2016/017

[LP09] Lindell, Y., Pinkas, B.: A proof of security of Yao's protocol for two-party computation. J. Cryptol. **22**(2), 161–188 (2009). https://doi.org/10.1007/s00145-008-9036-8

[LPR10] Lyubashevsky, V., Peikert, C., Regev, O.: On ideal lattices and learning with errors over rings. In: Gilbert, H. (ed.) EUROCRYPT 2010. LNCS, vol. 6110, pp. 1–23. Springer, Heidelberg (2010). https://doi.org/10.1007/978-3-642-13190-5_1

[Mil86] Miller, V.S.: Use of elliptic curves in cryptography. In: Williams, H.C. (ed.) CRYPTO 1985. LNCS, vol. 218, pp. 417–426. Springer, Heidelberg (1986). https://doi.org/10.1007/3-540-39799-X_31

[MS13] Mohassel, P., Sadeghian, S.: How to hide circuits in MPC an efficient framework for private function evaluation. In: Johansson, T., Nguyen, P.Q. (eds.) EUROCRYPT 2013. LNCS, vol. 7881, pp. 557–574. Springer, Heidelberg (2013). https://doi.org/10.1007/978-3-642-38348-9_33

[MSS14] Mohassel, P., Sadeghian, S., Smart, N.P.: Actively secure private function evaluation. In: Sarkar, P., Iwata, T. (eds.) ASIACRYPT 2014. LNCS, vol. 8874, pp. 486–505. Springer, Heidelberg (2014). https://doi.org/10.1007/978-3-662-45608-8_26

[Nik+14] Niksefat, S., Sadeghiyan, B., Mohassel, P., Sadeghian, S.: ZIDS: a privacy-preserving intrusion detection system using secure two-party computation protocols. Comput. J. $\mathbf{57}$(4), 494–509 (2014)

[NPS99] Naor, M., Pinkas, B., Sumner, R.: Privacy preserving auctions and mechanism design. In: ACM Conference on Electronic Commerce (EC 1999), pp. 129–139. ACM (1999)

[Pai99] Paillier, P.: Public-key cryptosystems based on composite degree residuosity classes. In: Stern, J. (ed.) EUROCRYPT 1999. LNCS, vol. 1592, pp. 223–238. Springer, Heidelberg (1999). https://doi.org/10.1007/3-540-48910-X_16

[Pin+09] Pinkas, B., Schneider, T., Smart, N.P., Williams, S.C.: Secure two-party computation is practical. In: Matsui, M. (ed.) ASIACRYPT 2009. LNCS, vol. 5912, pp. 250–267. Springer, Heidelberg (2009). https://doi.org/10.1007/978-3-642-10366-7_15

[PSS09] Paus, A., Sadeghi, A.-R., Schneider, T.: Practical secure evaluation of semi-private functions. In: Abdalla, M., Pointcheval, D., Fouque, P.-A., Vergnaud, D. (eds.) ACNS 2009. LNCS, vol. 5536, pp. 89–106. Springer, Heidelberg (2009). https://doi.org/10.1007/978-3-642-01957-9_6

[Reg05] Regev, O.: On lattices, learning with errors, random linear codes, and cryptography. In: STOC 2005, pp. 84–93. ACM (2005)

[Sea19] Microsoft SEAL (release 3.3) (2019). https://github.com/Microsoft/SEAL

[Val76] Valiant, L.G.: Universal circuits (preliminary report). In: STOC 1976, pp. 196–203. ACM (1976)

[Yao82] Yao, A.C.: Protocols for secure computations (extended abstract). In: FOCS 1982, pp. 160–164. IEEE (1982)

[Yao86] Yao, A.C.-C.: How to generate and exchange secrets. In: FOCS 1986, pp. 162–167. IEEE (1986)

[Zha+19] Zhao, S., Yu, Yu., Zhang, J., Liu, H.: Valiant's universal circuits revisited: an overall improvement and a lower bound. In: Galbraith, S.D., Moriai, S. (eds.) ASIACRYPT 2019. LNCS, vol. 11921, pp. 401–425. Springer, Cham (2019). https://doi.org/10.1007/978-3-030-34578-5_15

[ZRE15] Zahur, S., Rosulek, M., Evans, D.: Two halves make a whole. In: Oswald, E., Fischlin, M. (eds.) EUROCRYPT 2015. LNCS, vol. 9057, pp. 220–250. Springer, Heidelberg (2015). https://doi.org/10.1007/978-3-662-46803-6_8

Certifying Decision Trees Against Evasion Attacks by Program Analysis

Stefano Calzavara$^{(\boxtimes)}$, Pietro Ferrara, and Claudio Lucchese

Università Ca' Foscari, Venezia, Italy
`stefano.calzavara@unive.it`

Abstract. Machine learning has proved invaluable for a range of different tasks, yet it also proved vulnerable to evasion attacks, i.e., maliciously crafted perturbations of input data designed to force mispredictions. In this paper we propose a novel technique to verify the security of decision tree models against evasion attacks with respect to an expressive threat model, where the attacker can be represented by an arbitrary imperative program. Our approach exploits the interpretability property of decision trees to transform them into imperative programs, which are amenable for traditional program analysis techniques. By leveraging the abstract interpretation framework, we are able to soundly verify the security guarantees of decision tree models trained over publicly available datasets. Our experiments show that our technique is both precise and efficient, yielding only a minimal number of false positives and scaling up to cases which are intractable for a competitor approach.

Keywords: Adversarial machine learning · Decision trees · Security of machine learning · Program analysis

1 Introduction

Machine learning (ML) learns predictive models from data and has proved invaluable for a range of different tasks, yet it also proved vulnerable to *evasion attacks*, i.e., maliciously crafted perturbations of input data designed to force mispredictions [25]. To exemplify, let us assume a credit company decides to use a ML model to automatically assess whether customers qualify for a loan or not. A malicious customer who somehow realises or guesses that the model privileges unmarried people over married people could cheat about her marital status to improperly qualify for a loan.

The research community recently put a lot of effort in the investigation of *adversarial* ML, e.g., techniques to train models which are resilient to attacks or assess the security properties of models. In the present paper we are interested in the security certification of a popular class of models called *decision trees*, i.e., we investigate formally sound techniques to quantify the resilience of such models against evasion attacks. Specifically, we propose the first *provably sound* certification technique for decision trees with respect to an expressive threat model,

© Springer Nature Switzerland AG 2020
L. Chen et al. (Eds.): ESORICS 2020, LNCS 12309, pp. 421–438, 2020.
https://doi.org/10.1007/978-3-030-59013-0_21

where the attacker can be represented by an arbitrary imperative program. Verifying ML techniques with respect to highly expressive threat models is nowadays one of the most compelling research directions of adversarial ML [12,16]. This is an important step forward over previous work, which either proposed empirical techniques without formal guarantees or only focused on artificial attackers expressed as mathematical distances (see Sect. 6 for full details).

Our approach exploits the *interpretability* property of decision trees, i.e., their amenability to be easily understood by human experts, which makes their translation into imperative programs a straightforward task. Once a decision tree is translated into an imperative program, it is possible to leverage state-of-the-art program analysis techniques to certify its resilience to evasion attacks. In particular we leverage the *abstract interpretation* framework [9,10] to automatically extract a sound abstraction of the behaviour of the decision tree under attack. This allows us to efficiently compute an over-approximated, yet precise, estimate of the resilience of the decision tree against evasion attacks.

Contributions. We specifically contribute as follows:

1. We propose a general technique to certify the security guarantees of decision trees against evasion attacks attempted by an attacker expressed as an arbitrary imperative program. We exemplify the technique at work on an expressive threat model based on rewriting rules (Sect. 3).
2. We implement our technique into a new tool called TreeCert. Given a decision tree, an attacker and a test set of instances used to estimate prediction errors, TreeCert outputs an over-approximation of the error rate that the attacker can force on the decision tree. TreeCert implements a *context-insensitive* analysis computing a single over-approximation of the attacker's behavior and reuses it in the analysis of all the test instances, thus boosting efficiency without missing attacks (Sect. 4).
3. We experimentally prove the effectiveness of TreeCert against publicly available datasets. Our results show that TreeCert is extremely precise, since it can compute tight over-approximations of the actual error rate under attack, with a difference of at most 0.02 over it on cases which are small enough to be analyzed without approximated techniques. Moreover, TreeCert is much faster than a competitor approach [5] and scales to intractable cases, avoiding the exponential blow-up of non-approximated techniques (Sect. 5).

2   Background

2.1   Security of Supervised Learning

In this paper, we deal with the security of *supervised learning*, i.e., the task of learning a classifier from a set of labeled data. Formally, let $\mathcal{X} \subseteq \mathbb{R}^d$ be a d-dimensional space of real-valued features and $\mathcal{Y}$ be a finite set of class labels; a *classifier* is a function $f : \mathcal{X} \to \mathcal{Y}$ which assigns a class label to each element of the vector space (also called *instance*). The correct label assignment for each instance is modeled by an unknown function $g : \mathcal{X} \rightarrow \mathcal{Y}$, called *target* function.

Given a *training set* of labeled data $\mathcal{D}_{train} = \{(\mathbf{x}_1, g(\mathbf{x}_1)), \ldots, (\mathbf{x}_n, g(\mathbf{x}_n))\}$ and a *hypothesis space* $\mathcal{H}$, the goal of supervised learning is finding the classifier $\hat{h} \in \mathcal{H}$ which best approximates the target function g. Specifically, we let $\hat{h} = \text{argmin}_{h \in \mathcal{H}} \mathcal{L}(h, \mathcal{D}_{train})$, where $\mathcal{L}$ is a *loss* function which estimates the cost of the prediction errors made by h on $\mathcal{D}_{train}$. Once $\hat{h}$ is found, its performance is assessed by computing $\mathcal{L}(\hat{h}, \mathcal{D}_{test})$, where $\mathcal{D}_{test}$ is a *test set* of labeled, held-out data drawn from the same distribution of $\mathcal{D}_{train}$.

Within the context of security certification, one should measure the accuracy of $\hat{h}$ by taking into account all the actions that an attacker could take to fool the classifier into mispredicting, i.e., the so-called *evasion attacks* [1,2]. To provide a more accurate evaluation of the performance of the classifier under attack, the loss $\mathcal{L}$ can thus be replaced by the *loss under attack* $\mathcal{L}^A$ [21]. Formally, the attacker can be modeled as a function $A : \mathcal{X} \rightarrow 2^{\mathcal{X}}$ mapping each instance into a set of *perturbed* instances which might fool the classifier. The test set $\mathcal{D}_{test}$ can thus be corrupted into any dataset obtained by replacing each $(\mathbf{x}_i, y_i) \in \mathcal{D}_{test}$ with any $(\mathbf{x}_i', y_i)$ such that $\mathbf{x}_i' \in A(\mathbf{x}_i)$; we let $A(\mathcal{D}_{test})$ stand for the set of all such datasets. The loss under attack $\mathcal{L}^A$ is thus defined by making the pessimistic assumption that the attacker is able to craft the most damaging perturbations, as follows:

$$\mathcal{L}^A(\hat{h}, \mathcal{D}_{test}) = \max_{\mathcal{D}' \in A(\mathcal{D}_{test})} \mathcal{L}(\hat{h}, \mathcal{D}').$$

Unfortunately, computing $\mathcal{L}^A$ by enumerating $A(\mathcal{D}_{test})$ is intractable, given the huge number of perturbations available to the attacker: for example, if the attacker can flip K binary features, then each instance can be perturbed in 2^K different ways, leading to $2^K \cdot |\mathcal{D}_{test}|$ possible attacks.

2.2   Decision Trees

A powerful set of hypotheses $\mathcal{H}$ is the set of the *decision trees* [4]. We focus on traditional binary decision trees, whose internal nodes perform thresholding over feature values. Such trees can be inductively defined as follows: a decision tree t is either a leaf $\lambda(\hat{y})$ for some label $\hat{y} \in \mathcal{Y}$ or a non-leaf node $\sigma(f, v, t_l, t_r)$, where $f \in [1, d]$ identifies a feature, $v \in \mathbb{R}$ is the threshold for the feature f and t_l, t_r are decision trees. At test time, an instance $\mathbf{x} = (x_1, \ldots, x_d)$ traverses the tree t until it reaches a leaf $\lambda(\hat{y})$, which returns the *prediction* $\hat{y}$, denoted by $t(\mathbf{x}) = \hat{y}$. Specifically, for each traversed tree node $\sigma(f, v, t_l, t_r)$, $\mathbf{x}$ falls into the left tree t_l if $x_f \leq v$, and into the right tree t_r otherwise.

Figure 1 represents an example decision tree, which assigns the instance $(6,8)$ with label -1 to its correct class. In fact, (i) the first node checks whether the second feature (whose value is 8) is less than or equal to 10 and then takes the left sub-tree, and (ii) the second node checks whether the first feature (whose value is 6) is less than or equal to 5 and then takes the right leaf, classifying the instance with label -1. However, note that an attacker who was able to corrupt

(6,8) into (5,8) could force the decision tree into changing its output, leading to the prediction of the wrong class +1.

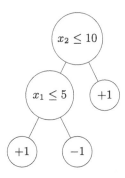

Fig. 1. Example of decision tree.

2.3   Abstract Interpretation

In the abstract interpretation framework, the behavior of a program is approximated through *abstract values* of a given *abstract domain* with a lattice structure, rather than concrete values. For example, the Sign domain abstracts numbers just with their sign, as formalized by the following *abstraction* and *concretization* functions (α and γ respectively):

$$\alpha(V) = \begin{cases} \bot & \text{if } V = \emptyset \\ + & \text{if } \forall v \in V : v > 0 \\ 0 & \text{if } \forall v \in V : v = 0 \\ - & \text{if } \forall v \in V : v < 0 \\ \top & \text{otherwise} \end{cases} \qquad \gamma(a) = \begin{cases} \mathbb{R} & \text{if } a = \top \\ \{n \in \mathbb{R} \mid n > 0\} & \text{if } a = + \\ \{0\} & \text{if } a = 0 \\ \{n \in \mathbb{R} \mid n < 0\} & \text{if } a = - \\ \emptyset & \text{if } a = \bot \end{cases}$$

Notice that for all sets of concrete values $V \subseteq \mathbb{R}$ we have $V \subseteq \gamma(\alpha(V))$, i.e., the abstraction function provides an over-approximation of the concrete values. Operations over concrete values like the sum operation $+$ are over-approximated by abstract counterparts $\oplus$ over the abstract domain, which define the *abstract semantics*. For example, the sum of two positive numbers is certainly positive, while the sum of a positive number and a negative number can be positive, negative or 0; this lack of information is modeled by $\top$. Hence, $\oplus$ is defined such that $+ \oplus + = +$ and $+ \oplus - = \top$. A sound definition of $\oplus$, here omitted, must ensure that $\forall V_1, V_2 \subseteq \mathbb{R} : \{v_1 + v_2 \mid v_1 \in V_1 \wedge v_2 \in V_2\} \subseteq \gamma(\alpha(V_1) \oplus \alpha(V_2))$, i.e., abstract operations must over-approximate operations over concrete values. By simulating the program over the abstract domain, abstract interpretation ensures a fast convergence to an over-approximation of all the reachable program states. In particular, the analysis consists in computing the fixpoint of the abstract semantics over the abstract domain, making use of a *widening* operator – usually if the upper bound operator does not converge within a given threshold [9,10].

Thanks to its modular approach, abstract interpretation allows one to define multiple abstractions of the same concrete domain. Therefore, several abstract domains approximating numerical values have been proposed in the literature. For instance Octagons [22] and Polyhedra [11] track different types of (linear) relations among numerical variables, and have been fruitfully applied to different contexts. Apron [18] is a library of numerical abstract domains comprising the main domains leveraged in this work.

3   Security Verification of Decision Trees

3.1   Threat Model

Our approach is general enough to be applied to attackers represented as arbitrary imperative programs. To exemplify it, we show how it can be applied to an expressive threat model based on *rewriting rules* [5]. This relatively new threat model goes beyond traditional distance-based models, which are plausible for perceptual tasks like image recognition, but are inappropriate for non-perceptual tasks (e.g., loan assignment) where mathematical distances do not capture useful semantic properties of the domain of interest.

We model the attacker A as a pair (R, K), where R is a set of *rewriting rules*, defining how instances can be corrupted, and $K \in \mathbb{R}^+$ is a *budget*, limiting the amount of alteration the attacker can apply to each instance. Each rule $r \in R$ has form:

$$[a, b] \xrightarrow{f}_k [\delta_l, \delta_u],$$

where: (i) $[a, b]$ and $[\delta_l, \delta_u]$ are intervals on $\mathbb{R} \cup \{-\infty, +\infty\}$, with the former defining the *precondition* for the application of the rule and the latter defining the *magnitude* of the perturbation enabled by the rule; (ii) $f \in [1, d]$ is the index of the feature to perturb; and (iii) $k \in \mathbb{R}^+$ is the *cost* of the rule. The semantics of the rewriting rule can be explained as follows: if an instance $\mathbf{x} = (x_1, \ldots, x_d)$ satisfies the condition $x_f \in [a, b]$, then the attacker can corrupt it by adding any $v \in [\delta_l, \delta_u]$ to x_f and spending k from the available budget. The attacker can corrupt each instance by using as many rewriting rules as desired in any order, possibly multiple times, up to budget exhaustion.

According to this attacker model, we can define $A(\mathbf{x})$, the set of the attacks against the instance $\mathbf{x}$, as follows.

Definition 1 (Attacks). *Given an instance $\mathbf{x}$ and an attacker $A = (R, K)$, we let $A(\mathbf{x})$ be the set of the attacks that can be obtained from $\mathbf{x}$, i.e., the set of the instances $\mathbf{x}'$ such that there exists a sequence of rewriting rules $r_1, \ldots, r_n \in R$ and a sequence of instances $\mathbf{x}_0, \ldots, \mathbf{x}_n$ where:*

1. *$\mathbf{x}_0 = \mathbf{x}$ and $\mathbf{x}_n = \mathbf{x}'$;*
2. *for all $i \in [1, n]$, the instance $\mathbf{x}_{i-1}$ can be corrupted into the instance $\mathbf{x}_i$ by using the rewriting rule r_i, as described above;*

3. the sum of the costs of $r_1, \ldots, r_n$ is not greater than K.

Notice that $\mathbf{x} \in A(\mathbf{x})$ for any A by picking an empty sequence of rewriting rules, i.e., the attacker can always leave the instance uncorrupted.

Example 1. Consider the attacker $A = (\{r_1, r_2\}, 10)$, where:

- $r_1 = [0, 10] \xrightarrow{1}_5 [-1, 0]$ allows the attacker to corrupt the first feature by adding any value in $[-1, 0]$, provided that the feature value is in $[0, 10]$ and the available budget is at least 5;
- $r_2 = [5, 10] \xrightarrow{2}_4 [0, 1]$ allows the attacker to corrupt the second feature by adding any value in $[0, 1]$, provided that the feature value is in $[5, 10]$ and the available budget is at least 4.

The attacker A can force the decision tree in Fig. 1 to change its original prediction (-1) on the instance $(6, 8)$. In particular, we can show that $(5, 8)$ is a possible attack against $(6, 8)$, since A can apply r_1 once by spending 5 from the budget, and $(5, 8)$ is classified as $+1$ by the decision tree.

3.2 Conversion to Imperative Program

Our analysis technique exploits the *interpretability* property of decision trees, i.e., their amenability to be easily understood by human experts. In particular, it is straightforward to convert any decision tree into an equivalent, loop-free imperative program. To exemplify, Fig. 2 shows the translation of the decision tree in Fig. 1 into an equivalent function.

```
1   int predict (float[] x) {
2       if (x[2] <= 10) {
3           if (x[1] <= 5)
4               return +1;
5           else
6               return -1;
7       }
8       else
9           return +1;
10  }
```

Fig. 2. Translation of the decision tree in Fig. 1 into an imperative program.

We can then model the attacker as an imperative program which has access to the function representing the decision tree to analyse. In particular, we observe that the attacker $A = (R, K)$ can be represented by means of a *non-deterministic* program which behaves as follows:

1. Select a random rewriting rule $r \in R$.

2. Let $[a, b] \xrightarrow{f}_k [\delta_l, \delta_u]$ be the selected rule r and let $\mathbf{x} = (x_1, \ldots, x_d)$ be the instance to perturb. If $x_f \in [a, b]$ and the available budget is at least k, then select a random $\delta \in [\delta_l, \delta_u]$, replace x_f with $x_f + \delta$ and subtract k from the available budget.
3. Non-deterministically go to step 1 or terminate the process. This stop condition allows the attacker to spare part of the budget, which is needed to enforce termination when the entire budget cannot be spent (or does not need to be spent).

This encoding is exemplified in Fig. 3, where lines 1–27 show how the attacker of Example 1 can be modeled as an imperative program, using standard functions for random number generation. Once the attacker has been modeled, we can finally encode the behavior of the decision tree under attack: this is shown in lines 29–32, where we let the attacker corrupt the input instance before it is fed to the decision tree for prediction.

3.3 Proving Security by Program Analysis

Given a decision tree t, an attacker A and a test set $\mathcal{D}_{test}$, we can compute an over-approximation of $\mathcal{L}^A(t, \mathcal{D}_{test})$ as follows.

We first translate the decision tree t together with the attacker A into an imperative program P modeling the decision tree under attack, as discussed in Sect. 3.2. For each instance $(\mathbf{x}_i, y_i) \in \mathcal{D}_{test}$, we build an abstract state $\alpha(\{\mathbf{x}_i\})$ representing $\mathbf{x}_i$ in the chosen abstract domain and we analyze P with such entry state. Then, the output of the analysis might be either of the following:

1. only leaves of the decision tree with the correct class label y_i are reachable. This means that, for all possible attacks against $\mathbf{x}_i$, the decision tree always classifies the instance correctly;
2. leaves with the wrong label are reachable as well. If t correctly classifies the instance in the unattacked setting, this might happen either because there is indeed an attack leading to a misprediction or for a loss of precision due to the over-approximation performed by the static analysis.

Since our approach relies on sound static analysis engines, it is not possible to miss attacks, i.e., every instance which can be mispredicted upon attack must fall in the second case of our analysis. Let $P^\#(\mathbf{x}_i) = Y_i$ stand for the set of labels Y_i returned by the analysis of P on the instance $\mathbf{x}_i$.

By using this information, we can construct an *abstraction* of the behaviour of t under attack on $\mathcal{D}_{test}$ defined as follows:

$$\forall (\mathbf{x}_i, y_i) \in \mathcal{D}_{test} : t^\#(\mathbf{x}_i) = \begin{cases} y_i & \text{if } P^\#(\mathbf{x}_i) = \{y_i\} \\ y \neq y_i & \text{otherwise} \end{cases}$$

By construction, we have that $\mathcal{L}^A(t, \mathcal{D}_{test}) \leq \mathcal{L}(t^\#, \mathcal{D}_{test})$ for any loss function which depends just on the number of mispredictions, like the *error rate*, i.e., the fraction of wrong predictions among all the performed predictions.

```
1   float[] attack (float[] x) {
2       float K = 10;
3       boolean done = false;
4       while (!done) {
5           int rule = random_int(1,3);
6           switch (rule) {
7               case 1:
8                   if (x[1] >= 0 && x[1] <= 10 && K >= 5) {
9                       float delta = random_float(-1,0);
10                      x[1] = x[1] + delta;
11                      K = K - 5;
12                  }
13                  break;
14              case 2:
15                  if (x[2] >= 5 && x[2] <= 10 && K >= 4) {
16                      float delta = random_float(0,1);
17                      x[2] = x[2] + delta;
18                      K = K - 4;
19                  }
20                  break;
21              case 3:
22                  // this models non-deterministic termination
23                  done = true;
24          }
25      }
26      return x;
27  }
28
29  int predict_under_attack (float[] x) {
30      float[] x' = attack(x);
31      return predict(x');
32  }
```

Fig. 3. Encoding predictions under attack into an imperative program.

This means that after building $t^{\#}$ we have an efficient way to over-approximate the loss under attack $\mathcal{L}^A$ by computing just a traditional loss $\mathcal{L}$, which does not require the computation of the set of attacks.

3.4   Extensions

We discuss here possible extensions of our approach to different popular settings. We leave the implementation of these extensions to future work, since they are essentially an engineering effort.

Regression. The *regression* task requires one to learn a regressor rather than a classifier from the training data. The key difference between a regressor and a classifier is that the former does not assign a class from a finite set $\mathcal{Y}$, but rather infers a numerical quantity from an unbound set, e.g., estimates the salary of an employee based on her features. Regression can be modeled by revising the abstraction $t^{\#}$ such that it returns an abstract value over-approximating all the values of the predictions found in the leaves which are reachable upon attack. Formally, this means requiring $t^{\#}(\mathbf{x}_i) = \bigsqcup_{y_i \in P^{\#}(\mathbf{x}_i)} \alpha(\{y_i\})$, where $\sqcup$ stands for the upper bound operator on the abstract domain.

Tree Ensembles. Ensemble methods train multiple decision trees and combine them to improve prediction accuracy. Traditional ensemble approaches include random forest [3] and gradient boosting [14]. Irrespective of how an ensemble is trained, its final predictions are performed just by aggregating the predictions of the individual trees, e.g., using majority voting or averaging. This means that it is possible to readily generalize our analysis technique to ensembles by translating each tree therein and by aggregating their predictions in the generated imperative program.

4   Implementation

Figure 4 depicts the architecture of TreeCert. The inputs are: (i) the attacker, expressed in the threat model of Sect. 3.1 using a JSON file, (ii) a decision tree to analyse, serialized through the `joblib` library, and (iii) a test set in CSV format. TreeCert reports for each test instance whether it is correctly classified for each possible attack or it might be wrongly classified. The analysis is performed along three different modules, called TreeCoder, AttackerAnalyzer and TreeAnalyzer respectively, which we detail in the following.

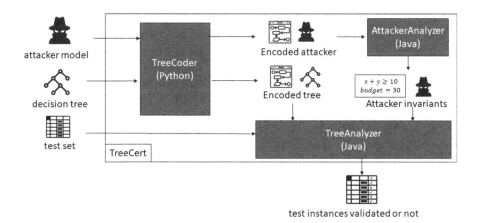

Fig. 4. The architecture of TreeCert.

4.1   TreeCoder

The first step of TreeCert is to encode the attacker and the decision tree as Java programs through the module TreeCoder, as described in Sect. 3.2. TreeCoder is a Python script that, given an attacker model and a decision tree, produces two distinct Java files encoding the attacker (see method `attack` in Fig. 3) and the decision tree (see method `predict` in Fig. 2).

There are only two small technical differences over the previous presentation. First, given that all instances of the same dataset share the same set of features, instances are not encoded as arrays, but rather modeled using a distinct local variable for each feature, which simplifies the static analysis; specifically, we let variable x_i represent the initial value of the i-th feature and variable x_i' represent its value after the attack. In addition, each time a rewriting rule r is applied, we increment a counter r_counter, initially set to 0, which allows one to capture useful analysis invariants. Clearly, these changes do not affect the semantics of the generated program, so we did not include them in Fig. 3 for simplicity.

4.2   AttackerAnalyzer

The encoded attacker is then passed to the AttackerAnalyzer module, a static analyzer based on abstract interpretation. The analyzer interfaces with Apron, a standard library implementing many popular abstract domains. The analyzer then computes a fixpoint over the Java program representing the attacker, using the Polka implementation[1] of the Polyhedra domain [11].

Polka tracks linear equalities and inequalities over an arbitrary number of variables. These invariants allow AttackerAnalyzer to infer the upper and lower bounds of each attacked feature, based on how many times a feature can be attacked using the available budget. To exemplify, pick the attacker in Fig. 3. AttackerAnalyzer infers on such program that, after the attack has been performed: (i) the value of the first feature may have been decreased by at most r1_counter (formally, $x_1' \in [x_1 - 1 * \text{r1\_counter}, x_1]$), (ii) the second feature may have been increased by at most r2_counter ($x_2' \in [x_2, x_2 + 1 * \text{r2\_counter}]$), (iii) both the counters are non-negative (r1_counter $\geq 0 \land$ r2_counter ≥ 0), and (iv) the budget spent in the application of the two rewriting rules is less than or equal to the initial budget ($5 * \text{r1\_counter} + 4 * \text{r2\_counter} \leq 10$). Note that the last invariant is inferred only if the calculation of a fixpoint over the abstract semantics did not require to apply the Polyhedra widening operator to convergence. Otherwise, the analysis would drop such information to ensure termination.

4.3   TreeAnalyzer

The attacker invariants are then passed to the TreeAnalyzer module together with the test set. Like AttackerAnalyzer, TreeAnalyzer performs a static analysis using the Polka implementation of the Polyhedra abstract domain. For each test

---

[1] http://apron.cri.ensmp.fr/library/0.9.10/mlapronidl/Polka.html.

instance $\mathbf{x}$, TreeAnalyzer (i) adds the initial values of the features of $\mathbf{x}$ to the attacker invariants, (ii) computes the fixpoint over the program encoding the decision tree t under attack, and (iii) uses it to return the output $t^{\#}(\mathbf{x})$.

To clarify, consider again Example 1, where the test instance $(6, 8)$ is correctly classified as -1 by the decision tree in Fig. 1, but can be misclassified upon attack. First of all, TreeAnalyzer adds the invariants $x_1 = 6$ and $x_2 = 8$ to the inferred attacker invariants, leading to an initial Polyhedra state tracking that $x_1' \in [6 - \mathsf{r1\_counter}, 6]$ and $x_2' \in [8, 8 + \mathsf{r2\_counter}]$ with $5 * \mathsf{r1\_counter} + 4 * \mathsf{r2\_counter} \leq 10$. Then the static analysis of the encoded tree starts with the evaluation of the condition $x_2' \leq 10$, inferring that such condition is always evaluated to true: indeed, x_2 could become greater than 10 only if $\mathsf{r2\_counter}$ was strictly greater than 2, but then $5 * \mathsf{r1\_counter} + 4 * \mathsf{r2\_counter} \leq 10$ could not hold since $\mathsf{r1\_counter} \geq 0$. TreeAnalyzer then analyzes the condition $x_1' \leq 5$. In this case, it cannot definitely conclude that the condition is always evaluated to false, since x_1 can become less than or equal to 5 if $\mathsf{r1\_counter} \geq 1$, which is allowed by the invariant $5 * \mathsf{r1\_counter} + 4 * \mathsf{r2\_counter} \leq 10$. TreeAnalyzer then concludes that the test instance might be wrongly classified, since a branch that classifies it as $+1$ could be reached.

5   Experimental Evaluation

5.1   Methodology

We evaluate our proposal on three public datasets: Census, House and Wine, which are described in Sect. 5.2. Our methodology includes multiple steps. We start with a preliminary *threat modeling* phase, where we define the attacker's capabilities by means of a set of rewriting rules R and a set of possible budgets $\{K_1, \ldots, K_n\}$, as explained in Sect. 3.1. Our attackers are primarily designed to perform an experimental evaluation of TreeCert, yet they are representative of plausible attack scenarios which do not fit traditional distance-based models and are instead readily supported by the expressiveness of our threat model.

Datasets are divided into $\mathcal{D}_{train}$ and $\mathcal{D}_{test}$ by using a 90-10 splitting with stratified sampling (80-20 splitting is used for the smaller Wine dataset). We first train a decision tree t on $\mathcal{D}_{train}$ using the popular `scikit-learn` library, tuning the maximum number of leaves in the set $\{2^1, 2^2, \ldots, 2^{10}\}$ through cross validation on $\mathcal{D}_{train}$. We then evaluate the tree resilience to attacks against each attacker $A = (R, K_i)$ on $\mathcal{D}_{test}$, using a non-approximated technique. Given the expressiveness of our threat model, the only available solution for this is the algorithm in [5]. In particular, the algorithm computes $\mathbb{A}(\mathbf{x}_i)$, the set of *representative* attacks against t, for each instance $\mathbf{x}_i$ in $\mathcal{D}_{test}$. This is a comparatively small subset of the attacks $A(\mathbf{x}_i)$, which suffices to detect the successful evasions attacks without any loss of soundness or precision. We refer to this method as *Representative Attacks*. We observe and we experimentally confirm that computing even the representative attacks is intractable in general, which motivates the need for approximated analyses like ours; yet, being able to deal with this in a few cases is useful to assess the precision of TreeCert against a ground truth.

Finally, we compute the abstraction $t^\#$ on $\mathcal{D}_{test}$ for each attacker $A = (R, K_i)$ by using TreeCert. This allows us to classify each $(\mathbf{x}_i, y_i) \in \mathcal{D}_{test}$ as follows:

- *True Positive* (*TP*): TreeCert states that the instance $\mathbf{x}_i$ can be misclassified upon attack and this conclusion is correct. Formally, $t^\#(\mathbf{x}_i) \neq y_i \wedge \exists \mathbf{x}_i' \in \mathbb{A}(\mathbf{x}_i) : t(\mathbf{x}_i') \neq y_i$.
- *False Positive* (*FP*): TreeCert states that the instance $\mathbf{x}_i$ can be misclassified upon attack, but this conclusion is wrong. Formally, $t^\#(\mathbf{x}_i) \neq y_i \wedge \forall \mathbf{x}_i' \in \mathbb{A}(\mathbf{x}_i) : t(\mathbf{x}_i') = y_i$.
- *True Negative* (*TN*): TreeCert states that the instance $\mathbf{x}_i$ cannot be misclassified upon attack and this conclusion is correct. Formally, $t^\#(\mathbf{x}_i) = y_i \wedge \forall \mathbf{x}_i' \in \mathbb{A}(\mathbf{x}_i) : t(\mathbf{x}_i') = y_i$.
- *False Negative* (*FN*): TreeCert states that the instance $\mathbf{x}_i$ cannot be misclassified upon attack, but this conclusion is wrong. Formally, $t^\#(\mathbf{x}_i) = y_i \wedge \exists \mathbf{x}_i' \in \mathbb{A}(\mathbf{x}_i) : t(\mathbf{x}_i') \neq y_i$.

Since our analysis is sound, we cannot have *FN*. We then assess the quality of TreeCert by computing its *False Positive Rate FPR* and *False Discovery Rate FDR* as follows:

$$FPR = \frac{FP}{FP + TN}, \quad FDR = \frac{FP}{FP + TP}.$$

We also compare the value of the loss under attack $\mathcal{L}^A(t, \mathcal{D}_{test})$ against its over-approximation $\mathcal{L}(t^\#, \mathcal{D}_{test})$, focusing on the *error rate*, i.e., the fraction of wrong predictions. Finally, we compare the execution time of TreeCert against the time spent in the computation of the set of the representative attacks.

5.2   Datasets

We perform our experiments on three publicly available datasets, whose key statistics are shown in Table 1. The preconditions of the rewriting rules and the magnitude of the perturbations have been set after a preliminary data exploration step, based on the observed data distribution in the dataset. A real-world application of our analysis technique would require input from domain experts to define the relevant threats, which is beyond the scope of our evaluation.

Census. The Census[2] dataset includes demographic information about American citizens. The prediction task is estimating whether the income of a citizen is above 50,000\$ per year. For this dataset, we define four rewriting rules:

- cost 5: if the capital gain is in $[0,100000]$, a citizen can raise it by 200;
- cost 5: if the capital loss is in $[0,100000]$, a citizen can lower it by 200;
- cost 10: if the number of work hours is in $[0,40]$, a citizen can raise it by 1;
- cost 10: if the age is in $[0,40]$, a citizen can raise it by 1.

We consider 20, 40, 60, 80 as possible values of the attacker's budget.

---

[2] http://archive.ics.uci.edu/ml/machine-learning-databases/adult.

Table 1. Properties of datasets used in the experiments.

Dataset	#Instances	#Features	Maj. class
Census	29169	51	0.75
House	21613	19	0.51
Wine	6497	12	0.63

House. The House[3] dataset contains house sale prices for the King County area. The prediction task is inferring whether a house costs at least as the median house price. For this dataset, we define four rewriting rules:

- cost 5: if the square footage of the living space of the house is in [0,3000], it can be increased by 50;
- cost 5: if the square footage of the land space is in [0,2000], it can be increased by 50;
- cost 5: if the average square footage of the living space of the 15 closest houses is in [0,2000], it can be increased by 50;
- cost 5: if the construction year is in [1900,1970], it can be increased by 10.

We consider 10, 20, 30, 40 as possible values of the attacker's budget.

Wine. The Wine[4] dataset represents different types of wines. The prediction task is detecting whether a wine has quality score at least 6 on a scale 0–10. For this dataset, we define four rewriting rules:

- cost 2: if the residual sugar is in [2,4], it can be lowered by 0.01;
- cost 5: if the alcohol level is in [0,11], it can be increased by 0.01;
- cost 5: if the volatile acidity is in [0,1], it can be lowered by 0.01;
- cost 5: if the free sulfur dioxide is in [20,40], it can be lowered by 0.1.

We consider 20, 30, 40, 50, 60 as possible values of the attacker's budget.

5.3   Experimental Results

Precision. Table 2 reports for all datasets and budgets a number of measures computed for the trained decision tree t:

1. the traditional loss in absence of attacks $\mathcal{L}(t, \mathcal{D}_{test})$. This is the fraction of wrong predictions returned by t on $\mathcal{D}_{test}$ in the unattacked setting;
2. the loss under attack $\mathcal{L}^A(t, \mathcal{D}_{test})$, computed by enumerating all the representative attacks using the algorithm in [5]. This is the fraction of wrong predictions returned by t on $\mathcal{D}_{test}$ upon attack;
3. the over-approximation of the loss under attack $\mathcal{L}(t^\#, \mathcal{D}_{test})$, computed using the program analysis of TreeCert;

---

[3] https://www.kaggle.com/harlfoxem/housesalesprediction.
[4] https://www.openml.org/data/get_csv/49817/wine_quality.arff.

4. the false positive rate of TreeCert, noted *FPR*;
5. the false discovery rate of TreeCert, noted *FDR*.

Table 2. Accuracy results across datasets.

Dataset	Budget	$\mathcal{L}(t, \mathcal{D}_{test})$	$\mathcal{L}^A(t, \mathcal{D}_{test})$	$\mathcal{L}(t^\#, \mathcal{D}_{test})$	FPR	FDR
Census	20	0.14	0.17	0.17	0.00	0.00
	40	0.14	0.17	0.17	0.00	0.01
	60	0.14	0.18	0.18	0.00	0.01
	80	0.14	0.20	0.21	0.00	0.01
House	10	0.10	0.12	0.12	0.00	0.02
	20	0.10	0.14	0.15	0.01	0.04
	30	0.10	0.16	0.17	0.01	0.06
	40	0.10	0.18	0.19	0.02	0.08
Wine	20	0.24	0.30	0.31	0.01	0.02
	30	0.24	0.34	0.35	0.02	0.03
	40	0.24	0.36	0.37	0.02	0.04
	50	0.24	0.37	0.39	0.03	0.05
	60	0.24	0.38	0.40	0.03	0.05

The experimental results clearly confirm the quality of the analysis performed by TreeCert. In particular, we observe that the *FPR* is remarkably low, standing well below 5%, where 10% is considered a state-of-the-art reference for static analysis techniques [24]. Indeed, in Census we measured an absolute number of false positives never greater than 5. This is interesting, because it shows that for many instances there is a simple security proof, i.e., TreeCert is able to prove that they cannot be successfully attacked (i.e., they are *TN*), which significantly drops the *FPR*. As to the *FDR*, we observe that it also scores extremely well on all datasets, though it tends to be slightly higher than *FPR*. However, this is not a major problem in our application setting: contrary to what happens in traditional program analysis, where users are forced to investigate all false alarms to identify possible bugs, here we are rather interested in the aggregated analysis results, i.e., the final over-approximation of the loss under attack. Even on the House dataset, where *FDR* tends to be higher, we observe that the loss under attack is appropriately approximated by TreeCert, since there is a difference of at most 0.01 between the actual value of the loss under attack and its over-approximation. Remarkably, our experiments also show that the quality of the over-approximation is not significantly affected by the attacker's budget, which is important because it suggests that TreeCert likely generalizes to cases where computing the actual value of the loss under attack is computationally intractable, which is the intended use case of our analysis tool.

Efficiency. To show the efficiency of our approach, we compare in Fig. 5 the running time of TreeCert against the time taken to compute the full set of the representative attacks. It is possible to clearly see that the two curves exhibit completely different trends. The time taken to construct the representative attacks has an *exponential* trend: the approach is efficient and feasible when the attacker's budget is low, but blows up to intractability very quickly. For example, each increase in the attacker's budget multiplies the execution time of a 3x factor in the case of Census and we experimentally confirmed that more than 12 h of computation are needed when the budget grows to 100 (not plotted). Conversely, the execution time of TreeCert is only marginally affected when increasing the attacker's budget, since the analysis always converges in less than one hour. In the case of the House dataset, computing the set of the representative attacks is even less feasible: even for small budgets, the running time is remarkably high, due to the fact that the trained decision tree uses many different thresholds, which makes the number of representative attacks blow up. Finally, also the Wine dataset shows similar figures, though the execution times there are lower due to its smaller size. This confirms that brute-force approaches based on the exhaustive enumeration of the representative attacks do not scale, yet luckily they can be replaced by more efficient abstraction techniques with very good precision.

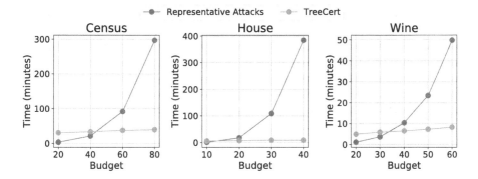

Fig. 5. Running time of TreeCert against the enumeration of representative attacks.

6   Related Work

Verifying the security guarantees of machine learning models is an important task, which received significant attention by the research community in the last few years. In particular, many papers proposed techniques to verify the security of deep neural networks [15,17,20,27,28]; we refer to a recent survey for more work in this research area [29]. As of now, however, comparatively less attention has been received by the security verification of decision trees models.

The closest related work to our approach is a very recent paper by Ranzato and Zanella [23]. Their work also focuses on decision trees and builds on the abstract interpretation framework. However, their approach can only be applied to attackers who admit a simple mathematical characterization as a set of perturbations, e.g., based on distances. In particular, their soundness theorem relies on the hypothesis that, for each test instance $\mathbf{x}$, one has $A(\mathbf{x}) \subseteq \gamma(\alpha(\{\mathbf{x}\}))$, i.e., the abstraction of $\mathbf{x}$ must cover all the possible attacks. Checking this condition for distance-based attackers is straightforward, yet it is computationally infeasible in general. For example, in the case of the rewriting rules we considered, $A(\mathbf{x})$ is unknown *a priori*, but is induced by the application of the rules. Indeed, their tool *silva* only supports attackers based on the infinity-norm L_∞, which has a compact mathematical characterization as a set, but falls short of representing realistic threats. Instead, our approach is general enough to work on attackers modeled as arbitrary imperative programs.

Other approaches also deal with the verification of decision trees, but are not based on abstract interpretation. For example, Einzinger et al. use SMT solving to verify the robustness of gradient-boosted models [13]. Their approach also requires to explicitly encode the set of attacks $A(\mathbf{x})$ in closed form, which is only easily doable for artificial distance-based attackers. Moreover, SMT solving suffers from scalability issues, which required the authors to develop custom optimizations to make their approach practical. It is unclear whether this line of work can be adapted and scale to more expressive attackers or not, also because their tool is not publicly available. Other notable work includes the robustness verification algorithm by Chen et al. [8], which only works for attackers based on the infinity-norm L_∞, and the abstraction-refinement approach by Törnblom and Nadjm-Tehrani [26], which is not proved sound.

Finally, it is worth mentioning adversarial learning algorithms which train decision trees more resilient to evasion attacks by construction [5–7,19]. This line of work is orthogonal to the security verification of decision trees, i.e., our approach can also be applied to estimate the improved robustness guarantees of trees trained using such algorithms.

7   Conclusion

We proposed a technique to certify the security of decision trees against evasion attacks by leveraging the abstract interpretation framework. This is the first solution which is both sound and expressive enough to deal with sophisticated attackers represented as arbitrary imperative programs. Our experiments showed that our technique is both precise and efficient, yielding only a minimal number of false positives and scaling up to cases which are intractable for a competitor [5].

We foresee several avenues for future work. First, we plan to extend our approach to the analysis of regression tasks and tree ensembles: though this is straightforward from an engineering perspective, we want to analyze the precision and the efficiency of our solution in such settings. Moreover, we will investigate techniques to automatically infer the minimal attacker's budget required to induce a given error rate on the test set, so as to efficiently provide security analysts with this useful information. Finally, we will investigate the trade-off between the precision and the efficiency of TreeCert by testing more sophisticated abstract domains and analysis techniques, e.g., trace partitioning.

References

1. Biggio, B., et al.: Evasion attacks against machine learning at test time. In: Blockeel, H., Kersting, K., Nijssen, S., Železný, F. (eds.) ECML PKDD 2013. LNCS (LNAI), vol. 8190, pp. 387–402. Springer, Heidelberg (2013). https://doi.org/10.1007/978-3-642-40994-3_25
2. Biggio, B., Roli, F.: Wild patterns: ten years after the rise of adversarial machine learning. Pattern Recognit. **84**, 317–331 (2018)
3. Breiman, L.: Random forests. Mach. Learn. **45**(1), 5–32 (2001). https://doi.org/10.1023/A:1010933404324
4. Breiman, L., Friedman, J.H., Olshen, R.A., Stone, C.J.: Classification and Regression Trees. Wadsworth, Belmont (1984)
5. Calzavara, S., Lucchese, C., Tolomei, G.: Adversarial training of gradient-boosted decision trees. In: Proceedings of CIKM. ACM (2019)
6. Calzavara, S., Lucchese, C., Tolomei, G., Abebe, S.A., Orlando, S.: TREANT: training evasion-aware decision trees. Data Min. Knowl. Discov. (2020, to appear). https://doi.org/10.1007/s10618-020-00694-9
7. Chen, H., Zhang, H., Boning, D.S., Hsieh, C.: Robust decision trees against adversarial examples. In: Proceedings of ICML. PMLR (2019)
8. Chen, H., Zhang, H., Si, S., Li, Y., Boning, D.S., Hsieh, C.: Robustness verification of tree-based models. In: Proceedings of NeurIPS, pp. 12317–12328 (2019)
9. Cousot, P., Cousot, R.: Abstract interpretation: a unified lattice model for static analysis of programs by construction or approximation of fixpoints. In: Proceedings of POPL. ACM (1977)
10. Cousot, P., Cousot, R.: Systematic design of program analysis frameworks. In: Proceedings of POPL. ACM (1979)
11. Cousot, P., Halbwachs, N.: Automatic discovery of linear restraints among variables of a program. In: Proceedings of POPL. ACM Press (1978)
12. Dreossi, T., Jha, S., Seshia, S.A.: Semantic adversarial deep learning. In: Chockler, H., Weissenbacher, G. (eds.) CAV 2018. LNCS, vol. 10981, pp. 3–26. Springer, Cham (2018). https://doi.org/10.1007/978-3-319-96145-3_1
13. Einziger, G., Goldstein, M., Sa'ar, Y., Segall, I.: Verifying robustness of gradient boosted models. In: Proceedings of AAAI, pp. 2446–2453. AAAI Press (2019)
14. Friedman, J.H.: Greedy function approximation: a gradient boosting machine. Ann. Stat. **29**, 1189–1232 (2001)
15. Gehr, T., Mirman, M., Drachsler-Cohen, D., Tsankov, P., Chaudhuri, S., Vechev, M.T.: AI2: safety and robustness certification of neural networks with abstract interpretation. In: Proceedings of Security and Privacy. IEEE Computer Society (2018)
16. Goodfellow, I., McDaniel, P., Papernot, N.: Making machine learning robust against adversarial inputs. Commun. ACM **61**(7), 56–66 (2018)
17. Huang, X., Kwiatkowska, M., Wang, S., Wu, M.: Safety verification of deep neural networks. In: Majumdar, R., Kunčak, V. (eds.) CAV 2017. LNCS, vol. 10426, pp. 3–29. Springer, Cham (2017). https://doi.org/10.1007/978-3-319-63387-9_1

18. Jeannet, B., Miné, A.: APRON: A library of numerical abstract domains for static analysis. In: Bouajjani, A., Maler, O. (eds.) CAV 2009. LNCS, vol. 5643, pp. 661–667. Springer, Heidelberg (2009). https://doi.org/10.1007/978-3-642-02658-4_52

19. Kantchelian, A., Tygar, J.D., Joseph, A.D.: Evasion and hardening of tree ensemble classifiers. In: Proceedings of ICML. JMLR.org (2016)

20. Katz, G., Barrett, C., Dill, D.L., Julian, K., Kochenderfer, M.J.: Reluplex: an efficient SMT solver for verifying deep neural networks. In: Majumdar, R., Kunčak, V. (eds.) CAV 2017. LNCS, vol. 10426, pp. 97–117. Springer, Cham (2017). https://doi.org/10.1007/978-3-319-63387-9_5

21. Madry, A., Makelov, A., Schmidt, L., Tsipras, D., Vladu, A.: Towards deep learning models resistant to adversarial attacks. In: Proceedings of ICLR. OpenReview.net (2018)

22. Miné, A.: The octagon abstract domain. Higher-Order Symb. Comput. **19**, 31–100 (2006). https://doi.org/10.1007/s10990-006-8609-1

23. Ranzato, F., Zanella, M.: Abstract interpretation of decision tree ensemble classifiers. In: Proceedings of AAAI. AAAI Press (2020)

24. Sadowski, C., Aftandilian, E., Eagle, A., Miller-Cushon, L., Jaspan, C.: Lessons from building static analysis tools at google. Commun. ACM **61**(4), 58–66 (2018)

25. Szegedy, C., et al.: Intriguing properties of neural networks. In: Proceedings of ICLR (2014)

26. Törnblom, J., Nadjm-Tehrani, S.: An abstraction-refinement approach to formal verification of tree ensembles. In: Romanovsky, A., Troubitsyna, E., Gashi, I., Schoitsch, E., Bitsch, F. (eds.) SAFECOMP 2019. LNCS, vol. 11699, pp. 301–313. Springer, Cham (2019). https://doi.org/10.1007/978-3-030-26250-1_24

27. Wang, S., Pei, K., Whitehouse, J., Yang, J., Jana, S.: Efficient formal safety analysis of neural networks. In: Proceedings of NeurIPS 2018 (2018)

28. Wang, S., Pei, K., Whitehouse, J., Yang, J., Jana, S.: Formal security analysis of neural networks using symbolic intervals. In: Proceedings of USENIX Security. USENIX Association (2018)

29. Xiang, W., et al.: Verification for machine learning, autonomy, and neural networks survey. CoRR abs/1810.01989 (2018). http://arxiv.org/abs/1810.01989

They Might NOT Be Giants Crafting Black-Box Adversarial Examples Using Particle Swarm Optimization

Rayan Mosli[1,2(✉)], Matthew Wright[1], Bo Yuan[1], and Yin Pan[1]

[1] Golisano College of Computing and Information Sciences, Rochester Institute of
Technology, Rochester, NY 14623, USA
{rhm6501, matthew.wright, bo.yuan, yin.pan}@rit.edu
[2] Faculty of Computing and Information Technology, King Abdul-Aziz University,
Jeddah, Saudi Arabia

Abstract. As machine learning is deployed in more settings, including
in security-sensitive applications such as malware detection, the risks
posed by adversarial examples that fool machine-learning classifiers have
become magnified. *Black-box* attacks are especially dangerous, as they
only require the attacker to have the ability to query the target model and
observe the labels it returns, without knowing anything else about the
model. Current black-box attacks either have low success rates, require a
high number of queries, produce adversarial images that are easily distinguishable from their sources, or are not flexible in controlling the outcome
of the attack. In this paper, we present AdversarialPSO, (Code available: https://github.com/rhm6501/AdversarialPSOImages) a black-box
attack that uses few queries to create adversarial examples with high
success rates. AdversarialPSO is based on Particle Swarm Optimization,
a gradient-free evolutionary search algorithm, with special adaptations
to make it effective for the black-box setting. It is flexible in balancing the number of queries submitted to the target against the quality
of the adversarial examples. We evaluated AdversarialPSO on CIFAR-
10, MNIST, and Imagenet, achieving success rates of 94.9%, 98.5%, and
96.9%, respectively, while submitting numbers of queries comparable to
prior work. Our results show that black-box attacks can be adapted to
favor fewer queries or higher quality adversarial images, while still maintaining high success rates.

1 Introduction

Deep learning (DL) is being used to solve a wide variety of problems in many different domains, such as image classification [20], malware detection [18], speech
recognition [23], and medical imaging based diagnosis [4]. Despite state-of-the-
art performance, DL models have been shown to suffer from a general flaw that
makes them vulnerable to external attack. Adversaries can manipulate models to
misclassify inputs by applying small perturbations to samples at test time [22].
These *adversarial examples* have also been successfully demonstrated against

L. Chen et al. (Eds.): ESORICS 2020, LNCS 12309, pp. 439–459, 2020.
https://doi.org/10.1007/978-3-030-59013-0_22

real-world black-box targets, where adversaries would perform remote queries on a classifier to develop and verify their attack samples [16]. The possibility of such attacks poses a significant risk to any ML application, especially in security-critical settings or life-threatening environments.

Early adversarial attacks relied on model gradients to create examples [3,7,17], which requires internal knowledge of the target model. Since some adversarial examples transfer from one model to another [16], limited black-box attacks are possible using model gradients, but with low success rates [5]. More recent approaches either estimate the model's gradients [2,5,9,10] or iteratively apply perturbations to the input [1,8,15]. As demonstrated by Moon et al., however, the success rate of gradient-estimation approaches depends heavily on the choice of hyperparameters [15]. Consequently, attack methods with fewer hyperparameters to set or potentially tune would be less sensitive to hyperparameter values and thus more practical in a black-box setting where tuning might be impossible.

In practice, the feasibility of a black-box attack also depends greatly on the number of required queries submitted to the model. Against machine-learning-as-a-service (MLaaS) platforms like Google Vision, each query has a monetary cost. Too many queries make the attack costly. Perhaps more importantly, needing too many queries could trigger a monitor to detect an attack underway by observing many subtly modified versions of the same image submitted to the system in a short period. To evade such a monitor, one could conduct the attack very slowly or use a large number of accounts that all have different credit cards attached and different IP addresses. Either approach would significantly add to the real-world costs of conducting the attack.

In this paper, we examine how an adversary could generate adversarial examples with a *controllable trade-off* between the number of queries and the quality of the adversarial examples. In particular, we propose the use of Particle Swarm Optimization (PSO)—a gradient-free optimization technique—to craft adversarial examples. PSO maintains a population of candidate solutions called particles. Each particle moves in the search space to find better solutions based on a fitness function that we have designed for finding adversarial examples.

In our attack, called AdversarialPSO, we specify that particles move by making small perturbations to the input image that are virtually imperceptible to a human observer. PSO has been shown to quickly converge on good (though not globally optimal) solutions [19], making it very suitable for finding adversarial examples in a black-box setting, as it can identify sufficiently good examples with few queries. In AdversarialPSO, we also propose numerous adaptations to fit the black-box setting, including a novel method to minimize redundancy among the particles that greatly reduces the number of queries. We test the effectiveness of this approach on three image classification datasets—MNIST, CIFAR-10, and Imagenet—and find that AdversarialPSO attains high success rates with queries comparable to state-of-the-art attacks.

In a real attack, the adversary may be constrained to making fewer queries or, alternatively, be able to make more queries and want to improve the quality of the images further. AdversarialPSO allows the attacker to tune the number of queries against the quality of images by simply changing the number of particles in the swarm. By using bigger swarms, more queries would be submitted to the model in exchange for higher-quality adversarial examples.

In addition to the flexibility offered by AdversarialPSO, due the gradient-free nature of the attack, no hyperparameters require tuning for the attack to be successful. As shown in Sect. 3.2, the attack only requires the number of particles and the initial block-size used in the attack. The two hyperparameters affect the quality vs number of queries trade-off and can be roughly estimated based on the dimensions of the input.

Contributions. In summary, we have made the following contributions:

- We present AdversarialPSO, a gradient-free black-box attack with controllable trade-offs between the number of queries and the quality of adversarial examples.
- We demonstrate the effectiveness of AdversarialPSO on both low-dimensional and high-dimensional datasets by empirically evaluating the attack on the MNIST, CIFAR-10, and Imagenet datasets. We show that AdversarialPSO produces adversarial examples comparable to the state-of-the-art.
- We show how AdversarialPSO can be adjusted to trade-off the number of queries against the quality of the images.

2 Related Work

In this section, we discuss related work in both the white-box and black-box settings.

2.1 White-Box Attacks

Szegedy et al. were the first to discuss the properties of neural networks that make adversarial attacks possible [22]. They show that imperceptible non-random perturbations of an image can cause an otherwise accurate DL model to misclassify it. The authors also discuss the transferability of adversarial examples from one model to another, including scenarios where models may have different architectures or are trained using different subsets of training data.

Goodfellow et al. [7] presented an explanation as to why DL models are susceptible to adversarial examples. They argue that the linearity of neural networks is what leads to their sensitivity to small and directed changes in input. They also present the Fast Gradient Sign Method (FGSM), which calculates the perturbations needed to transform inputs to adversarial examples. FGSM determines the direction of perturbations according to model gradients with respect to input and adds minuscule values in that direction. Kurakin et al. [13] extend this approach by introducing IGSM, an iterative variant of FGSM that takes several smaller steps instead of one relatively large step. The authors printed the images of the adversarial examples and fed them to a model through a camera. The results demonstrate that adversarial examples can work in the physical world, and that these types of attacks are practical.

Papernot et al. take a different approach to find adversarial examples [17]. Instead of taking multiple small steps, they construct a saliency map that maintains relevant input features with a high impact on model outputs. They utilize the saliency map to perturb specific features and create adversarial examples. This approach allows an adversarial example constructed towards a target label specified by the attacker. In a later paper, Papernot et al. extended the techniques of both Goodfellow et al. and Papernot et al. to launch black-box attacks against remotely hosted targets [16]. As both attacks require knowledge of model internals—information that is not available in a black-box setting—the authors used a local white-box surrogate that approximates the black-box target. The surrogate is trained using the Jacobian-based Dataset Augmentation method, which expands the training set used to train the surrogate with data points that allow the surrogate to approximate the target's decision boundary closely.

Another approach was employed by Carlini and Wagner [3], who search for adversarial examples by iteratively performing $minimize\, \mathcal{D}(x, x + \delta)$, where $\mathcal{D}$ is either an L_0, L_2, or L_∞ distance metric. The attack finds the minimum distance required to generate an adversarial example according to the distance metric being minimized. To use it as a black-box attack, it can be launched on a surrogate model, where only examples with high confidence are likely to transfer to the target model.

2.2   Black-Box Attacks

In a black-box attack, the attacker does not know the internals of a target model. Instead, the attacker can query the target with specially crafted inputs meant to help estimate the gradient or lead gradually to misclassified samples. Target models are typically assumed to return confidence scores along with each classification, and these are used in constructing the inputs for subsequent queries.

Gradient-Estimation Attacks. To launch black-box attacks, Chen et al. propose ZOO [5], a method to estimate model gradients using only the model inputs and the corresponding confidence scores provided by the model. The approach employs a finite difference method that evaluates image coordinates after adding a small perturbation to estimate the direction of the gradient for each coordinate. Since examining every coordinate requires a huge number of queries to the model, the authors applied the stochastic coordinate descent algorithm and attack-space dimension reduction to reduce the number of queries needed to approximate gradients. Moderate perturbations in the direction of the gradient are, as shown in the FGSM attack, sufficient to obtain an adversarial example from the input. Although ZOO can successfully create adversarial examples indistinguishable from the inputs, it requires up to a million queries for high-dimensional samples, such as from Imagenet. With so many queries, the attack could be easily detectable, and the cost could be prohibitive and impractical in a real-world setting for a single image.

To reduce the number of queries, Bhagoji et al. estimate the gradient of groups of features or coordinates instead of estimating one coordinate at a time [2]. Although the attack was not evaluated on a high-dimensional dataset, it outperformed ZOO on low-dimensional datasets such as CIFAR-10 and MNIST. The proposed Gradient Estimation (GE) approach by the authors still requires up to 10,000 queries to generate an adversarial example. The authors considered PSO as a possible approach for searching adversarial examples but found it to be slow and not as useful as GE. As we show in Sect. 4.2, however, our modifications to the basic PSO algorithm enable it to outperform GE. Our version of PSO does not require a swarm of 100 particles to be effective, which would be slow as per Bhagoji et al.'s experience. Instead, it can search for adversarial examples with high success rates using swarms with as few as five particles.

Ilyas et al. propose Natural Evolutionary Strategies (NES) to estimate gradients of the model, and then use projected gradient descent on the estimated gradients to craft adversarial examples [9]. They also extend the approach in [10] to utilize the bandit optimization method to exploit prior information when estimating the gradients. Specifically, they incorporate a data-dependent prior, which exploits the similarity in gradient information exhibited by adjacent pixels. Furthermore, they also incorporate a time-dependent prior that utilizes the high correlation between gradients estimated in successive steps. Although the attack can generate high-quality adversarial examples with few queries, the approach has been shown to be very sensitive to changes in hyperparameter values. Moon et al. [15] have shown that having too many hyperparameters could lead to significant variability in attack performance, creating dependability on the values chosen for those hyperparameters. Gradient-estimation based approaches commonly have multiple hyperparameters that are necessary for the execution of attacks, such as the learning rate, search variance, decay rate, and update rules – in a real-world black-box setting, tuning these hyperparameters would either incur additional queries or might not be possible at all in many cases. In our approach, there are only two hyperparameters with predictable effects on the outcome of the attack.

Gradient-Free Attacks. Moon et al. formulate the problem of crafting adversarial examples as a set maximization problem that searches for the set of positive and negative perturbations that maximizes an objective function [15]. Similar to [10], the authors exploit the spatial regularity exhibited by adjacent pixels by searching for perturbations in blocks instead of individual pixels. They increase the granularity of the blocks as the search progresses. Our AdversarialPSO attack searches for perturbations in blocks as well and yields comparable results as Moon et al.'s approach. However, our approach is capable of adjusting hyperparameter values effectively for the trade-off between L2 and queries as we show in Sect. 4.6.

Guo et al. explore a simple attack that crafts adversarial examples by randomly sampling a set of orthonormal vectors and adding or subtracting them from the input [8]. The attack is shown to be successful in crafting adversarial examples despite its simplicity. However, the success of the attack diminishes as dimensionality increases, as shown when targeting InceptionV3, which expects inputs (299×299) with higher dimensionality than that of ResNet and DenseNet (224×224). As the perturbations are applied randomly, many queries are wasted by the approach until a solution is found.

By utilizing Differential Evolution (DE), Su et al. show that some test samples can be misclassified by changing a single pixel [21]. Similar to the PSO algorithm used in this paper, DE is a population-based algorithm that maintains and manipulates a set of candidate solutions until an acceptable outcome is found. The objective of this one-pixel attack is to better understand the geometry of adversarial space and proximity of adversarial examples to their corresponding inputs. The attack does not achieve high success rates due to the tight constraints used in the study.

Another population-based black-box attack is GenAttack [1], which uses a *Genetic Algorithm (GA)* to find adversarial examples. This attack iteratively performs the three genetic functions–*selection, crossover*, and *mutation*–where selection extracts the fittest candidates in a population, crossover produces a child from two parents, and mutation encodes diversity to the population by applying small random perturbations. The authors propose two heuristics to reduce the number of queries used by GenAttack, namely dimensionality reduction and adaptive parameter scaling. Although the authors propose two heuristics to reduce the numbers of queries used by their approach, GenAttack uses a higher number of queries compared to our approach.

3   Particle Swarm Optimization

In this section, we provide an overview of the PSO algorithm and describe how we adapt it to generate adversarial examples against image classification models.

3.1   Conventional PSO

Kennedy and Eberhart first proposed PSO as a model to simulate how flocks of birds forage for food [12]. It has since been adapted to address a multitude of problems, such as text feature selection [14], grid job scheduling [11], and optimizing the generation of electricity [6]. The algorithm works by dispersing particles in a search space and moving them until a solution is found. The search space is assumed to be d-dimensional, where the position of each particle i is a d-dimensional vector $X_i = (x_{i,1}, x_{i,2}, x_{i,3}, \ldots, x_{i,d})$. The position of each particle is updated according to a velocity vector V_i where $V_i = (v_{i,1}, v_{i,2}, v_{i,3}, \ldots, v_{i,d})$. In each time-step or iteration, denoted as t, the velocity vector is used to update the particle's next position, calculated as:

$$x_i(t+1) = x_i(t) + v_i(t+1) \tag{1}$$

$$v_i(t+1) = wv_i(t) + c_1 R_1(p_g - x_i(t)) + c_2 R_2(p_i - x_i(t)) \tag{2}$$

Equation 2 contains three terms. The first term controls how much influence the current velocity has when calculating the next velocity and is constrained with the *inertia* weight w. The second term, with weight c_1, is referred to as *exploration*, as it allows particles to explore further regions in the search space in the direction of the best position found by the swarm, denoted by p_g. The third term, with weight c_2, is referred to as *exploitation*, and it is based on the best position found by this particle, denoted by p_i. R_1 and R_2 are d-dimensional vectors containing uniformly distributed random numbers that are calculated for each iteration to encode randomness in the search process. Early implementations of PSO assigned a fixed value to w. Shi and Eberhart, however, found that linearly decreasing the inertia weight w improved PSO performance [19]. In each iteration, fixed values w_{start} and w_{end} together with a maximum number of iterations t_{max} were used to calculate the inertia as:

$$w(t) = w_{\text{end}} + (w_{\text{start}} - w_{\text{end}}) \left(\frac{t_{\text{max}} - t}{t_{\text{max}}} \right) \tag{3}$$

In the case of black-box adversarial attacks, however, the number of queries is a more appropriate measure for how much the attack has progressed. We thus modify Eq. 3 to compute w with respect to the number of queries instead of number of iterations as:

$$w(t) = w_{\text{end}} + (w_{\text{start}} - w_{\text{end}}) \left(\frac{q_{\text{max}} - q}{q_{\text{max}}} \right), \tag{4}$$

where q_{max} is the query budget used in the attack and q is the number of queries submitted to the model. We set $w_{\text{start}} = 1$ and $w_{\text{end}} = 0$.

3.2   Adversarial PSO

Among the many applications of PSO, we show in this paper that it can also be used to craft adversarial examples for images. Shi and Eberhart [19] found that PSO is quick to converge on a solution and scales well to large dimensions, at the cost of slower convergence to global optima. This makes PSO an excellent fit for finding adversarial examples in the black-box setting, as it suggests that it can identify sufficiently good examples with few queries, even for high-dimensional image data.

In this section, we first describe the key adaptations we used to make PSO effective and query-efficient for black-box attacks, and especially highlight our technique for minimizing redundancy in the query process. We then lay out the overall algorithm.

PSO Adaptations. Our PSO includes several key adaptations for our problem:

Fitness Function. To adapt PSO to the problem of creating adversarial examples, we define a fitness function that measures the change in model output when perturbations are added to the input. In both targeted and untargeted attacks, the fitness function measures how much the model's confidence in the target label rises or drops, respectively. When performing untargeted attacks, the fitness for each candidate solution is the confidence drop in the original class predicted by the model. Given the original image x, the perturbed image x', the model parameters θ, and the original label y we compute confidence $f(x, y, \theta)$. We then calculate the fitness using fitness $= f(x, y, \theta) - f(x', y, \theta)$. In targeted attacks, fitness is given by the *increase* in confidence in the desired class. For the target label y', we compute confidence $f(x, y', \theta)$ and fitness $= f(x', y', \theta) - f(x, y', \theta)$.

Constraints. To further control the perturbations added to the input image, we define an upper bound value B of maximum change to limit the L_∞ distance between the adversarial image and the original image. L_∞ measures the maximum change to any of the coordinates, where $L_\infty = max(|x_1 - x_1'|, |x_2 - x_2'|, \ldots, |x_d - x_d'|)$. To ensure the upper bound, we use the clip operator to get $x' = clip(x_i + v_i, x_i - B, x_i + B)$. Additionally, we apply box constraints to maintain valid image values when adding perturbations. These constraints are applied to Eq. 1 to yield:

$$x_i(t + 1) = clip(clip(x_i(t) + v_i(t + 1), x_i - B, x_i + B), 0, 1) \qquad (5)$$

Block-Based Perturbation. Similar to related work [2,9,15], we exploit the spatial regularity of adjacent pixels by splitting the input into blocks and perturbing all the pixels in each block en masse. Perturbing pixels in blocks utilizes the gradient similarities that are shared between adjacent pixels. Essentially, as such pixels would have similar effects on the outcome of the prediction, perturbing them as a group would have a larger impact on the rise (or drop) on the model's confidence, which translates to requiring fewer queries to generate adversarial examples.

Reversals. Since we have a relatively small number of blocks, and thus a limited number of perturbations, we can examine the results of each modification separately. We take advantage of this by reversing all the perturbations that have caused a negative impact on the fitness with the goal of finding improvements. Note that instead of just undoing the perturbation, we actually move the particle in the opposite direction. In essence, this is similar to inferring the gradient, as we assume that the opposite of a bad direction will be a good direction. We note that this is different from the approach of Moon et al. of alternating between adding perturbations and removing perturbations [15], which just undoes some of the prior steps. In our tests, we find that our reversals do indeed lead to a better position in many cases.

Following the Edge of the L_∞ Ball. As observed by Moon et al. [15], the optimal solution when crafting adversarial examples often reside at the edges of the L_∞ ball. Based on this observation, when initializing and randomizing particles, we set their positions at the edge of the L_∞ ball to observe the highest (or lowest) fitness for each dimension. Particles are then moved inwards using Eqs. 2 and 5. Moving inwards from the edge ensures that particles get enough velocity to reach the other end quickly if the opposite position was found to have better fitness. Otherwise, particles would waste queries moving around the center of the ball until they eventually build enough velocity towards the position with the highest fitness.

The Particle Explosion Problem. For long running attacks, the velocity would eventually become so large that it would overpower the exploration and exploitation terms in Eq. 2. This would cause particles to get stuck at the edges of the L_∞ ball as the ever-increasing velocity would continuously push them to locations outside the search space. This is a well known problem in PSO, and although the inertia weight is meant to mitigate it, it does not completely solve the problem. Therefore, in addition to the inertia weight, we perform *velocity clamping* to limit the growth of the velocity vector, again leveraging the `clip` operator:

$$v_i(t) = clip(v_i(t), -B, B). \tag{6}$$

This is performed in every iteration for each particle before updating the particle positions.

Redundancy Minimization. Beyond these other adaptations to PSO, we found it very effective to minimize the redundancy across particles, which helps to minimize the number of particles and the number of queries to find good examples. The key insight of this approach is that relatively few of the possible changes to the image are going to be especially valuable to changing the classification result. If one of the particles includes one of these useful changes, then that benefit is likely to be seen in the query result. Having found that effective change in one particle, other particles can take advantage of this through the exploration attribute in the PSO algorithm, which moves particles towards the best position in the swarm. We thus aim to limit the possibility of redundant checks on already perturbed blocks. Essentially, if one of the particles has modified one of the blocks in a given way, e.g. it increased the red channel on all pixels in that block, then we prevent other particles from making the same modification. To do this, we first define a set β with all *available* blocks (which are still eligible to be modified), $\beta = (b_1, b_2, b_3, \ldots, b_n)$. Then, for each block in the set, we create a list of all possible directions containing the positive and negative directions for each channel in the block. For grayscale images, which contain only a single channel, the list of possible channel directions cd is given by $cd = \{(1), (-1)\}$. For RGB images, it is

$$\begin{aligned} cd = \{ &(1, 0, 0), (-1, 0, 0), \\ &(0, 1, 0), (0, -1, 0), \\ &(0, 0, 1), (0, 0, -1) \}. \end{aligned}$$

In other words, any single channel could be increased or decreased.

When a direction in a block is assigned to a particle, that direction is then removed from the list to avoid multiple particles perturbing the same block in the same direction. When all the directions in a block are assigned to particles, we remove that block from the set β. When there are no more blocks in the set, we increase the granularity of the blocks by dividing the block-size by half and recreate the block set to contain the smaller blocks.

For each particle, we maintain a list of all the blocks and directions assigned to it. This list is used to avoid assigning an opposite direction to the particle which would cancel out a direction that it was previously assigned. Section 3.2 discusses how this list is used.

PSO Algorithm. The threat model we assume for this attack consists of an attacker with exploratory capabilities that permits submissions to a remote black-box model, which returns confidence scores with each prediction. The attacker has no influence on the training process and has no access to internal model information. The attack is based solely on the confidence scores returned by the model.

The search for adversarial examples is performed in two stages: *initialization* and *optimization*. The *initialization* stage disperses the particles in the search space and tests the initial fitness for the starting point of each particle. The *optimization* stage moves the particles according to Eqs. 1 and 2, and tests the fitness for each new position until either an adversarial example is found or the query budget is exhausted, whichever comes first. The overall process of AdversarialPSO (Algorithm 1), and all other algorithms discussed in this section, can be seen in the appendix.

Initialization. For each image, the search process starts with initializing the particles by randomizing their positions in the search space (Algorithm 2). Particles are initialized by randomly assigning an equal number of blocks to each particle, without replacement to minimize redundancy (see Sect. 3.2). In large swarms, each particle is assigned relatively few blocks, resulting in a more fine-grained search for adversarial examples.

Two hyperparameters control how the swarm is initialized: the number of particles in the swarm P and the initial block-size b, which determines the number of initial blocks created and the number of blocks assigned to each particle. Each particle begins with the input image x and the set of blocks β with a single direction for each block. Particles are then dispersed in the search space by perturbing all the blocks assigned to them to the edge of the L_∞ ball according to the directions they were given. Once the particles are created and dispersed, their fitness is calculated and subsequently used in the optimization step.

Optimization. The optimization step of AdversarialPSO (Algorithm 3) is an iterative process that moves the particles in search of better fitness. Particle positions are updated using the velocity vector, which is calculated for each particle in every iteration. After moving the particles, their fitness is calculated and compared against the particle's best fitness to determine which particle position will be used to calculate future particle movements. The particle's fitness is also compared against the best fitness achieved in the swarm as a whole (i.e, best swarm fitness), and if the particle fitness was found to be better, the swarm is updated to account for the position with the highest fitness. The process is repeated until an adversarial example is found or when the process exhausts the allowed number of queries.

In every iteration, in addition to particle movements, each particle is assigned the next set of blocks and directions as was done in the initialization stage. Again, the assignment is designed to minimize redundancy (see Sect. 3.2). This randomization is performed after the particles are moved according to their calculated velocity vectors to allow the exploration of additional regions of the search space (Algorithm 4).

After some number of iterations, all the directions in all the blocks will have been assigned to a particle. At that point, the granularity of the blocks is increased, and the particles are re-initialized with the swarm best position as a starting point. When re-initializing the particles, we also reset their best positions. We do this to prevent the particles from retracting to the previous granularity level.

After all the blocks are assigned to particles and before increasing the granularity of the blocks, we perform the reversal operation (see Sect. 3.2 on *Reversals*). The reversal is performed on the swarm best position by iterating through the past positions of each particle and applying an opposite step for any movement that caused a negative fitness for the particle (Algorithm 5).

4   Evaluation

4.1   Setup

To evaluate AdversarialPSO, we consider the the success rate (i.e., the ratio of successfully generated adversarial examples over the total number of samples) and the average number of queries needed to generate adversarial examples. We compare our results against the Parsimonious Black-Box Adversarial Attack [15], NES [9] and Bandits [10] using the benchmark dataset Imagenet. We use the results reported in the Parsimonious attack paper [15] for our comparison, and as L_2 distances were not reported by the authors for all three attacks, we omit this metric from our evaluation. Nonetheless, the same L_∞ bound was used in our experiments as the other three attacks. Furthermore, similar to the related work, we evaluate the attack using InceptionV3. The Imagenet results for both untargeted and targeted attacks are obtained from running AdversarialPSO on 1,000 correctly classified samples from the indices list provided in the Parsimonious attack. The same target labels used in [15] and [10] are used for the targeted experiment. Also, for related work that utilize block-based perturbations, we use the same initial block-sizes as related work. If not, we use block-size that are adequate to the dimensions of the input samples. The results for the untargeted and targeted Imagenet attacks are reported in Sects. 4.3 and 4.4, respectively.

We also test the attack on an adversarially trained CIFAR-10 ResNet classier as was done in [15], by using the same pretrained network provided by MadryLab.[1] The results for this test are reported in Sect. 4.5.

---

[1] https://github.com/MadryLab/cifar10_challenge.

We compare the AdversatialPSO attack on MNIST and CIFAR-10 against the approach used by Bhagoji et al. [2] to show the improvements attained from our modifications to the PSO algorithm. Similar to the models used in [2], we use ResNet-32 and a two-layer convolutional neural network for CIFAR-10 and MNIST respectively. Furthermore, we use the same L_∞ limits of $L_\infty = 0.3$ for MNIST $L_\infty = 8/255$ for CIFAR-10. Unlike Bhagoji et al., who used 100 particles, we only use 5 particles. Using fewer particles translates to fewer queries being submitted to the model and a less resource intensive attack. As we show in Sect. 4.2, we achieve higher success rates with much smaller swarms. For all MNIST evaluations, due to the low dimensionality of the inputs, we use an initial block-size of 2 without increasing the granularity. For CIFAR-10, we use an initial block-size of 8.

Finally, we explore the effect of using different-sized swarms on ImageNet. We report the average per-pixel L_2 distance between input images and their adversarial counterparts. As using more particles enables us to increase the granularity, we find that larger swarms produce better adversarial examples with a lower L_2 average. We show the results of this analysis in Sect. 4.6.

Table 1. Results comparison: Untargeted attack on MNIST and CIFAR-10 against the PSO and GE attacks of Bhagoji et al. [2]. The results we list for the Bhagoji attacks are obtained from their paper

Attack	MNIST			CIFAR-10		
	Succ. rate	L2	Queries	Succ. rate	L2	Queries
Finite Diff	92.9%	6.1	1568	86%	410.3	6144
GE	61.5%	6.0	196	66.8%	402.7	768
IFD	**100%**	2.1	62720	**100%**	65.7	61440
Iterative GE	98.4%	**1.9**	8000	99.0%	80.5	7680
Their PSO	84.1%	5.3	10000	89.2%	262.3	7700
SPSA	96.7%	3.9	8000	88.0%	**44.4**	7680
AdversarialPSO	98.52%	5.3	**183**	94.92%	338.2	**129**

4.2 Untargeted MNIST and CIFAR-10

To demonstrate the effectiveness of AdversarialPSO, we compare our attack against the approach used by Bhagoji et al. [2]. As shown in Table 1, AdversarialPSO not only outperforms the standard PSO used by Bhagoji et al., it also outperforms the GE approach used by the authors. For MNIST, the only approach to have a higher success-rate is the Iterative Finite Difference (IFD) attack at 100%, however the average number of queries was above 60K. In our implementation, we set a maximum budget of 10K queries, which led to a handful of failures.

Regarding the average L_2, using a swarm with 5 particles produces adversarial examples with comparable distances. However, by increasing the number of particles in the swarm, better quality adversarial examples could be generated at the expense of more queries. Repeating the same experiment but with 10 particles produces an average L_2 of 4.9, but with an average of 296 queries.

Similarly for CIFAR-10, the only two approaches to have higher success rates are Iterative GE and IFD. Both of these, however, require many more queries on average (over 7500) than AdversarialPSO (under 200).

In examining the failed instances of the CIFAR-10 ResNet-32 model, we find that samples that failed were resistant to small perturbations. Particle movements had a low impact on the model's confidence scores and as such, executed for a large number of iterations until the query budget was exhausted. For a majority of the samples, the adversarial examples were crafted rather quickly without using many queries. We speculate that the failed instances were far from the decision boundary, thus requiring large changes to be misclassified. Figure 1 shows randomly chosen examples of our attack on both CIFAR-10 and MNIST.

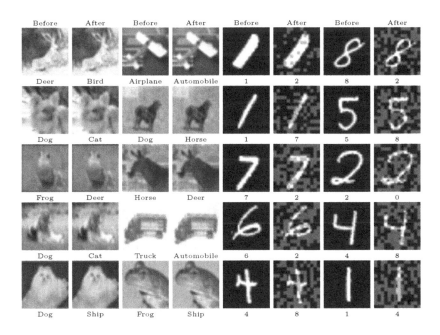

Fig. 1. Untargeted attack using AdversarialPSO on MNIST and CIFAR-10

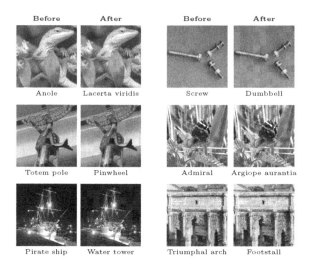

Fig. 2. Untargeted attacks on InceptionV3 (randomly selected samples)

Table 2. Untargeted and targeted attacks on Imagenet

Attack	Untargeted		Targeted	
	Success rate	Avg. queries	Success rate	Avg. queries
NES	80.3%	1660	99.7%	16284
Bandits	94.9%	1030	92.3%	26421
Parsimonious attack	**98.5%**	**722**	**99.9%**	**7485**
AdversarialPSO	96.9%	837	98.6%	14959

4.3 Untargeted Imagenet

To evaluate the attack on the Imagenet dataset, we use the InceptionV3 model provided by Keras[2]. As per the Keras implementation, inputs are scaled to $[-1,1]$, so we set the L_∞ bound to 0.1 (equivalent to the 0.05 L_∞ used by prior work). We choose the first 1000 samples from the indices list found in the Parsimonious Black-Box Attack GitHub page[3] and attack each sample with a query budget of 10,000 queries. We also use 32 for an initial block-size, similar to Moon et al. [15], and 5 particles in the swarm. Figure 2 shows randomly chosen examples of images generated from the attack, which we find have similar quality to those shown by Moon et al. [15]. As shown in Table 2, our attack achieves comparable success rates and number of queries as the related work, but with the advantage of providing controllable trade-offs between the number of queries and the quality of the adversarial examples.

---

[2] https://keras.io/applications/#inceptionv3.

[3] https://github.com/snu-mllab/parsimonious-blackbox-attack.

4.4   Targeted Imagenet

To evaluate AdversarialPSO in a targeted attack, we use samples from the Parsimonious Black-box Attack's list of sample indices and we use the same labels as in [15]. Furthermore, similar to [15], we use an initial block-size of 32 and a query budget of 100,000 queries. Unlike the untargeted attack however, we use 10 particles to accommodate the more difficult attack setting. Table 2 summarizes our results and Fig. 3 shows randomly chosen examples of the attack. Similar to the untargeted attack, we outperform both GE-based attacks. The Parsimonious attack however, generates adversarial examples with fewer queries.

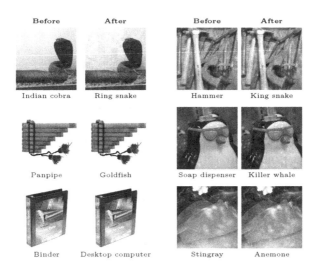

Fig. 3. Targeted attacks on InceptionV3 (randomly selected samples)

Table 3. Untargeted attack on adversarially trained CIFAR-10 ResNet classier

Attack	Success rate	Avg. queries
NES	29.5%	2872
Bandits	38.6%	1877
Parsimonious attack	**48%**	**1261**
AdversarialPSO	45.4%	2341

4.5   AdversarialPSO on Adversarially Trained Models

To test the attack against defended models, we evaluate AdversarialPSO against the adversarially trained CIFAR-10 model provided by MadryLabs. We use the same samples, L_∞ bound, and query budgets as used by Moon et al. [15]. As shown in Table 3, AdversarialPSO outperforms both Bandits and NES. Although

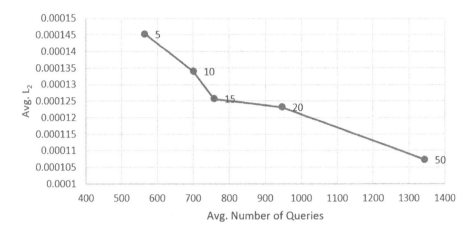

Fig. 4. The effect of swarm size on the average number of queries and per-pixel L_2 distance. In the figure, the x-axis represents the number of queries, the y-axis represents the per-pixel L_2, and the number of particles are shown by the markers

the Parsimonious Black-box attack remains the highest in success rate, AdversarialPSO performs comparably with the added advantage of providing a trade-off between queries and L_2.

4.6 Swarm-Size Analysis

By re-running the untargeted Imagenet attack using swarms with different sizes, we show that increasing the number of particles lowers the average L_2 at the expense of more queries. The results are based on samples that were successfully attacked by all swarm sizes. As shown in Fig. 4, there is a 26% improvement in adversarial example quality when increasing the number of particles from 5 to 50. With this trade-off, an attacker that favors adversarial example quality over number of queries can use larger swarms. On the other hand, if fewer queries is more important to the attacker, then smaller swarms would be more beneficial.

5 Conclusions

This paper presented a black-box attack based on the evolutionary search algorithm: Particle Swarm Optimization. The attack we call AdversarialPSO, adapts the traditional PSO algorithm to produce adversarial examples from images. Our experimental evaluations on the MNIST, CIFAR10, and Imagenet datasets suggest that AdversarialPSO can effectively generate adversarial examples in practical black-box settings with a limited number of queries to the target model. Furthermore, we demonstrate how the attack can be adjusted to control the trade-off between the number of queries submitted to the model and the L_2 distance between the original inputs and the generated adversarial examples.

The purpose of the attack is to help evaluate security-critical models against black-box attacks and to promote the search for robust defenses.

Acknowledgment. We would like to thank the reviewers for their constructive comments that helped clarify and improve this paper. This material is based upon work supported by the National Science Foundation under Awards No. 1816851, 1433736, and 1922169.

A   Appendix

As discussed in Sect. 3.2, the AdversarialPSO attack iteratively performs several operations to generate adversarial examples from images. Algorithm 1 provides a high-level view of the main AdversarialPSO loop that is responsible for initializing the swarm, moving the particles, randomizing the particles, increasing the granularity of the search space, and reversing any movement with a negative fitness:

Algorithm 1.   AdversarialPSO

1: **Input:** maximum queries q_{max}, block-set B
2: *Initialize swarm* (See Algorithm 2)
3: **while** $q < q_{max}$ **do**
4:    **if** *Success* **then**
5:       **return** *bestPosition*
6:    **end if**
7:    *Move Particles* (See Algorithm 3)
8:    **if** B *is empty* **then**
9:       *performReversal* (See Algorithm 5)
10:       *increaseGranularity*
11:       *initializeParticles(bestPosition)*
12:    **else**
13:       *randomizeParticles* (See Algorithm 4)
14:    **end if**
15: **end while**
16: **return** *bestPosition*

In preparation for the attack, AdversarialPSO initializes the swarm by separating the image into blocks and assigning a different set of blocks to each particle. The attack then moves the particles according to the blocks they were assigned and evaluates the new position to calculate the fitness of each new position. Algorithm 2 provides the steps for the initialization process:

Algorithm 2. Initializing the swarm

1: **Input:** input image x, particle array par, block-set B, and maximum change m.
2: $n \leftarrow int(length(B)/P)$ # blocks per particle
3: **for** p in par **do**
4: 　$blocks \leftarrow$ select random n elements from B
5: 　$p.pos \leftarrow x$
6: 　**for** $block$ in $blocks$ **do**
7: 　　$direction \leftarrow$ select random direction from $B[block]$
8: 　　pop direction from $B[block]$ and $push$ direction to $p.blockList[block]$
9: 　　**for** i in $block$ **do**
10: 　　　$p.pos_i \leftarrow p.pos_i + m * direction$
11: 　　**end for**
12: 　**end for**
13: 　$fitness \leftarrow calculateFitness$ #includes update to q
14: 　Compare new fitness against particle best and swarm best
15: **end for**
16: **return** par, $bestPosition$, $bestFitness$

In each iteration, particles are moved using traditional PSO operations, which consist of calculating the velocity of each particle and adding that velocity to the particle's current position. After each movement, the fitness for the new position is calculated and compared against the particle's best fitness and the swarn-wide best fitness. Future particle movements depend on the outcome of each fitness comparison. Algorithm 3 provides the steps for the velocity-based particle movements:

Algorithm 3. Move Particles

1: **Input:** particle array par, swarm-wide best fitness $bestFitness$, and swarm-wide best position $bestPosition$
2: **for** p in par **do**
3: 　$v \leftarrow calculateVelocity$
4: 　$p.pos \leftarrow updatePosition$
5: 　$fitness \leftarrow calculateFitness$ #includes update to q
6: 　Compare new fitness against particle best and swarm best
7: **end for**
8: **return** $bestPosition$

In addition to velocity-based movements, in every iteration, each particles is assigned new blocks with directions that are unique to that particle. Algorithm 4 shows the process of assigning blocks and directions to particles:

Algorithm 4.   Randomize Particles

1: **Input:** particle list par, block-set B, change rate cr, and maximum change m.
2: **for** p in par **do**
3:     $blocks \leftarrow$ select random cr elements from B
4:     **for** $block$ in $blocks$ **do**
5:         **if** $block$ in $p.blockList$ **then**
6:             $d \leftarrow p.blockList[block]$
7:             $direction \leftarrow$ select direction from $B[block]$ where $direction\,! = \{d, -d\}$
8:         **else**
9:             $push$ $block$ to $p.blockList$
10:            $direction \leftarrow$ select random direction from $B[block]$
11:        **end if**
12:        pop direction from $B[block]$ and $push$ direction to $p.blockList[block]$
13:        **for** i in $block$ **do**
14:            $p.pos_i \leftarrow p.pos_i + m * direction$
15:        **end for**
16:    **end for**
17:    $fitness \leftarrow calculateFitness$ #includes update to q
18:    Compare new fitness against particle best and swarm best
19: **end for**

If a given particle movement produced a negative fitness, we observed that moving in the opposite direction would most likely produce a positive fitness. Algorithm 5 provides the steps for these reversal operations:

Algorithm 5.   Reverse movements with negative fitness

1: **Input:** best position $bestPosition$ and Particle list par
2: **for** p in par **do**
3:     **for** $pastPos$ in $p.pastPos$ **do**
4:         **if** $pastPos.fitness < 0$ **then**
5:             $bestPosition \leftarrow bestPosition - pastPos.pos$
6:             **if** Fitness did not improve **then**
7:                 Undo last changes
8:             **end if**
9:             pop $pastPos$ $from$ $p.pastPos$
10:        **end if**
11:    **end for**
12: **end for**
13: **return** $bestPosition$

References

1. Alzantot, M., Sharma, Y., Chakraborty, S., Srivastava, M.B.: Genattack: practical black-box attacks with gradient-free optimization. CoRR, abs/1805.11090 (2018)

2. Bhagoji, A.N., He, W., Li, B., Song, D.: Practical black-box attacks on deep neural networks using efficient query mechanisms. In: Ferrari, V., Hebert, M., Sminchisescu, C., Weiss, Y. (eds.) ECCV 2018. LNCS, vol. 11216, pp. 158–174. Springer, Cham (2018). https://doi.org/10.1007/978-3-030-01258-8_10

3. Carlini, N., Wagner, D.: Towards evaluating the robustness of neural networks. In: IEEE Symposium on Security and Privacy (SP), pp. 39–57 (2017)

4. Carneiro, G., Zheng, Y., Xing, F., Yang, L.: Review of deep learning methods in mammography, cardiovascular, and microscopy image analysis. In: Lu, L., Zheng, Y., Carneiro, G., Yang, L. (eds.) Deep Learning and Convolutional Neural Networks for Medical Image Computing. ACVPR, pp. 11–32. Springer, Cham (2017). https://doi.org/10.1007/978-3-319-42999-1_2

5. Chen, P.-Y., Zhang, H., Sharma, Y., Yi, J., Hsieh, C.-J.: Zoo: zeroth order optimization based black-box attacks to deep neural networks without training substitute models. CoRR, abs/1708.03999v2 (2017)

6. Gaing, Z.-L.: Particle swarm optimization to solving the economic dispatch considering the generator constraints. IEEE Trans. Power Syst. **18**(3), 1187–1195 (2003)

7. Goodfellow, I., Shlens, J., Szegedy, C.: Explaining and harnessing adversarial examples. In: International Conference on Learning Representations (2015)

8. Guo, C., Gardner, J.R., You, Y., Wilson, A.G., Weinberger, K.Q.: Simple black-box adversarial attacks. CoRR, abs/1905.07121 (2019)

9. Ilyas, A., Engstrom, L., Athalye, A., Lin, J.: Black-box adversarial attacks with limited queries and information. CoRR, abs/1804.08598 (2018)

10. Ilyas, A., Engstrom, L., Madry, A.: Prior convictions: black-box adversarial attacks with bandits and priors. CoRR, abs/1807.07978 (2018)

11. Izakian, H., Tork Ladani, B., Zamanifar, K., Abraham, A.: A novel particle swarm optimization approach for grid job scheduling. In: Prasad, S.K., Routray, S., Khurana, R., Sahni, S. (eds.) ICISTM 2009. CCIS, vol. 31, pp. 100–109. Springer, Heidelberg (2009). https://doi.org/10.1007/978-3-642-00405-6_14

12. James Kennedy and Russell Eberhart. Particle swarm optimization. In: Proceedings of ICNN'95 - International Conference on Neural Networks, vol. 4, pp. 1942–1948 (1995)

13. Kurakin, A., Goodfellow, I., Bengio, S.: Adversarial examples in the physical world. CoRR, abs/1607.02533 (2016)

14. Yonghe, L., Liang, M., Ye, Z., Cao, L.: Improved particle swarm optimization algorithm and its application in text feature selection. Appl. Soft Comput. **35**, 629–636 (2015)

15. Moon, S., An, G., Song, H.O.: Parsimonious black-box adversarial attacks via efficient combinatorial optimization. In: ICML (2019)

16. Papernot, N., McDaniel, P., Goodfellow, I., Jha, S., Celik, Z.B., Swami, A.: Practical black-box attacks against machine learning. In: Proceedings of the 2017 ACM on Asia Conference on Computer and Communications Security, ASIA CCS 2017, pp. 506–519. ACM, New York (2017)

17. Papernot, N., McDaniel, P., Jha, S., Fredrikson, M., Celik, Z.B., Swami, A.: The limitations of deep learning in adversarial settings. In: IEEE European Symposium on Security and Privacy (EuroSP), pp. 372–387, November 2016

18. Raff, E., Barker, J., Sylvester, J., Brandon, R., Catanzaro, B., Nicholas, C.: Malware detection by eating a whole exe. In: The Workshops of the Thirty-Second AAAI Conference on Artificial Intelligence (2018)

19. Shi, Y., Eberhart, R.C.: Empirical study of particle swarm optimization. In: Proceedings of the 1999 Congress on Evolutionary Computation-CEC99 (Cat. No. 99TH8406), vol. 3, pp. 1945–1950, February 1999

20. Simonyan, K., Zisserman, A.: Very deep convolutional networks for large-scale image recognition. CoRR, abs/1409.1556 (2015)
21. Su, J., Vargas, D.V., Sakurai, K.: One pixel attack for fooling deep neural networks. CoRR, abs/1710.08864 (2017)
22. Szegedy, C., et al.: Intriguing properties of neural networks. CoRR, abs/1312.6199v4 (2014)
23. Zhang, Y., et al.: Towards end-to-end speech recognition with deep convolutional neural networks. CoRR, abs/1701.02720 (2017)

Understanding Object Detection Through an Adversarial Lens

Ka-Ho Chow[✉], Ling Liu, Mehmet Emre Gursoy, Stacey Truex, Wenqi Wei, and Yanzhao Wu

Georgia Institute of Technology, Atlanta, GA, USA
{khchow,ling.liu,memregursoy,staceytruex,wenqiwei,yanzhaowu}@gatech.edu

Abstract. Deep neural networks based object detection models have revolutionized computer vision and fueled the development of a wide range of visual recognition applications. However, recent studies have revealed that deep object detectors can be compromised under adversarial attacks, causing a victim detector to detect no object, fake objects, or mislabeled objects. With object detection being used pervasively in many security-critical applications, such as autonomous vehicles and smart cities, we argue that a holistic approach for an in-depth understanding of adversarial attacks and vulnerabilities of deep object detection systems is of utmost importance for the research community to develop robust defense mechanisms. This paper presents a framework for analyzing and evaluating vulnerabilities of the state-of-the-art object detectors under an adversarial lens, aiming to analyze and demystify the attack strategies, adverse effects, and costs, as well as the cross-model and cross-resolution transferability of attacks. Using a set of quantitative metrics, extensive experiments are performed on six representative deep object detectors from three popular families (YOLOv3, SSD, and Faster R-CNN) with two benchmark datasets (PASCAL VOC and MS COCO). We demonstrate that the proposed framework can serve as a methodical benchmark for analyzing adversarial behaviors and risks in real-time object detection systems. We conjecture that this framework can also serve as a tool to assess the security risks and the adversarial robustness of deep object detectors to be deployed in real-world applications.

Keywords: Adversarial robustness · Object detection · Attack evaluation framework · Deep neural networks

1 Introduction

Empowered by deep structures, nonlinear activation, and high-performance GPUs, deep neural networks (DNNs) have monopolized object detection systems [14, 21, 22], enabling the development of many security-critical applications, such as traffic sign detection on autonomous vehicles [23] and intrusion detection on surveillance systems [6]. While deep object detection algorithms offer

© Springer Nature Switzerland AG 2020
L. Chen et al. (Eds.): ESORICS 2020, LNCS 12309, pp. 460–481, 2020.
https://doi.org/10.1007/978-3-030-59013-0_23

real-time performance with high accuracy over traditional techniques [17,26], recent studies have revealed that well trained deep object detectors are vulnerable to adversarial inputs that are maliciously modified but visually imperceptible from the original benign input [2,12,27,28]. Table 1 illustrates such vulnerabilities. With no attack, the object detector can accurately identify the person, the car, and the stop sign on the two benign images (1st column). However, the *same* detector is fooled blindly by the adversarial examples (2nd-5th columns) that are perturbed malignantly but indistinguishable from the benign images by human-perception.

Table 1. Detection on two examples by the TOG family of attacks [2].

1.1   Related Work and Problem Statement

Object detection is the core task in computer vision, which takes an input image or video frame and detects multiple instances of semantic objects according to known categories [17,26]. Although some may view object detection as a generalization of the image classification task, a deep object detector is a multi-task learner and performs two unique learning tasks that make attacking object detection more complex and challenging than image classification: (1) Object detection should detect and identify instances of multiple semantic objects encapsulated in a single image or video frame, whereas a vanilla image classifier deals with the classification of each image into one of the known classes. (2) Object detection performs localization and classification of multiple instances of multiple semantic objects in a single image, and the localization accuracy of each instance may influence the classification accuracy of the instance. Thus, the adversarial attack techniques for image classifiers [10,24] are not applicable to attacking deep object detectors. The adversarial examples to attack object detection models are generated using more complex attack techniques, which compute and inject adversarial perturbations to the benign input by maximizing objectness loss, localization loss and classification loss simultaneously and iteratively [2,27].

Existing object detection models are broadly classified into two categories: (1) the proposal-based two-phase learning and (2) the regression-based single-phase learning. The proposal-based approach uses a two-phase procedure by first detecting proposal regions with a region proposal network (RPN), and then refining them with bounding box and class label prediction. This category is dominated by Faster R-CNN [22], and also includes R-CNN [7,8] and Mask R-CNN [11]. The regression-based single-phase learning formulates the detection task as a regression problem. It jointly estimates the bounding box and class label of objects by directly predicting the coordinates of bounding boxes. This category is represented by YOLO [19–21,23] and SSD [14]. Moreover, different object detectors, even from the same family (e.g., Faster R-CNN), may use different neural networks as the backbone, and some additionally utilize different input resolutions [21,22] to optimize their detection performance. Several white-box attacks are developed to attack Faster R-CNN by utilizing proposal regions, such as DAG [28], UEA [27], and other similar methods [1,12]. For example, DAG first assigns an adversarial label (at random) to each proposal region detected and then performs iterative gradient backpropagation to misclassify the proposals. However, DAG attack with Faster R-CNN as the victim detector cannot be applied or extended to attacking single-phase detectors, which do not use proposal regions. Similar to the black-box transfer attacks to image classifiers [18], UEA [27] studied the transferability of attacks by using the adversarial examples generated from a Faster R-CNN detector to attack SSD detectors.

1.2   Scope and Contribution

In this paper, we develop an attack evaluation framework to rigorously analyze the vulnerabilities and security risks of deep object detection systems. The paper makes three original contributions. (1) We take a holistic approach to analyzing and characterizing adversarial attacks to object detection models from three dominant families: YOLOv3 [21], SSD [14], and Faster R-CNN [8,22], including attack generalization, untargeted random attacks, targeted specificity attacks, such as object-vanishing, object-fabrication, and targeted object-mislabeling. We develop the TOG family of attacks, which on one hand show the feasibility of attacking one-phase regression-based and two-phase proposal-based detectors using the same attack framework, and on the other hand provide a broader coverage of vulnerabilities for analyzing and understanding object detection through an adversarial lens. (2) Our evaluation framework provides two main building blocks: the attack module, which incorporates the state-of-the-art attack algorithms, and the evaluation module, which includes a set of quantitative metrics to measure, compare and analyze different attack algorithms in terms of adversarial effectiveness and costs, and attack transferability. We define cross-model transferability in terms of both algorithm and backbone of the detectors and introduce cross-resolution transferability to enrich our analysis on adversarial robustness of deep object detection models. (3) We conduct comprehensive experimental analysis on six object detectors from three dominant families of object detection algorithms (YOLOv3, SSD, and Faster R-CNN), with four representative attack methods: DAG [28], RAP [12], UEA [27], and TOG [2], on two benchmark datasets: PASCAL VOC [4] and MS COCO [13]. Our experimental results further demonstrate the utility of the proposed framework as a methodical benchmark platform for evaluating adversarial robustness of deep object detectors, and assessing the security risks and the attack resilience of deep object detectors to be deployed in real-world applications.

2   Proposed Framework - Attack Module

Figure 1 gives an overview of the proposed framework. This section is dedicated to the attack module, a collection of attack algorithms for comparisons and analysis. We first give an algorithmic overview of deep object detection algorithms and adversarial attacks. Then, we provide the formal analysis on the four state-of-the-art attack algorithms (TOG [2], UEA [27], RAP [12], and DAG [28]).

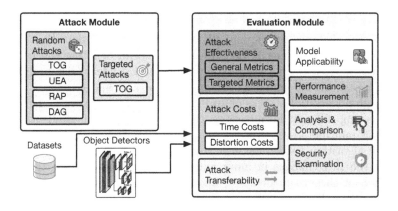

Fig. 1. The overview of the evaluation framework.

2.1   DNN-based Object Detection and Adversarial Attacks

DNN-based object detection is a multi-task learning problem, aiming to minimize the prediction error of (1) object existence, (2) bounding boxes, and (3) class labels of detected objects. Given an input image x with resolution $(H \times W)$, a K-class object detector f_θ, parameterized by θ, generates a large number of S candidate objects $\{\hat{o}_1, \ldots, \hat{o}_S\}$ where $\hat{o}_i = (\hat{b}_i^x, \hat{b}_i^y, \hat{b}_i^w, \hat{b}_i^h, \hat{C}_i, \hat{p}_i)$ represents a candidate centered at coordinates $(\hat{b}_i^x, \hat{b}_i^y)$ having a dimension $(\hat{b}_i^w, \hat{b}_i^h)$ with an objectness probability of $\hat{C}_i \in [0, 1]$ to be a real object, and a K-class probability vector $\hat{p}_i = (\hat{p}_i^1, \hat{p}_i^2, \ldots, \hat{p}_i^K)$. This is often done by dividing the input into mesh grids in different scales (resolutions). Each grid cell is responsible for locating objects centered at the cell. The final detection results $\hat{\mathcal{O}}$ are obtained by applying confidence thresholding to remove candidates with low prediction confidence and non-maximum suppression to exclude those with high overlapping.

To train a deep object detection neural network, every ground-truth object in a training sample $\tilde{x}$ is assigned to one of the S candidates according to their center coordinates. Let $\mathcal{O}$ be the set of ground-truth objects of $\tilde{x}$. The object detector can be trained by optimizing the following multi-task learning objective:

$$\mathcal{L}(\tilde{\mathcal{D}}; \theta) = \mathbb{E}_{(\tilde{x}, \mathcal{O}) \in \tilde{\mathcal{D}}}[\mathcal{L}_{\text{obj}}(\tilde{x}, \mathcal{O}; \theta) + \mathcal{L}_{\text{bbox}}(\tilde{x}, \mathcal{O}; \theta) + \mathcal{L}_{\text{class}}(\tilde{x}, \mathcal{O}; \theta)] \quad (1)$$

where $\tilde{\mathcal{D}}$ is the training set, $\mathcal{L}_{\text{obj}}$, $\mathcal{L}_{\text{bbox}}$, and $\mathcal{L}_{\text{class}}$ represent the loss function of the three prediction tasks: object existence (objectness), object localization (bounding box), and object class label respectively. In the rest of this paper, we use $\mathcal{O}$ and $\hat{\mathcal{O}}$ to distinguish between ground-truth and predicted detection, and we only specify the argument (e.g., $\mathcal{O}(x)$) to emphasize the input if necessary.

An adversarial example x' is generated by perturbing a benign input x sent to the victim detector, aiming to fool the victim to misdetect randomly or purposefully. The generation process can be conceptually formulated as

$$\min \|x' - x\|_p \quad s.t. \ \hat{\mathcal{O}}(x') \neq \hat{\mathcal{O}}(x), \hat{\mathcal{O}}(x') = \mathcal{O}^*(x) \quad (2)$$

where p is the distance metric and $\mathcal{O}^*(x)$ is the incorrect detection. Popular choices for the distance metric include the L_∞ norm, denoting the maximum change to any pixel, the L_2 norm, computing the Euclidean distance, and the L_0 norm, measuring the number of the pixels that are changed.

Although adversarial attacks on object detection systems are more sophisticated, adopting different formulations, they generally exploit gradients derived from one or multiple losses in Eq. 1 (i.e., $\mathcal{L}_{\text{obj}}$, $\mathcal{L}_{\text{bbox}}$, and $\mathcal{L}_{\text{class}}$). This allows the attack algorithm to meticulously inject perturbations to the input image, such that the tiny changes in input will be amplified throughout the forward propagation of the victim detector, and become large enough to alter one or more types of prediction results (i.e., object existence, bounding box, and class probability), depending on the composition of gradients. We analyze below the four representative attack algorithms on object detection systems, understanding their properties and demystifying their working principles.

2.2   TOG: Targeted Objectness Gradient Attacks

We develop the TOG family of attacks [2] based on an iterative gradient approach to obtain the malicious perturbation fooling the victim detector to give the desired erroneous detection. With a proper setting of the designated detection $\mathcal{O}^*(x)$ and the attack loss $\mathcal{L}^*$, TOG can be generally formulated as:

$$x'_{t+1} = \prod_{x, \epsilon} [x'_t - \alpha_{\text{TOG}} \Gamma(\nabla_{x'_t} \mathcal{L}^*(x'_t, \mathcal{O}^*(x); \theta))] \quad (3)$$

where x'_t is the adversarial example at the t-th iteration, $\prod_{x, \epsilon}[\cdot]$ is the projection onto a hypersphere with a radius ϵ centered at x in L_p norm, Γ is a sign function, and α_{TOG} is the attack learning rate. With this formulation, TOG allows adversaries to specify the effect imposed on victim's detection accuracy and correctness, including untargeted random attacks and three types of targeted specificity attacks: object-vanishing, object-fabrication, and targeted object-mislabeling.

Untargeted attacks fool the victim detector to *randomly* misdetect without targeting at any specific object. This class of attacks succeeds if the adversarial example fools the victim detector to give incorrect result of any form, such as having objects vanished, fabricated, or mislabeled randomly. TOG exploits gradients from both $\mathcal{L}_{\text{obj}}$, $\mathcal{L}_{\text{bbox}}$, and $\mathcal{L}_{\text{class}}$ and formulates the attack to be

$$x'_{t+1} = \prod_{x,\epsilon} \left[x'_t + \alpha_{\text{TOG}} \Gamma \left(\nabla_{x'_t} \mathcal{L}(x'_t, \mathcal{O}(x); \theta) \right) \right]. \tag{4}$$

As shown in the 2nd column in Table 1, the victim detector cannot identify any correct objects that were detected on benign inputs (1st column) but the exact effect varies across input images and attack algorithms.

Object-vanishing attacks *consistently* disable the victim detector to locate and recognize any object. TOG-vanishing utilizes gradients from $\mathcal{L}_{\text{obj}}$ as it dominates the decision on object existences and formulates the attack as follows:

$$x'_{t+1} = \prod_{x,\epsilon} \left[x'_t - \alpha_{\text{TOG}} \Gamma \left(\nabla_{x'_t} \mathcal{L}_{\text{obj}}(x'_t, \varnothing; \theta) \right) \right] \tag{5}$$

By targeting specifically at object-vanishing, this attack if successful will make the victim detector fail to detect any object as shown in the 3rd column in Table 1 where no object is detected in both examples.

Object-fabrication attacks *consistently* fool the victim to mistakenly recognize false objects. TOG-fabrication leverages gradients from $\mathcal{L}_{\text{obj}}$ with formulation:

$$x'_{t+1} = \prod_{x,\epsilon} \left[x'_t + \alpha_{\text{TOG}} \Gamma \left(\nabla_{x'_t} \mathcal{L}_{\text{obj}}(x'_t, \varnothing; \theta) \right) \right]. \tag{6}$$

This attack makes the victim to drastically increase the number of detected objects by introducing fake objects, as illustrated in the 4th column in Table 1.

Targeted object-mislabeling attacks *consistently* cause the victim detector to misclassify the objects detected on the input image by replacing their source class label with the maliciously chosen target class label, while maintaining the same set of correct bounding boxes. By focusing on the classification loss (i.e., $\mathcal{L}_{\text{class}}$) and keeping the gradients of the other two parts unchanged, TOG-mislabeling assigns the target class label to each object in $\mathcal{O}(x)$ to form $\mathcal{O}^*(x)$ and generate adversarial examples with

$$x'_{t+1} = \prod_{x,\epsilon} \left[x'_t - \alpha_{\text{TOG}} \Gamma \left(\nabla_{x'_t} \mathcal{L}(x'_t, \mathcal{O}^*(x); \theta) \right) \right]. \tag{7}$$

For instance, the object-mislabeling attack in the 5th column in Table 1 is configured to fool the victim to mislabel any stop sign as an umbrella. Note that the person (top) and the car (bottom) can still be detected under this attack as they are not the objects of attack interest and only stop signs will be mislabeled.

As TOG does not attack a special structure (e.g., RPN) in an object detector, it is applicable to both one-phase and two-phase techniques. Inspired by the universal perturbations to attack image classifiers [16], TOG also develops universal perturbations to attack deep object detectors in terms of object-vanishing or object-fabrication attack [2]. By training the universal perturbation offline on a training set and a victim detector, the universal perturbation can be applied during the online detection phase to any input sent to the victim.

2.3   DAG: Dense Adversary Generation

DAG [28] is an untargeted random attack and begins with manually assigning the IOU threshold to 0.90 in non-maximum suppression (NMS) in the RPN of a given two-phase model. This attack setting requires one proposal region to be highly overlapped (>90%) with the other proposal region in order to be pruned. Hence, a large amount of proposal regions remain unpruned. After the refinement by the subsequent network for bounding box and class label prediction, DAG assigns a randomly selected label for each proposal region and then performs the iterative gradient attack to misclassify the proposals with the following formulation:

$$r_t = \nabla_{x'_t} \sum_{j=1}^{J} z_j [p_j^c - p_j^{c'}], \quad x'_{t+1} = x'_t - \frac{\alpha_{\text{DAG}}}{||r_t||_\infty} r_t \qquad (8)$$

where $z_j = 1$ if the j-th proposal on x'_t from RPN is foreground and 0 otherwise, p_j^c and $p_j^{c'}$ are the prediction confidence of the correct class c and randomly selected incorrect class c' of the j-th proposal and α_{DAG} is the attack learning rate. This is equivalent to exploiting gradients derived from the classification loss $\mathcal{L}_{\text{class}}$. As DAG requires to manipulate the RPN to generate a large number of proposals, it can only be directly applicable to two-phase detection models.

2.4   RAP: Robust Adversarial Perturbation

RAP [12] is an untargeted random attack and focuses on collapsing the function of the RPN in two-phase algorithms. It exploits the composite gradients from (i) the objectness loss, i.e., $\mathcal{L}_{\text{obj}}$, that fools the RPN to not returning foreground objects, and (ii) the localization loss, i.e., $\mathcal{L}_{\text{bbox}}$, that causes the bounding box estimation to be incorrect even if foreground objects are proposed:

$$r_t = \nabla_{x'_t} \sum_{j=1}^{J} z_j [\log(\hat{C}_j) + \ell_{\text{SE}}(\hat{b}_j, \tau)], \quad x'_{t+1} = x'_t - \frac{\alpha_{\text{RAP}}}{||r_t||_2} r_t \qquad (9)$$

where ℓ_{SE} is the squared error, $\hat{b}_j$ and τ are quadruples of the proposed bounding box and large offsets respectively, and α_{RAP} is the attack learning rate.

2.5 UEA: Unified and Efficient Adversary

UEA [27] is an untargeted random attack. It trains a conditional generative adversarial network (GAN) [9] to craft adversarial examples. In deep object detectors, the backbone network plays an important role in feature extraction for region proposals in two-phase algorithms or object recognition in one-phase techniques. In practice, it is often one of the popular architectures (e.g., VGG16) that perform well in large-scale image classification and is pretrained with the ImageNet dataset for transfer learning. UEA designs a multi-scale attention feature loss, encouraging the GAN to create adversarial examples that can corrupt the feature map extracted by the backbone network in the victim detector:

$$\mathcal{L}_{\text{UEA}}^{\text{Fea}} = \mathbb{E}_{(\tilde{x}, \mathcal{O}) \in \mathcal{D}} [\sum_{m=1}^{M} ||\mathbf{A}_m \circ (\tilde{x}_m - \mathbf{R}_m)||_2] \tag{10}$$

where $\tilde{x}_m$ is the extracted feature map of the training example $\tilde{x}$ in the m-th layer of the backbone network, $\mathbf{R}_m$ is a randomly predefined feature map, and $\mathbf{A}_m$ is the attention weight computed based on the proposal regions from the RPN. Whenever another detector is equipped with the same backbone, the adversarial examples are likely to be effective. Equation 10 is jointly optimized with the DAG formulation (Eq. 8), requiring the manipulation of the RPN. Hence, it is unable to directly attack one-phase algorithms.

3 Proposed Framework - Evaluation Module

The evaluation module is the second building block of the proposed framework (Fig. 1), providing experimental testbed to measure, evaluate and analyze attacks and adversarial robustness of an object detector from four perspectives.

3.1 Attack Effectiveness

mean Average Precision (mAP). The interpolated average precision (AP) has been used by major object detection competitions [4,13]. For a given class, the precision/recall curve is computed from the detector's output, ranked by the detected confidence. The AP summarizes the shape of the precision/recall curve by taking the mean precision at a set of equally spaced recall levels. Then, the mean Average Precision (mAP) that quantifies the overall detection quality of a detector is computed by taking the mean of APs of all classes. The general attack performance can be analyzed on two sets of mAP (or AP), one on benign examples and another on adversarial examples. A low adversarial mAP implies the power of the attack but reveals the vulnerability of the victim model.

Attack Success Rate (ASR). In addition to comparing mAPs to reveal the impact on overall performance of the victim, we further define the attack success rate (ASR) for each targeted specificity attack, to capture their capability to fool the victim to misbehave with the designated effect (e.g., object-vanishing).

For object-vanishing attacks, we define the ASR as the proportion of objects detected on benign examples that are not covered by any objects detected on their adversarial counterparts:

$$\text{ASR} = \frac{\sum_{x \in \mathcal{D}} \sum_{\hat{o} \in \hat{\mathcal{O}}(x)} \mathbb{1}[\neg \exists \hat{o}' \in \hat{\mathcal{O}}(x')(\text{IOU}(\hat{o}_{[\text{bbox}]}, \hat{o}'_{[\text{bbox}]}) \geq t_{\text{IOU}})]}{\sum_{x \in \mathcal{D}} ||\hat{\mathcal{O}}(x)||}, \quad (11)$$

where $\mathbb{1}[\text{condition}] = 1$ if the condition is met and 0 otherwise, $\text{IOU}(\hat{o}_{[\text{bbox}]}, \hat{o}'_{[\text{bbox}]})$ computes the intersection over union of the two bounding boxes $\hat{o}_{[\text{bbox}]}$ and $\hat{o}'_{[\text{bbox}]}$, and t_{IOU} is a predefined threshold controlling the amount of overlapping required for two bounding boxes to be considered as referring to the same entity.

For object-fabrication attacks, the ASR is defined as the proportion of test examples where additional false objects are mistakenly detected by the victim detector under attacks:

$$\text{ASR} = \frac{1}{||\mathcal{D}||} \sum_{x \in \mathcal{D}} \mathbb{1}[||\hat{\mathcal{O}}(x')|| > ||\hat{\mathcal{O}}(x)||]. \quad (12)$$

For object-mislabeling attacks, we define the ASR to be the proportion of objects detected on benign examples that are mislabeled as the target label by the victim detector on their adversarial counterparts:

$$\text{ASR} = \frac{\sum_{x \in \mathcal{D}} \sum_{\hat{o} \in \hat{\mathcal{O}}(x)} \mathbb{1}[\exists \hat{o}' \in \hat{\mathcal{O}}(x')(\text{IOU}(\hat{o}_{[\text{bbox}]}, \hat{o}'_{[\text{bbox}]}) \geq t_{\text{IOU}} \wedge \hat{o}'_{[\text{class}]} = \mathcal{T}(\hat{o}_{[\text{class}]}))]}{\sum_{x \in \mathcal{D}} ||\hat{\mathcal{O}}(x)||} \quad (13)$$

where $\mathcal{T}(\hat{o}_{[\text{class}]})$ is a mapping from a source class to a target class. Under this setting, we consider the attack succeeds only if it (i) does not alter the bounding box significantly and (ii) fools the detector to give a designated wrong label.

3.2   Attack Cost

Time Cost. We measure time cost using two metrics: (i) the attack time, which measures the additional time introduced by the attack, excluding the inference of the victim detector to obtain the final detection results; and (ii) the total time cost, which considers both attack time and (benign) detection time.

Distortion Cost. Remaining human-imperceptible is an important factor in adversarial attacks as significant distortion naturally mislead a deep learning model to misbehave. A robust object detection model should be resilient against adversarial examples that are visually identical to their benign counterparts.

L_0, L_2, and L_∞ distances have been popularly used in adversarial learning. They are used as a constraint to limit the maximum perturbation introducible to the benign example. Note that a low L_p distance means a high imperceptibility.

Structural Similarity (SSIM) has become an important metric to quantify the similarly between two images in computer vision:

$$\text{SSIM}(\boldsymbol{x}, \boldsymbol{x}') = \sum_{i=1}^{I} \frac{(2\mu_{\boldsymbol{x}[i]}\mu_{\boldsymbol{x}'[i]} + \kappa_1)(2\sigma_{\boldsymbol{x}[i]\boldsymbol{x}'[i]} + \kappa_2)}{(\mu^2_{\boldsymbol{x}[i]} + \mu^2_{\boldsymbol{x}'[i]} + \kappa_1)(\sigma^2_{\boldsymbol{x}[i]} + \sigma^2_{\boldsymbol{x}'[i]} + \kappa_2)} \tag{14}$$

where $\boldsymbol{x}[i]$ denotes the i-th channel of image $\boldsymbol{x}$, $\mu_{\boldsymbol{x}}$ and $\sigma_{\boldsymbol{x}}$ are the average and variance of $\boldsymbol{x}$ respectively, $\sigma_{\boldsymbol{x}\boldsymbol{x}'}$ is the covariance of $\boldsymbol{x}$ and $\boldsymbol{x}$', and κ_1 and κ_2 are two variables for numerical stability. It has a range from -1.00 (the least similar) to 1.00 (the most similar) and is considered to be more consistent to human visual perception than L_p distances. As attacks optimize different L_p distances, SSIM offers an objective comparison on the imperceptibility of adversarial examples.

3.3   Attack Transferability

All adversarial attacks on deep object detectors are white-box attacks as they require model weights to optimize the generation of adversarial perturbation against a victim detector. The transferability of adversarial examples generated against one victim detector can be utilized to launch black-box attacks to other detectors, in a similar way as the transferability of adversarial examples to attack different image classifiers [18]. For object detection, we propose to study not only the cross-model transferability, but also the cross-resolution transferability.

Cross-model transferability in object detection can be further broken down into (i) cross-algorithm transferability that the source and the target models use different detection algorithms and (ii) cross-backbone transferability that examines the transferability between different backbones of the same detection algorithm and between different detection algorithms with the same backbone.

Cross-resolution transferability covers a characteristic unique to those object detection algorithms (e.g., YOLO and Faster R-CNN) that allow variable input resolutions. In contrast to image classification networks where the resolution of the input image is fixed due to the fully-connected layer for the final softmax, for object detection, increasing input resolution can generate more candidate objects with a potentially better detection quality with the cost of slowing down the detection. The cross-resolution transferability reveals whether the adversarial examples generated by an attack algorithm on a source resolution can be robust and survive under resizing and interpolation to the target resolution.

3.4   Model Applicability

From a macroscopic perspective, all object detection systems take an input image and output a set of detected objects. They may appear to be similar, but their internal learn-to-detect mechanisms can be very different. Some existing attacks are designed by exploiting the vulnerability of a particular structure, e.g., the region proposal network (RPN) in Faster R-CNN detectors. Hence, not all attack techniques are universally applicable. RAP [12] is an example, which perturbs the benign image to disable the functionality of the RPN in two-phase algorithms and cannot be used on one-phase detectors where no RPN is used. We also leverage model-applicability as an evaluation aspect on attack algorithms.

4 Experimental Analysis

Extensive experiments are conducted on two benchmark datasets: PASCAL VOC [4] and MS COCO [13]. All results are based on the entire test set, and we preprocess images by padding to preserve the aspect ratio of objects. We consider six models from three dominant detection algorithms. YOLOv3-D and YOLOv3-M are two YOLOv3 [21] models with a Darknet53 and a MobileNetV1 backbone respectively. For SSD [14], we have SSD300 and SSD512 corresponding to two models with different input resolutions. Finally, FRCNN denotes the Faster R-CNN [22] model. As experimental results on COCO are highly similar to VOC, we provide only YOLOv3-D on COCO due to the space constraint. We provide more experimental configuration details in Appendix A.

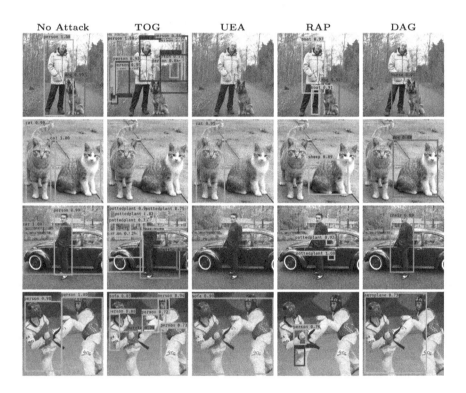

Fig. 2. Four visual examples of the untargeted attacks by different algorithms.

4.1 Untargeted Random Attacks

This section reports the set of experiments to compare the four attack algorithms: TOG, UEA, RAP, and DAG in terms of effectiveness and time cost of untargeted attacks. Figure 2 provides a visualization of four benign images (left most column) and their four adversarial examples generated by TOG, UEA, RAP, and DAG. Four attack algorithms fool the same victim detector FRCNN to misdetect on the same query image in different ways. TOG deceives the victim detector to return false objects on the 1st, 3rd and 4th examples with no correct objects detected. For the 2nd example with two cats, TOG succeeds by fooling the victim to detect no object at all. This shows that different images may respond to the same attack differently, such as missing cats by TOG in the 2nd example compared with fabricating fake objects in the other examples. Similarly, UEA misses both the person and the dog for the 1st example, detects one cat correctly and misses the other cat on the 2nd example, misses both person and car for the 3rd example, and misdetect all objects on the 4th example. RAP and DAG fail the detection on all four examples differently.

Table 2. Untargeted attacks on different datasets and victim detectors.

Dataset	Random attack	Victim detector	mAP (%)		Time cost (s)		Distortion cost			
			Benign	Adv.	Benign	Adv.	L_∞	L_2	L_0	SSIM
VOC	TOG	YOLOv3-D	83.43	0.56	0.03	0.98	0.031	0.083	0.984	0.875
VOC	TOG	YOLOv3-M	71.84	0.43	0.02	0.59	0.031	0.083	0.978	0.876
VOC	TOG	SSD300	76.11	0.86	0.02	0.39	0.031	0.120	0.975	0.879
VOC	TOG	SSD512	79.83	0.74	0.03	0.69	0.031	0.070	0.974	0.869
VOC	TOG	FRCNN	67.37	2.64	0.14	1.68	0.031	0.058	0.976	0.862
VOC	UEA	FRCNN	67.37	18.07	0.14	0.17	0.343	0.191	0.959	0.652
VOC	RAP	FRCNN	67.37	4.78	0.14	4.04	0.082	0.010	0.531	0.994
VOC	DAG	FRCNN	67.37	3.56	0.14	7.99	0.024	0.002	0.493	0.999
COCO	TOG	YOLOv3-D	54.16	3.52	0.03	1.02	0.031	0.083	0.986	0.872

Table 2 provides the quantitative measurements on all victim detectors under the four attack algorithms. The first metric is the mAP in percentage, including benign mAP with no attacks and adversarial mAP given adversarial examples. The second metric measures the detection time on benign inputs and attack total cost (both generation and detection). The third metric is the distortion cost measured in L_∞, L_2, L_0 distances, and SSIM. L_2 and L_0 costs reported here are normalized by the number of pixels and the L_2 cost has a magnitude of 10^{-3}. Note that UEA, RAP, and DAG can only attack FRCNN, and hence we do not evaluate them on YOLOv3, SSD300 and SSD512. We make two observations from Table 2. First, all attacks successfully bring down the mAP of the victim. Considering the TOG attack, the benign mAP of any victim detector is drastically reduced to less than 3.52% with four victims having a close to zero adversarial mAP. This indicates that the victims fail miserably with no detection capability. Second, we compare four different attacks on FRCNN, which has a benign mAP of 67.37%. TOG is the most powerful attack with the lowest adversarial mAP of 2.64%, followed by DAG (3.56%), RAP (4.78%), and UEA (18.07%). By default, UEA generates adversarial examples with a fixed resolution of 300 × 300. When attacking FRCNN taking inputs with resolution of 600 × 600, resizing and interpolation are required. Hence, the effectiveness of UEA is hindered. In comparison, TOG, RAP and DAG are much more adaptive, and capable of generating adversarial examples that fit the input resolution, as they do not rely on additional networks.

Apart from attack effectiveness, attack costs are equally important. UEA has the lowest time cost with only 0.17 s attack total time because the generation of adversarial examples does not use the victim model but the GAN, which can have much lower complexity. TOG has a reasonable range of attack total time but RAP and DAG have prohibitively high time cost (4.04 s and 7.99 s). This can be explained by the number of iterations required to succeed the attack in RAP and DAG. TOG needs 10 iteration while RAP and DAG need to run more than 30 rounds. Interestingly, spending more iterations allows RAP and DAG to have a much lower distortion cost and exceptionally high SSIM measures of 0.994 and 0.999 respectively. TOG also has a high imperceptibility with SSIM higher than 0.862, while adversarial perturbation generated by UEA is significantly more perceptible, having a low SSIM of 0.652. Furthermore, RAP and DAG have a low L_0 cost, which implies their perturbations are more localized. In comparison, both TOG and UEA have the L_0 cost close to 1.000, indicating that most pixels are modified by the adversarial perturbation.

4.2 Targeted Specificity Attacks

We evaluate the three targeted specificity attacks using TOG. For targeted mislabeling attacks, without loss of generality, we choose two representative attack targets: the most-likely (ML) and the least-likely (LL), which correspond to the incorrect class label of an object detected on benign example with the highest and the lowest prediction confidence respectively [3]. The TOG-mislabeling allows objects of any class to be attacked. Figure 3 shows the benign and adversarial AP of each class on YOLOv3-M. All targeted attacks by TOG drastically reduce the average precision of *every* class supported by the victim to almost zero, showing the severity of the targeted attacks. We provide more experimental measurements on all 24 cases (four attacks on six detectors) in Appendix B.

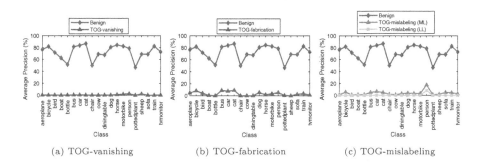

(a) TOG-vanishing   (b) TOG-fabrication   (c) TOG-mislabeling

Fig. 3. The AP of each class under TOG targeted attacks on YOLOv3-M

Recall Fig. 2, each of the four input images responds to the same untargeted random attack differently. Figure 4 provides a visualization of the same set of images attacked by TOG with different targeted specificity effects. This qualitatively validates that all targeted attacks in TOG are goal-driven, which can be more detrimental to victim detector. For example, with TOG-vanishing attack (2nd column), all four adversarial examples fool the victim detector FRCNN to misdetect with no object recognized. For TOG-mislabeling attacks, the person and the dog on the 1st row are purposefully mislabeled as the dog and the cat respectively in the ML case and both aeroplanes in the LL case. In comparison with Fig. 2, UEA, RAP, DAG and general TOG are untargeted: each of the four input images responds to attacks under the same attack algorithm (be it TOG, UEA, RAP and DAG) quite differently, showing random ways to fool a victim detector. We provide more experimental analysis on each targeted attack in Appendix B.

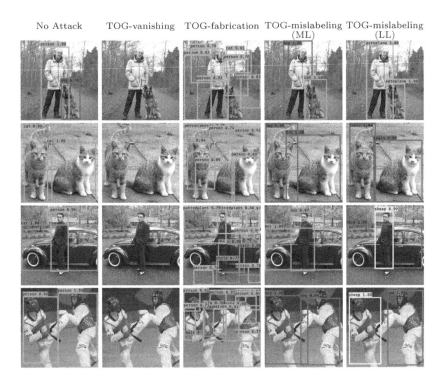

Fig. 4. Four visual examples of different targeted specificity attacks by TOG.

4.3 Transferability of Attacks

We conduct quantitative analysis on the transferability of all four untargeted attacks: TOG, UEA, RAP and DAG. Table 3 reports the results for the cross-model transferability, measured in adversarial mAP. Using the same model to craft adversarial examples always achieves the highest transferability, as indicated in boldface. We first consider the adversarial examples generated on different source models and measure their transferability to different target models using TOG (the 2nd-6th rows). First, we observe that having the same backbone architecture does not necessarily lead to high transferability. FRCNN, SSD300

Table 3. Cross-model transferability.

Transfer attack	Source model	Target model				
		YOLOv3-D	YOLOv3-M	SSD300	SSD512	FRCNN
Benign (No Attack)		83.43	71.84	76.11	79.83	67.37
TOG	YOLOv3-D	**0.56**	60.13	72.70	73.86	55.57
TOG	YOLOv3-M	74.62	**0.43**	73.27	75.27	59.1
TOG	SSD300	56.87	42.85	**0.86**	38.79	50.36
TOG	SSD512	56.21	46.00	58.00	**0.74**	35.98
TOG	FRCNN	79.47	68.60	75.80	78.09	**2.64**
UEA	FRCNN	51.92	31.88	47.08	47.66	**18.07**
RAP	FRCNN	81.80	69.45	75.77	76.84	**4.78**
DAG	FRCNN	81.21	70.37	75.15	78.38	**3.56**

and SSD512 all use VGG16 as the backbone network. Yet, the adversarial examples generated on FRCNN have very low transferability to SSD300 and SSD512, reducing their mAP from 76.11% to 75.80% and from 79.83% to 78.09% respectively. Second, the adversarial examples generated on SSD have relatively higher transferability compared to other source models. For instance, adversarial examples from SSD300 and SSD512 can reduce the mAP of YOLOv3-D from 83.43% to 56.87% and 56.21%, much better than YOLOv3-M and FRCNN that only reduction to 74.62% and 79.47% are recorded. Finally, considering the transferability of different attack algorithms with the same source model FRCNN (the last four rows), we find that adversarial examples by UEA exhibit a higher transferability consistently. This can be attributed to its high distortion cost incurred to perturb each adversarial example (recall Table 2).

Table 4. Cross-resolution transferability.

(a) FRCNN

Transfer attack	Source resolution	Target resolution					
		300×300	400×400	500×500	600×600	700×700	800×800
Benign (No Attack)		65.33	67.85	68.00	67.37	67.91	67.76
TOG	600×600	50.15	29.50	15.07	**2.64**	6.84	3.86
UEA	300×300	**3.86**	11.88	18.61	18.07	16.32	17.34
RAP	600×600	58.45	54.32	56.96	**4.78**	53.21	50.12
DAG	600×600	62.89	59.82	46.58	**2.84**	30.96	13.75

(b) YOLOv3

Model	Transfer attack	Source resolution	Target resolution				
			352×352	384×384	416×416	448×448	480×480
YOLOv3-D	Benign (No Attack)		82.71	83.25	83.43	83.63	83.65
	TOG	416×416	25.26	14.93	**0.56**	11.02	12.16
YOLOv3-M	Benign (No Attack)		69.98	71.13	71.84	73.10	72.72
	TOG	416×416	33.41	20.61	**0.43**	15.62	19.16

Table 4a and b report the cross-resolution transferability on FRCNN and YOLOv3 respectively. Note that only TOG can directly attack YOLOv3 (one-phase detectors), and SSD does not support variable input resolutions.

We use nearest neighbor interpolation during resizing as we find empirically that it can better preserve the malicious pattern. For victim detector FRCNN, we observe that TOG and UEA have higher cross-resolution transferability than RAP and DAG. The same observation can be made in both YOLOv3 detectors. For instance, TOG can still effectively reduce the mAP from more than 82% to less than 26% in all target resolutions evaluated on YOLOv3-D. This is because adversarial examples generated by TOG and UEA have a higher robustness under resizing and interpolation to fit the target resolution. Also, upsizing to a higher target resolution is always better than downsizing, causing a higher mAP drop in the target victim model, which can be explained by the fact that downsizing loses the fine details of malicious perturbation.

Table 5. Transferring targeted attacks on SSD300 to three other detectors.

Detection results under four TOG targeted attacks				
Benign (No Attack)	TOG-vanishing	TOG-fabrication	TOG-mislabeling (ML)	TOG-mislabeling (LL)

Detection results *transferred* from SSD300 to other victim detectors				
Benign (No Attack)	TOG-vanishing	TOG-fabrication	TOG-mislabeling (ML)	TOG-mislabeling (LL)

Table 5 provides a visualization to illustrate the transferability of four TOG targeted attacks by generating adversarial examples on SSD300 and evaluating their cross-model transferability to the other three detectors: SSD512, YOLOv3-D, and YOLOv3-M. Consider the SSD300 row, the detector can correctly identify the person and the bicycle on the benign input (1st column). The targeted attacks by TOG successfully fool the victim to misdetect with designated attack specificity effects: the two objects are missed in TOG-vanishing, false objects are detected in TOG-fabrication, and the person and the bicycle are mislabeled as a dog and a horse in the ML case of TOG-mislabeling and both buses in the LL case. We analyze the transferability by observing the other three rows. Given that all three detectors can successfully identify the two objects on the benign image, we find different degrees of adversarial transferability. For instance, TOG-vanishing and TOG-fabrication can be successfully transferred to SSD512, which has the same backbone (i.e., VGG16) and detection algorithm as the source detector SSD300. TOG-fabrication can also be transferred to YOLOv3-M with the same effect. However, even some adversarial examples may fool other detectors (e.g., TOG-vanishing to YOLOv3-M), they fail in transferring attacks with the same effect. Note that with adversarial transferability, the attacks are blackbox, generated and launched without any prior knowledge of the three victim detectors. We provide more discussion in Appendix C.

4.4   Model Applicability and Physical Attacks

We provide a comparison of seven representative attack algorithms, including two physical attacks, to deep object detectors in Table 6.

Table 6. Characteristics of seven representative attacks.

	Attack effect				Model-applicability		
	Random	Object-vanishing	Object-fabrication	Object-mislabeling	Two-phase	One-phase	
					FRCNN	YOLO	SSD
TOG [2]	✓	✓	✓	✓	✓	✓	✓
UEA [27]	✓	✗	✗	✗	✓	✗	✗
RAP [12]	✓	✗	✗	✗	✓	✗	✗
DAG [28]	✓	✗	✗	✗	✓	✗	✗
DPATCH [15]	✗	✗	✓	✗	✓	✓	✓
Extended-RP$_2$ [5]	✗	✓	✓	✗	✓	✓	✓
Thys's Patch [25]	✗	✓	✗	✗	✓	✓	✓

TOG [2], UEA [27], RAP [12] and DAG [28] are the representative digital attacks against a victim detector by perturbing pixel values of a benign image while maximizing one or more of the three loss functions: objectness, bounding box, and classification. All four can perform untargeted random attacks, and TOG also provides additional three targeted specificity attacks. For model-applicability, UEA, RAP and DAG by design depend on the RPN structure, and can only be employed to generate adversarial examples against FRCNN (two-phase detectors). TOG is a general attack framework without dependency on any special structure and can be used to fool object detectors from both one-phase (YOLO and SSD families) and two-phase algorithms (e.g., FRCNN).

In addition to perturbing the entire image, adversarial patches are also proposed in either a digital (DPATCH) or physical (Extended-RP$_2$ and Thys's Patch) form. DPATCH puts a small patch (e.g., 40×40) on a benign example, fooling the victim to fabricate objects at random position or the location where the patch is placed. Extended-RP$_2$ and Thys's Patch propose printable adversarial patches. If the adversarial patch is presented physically in the scene captured by the camera, the captured image will become adversarial input, which will fool a victim detector to misdetect. Extended-RP$_2$ supports "disappearance" and "creation", corresponding to the object-vanishing and object-fabrication effects, while Thys's Patch aims to make the object vanishing from the detector. Similar to TOG, all physical attack and digital patch algorithms can be employed on both two-phase and one-phase detection techniques.

5 Conclusion

We witnessed a growing number of digital or physical adversarial attacks to object detection systems recently [2,5,12,15,25,27,28]. To gain an in-depth understanding of the security risks of employing object detection intelligence in security-critical applications, in this paper, we develop a principled evaluation framework to analyze vulnerabilities of object detection systems through an adversarial lens, with three original contributions. First, we examine and compare the state-of-the-art attacks through our proposed evaluation framework. Second, to provide broader coverage of security risks in deep object detection systems, we present a family of TOG attack algorithms, capable of attacking both proposal-based two-phase detectors (e.g., FRCNN) and regression-based one-phase techniques (e.g., SSD, YOLOv3), supporting a general form of untargeted random attacks, and three targeted attacks, geared specifically to object detection. Third but not least, we introduce a set of quantitative metrics, including cross-resolution transferability and cross-model transferability w.r.t. algorithms and DNN backbones, to evaluate the effectiveness and cost of four representative methods of digital attacks, and using model-applicability to compare digital attacks with physical patch attacks. Our evaluation framework can serve as a tool for analyzing adversarial attacks, assessing security risks and adversarial robustness of deep object detectors deployed in real-world applications.

Acknowledgment. This research is partially sponsored by National Science Foundation under grant NSF 1564097, NSF 2038029 and an IBM faculty award. Any opinions, findings, and conclusions or recommendations expressed in this material are those of the author(s) and do not necessarily reflect the views of the National Science Foundation or other funding agencies and companies mentioned above.

A   Appendix

A. Background. The VOC 2007+2012 dataset has 16,551 training images and 4,952 testing images, while the COCO 2014 dataset has 117,264 training images and 5,000 testing images. The configuration and detection performance of the six detectors under no attack are reported in Table 7. All measurements are recorded on NVIDIA RTX 2080 SUPER (8 GB) GPU, Intel i7-9700K (3.60GHz) CPU, and 32 GB RAM on Ubuntu 18.04.

Table 7. A summary of victim detectors under no attack.

Dataset	Detector identifier	Algorithm	Backbone	Input resolution	Benign mAP(%)	Detection time(s)
VOC	YOLOv3-D	YOLOv3	Darknet53	416 × 416	83.43	0.0328
	YOLOv3-M	YOLOv3	MobileNetV1	416 × 416	71.84	0.0152
	SSD300	SSD	VGG16	300 × 300	76.11	0.0208
	SSD512	SSD	VGG16	512 × 512	79.83	0.0330
	FRCNN	Faster R-CNN	VGG16	600 × 600	67.37	0.1399
COCO	YOLOv3-D	YOLOv3	Darknet53	416 × 416	54.16	0.0337

B. Analysis on Targeted Specificity Attacks. Table 8 reports the results of four TOG targeted attacks on six victim detectors (24 cases). TOG targeted attacks effectively bring down the mAP of all victim detectors, with any attack specificity. For instance, YOLOv3-D on VOC has a high mAP of 83.43% given benign images but, under attacks, it becomes less than 3.15%. Even though the adversarial examples in targeted attacks can fool the victim detectors to misdetect with the targeted specificity effects, such attack sophistication does not drastically incur additional attack time cost and distortion cost, compared with the TOG untargeted attack scenario in Table 2.

Figure 5 compares the four targeted attacks with respect to the number of object detected by three victim detectors (YOLOv3-D, SSD512 and FRCNN) with different settings of the confidence threshold. The benign case (the blue solid curve) indicates the number of objects detected by the victims under no attacks. Confidence thresholding is used by object detection algorithms as a post-processing step to return only detected objects with high confidence (Sect. 2.1), and the threshold is a hyperparameter defined by the system owner (e.g., FRCNN uses 0.70 by default). We find that all trends are consistent across both detectors: Fig. 5 experimentally confirms that (i) the TOG-vanishing attacks significantly lower the number of detected objects with any setting of confidence threshold, (ii) the number of detected objects is drastically increased in TOG-fabrication attacks, and (iii) the TOG-mislabeling attacks (both ML and LL) have almost the same number of objects detected on benign examples.

Figure 6 further analyzes the two targeted mislabeling attacks of TOG in terms of ASR according to Eq. 13. With a similar formulation, we also introduce misdetection rate (MR) to compute the portion of objects that are mislabeled under TOG-mislabeling attacks. Note that MR still requires the detected

Table 8. Targeted attacks by TOG on different datasets and victim detectors.

Detector (Dataset)	Targeted attack	mAP (%)		Time cost (s)		Distortion cost			
		Benign	Adv.	Benign	Adv.	L_∞	L_2	L_0	SSIM
YOLOv3-D (VOC)	TOG-vanishing	83.43	0.32	0.03	**0.77**	0.031	0.082	0.983	0.877
	TOG-fabrication	83.43	**0.25**	0.03	0.93	0.031	0.084	0.984	0.873
	TOG-mislabeling (ML)	83.43	3.15	0.03	0.95	0.031	0.080	0.972	**0.879**
	TOG-mislabeling (LL)	83.43	2.80	0.03	0.96	0.031	0.081	0.972	**0.879**
YOLOv3-M (VOC)	TOG-vanishing	71.84	0.36	0.02	**0.37**	0.031	0.082	0.978	0.878
	TOG-fabrication	71.84	**0.17**	0.02	0.57	0.031	0.084	0.976	0.873
	TOG-mislabeling (ML)	71.84	2.67	0.02	0.56	0.031	0.079	0.953	**0.882**
	TOG-mislabeling (LL)	71.84	1.60	0.02	0.56	0.031	0.079	0.953	0.881
SSD300 (VOC)	TOG-vanishing	76.11	5.54	0.02	**0.36**	0.031	0.120	0.978	0.880
	TOG-fabrication	76.11	**0.57**	0.02	0.37	0.031	0.122	0.978	0.877
	TOG-mislabeling (ML)	76.11	2.53	0.02	0.37	0.030	0.110	0.945	**0.891**
	TOG-mislabeling (LL)	76.11	1.44	0.02	0.37	0.030	0.111	0.945	0.889
SSD512 (VOC)	TOG-vanishing	79.83	6.23	0.03	**0.62**	0.031	0.071	0.975	0.868
	TOG-fabrication	79.83	**0.50**	0.03	0.69	0.031	0.071	0.976	0.866
	TOG-mislabeling (ML)	79.83	2.53	0.03	0.65	0.031	0.065	0.957	**0.878**
	TOG-mislabeling (LL)	79.83	1.20	0.03	0.65	0.031	0.066	0.956	0.877
FRCNN (VOC)	TOG-vanishing	67.37	**0.14**	0.14	**1.66**	0.031	0.058	0.975	0.862
	TOG-fabrication	67.37	1.24	0.14	1.68	0.031	0.057	0.977	0.866
	TOG-mislabeling (ML)	67.37	2.14	0.14	1.64	0.030	0.054	0.935	**0.873**
	TOG-mislabeling (LL)	67.37	1.44	0.14	1.60	0.030	0.054	0.935	0.872
YOLOv3-D (COCO)	TOG-vanishing	54.16	**0.41**	0.03	**0.78**	0.031	0.082	0.986	0.874
	TOG-fabrication	54.16	1.46	0.03	**0.78**	0.031	0.083	0.986	0.871
	TOG-mislabeling (ML)	54.16	5.43	0.03	1.00	0.031	0.080	0.968	**0.878**
	TOG-mislabeling (LL)	54.16	0.76	0.03	1.00	0.031	0.080	0.968	0.877

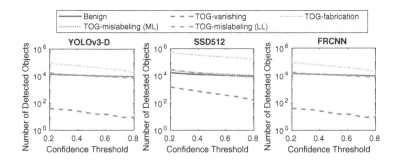

Fig. 5. Number of detected objects under no attack and TOG targeted attacks.

bounding box to be correct, but the predicted class label of the object can be any class but not the correct one. We observe that a large portion of objects are successfully mislabeled as the maliciously targeted class (ASR), and only small portion is randomly mislabeled instead (MR - ASR), especially for the ML targets (Fig. 6a). For the LL attack targets (Fig. 6b), the ASR is less than 80%, but the misdetection rate (MR) is close to 100% in all five victim detectors, indicating that almost all objects in all test examples are mislabeled though only less than 80% LL targeted mislabeling attacks succeeded.

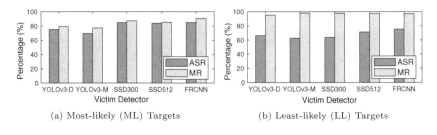

(a) Most-likely (ML) Targets   (b) Least-likely (LL) Targets

Fig. 6. ASR and MR of TOG-mislabeling attacks.

C. Transferability of Targeted Specificity Attacks. Consider in Table 5 the victim detector SSD512 with the same backbone and detection algorithm as SSD300, TOG-vanishing can perfectly transfer the attack to SSD512 with the same effect (i.e., no object is detected). For TOG-fabrication, we observe that while the number of false objects is not as much as in the SSD300 case, a fairly large number of fake objects are wrongly detected by SSD512. The TOG-mislabeling (LL) attack transfers to SSD512 but with the object-fabrication effect instead, while the TOG-mislabeling (ML) attack failed to transfer for this example. Now consider YOLOv3-D and YOLOv3-M, the TOG-mislabeling (LL) attack is successful in transferability for both victims but with different attack effects, such as wrong or additional bounding boxes or wrong labels. Also, the attacks from SSD300 can successfully transfer to YOLOv3-M with different attack effects compared to the attack results in SSD300, but not to YOLOv3-D for this example.

References

1. Chen, K., et al.: Optimizing video object detection via a scale-time lattice. In: CVPR (2018)
2. Chow, K.H., Liu, L., Gursoy, E., Truex, S., Wei, W., Wu, Y.: TOG: targeted adversarial objectness gradient attacks on real-time object detection systems. arXiv preprint arXiv:2004.04320 (2020)
3. Chow, K.H., Wei, W., Wu, Y., Liu, L.: Denoising and verification cross-layer ensemble against black-box adversarial attacks. In: IEEE BigData (2019)
4. Everingham, M., Eslami, S.A., Van Gool, L., Williams, C.K., Winn, J., Zisserman, A.: The pascal visual object classes challenge: a retrospective. IJCV **111**(1), 98–136 (2015). https://doi.org/10.1007/s11263-014-0733-5
5. Eykholt, K., et al.: Physical adversarial examples for object detectors. arXiv preprint arXiv:1807.07769 (2018)
6. Gajjar, V., Gurnani, A., Khandhediya, Y.: Human detection and tracking for video surveillance: A cognitive science approach. In: ICCV (2017)
7. Girshick, R.: Fast R-CNN. In: ICCV (2015)
8. Girshick, R., Donahue, J., Darrell, T., Malik, J.: Rich feature hierarchies for accurate object detection and semantic segmentation. In: CVPR (2014)
9. Goodfellow, I., et al..: Generative adversarial nets. In: NIPS (2014)

10. Goodfellow, I.J., Shlens, J., Szegedy, C.: Explaining and harnessing adversarial examples. In: ICLR (2015)
11. He, K., Gkioxari, G., Dollár, P., Girshick, R.: Mask R-CNN. In: ICCV (2017)
12. Li, Y., Tian, D., Bian, X., Lyu, S., et al.: Robust adversarial perturbation on deep proposal-based models. arXiv preprint arXiv:1809.05962 (2018)
13. Lin, T.Y., et al.: Microsoft COCO: common objects in context. In: ECCV (2014)
14. Liu, W., et al.: SSD: single shot MultiBox detector. In: Leibe, Bastian, Matas, Jiri, Sebe, Nicu, Welling, Max (eds.) ECCV 2016. LNCS, vol. 9905, pp. 21–37. Springer, Cham (2016). https://doi.org/10.1007/978-3-319-46448-0_2
15. Liu, X., Yang, H., Liu, Z., Song, L., Li, H., Chen, Y.: DPatch: an adversarial patch attack on object detectors. arXiv preprint arXiv:1806.02299 (2018)
16. Moosavi-Dezfooli, S.M., Fawzi, A., Fawzi, O., Frossard, P.: Universal adversarial perturbations. In: CVPR (2017)
17. Papageorgiou, C.P., Oren, M., Poggio, T.: A general framework for object detection. In: ICCV. IEEE
18. Papernot, N., McDaniel, P., Goodfellow, I.: Transferability in machine learning: from phenomena to black-box attacks using adversarial samples. arXiv preprint arXiv:1605.07277 (2016)
19. Redmon, J., Divvala, S., Girshick, R., Farhadi, A.: You only look once: Unified, real-time object detection. In: CVPR (2016)
20. Redmon, J., Farhadi, A.: YOLO9000: better, faster, stronger. In: CVPR (2017)
21. Redmon, J., Farhadi, A.: YOLOv3: an incremental improvement. arXiv preprint arXiv:1804.02767 (2018)
22. Ren, S., He, K., Girshick, R., Sun, J.: Faster R-CNN: towards real-time object detection with region proposal networks. In: NIPS (2015)
23. Simon, M., et al.: Complexer-YOLO: real-time 3D object detection and tracking on semantic point clouds. In: CVPRW (2019)
24. Szegedy, C., et al..: Intriguing properties of neural networks. arXiv preprint arXiv:1312.6199 (2013)
25. Thys, S., Van Ranst, W., Goedemé, T.: Fooling automated surveillance cameras: adversarial patches to attack person detection. In: CVPRW (2019)
26. Viola, P., Jones, M.: Rapid object detection using a boosted cascade of simple features. In: CVPR. IEEE (2001)
27. Wei, X., Liang, S., Chen, N., Cao, X.: Transferable adversarial attacks for image and video object detection. arXiv preprint arXiv:1811.12641 (2018)
28. Xie, C., Wang, J., Zhang, Z., Zhou, Y., Xie, L., Yuille, A.: Adversarial examples for semantic segmentation and object detection. In: ICCV (2017)

Applied Cryptography II

Signatures with Tight Multi-user Security from Search Assumptions

Jiaxin Pan and Magnus Ringerud$^{(\boxtimes)}$

Department of Mathematical Sciences,
NTNU – Norwegian University of Science and Technology, Trondheim, Norway
{jiaxin.pan,magnus.ringerud}@ntnu.no

Abstract. We construct two tightly secure signature schemes based on the computational Diffie-Hellman (CDH) and factoring assumptions in the random oracle model. Our schemes are proven secure in the multi-user setting, and their security loss is constant and does not depend on the number of users or signing queries. They are the first schemes that achieve this based on standard search assumptions, as all existing schemes we are aware of are either based on stronger decisional assumptions, or proven tightly secure in the less realistic single-user setting. Under a concrete estimation, in a truly large scale, the cost of our CDH-based scheme is about half of Schnorr and DSA (in terms of signature size and running time for signing).

Keywords: Digital signature · Tight reduction · Multi-user security · Search assumption

1 Introduction

In modern public-key cryptography, a scheme is usually proposed together with a reduction-based security analysis. In such an analysis, a security model is defined to capture the security required in the real world. Then a reduction is constructed to show that if there is an adversary can break the security of the scheme, then the reduction can use this adversary to break some well-studied hardness assumption.

This analysis provides not only a mathematical proof for the security of a scheme, but also guidelines for theoretically sound parameter setup, namely, setting up parameters for a scheme so that it can offer the proven security guarantee.

CONCRETE SECURITY. To deploy a scheme in a theoretically sound manner, we need to know the scheme's concrete security. The reduction-based analysis offers a way to do so. More precisely, it establishes the following relation between the success ratio $\Gamma_{\mathcal{A}}$ of an adversary $\mathcal{A}$ (which is defined as the quotient of its success probability and running time) attacking scheme S, and that of a reduction $\mathcal{B}$ breaking the underlying assumption P:

$$\Gamma_{\mathcal{A}} \leq L \cdot \Gamma_{\mathcal{B}}. \tag{1}$$

© Springer Nature Switzerland AG 2020
L. Chen et al. (Eds.): ESORICS 2020, LNCS 12309, pp. 485–504, 2020.
https://doi.org/10.1007/978-3-030-59013-0_24

The parameter L is called the security loss. Equation 1 guides us in deriving parameters that can provably guarantee a *k-bit security* for the scheme[1]. According to the current cryptanalysis results, we derive suitable parameters for the hardness problem P to compensate the security loss L and have $\Gamma_{\mathcal{A}} \leq L \cdot \Gamma_{\mathcal{B}} \leq 2^{-k}$. Thus a smaller L can give us shorter key lengths, and potentially more efficient schemes.

We call a reduction (or the scheme's security) *tight* if L is a small constant. Recently, a relaxed notion, called almost tight security, was considered in [18,25,26], where L could be a linear or logarithmic function of the security parameter. In this paper, we only consider fully tight security. In non-tight schemes, the security loss can depend on the scale of applications, for instance the number of users and/or issued signatures for digital signatures. To provide the same level of security guarantee, one needs to reasonably estimate the scale of an application and derive larger parameters to compensate for the security loss. Such an increase in parameters will inevitably slow down computations.

Thus, a large amount of attention has recently been drawn towards research on tight security, which has spanned from theoretical (such as [4,13,31]) to more practical aspects (such as [20,27], and covered different primitives including (identity-based) encryption [14,18,25], digital signatures [26–28,30,31] and non-interactive zero-knowledge proofs [2,3].

In this paper we focus on digital signatures, which has numerous applications both on its own, and as a basic building block for advanced cryptographic protocols (for instance, TLS).

MULTI-USER SECURITY. The classical security model (or definition) for signature schemes is unforgeability against chosen-message attacks (UF-CMA) [29], where an adversary attempts to forge a signature on a fresh message after it adaptively asks for signatures on multiple different messages. The UF-CMA security is defined in the *single-user* setting, namely, an adversary can only see the public key of a single user. We believe this is less desirable in practice.

In practice, (independent) public keys of multiple users are exposed to an adversary. Presumably, it will output a valid forgery under one of these public keys in a meaningful way after asking multiple signatures. This is captured by the UF-CMA security in the multi-user setting (denoted by MU-UF-CMA).

Although the MU-UF-CMA security is more desirable than the UF-CMA security, most signature schemes are typically proven in the UF-CMA model. We believe there are two main reasons: Firstly, adversaries in the UF-CMA model have less capabilities and thus the security proof in this model is easier; secondly, asymptotically speaking, the UF-CMA security implies MU-UF-CMA according to a generic reduction in [24]. However, this is problematic when we consider concrete security and derive theoretically sound parameters for the scheme in practice, since the generic reduction in [24] is not tight.

Concretely, it loses a factor of ℓ, which is the number of users: It only proves that attacking a scheme in the MU-UF-CMA model with ℓ users does not increase

---

[1] Usually, "k-bit security" means that there is no adversary can break the scheme with success ratio larger than 2^{-k} (see discussions in [7,17]).

the success ratio of the adversary by more than a factor of ℓ, compared to attacking the same scheme in the UF-CMA model. Thus, via this non-tight generic reduction, a signature scheme with k-bit security guarantee in the UF-CMA model does not gives us the same level of provable security guarantee in the MU-UF-CMA model.

As a concrete example, we reasonably assume $\ell := 2^{30}$ (about 1 billion)[2]. For a signature scheme, if the best adversary attacking it in the UF-CMA model has success ratio $\Gamma_U := 2^{-80}$ (i.e. 80-bit UF-CMA security), then the argument in [24] shows that the best adversary against the same scheme in the MU-UF-CMA model has success ratio $\Gamma_{MU} = 2^{30} \cdot 2^{-80} = 2^{-50}$, which is not a safe margin for current large-scale applications. To provide the same level of security in the MU-UF-CMA model, we need to increase the key length accordingly to compensate the security loss, which is $\ell := 2^{30}$ in the above case.

DIFFICULTY: TIGHT SECURITY FROM SEARCH ASSUMPTIONS. In recent years, several signature schemes with tight security in the single-user setting (aka. UF-CMA security) have been created, such as [13,14,18,26,28,30,31,34]. The schemes in [4,27,38,43,44] are the only ones we know of that have tight security in the multi-user setting (aka. MU-UF-CMA security). We note that [43] is based on the one-more CDH assumption, which is a non-static interactive assumption in pairing groups.

Furthermore, most of all the known tightly secure schemes (in both single-user and multi-user settings) require decisional assumptions. Inherently, decisional assumptions seem crucial for tight security. Different to the non-tight and guessing proof strategy, decisional assumptions and their random self-reducibility give security reductions the advantage to switch the distribution of signatures to random "at once", and then argue that even for an unbounded adversary there is no chance to win. This advantage cannot be easily achieved by search assumptions (such as the Computational Diffie-Hellman (CDH) and Factoring (FAC) assumptions), although search assumptions are more standard and reliable. For instance, the CDH assumption is more standard and weaker than the Decisional Diffie-Hellman assumption. It is similar for the FAC and the decisional Phi-Hiding assumption used in [34].

There are a few notable exceptions including the Rabin-William scheme [11] and the Micali-Reyzin scheme [6,40] based on FAC, the "selector bit" variants of RSA-PSS [35], and the Chevallier-Mames [19] and its later abstraction by Kiltz, Loss, and Pan [37]. However, their tight security is established in the less realistic single-user setting.

As a result of the above discussion, we raise the question of whether it is possible to construct an efficient and tightly MU-UF-CMA-secure signature scheme based on standard search assumptions. We are interested in schemes in the random oracle model [8]. In the random oracle model, a cryptographic hash function is modeled as an oracle that responds a random value in its output domain for each unique query. Although there is some limitation with the model [16],

---

[2] Nowadays many applications involve billions of users. For instance, Facebook has about 2 billion active users daily, according to https://about.fb.com/company-info/.

security proofs in the model still give strong evidence of the scheme's practical security. Moreover, schemes in the random oracle model are usually more efficient than their counterparts in the standard model.

1.1 Our Contribution: Multi-User Security from Search Assumptions

We construct two tightly secure signature schemes from standard (static) search assumptions (namely, CDH and FAC) in the multi-user setting. The security is proven in the random oracle model and the security loss is the constant 1. Our schemes improve upon those from the framework of Kiltz, Loss, and Pan at Asiacrypt 2017 [37] in the sense that our schemes have tight multi-user security. Asymptotically, our schemes have the same number of elements in a signature as [37], but, since our schemes are tightly secure in the multi-user setting, at the concrete security level our elements will be shorter and our schemes will have smaller signature size and achieve more efficient computation, in particular, for settings with large number of users. In fact, our CDH-based scheme is the Chevallier-Mames scheme [19]. Another interpretation of it is that we give a new tight security proof of the original Chevallier-Mames scheme in the multi-user setting.

In the following efficiency analysis, it shows that our CDH-based scheme is more efficient than Schnorr and DSA in a truly large setting. Moreover, our CDH-based scheme can offer offline pre-computation to speed up signing, namely, most of the work can be done offline before receiving the signing messages.

EFFICIENCY ANALYSIS. We compare the asymptotic efficiency of known tightly secure signature schemes (in both single-user and multi-user settings) in the random oracle model in Table 1. We are precise about the security loss from the single-user to the multi-user setting. The multi-user security of some schemes is established by the non-tight reduction in [24] and thus we need to choose a larger group to compensate the non-trivial security loss. We will mark those group sizes with G_ℓ. We also include the two famous signature schemes Schnorr and DSA in our comparison. By the optimal security proof in [38], the security loss of Schnorr is $12Q_h$, where Q_h is the number of hash queries an adversary makes, and the loss of the Katz-Wang scheme (KW) [28] is 4. We note a recent work on Schnorr in the (idealized) generic group model (GGM) [15]. While a proof in the GGM certainly provides certain degree of confidence in the scheme's security, its scope is rather limited, for instance, it does not capture algorithms that make use of the representation of the group. Thus, we do not include their result in our comparison. The provable security result for DSA [36] is established by [22] in the single-user setting, and we believe it is hard to prove it tightly in the multi-user setting. We will give more details about this in Appendix A.

To provide the concrete efficiency comparison, we estimate the schemes based on the DLOG and Diffie-Hellman assumptions in Table 2. We consider exponentiation as the dominating factor in the running time cost. We use elliptic curves when estimating the schemes, as group elements have a much shorter representation there than over finite fields. To have a k-bit secure DLOG problem, we need

Table 1. Comparison between some known signature schemes in the random oracle model. Top: schemes in a cyclic group $\mathbb{G}$ of prime order p. Bottom: schemes over $\mathbb{Z}_N$ for composite N. We detail the security loss of the schemes in the multi-user setting with ℓ users. Q_h is the maximum number of hash queries an adversary can make. Elements of $\mathbb{G}$ have bit length G and n denotes the security parameter. We take the security loss into account, and, for non-tight schemes, we write their group size as G_ℓ. G' denotes the bit length of a pairing-friendly group. $c < |p|$ is a parameter for the short Diffie-Hellman assumptions. We count the numbers of offline ("Off-line Exp.") and online exponentiation ("On-line Exp.") during signing, respectively.

Scheme	Approx. Size	Off-line Exp.	On-line Exp.	Loss	Ass.	Search?
Schnorr [42]	$n + |p|$	1	0	$12Q_h$	DLOG	✓
DSA [36]	$2|p|$	1	0	ℓQ_h	DLOG	✓
KW [28,38]	$n + |p|$	2	0	4	DDH	✗
GJKW [28]	$G_\ell + n + |p|$	1	2	ℓ	CDH	✓
FS$_{\text{CDH}}$ [37]	$G_\ell + n + |p|$	1	2	ℓ	CDH	✓
OF$_{\text{CDH}}$ [37]	$G_\ell + n + |p|$	3	0	ℓ	CDH	✓
AFLT [1]	$2n + c$	1	0	ℓ	DSDL	✗
FS$_{\text{SCDH}}$ [37]	$G_\ell + 2n + c$	1	2	ℓ	SCDH	✓
OF$_{\text{SCDH}}$ [37]	$G_\ell + 2n + c$	3	0	ℓ	SCDH	✓
GJ [27]	$2G + n + 4|p|$	0	7	3	CDH&DDH	✗
WLGSZ [43]	$2G' + 1$	1	1	1	OMCDH	(✓)
Ours (Fig. 2)	$G + n + |p|$	3	0	1	CDH	✓
MR [40, §4.3]	$n + |N|$	1	1	ℓ	FAC	✓
BR [9]	$n + |N|$	0	0	ℓ	FAC	✓
RSA-FDH [33]	$|N|$	0	1	ℓ	ΦH	✗
FS$_{\text{FAC}}$ [37]	$G_\ell + n + |N|$	1	2	ℓ	FAC	✓
Ours (Fig. 4)	$G + n + |N|$	1	2	1	FAC	✓

to choose a $2k$-bit elliptic curve, according to the baby-step giant-step algorithm. As in [27], we assume $k+1$ bits to represent a k-bit elliptic curve group element, and k bits to represent the corresponding discrete log. Thus, we need 257 bits to represent a group element of the NIST P256 curve.

For the running time in Table 2, similar to [27], we run "openssl speed ecdh" on a computer with a 2.4 GHz Quad-Core Intel Core i5 CPU, 16 GB RAM and MacOS 10.15.3. This command offers speed estimation for one operation (namely, exponentiation in the language of this paper) for curves NIST P192 (takes 0.3 ms), P224 (0.4 ms), P256 (0.4 ms), P384 (1.0 ms), P521 (2.2 ms), K233 (2.6 ms), B163 (1.3 ms) and so on. We use NIST P-curves for estimation, as they are more efficient than the other curves providing the same security level. We note that the security of Schnorr and DSA is dependent on Q_h, which is problematic, since an adversary can compute as many hash values as he would like offline. Computing hash functions is very cheap, and for instance, one can easily compute 2^{29} (≈ 0.5 billion) SHA-512 of 8192 byte messages per second with a normal PC. This is estimated by running "openssl speed sha". Thus, Q_h can be much larger than the number of users. According to [38], Q_h is estimated in the range between 2^{40} to 2^{80}. We consider a setting with roughly a billion users ($\ell := 2^{30}$), and take DSA as an example to show how we estimate: For $(\ell, Q_h) = (2^{30}, 2^{40})$ and 128-bit security, the security loss is 2^{70}, and we require a 198-bit secure DLOG. Thus we need a 396-bit curve, and we suggest NIST P521 as the appropriate choice, for which one signing (which requires 1 operation) takes 2.2 ms.

We note that the WLGSZ scheme uses Type 1 (symmetric) pairings [23]. Usually, in pairing-friendly groups, the group size is larger and operations (in particular, computing pairings) are less efficient than those in groups without pairings. For 128-bit security of WLGSZ, we should choose a Supersingular Curve over $GF(2^{1223})$, where 1 group operation takes 2.57 ms, and 1 pairing takes 19.00 ms.[3] We also put the estimation of it in Table 2.

Table 2. Concrete efficiency estimation of some known signature schemes based on the DLOG-related assumptions for 128-bit security and 2^{30} ($\approx$ 1 billion) users. Top: schemes using search assumptions. Bottom: schemes using decisional assumptions. For the same security level, we focus on the signature size ("Sig. Size") and running time for signing ("Sig. Time"). '–' means the security of the corresponding scheme is independent of that parameter.

Scheme	Q_h	Curve	Sig. Size (in bits)	Sig. Time (in milliseconds)
Schnorr [42]	2^{40}	P384	768	1.0
Schnorr [42]	2^{80}	P521	1024	2.2
DSA [36]	2^{40}	P521	1024	2.2
DSA [36]	2^{80}	P521	1024	2.2
GJKW [28]	–	P384	1153	3.0
FS$_{CDH}$ [37]	–	P384	1153	3.0
OF$_{CDH}$ [37]	–	P384	1153	3.0
WLGSZ [43]	–	SS	2447	5.14
Ours (Fig. 2)	–	P256	769	1.2
KW [28,38]	–	P256	512	0.4
GJ [27]	–	P256	1794	2.8

INTERPRETATION AND OPEN PROBLEMS. According to Table 2, for a medium scale $((\ell, Q_h) = (2^{30}, 2^{40}))$, our scheme based on CDH (cf. PF-OF$_{CDH}$ in Fig. 2) is comparable to the Schnorr signature, but for a truly large scale $((\ell, Q_h) = (2^{30}, 2^{80}))$ our scheme is significantly more efficient than other schemes based on search assumptions (either DLOG or CDH).

It is worth mentioning that the KW scheme achieves the best efficiency at the cost of using a stronger assumption (DDH). CDH is more standard and weaker

---

[3] Taken from the benchmarks in https://github.com/miracl/MIRACL/blob/master/docs/miracl-explained/benchmarks.md (2020-03-26).

than DDH. For instance, in symmetric pairing groups, CDH is still hard, while DDH is easy. In fact, for certain primes, CDH is equivalent to DLOG [21,39].

Our schemes live in harmony with the existing impossibility results about tightness [5,20,41]. Firstly, our schemes are not unique with respect to [5, Definition 1] and [41, Definition 1], and thus we do not contradict their results. Secondly, Cohn-Gordon et al. [20] showed the tightness impossibility result about authenticated key exchange protocols in a model where an adversary is allowed to corrupt a user's secret key, while our model does not allow signing key corruptions. This is a disadvantage of our schemes, since if one combines our schemes with the framework in [27] to construct an AKE protocol, the resulting protocol cannot provide any tight forward secrecy. We leave improving our schemes to allow signing key corruptions in a tight manner as the main open problem.

Another natural open problem is to further improve the efficiency of our schemes.

OUR APPROACH. We provide a brief overview of our technique. The starting point of our work is the work of Kiltz, Loss, and Pan (KLP) [37], which tightly transforms a five-move identification (ID) scheme into a signature scheme with programmable random oracles in the single-user setting. Before them, a similar work of Kiltz, Masny, and Pan (KMP) [38] has been done for the three-move identification schemes in the *multi-user* setting, and the Schnorr signature is a well-known example from this transformation. In particular, the KMP framework proves that the UF-KOA security implies the MU-UF-CMA security for signatures (cf. Appendix B and Theorem 3.2 in [38]). The UF-KOA security is the same as UF-CMA, except that an adversary cannot ask any signing queries. Naturally, one is tempted to transform the single-user security (UF-KOA) to multi-user (MU-UF-CMA) one for KLP signatures by using the KMP method.

In the "UF-KOA → MU-UF-CMA" for SIG[ID][4], the security reduction gets a public key pk from the UF-KOA challenger. By the random self-reducibility (RSR) of ID, the reduction can randomize pk and derive public keys $(pk_1, ..., pk_\ell)$, which is given to the adversary $\mathcal{A}$ against the MU-UF-CMA security. Due to some technical reason, only about half of $(pk_1, ..., pk_\ell)$ are computed using pk and the other half are generated honestly. Signing queries from $\mathcal{A}$ is generated by the honest-verifier zero-knowledge property of ID and programming the random oracle. To correctly map a MU-UF-CMA forgery to a UF-KOA one, the RSR property of ID allows, given the randomization trapdoor τ_i (for a $1 \leq i \leq \ell$), a valid transcript $\mathbf{t}_1 := (R, h, s)$ under $\boxed{pk_i}$ to be turned into another valid transcript $\mathbf{t}_2 := (R, h, s^*)$ under $\boxed{pk}$. The reduction crucially requires that only the value s^* in $\mathbf{t}_2$ is different to s in $\mathbf{t}_1$.

The five-move ID schemes in KLP only have a weaker form of RSR, namely, given τ_i, a valid transcript $(R_1, h_1, \boxed{R_2}, h_2, s)$ under pk_i can be converted to another valid transcript $(R_1, h_1, \boxed{R_2'}, h_2, s^*)$ under pk for $R_2 \neq R_2'$, since R_2 is dependent of pk_i. Unfortunately, this is problematic for converting a valid

---

[4] SIG[ID] is the signature scheme constructed from a three-move identification scheme ID via the Fiat-Shamir transformation.

MU-UF-CMA forgery to a UF-KOA one: For a valid UF-KOA forgery under pk, h_2 has to be equal to $H_2(R'_2, m)$ and, in particular, H_2 is simulated by the UF-KOA challenger; However, before the reduction receives $\mathcal{A}$'s MU-UF-CMA forgery of message m under public key pk_i, h_2 has been defined as $h_2 := H_2(R_2, m)$ in one of the random oracle queries. Clearly, $H_2(R_2, m) \neq H_2(R'_2, m)$ with overwhelming probability. Our solution is to apply the key-prefixing technique [12] and append R_1 and a public key in H_2, namely, we compute $H_2(R_1, R_2, pk, m)$ in our schemes. By knowing this additional information, we can carefully modify how the reduction queries the random oracle H_2, and make sure that $h_2 = H_2(R_1, R'_2, pk, m)$. We will refer to Sects. 3 and 4 for technical details.

2   Preliminaries

NOTATIONS. For a prime p, $\mathbb{Z}_p$ is the residual ring $\mathbb{Z}/p\mathbb{Z}$. If A is a set, then $a \xleftarrow{\$} A$ denotes picking a from A according to the uniform distribution. All our algorithms are probabilistic polynomial time, otherwise, we will state it. Let A be an algorithm and $a \xleftarrow{\$} A(b)$ denote the output of A on input b.

We present our definitions and proofs in the code-based game-playing framework [10,14]. A game G contains procedures INITIALIZE and FINALIZE, and some additional procedures $P_1, \ldots, P_n$, which are defined in pseudo-code. Initially all variables in a game are undefined (denoted by $\perp$) and all sets are empty (denoted by $\emptyset$). An adversary $\mathcal{A}$ is executed in game G (denoted by $G^{\mathcal{A}}$) if it first calls INITIALIZE, obtaining its output. Next, it may make arbitrary queries to P_i (according to their specification), again obtaining their output. Finally, it makes one single call to FINALIZE$(\cdot)$ and stops. We use $G^{\mathcal{A}} \Rightarrow d$ to denote that G outputs d after interacting with $\mathcal{A}$, and d is the output of FINALIZE.

2.1   The Computational Diffie-Hellman Assumption

A cyclic group generator $\mathcal{G}$ is an algorithm that takes 1^n as input (where n is the security parameter), and returns a n-bit prime p, a cyclic group $\mathbb{G}$ of order p, and a generator of the group. We denote the output as $(p, g, \mathbb{G}) \xleftarrow{\$} \mathcal{G}(1^n)$.

Definition 1 (Computational Diffie-Hellman Assumption). *The computational Diffie-Hellman problem* CDH *is* (t, ε)-*hard with respect to* $\mathcal{G}$ *if for all adversaries* $\mathcal{A}$ *running in time at most* t, *we have*

$$\Pr[Z = g^{xy} \mid \mathsf{par} := (p, g, \mathbb{G}) \xleftarrow{\$} \mathcal{G}(1^n); x, y \xleftarrow{\$} \mathbb{Z}_p, Z \leftarrow \mathcal{A}(\mathsf{par}, g^x, g^y)] \leq \varepsilon.$$

2.2   The Factoring Assumption

The factoring-based scheme in [37] is proven based on the CDH assumption in the group of signed quadratic residues [32], which is tightly implied by the factoring assumption. We recall necessary background here. It is almost verbatim to the definitions in Sect. 4.3 of [37].

For $n \in \mathbb{N}$, we denote $\mathbb{P}_{n/2}$ as the set of $n/2$ bit primes, and $\mathsf{Blum}_n := \{N \mid N = (2p+1)(2q+1) \wedge (2p+1), (2q+1), p, q \in \mathbb{P}_{n/2} \wedge p \neq q\}$. The factoring assumption is defined as follows.

Definition 2 (Factoring Assumption). *The factoring problem* FAC *is* (t, ε) *hard for* Blum_n *if for all adversaries* $\mathcal{A}$ *running in time at most* t,

$$\Pr\left[N = PQ \wedge P, Q \in \mathbb{P}_{n/2} \mid N \xleftarrow{\$} \mathsf{Blum}_n; (P, Q) \leftarrow \mathcal{A}(N)\right] \leq \varepsilon. \qquad (2)$$

For an element $a \in \mathbb{Z}_N$, we define the absolute value

$$|x| := \begin{cases} x & \text{if } x \leq (N-1)/2 \\ -x & \text{otherwise} \end{cases}.$$

We define the group of signed quadratic residues as $\mathbb{QR}_N^+ := \{|x| : x \in \mathbb{QR}_N\}$. We have that $(\mathbb{QR}_N^+, \circ)$ is a cyclic group with order $|\mathbb{QR}_N^+| = \varphi(N)/4$, where, for all $a, b \in \mathbb{QR}_N^+$ and $x \in \mathbb{Z}_N$, group operations are defined as follows:

$$a \circ b := |a \cdot b \bmod N|, \quad a^x := \underbrace{a \circ a \circ \ldots \circ a}_{x \text{ times}} = |a^x \bmod N|, \quad a^{-1} := |a^{-1} \bmod N|.$$

Lemma 1 (Lemma 7, [37]). *Let* $N' := \lceil N/4 \rceil$, $\mathbb{G} := \mathbb{QR}_N^+$, *and* $X \xleftarrow{\$} \mathbb{Z}_{N'}, Y \xleftarrow{\$} \mathbb{Z}_{|\mathbb{G}|}$. *Then the statistical distance* $D(X, Y)$ *satisfies* $D(X, Y) \leq \frac{2(P+Q)}{PQ}$.

2.3 Digital Signature

Definition 3 (Syntax of Digital Signature). *A digital signature scheme* SIG *is a tuple of algorithms* (Setup, Gen, Sign, Ver) *where*

- *The setup algorithm* Setup *takes as input a security parameter* 1^n, *and outputs system parameters* par.
- *The key generation algorithm* Gen *takes as input the system parameters* par, *and returns public and secret keys* (pk, sk). *We assume that* pk *defines a message space* $\mathcal{M}$ *and a signature space* Σ.
- *The signing algorithm* Sign *takes the secret key* sk *and a message* $m \in \mathcal{M}$ *as inputs, and returns a signature* $\sigma \in \Sigma$.
- *The* deterministic *verification algorithm* Ver *takes a public key* pk, *a message* m *and a signature* σ *as inputs and returns 1 (accept) or 0 (reject).*

For correctness, we require that $\Pr[\mathsf{Ver}(pk, m, \mathsf{Sign}(sk, m)) = 1] = 1$.

Definition 4 (MU-UF-CMA Security). *A signature scheme* SIG *is said to be* $(t, \varepsilon, \ell, Q_s)$-MU-UF-CMA *secure (multi-user unforgeable against chosen message attacks), if for all adversaries* $\mathcal{A}$ *that run in time* t *and makes at most* Q_s *queries to the signature oracle in the security game in Fig. 1, we have*

$$\Pr\left[\mathsf{MU\text{-}UF\text{-}CMA}^{\mathcal{A}} \Rightarrow 1\right] \leq \varepsilon.$$

Oracle INITIALIZE:	Oracle SIGN(i, m):
par $\overset{\$}{\leftarrow}$ Setup(1^n)	$M \leftarrow M \cup \{(i, m)\}$
For $i = 1, \ldots, \ell$: $(pk_i, sk_i) \overset{\$}{\leftarrow}$ Gen(par)	ctr := ctr + 1
$M := \emptyset$; ctr := 0	$\sigma \leftarrow$ Sign(sk_i, m)
Return (par, $pk_1, \ldots, pk_\ell$)	Return σ
Oracle FINALIZE(i^*, m^*, σ^*):	
Return $((\text{ctr} \leq Q_s) \wedge \text{Ver}(pk_{i^*}, m^*, \sigma^*) \wedge (i^*, m^*) \notin M)$	

Fig. 1. Security game for MU-UF-CMA security with ℓ users.

3   Construction from the CDH Assumption

Our construction here is based on the CDH-based online/offline signature scheme in [37]. We apply the key-prefixing technique [12] on it.

Let $H_1: \{0, 1\}^* \to \mathbb{G}$ and $H_2: \{0, 1\}^* \to \{0, 1\}^n$ be two hash functions. We recall the signature scheme $\mathsf{OF_{CDH}} := (\mathsf{Setup}, \mathsf{Gen}, \mathsf{Sign}, \mathsf{Ver})$ from [37] and define our key-prefixing variant $\mathsf{PF\text{-}OF_{CDH}} := (\mathsf{Setup}, \mathsf{Gen}, \mathsf{Sign_{pf}}, \mathsf{Ver_{pf}})$ of it in Fig. 2. We highlight the differences with grey. By additionally hashing R_1 in H_2, we can prove that the multi-user (MU-UF-CMA) security of our $\mathsf{PF\text{-}OF_{CDH}}$ can be tightly implied by the single-user security of $\mathsf{OF_{CDH}}$ in the programmable random oracle model. Interestingly, $\mathsf{PF\text{-}OF_{CDH}}$ is the same as the original Chevallier-Mames scheme [19]. Our proof can be seen as a new, tight proof of the scheme in the multi-user setting, while the original proof is only tight in the single-user setting.

Setup(1^n):	Sign $_{pf}$ (sk, m):	Ver $_{pf}$ (pk, m, σ):
par := $(p, g, \mathbb{G}) \overset{\$}{\leftarrow} \mathcal{G}(1^n)$	$r \overset{\$}{\leftarrow} \mathbb{Z}_p$; $R_1 := g^r$	Parse $\sigma := (R_L, h_2, s)$
Return par	$h_1 := H_1(R_1)$	$R_1 := g^s \cdot X^{-h_2}$
	$R_L := h_1^x \in \mathbb{G}$; $R_R := h_1^r$	$h_1 := H_1(R_1)$
Gen(par):	$R_2 := (R_L, R_R)$	$R_R := h_1^s \cdot R_L^{-h_2}$
$sk := x \overset{\$}{\leftarrow} \mathbb{Z}_p$	$h_2 := H_2(R_1, R_2, pk, m)$	$R_2 := (R_L, R_R)$
$pk := X = g^x$	$s := x \cdot h_2 + r \in \mathbb{Z}_p$	If $h_2 = H_2(R_1, R_2, pk, m)$
Return (pk, sk)	$\sigma := (R_L, h_2, s)$	Return 1
	Return σ	Else return 0

Fig. 2. Signature schemes $\mathsf{OF_{CDH}}$ and $\mathsf{PF\text{-}OF_{CDH}}$. We highlight the difference with grey. Both schemes execute all the codes, while the codes with grey are only executed in $\mathsf{PF\text{-}OF_{CDH}}$.

We recall the security of $\mathsf{OF_{CDH}}$ from [37].

Lemma 2 (Security of $\mathsf{OF_{CDH}}$, Theorem 2 of [37]). *If CDH is (t, ε)-hard w.r.t $\mathcal{G}$, then $\mathsf{OF_{CDH}}$ is $(t', \varepsilon', Q_s, Q_1, Q_2)$-UF-CMA secure in the programmable* *random oracle model, where*

$$\varepsilon' \le \varepsilon + \frac{Q_2 + 2}{2^n} + \frac{(Q_1 + Q_2)Q_s}{2^n} + \frac{1}{2^n}, \quad t' \approx t. \tag{3}$$

where Q_s, Q_1 and Q_2 are upper bounds on the number of signature and hash queries to H_1 and H_2 in the UF-CMA-experiment.

Lemma 3 (UF-CMA of $\mathsf{OF_{CDH}}$ $\rightarrow$ MU-UF-CMA of $\mathsf{PF\text{-}OF_{CDH}}$). *If $\mathsf{OF_{CDH}}$ is $(t, \varepsilon, Q_s, Q_1, Q_2)$-UF-CMA secure, then $\mathsf{PF\text{-}OF_{CDH}}$ is $(t', \varepsilon', \ell, Q'_s, Q'_1, Q'_2)$-MU-UF-CMA secure in the programmable random oracle model, where*

$$\varepsilon' \le \varepsilon + \frac{Q'_2 Q'_s}{2^n}, \quad Q'_s = Q_s, \quad Q'_1 = Q_1 - 1, \quad Q'_2 = Q_2 - 1, \ and \ t' \approx t. \tag{4}$$

Here Q_s, Q_1 and Q_2 are upper bounds on the number of signature and hash queries to H_1 and H_2 in the UF-CMA-experiment. Similarly, Q'_s, Q'_1 and Q'_2 are upper bounds on the number of signature and hash queries to H'_1 and H'_2 in the MU-UF-CMA-experiment.

Combining Lemmata 3 and 2, we get the following theorem.

Theorem 1 (Security of $\mathsf{PF\text{-}OF_{CDH}}$). *If CDH is (t, ε)-hard with respect to $\mathcal{G}$, then $\mathsf{PF\text{-}OF_{CDH}}$ is $(t', \varepsilon', \ell, Q_s, Q_1, Q_2)$-MU-UF-CMA secure in the programmable random oracle model, where*

$$\varepsilon' \le \varepsilon + \frac{Q_2 + 3}{2^n} + \frac{(Q_1 + Q_2 + 2)Q_s}{2^n} + \frac{1}{2^n} + \frac{Q_2 Q_s}{2^n}, \quad t' \approx t. \tag{5}$$

where Q_s, Q_1 and Q_2 are upper bounds on the number of signature and hash queries to H_1 and H_2 in the MU-UF-CMA-experiment.

Thus, we only need to prove Lemma 3.

3.1   Proof of Lemma 3

Let $\mathcal{A}$ be an adversary that $(t', \varepsilon', \ell, Q'_s, Q'_1, Q'_2)$-breaks the MU-UF-CMA security of $\mathsf{PF\text{-}OF_{CDH}}$. We prove Lemma 3 by constructing a reduction $\mathcal{B}$ that $(t, \varepsilon, Q_s, Q_1, Q_2)$-breaks the UF-CMA security of $\mathsf{OF_{CDH}}$ and provides oracle access for $\mathcal{A}$ as in Fig. 3.

The reduction $\mathcal{B}$ gets oracle access to INITIALIZE$_U$, SIGN$_U$, and FINALIZE$_U$ and random oracles HASH$_1$ and HASH$_2$ (for hash function H_1 and H_2 in $\mathsf{OF_{CDH}}$) from the UF-CMA security experiment. Moreover, $\mathcal{B}$ simulates oracles INITIALIZE$_{MU}$, SIGN$_{MU}$, FINALIZE$_{MU}$ and random oracles HASH$'_1$ and HASH$'_2$ (for hash functions H_1 and H_2 in $\mathsf{PF\text{-}OF_{CDH}}$) for adversary $\mathcal{A}$.

ANALYSIS. We show that $\mathcal{B}$ simulates a distribution statistically close to the real one for $\mathcal{A}$. It is trivial to see that the output of INITIALIZE$_{MU}$ distributes the same as the real one, since X_i is uniformly random over $\mathbb{G}$. Random oracles HASH$_1$ and HASH$_2$ are provided by the UF-CMA challenger and thus HASH$'_1$ and HASH$'_2$ are simulated properly.

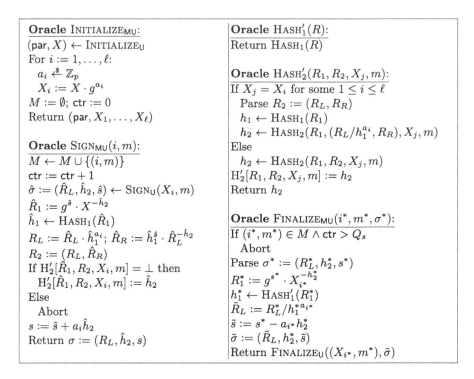

Oracle INITIALIZE_MU:
$(\mathsf{par}, X) \leftarrow$ INITIALIZE_U
For $i := 1, \ldots, \ell$:
$\quad a_i \overset{\$}{\leftarrow} \mathbb{Z}_p$
$\quad X_i := X \cdot g^{a_i}$
$M := \emptyset;\ \mathsf{ctr} := 0$
Return $(\mathsf{par}, X_1, \ldots, X_\ell)$

Oracle SIGN_MU(i, m):
$M \leftarrow M \cup \{(i, m)\}$
$\mathsf{ctr} := \mathsf{ctr} + 1$
$\hat{\sigma} := (\hat{R}_L, \hat{h}_2, \hat{s}) \leftarrow$ SIGN_U(X_i, m)
$\hat{R}_1 := g^{\hat{s}} \cdot X^{-\hat{h}_2}$
$\hat{h}_1 \leftarrow$ HASH_1$(\hat{R}_1)$
$R_L := \hat{R}_L \cdot \hat{h}_1^{a_i};\ R_R := \hat{h}_1^{\hat{s}} \cdot \hat{R}_L^{-\hat{h}_2}$
$R_2 := (R_L, \hat{R}_R)$
If $\mathsf{H}'_2[\hat{R}_1, R_2, X_i, m] = \bot$ then
$\quad \mathsf{H}'_2[\hat{R}_1, R_2, X_i, m] := \hat{h}_2$
Else
$\quad$ Abort
$s := \hat{s} + a_i \hat{h}_2$
Return $\sigma := (R_L, \hat{h}_2, s)$

Oracle HASH'_1(R):
Return HASH_1(R)

Oracle HASH'_2(R_1, R_2, X_j, m):
If $X_j = X_i$ for some $1 \le i \le \ell$
$\quad$ Parse $R_2 := (R_L, R_R)$
$\quad h_1 \leftarrow$ HASH_1(R_1)
$\quad h_2 \leftarrow$ HASH_2$(R_1, (R_L/h_1^{a_i}, R_R), X_j, m)$
Else
$\quad h_2 \leftarrow$ HASH_2(R_1, R_2, X_j, m)
$\mathsf{H}'_2[R_1, R_2, X_j, m] := h_2$
Return h_2

Oracle FINALIZE_MU(i^*, m^*, σ^*):
If $(i^*, m^*) \in M \wedge \mathsf{ctr} > Q_s$
$\quad$ Abort
Parse $\sigma^* := (R_L^*, h_2^*, s^*)$
$R_1^* := g^{s^*} \cdot X_{i^*}^{-h_2^*}$
$h_1^* \leftarrow$ HASH'_1(R_1^*)
$\tilde{R}_L := R_L^*/h_1^{*a_{i^*}}$
$\tilde{s} := s^* - a_{i^*} h_2^*$
$\tilde{\sigma} := (\tilde{R}_L, h_2^*, \tilde{s})$
Return FINALIZE_U$((X_{i^*}, m^*), \tilde{\sigma})$

Fig. 3. Security reduction $\mathcal{B}$ to break the UF-CMA security of OF_CDH, and simulate oracles for adversary $\mathcal{A}$ against the MU-UF-CMA security of PF-OF_CDH. H'_2 is a list that keeps track of the inputs and outputs of random oracle HASH'_2.

Our focus is to show that signatures simulated by SIGN_MU are statistically close to those outputted by Sign_pf of PF-OF_CDH. Given $\hat{\sigma} := (\hat{R}_L, \hat{h}_2, \hat{s}) \leftarrow$ SIGN_U(X_i, m), $\hat{\sigma}$ is a valid signature w.r.t. the verification of OF_CDH (defined in Fig. 2) and $\hat{s}$ distributes uniformly at random, namely, the following equation holds:

$$\hat{h}_2 = \text{HASH}_2(\hat{R}_2, X_i, m),$$

where $\hat{R}_2 = (\hat{R}_L, \hat{R}_R), \hat{R}_R = \hat{h}_1^{\hat{s}} \cdot \hat{R}_L^{-\hat{h}_2}, \hat{h}_1 = \text{HASH}_1(\hat{R}_1)$ and $\hat{R}_1 = g^{\hat{s}} \cdot X^{-\hat{h}_2}$.

If SIGN_MU(i, m) does not abort, the signature $\sigma := (R_L, \hat{h}_2, s)$ with $s = \hat{s} + a_i \hat{h}_2$ output by SIGN_MU(i, m) has the right distribution, namely, s is uniformly random (which is trivial due to the random $\hat{s}$) and σ will pass the verification Ver_pf of PF-OF_CDH: Firstly, Ver_pf will compute values R_1 and $R_2 := (R_L, R_R)$ according to its definition in Fig. 2, and, by our simulation of INITIALIZE_MU and SIGN_MU, the following holds

$$R_1 := g^s \cdot X_i^{-\hat{h}_2} = g^{\hat{s} + a_i \hat{h}_2} \cdot (X \cdot g^{a_i})^{-\hat{h}_2} = g^{\hat{s}} \cdot X^{-\hat{h}_2} = \hat{R}_1$$
$$R_R := h_1^s \cdot R_L^{-\hat{h}_2} = \hat{h}_1^{\hat{s} + a_i \hat{h}_2} \cdot (\hat{R}_L \cdot \hat{h}_1^{a_i})^{-\hat{h}_2} = \hat{h}_1^{\hat{s}} \cdot \hat{R}_L^{-\hat{h}_2} = \hat{R}_R$$

where $h_1 = \text{HASH}_1(R_1) = \text{HASH}_1(\hat{R}_1) = \hat{h}_1$. Thus, $\hat{h}_2$ in σ returned by $\text{SIGN}_{\text{MU}}(i, m)$ will have $\hat{h}_2 = \text{HASH}'_2(R_1, R_2, X_i, m)$ and $\text{Ver}_{\text{pf}}(X_i, m, \sigma) = 1$.

Moreover, since $\hat{s}$ is uniform, $\hat{R}_1$ distributes uniformly over $\mathbb{G}$ and the probability that $\text{H}'_2[\hat{R}_1, R_2, X_i, m]$ has been defined is at most $Q'_2/|\mathbb{G}|$. By applying the union bound on the number of signing queries, $\mathcal{B}$ will abort its simulation with probability at most $Q_s Q'_2/|\mathbb{G}|$.

A VALID FORGERY. To see that $\mathcal{B}$ produces a valid forgery, we first assume that the forgery $(i^*, m^*, \sigma^* = (R_L^*, h_2^*, s^*))$ made by $\mathcal{A}$ is a valid forgery in the MU-UF-CMA-experiment under the public key X_{i^*}, meaning that for

$$R_1^* := g^{s^*} \cdot X_{i^*}^{-h_2^*}, \quad h_1^* := \text{HASH}_1(R_1^*) \quad \text{and} \quad R_R^* := h_1^{*s^*} \cdot R_L^{*-h_2^*},$$

we have $h_2^* = \text{HASH}'_2(R_1^*, R_L^*, R_R^*, X_{i^*}, m^*)$. In addition, it satisfies the freshness condition that (i^*, m^*) has not been queried in a previous signature query. For the signature $\tilde{\sigma} = (\tilde{R}_L, h_2^*, \tilde{s})$, we compute

$$\tilde{R}_1 := g^{\tilde{s}} \cdot X^{-h_2^*} = g^{s^* - a_{i^*} h_2^*} \cdot X^{-h_2^*} = g^{s^*} \cdot X_{i^*}^{-h_2^*} = R_1^*.$$

We set $\tilde{h}_1 := \text{HASH}_1(\tilde{R}_1) = \text{HASH}_1(R_1^*) = h_1^*$ and compute

$$\tilde{R}_R := \tilde{h}_1^{\tilde{s}} \cdot \tilde{R}_L^{-h_2^*} = \tilde{h}_1^{s^* - a_{i^*} h_2^*} \cdot \left(R_L^*/\tilde{h}_1^{a_{i^*}}\right)^{-h_2^*} = \tilde{h}_1^{s^*} \cdot R_L^{*-h_2^*} = R_R^*.$$

Then, by the simulation of $\text{HASH}'_2(R_1^*, R_2^*, X_{i^*}, m^*)$ and $\tilde{R}_L = R_L^*/h_1^{a_{i^*}}$, we have that

$$h_2^* = \text{HASH}'_2(R_1^*, R_2^*, X_{i^*}, m^*) = \text{HASH}'_2(R_1^*, (R_L^*, R_R^*), X_{i^*}, m^*)$$
$$= \text{HASH}_2(R_1^*, (R_L^*/h_1^{a_{i^*}}, R_R^*), X_{i^*}, m^*) = \text{HASH}_2(\tilde{R}_1, (\tilde{R}_L, \tilde{R}_R), X_{i^*}, m^*) = \tilde{h}_2$$

and hence $\text{Ver}(X, \tilde{m}, \tilde{\sigma}) = 1$ where $\tilde{m} := (X_{i^*}, m^*)$. Since σ^* was a fresh signature on (i^*, m^*), $\tilde{m}$ has never been queried to the UF-CMA signature oracle, and hence $\tilde{\sigma}$ is a fresh signature on the message $\tilde{m}$.

4   Construction from the Factoring Assumption

We can also apply our method to FS_{FAC} in [37] to get tight MU-UF-CMA security from the FAC assumption. We refer readers to Sect. 2.2 for necessary mathematical background of this section.

Let $H_1 : \{0,1\}^* \to \mathbb{QR}_N^+$ and $H_2 : \{0,1\}^* \to \{0, \dots, 2^k - 1\}$ be hash functions, and let g be a generator of $\mathbb{QR}_N^+$. As before, in Fig. 4 we have the original scheme FS_{FAC} and its prefixed variant $\text{PF-FS}_{\text{FAC}}$. To give a syntactically correct definition, we require that Setup outputs a private parameter sp that only inputs to Gen.

By combining Corollary 1, Lemma 8[5] and Lemma 1 of [37], we get the following result.

---

[5] We use the result derived in the reduction, not the statement of the lemma, as they are not the same.

Setup(1^n):	Sign $_{pf}$ (sk, m):	Ver $_{pf}$ (pk, m, σ):
$p, q \xleftarrow{\$} \mathbb{P}_{n/2}$ s.t.	$r \xleftarrow{\$} \mathbb{Z}_{N/4}; R_1 := g^r$	Parse $\sigma := (R_L, h_2, s)$
$P := 2p + 1 \in \mathbb{P}_{n/2}$	$h_1 := H_1(R_1, \boxed{pk}, m) \in \mathbb{QR}_N^+;$	$R_1 := g^s \circ X^{-h_2}$
$Q := 2q + 1 \in \mathbb{P}_{n/2}$	$R_L := h_1^x; R_R := h_1^r$	$h_1 := H_1(R_1, \boxed{pk}, m)$
$N := PQ$	$R_2 := (R_L, R_R)$	$R_R := h_1^s \circ R_L^{-h_2}$
par $:= (N, g)$	$h_2 := H_2(\boxed{R_1, R_2, pk}, m)$	$R_2 := (R_L, R_R)$
sp $:= (p, q)$	$s :=$	If $h_2 = H_2(\boxed{R_1, R_2, pk}, m)$
Return (par, sp)	$\quad x \cdot h_2 + r \mod (\varphi(N)/4)$	$\quad$ Return 1
	$\sigma := (R_L, h_2, s)$	Else return 0
Gen(par, sp):	Return σ	
$x \xleftarrow{\$} \mathbb{Z}_{N/4}; X := g^x$		
$sk := (x, p, q)$		
$pk := X$		
Return (pk, sk)		

Fig. 4. Signature schemes FS$_\mathsf{FAC}$ and PF-FS$_\mathsf{FAC}$. We highlight the difference with grey. Both schemes execute all the codes, while the codes with grey are only executed in PF-FS$_\mathsf{FAC}$.

Lemma 4 (Security of FS$_\mathsf{FAC}$). *If* FAC *is* (t, ε)*-hard for* Blum$_n$*, then* FS$_\mathsf{FAC}$ *is* $(t', \varepsilon', Q_1, Q_2)$*-UF-KOA secure in the random oracle model, where*

$$\varepsilon' \leq \varepsilon + \frac{1}{2^{n/2}} + \frac{Q_2 + 1}{2^k}, \quad t' \approx t.$$

Lemma 5 (UF-KOA of FS$_\mathsf{FAC}$ → MU-UF-CMA of PF-FS$_\mathsf{FAC}$). *If* FS$_\mathsf{FAC}$ *is* $(t, \varepsilon, Q_1, Q_2)$*-UF-KOA secure, then* PF-FS$_\mathsf{FAC}$ *is* $(t', \varepsilon', \ell, Q_s, Q_1', Q_2')$*-MU-UF-CMA secure in the programmable random oracle model, where*

$$\varepsilon' \leq \varepsilon + \frac{1}{2^{n/2-2}} + Q_s \left(\frac{Q_1'}{2^n} + \frac{Q_2'}{2^k} \right), \quad Q_1' = Q_1 - 1, \ Q_2' = Q_2 - 1, \ and \ t' \approx t. \quad (6)$$

Here Q_1 and Q_2 are upper bounds on the number of hash queries to H_1 and H_2 in the UF-KOA*-experiment. Similarly, Q_s, Q_1' and Q_2' are upper bounds on the number of signature and hash queries to H_1' and H_2' in the* MU-UF-CMA*-experiment.*

Combining Lemmata 4 and 5, we get the following theorem.

Theorem 2 (Security of PF-FS$_\mathsf{FAC}$). *If* FAC *is* (t, ε)*-hard for* Blum$_n$*, then* PF-FS$_\mathsf{FAC}$ *is* $(t', \varepsilon', Q_s, Q_1, Q_2)$*-MU-UF-CMA secure in the programmable random oracle model, where*

$$\varepsilon' \leq \varepsilon + \frac{1}{2^{n/2}} + \frac{Q_2 + 2}{2^k} + \frac{1}{2^{n/2-2}} + Q_s \left(\frac{Q_1}{2^n} + \frac{Q_2}{2^k} \right), \quad t' \approx t. \quad (7)$$

As before, we now only need to prove Lemma 5.

Oracle INITIALIZE$_{\text{MU}}$:	**Oracle** HASH$'_1(R, X_j, m)$:
$(\text{par}, X) \leftarrow$ INITIALIZE$_{\text{U}}$	If H$'_1[R, X_j, m] \neq \perp$
For $i := 1, \ldots, \ell$	$\quad$ Return H$'_1[R, X_j, m]$
$\quad a_i \overset{\$}{\leftarrow} \mathbb{Z}_{\lceil N/4 \rceil}$	$h_1 \leftarrow$ HASH$_1(R, X_j, m)$
$\quad X_i := X \circ g^{a_i}$	H$'_1[R, X_j, m] := h_1$
$\quad pk_i := X_i$	Return h_1
$M := \emptyset;\ \text{ctr} := 0$	
Return $(\text{par}, pk_1, \ldots, pk_\ell)$	**Oracle** HASH$'_2(R_1, R_2, X_j, m)$:
	If H$'_2[R_1, R_2, X_j, m] \neq \perp$
	$\quad$ Return H$'_2[R_1, R_2, X_j, m]$
Oracle SIGN$_{\text{MU}}(i, m)$:	If $X_j = X_i$ for some $1 \leq i \leq \ell$
$M \leftarrow M \cup \{(i, m)\}$	$\quad$ Parse $R_2 := (R_L, R_R)$
$\text{ctr} := \text{ctr} + 1$	$\quad h_1 \leftarrow$ HASH$'_1(R_1, X_i, m)$
$\hat{s}, w, \hat{h}_2 \overset{\$}{\leftarrow} \mathbb{Z}_{\lceil N/4 \rceil}$	$\quad h_2 \leftarrow$ HASH$_2(R_1, (R_L \circ h_1^{-a_i}, R_R), X_i, m)$
$\hat{h}_1 := g^w;\ \hat{R}_1 := g^{\hat{s}} \circ X_i^{-\hat{h}_2}$	Else
$\hat{R}_L := X_i^w;\ \hat{R}_R := \hat{R}_1^w$	$\quad h_2 \leftarrow$ HASH$_2(R_1, R_2, X_j, m)$
If H$'_1[\hat{R}_1, X_i, m] = \perp$ then	H$'_2[R_1, R_2, X_j, m] := h_2$
$\quad$ H$'_1[\hat{R}_1, X_i, m] := h_1$	Return h_2
Else	
$\quad$ Abort	**Oracle** FINALIZE$_{\text{MU}}(i^*, m^*, \sigma^*)$:
$\hat{R}_2 = (\hat{R}_L, \hat{R}_R)$	If $((i^*, m^*) \in M \wedge \text{ctr} > Q_s)$
If H$'_2[\hat{R}_1, \hat{R}_2, X_i, m] = \perp$ then	$\quad$ Abort
$\quad$ H$'_2[\hat{R}_1, \hat{R}_2, X_i, m] := \hat{h}_2$	Parse $\sigma^* := (R_L^*, h_2^*, s^*)$
Else	$R_1^* := g^{s^*} \circ X_{i^*}^{-h_2^*}$
$\quad$ Abort	$h_1^* \leftarrow$ HASH$'_1(R_1^*, X_{i^*}, m^*)$
Return $\sigma := (\hat{R}_L, \hat{h}_2, \hat{s})$	$\tilde{R}_L := R_L^* \circ (h_1^*)^{-a_{i^*}}$
	$\tilde{s} := s^* - a_{i^*} h_2^*$
	$\tilde{\sigma} := (\tilde{R}_L, h_2^*, \tilde{s})$
	Return FINALIZE$_{\text{U}}((X_{i^*}, m^*), \tilde{\sigma})$

Fig. 5. Security reduction $\mathcal{B}$ to break the UF-KOA security of FS$_{\text{FAC}}$, and simulate oracles for adversary $\mathcal{A}$ against the MU-UF-CMA security of PF-FS$_{\text{FAC}}$. Operations denoted with $\circ$ are performed in $\mathbb{QR}_N^+$, while other operations are performed over the integers.

4.1 Proof of Lemma 5

Let $\mathcal{A}$ be an adversary that breaks the $(t', \varepsilon', \ell, Q_s, Q'_1, Q'_2)$-MU-UF-CMA-security of PF-FS$_{\text{FAC}}$. We construct a reduction $\mathcal{B}$ that breaks the $(t, \varepsilon, Q_1, Q_2)$-UF-KOA-security of FS$_{\text{FAC}}$ as in Fig. 5. As before, the reduction $\mathcal{B}$ gets oracle access to INITIALIZE$_{\text{U}}$, FINALIZE$_{\text{U}}$ and random oracles HASH$_1$ and HASH$_2$ (for hash function H_1 and H_2 in FS$_{\text{FAC}}$) from the UF-KOA security experiment. Moreover, $\mathcal{B}$ simulates oracles INITIALIZE$_{\text{MU}}$, SIGN$_{\text{MU}}$, FINALIZE$_{\text{MU}}$ and random oracles HASH$'_1$ and HASH$'_2$ (for hash functions H_1 and H_2 in PF-FS$_{\text{FAC}}$) for adversary $\mathcal{A}$.

ANALYSIS. We again want to show that $\mathcal{B}$ simulates a distribution statistically close to the real one for $\mathcal{A}$. It is trivial to see that the output of INITIALIZE$_{\text{MU}}$ has the same distribution as in the real case, since X_i is uniformly random over

$\mathbb{QR}_N^+$. The random oracles are provided by the UF-KOA challenger and thus HASH_1' and HASH_2' are properly simulated.

If SIGN_{MU} does not abort, the signature $\sigma = (\hat{R}_L, \hat{h}_2, \hat{s})$ is within statistical distance $2(P + Q)/PQ \le 2^{2-n/2}$ from a real distribution, and it passes the verification Ver_{pf} of $\text{PF-FS}_{\text{FAC}}$. To show this, we use Lemma 1 and a result from Lemma 8 in [37]. Combined, these show that when simulating a signature like we do in SIGN_{MU}, the returned transcript $(\hat{R}_1, \hat{h}_1, \hat{R}_2, \hat{h}_2, \hat{s})$ is within statistical distance at most $2(P + Q)/PQ$ from a real distribution. This is so because $\hat{s}$ has statistical distance at most $2(P+Q)/PQ$ from a uniformly random variable over $\mathbb{Z}_{|\mathbb{QR}_N^+|}$ by Lemma 1, and $\hat{R}_1, \hat{R}_L, \hat{R}_R$ are determined by $\hat{s}, \hat{h}_2$ and X_i, since they are the unique values that satisfy $\hat{R}_1 = g^{\hat{s}} \circ X_i^{-\hat{h}_2}$ and $\hat{R}_R = \hat{h}_1^{\hat{s}} \circ \hat{R}_L^{-\hat{h}_2}$.

For the verification, we proceed as we did for $\text{PF-OF}_{\text{CDH}}$. The Ver_{pf} algorithm computes R_1 and R_R as described in Fig. 4, and from our simulation of $\text{INITIALIZE}_{\text{MU}}$ and SIGN_{MU} we get

$$R_1 := g^{\hat{s}} \circ X_i^{-\hat{h}_2} = \hat{R}_1$$
$$R_R := h_1^{\hat{s}} \circ \hat{R}_L^{-\hat{h}_2} = g^{w\hat{s}} \circ X_i^{-w\hat{h}_2} = \left(g^{\hat{s}} \circ X_i^{-\hat{h}_2}\right)^w = \hat{R}_1^w = \hat{R}_R,$$

where we after the programming have $h_1 := \text{HASH}_1(R_1, X_i, m) = \hat{h}_1 = g^w$. Thus, $\hat{h}_2$ in σ returned by $\text{SIGN}_{\text{MU}}(i, m)$ will satisfy

$$\hat{h}_2 := \text{HASH}_2'(R_1, \hat{R}_L, R_R, X_i, m),$$

and therefore $\text{Ver}_{\text{pf}}(X_i, m, \sigma) = 1$. In the simulation we randomly choose $\hat{s} \xleftarrow{\$} \mathbb{Z}_{\lceil N/4 \rceil}$, which means that R_1 will be uniformly random over $\mathbb{QR}_N^+$, and the probability that $\text{H}_1'[\hat{R}_1, X_i, m]$ has been defined is at most $Q_1'/|\mathbb{QR}_N^+| \le Q_1'/2^n$. A similar argument shows that the probability that $\text{H}_2'[\hat{R}_1, R_2, X_i, m]$ has been defined is at most $Q_2'/2^k$. The union bound applied on the number of signing queries shows that $\mathcal{B}$ will abort its simulation with probability at most $Q_s(Q_1'/2^n + Q_2'/2^k)$.

A VALID FORGERY. To show that $(X_{i^*}, m^*, \tilde{\sigma} = (\tilde{R}_L, h_2^*, \tilde{s}))$ is a valid forgery in the UF-KOA-experiment, we first assume that $(i^*, m^*, \sigma^* := (R_L^*, h_2^*, s^*))$ is a valid signature in the MU-UF-CMA-experiment, meaning that for

$$R_1^* := g^{s^*} \circ X_{i^*}^{-h_2^*}, \quad h_1^* := \text{HASH}_1'(R_1^*, X_{i^*}, m^*) \quad \text{and} \quad R_R^* := h_1^{*s^*} \circ R_L^{*-h_2^*},$$

we have $h_2^* = \text{HASH}_2'(R_1^*, R_L^*, R_R^*, X_{i^*}, m^*)$. It also satisfies the freshness condition that (i^*, m^*) has not been queried in a previous signature query in the MU-UF-CMA game. This means that if $h_1^* = \text{H}_1'[R_1^*, X_{i^*}, m^*]$ or $h_2^* = \text{H}_2'[R_1^*, R_2^*, X_{i^*}, m^*]$ are defined, it was not done by SIGN_{MU}, and hence the value was returned by an UF-KOA hash oracle, as required. For the signature $\tilde{\sigma} = (\tilde{R}_L, h_2^*, \tilde{s})$ generated in $\text{FINALIZE}_{\text{MU}}$, we compute $\tilde{R}_1 := g^{\tilde{s}} \circ X^{-h_2^*} = g^{s^* - a_{i^*} h_2^*} \circ X^{-h_2^*} = g^{s^*} \circ X_{i^*}^{-h_2^*} = R_1^*$. We set $\tilde{h}_1 = \text{HASH}_1(\tilde{R}_1, X_{i^*}, m^*) = \text{HASH}_1(R^*, X_{i^*}, m^*) = h_1^*$, and compute

$$\tilde{R}_R := \tilde{h}_1^{\tilde{s}} \circ \tilde{R}_L^{-h_2^*} = \tilde{h}_1^{s^* - a_{i^*} h_2^*} \circ \left(R_L^* \circ (\tilde{h}_1)^{-a_{i^*}}\right)^{-h_2^*} = \tilde{h}_1^{s^*} \circ R_L^{*-h_2^*} = R_R^*.$$

Then, by the simulation of $\text{HASH}'_2(R_1^*, R_2^*, X_{i^*}, m^*)$, we have that

$$\tilde{h}_2 := \text{HASH}_2(\tilde{R}_1, (\tilde{R}_L, \tilde{R}_R), X_{i^*}, m^*) = \text{HASH}'_2(R_1^*, R_2^*, X_{i^*}, m^*) = h_2^*, \quad (8)$$

and hence $\text{Ver}(X, \tilde{m}, \tilde{\sigma}) = 1$ where $\tilde{m} := (X_{i^*}, m^*)$. The running time is that of $\mathcal{A}$ plus the Q_s simulations of SIGN_{MU}, and we write $t' \approx t$.

A   On the Multi-user Security of DSA

We show why it is difficult to show tight implication from the single-user security to the multi-user security for DSA. We first recall the scheme. Let p be an L-bit prime, and q be an N-bit prime such that $q \mid (p - 1)$. For specifications on L and N, see the DSA documentation [36]. Let g be a generator of a subgroup of order q in $\mathbb{Z}_p^*$. The Gen, Sign and Ver can then be described as follows.

Gen(par):	Sign(sk, m):	Ver(X, m, σ):
$sk := x \stackrel{\$}{\leftarrow} \mathbb{Z}_q$	$r \stackrel{\$}{\leftarrow} \mathbb{Z}_q^*$	Parse $\sigma := (R, s)$
$X := g^x \mod p$	$R := (g^r \mod p) \mod q$	If $R = 0 \vee s = 0$
$pk := X$	$s :=$	Return 0
Return (pk, sk)	$\quad (r^{-1}(H(m) + xR)) \mod q$	$w := s^{-1} \mod q$
	Return $\sigma := (R, s)$	$u_1 := H(m) \cdot w \mod q$
		$u_2 := R \cdot w \mod q$
		$v :=$
		$\quad (g^{u_1} X^{u_2} \mod p) \mod q$
		If $v = R$
		Return 1
		Else return 0

Different to the Schnorr signature, given a valid signature $\sigma := (R, s)$ under public key X, it is not possible to convert it to a valid signature under public key $X \cdot g^{a_i}$ for $a_i \stackrel{\$}{\leftarrow} \mathbb{Z}_q^* = \mathbb{Z}_q \setminus \{0\}$ using methods in [12,38], since we do not have the discrete log of R, namely, $r \in \mathbb{Z}_q^*$.

References

1. Abdalla, M., Fouque, P.-A., Lyubashevsky, V., Tibouchi, M.: Tightly-secure signatures from lossy identification schemes. In: Pointcheval, D., Johansson, T. (eds.) EUROCRYPT 2012. LNCS, vol. 7237, pp. 572–590. Springer, Heidelberg (2012). https://doi.org/10.1007/978-3-642-29011-4_34
2. Abe, M., Jutla, C.S., Ohkubo, M., Pan, J., Roy, A., Wang, Y.: Shorter QA-NIZK and SPS with tighter security. In: Galbraith, S.D., Moriai, S. (eds.) ASIACRYPT 2019. LNCS, vol. 11923, pp. 669–699. Springer, Cham (2019). https://doi.org/10.1007/978-3-030-34618-8_23
3. Abe, M., Jutla, C.S., Ohkubo, M., Roy, A.: Improved (almost) tightly-secure simulation-sound QA-NIZK with applications. In: Peyrin, T., Galbraith, S. (eds.) ASIACRYPT 2018. LNCS, vol. 11272, pp. 627–656. Springer, Cham (2018). https://doi.org/10.1007/978-3-030-03326-2_21

4. Bader, C., Hofheinz, D., Jager, T., Kiltz, E., Li, Y.: Tightly-secure authenticated key exchange. In: Dodis, Y., Nielsen, J.B. (eds.) TCC 2015. LNCS, vol. 9014, pp. 629–658. Springer, Heidelberg (2015). https://doi.org/10.1007/978-3-662-46494-6_26

5. Bader, C., Jager, T., Li, Y., Schäge, S.: On the impossibility of tight cryptographic reductions. In: Fischlin, M., Coron, J.-S. (eds.) EUROCRYPT 2016. LNCS, vol. 9666, pp. 273–304. Springer, Heidelberg (2016). https://doi.org/10.1007/978-3-662-49896-5_10

6. Bellare, M., Poettering, B., Stebila, D.: From identification to signatures, tightly: a framework and generic transforms. In: Cheon, J.H., Takagi, T. (eds.) ASIACRYPT 2016. LNCS, vol. 10032, pp. 435–464. Springer, Heidelberg (2016). https://doi.org/10.1007/978-3-662-53890-6_15

7. Bellare, M., Ristenpart, T.: Simulation without the artificial abort: simplified proof and improved concrete security for Waters' IBE scheme. In: Joux, A. (ed.) EUROCRYPT 2009. LNCS, vol. 5479, pp. 407–424. Springer, Heidelberg (2009). https://doi.org/10.1007/978-3-642-01001-9_24

8. Bellare, M., Rogaway, P.: Random oracles are practical: a paradigm for designing efficient protocols. In: Denning, D.E., Pyle, R., Ganesan, R., Sandhu, R.S., Ashby, V. (eds.) ACM CCS 1993, pp. 62–73. ACM Press, November 1993

9. Bellare, M., Rogaway, P.: The exact security of digital signatures-how to sign with RSA and Rabin. In: Maurer, U. (ed.) EUROCRYPT 1996. LNCS, vol. 1070, pp. 399–416. Springer, Heidelberg (1996). https://doi.org/10.1007/3-540-68339-9_34

10. Bellare, M., Rogaway, P.: The security of triple encryption and a framework for code-based game-playing proofs. In: Vaudenay, S. (ed.) EUROCRYPT 2006. LNCS, vol. 4004, pp. 409–426. Springer, Heidelberg (2006). https://doi.org/10.1007/11761679_25

11. Bernstein, D.J.: Proving tight security for Rabin-Williams signatures. In: Smart, N. (ed.) EUROCRYPT 2008. LNCS, vol. 4965, pp. 70–87. Springer, Heidelberg (2008). https://doi.org/10.1007/978-3-540-78967-3_5

12. Bernstein, D.J.: Multi-user Schnorr security, revisited. Cryptology ePrint Archive, Report 2015/996 (2015). http://eprint.iacr.org/2015/996

13. Blazy, O., Kakvi, S.A., Kiltz, E., Pan, J.: Tightly-secure signatures from Chameleon hash functions. In: Katz, J. (ed.) PKC 2015. LNCS, vol. 9020, pp. 256–279. Springer, Heidelberg (2015). https://doi.org/10.1007/978-3-662-46447-2_12

14. Blazy, O., Kiltz, E., Pan, J.: (Hierarchical) identity-based encryption from affine message authentication. In: Garay, J.A., Gennaro, R. (eds.) CRYPTO 2014. LNCS, vol. 8616, pp. 408–425. Springer, Heidelberg (2014). https://doi.org/10.1007/978-3-662-44371-2_23

15. Blocki, J., Lee, S.: On the multi-user security of short Schnorr signatures. Cryptology ePrint Archive, Report 2019/1105 (2019). https://eprint.iacr.org/2019/1105

16. Canetti, R., Goldreich, O., Halevi, S.: The random oracle methodology, revisited (preliminary version). In: 30th ACM STOC, pp. 209–218. ACM Press, May 1998

17. Chatterjee, S., Koblitz, N., Menezes, A., Sarkar, P.: Another look at tightness II: practical issues in cryptography. Cryptology ePrint Archive, Report 2016/360 (2016). http://eprint.iacr.org/2016/360

18. Chen, J., Wee, H.: Fully, (almost) tightly secure IBE and dual system groups. In: Canetti, R., Garay, J.A. (eds.) CRYPTO 2013. LNCS, vol. 8043, pp. 435–460. Springer, Heidelberg (2013). https://doi.org/10.1007/978-3-642-40084-1_25

19. Chevallier-Mames, B.: An efficient CDH-based signature scheme with a tight security reduction. In: Shoup, V. (ed.) CRYPTO 2005. LNCS, vol. 3621, pp. 511–526. Springer, Heidelberg (2005). https://doi.org/10.1007/11535218_31

20. Cohn-Gordon, K., Cremers, C., Gjøsteen, K., Jacobsen, H., Jager, T.: Highly efficient key exchange protocols with optimal tightness. In: Boldyreva, A., Micciancio, D. (eds.) CRYPTO 2019. LNCS, vol. 11694, pp. 767–797. Springer, Cham (2019). https://doi.org/10.1007/978-3-030-26954-8_25

21. Boer, B.: Diffie-Hellman is as strong as discrete log for certain primes. In: Goldwasser, S. (ed.) CRYPTO 1988. LNCS, vol. 403, pp. 530–539. Springer, New York (1990). https://doi.org/10.1007/0-387-34799-2_38

22. Fersch, M., Kiltz, E., Poettering, B.: On the provable security of (EC) DSA signatures. In: Weippl, E.R., Katzenbeisser, S., Kruegel, C., Myers, A.C., Halevi, S. (eds.) ACM CCS 2016, pp. 1651–1662. ACM Press, October 2016

23. Galbraith, S., Paterson, K., Smart, N.: Pairings for cryptographers. Cryptology ePrint Archive, Report 2006/165 (2006). http://eprint.iacr.org/2006/165

24. Galbraith, S.D., Malone-Lee, J., Smart, N.P.: Public key signatures in the multiuser setting. Inf. Process. Lett. **83**(5), 263–266 (2002). https://doi.org/10.1016/S0020-0190(01)00338-6

25. Gay, R., Hofheinz, D., Kiltz, E., Wee, H.: Tightly CCA-secure encryption without pairings. In: Fischlin, M., Coron, J.-S. (eds.) EUROCRYPT 2016. LNCS, vol. 9665, pp. 1–27. Springer, Heidelberg (2016). https://doi.org/10.1007/978-3-662-49890-3_1

26. Gay, R., Hofheinz, D., Kohl, L., Pan, J.: More efficient (almost) tightly secure structure-preserving signatures. In: Nielsen, J.B., Rijmen, V. (eds.) EUROCRYPT 2018. LNCS, vol. 10821, pp. 230–258. Springer, Cham (2018). https://doi.org/10.1007/978-3-319-78375-8_8

27. Gjøsteen, K., Jager, T.: Practical and tightly-secure digital signatures and authenticated key exchange. In: Shacham, H., Boldyreva, A. (eds.) CRYPTO 2018. LNCS, vol. 10992, pp. 95–125. Springer, Cham (2018). https://doi.org/10.1007/978-3-319-96881-0_4

28. Goh, E.J., Jarecki, S., Katz, J., Wang, N.: Efficient signature schemes with tight reductions to the Diffie-Hellman problems. J. Cryptol. **20**(4), 493–514 (2007). https://doi.org/10.1007/s00145-007-0549-3

29. Goldwasser, S., Micali, S., Rivest, R.L.: A digital signature scheme secure against adaptive chosen-message attacks. SIAM J. Comput. **17**(2), 281–308 (1988). https://doi.org/10.1137/0217017

30. Guo, F., Chen, R., Susilo, W., Lai, J., Yang, G., Mu, Y.: Optimal security reductions for unique signatures: bypassing impossibilities with a counterexample. In: Katz, J., Shacham, H. (eds.) CRYPTO 2017. LNCS, vol. 10402, pp. 517–547. Springer, Cham (2017). https://doi.org/10.1007/978-3-319-63715-0_18

31. Hofheinz, D., Jager, T.: Tightly secure signatures and public-key encryption. In: Safavi-Naini, R., Canetti, R. (eds.) CRYPTO 2012. LNCS, vol. 7417, pp. 590–607. Springer, Heidelberg (2012). https://doi.org/10.1007/978-3-642-32009-5_35

32. Hofheinz, D., Kiltz, E.: Programmable hash functions and their applications. In: Wagner, D. (ed.) CRYPTO 2008. LNCS, vol. 5157, pp. 21–38. Springer, Heidelberg (2008). https://doi.org/10.1007/978-3-540-85174-5_2

33. Kakvi, S.A., Kiltz, E.: Optimal security proofs for full domain hash, revisited. In: Pointcheval, D., Johansson, T. (eds.) EUROCRYPT 2012. LNCS, vol. 7237, pp. 537–553. Springer, Heidelberg (2012). https://doi.org/10.1007/978-3-642-29011-4_32

34. Kakvi, S.A., Kiltz, E.: Optimal security proofs for full domain hash, revisited. J. Cryptol. **31**(1), 276–306 (2018). https://doi.org/10.1007/s00145-017-9257-9

35. Katz, J., Wang, N.: Efficiency improvements for signature schemes with tight security reductions. In: Jajodia, S., Atluri, V., Jaeger, T. (eds.) ACM CCS 2003, pp. 155–164. ACM Press, October 2003

36. Kerry, C.F., Director, C.R.: FIPS PUB 186–4 federal information processing standards publication digital signature standard (DSS) (2013)

37. Kiltz, E., Loss, J., Pan, J.: Tightly-secure signatures from five-move identification protocols. In: Takagi, T., Peyrin, T. (eds.) ASIACRYPT 2017. LNCS, vol. 10626, pp. 68–94. Springer, Cham (2017). https://doi.org/10.1007/978-3-319-70700-6_3

38. Kiltz, E., Masny, D., Pan, J.: Optimal security proofs for signatures from identification schemes. In: Robshaw, M., Katz, J. (eds.) CRYPTO 2016. LNCS, vol. 9815, pp. 33–61. Springer, Heidelberg (2016). https://doi.org/10.1007/978-3-662-53008-5_2

39. Maurer, U.M., Wolf, S.: Diffie-Hellman oracles. In: Koblitz, N. (ed.) CRYPTO 1996. LNCS, vol. 1109, pp. 268–282. Springer, Heidelberg (1996). https://doi.org/10.1007/3-540-68697-5_21

40. Micali, S., Reyzin, L.: Improving the exact security of digital signature schemes. J. Cryptol. **15**(1), 1–18 (2002). https://doi.org/10.1007/s00145-001-0005-8

41. Morgan, A., Pass, R.: On the security loss of unique signatures. In: Beimel, A., Dziembowski, S. (eds.) TCC 2018. LNCS, vol. 11239, pp. 507–536. Springer, Cham (2018). https://doi.org/10.1007/978-3-030-03807-6_19

42. Schnorr, C.P.: Efficient signature generation by smart cards. J. Cryptol. **4**(3), 161–174 (1991). https://doi.org/10.1007/BF00196725

43. Wu, G., Lai, J.-C., Guo, F.-C., Susilo, W., Zhang, F.-T.: Tightly secure public-key cryptographic schemes from one-more assumptions. J. Comput. Sci. Technol. **34**(6), 1366–1379 (2019). https://doi.org/10.1007/s11390-019-1980-2

44. Zhang, X., Liu, S., Gu, D., Liu, J.K.: A generic construction of tightly secure signatures in the multi-user setting. Theor. Comput. Sci. **775**, 32–52 (2019). https://doi.org/10.1016/j.tcs.2018.12.012

Biased RSA Private Keys: Origin Attribution of GCD-Factorable Keys

Adam Janovsky[1,2](✉), Matus Nemec[3], Petr Svenda[1], Peter Sekan[1], and Vashek Matyas[1]

[1] Masaryk University, Brno, Czech Republic
adamjanovsky@mail.muni.cz
[2] Invasys, Brno, Czech Republic
[3] Linköping University, Linköping, Sweden

Abstract. In 2016, Švenda et al. (USENIX 2016, The Million-key Question) reported that the implementation choices in cryptographic libraries allow for qualified guessing about the origin of public RSA keys. We extend the technique to two new scenarios when not only public but also private keys are available for the origin attribution – analysis of a source of GCD-factorable keys in IPv4-wide TLS scans and forensic investigation of an unknown source. We learn several representatives of the bias from the private keys to train a model on more than 150 million keys collected from 70 cryptographic libraries, hardware security modules and cryptographic smartcards. Our model not only doubles the number of distinguishable groups of libraries (compared to public keys from Švenda et al.) but also improves more than twice in accuracy w.r.t. random guessing when a single key is classified. For a forensic scenario where at least 10 keys from the same source are available, the correct origin library is correctly identified with average accuracy of 89% compared to 4% accuracy of a random guess. The technique was also used to identify libraries producing GCD-factorable TLS keys, showing that only three groups are the probable suspects.

Keywords: Cryptographic library · RSA factorization · Measurement · RSA key classification · Statistical model

1 Introduction

The ability to attribute a cryptographic key to the library it was generated with is a valuable asset providing direct insight into cryptographic practices. The slight bias found specifically in the primes of RSA private keys generated by the OpenSSL library [14] allowed to track down the devices responsible for keys found in TLS IPv4-wide scans that were in fact factorable by distributed GCD algorithm. Further work [23] made the method generic and showed that many

---

Full details, datasets and paper supplementary material can be found at https://crocs.fi.muni.cz/papers/privrsa_esorics20.

© Springer Nature Switzerland AG 2020
L. Chen et al. (Eds.): ESORICS 2020, LNCS 12309, pp. 505–524, 2020.
https://doi.org/10.1007/978-3-030-59013-0_25

other libraries produce biased keys allowing for the origin attribution. As a result, both separate keys, as well as large datasets, could be analyzed for their origin libraries. The first-ever explicit measurement of cryptographic library popularity was introduced in [18], showing the increasing dominance of the OpenSSL library on the market. Furthermore, very uncommon characteristics of the library used by Infineon smartcards allowed for their entirely accurate classification. Importantly, this led to a discovery that the library is, in fact, producing practically factorable keys [19]. Consequently, more than 20 million of eID certificates with vulnerable keys were revoked just in Europe alone. The same method allowed to identify keys originating from unexpected sources in Estonian eIDs. Eventually, the unexpected keys were shown to be injected from outside instead of being generated on-chip as mandated by the institutional policy [20].

While properties of RSA primes were analyzed to understand the bias detected in public keys, no previous work addressed the origin attribution problem *with* the knowledge of private keys. The reason may sound understandable – while the public keys are readily available in most usage domains, the private keys shall be kept secret, therefore unavailable for such scrutiny. Yet there are at least two important scenarios for their analysis: 1) Tracking sources of GCD-factorable keys from large TLS scans and 2) a forensic identification of black-box devices with the capability to export private keys (e.g., unknown smartcard, remote key generation service, or in-house investigation of cryptographic services). The mentioned case of unexpected keys in Estonian eIDs [20] is a practical example of a forensic scenario, but with the use of public keys only. The analysis based on private keys can spot even a smaller deviance from the expected origin as the bias is observed closer to the place of its inception. This work aims to fill this gap in knowledge by a careful examination of both scenarios.

We first provide a solid coverage of RSA key sources used in the wild by expanding upon the dataset first released in [23]. During our work, we more than doubled the number of keys in the dataset, gathered from over 70 distinct cryptographic software libraries, smartcards, and hardware security modules (HSMs). Benefiting from 158.8 million keys, we study the bias affecting the primes p and q. We transform known biased features of public keys to their private key analogues and evaluate how they cluster sources of RSA keys into groups. We use the features in multiple variants of Bayes classifier that are trained on 157 million keys. Subsequently, we evaluate the performance of our classifiers on further 1.8 million keys isolated from the whole dataset. By doing so, we establish the reliability results for the forensic case of use, when keys from a black-box system are under scrutiny. On average, when looking at just a single key, our best model is able to correctly classify 47% of cases when all libraries are considered and 64.6% keys when the specific sub-domain of smartcards is considered. These results allow for much more precise classification compared to the scenario when only public keys are available.

Finally, we use the best-performing classification method to analyze the dataset of GCD-factorable RSA keys from the IPv4-wide TLS scan collected by Rapid7 [21].

The main contributions of this paper are:

– A systematic mapping of biased features of RSA keys evaluated on a more exhaustive set of cryptographic libraries, described in Sect. 2. The dataset (made publicly available for other researchers) lead to 26 total groups of libraries distinguishable based on the features extracted from the value of RSA private key(s).
– Detailed evaluation of the dataset on Bayes classifiers in Sect. 3 with an average accuracy above 47% where only a single key is available, and almost 90% when ten keys are available.
– An analysis of the narrow domain of cryptographic smartcards and libraries used for TLS results in an even higher accuracy, as shown in Sect. 4.
– Practical analysis of real-world sources of GCD-factorable RSA keys from public TLS servers obtained from internet-wide scans in Sect. 5.

The paper roadmap has been partly outlined above, Sect. 7 then shows related work and Sect. 8 concludes our paper.

2   Bias in RSA Keys

Various design and implementation decisions in the algorithms for generating RSA keys influence the distributions of produced RSA keys. A specific type of bias was used to identify OpenSSL as the origin of a group of private keys [17]. Systematic studies of a wide range of libraries [18,23] described more reasons for biases in RSA keys in a surprising number of libraries. In the majority of cases, the bias was not strong enough to help factor the keys more efficiently. Previous research [23] identified multiple sources of bias that our observations from a large dataset of private RSA keys confirm:

1. **Performance optimizations**, e.g., most significant bits of primes set to a fixed value to obtain RSA moduli of a defined length.
2. **Type of primes**: probable, strong, and provable primes:
    – For probable primes, whether candidate values for primes are chosen randomly or a single starting value is incremented until a prime is found.
    – When generating candidates for probable primes, small factors are avoided in the value of $p-1$ by multiple implementations without explaining.
    – Blum integers are sometimes used for RSA moduli – both RSA primes are congruent to 3 modulo 4.
    – For strong primes, the size of the auxiliary prime factors of $p-1$ and $p+1$ is biased.
    – For provable primes, the recursive algorithm can create new primes of double to triple the binary length of a given prime; usually one version of the algorithm is chosen.
3. **Ordering of primes**: are the RSA primes in private key ordered by size?
4. **Proprietary algorithms**, e.g., the well-documented case of Infineon fast prime key generation algorithm [19].

5. **Bias in the output of a PRNG**: often observable only from a large number of keys from the same source;
6. **Natural properties of primes** that do not depend on the implementation.

2.1 Dataset of RSA Keys

We collected, analyzed, and published the largest dataset of RSA keys with a known origin from 70 libraries (43 open-source libraries, 5 black-box libraries, 3 HSMs, 19 smartcards). We both expanded the datasets from previous work [18,23] and generated new keys from additional libraries for the sake of this study. We processed the keys to a unified format and made them publicly available. Where possible, we analyzed the source code of the cryptographic library to identify the basic properties of key generation according to the list above.

We are primarily interested in 2048-bit keys, what is the most commonly used key length for RSA. As in previous studies [18,23], we also generate shorter keys (512 and 1024 bits) to speed up the process, while verifying that the chosen biased features are not influenced by the key size. This makes the keys of different sizes interchangeable for the sake of our study. We assume that repeatedly running the key generation locally approximates the distributed behaviour of many instances of the same library. This model is supported by the measurements taken in [18] where distributions of keys collected from the Internet exhibited the same biases as locally generated keys.

2.2 Choice of Relevant Biased Features

We extended the features used in previous work on public keys to their equivalent properties of private keys:

Feature '5p and 5q': Instead of the most significant bits of the modulus, we use five most significant bits of the primes p and q. The modulus is defined by the primes, and the primes naturally provide more information. We chose 5 bits based on a frequency analysis of high bits. Further bits are typically not biased and reducing the size of this feature prevents an exponential growth of the feature space.

Feature 'blum': We replaced the feature of second least significant bit of the modulus by the detection of Blum integers. Blum integers can be directly identified using the two prime factors. When only the modulus is available, we can rule out the usage of Blum integers, but not confirm it.

Feature 'mod': Previous work used the result of modulus modulo 3. It was known that primes can be biased modulo small primes (due to avoiding small factors of $p-1$ and $q-1$). The authors only used the value 3, because it is possible to rule out that 3 is being avoided as a factor of $p-1$, when the modulus equals 2 modulo 3 [23]. It is not possible to rule out higher factors from just a single modulus. With the access to the primes we can directly check for this bias for all factors. We detected four categories of such bias, each avoiding all small odd

Dendrogram for all groups

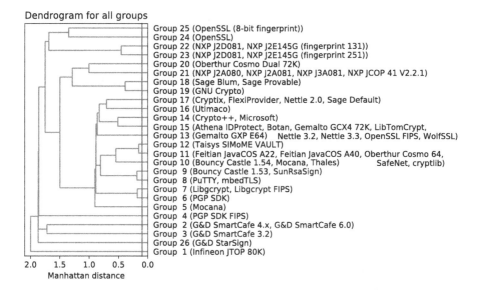

Fig. 1. How the keys from various libraries differ can be depicted by a dendrogram. It tells us, w.r.t. our feature set, how far from each other the probability distributions of the sources are. We can then hierarchically cluster the sources into groups that produce similar keys. The blue line at 0.085 highlights the threshold of differentiating between two sources/groups. This threshold yields 26 groups using our feature set.

prime factors up to a threshold. We use these categories directly by looking at small odd divisors of $p - 1$ and $q - 1$ and note if none were detected: 1) up to 17863, 2) up to 251, 3) up to 5, 4) none – at least one value is divisible by 3.

Feature 'roca': We use a specific fingerprint of factorable Infineon keys published in [19].

2.3   Clustering of Sources into Groups

Since it is impossible to distinguish sources that produce identically distributed keys, we introduce a process of clustering to merge similar sources into groups. We cluster two sources together if they appear to be using identical algorithms based on the observation of the key distributions. We measure the difference in the distributions using the Manhattan distance[1]. The absolute values of the distances depend on the actual distributions of the features. Large distances correlate with significant differences in the implementations. Note, that very

---

[1] We experimented with Euclidean distance and fractional norms. While Euclidean distance is a proper metric, our experiments showed that it is more sensitive to the noise in the data, creating separable groups out of sources that share the same key generation algorithms. On the other hand, fractional norms did not highlight differences between sources that provably differ in the key generation process.

small observed distances may be only the result of noise in the distributions instead of a real difference, e.g., due to a smaller number of keys available.

We attempt to place the clustering threshold as low as possible, maximizing the number of meaningful groups. If we are not able to explain why two clusters are separated based on the study of the algorithms and distributions of the features, the threshold needs to be moved higher to join these clusters. We worked with distributions that assume all features correlated (as in [23]).

The resulting classification groups and the dendrogram is shown in Fig. 1. We placed the threshold value at 0.085. By moving it higher than to 0.154, we would lose the ability to distinguish groups 11 and 12. It would be possible to further split group 14, as there is a slight difference in the prime selection intervals used by Crypto++ and Microsoft [23]. However, the difference manifests less than the level of noise in other sources, requiring the threshold to be put at 0.052, what would create several false groups. We use the same clustering throughout the paper, although the value of the threshold would change when the features change. Note that different versions of the same library may fall into different groups, mostly because of the algorithm changes between these versions. This, for instance, is the case of the Bouncy Castle 1.53, and 1.54.

3   Model Selection and Evaluation

How accurately we can classify the keys depends on several factors, most notably on: the libraries included in the training set, number of keys available for classification, features extracted from the classified keys, and on the classification model. In this section, we focus on the last factor.

3.1   Model Selection

As generating the RSA keys is internally a stochastic process, we choose the family of probabilistic models to address the source attribution problem. Since there is no strong motivation for complex machine learning models, we utilize simple classifiers. More sophisticated classifiers could be built based on our findings when the goal is to reach higher accuracy or to more finely discriminate sources within a group. The rest of this subsection describes the chosen models.

Naïve Bayes Classifier. The first investigated model is a *naïve Bayes classifier*, called naïve because it assumes that the underlying features are conditionally independent. Using this model, we apply the maximum-likelihood decision rule and predict the label as $\hat{y} = \text{argmax}_y P(X = x \mid y)$. Thanks to the naïve assumption, we may decompose this computation into $\hat{y} = \text{argmax}_y \prod_{i=1}^n P(x_i \mid y)$ for the feature vector $x = (x_1, \ldots, x_n)$.

Bayes Classifier. We continue to develop the approach originally used in [23] that used the *Bayes classifier* without the naïve assumption. Several reasons motivate this. First, it allows to evaluate how much the naïve Bayes model suffers from the violated independence assumption (on this specific dataset). Secondly, it enables us to access more precise probability estimates that are needed to classify real-world GCD-factorable keys. Additionally, we can directly compare the classification accuracy of private keys with the case of the public keys from [23]. However, one of the main drawbacks of the Bayes classifier is that it requires exponentially more data with the growing number of features. Therefore, when striving for high accuracy achievable by further feature engineering, one should consider the naïve Bayes instead.

Naïve Bayes Classifier with Cross-Features. The third investigated option is the naïve Bayes classifier, but we merged selected features that are known to be correlated into a single feature. In particular, we merged the features of the most significant bits (of p, q) into a single cross-feature. Subsequently, the naïve Bayes approach is used. This enables us to evaluate whether merging clearly interdependent features into one will affect the performance of naïve Bayes classifier w.r.t. this specific dataset.

3.2   Model Evaluation

Methodology of Classification and Metrics. Our training dataset contains 157 million keys and the test set contains 1.8 million keys. We derived the test set by discarding 10 thousand keys of each source from the complete dataset before clustering. This assures that each group has the test set with at least 10 thousand keys. Accordingly, since the groups differ in the number of sources involved, the resulting test dataset is imbalanced. For this reason, we employ the metrics of precision and recall when possible. However, we represent the model performance by accuracy measure in the tables and in more complex classification scenarios.

For *group X*, the precision can be understood as a fraction of correctly classified keys from *group X* divided by the number of keys that were marked as *group X* by our classifier. Similarly, the recall is a fraction of correctly classified keys from *group X* divided by a total number of keys from *group X* [11]. We also evaluate the performance of the models under the assumption that the user has a *batch* of several keys from the same source at hand. This scenario can arise, e.g., when a security audit is run in an organization and all keys are being tested. Furthermore, to react to some often misclassified groups, we additionally provide the answer "this key originates from *group X* or *group Y*" to the user (and we evaluate the confidence of these answers).

Table 1. Performance comparison of different models on the dataset with all libraries. Note that the precision of a random guess classifier is 3.8% when considering 26 groups.

Model	Avg. precision	Avg. recall
Bayes classifier	43.2%	47.6%
Naïve Bayes classifier	40.9%	46.2%
Cross-feature naïve B	41.7%	47.6%

Comparison of the Models. The overall comparison of all three models can be seen in Table 1. If the precision for some group is undefined, i.e., no key is allegedly originating from this group, we say that the precision is 0. We evaluate the naïve Bayes classifier on the same features that were used for Bayes classifier to measure how much classification performance is lost by introducing the feature independence assumption. A typical example of interdependent features is that the most significant bits of primes p and q are intentionally correlated to preserve the expected length of the resulting modulus n. Pleasantly, the observed precision (recall) decrease is only 2.3% (1.4%) when compared to the Bayes classifier. Accordingly, this suggests that a larger number of different features than usable with the Bayes classifier (due to exponential growth in complexity) can be considered when the naïve Bayes classifier is used. As a result, further improvement of the performance might be achieved, despite ignoring the dependencies among features. Overall, the Bayes classifier shows the best results. When a single key is classified, the average success rate for the 26 groups is captured by precision of 43.2% and a recall of 47.6%. Still, there is a wide variance between the performance in specific groups. A detailed table of results together with a discussion is presented in Appendix A.

4   Classification with Prior Information

Section 2 outlined the process of choosing a threshold value that determines the critical distance for distinguishing between distinct groups. Inevitably, the same threshold value directly influences the number of groups after the clustering task. As such, the threshold introduces a trade-off between the model performance and the number of discriminated groups. The smaller the difference between group distributions is, the more they are similar, and the model performance is lower as more misclassification errors occur. The objective of this section is to examine the classification scenario when some prior knowledge is available to the analyst, limiting the origin of keys to only a subset of all libraries or increase the likelihood of some. Since Sect. 3 showed that the Bayes classifier provides the best performance, this chapter considers only this model.

Prior knowledge can be introduced into the classification process in multiple ways, e.g., by using a prior probability vector that considers some groups more prevalent. We also note that the measurement method of [18] can be used to obtain such prior information, but a relatively large dataset (around 10^5 private keys) is required that may not be available. Our work, therefore, considers a different setting when some sources of the keys are ruled-out *before* the classifier is constructed. Such scenario arises e.g., when the analyst knows that the scrutinized keys were generated in an unknown cryptographic smartcard. In such case, HSMs and other sources of keys can thus be omitted from the model altogether what will arguably increase the performance of the classification process. Another example is leaving out libraries that were released after the classified data sample was collected.

Table 2. Bayes classifier performance on three analyzed partitionings of the dataset – complete dataset with all libraries (*All libraries*), smartcards only (*Smartcards domain*), libraries and HSMs expected to be used for TLS (*TLS domain*) and specific subset of TLS domain where only single prime is available due to the nature of results obtained by GCD factorization method (*Single-prime TLS domain*). Comparison with the random guess as a baseline is provided (here, accuracy equals precision and recall).

Dataset	Avg. precision	Avg. recall	Random guess (baseline)
All libraries	43.2%	47.6%	3.8%
Smartcards domain	61.9%	64.6%	8.3%
TLS domain	45.5%	42.2%	7.7%
Single-prime TLS domain	28.8%	36.2%	11.1%

We present the classification performance results for three scenarios with a limited number of sources – 1) cryptographic smartcards (Sect. 4.1), 2) sources likely to be used in the TLS domain (Sect. 4.2) and 3) a specific case of GCD-factorable keys from the TLS domain, where only one out of two primes can be used for classification (see Sect. 4.3 for more details). The comparison of models for these scenarios can be seen in Table 2.

To compute these models we first, discard the sources that cannot be the origin of the examined keys according to the prior knowledge of the domain (e.g., smartcards are not expected in TLS). Next, we re-compute the clustering task to obtain fewer groups than on the dataset with all libraries. Finally, we compute the classification tables for the reduced domain and evaluate the performance.

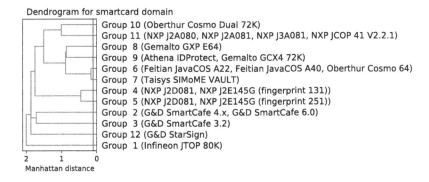

Fig. 2. The clustering of smartcard sources yields 12 separate groups.

4.1   Performance in the Smartcards Domain

The clustering task in the smartcards domain yields 12 recognizable groups for 19 different smartcard models as shown in Fig. 2. The training set for this limited domain contains 20.6 million keys, whereas the test set contains 340 thousand keys. On average, 61.9% precision and 64.6% recall is achieved. Moreover, 8 out of 12 groups achieve > 50% precision. Additionally, the classifier exhibits 100% recall on 3 specific groups: a) Infineon smartcards (before 2017 with the ROCA vulnerability [19]), b) G&D Smartcafe 4.x and 6.0, and c) newer G&D Smartcafe 7.0. Figure 3 shows so-called confusion matrix where each row corresponds to percentage of keys in an actual group while each column represents percentage of keys in a predicted group.

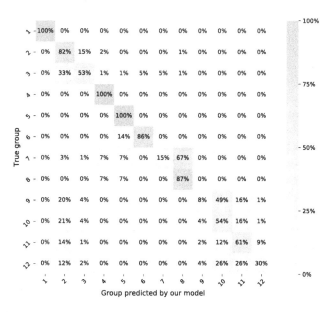

Fig. 3. The confusion matrix for the classifier of a single private key generated in the smartcards domain. A given row corresponds to a vector of observed relative frequencies with which keys generated by a specific group (True group) are misclassified as generated by other groups (Group predicted by our model). For example, group 1 and group 2 have no misclassifications (high accuracy), while keys of group 3 are in 33% cases misclassified as keys from group 2. On average, we achieve 64.6% accuracy. The darker the cell is, the higher number it contains. This holds for all figures in this paper.

As expected, the results represent an improvement when compared to the dataset with all libraries. When one has ten keys of the same card at hand, the expected recall is over 90% on 10 out of 12 groups. The full table of results can be found in the project repository.

Interestingly, 512- and 1024-bit keys generated by the same NXP J2E145G card (similarly also for NXP J2D081) fall into different groups[2]. The main difference is in the modular fingerprint (avoidance of small factors in $p-1$ and $q-1$). We hypothesize that on-card key generation avoids more small factors for

---

[2] This is an exception to the observation that the selected features behave independently of key length. Otherwise, keys of different length can be used interchangeably.

larger keys. Such behaviour was not observed for other libraries but highlights the necessity of collecting different key lengths in the training dataset when one analyzes black-box proprietary devices or closed-source software libraries.

To summarize, the classification of private keys generated by smartcards is very accurate due to the significant differences resulting from the proprietary, embedded implementations among the different vendors. The differences observed likely results from the requirements to have a smaller footprint required by low-resources devices.

4.2 Performance in the TLS Domain

For the TLS domain, we excluded all the libraries and devices unlikely to be used to generate keys then used by TLS servers. All smartcards are excluded, together with highly outdated or purpose-specific libraries like PGP SDK 4. All hardware security modules (HSMs) are present as they may be used as TLS accelerators or high-security key storage. Summarized, we started with 17 separate cryptographic libraries and HSMs, inspected in a total of 134 versions. The clustering resulted in 13 recognizable groups as shown in Fig. 4.

The domain training set contains 121.8 million keys and the test set contains 1.3 million keys. On average, the classifier achieves 45.5% precision and 42.2% recall. The decrease in average recall compared to the full domain may look surprising, but averaging is deceiving in this context. In fact, recall improved for 10 out of 13 groups that are both in the full set and the TLS domain set, with the precision improving for 9 groups. The mean values of the full dataset are being uplifted by a generally better performance of the model outside the TLS domain. Five groups have >50% precision. OpenSSL (by far the most popular library used by servers for TLS [18]) has 100% recall, making the classification of OpenSSL keys very reliable. Complete results can be found in the project repository.

To summarize, we correctly classify more keys in a more specific TLS domain than with the full dataset classifier. Additionally, the user can be more confident about the decisions of the TLS-specific classifier.

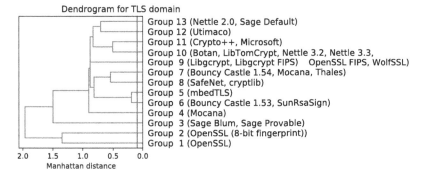

Fig. 4. The clustering of the sources from the TLS domain yields 13 separate groups.

4.3 Performance in the Single-Prime TLS Domain

The rest of this section is motivated by a setting when one wants to analyze a batch of correlated keys. Specifically, we assume a case of $k \geq 1$ keys $(p_1, q_1), \ldots, (p_k, q_k)$ generated by the same source, where $p_1 = p_2 = \cdots = p_k$. This scenario emerges in Sect. 5 and cannot be addressed by previously considered classifiers. If applied, the results would be drastically skewed since the classifier would consider each of p_i separately, putting half of the weight on the shared prime. For that reason, we train a classifier that works on single primes rather than on complete private keys. Instead of feeding the classifier with a batch of k private keys, we supply it with a batch of $k + 1$ unique primes from those keys. The selected features were modified accordingly: we extract the 5 most significant bits from the unique prime, its second least significant bit, and compute the ROCA and modular fingerprint for the single prime. We trained the classifier on the learning set limited to the TLS domain, as in Sect. 4.2.

On average, we achieve 28.8% precision and 36.2% recall when classifying a single prime. Table 3 shows the accuracy results in more detail. It should, however, be stressed that this classifier is meant to be used for batches of many keys at once. When considering a batch of $k \geq 10$ primes, the accuracy is more than 77%. The decrease in accuracy compared to Sect. 4.2 can be explained by the loss of information from the second prime. The features **mod** and **blum** are much less reliable when using only one prime. Since we can compute the most significant bits from a single prime at a time, we lost the information about the ordering of primes (since features **5p** and **5q** are correlated). These facts resulted in only nine separate groups of libraries being distinguishable. The following groups from the TLS domain are no longer mutually distinguishable: 5 and 13, 7 and 11, 8 and 9 and 10.

4.4 Methodology Limitations

The presented methodology has several limitations:

Table 3. Classification accuracy for single-prime features evaluated on TLS domain.

Number of primes in a batch	1	10	20	30	100
Group 1	100.0%	100.0%	100.0%	100.0%	100.0%
Group 2	42.8%	99.7%	100.0%	100.0%	100.0%
Group 3	78.0%	100.0%	100.0%	100.0%	100.0%
Group 4	47.5%	90.3%	95.8%	98.7%	100.0%
Group 5|13	1.8%	30.8%	43.7%	51.8%	74.7%
Group 6	5.2%	48.9%	61.0%	64.8%	76.7%
Group 7|11	0.0%	67.3%	92.3%	97.4%	100.0%
Group 8|9|10	37.9%	99.9%	100.0%	100.0%	100.0%
Group 12	12.8%	61.8%	77.7%	83.9%	97.2%
Average	**36.2%**	77.6%	85.6%	88.5%	94.3%

Classification of an Unseen Source. Not all existing sources of RSA keys are present in our dataset for clustering analysis and classification. This means that attempting to classify a key from a source not considered in our study will bring unpredictable results. The new source may either populate some existing group or have a unique implementation, thus creating a new group. In both cases, the behaviour of the classifier is unpredictable.

Granularity of the Classifier. There are multiple libraries in a single group. The user is therefore not shown the exact source of the key, but the whole group instead. This limitation has two main reasons: 1) Some sources share the same implementation and thus cannot be told apart. 2) The list of utilized features is narrow. There are infinitely many possible features in principle and some may hide valuable information that can further help the model performance. Nevertheless, the proposed methodology allows for an automatic evaluation of features using the naïve Bayes method which shall be considered in future work.

Human Factor. The clustering task in our study requires human knowledge. To be specific, the value of the threshold that splits the libraries into groups (for a particular feature) is established only semi-automatically. We manually confirmed the threshold – when we could explain the difference between the libraries, or moved it otherwise. Summarized, this complicates the fully automatic evaluation on a large number of potential features. Once solved, the relative importance of the individual features could be measured.

5   Real-World GCD-Factorable Keys Origin Investigation

Previous research [2,13,14,16] demonstrated that a non-trivial fraction of RSA keys used on publicly reachable TLS servers is generated insecurely and is practically factorable. This is because the affected network devices were found to independently generate RSA keys that share a single prime or both primes. While an efficient factorization algorithm for RSA moduli is unknown, when two keys accidentally share one prime, the efficient factorization is possible using the Euclidean algorithm to find their GCD[3]. Still, the current number of public keys obtained from crawling TLS servers is too high to allow for the investigation of all possible pairs. However, the distributed GCD algorithm [15] allows analyzing hundreds of millions of keys efficiently. Its performance was sufficient to analyze all keys collected from IPv4-wide TLS scans [5,21] and resulted in almost 1% of factorable keys in the scans collected at the beginning of the year 2016.

After the detection of GCD-factorable keys, the question of their origin naturally followed. Previous research addressed it using two principal approaches: 1) an analysis of the information extractable from the certificates of GCD-factorable keys, and 2) matching specific properties of factored primes with primes generated by a suspected library – OpenSSL. The first approach allowed to detect a range of network routers that seeded their PRNG shortly after boot without

---

[3] Note that the keys sharing both primes are not susceptible to this attack but reveal their private keys to all other owners of the same RSA key pair.

enough entropy, what caused them to occasionally generate a prime shared with another device. These routers contained a customized version of the OpenSSL library, what was confirmed with the second approach, since OpenSSL code intentionally avoids small factors of $p - 1$ as shown by [17].

While this suite of routers was clearly the primary source of the GCD-factorable keys, are they the sole source of insecure keys? The paper [13] identified 23 router/device vendors that used the code of OpenSSL (using specific OpenSSL fingerprint based on avoidance of small factors in $p - 1$ and information extracted from the certificates). Eight other vendors (DrayRek, Fortinet, Huawei, Juniper, Kronos, Siemens, Xerox, and ZyXEL) produced keys without such OpenSSL fingerprint, and the underlying libraries remained unidentified. In the rest of this section, we build upon the prior work to identify probable sources of the GCD-factorable keys that *do not* originate from the OpenSSL library.

Two assumptions must be met to employ the classifier studied in Sect. 4.3. First, we assume that *when a batch of GCD-factored keys shares a prime, they were all generated by sources from a single classification group*. This conjecture is suggested in [13,14] and supported by the fact that when distinct libraries differ in their prime generation algorithm, they will produce different primes even when initialized from the same seed. On the other hand, when they share the same generation algorithm, they inevitably fall into the same classification group. Second, we assume that *if the malformed keys share only single prime, the PRNG was reseeded with enough entropy before the second prime got generated*. This is suggested by the failure model studied for OpenSSL in [14] and implies that the second prime is generated as it normally would be.

Leveraging these conjectures, the rest of this section tracks the libraries responsible for GCD-factorable keys while not relying on the information in the certificates. First, we describe the dataset gathering process, as well as the factorization of the RSA public keys. Later, successfully factored keys are analyzed, followed with a discussion of findings.

6   Datasets of GCD-Factorable TLS Keys

The input dataset with public RSA keys (both secure and vulnerable ones) was obtained from the Rapid7 archive. All scans between October 2013 and July 2019 (mostly in one or two weeks period) were downloaded and processed, resulting in slightly over 170 million certificates. Only public RSA keys were extracted, and duplicates removed, resulting in 112 million unique moduli. On this dataset, the *fastgcd* [15] tool based on [3] was used to factorize the moduli into private keys. A detailed methodology of this procedure is discussed in Appendix B.

6.1   Batching of GCD-Factorable Keys

Would the precision and recall of our classifier be 100%, one could process the factored keys one by one, establish their origin library and thus detect all sources of insecure keys. But since the classification accuracy of the single-prime TLS classifier[4] with a single key is only 36%, we apply three adjustments: 1) batch the GCD-factorable keys sharing the same prime (believed to be produced by the same library); 2) analyze only the batches with at least 10 keys (therefore with high expected accuracy); 3) limit the set of the libraries considered for classification only to the single-prime TLS domain. Since the keys from the OpenSSL library were already extensively analyzed by [13], we use the **mod** feature to reliably mark and exclude them from further analysis. By doing so, we concentrate primarily on the non-OpenSSL keys that were not yet attributed. The exact process for classification of factored keys in batches is as follows:

1. Factorize public keys from a target dataset (e.g., Rapid7) using *fastgcd* tool.
2. Form batches of factored keys that share a prime and assume that they originate from the same classification group.
3. Select only the batches with at least k keys (e.g., 10).
4. Separate batches of keys that all carry the OpenSSL fingerprint. As a control experiment, they should classify only to a group with the OpenSSL library.
5. Separate batches without the OpenSSL fingerprint. This cluster contains yet unidentified libraries.
6. Classify the non-OpenSSL cluster using a single-prime TLS classifier.

6.2   Source Libraries Detected in GCD-Factorable TLS Keys

In total, we analyzed more than 82 thousand primes divided into 2511 batches. While each batch has at least 10 keys in it, the median of the batch size is 15. Among the batches, 88.8% of them exhibit the OpenSSL fingerprint. This number well confirms the previous finding by [13] that also captured the OpenSSL-specific fingerprint in a similar fraction of keys. We attribute three other batches as coming from the OpenSSL (8-bit fingerprint), an OpenSSL library compiled to test and avoid divisors of $p-1$ only up to 251. Importantly, slightly more than 11% of batches were generated by some library from groups 8, 9, or 10, which are not mutually distinguishable when only a single prime is available. There are also negative results to report. With the accuracy over 80% (for a batch size of

Table 4. Keys that share a prime factor belong to the same batch. Classification of most batches resulted in OpenSSL as the likely source. The rest of the batches were likely generated by libraries in the combined group 8 | 9 | 10.

Group(s)	# batches
1 (OpenSSL)	2230
2 (8-bit OpenSSL)	3
8 | 9 | 10 (various libraries, see Fig. 4)	278
3; 4; 6; 12; 5 | 13; 7 | 11	0 (*improbable*)

---

[4] Note that without using single-prime model, the results are biased as the shared prime is considered multiple times in the classification process.

15) and no batches attributed to any of groups 3, 4, 6, 12, 5 | 13, or 7 | 11, it is very improbable that any GCD-factorable keys originate from the respective sources in these libraries (Table 4).

7 Related Work

The fingerprinting of devices based on their physical characteristics, exposed interfaces, behaviour in non-standard or undefined situations, errors returned, and a wide range of various other side-channels is a well-researched area. The experience shows that finding a case of a non-standard behaviour is usually possible, while making a group of devices indistinguishable is very difficult due to an almost infinite number of observable characteristics, resulting in an arms race between the device manufacturers and fingerprinting observers.

Having the device fingerprinted is helpful to better understand the complex ecosystem like quantifying the presence of interception middle-boxes on the internet [9], types of clients connected or version of the operating system. Differences may help point out subverted supply chains or counterfeit products.

When applied to the study of cryptographic keys and cryptographic libraries, researchers devised a range of techniques to analyze the fraction of encrypted connections, the prevalence of particular cryptographic algorithms, the chosen key lengths or cipher suites [1,2,4,8,10,12,24]. Information about a particular key is frequently obtained from the metadata of its certificate.

Periodical network scans allow to assess the impact of security flaws in practice. The population of OpenSSL servers with the Heartbleed vulnerability was measured and monitored by [7], and real attempts to exploit the bug were surveyed. If the necessary information is coincidentally collected and archived, even a backward introspection of a vulnerability in time might be possible.

The simple test for the ROCA vulnerability in public RSA keys allowed to measure the fraction of citizens of Estonia who held an electronic ID supported by a vulnerable smartcard, by inspecting the public repository of eID certificates [19]. The fingerprinting of keys from smartcards was used to detect that private keys were generated outside of the card and injected later into the eIDs, despite the requirement to have all keys generated on-card [20].

The attribution of the public RSA key to its origin library was analyzed by [23]. Measurements on large datasets were presented in [18], leading to accurate estimation of the fraction of cryptographic libraries used in large datasets like IPv4-wide TLS. While both [23] and [18] analyze the public keys, private keys can be also obtained under certain conditions of faulty random number generator [6,13,14,16,22]. The origin of weak factorable keys needs to be identified in order to notify the maintainers of the code to fix underlying issues. A combination of key properties and values from certificates was used.

8 Conclusions

We provide what we believe is the first wide examination of properties of RSA keys with the goal of attribution of private key to its origin library.

The attribution is applicable in multiple scenarios, e.g., to the analysis of GCD-factorable keys in the TLS domain. We investigated the properties of keys as generated by 70 cryptographic libraries, identified biased features in the primes produced, and compared three models based on Bayes classifiers for the private key attribution.

The information available in private keys significantly increases the classification performance compared to the result achieved on public keys [23]. Our work enables to distinguish 26 groups of sources (compared to 13 on public keys) while increasing the accuracy more than twice w.r.t. random guessing. When 100 keys are available for the classification, the correct result is almost always provided (>99%) for 19 out of 26 groups.

Finally, we designed a method usable also for a dataset of keys where one prime is significantly correlated. Such primes are found in GCD-factorable TLS keys where one prime was generated with insufficient randomness and would introduce a high classification error in the unmodified method. As a result, we can identify libraries responsible for the production of these GCD-factorable keys, showing that only three groups are a relevant source of such keys. The accurate classification can be easily incorporated in forensic and audit tools.

While the bias in the keys usually does not help with factorization, the cryptographic libraries should approach their key generation design with a great care, as strong bias can lead to weak keys [19]. We recommend to follow a key generation process with as little bias present as possible.

Acknowledgements. The authors would like to thank anonymous reviewers for their helpful comments. P. Svenda and V. Matyas were supported by Czech Science Foundation project GA20-03426S. Some of the tools used and other people involved were supported by the CyberSec4Europe Competence Network. Computational resources were supplied by the project e-INFRA LM2018140. This work was partially supported by the Wallenberg AI, Autonomous Systems and Software Program (WASP) funded by the Knut and Alice Wallenberg Foundation.

A   Classifier Results Discussion and Datasets Preparation

Some groups are accurately classified and rarely misclassified even with a single key available: namely group 1 (Infineon prior 2017, distinct because of the ROCA fingerprint), group 2 (Giesecke&Devrient SmartCafe 4.x and 6.0), group 24 (standard OpenSSL *without* the FIPS module enabled) and group 26 (Giesecke&Devrient SmartCafe 7.0) are all classified with more than 96% recall. Groups 1, 2, and 26 are rarely misclassified as origin library (false positive). The keys from group 25 (OpenSSL avoiding only 8-bit small factors in $p - 1$) are misclassified as group 24 (standard OpenSSL) in 31.6% cases, which still identifies the origin library correctly, only misidentifies the OpenSSL compile-time configuration.

In contrast, keys from groups 7, 10, 11, 14, 15, and 17 are almost always misclassified (less than 8% recall, some even less than 1%). However, as dis-

Table 5. The average classification accuracy of the best performing Bayes classifier. In the i-th column we consider a classifier successful if the true source of the key is among i best guesses of our model. Similarly, for each of the 3 columns we evaluate the success rate when $1, 2, 3, 5$ or 10 keys from the same group are available.

#keys in batch	Top 1 match					Top 2 match					Top 3 match				
	1	2	3	5	10	1	2	3	5	10	1	2	3	5	10
Group 1	100.0%	100.0%	100.0%	100.0%	100.0%	100.0%	100.0%	100.0%	100.0%	100.0%	100.0%	100.0%	100.0%	100.0%	100.0%
Group 2	100.0%	100.0%	100.0%	100.0%	100.0%	100.0%	100.0%	100.0%	100.0%	100.0%	100.0%	100.0%	100.0%	100.0%	100.0%
Group 3	86.3%	98.1%	99.8%	100.0%	100.0%	98.2%	100.0%	100.0%	100.0%	100.0%	98.2%	100.0%	100.0%	100.0%	100.0%
Group 4	92.7%	99.3%	99.9%	100.0%	100.0%	94.8%	99.7%	100.0%	100.0%	100.0%	96.4%	99.9%	100.0%	100.0%	100.0%
Group 5	60.8%	76.3%	79.8%	99.9%	96.6%	71.5%	90.1%	93.6%	98.7%	99.9%	73.0%	91.3%	97.6%	98.8%	100.0%
Group 6	73.0%	88.1%	88.5%	83.5%	69.8%	92.8%	92.8%	97.7%	98.2%	99.9%	96.5%	97.0%	99.5%	99.8%	100.0%
Group 7	7.6%	18.9%	30.0%	47.9%	73.6%	77.3%	95.5%	98.8%	99.9%	100.0%	92.7%	99.3%	99.9%	100.0%	100.0%
Group 8	16.3%	33.5%	44.2%	54.6%	62.8%	27.5%	56.2%	73.5%	91.3%	99.2%	38.6%	63.9%	81.7%	94.2%	99.5%
Group 9	12.8%	28.3%	38.9%	50.9%	61.1%	37.7%	65.7%	79.1%	90.4%	99.0%	48.3%	75.9%	87.8%	96.8%	99.8%
Group 10	0.0%	24.7%	47.7%	67.9%	92.0%	18.4%	44.1%	60.8%	79.8%	96.1%	52.7%	87.6%	92.5%	98.5%	100.0%
Group 11	6.9%	21.8%	34.2%	51.6%	63.1%	56.7%	87.2%	95.9%	99.4%	100.0%	73.2%	95.2%	99.2%	100.0%	100.0%
Group 12	54.9%	75.4%	78.2%	71.5%	65.8%	72.2%	85.0%	95.4%	98.1%	100.0%	89.5%	95.7%	99.0%	99.8%	100.0%
Group 13	47.2%	57.0%	69.6%	84.8%	96.3%	52.9%	68.6%	80.9%	93.8%	99.5%	66.4%	82.9%	91.4%	98.0%	99.8%
Group 14	6.9%	22.4%	40.8%	70.5%	93.6%	7.7%	41.0%	69.7%	90.8%	99.3%	12.4%	53.7%	78.9%	95.4%	99.9%
Group 15	0.2%	28.0%	52.7%	80.0%	96.5%	2.5%	43.4%	65.4%	90.2%	99.4%	28.2%	64.6%	81.0%	94.4%	99.7%
Group 16	31.4%	63.6%	79.4%	91.1%	99.4%	40.9%	70.6%	85.4%	96.5%	100.0%	48.3%	80.0%	92.1%	98.8%	100.0%
Group 17	5.1%	28.6%	50.2%	78.0%	97.6%	18.3%	51.2%	71.9%	92.0%	99.7%	37.7%	73.0%	89.0%	98.1%	100.0%
Group 18	12.2%	55.1%	70.5%	78.5%	84.7%	45.2%	91.0%	98.2%	100.0%	100.0%	76.3%	96.1%	99.4%	100.0%	100.0%
Group 19	44.0%	54.4%	59.7%	67.3%	78.5%	54.5%	88.3%	97.3%	99.9%	100.0%	62.1%	93.8%	99.1%	100.0%	100.0%
Group 20	81.5%	95.2%	98.7%	99.9%	100.0%	97.2%	100.0%	100.0%	100.0%	100.0%	98.9%	100.0%	100.0%	100.0%	100.0%
Group 21	53.0%	77.9%	88.4%	97.0%	99.9%	95.2%	99.7%	100.0%	100.0%	100.0%	97.6%	100.0%	100.0%	100.0%	100.0%
Group 22	14.6%	39.2%	53.5%	72.5%	92.3%	78.0%	98.2%	99.8%	100.0%	100.0%	97.2%	99.9%	100.0%	100.0%	100.0%
Group 23	77.4%	98.0%	99.9%	100.0%	100.0%	96.8%	99.9%	100.0%	100.0%	100.0%	100.0%	100.0%	100.0%	100.0%	100.0%
Group 24	96.8%	99.9%	100.0%	100.0%	100.0%	100.0%	100.0%	100.0%	100.0%	100.0%	100.0%	100.0%	100.0%	100.0%	100.0%
Group 25	58.3%	86.7%	96.1%	99.7%	100.0%	87.6%	97.9%	99.6%	100.0%	100.0%	93.9%	99.7%	100.0%	100.0%	100.0%
Group 26	100.0%	100.0%	100.0%	100.0%	100.0%	100.0%	100.0%	100.0%	100.0%	100.0%	100.0%	100.0%	100.0%	100.0%	100.0%
Average	**47.7%**	64.2%	73.1%	82.2%	89.4%	**66.3%**	83.3%	90.9%	96.9%	99.7%	**76.1%**	90.4%	95.7%	98.9%	100.0%

cussed in the next section, if some additional information is available and can be considered, this misclassification can be largely remediated.

Keys from group 7 (Libgcrypt) are mostly misclassified as group 6 (PGP SDK 4, 64.5%) or group 13 (Gemalto GXP E64, 20.2%). As libgcrypt is a commonly used library while groups 6 and 13 correspond to a very old library and card, this case demonstrates the possibility for further classifier improvement when some prior knowledge is available. E.g., for the TLS domain, groups corresponding to old smartcards or non-TLS libraries can be ruled out from the process.

Group 10 (Bouncy Castle since 1.54, Mocana 7.x or HSM Thales nShieldF3) is misclassified as group 12 (smartcard Taisys SIMoME, 36.3%) or group 5 (Mocana 6.x 21.0%). Additional information can improve classification accuracy as the Taisys smartcard is unlikely source for the most usage domains. If Mocana library actually generated the key, only the identified version is incorrect.

Group 11 (cryptlib, Safenet HSM Luna SA-1700, and Feitian and Oberthur cards) is misclassified as group 12 (smartcard Taisys, 50.2%) or group 20 (Oberthur Cosmo Dual, 20.4%). This is a very similar case as for group 10.

Group 14 (Microsoft and Crypto++, prevalent group) is misclassified as group 6 (PGP SDK 4, 23.9%), group 12 (card Taisys, 20.1%), group 13 (card Gemalto GXP E64, 13.5%) or group 5 (Mocana 6.x, 10.7%). Again, for the TLS domain, the only real misclassification problem is with the Mocana 6.x library.

Group 15 (large group with multiple frequently used libraries) is misclassified as group 12 (card Taisys, 27.2%), group 13 (card Gemalto GXP E64, 18.1%), group 20 (card Oberthur, 11.7%) or group 6 (PGP SDK 4, 32.3%). For the TLS domain, no group from the misclassified ones is likely.

Group 17 (Nettle, Cryptix, FlexiProvider) is misclassified as multiple other groups where only groups 5 (Mocana 6.x) and 9 (Bouncy Castle prior 1.54 and SunRsaSign OpenJDK 1.8) cannot be ruled out as unlikely for the TLS domain (Table 5).

B   Obtaining Dataset of GCD-Factorable Keys

The *fastgcd* [15] tool based on [3] was used to perform the search for the GCD-factorable keys. Only valid RSA keys were considered[5]. Running the *fastgcd* tool for a high number of keys (around 112 million for Rapid7 dataset) requires an extensive amount of RAM. Running the tool on a machine with 500 GB of RAM resulted in only a few factored keys, all sharing just tiny factors, while the tool did not produce any errors or warnings. The same computation on a subset of 10 million keys revealed a substantial number of large factors. Likely, the *fastgcd* tool requires even more RAM for the correct functioning with such a large number of keys. To solve the problem, we partitioned the time-ordered dataset into two subsets of 50 and 62 million keys with an additional third subset with 50 million keys that partially overlapped both previous partitions. By doing so, we miss GCD-factorable keys that appeared in the dataset separated by a considerable time distance (2–3 years). We hypothesise that if a prevalent source starts producing GCD-factorable keys, we capture a sufficiently large batch of them within a single subset. In total, we have acquired 114 thousand unique factors from the whole dataset.

References

1. Albrecht, M.R., Degabriele, J.P., Hansen, T.B., Paterson, K.G.: A surfeit of SSH cipher suites. In: Proceedings of the 2016 ACM SIGSAC Conference on Computer and Communications Security, pp. 1480–1491. ACM (2016)
2. Barbulescu, M., Stratulat, A., Traista-Popescu, V., Simion, E.: RSA weak public keys available on the internet. In: Bica, I., Reyhanitabar, R. (eds.) SECITC 2016. LNCS, vol. 10006, pp. 92–102. Springer, Cham (2016). https://doi.org/10.1007/978-3-319-47238-6_6
3. Bernstein, D.J.: How to find smooth parts of integers (2004). [cit. 2020-07-13]. http://cr.yp.to/papers.html#smoothpart
4. Cangialosi, F., et al.: Measurement and analysis of private key sharing in the https ecosystem. In: Proceedings of the 2016 ACM SIGSAC Conference on Computer and Communications Security, pp. 628–640. ACM (2016)
5. Censys: Censys TLS Full IPv4 443 Scan (2015). [cit. 2020-07-13]. https://censys.io/data/443-https-tls-full_ipv4/historical
6. Batch-GCDing Github SSH Keys (2015). [cit. 2020-07-13]. https://cryptosense.com/batch-gcding-github-ssh-keys/

---

[5] The factorization occasionally finds small prime factors up to 2^{16}, likely because the public key (certificate) was damaged, e.g., by a bit flip.

7. Durumeric, Z., et al.: The matter of heartbleed. In: Proceedings of the 2014 Conference on Internet Measurement Conference, pp. 475–488. ACM (2014)
8. Durumeric, Z., Kasten, J., Bailey, M., Halderman, J.A.: Analysis of the HTTPS certificate ecosystem. In: Proceedings of the 2013 ACM Internet Measurement Conference, pp. 291–304. ACM (2013)
9. Durumeric, Z., et al.: The security impact of https interception. In: Network and Distributed Systems Symposium. The Internet Society (2017)
10. Electronic Frontier Foundation: The EFF SSL Observatory (2010). [cit. 2020–07-13]. https://www.eff.org/observatory
11. Flach, P.: Machine Learning: The Art and Science of Algorithms that Make Sense of Data, Chap. 2, pp. 57–58. Camridge University Press (2012)
12. Gustafsson, J., Overier, G., Arlitt, M., Carlsson, N.: A first look at the CT landscape: certificate transparency logs in practice. In: Kaafar, M.A., Uhlig, S., Amann, J. (eds.) PAM 2017. LNCS, vol. 10176, pp. 87–99. Springer, Cham (2017). https://doi.org/10.1007/978-3-319-54328-4_7
13. Hastings, M., Fried, J., Heninger, N.: Weak keys remain widespread in network devices. In: Proceedings of the 2016 ACM on Internet Measurement Conference, pp. 49–63. ACM (2016)
14. Heninger, N., Durumeric, Z., Wustrow, E., Halderman, J.A.: Mining your Ps and Qs: detection of widespread weak keys in network devices. In: Proceeding of USENIX Security Symposium, pp. 205–220. USENIX (2012)
15. Heninger, N., Halderman, J.A.: Fastgcd (2015). [cit. 2020-07-13]. https://github.com/sagi/fastgcd
16. Lenstra, A.K., Hughes, J.P., Augier, M., Bos, J.W., Kleinjung, T., Wachter, C.: Ron was wrong, whit is right. Cryptology ePrint Archive, Report 2012/064 (2012). [cit. 2020-07-13]. https://eprint.iacr.org/2012/064
17. Mironov, I.: Factoring RSA Moduli II (2012). [cit. 2020–07-13]. https://windowsontheory.org/2012/05/17/factoring-rsa-moduli-part-ii/
18. Nemec, M., Klinec, D., Svenda, P., Sekan, P., Matyas, V.: Measuring popularity of cryptographic libraries in internet-wide scans. In: Proceedings of the 33rd Annual Computer Security Applications Conference, pp. 162–175. ACM (2017)
19. Nemec, M., Sys, M., Svenda, P., Klinec, D., Matyas, V.: The return of coppersmith's attack: practical factorization of widely used RSA Moduli. In: 24th ACM Conference on Computer and Communications Security (CCS 2017), pp. 1631–1648. ACM (2017)
20. Parsovs, A.: Estonian electronic identity card: security flaws in key management. In: 29th USENIX Security Symposium. USENIX Association (2020)
21. Rapid7: Rapid 7 Sonar SSL full IPv4 scan (2019). [cit. 2020-07-13]. https://opendata.rapid7.com/sonar.ssl/
22. Software in the Public Interest: DSA-1571-1 openssl - predictable random number generator (2008). [cit. 2020-07-13]. https://www.debian.org/security/2008/dsa-1571
23. Svenda, P., et al.: The million-key question—investigating the origins of RSA public keys. In: Proceeding of USENIX Security Symposium, pp. 893–910 (2016)
24. VanderSloot, B., Amann, J., Bernhard, M., Durumeric, Z., Bailey, M., Halderman, J.A.: Towards a complete view of the certificate ecosystem. In: Proceedings of the 2016 ACM on Internet Measurement Conference, pp. 543–549. ACM (2016)

MAC-in-the-Box: Verifying a Minimalistic Hardware Design for MAC Computation

Robert Küennemann[(⊠)] and Hamed Nemati

Helmholtz Center for Information Security (CISPA), Saarbrücken, Germany
{robert.kuennemann,hamed.nemati}@cispa.saarland

Abstract. We study the verification of security properties at the state machine level of a minimalistic device, called the MAC-in-the-Box (MITB). This device computes a message authentication code based on the SHA-3 hash function and a key that is stored on device, but never output directly. It is designed for secure password storage, but may also be used for secure key-exchange and second-factor authentication. We formally verify, in the HOL4 theorem prover, that no outside observer can distinguish this device from an ideal functionality that provides only access to a hashing oracle. Furthermore, we propose protocols for the MITB's use in password storage, key-exchange and second-factor authentication, and formally show that it improves resistance against host-compromise in these three application scenarios.

1 Introduction

Practically all large providers of communication and banking services employ cryptographic hardware in their critical infrastructure. This ranges from expensive hardware security modules, used in the web's public-key infrastructure and the banking network, to low-cost devices like smart cards, used in mobile communication and health care. Their purpose is to separate and encapsulate sensitive cryptographic operations in a device that is (a) designed for security and (b) small enough to be audited. By encapsulating sensitive information within these small, purportedly secure devices, the surrounding system can exploit the flexibility of general-purpose operating systems to interoperate with its complex environment.

Despite this simplicity, and even despite their ubiquity—it is estimated that there are at least 30 billion smart cards in circulation [30]—the formal verification of security properties in cryptographic hardware designs (i.e., at the state machine level) has received little attention. So far, formal verification focused on functional correctness, i.e., the correctness w.r.t. the mathematical description of the algorithm, while the security of the algorithm was (hopefully) shown in a pen-and-paper proof. Historically, this was due to a lack of support for reasoning over probabilistic systems. Over the last years, this support was continuously improved with standalone proof assistants [5], as well as frameworks for Coq [5,32] and Isabelle/HOL [3,29]. They were successfully used to show security

© Springer Nature Switzerland AG 2020
L. Chen et al. (Eds.): ESORICS 2020, LNCS 12309, pp. 525–545, 2020.
https://doi.org/10.1007/978-3-030-59013-0_26

properties for mathematical algorithms and even for software implementations, but not for hardware, due to their focus on probabilistic programs. By contrast, hardware is typically verified in higher-order logic, using mathematical functions to model its components [11].

In this work, we demonstrate the practicability of traditional hardware verification techniques for providing strong security guarantees, even when probabilistic reasoning is not available.[1] We develop a minimalistic device for the computation of *message authentication codes* (MACs) based on the recently standardized SHA-3 hash function. We call it *MAC-in-the-box* (MITB).

This device stores and protects a user-generated key. We can show that this minimalistic device provides strong guarantees such as confidentiality and unpredictability, given the usual assumption that the hash function behaves like a so-called *random oracle*. This holds even if its computing environment is under attack: In HOL4, we formally verify that, to any outside observer, the information gathered by an active attacker capable of compromising the MITB's host is limited by the information that can be gained from accessing a hashing oracle. In the random oracle model, this provides the desired guarantees by construction. This case study in security hardware design also shows the potential of formal analysis of hardware in the security setting: the verification helped us to identify three bugs in the early design of the MITB. We elaborate on these discovered issues in Sect. 7.

Despite its minimalism, the MITB can be used for various applications, e.g., establishment of secure channels and second-factor authentication. Its main application is to secure password databases. Password databases are frequently targeted to expose millions of passwords and exploit their reuse on other web pages. The MITB is initialized with a cryptographic key and stores a MAC of the password instead of the password itself. Even if this MAC is leaked, it is neither possible to recover the password from it, nor to guess popular passwords ('12345') without online access to the MITB. We formalize the password storage protocol, and protocols for two further applications, showing their security against host compromise in the symbolic model. Proof scripts and case studies are available online (https://bit.ly/32cu17B).

Paper Organization: In Sect. 2, we discuss related work on formally verified cryptographic implementations. In Sect. 3 we introduce the MITB. We define the security goal in Sec. 4. Sect. 5 to 7 describe the formalization of the MITB, the threat model and the proof. Before we conclude, we outline three applications where the MITB improves the security after host compromise in Sect. 8.

2   Related Work

There are various approaches to support cryptographic reasoning in mainstream theorem provers. The most important aspects here are reasoning about outcome

---

[1] We verify the MITB at the state machine level. Proof-producing synthesis (e.g. [36]) can be used to refine this to the gate-level for future work.

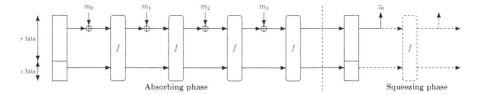

Fig. 1. Sponge construction as in SHA-3 (adapted from [23]). The final output consists of the first n bits of z_0.

distributions of random processes described in terms of simple probabilistic programming languages, and reasoning about their runtime. Both CertiCrypt [4] and Verypto [3] were the pioneers in this regard, providing a deep embedding in Coq and Isabelle, respectively. EasyCrypt [5] is CertiCrypt's successor and provides better automation by calling external SMT solvers. It is essentially a theorem prover on its own, but unlike Coq, Isabelle or HOL-4, it does not strive to have a small trusted kernel that tactics derive from—a trade-off to speed up development. More recent approaches prefer a (semi-) shallow embedding to make it easier to use the theorem prover's libraries and reasoning infrastructure. The Foundational Cryptography Framework (FCF) extends Coq's built-in functional language Gallina with probabilistic semantics [32]. CryptoHOL [29] provides a shallow embedding in Isabelle/HOL. All of these approaches have not been designed to reason about hardware designs, which are typically described in terms of higher-order functions [11]. We side-step the need for probabilistic reasoning in this work and exemplify that, for some cases, it is possible to describe and prove cryptographic properties like secrecy with standard techniques. While FCF and CryptoHOL would certainly be useful to formalize surrounding protocols using the MITB, they currently both have drawbacks preventing that use. FCF's probabilistic semantics do not allow for recursions or exceptions, which would be used for modeling network routing and communication between the MITB and the protocol using it. CryptoHOL cannot express polynomial runtime, which is a prerequisite to formalizing the threat model.

   To our knowledge, all approaches for formal verification on the hardware level were showing the correctness w.r.t. a functional specification, i.e., in absence of an adversary [17,19]. There are, however, formalized proofs for implementations written in C, e.g., for the random number generator HMAC-DRBG [38] and the HMAC construction in OpenSSL [6], and even for an x86-64 implementation of SHA-3 [2]. This line of work separates the probabilistic reasoning about the cryptographic algorithm from the correctness of its implementation in presence of an adversary. Almeida et al. [2], e.g., use Easycrypt to show the indistinguishability of the Sponge construction from a random oracle, and the Jasmin framework [1] to show the correctness, as well as the side-channel resistance, of a highly-optimized implementation. Our main result (Theorem 1) categorizes as a correctness result, in the sense that it talks about equivalences modulo abstraction, however, our verificationx objective is not a straight-forward *implementation* of SHA-3, i.e.,

Fig. 2. MITB: inputs and outputs

with the same or a similar interface, but a hardware design that *uses* SHA-3 to achieve higher-level properties. Furthermore, our goals are orthogonal: first, we want guarantees for a hardware design, not a software implementation. Second, we want to demonstrate how probabilistic reasoning can be avoided and traditional theorem provers be used (Fig. 2).

Existing work on cryptographic hardware like the TPM [14,15,35], hardware security modules [10,13,16,25,33] or authentication tokens [22,27] operate on the specification level, abstracting cryptographic bitstrings using a term algebra. Implementation-specific aspects like the complicated state-machine needed to correctly apply padding or the low-level access available to an adversary after compromise are not represented in these models.

3 Hardware Design

The MITB is a standalone device that computes a MAC using the KECCAK family of hash functions [8], which NIST standardized as SHA-3 [18]. A nice feature of SHA-3 is that it can serve as a message authentication code (MAC) by simply prepending a secret key to the message, i.e., the function:

$$mac(k, m) := \mathsf{SHA3}(k\|m)$$

is a valid MAC [7]. MACs operate as follows: to ensure the integrity of a message m, one computes $mac(k, m)$ and attaches it to the message. The communication partner, who also knows k, can recompute this function and compare the result to the MAC received. If the result is the same, the communication partner can be sure the message was created by a party that knows k (typically either the sender or the receiver himself) and that m was not modified in transit. Previous hash functions like SHA-1, SHA-2 and MD5 were vulnerable to length-extension attacks and thus required more complicated constructions like HMAC to serve as MACs. (Cryptographic) hash functions themselves are functions that are difficult to invert and are resistant to collision attacks. In contrast to unforgeability, the main property of a MAC, it is difficult to formalize these properties, hence hash functions are often abstracted in terms of random oracles. A random oracle is a randomly chosen function from $\{0,1\}^* \to \{0,1\}^n$ where n is the length of the hash, i.e., each new input appears to be freshly sampled, but the function itself is deterministic.

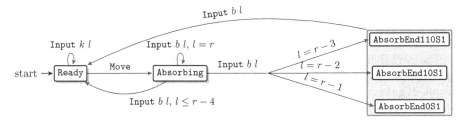

Fig. 3. State transition diagram. Not shown: (a) `Skip` preserves state. (b) In any absorbing state, `Move` returns to `Ready`, but resets volatile memory to 0^{r+c}. Here, k and b are input blocks and l represent input size.

The Sponge Construction. SHA-3 is based on the 'sponge construction' in which an arbitrary length message is iteratively 'absorbed' into a finite state (see Fig. 1). The number of iterations depends on the length of the message. Once all message blocks have been absorbed, the resulting state can be 'squeezed' to extract a digest. In general, this squeezing can be used to derive a digest of any desired length, however, all instances of fixed-length SHA-3 require only a single squeeze operation.

SHA-3 defines four instances of this construction, but recommends only one (the others are for testing and light-weight hashing). This instance is defined by a *bitrate* of $r = 576$, a *capacity* of $c = 1024$ and an *output size* $n = 512 < r$, i.e., the number of bits to which the output is truncated. The state of the SHA-3 sponge algorithm thus consists of $r + c = 1600$ bits. Initially, the state is 0^{r+c}, i.e. each of the 1600 state bits is 0. In each iteration, a state permutation $f : \mathbb{Z}_2^{r+c} \rightarrow \mathbb{Z}_2^{r+c}$ is applied on the state. A detailed formal specification of f is not given here; f is treated as an uninterpreted parameter in the specification and proofs. That is, we do not make any assumptions about f itself other than that the sponge construction with f can be abstracted by a random oracle. The attacker can compute f on inputs of her choice.

By itself, the sponge construction is only defined for input sizes that are multiples of r. Therefore, a 10*1 padding is used, i.e., a bitstring with 1 at the beginning and end, and sufficiently many 0s in between. In addition, the SHA-3 specification requires two bits 01 to be added to distinguish fixed-length SHA-3 from its variable-length siblings SHAKE-128 and SHAKE-256. Hence any message m is padded to a multiple of r bits by appending at least four bits: first 011, then sufficiently many ($|m| + 4 \mod r$) zeroes, and finally a trailing 1. An empty message, e.g., is padded to a block $0110^{r-4}1$.

State Machine. The MITB computes $mac(k, m)$, but keeps k secret. It provides two operations: overwriting k (reading is not possible by an outsider), and computing $mac(k, m)$ for a given m. As we detail in Sect. 8, this functionality by itself is sufficient to improve the resilience of password databases, secure channel establishment and two-factor authentication against host compromise. As m can be arbitrarily long, the device operates in a blockwise fashion, absorbing 512 bits per call. Each full block is applied to the current state. If the user indicates an input of shorter length, a padding is applied and the operation finalized. Only if the padding was correctly applied, the state may be output.

The MITB has two 1-bit control inputs skip_inp and move_inp, two data inputs block_inp and size_inp, a 1-bit control output ready_out and a data output digest_out. It is parametrized on three numbers (r, c, n) and a permutation function f. These are part of the KECCAK specification. An actual device would be manufactured with specific values for the parameters, and we require that $4 < r$, $0 < c$ and $n \leq r$.

The input block_inp is r-bits wide and the output digest_out is n-bits wide. The input size_inp has sufficient bits to represent a number of size r or less. For convenience, it is modeled as a number rather than a bitstring. The truth values T, F model bits 1, 0, respectively. The MITB runs continuously after being switched on. It is implemented as a state machine using combinational logic and registers (see Sect. 5). All a user can observe (assuming tamper-resistant manufacture) are the sequences of values appearing on the outputs ready_out and digest_out, which depend on the values input via skip_inp, move_inp, block_inp and size_inp. From a user's point of view, the MITB can be in either of two states: Ready or Absorbing. It powers up into state Ready. The 1-bit output ready_out indicates whether the state is Ready (ready_out = T) or in some absorbing state (ready_out = F).

The input skip_inp 'freezes' the MITB: holding it T stops the state changing on successive cycles. If skip_inp is F, then input move_inp causes the state to change on the next cycle; in particular it is used to signal that MITB should start absorbing a message. In the state machine, this is represented as a transition Move, no matter what values block_inp and size_inp have. If both move_inp and skip_inp are F, we consider this as a transition Input block_inp size_inp.

MITB has a permanent memory for holding an r-bit secret key. The key can be set or changed by holding both skip_inp and move_inpF in the Ready state. The data being input on block_inp then overwrites the stored key. In the Absorbing state, if both move_inp and skip_inp are F, we absorb block_inp to compute the MAC in a blockwise fashion. Depending on the message length, the padding might cause the message to extend to another block, in which case this additional block needs to be absorbed. As described in the previous section, the padding adds at least four bits, so a message that is 1, 2 or 3 bits short to the block length needs to have an extra block for the parts of the padding. Thus the need for three states that finalize the padding block. E.g., if the message is two bits short, i.e., size_inp is $r - 2$ in Absorbing, then 01 is appended to the last block before absorbing it, and MITB moves into state AbsorbEnd10S1 (the 'S' can be read as '*'). There, a block $10^{r-2}1$ is absorbed (inputs block_inp and size_inp are ignored) before moving to Ready in the next cycle. Note that Absorbing also moves back to Ready if size_inp $\leq r - 4$.

The main correctness property of the device is that if the specified protocol is used to input a message, then its MAC will appear on digest_out. The main security property is that no matter what inputs are supplied, the secret key cannot be revealed nor any other information than a valid MAC. In particular, no chain of inputs can leak parts of the state of the sponge construction before the padding has been completed.

MAC Computation Protocol. The MAC of m, i.e., the SHA-3 hash of $k\|m$, is computed as follows:

1. If $\texttt{ready\_out} = 0$, i.e., the device is not in Ready state, transition to the Ready state using Move, i.e., by inputting F on $\texttt{skip\_inp}$ and T on $\texttt{move\_inp}$ ($\texttt{block\_inp}$ and $\texttt{size\_inp}$ are ignored during this step).
2. The device is put into Absorbing state using another Move.
3. The user splits m into a sequence of blocks, $m = b_1\|b_2\|\cdots\|b_{n-1}\|b_n$, such that all blocks except the last one are r-bits wide, i.e., $|b_i| = r$ for $1 \le i < n$ and $|b_n| < r$. If r divides exactly into $|m|$, then b_n is taken to be the empty block (so $|b_n| = 0$).
4. Starting on the next cycle, and continuing for n cycles, the user performs transitions Input b_i $|b_i|$, i.e., inputs F on both $\texttt{move\_inp}$ and $\texttt{skip\_inp}$, b_i on $\texttt{block\_inp}$ and $|b_i|$ on $\texttt{size\_inp}$, where $1 \le i \le n$. During this time F will be output on $\texttt{ready\_out}$.
5. After inputting b_n, the user keeps inputting F on $\texttt{skip\_inp}$ and $\texttt{move\_inp}$ for one more cycle until $\texttt{ready\_out}$ becomes T. On the cycle when this happens, the hash of $k\|n$ will appear on $\texttt{digest\_out}$. The number of cycles taken depends on $|b_n|$. If $|b_n| \le r-4$ then $\texttt{ready\_out}$ will become T on the cycle after b_n is input. If $r-4 < |b_n| < r$, then $\texttt{ready\_out}$ will become T the cycle after b_n is input.

Key Update Protocol. The key is updated to value k in two steps.

1. Exactly as step 1 in the MAC computation protocol.
2. Perform transitions Input k 576 by setting both $\texttt{move\_inp}$ and $\texttt{skip\_inp}$ to F, $\texttt{block\_inp}$ to k and $\texttt{size\_inp}$ to 576.

4 Security Goals

The MITB is designed to protect password databases in case of a server breach, but can be used for many other different applications (see Sect. 8). We assume that an attacker may eventually gain control over this server, in which case the secrecy of the key should be preserved, but the attacker can compute MACs of her choice, re-set the key or send arbitrary other commands to the MITB. Before the attacker gains control, she shall not be able to compute or predict MACs.

Real-World/Ideal-World Formulation. Complex cryptographic properties are often formulated using the real-world/ideal-world paradigm. The real world describes how the cryptographic primitive or protocol interacts with the adversary, i.e., the threat model. The ideal world describes an idealised setup that provides the necessary guarantees by construction. In the case of signatures, e.g., all signatures are created by a central authority that keeps a list of message-signature pairs, so only message-signature pairs that it constructed itself are accepted, thus providing unforgeability by construction. Or, for encryption schemes, it outputs random bitstrings instead of a ciphertexts, thus providing confidentiality by construction. If it is not possible to distinguish both worlds, then the real-world scenario must be sufficiently close to the ideal world that it can be considered secure.

In our case, the real world consists of the MITB in communication with some environment, e.g., one of the applications in Sect. 8. The environment uses the protocol from Sect. 3 to compute a MAC or update the key, but can also bypass this protocol by declaring the host computer corrupted. In this case, the environment's inputs are directly transferred to the MITB.

The ideal world is specified by a simple machine that (a) stores or overwrites a key k; (b) for every MAC request m, calls a hash oracle with $k\|m$. (c) If the environment declares the host system corrupted, the attacker can do nothing more than to continue to query this oracle, in particular, she does not get access to k. Our security result in Theorem 1 can thus be informally stated as follows:

For all parameters r, c and n such that $r > 4$, $c > 0$ and $n \leq r$, and any sequence of inputs i, the sequence of outputs obtained by sending i to the real-world is equal to the sequence of outputs obtained by sending i to the ideal-world.

Hash Functions and the Random Oracle Model. So far, a security definition for cryptographic hash functions that is both formal and directly applies to real-life hash functions has not been found. Properties like collision resistance postulate that there is no *known* adversary that can provoke a collision, but fundamentally, there are adversaries that can create collisions, due to the pigeonhole principle. We cannot formally reason about all known algorithms.

In cryptographic proofs, hash functions are thus usually abstracted using random oracles (ROs). A RO has two properties: First, when queried for a new bitstring m, RO draws a bitstring from the uniform distribution of bitstrings of length n. Second, if m was queried before, the RO responds with the same bitstring as before. Since hash functions are deterministic, a RO can be distinguished from any fixed hash function. Cryptographic results, e.g., indifferentiability [7] or PRF security [20] hence consider a sponge construction that calls an oracle to evaluate a randomly chosen permutation (and/or a keyed variant of the construction [20]). But in SHA-3, the permutation is public and fixed.

Theorem 1 *complements* these result. It relates the MITB to the ideal world with the sponge construction for an arbitrary, but fixed permutation. Indifferentiability relates the ideal world with a randomized sponge construction (keyed or with a randomly chosen permutation) to the ideal world with a random oracle, within certain bounds on the adversary's running time and the number of oracle queries. Observe, however, that the step from the deterministic sponge construction (with a fixed permutation) to the randomised construction used in cryptographic proofs remains a heuristic; it is (provably) incorrect.

Guarantees Provided by Construction. Once we (heuristically) instantiate the hash function in the ideal world with a randomly chosen hash function, as in the RO model,[2] we obtain a very clear interpretation of the guarantees that the ideal world we previously described provides.

1. *Confidentiality:* The output contains neither information about k, nor the message m (as it is merely a randomly chosen bitstring).
2. *Unpredictability:* The MAC computation yields unpredictable values for each k and m, as long as (k, m) were not queried before (as the result is chosen freshly).
3. *Determinism:* If (k, m) were previously queried, the MAC will be the same (as the RO is deterministic and $k\|m$ constitutes the query). This guarantees that a MAC can be verified later.
4. *Resistance against compromise:* The above guarantees hold even if the host system is compromised.

These guarantees go beyond the guarantees of message authentication codes (which are allowed to leak information about the authenticated message) or hash functions (which may leak information about the hashed message, but can be forged by everyone). We have designed the functionality specifically to suit secure password storage, our main application.

5   Formalising the MITB

We base the MITB's definition on the function MITB_FUN, which specifies the behaviour abstractly. MITB_FUN takes an abstract state $s \in \mathbb{S}$ and an input i, and returns the next state. The abstract state $s = \langle \text{cntl}, \text{pmem}, \text{vmem} \rangle$ consists of the value of the control register $\text{cntl} \in \{\text{Ready}, \text{Absorbing}, \text{AbsorbEnd}(\text{0S1}|\text{10S1}|\text{110S1})\})$ and a permanent (pmem) and volatile (vmem) memory, which are both bit-strings of length $r + c$. The control flags correspond to the states described in Sect. 3. An input i can either be Move, Skip or Input bk len, where bk is a bitstring of size r and len corresponds to the number of bits of bk that constitutes the input block (thus $len \leq r$). The bitstring bk and number len represent inputs on block_inp and size_inp.

---

[2] A randomly chosen hash function or an oracle that samples random hash values on demand are equivalent formulations of the RO model.

The definition of MITB_FUN uses ML-style pattern matching. Due to lack of space we skip presenting MITB_FUN's formal definition here. However, its possible transitions are depicted in Fig. 3. The most complex part of MITB_FUN specifies the state transition corresponding to absorbing a block. What happens depends on the input length. The complexity here is due to the padding applied by the devices, as described in Sect. 3. If the block length is less or equal to $r - 4$, e.g. 0, the device applies the padding and sets cntl to Ready. If the last block is one bit short of being a full block ($len = r - 1$) then one bit of padding is added and the device enters an absorbing state with cntl = AbsorbEndOS1. On the next cycle, the remaining padding (i.e. $r - 1$ zeros and a final T) is added and the permutation f is applied to vmem before transitioning back to the ready state. Similar steps are taken if the input block length is equal to $r - 2$ or $r - 3$. When the block size is exactly r, the device starts absorbing a non-final block, which is done by: (i) appending zero to it, (ii) XOR-ing the result with the current value of the volatile memory vmem, (iii) applying the KECCAK permutation f to the result of the XOR-ing, and finally, (iv) updating the volatile memory with the result of applying the function f.

Figure 4 shows the definition of the function MITB which decodes the inputs into abstract commands Skip, Move and Input and calls MITB_FUN.

MITB f $(cntl, pmem, vmem)$
$\quad$ $(skip, move, block, size)$ $\quad=$
$\quad$ MITB_FUN f $(cntl, pmem, vmem)$
$\quad\quad$ (**if** $skip$ = T **then** Skip
$\quad\quad$ **else if** $move$ = T **then** Move
$\quad\quad$ **else if** $size \leq r$ **then**
$\quad\quad\quad$ Input $block$ $size$
$\quad\quad$ **else** Skip)

MITB_STEP f s i $=$
$\quad$ **let** $(cntl', pmem', vmem')$ = MITB f s i;
$\quad\quad$ $digest$ $=$
$\quad\quad\quad$ (**if** $cntl'$ = Ready
$\quad\quad\quad\quad$ **then** (T, $(r - 1 >< 0)$ $vmem'$)
$\quad\quad\quad\quad$ **else** (F, ZERO))
$\quad$ **in** $\quad$ (($cntl', pmem', vmem'$), $digest$)

Fig. 4. Definition of MITB function.   **Fig. 5.** Definition of step function.

We also define a *step function* (Fig. 5) which yields the next state of the system. The step function behaves like the MITB, but defines the output, too. The step function takes a permutation f, the current state of the MITB, denoted as s, and the input $i = ($skip_inp, move_inp, block_inp, size_inp$)$. It returns the next state of the MITB together with an output. The returned output depends on the value of cntl in that cycle. In the definition, $(h >< l)$ w represents the HOL4 *bit extraction* function for input word w, and h and l are the upper and lower bound for the number of extracted bits, respectively.

6   Formalizing Security

We define the security of the MITB in terms of a *functionality*, an idealized specification of both the functional correctness of the device, and the information the adversary can learn from it. The popular 'universal composability' framework defines how the MITB ought to relate to this functionality (Fig. 6).

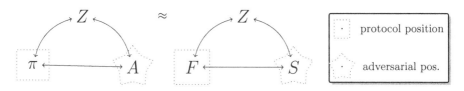

Fig. 6. π (perfectly) emulates F iff, for all A, there exists S such that for all Z, the lhs network is indistinguishable (or instead: identical) from the rhs.

6.1   Universal Composability

Our security definition follows the real-world/ideal-world paradigm, which can be generalized into a security notion called *emulation*.[3] Emulation provides properties similar to refinement and entails a property called *universal composability*. Canetti introduced universal composability (UC) in a framework that goes by the same name [12], but there are several variations of it [21,28]. If a protocol or cryptographic primitive π UC emulates an 'ideal-world' system F (called the *functionality*), then π provides universal composability w.r.t. F. This means that for the analysis of any higher-level system ρ that uses π, it is sufficient to analyze the more abstract and thus simpler system where ρ interacts with F instead—even if multiple copies of π run in parallel.

To formulate the security property, we formalize UC's communication framework and *perfect emulation*, the strongest variant of their refinement notion. We did not seek to prove that UC emulation implies universal composability.

The *real world* is characterized by the protocol π communicating on two interfaces, the honest and the adversarial interface. The honest interface provides inputs, possibly from higher level protocols. A secure channel protocol like TLS, e.g., receives the instruction 'Party A requests sending m to Party B' and may later output 'Party B received m from A'. The adversarial interface models the network: all network communication, e.g., the encrypted TLS records, is sent to and received from an *adversary* A. The attacker can hence eavesdrop messages, but also drop or modify them.

In the *ideal world*, the functionality F receives the same high-level instructions on the honest interface.[4] Ideally, the messages on the network provide no

---

[3] Also called 'realization' [12].
[4] More precisely, F specifies this interface, and π tries to implement it accordingly.

useful information for the adversary. However, often enough this is impossible; encryption, e.g., reveals the length of the plain text. Therefore, the functionality makes this so-called leakage explicit by outputting, e.g., the length of the plaintext on the adversarial interface. To show that the network traffic leaks no information besides F's output on the dishonest interface, most emulation proofs construct a simulator S that imitates A's behavior using only this intended leakage. Thus, to an outsider, no matter what inputs the protocol receives, for every attacker A there should be a simulator S such that π interacting with A is indistinguishable from F interacting with S. The comparison assures *correctness* (as any difference between the honest protocol and the ideal functionality on the honest interface can be observed) and *confidentiality up to the leakage in F* (if the adversary can learn something that the simulator cannot reproduce from the input provided by F, then there would not be a simulator that achieves indistinguishability). The inputs to the protocol can come from a high-level protocol using it (e.g., a p2p system using TLS for communication between peers), and are abstracted as a Turing Machine Z. In the real world, Z interacts with π (on the honest interface) and with A (on the adversarial interface). In the ideal world, Z interacts with F and S.

It was shown[5] that for any environment Z and adversary A that are successful in distinguishing real world and ideal world, a new environment Z' can be constructed that simulates A and only relies on a special attacker A_d, the so-called *dummy adversary*. The dummy adversary only forwards messages between Z' and π. Thus, in practice, one shows the existence of a simulator S such that for all environments Z, π and A_d are indistinguishable from F and S.

We formalize the communication structure in UC as follows. A message datatype indicates the routing for messages between the protocol position (occupied by π in real world, F in the ideal world), the adversary position (occupied by A_d in the real word, S in the ideal world) and the environment position (occupied by Z in both cases).

Message = EnvtoP of α | EnvtoA of β | PtoEnv of γ | PtoA of δ | AtoEnv of η | AtoP of ϕ

Initially, the environment sends a message of type EnvtoP or EnvtoA to either the adversary or the protocol. The function ROUTE $p\ a$, for a protocol step function p and an adversary step function a, expects the previous state of p and a and a value of type Message to be routed. It computes the next state of the protocol and adversary and the next message to be routed. If the message matches EnvtoP or AtoP, the protocol step function is applied, the protocol's state updated, and the output converted into type Message, e.g.:

$$\text{ROUTE } p\ a\ ((state\_p, state\_a), \text{EnvtoP } m) =$$
$$(\textbf{let } (state\_p\_n, out) = p\ state\_p\ (\text{EnvtoP } m)$$
$$\textbf{in } ((state\_p\_n, state\_a), \text{Proto\_Wrapper } out))$$

---

[5] This simplification was proven sound for the UC framework [12], GNUC framework [21] and the IITM framework [28], so for brevity, we will assume it part of the definition.

The wrapper Proto_Wrapper transforms a datatype for protocol output into Message, i.e., values that match either PtoEnv or PtoA. This ensures that the protocol cannot send messages that appear to originate from the adversary, and vice versa. Messages addressing the adversary are handled analogously.

Before the environment is addressed again, there can be additional routing steps between the protocol and the adversary. Messages to the environment, however, terminate a routing step and are returned. We will later restrict the communication to three routing steps before the environment is again in control, which is sufficient for our case (otherwise, a routing error is produced).

$$\text{ROUTE } p \ a \ ((\mathit{state\_p}, \mathit{state\_a}), \text{PtoEnv } m) \ = \ ((\mathit{state\_p}, \mathit{state\_a}), \text{PtoEnv } m)$$

Note that the scheduling model of UC gives control to the party that received a message. More elaborate scheduling mechanisms are modeled by including scheduling requests to the adversary in the protocol.

In UC, the environment is a Turing Machine, however, in this work, we consider the strongest notion of emulation, called *perfect emulation*. Here, the sequence of messages the environment receives is the same (rather than indistinguishable to all polynomial time environments). We, furthermore, do not assume any runtime bounds on the participants.[6] This simplifies the analysis: We can model the set of environments as the set of input sequences and consider all other participants in terms of mathematical functions, and thus avoid probabilistic reasoning altogether. This is sufficient for the MITB because it is entirely deterministic, due to the key being generated outside the device and the deterministic nature of the hash function. We hence define (EXEC p a), again on protocol and adversary step functions p and a, that applies a sequence of inputs i to an initial protocol and adversary state $s = (s_a, s_p)$ until one of these two parties outputs a message addressed to the environment.

The environment is fully described by the sequence of inputs it sends to the protocol or the adversary, hence we define an execution as follows:

EXEC $p \ a \ s \ [] \ = \ []$
EXEC $p \ a \ s \ (i :: il) \ = (\textbf{let} \ (s', out) = \text{EXEC\_STEP } p \ a \ (s, i) \ \textbf{in} \ (s', out) :: \text{EXEC } p \ a \ s' \ il)$

In this definition the EXEC_STEP function defines a single execution step from the perspective of the environment.

6.2   Security Definition

The Real World. The environment Z communicates with parties that compute MACs using the MITB via a library, as well as an attacker, who can take control over the machine the MITB is attached to and thus bypass this library. The attacker also communicates with Z and can thus provide Z with information that allows it to distinguish real world and ideal world. As the attacker is

---

[6] This is w.l.o.g. for all participants except for the simulator, which, however, is obvious to run in polynomial time in our case.

instantiated with the dummy attacker, which is defined as follows, Z can access the adversarial interface, in this case the MITB, via this indirection.

$$\text{DUMMY\_ADV } v_0 \ (\text{EnvtoA } m) \ = \ (0, \text{Adv\_toP } m)$$
$$\text{DUMMY\_ADV } v_1 \ (\text{PtoA } m) \ = \ (0, \text{Adv\_toEnv } m)$$

For messages from the environment, PROTO models the protocols for MAC computation and key updates we defined in Sect. 3 (see Appendix B in [26] for the precise modeling).

The Ideal World. In the ideal world, Z receives 'correct' output for whatever message it inputs. 'Correct' means the following: given a message $(SetKey, k)$, it stores k. For any subsequent message (Mac, m), it outputs $\mathcal{H}(k\|m)$, where $\mathcal{H}$ is a hash function. The function (FMAC H s) describes the output and next state of the ideal-world functionality in state s, parametrized with the hash function H to represent the hashing oracle $\mathcal{H}$. The only state that FMAC holds is the stored key k and the corruption status (T iff corrupted).

$$\text{FMAC } H \ (K', \text{F}) \ (\text{EnvtoP } (\text{SetKey } k)) \ = \ ((k, \text{F}), \text{Proto\_toEnv } 0w)$$
$$\text{FMAC } H \ (K', \text{F}) \ (\text{EnvtoP } (\text{Mac } m)) \ =$$
$$((K', \text{F}), \text{Proto\_toEnv } (H \ (\text{word\_to\_bits } K' \ \| \ m)))$$

After the corruption signal was received (and forwarded to the adversary), FMAC responds to oracle queries, computing $\mathcal{H}(k\|m)$:

$$\text{FMAC } H \ (K', \text{F}) \ (\text{EnvtoP Corrupt}) \ = ((K', \text{T}), \text{Proto\_toA WasCorrupted})$$
$$\text{FMAC } H \ (K', \text{T}) \ (\text{AtoP CorruptACK}) \ = ((K', \text{T}), \text{Proto\_toEnv } 0w)$$
$$\text{FMAC } H \ (K', \text{T}) \ (\text{AtoP } (\text{OracleQuery } m)) \ =$$
$$((K', \text{T}), \ \text{Proto\_toA } (\text{OracleResponse } (H \ (\text{word\_to\_bits } K' \ \| \ m))))$$

The responses on the attacker interface formalize that the attacker does not receive information beyond the ability to compute MACs: Via the adversarial interface of FMAC, the simulator has access to the hash function $\mathcal{H}$, but not to the MITB. Note that, in contrast to the real world, FMAC notifies the simulator that it was corrupted, so the simulator knows whether it has to deny or simulate direct access to the MITB. After corruption, all honest queries are ignored:

$$\text{FMAC } H \ (K', \text{T}) \ (\text{EnvtoP } (\text{SetKey } v_{16})) \ = ((K', \text{T}), \text{Proto\_toEnv } 0w)$$
$$\text{FMAC } H \ (K', \text{T}) \ (\text{EnvtoP } (\text{Mac } v_{17})) \ = ((K', \text{T}), \text{Proto\_toEnv } 0w)$$

Our main result is that, no matter which inputs the environment sends, the outputs are the same. In the next section, we will define a simulator SIM that mimics the behavior of the MITB with access only to the hashing oracle provided by FMAC. We establish its existence by constructing it so that:

Theorem 1. *For all parameters r, c and n such that $r > 4$, $c > 0$ and $n \leq r$ and permutations $f : \{0,1\}^{r+c} \to \{0,1\}^{r+c}$, if the protocol and dummy adversary, as well as the functionality FMAC and the simulator are in their respective initial states s and s', then, for any sequence of inputs i, the output sequences $trace_{\text{real}} = EXEC \ (PROTO \ (MITB\_STEP \ f)) \ DUMMY\_ADV \ s \ i$, and $trace_{\text{ideal}} = EXEC \ (FMAC \ (Hash \ f \ 0)) \ (SIM \ MITB\_STEP \ f) \ s' \ i$ are equal.*

Note that f is a free variable in this theorem, and can stand for any permutation. The function $(\mathsf{Hash}\ f\ 0)$ formalizes the sponge construction with permutation f and initial state 0^{r+c}, including the SHA-3 padding and the truncation to n bits. For lack of space, we will not elaborate on its formalization. The protocol, which is parametric in the MITB step function, is instantiated with $\mathsf{MITB\_STEP}$ from Sect. 5, which itself is parametric in the underlying permutation f.

7 Proof Overview

We proceed to outline the proof of Theorem 1. To this end, we first present the simulator and the relational invariant used to characterize possible states that the system can enter at runtime.

The simulator pretends to be the attacker from the real world, i.e., the dummy adversary. It simulates the information the functionality outputs in the ideal world, in particular the MITB's output after corruption. To imitate the MITB, without knowing the last key that was stored, the simulator uses the oracle $\mathcal{H}(k\|m)$, where $\mathcal{H}$ is a hash function and $\|$ denotes the bit-string concatenation function. The simulator SIM ignores queries until the variable *corrupted* is set. Afterwards, it parses each message m sent by the environment into an input $(\mathsf{skip\_inp}, \mathsf{move\_inp}, \mathsf{block\_inp}, \mathsf{size\_inp}) \in \mathbb{B} \times \mathbb{B} \times \{0,1\}^r \times \mathbb{N}^r$. We formulate the behavior of SIM for the case where *Corrupt* $= \mathsf{T}$ as a function on its state $(\mathsf{cntl}, \mathsf{vmem}, m, \mathsf{overwt}, s) \in \{\mathsf{Ready}, \mathsf{Absorbing}, \mathsf{AbsorbEnd}(0\mathsf{S1}|10\mathsf{S1}|110\mathsf{S1})\} \times \{0,1\}^n \times \{0,1\}^* \times \mathbb{B} \times \mathbb{S}$ and the input $(\mathsf{skip\_inp}, \mathsf{move\_inp}, \mathsf{block\_inp}, \mathsf{size\_inp})$. The output of the function is a new state, and the simulated output of the MITB, i.e., $(\mathsf{ready\_out}, \mathsf{digest\_out}) \in \mathbb{B} \times \{0,1\}^n$. Due to lack of space, the detailed definition of SIM is included in Appendix C in [26].

Our invariant to prove emulation (i) relates the permanent and volatile memory in the real world to the key and the messages received so far in the real world, in case the MITB was corrupted; and guarantees that (ii) corruption status in real and ideal world correspond; and that (iii) if the real world is corrupted, the control state of the MITB simulated by SIM and the actual MITB in the real world correspond. The proof of Theorem 1 proceeds by induction on the length of the input i. Table 1 gives details on the specification and proof size.

Table 1. Size of formal proof in lines of code (loc).

	Definitions (loc)	Theorems incl. proofs (loc)
Universal composability	137	—
Sponge construction	58	512
MITB	547	1962

Intuitively, the existence of the simulator shows that all outputs of the MITB are hashes of correctly padded messages, and therefore non-revealing. The construction of the simulator pointed us to the need of an extra absorbing state—our initial design trusted the library to remember to request a final block. Later, we incorporated the two bits that are meant to distinguish SHA-3 from the SHAKE family, hoping the proof would not be affected. On the contrary, it required the introduction of another two absorbing states, which manifested in the impossibility of proving the memory invariant with only one absorbing state. Finally, failed attempts in showing the state invariant indicated the need for an initialization procedure in MAC computation protocol (as well as the key update protocol), to ensure that the device is indeed in `Ready` state. These three flaws, which we discovered early on, while proving emulation of the ideal functionality, seem to be stereotypical flaws when designing hardware for a hostile environment. None of them would have been discovered by tests for functional correctness.

8   Applications

We propose three applications for the MITB. Each provides improved resilience against host compromise. All properties we mention have been verified using off-the-shelf protocol verification tools. As protocols are notorious for their complex interleaving of a possibly unbounded number of small programs running in concurrency, these are the right tool for the job, as they have a large degree of automation. These tools operate in the symbolic model, where cryptographic outputs are abstracted using a term algebra, e.g., a MAC is a term of form $mac(k, m)$, where mac is a function symbol, and k, m themselves are terms. The MITB is reflected in these models by the simple fact that the term k used in the key-position remains secret even if the attacker gains control over its host system (see Appendix D in [26] for the models).

Secure Password Storage: All businesses that store password data need to secure these password databases for the case where they get stolen. To store passwords securely, the MITB is initialized with a fresh key during set-up, then used to compute MACs on the hashed and salted password. We used ProVerif's diff-equivalence [9] to show strong secrecy, i.e., resistance against offline password guessing. The verification takes less than a second for an unbounded number of passwords[7]. Furthermore, the MITB could replace the YubiHSM, which costs about $ 650,[8] in an even more elaborate password storage scheme by Almeshekah et. al.

Establishing a Secure Channel: The MITB can harden a variation of the signed Diffie-Hellman key-exchange protocol, which is used, e.g., in TLS and IPsec. Due to the MITB, this protocol provides *perfect forward secrecy* (even if the adversary gains control over one of the MITBs, all session keys established

---

[7] Computed on a MacBook Pro with 3,1 GHz Intel i7 and 16 GB RAM.

[8] Pessl et al. estimate a SHA-3 implementation on an RFID token to cost about $ 0.05 [31]. As the MITB's state machine and key storage do not fundamentally add to that, production cost will likely be dominated by the bus technology, e.g., USB.

prior to this event remain secret) and *post-compromise security* (even if the adversary temporarily gains control over one of the MITBs, once the participants come together and set up a new key, future session keys will again remain secure.) Using the tamarin/SAPIC [24, 34] toolchain, we establish both properties for an unbounded number of sessions. The proof terminates in1516 s (See footnote 7).

Two-Factor Authentication: We demonstrate that the MITB is compatible with the FIDO standard for universal 2nd factor authentication [37] (see Fig. 7 in Appendix A). With tamarin/SAPIC, we establish perfect forward security and post-compromise security for authentication, i.e., the property that any successful login on the web server was initiated by the user. The proof terminates within 9 s (See footnote 7).

9   Conclusion

With the *MAC-in-the-box* we presented the first full-fledged formal security argument for a hardware design. Despite its simplicity, the device has various applications. It also demonstrates that interactive theorem provers, which have an excellent track record for hardware verification, can in some cases be directly applied to the analysis of cryptographic constructions—even if support for probabilistic reasoning is missing or insufficient.

Our technique applies when common abstractions in cryptography are heuristics rather than mathematically valid simplifications. Examples are random oracles for hash functions, or pseudorandom functions for block ciphers. Designs based on these primitives essentially argue that they provide proper access to these abstractions. For cases where this property holds unconditionally, our approach has advantages over cryptographic frameworks that come with additional proof obligations, or are not available for the theorem prover of choice.

Acknowledgements. This project was Graham Steel's and Michael J. C. Gordon's idea, who both supported it in its early stages. A substantial part of the MITB's formalisation was contributed by Mike, who this paper is dedicated to. The first author is grateful for his guidance and his kindness in difficult times. This work was carried out in the framework of the French-German-Center for Cybersecurity, a collaboration of CISPA and LORIA. The second author is supported by the German Federal Ministry of Education and Research (BMBF) through funding for the CISPA-Stanford Center for Cybersecurity (FKZ: 16KIS0762).

A   Two-Factor Authentication

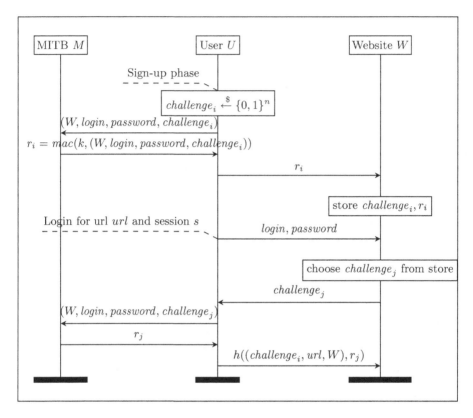

Fig. 7. U2F protocol for user U using MITB M to sign up and login on website W, simplified.

References

1. Almeida, J.B., et al.: Jasmin: high-assurance and high-speed cryptography. In: Proceedings of the 2017 ACM SIGSAC Conference on Computer and Communications Security, CCS 2017, Dallas, TX, USA, 30 October–03 November 2017, pp. 1807–1823. ACM (2017)
2. Almeida, J.B., et al.: Machine-checked proofs for cryptographic standards: indifferentiability of sponge and secure high-assurance implementations of SHA-3. In: Proceedings of the 2019 ACM SIGSAC Conference on Computer and Communications Security, CCS 2019, London, UK, 11–15 November 2019, pp. 1607–1622. ACM (2019)

3. Backes, M., Berg, M., Unruh, D.: A formal language for cryptographic pseudocode. In: Cervesato, I., Veith, H., Voronkov, A. (eds.) LPAR 2008. LNCS (LNAI), vol. 5330, pp. 353–376. Springer, Heidelberg (2008). https://doi.org/10.1007/978-3-540-89439-1_26

4. Barthe, G., Grégoire, B., Béguelin, S.Z.: Formal certification of code-based cryptographic proofs. In: Proceedings of the 36th ACM SIGPLAN-SIGACT Symposium on Principles of Programming Languages, POPL 2009, Savannah, GA, USA, 21–23 January 2009, pp. 90–101. ACM (2009)

5. Barthe, G., Grégoire, B., Heraud, S., Béguelin, S.Z.: Computer-aided security proofs for the working cryptographer. In: Rogaway, P. (ed.) CRYPTO 2011. LNCS, vol. 6841, pp. 71–90. Springer, Heidelberg (2011). https://doi.org/10.1007/978-3-642-22792-9_5

6. Beringer, L., Petcher, A., Katherine, Q.Y., Appel, A.W.: Verified correctness and security of OpenSSL HMAC. In: USENIX Security Symposium, pp. 207–221 (2015)

7. Bertoni, G., Daemen, J., Peeters, M., Van Assche, G.: On the indifferentiability of the sponge construction. In: Smart, N. (ed.) EUROCRYPT 2008. LNCS, vol. 4965, pp. 181–197. Springer, Heidelberg (2008). https://doi.org/10.1007/978-3-540-78967-3_11

8. Bertoni, G., Daemen, J., Peeters, M., and Assche, G.V.: Online Keccak Specifications (2009). http://keccak.noekeon.org/

9. Blanchet, B., Abadi, M., Fournet, C.: Automated verification of selected equivalences for security protocols. In: Symposium on Logic in Computer Science (LICS 2005), pp. 331–340. IEEE Computer Society (2005)

10. Bortolozzo, M., Centenaro, M., Focardi, R., Steel, G.: Attacking and fixing PKCS#11 security tokens. In: 17th ACM Conference on Computer and Communications Security (CCS 2010), pp. 260–269. ACM (2010)

11. Camilleri, A., Gordon, M., Melham, T.: Hardware verification using higher-order logic. Technical report, University of Cambridge, Computer Laboratory (1986)

12. Canetti, R.: Universally composable security: a new paradigm for cryptographic protocols. In: Foundations of Computer Science, pp. 136–145. IEEE Computer Society (2001)

13. Dax, A., Tangermann, S., Künnemann, R., Backes, M.: How to wrap it up - a formally verified proposal for the use of authenticated wrapping in PKCS#11. In: Computer Security Foundations Symposium (2019)

14. Delaune, S., Kremer, S., Ryan, M.D., Steel, G.: Formal analysis of protocols based on TPM state registers. In: 24th IEEE Computer Security Foundations Symposium (CSF 2011), pp. 66–82. IEEE Computer Society (2011)

15. Delaune, S., Kremer, S., Ryan, M.D., Steel, G.: A formal analysis of authentication in the TPM. In: Degano, P., Etalle, S., Guttman, J. (eds.) FAST 2010. LNCS, vol. 6561, pp. 111–125. Springer, Heidelberg (2011). https://doi.org/10.1007/978-3-642-19751-2_8

16. Delaune, S., Kremer, S., Steel, G.: Formal analysis of PKCS#11 and proprietary extensions. J. Comput. Secur. **18**(6), 1211–1245 (2010)

17. Deschamps, J.-P.: Hardware Implementation of Finite-Field Arithmetic. McGraw-Hill Inc., New York (2009)

18. Dworkin, M.J.: SHA-3 Standard: Permutation-Based Hash and Extendable-Output Functions. Technical report (2015)

19. Erkök, L., Carlsson, M., Wick, A.: Hardware/software co-verification of cryptographic algorithms using cryptol. In: Formal Methods in Computer-Aided Design, 2009. FMCAD 2009, pp. 188–191 (2009)

20. Gaži, P., Pietrzak, K., Tessaro, S.: The exact PRF security of truncation: tight bounds for keyed sponges and truncated CBC. In: Gennaro, R., Robshaw, M. (eds.) CRYPTO 2015. LNCS, vol. 9215, pp. 368–387. Springer, Heidelberg (2015). https://doi.org/10.1007/978-3-662-47989-6_18
21. Hofheinz, D., Shoup, V.: GNUC: a new universal composability framework. Cryptology ePrint Archive (2011). http://eprint.iacr.org/
22. Jacomme, C., Kremer, S.: An extensive formal analysis of multi-factor authentication protocols. In: 31st IEEE Computer Security Foundations Symposium, CSF 2018, Oxford, United Kingdom, 9–12 July 2018, pp. 1–15. IEEE Computer Society (2018)
23. Jean, J.: TikZ for Cryptographers (2016). https://www.iacr.org/authors/tikz/
24. Kremer, S., Künnemann, R.: Automated analysis of security protocols with global state. J. Comput. Secur. **24**, 583–616 (2016)
25. Kremer, S., Künnemann, R., Steel, G.: Universally composable key-management. In: Crampton, J., Jajodia, S., Mayes, K. (eds.) ESORICS 2013. LNCS, vol. 8134, pp. 327–344. Springer, Heidelberg (2013). https://doi.org/10.1007/978-3-642-40203-6_19
26. Künnemann, R., Nemati, H.: MAC-in-the-Box: Verifying a Minimalistic Hard- ware Design for MAC Computation (extended). https://bit.ly/2yyttvL
27. Künnemann, R., Steel, G.: YubiSecure? Formal security analysis results for the Yubikey and YubiHSM. In: Jøsang, A., Samarati, P., Petrocchi, M. (eds.) STM 2012. LNCS, vol. 7783, pp. 257–272. Springer, Heidelberg (2013). https://doi.org/10.1007/978-3-642-38004-4_17
28. Küsters, R., and Tuengerthal, M.: The IITM model: a simple and expressive model for universal composability. Technical report 2013/025, Cryptology ePrint Archive (2013)
29. Lochbihler, A.: Probabilistic functions and cryptographic oracles in higher order logic. In: Thiemann, P. (ed.) ESOP 2016. LNCS, vol. 9632, pp. 503–531. Springer, Heidelberg (2016). https://doi.org/10.1007/978-3-662-49498-1_20
30. NV, G.: Smart card basics - A short guide (2019). https://www.gemalto.com/companyinfo/smart-cards-basics
31. Pessl, P., Hutter, M.: Pushing the limits of SHA-3 hardware implementations to fit on RFID. In: Bertoni, G., Coron, J.-S. (eds.) CHES 2013. LNCS, vol. 8086, pp. 126–141. Springer, Heidelberg (2013). https://doi.org/10.1007/978-3-642-40349-1_8
32. Petcher, A., Morrisett, G.: The foundational cryptography framework. In: Focardi, R., Myers, A. (eds.) POST 2015. LNCS, vol. 9036, pp. 53–72. Springer, Heidelberg (2015). https://doi.org/10.1007/978-3-662-46666-7_4
33. Scerri, G., Stanley-Oakes, R.: Analysis of KeyWrapping APIs: generic policies, computational security. In: 29th Computer Security Foundations Symposium, pp. 281–295. IEEE Computer Society (2016)
34. Meier, S., Schmidt, B., Cremers, C., Basin, D.: The TAMARIN prover for the symbolic analysis of security protocols. In: Sharygina, N., Veith, H. (eds.) CAV 2013. LNCS, vol. 8044, pp. 696–701. Springer, Heidelberg (2013). https://doi.org/10.1007/978-3-642-39799-8_48
35. Shao, J., Qin, Y., Feng, D., Wang, W.: Formal analysis of enhanced authorization in the TPM 2.0. In: 10th ACM Symposium on Information, Computer and Communications Security (ASIA CCS 2015), pp. 273–284. ACM (2015)
36. Slind, K., Owens, S., Iyoda, J., Gordon, M.: Proof producing synthesis of arithmetic and cryptographic hardware. Form. Asp. Comput. **19**(3), 343–362 (2007)

37. Srinivas, S., Balfanz, D., Tiffany, E., Alliance, F., Czeskis, A.: Universal 2nd factor (U2F) overview. FIDO Alliance Proposed Standard (2015)
38. Ye, K.Q., Green, M., Sanguansin, N., Beringer, L., Petcher, A., Appel, A.W.: Verified correctness and security of mbedTLS HMAC-DRBG. In: Proceedings of the 2017 ACM SIGSAC Conference on Computer and Communications Security (CCS 2017), pp. 2007–2020. ACM (2017)

Evaluating the Effectiveness of Heuristic Worst-Case Noise Analysis in FHE

Anamaria Costache[1(✉)], Kim Laine[2], and Rachel Player[1]

[1] Royal Holloway, University of London, Egham, UK
{anamaria.costache,rachel.player}@rhul.ac.uk
[2] Microsoft Research, Seattle, USA
kim.laine@microsoft.com

Abstract. The purpose of this paper is to test the accuracy of worst-case heuristic bounds on the noise growth in ring-based homomorphic encryption schemes. We use the methodology of Iliashenko (Ph.D. thesis, 2019) to provide a new heuristic noise analysis for the BGV scheme. We demonstrate that for both the BGV and FV schemes, this approach gives tighter bounds than previous heuristic approaches, by as much as 10 bits of noise budget. Then, we provide experimental data on the noise growth of HElib and SEAL ciphertexts, in order to evaluate how well the heuristic bounds model the noise growth in practice. We find that, in spite of our improvements, there is still a gap between the heuristic estimate of the noise and the observed noise in practice. We extensively justify that a heuristic worst-case approach inherently leads to this gap, and hence leads to selecting significantly larger parameters than needed. As an additional contribution, we update the comparison between the two schemes presented by Costache and Smart (CT-RSA, 2016). Our new analysis shows that the practical crossover point at which BGV begins to outperform FV occurs for very large plaintext moduli, well beyond the crossover point reported by Costache and Smart.

1 Introduction

Fully homomorphic encryption enables the evaluation of arbitrary polynomials on encrypted data, without requiring access to the secret key. In contrast, somewhat homomorphic encryption enables the evaluation of limited functions on encrypted data; this is usually characterised by a bound of the depth of the circuits that can be evaluated. The first fully homomorphic encryption scheme was presented by Gentry [22], whose construction augmented a somewhat homomorphic encryption scheme with a technique known as bootstrapping.

In all homomorphic encryption schemes ciphertexts contain noise that grows during homomorphic evaluation operations. Once the noise exceeds a certain threshold, decryption will fail. In practice, managing the noise to ensure it is always below the threshold can be done in two ways. The first approach uses the bootstrapping procedure, which takes as input a ciphertext with large noise, and outputs a new ciphertext which has less noise and can be further computed on.

© Springer Nature Switzerland AG 2020
L. Chen et al. (Eds.): ESORICS 2020, LNCS 12309, pp. 546–565, 2020.
https://doi.org/10.1007/978-3-030-59013-0_27

Hence by bootstrapping at appropriate points, the entire evaluation can be performed. The second approach is to pre-determine the function to be evaluated and set the parameters so as to allow for the noise growth that this specific function will incur. Using this method, we are sure that the output ciphertext at the end of the evaluation will have noise below the threshold, thus no bootstrapping will be necessary and correct decryption is ensured. In either case, good understanding of the noise growth behaviour is essential to achieve correctness and optimal performance. In fact, a good understanding of the noise growth in any scheme is crucial to parameter setting, large parameters remaining one of the main hurdles in homomorphic encryption development.

Contributions. This paper presents two main contributions. Firstly, we evaluate the effectiveness of the heuristic worst-case method. We do so by reworking the noise growth estimates produced by this method for the somewhat homomorphic encryption (SHE) schemes BGV [10] and FV[1] [21]. We use the Iliashenko method [27] for obtaining the heuristic bounds. The bounds for FV were presented in [27], with the exception of modulus switching, while the BGV bounds we present using this method are new. We compare these new bounds against the previous heuristic analyses [18,23,24], and show that Iliashenko's approach improves on the previous approach by as much as 10 bits of noise budget in certain settings, particularly so for the FV scheme. To demonstrate this, we provide the noise estimated by the old bounds and the new approach in Tables 1, 2, 3, and 4.

Next, we evaluate the practical noise growth incurred when evaluating homomorphic operations in BGV and FV by looking at their implementations in the HElib [26] and SEAL [36] libraries, respectively. The first HElib noise results concern the growth of the *critical quantity* [18] and can be found in Table 1. In order to facilitate comparison, we define and implement in HElib a noise budget for the critical quantity for BGV, analogous to the *invariant noise budget* [36] for FV that is implemented in SEAL. The results in terms of the noise budget are presented in Table 2. Our SEAL noise results are presented in Tables 3 and 4, for the binary encoding and batch settings, respectively. We find that, despite the improvements mentioned above, the predictions are not tight, and that a significant gap between the predicted noise and the actual noise remains. We will refer to this gap as the *heuristic-to-practical gap*.

We conclude that a worst-case heuristic estimate of homomorphic noise growth is inadequate. That is to say, we conjecture that the theoretical bounds we present in this work cannot be made tighter. We give an extensive justification for this conjecture, and comment on other methods we attempted for improvement, in Sect. 6. Therefore, we propose further tightening the heuristic-to-practical gap as an open problem. We believe that a better model of the noise growth behaviour can only be achieved by fine-tuning the analysis of a specific scheme to its specific implementation.

Our second main contribution, which can be of independent interest, is to use our improved analysis to update the Costache-Smart [18] comparison of the

---

[1] FV is based on a scheme of Brakerski [9] and hence is sometimes referred to as BFV.

BGV and FV schemes. We improve upon the previous work of Costache-Smart in several ways. As well as applying the updated noise analysis following [27], we use a different notion of noise for FV than that used in [18], namely the invariant noise. In addition, our comparison relies on an up-to-date security analysis conforming to HE standards [1]. Indeed, it has since been shown [17] that parameters used in [18] that were estimated to have 80 bits of security are now estimated to have as little as 50. In contrast, the HE standards security recommendations start at the level of 128 bits [1].

The BGV and FV schemes remain two of the most popular SHE schemes, as they continue to see many performance improvements and optimisations and are implemented in several actively maintained homomorphic encryption libraries, including PALISADE[2] as well as SEAL and HElib. It is therefore an important question to accurately assess how they perform and compare them against one another.

We conduct our comparison for a range of plaintext moduli t and present our results in Tables 5, 6, 7, 8 and 9. We expect that BGV will outperform FV asymptotically and our results remain consistent with this. An important issue in practice is to understand where the crossover point is, and our key conclusion is that the crossover point is somewhere between $t = 2^{32}$ and $t = 2^{64}$, far beyond the crossover point $t \approx 2^8$ reported in [18].

In most cases, our results show that BGV and FV present only minor performance differences in terms of supporting a specific homomorphic evaluation. We can conclude that, from the perspective of computational capabilities, the question of whether or not BGV should be preferred to FV should not be an important one when deciding between the two schemes.

Related Work. The BGV and FV schemes are among the primary schemes being considered in the ongoing effort to standardise homomorphic encryption[3]. Indeed, the Homomorphic Encryption Security Standard [1] explicitly mentions the comparison of BGV and FV as an open problem, and motivates the present work. The analysis presented in our work should be expected to feed into the ongoing effort of the standardisation consortium [11] towards automation such as compilers or optimiser toolchains. An accurate noise growth estimator is likely to be a central component of any such tool.

A comparison of BGV as implemented in HElib and FV as implemented in SEAL was identified as an interesting and challenging open problem in [13]. Al Badawi et al. [35] investigate the behaviour of the BEHZ [5] and HPS [25] variants of FV[4], and call for further study on BEHZ-FV noise growth, which further motivates the present work.

Previous comparisons of homomorphic encryption schemes include [18,28,30]. In our comparison, we do not consider newer schemes such as CKKS [15] or TFHE [16], which come with entirely different trade-offs. We also do not consider

---

[2] https://git.njit.edu/palisade/PALISADE.

[3] HomomorphicEncryption.org.

[4] The results of [35] were recently revisited by Bajard et al. [6].

the NTRU-based schemes YASHE [8] and LTV [32], which are vulnerable to attacks in "overstretched" parameter settings of interest [4, 29].

2   Preliminaries

For reasons of space, we recall the BGV scheme in Appendix A and the FV scheme in Appendix B. As in prior work [18], we deviate from the original description of FV by also defining a modulus switching operation. In particular, we describe switching from a modulus q to a modulus p.

Parameters. A Ring-LWE-based (levelled) FHE scheme is parameterised by L, n, Q, t, χ, S, w, ℓ and λ. There are L primes $p_0, \ldots, p_{L-1}$ which are used to form the chain of moduli $q_0, \ldots, q_{L-1}$. Elements in the chain of moduli are formed as $q_k = \prod_{j=0}^{k} p_j$. The dimension n is a typically chosen as a power of two, and we will only use such n in this work. The dimension n, plaintext modulus t and the chain of moduli parameterise the underlying plaintext and ciphertext rings. In particular, the ciphertext modulus $Q = q_{L-1} = \prod_{j=0}^{L-1} p_j$ is the product of all the primes. Each intermediate prime q_j corresponds to a level and all ciphertexts are with respect to a specific level. We denote by q some fixed level when describing the schemes, so that the ciphertext space at any given moment is $R_q = \mathbb{Z}_q[x]/(x^n + 1)$. Note that for key generation and for fresh ciphertexts, we always have $q = Q$. The plaintext space is always $R_t = \mathbb{Z}_t[x]/(x^n + 1)$. Let w be a base, then $\ell + 1 = \lfloor \log_w q \rfloor + 1$ is the number of terms in the decomposition into base w of an integer in base q. The security parameter is λ.

The Ring-LWE error distribution is denoted χ and is typically a discrete gaussian with standard deviation $\sigma = 3.2$ [1]. The underlying Ring-LWE problem, parameterised by n, Q and σ, is a variant with small secret. The parameter S denotes the secret key distribution. In the FV scheme [21] the distribution S is the uniform distribution on the subspace of R_q consisting of polynomials whose coefficients are in the set $\{0, 1\}$. In the SEAL implementation [36] the distribution S is the uniform distribution on the subspace of R_q consisting of polynomials whose coefficients are in the set $\{-1, 0, 1\}$. In the BGV scheme [10], the distribution S is the same as the error distribution χ. In the HElib[5] implementation [26], S is the distribution on the subspace of R_q consisting of polynomials whose coefficients are in the set $\{-1, 0, 1\}$ where each coefficient is sampled as follows: the element 0 is sampled with probability 0.5 and the elements ± 1 are each sampled with probability 0.25. To obtain the heuristic bounds for both BGV and FV, we take S to be the uniform distribution on the subspace of R_q consisting of polynomials whose coefficients are in the set $\{-1, 0, 1\}$. This ensures our comparison of the two schemes in Sect. 5 is fair.

Canonical Embedding Norm. Following previous work [18, 23, 24, 27], we will present heuristic bounds for the noise growth behaviour of FV and BGV with respect to the canonical embedding norm $\|\cdot\|^{\mathrm{can}}$. Throughout this work, the

---

[5] Since January 2019 the HElib default secret distribution is no longer sparse.

notation $\|a\|$ refers to the infinity norm of a, while $\|a\|^{\mathrm{can}}$ refers to the canonical embedding norm. The canonical embedding norm of an element a is defined to be the infinity norm of the canonical embedding[6] $\sigma(a)$ of a, so $\|a\|^{\mathrm{can}} = \|\sigma(a)\|$.

We will use the following properties of the canonical embedding norm. For any polynomial $a \in R$ we have $\|a\| \le c_m \|a\|^{\mathrm{can}} \le \|a\|_1$ where c_m is a constant known as the ring expansion factor (see [20]). We have $c_m = 1$ when the dimension n is a power of two [20]. In this case, it suffices for correctness to ensure that $\|v\|^{\mathrm{can}}$ is less than the maximal value of $\|v\|$ such that decryption succeeds. For any polynomials a, b we have $\|ab\|^{\mathrm{can}} \le \|a\|^{\mathrm{can}} \|b\|^{\mathrm{can}}$.

For our bounds, we use the method presented in [27]. This allows us to improve our noise bounds compared to previous ones [18,23,24] by as much as 10 bits of noise budget in certain settings. Therefore, the noise bounds we present in this work are much tighter than ones presented in previous works.

Let $R = \mathbb{Z}[x]/(x^n + 1)$ and let ζ be a primitive $2n^{th}$ root of unity (it does not matter which one, by the definition of the canonical embedding norm). Let $a \in R$ be a polynomial for which the variance of each coefficient is V_a. Then, the variance of the random variable $a(\zeta)$ is nV_a [18,24,27]. We use the fact that $\mathrm{erfc}(6) \approx 2^{-55}$ to obtain the following bound $\|a\|^{\mathrm{can}} \le 6\sqrt{n}\sqrt{V_a}$.

We also use the following facts. Let V_a and V_b the variances of the coefficients of two polynomials $a \in R$ and $b \in R$ chosen from zero-mean distributions, and let γ be a constant. The variance of the coefficients of the polynomial $a + b$ is $V_{a+b} = V_a + V_b$. The variance of the coefficients of the polynomial γa is $V_{\gamma a} = \gamma^2 V_a$. The variance of the coefficients of the polynomial ab is $V_{ab} = nV_a V_b$ (see [27] for a proof).

The variances in situations of interest for this paper are as follows. The coefficients of a polynomial f that are distributed uniformly in $[-\frac{k}{2}, \frac{k}{2}]$ have variance $V_f \approx \frac{k^2}{12}$. The coefficients of a polynomial e that are drawn from an error distribution χ, which has standard deviation σ, have variance $V_e = \sigma^2$. The coefficients of a polynomial s that are drawn from the uniform distribution on the ternary set $\{-1, 0, 1\}$ have variance $V_s = \frac{2}{3}$.

3   BGV Noise Growth in Practice

3.1   Noise Growth Behaviour

In this section we present new heuristic bounds on the noise growth behaviour of BGV, developed using the methodology of [27]. In Sect. 3.2 we compare our bounds with those that would be obtained following the methodology presented in prior work [18,23,24], and show that our analysis provides a better estimate of the noise growth.

Our bounds use the *critical quantity* [18] definition of noise, which is the notion of noise used in the HElib implementation of BGV. We assume that the plaintext is chosen uniformly at random from the plaintext space. We further assume that the secret key distribution S is the uniform ternary distribution.

---

[6] For a definition of the canonical embedding and other algebraic background, see [33].

Earlier heuristic bounds for BGV [18,23,24] were presented assuming a sparse secret distribution, in line with earlier versions of HElib. For comparison with our new bounds, we redo the prior analysis so that in Tables 1 and 2, the '[18]' column refers to bounds that would be obtained using the heuristic method presented in [18] and assuming a uniform ternary distribution for the secret key.

Definition 1 (BGV critical quantity [18]). *Let* $ct = (c_0, c_1)$ *be a BGV ciphertext encrypting the message* $m \in R_t$. *Its* critical quantity v *is the polynomial*

$$v = [ct(s)]_q = (c_0 + c_1 s) \pmod{q}.$$

During decryption, we first compute the critical quantity and then take the result modulo t. If there is no wraparound modulo q then for some integer polynomial k, the critical quantity satisfies $[ct(s)]_q = m + tk$. The reduction modulo t hence returns m. Therefore for correctness, we require that $\|v\| \le q/2$.

Lemma 1 (Maximal noise [18]). *A BGV ciphertext* ct *encrypting a message* m *can be correctly decrypted if the critical quantity* v *satisfies* $\|v\| < q/2$.

Encrypt: Let ct be a fresh BGV encryption of a message $m \in R_t$. With high probability, the critical quantity v in ct satisfies

$$\|v\|^{\mathrm{can}} \le 6t \sqrt{\frac{n}{12} + n\sigma^2 \left(\frac{4}{3}n + 1\right)}.$$

To see this, we use that for a polynomial a with coefficients with variance V_a, and a scalar t, the polynomial ta has coefficients with variance $V_{at} = t^2 V_a$. The noise polynomial is $v = m + t(e_1 + e_2 s - eu)$. Its coefficients have variance

$$V_v = V_{m+t(e_1+e_2s-eu)} = V_m + t^2 V_{e_1+e_2s-eu} = t^2 \left(\frac{1}{12} + \sigma^2 \left(\frac{4}{3}n + 1\right)\right).$$

Hence $\|v\|^{\mathrm{can}} \le 6\sqrt{nV_v} = 6\sqrt{nt^2 \left(\frac{1}{12} + \sigma^2 \left(\frac{4}{3}n + 1\right)\right)}$.

Add [18]: Let ct_1 and ct_2 be two BGV ciphertexts encrypting $m_1, m_2 \in R_t$, and having critical quantities v_1, v_2, respectively. Then the critical quantity v_{add} in their sum ct_{add} satisfies $\|v_{\mathrm{add}}\|^{\mathrm{can}} \le \|v_1\|^{\mathrm{can}} + \|v_2\|^{\mathrm{can}}$.

Mult [18]: Let ct_1 and ct_2 be two BGV ciphertexts encrypting $m_1, m_2 \in R_t$, and having critical quantities v_1, v_2, respectively. Then the critical quantity v_{mult} in their product ct_{mult} satisfies $\|v_{\mathrm{mult}}\|^{\mathrm{can}} \le \|v_1\|^{\mathrm{can}} \cdot \|v_2\|^{\mathrm{can}}$.

Relinearize: Let ct be a BGV ciphertext encrypting m and having noise v. Let ct_{relin} be the ciphertext obtained by the relinearization of ct. Then with high probability, the critical quantity v_{relin} in ct_{relin} satisfies

$$\|v_{\mathrm{relin}}\|^{\mathrm{can}} \le \|v\|^{\mathrm{can}} + t\sqrt{(\ell + 1)}nw\sigma\sqrt{3}.$$

The justification is analogous to the FV relinearization bound proved in [27].

ModSwitch: Let ct be a BGV ciphertext encrypting m with critical quantity v with respect to a modulus q. Let ct_{mod} be the ciphertext encrypting m obtained by modulus switching to the modulus p. Then with high probability, the critical quantity v_{mod} in ct_{mod} satisfies

$$\|v_{\text{mod}}\|^{\text{can}} \leq \frac{p}{q} \|v\|^{\text{can}} + t\sqrt{3n + 2n^2}.$$

Let $\text{ct}_{\text{mod}} = (c_0', c_1')$, the result of the modulus switching operation applied to $\text{ct} = (c_0, c_1)$. As in [18], we let τ_i be the rounding error of $\frac{p}{q} \cdot \delta_i$. Then:

$$\|c_0' + c_1's\|^{\text{can}} \leq \frac{p}{q}\left(\|c_0 + c_1s\|^{\text{can}} + \|\delta_0 + \delta_1 s\|^{\text{can}}\right) \leq \frac{p}{q}\|v\|^{\text{can}} + \|\tau_0 + \tau_1 s\|^{\text{can}}$$

$$\leq \frac{p}{q}\|v\|^{\text{can}} + 6t\sqrt{\frac{n}{12}\left(1 + \frac{2n}{3}\right)}.$$

3.2   Practical Experiments

In this section we compare the observed critical quantity in HElib ciphertexts formed as a result of certain homomorphic evaluation operations with expected estimates on the noise growth from the heuristic upper bounds. We run the following experiment for a certain number of trials: we step through a specific homomorphic evaluation, and for each operation, we record the observed noise growth. We then output the mean of the observed noise. Separately, we compute an estimate of the noise growth using the heuristic bounds presented in Sect. 3.1.

HElib offers a debugging function[7] that implements an augmented decryption, which also returns the critical quantity v. We modify this to create a function that returns $\|v\|$.

Table 1. The column $\overline{x}$ gives the logarithm to base 2 of the observed mean of the noise in HElib ciphertexts over 10000 trials of a specific homomorphic evaluation for parameter sets with dimension $n \in \{2048, 4096, 8192, 16384\}$. The column E gives an estimate of the noise growth using heuristic bounds obtained following our analysis. The remaining column gives an estimate of the noise growth using heuristic bounds obtained following an analysis as in [18].

n	Enc			Add			Mult			ModSwitch		
	[18]	E	$\overline{x}$	[18]	E	$\overline{x}$	[18]	E	$\overline{x}$	[18]	E	$\overline{x}$
2048	19.0	17.1	5.12	20.0	18.1	5.62	39.0	35.1	14.7	–	–	–
4096	20.0	18.1	5.19	21.0	19.1	5.69	40.9	37.1	15.3	15.5	14.1	3.62
8192	21.0	19.1	5.25	22.0	20.1	5.76	42.9	39.1	15.8	16.5	15.1	3.65
16384	22.0	20.1	5.31	23.0	21.1	5.81	44.9	41.1	16.4	17.5	16.1	3.70

---

[7] decryptAndPrint.

Table 2. The column $\bar{x}$ gives the observed mean of the noise budget in HElib ciphertexts over 10000 trials of a specific homomorphic evaluation for parameter sets with dimension $n \in \{2048, 4096, 8192, 16384\}$. The column E gives an estimate of the noise budget using heuristic bounds obtained following our analysis. The remaining column gives an estimate of the noise budget using heuristic bounds obtained following an analysis as in [18].

n	Enc			Add			Mult			ModSwitch		
	[18]	E	$\bar{x}$	[18]	E	$\bar{x}$	[18]	E	$\bar{x}$	[18]	E	$\bar{x}$
2048	34.0	35.0	41.1	33.0	34.0	40.2	14.0	17.0	26.0	–	–	–
4096	88.0	89.0	97.9	87.0	88.0	97.0	67.0	70.0	82.4	38.0	39.0	38.1
8192	196	197	209	195	196	209	174	177	194	146	147	150
16384	415	416	433	414	415	432	392	395	416	365	366	373

The evaluation is as follows in the i-th trial. We first generate fresh ciphertexts ct_1 and ct_2 encrypting $i+1$ and i. Next, generate ct_3 as the homomorphic addition of ct_1 and ct_2. Next, generate ct_4 as the homomorphic multiplication of ct_3 and ct_2. Finally, generate ct_5 by modulus switching ct_4 down to the next prime in the chain.

Relinearization for BGV as defined in Appendix A above is not implemented in HElib. Instead, a different variant is implemented (see [24]). Indeed, relinearization can be (and, in practice, is) implemented in a number of ways, all with easy-to-understand additive noise growth. Therefore, we do not investigate the noise growth behaviour during relinearization in our practical experiments.

Table 1 gives the results of this experiment for 10000 trials. We used the follow default parameter settings in HElib: we set the standard deviation of the error distribution as $\sigma = 3.2$ and the security parameter[8] $\lambda = 80$. The HElib parameter c, which relates to relinearization, was set as a default value $c = 2$. We set the number of plaintext slots as $s = 1$ as we did not require batching functionality. We used the default HElib secret distribution, which slightly differs from a uniform ternary secret distribution, as discussed in Sect. 2.

We set the dimension[9] $n \in \{2048, 4096, 8192, 16384\}$. The HElib parameter nBits is passed to the function buildModChain which sets an appropriate chain of moduli for which the product of all the primes, Q, satisfies $Q \approx 2^{nBits}$. We set nBits $\in \{54, 109, 218, 438\}$, which are the same values as for the default Q in SEAL [36]. The parameters for $n = 2048$ were not large enough to perform modulus switching. We set the plaintext modulus[10] as $t = 3$. Such a small plaintext modulus means that the values encrypted in our trials 'cover' the whole

---

[8] In HElib, the security parameter is typically denoted as k. This may not be an accurate security estimate [3].

[9] In HElib, the dimension is selected as m where $n = \varphi(m)$ and $\varphi(\cdot)$ is the Euler totient function. Hence, we set $m \in \{4096, 8192, 16384, 32768\}$. We verified that our other choices allowed for these m using the function FindM.

[10] In HElib, the plaintext modulus is parameterised as p^r hence we set $p = 3$ and $r = 1$.

plaintext space and hence the assumption used in the noise bounds that m is a random plaintext is reasonable.

Table 1 shows that the heuristic bounds hold on average: the actual observed mean noise is less than the estimated noise. However, it will be difficult to directly compare these results with those for experiments in SEAL, which are given in terms of a *noise budget*, rather than the noise itself [36]. In order to facilitate an easier comparison, we define a noise budget for BGV that is analogous to the invariant noise budget in FV.

Definition 2 (BGV noise budget). *Let* ct *be a BGV ciphertext with respect to modulus q having critical quantity v. The* noise budget *for this ciphertext is defined as*

$$\log_2(q) - \log_2(\|v\|) - 1.$$

To see that this is an analogous definition, note that for FV the invariant noise budget is defined in [36] as $-\log_2(2 \cdot \|v\|) = \log_2(q) - \log_2(q \cdot \|v\|) - 1$. This captures that for correctness in FV, we require that $q \cdot \|v\| < \frac{q}{2}$. Similarly, Definition 2 captures that for correctness in BGV, we require $\|v\| \le q/2$.

We implemented a function in HElib to measure the noise budget, and a function to estimate the noise budget using the heuristic bounds. We then ran the same experiment as detailed above to compare the growth of the observed noise budget in HElib ciphertexts with that predicted from the heuristic bounds. Table 2 gives the results of this experiment for 10000 trials.

We see from Tables 1 and 2 that the heuristic bounds hold: the observed mean noise is less than the estimated noise, so the observed mean noise budget is more than the estimated noise budget. Moreover, we see that using our new analysis to obtain the heuristic bounds gives an estimate closer to the observed noise than an analysis as in the line of prior work [18,23,24].

Despite this improvement, the heuristic bounds are still not tight[11]. For example, for fresh ciphertexts, our heuristic bound predicts 6 to 17 fewer bits of remaining noise budget than the mean observed. We see that the gap compounds as we move through the computation: after multiplication, the gap is 9 to 21 bits. The gap narrows after modulus switching, to below 7 bits. Although the HElib implementation uses a secret key distribution that is slightly different from the uniform ternary distribution assumed in the heuristic bounds, we do not expect this to significantly contribute to the gap.

We also found that the observed noise budgets follow narrow distributions, which gives us confidence that the heuristic bounds will hold very often, and so could be relied upon to set parameters for correctness. However, since the heuristic bounds are not tight, they may lead us to choose larger parameters than is necessary. It is not clear that choosing BGV parameters using the heuristic bounds will be optimal for performance.

---

[11] An exception is modulus switching for $n = 4096$, which seems to be well-modelled by both approaches for obtaining heuristic bounds.

4   FV Noise Growth in Practice

4.1   Heuristic Upper Bounds

To evaluate the effectiveness of heuristic worst-case noise analyses for FV, we will use the heuristic upper bounds for FV presented by Iliashenko [27]. For reasons of space we do not reproduce these bounds, except for modulus switching, for which a bound was not presented in [27]. In Sect. 4.2 we compare these bounds with those that would be obtained following the methodology of previous work [14, 18,23,24], and show that the Iliashenko method provides a better estimate of the noise growth.

The bounds use the *invariant noise* definition for noise [14], as used in the SEAL [36] implementation of FV. We assume that the secret key distribution S is the uniform ternary distribution, as in SEAL [36], and that plaintexts are chosen uniformly at random in the plaintext space.

Definition 3 (FV invariant noise [36]). *Let* $ct = (c_0, c_1)$ *be an FV ciphertext encrypting the message* $m \in R_t$. *Its* invariant noise v *is the polynomial with the smallest infinity norm such that, for some integer coefficient polynomial* a,

$$\frac{t}{q} ct(s) = \frac{t}{q}(c_0 + c_1 s) = m + v + at.$$

The intuition for this definition of noise is that v is exactly the term which will be removed by the rounding in a successful decryption. Therefore for correctness, we require that $\|v\| < \frac{1}{2}$ [36].

ModSwitch: Let ct be an FV ciphertext encrypting m with invariant noise v with respect to a modulus q. Let ct_{mod} be the ciphertext encrypting m obtained by modulus switching to the modulus p. Then with high probability, the invariant noise v_{mod} in ct_{mod} satisfies

$$\|v_{\mathrm{mod}}\|^{\mathrm{can}} \leq \|v\|^{\mathrm{can}} + \frac{t}{p} \cdot \sqrt{3n + 2n^2}.$$

The bound can be seen as analogous to the BGV modulus switching bound (Sect. 3.1) and is justified by a similar argument.

4.2   Practical Experiments

In this section we compare the observed noise in SEAL ciphertexts formed as a result of certain homomorphic evaluation operations with expected estimates on the noise growth from the heuristic upper bounds. We run the following experiment for a certain number of trials: we step through a specific homomorphic evaluation and for each operation we record the observed noise growth. We then output the mean of the observed noise. Separately, we compute an estimate of the noise growth using the heuristic bounds.

Recall that since $\|v\| \leq \|v\|^{\mathrm{can}}$, we can use the bounds presented in Sect. 4.1 as upper bounds for the infinity norm $\|v\|$ of the invariant noise v. Rather than working with the invariant noise v directly, since it can be an extremely small quantity, SEAL instead uses the current *invariant noise budget* [36], which is defined as $-\log_2(2 \cdot \|v\|)$.

We conduct the same evaluation in SEAL as we did in Sect. 3.2 for HElib. In particular, this means we do not measure the noise growth in relinearization. Apart from the reasons discussed in Sect. 3.2, this is also necessary for two reasons. Firstly, the choice of the parameter w is no longer part of the API in SEAL, so it is difficult to compare to the relinearization heuristic bound. Secondly, SEAL reserves one of the chain of moduli as 'special prime' used both in relinearization and in a modulus switching implemented as part of the encryption operation. This reduces noise in a fresh SEAL ciphertext, but deviates from a plain FV encryption, and hence would not be accurately captured by the fresh noise bound presented in [27]. We modify SEAL to disable this special prime functionality. This enables us to obtain data on the noise growth in an implementation of plain FV encryption, at the cost of being unable to investigate relinearization.

The evaluation is as follows in the i-th trial. First, generate fresh ciphertexts $\mathtt{ct}_1$ and $\mathtt{ct}_2$ encrypting $i + 1$ and i. Next, generate $\mathtt{ct}_3$ as the homomorphic addition of $\mathtt{ct}_1$ and $\mathtt{ct}_2$. Next, generate $\mathtt{ct}_4$ as the homomorphic multiplication of $\mathtt{ct}_3$ and $\mathtt{ct}_2$. Finally, generate $\mathtt{ct}_5$ by modulus switching $\mathtt{ct}_4$ down to the next prime in the chain. We ran this evaluation over 10000 trials, using the SEAL default parameters n, Q, σ for the 128-bit security level for dimensions $n \in \{2048, 4096, 8192, 16384\}$. The SEAL default parameters for $n = 2048$ correspond to a chain of only one modulus, and hence we cannot perform modulus switching in this case. We used a plaintext modulus $t = 256$. Such a plaintext modulus means that the values encrypted in our trials 'cover' the whole plaintext space and hence the assumption used in the noise bounds that m is a random plaintext is reasonable. To generate the plaintexts encoding $i + 1$ and i, we used the default binary encoder. Table 3 reports on the results of this experiment[12].

In a second experiment, we repeated the above evaluation using a batch encoder. In each trial we generate two plaintexts, encoding the values j and $j + 1$ for $j \in \{0, 1, \ldots, n\}$ respectively in each of the n slots. To enable batching, we changed the plaintext modulus to be $t = 65537$, a prime congruent to 1 modulo $2n$. All other parameters were kept the same. Table 4 reports on the results of this experiment for 10000 trials.

Tables 3 and 4 show that the heuristic bounds indeed hold: the observed mean noise is less than the estimated noise, so the observed mean noise budget is more than the estimate obtained using the heuristic bounds. This gives us confidence that the heuristic bounds will hold very often, and so can be used reliably to

---

[12] Bajard *et al.* [6] recently identified a bug in the implementation of multiplication in SEAL, resulting in a ciphertext that is has more noise than expected when the plaintext modulus is large. Our experiments, using a small plaintext modulus $t = 256$, are not affected. This bug is expected to be fixed in SEAL v3.5.

Table 3. Binary encoder setting. The column $\bar{x}$ gives the observed mean of the invariant noise budget in SEAL ciphertexts over 10000 trials of a specific homomorphic evaluation for parameter sets with dimension $n \in \{2048, 4096, 8192, 16384\}$. The column E gives an estimate of the noise budget using heuristic bounds obtained following our analysis. The remaining column gives an estimate of the noise budget using heuristic bounds obtained following an analysis as in prior work [14].

n	Enc			Add			Mult			ModSwitch		
	[14]	E	$\bar{x}$	[14]	E	$\bar{x}$	[14]	E	$\bar{x}$	[14]	E	$\bar{x}$
2048	27.0	29.0	35.4	26.0	28.0	35.0	0.000	8.00	16.9	–	–	–
4096	81.0	83.0	90.0	80.0	82.0	89.1	51.0	61.0	69.8	31.0	33.0	50.2
8192	189	191	198	188	190	198	157	168	178	139	141	151
16384	408	410	418	407	409	417	375	386	396	358	360	365

Table 4. Batching setting. The column $\bar{x}$ gives the observed mean of the invariant noise budget in SEAL ciphertexts over 10000 trials of a specific homomorphic evaluation for parameter sets with dimension $n \in \{2048, 4096, 8192, 16384\}$. The column E gives an estimate of the noise budget using heuristic bounds obtained following our analysis. The remaining column gives an estimate of the noise budget using heuristic bounds obtained following an analysis as in prior work [14].

n	Enc			Add			Mult			ModSwitch		
	[14]	E	$\bar{x}$	[14]	E	$\bar{x}$	[14]	E	$\bar{x}$	[14]	E	$\bar{x}$
2048	19.0	21.0	27.4	18.0	20.0	27.0	0.000	0.00	1.00	–	–	–
4096	71.0	71.0	82.0	70.0	70.0	81.1	32.0	41.0	54.0	23.0	25.0	42.3
8192	179	179	190	178	178	190	139	148	161	131	133	143
16384	398	398	410	397	397	409	356	366	380	350	352	357

set parameters to ensure correctness. However, the bounds do not appear to be tight. Indeed, for encryption, the heuristic bound predicts 6 to 8 (respectively 6 to 12) fewer bits of remaining noise budget than the mean observed in Table 3 (respectively Table 4). This gap is compounded as the number of operations increases, reaching 8 to 17 (respectively 7 to 14) bits after multiplication in Table 3 (respectively Table 4, for $n = 4096$ and above). It appears that the gap reduces after modulus switching, with 8 or 9 fewer bits of remaining noise budget than the mean observed in both Table 3 and Table 4. Comparing to Table 2 we see that these trends are all similar to the HElib case. Finally, notice that while the new method tightens the bounds by up to 3 bits for BGV as seen in Tables 1 and 2, for FV the improvement is more dramatic. Indeed, the new analysis tightens the bounds by as much as 10 bits in the case of the multiplication operation, as seen in Tables 4 and 3. This difference can be explained by looking at the multiplication bounds. The BGV bound is very simple (recall Sect. 3.1) while the complexity of the FV bound implies that this scheme has a much larger benefit from a tighter analysis.

Table 5. Logarithm to base 2 of the minimal ciphertext size in kilobytes required in the BGV and FV schemes to support the described homomorphic evaluation for L levels, for plaintext modulus $t = 3$.

Scheme	Level L														
	2	4	6	8	10	12	14	16	18	20	22	24	26	28	30
BGV	4.75	6.77	8.77	8.77	10.8	10.8	10.8	10.8	12.8	12.8	12.8	12.8	12.8	12.8	12.8
FV	4.75	6.77	8.77	8.77	8.77	10.8	10.8	10.8	10.8	12.8	12.8	12.8	12.8	12.8	12.8

Table 6. Logarithm to base 2 of the minimal ciphertext size in kilobytes required in the BGV and FV schemes to support the described homomorphic evaluation for L levels, for plaintext modulus $t = 256$. The symbol '-' indicates that the computation was too large to be supported by any parameter set.

Scheme	Level L														
	2	4	6	8	10	12	14	16	18	20	22	24	26	28	30
BGV	6.77	8.77	8.77	10.8	10.8	10.8	10.8	12.8	12.8	12.8	12.8	12.8	12.8	–	–
FV	4.75	6.77	8.77	8.77	10.8	10.8	10.8	12.8	12.8	12.8	12.8	12.8	12.8	12.8	12.8

Table 7. Logarithm to base 2 of the minimal ciphertext size in kilobytes required in the BGV and FV schemes to support the described homomorphic evaluation for L levels, for plaintext modulus $t = 32768$. The symbol '-' indicates that the computation was too large to be supported by any parameter set.

Scheme	Level L														
	2	4	6	8	10	12	14	16	18	20	22	24	26	28	30
BGV	6.77	8.77	10.8	10.8	10.8	12.8	12.8	12.8	12.8	12.8	12.8	–	–	–	–
FV	6.77	8.77	8.77	10.8	10.8	10.8	12.8	12.8	12.8	12.8	12.8	12.8	–	–	–

5   Updated Comparison Between BGV and FV

In this section we compare the BGV and FV schemes, improving on a prior comparison by Costache and Smart [18]. Our first main improvement is to select parameters that achieve a security level $\lambda = 128$ according to the Homomorphic Encryption Standard [1]. In contrast, the prior work [18] relied on a security analysis by Lindner and Peikert [31], which has been shown to be incorrect [2,3]. In fact, as shown in [17], FHE parameters which were estimated by [31] to have 80 bits of security had as little as 51 bits of security according to [2,3]. Our second main improvement is to use a heuristic noise analysis following the methodology of Iliashenko [27]. Our experimental results in Sects. 3 and 4 show that this analysis more closely represents the noise growth in implementations than the heuristic analysis that was used in [18].

Methodology. We now describe the homomorphic evaluation function used in our comparison, which is the same as was used in [18]. We begin by guessing the dimension n. We go through a pre-determined circuit as follows: we take a fresh ciphertext, perform ζ additions, followed by a multiplication, and a relinearization.

Table 8. Logarithm to base 2 of the minimal ciphertext size in kilobytes required in the BGV and FV schemes to support the described homomorphic evaluation for L levels, for plaintext modulus $t = 2^{32}$. The symbol '-' indicates that the computation was too large to be supported by any parameter set.

Scheme	Level L														
	2	4	6	8	10	12	14	16	18	20	22	24	26	28	30
BGV	6.77	8.77	10.8	12.8	12.8	12.8	12.8	–	–	–	–	–	–	–	–
FV	8.77	10.8	10.8	10.8	12.8	12.8	12.8	12.8	–	–	–	–	–	–	–

Table 9. Logarithm to base 2 of the minimal ciphertext size in kilobytes required in the BGV and FV schemes to support the described homomorphic evaluation for L levels, for plaintext modulus $t = 2^{64}$. The symbol '-' indicates that the computation was too large to be supported by any parameter set.

Scheme	Level L														
	2	4	6	8	10	12	14	16	18	20	22	24	26	28	30
BGV	8.77	10.8	12.8	12.8	12.8	–	–	–	–	–	–	–	–	–	–
FV	10.8	10.8	12.8	12.8	–	–	–	–	–	–	–	–	–	–	–

We then modulus switch down to the next prime in the chain, perform ζ additions, followed by a multiplication and relinearization, and so on. After modulus switching to the smallest prime, we check if we get a decryption error. If that is the case, we increase the guess, and repeat the procedure until decryption succeeds. Each of the circuits we consider in this work is parameterised by a number of additions ζ and a multiplicative depth L. Any circuit that is to be homomorphically evaluated consists of additions and/ or multiplications, thus this approach is as comprehensive as can be. We refer to the reader to [19] for real-life applications of such circuits.

Parameter Selection. For the given circuit, and for a fixed level L, plaintext modulus t, and security level λ, our goal is to find the smallest parameter set, in terms of ciphertext size in kilobytes, such that decryption succeeds. While we could have considered other criteria such as key size, it is ciphertexts which are sent over networks and computed on, thus a very large ciphertext could present the biggest overhead in an implementation. Therefore, we believe ciphertext size is the most relevant criterion.

To keep the comparison fair, we assume a uniform ternary distribution for the secret keys, as well for the ephemeral keys sampled in encryption, in both BGV and FV. Following the choice in [18], we perform $\zeta = 8$ additions before each multiplication. The ring constant is set to $c_m = 1$, as n (and hence m) is always a power of two. We consider a range of levels L of circuits, choosing $L \in \{2, 4, 6, \ldots, 30\}$. We set the standard deviation $\sigma = 3.2$, which follows the recommendation in the Homomorphic Encryption Standard [1]. We set the parameters n and (top modulus) Q as those recommended in the Homomorphic

Encryption Standard [1] to achieve a security level $\lambda = 128$ when the secret follows a uniform ternary distribution.

Asymptotically, we expect that BGV will outperform FV. We investigate a range of plaintext moduli to understand where the practical crossover point is. We first perform the comparison using plaintext modulus $t = 3$, which was shown to be optimal among integral bases for encoding by Costache *et al.* [19], and is well within the regime for which FV is reported to be more performant in [18]. We then consider a plaintext modulus $t = 256$, a choice slightly beyond the crossover point according to [18]. We also perform the comparison with the plaintext moduli $t = 32768$, $t = 2^{32}$ and $t = 2^{64}$, which are all well beyond the reported crossover point.

Results and Analysis. Table 5 presents the results of the comparison for plaintext modulus $t = 3$. We see that, as the level increases, the point at which we need to switch to the next parameter set is often the same for both schemes. However, for $L \in \{10, 18\}$ we see that BGV required a larger parameter set than FV. This would suggest that for small plaintext modulus, FV is sometimes preferable to BGV. This is in agreement with the findings of [18].

Table 6 presents the results of the comparison for plaintext modulus $t = 256$. Again, for most values of L, the ciphertext sizes were the same for both BGV and FV. However, for $L \in \{2, 4, 8, 28, 30\}$ we see from Table 6 that BGV required a larger parameter set than FV. Indeed, the computation for $L \in \{28, 30\}$ could not be supported for BGV using any parameter set. The results for plaintext modulus $t = 32768$, presented in Table 7, are similar. This would suggest that FV continues to outperform BGV even after the crossover point reported in [18].

In Table 8, for plaintext modulus $t = 2^{32}$, we see that depending on the level, sometimes BGV outperforms FV and sometimes vice versa. In Table 9, for plaintext modulus $t = 2^{64}$, we see that FV required a larger parameter set than BGV for $L = 2$ and BGV could support up to $L = 10$ levels while FV could only support $L = 8$. This would suggest that by plaintext modulus $t = 2^{64}$ we have entered the regime in which BGV outperforms FV.

In summary, our results are consistent with the asymptotic expectation that BGV will outperform FV. However, they also indicate that the practical crossover point is far beyond that reported in [18], being somewhere between $t = 2^{32}$ and $t = 2^{64}$. Across all tables, we see that for most values of L, both BGV and FV required the same minimal values of n and Q to support the computation and hence the ciphertext sizes were the same. We can additionally conclude that BGV and FV present only minor performance differences from the point of view of computational capabilities.

Limitations. We stress that this is a comparison of how the noise growth behaviour impacts correctness in the BGV and FV schemes: we ignore correctness issues coming from decoding failure. Our comparison is naturally limited in several other aspects. For example, we only consider a certain specific computation, for which we do not attempt to make any scheme-specific optimisations that may be possible. Also, we note that while the choice of plaintext modulus $t = 3$

is optimal for integral bases, recent work has demonstrated the benefits of using non-integral bases [7,12] or using t a polynomial rather than an integer [14].

6   Improving the Heuristic-to-practical Gap

In this section, we present additional supporting evidence for our main conclusion that the worst-case heuristic approach is inadequate.

Different Definitions of Noise Result in a Similar Gap. In a fresh FV encryption (see Appendix B), the message m is scaled up by $\Delta = \lfloor q/t \rfloor$ to put it in the high-order bits. In decryption, we cancel Δ by multiplying by t/q, but this introduces a rounding term of the form $r_t(q) \cdot m$, since typically q is not exactly divisible by t. The invariant noise, defined such that $t/q \cdot (\mathtt{ct}(s)) = m + v + at$, folds this rounding term into the noise. However, notice that this $r_t(q) \cdot m$ term is only introduced by the decryption process: this term is not a part of the noise that the ciphertext carries before a decryption is performed. Therefore, including this term in every intermediate ciphertext will lead to overestimates that compound. We modified our experiments to take this into account and found that while this would represent a slight improvement for modelling the noise in fresh ciphertexts, it does not significantly improve the heuristic-to-practical gap.

Worst-Case Bounds are Inherently Loose. Our approach to obtain heuristic bounds requires us to bound Gaussian random variables in the canonical embedding. For example, a Gaussian random variable e, with mean zero and standard deviation σ is bounded as $\|e\|^{\mathrm{can}} \leq B \cdot \sigma_e$, for some B, where $\sigma_e = \sigma\sqrt{n}$. Following [18], we use $B = 6$, while HElib uses $B = 10$ as a default [26]. On the one hand, we never see $\|e\|^{\mathrm{can}}$ this large in experiments, which is not surprising because the probability of $\|e\|^{\mathrm{can}} > B \cdot \sigma_e$ is extremely low. On the other hand, to prove a heuristic bound of this type in theory, we need to ensure B is large enough (such as $B = 5$ or $B = 6$) to obtain a 'reasonable' failure probability. For example, we have $\mathrm{erfc}(5) \approx 2^{-40}$, while $\mathrm{erfc}(6) \approx 2^{-50}$.

An Average-Case Analysis Would be Complicated by Nonlinearity. The TFHE scheme [16] uses an appealing average-case approach to estimate noise growth, rather than worst-case bounds. In this approach, the coefficients of the noise in a TFHE ciphertext are modelled as independent subgaussians, and the variance of these subgaussians is traced through the homomorphic evaluation operations. This heuristic has been experimentally verified for the gate bootstrapping operation [16, Figure 10], showing in this case the noise in an output ciphertext can be modelled as a Gaussian of a certain variance. Moreover, every elementary operation in TFHE can be implemented via gate bootstrapping on a linear combination of ciphertexts [16, Table 1]. Hence, by linearity, all noises in TFHE ciphertexts can be modelled as subgaussian and it is easy to follow through the analysis of the variances.

In contrast, in the case of BGV and FV, we have a nonlinear noise growth in multiplication. In [34] it was shown that while a Central Limit argument could be used to approximate the noise in a BGV-like ciphertext as Gaussian, the quality of such an approximation would tend to decrease after many multiplications because the true noise distribution would have heavier and heavier tails. Hence it is not clear if an average-case approach as used in [16] would tightly model the noise growth in BGV or FV after many multiplications. Resolving this would be an interesting direction for future work.

Acknowledgements. Player was partially supported by the French Programme d'Investissement d'Avenir under national project RISQ P141580. Player and Costache were partially supported by the European Union PROMETHEUS project (Horizon 2020 Research and Innovation Program, grant 780701). Most of this work was done while Costache was at Intel AI, San Diego. We thank Ilia Iliashenko, Shai Halevi and Nigel Smart for helpful comments.

A   The BGV scheme

In this section we introduce the BGV scheme [10]. The BGV scheme is comprised of the `SecretKeyGen`, `PublicKeyGen`, `EvaluationKeyGen`, `Encrypt`, `Decrypt`, `Add`, `Multiply`, `Relinearize`, and `ModSwitch` algorithms.

In the `ModSwitch` algorithm, we describe switching from a modulus q to a modulus p where, for correctness, we require that $p = q = 1 \mod t$ [10,23]. For the algorithm as described here, we also need $p \mid q$, which will be the case when moving down the chain of moduli.

- `SecretKeyGen`(λ): Sample $s \leftarrow S$ and output $\mathsf{sk} = s$.
- `PublicKeyGen`(sk): Set $s = \mathsf{sk}$ and sample $a \leftarrow R_q$ uniformly at random and $e \leftarrow \chi$. Output $\mathsf{pk} = ([-(as + te)]_q, a)$.
- `EvaluationKeyGen`(sk, w): Set $s = \mathsf{sk}$. For $i \in \{0, \dots, \ell\}$, sample $a_i \leftarrow R_q$ uniformly at random and $e_i \leftarrow \chi$. Output $\mathsf{evk} = ([-(a_i s + te_i) + w^i s^2]_q, a_i)$.
- `Encrypt`(pk, m): For the message $m \in R_t$. Let $\mathsf{pk} = (p_0, p_1)$, sample $u \leftarrow S$ and $e_1, e_2 \leftarrow \chi$. Output $\mathsf{ct} = ([m + p_0 u + te_1]_q, [p_1 u + te_2]_q)$.
- `Decrypt`(sk, ct): Let $s = \mathsf{sk}$ and $\mathsf{ct} = (c_0, c_1)$. Output $m' = [[c_0 + c_1 s]_q]_t$.
- `Add`($\mathsf{ct}_0, \mathsf{ct}_1$): Output $\mathsf{ct} = ([\mathsf{ct}_0[0] + \mathsf{ct}_1[0]]_q, [\mathsf{ct}_0[1] + \mathsf{ct}_1[1]]_q)$.
- `Multiply`($\mathsf{ct}_0, \mathsf{ct}_1$): Set $c_0 = [\mathsf{ct}_0[0]\mathsf{ct}_1[0]]_q$, $c_1 = [\mathsf{ct}_0[0]\mathsf{ct}_1[1] + \mathsf{ct}_0[1]\mathsf{ct}_1[0]]_q$, and $c_2 = [\mathsf{ct}_0[1]\mathsf{ct}_1[1]]_q$. Output $\mathsf{ct} = (c_0, c_1, c_2)$.
- `Relinearize`($\mathsf{ct}, \mathsf{evk}$) : Let $\mathsf{ct}[0] = c_0$, $\mathsf{ct}[1] = c_1$ and $\mathsf{ct}[2] = c_2$. Let $\mathsf{evk}[i][0] = [-(a_i s + te_i) + w^i s^2]_q$ and $\mathsf{evk}[i][1] = a_i$. Express c_2 in base w as $c_2 = \sum_{i=0}^{\ell} c_2^{(i)} w^i$. Set $c_0' = c_0 + \sum_{i=0}^{\ell} \mathsf{evk}[i][0] c_2^{(i)}$, and $c_1' = c_1 + \sum_{i=0}^{\ell} \mathsf{evk}[i][1] c_2^{(i)}$. Output $\mathsf{ct}' = (c_0', c_1')$.
- `ModSwitch`(ct, p) : Let $\mathsf{ct} = (c_0, c_1)$. Fix δ_i such that $\delta_i = -c_i \pmod{\frac{q}{p}}$ and $\delta_i = 0 \pmod{t}$. Set $c_0' = \frac{p}{q}(c_0 + \delta_0)$ and $c_1' = \frac{p}{q}(c_1 + \delta_1)$. Output $\mathsf{ct} = (c_0', c_1')$.

B   The FV scheme

In this section we introduce the FV scheme [21], comprised of the algorithms `SecretKeyGen`, `PublicKeyGen`, `EvaluationKeyGen`, `Encrypt`, `Decrypt`, `Add`,

Multiply, Relinearize and ModSwitch. Unlike for BGV, the constraint on the chain of moduli that $p_i = 1 \mod t$ is not required, though was enforced for FV in [18]. Imposing this constraint may result in unfairly large parameters for FV, hence our updated comparison can be seen as allowing a more flexible modulus switching.

In order to define Encrypt, we must first define $\Delta = \left\lfloor \frac{q}{t} \right\rfloor$, where q is the current ciphertext modulus, and t is the plaintext modulus. We also define $r_t(q)$ as the remainder of q on division by t, so that $q = \Delta t + r_t(q)$.

- SecretKeyGen(λ): Sample $s \leftarrow S$ and output sk $= s$.
- PublicKeyGen(sk): Set $s =$ sk and sample $a \leftarrow R_q$ uniformly at random and $e \leftarrow \chi$. Output pk $= ([-(as + e)]_q, a)$.
- EvaluationKeyGen(sk, w): Set $s =$ sk. For $i \in \{0, \ldots, \ell\}$, sample $a_i \leftarrow R_q$ uniformly at random and $e_i \leftarrow \chi$. Output evk $= ([-(a_i s + e_i) + w^i s^2]_q, a_i)$.
- Encrypt(pk, m): For the message $m \in R_t$. Let pk $= (p_0, p_1)$, sample $u \leftarrow S$ and $e_1, e_2 \leftarrow \chi$. Output ct $= ([\Delta m + p_0 u + e_1]_q, [p_1 u + e_2]_q)$.
- Decrypt(sk, ct): Let $s =$ sk and ct $= (c_0, c_1)$. Output $m' = \left[\left\lfloor \frac{t}{q}[c_0 + c_1 s]_q \right\rceil \right]_t$.
- Add(ct$_0$, ct$_1$): Output ct $= ([\text{ct}_0[0] + \text{ct}_1[0]]_q, [\text{ct}_0[1] + \text{ct}_1[1]]_q)$.
- Multiply(ct$_0$, ct$_1$): Compute $c_0 = \left[\left\lfloor \frac{t}{q} \text{ct}_0[0] \text{ct}_1[0] \right\rceil \right]_q$,
$c_1 = \left[\left\lfloor \frac{t}{q} (\text{ct}_0[0] \text{ct}_1[1] + \text{ct}_0[1] \text{ct}_1[0]) \right\rceil \right]_q$, and $c_2 = \left[\left\lfloor \frac{t}{q} \text{ct}_0[1] \text{ct}_1[1] \right\rceil \right]_q$.
Output ct $= (c_0, c_1, c_2)$.
- Relinearize(ct, evk) : Let ct$[0] = c_0$, ct$[1] = c_1$ and ct$[2] = c_2$. Let evk$[i][0] = [-(a_i s + e_i) + w^i s^2]_q$ and evk$[i][1] = a_i$. Express c_2 in base w as $c_2 = \sum_{i=0}^{\ell} c_2^{(i)} w^i$. Set $c_0' = [c_0 + \sum_{i=0}^{\ell} \text{evk}[i][0] c_2^{(i)}]_q$, and $c_1' = [c_1 + \sum_{i=0}^{\ell} \text{evk}[i][1] c_2^{(i)}]_q$. Output ct$' = (c_0', c_1')$.
- ModSwitch(ct, p) : Let ct$[0] = c_0$ and ct$[1] = c_1$. Set $c_0' = \left[\left\lfloor \frac{p}{q} c_0 \right\rceil \right]_p$ and $c_1' = \left[\left\lfloor \frac{p}{q} c_1 \right\rceil \right]_p$. Output ct$' = (c_0', c_1')$.

References

1. Albrecht, M., et al.: Homomorphic encryption security standard. HomomorphicEncryption.org, Technical report (2018)
2. Albrecht, M.R., Player, R., Scott, S.: On the concrete hardness of learning with errors. J. Math. Cryptol. 9(3), 169–203 (2015)
3. Albrecht, M.R.: On dual lattice attacks against small-secret LWE and parameter choices in HElib and SEAL. In: Coron, J.-S., Nielsen, J.B. (eds.) EUROCRYPT 2017. LNCS, vol. 10211, pp. 103–129. Springer, Cham (2017). https://doi.org/10.1007/978-3-319-56614-6_4
4. Albrecht, M., Bai, S., Ducas, L.: A subfield lattice attack on overstretched NTRU assumptions. In: Robshaw, M., Katz, J. (eds.) CRYPTO 2016. LNCS, vol. 9814, pp. 153–178. Springer, Heidelberg (2016). https://doi.org/10.1007/978-3-662-53018-4_6

5. Bajard, J.-C., Eynard, J., Hasan, M.A., Zucca, V.: A full RNS variant of FV like somewhat homomorphic encryption schemes. In: Avanzi, R., Heys, H. (eds.) SAC 2016. LNCS, vol. 10532, pp. 423–442. Springer, Cham (2017). https://doi.org/10.1007/978-3-319-69453-5_23

6. Bajard, J.C., Eynard, J., Martins, P., Sousa, L., Zucca, V.: An HPR variant of the FV scheme: Computationally cheaper, asymptotically faster. IACR Cryptology ePrint Archive 2019, vol. 500 (2019)

7. Bonte, C., Bootland, C., Bos, J.W., Castryck, W., Iliashenko, I., Vercauteren, F.: Faster homomorphic function evaluation using non-integral base encoding. In: Fischer, W., Homma, N. (eds.) CHES 2017. LNCS, vol. 10529, pp. 579–600. Springer, Cham (2017). https://doi.org/10.1007/978-3-319-66787-4_28

8. Bos, J.W., Lauter, K., Loftus, J., Naehrig, M.: Improved security for a ring-based fully homomorphic encryption scheme. In: Stam, M. (ed.) IMACC 2013. LNCS, vol. 8308, pp. 45–64. Springer, Heidelberg (2013). https://doi.org/10.1007/978-3-642-45239-0_4

9. Brakerski, Z.: Fully homomorphic encryption without modulus switching from classical GapSVP. In: Safavi-Naini, R., Canetti, R. (eds.) CRYPTO 2012. LNCS, vol. 7417, pp. 868–886. Springer, Heidelberg (2012). https://doi.org/10.1007/978-3-642-32009-5_50

10. Brakerski, Z., Gentry, C., Vaikuntanathan, V.: (Leveled) fully homomorphic encryption without bootstrapping. In: Goldwasser, S (ed.) ITCS 2012, pp. 309–325. ACM, January 2012

11. Brenner, M., et al.: A standard API for RLWE-based homomorphic encryption. HomomorphicEncryption.org, Technical report (2017)

12. Castryck, W., Iliashenko, I., Vercauteren, F.: Homomorphic SIM^{2}D operations: single instruction much more data. In: Nielsen, J.B., Rijmen, V. (eds.) EUROCRYPT 2018. LNCS, vol. 10820, pp. 338–359. Springer, Cham (2018). https://doi.org/10.1007/978-3-319-78381-9_13

13. Chen, H., Laine, K., Player, R.: Simple encrypted arithmetic library - SEAL v2.1. In: Brenner, M., Rohloff, K., Bonneau, J., Miller, A., Ryan, P.Y.A., Teague, V., Bracciali, A., Sala, M., Pintore, F., Jakobsson, M. (eds.) FC 2017. LNCS, vol. 10323, pp. 3–18. Springer, Cham (2017). https://doi.org/10.1007/978-3-319-70278-0_1

14. Chen, H., Laine, K., Player, R., Xia, Y.: High-precision arithmetic in homomorphic encryption. In: Smart, N.P. (ed.) CT-RSA 2018. LNCS, vol. 10808, pp. 116–136. Springer, Cham (2018). https://doi.org/10.1007/978-3-319-76953-0_7

15. Cheon, J.H., Kim, A., Kim, M., Song, Y.: Homomorphic encryption for arithmetic of approximate numbers. In: Takagi, T., Peyrin, T. (eds.) ASIACRYPT 2017. LNCS, vol. 10624, pp. 409–437. Springer, Cham (2017). https://doi.org/10.1007/978-3-319-70694-8_15

16. Chillotti, I., Gama, N., Georgieva, M., Izabachène, M.: TFHE: fast fully homomorphic encryption over the torus. J. Cryptol. **33**(1), 34–91 (2019). https://doi.org/10.1007/s00145-019-09319-x

17. Costache, A.: On the practicality of ring-based fully homomorphic encryption schemes. Ph.D. thesis, University of Bristol (2018)

18. Costache, A., Smart, N.P.: Which ring based somewhat homomorphic encryption scheme is best? In: Sako, K. (ed.) CT-RSA 2016. LNCS, vol. 9610, pp. 325–340. Springer, Cham (2016). https://doi.org/10.1007/978-3-319-29485-8_19

19. Costache, A., Smart, N.P., Vivek, S., Waller, A.: Fixed-point arithmetic in SHE schemes. In: Avanzi, R., Heys, H. (eds.) SAC 2016. LNCS, vol. 10532, pp. 401–422. Springer, Cham (2017). https://doi.org/10.1007/978-3-319-69453-5_22

20. Damgård, I., Pastro, V., Smart, N., Zakarias, S.: Multiparty computation from somewhat homomorphic encryption. In: Safavi-Naini, R., Canetti, R. (eds.) CRYPTO 2012. LNCS, vol. 7417, pp. 643–662. Springer, Heidelberg (2012). https://doi.org/10.1007/978-3-642-32009-5_38

21. Fan, J., Vercauteren, F.: Somewhat practical fully homomorphic encryption. Cryptology ePrint Archive, Report 2012/144 (2012). http://eprint.iacr.org/2012/144

22. Gentry, C.: Fully homomorphic encryption using ideal lattices. In: Mitzenmacher, M., (ed.) 41st ACM STOC, pp. 169–178. ACM Press, May/June 2009

23. Gentry, C., Halevi, S., Smart, N.P.: Fully homomorphic encryption with polylog overhead. In: Pointcheval, D., Johansson, T. (eds.) EUROCRYPT 2012. LNCS, vol. 7237, pp. 465–482. Springer, Heidelberg (2012). https://doi.org/10.1007/978-3-642-29011-4_28

24. Gentry, C., Halevi, S., Smart, N.P.: Homomorphic evaluation of the AES circuit. In: Safavi-Naini, R., Canetti, R. (eds.) CRYPTO 2012. LNCS, vol. 7417, pp. 850–867. Springer, Heidelberg (2012). https://doi.org/10.1007/978-3-642-32009-5_49

25. Halevi, S., Polyakov, Y., Shoup, V.: An improved RNS variant of the BFV homomorphic encryption scheme. In: Matsui, M. (ed.) CT-RSA 2019. LNCS, vol. 11405, pp. 83–105. Springer, Cham (2019). https://doi.org/10.1007/978-3-030-12612-4_5

26. HElib, January 2019. https://github.com/shaih/HElib,

27. Iliashenko, I.: Optimisations of fully homomorphic encryption. Ph.D. thesis, KU Leuven (2019)

28. Kim, M., Lauter, K.: Private genome analysis through homomorphic encryption. BMC Med. Inform. Decis. Mak. **15**(5), S3 (2015). https://doi.org/10.1186/1472-6947-15-S5-S3

29. Kirchner, P., Fouque, P.-A.: Revisiting lattice attacks on overstretched NTRU parameters. In: Coron, J.-S., Nielsen, J.B. (eds.) EUROCRYPT 2017. LNCS, vol. 10210, pp. 3–26. Springer, Cham (2017). https://doi.org/10.1007/978-3-319-56620-7_1

30. Lepoint, T., Naehrig, M.: A comparison of the homomorphic encryption schemes FV and YASHE. In: Pointcheval, D., Vergnaud, D. (eds.) AFRICACRYPT 2014. LNCS, vol. 8469, pp. 318–335. Springer, Cham (2014). https://doi.org/10.1007/978-3-319-06734-6_20

31. Lindner, R., Peikert, C.: Better key sizes (and Attacks) for LWE-based encryption. In: Kiayias, A. (ed.) CT-RSA 2011. LNCS, vol. 6558, pp. 319–339. Springer, Heidelberg (2011). https://doi.org/10.1007/978-3-642-19074-2_21

32. López-Alt, A., Tromer, E., Vaikuntanathan, V.: On-the-fly multiparty computation on the cloud via multikey fully homomorphic encryption. In: Karloff, H.J., Pitassi, T., (eds.) 44th ACM STOC, pp. 1219–1234. ACM Press, May 2012

33. Lyubashevsky, V., Peikert, C., Regev, O.: A toolkit for ring-LWE cryptography. In: Johansson, T., Nguyen, P.Q. (eds.) EUROCRYPT 2013. LNCS, vol. 7881, pp. 35–54. Springer, Heidelberg (2013). https://doi.org/10.1007/978-3-642-38348-9_3

34. Murphy, S., Player, R.: Discretisation and product distributions in Ring-LWE. MathCrypt 2019, to appear (2019)

35. Al Badawi, A.Q.A., Polyakov, Y., Aung, K.M.M., Veeravalli, B., Rohloff, K.: Implementation and performance evaluation of RNS variants of the BFV homomorphic encryption scheme. IEEE Trans. Emerg. Top. Comput., 1 (2019). https://doi.org/10.1109/TETC.2019.2902799

36. Microsoft SEAL (release 3.4), Microsoft Research, Redmond, WA, October 2019. https://github.com/Microsoft/SEAL

Blockchain I

How to Model the Bribery Attack: A Practical Quantification Method in Blockchain

Hanyi Sun[1], Na Ruan[1(✉)], and Chunhua Su[2]

[1] Shanghai Jiao Tong University, Shanghai, China
sunhanyi2015@sjtu.edu.cn, naruan@cs.sjtu.edu.cn
[2] University of Aizu, Aizuwakamatsu, Japan
chsu@u-aizu.ac.jp

Abstract. Due to substantial profit gain and economic rewards, decentralized cryptocurrency systems have become primary targets for attackers. Double-spending is one of the most rudimentary and collective risks. Even without high hash power, attackers can still increase the probability of double-spending by bribing other miners to subvert the consensus agreement. This kind of attack is called bribery attack and a number of bribery attack models have been proposed during last few years. The evaluation and comparison of bribery attack models remain problematic due to the lack of systematic methods to quantify them. In particular, the costs and benefits of attackers are rarely considered which influenced by many factors. We propose a quantitative analysis method for previous bribery attack models. For further exploration, we design a bribery attack model and introduce profit formulations based on our analysis method. We experimentally prove that our model can reduce costs and increase benefits of bribery attacks compared with comparable models. The result shows our quantitative method is instructive both for bribery attack designing and analyzing.

Keywords: Blockchain · Quantified model · Bribery attack · Mechanism design

1 Introduction

In recent years, decentralized cryptocurrencies have not only become a heated topic in the economic sphere, but also the focus of attackers who tend to gain direct economic interest or undermine the cryptocurrency systems. Bitcoin [1], launched as the first cryptocurrency based on blockchain in 2009, has now achieved a market value of more than 100 billion dollars. Its core rule, known as Nakamoto Consensus, mentioned that the Bitcoin uses a computational puzzle system Proof-of-Work (POW) to guarantee the consensus of the whole Bitcoin system and continuously generate new blocks. Those who work out the computational puzzle, also called miners, can get block reward if they generate a new block.

© Springer Nature Switzerland AG 2020
L. Chen et al. (Eds.): ESORICS 2020, LNCS 12309, pp. 569–589, 2020.
https://doi.org/10.1007/978-3-030-59013-0_28

Preventing double-spending is very important in all cryptocurrencies. Attackers retrieve the cryptocurrency in some previous transactions by invalidating them. Nakamoto consensus provides a probability guarantee to prevent double-spending. Miners try to work out a computational puzzle and the first miner to resolve it will get block reward. The new block will be added to the chain and chain may fork since the mining process is performed simultaneously. Miners solve the branches problem by mining on the longest branch. In the process, shorter branches will be isolated and any transaction that conflicts with the main branch will be considered invalid. At the same time, participants accept a transaction with six confirmations which means six blocks past since its first appearing block to prevent double-spending. In this case, as long as most of the miners in the blockchain are honest and control more than half of hash power, double-spending will not happen.

However, double-spending still happened in the cryptocurrencies. For example, in May 2018, a Bitcoin hard fork BTG suffered a double-spending through 51% attack and lost nearly 388200 BTGs. On January 2019, another cryptocurrencie ETC has also suffered a double-spending and lost 54200 ETCs, nearly 2.7 million dollars. Although getting 51% hash power is difficult, attackers can increase the probability of double-spending by bribing other miners to subvert the consensus agreement. This kind of attack is called bribery attack and first proposed by Bonneau J. [2] and the first practical example of this type of attack is implemented in [17].

Bribery attacks assume that at least some miners in the blockchain act rationally. These miners accept bribes from attackers to maximize their profit. If the attacker and rational miners can get a high percentage of hash power, they may be able to carry out a successful attack such as double-spending. Due to the danger of bribery attack and lack of a practical model to analyze it, we aim at proposing a new model to quantify the bribery attack with assumptions suitable for a real scenario. At the same time, we translate the miner's strategy into a Markov decision process while rational miners in other models only consider the current state to make their decisions.

Our contributions in this work are listed as follows:

- We propose a quantitative analysis method for previous bribery attack models. We analyze the previous models through different aspects, such as hash power, smart contract and the benefits or costs of attackers. And we discuss the feasibility of these models based on our analysis.
- We establish a new model of bribery attack with practical assumptions and introduce profit formulations based on our analysis method. We translate the miner's strategy into a Markov decision process. And we experimentally prove that our model can reduce costs and increase benefits of bribery attacks compared with comparable models.
- We discuss the possibility of preventing bribery attacks give a defensive strategy.

The rest of our work is organized as follows: In Sect. 2, we introduce basic concepts. In Sect. 3, we briefly summarize researches on bribery attacks on blockchain and make quantitative analysis. In Sect. 4, we introduce our model, strategies of attackers and miners and profit calculation. In Sect. 5, we simulate and analyze our model. In Sect. 6, we propose possible defense strategy. In Sect. 7, we conclude our work.

2   Background

2.1   Bitcoin Mining Process

Bitcoin system can be briefly described as followed. A decentralized economy system requires the data to be kept on the public ledger. In Bitcoin system, merchants or buyers produce transactions with Bitcoins. These transactions would be recorded by block underlying Bitcoin.

When transactions emerge, all of the miners on the Bitcoin network try to collect a set of valid transactions and form them into a block. The generation process of a block is to solve a computational puzzle, a process called Proof-of-Work (POW). The puzzle can be abstracted as follows [18]:

$$\texttt{SHA-256}^2\{v \,\|\, B_l \,\|\, k \,\|\, MR(TR_1, ..., TR_n) \,\|\, T \,\|\, n\,\} \leq target \qquad (1)$$

Where v is a version number, B_l denotes the last generated block, $TR_1, ...TR_n$ is the set of valid transactions not yet confirmed, $MR(x)$ denotes the root of the Merkle tree over transactions x, T is the current Unix timestamp, n is a nonce in the space N, and the target is a 256-bit value that determines the difficulty of the mining operation. What miners want to do is finding that n which satisfies this inequality.

Once a miner completes the calculation, it sends this block to all its neighbor nodes. These nodes will continue to propagate this block after receiving and verifying it. Other miners in the network begin to work on the next puzzle for the next block based on B_{l+1} to show that they confirm the block. After the block has six confirmations which means six blocks added since its first appearing, the block and transactions in it can be regarded as valid. The consensus means all the participants in the network believes the longest chain is the main one.

2.2   Double-Spending

Some researches about the double-spending focus on fast payments [8,13]. Fast payments refer to a transaction which does not need six confirmations since the transaction payment is not high enough to attract an attack in real transactions in life. For example, shopping in a supermarket or have a lunch in restaurants. Pinzn C. and Rocha C. [19] proves the feasibility of double-spending and establish better double-spending model in mathematical ways.

In the mining process, the core mechanism POW provides the miner with profits by rewarding the minted bitcoins and embedded transaction fees in the newly confirmed block to the miner who first figures out the answer to the puzzle. Since mining is performed simultaneously, the main chain will fork and some branches will be generated. Eventually, one branch will be extended longer than the others because of the random nature of the computational puzzle [6] and the only way to solve the puzzle is to try random nounces [12]. That longer branch will be considered as the main chain. However, the randomness of the puzzle and its economic incentive leads to a double-spending risk.

When an attacker wants to launch a double-spending [7], he needs to make a fork chain longer than the main one. Then blocks on the main chain since the forked block and transactions on them will be abandoned. At that time, attackers can retrieve the payment of the abandoned transaction and use it twice. If the transaction has already been confirmed, the destination of the transaction can never notice that the payment is sent back. The double-spending aims to retrieve the transaction, which means an attacker can both get the commodity and retrieve the payment, or in other words, use the payment twice. We explain it in Fig. 1.

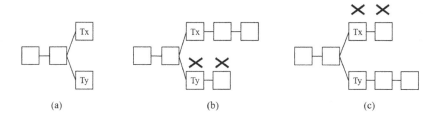

(a)   (b)   (c)

Fig. 1. Double-spending

In Fig. 1, state(a) refers to the beginning of a double-spending, in which an attacker produces a conflicting transaction T_y. T_x and T_y are the same except for different destination of the transaction—payment of T_x will send to the merchant while T_y to the attacker. State(b) refers to the condition when the attack fails and T_y is abandoned. State(c) is the opposite one, which means T_x is abandoned, and the attack succeed.

In such circumstances, a merchant can never ensure whether the transaction is abandoned by a very deep fork [9]. In Bitcoin, the consensus system is robust, and the network gradually reaches consensus if no more than half of the hash power fork the main chain on purpose [10,11]. However, even if the attacker does not hold more than half of the hash power, he can still increase the probability of double-spending by bribing other miners.

2.3   Bribery Attack

Since Nakamoto consensus requires most hash power to keep mining on the most extended branch, some researchers suggest bribing other hash power to mine for attackers, attempting to catch up and overtake the main branch to launch a double-spending. Bonneau J. [2] assumes bribing more than half of the hash power and lists several reasons why bribery attack may not be effective but does not give a quantitative or detailed analysis and it lacks experimental simulations.

Liao K. and Katz J. [3] describe the process of bribery attack and give some defensive suggestions. M. Rosenfeld [5] focus on the economic profit of hash-based double-spending but does not apply it to bribery attacks. J. Garay [17] presents three smart contracts that allow a briber to fairly exchange bribes to miners who pursue a mining strategy benefiting the briber. They can be combined with any model on bribery attack and put into practice.

Bribery Attack is targeting incentive compatibility. In Nakamoto consensus, when most of the miners in the blockchain are honest and control more hash power than attackers, double-spending will not happen. However, some miners act rationally in the actual blockchain. Bribery attack assume that those miners are not interested in the cryptocurrency long-term health and accept bribery to maximize their profit. If the attacker and all bribe miners can obtain a significant portion of the hash power in the blockchain for a short period of time, the attack is likely to succeed and double-spending may happen.

There are mainly two forms of bribery attacks:

- In-band. Most bribery attacks focus on optimizing the earnings of miners by accepting in-band bribes. It contains large fees in block reward and cryptocurrency payments in the same cryptocurrency. Some miners will choose to mine on attacker's branch when they can get higher returns.
- Out-of-band. Another form of bribery attacks is the Out-of-band. The attacker's goal is to disrupt competing cryptocurrencies to gain utility. The first practical example of this type of attack is implemented in [17].

Out-of-band bribery attacks need bank transfer or payment in another cryptocurrency. In comparison, in-band bribery attacks directly aim at gaining direct profit. Therefore, in our work, we do not consider the second form of bribery attack and only consider the in-band profit that the miners and attackers can get. In Sect. 3, we make quantitative analysis for existing bribery attack models. And in Sect. 4, we establish our model with practical assumptions.

3   Quantitative Analysis

3.1   General Model

For all analyzed and presented bribery attacks we adopt the following general attack model. We divided the participating miners into three categories, and their roles remained unchanged for the duration of the attack.

- Attacker: The attacker A wants to launch a double-spending through bribery attack. Attacker A controls hashrate α in the cryptocurrency and makes a transaction payment value v for double-spending. In addition to this, the attacker has a sum of cryptocurrency to bribe rational miners.
- Honest miner: The honest miner H always abides by the rules of the agreement, and they will not accept bribes to jeopardize the security of the cryptocurrency. H controls hashrate λ in the cryptocurrency.

– Rational miner: The rational miner R aims to maximize its short-term profits. As long as the gains obtained through bribery attacks are higher than following the rules, they will accept bribes and cooperate with the attackers. R controls hashrate β in the cryptocurrency. For our analysis, we assume that rational miners will not engage in other attacks, such as selfish mining.

It holds that $\alpha + \beta + \lambda = 1$. In general, suppose that the reward for mining a block is 1, then the expected return of the rational miner on main chain is β. Only when the expected return is greater than β, the rational miner will choose to cooperate with the attacker to mine on the attacker's private chain.

In general, the process a double-spending launched by bribery attack is shown in Fig. 2:

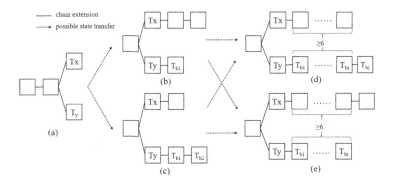

Fig. 2. Possible states during attack

In Fig. 2, state (a) refers to the beginning state. After the intended double-spend transaction T_x was included in a block, the attacker uses the last block as the previous one of his private chain. As soon as he gets a new block, he contains a conflict transaction T_y into it – a transaction same as the transaction T_x but sent the cryptocurrency to the account controlled by the briber. States (b) and (c) represent the possible cases when the main chain does not reach six confirmations, attacker. Whenever a new block is added to the private chain, the attacker will pay a bribe to the rational miner which is presented as $T_{b1}, ..., T_{bk}$. States (d) and (e) are under conditions where the intended transaction has been confirmed. When the length of the private chain overtakes the main one and intended transaction has been confirmed on the main chain as shown in State (d), the briber can public the private chain and abolish the intended transaction without the notice of merchants. In which case, the attack succeeds.

In the attack process, Liao K. and Katz J. [3] give the conclusion that the probability of private chain getting longer than the main one is:

$$a_z = min(\frac{q}{p}, 1)^{max(z+1,0)} = \begin{cases} 1, & z < 0 \ or \ q > p \\ (\frac{q}{p})^{z+1}, & z \geqq 0 \ and \ q \leqq p \end{cases} \quad (2)$$

q refers to hash power on the private chain, and p refers to hash power on the main chain. z refers to length difference between private chain and main chain.

When $z \geq 0$:

If miner choosing to keep mining on briber's branch, then $q = \alpha + \beta$, $p = 1 - \alpha - \beta$, α is briber's hash power proportion, β is miner's hash power proportion. The possibility of private branch overtaking the main branch:

$$P_b = (\frac{\alpha + \beta}{1 - \alpha - \beta})^{z+1} \tag{3}$$

If miner choosing to keep mining on the main branch, then $q = \alpha$, $p = 1 - \alpha$. The possibility of private branch overtaking the main branch:

$$P_m = (\frac{\alpha}{1 - \alpha})^{z+1} \tag{4}$$

The important principle of designing a bribery attack is: suppose δ is the bribery value attacker can give. And ζ is the income of miners mining on the main chain. Rational miners will choose to mine on private chain when:

$$P_b \cdot \delta > P_m \cdot \zeta \tag{5}$$

When α and β are fixed, what an attacker wants to do is to reduce δ to make himself profitable.

3.2 Analysis of Existing Models

The previous researches on double-spending and bribery attack do have some valuable points. However, there still lacks a quantitative or detailed analysis. In order to fill this gap, we conduct a systematic quantitative analysis of the previous bribery attack models in this section.

Table 1 presents an overview of our analysis of representative previous related works, each row represents a different attack and each columns represents a different property. Suppose the reward for a new block is b, and the attack lasted k blocks in private chain. ϵ is a coefficient which determines the value of the bribe fee which is not exactly the same in all attacks. c is the operational fee if the attack needs smart contract. Symbol/means the model only gives idea but not design specific details. Due to space reasons, we use the source to represent each model.

Attacker hashrate α is the need of attacker's hashrate to launch a bribery attack. Some bribery attacks can be executed when the attacker has no hashrate such as model [2,20]. However, a low hashrate α means more bribery fees which has a great effect of attacker's benefits. In order to avoid the impact of the 51% attack, the previous models limit the briber's hashrate $\alpha < \frac{1}{2}$.

Malicious miner hashrate $\alpha + \beta$ is the total hashrate of rational miner and attacker. Generally, all bribing attacks assume that at least some of the miners in the blockchain are rational and accept bribes. However, some works like model [15] and [16] assume that $\alpha + \beta = 1$ which is difficult to achieve in

Table 1. Quantitative analysis of related works, each model is represented by reference source id.

Model	Attacker hashrate α	Malicious hashrate $\alpha + \beta$	Smart contract	Payment	Expected gains	Expected costs	Repay if attack fail
[2]	/	$[\frac{1}{2}, 1]$	No need	in-band	v	$k \cdot \epsilon \cdot b$	No
[3]	/	$[\frac{1}{2}, 1]$	No need	in-band	/	$k \cdot B_e$	No
[15]	$(0, \frac{1}{2})$	1	No need	in-band	v	$k \cdot \frac{1+\epsilon-0.02}{\epsilon} \cdot b$	No
[17]	$[\frac{1}{3}, \frac{1}{2})$	$[\frac{2}{3}, 1)$	Need	in-band	/	$k \cdot (1 - \frac{\epsilon}{8}) \cdot b$	No
[14]	/	$(\frac{1}{3}, 1]$	No need	out-band	/	/	No
[16]	/	1	Need	in-band	/	$k \cdot (\epsilon \cdot b + \delta)$	Yes
[20]	/	$[\frac{1}{2}, 1]$	Need	out-band	$v - c$	$k \cdot \epsilon \cdot b + c$	Yes

reality. This assumption makes these attacks difficult to perform. Overall, it is a reasonable assumption that $\alpha + \beta$ is around 0.5.

Smart contract shows whether the attack requires a smart contract to launch. Models [16,17,20] use smart contract in the attacks. If the target cryptocurrency does not support smart contracts, this kind of attacks are difficult to play a role. At the same time, using smart contracts for attack requires additional fees to execute.

Payment means where the bribery fees to pay. Payment is in-band (in the target cryptocurrency) or out-of-band (in a different cryptocurrency). Obviously, in order to avoid the influence of other factors, the rational miner prefers in-band payment. In-band transactions are more convenient, and rational miners can more accurately calculate their expected returns.

Expected gains means how much can an attacker benefit from a successful attack. In many previous works, the models do not take into account the attacker's benefits. It is true that paying a large bribery fees such as [3] can increase the success rate of bribery attack, but attacker cannot obtain any substantial benefits or the cost of bribery far exceeds the value v in the double-spend transaction. This is inconsistent with the attacker's desire to profit. The final gain of attacker is expected gain minus expected cost.

Expected costs means the cost of the attacker to launch a bribery attack. The cost contains the bribery fees to miner and operation fees for smart contracts if needed. The cost of an attack is also a factor considered by the attacker. With a similar success rate, attackers would consider using a bribery attack model that costs less. Take [3] as a example, the expected cost for a bribery attack may more than hundreds of Bitcions which is difficult for an attacker to bear.

Repay if attack fails means at least some bribes is paid whether the attack is successful such as [20]. Some definite benefits can increase the probability of rational miners participating in the attack, but obviously this is a undesirable choice for attackers.

3.3   Observation

In existing bribery attacks, the attacker's benefits were rarely considered. The attacker pays huge bribes but has no real gains, which is untenable in reality. So in our model, we think more about whether attackers can benefit from bribery attacks. At the same time, we prove the profitability of our model through experimental simulation.

Previous models rarely considered rational miners' decision-making process. If we want to guarantee the profit of the attacker, the bribery costs need to be carefully calculated. In this case, the rational miner compares the expected benefits of two actions (cooperating with attacker, or mining with honest miners) to take their own actions. In Sect. 4, we translate this behavior into a Markov decision process. We calculate the profit formula of the attacker and the rational miner, and give the bribery process.

We consider including bribery fees in the form of transactions on the blocks of the private chain. If bribery attack fails, the fees in these transactions will also lapse. This can reduce the cost of bribery attacks, and greatly encourage rational miners to mine on attacker's private chain. In short, we leave the risk of decision to rational miners, which are continuing to mine on the private chain to obtain the previous bribery fees or mining on main chain with honest miners.

4   Model Design

In this section, we elaborate on our model. In the following, for the convenience of description, we will call the attacker as the **briber**, and rational miners who accepts the bribery as **miner**. Section 4.1 talks about the assumptions on which our model is based. Section 4.2 shows both the briber's and the miner's decision-making strategies. Section 4.3 does profit calculation for our model, based on which we can analyze the profit of the bribery attack.

4.1   Assumptions

The amount of bribery cost for successfully carrying out an attack depends on the assumption of hash power entities' behavior pattern. That contains miners' tolerance to the risk of failure, judgment on whether bribers would go on to attack or give up and consideration of the long-term benefit. Even worse, miners' may not share the block with the bribers and may withhold blocks on the bribers' chain to get more revenue if they confirm that the briber would not readily give up the attack. To simplify the model and show our originality, we make the following assumptions:

Less Hash Power. Both sides of the attack are the entities with less than 50% hash power. What is more, when simulating the model, we only consider the conditions where dishonest hash power (bribers and miners together) is less than 50%. Since if dishonest hash power is more than half, the attacker is easily to lauch a double-spending attack which is also called 51 attacks [4]. What we discuss is a worse condition for the attacker.

One Briber and One Miner. The model is under the condition with one miner. The miner can be a miner or a mining pool, and the latter one seems a better choice because they have much hash power. During the process of bribery, no other bribers or miners will participate in the attack. In the mining process, the probability of an attacker finding a new block is only affected by the hash power of himself and the miner.

A Persistent Attack. When miners make their choices, they will not consider the bribers' sudden giving up. Given the condition where bribers find that the private chain has fallen too far behind the main chain and quit the attack, which leads to influence on miners' decision, our model is more straightforward. Meanwhile, briber will put bribery in every new block in private branch to attract the miner.

Practical Profit Calculation. In our simulation, Bribery means to contain a transaction in private chain where the briber sends some cryptocurrency to the miners. To attract the miners, the briber should contain such transactions every time private chain gets longer. Different from previous works, the profit of briber and miner consider the entire bribery process. When miners are making decisions on which chain to mine, he not only consider the status next but also previous blocks the miner has mined and bribery he can get.

Markov Decision Process. Based on assumption ahead, the briber and miner predict the possibility of success under consideration that there will not be hash power on this fork other than the miner and the briber. Miners' decisions of which chain to mine depends on the expectation of revenue in the next period of mining, and the status at present including the previous blocks the miner has mined (Markov decision process).

Normalized Unit. We set the block reward as 1. It is a unit to simplify our calculations.

4.2 Strategies

In this section, we analyze briber's and miner's decision-making strategies. Then we summarize the attack process in the form of algorithm. In the attack process, miners and bribers have different decision-making process.

Miners' Decision-Making Process. The core gist of this process is the difference of expectation reward between the main chain and the private one. To be specific, if revenue on the main chain R_m > revenue on briber's chain R_b, the miners will choose the main chain, and if not, they will choose the briber's chain. We use this to establish the miners' decision-making strategy. Whenever the miner (miner) receives a bribery transaction which includes some bribery fee, he should compare R_m and R_b to find which chain to choose. If he finds there is more profit mining on R_m, then he will choose the main chain. And he begins to compete on the main chain with the honest hash power for a new block. Oppositely, if he finds there is more profit mining on R_b, he will mine on the briber's chain with the bribers in order to make the briber's chain longer than the main one.

Bribers' Decision-Making Process. As is discussed in Sect. 4.1, after the intended double-spend transaction was included in a block, the briber begins to mine the first block on his briber's chain using the last block as the head while doing the hash calculation. Then, he will take several factors which are related to his attack revenue into account and accordingly work out the bribery fee he should give to the miner.

Algorithm 1: Bribery Attacking Process

Input: Hash Power α, β; Transaction Payment v; Revenue Coefficient θ
Output: Sum of Bribery Fee δ_i
Result: Succeed or Fail

1   Initialize $t = 1$, $z = $ add_to_main(α,β), $n = 6$ (n is confirmation blocks which is now six);
2   **while** *True* **do**
3   **if** $z \geq 0$ **then**
4   Use Equation 8 to figure out δ;
5   Record $\theta\delta$ as δ_i in Array1;
6   **if** *profit on private > profit on main* **then**
7   Mine on the private chain;
8         $t = t + $ add_to_main(α,β);
9   miner competes with the briber for a new block on the private chain;
10   **end**
11   **if** *profit on private $\leq$ profit on main* **then**
12   Mine on the main chain;
13         $t = t + $ add_to_main($\alpha,0$);
14   miner competes with the honest for a new block on the main chain;
15         $k = k + $ add_reward();
16   **end**
17   **end**
18   **if** $z < 0$ **then**
19   Mine on the private chain;
20       $t = t + $ add_to_main(α,β);
21   miner competes with the briber for a new block on the private chain;
22   **end**
23   **if** $z = -1$ *and* $t > n$ **then**
24   Break; The attack succeeds;
25   **end**
26   **end**

Our model is to combine the two strategies profit analysis explained in Sect. 4.3, and have a simulation of the whole process. We clarify our model in the form of pseudo-code as Algorithm 1. Related symbols are explained in Table 2. The algorithm omits the following details. Different from previous works, in our algorithm, the decisions of the miner are constantly changing. When a new block generated, the miner decides which chain to mine based on the expected profit he can get.

Beginning of Attack. The briber publics the intended transaction and mines the first block on the private chain using the last block on the main chain as the hash head. Suppose at that time the private chain has already fallen z blocks behind the main one.

Process of Attack. During the simulation, we always stand on the private chain to evaluate the situation. From the model above, the private chain gets one block longer while the main chain gets several blocks longer each loop. The function *add_to_main* returns the number of additional blocks on main chain after the private chain gets one block longer. We assume that the hash power of the main chain is a and private is b. Adding n blocks after the private chain's one block extension equals the case in which miners successively mine $n+1$ blocks and the front n blocks are main chain blocks, and the last block belongs to the private one. Thus, the probability of n can be figured out. The function *Add_Reward* is the number of blocks found by the miner on the main chain when competing with the honest miners. It can be abstracted to a probability problem, totally n blocks have been generated, and among them, k blocks belong to the miner. It is a binomial distribution, so the probability of k can be calculated.

Markov Decision Process. Just as what mentioned in the assumption part, when the miner is making his choice, he only compares the expected revenue between the private chain and the main one, regardless of any other external factor like the briber's quit or decrease in Bitcoin's value resulting from the attack. The expectation of the private revenue is only concerned with past bribery fee, past mining conditions and the current possibility of attacking successfully.

4.3   Profit Calculations

In this part, we show how briber and miner work out their profit and accordingly make their decisions. We list and explain the symbols in the model in Table 2. Based on that, we show how briber and miner work out their profit and accordingly make their decisions.

Calculations of Miner's Mining Profit
In the expression of mathematics formula, we define symbols in Table 2. We consider the miner's mining profit in two situation:

- If miner choose keeping mining on the main branch and attack failed, the expected reward:

$$R_m = [1 - (\frac{\alpha}{1-\alpha})^{z+1}] * (k + \frac{\beta}{1-\alpha}) \tag{6}$$

Table 2. Symbols and explanation for calculation

Symbol	Explanation
α	Briber's hash power proportion
β	Miner's hash power proportion
z	Length difference between two chains
δ	Bribery transaction value in the current block
δ_i	Bribery transaction value in the previous i-th block
k	Blocks on the main chain already mined by miner
l	Blocks on the private chain already mined by miner
r	Length of the private chain
t	Length of the main chain
v	Transaction payment for double-spending
θ	Revenue coefficient

Left of the multiple sign is the possibility of a fail attack. If the attack failed, miner can only get reward from the main branch—previous acquired reward k and possible next block reward.

– If miner choose keeping mining on the briber's branch and attack succeed, the expected reward:

$$R_b = (\frac{\alpha + \beta}{1 - \alpha - \beta})^{z+1} * [\sum_{i=1}^{r} \delta_i + l + \frac{\beta}{\alpha + \beta} + \delta] \tag{7}$$

Left of the multiple sign is the possibility of a successful attack, in which miner can only get the reward from briber's branch—previously acquired block reward l, acquired bribery fee and possible next block reward.

When making decision, miner only considers the expected profit if keeping mining on the main branch and attack failed and if keeping mining on the briber's branch and attack succeed.

Calculations of Briber's Attack Profit. The revenue of one briber get from briberry attack equals the intended transaction fee for double-spending minus bribery fee when attack succeeds and minus any reward the briber will lost when attack fails. Here, we get a equation, which illuminated by Meni Rosenfeld [5], the profit R of Briber is:

$$R = v - (1 - P_b)(v + r - l) - P_b(\delta + \delta_i) \tag{8}$$

v is the transaction payment for double-spending. P_b is the possibility of a successful bribery attack which defined in Sect. 3.1. r is length of the private chain. δ is bribery transaction value in the current block and δ_i is the bribery transaction value in the previous i-th block.

To benefit from the attack, the briber must surely guarantee the profit to be more than 0, that is

$$v - \delta - \delta_i > \frac{(1 - P_b)(r - l)}{P_b} \tag{9}$$

When setting the profit to 0, the briber can get the max bribery fee δ_{max} in next block he can give to the miner. However, bribe obviously does not want to do so because the attack has no gain in this way. In our model, we assume a unique parameter θ ($0 < \theta < 1$) which we call revenue coefficient to measure how much profit can the briber get from the attack. After getting the δ_{max} according to the above inequation and the briber set real bribery fee δ to $\delta = \theta\delta_{max}$. The bigger the θ is, the more bribery fees and thus the less attack revenue. δ is also a important effect of attacker's profit.

After sending the bribery transaction to the miner, briber will mine on the private branch and sending bribery fee δ to miner. Then he will check whether the main branch is far ahead or z is less than 0 to determine the attack succeed or to give up this attack.

5   Simulation and Analysis

In this section, we simulate our model and achieve several conclusions. Section 5.1 shows the parameters of our simulation and carry out our simulation in Python program. Section 4.2 presents the relationship between hash power, transaction payment, revenue coefficient and revenue based on our simulation and shows our analysis for the simulation result. Through simulation and analysis, we find that bribers can get 90% of transaction payment revenue with our strategies.

5.1   Scenario

The experiment emulates the whole process of the bribery attacks based on the model we designed and the miner's mining profit and briber's attack profit. We set the simulation and the details are as follows:

- The input of each attack simulation is transaction payment v, revenue coefficient θ and the hash power α and β.
- For each group of input, we simulate the bribery attack for 10000 times.
- we count the number of failure bribery attacks (which called error number below) among them.
- We count the total bribery fee of those successful attacks. Then we calculate the average bribery fee and average revenue of the successful trails.
- For those 10000 bribery attack simulations, we calculate the briber's absolute gains (the frequency of the successful attack multiplies the average revenue) and briber's relative gains (the absolute revenue divided by the intended transaction fee).

Hash Power $\alpha + \beta$. The choice of $\alpha + \beta$ is much closer to ideal conditions, with the range of $0.33-0.49$. If $\alpha + \beta$ is smaller than 0.33, the final possibility of successful attacks would be too little to get any valid data. In real conditions, the briber can hardly carry out a successful attack with little hash power. Given the existence of mining pools, a sum of $0.33-0.49$ power hash is possible. To present the proportion of α and β, which refers to briber's and miner's hash power relatively, we choose $0.25 + 0.24 = 0.49$ and $0.15 + 0.34 = 0.49$, two conditions when $\alpha + \beta = 0.49$, and choose the same when $\alpha + \beta = 0.4$: $0.1 + 0.3 = 0.4$ and $0.2 + 0.2 = 0.4$.

Transaction Payment v. The choice of v refers to transaction fees in reality. We check the transactions and find that the biggest transaction is no more than 50 Bitcoins and most transactions fee is small, so v should be as small as possible. Since the block reward as 1, which now equals 12.5 Bitcoins, our result of the simulation should regard one block reward as the unit and the real value of these result should be 12.5 times bigger.

The v we choose for the simulation is $0-100$, which is more in line with the situation in the actual blockchain.

Revenue Coefficient θ. In the model, we assume a parameter θ $(0 < \theta < 1)$ which we can call revenue coefficient when calculating the bribery cost. After getting the δ_{max} according to the above Inequation 7 and the briber set the real bribery fee δ to $\delta = \theta\delta_{max}$ in the recent block. For the convenience of simulation, we set θ to a fixed value in every same bribery attack, and simulate the profit of the briber can get through different θ in different bribery attack.

When simulating the whole model process, we may get a bribery fee δ below 0. In such case, we set δ to 0. The meaning of it, in reality, is that at that time the briber considers continue bribing as unprofitable, so he will stop sending bribery fee but not stop mining on the private branch. However, if the previous bribery money is more than profit on the main branch, the miner may still mine on the private branch to take back their previous bribery money even though he does not receive any new bribery money. θ has a great impact on the success rate of the attack, which will ultimately affect the profit of the attacker.

5.2 Result and Analysis

We collect all the data in the simulation and analyze them. We first confirm that high hash power of bribery and miner is beneficial for an bribery attack. Then we discover the relationship between transaction payment v, revenue coefficient θ and revenue of the attack to verify that our model is practical. Based on that, we propose a strategy for bribers to gain maximum revenue.

In the simulation result, we find that hash power $a + b$, transaction v and revenue coefficient θ can greatly influence the revenue.

Impact of Hash Power $\alpha + \beta$ **on Revenue.** In order to get a general conclusion, we set the transaction Payment v and the revenue coefficient θ in two situations, where $v = 1$ and $\theta = 0.1$ and $v = 3$ and $\theta = 0.2$.

Table 3. Simulation results with v = 1, $\theta = 0.1$ and different $\alpha + \beta$.

Sum = $\alpha + \beta$	Average bribery fee	Error number	Absolute gains	Relative gains
0.49	0.285146072	1145	0.633003154	0.633003154
0.49	0.323679056	1192	0.595703488	0.595703488
0.47	0.171929098	3284	0.556132418	0.556132418
0.45	0.118794884	5185	0.424300263	0.424300263
0.43	0.086186667	6835	0.28922192	0.28922192
0.4	0.051793966	8327	0.158634869	0.158634869
0.4	0.059810257	7826	0.20439725	0.20439725
0.37	0.039667427	9100	0.086429932	0.086429932
0.35	0.016023851	9333	0.065631209	0.065631209
0.33	0	9600	0.04	0.04

Table 4. Simulation results with v = 3, $\theta = 0.2$ and different $\alpha + \beta$.

Sum = $\alpha + \beta$	Average bribery fee	Error number	Absolute gains	Relative gains
0.49	1.733100993	1133	1.12335935	0.374453117
0.49	1.819382873	1201	1.03882501	0.346275003
0.47	1.37117179	2867	1.161843162	0.387281054
0.45	1.136255103	4693	0.989089417	0.329696472
0.43	0.96314839	6202	0.773596241	0.257865414
0.4	0.767397473	7781	0.495414501	0.165138167
0.4	0.901051675	7881	0.44476715	0.148255717
0.37	0.739853301	8691	0.295853203	0.098617734
0.35	0.5603207	9291	0.172973262	0.057657754
0.33	0.528124165	9555	0.109998475	0.036666158

From the data above in Table 3 and 4, the less the hash power $\alpha + \beta$, the more error times, the fewer the absolute and relative gains. Thus, from the practical point of view, if the briber wants more gains, he should raise the sum hash power with rational miners. No matter the absolute gains (the attack revenue that briber actually gets), or relative gains (the proportion of gains and costs), they are all based on increasing the hash power, which is rational in the real Bitcoin. Since the choice of v and θ is random, such a conclusion is applicable for all v and θ.

Impact of Transaction Payment v on Revenue. With a definite $\alpha + \beta$, we inspect the impact of v on absolute and relative gains with different θ through line charts. To be clearer, we only choose $\alpha + \beta$ as $0.15 + 0.34 = 0.49$, $0.1 + 0.23 = 0.33$ and θ as 0.01, 0.1, 0.3, 0.5.

From with Fig. 3 (a) and Fig. 3 (c), we can see that with the increasing of v, the absolute gains increase. The smaller the θ, the bigger the slope of the curve, which means faster growth of absolute gains and more absolute gains.

From Fig. 3 (b), we can see that the relative gains decrease with the increasing v. And when v is fixed, the relative gains decrease with the increasing θ. However, in Fig. 3 (d), the relative gains can also increase wity. That is because the success rate.

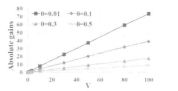

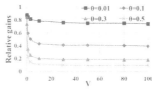

(a) Absolute gains and v when $\alpha + \beta = 0.49$(b) Relative gains and v when $\alpha + \beta = 0.49$

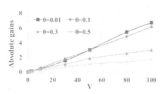

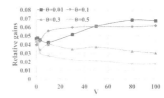

(c) Absolute gains and v when $\alpha + \beta = 0.33$ (d) Relative gains and v when $\alpha + \beta = 0.33$

Fig. 3. The impact of v on gains

All the curves will approach their respective value, a value concerned with θ—a bigger θ means a smaller revenue. The tendency of the relative curves can be explained by reality: when v is small, block reward becomes the main

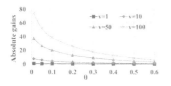

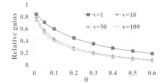

(a) Absolute gains and θ when $\alpha + \beta = 0.49$(b) Relative gains and θ when $\alpha + \beta = 0.49$

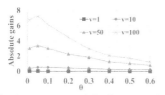

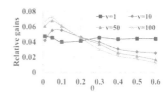

(c) Absolute gains and θ when $\alpha + \beta = 0.33$ (d) Relative gains and θ when $\alpha + \beta = 0.33$

Fig. 4. The impact of θ on gains

revenue; while v gets bigger, v dominates the revenue, and thus relative gains will be stable. As a conclusion, with enough hash power, bribers should raise the intended transaction value v if he needs more absolute gains, or decreases the transaction value v to get bigger relative gains.

Impact of Revenue Coefficient θ on Revenue. With a definite $\alpha + \beta$, we inspect the performance of θ on absolute and relative gains with different v through line charts. To be clearer, we also choose $\alpha + \beta$ as $0.15 + 0.34 = 0.49$, $0.1 + 0.23 = 0.33$, v as $1, 10, 50, 100$ and θ as $0.01, 0.1, 0.3, 0.5, 0.6$.

From Fig. 4 (a) and Fig. 4 (c), we can see that the absolute gains decrease with the increasing of θ. It is reasonable because the bigger θ, the more bribery fee should the attack pay. When considering about v, in most cases the bigger the v, the more absolute gains. However, when θ is reached to 0.6, the absolute gains is smaller enough even v is 100. In this case, the attacker can get little profit even the attack succeed.

From Fig. 4 (b), we can see that the relative gains decrease with the increasing of θ. However, in Fig. 4 (d), the relative gains may increase with the increasing of θ. This is because the success rate which influenced by θ.

The fluctuation is serious when the hash power is only 0.33. As a conclusion, with enough hash power, bribers should decrease θ in order to get more gains, both absolute gains and relative gains.

Strategy to Get Maximum Revenue. According to the analysis above, the briber should first guarantee enough hash power with the intended miners in order to get the maximum absolute and relative gains. With this premise, the fluctuation of expectation revenue will be smoother, and the model is more controllable. If the attacker is eager for higher absolute gains, he can choose transaction with a higher fee and a smaller revenue coefficient θ. However, if briber seeks for higher relative gains, he should choose a smaller v and θ. Since the maximum relative gain can be nearly 90% through the data from the experiment, which means the briber making a transaction with 1 pay can retrieve 90% of the transaction through bribery attack at most, the attack is a profitable one.

6   Defensive Strategy for Bribery Attack

Based on the analysis above, we give some defensive strategy mainly on both the transaction and the confirmation of a block.

Take Bitcoin for an example, we suggest increasing the blocks needed to confirm a transaction when the transaction fee is high. When waiting for the six blocks, the private chain falls behind the main one with a high possibility. Assuming that bribers need to wait for more than six blocks, the length difference between the main and private chain is even larger, which is adverse for the briber: less attack revenue and less probability of success. We carry out a simple

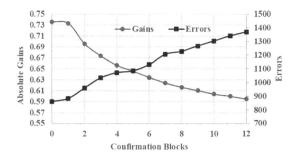

Fig. 5. Absolute gains and errors with confirmation blocks

experiment followed to verify that increasing the number of confirmed blocks is effective, as shown in Fig. 5. The figure shows the relationship of gains and errors with confirmation blocks when $v = 1, \theta = 0.1, a + b = 0.25 + 0.24 = 0.49$. With the increase of confirmation blocks from 0 to 12, absolute gains decrease with inverse proportional function and errors obviously increase.

The transaction payment v is a key factor which can directly influence the attack revenue. Transactions with a high fee are needed for the briber to get the maximum revenue. Bitcoin can have an exact upper threshold value for the transaction payment. We can not verify this through our experiment since the block reward, which is our unit of gains, will change in the future and accordingly the transaction payment will change, but this suggestion is effective. At the same time, we should consider the briber's trick to avoid this threshold value limitation: he has many transactions with the same input (the briber) and double spends all these transactions to surpass the limitation value. Hence, we suggest that besides the threshold value for the transaction payment, several transactions with the same input cannot be present in a block during a short period time. These limitations do not have any negative influence on the normal transaction and two honest parties of the transaction, because they are unlikely to send many transactions in a short period time, and even when this happens, some of these transactions will be delayed to the next block, which will not lead much influence.

7   Conclusion

In this work, we proposed a quantitative analysis method for previous bribery attack models. For further exploration, we design a new bribery attack model with more practical assumptions and propose decision-making strategies for mercenary briber and miners. We simulated the whole process of bribery to find how much the bribers should pay to attract miners to mine for them and how much they can get from one attack. Our model is practical via analysis on simulation. In the last part, we presented the defense strategy to control this bribery attack with limitation of transaction payment and high confirmation blocks. It is noteworthy that our model is suitable for all POW based cryptocurrencies, not only Bitcoins.

Acknowledgments. Our work is supported by National Nature Science Foundation of China (NSFC) No. 61702330, JSPS Kiban(B) 18H03240 and JSPS Kiban(C) 18K11298.

References

1. Nakamoto, S.: Bitcoin: a peer-to-peer electronic cash system (2008)
2. Bonneau, J.: Why buy when you can rent? In: Clark, J., Meiklejohn, S., Ryan, P.Y.A., Wallach, D., Brenner, M., Rohloff, K. (eds.) FC 2016. LNCS, vol. 9604, pp. 19–26. Springer, Heidelberg (2016). https://doi.org/10.1007/978-3-662-53357-4_2
3. Liao, K., Katz, J.: Incentivizing blockchain forks via whale transactions. In: Brenner, M., et al. (eds.) FC 2017. LNCS, vol. 10323, pp. 264–279. Springer, Cham (2017). https://doi.org/10.1007/978-3-319-70278-0_17
4. Bradbury, D.: The problem with bitcoin. Comput. Fraud Secur. **2013**(11), 5–8 (2013)
5. Rosenfeld, M.: Analysis of hashrate-based double-spending. arXiv preprint, arXiv: 1402.2009 [cs.CR] (2014)
6. Bonneau, J., Miller, A., Clark, J., Narayanan, A., Kroll, J.A., Felten, E.W.: SoK: research perspectives and challenges for bitcoin and cryptocurrencies. In: Proceedings of IEEE Symposium on Security and Privacy, pp. 104–121 (2015)
7. Bamert, T., Decker, C., Elsen, L., Wattenhofer, R., Welten, S.: Have a snack, pay with bitcoins. In: Proceedings of IEEE P2P (2013)
8. Karame, G.O., Androulaki, E., Capkun, S.: Double-spending fast payments in bitcoin. In: Proceedings of the ACM Conference on Computer and Communications Security, pp. 906–917 (2012)
9. Barber, S., Boyen, X., Shi, E., Uzun, E.: Bitter to better—how to make bitcoin a better currency. In: Keromytis, A.D. (ed.) FC 2012. LNCS, vol. 7397, pp. 399–414. Springer, Heidelberg (2012). https://doi.org/10.1007/978-3-642-32946-3_29
10. Garay, J., Kiayias, A., Leonardos, N.: The bitcoin backbone protocol: analysis and applications. In: Oswald, E., Fischlin, M. (eds.) EUROCRYPT 2015. LNCS, vol. 9057, pp. 281–310. Springer, Heidelberg (2015). https://doi.org/10.1007/978-3-662-46803-6_10
11. Miller, A., LaViola Jr., J.J.: Anonymous byzantine consensus from moderately-hard puzzles: a model for bitcoin (2014)
12. Courtois, N.T., Grajek, M., Naik, R.: Optimizing SHA256 in bitcoin mining. In: Kotulski, Z., Księżopolski, B., Mazur, K. (eds.) CSS 2014. CCIS, vol. 448, pp. 131–144. Springer, Heidelberg (2014). https://doi.org/10.1007/978-3-662-44893-9_12
13. Karame, G.O., Androulaki, E., Roeschlin, M., Gervais, A., Čapkun, S.: Misbehavior in bitcoin: a study of double-spending and accountability. ACM Trans. Inf. Syst. Secur. (TISSEC) **18**(1), Article no. 2 (2015)
14. Judmayer, A., Stifter, N., Schindler, P., Weippl, E.: Pitchforks in cryptocurrencies. In: Garcia-Alfaro, J., Herrera-Joancomartí, J., Livraga, G., Rios, R. (eds.) DPM/CBT-2018. LNCS, vol. 11025, pp. 197–206. Springer, Cham (2018). https://doi.org/10.1007/978-3-030-00305-0_15

15. Teutsch, J., Jain, S., Saxena, P.: When cryptocurrencies mine their own business. In: Grossklags, J., Preneel, B. (eds.) FC 2016. LNCS, vol. 9603, pp. 499–514. Springer, Heidelberg (2017). https://doi.org/10.1007/978-3-662-54970-4_29
16. Winzer, F., Herd, B., Faust, S.: Temporary censorship attacks in the presence of rational miners. In: IEEE European Symposium on Security and Privacy Workshops (EuroS&PW), pp. 357–366. IEEE (2019)
17. McCorry, P., Hicks, A., Meiklejohn, S.: Smart contracts for bribing miners. In: Zohar, A., et al. (eds.) FC 2018. LNCS, vol. 10958, pp. 3–18. Springer, Heidelberg (2019). https://doi.org/10.1007/978-3-662-58820-8_1
18. Daian, P., Eyal, I., Juels, A., Sirer, E.G.: (Short paper) PieceWork: generalized outsourcing control for proofs of work. In: Brenner, M., et al. (eds.) FC 2017. LNCS, vol. 10323, pp. 182–190. Springer, Cham (2017). https://doi.org/10.1007/978-3-319-70278-0_11
19. Pinzón, C., Rocha, C.: Double-spend attack models with time advantage for bitcoin. Electron. Notes Theor. Comput. Sci. **329**(9), 79–103 (2016)
20. Judmayer, A., Stifter, N., Zamyatin, A., et al.: Pay-to-win: incentive attacks on proof-of-work cryptocurrencies. Cryptology ePrint Archive, Report 2019/775 (2019)

Updatable Blockchains

Michele Ciampi[2(✉)], Nikos Karayannidis[1], Aggelos Kiayias[1,2],
and Dionysis Zindros[3]

[1] Input Output HK Limited, Hong Kong, People's Republic of China
`nikos.karagiannidis@iohk.io`
[2] The University of Edinburgh, Edinburgh, UK
`mciampi@ed.ac.uk, akiayias@inf.ed.ac.uk`
[3] National and Kapodistrian University of Athens, Athens, Greece
`dionyziz@gmail.com`

Abstract. Software updates for blockchain systems become a real challenge when they impact the underlying consensus mechanism. The activation of such changes might jeopardize the integrity of the blockchain by resulting in chain splits. Moreover, the software update process should be handed over to the community and this means that the blockchain should support updates without relying on a trusted party. In this paper, we introduce the notion of *updatable blockchains* and show how to construct blockchains that satisfy this definition. Informally, an updatable blockchain is a secure blockchain and in addition it allows to update its protocol preserving the history of the chain. In this work, we focus only on the processes that allow securely switching from one blockchain protocol to another assuming that the blockchain protocols are correct. That is, we do not aim at providing a mechanism that allows reaching consensus on what is the code of the new blockchain protocol. We just assume that such a mechanism exists (like the one proposed in NDSS 2019 by Zhang et al.), and show how to securely go from the old protocol to the new one. The contribution of this paper can be summarized as follows. We provide the first formal definition of updatable ledgers and propose the description of two compilers. These compilers take a blockchain and turn it into an updatable blockchain. The first compiler requires the structure of the current and the updated blockchain to be very similar (only the structure of the blocks can be different) but it allows for an update process more simple, efficient. The second compiler that we propose is very generic (i.e., makes few assumptions on the similarities between the structure of the current blockchain and the update blockchain). The drawback of this compiler is that it requires the new blockchain to be resilient against a specific adversarial behaviour and requires all the honest parties to be online during the update process. However, we show how to get rid of the latest requirement (the honest parties being online during the update) in the case of proof-of-work and proof-of-stake ledgers.

Keywords: Blockchain · Update · Ledger

Research partly supported by H2020 project PRIVILEDGE #780477.

L. Chen et al. (Eds.): ESORICS 2020, LNCS 12309, pp. 590–609, 2020.
https://doi.org/10.1007/978-3-030-59013-0_29

1   Introduction

Most of the existing software requires to be updated (or replaced) at some point. Indeed, the most vital aspect for the sustainability of any software system is its ability to effectively and swiftly adapt to changes; one basic form of which are software updates. Therefore the adoption of software updates is at the heart of the lifecycle of any system, and blockchain systems are no exception. Software updates might be triggered by a plethora of different reasons: change requests, bug-fixes, security holes, new-feature requests, various optimizations, code refactoring etc. More specifically, for blockchain systems, a typical source of change is the enhancements at the consensus protocol level. There might be changes to the values of specific parameters (e.g., the maximum block size, or the maximum transaction size etc.), changes to the validation rules at any level (transaction, block, or blockchain), or even changes at the consensus protocol itself. Usually, the reason for such changes is the reinforcement of the protocol against a broader scope of adversary attacks, or the optimization of some aspect of the system like the transaction throughput, or the storage cost etc. A software update's lifecycle comprises of three important decision points: a) What update proposal should be implemented, b) is a specific implementation appropriate to be deployed and c) when and how the changes should be activated on the blockchain. A fully decentralized approach should decentralize all of these three decisions. Indeed, there are already proposals on how to update specific blockchain protocols in a decentralized way [8,9,14]. Moreover, Bingsheng et al. [16], proposes a complete treasury system in order to solve the funding problem for software updates. The decentralization of such decisions is usually called in short *decentralized governance*. This paper does not focus on how to achieve decentralized governance for software updates. Indeed, we assume that appropriate decentralized governance processes (e.g., voting, delegation of voting, upgrade-readiness signaling etc.) are in place and the community has already reached a consensus on what specific update should be activated and this information is *written* on the blockchain. Moreover, we assume that a sufficient percent of honest parties have expressed (e.g. through a signaling mechanism) their readiness to upgrade to the new ledger. This is exactly the point from where our focus begins. In particular, we deal with the *secure activation* of software update changes on the blockchain in a fully decentralized setting and essentially provide a way to safely transition from the old ledger to the upgraded ledger without the need of a trusted third party. Moreover, we define what is a secure activation of changes by introducing the notion of *updatable blockchains*. To the best of our knowledge, our approach is the first that treats the problem of decentralized activation of updates for blockchains in such a formal way providing a security definition for updatable blockchain and generic constructions (more details will be provided in the next section).

1.1 Our Contributions

In our work, we try to define what is a ledger[1] that supports updates and refer to it as an *updatable ledger*.

Then we propose a generic compiler that takes a ledger $\mathcal{L}_1$ and turns it into an updatable ledger that tolerates updates only with respect to ledgers that follow the same consensus rule as $\mathcal{L}_1$ but have different blocks structure. We then propose another (more generic) compiler that, always starting from $\mathcal{L}_1$, turns $\mathcal{L}_1$ it into a ledger $\mathcal{L}^{\mathsf{UPD}}$ that can be updated to the code of a ledger $\mathcal{L}_2$. This compiler works assuming only few similarities between $\mathcal{L}_1$ and $\mathcal{L}_2$, but it is more complicated and decreases the throughput of the ledger during the update. All our constructions do not rely on any trusted third party (TTP).

1.2 Our Techniques

Our definition of updatable ledgers is quite intuitive. We require an updatable ledger $\mathcal{L}^{\mathsf{UPD}}$ to be secure under the standard definition of security (i.e., it has to enjoy consistency and liveness) but on top of this, it has to support the property of *updatability*. This property guarantees that, in the case there are enough parties that are willing to upgrade the code of $\mathcal{L}^{\mathsf{UPD}}$ to the code of a new ledger $\mathcal{L}_2$, the honest parties can securely run $\mathcal{L}_2$ and preserve the state of $\mathcal{L}^{\mathsf{UPD}}$.

Clearly, (almost) any ledger $\mathcal{L}_1$ can be turned into an updatable ledger $\mathcal{L}^{\mathsf{UPD}}$ if we can rely on a TTP. Indeed, in this case the TTP can issue a genesis block for $\mathcal{L}_2$ which incorporates the state of $\mathcal{L}_1$ (or just the hash of it), and then the parties that where running $\mathcal{L}_1$ can abandon it and start running $\mathcal{L}_2$ using the genesis block issued by the TTP.

We show how to construct an updatable ledger without relying on a TTP. The starting point for our construction is a standard ledger $\mathcal{L}_1$ that we enhance with the following mechanism. At time T_0 (when enough parties are assumed to be willing to update to $\mathcal{L}_2$) a block of $\mathcal{L}_1$ is chosen and *translated* into a genesis block for $\mathcal{L}_2$. All the parties that wanted to update can now simply run $\mathcal{L}_2$ on the chosen genesis block. This approach clearly requires that there is an efficient way to translate a block of $\mathcal{L}_1$ into a block for $\mathcal{L}_2$, and this might limit the class of ledgers to which $\mathcal{L}^{\mathsf{UPD}}$ can be updated.

Even though the above approach seems to work, there are unfortunately many subtleties that we need to deal with. The first is that the adversary might be able to see the genesis block for $\mathcal{L}_2$ before any other honest parties do, and therefore he can take advantage in the generation of the blocks of $\mathcal{L}_2$ thus compromising the security of the system. The second issue is that the adversary might influence the choice of the genesis block. Indeed, we do not know how the consensus algorithm of $\mathcal{L}_1$ works and what is the power of the adversary in biasing the content of $\mathcal{L}_1$'s blocks. We note that this scenario (where there are

---

[1] With slight abuse of terminology we use the words ledger and blockchain interchangeably.

many candidates blocks and the adversary can decide which block is added to the final chain) is well studied (see [11]) and many blockchain protocols allow this kind of adversarial behaviour (i.e., an adversary can create forks and influence the decision on what fork will become part of the stable chain). To tackle these issues, we further shrink the class of ledgers to which $\mathcal{L}^{\mathsf{UPD}}$ can be updated, and require $\mathcal{L}_2$ to retain its security even in the case the genesis block can be seen by the adversary before that the hones parties can see it, and even if the adversary can pick the genesis block from a set of candidate genesis blocks. Despite being quite general, this compiler has the drawback that the honest parties need to be online during the update. Indeed, if an honest party is offline before T_0 and comes online after the update then no security can be guaranteed for this party. However, we show how to relax the requirement on the honest parties being online during the update by relying on a *2-for-1 mining* approach (more details are provided in the end of Sect. 4.2).

The second scheme that we propose requires $\mathcal{L}^{\mathsf{UPD}}$ and $\mathcal{L}_2$ to be the same (i.e., they use the same consensus rules) but might have a different block structure. In this case, the update process is even simpler, the parties, starting from a pre-agreed block index j, start extending the state of $\mathcal{L}^{\mathsf{UPD}}$ using the rules of $\mathcal{L}_2$ even if the block in position j is not stable. That is, it might happen that different honest parties start running $\mathcal{L}_2$ using a different starting block given that the block j does not belong to the common prefix. We prove that this does not cause issues even in the case when not all the honest parties participate to the update (i.e., some honest parties are offline or decided to not participate to the update). The advantage of this approach over the first that we have proposed is that we do not require all the honest parties to be online during the update, and the throughput is not affected by the update process.

2   The Model

Protocol participants are represented as parties—formally Interactive Turing Machine instances (ITIs)—in a multi-party computation. We assume a central adversary who corrupts miners and uses them to attack the protocol. The adversary is *adaptive*, i.e., can corrupt (additional) parties at any point and depending on his current view of the protocol execution. Our protocols are synchronous (G)UC protocols [4,15]: parties have access to a (global) clock setup, denoted by $\mathcal{G}_{\mathsf{clock}}$, and can communicate over a network of authenticated multicast channels. We note that the assumption on the existence of a global clock has been used to prove the security of Bitcoin [4] and we are not aware of any other formal proof that relies on weaker notion of "time". For this reason we believe that the use of the functionality $\mathcal{G}_{\mathsf{clock}}$ in this work is without loss of generality.

We assume instant and *fetch-based* delivery channels [7,15]. Such channels, whenever they receive a message from their sender, they record it and deliver it to the receiver upon his request with a "fetch" command. In fact, all functionalities we design in this work will have such fetch-based delivery of their outputs. We remark that the instant-delivery assumption is without loss of generality as the channels are only used for communicating the timestamped object to the verifier which can anyway happen at any point after its creation. However, our treatment trivially applies also to the setting where parties communicate over bounded-delay channels as in [4].

We adopt the *dynamic availability* model implicit in [4] which was fleshed out in [3]. We next sketch its main components: All functionalities, protocols, and global setups have a dynamic party set. i.e., they all include special instructions allowing parties to register, deregister, and allowing the adversary to learn the current set of registered parties. Additionally, global setups allow any other setup (or functionality) to register and deregister with them, and they also allow other setups to learn their set of registered parties. For more details on the registration process we refer the reader to Appendix B.

The Clock Functionality $\mathcal{G}_{\texttt{clock}}$ (cf. Fig. 4). The *clock functionality* was initially proposed in [15] to enable synchronous execution of UC protocols. Here we adopt its global-setup version, denoted by $\mathcal{G}_{\texttt{clock}}$, which was proposed by [4] and was used in the (G)UC proofs of the ledger's security.[2] $\mathcal{G}_{\texttt{clock}}$ allows parties (and functionalities) to ensure that the protocol they are running proceeds in synchronized rounds; it keeps track of round variable whose value can be retrieved by parties (or by functionalities) via sending to it the pair: CLOCK-READ. This value is increased when every honest party has sent to the clock a command CLOCK-UPDATE. The parties use the clock as follows. Each party starts every operation by reading the current round from $\mathcal{G}_{\texttt{clock}}$ via the command CLOCK-READ. Once any party has executed all its instructions for that round it instructs the clock to advance by sending a CLOCK-UPDATE command, and gets in an idle mode where it simply reads the clock time in every activation until the round advances. To keep more compact the description of our functionalities that rely on $\mathcal{G}_{\texttt{clock}}$, we implicitly assume that whenever an input is received the command CLOCK-READ is sent to $\mathcal{G}_{\texttt{clock}}$ to retrieve the current round. Moreover, before giving the output, the functionalities request to advance the clock by sending CLOCK-UPDATE to $\mathcal{G}_{\texttt{clock}}$.

2.1   Ledger Consensus: Model

In this section, we define our notion of protocol execution following [5,11]. The execution of a protocol Π is driven by an environment program $\mathcal{Z}$ that may spawn multiple instances running the protocol Π. The programs in question can be thought of as interactive Turing machines (ITM) that have communication, input and output tapes. An instance of an ITM running a certain program will be referred to as an interactive Turing machine instance or ITI. The spawning of new ITI's by an existing ITI as well as the interaction between them is at the discretion of a control program which is also an ITM and is denoted by C. The pair $(\mathcal{Z}, C)$ is called a system of ITM's, cf. [5]. Specifically, the execution driven

---

[2] As a global setup, $\mathcal{G}_{\texttt{clock}}$ also exists in the ideal world and the ledger connects to it to keep track of rounds.

by $\mathcal{Z}$ is defined with respect to a protocol Π, an adversary $\mathcal{A}$ (also an ITM) and a set of parties $P_1, \ldots, P_n$; these are hardcoded in the control program C. Initially, the environment $\mathcal{Z}$ is restricted by C to spawn the adversary $\mathcal{A}$. Each time the adversary is activated, it may send one or more messages of the form (corrupt, P_i) to C. The control program C will register party P_i as corrupted, only provided that the environment has previously given an input of the form (corrupt, P_i) to $\mathcal{A}$ and that the number of corrupted parties is less or equal tc, a bound that is also hardcoded in C.

We divide time into discrete units called *time slots* or *round*. Players are equipped with (roughly) synchronized clocks $\mathcal{G}_{\text{clock}}$ that indicate the current slot: we assume that any clock drift is subsumed in the slot length.

Ledger Consensus. Ledger consensus (a.k.a. "Nakamoto consensus") is the problem where a set of nodes (or parties) operate continuously accepting inputs that are called transactions and incorporate them in a public data structure called the *ledger*. A ledger (denoted in calligraphic-face, e.g. $\mathcal{L}$) is a mechanism for maintaining a sequence of transactions, often stored in the form of a blockchain. In this work, we denote with $\mathcal{L}$ the algorithms used to maintain the sequence, and with L all the views of the participants of the state of these algorithms when being executed. For example, the (existing) ledger Bitcoin consists of the set of all transactions that ever took place in the Bitcoin network, the current UTXO set, as well as the local views of all the participants. In contrast, we call a *ledger state* a concrete sequence of transactions $\mathsf{Tx}_1, \mathsf{Tx}_2, \ldots$ stored in the stable part of a ledger state L, typically as viewed by a particular party. Hence, in every blockchain-based ledger $\mathcal{L}$, every fixed chain $\mathcal{C}$ defines a concrete ledger state by applying the interpretation rules given as a part of the description of $\mathcal{L}$. In this work, we assume that the ledger state is obtained from the blockchain by dropping the last k blocks and serializing the transactions in the remaining blocks. We refer to k as the *common-prefix parameter*. We denote by $\mathsf{L}^P[t]$ the ledger state of a ledger $\mathcal{L}$ as viewed by a party P at the beginning of a time slot t and by $\check{\mathsf{L}}^P[t]$ the complete state of the ledger (at time t) including all pending transactions that are not stable yet. $\mathsf{L}^P[t]$ can be obtained from $\check{\mathsf{L}}^P[t]$ by dropping the last k block.

For two ledger states (or, more generally, any sequences), we denote by $\preceq$ the prefix relation. Recall the definition of secure ledger protocol given in [10].

Definition 1. *A ledger protocol $\mathcal{L}$ is secure if it enjoys the following properties.*

> **Consistency.** *For any two honest parties P_1, P_2 and two time slots $t_1 \leq t_2$, it holds $\mathsf{L}^{P_1}[t_1] \preceq \check{\mathsf{L}}^{P_2}[t_2]$.*
> **Liveness.** *If all honest parties in the system attempt to include a transaction Tx then, at any slot t after s slots (called the liveness parameter), any honest party P, if queried, will report $\mathsf{Tx} \in \mathsf{L}^P[t]$.*

In this work we also explicitly rely on the properties of *Common Prefix (CP)*, *Chain Growth (CG)* and *Chain Quality (CQ)*.

Common Prefix (CP); with parameters $k \in \mathbb{N}$ states that for any pair of honest players P_1, P_2 at rounds $r_1 \leq r_2$ respectively, it holds that $\mathsf{L}^{P_1}[r_1] \preceq \check{\mathsf{L}}^{P_2}[r_2]$.

Chain Growth (CG); with parameters $\tau \in (0,1]$ **and** $s \in \mathbb{N}$. Consider the chain $\mathcal{C}$ adopted by an honest party at the onset of a slot and any portion of $\mathcal{C}$ spanning s prior slots; then the number of blocks appearing in this portion of the chain is at least τs.

Chain Quality (CQ) with parameters $\mu \in \mathbb{R}$ **and** $\ell \in \mathbb{N}$. For any honest party P with chain $\mathcal{C}$ it holds that for any ℓ consecutive blocks of $\mathcal{C}$ the ratio of honest blocks is at least μ.

We consider a setting where a set of parties run a protocol maintaining a ledger $\mathcal{L}_1$. Following [13], we denote by $\mathbb{A}_1$ the assumptions for $\mathcal{L}_1$. That is, if the assumption $\mathbb{A}_1$ holds, then ledger $\mathcal{L}_1$ is secure under the Definition 1. Formally, $\mathbb{A}_i$ for a ledger $\mathcal{L}_i$ is a sequence of events $\mathbb{A}_i[t]$ for each time slot t that can assume value 1, if the assumption is satisfied, and 0 otherwise. For example, $\mathbb{A}_i$ may denote that there has never been a majority of hashing power (or stake in a particular asset, on this ledger or elsewhere) under the control of the adversary; that a particular entity (in case of a centralized ledger) was not corrupted; and so on. Without loss of generality, we say that the assumption $\mathbb{A}_1$ for the ledger $\mathcal{L}_1$ holds if and only if the fraction of corrupted parties (the parties that received the input $(\mathsf{corrupt}, \cdot)$) is below the threshold tc_1 (where tc_1 is part of the control function as described in the beginning of this section).

Chain Selection Rule and Block Validation. We sometimes assume that a ledger protocol describes a *chain selection rule* that we denote with ChainSel. That is, we assume that each party in each round of the execution of the protocol collects all chains that come from the network and runs the algorithm ChainSel to decide whether to keep his current local chain $\mathsf{C}_{\mathsf{loc}}$, or adopt one of the newly received chains. Following [4] we also assume that before applying the chain-selection rule, any given chain is tested using the procedure IsValidChain. IsValidChain checks filters the valid chains among all the chain received from the network and only the valid chain are used as input for ChainSel. ChainSel in turns rely on the algorithm IsValidBlock. IsValidBlock take as input a block B of $\mathsf{C}_{\mathsf{loc}}$ and outputs 1 if B is a valid block (i.e., the structure of the block is correct) and 0 otherwise.

We note that by assuming that a ledger protocol is always equipped with the algorithms ChainSel, IsValidChain and IsValidBlock make some of our results less general. However, we will show that it is possible to obtain a better updatable ledger in the case when the two ledgers (the current ledger) and the new ledger have the same chain selection rule (among other similarities).

2.2   Genesis Block Functionality

The ledger protocols that we consider in this work are equipped with the description of an algorithm genesis that, on input a random value of appropriate length, outputs a valid genesis block (i.e., the first block of the chain). The security of most of the known ledger protocols holds under the additional assumption that the genesis block is correct. That is, the genesis block has been generated accordingly to **genesis** using appropriate randomness. Multiple ways have been presented to generate a correct genesis block in the literature (i.e., by relying on a trusted authority, use unpredictable information (like in bitcoin), run a multi-party computation (MPC) protocol [1], rely on PoW [12] assumptions and so on and so forth). In this work we abstract the generation of the genesis block by means of an ideal functionality. The ideal functionality that one might expect, upon being activated from the adversary or from an honest party, should sample a random string and use it to run the algorithm **genesis**. Unfortunately this simple functionality does not cover real world scenarios where an adversarial party might see the genesis block before the honest parties do. This, for example, can happen in the case when **genesis** is realized via an MPC protocol and a rushing adversary[3] could hold the genesis block (the output of the computation) for some bounded amount of time τ^{max} before the honest parties can see it. We note that an adversary can use this strategy to take an advantage on the generation of the blocks that extend the genesis block. Therefore, the first modification that we consider for our ideal functionality is to allow the adversary to see the genesis block up to τ^{max} rounds earlier than the honest parties. The second relaxation allows the adversary to see up to m honestly generated genesis blocks and consequently decide which of these blocks will become the genesis block. We propose the formal description of our genesis functionality $\mathcal{F}^{\mathsf{gen}}$ in Fig. 1. We note that the case where $\tau^{\mathsf{max}} = 0$ and $m = 1$ corresponds to the case where there is only one candidate genesis block and all the parties can see it at the same round.

3   Secure Updatable Ledgers

3.1   Defining Secure Updatable Ledgers

In this section, we provide the definition of updatable ledgers. Our definition is generic in the sense that can be applied to a large class of ledgers (e.g., PoS, PoW and so on). Let $\mathcal{L}^{\mathsf{UPD}}$ and $\mathcal{L}_2$ be the two ledgers with the respective assumptions $\mathbb{A}_1$ and $\mathbb{A}_2$. Assuming that $\mathbb{A}_1$ holds, then among the parties that are running $\mathcal{L}^{\mathsf{UPD}}$ we could have up to a fraction of tc_1 corrupted parties (i.e., parties that have received the command **corrupt**). Analogously, the assumption $\mathbb{A}_2$ for the ledger $\mathcal{L}_2$ holds if the number of corrupted parties divided by the number of honest party is below the threshold tc_2.

The interface of an updatable ledger extends the interface of a standard ledger by adding the command (**activate**, $\mathcal{L}_2$). That is, each party that runs an updatable ledger $\mathcal{L}^{\mathsf{UPD}}$ can receive the command (**activate**, $\mathcal{L}_2$) from the environment to enable the update procedure. Let t_{P_i} denote the time in which a party P_i receives the activation command and let $\mathcal{P}^{\mathsf{u}}$ be the set of parties that received this

---

[3] A rushing adversary waits to receive the messages from all the honest parties and then computes its reply. Note that this means that, in general, the adversary is always able to see the output of the computation before the honest parties do.

Genesis Functionality for $\mathcal{L}$

Parameters. The functionality is parametrized by $\tau^{\max}$, the maximum number of candidate genesis block m, the genesis block B^{gen} initialized with a default value $\perp$ and the procedure **genesis**(). We assume the functionality to be registered to $\mathcal{G}_{\text{clock}}$ and that it maintains a set of registered parties $\mathcal{P}$. On any input I the functionality queries $\mathcal{G}_{\text{clock}}$, and we denote with R be the response obtained by $\mathcal{G}_{\text{clock}}$.

- If $I = \texttt{GEN\_GENESIS}$ is received from the adversary $\mathcal{A}$ then set $\tau := R$, generate m genesis blocks (each block is generated by running the procedure **genesis**()) $\mathsf{GB} := \{B_1^{\text{gen}}, \ldots, B_m^{\text{gen}}\}$ for $\mathcal{L}$, and send GB to the adversary.
- If $I = \texttt{GET\_GENESIS}$ is received from an honest party $p_i \in \mathcal{P}$ do the following
    - If $B^{\text{gen}} \neq \perp$ then return B^{gen} to p_i.
    - If $B^{\text{gen}} = \perp$ and $R - \tau > \tau^{\max}$ then set generate a genesis block $\tilde{B}^{\text{gen}}$ by running **genesis**, set $B^{\text{gen}} \leftarrow \tilde{B}^{\text{gen}}$ and send B^{gen} to p_i.
- If $I = (\texttt{GET\_GENESIS}, B^{\text{gen}\prime})$ is received from the adversary do the following
    - If $(R - \tau) \leq \tau^{\max}$ and $B^{\text{gen}\prime} \in \mathsf{GB}$ then set $B^{\text{gen}} := B^{\text{gen}\prime}$.
    - Else, return $\perp$ to the adversary.

Fig. 1. The genesis functionality $\mathcal{F}^{\text{gen}}$.

command. Informally, an updatable ledger guarantees that if the set of honest parties that are willing to run $\mathcal{L}_2$ (i.e., the number of parties that received (activate, $\mathcal{L}_2$)) is such that $\mathbb{A}_2[\tau] = 1$ for all $\tau \geq T_0$ for some $T_0 \in \mathbb{N}$, then the state of $\mathcal{L}_2$ at time $T_0 + \Delta$ corresponds to the state of $\mathcal{L}^{\text{UPD}}$ at some time $T \in [T_0, T_0 + \Delta]$. The parameter Δ represents the time required for the update process to be completed. The above implies that L_2 extends L_1 and that $\mathcal{L}_2$ is secure (i.e., it enjoys consistency and liveness). In a nutshell, a secure update process guarantees that the state of the old ledger is moved into the new ledger, and that the new ledger is secure. We now give a more formal definition.

Definition 2 (Updatable Ledger). *We say that a ledger $\mathcal{L}^{\text{UPD}}$ is updatable with activation parameter Δ (where $\Delta \in \mathbb{N}$) if it is a secure ledger according to Definition 1 and it enjoys the following property.*

Updatability. *Let $\mathcal{L}_2$ be a secure ledger (always according to Definition 1). Let $\mathcal{P}^{\text{u}}$ be the set of parties that received the input (activate, $\mathcal{L}_2$). If $\mathcal{P}^{\text{u}}$ is such that $\mathbb{A}_2[\tau] = 1$ for all $\tau \geq T_0$ for some $T_0 \in \mathbb{N}$ and $\mathbb{A}_1[\tau'] = 1$ for all $\tau' \leq T_1 = T_0 + \Delta$, then*

1. $\mathsf{L}_1^{P_i}[T'] \preceq \mathsf{L}_2$ for some $P_i \in \mathcal{P}^{\text{u}}$ with $T_0 \leq T' \leq T_1$.
2. for all $\tau'' \geq T_1$ $\mathcal{L}_2$ enjoys consistency and liveness

We note that this definition says nothing on the security of $\mathcal{L}^{\text{UPD}}$ after the time $T_1 = T_0 + \Delta$. Indeed, the Definition 2 implies that if after this time slot $T_0 + \Delta$ $\mathcal{L}^{\text{UPD}}$ becomes insecure (e.g., because $\mathbb{A}_1$ does not hold) then the security of $\mathcal{L}_2$ is not compromised.

We relax the above definition by introducing the notion of updatable ledger in the *semi-online* setting. An updatable ledger in the semi-online setting guarantees the properties of updatability only for the honest parties that where active during the activation period $[T_0, T_1]$. That is, if an honest party P is offline before time T_0, and comes online after at time T_1 then no security is guaranteed with respect to P.

4   Our Constructions

In this section we propose two main approaches to turn a ledger $\mathcal{L}_1$ into an updatable ledger $\mathcal{L}^{\mathsf{UPD}}$. That is, we show how to make $\mathcal{L}_1$ able to self-update to the code of a new ledger $\mathcal{L}_2$. The first approach proposed requires $\mathcal{L}_1$ and $\mathcal{L}_2$ to be the same (i.e., they use the same consensus rules) but might have a different block structure. The advantage in this approach is that we get a very simple updatable ledger, that does not decrease the throughput of $\mathcal{L}^{\mathsf{UPD}}$ during the update and does not require all the honest parties to be online during the update[4]. The second approach requires fewer similarities between the two ledgers, but it is proven secure only in the semi-online. We also show that we can relax the requirement on the honest parties being online during the update by relying on a *2-for-1 mining* approach (more details are provided in the end of Sect. 4.2).

We now provide a detailed description of our approaches and formally prove their security.

4.1   First Approach

In this section we consider a simplified scenario where the two ledgers, $\mathcal{L}_1$ and $\mathcal{L}_2$, are the same except for the block format (i.e., $\mathcal{L}_1$ and $\mathcal{L}_2$ might have a different block size). Moreover, we assume that a block valid for $\mathcal{L}_1$ is valid for $\mathcal{L}_2$ as well (but the vice versa does not necessarily hold). Formally, this means that if the block validation algorithm $\mathsf{IsValidBlock}_1$ of $\mathcal{L}_1$ outputs 1 on some input B, then also the block validation algorithm $\mathsf{IsValidBlock}_2$ of $\mathcal{L}_2$ outputs 1 (see Sect. 2.1 for more details). We now prove the following theorem

Theorem 1. *If $\mathcal{L}_1$ and $\mathcal{L}_2$ are secure ledgers with block validation rules respectively $\mathsf{IsValidBlock}_1$ and $\mathsf{IsValidBlock}_2$ such that:*

1. *$\mathcal{L}_1$ and $\mathcal{L}_2$ are the same except with respect to the block validation rules;*
2. *for every block B such that if $\mathsf{IsValidBlock}_1(B) = 1$ then $\mathsf{IsValidBlock}_2(B) = 1$,*
3. *$\mathcal{L}_1$ (resp. $\mathcal{L}_2$) has common-prefix parameter k, chain-growth parameter (τ, s) and assumption $\mathbb{A}_1$ (resp. $\mathbb{A}_2$) with $\mathbb{A}_1 = \mathbb{A}_2$,*

then there exists an updatable ledger $\mathcal{L}^{\mathsf{UPD}}$ with update parameter $\Delta := (k + 1)\tau^{-1} + s$.

---

[4] We also show that we can relax the requirement on the honest parties being online during the update for the case of PoW ledgers.

Proof. We assume that enough parties have received the command (activate, $\mathcal{L}_2$) such that $\mathbb{A}_2$ holds and denote the time when this happen with T_0. Our updatable ledger $\mathcal{L}^{\mathsf{UPD}}$ works as follows.

Each party $P_i \in \mathcal{P}^u$ does the following steps.

1. Use IsValidBlock$_2$ as a block validation algorithm.
2. Create and post a transaction that contains an *activation flag*.
3. Let i_f be the index of the block that will contain the first transaction with an activation flag.
4. Let $j := i_f + k + 1$, run $\mathcal{L}_1$ and when the j-th block B_j^i becomes part of $\check{\mathsf{L}}_1^{P_i}[\tau_i]$ for some $\tau_i \geq T_0$ start extending B_j^i using the rules of $\mathcal{L}_2$ instead of the rules of $\mathcal{L}_1$ (we recall that a valid block for $\mathcal{L}_1$ is also a valid block for $\mathcal{L}_2$)

We provide a pictorial description of what happens to the ledger state during the update in Fig. 2. We note that two honest parties P_1 and P_2 might have different $\check{\mathsf{L}}_1^{P_1}[\tau]$ and $\check{\mathsf{L}}_1^{P_2}[\tau]$ at any time τ. The Fig. 2 describe the scenario where P_1 might start to run $\mathcal{L}_2$ starting from an unstable block (i.e. a block of $\check{\mathsf{L}}_1^{P_1}[\tau]$ with $\tau \geq T_0 + s$) which is different from the block that P_2 is using. However, after sufficiently many rounds (at some round $\tau' \leq T_0 + s + (k_1 + 1)\tau_1^{-1}$ to be precise) P_1 and P_2 will agree on what is the last block of $\mathcal{L}_1$ and what is the first bock of $\mathcal{L}_2$.

To complete the proof we need to show that $\mathcal{L}_2$ enjoys consistency and liveness and that the state $\mathcal{L}_1$ at some time $\tau \in [T_0, T_1]$ is a prefix of $\mathcal{L}_2$'s state.

Before doing that, we introduce the notion of *canonical execution* for the ledger $\mathcal{L}_2$. A canonical execution represents a standalone execution of $\mathcal{L}_2$. More precisely, we assume the existence of a genesis block for $\mathcal{L}_2$ (that the adversary and the honest party see at the round 0) and that $\mathbb{A}_2[\tau] = 1$ for all $\tau \geq 0$. Let $\mathcal{P}$ be the set of parties that is running $\mathcal{L}_2$. Also, let t be the smallest time slot in which B_{i_f} appears in $\mathsf{L}_2^{P_i}[t]$ for all $P_i \in \mathcal{P}$ and let $\tilde{t}_{i,j}$ be the smallest time slot in which B_j^i appears in $\check{\mathsf{L}}_2^{P_i}[t_{i,j}]$ for each $P_i \in \mathcal{P}$ with $j := i_f + k + 1$.

We now go back to our updatable ledger protocol. In the protocol that we have described, by assumption, we have that $\mathbb{A}_2[T_0] = 1$ for all $\tau \geq T_0$. From the moment when $\mathbb{A}_2$ becomes true the activation process takes $\Delta \leq (k+1)\tau^{-1} + s$ time slots to be completed.

This is because the parties need to wait for the block i_f to be part of all the honest parties stable view and wait for the j-th block (with $j := i_f + k + 1$) of to be part of $\check{\mathsf{L}}_1^{P_i}[t_{i,j}]$ for all P_i with $t_{i,j} \in \mathbb{N}$. Note that in the moment that the block B_j^i becomes available to an honest party $P_i \in \mathcal{P}^u$ (i.e., B_j^i is part of $\check{\mathsf{L}}_1^{P_i}$) then the party starts running $\mathcal{L}_2$ to extend B_j^i as described earlier (we recall that at this time slot the assumption $\mathbb{A}_2$ holds). Let $t'_{i,j}$ be the smallest time slot in which B_j^i appears in $\check{\mathsf{L}}_2^{P_i}[t'_{i,j}]$ for each $P_i \in \mathcal{P}$ with $t'_{i,j} \in \mathbb{N}$. If we consider the execution of the protocol from time T_0 and $T_0 + \Delta$ this can be seen as a canonical execution of $\mathcal{L}_2$ given that $\mathcal{L}_1$ and $\mathcal{L}_2$ follow the same rules and the same assumption, and given that $\check{\mathsf{L}}_1^{P_i}$ (and $\check{\mathsf{L}}_2^{P_i}$) contains at most k blocks more than $\mathsf{L}_1^{P_i}$ (and $\mathsf{L}_2^{P_i}$) for all $P_i \in \mathcal{P}^u$. Hence, any advantage that the adversary has on our updatable ledger can be translated into an advantage for an adversary

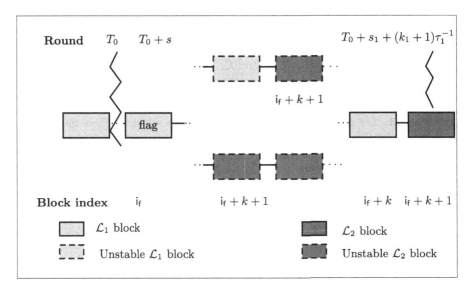

Fig. 2. Transition from $\mathcal{L}_1$ to $\mathcal{L}_2$. Note that different honest parties might have different views (i.e., forks) of the unstable part of the chain which have also different lengths.

that is attacking $\mathcal{L}_2$, which is assumed to be secure. Note that it is crucial that the assumption that underlines the two ledger is the same. Indeed, we note that the number of honest parties that received (activate, $\mathcal{L}_2$) might be lower than the overall number of honest parties. Hence, the honest parties that are running the update procedure are less than the parties that are running $\mathcal{L}_1$ (this might happen as we do not require all the honest parties to update). However, given that $\mathbb{A}_1 = \mathbb{A}_2$, we can see the honest parties that did not receive the command (activate, $\mathcal{L}_2$) as parties controlled by the adversary as they are not following the update procedure. Luckily, this does not cause problems as even if we consider these parties as adversarial, $\mathbb{A}_1$ would still hold (given that $\mathbb{A}_1 = \mathbb{A}_2$). Hence, we can claim that in the worst case everything that can be done by the adversary during the update can be done also in the canonical execution given that the number of honest parties in the canonical execution is the same as the number of honest parties that are performing the update.

We remark that the only difference between this and the canonical execution described above is that the blocks $B_{i_f}, \ldots, B_{j-2}, B_{j-1}$ are generated using $\mathcal{L}_1$, but this does not represent an issue since we are assuming that any block of $\mathcal{L}_1$ is valid for $\mathcal{L}_2$. □

We finally note that this protocol does not put any restriction on whether an honest party needs to be online or not during an update given that $\mathcal{L}_1$ and $\mathcal{L}_2$ have the same chain selection rule (only the block selection rule is different). One practical advantage of our approach is that if $\mathcal{L}_1$ (and $\mathcal{L}_2$) allows bootstrapping from the genesis block (like in [3]) so does our updatable ledger.

4.2   Second Approach

Before providing our construction we introduce the notion of *genesis-compatible* ledgers. We say that two ledgers $\mathcal{L}_1$ and $\mathcal{L}_2$ are genesis-compatible if a block of $\mathcal{L}_1$ can be turned into a valid candidate genesis block for $\mathcal{L}_2$. We now propose a formal definition.

Definition 3. *Let $\mathcal{L}_1$ and $\mathcal{L}_2$ be two secure ledgers where $\mathcal{F}^{\mathsf{gen}}$ is the genesis functionality of $\mathcal{L}_2$ parameterized by the algorithm* genesis() *(see Fig. 1).*

We say that $\mathcal{L}_1$ is genesis-compatible with $\mathcal{L}_2$ if there exists a deterministic polynomial time algorithm $\Pi^{1\rightarrow 2}$ that, on input a valid block B of $\mathcal{L}_1$ outputs a valid genesis block $\tilde{B}$ for $\mathcal{L}_2$. Moreover, the output of $\Pi^{1\rightarrow 2}$ is identically distributed to the output of the procedure genesis().

We note that $\Pi^{1\rightarrow 2}$ could be a very simple protocol. For example, if we consider two PoW ledgers that use the same puzzles, then $\mathcal{L}_1$ is genesis-compatible with $\mathcal{L}_2$ since the $\Pi^{1\rightarrow 2}$ can simply take a block of $\mathcal{L}_1$ and use it as a candidate genesis block for $\mathcal{L}_2$. We note that the definition of genesis-compatibility only tells that it is possible to generate a genesis block for $\mathcal{L}_2$ with a valid structure. That is, it does not imply that $\mathcal{L}_2$ can be securely run using any genesis block generated using $\Pi^{1\rightarrow 2}$ as, for example, using an old block of $\mathcal{L}_1$ could give an advantage to the adversary over the honest parties. More details follow.

We now propose our first compiler that turns a ledger $\mathcal{L}_1$ that is genesis-compatible with $\mathcal{L}_2$, into an updatable ledger. At a very high level our approach is the following. We use $\mathcal{L}_1$ to realize the genesis functionality of $\mathcal{L}_2$, and then we use the output of the genesis functionality to execute $\mathcal{L}_2$. We note that it is easy to create a candidate genesis block from $\mathcal{L}_1$ because it is genesis-compatible with $\mathcal{L}_2$. To complete the description of our compiler, we need to specify what block of $\mathcal{L}_1$ will be chosen, and argue that this process is indeed sufficient to realize the genesis functionality for $\mathcal{L}_2$. In our approach the parties that are running $\mathcal{L}_1$ agree on the index j of a block that will be used as a genesis block (this block can be decided using the consensus algorithm of $\mathcal{L}_1$, more details will be provided). When the block of position j, that we denote with B_j, becomes stable for all the honest parties that decided to update, then these parties use $\Pi^{1\rightarrow 2}$ to turn B_j into a genesis block for $\mathcal{L}_2$ thus obtaining B^{gen}. At this point B^{gen} is used to run $\mathcal{L}_2$ and $\mathcal{L}_1$ can be abandoned. Even though the above approach seems to work, there are many subtleties. The first is that the adversary might be able to see the block B_j before any other honest parties do, and therefore he can take an advantage in the generation of the blocks of $\mathcal{L}_2$. The second issue is that the adversary might influence the choice of the block that will appear in position j. Indeed, we do not know how the consensus algorithm of $\mathcal{L}_1$ works and what is the power of the adversary in biasing the content of B_j. We denote with $\tau^{\mathsf{max}'}$ the upper bound on the number of rounds that pass between the time at which the adversary can see a candidate block for $\mathcal{L}_1$ for a position j, and the time at which all the honest parties see B_j as part of the stable chain. We refer to this parameter $\tau^{\mathsf{max}'}$ as the *prediction* parameter. We also denote with m' the upper bound on the number of valid chains that are broadcasted on the network that contain a block in position j and refer to this parameter as *maximum forks* parameter.

Coming back to our protocol, we note that if the genesis functionality of $\mathcal{L}_2$ is parameterized with $\tau^{\mathsf{max}} = \tau^{\mathsf{max}\prime}$ and $m = m'$ then we can prove that the solution we proposed works.

We are now ready to state formally our theorem and prove it.

Theorem 2. *If $\mathcal{L}_1$ and $\mathcal{L}_2$ are secure ledgers and:*

1. *$\mathcal{L}_1$ has common-prefix parameter k_1, chain-growth parameter (τ_1, s_1) and assumption $\mathbb{A}_1$;*
2. *$\mathcal{L}_2$ has common-prefix parameter k_2, chain-growth parameter (τ_2, s_2) and assumption $\mathbb{A}_2$;*
3. *the prediction parameter of $\mathcal{L}_1$ is $\tau^{\mathsf{max}\prime}$ and the maximum forks parameter is m';*
4. *the genesis functionality $\mathcal{F}^{\mathsf{gen}}$ of $\mathcal{L}_2$ is parametrized by $\tau^{\mathsf{max}} = \tau^{\mathsf{max}\prime}$ and $m = m'$;*
5. *$\mathcal{L}_1$ is genesis-compatible with $\mathcal{L}_2$.*

then there exists an updatable ledger $\mathcal{L}^{\mathsf{UPD}}$ with update parameter $\Delta := 2k_1\tau_1^{-1} + s_1$ in the semi-online setting.

Proof. We start the proof by describing how formally our protocol works. Let T_0 be such that $\mathbb{A}_2$ holds. At time T_0 each party in $P_i \in \mathcal{P}^{\mathsf{u}}$ does the following steps.

1. Create and post a transaction that contains an *activation flag*, let i_f be the index of the block that will contain the first transaction with an activation flag (note that there might be more than one of such a transactions).
2. Keep running $\mathcal{L}_1$ until the block with index $j = \mathsf{i}_\mathsf{f} + k_1$ becomes stable (i.e., becomes part of $\mathsf{L}_1^P[\tau]$ for all $P \in \mathcal{P}^{\mathsf{u}}$ for some $\tau \geq T_0$) and stop issuing transaction for $\mathcal{L}_1$ (if any).
3. When the j-th block B_j becomes stable then stop running $\mathcal{L}_1$ and start running $\mathcal{L}_2$ using $B^{\mathsf{gen}} \leftarrow \varPi^{1 \rightarrow 2}(B_j)$ as the genesis block.

We provide a pictorial description of what happens to the ledger state during the update in Fig. 3. The activation flag is used by the honest parties to reach an agreement on what it will be the index of the block used as a genesis block. We note that the blocks of $\mathcal{L}_1$ that extend B_j might be unstable, moreover after the update has been completed the parties in $\mathcal{P}^{\mathsf{u}}$ will ignore the blocks of $\mathcal{L}_1$ that extend B_j (since after the update all the parties in $\mathcal{P}^{\mathsf{u}}$ will be using the rules $\mathcal{L}_2$, hence its chain selection rule). The reason why the parties in $\mathcal{P}^{\mathsf{u}}$ will stop issuing transactions for $\mathcal{L}_1$ is that these transactions might be included in blocks that extend B_j, which will be ignored after $T_0 + \Delta$ rounds. This clearly affects the throughput of the ledger in the interval $[T_0 + k_1\tau_1^{-1} + s_1, T_0 + 2k_1\tau_1^{-1} + s_1]$ (Fig. 3). We now continue with the proof. Let T_0 be the time at which we know that $\mathcal{P}^{\mathsf{u}}$ is such that $\mathbb{A}_2$ holds. In the worst case, the time required for an honest party to post a transaction that contains the activation flag takes time s_1 rounds

(s_1 comes from the liveness of $\mathcal{L}_1$). The number of rounds required for j to be stable in the view of all the honest parties is $2k_1\tau_1^{-1}$ rounds. This is because to generate the block B_j are required at least $k_1\tau_1^{-1}$ rounds, and B_j has to be extended with at least k_1 blocks to be part of all the honest parties view (and this takes additional $k_1\tau_1^{-1}$ rounds) Hence, the time required to complete the update is $\Delta = 2k_1\tau_1^{-1} + s_1$. Once the block B_j becomes stable, the parties in $\mathcal{P}^u$ can start running $\mathcal{L}_2$, and we are guaranteed that $\mathcal{L}_2$ enjoys liveness and consistency because the genesis block for $\mathcal{L}_2$ is created accordingly to $\mathcal{F}^{\mathsf{gen}}$ and by assumption $\mathbb{A}_2$ holds. Therefore, everything that appears before B^{gen} is preserved due to the consistency of $\mathcal{L}_2$. We refer to the state of $\mathcal{L}_1$ before B^{gen} as $\tilde{\mathsf{L}}_1$, and to the state of the ledger after the update as $\tilde{\mathsf{L}}_1\|\mathsf{L}_2$. We finally note that we guarantee no security for the honest parties that were not online during the update. The reason is that after T_1 the honest parties abandon $\mathcal{L}_1$ and the adversary could compromise it. For example, an adversary could potentially keep extending L_1 after the block j, and create a very long chain, even longer that $\tilde{\mathsf{L}}_1\|\mathsf{L}_2$. Hence, if the chain selection rule of $\mathcal{L}_1$ prescribes to take the longest chain, then a party that comes online at time T_1 might take the chain L_1 (which is compromised). $\qquad\square$

We remark that our construction requires the parties to generate empty blocks for $\mathcal{L}_1$ from block index $j+1$ and until block B_j becomes stable. This is required as the honest parties, after the update completes, will ignore any block generated using the rules of $\mathcal{L}_1$ that comes after B_j.

Practical Implications. The updatable ledger that we have described can be updated to any ledger $\mathcal{L}_2$ under the condition that the genesis functionality of $\mathcal{L}_2$ tolerates an adversary that can see the genesis block τ^{max} rounds before the honest parties and decide the genesis block among a set of m candidate genesis blocks. This requirement might look strong, but we note that the problem of constructing a ledger that is secure in such a scenario is simpler than the problem of constructing a ledger that supports temporary dishonest majority [2]. A ledger with security assumption $\mathbb{A}$ that tolerates temporary dishonest majority is such that its security properties (liveness and consistency) become valid again when $\mathbb{A}[\tau_1] = 1$, even if $\mathbb{A}[\tau'] = 0$ for all $\tau' \in [\tau_0, \tau_1 - \delta]$ for some $\tau_0, \tau_1, \delta \in \mathbb{N}$ such that $\tau_1 - \delta \geq \tau_0$. That is, the ledger become secure again when there is honest majority (i.e., $\mathbb{A}$ holds) even if there was an interval of time when there was no honest majority (i.e., $\mathbb{A}$ did not hold). Therefore, if we consider the extreme case where $\tau_0 = 0$, we can assume without loss of generality that the ledger admits a genesis functionality parametrized by $\tau^{\mathsf{max}} = \delta$, and by m that depends on the upper bound on the number of forks that the adversary can create. Hence, there are already ledgers that might fit our requirements for $\mathcal{L}_2$, and all the advancement in the research that concerns the security of ledgers in the case of temporary dishonest majority can be used to construct good candidates of updated ledgers ($\mathcal{L}_2$) for existing ledgers ($\mathcal{L}_1$) that can be used in our compiler.

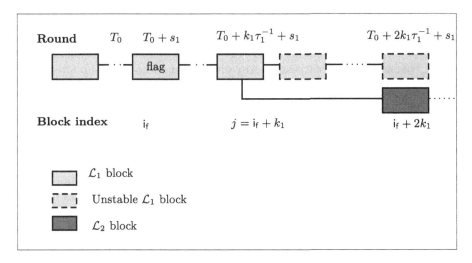

Fig. 3. Transition from $\mathcal{L}_1$ to $\mathcal{L}_2$. Note that the empty blocks of $\mathcal{L}_1$ might be non-stable.

Security for Offline Parties. Our security notion above is ensured for parties that are online during the upgrade process. Clearly it is necessary that the majority of the population's consensus-maintaining parties are honest and online, as the honest majority assumption mandates. Nevertheless, practical blockchain systems often have a large number of *consumer* parties by count who have a very small contribution to the total computational power of network, if at all, and are not significantly contributing to the maintenance of the consensus. These nodes can be wallets and other clients who mainly consume, rather than maintain, the blockchain, and are often offline for longer periods of time. Regardless, these nodes constitute the economic majority of the nodes and we must ensure they can also upgrade safely. The critical situation arises when such a party goes offline prior to an upgrade, remains offline during every phase of the upgrade, and comes online long after the rest of the population has successfully upgraded. Before describing how to construct a protocol that can protect these parties, let us briefly observe why an attack is easily possible by a minority adversary in a construction with no relevant protective mechanism. Consider a situation where a hard-fork-style change takes place and that blocks mined by upgraded parties after the upgrade are incompatible with blocks mined prior to the upgrade, i.e., after the upgrade, an unupgraded party will not consider an upgraded block as valid and an upgraded party will not consider an unupgraded block as valid. After the upgrade has been completed, the majority of the population will shift their mining power to mining new-style blocks. The adversary can take advantage of this situation to *ex post facto* attack the old system, which now remains unprotected as no significant mining power remains to secure it. As such, she can break the *common prefix* property, rewrite history, and subvert the upgrade signaling mechanism itself. More concretely, an adversary in this situation forks the old chain from the parent of the block in which upgrade information appeared for the first time and continues mining a chain parallel to the one that yielded the upgrade. As soon as that alternative history overtakes the old chain in terms of work, the adversary is successful. Any offline party who wakes up afterwards will use the old-style consensus rules to choose the blockchain and hence the upgrade will not appear in its view. The adversary has succeeded in isolating the offline party from the rest of the network. To rectify the above issue, a practical implementation of the protocol must leverage the mining power of the upgraded population to maintain *both* the new chain while at the same time securing the old chain. We propose a solution for the case where $\mathcal{L}_1$ and $\mathcal{L}_2$ are two proof-of-work or two proof-of-stake type of ledgers. Our solution leverages on a variation of 2-for-1 mining [11]. An upgraded miner works as follows. They maintain the longest chain C in view of the new protocol rules, but also the longest chain C' in the view of an unupgraded party. In case of hard fork, these two chains will differ. When they are about to mine a new block on top of the upgraded chain, they construct a new-style candidate block b extending C as usual. In addition, they also construct an empty (transactionless) old-style block b' on top of the best unupgraded chain C'. In a commentary section of the old-style candidate block b', such as the coinbase transaction, the miner places the hash $H(b)$ of the new-style candidate block. The miner then attempts to find proof-of-work for the old-style block, i.e., some nonce ctr that satisfies the proof-of-work equation $H(b' \| \text{ctr}) \leq T$ for the mining target T. If such proof-of-work is found, then the block b' is broadcast to the network and adopted as the tip of the longest unupgraded chain by the rest of the (upgraded or unupgraded) miners. Note that this block is designed to be backwards-compatible in the sense that it will be accepted by unupgraded miners even though they remain unaware of the upgrade. On the other hand, if the *reverse proof-of-work equation* $H(b' \| \text{ctr})^R \leq T$ is satisfied (where $H(\cdot)^R$ denotes the reversed bitstring of $H(\cdot)$), then b' and the respective proof-of-work and blocks b', b are broadcast to the network. This time unupgraded miners will not consider this a valid block. However, upgraded miners examine the validity of the block b contained within the commentary section of b' and check that the reverse proof-of-work equation is satisfied. If so, they adopt the block b as the next block in their upgraded blockchain. The above mechanism is the only mechanism by which new-style blocks are accepted by upgraded honest miners. The protocol just described has two advantages. Firstly, the upgraded honest miners make use of their mining power to contribute to the security of both the old and the new-style chain simultaneously. Therefore, an adversary cannot attack the old chain *ex post facto*. Secondly, instead of *dividing* their mining power between the two chains, the honest parties only use their mining power *once* to mine on *both* networks, because the hash function is only evaluated once. As such, the honest mining power is not diminished by the use of this mechanism. We observe that, in the Random Oracle model, the last bits of the hash output remain uniformly distributed conditioned on the fact that the proof-of-work equation has a solution. Therefore, finding a solution of the proof-of-work equation and finding a solution of the reverse proof-of-work equation are two independent events (they will occur simultaneously so rarely that the honest parties can ignore this possibility). Lastly, note that this scheme can be used repeatedly when multiple upgrades have occurred on top of one another, simply by treating a portion of the bits of the hash as the significant bits to test against the proof-of-work equation (e.g., for a second upgrade, the hash output can be split in three equal parts to be tested against the proof-of-work equation). This scheme therefore theoretically resolves the question of securing offline parties. In practice, because the scheme adds significant implementation complexity, implementors may elect to maintain this backwards-compatibility mechanism for a limited amount of time. In that case, parties who have remained offline longer than the backwards-compatibility mechanism is maintained, will have no guarantees for security, similarly to a classical system whose long-term support window has expired. The scheme requires the added complexity of mining two blocks simultaneously only in the case of proof-of-work. This is due to the nature of proof-of-work and specifically the fact that each query counted towards the proof-of-work quota can only be devoted to a specific message. In proof-of-stake blockchains, the solution for maintaining the security of offline unupgraded parties is the obvious one and allows for a much simpler implementation: We require upgraded parties to mint, alongside their new-style blocks extending the longest upgraded chain and containing transactions, also empty old-style blocks extending the longest unupgraded chain, to ensure the security of their unupgraded counterparts.

A   Modeling Synchrony

We refer to Fig. 4 for the formal description of the functionality $\mathcal{G}_{\texttt{clock}}$.

B   Functionalities with Dynamic Party Sets

UC provides support for functionalities in which the set of parties that might interact with the functionality is dynamic. We make this explicit by means of the following mechanism (that we describe almost verbatim from [4, Sec. 3.1]): All the functionalities considered here include the following instructions that allow honest parties to join or leave the set $\mathcal{P}$ of players that the functionality interacts with, and inform the adversary about the current set of registered parties:

- Upon receiving (REGISTER, sid) from some party p_i (or from $\mathcal{A}$ on behalf of a corrupted p_i), set $\mathcal{P} := \mathcal{P} \cup \{p_i\}$. Return (REGISTER, sid, p_i) to the caller.
- Upon receiving (DE-REGISTER, sid) from some party $p_i \in \mathcal{P}$, the functionality updates $\mathcal{P} := \mathcal{P} \setminus \{p_i\}$ and returns (DE-REGISTER, sid, p_i) to p_i.
- Upon receiving (IS-REGISTERED, sid) from some party p_i, return (REGISTER, sid, b) to the caller, where the bit b is 1 if and only if $p_i \in \mathcal{P}$.
- Upon receiving (GET-REGISTERED, sid) from $\mathcal{A}$, the functionality returns the response (GET-REGISTERED, $sid, \mathcal{P}$) to $\mathcal{A}$.

The functionality is available to all participants. The functionality is parametrized with variable τ, a set of parties $\mathcal{P} = p_1, \ldots, p_n$, and a set F of functionalities. For each party $p_i \in \mathcal{P}$ it manages variable d_i. For each $\mathcal{F} \in F$ it manages variable $d_{\mathcal{F}}$
Initially, $\tau = 0$, $\mathcal{P} = \emptyset$ and $F = \emptyset$.

- Upon receiving (CLOCK-UPDATE, sid) from some party $p_i \in \mathcal{P}$ set $d_i = 1$ execute *Round-Update* and forward (CLOCK-UPDATE, sid, p_i) to $\mathcal{A}$.
- Upon receiving (CLOCK-UPDATE, sid) from some functionality $\{ \in F$ set $d_{\mathcal{F}} = 1$, execute *Round-Update* and return (CLOCK-UPDATE, sid, F) to F.
- Upon receiving (CLOCK-READ, sid) from any participant (including the environment, the adversary, or any ideal-shared or local-functionality) return (CLOCK-READ, sid, τ) to the requester.

Procedure *Round-Update*: If $d_{\mathcal{F}} = 1$ for all $\mathcal{F} \in F$ and $d_i = 1$ for all honest $p_i \in \mathcal{P}$, then set $\tau = \tau + 1$ and reset $d_{\mathcal{F}} = 0$ and $d_i = 0$ for all parties in $\mathcal{P}$.

Fig. 4. The functionality $\mathcal{G}_{\texttt{clock}}$

In addition to the above registration instructions, global setups, i.e., shared functionalities that are available both in the real and in the ideal world and allow parties connected to them to share state [6], allow also UC functionalities to register with them. Concretely, global setups include, in addition to the above party registration instructions, two registration/de-registration instructions for functionalities:

- Upon receiving (REGISTER, sid_G) from a functionality F (with session-id sid), update $F := F \cup \{(F, sid)\}$.
- Upon receiving (DE_REGISTER, sid_G) from a functionality F (with session-id sid), update $F := F\{(F, sid)\}$.
- Upon receiving (GET_REGISTERED$_F$, sid_G) from $\mathcal{A}$, return (GET_REGISTERED$_F$, sid_G, F) to $\mathcal{A}$.

We use the expression sid_G to refer to the encoding of the session identifier of global setups. By default (and if not otherwise stated), the above four (or seven in case of global setups) instructions will be part of the code of all ideal functionalities considered in this work. However, to keep the description simpler we will omit these instructions from the formal descriptions unless deviations are defined.

References

1. Zcash. https://z.cash/
2. Avarikioti, G., Käppeli, L., Wang, Y., Wattenhofer, R.: Bitcoin security under temporary dishonest majority. In: Goldberg, I., Moore, T. (eds.) FC 2019. LNCS, vol. 11598, pp. 466–483. Springer, Cham (2019). https://doi.org/10.1007/978-3-030-32101-7_28
3. Badertscher, C., Gazi, P., Kiayias, A., Russell, A., Zikas, V.: Ouroboros genesis: composable proof-of-stake blockchains with dynamic availability. In: Lie, D., Mannan, M., Backes, M., Wang, X. (eds.) ACM CCS 2018, pp. 913–930. ACM Press, October 2018. https://doi.org/10.1145/3243734.3243848
4. Badertscher, C., Maurer, U., Tschudi, D., Zikas, V.: Bitcoin as a transaction ledger: a composable treatment. In: Katz, J., Shacham, H. (eds.) CRYPTO 2017. LNCS, vol. 10401, pp. 324–356. Springer, Cham (2017). https://doi.org/10.1007/978-3-319-63688-7_11
5. Canetti, R.: Universally composable security: a new paradigm for cryptographic protocols. In: 42nd FOCS, pp. 136–145. IEEE Computer Society Press, October 2001. https://doi.org/10.1109/SFCS.2001.959888
6. Canetti, R., Dodis, Y., Pass, R., Walfish, S.: Universally composable security with global setup. In: Vadhan, S.P. (ed.) TCC 2007. LNCS, vol. 4392, pp. 61–85. Springer, Heidelberg (2007). https://doi.org/10.1007/978-3-540-70936-7_4
7. Coretti, S., Garay, J., Hirt, M., Zikas, V.: Constant-round asynchronous multi-party computation based on one-way functions. In: Cheon, J.H., Takagi, T. (eds.) ASIACRYPT 2016. LNCS, vol. 10032, pp. 998–1021. Springer, Heidelberg (2016). https://doi.org/10.1007/978-3-662-53890-6_33
8. Decred: Decred white paper (2019). https://docs.decred.org/
9. Duffield, E., Diaz, D.: Dash: a payments-focused cryptocurrency (2018). https://github.com/dashpay/dash/wiki/Whitepaper
10. Garay, J., Kiayias, A.: SoK: a consensus taxonomy in the blockchain era. In: Jarecki, S. (ed.) CT-RSA 2020. LNCS, vol. 12006, pp. 284–318. Springer, Cham (2020). https://doi.org/10.1007/978-3-030-40186-3_13
11. Garay, J., Kiayias, A., Leonardos, N.: The bitcoin backbone protocol: analysis and applications. In: Oswald, E., Fischlin, M. (eds.) EUROCRYPT 2015. LNCS, vol. 9057, pp. 281–310. Springer, Heidelberg (2015). https://doi.org/10.1007/978-3-662-46803-6_10
12. Garay, J.A., Kiayias, A., Leonardos, N., Panagiotakos, G.: Bootstrapping the blockchain, with applications to consensus and fast PKI setup. In: Abdalla, M., Dahab, R. (eds.) PKC 2018. LNCS, vol. 10770, pp. 465–495. Springer, Cham (2018). https://doi.org/10.1007/978-3-319-76581-5_16
13. Gazi, P., Kiayias, A., Zindros, D.: Proof-of-stake sidechains. In: 2019 IEEE Symposium on Security and Privacy, pp. 139–156. IEEE Computer Society Press, May 2019. https://doi.org/10.1109/SP.2019.00040
14. Goodman, L.: Tezos—a self-amending crypto-ledger white paper (2014). https://tezos.com/static/white_paper-2dc8c02267a8fb86bd67a108199441bf.pdf
15. Katz, J., Maurer, U., Tackmann, B., Zikas, V.: Universally composable synchronous computation. In: Sahai, A. (ed.) TCC 2013. LNCS, vol. 7785, pp. 477–498. Springer, Heidelberg (2013). https://doi.org/10.1007/978-3-642-36594-2_27
16. Zhang, B., Oliynykov, R., Balogun, H.: A treasury system for cryptocurrencies: enabling better collaborative intelligence. In: NDSS 2019. The Internet Society, February 2019

PrivacyGuard: Enforcing Private Data Usage Control with Blockchain and Attested Off-Chain Contract Execution

Yang Xiao[1(✉)], Ning Zhang[2], Jin Li[3], Wenjing Lou[1], and Y. Thomas Hou[1]

[1] Virginia Polytechnic Institute and State University, Blacksburg, VA, USA
xiaoy@vt.edu
[2] Washington University in St. Louis, St. Louis, MO, USA
[3] Guangzhou University, Guangzhou, China

Abstract. The abundance and rich varieties of data are enabling many transformative applications of big data analytics that have profound societal impacts. However, there are also increasing concerns regarding the improper use of individual data owner's private data. In this paper, we propose PrivacyGuard, a system that leverages blockchain smart contract and trusted execution environment (TEE) to enable individual's control over the access and usage of their private data. Smart contracts are used to specify data usage policy, i.e., who can use what data under which conditions and what analytics to perform, while the distributed blockchain ledger is used to keep an irreversible and non-repudiable data usage record. To address the efficiency problem of on-chain contract execution and to prevent exposing private data on the publicly viewable blockchain, PrivacyGuard incorporates a novel TEE-based off-chain contract execution engine along with a protocol to securely commit the execution result onto blockchain. We have built and deployed a prototype of PrivacyGuard with Ethereum and Intel SGX. Our experiment result demonstrates that PrivacyGuard fulfills the promised privacy goal and supports analytics on data from a considerable number of data owners.

Keywords: Privacy · Data access and usage control · Trusted execution · Blockchain · Smart contract

1 Introduction

The recent emergence of big data analytics and artificial intelligence has made life-impacting changes in many sectors of society. One of the fundamental enabling components for the recent advancements in artificial intelligence is the abundance of data. However, as more information on individuals is collected, shared, and analyzed, there is an increasing concern on the privacy implication. In the 2018 Facebook-Cambridge Analytica data scandal, an API, originally designed to allow a third party app to access the personality profile of limited participating users, was misused by Cambridge Analytica to collect information on 87 million of Facebook profiles without the consent of the users. These illicitly harvested private data were later used to create personalized psychology profiles for political purposes [21]. With increasing exposure to the

© Springer Nature Switzerland AG 2020
L. Chen et al. (Eds.): ESORICS 2020, LNCS 12309, pp. 610–629, 2020.
https://doi.org/10.1007/978-3-030-59013-0_30

privacy risks of big data, many now consider the involuntary collection of personal information a step backward in the fundamental civil right of privacy [19], or even in humanity [43,44]. Yet, driven by economic incentives, the collection and analysis of the personal data continue to grow at an amazing pace.

Individuals share personal information with people or organizations within a particular community for specific purposes; this is often referred to as the context of privacy [33]. For example, individuals may share their medical status with healthcare professionals, product preferences with retailers, and real-time whereabouts with their loved ones. When information shared within one context is exposed in another unintended one, people may feel a sense of privacy violation [32]. The purposes and values of those contexts are also undermined. The contextual nature of privacy implies that privacy protection techniques need to address at least two aspects: 1) what kind of information can be exposed to whom, under what conditions; and 2) what is the "intended purpose" or "expected use" of this information.

Much research has been done to address the first privacy aspect, focusing on data access control [4,23,49,53] and data anonymization [16,28,29,41]. Only recently, there have been a few works that attempted to address the second aspect of privacy from the architecture perspective [6,14,17,38,60,61]. In fact, many believe that the prevention of this kind of "second-hand" data (mis)use can only be enforced by legal methods [13]. Under the current practice, once an authorized user gains access to the data, there is little control over how this user would use the data. Whether he would use the data for purposes not consented by the original data owner, or pass the data to another party (i.e., data monetization) is entirely up to this new "data owner", and is no longer enforceable by the original data owner.

Our Contribution. Building upon our previous work [55], we present the design, implementation and evaluation of *PrivacyGuard* in this paper. PrivacyGuard empowers individuals with full control over the access and usage of their private data in a data market. The data owner is not only able to control who can have access to their private data, but also ensured that the data are used only for the intended purpose. To realize this envisioned functionalities of PrivacyGuard, three key requirements need to be met. First, users should be able to define their own data access and usage policy in terms of to whom they will share the data, at what price, and for what purpose. Second, data usage should be recorded in a platform that offers non-repudiation. Third, the actual usage of data should have a verifiable proof to show its compliance to the policy.

Blockchain, the technology behind Bitcoin [31] and Ethereum [18], has exhibited great potential in providing security and privacy services. Smart contract is a program that realizes a global state machine atop the blockchain and has its correct execution enforced by the blockchain's consensus protocol. PrivacyGuard enables individual users to control the access and usage of their data via smart contract and leverages the blockchain ledger for transparent and tamper-proof recording of data usage.

While smart contract and blockchain appear to be the perfect solution, there are fundamental limitations if applied directly. First, data used by smart contracts are uploaded in the form of blockchain transaction payload, which is not designed to hold arbitrarily large amount of data due to communication burden and scalability concerns [12,31]. Second, smart contracts are small programs that have to be executed by all participants in the network, which raises serious computational efficiency concerns. For the same reason, existing platforms such as Ethereum are not purposed to handle complex contract programs [51]. Last but not least, data used by smart contracts are available to every participant on blockchain by design, which conflicts with the confidentiality requirement of user data. Existing secure computation techniques for preserving confidentiality and utility of data, such as functional encryption [5], can nonetheless be prohibitively expensive for the network.

To tackle data and computation scalability problems, PrivacyGuard splits the private data usage enforcement problem into two domains: the control plane and the data plane. In the control plane, individual users publish the availability as well as the usage policy of their private data as smart contracts on blockchain. Data consumers interact with the smart contract to obtain authorization to use the data. Crucially, the actual data of the users are never exposed on the blockchain. Instead, they are stored in the cloud in encrypted forms. Computation on those private user data as well as the provision of secret keys are accomplished off-chain in the data plane with a trusted execution environment (TEE) [2,30] on the cloud.

When a data contract's execution is split into control and computation, where the computation actually takes place off-chain, several challenges occur. First, the correctness of the contract execution can no longer be guaranteed by the blockchain consensus. To this end, we propose "local consensus" for the contracting parties to establish trust on the off-chain computation via remote attestations. Second, the execution of contract is no longer atomic when the computation part is executed off-chain. We design a multistep commitment protocol to ensure that result release and data transaction remain an atomic operation, where if the computation results were tampered with, the data transaction would abort gracefully. Lastly, private data are protected inside the TEE enclave and secrets are only provisioned when approved according to the contract binding.

We implemented a prototype of PrivacyGuard using Intel SGX as the TEE technology and Ethereum as the smart contract platform. We chose these two technologies for implementation due to their wide adoption. Our design generally applies to other types of trusted execution environments and blockchain smart contract platforms. The platform fulfills the goal of user-define data usage control at reasonable cost and we show that it is feasible to perform complex data operations with the security and privacy protection as specified by the data contract.

To summarize, we make the following contributions in this paper:

- We propose PrivacyGuard, a platform that combines blockchain smart contract and trusted execution environment to address one of the most pressing problems in big data analytics—trustworthy private data computation and usage control. PrivacyGuard essentially allows data owners to contribute their data into the data market and specify the context under which their data can be used.
- We propose a novel construction of off-chain contract execution environment to support the vision of PrivacyGuard, which is the key to improving the execution efficiency of smart contract technology and enabling trustworthy execution of complex contract program without solely relying on costly network consensus.
- We implemented a prototype of PrivacyGuard using Intel SGX and Ethereum smart contract and deployed it in a simulated data market. Our evaluation shows that

PrivacyGuard is capable of processing considerable volumes of data transactions on existing public blockchain infrastructure with reasonable cost.

2   Background

Blockchain and Smart Contract. Blockchain is a recently emerged technology used in popular cryptocurrencies such as Bitcoin [31] and Ethereum [18]. It enables a wide range of distributed applications as a powerful primitive. With a blockchain in place, applications that could previously run only through a trusted intermediary can now operate in a fully decentralized fashion and achieve the same functionality with comparable reliability. When the majority of the network's voting power (hashing power, stake value, etc.) are controlled by honest participants, the shared blockchain becomes a safe and timestamped record of the network's activities. The conceptual idea of programmable electronic "smart contracts" dates back nearly twenty years [42]. When implemented in the blockchain platform (e.g. Ethereum), smart contracts are account-like entities that can receive transfers, make decisions, store data or even interact with other contracts. The blockchain and the smart contract platform however have several drawbacks in transaction capacity [12], computation cost [9,26], as well as privacy of user and data [26,27].

Trusted Execution Environment. Creating vulnerability-free software has long been considered a very challenging problem [40]. Researchers in the architecture community in both academia [11] and industry [2,30] have embraced a new paradigm of limiting the trusted computing base (TCB) to only the hardware, realizing a trusted execution environment (TEE). The well-known Intel SGX [30] is an instruction set extension to provide TEE functionalities. Applications are executed in secure containers called *enclaves*. The hardware guarantees the integrity and confidentiality of the protected application, even if the platform software is compromised. TEE has recently been adapted as a powerful tool to support blockchain-based applications [9,22,25,54].

3   PrivacyGuard Overview

3.1   System Goal and Architecture

The vision of PrivacyGuard is to not only protect data owner privacy but also promote a vibrant data sharing economy, in which data owners can confidently sell the right to use their data to data consumers for profits without worrying about data misuse. To realize this, there are three specific goals. First, data encryption/decryption are fully controlled by data owners. Untrusted parties (e.g. cloud storage and data consumers) can not obtain or possess data owners' plaintext data. Second, Data owners are able to control who can access which data items under what conditions for what usage. The data usage records should be non-repudiable and auditable by data owners. Third, the security mechanism of our system should be able to capture user-defined policies and enforce the compliance of the policies during the execution of data access.

Figure 1 shows the system architecture of PrivacyGuard. Although we have been using the term *users* to refer to both individuals and organizations, we differentiate two

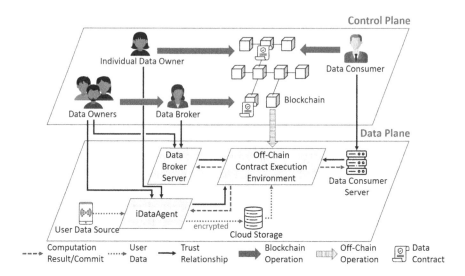

Fig. 1. System architecture for PrivacyGuard framework.

roles that an user in the data market can take. We refer to the individual or organization that owns the data as *data owner (DO)* and the entity that needs to access the data as *data consumer (DC)*. Classified by the assigned responsibility, there are three main functional components in the PrivacyGuard framework:

Data Market. Data market is an essential PrivacyGuard subsystem that supports the supply, demand and exchange of data on top of blockchain. For data access and usage control, DO can encode the terms and conditions pertaining to her personal data in a data contract, and publish it on a blockchain platform such as Ethereum. Data usage by DC is recorded via transactions that interact with the data contract.

iDataAgent (iDA) and Data Broker (DB). iDA is a trusted entity representing an individual DO and responsible for key management for the DO. It also participates in contract execution by only provisioning the data key material to attested remote entities. Since it is often not realistic to expect individual DO to be connected all the time, iDA can also be instantiated as a trusted program in a TEE-enabled cloud server. To address the inherent transaction bandwidth limit of the blockchain network, DB is introduced to collectively represent a group of users.

Off-Chain Contract Execution Environment (CEE). This off-chain component executes data operations contracted between DO(s) and DC in a TEE enclave. The trusted execution guarantees correctness as if it was executed on-chain. The computation result is securely committed to DC while enforcing the contract obligation.

3.2   PrivacyGuard High-Level Workflow

The workflow of PrivacyGuard proceeds in three stages which can function concurrently. Stage 1 and 2 involve the supply side (DO, iDA, DB) that prepares the data items and usage contracts while stage 3 characterizes the regular operation.

Stage 1: Data Generation, Encryption, and Key Management. In this stage, a DO's data are generated by its data sources and collected by its iDA, who passes the encrypted data to the cloud storage. Keys for data en/decryption are generated by the DO via interface to iDA and managed by iDA. For a group of users with common data types, they can delegate their trust to a DB by remote-attesting the DB's enclave and provision data keys to the enclave.

Stage 2: Policy Generation with Smart Contract. In PrivacyGuard, individual DOs can define their own usage policies for their private data in DO contract (C_{DO}). The policies encoded usually includes the essential components for privacy context, such as *data type, data range, operation, cost, consumer, expiration*, etc. The operation, which specifies intended usage of the targeted data, can be an arbitrary attestable computer program. This paradigm grants DOs fine-grained control on the data usage policy and the opportunity to participate in the data market independently. However, it requires ample transaction processing capacity from the blockchain network that scales in the number of DOs. Alternatively, the DB-based paradigm uses DB as a trusted delegate for a large number of DOs. DB represents the DOs in the blockchain by curating a DB contract (C_{DB}) that accepts data registries from DOs and advertising their data in bundles. The encoding of C_{DO} and C_{DB} will be elaborated in Sect. 4.

Stage 3: Data Utilization and Contract Execution. DC invokes a C_{DO} (or C_{DB}) for permission to use certain private data of the targeted DO(s) for a specific operation, and deposits payment onto the contract. If permission is granted on the blockchain, DC instructs CEE to load the enclave program for the contracted operation whose checksum is specified in the contract. Then both the DC and iDA (or DB) proceed to remote-attest the CEE enclave. This essentially allows the two parties to reach a "local consensus" on CEE's trustworthiness that enables the *off-chain execution* of the on-chain contract. When the attestations succeed, iDA (or DB) provisions data decryption keys to the CEE enclave to enable data operation within the enclave. When the operation finishes, the enclave releases the result in encrypted form and erases all the associated data and keying materials. To achieve a fair and atomic exchange that DC gets the decrypted result while DO(s) get the payment, we propose a commitment protocol for the two sides which ensures the atomic exchange only when they agree upon each other. The detailed design of the commitment protocol will be explained in Sect. 5.

3.3   Threat Model and Assumptions

We assume all entities act based on self-interest and may not follow the protocol. However, to maintain a reasonable scope for the paper, we assume DO will not provide meaningless or falsified data intentionally. It is possible to encode rules in smart contract to penalize DOs for abusing the system with bad data. Furthermore, we assume the security systems, i.e. the blockchain and TEE, are trustworthy and are free of vulnerability. Specifically, in the control plane, we assume the blockchain infrastructure is secure that adversaries do not control enough resources to disrupt distributed consensus. We also assume smart contract implementations are free of software vulnerability. In the data plane, we assume the TEE is up to date, and particularly, Intel SGX, is secure against malicious attack from the operating system. We recognize that TEE implementations are not always perfect, and previous work has demonstrated side channel information leakage on the SGX platform alone [45,46,50,52,56–58], preventing such attacks is an important but orthogonal task. We also assume that all data operations requested by DC have been ratified by trusted sources and a cryptographic checksum of the program binary is sufficient for PrivacyGuard to check the data operation integrity.

4   Data Market of User-Defined Usage with Blockchain

The intuition behind the data market is to enable fair and transparent data transactions between DO and DC. In PrivacyGuard, DOs advertise private data items available for knowledge extraction on blockchain smart contracts. DC shops for a desirable data set and contract for his analytics. To start the data transaction, DC invokes the data contract and deposits a payment. The sales of knowledge extraction rights on private data are fulfilled that DO obtains the payment while the DC obtains the knowledge. The data transaction is then recorded in the blockchain with transparency. To enable user-defined access and usage control, the data contract, needs to encode DO's data usage policy including how data can be used by which DC at what cost. Next we present the our data contract design in PrivacyGuard in a constructive manner.

4.1   Encoding Data Usage Policy with Smart Contract

Basic Data Usage Contract. In the conventional data sharing scenario, the data access policy often includes attributes such as type of the data, range or repository of the data, DO and DC credentials. For example, we assume patient X with public key pair (pk_X, sk_X) has three types of medical data: radiology data, blood test data and mental record data. X is only willing to share his radiology data (with descriptor $pData$) with urology specialist S with public key pk_S. X can treat S as a DC and specify an access policy P in a *data access* contract: $\mathbf{C_{X(DA)}} = \{P = \{pData, pk_S\}, Sig_{sk_X}(P)\}$. This encoding, however, specifies only data access but no obligation of the DC once access is granted. The DC could share the data with other parties against the original intention of the DO. To enable fine-grained control on how data is used, obligations need to be attached to the policy. For instance, if X only wants S to run a certain operation op on the data, then X can encode a new *data usage* contract in the following form: $\mathbf{C_{X(DU)}} = \{P = \{pData, op, pk_S\}, Sig_{sk_X}(P)\}$.

Enabling Data Market Economy. A key feature of PrivacyGuard is to encourage DOs to share private data for public welfare as well as financial rewards without concerning privacy leakage or data misuse. Building on top of the success of cryptocurrency, the blockchain smart contract platform allows DO and DC to transact on the usage of data with financial value attached. DO can specify a price tag $\$pr$

(in cryptocurrency) in the policy. To further ensure a fair exchange that DC gets the knowledge and DO gets the payment, certain control logic should be instated in the form of smart contract functions. We call these functions and other contract meta-data the contextual information, denoted ctx. Back to the previous example, we now have $\mathbf{C}_{\mathbf{X}(\mathbf{DU})} = \{P = \{pData, op, \$pr, pk_S\}, ctx, Sig_{sk_X}(P\|ctx)\}$. In blockchain domain, the signature is conveniently fulfilled by X's signature in the contract creation transaction.

Transparent Tracking of Data Utilization. For the system to provide transparent data utilization tracking and policy compliance auditing, each data transaction needs to be recorded in a tamper-resistant and non-repudiable manner. In PrivacyGuard, contract functions (part of ctx, invoked via blockchain transactions) are used to facilitate the recording of data utilization. Since the blockchain ledger is publicly managed via global consensus and unforgeable, contract function invocations in blockchain transactions can provide non-repudiable records on data utilization.

Algorithm 1: Data Owner's Smart Contract $\mathbf{C}_{\mathbf{DO}}$ Pseudocode

---

Function *Constructor()*   `// Contract creation by DO with a policy`
    Parse *policy* as $(dataset, price, operation, DCList, requestTimeout)$;
    $pDS \leftarrow policy.dataset$;
    $pPrice \leftarrow policy.price$;
    $pOP \leftarrow policy.operation$;
    $pDCL \leftarrow policy.DCList$;
    $pRTO \leftarrow policy.requestTimeout$;
    $R \leftarrow [\,]$ `// Usage records`;
    $DO \leftarrow creator$;

Function *Request(op, data, \$f)*   `// Callable by DC`
    if $op = pOP$ **and** $sender \in pDCL$ **and** $data \subset pDS$ **and** $f \geq pPrice$ **then**
        Create a record entry $R[idx]$ with index idx for this new data transaction;
        $R[idx].\{data, DC, reqTime\} \leftarrow \{data, sender, sys.time\}$;
        $R[idx].status \leftarrow$ WAIT_COMPUTATION;
    else
        Return $\$f$ to $sender$ and terminate;

Function *ComputationComplete(idx, $K_{result}Hash$)*   `// Callable by DC`
    $R[idx].krHash \leftarrow K_{result}Hash$;
    $R[idx].status \leftarrow$ WAIT_COMPLETE;

Function *CompleteTransaction(idx, K_{result})*   `// Callable by DO`
    if $Hash(K_{result}) = R[idx].krHash$ **then**
        Send $\$f$ to DO;
        $R[idx].kr \leftarrow K_{result}$;
        $R[idx].status \leftarrow$ COMPLETE   `// Data transaction complete`;

Function *Cancel(idx)*   `// Callable by DC`
    if $sender = R[idx].DC$ **and** $(sys.time - R[idx].reqTime) > pRTO$ **then**
        Return $\$f$ to $R[idx].DC$;;
        $R[idx].status =$ CANCELED;

Function *Revoke()*   `// Callable by DO`
    if $sender = DO$ **then**
        contract selfdestruct;

Data Owner's Smart Contract $\mathbf{C}_{\mathbf{DO}}$. We design $\mathbf{C}_{\mathbf{DO}}$ to capture the functionalities discussed above. The pseudo code of $\mathbf{C}_{\mathbf{DO}}$ in shown in Algorithm 1. In addition to the policy variables, $\mathbf{C}_{\mathbf{DO}}$ encodes functions for enforcing the control logic. *Constructor* initializes the policy at contract creation. *Request* takes a payment deposit from DC along with the requested operation op, the requested data descriptor D_{target}, and authorizes this data transaction. *ComputationComplete* is called by DC to signal the completion of the off-chain data execution. *CompleteTransaction* is called by DO to record the data usage and completes the transaction. The deposited payment is then redistributed to DO. We will cover more details on them along with the result commitment process in Sect. 5. *Cancel* is called by DC to abort the current transaction if the timeout passes. Lastly, *Revoke* invalidates the contract and can be called only by DO.

4.2   Using Data Broker to Address the On-Chain Scalability Challenge

While C_{DO} allows individual DOs to have fine-grained control over data usage policy and participate in data market independently, this paradigm puts heavy pressure on the blockchain transaction processing capability when the number of DOs is huge. In the meantime limited transaction throughput is a known problem for major public blockchains [7, 12, 20]. While there are many ongoing efforts to scale up transaction throughput [1, 36], we take a different but complementary approach to address this issue in PrivacyGuard's scenario. A trusted delegate, namely data broker (DB), is used to represent a group of users and curates a DB's contract (C_{DB}). C_{DB} allows individual DOs to register data entries and operations for DB to moderate. DB then participates in the data market on behalf of the registered DOs. We call this paradigm the DB-based system in our later implementation, in contrast to the iDA-based system.

The pseudo code of C_{DB} is provided in Appendix A. C_{DB} emulates C_{DO} for most parts but with extra global variables for data source management and two more functions: *Register* and *Confirm*. When a DO wants to make use of the DB, she first invokes *Register* function to register her data with the C_{DB}. In the data plane, the DO needs to remotely attest the DB to establish trust, then provisions the data keys to the DB enclave. This, however, is not the end of data registration, because the data source and quality still need to be verified by the DB. Once verified, DB invokes *Confirm* function to complete the data registration. Furthermore, result commitment is also slightly different for C_{DB}. The *CompleteTransaction* function is now callable by DB and needs to distribute payments to all involved DOs.

5   Off-Chain Contract Execution

PrivacyGuard leverages blockchain smart contract to provide the control mechanisms for valued data exchanges. While the technology offers a distributed time-stamped ledger which is ideal in providing a transparent recording of data usage, smart contract suffers from several prohibiting drawbacks when it comes to confidential data computation purely on-chain. First, the smart contract invocation and the ensuing computation is executed and repeated by all nodes in the blockchain network. The cost to run complex algorithms on-chain can be prohibitive even assuming data storage is not an issue. Second, data has to be decrypted and stored on the chain, causing confidentiality problems.

To tackle this problem, we introduce the concept of *off-chain contract execution* in PrivacyGuard and introduce an entity called off-chain contract execution environment (CEE) to bring both the computation and data provisioning off-chain. Particularly, we decompose a data usage contract into two portions, the control part and the computation

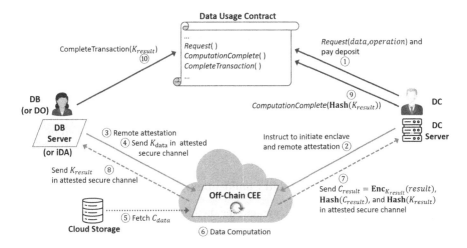

Fig. 2. Off-chain contract execution and result commitment

part. The control flow starts with invoking the contract and stops at the contracted computation task which switched to off-chain. The control flow is resumed with another contract invocation when the off-chain computation task is finished. Accordingly, we propose a novel off-chain contract execution and result commitment protocol, as is shown in Fig. 2. Note that both DB and iDA can represent a DO. Here we resort to the DB-based paradigm for convenience of presentation. We defer the discussion on DB's role in the data plane to the end of this section. Next we elaborate on the important features of off-chain contract execution in a constructive manner.

5.1 Establishing Trust on the Execution of Contracted Operation Through "Local Consensus"

The first challenge is the correct execution of the contracted task. As we have mentioned, when smart contracts are executed on blockchain platform, the correctness of the execution is guaranteed by the entire network through global consensus, which suffers from high on-chain cost. Our observation is that the correctness of one particular computation instance only matters to the stakeholders of the data transaction, i.e. the DOs, DB, and DC. And we do not need the entire network to verify the correctness.

In the conventional setting of distributed computing, both the DC and DO would perform the data computation task and expect the same result from each other. However, it contradicts DO's goal of fine-grained control on data usage if the data are directly provided to DC. Instead, we rely on software remote attestation, which is a widely available primitive with TEEs [2,30], for securely delegating the computation task to CEE. In this paper we opt for Intel SGX [30]. First of all, the designated computation program should pre-ratified with its program (binary) hash published in the data contract along side "authorized operations". When instructed by DC for a specific computation task, CEE loads the corresponding enclave program for that task. Then the two transacting sides in the data plane, DB and DC, remotely attest the enclave program to verify its authenticity and integrity with the program hash in the contract. As a result, as shown in Fig. 2, the immediate steps after data transaction request is to have CEE load the enclave program and DC and DB remotely attest the CEE enclave. Once correctly CEE enclave is verified with attestation reports, both sides of the contract can then extend their trust to CEE, knowing the attested program will execute securely in the enclave till termination, and the computation result will be genuine even if an adversary compromises CEE's untrusted platform (i.e., "normal world" in TEE terminology, which includes the operating system and non-enclave programs). And finally the result produced by CEE will be the "local consensus" between the two sides.

5.2   Enforcing Data Obligation and Confidentiality

The local consensus mechanism guarantees the data intensive computation task can be offloaded to the off-chain entity CEE for execution while maintaining the correctness of computation. However, in order to achieve the privacy goals of PrivacyGuard, computation itself has to fulfill the *data obligation*, which we refer to as the obligations of DC for utilizing DO's data. More specifically, it follows the general requirement of secure computation, wherein only the computation result is accessible by the DC, not the plaintext source data. First, the computation process should not output any plaintext source data or any intermediate results that are derived from the source data. Second, at the end of the computation, all decrypted data and intermediate results should be sanitized. Despite recent breakthrough in fully homomorphic encryption, performing arbitrary computation over encrypted data remains impractical for generic computation. In PrivacyGuard, we make use of TEE enclaves to create the environment for confidential computing. As is illustrated by step 3 and 4 in Fig. 2, DO's data en/decryption key K_{data} can be provisioned to CEE's enclave only if the latter can be cryptographically verified via remote attestation and a secure channel is established. This comes as an integral part of the local consensus. The hardware of CEE, the processor specifically, enforces the isolation between the untrusted platform and the enclave. We require the enclave program to include steps to sanitize intermediate results and keying materials. Since memory contents are encrypted in Intel SGX, once the keying material is removed, the data can be considered effectively sanitized. This also ensures that the program inside the enclave will terminate once the contracted task is completed.

5.3   Ensuring Atomicity in Contract Execution and Result Commitment

The last challenge is ensuring the atomicity of the contract, which arises from the split of control between on-chain off-chain. Contract functions that were previously executed in a single block are now completed via multiple function invocations that are executed in multiple blocks. Furthermore, there is no guarantee on the execution time of the off-chain computation, because an adversary controlling the platform can interrupt the computation and cause delays. Specifically, two issues need to be addressed.

The first issue is the contract function runtime. When the adversary has control of the off-chain computation platform of CEE, he can pause or delay the computation. For many data computations, the result can be time-sensitive. To tackle this problem, we add a timeout mechanism in the data contract to allow DC to cancel the request after timeout and have the deposit refunded (see Algorithm 1).

The second issue is the atomic completion of the contract. We want both the DOs to get the payment in the control plane while allowing DC to get the computation results in the data plane. This is particularly challenging due to the lack of availability guarantee on the CEE platform. When the platform is compromised, the adversary can intercept and modify any external I/O from the enclave, including both the network and storage. Our design for the atomic completion and result commitment can be observed from step 7 to 10 in Fig. 2. The key idea is that result release and contract completion should be done as a single message in the control plane. To prevent DC from getting the result without completing the payment to DOs, the result are encrypted into C_{result} with a random result key K_{result}, before being sent to DC in the attested secure channel. Since the platform can corrupt any output from CEE, the CEE enclave also sends DC the hash of the encrypted result and key, i.e., $\mathbf{Hash}(C_{result})$ and $\mathbf{Hash}(K_{result})$, which will be later used by DC for integrity check on the result and the key. K_{result} is passed to DB in the attested secure channel. To prevent DB from completing the transaction without releasing the correct result key, DC needs to initiate the commitment procedure in the control plane by invoking the contract function *ComputationComplete* with $\mathbf{Hash}(K_{result})$, indicating it has the encrypted result and is ready to finish the data transaction if and only if the correct result key K_{result} is released. Upon observing the message from DC, DB then invokes the smart contract function *CompleteTransaction* with the result key K_{result}. Only when the hash of K_{result} matches the previously received $\mathbf{Hash}(K_{result})$, will the contract write the data usage into records, release the payment to DOs, and finally conclude the data transaction. Note that our commitment protocol design does not need to protect the confidentiality of K_{result} (thus enabling the on-chain hash check). This is because the encrypted result C_{result} is passed directly from CEE enclave to DC via the attested secure channel. Finally, DC has the full discretion in deciding whether to publish the computation result afterwards.

5.4   Data Broker for Scalability in the Data Plane

In the iDA-based paradigm, when DC needs to use the data from a large number of DOs, the naive use of remote attestation on the CEE would require each iDA to individually attest and verify the CEE enclave, resulting in linearly growing computation overhead and network traffic. To address this challenge, in the DB-based paradigm, DB can be re-purposed as a trusted intermediary between the CEE and all relevant DOs in the data plane during the preparation stage, similar to its control plane role. Essentially, DB is also deployed on a TEE-enabled machine and instantiates an enclave for secure handling of DOs' data. The enclave is attested to every new DO only once after the DO registers with DB. During the normal operation, DB attests CEE on behalf of all relevant DOs for each DC request, saving the need for individual DOs to attest CEE. To accommodate the extreme case when a large number of DOs registers with DB simultaneously, we will explore parallel remote attestation solutions in Subsect. 6.1.

6   Implementation and Evaluation

We implemented a prototype of PrivacyGuard using Intel SGX as the TEE technology and Ethereum as the smart contract platform. Source code with documentation is available at https://github.com/yang-sec/PrivacyGuard. The on-chain components, namely the DO contract and the DB contract, were implemented in Solidity with 144 and 162 software lines of code (SLOC) respectively. The data usage price was set at 0.01 ethers per user data. The off-chain components include five PrivacyGuard applications, namely *iDataAgent (iDA), Data Broker (DB), Data Owner (DO), Data Consumer (DC), Contract Execution Environment (CEE)*. They were implemented in C++ with Intel SGX SDK v2.3.1 on top of Ubuntu 16.04 LTS. The total SLOC for off-chain components is about 37,000.

We deployed the contracts onto Ethereum Rinkeby testnet for evaluation, though our system is fully compatible with Ethereum mainnet. We used a fixed gas price of 10^{-9} ethers. PrivacyGuard applications were deployed in a LAN scenario. 1 DB, 1 iDataAgent, and 1 CEE ran on a SGX-enabled Linux machine with Intel Core i5-7260U CPU (2 cores 4 threads, 3.5 5 GHz). Up to 160 DOs and 1 DC ran on a Linux machine with AMD FX-8320 CPU (4 cores 8 threads, 3.5 5 GHz). We note that this setup aims for feasibility demonstration; in real-world deployment each application will most likely reside in a different machine. We used the *adult* dataset from UCI Machine Learning Repository [15] to simulate the data source. Each DO randomly drew 500 data points from the dataset as its private data. We have tested the entire PrivacyGuard workflow in multiple runs and the data usage history has been recorded in the deployed contracts. Our evaluation focuses on the system's scalability and consists of three parts: control plane runtimes, control plane costs, and data plane runtimes.

6.1   Control Plane Runtimes

To accommodate the scenario where N DOs simultaneously attest the DB enclave in the DB-based system, we experimented with a parallel attestation scheme in DB that each of the N attestation instances is handled by one of the T software threads, which invokes a new attestation context of the enclave and a dedicated enclave thread control structure (TCS) (thus TCSNUM = T). The experiment was repeated under different T. To avoid congesting the Intel Attestation Service (IAS) which may violate the terms of service, we instead used a simulated IAS that responds to EPID signature revocation list request and attestation report request with 0.1 s and 0.5 s delays respectively. The result is shown in Fig. 3(a). We observe that the parallel scheme is indeed a promising solution for scaling up attestation capacity, at the cost of enlarged enclave memory footprint. When $N = 160$, it takes the 64-thread DB about a tenth the attestation time of its sequential counterpart. We remark that efficient and scalable remote attestation is an interesting standalone topic to explore in future work.

To further evaluate the performance constraints imposed by the blockchain network, we measured the average transaction finalization delay in a congested environment. We set up 160 DOs to simultaneously send out a transaction calling the *Register()* function in the DB contract and their own DO contracts. we use *receipt* as the finalization response of the Ethereum transaction that makes the function call. The result is shown in Fig. 3(b). As more DOs send transactions at the same time, the average time to finalize a transaction increases dramatically. A straightforward workaround is to require DOs to call *Register()* according to a time schedule that minimizes congestion.

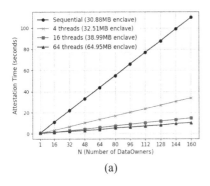
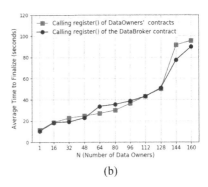

Fig. 3. (a) Attestation times of DB when N DOs simultaneously initiate attestation. (b) Average transaction finalization delay when N DOs simultaneously call a contract function.

6.2 Control Plane Cost

The monetary cost of the control plane mainly comes from the gas cost of operating smart contracts in Ethereum. At the beginning, every DO registers its data items on its own DO contract and the DB contract. DB fetc.hes data from whoever registered with its contract and routinely confirms new registries. DC then requests for the data items from N DOs by sending a request transaction to the DB contract (or separate requests to all related DO contracts) with a sufficient deposit to cover the price before proceeding to attesting CEE. We repeated the experiment for $N = 1 \rightarrow 10$ and obtained the gas costs and dollar equivalents for each contract function call, based on the ether price on 03/31/2019, which was $141.51 (source: https://coinmarketcap.com/).

Table 1. Cost of the data contract's scale-independent functions

Function	DO Contract		DB Contract	
	Gas Cost	USD Equiv.	Gas Cost	USD Equiv.
constructor()	951747	0.13468	846794	0.11983
Register() (new)	156414	0.02213	125392	0.01774
Register() (update)	30121	0.00426	45177	0.00639
Cancel()	81998	0.01160	66954	0.00947

We find that in both DB and DO contracts the costs of calling *constructor()* (contract creation), *Register()* and *Cancel()* do not depend on the number of registered DOs. We call these type of function calls scale-independent; otherwise scale-dependent. The costs of calling scale-independent functions and scale-dependent functions are shown in Table 1 and Fig. 4(a). Notably, the costs of calling *Request()* and *ComputationComplete()* grow faster than the costs of calling *Confirm()* and *CompleteTransaction()*. This implies the total cost will increasingly shift to the DC side, which is a scalable trend for the system as the DC has incentives to pay for more data usage.

To evaluate the scalability gain brought by DB, we compare the case wherein individual DOs share data via their own DO contracts versus via the DB contract. In both cases, the total amount of data requested by the DC and subsequently operated with by the CEE are the same. We summed the costs of all function calls except for the contract creation (calling *constructor()*) and extrapolated over different N. Figure 4(b) shows that it costs the DB-based system much less to accommodate one extra DO ($0.0304) compared to the iDataAgent-based system ($0.06096). This result together with control plane runtimes (Fig. 3(a)) demonstrate DB's ability to provide PrivacyGuard with financial and performance scalability when facing a growing number of DOs.

6.3   Data Plane Runtimes

To evaluate CEE's performance in off-chain contract execution, we experimented with a demonstrative, reasonably complex computation task: training four parallel instances of a neural network classifier. Detailed hyperparameters can be found in our source code. The training functions were ported to the SGX enclave from the Fast Artificial Neural Network (FANN) Library (https://github.com/libfann/fann). To evaluate enclave overhead, we also implemented an untrusted version (executed outside enclave) of the computation task that ran on the same machine. We noticed that recent work showed Intel's Hyperthreading Technology (HTT) has flaws that may impair the security of SGX enclaves [45]. Therefore, we tested the computation task under different hardware options with respect to the usage of SGX enclave and HTT. The Intel CPU's TurboBoost feature was turned off to avoid unexpected performance gain.

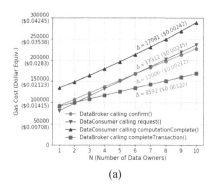
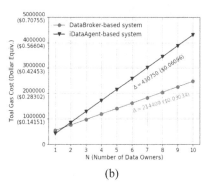

(a)   (b)

Fig. 4. (a) Gas costs of the DB contract's scale-dependent function calls. (b) Total gas costs of the DB based system and the iDataAgent based system.

The experiment results is shown in Fig. 5. We find that the overhead caused by disabling HTT is 48.84% for inside enclave and 17.99% for outside-enclave. This indicates disabling HTT will drag down in-enclave performance more significantly. The overheads caused by enclave are 196.55% and 274.13% for HTT-enabled and HTT-disabled respectively. We speculate that the big enclave overhead is related to the enclave's secure function calls and our imperfect porting of the training program. We leave the performance caveats of Intel SGX and possible solutions to future work.

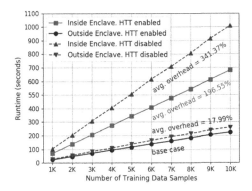

Fig. 5. Runtimes of training an example neural network classifier under four hardware options.

7 Related Work

Privacy Protection. Privacy-preserving computation has been an active area of research in the past decade [8,25,34,37,47,55]. With the increasing reliance on rich data, there has been a significant amount of research on applying cryptographic techniques to perform privacy preserving computation and data access control [3,5,8,35,47, 48]. Recently, hardware-assisted TEE has been adapted in numerous works to achieve privacy-preserving computation [22,24,25,34,37,59]. Specially, Ryoan [25] is closely related to PrivacyGuard. It combines native client sandbox and Intel SGX to confine data processing module and provide confidentiality. However, Ryoan aims to achieve data confinement with a user-defined directed acyclic graph that specifies information flow. In comparison, PrivacyGuard allows data user and consumer to negotiate data usage using smart contract with non-repudiable usage recording.

Blockchain and TEE. The idea of moving computation off-chain to improve the performance and security is mentioned in [6,9,10,26,39,51]. Choudhuri et al. [10] combines blockchain with TEE to build one-time programs that resemble to smart contracts but only aim for a restricted functionality. Ekiden [9] and the Intel Private Data Object (PDO) project [6] are two concurrently developed projects that are closely related to our work. Similar to PrivacyGuard, Ekiden harmonizes trusted computing and distributed ledger to enable confidential contract execution. Ekiden offloads computation from consensus nodes to a collection computing nodes in the aim of improving the ecosystem. In comparison, PrivacyGuard is designed to fit existing blockchain infrastructure. The Intel PDO project aims to combine Intel SGX and distributed ledger to allow distrustful parties to work on the data in a confidential manner. However, the system focuses heavily on a permissioned model with significant overhead for bootstrapping trust.

8 Conclusion

In this paper, we proposed PrivacyGuard, a platform that combines blockchain smart contract and TEE to enable transparent enforcement of private data computation and fine-grained usage control. Blockchain can not only be used as a tamper-proof distributed ledger that records data usage, but also facilitate financial transactions to incentivize data sharing. To enable complex and confidential operations on private data, PrivacyGuard splits smart contract functionalities into control operations and data operations. Remote attestation and TEE are used to achieve local consensus of the contract participants on the trustworthiness of the off-chain contract execution environment. Atomicity of the contract completion and result release is facilitated by a commitment protocol. We implemented a prototype of PrivacyGuard platform and evaluated it in a simulated data market. The results show the reasonable control plane costs and feasibility of executing complex data operations in a confidential manner using the platform.

Acknowledgment. This work was supported in part by US National Science Foundation under grants CNS-1916902 and CNS-1916926.

A   Data Broker Contract C_{DB}

Algorithm 2: Data Broker's Smart Contract C_{DB} Pseudocode

Function *Constructor()*   // Contract creation by DB with config
   Parse $config$ as $(operationList, requestTimeout)$;
   $cOPL \leftarrow config.operationList$;
   $cRTO \leftarrow config.requestTimeout$;
   $\{DO, DS, R\} \leftarrow \{[[]], [], []\}$ // DOs, data sources, data usage records;
   $DB \leftarrow creator$;

Function *Register(op, DC, price)*   // Callable by a DO
   Create a DO entry $DO[ido, op]$ with index ido for this new DO;
   $DO[ido, op].\{DO, DC, price\} \leftarrow \{sender, DC, price\}$;

Function *Confirm(cfDOs)*   // Callable by DB
   for all $\{ido, op\}$ **that** $ido \in cfDOs$ **and** $op \in cOPL$ **and** $DO[ido, op] \neq null$ **do**
      Append ido to $DS[op].DOList$;
      Append $DO[ido, op].DC$ to $DS[op].DCList$;
      $DS[op].price \leftarrow DS[op].price + DO[ido, op].price$;

Function *Request(op, targetDOs, \$f)*   // Callable by DC
   if $op \in cOPL$ **and** $sender \in DS[op].DCList$ **and** $targetDOs \subset DS[op].DOList$ **and** $f \geq DS[op].price$ **then**
      Create a record entry $R[idx]$ with index idx for this new data transaction;
      $R[idx].\{targetDOs, DC, reqTime\} \leftarrow \{targetDOs, sender, sys.time\}$;
      $R[idx].status \leftarrow$ WAIT_COMPUTATION;
   else
      Return $\$f$ to $sender$ and terminate;

Function *ComputationComplete(idx, $K_{result}Hash$)*
   (same as in C_{DO}, see Algorithm 1)

Function *CompleteTransaction(idx, K_{result})*   // Callable by DB
   if $Hash(K_{result}) = R[idx].krHash$ **then**
      for all $ido \in DS[R[idx].op].DOList$ **do**
         Send $\$DO[ido, R[idx].op].price$ to $DO[ido].DO$;
      $R[idx].kr \leftarrow K_{result}$;
      $R[idx].status \leftarrow$ COMPLETE   // Data transaction complete;

Function *Cancel(idx)*
   (same as in C_{DO})

Function *Revoke()*
   (same as in C_{DO}, except callable by DB)

References

1. Brainbot technologies AG: raiden network. https://raiden.network/
2. ARM: Security technology building a secure system using trustzone technology (2009)
3. Bacis, E., De Capitani di Vimercati, S., Foresti, S., Paraboschi, S., Rosa, M., Samarati, P.: Mix & slice: efficient access revocation in the cloud. In: Proceedings of the 2016 ACM SIGSAC Conference on Computer and Communications Security, pp. 217–228 (2016)
4. Bethencourt, J., Sahai, A., Waters, B.: Ciphertext-policy attribute-based encryption. In: 2007 IEEE Symposium on Security and Privacy (SP 2007), pp. 321–334. IEEE (2007)
5. Boneh, D., Sahai, A., Waters, B.: Functional encryption: definitions and challenges. In: Ishai, Y. (ed.) TCC 2011. LNCS, vol. 6597, pp. 253–273. Springer, Heidelberg (2011). https://doi.org/10.1007/978-3-642-19571-6_16
6. Bowman, M., Miele, A., Steiner, M., Vavala, B.: Private data objects: an overview (2018). https://arxiv.org/pdf/1807.05686.pdf
7. Buterin, V.: Privacy on blockchain. https://blog.ethereum.org/2016/01/15/privacy-on-the-blockchain/
8. Cao, N., Wang, C., Li, M., Ren, K., Lou, W.: Privacy-preserving multi-keyword ranked search over encrypted cloud data. IEEE Trans. Parallel Distrib. Syst. **25**(1), 222–233 (2014)
9. Cheng, R., et al.: Ekiden: a platform for confidentiality-preserving, trustworthy, and performant smart contracts. In: 2019 IEEE European Symposium on Security and Privacy (EuroS&P), pp. 185–200. IEEE (2019)
10. Choudhuri, A.R., Green, M., Jain, A., Kaptchuk, G., Miers, I.: Fairness in an unfair world: Fair multiparty computation from public bulletin boards. In: Proceedings of the 2017 ACM SIGSAC Conference on Computer and Communications Security, pp. 719–728. ACM (2017)
11. Costan, V., Lebedev, I.A., Devadas, S.: Sanctum: minimal hardware extensions for strong software isolation. In: USENIX Security Symposium, pp. 857–874 (2016)
12. Croman, K., et al.: On scaling decentralized blockchains. In: Clark, J., Meiklejohn, S., Ryan, P.Y.A., Wallach, D., Brenner, M., Rohloff, K. (eds.) FC 2016. LNCS, vol. 9604, pp. 106–125. Springer, Heidelberg (2016). https://doi.org/10.1007/978-3-662-53357-4_8
13. Custers, B., Uršič, H.: Big data and data reuse: a taxonomy of data reuse for balancing big data benefits and personal data protection. Int. Data Privacy Law **6**(1), 4–15 (2016)
14. Datta, A., Fredrikson, M., Ko, G., Mardziel, P., Sen, S.: Use privacy in data-driven systems: theory and experiments with machine learnt programs. In: Proceedings of the 2017 ACM SIGSAC Conference on Computer and Communications Security, pp. 1193–1210. ACM (2017)
15. Dheeru, D., Karra Taniskidou, E.: UCI machine learning repository (2017). http://archive.ics.uci.edu/ml
16. Dwork, C.: Differential privacy: a survey of results. In: Agrawal, M., Du, D., Duan, Z., Li, A. (eds.) TAMC 2008. LNCS, vol. 4978, pp. 1–19. Springer, Heidelberg (2008). https://doi.org/10.1007/978-3-540-79228-4_1
17. Elnikety, E., Mehta, A., Vahldiek-Oberwagner, A., Garg, D., Druschel, P.: Thoth: comprehensive policy compliance in data retrieval systems. In: USENIX Security Symposium, pp. 637–654 (2016)
18. Ethereum: Blockchain app platform. https://www.ethereum.org/
19. General data protection regulation (GDPR) (2016). https://eur-lex.europa.eu/eli/reg/2016/679/oj
20. Eyal, I., Gencer, A.E., Sirer, E.G., Van Renesse, R.: Bitcoin-NG: a scalable blockchain protocol. In: NSDI, pp. 45–59 (2016)
21. Facebook-cambridge analytica data scandal. https://en.wikipedia.org/wiki/Facebook%E2%80%93Cambridge_Analytica_data_scandal

22. Fisch, B., Vinayagamurthy, D., Boneh, D., Gorbunov, S.: Iron: functional encryption using intel sgx. In: Proceedings of the 2017 ACM SIGSAC Conference on Computer and Communications Security, pp. 765–782. ACM (2017)

23. Goyal, V., Pandey, O., Sahai, A., Waters, B.: Attribute-based encryption for fine-grained access control of encrypted data. In: Proceedings of the 13th ACM Conference on Computer and Communications Security, pp. 89–98 (2006)

24. Hunt, T., Song, C., Shokri, R., Shmatikov, V., Witchel, E.: Chiron: privacy-preserving machine learning as a service (2018). https://arxiv.org/pdf/1803.05961.pdf

25. Hunt, T., Zhu, Z., Xu, Y., Peter, S., Witchel, E.: Ryoan: a distributed sandbox for untrusted computation on secret data. In: OSDI, pp. 533–549 (2016)

26. Kalodner, H., Goldfeder, S., Chen, X., Weinberg, S.M., Felten, E.W.: Arbitrum: scalable, private smart contracts. In: Proceedings of the 27th USENIX Conference on Security Symposium, pp. 1353–1370. USENIX Association (2018)

27. Kosba, A., Miller, A., Shi, E., Wen, Z., Papamanthou, C.: Hawk: the blockchain model of cryptography and privacy-preserving smart contracts. In: 2016 IEEE Symposium on Security and Privacy (SP), pp. 839–858. IEEE (2016)

28. Li, N., Li, T., Venkatasubramanian, S.: t-closeness: privacy beyond k-anonymity and l-diversity. In: 2007 IEEE 23rd International Conference on Data Engineering, pp. 106–115. IEEE (2007)

29. Machanavajjhala, A., Kifer, D., Gehrke, J., Venkitasubramaniam, M.: l-diversity: privacy beyond k-anonymity. ACM Trans. Knowl. Discov. Data (TKDD) 1(1), 3-es (2007)

30. McKeen, F., et al.: Innovative instructions and software model for isolated execution. In: HASP@ ISCA, p. 10 (2013)

31. Nakamoto, S.: Bitcoin: A Peer-to-Peer Electronic Cash System (2008)

32. National Science and Technology Council: National privacy research strategy. https://www.nitrd.gov/PUBS/NationalPrivacyResearchStrategy.pdf

33. Nissenbaum, H.: Privacy as contextual integrity. Wash. Law Rev. 79, 119 (2004)

34. Ohrimenko, O., et al.: Oblivious multi-party machine learning on trusted processors. In: USENIX Security Symposium, pp. 619–636 (2016)

35. Pass, R., Shi, E., Tramèr, F.: Formal abstractions for attested execution secure processors. In: Coron, J.-S., Nielsen, J.B. (eds.) EUROCRYPT 2017. LNCS, vol. 10210, pp. 260–289. Springer, Cham (2017). https://doi.org/10.1007/978-3-319-56620-7_10

36. Poon, J., Dryja, T.: The bitcoin lightning network: scalable off-chain instant payments (2016). https://www.bitcoinlightning.com/wp-content/uploads/2018/03/lightning-network-paper.pdf

37. Schuster, F., et al.: Vc3: trustworthy data analytics in the cloud using SGX. In: 2015 IEEE Symposium on Security and Privacy (SP), pp. 38–54. IEEE (2015)

38. Sen, S., Guha, S., Datta, A., Rajamani, S.K., Tsai, J., Wing, J.M.: Bootstrapping privacy compliance in big data systems. In: 2014 IEEE Symposium on Security and Privacy (SP), pp. 327–342. IEEE (2014)

39. Sinha, R., Gaddam, S., Kumaresan, R.: Luciditee: policy-compliant fair computing at scale (2019). https://eprint.iacr.org/2019/178.pdf

40. Song, D., et al.: SoK: sanitizing for security. In: 2019 IEEE Symposium on Security and Privacy (SP), pp. 1275–1295. IEEE (2019)

41. Sweeney, L.: k-anonymity: a model for protecting privacy. Int. J. Uncertainty, Fuzziness Knowl. Based Syst. 10(05), 557–570 (2002)

42. Szabo, N.: Formalizing and securing relationships on public networks. First Monday 2(9) (1997). https://firstmonday.org/article/view/548/469

43. TED Talk: how tech companies deceive you into giving up your data and privacy. https://goo.gl/hSfaUX

44. Tim cook: personal data collection is being 'weaponized against us with military efficiency'. https://goo.gl/BsWB3k
45. Van Bulck, J., Piessens, F., Strackx, R.: Foreshadow: extracting the keys to the intel {SGX} kingdom with transient out-of-order execution. In: 27th USENIX Security Symposium (USENIX Security 18) (2018)
46. Van Bulck, J., Weichbrodt, N., Kapitza, R., Piessens, F., Strackx, R.: Telling your secrets without page faults: stealthy page table-based attacks on enclaved execution. In: 26th USENIX Security Symposium (USENIX Security 17), pp. 1041–1056 (2017)
47. Verykios, V.S., Bertino, E., Fovino, I.N., Provenza, L.P., Saygin, Y., Theodoridis, Y.: State-of-the-art in privacy preserving data mining. ACM Sigmod Rec. **33**(1), 50–57 (2004)
48. Vimercati, S.D.C.D., Foresti, S., Jajodia, S., Paraboschi, S., Samarati, P.: Encryption policies for regulating access to outsourced data. ACM Trans. Database Syst. (TODS) **35**(2), 12 (2010)
49. Wang, G., Liu, Q., Wu, J.: Hierarchical attribute-based encryption for fine-grained access control in cloud storage services. In: Proceedings of the 17th ACM Conference on Computer and Communications Security, pp. 735–737 (2010)
50. Wang, W., et al.: Leaky cauldron on the dark land: understanding memory side-channel hazards in SGX. In: Proceedings of the 2017 ACM SIGSAC Conference on Computer and Communications Security, pp. 2421–2434. ACM (2017)
51. Wüst, K., Matetic, S., Egli, S., Kostiainen, K., Capkun, S.: Ace: asynchronous and concurrent execution of complex smart contracts. (2019). https://eprint.iacr.org/2019/835.pdf
52. Xu, Y., Cui, W., Peinado, M.: Controlled-channel attacks: deterministic side channels for untrusted operating systems. In: 2015 IEEE Symposium on Security and Privacy, pp. 640–656. IEEE (2015)
53. Yu, S., Wang, C., Ren, K., Lou, W.: Achieving secure, scalable, and fine-grained data access control in cloud computing. In: Infocom, 2010 proceedings IEEE, pp. 1–9. IEEE (2010)
54. Zhang, F., Cecchetti, E., Croman, K., Juels, A., Shi, E.: Town crier: an authenticated data feed for smart contracts. In: Proceedings of the 2016 ACM SIGSAC Conference on Computer and Communications Security, pp. 270–282. ACM (2016)
55. Zhang, N., Li, J., Lou, W., Hou, Y.T.: PrivacyGuard: enforcing private data usage with blockchain and attested execution. In: Garcia-Alfaro, J., Herrera-Joancomartí, J., Livraga, G., Rios, R. (eds.) DPM/CBT -2018. LNCS, vol. 11025, pp. 345–353. Springer, Cham (2018). https://doi.org/10.1007/978-3-030-00305-0_24
56. Zhang, N., Sun, H., Sun, K., Lou, W., Hou, Y.T.: Cachekit: evading memory introspection using cache incoherence. In: 2016 IEEE European Symposium on Security and Privacy (EuroS&P), pp. 337–352. IEEE (2016)
57. Zhang, N., Sun, K., Lou, W., Hou, Y.T.: Case: cache-assisted secure execution on arm processors. In: 2016 IEEE Symposium on Security and Privacy (SP), pp. 72–90. IEEE (2016)
58. Zhang, N., Sun, K., Shands, D., Lou, W., Hou, Y.T.: Trusense: information leakage from trustzone. In: IEEE INFOCOM 2018-IEEE Conference on Computer Communications, pp. 1097–1105. IEEE (2018)
59. Zheng, W., Dave, A., Beekman, J.G., Popa, R.A., Gonzalez, J.E., Stoica, I.: Opaque: an oblivious and encrypted distributed analytics platform. In: 14th USENIX Symposium on Networked Systems Design and Implementation (NSDI 17), pp. 283–298. USENIX Association, Boston, MA (2017)
60. Zyskind, G., Nathan, O., Pentland, A.: Enigma: decentralized computation platform with guaranteed privacy (2015). https://arxiv.org/pdf/1506.03471.pdf
61. Zyskind, G., Nathan, O., Pentland, A.S.: Decentralizing privacy: using blockchain to protect personal data. In: Security and Privacy Workshops (SPW). IEEE (2015)

Applied Cryptography III

Identity-Based Authenticated Encryption with Identity Confidentiality

Yunlei Zhao[1,2(✉)]

[1] School of Computer Science, Fudan University, Shanghai, China
ylzhao@fudan.edu.cn
[2] State Key Laboratory of Integrated Services Networks, Xidian University, Xi'an, China

Abstract. Identity-based cryptography (IBC) is fundamental to security and privacy protection. Identity-based authenticated encryption (i.e., signcryption) is an important IBC primitive, which has numerous and promising applications. After two decades of research on signcryption, recently a new cryptographic primitive, named higncryption, was proposed. Higncryption can be viewed as privacy-enhanced signcryption, which integrates public key encryption, entity authentication, and identity concealment (which is not achieved in signcryption) into a monolithic primitive. Here, briefly speaking, identity concealment means that the transcript of protocol runs should not leak participants' identity information.

In this work, we propose the first identity-based higncryption (IBHigncryption). The most impressive feature of IBHigncryption, among others, is its simplicity and efficiency. The proposed IBHigncryption scheme is essentially as efficient as the fundamental CCA-secure Boneh-Franklin IBE scheme [12], while offering entity authentication and identity concealment simultaneously. Compared to the identity-based signcryption scheme [8], which is adopted in the IEEE P1363.3 standard, our IBHigncryption scheme is much simpler, and has significant efficiency advantage in total. Besides, our IBHigncryption enjoys forward ID-privacy, receiver deniability and x-security simultaneously. In addition, the proposed IBHigncryption has a much simpler setup stage with smaller public parameters, which in particular does not have the traditional master public key.

1 Introduction

Identity-based cryptography (ID-based) was proposed by Shamir in 1984 [45], with the motivation to simplify certificate management in traditional public-key

This work is supported in part by National Key Research and Development Program of China under Grant No. 2017YFB0802000, National Natural Science Foundation of China under Grant Nos. 61877011 and 61472084, and Shandong Provincial Key Research and Development Program of China under Grant Nos. 2017CXG0701 and 2018CXGC0701.

© Springer Nature Switzerland AG 2020
L. Chen et al. (Eds.): ESORICS 2020, LNCS 12309, pp. 633–653, 2020.
https://doi.org/10.1007/978-3-030-59013-0_31

cryptography. In an ID-based cryptosystem, the identity of a user acts as its public key, so the certificate issuance and management problem is simplified in an ID-based system. In general, ID-based cryptography includes identity-based signature (IBS), identity-based encryption (IBE), etc. Though ID-based signature schemes appeared much earlier [45]. However, the first practical and fully functional identity-based encryption scheme was only proposed by Boneh and Franklin [12] in 2001 based on bilinear maps. The Boneh-Franklin's IBE scheme is further standardized with ISO/IEC 18033-5 and IETF RFC 5091 [15], and is now widely deployed (e.g., in HPE Secure Data by Voltage security [3]).[1]

Authenticated encryption in the public-key setting, i.e., signcryption, was proposed by Zheng [48]. It enables the sender to send an encrypted message such that only the intended receiver can decrypt it, and meanwhile, the intended receiver has the ability to authenticate that the message is indeed from the specified sender. It provides a more economical and safer way to integrate encryption and signature, compared to the sequential composition of them. Since its introduction, research and development (including international standardizations) of signcryption have been vigorous. In particular, a list of public-key signcryption schemes were standardized with ISO 29150.

Identity-based signcryption was first proposed by Malone-Lee [37], and was then intensively studied thereafter (e.g., [8,14,18,34]). The reader is referred to [13,29] for a good survey on ID-based signcryption and key establishment. Identity-based signcryption has numerous promising applications. For example, it is used in secure and privacy-preserving protocols for vehicular ad hoc networks (VANET) [36], for beyond 5G mobile small cells [20], for big data [46], for cloud data access control [21], for industrial Internet of things [29], and more. In particular, as shown in [24,39], signcryption and one-pass authenticated key establishment (AKE) are functionally equivalent, and identity-based one-pass AKE is critically used in the standards for 4G/5G mission critical services as specified by 3GPP [2], which involves the *sequential* composition of an identity-based encryption scheme [27] and an identity-based signature scheme [25]. To our knowledge, the ID-based signcryption scheme proposed in [8] is one of the most efficient up to now, which was also adopted as IEEE P1363.3 standard.

For almost all the existing identity-based signcryption schemes, the sender's identity information has to be exposed; otherwise, the ciphertext cannot be decrypted and the authentication cannot be verified. However, identity concealment is a fundamental privacy concern. Identity confidentiality is now mandated by a list of prominent standards such as TLS1.3 [41], EMV [16], QUIC [43], and the 5G telecommunication standard [2] by 3GPP, etc., and is enforced by General Data Protection Regulation (GDPR) of EU. Under this motivation, a new cryptographic primitive called identity-hiding signcryption (higncryption, for short) was introduced in [47]. Higncryption can be viewed as a novel monolithic integration of public key encryption, entity authentication, and identity concealment.

---

[1] The HPE IBE (including BF01 [12] and BB1 [11]) technology developed by Voltage provides plug-ins for Outlook, Pine, Hotmail, Yahoo, etc., and is reported to be used by over 200 million users and more than 1,000 enterprises worldwide.

Here, identity concealment means that the transcript of protocol runs should not leak participants' identity information. Moreover, a higncryption scheme satisfies the following features simultaneously:

- Forward ID-privacy, which means that the player's ID-privacy is preserved even when its static secret key is compromised.
- Receiver deniability [28], in the sense that the session transcript can be simulated from the public parameters and the receiver's secret-key.
- x-security [28], in the sense that the leakage of some critical intermediate randomness (specifically, DH-exponent x) does not cause the exposure of the sender's static secret key or the primary secret (from which session-key is derived).

We note that the work in [47] only considered higncryption in the traditional public-key setting. In this work, we study identity-based higncryption and its applications. A natural way to achieve identity-based higncryption is the sign-then-encrypt approach: i.e., first employing an identity-based signature then encrypt the message together with the signature and identity information by running an identity-based encryption. With this approach, some careful considerations are needed for security issues. The identity-based signcryption proposed in [18] adopts this sign-then-encrypt approach. But the resultant scheme is less efficient: it requires the generation of traditional master public key, and performs four pairs and four exponentiations in total in signcryption and de-signcryption. In addition, we note that the security analysis in [18] assumes that the challenger can successfully guess the target sender and the target receiver in advance, and does not consider the case that the sender and the receiver are the same party.

1.1 Motivational Applications

5G is the fifth generation of cellular mobile communication, which succeeds the 4G (LTE/WiMax), 3G (UMTS) and 2G (GSM) systems. 5G performance targets include high data rate, reduced latency, and massive device connectivity (for low-power sensors and smart devices), which are far beyond the levels 4G technologies can achieve. Among the services 5G supported, mission critical services and communications require ultra reliability and virtual zero latency. The platform for mission critical (MC) communications and MC services has been a key priority of 3GPP in recent years, and is expected to evolve further in the future [33]. In June 2018, 3GPP has identified the following essential requirements related to user privacy [1,30] for 5G communications.

- User identity confidentiality: The permanent identity of a user to whom a service is delivered cannot be eavesdropped on the radio access link.
- User untraceability: An intruder cannot deduce whether different services are delivered to the same user by eavesdropping on the radio access link.
- User location confidentiality: The presence or the arrival of a user in a certain area cannot be determined by eavesdropping on the radio access link.

At the heart of the security architecture, specified by 3GPP [2] for 5G mission critical communications and services, is an identity-based authenticated key transport (IB-AKT) protocol inherited from 4G, which is the identity-based version of Multimedia Internet KEYing (MIKEY) specified in IETF RFC 3830 [4]. This IB-AKT protocol involves the *sequential* composition of an identity-based encryption scheme (specifically, SAKKE specified in IETF RFC 6508 [27] and 6509 [26]) and an identity-based signature scheme (specifically, ECCSI specified in IETF RFC 6507 [25]). In MIKEY-SAKKE, the user's identity ID takes the form of a constrained telephone URI (universal resource identifier), in front of which there is a monthly-updated time stamp for periodically refreshing the key of the user. It also provides a simple mechanism for masking identity; Briefly speaking, for MIKEY-SAKKE with identity masking, a user's URI is replaced by $UID = H(S)$, where H is the SHA-256 hash function and S is some information related to the identifiers of the user and the key management server (KMS). Further, UID shall be used as the identifier within MIKEY-SAKKE with identity masking. Clearly, MIKEY-SAKKE does not satisfy the above requirements on identity privacy mandated by 5G now.

Considering that the *sequential* composition of an identity-based encryption scheme and an identity-based signature scheme is less efficient, identity-based signcryption may be a promising candidate for mission critical services. We note that there already exists IEEE P1363.3 standard for ID-based signcryption [8]. However, as mentioned ahead, the sender's identity has to be exposed [8]. In this sense, ID-based identity-concealed signcryption (IBHigncryption) takes place. Moreover, for enhancing privacy and strengthening security, forward ID-privacy, receiver deniability, and x-security are all desirable in such settings.

Identity-based cryptography is fundamental to security and privacy protection. We remark that though 5G mission critical service is introduced as an illustrative application of IBHigncryption, IBHigncryption can actually have much more applications beyond that. It can find applications wherever identity-based encryption, authentication, and identity concealment are needed simultaneously. Some other promising applications include secure and privacy-preserving protocols for vehicular ad hoc networks (VANET) [36], for beyond 5G mobile small cells [20], for big data [46], for cloud data access control [21], for industrial IoTs [29], etc.

1.2   Contribution

In this work, we propose the first identity-based higncryption (IBHigncryption, for short). We present the formal security model of IBHigncryption, and the detailed security proofs for the proposed scheme. The difficulty and non-triviality in achieving secure and efficient IBHigncryption is witnessed by the intensive study history of identity-based signcryption, and lies in that we actually cannot adapt the higncryption construction in the public-key setting [47] into the identity-based setting. The higncryption construction proposed in [47] is actually the dual of a protocol variant of HMQV [28,31]. We note that directly transforming the higncryption construction of [47] into the identity-based setting, if possible, is at least less efficient. The highly practical construction of IBHigncryption proposed in this work involves a novel combination of Boneh-Franklin IBE and Fujisaki-Okamoto (FO) transformation [22] in the authenticated encryption setting. In addition, the security definition and analysis of higncryption in [47] assumes that the players in the system are fixed at the onset. In this work, we do not make such an unreasonable restriction in security definition and analysis.

The most impressive feature of IBHigncryption, among others (including the desirable properties it offers, such as forward ID-privacy, receiver deniability, and x-security), is its simplicity and efficiency, which might be somewhat surprising in retrospect. The proposed IBHigncryption scheme is essentially as efficient as the fundamental CCA-secure Boneh-Franklin IBE scheme [12], while offering entity authentication and identity concealment simultaneously. Compared to the identity-based signcryption scheme [8], which is adopted in the IEEE P1363.3 standard, our IBHigncryption scheme is much simpler, and has significant efficiency advantage in total (particularly on the receiver side). Besides, our IBHigncryption enjoys forward ID-privacy, receiver deniability and x-security simultaneously, while the IEEE 1363.3 standard of ID-based signcryption satisfies none of them.

In addition, our IBHigncryption has a much simpler setup stage with smaller public parameters, which in particular *does not need to generate the traditional master public key*. To the best of our knowledge, this is the first identity-based cryptographic scheme of this type (i.e., without master public key). The much simpler setup stage of IBHigncryption, particularly waiving the master public key, brings the following advantages:

- The computational and space complexity for generating and storing the system parameters is reduced.
- The attack vector (for recovering the master secret key) is decreased, e.g., for some mission critical applications.
- It eases deployment and compatibility with existing ID-based cryptosystems. Specifically, when deploying our IBHigncryption scheme in reality with other existing identity-based cryptosystems, the system parameters and particularly the master public key can remain unchanged.

We implement the IBHigncryption scheme, where the codes are available from https://github.com/IBHigncryption2018/IBHigncryption. The implementations use the PBC (pairing-based cryptography) library of Stanford University http://crypto.stanford.edu/pbc, and the underlying authenticated encryption is implemented with AES-GCM-256.

2   Preliminaries

2.1   Authenticated Encryption

Briefly speaking, an *authenticated encryption* (AE) scheme transforms a message M and a public header information H (e.g., a packet header, an IP address, some predetermined nonce or initial vector) into a ciphertext C in such a way that C provides both privacy (of M) and authenticity (of C and H) [9,10,32,42]. In practice, when AE is used within cryptographic systems, the associated data H is usually implicitly determined from the context (e.g., the hash of the transcript of the protocol run or some pre-determined states).

Let $\mathsf{SE} = (\mathsf{K}_{se}, \mathsf{Enc}, \mathsf{Dec})$ be a symmetric encryption scheme. The probabilistic polynomial-time (PPT) algorithm K_{se} takes the security parameter κ as input and samples a key K from a finite and non-empty set $\mathcal{K} \bigcap \{0,1\}^\kappa$. For presentation simplicity, we assume $K \leftarrow \mathcal{K} = \{0,1\}^\kappa$. The polynomial-time (randomized or stateful)[2] encryption algorithm $\mathsf{Enc} : \mathcal{K} \times \{0,1\}^* \times \{0,1\}^* \rightarrow \{0,1\}^* \cup \{\bot\}$, and the (deterministic) polynomial-time decryption algorithm $\mathsf{Dec} : \mathcal{K} \times \{0,1\}^* \rightarrow \{0,1\}^* \cup \{\bot\}$ satisfy: for any $K \leftarrow \mathcal{K}$, any associated data $H \in \{0,1\}^*$ and any message $M \in \{0,1\}^*$, if $\mathsf{Enc}_K(H, M)$ outputs $C \neq \bot$, $\mathsf{Dec}_K(C)$ always outputs M. Here, for presentation simplicity, we assume that the ciphertext C bears the associated data H in plain.

Let $\mathcal{A}$ be an adversary. Table 1 describes the security game for authenticated encryption. We define the advantage of $\mathcal{A}$ to be

$$\mathbf{Adv}_{\mathsf{SE}}^{\mathsf{AE}}(\mathcal{A}) = \left| 2 \cdot \Pr[\mathrm{AE}_{\mathsf{SE}}^{\mathcal{A}} \ returns \ \mathsf{true}] - 1 \right|.$$

We say that the SE scheme is AE-secure, if for any sufficiently large κ, the advantage of any probabilistic polynomial-time (PPT) algorithm adversary is negligible. We say the SE scheme is (t_{AE}, ϵ_{AE})-secure, if for any sufficiently large κ and any PPT adversary $\mathcal{A}$ of running time t, $\mathbf{Adv}_{\mathsf{SE}}^{\mathsf{AE}}(\mathcal{A}) < \epsilon_{AE}$.

The above AE definition is based on that given in [9,10], but with the public header data H explicitly taken into account. The definition of *authenticated encryption with associated data* (AEAD) given in [32] is stronger than ours in that: (1) it is length-hiding; and (2) both the encryption and the decryption algorithms are stateful.

Table 1. AE security game

main $\mathrm{AE}_{\mathsf{SE}}^{\mathcal{A}}$:	**proc.** $\mathsf{Enc}(H, M_0, M_1)$:	**proc.** $\mathsf{Dec}(C')$:
$K \leftarrow \mathcal{K}_{\mathsf{se}}$	If $\|M_0\| \neq \|M_1\|$, Ret $\bot$	If $\sigma = 1 \wedge C' \notin \mathcal{C}$
$\sigma \leftarrow \{0,1\}$	$C_0 \leftarrow \mathsf{Enc}_K(H, M_0)$	Ret $\mathsf{Dec}_K(C')$
$\sigma' = \mathcal{A}^{\mathbf{Enc},\mathbf{Dec}}$	$C_1 \leftarrow \mathsf{Enc}_K(H, M_1)$	Ret $\bot$
Ret $(\sigma' = \sigma)$	If $C_0 = \bot$ or $C_1 = \bot$	
	Ret $\bot$	
	$\mathcal{C} \xleftarrow{\cup} C_\sigma$; Ret C_σ	

---

[2] If randomized, it flips coins anew on each invocation. If stateful, it uses and then updates a state that is maintained across invocations.

The above AE security is quite strong. In particular, it means that, after adaptively seeing a polynomial number of ciphertexts, an efficient adversary is unable to generate a new valid ciphertext in the sense that its decryption is not "$\perp$". Also, for two independent keys $K, K' \leftarrow \mathcal{K}$ and any message M and any header information H, $\Pr[\mathsf{Dec}_{K'}(\mathsf{Enc}_K(H, M)) \neq \perp]$ is negligible.

2.2 Bilinear Pairings, and Hard Problems

Definition 1 (Bilinear Pairing [12,44]). *Let $\mathbb{G}_1, \mathbb{G}_2$ and $\mathbb{G}_\mathsf{T}$ be three multiplicative groups of the same prime order q, and let g_1, g_2 be generators of $\mathbb{G}_1$ and $\mathbb{G}_2$, respectively. Assume that the discrete logarithm problems in $\mathbb{G}_1, \mathbb{G}_2$ and $\mathbb{G}_\mathsf{T}$ are intractable. We say that $e : \mathbb{G}_1 \times \mathbb{G}_2 \to \mathbb{G}_\mathsf{T}$ is an admissible bilinear pairing, if it satisfies the following properties:*

1. *Bilinear: For all a, $b \leftarrow \mathbb{Z}_q^*, \hat{g}_1 \leftarrow \mathbb{G}_1, \hat{g}_2 \leftarrow \mathbb{G}_2, e(\hat{g}_1{}^a, \hat{g}_2{}^b) = e(\hat{g}_1, \hat{g}_2)^{ab}$.*
2. *Non-degenerate: For each $\hat{g}_1 \in \mathbb{G}_1/\{1\}$, there exists $\hat{g}_2 \in \mathbb{G}_2$, such that $e(\hat{g}_1, \hat{g}_2) \neq 1$.*
3. *Computable: For all $\hat{g}_1 \leftarrow \mathbb{G}_1, \hat{g}_2 \leftarrow \mathbb{G}_2, e(\hat{g}_1, \hat{g}_2)$ is efficiently computable.*

Bilinear pairings are powerful mathematical tools for numerous cryptographic applications. Generally, there are three types of bilinear pairing [17,23]:

Type 1: $\mathbb{G}_1 = \mathbb{G}_2$, it is also called symmetric bilinear pairing.
Type 2: There is an efficiently computable isomorphism either from $\mathbb{G}_1$ to $\mathbb{G}_2$ or from $\mathbb{G}_2$ to $\mathbb{G}_1$.
Type 3: There exists no efficiently computable isomorphism between $\mathbb{G}_1$ and $\mathbb{G}_2$.

A brief history of pairings is presented in [6]. In recent years, much progress on number field sieve (NFS) has been made against pairing-friendly curves, which imposes new estimation of the security of parings. The reader is referred to [7] for updated key size estimation of some popular pairing-friendly curves (e.g., BN, BLS, KSS).

The computationally *intractable* problems considered in this work are defined as follows, which are described w.r.t. Type 1 pairings for presentation simplicity. Let $\mathbb{G}_1, \mathbb{G}_\mathsf{T}$ be two multiplicative groups of the same prime order q, g be a generator of $\mathbb{G}_1$, $e : \mathbb{G}_1 \times \mathbb{G}_1 \to \mathbb{G}_\mathsf{T}$ be an admissible symmetric bilinear pairing.

Definition 2 (Bilinear Diffie-Hellman (BDH)). *The bilinear Diffie-Hellman (BDH) problem [35] in $\langle \mathbb{G}_1, \mathbb{G}_\mathsf{T}, e \rangle$ is to compute $e(g, g)^{abc} \in \mathbb{G}_\mathsf{T}$, given $(g, g^a, g^b, g^c) \in \mathbb{G}_1^4$, where $a, b, c \leftarrow \mathbb{Z}_q^*$. The BDH assumption says that no PPT algorithm can solve the BDH problem with non-negligible probability.*

Definition 3 (Square Bilinear Diffie-Hellman (SBDH)). *The square bilinear Diffie-Hellman (SBDH) problem in $\langle \mathbb{G}_1, \mathbb{G}_\mathsf{T}, e \rangle$ is to compute $e(g, g)^{a^2 b} \in \mathbb{G}_\mathsf{T}$, given $(g, g^a, g^b) \in \mathbb{G}_1^3$, where $a, b \leftarrow \mathbb{Z}_q^*$. The SBDH assumption says that no PPT algorithm can solve the SBDH problem with non-negligible probability.*

Below, we show that the SBDH assumption is equivalent to the BDH assumption. Due to space limitation, the proof details are given in the full version.

Theorem 1. *The* BDH *assumption and the* SBDH *assumption are equivalent.*

Definition 4 (Gap Bilinear Diffie-Hellman (Gap-BDH)). *The gap bilinear Diffie-Hellman (*Gap-BDH*) problem [5, 35] is to compute* $e(g, g)^{abc} \in \mathbb{G}_T$*, given* $(g, g^a, g^b, g^c) \in \mathbb{G}_1^4$*, where* $a, b, c \leftarrow \mathbb{Z}_q^*$*, but with the help of a decisional bilinear Diffie-Hellman (*DBDH*) oracle for* $\mathbb{G}_1 = \langle g \rangle$ *and* $\mathbb{G}_T$*. Here, on arbitrary input* $(A = g^a, B = g^b, C = g^c, T) \in \mathbb{G}_1^3 \times \mathbb{G}_T$*, the* DBDH *oracle outputs 1 if and only if* $T = e(g, g)^{abc}$*. The* Gap-BDH *assumption says that no PPT algorithm can solve the* Gap-BDH *problem with non-negligible probability.*

Definition 5 (Gap Square Bilinear Diffie-Hellman). *The gap square bilinear Diffie-Hellman (*Gap-SBDH*) problem is to compute* $e(g, g)^{a^2 b} \in \mathbb{G}_T$*, given* $(g, g^a, g^b) \in \mathbb{G}_1^3$*, where* $a, b \leftarrow \mathbb{Z}_q^*$*, but with the help of a decisional bilinear Diffie-Hellman (*DBDH*) oracle for* $\mathbb{G}_1 = \langle g \rangle$ *and* $\mathbb{G}_T$*. Here, on arbitrary input* $(A' = g^{a'}, B' = g^{b'}, C' = g^{c'}, T) \in \mathbb{G}_1^3 \times \mathbb{G}_T$*, the* DBDH *oracle outputs 1 if and only if* $T = e(g, g)^{a'b'c'}$*. The* Gap-SBDH *assumption says that no PPT algorithm can solve the* Gap-SBDH *problem with non-negligible probability.*

Clearly, by Theorem 1, the Gap-BDH assumption and the Gap-SBDH assumption are equivalent.

3   Identity-Based Higncryption: Definition and Security Model

3.1   Definition of IBHigncryption

In an identity-based identity-concealed signcryption scheme (IBHigncryption) (denoted by IBHC), there is a private key generator (PKG) who is responsible for the generation of private keys for the users in the system. The PKG computes the private key for each user using its master secret key on the user's public identity. Next, we give the formal definition of an IBHigncryption.

Definition 6 (IBHigncryption). *An* IBHigncryption *scheme* IBHC *with associated data, consists of the following four polynomial-time algorithms:* Setup, KeyGen, IBHigncrypt, *and* UnIBHigncrypt.

– Setup(1^κ) → (par, msk)*: The algorithm is run by the PKG. On input of the security parameter* κ*, it outputs the system's common parameters* par *and the master secret key* msk*. Finally, the PKG outputs* par*, and it keeps the master secret key* msk *in private. We assume that the security parameter and an admissible identity space* $\mathcal{ID}$ *are always (implicitly) encoded in* par*.*
– KeyGen(par, msk, ID) → sk*: On input of the system's public parameters* par*, the master secret key* msk *of the PKG, and a user's identity* ID*, the PKG computes and outputs the private key* sk *of* ID *using* msk *if* ID $\in \mathcal{ID}$*. The public identity and its private key are for algorithm* IBHigncrypt *and algorithm* UnIBHigncrypt *respectively.*

- IBHigncrypt(par, sk_s, ID$_s$, ID$_r$, H, M) → $(C, \perp)$: *It is a* PPT *algorithm. On input of the system's public parameters* par, *a sender's private key* sk_s, *and his public identity* ID$_s \in \mathcal{ID}$, *a receiver's public identity* ID$_r \in \mathcal{ID}$, *a message* $M \in \{0,1\}^*$ *and its associated data* $H \in \{0,1\}^*$ *to be* IBHigncrypted, *it outputs an* IBHigncryptext $C \in \{0,1\}^*$, *or* $\perp$ *indicating* IBHigncrypt*'s failure. The associated data* H, *if there is any, appears in clear in the* IBHigncryptext C, *when* $C \neq \perp$.
- UnIBHigncrypt(par, sk_r, ID$_r$, C) → $((\text{ID}_s, M), \perp)$: *It is a deterministic algorithm. On input of the system's public parameters* par, *the receiver's private key* sk_r, *the receiver's public identity* ID$_r \in \mathcal{ID}$, *and an* IBHigncryptext C, *it outputs* (ID$_s$, M) *if the verification is successful, or* $\perp$ *indicating an error, where* ID$_s \in \mathcal{ID}$ *is the sender's public identity, and* $M \in \{0,1\}^*$ *is the message* IBHigncrypted *by* ID$_s$. *It is different from the traditional identity-based signcryption in that* UnIBHigncrypt *does not need to take the sender's public identity* ID$_s$ *as input.*

Definition 7 (correctness). *We say an* IBHigncryption *scheme* IBHC *is correct, if for any sufficiently large security parameter* κ, *any key pairs* (ID$_s$, sk_s), *and* (ID$_r$, sk_r), *where* sk_s *and* sk_r *are output by* KeyGen *on* ID$_s$ *and* ID$_r$ *respectively, it holds that* UnIBHigncrypt(par, sk_r, ID$_r$, IBHigncrypt(par, sk_s, ID$_s$, ID$_r$, H, M)) = (ID$_s$, M) *for any* $H, M \in \{0,1\}^*$ *such that* IBHigncrypt(par, sk_s, ID$_s$, ID$_r$, H, M) $\neq \perp$.

Definition 8 (receiver deniability). *We say that an* IBHigncryption *scheme* IBHC *has receiver deniability, if the same* IBHigncryptext *can be generated either by the sender or the receiver. Specifically, there exists a PPT algorithm* IBHigncrypt′(par, sk_r, ID$_s$, ID$_r$, H, M) → $(C, \perp)$, *satisfying: the output of* IBHigncrypt′(par, sk_r, ID$_s$, ID$_r$, H, M) *has the same distribution as that of* IBHigncrypt(par, sk_s, ID$_s$, ID$_r$, H, M), *for any security parameter* κ, *any* $H, M \in \{0,1\}^*$, *and any key pairs* (ID$_s$, sk_s) *and* (ID$_r$, sk_r) *where* sk_s *and* sk_r *are output by* KeyGen *on* ID$_s$ *and* ID$_r$ *respectively.*

Remark 1. Deniability has always been a central privacy concern in personal and business communications, with off-the-record communication serving as an essential social and political tool [40]. Given that many of these interactions now happen over digital media (e.g., email, instant messaging, web transactions, virtual private networks), it is critically important to provide these communications with "off-the-record" or deniability capability to protocol participants.[3] For these applications, we may only concern about the authentication of the communication, and less care about the non-repudiation of the communication.

---

[3] Needless to say, there are special applications where non-repudiable communication is essential. But this is not the case for most of our nowaday communications over Internet, where deniable authentication is much more desirable than non-repudiable one [40].

3.2   Security Model for IBHigncryption

We focus on the security model for IBHigncryption in the multi-user environment, where each user possesses a single key pair for both IBHigncrypt and UnIBHigncrypt, and the sender can IBHigncrypt messages to itself. Our security model is stronger than that of an identity-based signcryption, since it allows the adversaries to access more oracles.

The private keys of all the users in the system are generated by the challenger by running the specified key generation algorithm KeyGen. All the users' public identities are given to the adversary initially. Throughout this work, denote by ID_i, the public identity of user i, and denote by ID_s (resp., ID_r) the public identity of the sender (resp., the receiver). For presentation simplicity, throughout this work we assume that all the users in the system have public identity information of equal length. But our security model and protocol construction can be extended to the general case of different lengths of identities, by incorporating length-hiding authenticated encryption [38] in the underlying security model and protocol construction.

The security of an IBHigncryption includes two parts: outsider unforgeability (OU) and insider confidentiality (IC). In order to formally define the above security, we introduce two types of adversaries in our system, one is called OU-adversary, $\mathcal{A}_{IBHC}^{OU}$, and the other is called IC-adversary, $\mathcal{A}_{IBHC}^{IC}$. The goal of an $\mathcal{A}_{IBHC}^{OU}$ is to forge a valid IBHigncryptext on behalf of an uncorrupted sender ID_{s*} to an uncorrupted receiver ID_{r*}, where ID_{s*} may be equal to ID_{r*}. The goal of an $\mathcal{A}_{IBHC}^{IC}$ adversary is to break the confidentiality of the message or the privacy of the sender's identity for any IBHigncryptext from any (even corrupted) sender to any uncorrupted receiver, even if $\mathcal{A}_{IBHC}^{IC}$ is allowed to corrupt the sender and to expose the intermediate randomness used for generating other IBHigncryptexts. Likewise, here the sender may be equal to the receiver. The terminology "insider" (resp., "outsider"), which is traditional in this literature, refers to the situation that the target sender can (resp., cannot) be corrupted.

Now, we describe the oracles to which $\mathcal{A}_{IBHC}^{OU}$ or $\mathcal{A}_{IBHC}^{IC}$ gets access in our security model for IBHigncryption.

- HO Oracle : This oracle is used to respond to the IBHigncrypt queries made by an adversary, including $\mathcal{A}_{IBHC}^{OU}$ or $\mathcal{A}_{IBHC}^{IC}$. On input (ID_s, ID_r, H, M) by an adversary, where $ID_r \in \mathcal{ID}$ may be equal to $ID_s \in \mathcal{ID}$, and $H, M \in \{0,1\}^*$, this oracle returns $C = $ IBHigncrypt$(par, sk_s, ID_s, ID_r, H, M)$ to the adversary. In order to respond to some EXO queries against C by the adversary, the HO Oracle needs to store some specified offline-computable intermediate randomness (which is used in generating C) into an initially empty table ST_C privately.
- UHO Oracle: This oracle is used to respond to the UnIBHigncrypt queries made by an adversary, including $\mathcal{A}_{IBHC}^{OU}$ or $\mathcal{A}_{IBHC}^{IC}$. On input (ID_r, C) by an adversary, this oracle returns UnIBHigncrypt(par, sk_r, ID_r, C) to the adversary, where sk_r is the private key of the receiver $ID_r \in \mathcal{ID}$.
- EXO Oracle: This oracle is used to respond to the intermediate randomness used in generating an IBHigncryptext of an earlier HO query. It is an additional

oracle in our security model that makes our security stronger than the traditional security for signcryption; This feature is considered and named as x-security in [28]. On input an IBHigncryptext C, this oracle returns the value (i.e., the offline-computable intermediate randomness used in generating C) stored in the table ST_C, if $C \neq \perp$ and C was an output of an earlier HO query. If there is no such a record in ST_C, this oracle returns $\perp$ to the adversary.

- CORRUPT Oracle: This oracle is used to respond to the private key queries for any user in the system. On input a user's identity $\mathsf{ID}_i \in \mathcal{ID}$, this oracle returns the private key $sk_i = \mathsf{KeyGen}(\mathsf{par}, \mathsf{msk}, \mathsf{ID}_i)$, and ID_i is then marked as a corrupted user. Denote by $\mathsf{S}_{\mathrm{corr}}$ the set of corrupted users in the system, which is initially empty. This oracle updates $\mathsf{S}_{\mathrm{corr}}$ with $\mathsf{S}_{\mathrm{corr}} := \mathsf{S}_{\mathrm{corr}} \bigcup \{\mathsf{ID}_i\}$ whenever the private key of ID_i is returned to the adversary.

Next, we describe the security games for insider confidentiality (IC) and outsider unforgeability (OU).

Definition 9 (Insider Confidentiality (IC)). *Let $\mathcal{A}_{\mathsf{IBHC}}^{\mathsf{IC}}$ be an IC-adversary against IBHC. We consider the following game, denoted by $\mathrm{GAME}_{\mathsf{IBHC}}^{\mathcal{A}^{\mathsf{IC}}}$, in which an adversary $\mathcal{A}_{\mathsf{IBHC}}^{\mathsf{IC}}$ interacts with a challenger $\mathcal{C}$.*

- Setup: *The challenger $\mathcal{C}$ runs* Setup *to generate the system public parameters* par *and a master secret key* msk. *The challenger returns* par *to the adversary $\mathcal{A}_{\mathsf{IBHC}}^{\mathsf{IC}}$, and keeps the* msk *secretly for itself.*
- Phase 1: *In this phase, $\mathcal{A}_{\mathsf{IBHC}}^{\mathsf{IC}}$ issues any polynomial number of queries, including HO, UHO, EXO, and CORRUPT.*
- Challenge: *At the end of* phase 1, *$\mathcal{A}_{\mathsf{IBHC}}^{\mathsf{IC}}$ selects in the identity space $\mathcal{ID}$ two different target senders, $\mathsf{ID}_{s_0^*}$ and $\mathsf{ID}_{s_1^*}$, and an uncorrupted target receiver ID_{r^*}, a pair of messages (M_0^*, M_1^*) of equal length from the message space, and associated data H^*. $\mathcal{A}_{\mathsf{IBHC}}^{\mathsf{IC}}$ submits (M_0^*, M_1^*), H^*, and $(\mathsf{ID}_{s_0^*}, \mathsf{ID}_{s_1^*}, \mathsf{ID}_{r^*})$ to the challenger $\mathcal{C}$.*
  The challenger $\mathcal{C}$ chooses $\sigma \leftarrow \{0, 1\}$, and gives the challenge IBHigncryptext

$$C^* = \mathsf{IBHigncrypt}(\mathsf{par}, sk_{s_\sigma^*}, \mathsf{ID}_{s_\sigma^*}, \mathsf{ID}_{r^*}, H^*, M_\sigma^*)$$

  to the adversary $\mathcal{A}_{\mathsf{IBHC}}^{\mathsf{IC}}$. Here, we stress that there is no restriction on selecting the target senders $\mathsf{ID}_{s_0^*}$ and $\mathsf{ID}_{s_1^*}$. It implies that both target senders can be corrupted, which captures forward ID-privacy; And either one of the target senders can be the target receiver (i.e., it may be the case that $\mathsf{ID}_{s_\sigma^*} = \mathsf{ID}_{r^*}$).
- Phase 2: *$\mathcal{A}_{\mathsf{IBHC}}^{\mathsf{IC}}$ continues to make queries as in* phase 1 *with the following restrictions:*
  1. *$\mathcal{A}_{\mathsf{IBHC}}^{\mathsf{IC}}$ is not allowed to issue $\mathsf{CORRUPT}(\mathsf{ID}_{r^*})$.*
  2. *$\mathcal{A}_{\mathsf{IBHC}}^{\mathsf{IC}}$ is not allowed to issue $\mathsf{UHO}(\mathsf{ID}_{r^*}, C^*)$.*
  3. *$\mathcal{A}_{\mathsf{IBHC}}^{\mathsf{IC}}$ is not allowed to issue $\mathsf{EXO}(C^*)$.*
- Guess: *Finally, $\mathcal{A}_{\mathsf{IBHC}}^{\mathsf{IC}}$ outputs $\sigma' \in \{0, 1\}$ as his guess of the random bit σ. $\mathcal{A}_{\mathsf{IBHC}}^{\mathsf{IC}}$ wins the game if $\sigma' = \sigma$.*

With respect to the above security game $\mathsf{GAME}_{\mathsf{IBHC}}^{\mathcal{A}^{\mathsf{IC}}}$, we define the advantage of an $\mathcal{A}_{\mathsf{IBHC}}^{\mathsf{IC}}$ adversary in $\mathsf{GAME}_{\mathsf{IBHC}}^{\mathcal{A}^{\mathsf{IC}}}$ as:

$$\mathsf{Adv}_{\mathsf{IBHC}}^{\mathcal{A}^{\mathsf{IC}}} = |2 \cdot \mathsf{Pr}[\sigma' = \sigma] - 1|.$$

We say that an IBHigncryption scheme IBHC has insider confidentiality, if for any PPT adversary $\mathcal{A}_{\mathsf{IBHC}}^{\mathsf{IC}}$, its advantage $\mathsf{Adv}_{\mathsf{IBHC}}^{\mathcal{A}^{\mathsf{IC}}}$ is negligible for any sufficiently large security parameter.

Definition 10 (Outsider Unforgeability (OU)). Let $\mathcal{A}_{\mathsf{IBHC}}^{\mathsf{OU}}$ be an OU-adversary against IBHC. We consider the following game, denoted by $\mathsf{GAME}_{\mathsf{IBHC}}^{\mathcal{A}^{\mathsf{OU}}}$, in which an adversary $\mathcal{A}_{\mathsf{IBHC}}^{\mathsf{OU}}$ interacts with a challenger $\mathcal{C}$.

- Phase 1: The challenger $\mathcal{C}$ runs Setup to generate the system public parameters par and a master secret key msk. The challenger returns par to the adversary $\mathcal{A}_{\mathsf{IBHC}}^{\mathsf{OU}}$, and keeps the msk for itself in private.
- Phase 2: In this phase, $\mathcal{A}_{\mathsf{IBHC}}^{\mathsf{OU}}$ issues any polynomial number of queries, including HO, UHO, EXO, and CORRUPT.
- Phase 3: In this phase, $\mathcal{A}_{\mathsf{IBHC}}^{\mathsf{OU}}$ outputs (ID_{r^*}, C^*) as its forgery, where $\mathsf{ID}_{r^*} \notin S_{\mathsf{corr}}$ and the associated data contained in C^* in clear is denoted by H^*. We say the forgery (ID_{r^*}, C^*) is a valid IBHigncryptext created by an uncorrupted sender $\mathsf{ID}_{s^*} \in \mathcal{ID}$ for an uncorrupted receiver $\mathsf{ID}_{r^*} \in \mathcal{ID}$ if and only if the following conditions hold simultaneously:
  1. $\mathsf{UnIBHigncrypt}(sk_{r^*}, \mathsf{ID}_{r^*}, C^*) = (\mathsf{ID}_{s^*}, M^*)$, where $\mathsf{ID}_{s^*} \in \mathcal{ID} \setminus S_{\mathsf{corr}}$, $M^* \in \{0,1\}^*$, and ID_{s^*} may be equal to ID_{r^*}.
  2. $\mathcal{A}_{\mathsf{IBHC}}^{\mathsf{OU}}$ is not allowed to issue CORRUPT queries on ID_{s^*} or ID_{r^*}.
  3. $\mathcal{A}_{\mathsf{IBHC}}^{\mathsf{OU}}$ is allowed to issue $\mathsf{HO}(\mathsf{ID}_{s'}, \mathsf{ID}_{r'}, H', M')$ for any $(\mathsf{ID}_{s'}, \mathsf{ID}_{r'}, H', M') \neq (\mathsf{ID}_{s^*}, \mathsf{ID}_{r^*}, H^*, M^*)$. In particular, $\mathcal{A}_{\mathsf{IBHC}}^{\mathsf{OU}}$ can make an HO query on $(\mathsf{ID}_{s^*}, \mathsf{ID}_{r^*}, H', M^*)$, where $H' \neq H^*$. It can even make the query $\mathsf{HO}(\mathsf{ID}_{s^*}, \mathsf{ID}_{r^*}, H^*, M^*)$, as long as the output returned is not equal to C^*.

Let $\mathsf{Adv}_{\mathsf{IBHC}}^{\mathcal{A}^{\mathsf{OU}}}$ denote the advantage that $\mathcal{A}_{\mathsf{IBHC}}^{\mathsf{OU}}$ outputs a valid forgery in the above security game $\mathsf{GAME}_{\mathsf{IBHC}}^{\mathcal{A}^{\mathsf{OU}}}$. We say an IBHigncryption scheme IBHC has outsider unforgeability, if for any PPT adversary $\mathcal{A}_{\mathsf{IBHC}}^{\mathsf{OU}}$, its advantage $\mathsf{Adv}_{\mathsf{IBHC}}^{\mathcal{A}^{\mathsf{OU}}}$ is negligible for any sufficiently large security parameter.

Remark 2. Note that the above definition of outsider unforgeability implies the x-security considered and named in [28]. Specifically, getting access to the oracle EXO in an arbitrary way does not allow the adversary to forge IBHigncryptext (in particular, to recover the secret key of any uncorrupted user).

4   IBHigncryption: Construction and Discussion

For presentation simplicity, below we present the construction of IBHigncryption based on bilinear pairings of Type 1. The straightforward extensions to Type 2 and 3 pairings are presented in Appendix A.

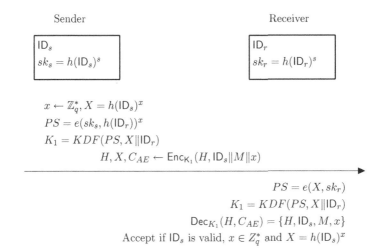

Fig. 1. Protocol Structure of IBHigncryption

Our IBHigncryption scheme consists of the following four algorithms:

- Setup(1^κ): The algorithm is run by the PKG in order to produce the system's public parameters and the master secret key. On input of the security parameter κ, it chooses two multiplicative bilinear map groups $\mathbb{G}_1 = \langle g \rangle$ and $\mathbb{G}_T$ of the same prime order q such that the discrete logarithm problems in both $\mathbb{G}_1$ and $\mathbb{G}_T$ are intractable. The algorithm constructs a bilinear pairing $e : \mathbb{G}_1 \times \mathbb{G}_1 \to \mathbb{G}_T$, and chooses $s \leftarrow \mathbb{Z}_q^*$. Additionally, it selects a one-way collision-resistant cryptographic hash function, $h : \{0,1\}^* \to \mathbb{G}_1$. Finally, the algorithm outputs the public parameters $\mathsf{par} = (q, \mathbb{G}_1, \mathbb{G}_T, e, g, h)$, and the PKG's master secret key $\mathsf{msk} = s$. The PKG makes par public to the users in the system, but keeps msk secret for itself. Note that the setup stage is much simpler, where in particular no modular exponentiation is performed in order to generate a traditional master public key as in [12] and [8]. For presentation simplicity, we assume the admissible identity space $\mathcal{ID} = \{0,1\}^*$.
- KeyGen($\mathsf{par}, \mathsf{msk}, \mathsf{ID}$): On input of the system's public parameters par, the master secret key msk of PKG, and a user's identity $\mathsf{ID} \in \{0,1\}^*$, the PKG computes $sk = h(\mathsf{ID})^{\mathsf{msk}} = h(\mathsf{ID})^s$, and outputs sk_{ID} as the private key associated with identity ID.
- IBHigncrypt($\mathsf{par}, sk_s, \mathsf{ID}_s, \mathsf{ID}_r, H, M$): Let $\mathsf{SE} = (\mathsf{K_{se}}, \mathsf{Enc}, \mathsf{Dec})$ be an authenticated encryption (AE) scheme as defined in Sect. 2.1, $M \in \{0,1\}^*$ be the message to be IBHigncrypted with associated data $H \in \{0,1\}^*$, and $\mathsf{KDF} : \mathbb{G}_T \times \{0,1\}^* \to \mathcal{K}$ be a key derivation function that is modelled to be a random oracle, where $\mathcal{K}$ is the key space of $\mathsf{K_{se}}$. For presentation simplicity, we denote by ID_s the sender's public identity whose private key is $sk_s = h(\mathsf{ID}_s)^s$, and by ID_r the receiver's public identity whose private key is $sk_r = h(\mathsf{ID}_r)^s$.

To IBHigncrypt a message $M \leftarrow \{0,1\}^*$ with the sender's identity ID_s concealed, the sender ID_s runs the following steps: (1) selects $x \leftarrow \mathbb{Z}_q^*$, and computes $X = h(\mathsf{ID}_s)^x \in \mathbb{G}_1$; (2) computes the pre-shared secret $PS = e(sk_s, h(\mathsf{ID}_r))^x \in \mathbb{G}_\mathsf{T}$; (3) derives the AE key $K_1 = KDF(PS, X\|\mathsf{ID}_r) \in \mathcal{K}$; (4) computes $C_{AE} \leftarrow \mathsf{Enc}_{K_1}(H, \mathsf{ID}_s\|M\|x)$; and finally (5) sends the IBHigncryptext $C = (H, X, C_{AE})$ to the receiver ID_r.

- UnIBHigncrypt($\mathsf{par}, sk_r, \mathsf{ID}_r, C$): On receiving $C = (H, X, C_{AE})$, the receiver ID_r with private key sk_r does the following: (1) computes the pre-shared secret $PS = e(X, sk_r) \in \mathbb{G}_\mathsf{T}$, and derives the key $K_1 = KDF(PS, X\|\mathsf{ID}_r) \in \mathcal{K}$; (2) runs $\mathsf{Dec}_{K_1}(H, C_{AE})$. If $\mathsf{Dec}_{K_1}(H, C_{AE})$ returns $\perp$, it aborts; Otherwise, the receiver gets $\{\mathsf{ID}_s, M, x\}$, and outputs (ID_s, M) if $\mathsf{ID}_s \in \mathcal{ID}$, $x \in Z_q^*$, and $X = h(\mathsf{ID}_s)^x$. Otherwise, it outputs "$\perp$" and aborts.

Remark 3. The correctness and the property of receiver deniability of the above IBHigncryption are straightforward. It also enjoys x-security and forward ID-privacy, which are implied by the formal analyses of outsider unforgeability and insider confidentiality to be given in Sect. 5.

Remark 4. The construction of IBHigncryption is fundamentally different from the PKI-based higncrypiton from [47], and cannot be transformed each other. Briefly recall the construction by directly transforming the higncryption scheme from [47] into ID-based setting. Let $S = g^s$ and $s \leftarrow Z_q^*$ be the master public and private keys of PKG. Let $sk_s = h(\mathsf{ID}_s)^s$ and $sk_r = h(\mathsf{ID}_r)^s$ be the private keys of sender ID_s and receiver ID_r respectively. Let $x \leftarrow Z_q^*$, $X = g^x$, $\bar{X} = h(\mathsf{ID}_s)X^d$, where $d = h'(\mathsf{ID}_s, \mathsf{ID}_r, X)$ and $h' : \{0,1\}^* \rightarrow Z_q^*$ is a cryptographic hash function. Let $PS = e(sk_s, h(\mathsf{ID}_r))e(S^{xd}, h(\mathsf{ID}_r)) = e(\bar{X}, sk_r)$. The sender computes and sends $\{\bar{X}, C_{AE} = \mathsf{Enc}_{K_1}(\mathsf{ID}_s, M, X)\}$. The receiver decrypts C_{AE} and checks whether $\bar{X} = h(\mathsf{ID}_s)X^d$. This is indeed the starting point of our design of IBHigncryption. This straightforward design is much less efficient, and has the traditional master public key. Our actual design of IBHigncryption embeds a technique similar to the FO-transformation [22], and critically relies on the properties of pairings. So, the construction of IBHigncryption is fundamentally different from the direct transformation of the higncryption scheme [47].

4.1   Comparison and Discussion

In this section, we briefly compare our IBHigncryption scheme with the CCA-secure Boneh-Franklin IBE [12] (referred to as BF-IBE), and the IEEE P1363.3 standard of ID-based signcryption [8] (referred to as IEEE P1363.3 for simplicity). The schemes of CCA-secure BF-IBE and IEEE P1363.3 will be presented in the full version due to space limitation.

The comparisons between our IBHigncryption scheme based on symmetric bilinear pairings of Type 1 and BF-IBE [12], and our IBHigncryption scheme based on asymmetric bilinear pairings of Type 2 and the IEEE P1363.3 standard [8], are briefly summarized in Table 2 and Table 3 respectively. Therein, $\perp$ denotes "unapplicable", "-" denotes no exponentiation operation, "E" denotes

Table 2. Brief comparison between IBHigncryption and CCA-secure BF-IBE

par		IBHigncryption	BF-IBE [12]
		$(q, \mathbb{G}_1, \mathbb{G}_T, e, g, h)$	$(q, \mathbb{G}_1, \mathbb{G}_T, e, n, g, P_{\mathsf{pub}}, h_1, h_2, h_3, h_4)$
Efficiency	Setup	-	1 E
	KeyGen	1 E + 1 H_2	1 E + 1 H_2
	Sender	2 E + 1 P + 2 H_2 + 1 Enc	2 E + 1 P + 1 H_2 + 3 H_1
	Receiver	1 E + 1 P + 1 H_2 + 1 Dec	1 E + 1 P + 3 H_1
Message space		$\{0,1\}^*$	$\{0,1\}^n$
Assumption		Gap-SBDH	BDH

Table 3. Brief comparison between IBHigncryption and IEEE P1363.3

par		IBHigncryption	IEEE P1363.3 [8]
		$(q, \mathbb{G}_1, \mathbb{G}_2, \mathbb{G}_T, g_1, g_2, e, \psi, h)$	$(q, \mathbb{G}_1, \mathbb{G}_2, \mathbb{G}_T, g_1, g_2, g, Q_{\mathsf{pub}}, e, \psi, h_1, h_2, h_3)$
Efficiency	Setup	1 ψ	1 E + 1 P + 1 ψ
	KeyGen	1 E + 1 H_2	1 E + 1 INV + 1 H_1 + 1 A
	Sender	2 E + 1 P + 2 H_2 + 1 ψ + 1 Enc	4 E + 2 ψ + 3 H_1 + 1 M + 1 A
	Receiver	1 E + 1 P + 1 H_2 + 1 ψ + 1 Dec	2 E + 2 P + 3 H_1 + 1 M_T + 1 M + 1 A
Message space		$\{0,1\}^*$	$\{0,1\}^n$
Forward ID-privacy		✓	×
x-security		✓	×
Receiver deniability		✓	×
Consider $\mathsf{ID}_s = \mathsf{ID}_r$		✓	×
Assumption		Gap-SBDH	q-BDHIP

modular exponentiation, "P" denotes paring, "H_1" denotes a plain hashing, "H_2" denotes a hashing onto the bilinear group, "A" denotes modular addition, "M" (resp., M_T) denotes modular multiplication in G_1 or G_2 (resp., G_T), "INV" denotes modular inversion, and ψ denotes isomorphism. Note that modular inverse is a relatively expensive operation, which is typically performed by the extended Euclid algorithm.

In comparison with BF-IBE [12] and IEEE P1363.3 [8], IBHigncryption has a much simpler setup stage. Specifically, the setup stage of our IBHigncryption has much smaller public parameters, and actually does not need to perform exponentiation to generate the master public key (corresponding to P_{pub} in BF-IBE, and Q_{pub} in IEEE P1363.3). The much simpler setup stage of IBHigncryption, particularly waiving the master public key, brings the following advantages:

- The computational and space complexity for generating and storing the system parameters is reduced.
- The attack vector (for recovering the master secret key) is decreased, e.g., for some mission critical applications.
- It eases deployment and compatibility with existing identity-based cryptosystems. Specifically, when deploying our IBHigncryption scheme in reality with other existing identity-based cryptosystems, the system parameters and particularly the master public key can remain unchanged.

For IEEE P1363.3 [8], if the secret x is exposed one can compute from the corresponding signcryptext the following values: the message M being signcrypted, and more importantly the secret key value $\psi(sk_{\mathsf{ID_A}})$ which then allows the attacker to impersonate the sender in an arbitrary way. This shows that IEEE P1363.3 lacks the x-security (specifically, cannot be outsider unforgeable when getting access to the EXO oracle is allowed). We also note that the provable security of IEEE P1363.3 [8] does not consider the case of $\mathsf{ID}_s = \mathsf{ID}_r$.

For computational efficiency, briefly speaking, our IBHigncryption is essentially as efficient as BF-IBE [12], while providing the functionalities of encryption, authentication, and ID-privacy simultaneously and with a much simpler setup stage. In other words, compared with BF-IBE, the functionalities of authentication and ID-privacy are gotten almost for free with IBHigncryption. In comparison with IEEE P1363.3 [8], besides the extra properties of forward ID-privacy, x-security, receiver deniability, IBHigncryption is also computationally more efficient in total. Note that the plaintext spaces for BF-IBE and IEEE P1363.3 are pre-specified to be $\{0,1\}^n$. If one employs the hybrid encryption approach to encrypt messages of arbitrary length with BF-IBE or IEEE P1363.3, it also needs to employ some appropriate symmetric-key encryption scheme in reality.

5   Security Analysis of IBHigncryption

Due to space limitation, we focus on the security proof of our IBHigncryption construction with symmetric bilinear groups. The extension to the asymmetric bilinear groups is straightforward. In the following security analysis, KDF and the hash function h are modelled as random oracles (RO). The proof details of the following theorems are given in the full version.

Theorem 2. *The* IBHigncryption *scheme presented in Fig. 1 is outsider unforgeable in the random oracle model, under the AE security and the* Gap-SBDH *assumption.*

Theorem 3. *The* IBHigncryption *scheme presented in Fig. 1 has insider confidentiality in the random oracle model, under the AE security and the* Gap-SBDH *assumption.*

Acknowledgement. We are grateful to Hongbing Wang for many helpful discussions and for contributions in writing and presentation.

A   IBHigncryption Constructions with Asymmetric Bilinear Pairings

The construction of our IBHigncryption in this section, as well as the IEEE P1363.3 standard [8] for ID-Based signcryption, is based on asymmetric bilinear pairings of Type 2. The extension of our IBHigncryption construction to the Type 2 bilinear pairings is straightforward, which is described below from scratch for ease of reference.

- Setup(1^κ): On input of the security parameter κ, the algorithm chooses three multiplicative bilinear map groups $\mathbb{G}_1, \mathbb{G}_2$ and $\mathbb{G}_T$ of the same prime order q, generators $g_1 \in \mathbb{G}_1$, $g_2 = \psi(g_1) \in \mathbb{G}_2$, and a bilinear pairing $e : \mathbb{G}_1 \times \mathbb{G}_2 \to \mathbb{G}_T$ such that the discrete logarithm problems in $\mathbb{G}_1, \mathbb{G}_2$ and $\mathbb{G}_T$ are intractable, where $\psi : \mathbb{G}_1 \to \mathbb{G}_2$ is an efficient, publicly computable isomorphism. The algorithm chooses a master secret key $s \leftarrow \mathbb{Z}_q^*$. Additionally, it selects a one-way collision-resistant cryptographic hash function, $h : \{0,1\}^* \to \mathbb{G}_1$. Finally, the algorithm outputs the public parameters par $= (q, \mathbb{G}_1, \mathbb{G}_2, \mathbb{G}_T, e, g_1, g_2, \psi, h)$, and the PKG's master secret key msk $= s$. The PKG makes par public to the users in the system, but keeps msk secret for itself.
- KeyGen(par, msk, ID): On input of the system's public parameters par, the master secret key msk of the PKG, and a user's identity ID $\in \{0,1\}^*$, the PKG computes $sk = h(\mathsf{ID})^{\mathsf{msk}} = h(\mathsf{ID})^s$, and outputs sk as the private key associated with identity ID.
- IBHigncrypt(par, sk_s, ID_s, ID_r, H, M): Let SE $= (\mathsf{K}_{\mathsf{se}}, \mathsf{Enc}, \mathsf{Dec})$ be an authenticated encryption scheme, $M \in \{0,1\}^*$ be the message to be IBHigncrypted with associated data $H \in \{0,1\}^*$, and KDF $: \mathbb{G}_T \times \{0,1\}^* \to \{0,1\}^*$ be a key derivation function, where $\mathcal{K}$ is the key space of K_{se}. For presentation simplicity, we denote by ID_s the sender's public identity whose private key is $sk_s = h(\mathsf{ID}_s)^s$, and by ID_r the receiver's public identity whose private key is $sk_r = h(\mathsf{ID}_r)^s$.

  To IBHigncrypt a message $M \leftarrow \{0,1\}^*$ with the sender's identity ID_s concealed, the sender: (1) selects $x \leftarrow \mathbb{Z}_q^*$, and computes $X = h(\mathsf{ID}_s)^x \in \mathbb{G}_1$; (2) computes the primary secret $PS = e(sk_s, \psi(h(\mathsf{ID}_r)))^x$; (3) derives $K_1 = KDF(PS, X\|\mathsf{ID}_r) \in \mathcal{K}$; (4) computes $C_{AE} \leftarrow \mathsf{Enc}_{K_1}(H, \mathsf{ID}_s\|M\|x)$; and finally (5) sends the IBHigncryptext $C = (H, X, C_{AE})$ to the receiver ID_r.
- UnIBHigncrypt(par, sk_r, ID_r, C): Upon receiving $C = (H, X, C_{AE})$, the receiver: (1) computes the primary secret $PS = e(X, \psi(sk_r)) \in \mathbb{G}_T$, and derives the key $K_1 = KDF(PS, X\|\mathsf{ID}_r) \in \mathcal{K}$; (2) runs $\mathsf{Dec}_{K_1}(H, C_{AE})$. If $\mathsf{Dec}_{K_1}(H, C_{AE})$ returns $\bot$, it aborts; Otherwise, the receiver gets $\{\mathsf{ID}_s, M, x\}$, and outputs (ID_s, M) if $x \in Z_q^*$ and $X = h(\mathsf{ID}_s)^x$; Otherwise, it outputs "$\bot$" and aborts.

A.1 Construction with Bilinear Pairings of Type 3

The construction of our IBHigncryption in this subsection is based on the bilinear pairings of Type 3.

- Setup(1^κ): On input of the security parameter κ, the algorithm chooses three multiplicative bilinear map groups $\mathbb{G}_1, \mathbb{G}_2$ and $\mathbb{G}_T$ of the same prime order q, generators $g_1 \in \mathbb{G}_1$, $g_2 \in \mathbb{G}_2$, and a bilinear pairing $e : \mathbb{G}_1 \times \mathbb{G}_2 \to \mathbb{G}_T$ such that the discrete logarithm problems in $\mathbb{G}_1, \mathbb{G}_2$ and $\mathbb{G}_T$ are intractable. The algorithm chooses a master secret key $s \leftarrow \mathbb{Z}_q^*$. Additionally, it selects two one-way collision-resistant cryptographic hash functions, $h_1 : \{0,1\}^* \to \mathbb{G}_1$, and $h_2 : \{0,1\}^* \to \mathbb{G}_2$. Finally, the algorithm outputs the public parameters

$\mathsf{par} = (q, \mathbb{G}_1, \mathbb{G}_2, \mathbb{G}_\mathsf{T}, e, g_1, g_2, h_1, h_2)$, and the PKG's master secret key $\mathsf{msk} = s$. The PKG makes par public to the users in the system, but keeps msk secret for itself.

- KeyGen($\mathsf{par}, \mathsf{msk}, \mathsf{ID}$): On input of the system's public parameters par, and a user's identity $\mathsf{ID} \in \{0,1\}^*$, the PKG computes $sk = (sk_1, sk_2) = (h_1(\mathsf{ID})^s, h_2(\mathsf{ID})^s)$, and outputs sk as the private key associated with identity ID.

- IBHigncrypt($\mathsf{par}, sk_s = (sk_{s_1}, sk_{s_2}), \mathsf{ID}_s, \mathsf{ID}_r, H, M$): Let $\mathsf{SE} = (\mathsf{K}_\mathsf{se}, \mathsf{Enc}, \mathsf{Dec})$ be an authenticated encryption scheme, $M \in \{0,1\}^*$ be the message to be IBHigncrypted with associated data $H \in \{0,1\}^*$, and $\mathsf{KDF} : \mathbb{G}_\mathsf{T} \times \{0,1\}^* \to \{0,1\}^*$ be a key derivation function, where $\mathcal{K}$ is the key space of K_se. For presentation simplicity, we denote by ID_s the sender's public identity whose private key is $sk_s = (sk_{s_1}, sk_{s_2}) = (h_1(\mathsf{ID}_s)^s, h_2(\mathsf{ID}_s)^s)$, and by ID_r the receiver's public identity whose private key is $sk_r = (sk_{r_1}, sk_{r_2}) = (h_1(\mathsf{ID}_r)^s, h_2(\mathsf{ID}_r)^s)$. To IBHigncrypt a message $M \leftarrow \{0,1\}^*$ with the sender's identity ID_s concealed, the sender: (1) selects $x \leftarrow \mathbb{Z}_q^*$, and computes $X = h_1(\mathsf{ID}_s)^x \in \mathbb{G}_1$; (2) computes the primary secret $PS = e(sk_{s_1}, h_2(\mathsf{ID}_r))^x$; (3) derives $K_1 = KDF(PS, X \| \mathsf{ID}_r) \in \mathcal{K}$; (4) computes $C_{AE} \leftarrow \mathsf{Enc}_{K_1}(H, \mathsf{ID}_s \| M \| x)$; and finally (5) sends the IBHigncryptext $C = (H, X, C_{AE})$ to the receiver ID_r.

- UnIBHigncrypt($\mathsf{par}, sk_r = (sk_{r_1}, sk_{r_2}), \mathsf{ID}_r, C$): On receiving $C = (H, X, C_{AE})$, the receiver: (1) computes the primary secret $PS = e(X, sk_{r_2}) \in \mathbb{G}_\mathsf{T}$, and derives the key $K_1 = KDF(PS, X \| \mathsf{ID}_r) \in \mathcal{K}$; (2) runs $\mathsf{Dec}_{K_1}(H, C_{AE})$. If $\mathsf{Dec}_{K_1}(H, C_{AE})$ returns $\perp$, it aborts; Otherwise, the receiver gets $\{\mathsf{ID}_s, M, x\}$, and outputs (ID_s, M) if $x \in Z_q^*$ and $X = h_1(\mathsf{ID}_s)^x$; Otherwise, it outputs "$\perp$" and aborts.

Remark 5. For presentation simplicity, the above Type 3 pairing based implementation of IBHigncryption is described w.r.t. a pair of secret keys (sk_1, sk_2) for each user in the system. But from the protocol description, it is clear that: if a user only performs the role of sender (resp., receiver), it only needs a single secret key sk_1 (resp., sk_2).

References

1. 3GPP TS 33.180 v15.3.0 (2018–09), 3rd Generation Partnership Project: 3G Security; Security Architecture (3GPP TS 33.102 Version 15.0.0 Release 15)
2. 3GPP TS 33.180 v15.3.0 (2018–09), 3rd Generation Partnership Project; Technical Specification Group Services and System Aspects; Security of the mission critical service; (Release 15)
3. Voltage identity-based encryption-information encryption for email, files, documents and databases. https://www.voltage.com/technology/data-encryption/identity-based-encryption/
4. Arkko, J., Carrara, E., Lindholm, F., Naslund, M., Norrman, K.: Mikey: multimedia internet keying. RFC 3830, pp. 1–66 (2004)
5. Baek, J., Safavi-Naini, R., Susilo, W.: Efficient multi-receiver identity-based encryption and its application to broadcast encryption. In: Vaudenay, S. (ed.) PKC 2005. LNCS, vol. 3386, pp. 380–397. Springer, Heidelberg (2005). https://doi.org/10.1007/978-3-540-30580-4_26

6. Barbulescu, R.: A brief history of pairings. In: Duquesne, S., Petkova-Nikova, S. (eds.) WAIFI 2016. LNCS, vol. 10064, pp. 3–17. Springer, Cham (2016). https://doi.org/10.1007/978-3-319-55227-9_1

7. Barbulescu, R., Duquesne, S.: Updating key size estimations for pairings. J. Cryptol. **32**(4), 1298–1336 (2018). https://doi.org/10.1007/s00145-018-9280-5

8. Barreto, P.S.L.M., Libert, B., McCullagh, N., Quisquater, J.-J.: Efficient and provably-secure identity-based signatures and signcryption from bilinear maps. In: Roy, B. (ed.) ASIACRYPT 2005. LNCS, vol. 3788, pp. 515–532. Springer, Heidelberg (2005). https://doi.org/10.1007/11593447_28

9. Bellare, M., Namprempre, C.: Authenticated encryption: relations among notions and analysis of the generic composition paradigm. In: Okamoto, T. (ed.) ASIACRYPT 2000. LNCS, vol. 1976, pp. 531–545. Springer, Heidelberg (2000). https://doi.org/10.1007/3-540-44448-3_41

10. Bellare, M., Namprempre, C.: Authenticated encryption: relations among notions and analysis of the generic composition paradigm. J. Cryptol. **21**(4), 469–491 (2008). https://doi.org/10.1007/s00145-008-9026-x

11. Boneh, D., Boyen, X.: Efficient selective-id secure identity-based encryption without random oracles. In: Cachin, C., Camenisch, J.L. (eds.) EUROCRYPT 2004. LNCS, vol. 3027, pp. 223–238. Springer, Heidelberg (2004). https://doi.org/10.1007/978-3-540-24676-3_14

12. Boneh, D., Franklin, M.: Identity-based encryption from the weil pairing. In: Kilian, J. (ed.) CRYPTO 2001. LNCS, vol. 2139, pp. 213–229. Springer, Heidelberg (2001). https://doi.org/10.1007/3-540-44647-8_13

13. Boyd, C., Mathuria, A., Stebila, D.: Protocols for Authentication and Key Establishment. ISC. Springer, Heidelberg (2020). https://doi.org/10.1007/978-3-662-58146-9_9

14. Boyen, X.: Multipurpose identity-based signcryption. In: Boneh, D. (ed.) CRYPTO 2003. LNCS, vol. 2729, pp. 383–399. Springer, Heidelberg (2003). https://doi.org/10.1007/978-3-540-45146-4_23

15. Boyen, X., Martin, L.: Identity-based cryptography standard (IBCS) #1: Supersingular curve implementations of the BF and BB1 cryptosystems. RFC 5091, pp. 1–63 (2007)

16. Brzuska, C., Smart, N.P., Warinschi, B., Watson, G.J.: An analysis of the EMV channel establishment protocol. In: ACM CCS, pp. 373–386 (2013)

17. Chatterjee, S., Menezes, A.: On cryptographic protocols employing asymmetric pairings - the role of Ψ revisited. Discrete Appl. Math. **159**(13), 1311–1322 (2011)

18. Chen, L., Malone-Lee, J.: Improved identity-based signcryption. In: Vaudenay, S. (ed.) PKC 2005. LNCS, vol. 3386, pp. 362–379. Springer, Heidelberg (2005). https://doi.org/10.1007/978-3-540-30580-4_25

19. Coron, J.-S.: On the exact security of full domain hash. In: Bellare, M. (ed.) CRYPTO 2000. LNCS, vol. 1880, pp. 229–235. Springer, Heidelberg (2000). https://doi.org/10.1007/3-540-44598-6_14

20. De Ree, M., Mantas, G., Radwan, A., Mumtaz, S., Rodriguez, J., Otung, I.: Key management for beyond 5G mobile small cells: a survey. IEEE Access **7**, 59200–59236 (2019)

21. Debnath, S., Nunsanga, M.V.L., Bhuyan, B.: Study and scope of signcryption for cloud data access control. In: Biswas, U., Banerjee, A., Pal, S., Biswas, A., Sarkar, D., Haldar, S. (eds.) Advances in Computer, Communication and Control. LNNS, vol. 41, pp. 113–126. Springer, Singapore (2019). https://doi.org/10.1007/978-981-13-3122-0_12

22. Fujisaki, E., Okamoto, T.: Secure integration of asymmetric and symmetric encryption schemes. J. Cryptol. **26**(1), 80–101 (2013). https://doi.org/10.1007/s00145-011-9114-1
23. Galbraith, S.D., Paterson, K.G., Smart, N.P.: Pairings for cryptographers. Discrete Appl. Math. **156**(16), 3113–3121 (2008)
24. Gorantla, M.C., Boyd, C., González Nieto, J.M.: On the connection between signcryption and one-pass key establishment. In: Galbraith, S.D. (ed.) Cryptography and Coding 2007. LNCS, vol. 4887, pp. 277–301. Springer, Heidelberg (2007). https://doi.org/10.1007/978-3-540-77272-9_17
25. Groves, M.: Elliptic curve-based certificateless signatures for identity-based encryption (ECCSI). RFC 6507, pp. 1–17 (2012)
26. Groves, M.: MIKEY-SAKKE: sakai-kasahara key encryption in multimedia internet keying (MIKEY). RFC 6509, pp. 1–21 (2012)
27. Groves, M.: Sakai-kasahara key encryption (SAKKE). RFC 6508, pp. 1–21 (2012)
28. Halevi, S., Krawczyk, H.: One-pass HMQV and asymmetric key-wrapping. In: Catalano, D., Fazio, N., Gennaro, R., Nicolosi, A. (eds.) PKC 2011. LNCS, vol. 6571, pp. 317–334. Springer, Heidelberg (2011). https://doi.org/10.1007/978-3-642-19379-8_20
29. Karati, A., Islam., H, Biswas, G., Bhuiyan, M., Vijayakumar, P., Karuppiah, M: Provably secure identity-based signcryption scheme for crowdsourced industrial internet of things environments. IEEE Internet Things J. **5**(4), 2904–2914 (2018)
30. Khan, H., Dowling, B., Martin, K.M.: Identity confidentiality in 5G mobile telephony systems. IACR Cryptology ePrint Archive 2018, 876 (2018). https://eprint.iacr.org/2018/876
31. Krawczyk, H.: HMQV: a high-performance secure Diffie-Hellman protocol. In: Shoup, V. (ed.) CRYPTO 2005. LNCS, vol. 3621, pp. 546–566. Springer, Heidelberg (2005). https://doi.org/10.1007/11535218_33
32. Krawczyk, H., Paterson, K.G., Wee, H.: On the security of the TLS protocol: a systematic analysis. In: Canetti, R., Garay, J.A. (eds.) CRYPTO 2013. LNCS, vol. 8042, pp. 429–448. Springer, Heidelberg (2013). https://doi.org/10.1007/978-3-642-40041-4_24
33. Lair, Y., Mayer, G.: Mission critical services in 3GPP. IEEE Spectrum **6507**, 1–195 (2018)
34. Libert, B., Quisquater, J.: A new identity based signcryption scheme from pairings. In: IEEE Information Theory Workshop, pp. 155–158 (2003)
35. Libert, B., Quisquater, J.-J.: Identity based undeniable signatures. In: Okamoto, T. (ed.) CT-RSA 2004. LNCS, vol. 2964, pp. 112–125. Springer, Heidelberg (2004). https://doi.org/10.1007/978-3-540-24660-2_9
36. Lu, Z., Qu, G., Liu, Z.: A survey on recent advances in vehicular network security, trust, and privacy. IEEE Trans. Intell. Transp. Syst. **20**(2), 760–776 (2019)
37. Malone-Lee, J.: Identity-based signcryption. Public Key Cryptography - PKC 2002, pp. 362–379 (2002)
38. Paterson, K.G., Ristenpart, T., Shrimpton, T.: Tag size *does* matter: attacks and proofs for the TLS record protocol. In: Lee, D.H., Wang, X. (eds.) ASIACRYPT 2011. LNCS, vol. 7073, pp. 372–389. Springer, Heidelberg (2011). https://doi.org/10.1007/978-3-642-25385-0_20
39. Paterson, K.G., Srinivasan, S.: On the relations between non-interactive key distribution, identity-based encryption and trapdoor discrete log groups. Des. Codes Cryptogr. **52**(2), 219–241 (2009). https://doi.org/10.1007/s10623-009-9278-y
40. Raimondo, D., Gennaro, R., Krawczyk, H.: Deniable authentication and key exchange. ACM CCS, pp. 400–409 (2006)

41. Rescorla, E.: The Transport Layer Security (TLS) Protocol Version 1.3, RFC 8446 (2018)
42. Rogaway, P.: Authenticated-encryption with associated-data. In: Proceedings of the 9th ACM Conference on Computer and Communications Security, CCS 2002, pp. 98–107 (2002)
43. Roskind, J.: Quick UDP internet connections: Multiplexed stream transport over UDP. https://tools.ietf.org/html/draft-ietf-tls-tls-12 1(2), 77-94 (2012)
44. Sakai, R., Ohgishi, K., Kasahara, M.: Cryptosystem based on pairings. In: Symposium on Cryptography and Information Security (SCIS), pp. 26–28 (2000)
45. Shamir, A.: Identity-based cryptosystems and signature schemes. In: Advances in Cryptology, Proceedings of CRYPTO 1984, pp. 47–53 (1984)
46. Wei, G., Shao, J., Xiang, Y., Zhu, P., Lu, R.: Obtain confidentiality or/and authenticity in big data by ID-based generalized signcryption. Inf. Sci. **318**, 111–122 (2015)
47. Zhao, Y.: Identity-concealed authenticated encryption and key exchange. In: Proceedings of the 2016 ACM SIGSAC Conference on Computer and Communications Security, pp. 1464–1479 (2016)
48. Zheng, Yuliang: Digital signcryption or how to achieve cost(signature & encryption) cost(signature) + cost(encryption). In: Kaliski, Burton S. (ed.) CRYPTO 1997. LNCS, vol. 1294, pp. 165–179. Springer, Heidelberg (1997). https://doi.org/10.1007/BFb0052234

Securing DNSSEC Keys via Threshold ECDSA from Generic MPC

Anders Dalskov[1], Claudio Orlandi[1], Marcel Keller[2], Kris Shrishak[3(✉)], and Haya Shulman[4]

[1] Aarhus University, Aarhus, Denmark
[2] CSIRO's Data61, Sydney, Australia
[3] Technical University Darmstadt, Darmstadt, Germany
`kris.shrishak@sit.tu-darmstadt.de`
[4] Fraunhofer SIT, Darmstadt, Germany

Abstract. Deployment of DNSSEC, although increasing, still suffers from many practical issues that results in a false sense of security. While many domains outsource zone management, they also have to outsource DNSSEC key management to the DNS operator, making the operator an attractive target for attackers. Moreover, DNSSEC does not provide any sort of protection in the case the operator itself decides to serve false information, for example, if it gets compromised.

In this work, we show how to use techniques from threshold ECDSA: (1) to protect keys such that domains do not reveal their signing keys to a DNS operator, and (2) to protect the operational integrity of DNS operator. As a result of being highly specialized, prior work on threshold ECDSA has focused on a limited set of threat models, and none have so far considered techniques to amortize signature generation. Our work takes a different approach and presents a *generic* technique for obtaining a threshold ECDSA protocol from *any* secure multiparty computation protocol that works over an appropriate finite field. We show how this technique lends itself to very efficient threshold signing protocols by comparing it against state-of-the-art protocols from both academia and industry. For similar threat models, our protocols are as fast as the previous best protocol in terms of signing, and up to an order of magnitude faster for key generation on a fast network. Finally, we show how to integrate our application into a widely used DNS management software and demonstrate through experiments the overhead compared to traditional DNSSECs.

1 Introduction

The Domain Name System (DNS) [RFC1033, RFC1034], one of the core Internet protocols, performs lookup services and provides a platform for an increasing number of systems and applications. DNS was not designed with security in mind and is alarmingly vulnerable to DNS cache poisoning [2,6,9,22,23,36]. DNS Security extensions (DNSSEC) [RFC4033–RFC4035] was standardized to mitigate cache poisoning using cryptographic techniques. At a high level, DNSSEC

© Springer Nature Switzerland AG 2020
L. Chen et al. (Eds.): ESORICS 2020, LNCS 12309, pp. 654–673, 2020.
https://doi.org/10.1007/978-3-030-59013-0_32

enables certification of DNS records in a response such that the machine making the query can verify that it was not tampered with, assuming the DNS operator is trusted. A record is certified using a digital signature scheme, with RSA and ECDSA being the supported algorithms [RFC 5702, RFC 6605]. While RSA is the most commonly used scheme, the need to prevent fragmentation of UDP responses requires the signing keys to be short. ECDSA is the better choice moving forward as it provides the same level of security as RSA but with much smaller signatures. While DNSSEC prevents cache poisoning, this only holds insofar as the operator is trusted. Moreover, DNSSEC additionally requires the operator to manage cryptographic keys. Both these requirements manifest themselves as areas of insecurity in practice.

Centralization of Key Management. DNSSEC burdens the provider with the additional task of generating and managing the keys of their users. Recent work has demonstrated that a large number of domains share the same key [12]. Sharing the same key across multiple domains makes the DNSSEC provider a lucrative target. If the key of one domain is compromised, several *other* domains can be compromised as well. Another study [34] has shown issues with key generation that result in keys with inadequate security.

Centralization of Operation. A second issue that arises from the problem of the DNS operator being in-charge of key management is that the entire operation is centralized. In other words, any guarantee towards integrity of a DNS response to a query is lost if the operator cannot be trusted. This implies that DNSSEC does not prevent attacks from powerful adversaries on the operator, such as nation-state actors. In recent years, several examples of sophisticated attacks on DNS registrars have been observed in Germany [32], Greece [14] and Sweden [30] as part of attacks on DNS infrastructure [37].

1.1 Threshold Signing

Threshold signatures are a natural candidate to solve the issues outlined above. A threshold signature scheme distributes a signing key to n signers such that any subset of at least t signers can sign a message. Since the signing key is distributed among many signers, it will remain private as long as at least t servers remain uncompromised. Moreover, the threshold signing scheme can be made secure against tampering, i.e., a malicious operator cannot compromise the integrity of a response.

While threshold RSA has previously been studied for fault tolerance in DNSSEC, threshold ECDSA has not been used for DNSSEC in spite of an increased interest in threshold ECDSA in recent years [18,19,21,27,28]. All of these recent works motivate the problem of threshold ECDSA in the context of crypto-currencies, a problem that is substantially different from DNSSEC: First, recent work on threshold ECDSA focus on "full threshold", i.e., privacy of the signing key is maintained when up to $t = n - 1$ signers collaborate. Second, the focus has typically been on "malicious" security, i.e., signers are not assumed to behave according to the signing protocol. However, it is possible to design faster protocols by relaxing some of these security guarantees, e.g., by requiring an honest majority, or assuming that signers do not deviate from the signing protocol. The diverse context in which DNS is used can benefit from solutions that are not limited to a specific threat model.

In the real world application of DNSSEC where multiple operators (e.g., 3) serve a domain, the possibility of only one of them being controlled by an adversary is reasonable as operators are often corporations located in different parts of the world and adhere to different local laws. In such a setting, a "full threshold" protocol may not be necessary, and a protocol that assumes an honest-majority (i.e., with 3 servers this implies none of the servers collude) among the operators can be sufficient. Moreover, DNS operators are bound by legal contracts with their customers and they provide service according to this contract. These legal bounds allow us to consider operators that do not act maliciously since that would be a breach of contract. However, in such a case we will still be interested in protecting keys stored at the operator.

1.2   Contributions

A summary of our contributions:

- A generic transformation for secure multiparty computation (MPC) protocols over a field $\mathbb{Z}_p$ to protocols over an elliptic group of order p, such as one used in ECDSA.
- An implementation of this transformation in MP-SPDZ [17] to support threshold signing with ECDSA in many different threat models. We benchmark each instantiation against state-of-the-art protocols for threshold signing and show that they perform comparably.
- A measurement study to understand the extent to which multiple providers for a given domain is used on the Internet.
- A prototype of a full implementation, based on our implementation in MP-SPDZ and Knot, as well as experiments showing that threshold signing incurs only a minimal overhead.

1.3   Outline

Section 2 presents a measurement study we performed. We show that a significant number of domains use multiple operators, which allows them to easily use our solution. Section 3 outlines our system and threat model. Section 4 presents our technical contribution as well as our threshold signing protocol. Section 5 shows how we integrate our signing protocol into a well-known DNSSEC application. Section 6 presents a number of different experiments and comparisons to prior work. Section 7 discusses how our work relates to prior works before the conclusion is presented in Sect. 8.

2   Quantifying Multiple Operators

Since the large DDoS attacks on Dyn [20] and NS1 [5] in 2016, many domains are using more than one operator to increase the redundancy of the zone so that they do not fall victim to another DDoS attack. However, no recent work has measured the number of domains that make use of multiple operators. As we propose to use our multiparty ECDSA protocol for DNSSEC zone signing, we measure the extent to which multiple operators are used on the Internet. We consider a domain to have more than one operator if the DNS name servers of the same domain are hosted by an entirely different DNS operator.

2.1   Data Collection Methodology

If a domain name is configured to be served by three DNS name servers, we check whether it is managed by the same operator. For our purpose, we are interested in nameservers run by different operators and not necessarily name servers placed at different locations. For instance, some domains might use two operators who are geographically located in close proximity to each other; sometimes, even in the same data centre. We are interested in the setting with different operators as they do not trust each other with signing keys and they do not have a business relationship with each other that will allow them to pass on copies of signing keys. Hence, being geographically close does not eliminate the need to run a secure signing protocol. Some domains make use of a single operator which has name servers at different locations. In principle, a multiparty ECDSA protocols can be used in this setting as well because it provides better security than simply storing a copy of the signing key on each name server.

Our measurements were conducted using the Alexa Global Top 1 million list[1] as the dataset. The list was downloaded on 12 July 2019. We ran scans on the same date on all the domains in the dataset and requested its NS records. For each NS record we also obtain the first associated A record. On obtaining the NS record, we have the list of authoritative name servers. We compare the sub-domains of *country code TLDs* (ccTLDs), *country code second-level domains* (ccSLDs) and *generic TLDs* (gTLDs). E.g., if the two name servers of a domain are dns1.p09.nsone.net. and ns1.p43.dynect.net., then we compare nsone and dynect. However, we do not only compare the SLD names. For instance, if there is a third name server for the same domain at pdns6.ultradns.co.uk., then we compare ultradns with nsone and dynect.

To measure how many domains use multiple operators, we need to know the owners of the authoritative name servers. Though it is possible to obtain this information from the WHOIS database using the A records we collected, the information obtained does not have a consistent schema and is heavily rate limited [29]. Hence, we use the WHOIS database to only check information for Alexa Top-1k; for the rest of Alexa Top 1 million, we take an approach similar to [12] and rely on the NS records to indicate the DNS operator. We made manual

---

[1] https://www.alexa.com/topsites.

checks to make sure that subsidiaries of large corporations are not classified as separate operators. (For instance, Chinese online shopping website taobao.com is a subsidiary of the Alibaba group, and we found that one of their name servers is owned by Alibaba and hence, we classified them as the same operator.) Note that large organizations such as Facebook and Google run dedicated networks which provides DNS redundancy. However, as it is run by the same organization, we do not account for them in our list of domains with multiple operators.

2.2 Data Analysis

We classified domains as having a single operator (Only 1), multiple operators (More than 1), no response (NR) and misconfigured (Misconf). An NR classification refers to the case where, during our scans, we did not receive a response with the name server list within a 15-s timeout. Misconf refers to zones which are misconfigured due to mistakes and/or typos. More precisely, we first observed whether we received an A record for the NS record. If we instead receive an error, we then checked the NS record for completeness. If, during this check, we encouter mistakes or typos, the domain is marked as misconfigured. E.g., just ds0. was configured as one of the authoritative name servers for the domain oxfordlearnersdictionaries.com. See Fig. 1 for the result of classifying the Alexa

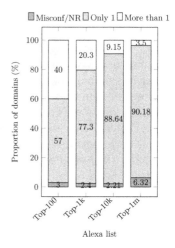

Fig. 1. Domains with multiple operators

Global Top 1 million, as well as its subsets, in this manner.

We did not receive a response to our queries from 3, 24, 208, 60775 domains in the Top-100, Top-1k, Top-10k and Top-1m respectively. Although we did not find any misconfigured domains in the Top-1k, we found 13 misconfigured domains in the Top-10k and 2483 domains in Top-1m. We observe that 40% of the domains in Alexa Top-100 have more than one operator while the proportion reduces as we move down the Top-1m list. 20.3%, 9.2% and 3.5% of the domains in the Top-1k, Top-10k and Top-1m have more than one operator for their domain. Hence, we conclude from our measurements that there are thousands of domains that use multiple operators and that can easily plug-in our threshold ECDSA protocols.

3 System and Threat Model

The diversity of the DNS ecosystem should be reflected in our system and threat model. For the system model, we assume a small number of operators that serve a single domain. As seen in the previous section, this setting is common in practice, in particular among popular domains. For the threat models, we take the two issues outlined in the introduction as our starting point. Before we continue, we describe the security properties that we address with our threat model:

1. **Key Privacy.** This is our baseline. *Key privacy* states that signing key remains private in the event that a server is compromised. We note that this property is relevant in a number of different contexts. For example, this property states that a signing key isn't exposed to a system administrator, or to anyone who obtains a decommissioned (but improperly cleaned) server.

2. **Operational Integrity.** Besides keeping keys secret, we may also want to uphold the *integrity* of operation. By operational integrity, we mean that only two situations can occur: Either operation proceeds as normal, that is, the right zone is signed, *or* nothing is signed. In other words, at best, a malicious operator can only disrupt operation, i.e., it performs a denial of service attack but it cannot sign zones with bogus information. Notice that key privacy is subsumed in operational integrity. If it is possible to extract the signing key, then no guarantee about the integrity can be made since a single operator can sign any zone it manages at will.

3.1 System and Communication Model

Intuitively, our system model can be viewed as distributing the task of a single operator among multiple operators. To simplify things, we assume that such a system has either $n = 2$ or $n = 3$ operators who maintain a fixed set of domains. These operators can be distributed in a single location, communicating over a LAN, or they can be distributed globally. Finally, we assume that the servers are sufficiently separated, that is, a compromise of one server does not automatically lead to a compromise of another server.

3.2 Threat Model

We consider an adversary that is capable of compromising a single server. Thus, when $n = 2$, the adversary controls half the servers, and when $n = 3$, the adversary controls a minority (since 2 servers remain honest). We distinguish between the two standard adversarial models from the MPC literature. The first type of adversary, called *passive*, is characterized by following the prescribed protocol. The second adversary, called *active*, may behave arbitrarily and not follow the protocol. Notice how these two adversarial types capture our security properties. If we only desire key privacy, then security against a passive adversary suffices. If we want operational integrity as well, then we must also secure ourselves against active adversaries. Indeed, it is exactly against such an adversary that the integrity of operation becomes an issue.

4 Threshold ECDSA

In this section we present a *generic* transformation of any secure computation protocol over a field $\mathbb{Z}_p$ into a protocol for a group of order p. In particular, this technique enables an efficient method to compute threshold ECDSA signatures.

Arithmetic black-box

- A command $([a], [b], [c]) \leftarrow \mathsf{RandMul}()$ that generates appropriate representations of a random tuple of secret shared values $a, b, c \in \mathbb{Z}_p$ with $c = ab$.
- A command $[c] \leftarrow \mathsf{Mul}([a], [b])$ that returns $c = ab$ (This is typically implemented using one invocation of $\mathsf{RandMul}$ and Beaver's re-randomization technique [4]).
- A command $[a] \leftarrow \mathsf{Rand}()$ that generates appropriate representation of a random value $a \in \mathbb{Z}_p$.
- A command $a \leftarrow \mathsf{Open}([a])$ that publicly reconstructs a (or outputs a special symbol $\perp$ denoting abort).
- Linear computation for the $[\cdot]$ representation: given the shares $[a]$, $[b]$ and public scalars $x, y \in \mathbb{Z}_p$, the parties can compute $[c] = x \cdot [a] + y \cdot [b]$ "for free", i.e., the computation does not involve communicating with the other parties.

Fig. 2. The arithmetic black-box functionality.

4.1   ECDSA Signing

ECDSA as standardized in [25] is parametrized by a curve $E(K)$ for a field K. Let $\mathcal{G} \subseteq E(K)$ be an additive subgroup group of order p with generator G, and let $\mathbb{Z}_p$ denote the field of size p. Given a message M, secret key $\mathsf{sk} \in \mathbb{Z}_p$, signing is performed as follows:

1. Sample $k \leftarrow \mathbb{Z}_p$ at random.
2. Compute $(r_x, r_y) = k \cdot G$.
3. Let $s = k^{-1}(H(M) + \mathsf{sk} \cdot r_x)$ where H is a hash function mapping messages into elements of $\mathbb{Z}_p$.
4. Output signature $\sigma = (r_x, s)$.

4.2   Secure Multiparty Computation

We assume a MPC engine supporting the standard commands of the *arithmetic black-box (ABB)* functionality as shown in Fig. 2, where the notation $[a]$ indicates that the value a is "secret-shared", i.e., no party has access to it. The security model of a MPC protocol is parametrized by two variables. First, whether the adversary can control at least half, or less than half the parties. The former is called dishonest majority, while the latter is called honest majority. Observe that an honest majority protocol would correspond a setting with $n = 3$ servers, while a dishonest majority protocol means $n = 2$. The second parameter is the corruption model: The two cases considered here—active and passive—correspond to our description in Sect. 3.2.

4.3   Secure Computation on Groups

We present an extension to the ABB that extends its capabilities to secure computation over an arbitrary Abelian group of order p. In some sense, this shows that the actual representation of the algebraic structure used to perform MPC is irrelevant as long as it is possible to perform linear operations. This generalization of arithmetic MPC has also been described independently by [35], and might have applications in other contexts. In this paper, we use this idea to perform MPC in subgroup $\mathcal{G}$. This extension comes at no extra cost in terms of communication and a small increase in computation complexity (corresponding to standard operations in the subgroup of the curve).

Consider a protocol implementing the ABB in Fig. 2 and assume that the shares $[a]$ are also elements of $\mathbb{Z}_p$. The idea is to let each party map their share of $[a]$ to a curve point of order p by locally computing $A_i = a_i \cdot G$, where a_i is party i's share of a. This mapping, being a homomorphism, preserves linearity and so A_i is a share of $a \cdot G$ with the same properties as the original $\mathbb{Z}_p$ sharing $[a]$. In the following, we write $\langle a \rangle$ to denote a share of $a \cdot G$, and we add the following two commands to the ABB in Fig. 2:

- A command $\langle a \rangle \leftarrow \mathsf{Convert}([a])$ that converts a representation of the shared value a in $\mathbb{Z}_p$ to a representation of the value $a \cdot G$ in the group $\mathcal{G}$.
- A command $a \cdot G \leftarrow \mathsf{Open}(\langle a \rangle)$ that recovers the secret shared point.

These two commands are sufficient to give us a protocol for secure computation over the group $\mathcal{G}$. If we consider the sharing $[a]$ as a vector with elements from $\mathbb{Z}_p$, we get the following useful properties:

- Linearity is preserved, i.e., given the shares $\langle a \rangle$, $\langle b \rangle$ and scalars $x, y \in \mathbb{Z}_p$, we can locally compute $\langle c \rangle = x\langle a \rangle + y\langle b \rangle$.
- If the Open procedure for $[\cdot]$ shares relies only on group operations in $\mathbb{Z}_p$, then we can implement Open for $\langle \cdot \rangle$ shares by using the corresponding group operations of $\mathcal{G}$. This property follows from the fact that $\mathsf{Convert}$ is structure preserving.
- Secret scalar multiplication by public point is possible by noting that $\mathsf{Convert}$ defines an action of $\mathbb{Z}_p$ on $\mathcal{G}$, i.e., $[a] \cdot P$ for a $P \in \mathcal{G}$ is a local operation that results in $\langle a \cdot \log_P(G) \rangle$. Note that opening this share will result in $a \cdot P$.
- Finally, given $[x]$ and $\langle y \rangle$ (and a multiplication tuple $[a], [b], [c]$) it is possible to compute $\langle xy \rangle$ using a slight tweak on Beaver's technique as follows: (1) $e = \mathsf{Open}([a]+[x])$, (2) $D = \mathsf{Open}(\mathsf{Convert}([b])+\langle y \rangle)$, (3) $\langle xy \rangle = \mathsf{Convert}([c])+ e\langle y \rangle + [x]D - eD$. Note that this property is not required for our application but could be of independent interest.

The properties of $\mathsf{Convert}$ and Open, as well as the functionality of the underlying ABB (which provide secure computation over $\mathbb{Z}_p$) is enough to give us a protocol for secure computation over $\mathcal{G}$. This extended ABB (which we will call ABB+) is shown in Fig. 3.

4.4 Active Security Using SPDZ Like MACs

The previous section showed that one can easily extend a protocol of $\mathbb{Z}_p$ with functionality for secure computation over a subgroup of $\mathcal{G} \subseteq E(K)$ of order p.

Extended Arithmetic black-box (ABB+)

- RandMul, Mul($[\cdot], [\cdot]$), Rand, Open($[\cdot]$) as described in Figure 2.
- A command $\langle a \rangle \leftarrow$ Convert($[a]$) that converts a representation of a secret $[a]$ over the field $\mathbb{Z}_p$ into a representation of the secret $\langle a \rangle$ over the group $\mathcal{G}$.
- A command $a \cdot G \leftarrow$ Open($\langle a \rangle$) that reconstructs a curve point $a \cdot G$ from a secret representation $\langle a \rangle$.

Fig. 3. ABB from Fig. 2 extended to support computation over elliptic curves.

A natural question to ask is whether the active security guarantees of the $\mathbb{Z}_p$ protocol extend to the $\mathcal{G}$ protocol. We answer this question in the affirmative by showing that the MAC scheme of SPDZ [16] can be used to provide authentication of shares in $\mathcal{G}$ (i.e., $\langle \cdot \rangle$ shares) as well.

SPDZ Recap. We recall the SPDZ protocol and its security using the description from [15]. In SPDZ a value $a \in \mathbb{Z}_p$ is shared as

$$[a] = ((a_1, \ldots, a_N), (\gamma(a)_i, \ldots, \gamma(a)_N)),$$

where party i holds the pair $(a_i, \gamma(a)_i)$, and where $a = \sum_i a_i$ and $\alpha \cdot a = \gamma(a) = \sum_i \gamma(a)_i$. The value $\alpha \in \mathbb{Z}_p$ is a global MAC key which is secret shared using a different scheme, $[\![\alpha]\!]$. (The details of this are not important for the following discussion; it suffices to say that each party has a share α_i, such that $\sum_i \alpha_i = \alpha$, as well as other information to make this sharing secure) The global MAC key is unknown to all parties and provide a notion of authentication of the shares.

We recap here the opening phase of the SPDZ protocol for a single value, i.e., the part where the parties check if the output was computed correctly[2]:

1. Each P_i has input α_i, their share of the global MAC key, and $\gamma(a)_i$, their share of the MAC on a partially opened value a[3].
2. Each P_i computes $\sigma_i = \gamma_i(a) - \alpha_i a$ and broadcasts a commitment com(σ_i).
3. All parties open com(σ_i), compute chk $= \sum_i \sigma_i$ and abort if chk $\neq 0$.

Suppose $a' = a + \epsilon$, i.e., the adversary adds an error $\epsilon \neq 0$ during the partial opening. If, in addition, the adversary lies about its MAC in Step 2 of SPDZ opening phase and let Δ denote this error, then the adversary is successful if $\Delta = \sum_i \sigma_i$. In this case, we have

$$\Delta = \sum_{i=1}^{n} \sigma_i = \sum_{i=1}^{n} \gamma_i(a) - \alpha_i a = \alpha \epsilon.$$

---

[2] Note that several openings can be batched at the same time, see the original paper [15] for more details.

[3] A partial opening reveals the value but not the MAC.

Since $\epsilon = (a - a') \neq 0$, then $\alpha = \Delta\epsilon^{-1}$ which happens with probability at most $1/p$ due to the random choice of α.

SPDZ-Like Computation Over an Elliptic Curve. In the remainder of this section, we will use the shorthand notation $cv(a) = Convert(a)$ interchangeably for convenience. Consider the most natural modification possible to obtain a notion of a SPDZ-sharing $\langle \cdot \rangle$ over $\mathcal{G}$, from a SPDZ-sharing $[\cdot]$ over $\mathbb{Z}_p$, by applying cv to all local shares. We define $\langle a \rangle$ as the vector

$$\langle a \rangle = ((cv(a_i), \ldots, cv(a_N)), (cv(\gamma(a)_i), \ldots, cv(\gamma(a)_N))),$$

where P_i holds $(cv(a_1), cv(\gamma(a)_i))$. Observe that the linearity of cv implies that $\sum_i(cv(a_i)) = cv(\sum_i a_i) = cv(a)$, which makes the above a valid sharing of $cv(a)$. In addition, the semantics of the MAC is preserved since

$$\sum_i cv(\gamma(a)_i) = cv(\sum_i \gamma(a)_i) = cv(\alpha \cdot a).$$

Therefore, we can use the same $[\![\alpha]\!]$ to authenticate the Converted share as well. More precisely, we consider a modified opening procedure that works as follows:[4]

1. Let α_i be the share of the key held by P_i, and $\Gamma_i = cv(\gamma(a)_i)$ be the shares of the MAC on $A = cv(a)$.
2. Each P_i computes $\Sigma_i = \Gamma_i - \alpha_i A$ and broadcasts a commitment $com(\Sigma_i)$.
3. Open $com(\Sigma_i)$, compute $chk = \Sigma_1 + \cdots + \Sigma_N$ and abort if $chk \neq 0$.

It follows that, due to the linearity of the group operations, if the adversary opens $A' \neq A$, then the check only passes with probability $1/p$. In a nutshell, we are taking a secure linear MAC procedure, and raising all the MACs and values in the exponent. Since the SPDZ MACs are information theoretic secure, the security of the "MAC in the exponent" can be reduced to the security of the regular MAC (as the reduction can run in unbounded time and retrieve the original MAC).

4.5 Multiparty ECDSA Protocol Using the ABB+

We recall the protocol of Gennaro and Goldfeder [21] and show that it can be computed by our extended arithmetic black box functionality. The main issue with computing ECDSA signatures securely is calculating k^{-1} such that it does not reveal information about k. However, the inversion trick by Bar-Ilan and Beaver [3] can be used here: Suppose each party has a share of two random values γ, k, and their product, i.e., $[\gamma]$, $[k]$, $[\delta]$ where $\delta = \gamma \cdot k$. The parties can then open δ and use it locally to compute their share of $[k^{-1}] = \delta^{-1}[\gamma]$. Thus the price to pay for the inversion (which is the most expensive part of every threshold ECDSA protocol) is essentially just generating a random multiplication triple

---

[4] Once again, the procedure is described for a single value, but it can be extended to support batched opening.

Threshold ECDSA in the ABB+ Hybrid Model

Key Generation. To generate a key for user U_j, either U_j supplies the sharing $[\mathsf{sk}_j]$, or the servers run $[\mathsf{sk}_j] \leftarrow \mathsf{Rand}()$. The public key is computed as $\mathsf{pk}_j = \mathsf{Open}(\mathsf{Convert}([\mathsf{sk}_j]))$.

User independent preprocessing. The goal is to generate a pair $(\langle k \rangle, [k^{-1}])$ for each signature in the following way.

1. The servers run $([a], [b], [c]) \leftarrow \mathsf{RandMul}()$.
2. Run $c \leftarrow \mathsf{Open}([c])$.
3. Let $[k^{-1}] = [a]$.
4. Define $\langle k \rangle \leftarrow \mathsf{Convert}([b]) \cdot c^{-1}$
5. Output $(\langle k \rangle, [k^{-1}])$.

User dependent preprocessing.

1. Take as input $[\mathsf{sk}_j]$ (the sharing of the secret key of user U_j) and $(\langle k \rangle, [k^{-1}])$ (an unused tuple from the previous phase).
2. Compute $[\mathsf{sk}'_j] = [\mathsf{sk}_j/k] \leftarrow \mathsf{Mul}([k^{-1}], [\mathsf{sk}_j])$
3. Output a final tuple $(\langle k \rangle, [k^{-1}], [\mathsf{sk}'_j])$.

Given a message to be signed M and preprocessed tuple $(\langle k \rangle, [k^{-1}], [\mathsf{sk}'_j])$ for U_j.

1. Run $R \leftarrow \mathsf{Open}(\langle k \rangle) = (bc^{-1}) \cdot G = a^{-1} \cdot G = k \cdot G$
2. Let $(r_x, r_y) \leftarrow R$.
3. Compute $[s] = H(M) \cdot [k^{-1}] + r_x \cdot [\mathsf{sk}'_j]$.
4. Open $s \leftarrow \mathsf{Open}([s])$ and output $\sigma = (r_x, s)$.

Fig. 4. Protocol with preprocessing computing threshold ECDSA signatures using our extended ABB.

using $\mathsf{RandMul}$, and using $\mathsf{Convert}$ to compute the value $R = \mathsf{Open}(\mathsf{Convert}([k]))$. The other value we need is a sharing of sk/k. Given $[k^{-1}]$ it is possible to compute $[\mathsf{sk}/k]$ very efficiently by performing a single secure multiplication.

The full protocol using the ABB+ now follows: We consider a setting with a number of servers $\mathcal{S} = \{S_1, \ldots, S_N\}$ and a number of users $\mathcal{U} = \{U_1, \ldots, U_\ell\}$. Our protocol has 4 phases: Key generation in which a random secret key is generated using $[\mathsf{sk}] = \mathsf{Rand}()$, and then converted into the public key by running $\mathsf{pk} = \mathsf{Open}(\mathsf{Convert}([\mathsf{sk}]))$. (Alternatively, users can pick their own keys and input them to the servers in $\mathcal{S}$). Next up are two preprocessing phases: One phase is independent of the users and the messages to be signed, and serves to generate the values $[k^{-1}]$ and $\langle k \rangle$ that are required for generating any signature; the other phase depends on the user and computes $[\mathsf{sk}_j/k]$, where sk_j is the signing key of user U_j. Finally, generating a signature using the output of the preprocessing and the user's signing key is just a matter of performing a linear computation followed by an opening. We show the details of the full protocol in Fig. 4.

Security Analysis. Security of the protocol in Fig. 4 follows directly from the security of the underlying ABB scheme, and from an assumption that ECDSA is a secure signature scheme (this assumption has also been used in [18] and [19]).

5 Multiparty Zone Signing System

In this section, we describe the integration of our threshold ECDSA implementation in a DNS name server before describing the important operations. We implement several variants of our threshold ECDSA protocol on top of MP-SPDZ [17] and have used Crypto++ as the library for computation over elliptic curves. We integrate MP-SPDZ with DNS administrative name servers. For DNS name server software, we use Knot DNS [26] as it has the possibility to perform automated key management and it comes with extensive documentation. For the setting where the registrar is the DNS operator, we propose that registrars interact with other registrars in the zone signing protocol. We describe the multi-operator setting in this section and, where necessary, we note the difference if the operators are also the registrar.

5.1 Setup

In our DNSSEC signing system, each operator serves a name server, runs a threshold ECDSA module and has two key stores: one to store the keys for particular zones and another to store the key material associated with other operators. We consider three name servers operated by independent DNS operators, all of which support ECDSA with SHA256 message digest. We do not change the operation of Knot DNS apart from the parts involved in DNSSEC key generation, key rollover and zone signing. Communication between the name server and the threshold ECDSA module is performed using a message queue.

5.2 Key Generation/Rollover

In the key generation/rollover phase, when new keys need to be generated, each operator generates a signing key sharing $[\mathsf{sk}_j]$ for the zone and runs the key generation as shown in Fig. 4. At the end of this phase, the public key is added to DNSKEY record of the zone at all the operators and the signing key share $[\mathsf{sk}_j]$ is stored in the keystore for the zones. In addition, a tag that indicates the DNS operators associated with this signing key share is stored. E.g., Operator A would store a tag $T(B, C)$ along with the key shares associated with Operator B and Operator C. This makes it easy for the threshold ECDSA module to contact the corresponding DNS operators during the signature generation phase. Note that the key generation for ZSK and KSK is the same except that in the case of KSK, the domain owner generates the DS record and sends it to the registrar, who then submits it to the registry. When the registrar is one of the DNS operators of the zone, then the registrar can directly submit the DS record.

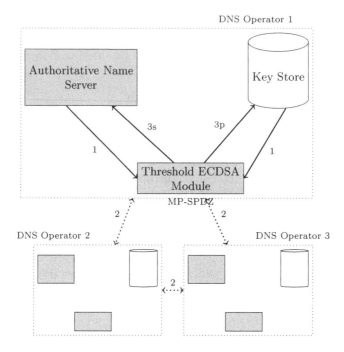

Fig. 5. Zone signing

5.3   Zone Signing

As shown in Fig. 4, our signing protocol has three phases: the first is independent of the zone to be signed, while the second is independent of the RRset, but dependent on the zone to be signed. Each of the three phases involve three steps that are shown in Fig. 5. In Step 1, the threshold ECDSA module receives the input for the phase from the name server and the tag from the key store. In Step 2, the MPC protocol for the phase is run between the threshold ECDSA module of the three operators. In Step 3, the output of the preprocessing phases are sent to the key store (Step 3p) while the output of the signing phase, RRSIG, is sent to the name server to store in the zone file (Step 3s). We note that the threshold ECDSA module runs in the background and periodically polls the name server so that it is always available to sign.

Implication for DNS Operators. In our system, the DNS operators do not need to be online any more than they already are in existing systems. DNS operators in existing systems remain online to respond to DNS queries. Many DNS operators sign DNS responses on-the-fly and, hence, they are already equipped with signing systems that are online. In our system they will not only respond to DNS queries, they will also run MPC with other registrar/operators to create RRSIG. Our threshold ECDSA protocols have an overhead—both in terms of communication and computation—that depends on the concrete threat and system model. We discuss the overheads as part of our benchmarks in Sect. 6.

It is also worth noting that the operators need not rely on secure hardware to store their user's keys anymore, which may bring down both the cost and complexity for a DNS operator.

Implication for DNS Resolvers. Proper functioning of the DNSSEC ecosystem requires both the signing and the validation to work. Deploying changes at DNS resolvers is extremely hard as numerous resolver software need to be changed. Fortunately, no change is required at the validating resolver to use our solution. Every time the domain is queried at the authoritative name server, the signatures for the zone need to be verified at the resolvers for the chain of trust to be established. Though three operators are involved in the signing process, the signature can be verified with the same DNSKEY, irrespective of the operator which initiated the signing process. If the DNS resolver obtains the DNSKEY records from Operator A and stores it in the cache, then it will be able to authenticate a response from Operator B for the same domain, as the two operators have the same DNSKEY for the zone. The resolver will be able to verify the chain of trust irrespective of the operator responded to the query.

6   Evaluation

In this section we report on several benchmarks of our protocol and compare with prior work of both signature generation and key generation times. We implement six varieties of our protocol (thus supporting different system and threat models) in MP-SDPZ [17]. For $n = 3$ we have *Rep3*, *Shamir* (passive security) and *Mal. Rep3* and *Mal. Shamir* (active security). We remark that only the Shamir protocols support $n > 3$. For $n = 2$, we use *MASCOT* and *MASCOT-* (MASCOT minus) where the latter is a heuristic optimization of the former. Many of these protocols have asymmetric communication patterns and thus we report the maximum execution time, instead of the average. All experiments were run on AWS c5.2xlarge instances in three settings: LAN, continental WAN and worldwide WAN. The maximum RTT between any two servers in these settings are 0.08 ms, 17 ms and 240 ms, respectively.

6.1   MASCOT- Optimizations

Our MASCOT- protocol is obtained by making a number of function specific optimizations to MASCOT [24]. Threshold signatures are a special case of MPC where the correctness of the output can trivially be determined by observing the output itself (by verifying the signature). This is a well known trick which has previously been used to optimize many threshold ECDSA protocols in the literature. We can similarly optimize our protocol by using an "optimistic" version of the Open command when running Step 3 of the *Signing* subroutine in Fig. 4.

SPDZ Opening. We save a round of communication during opening as we do not need to check correctness of the MACs. Omitting this attack permits the adversary to make an additive attack, which may result in an invalid signature, but does not leak anything about the secret key.

Beaver Multiplication. Suppose the adversary can perform an additive attack during multiplication. That is, $x + a + \epsilon_1$ and $y + b + \epsilon_2$ for independent ϵ_1 and ϵ_2. A multiplication becomes

$$(x+a+\epsilon_1)\cdot(y+b+\epsilon_2) - (x+a+\epsilon_1)\cdot b - (y+b+\epsilon_2)\cdot a + ab = xy + \epsilon_1 y + \epsilon_2 x + \epsilon_1\epsilon_2.$$

This permits a selective failure attack (e.g., $\epsilon_2 = 0$, $\epsilon_1 \neq 0$ then the multiplication is correct if and only if $y = 0$). However, multiplications are only used on k^{-1} and sk, both of which are of high entropy.

6.2   Comparison with Prior Work

We present a comparison of our protocols with two industry protocols from Unbound [38] and KZen [31], as well as the two-party protocol of Doerner et al. [18] (DKLS) in Table 1. The numbers reported for our protocols correspond to running all three phases in Fig. 4. We see that MASCOT– performs as well as the fastest prior protocol in DKLS, with the same security guarantees, in the LAN setting. However, with more servers, some of our protocols perform better in the LAN setting. In our two WAN settings, DKLS outperforms our protocols, a fact we attribute to the fact that DKLS requires only 2 messages (1 round of communication) whereas our fastest protocol (Rep3) requires 3. Interestingly, the simplicity of our key generation protocol is very apparent, and in all cases (except MASCOT–) key generation is faster than signing.

6.3   Key Generation

We also benchmark the key generation phase as that is typically the more expensive phase in prior works (e.g., [21,28]). With our approach, generating a shared key amounts to running any protocol for generating a secret shared field element [sk], followed by opening the result of Convert[sk]. Timings for key generation is shown in Table 2. For our honest majority protocol ($n = 3$) generating a secret key requires only 1 or 2 rounds of communication. MASCOT and MASCOT– is slightly different in that the opening procedure is more costly. Finally, notice that MASCOT– and MASCOT perform the same. Indeed, the heuristics used to obtain MASCOT– cannot be used when generating keys.

6.4   Amortizing Signing

Finally, we analyze the cost of signing when amortization is applied, something that no prior work has considered.[5] Table 3 shows how many signing tuples

---

[5] Although it might be possible to split some of the protocols in previous work into a preprocessing and signing phase, such a split has not been implemented and, hence, we cannot compare with it.

Table 1. Comparison with prior work. Numbers for our protocols are obtained by taking the mean over the maximum execution time over many runs.

	n	Colocation		Continent		World	
		Sig (ms)	KGen (ms)	Sig (ms)	KGen (ms)	Sig (ms)	KGen (ms)
Rep3	3	2.78	1.45	27.22	29.44	367.87	291.32
Shamir	3	3.02	1.39	78.75	35.52	1140.09	486.82
Mal. Rep3	3	3.45	1.57	82.14	39.97	1128.01	429.47
Mal. Shamir	3	4.43	1.89	174.95	37.35	2340.53	485.11
MASCOT	2	6.56	4.32	196.19	185.71	2688.92	2632.07
MASCOT–	2	3.61	4.41	54.38	181.12	729.08	2654.59
DKLS [18]	2	3.58	43.73	15.33	109.80	234.37	1002.97
Unbound [38]	2	11.33	315.96	31.08	424.02	490.73	1010.98
Kzen [31]	2	310.71	153.87	1282.81	577.67	14441.83	7237.93

Table 2. Breakdown of key generation benchmarks into the time it takes to generate the [sk] sharing, and the time it takes to run Open(Convert([sk])). Times are the maximum time that each step takes.

	Colocation		Continent		World	
	Secret (ms)	Public (ms)	Secret (ms)	Public (ms)	Secret (ms)	Public (ms)
Rep3	0.16	1.27	11.12	18.31	113.86	174.03
Shamir	0.25	1.13	17.17	18.09	243.00	243.82
Mal. Rep3	0.16	1.40	11.00	28.98	115.25	301.66
Mal. Shamir	0.25	1.62	16.90	18.32	241.78	243.18
MASCOT	2.34	1.91	149.26	33.01	2142.31	442.75
MASCOT–	2.40	1.92	145.48	33.21	2132.75	449.43

each protocol can generate per second. The signing times reported in this table correspond to computing a signature when amortization is taken into account. A signing tuple corresponds to the output of the *user dependent preprocessing* phase in Fig. 4. We note that, for almost all protocols, amortized signing corresponds essentially to a single round of communication.

6.5 Overhead for Operators

The storage overhead can be derived from the sizes of a share for a given protocol. For Mal. Rep3, MASCOT and Rep3 each share consists of two $\mathbb{Z}_p$ elements, while for the rest a share is a single element. Thus, for the former three the overhead for storing the signing keys is doubled. A signing tuple consists of two $\mathbb{Z}_p$ shares and one $\mathcal{G}$ share. For example, Rep3 needs to store roughly $2 \cdot 4 \cdot 32$ bytes per signature, assuming a 256-bit prime. Communication per party is between 177 and 354 bytes, depending on the protocol (this number was derived at experimentally).

Table 3. Throughput in signing tuples per second as well as signing time when amortization is taken into account.

	Colocation		Continent		World	
	Tuples per sec.	Sig (ms)	Tuples per sec.	Sig (ms)	Tuples per sec.	Sig (ms)
Rep3	922.27	2.49	898.25	19.91	715.54	247.13
Shamir	1829.69	2.37	1544.31	20.62	402.88	271.80
Mal. Rep3	914.65	2.52	806.13	20.07	309.76	245.14
Mal. Shamir	1792.30	2.91	1154.30	27.03	172.87	416.60
MASCOT	380.19	4.82	233.73	57.02	31.98	756.34
MASCOT−	700.94	2.75	447.85	20.37	68.31	258.85

7   Related Works

DNSSEC Deployment and Measurement. DNSSEC deployment heavily relies on DNS operators and registrars. Prior works have found issues such as reuse of signing keys by DNS operators for multiple domains[6] [12] and sharing of RSA modulus among multiple domains [34]. After the DDoS attacks of 2016, the impact of the attacks and the number of customers of DyN and NS1 that added another operator was measured [1]. However, only the domains that use DyN and NS1 were measured while we measure the use of multiple operators, not restricting our measurements to managed DNS providers.

Privacy in DNS. Though DNSSEC provides data integrity, it does not provide confidentiality. "Range queries" [39] and private information retrieval [40] have been proposed as a solution to hide queries. Recently, the Internet Engineering Task Force (IETF) has considered privacy issues in DNS and DNSSEC [7,8] and proposed DNS-over-TLS [RFC8310] and DNS-over-HTTPS [RFC8484]. While privacy of DNS queries has been considered, we address the issue of privacy of DNSSEC keys.

Threshold ECDSA. Protocols for computing ECDSA signatures in a threshold manner has seen a resurgence lately due to their relevance to crypto-currencies. Doerner et al. have developed threshold ECDSA protocols for both 2-parties [18] and multiple parties [19]. Another recent protocol for dishonest majority is due to Lindell [27]. Even more recently, Castagnos et al. developed a threshold ECDSA protocol from Hash Proof Systems [11].

Threshold Signatures for DNSSEC. Threshold RSA signatures for DNSSEC have been considered in the past. [10] proposed a distributed DNS to avoid single point of failure, which provides fault tolerance and security in the presence of corrupted servers. [13] emulate a HSM at an authoritative name server and they report timings on a LAN which range from tens to hundreds of milliseconds on commodity hardware. Both used RSA threshold signature scheme of [33].

---

[6] https://www.netnod.se/sites/default/files/2016-12/NETNOD2015_DNS_Martin_Levy_CloudFlare-2.pdf (Slide 28).

8   Conclusion

Deployment of DNSSEC is still an open problem. Current practices force the domain owners to "outsource" management of their DNSSEC keys to the operators, and trust them not to abuse that knowledge. We replace that *trust* with distributed mechanism that generates DNSSEC keys and signatures.

Our mechanism is based on a simple but powerful transformation that can be applied to a large class of protocols for secure computation over $\mathbb{Z}_p$ to obtain protocols for secure computation over an elliptic curve group. We demonstrated the appeal of such a transformation by obtaining several very efficient protocols for threshold ECDSA. Our protocols work in the preprocessing model, which allows us to obtain schemes for computing 100s to 1000s of signatures per second.

Our measurements demonstrate that multi-operator solutions for name servers and for domains are popular in the Internet. Finally, motivated by the aforementioned measurements, we show that our protocols provide an efficient solution to existing issues in DNSSEC. In particular, we demonstrate a system that allows multiple distinct operators to digitally sign zone (as required in DNSSEC) at essentially no cost compared to regular single-operator DNSSEC.

Acknowledgment. This work has been co-funded by: the Concordium Blockhain Research Center, Aarhus University, Denmark; the European Research Council (ERC) under the European Unions's Horizon 2020 research and innovation programme under grant agreement No 803096 (SPEC); the Danish Independent Research Council under Grant-ID DFF-6108-00169 (FoCC); the German Federal Ministry of Education and Research and the Hessen State Ministry for Higher Education, Research and Arts within their joint support of the National Research Center for Applied Cybersecurity ATHENE; the Deutsche Forschungsgemeinschaft (DFG, German Research Foundation): GRK 2050/251805230 and SFB 1119/236615297.

References

1. Abhishta, A., van Rijswijk-Deij, R., Nieuwenhuis, L.J.M.: Measuring the impact of a successful DDoS attack on the customer behaviour of managed DNS service providers. Comput. Commun. Rev. **48**(5), 70–76 (2018)
2. Atkins, D., Austein, R.: Threat analysis of the domain name system (DNS). RFC **3833**, 1–16 (2004)
3. Bar-Ilan, J., Beaver, D.: Non-cryptographic fault-tolerant computing in constant number of rounds of interaction. In: Proceedings of the Eighth Annual ACM Symposium on Principles of Distributed Computing, pp. 201–209. ACM (1989)
4. Beaver, D.: Efficient multiparty protocols using circuit randomization. In: Feigenbaum, J. (ed.) CRYPTO 1991. LNCS, vol. 576, pp. 420–432. Springer, Heidelberg (1992). https://doi.org/10.1007/3-540-46766-1_34
5. Beevers, K.: A note from NS1's CEO: How we responded to last week's major, multi-faceted DDoS attacks, 23 May 2016. https://ns1.com/blog/how-we-responded-to-last-weeks-major-multi-faceted-ddos-attacks
6. Bellovin, S.M.: Using the domain name system for system break-ins. In: USENIX Security Symposium. USENIX Association (1995)

7. Bortzmeyer, S.: DNS privacy considerations. RFC **7626**, 1–17 (2015)
8. Bortzmeyer, S.: DNS query name minimisation to improve privacy. RFC **7816**, 1–11 (2016)
9. Brandt, M., Dai, T., Klein, A., Shulman, H., Waidner, M.: Domain validation++ for MitM-resilient PKI. In: Proceedings of the 2018 ACM SIGSAC Conference on Computer and Communications Security, pp. 2060–2076. ACM (2018)
10. Cachin, C., Samar, A.: Secure distributed DNS. In: International Conference on Dependable Systems and Networks, 2004, pp. 423–432. IEEE (2004)
11. Castagnos, G., Catalano, D., Laguillaumie, F., Savasta, F., Tucker, I.: Two-party ECDSA from hash proof systems and efficient instantiations. In: Boldyreva, A., Micciancio, D. (eds.) CRYPTO 2019. LNCS, vol. 11694, pp. 191–221. Springer, Cham (2019). https://doi.org/10.1007/978-3-030-26954-8_7
12. Chung, T., et al.: A longitudinal, end-to-end view of the DNSSEC ecosystem. In: USENIX Security Symposium, pp. 1307–1322. USENIX Association (2017)
13. Cifuentes, F., Hevia, A., Montoto, F., Barros, T., Ramiro, V., Bustos-Jiménez, J.: Poor man's hardware security module (pmHSM): a threshold cryptographic backend for DNSSEC. In: LANC, pp. 59–64. ACM (2016)
14. Cimpanu, C.: Hackers breached Greece's top-level domain registrar, 9 July 2019. https://www.zdnet.com/article/hackers-breached-greeces-top-level-domain-registrar/
15. Damgard, I., Keller, M., Larraia, E., Pastro, V., Scholl, P., Smart, N.P.: Practical covertly secure MPC for dishonest majority - or: Breaking the SPDZ limits. Cryptology ePrint Archive, Report 2012/642 (2012). https://eprint.iacr.org/2012/642
16. Damgård, I., Pastro, V., Smart, N., Zakarias, S.: Multiparty computation from somewhat homomorphic encryption. In: Safavi-Naini, R., Canetti, R. (eds.) CRYPTO 2012. LNCS, vol. 7417, pp. 643–662. Springer, Heidelberg (2012). https://doi.org/10.1007/978-3-642-32009-5_38
17. Data61. MP-SPDZ - versatile framework for multi-party computation. https://github.com/data61/MP-SPDZ
18. Doerner, J., Kondi, Y., Lee, E., Shelat, A.: Secure two-party threshold ECDSA from ECDSA assumptions. In: 2018 IEEE Symposium on Security and Privacy, pp. 980–997. IEEE Computer Society Press, May 2018
19. Doerner, J., Kondi, Y., Lee, E., Shelat, A.: Threshold ECDSA from ECDSA assumptions: the multiparty case. In: 2019 IEEE Symposium on Security and Privacy, pp. 1051–1066. IEEE Computer Society Press, May 2019
20. DYN. DYN analysis summary of friday october 21 attack, 26 October 2016. https://dyn.com/blog/dyn-analysis-summary-of-friday-october-21-attack/
21. Gennaro, R., Goldfeder, S.: Fast multiparty threshold ECDSA with fast trustless setup. In: ACM Conference on Computer and Communications Security, pp. 1179–1194. ACM (2018)
22. Herzberg, A., Shulman, H.: Socket overloading for fun and cache-poisoning. In: ACSAC, pp. 189–198. ACM (2013)
23. Kaminsky, D.: Black ops 2008: It's the end of the cache as we know it. Black Hat USA (2008)
24. Keller, M., Orsini, E., Scholl, P.: MASCOT: faster malicious arithmetic secure computation with oblivious transfer. In: Weippl, E.R., Katzenbeisser, S., Kruegel, C., Myers, A.C., Halevi, S. (eds.) ACM CCS 2016, pp. 830–842. ACM Press, October 2016
25. Kerry, C.F., Gallagher, P.D.: FIPS pub 186–4 federal information processing standards publication digital signature standard (DSS) (2013)

26. Knot. Knot DNS. https://www.knot-dns.cz/
27. Lindell, Y.: Fast Secure Two-Party ECDSA Signing. In: Katz, J., Shacham, H. (eds.) CRYPTO 2017. LNCS, vol. 10402, pp. 613–644. Springer, Cham (2017). https://doi.org/10.1007/978-3-319-63715-0_21
28. Lindell, Y., Nof, A., Ranellucci, S.: Fast secure multiparty ECDSA with practical distributed key generation and applications to cryptocurrency custody. Cryptology ePrint Archive, Report 2018/987 (2018). https://eprint.iacr.org/2018/987
29. Liu, S., Foster, I.D., Savage, S., Voelker, G.M., Saul, L.K.: Who is .com?: learning to parse WHOIS records. In: Internet Measurement Conference, pp. 369–380. ACM (2015)
30. Netnod. Statement on man-in-the-middle attack against netnod, 5 February 2019. https://www.netnod.se/news/statement-on-man-in-the-middle-attack-against-netnod
31. Kzen networks. Rust implementation of t, n-threshold ecdsa (elliptic curve digital signature algorithm). https://github.com/KZen-networks/multi-party-ecdsa
32. Krebs on Security. A Deep Dive on the Recent Widespread DNS Hijacking Attacks, 18 February 2019. https://krebsonsecurity.com/2019/02/a-deep-dive-on-the-recent-widespread-dns-hijacking-attacks/
33. Shoup, V.: Practical threshold signatures. In: Preneel, B. (ed.) EUROCRYPT 2000. LNCS, vol. 1807, pp. 207–220. Springer, Heidelberg (2000). https://doi.org/10.1007/3-540-45539-6_15
34. Shulman, H., Waidner, M.: One key to sign them all considered vulnerable: evaluation of DNSSEC in the internet. In: NSDI, pp. 131–144. USENIX Association (2017)
35. Smart, N.P., Talibi Alaoui, Y.: Distributing any elliptic curve based protocol. In: Albrecht, M. (ed.) IMACC 2019. LNCS, vol. 11929, pp. 342–366. Springer, Cham (2019). https://doi.org/10.1007/978-3-030-35199-1_17
36. Son, S., Shmatikov, V.: The Hitchhiker's guide to DNS cache poisoning. In: Jajodia, S., Zhou, J. (eds.) SecureComm 2010. LNICSSITE, vol. 50, pp. 466–483. Springer, Heidelberg (2010). https://doi.org/10.1007/978-3-642-16161-2_27
37. Talos Intelligence. DNS hijacking abuses trust in core internet service, 17 April 2019. https://blog.talosintelligence.com/2019/04/seaturtle.html
38. Unbound Tech. blockchain-crypto-mpc. https://github.com/unbound-tech/blockchain-crypto-mpc
39. Zhao, F., Hori, Y., Sakurai, K.: Analysis of privacy disclosure in DNS query. In: MUE, pp. 952–957. IEEE Computer Society (2007)
40. Zhao, F., Hori, Y., Sakurai, K.: Two-servers PIR based DNS query scheme with privacy-preserving. In: IPC, pp. 299–302. IEEE Computer Society (2007)

On Private Information Retrieval Supporting Range Queries

Junichiro Hayata[1,2]($\boxtimes$), Jacob C. N. Schuldt[2], Goichiro Hanaoka[2],
and Kanta Matsuura[1]

[1] Institute of Industrial Science, The University of Tokyo, Meguro-Ku, Tokyo, Japan
{hayata,kanta}@iis.u-tokyo.ac.jp
[2] National Institute of Advanced Industrial Science and Technology (AIST),
Koto-Ku, Tokyo, Japan
{jacob.schuldt,hanaoka-goichiro}@aist.go.jp

Abstract. Private information retrieval (PIR) allows a client to retrieve data from a database without the database server learning what data is being retrieved. Although many PIR schemes have been proposed in the literature, almost all of these focus on retrieval of a single database element, and do not consider more flexible retrieval queries such as basic range queries. Furthermore, while practically-oriented database schemes aiming at providing flexible and privacy-preserving queries have been proposed, to the best of our knowledge, no formal treatment of range queries has been considered for these. In this paper, we firstly highlight that a simple extension of the standard PIR security notion to range queries, is insufficient in many usage scenarios, and propose a stronger security notion aimed at addressing this. We then show a simple generic construction of a PIR scheme meeting our stronger security notion, and propose a more efficient direct construction based on function secret sharing – while the former has a round complexity logarithmic in the size of the database, the round complexity of the latter is constant. Finally, we report on the practical performance of our direct construction.

Keywords: Private information retrieval · Range query · Function secret sharing

1 Introduction

An increasing number of applications and services rely on remotely stored data e.g. data stored in the cloud. While the data itself might not be private, the information regarding a client's queries might be. For example, investors searching information regarding companies and stock prices, might involuntarily leak their investment interests and intentions through their queries. It is conceivable that a malicious data manager collects statistical data from the client's queries and attempt to exploit this information. To prevent such attacks, private information retrieval (PIR) was proposed [1]. By using PIR, a client can retrieve data from

© Springer Nature Switzerland AG 2020
L. Chen et al. (Eds.): ESORICS 2020, LNCS 12309, pp. 674–694, 2020.
https://doi.org/10.1007/978-3-030-59013-0_33

a database without the database server learning what data is being retrieved. A trivial way to achieve PIR would be for the client to download all data from the database. However, since this trivial approach would incur communication cost $O(n)$ for the client, assuming the size of the database is n, this solution quickly becomes unreasonable when we consider larger databases. Hence, a PIR scheme is required to have communication cost lower than $O(n)$.

The first PIR scheme was proposed by Chor et al. [1]. Their construction assumed that many servers hold a replicated database, and that the servers do not communicate with each other. A PIR scheme constructed under these assumptions is called a multi-server PIR scheme. A PIR scheme relying on just a single server, which is technically more difficult to construct, was first achieved by Kushilevitz et al. [2]. After that, several works on constructing single-server PIR and multi-server PIR schemes have been introduced, gradually improving the communication cost of PIR [3–5]. However, while PIR provides strong security guarantees, the standard definition of PIR only consider queries that retrieve a single element, and do not consider other often used queries types, such as basic range queries.

In contrast, in the somewhat related area of encrypted databases, most schemes aims at providing functionality approaching standard SQL, including range queries [6,7]. However, note that even setting aside the problem of how data would be encrypted and decrypted, an encrypted database would not address the privacy concerns considered in a PIR scheme, as the aim is only to protect the confidentiality of the data against a malicious server, and no attempts are done in these scheme to hide the access pattern by clients. Furthermore, several attacks reconstructing the underlying data or partial information about this, based on the functionality of encrypted database schemes, have been discovered e.g. attacks based on information leakage in searchable encryption [8], and volume attacks based on observing only the volume of answers to the range queries [9–11].

An interesting recent scheme that provides a SQL-like functionality, but still aims at preserving the privacy of client queries, is the private query scheme by Wang et al. [14]. While the scheme does not directly support unbounded range queries, by combining the supported TOPK and COUNT queries of their scheme, we can implement the range query functionality we consider in this paper. The scheme is based on a two-server setup, and uses function secret sharing [18] to generate and respond to queries. Essentially, each server will only receive a share of a function that extracts the relevant information the client is interested in obtaining, and evaluate that share over his own copy of the database. By the security property of function secret sharing, the server will not learn what function is being evaluated, but correctness allows the client to combine the evaluation results from the two server, to obtain the output of the function. While Wang et al. [14] do not provide any formal security models or security proofs for their construction, it is plausible that their construction will satisfy our simple extension of PIR security to range queries, defined in Sect. 3. However, it is relatively easy to see that the structure of their scheme leaks the kind of queries a client is making, and for range queries, the number of elements returned be the server. As discussed below, this can potentially by problematic with respect to maintaining query privacy.

1.1   Our Contribution

In this paper, we focus on PIR schemes that simultaneously provide strong security and functionality beyond simple standard PIR. Specifically, we consider schemes supporting range queries, which is one of the most frequently used queries for online data analytics [12,13]. Only very few works seems to have a similar focus (Wang et al. [14] being an exception). In addition to this, to the best of our knowledge, all query privacy preserving schemes that do support some kind of range queries, are not formally shown secure.

Firstly, we formalize PIR schemes supporting both standard PIR queries as well as range queries, and introduce corresponding security models. More specifically, we define three security notions. The first notion captures ordinary PIR security i.e. when a client request just a single element at a given position in the database (which we denote an index query), the server(s) does not learn what element is being retrieved. The second notion, which is a simple extension of the first notion to range queries, captures that when a client request all database entries x satisfying $a \leq x \leq b$ for chosen bounds (a, b), the server(s) does not learn what elements are being retrieved i.e. the server cannot distinguish this query from any other range query containing the same number of elements. However, we note that this notion might not be sufficient to protect query privacy in some scenarios. For example, consider a simple database consisting of five elements; three distinct elements (x, y, z) as well as two additional elements (z', z'') identical to the third element i.e. $z = z' = z''$. For this particular database, any range query resulting in a three elements response, can only have been for ranges including z, but not x or y; any query resulting in two elements must have been for a range including x and y; and any query resulting in a single element, must have been for ranges include either x or y, but not both. In other words, the privacy of the range queries is almost completely lost, if the fact that a range query is made, and the number of elements in the response, leaks to the server. This is the case for the scheme by Wang et al. [14]. Furthermore, if additional information regarding the distribution of queries a client is likely to make, is available to the server, deriving what queries the client makes becomes even easier.

While this type of information leakage might seem inherent to range queries, we define a third notion aimed at addressing this. This notion, which we call query indistinguishability, captures that the server(s) cannot distinguish between range queries and an appropriate number of independent index queries. This adds an additional layer of security, in particular if multiple queries (ideally from multiple indistinguishable clients) are done simultaneously. In other words, this notion ensures that the server(s) cannot detect range queries (or the boundaries between different range queries), and that server(s) can only obtain an overall estimate of the size of the data transferred in all queries by the client(s).

This can greatly reduce the ability of the server(s) to infer information about client queries. We note that the definition of query indistinguishability addresses the *structural* information leakage wrt. range queries, but, like most other cryptographic security definitions, does not address *temporal* information leakage i.e. what servers might infer from the timing of the queries made by the clients. In Sect. 7 we discuss potential ways to address this dimension.

Having defined the above three notions of security, we show that query indistinguishability implies the other two i.e. schemes shown to satisfy query indistinguishability will also satisfy ordinary PIR security as well as the simple extension to range queries. We then show a simple generic construction of a PIR scheme satisfying query indistinguishability from a standard PIR scheme. This scheme has a range query round complexity with a multiplicative overhead of $O(k + \log n)$, where n is the size of the database and k is the number of elements retrieved in the range query, compared to the underlying PIR scheme. Lastly, we give a direct construction of a multi-server PIR scheme supporting range queries based on function secret sharing. Our construction takes a similar approach to the private query scheme of Wang et al. [14], but whereas the scheme from [14] is not formally shown secure, and can potentially only achieve the simple extension of PIR security to range queries, our construction is shown to satisfy query indistinguishability. In contrast to the generic constructions, the round complexity of the direct construction is $2 + k$. We additionally implemented the client and server components of our scheme, and performed various performance measurements. These show that the time required to process a range query containing 50 elements from a database containing 7.5 million elements, is about 200 s. The details of this are discussed in Appendix A.

1.2 Related Works

While most PIR schemes support only index queries, there are a few exception in the literature. Chor et al. [15] proposed a PIR scheme supporting keyword search queries. Tillem et al. [16] proposed a PIR scheme supporting range queries, and Wang et al. [14], highlighted above, proposed PIR schemes providing functionality approaching standard SQL, including range queries. We note that the latter two works do not formally define security and provide security proofs. Furthermore, neither of these schemes satisfy query indistinguishability, and it is unclear whether the scheme by Tillem et al. even satisfy our simple security notion for range queries.

The concept of multi-query PIR proposed by Groth et al. [17] allows multiple elements to be retrieved simultaneously. Groth et al. [17] gave an information-theoretic lower bound on the communication of any multi-query PIR scheme, as well as a construction matching this bound. We note, however, that in multi-query PIR, it is assumed that the client knows the (possibly independent) indices of the elements to be retrieved, whereas in a range query, no such assumption is made. Hence, multi-query PIR schemes and PIR schemes supporting range queries are not directly comparable.

1.3 Paper Organization

The structure of this paper is as follows. In Sect. 2, we introduce notation and preliminary definitions. In Sect. 3, we define the syntax and security models for multi-server PIR schemes supporting range queries, and in Sect. 4, we prove relations among the introduced security notions. In Sect. 5, we show a generic construction of a PIR scheme supporting range queries from a standard PIR scheme. In Sect. 6, we show our efficient constructions of a PIR scheme supporting range queries using function secret sharing. In Sect. 7, we discuss information leakage due to the timing of queries and how to address this. In Appendix A, we show experimental results regarding the efficiency of our scheme. Lastly, Appendix B contains omitted proofs.

2 Preliminaries

Parameters. We use the following parameters:

- ℓ: number of servers.
- n: size of the database (number of elements).
- V: size of each element.

Notation. We denote probabilistic polynomial time algorithm by PPTA, denote PIR supporting range queries by RQ-PIR, and for an algorithm A, we denote the procedure that A is given input a and outputs b by $b \leftarrow A(a)$. In addition, we use the notation $\overrightarrow{x}$ for vectors, and denote a vector with all elements being $\perp$ by $\overrightarrow{\perp}$.

Function Secret Sharing (FSS). Function secret sharing (FSS) was proposed by Boyle et al. [18], and a FSS scheme provides a means to split a function f into separate evaluation keys, where each party's key enables him to efficiently generate a standard secret share of the evaluation $f(x)$ for any input x, and yet each key individually does not reveal information about which function f has been shared.

In this paragraph, we define syntax, correctness, and a security model for FSS schemes. A FSS scheme is defined for a function family $\mathcal{F}$. Like Boyle et al. [18], we model $\mathcal{F}$ as an infinite collection of bit strings f, together with efficient procedures IdentityDomain and Evaluate, such that $D_f \leftarrow \mathsf{IdentityDomain}(1^\lambda, f)$ extracts from the string f an input domain space D_f, and $y \leftarrow \mathsf{Evaluate}(f, x)$, for any input $x \in D_f$, defines the output of f at x. By convention, we assume the description f includes also the input length and output length of f.

For simplicity of notation, in this paper, we will refer to the domain D_f of f without making explicit reference to the corresponding call to IdentityDomain, and will denote an evaluation $\mathsf{Evaluate}(f, x)$ by shorthand notation $f(x)$.

The syntax of a FSS scheme is as follows.

Definition 1. *For $p \in \mathbb{N}$, $T \subseteq [p]$, a p-party, T-secure function secret sharing (FSS) scheme $\mathcal{FSS}$ with respect to function class $\mathcal{F}$, is a pair of PPTA (Gen, Eval) with the following syntax:*

- $(k_1, \ldots, k_p) \leftarrow \mathsf{Gen}(1^\lambda, f)$: *Key Generation algorithm* Gen *takes as input the security parameter 1^λ and function description $f \in \mathcal{F}$, and outputs a p-tuple of keys $(k_1, \ldots, k_p)$.*
- $y_i \leftarrow \mathsf{Eval}(i, k_i, x)$: *Evaluation algorithm* Eval *takes as input a party index $i \in [p]$, key k_i and input string $x \in D_f$, and outputs a value y_i, corresponding to the party's share of $f(x)$.*

Correctness and secrecy requirements are as follows:

Correctness: For all $f \in \mathcal{F}, x \in D_f$,

$$\Pr\left[(k_1, \ldots, k_p) \leftarrow \mathsf{Gen}(1^\lambda, f) : \sum_{i=1}^{p} \mathsf{Eval}(i, k_i, x) = f(x)\right] = 1.$$

Security: Consider the following indistinguishability experiment for an adversary $\mathcal{A} = (\mathcal{A}_1, \mathcal{A}_2)$ and corrupted parties $T \subset [p]$:

1: The adversary outputs $(f^0, f^1, st) \leftarrow \mathcal{A}_1(1^\lambda)$, where $f^0, f^1 \in \mathcal{F}$ with $D_{f^0} = D_{f^1}$.
2: The challenger samples $b \leftarrow \{0, 1\}$ and computes $(k_1, \ldots, k_p) \leftarrow \mathsf{Gen}(1^\lambda, f^b)$.
3: Given the keys for corrupted parties T, the adversary outputs a guess $b' \leftarrow \mathcal{A}_2((k_i)_{i \in T}, st)$.

Denote by

$$\mathsf{Adv}_{\mathcal{FSS}}(1^\lambda, \mathcal{A}) := |\Pr[b = b'] - 1/2|$$

the advantage of $\mathcal{A}$ in guessing b in the above experiment, where the probability is taken over the randomness of the challenger and $\mathcal{A}$. We say the scheme (Gen, Eval) is T-secure if there exists a negligible function ϵ such that for all PPTA $\mathcal{A}$, it holds that $Adv(1^\lambda, \mathcal{A}) \leq \epsilon(\lambda)$.

Although it is possible to construct FSS for arbitrary functions, practical FSS protocols only exist for some functions, e.g. point and interval functions. These take the following forms [18, 19]:

- Point functions f_a are defined as $f_a(x) = 1$ if $x = a$ or 0 otherwise.
- Interval functions are defined as $f_{a,b}(x) = 1$ if $a < x < b$ or 0 otherwise.

Hereafter, for a function f, we denote by $(f_1, \ldots, f_p) \leftarrow \mathsf{Gen}(1^\lambda, f)$ the function shares described by the keys $(k_1, \ldots, k_\ell)$ generated by $\mathsf{Gen}(1^\lambda, f)$, and by $f_i(x)$ the output of $\mathsf{Eval}(i, k_i, \cdot)$.

3   Syntax and Security Models for PIR Schemes Supporting Range Queries

In this section, we define syntax and security models for PIR schemes supporting range queries. In the following, we will treat a database as consisting of an n-entry vector $\overrightarrow{x} = (x_1, \ldots, x_n)$, and each entry as a V-bit integer. Furthermore, we will assume that the entries in the database are sorted in ascending order i.e. it holds that $x_1 \leq x_2 \leq \cdots \leq x_n$.

3.1   Syntax of RQ-PIR

Our notion of a RQ-PIR scheme supports two types of queries: index queries and range queries. In an index query, the client specifies an index $i \in [n]$, and obtains the ith entry in the database i.e. x_i. However, in a range query, the client specifies a range by values $a, b \in \mathbb{N}$ ($a < b$), and obtains all entries x_j in the database satisfying $a \leq x_j \leq b$. Note that the client might be unaware of the indices j of the elements retrieved in a range query.

To capture interactive schemes, we define a RQ-PIR scheme via stateful algorithms. Note, however, that we only require the client to maintain state. Specifically, only the algorithms *Index* and *Range* defined below, which the client will run to make an index or range query, respectively, will be stateful, whereas the algorithm *Res* run by the servers to respond to the clients request, will be stateless.

$(q, st') \leftarrow Index(1^\lambda, \overrightarrow{ans}, st)$: The *Index* algorithm is a stateful interactive algorithm run by the client to execute an index query. The algorithm takes as input the security parameter 1^λ, potential previous answers $\overrightarrow{ans} := (ans_1, ans_2, \ldots, ans_\ell)$ from servers, where ans_j is the answer from server j, and state st. The algorithm outputs server queries $\overrightarrow{q} := (q_1, q_2, \ldots, q_\ell)$, and new state st'. The client sets the initial state to $st := \{i\}$, where i is the index of the entry in the database he would retrieve, and sets the initial $\overrightarrow{ans} \leftarrow \overrightarrow{\perp}$. When *Index* outputs $q = \overrightarrow{\perp}$, it indicates termination of the index query, and the client outputs st as the final output y.

$(q, st') \leftarrow Range(1^\lambda, \overrightarrow{ans}, st)$: The *Range* algorithm is a stateful interactive algorithm run by the client to execute a range query. The algorithm takes as input the security parameter 1^λ, potential previous answers $\overrightarrow{ans} := (ans_1, ans_2, \ldots, ans_\ell)$ from servers, where ans_j is the answer from server j, and state st. The algorithm outputs queries $\overrightarrow{q} := (q_1, q_2, \ldots, q_\ell)$, and new state st'. The client sets the initial state to $st := \{a, b\}$, where $a, b \in \mathbb{N}, a \leq b$ and $[a, b]$ is the range that client wants to retrieve from database, and sets the initial $\overrightarrow{ans} \leftarrow \overrightarrow{\perp}$. When *Range* outputs $q = \overrightarrow{\perp}$, it indicates termination of the range query, and client outputs st as a final output y.

$ans_j \leftarrow Res(1^\lambda, x, j, q)$: The *Res* algorithm is stateless and run by each server to respond to the clients queries. The algorithm takes as input the security parameter 1^λ, database x, the identifier of the server $j \in [\ell]$, and query q from the client, and outputs answer ans_j.

To simplify notation, we will often omit the security parameter 1^λ from the input of the above defined algorithms. In addition to this, we will use $Res_j(\boldsymbol{x}, q)$ to denote $Res(1^\lambda, \boldsymbol{x}, j, q)$.

Based on the above algorithms, we obtain protocols for index and range queries by respectively combining $Index$ and Res, and $Range$ and Res. We will use the following notation regarding these:

$(y, \overrightarrow{\perp}) \leftarrow \langle Index, Res_1, \ldots, Res_\ell \rangle(i, \boldsymbol{x}, \ldots, \boldsymbol{x})$: This denotes the client running the $Index$ algorithm with input the initial state $st_0 := \{i\}$, and server j replying to each query q_j from client by running $Res_j(\boldsymbol{x}, q_j)$, for all $j \in [\ell]$, until the $Index$ algorithm halts. After completing the protocol, the client outputs y and each server receives no output (i.e. $\perp$).

$(\boldsymbol{y}, \overrightarrow{\perp}) \leftarrow \langle Range, Res_1, \ldots, Res_\ell \rangle((a, b), \boldsymbol{x}, \ldots, \boldsymbol{x})$: This denotes the client running the $Range$ algorithm with input initial state $st_0 := \{a, b\}$, and server j replying to queries q_j from client by running $Res_j(\boldsymbol{x}, q_j)$, for all $j \in [\ell]$ until the $Range$ algorithm halts. After completing the protocol, the client outputs $\boldsymbol{y}$ and each server outputs $\perp$.

For the above protocols, we will consider the transcript of an interaction between a client and a server: for any $j \in [\ell]$ and for any $i \in [n]$, we denote by $\mathsf{Trans}_j(\langle Index, Res_1, \ldots, Res_\ell \rangle(i, \boldsymbol{x}, \ldots, \boldsymbol{x}))$ the messages sent between the client and server j when executing the above defined protocol for retrieving the database entry for index i (held by the client). Likewise, for any $j \in [\ell]$ and for any $a, b \in \mathbb{N}$, we denote by $\mathsf{Trans}_j(\langle Range, Res_1, \ldots, Res_\ell \rangle((a, b), \boldsymbol{x}, \ldots, \boldsymbol{x}))$ the messages sent between client and server j during the execution of the above defined protocol for retrieving values in the range $[a, b]$.

3.2   Security of RQ-PIR

We will now define three security models for PIR schemes that support index queries and range queries. In all of these models, we assume that serves do not collude, and there is a secure channel between the client and each server.

At first, we define security of index queries for RQ-PIR schemes. This security notion is equivalent to the computational notion normally considered for standard (multi-server) PIR, and captures that the servers do not learn anything regarding the element being retrieved in the index query.

Definition 2. *A RQ-PIR scheme provides secure index queries if for all $\lambda \in \mathbb{N}$, for any database $\boldsymbol{x} = (x_1, \ldots, x_n)$ of size n, for any server $m \in [\ell]$, for any indices $i, j \in [n]$, for any PPTA distinguisher $\mathcal{D}$,*

$$| \Pr[\mathcal{D}(\mathsf{View}_i^m) = 1] - \Pr[\mathcal{D}(\mathsf{View}_j^m) = 1]|$$

is negligible, where

$$\mathsf{View}_k^m \leftarrow \{\mathsf{Trans}_m(\langle Index, Res_1, \ldots, Res_\ell \rangle(k, \boldsymbol{x}, \ldots, \boldsymbol{x})), \boldsymbol{x}, r\}$$

for $k \in \{i, j\}$, and where r is the randomnesses used by server m during the execution of the protocol.

We now define a simple extension of the above security notion aimed at capturing security of range queries. This security notion captures that the servers do not learn the bounds (a, b) of the range query, and what elements are being retrieved via an indistinguishability requirement: any server should be unable to distinguish two different range queries as long as the number of elements in the query is the same.

Definition 3. *A RQ-PIR scheme provides secure range queries if for all $\lambda \in \mathbb{N}$, for any database $\boldsymbol{x} = (x_1, \ldots, x_n)$ of size n, for any server $m \in [\ell]$, for any bounds $a, b, c, d \in [n]$ such that $|\{x_i \mid a \leq x_i \leq b\}| = |\{x_i \mid c \leq x_i \leq d\}| = k$, for any PPTA distinguisher $\mathcal{D}$,*

$$| \Pr[\mathcal{D}(\mathsf{View}_{a,b}^m) = 1] - \Pr[\mathcal{D}(\mathsf{View}_{c,d}^m) = 1]|$$

is negligible, where

$$\mathsf{View}_{h_0,h_1}^m \leftarrow \{\mathsf{Trans}_m(\langle Range, Res_1, \ldots, Res_\ell\rangle((h_0, h_1), \boldsymbol{x}, \ldots, \boldsymbol{x})), \boldsymbol{x}, r\}$$

for $(h_0, h_1) \in \{(a, b), (c, d)\}$, and where r is the randomnesses of server m during the execution of the protocol.

While Definition 3 above intuitively guarantees the security of range queries, this security notion does not guarantee that the type of query being made, or the number of elements in a range query, are hidden. As discussed in the introduction, that might lead to the privacy of range queries being compromised. Thus, a stronger security notion is desirable.

Hence, we define query indistinguishability of a RQ-PIR scheme aimed at addressing this. This security notion captures that the servers cannot learn whether the client is performing a range query or a number of independent index queries for a set of arbitrary unrelated set of entries in the database.

Definition 4. *A RQ-PIR scheme provides query indistinguishability if there exists a polynomial time computable function $f : \mathbb{N} \to \mathbb{N}$ such that for all $\lambda \in \mathbb{N}$, for any database $\boldsymbol{x} = (x_1, \ldots, x_n)$ of size n, for any server $m \in [\ell]$, for any bounds $a, b \in \mathbb{N}$, for any st of indices $i_1, \ldots i_{f(k)} \in [n]$ where $k = |\{x_i \mid a \leq x_i \leq b\}|$, for any PPTA distinguisher $\mathcal{D}$,*

$$| \Pr[\mathcal{D}(\mathsf{View}_{range}^m) = 1] - \Pr[\mathcal{D}(\mathsf{View}_{index}^m) = 1]|$$

is negligible, where

$$\mathsf{View}_{range}^m \leftarrow \{\mathsf{Trans}_m(\langle Range, Res_1, \ldots, Res_\ell\rangle((a, b), \boldsymbol{x}, \ldots, \boldsymbol{x})), \boldsymbol{x}, r\},$$

and

$$\mathsf{View}_{index}^m \leftarrow \mathsf{View}_{i_1} || \cdots || \mathsf{View}_{i_{f(k)}},$$

where $\mathsf{View}_s \leftarrow \{\mathsf{Trans}_m(\langle Index, Res_1, \ldots, Res_\ell\rangle(k, \boldsymbol{x}, \ldots, \boldsymbol{x})), \boldsymbol{x}, r\}$, and $s \in \{i_1, \ldots, i_{f(k)}\}$ and r is the randomnesses of server m during the execution of the protocol.

Note that while Definition 4 guarantees that database server(s) cannot detect range queries (or boundaries between these) from the queries alone, the definition by itself does not address information derived from the timing of queries. In Sect. 7, we discuss ways to address this.

4   Relation Among Security Notions

In this section, we prove implications among the security notions introduced above. Specifically, we prove that query indistinguishability implies secure index queries, as well as secure range queries.

Theorem 1. *If RQ-PIR scheme Π provides query indistinguishability, then Π provides secure range queries.*

Due to the page limitation, we defer the full proof to Appendix B.

Then, we prove that query indistinguishability implies secure index queries. To show this implication, we introduce the security notion of secure index queries for sets. At first, we prove that query indistinguishability implies secure index queries for sets, and then show that index queries for sets implies secure index queries.

Definition 5. *A RQ-PIR scheme provides secure index queries for sets if for all $\lambda \in \mathbb{N}$, for any database $\boldsymbol{x} = (x_1, \ldots, x_n)$ of size n, for any server $m \in [\ell]$, for any set of indices $\boldsymbol{i}_1 = (i_{1_1}, \ldots, i_{1_k}), \boldsymbol{i}_2 = (i_{2_1}, \ldots, i_{2_k}) \in [n]^k$, for any PPTA distinguisher $\mathcal{D}$,*

$$| \Pr[\mathcal{D}(\mathsf{View}_{i_1}^m) = 1] - \Pr[\mathcal{D}(\mathsf{View}_{i_2}^m) = 1]|$$

is negligible, where

$$\mathsf{View}_k^m \leftarrow \{\mathsf{Trans}_m(\langle Index, Res_1, \ldots, Res_\ell\rangle(i_{t_1}, \boldsymbol{x}, \ldots, \boldsymbol{x})), \boldsymbol{x}, r_1\}|| \cdots$$
$$||\{\mathsf{Trans}_m(\langle Index, Res_1, \ldots, Res_\ell\rangle(i_{t_k}, \boldsymbol{x}, \ldots, \boldsymbol{x})), \boldsymbol{x}, r_k\}$$

for $t \in \{1, 2\}$, and where $r_1, \ldots, r_k$ is the randomnesses used by server m during the execution of the protocol.

Theorem 2. *If RQ-PIR scheme Π provides query indistinguishability, then Π provides secure index queries for sets.*

Theorem 3. *If RQ-PIR scheme Π provides secure index queries for sets, then Π provides secure index queries.*

Due to the page limitation, we omit proof of Theorems 2 and 3.

From Theorem 2 and 3, we can derive following theorem.

Theorem 4. *If RQ-PIR scheme Π provides query indistinguishability, then Π provides secure index queries.*

5   Generic Construction of RQ-PIR from PIR

Let $\Sigma = (Index, Res_1, \ldots, Res_\ell)$ be a PIR scheme that provides secure index queries. We give a simple generic construction of a RQ-PIR scheme Π from Σ.

Π simply uses the index query algorithm provided by the underlying Σ for index queries, and we omit the description of this. Likewise, Π uses the response algorithms from Σ, and we omit the description of these as well. However, how range queries are implemented does not follow immediately, and care must be taken to avoid these leaking information. We firstly discuss the intuition of our construction, and then provide the full details.

Note that when a client sends a range query, he does not know the indices corresponding to the elements he would like to retrieve. Thus, to retrieve these elements using Σ, he needs to obtain the relevant indices first. To do this, we use binary search. However, if binary search is used naively, it might terminate in less than $\log n$ rounds, which will leak information regarding the search, and prevent us from showing query indistinguishability, as the query size of range queries for a given number of elements is required to be constant. To prevent this, we adjust the communication rounds by sending dummy queries.

After the client has run binary searches for the bounds defining the range query, he obtains the corresponding indices. However, when the database contains elements with the same value, it is not guaranteed that the indices the client obtained cover all elements in the range. To address this, the client will query additional elements on either side of the obtained indices, until elements outside the desired range is obtained.

In the following, $[a, b]$ denotes a range query specified by the client.

$Range(\overrightarrow{ans}, st)$:
- Using binary search, the client searches for an index i such that $x_i = a$, by appropriately setting the queries $\overrightarrow{q}$, processing the corresponding $\overrightarrow{ans}$, and updating st. Each query in the search is done using $Index$ from Σ. The client additionally maintains a counter c during this execution, which represents the total number of queries made. If the index i is found, but $c < \log n$, the client chooses random index $i' \in [n]$ and runs additional $Index$ queries for i' until $c = \log n$.
- Then, if $x_i \geq a$, the client runs $Index$ queries for $i - k$ for $k = 1, 2, \dots$ until he retrieves an element such that $x_{i-k'} < a$ (i.e. $i - k' + 1$ is the smallest index of the elements with value a).
- The client then searches an index j such that $x_j = b$, using binary search as above.
- Then, if $x_j \leq b$, the client runs $Index$ queries for $j + t$ for $t = 1, 2, \dots$ until he retrieves an element such that $x_{j+t'} > b$ (i.e. $j - t' - 1$ is the largest index of the elements whose value is b).
- Finally, the client generates index queries for $i + 1$ to $j - 1$. Since the elements in the range from $i - k' + 1$ to i and j to $j + t' - 1$ have already been retrieved, the client obtains all elements within the range $[a, b]$.

Regardless of the type of queries executed by the client, only $Index$ queries from Σ is used when communicating with the server. In addition to this, when the client submits a range query, the number of elements retrieved is always $k + 2 + 2 \log n$, where k is the number of elements within $[a, b]$. Hence, the following theorem easily follows.

Theorem 5. *The RQ-PIR scheme Π above provides query indistinguishability.*

6   Construction of RQ-PIR Scheme from FSS

In this section, we give a construction of a two-server RQ-PIR scheme using function secret sharing. After that, we give a security proof for our construction. Our construction is more efficient than the scheme described in Sect. 5 in terms of communication complexity and the number of communication rounds.

6.1   Construction of Two-Server RQ-PIR Scheme

We construct a two-server RQ-PIR scheme $\Pi = (Index, Range, Res)$. Our construction is based on function secret sharing and we take a similar approach to the private query construction of Wang et al. [14]. While the scheme from [14] can be used for range queries as highlighted in the introduction, the scheme allows the server to distinguish whether the query from the client is an index query or range query. Our construction avoids this issue by computing a server response that the client can simultaneously used for both index and range queries, which leads to the server being unable to distinguish which query it receives. Our constructions of $Index, Range, Res_j$ ($j \in \{1,2\}$) are as follows:

$Index(\overrightarrow{ans}, st)$: This algorithm is stateless besides the initial state $st = i$ indicating the index i to retrieve, and allows a one-round index query protocol.
- On input $st = i$, the client computes $(f_1, f_2) \leftarrow \mathsf{Gen}(1^\lambda, f)$, where

$$f(x) = \begin{cases} 1 & i-1 < x < i+1 \\ 0 & \text{otherwise.} \end{cases}$$

  The client then output $(q, st') = ((f_1, f_2), \bot)$, implying that f_1 is sent to server 1 and f_2 to server 2 in the protocol.
- On input answers $\overrightarrow{ans} = ((a_{1,1}, a_{1,2}), (a_{2,1}, a_{2,2}))$ from server 1 and server 2 (and state $st = \bot$), the client computes $y \leftarrow a_{1,2} + a_{2,2}$, and outputs $(q, st') = ((\bot, \bot), y)$ indicating termination.

$Range(\overrightarrow{ans}, st)$: During the range query protocol, the client maintains state information $st := \{st_1, st_2, st_3, st_4\}$, and initial state is $st := \{\{a, b\}, \{\}, \bot, \{\}\}$ where a and b are the bounds in the range query.
- On input $st_1 = \{a, b\}$, the client computes $(f_1, f_2) \leftarrow \mathsf{Gen}(1^\lambda, f)$, where

$$f(x) = \begin{cases} 1 & 0 < x < a \\ 0 & \text{otherwise.} \end{cases}$$

  The client then outputs $(q, st') := ((f_1, f_2), \{\{b\}, \{\}, \bot, \{\}\})$, indicating that f_1 is sent to server 1 and f_2 to server 2 in the protocol.
- On input $st_1 = \{b\}$ and $\overrightarrow{ans} = ((a_{1,1}, a_{1,2}), (a_{2,1}, a_{2,1}))$ from server 1 and server 2, the client computes $y \leftarrow a_{1,1} + a_{2,1}$ and start index $s \leftarrow y+1$, and updates the state $st = \{\{\}, \{s\}, \bot, \{\}\}$. After that, the client computes $(g_1, g_2) \leftarrow \mathsf{Gen}(1^\lambda, g)$, where

$$g(x) = \begin{cases} 1 & 0 < x < b+1 \\ 0 & \text{otherwise.} \end{cases}$$

Finally, the client outputs $(\boldsymbol{q}, st') := ((g_1, g_2), st)$, indicating that g_1 is sent to server 1 and g_2 to server 2.

- On input $st_1 = \{\}$, $st_2 = \{s\}$, and $\overrightarrow{ans} = ((a_{1,1}, a_{1,2}), (a_{2,1}, a_{2,2}))$ from server 1 and server 2, the client computes $y' \leftarrow a_{1,1} + a_{2,1}$, sets the end index $t \leftarrow y'$, computes the number of elements in the range $k \leftarrow t - s$, and updates the state $st = \{\{\}, \{s, t\}, k\}$. After that, client computes $(h_1, h_2) \leftarrow \mathsf{Gen}(1^\lambda, h)$, where

$$h(x) = \begin{cases} 1 & t - 1 < x < t + 1 \\ 0 & \text{otherwise.} \end{cases}$$

The client outputs $(\boldsymbol{q}, st') := ((h_1, h_2), st)$, indicating that h_1 is sent to server 1 and h_2 to server 2.

- On input $st_1 = \{\}$, $st_2 = \{s, t\}$, $st_3 \neq 0$, and $\overrightarrow{ans} = ((a_{1,1}, a_{1,2}), (a_{2,1}, a_{2,2}))$ from server 1 and server 2, the client does the following: The client computes $y \leftarrow a_{1,2} + a_{2,2}$, $st_3 = st_3 - 1$, $st_4 = st_4 \| y$. After that, the client computes $(h'_1, h'_2) \leftarrow \mathsf{Gen}(1^\lambda, h')$, where

$$h'(x) = \begin{cases} 1 & st_3 - 1 < x < st_3 + 1 \\ 0 & \text{otherwise.} \end{cases}$$

The client outputs $(\boldsymbol{q}, st') := ((h'_1, h'_2), st)$, indicating that h'_1 is sent to server 1 and h'_2 to server 2.

- On input $st_1 = \{\}$, $st_2 = \{s, t\}$, $st_3 = 0$, and $\overrightarrow{ans} = ((a'_{1,1}, a'_{1,2}), (a'_{2,1}, a'_{2,2}))$ from server 1 and server 2, the client computes $y \leftarrow a'_{1,2} + a'_{2,2}$, $st_4 = st_4 \| y$, and outputs $(\boldsymbol{q}, \boldsymbol{y}) := ((\bot, \bot), st_4)$, indicating termination.

$Res_j(\boldsymbol{x}, f_j)$: In the above algorithms, the client sends a share of a function f_j to server j. Upon receiving this, the server computes $a_{j,1} = \sum_{i=1}^n f_j(x_i)$, $a_{j,2} = \sum_{i=1}^n f_j(i) \cdot x_i$, and sends these to the client. Note that the server response is the same whether the query from the client is a range query or an index query. Note also that the Res algorithm is deterministic.

In the following, we prove security of our RQ-PIR scheme Π. Since query indistinguishability implies secure index queries and secure range queries (as shown in Sect. 4), we only prove query indistinguishability. The main idea of the security proof is to use the security of the FSS scheme to gradually change the function shares sent from the client to the servers, transforming a range query into an appropriate number of index queries.

Theorem 6. *If FSS scheme $\mathcal{FSS} = (\mathsf{Gen}, \mathsf{Eval})$ is secure, then RQ-PIR scheme Π provides query indistinguishability.*

Proof. For the function $f(x) := x + 2$, for all λ, for any database $\boldsymbol{x} = (x_1, \ldots, x_n)$ of size n, for any $m \in [2]$, for any $a, b \in [n]$, for any $i_1, \ldots i_{f(k)} \in [n]$ where $k = |\{x_i \mid a \leq x_i \leq b\}|$, we consider a PPTA $\mathcal{D}$ against query indistinguishability in RQ-PIR scheme Π. The advantage of $\mathcal{D}$ is defined by

$$\mathsf{Adv}_{\mathcal{D},\Pi}^{ind} = |\Pr[\mathcal{D}(\mathsf{View}_{range}^m) = 1] - \Pr[\mathcal{D}(\mathsf{View}_{index}^m) = 1]|.$$

Since the *Res* algorithm in our RQ-PIR scheme Π is deterministic, $\mathsf{View}_{range_{a,b}}^m$ can be written as $\{\mathsf{Trans}_m(\langle Range, Res_1, Res_2\rangle((a,b), \boldsymbol{x}, \boldsymbol{x}), \boldsymbol{x}\} = \{(\boldsymbol{q}, \boldsymbol{a}), \boldsymbol{x}\}$, where $|\{x_i \mid a \leq x_i \leq b\}| = k$, $\boldsymbol{q} = (q_1, \ldots, q_{k+2})$ and the i-th element in $\boldsymbol{q}$ is a query for server m generated from some function f_i by the client, and $\boldsymbol{a} = ((a_{1,1}, a_{1,2}), \ldots, (a_{k+2,1}, a_{k+2,2}))$ and $(a_{i,1}, a_{i,2})$ is the reply from server m for query q_i.

To obtain a proof, we use a sequence of games (**Game** 0 to **Game** $k + 2$).

Game 0: This game corresponds to the client and servers running $\langle Range, Res_1, Res_2\rangle((a,b), \boldsymbol{x}, \boldsymbol{x})$.

Game r ($1 \leq r \leq k + 1$): The difference from **Game** $r - 1$ is that q_{r-1} is replaced with q'_{r-1} where q'_{r-1} is a function share for server m generated from a function $f_{r-1}(x) = \begin{cases} 1 & i_{r-1} - 1 < x < i_{r-1} + 1 \\ 0 & \text{otherwise} \end{cases}$.

Game $k + 2$: This game corresponds to the client and servers running $\langle Index, Res_1, Res_2\rangle(i_r, \boldsymbol{x}, \boldsymbol{x})$ for $r = 1, \ldots, f(k)$.

For all r, we denote by View_r^m the view for server m generated by the experiment **Game** r.

Lemma 1. *If FSS scheme $\mathcal{FSS} = (\mathsf{Gen}, \mathsf{Eval})$ is secure, then for any $1 \leq s \leq k + 2$ and for any PPTA $\mathcal{B}$, it holds that the difference between the probability that $\mathcal{B}$ outputs 1 in **Game** $s - 1$ and s is negligible.*

Proof. We consider a PPTA $\mathcal{B}$ who distinguishes View_{r-1}^m from View_r^m, and denote the advantage of $\mathcal{B}$ by

$$\mathsf{Adv}_{\mathcal{B},\Pi}^r = |\Pr[\mathcal{B}(\mathsf{View}_r^m) = 1] - \Pr[\mathcal{B}(\mathsf{View}_{r-1}^m) = 1]|.$$

Then, we construct an adversary $\mathcal{A}$ against $\mathcal{FSS}$ who uses $\mathcal{B}$ internally as shown in Fig. 1.

By the construction of $\mathcal{A}$, $\mathcal{A}$ simulates View_{r-1}^m for $\mathcal{B}$ when $\mathcal{A}$ receives a function share of f^0 in the FSS security experiment. Moreover, $\mathcal{A}$ outputs 1 only when $\mathcal{B}$ outputs 1. Thus the probability that $\mathcal{A}$ outputs 1 in the experiment that $\mathcal{A}$ receives a function share of f^0 is equal to $\Pr[\mathcal{B}(\mathsf{View}_{r-1}^m) = 1]$. Likewise, the

$\mathcal{A}_1(1^\lambda)$

Send $f^0 := f_{r-1}$ and $f^1 := f'_{r-1}$ to challenger,

where f_{r-1} is the $r-1$-th function used in the range protocol for $[a,b]$,

and $f^1(x) = \begin{cases} 1 & i_{r-1} - 1 < x < i_{r-1} + 1 \\ 0 & \text{otherwise.} \end{cases}$

Output $st := (\{(a,b),(i_1,\ldots,i_{f(k)})\}, \boldsymbol{x})$

$\mathcal{A}_2(f^b_m, st)$

Let $st := \{(a',b'),(i'_1,\ldots,i'_{f(k)}), \boldsymbol{x}'\}$

Compute $s = \sum_{i=1}^n f^b_m(x'_i), s' = \sum_{i=1}^n f^b_m(i) \cdot x'_i$

Run $(y_1||y_2||\ldots||y_{k+2}) \leftarrow \mathsf{Trans}_m(\langle Range, Res_1, Res_2\rangle((a',b'),\boldsymbol{x}',\boldsymbol{x}'))$,

where $y_t := q_t||a_{t,1}||a_{t,2}$ for $t = 1,\ldots,k+2$

For $u = 1$ to $r-2$

$\quad (q'_u, a'_{u,1}, a'_{u,2}) \leftarrow \mathsf{Trans}_m(\langle Index, Res_1, Res_2\rangle(i_u, \boldsymbol{x}', \boldsymbol{x}'))$

View $\leftarrow \{(y'_1||y'_2||\ldots||y'_{r-2}||q'_{r-2}||f^b_m||s||s'||y_r||\ldots||y_{k+2}), \boldsymbol{x}\}$,

where $y'_w := q'_w||a'_{w,1}||a'_{w,2}$ for $w = 1,\ldots,r-2$

$b' \leftarrow \mathcal{B}(\mathsf{View})$

Output b'

Fig. 1. Construction of $\mathcal{A}$ in Lemma 1

probability that $\mathcal{A}$ outputs 1 in the experiment that $\mathcal{A}$ receives a function share of f^1 is equal to $\Pr[\mathcal{B}(\mathsf{View}^m_r) = 1]$. Therefore, we obtain

$$\mathsf{Adv}^r_{\mathcal{B},\Pi} = |\Pr[\mathcal{B}(\mathsf{View}^m_r) = 1] - \Pr[\mathcal{B}(\mathsf{View}^m_{r-1}) = 1]| = \mathsf{Adv}_{\mathcal{FSS}}(1^\lambda, \mathcal{A}).$$

Since we assume $\mathcal{FSS}$ is secure i.e. that $\mathsf{Adv}_{\mathcal{FSS}}(1^\lambda, \mathcal{A})$ is negligible for all PTTA $\mathcal{A}$, we can conclude $\mathsf{Adv}^r_{\mathcal{B},\Pi}$ is negligible.   □

By using Lemma 1, we can derive

$$|\Pr[\mathcal{D}(\mathsf{View}^m_{range}) = 1] - \Pr[\mathcal{D}(\mathsf{View}^m_{index}) = 1]|$$

$$\leq \sum_{r=1}^{k+2} |\Pr[\mathcal{D}(\mathsf{View}^m_{r-1}) = 1] - \Pr[\mathcal{D}(\mathsf{View}^m_r) = 1]| \leq (k+2) \cdot negl.$$

□

Efficiency. We summarize the efficiency of the FSS-based RQ-PIR scheme in Fig. 2, and compare this to the generic constructions from Sect. 5. The RQ-PIR scheme requires a FSS scheme for interval functions, and the most efficient among these was proposed by Boyle et al. [19]. Specifically, let $G : \{0,1\}^\lambda \to \{0,1\}^{2\lambda+2}$ be a PRG, and $f_{a,b} : \mathbb{G}^{in} \to \mathbb{G}^{out}$ be an interval function. Then, in their construction, the key size (i.e. the size of the query sent in one round from the client to the servers in the RQ-PIR scheme) is $8m \cdot (\lambda + 1) + 2m\ell + 2\lambda$, and the size of the evaluation (i.e. the size of the response from servers to the client) is ℓ, where $m = \lceil \log_2 |\mathbb{G}^{in}| \rceil$ and $\ell = \lceil \log_2 |\mathbb{G}^{out}| \rceil$.

We note that for range queries in particular, the generic construction is less efficient, both in terms of communication cost and the number of communication rounds, compared to the FSS-based construction.

	Generic Construction	FSS based Construction
Com. Cost $Index$	cc_{pir}	cc_{fss}
Rounds $Index$	cr_{pir}	1
Com. Cost $Range$	$O(cc_{pir} \cdot (k + \log n))$	$(k + 2) \cdot cc_{fss}$
Rounds $Range$	$O(cr_{pir} \cdot (k + \log n))$	$(k + 2)$

Fig. 2. The figure above shows the efficiency of the RQ-PIR schemes from Sect. 5 and 6 in terms of communication cost and round complexity of the underlying PIR and FSS schemes, respectively. We denote communication cost by *Com. Cost*, and the communication cost of the PIR and FSS schemes cc_{pir} and cc_{fss}, respectively. The communication costs for the client and the servers are obtained simply by using the corresponding values of cc_{pir} and cc_{fss} (note that cc_{fss} corresponds to a FSS evaluation key when considering the communication cost of the client, and a FSS evaluation result when considering the communication cost of the servers). We denote the round complexity by *Rounds*, and the round complexity of the PIR scheme by cr_{pir}. The parameter k represents the number of data entries in the database hit by the range query.

7 Discussion

In both the introduction and in Sect. 3, it was highlighted that the definition of query indistinguishability addresses the structural part of the problem of hiding range queries, but does not, by itself, address information leakage due to the timing of queries. Furthermore, it was left open how to take advantage of multiple clients accessing the same server. In this section, we will provide an informal discussion of this.

Query indistinguishability guarantees that the server(s) cannot tell from the queries alone, whether a client makes a set of index queries, a single or multiple range queries, or a combination of these. However, under the assumption that a client will always wait a certain amount of time between each query, and that the individual steps that range queries are comprised of, are executed immediately, the server(s) will be able to infer from the timing of the queries whether a range query is being made or not, and potentially the amount of data transfer in the range query.

To address this, clients might adopt a number of different countermeasures. The perhaps simplest of these, is for the client to adopt a constant query rate, in which all index queries and each step of range queries, are executed at a constant rate. Additionally adding dummy queries to maintain the query rate in between real queries will eliminate information leakage due to the timing of queries. However, the drawback of this approach is that if the query rate is high, dummy queries might cause a significant overhead for servers, as these would have to be processed like ordinary queries, and if the query rate is low, a delay with respect to the completion of range queries will be introduced, which might be significant if large amounts of data are retrieved.

A different approach is to group queries from different clients via a mechanism that will hide from the server which queries belong to which clients. This will leave the server(s) unable to analyze the query pattern of individual clients, and given a sufficient number of clients generating various queries, this can prevent the server from inferring what type of queries clients are making.

An easily conceivable but naive approach to this, is to use a proxy server for queries. The clients submit their queries to the proxy server, which will group queries for a given time interval, and then forward these to the database server. When the database server responds, the proxy server would forward the appropriate responses to the appropriate clients. Note, however, this merely moves the problem of protecting query privacy from the database server itself to the proxy server. While a proxy server without access to the database itself might be able to infer less about the queries made by clients, it would still be able to detect whether or not range queries are made, and estimate the amount of data being retrieved.

A potential way to resolve this issue, is to use an approach similar to mix networks (e.g. the Tor network [20]). In a mix network, the origin of a message is disguised by routing it through various mixing servers, and each intermediate server will not be able to determine the source of the message. Note, however, that to avoid the same issue that arose when using a proxy server, client must distribute their index queries and range query steps across different entry nodes in the mix network. In order to maximize the number of mixing servers and entry points, it conceivable that each client would act as a mixing server, and randomly distribute his own queries among all participating clients and servers, who would then route the queries through the mix network to the database server. This is very similar to the approach taken in user-private information retrieval (UPIR) [21]. In UPIR, multiple clients form a P2P network with a shared memory, and the clients forward each other's queries to the database, thereby preventing the database from learning the identity of the user who sent a particular query. A full analysis of this type of construction is outside the scope of this paper, and is left as future work.

Lastly, note that query rate limitation and mixing of client queries can easily be combined.

Acknowledgment. A part of this work was supported by JST CREST Grant Number JPMJCR19F6, Japan, JSPS KAKENHI Grant Number 19H01109, Japan and JSPS KAKENHI Grant Number 17KT0081, Japan.

A   Experimental Results

We implemented the client query generation and server response computation of our RQ-PIR scheme in C++ using FSS library [22]. In our evaluation, we used a server with a 10-core Intel(R) Xeon(R) CPU E5-2640 v4 @ 2.40 GHz and 130 GB of RAM. As client, we used a 1.3 GHz Intel Core i5 machine with 8 GB of RAM.

A.1   Evaluation

Our evaluation was done using a databases with elements consisting of 24-bits integers, and a total database size of 5, 7.5 and 10 million elements. We measured the overall time of generating client queries and server responses in our scheme for range queries retrieving 10, 50 and 100 elements from the database. In addition to the above, we noted the size of the query that the client generates and the size of the response from servers.

In our implementation, in each communication round between client and servers, the client generates a query of size 144 bytes, whereas the size of the response from each server is 8 bytes. Since our RQ-PIR scheme requires $k + 2$ rounds of communication when the client makes a range query, the total communication cost for the client is $144 \cdot (k + 2)$ bytes per server, and each server needs to generate and send responses with a total size of $8 \cdot (k+2)$ bytes, where k is the number retrieved from the database by the range query. In our particular network setup, in which the client connected to the server via a Wifi router, the total round trip time for the client to send 144 bytes of data to the server, and the server to respond with a 8 byte response, was 24 ms.

The client side computations in each round consists of generating the keys for the function secret sharing, and retrieving and combining the values from the servers' responses. Our measurements show that those computations take less than 1 ms per communication round for the client to perform. In contrast, our measurements showed that the server side computation took several orders of magnitude longer to execute, even for our smallest test case. Hence, almost the entire execution time is occupied by server side computations, which is the most important factor when considering practicality.

Figure 3 shows the experimental results of the server side computation time during the execution of the protocol. Note that our scheme was implemented to perform parallel processing of the database on the server side to accelerate the protocol execution. In particular, the server used 20 threads when running the experiments.

B   Proof of Theorem 1

Proof. For all λ, for any database $\boldsymbol{x} = (x_1, \ldots, x_n)$ of size n, for any $m \in [\ell]$, for any $a, b, c, d \in [n]$ such that $|\{x_i \mid a \leq x_i \leq b\}| = |\{x_i \mid c \leq d \leq b\}| = k$, we consider a PPTA $\mathcal{D}$ against the security for range queries in RQ-PIR scheme Π. The advantage of $\mathcal{D}$ is defined by

$$\mathsf{Adv}_{\mathcal{D},\Pi}^{range} = |\Pr[\mathcal{D}(\mathsf{View}_{a,b}^m) = 1] - \Pr[\mathcal{D}(\mathsf{View}_{c,d}^m) = 1]|.$$

To obtain a proof, we use a sequence of games (**Game** 0 to **Game** 2).

Game 0: This game corresponds to the client and servers running $\langle Range, Res_1, \ldots, Res_\ell\rangle((a, b), \boldsymbol{x}, \ldots, \boldsymbol{x})$.

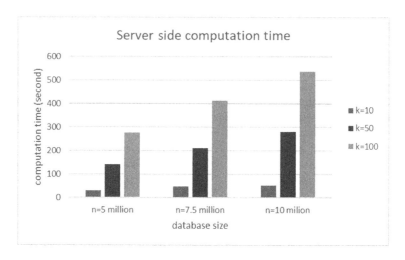

Fig. 3. Experimental result of server side computation time: n denotes the database size, and k denotes the number of element that client retrieves from database by range query.

Game 1: This game corresponds to the client and servers running $\langle Index, Res_1, \ldots, Res_\ell \rangle (i_1, \boldsymbol{x}, \ldots, \boldsymbol{x}), \ldots, \langle Index, Res_1, \ldots, Res_\ell \rangle (i_{f(k)}, \boldsymbol{x}, \ldots, \boldsymbol{x})$, where $k := |\{x_i \mid a \le x_i \le b\}|$ and $i_1, \ldots, i_{f(k)}$ are chosen randomly from $[n]$.

Game 2: This game corresponds to the client and servers running $\langle Range, Res_1, \ldots, Res_\ell \rangle ((c, d), \boldsymbol{x}, \ldots, \boldsymbol{x})$.

For all r, we denote by View_r^m the view for server m generated in **Game** r.

Lemma 2. *If RQ-PIR scheme Π provides query indistinguishability, then for any $r \in \{1, 2\}$ and for any PPTA $\mathcal{B}$, it holds that the difference between the probability that $\mathcal{B}$ outputs 1 in **Game** $r - 1$ and r is negligible.*

Proof. We consider a PPTA $\mathcal{B}$ who distinguishes View_{r-1}^m from View_r^m, and denote the advantage of $\mathcal{B}$ by

$$\mathsf{Adv}_{\mathcal{B}, \Pi}^r = |\Pr[\mathcal{B}(\mathsf{View}_r^m) = 1] - \Pr[\mathcal{B}(\mathsf{View}_{r-1}^m) = 1]|.$$

Then, since View_0^m and View_2^m are same as View_{range}^m in the definition of query indistinguishability, and View_1^m is same as View_{index}^m, we can see $\mathcal{B}$ as an adversary against query indistinguishability for Π. Thus, we can conclude

$$\mathsf{Adv}_{\mathcal{B}, \Pi}^r = |\Pr[\mathcal{B}(\mathsf{View}_r^m) = 1] - \Pr[\mathcal{B}(\mathsf{View}_{r-1}^m) = 1]|$$

is negligible.   □

By using Lemma 2, we can derive

$$|\Pr[\mathcal{D}(\mathsf{View}_{a,b}^m) = 1] - \Pr[\mathcal{D}(\mathsf{View}_{c,d}^m) = 1]|$$

$$\le \sum_{r=1}^{2} |\Pr[\mathcal{D}(\mathsf{View}_{r-1}^m) = 1] - \Pr[\mathcal{D}(\mathsf{View}_r^m) = 1]| \le 2 \cdot negl. \quad \Box$$

References

1. Chor, B., Goldreich, O., Kushilevitz, E., Sudan, M.: Private information retrieval. In: FOCS, pp. 41–50 (1995)
2. Kushilevitz, E., Ostrovsky, R.: Replication is NOT needed: SINGLE database, computationally-private information retrieval. In: FOCS, pp. 364–373 (1997)
3. Dvir, Z., Gopi, S.: 2-server PIR with sub-polynomial communication. In: STOC, pp. 577–584 (2015)
4. Cachin, Christian., Micali, Silvio, Stadler, Markus: Computationally private information retrieval with polylogarithmic communication. In: Stern, Jacques (ed.) EUROCRYPT 1999. LNCS, vol. 1592, pp. 402–414. Springer, Heidelberg (1999). https://doi.org/10.1007/3-540-48910-X_28
5. Dong, C., Chen, L.: A fast single server private information retrieval protocol with low communication cost. In: Kutyłowski, M., Vaidya, J. (eds.) ESORICS 2014. LNCS, vol. 8712, pp. 380–399. Springer, Cham (2014). https://doi.org/10.1007/978-3-319-11203-9_22
6. Hore, B., Mehrotra, S., Tsudik, G.: A privacy-preserving index for range queries. In: VLDB, pp. 720–731 (2004)
7. Kamara, S., Moataz, T.: SQL on structurally-encrypted databases. In: Peyrin, T., Galbraith, S. (eds.) ASIACRYPT 2018. LNCS, vol. 11272, pp. 149–180. Springer, Cham (2018). https://doi.org/10.1007/978-3-030-03326-2_6
8. Cash, D., Grubbs, P., Perry, J., Ristenpart, T.: Leakage-abuse attacks against searchable encryption. In: ACM Conference on Computer and Communications Security, pp. 668–679 (2015)
9. Kellaris, G., Kollios, G., Nissim, K., O'neill, A.: Adam: generic attacks on secure outsourced databases. In: ACM Conference on Computer and Communications Security, pp. 1329–1340 (2016)
10. Grubbs, P., Lacharité, M.S., Minaud, B., Paterson, K.G.: Pump up the volume: practical database reconstruction from volume leakage on range queries. In: ACM Conference on Computer and Communications Security, pp. 315–331 (2018)
11. Gui, Z., Johnson, O., Warinschi, B.: Encrypted databases: new volume attacks against range queries. In: ACM Conference on Computer and Communications Security, pp. 361–378 (2019)
12. Li, J., Omiecinski, E.R.: Efficiency and security trade-off in supporting range queries on encrypted databases. In: Jajodia, S., Wijesekera, D. (eds.) DBSec 2005. LNCS, vol. 3654, pp. 69–83. Springer, Heidelberg (2005). https://doi.org/10.1007/11535706_6
13. Chen, K., Kavuluru, R., Guo, S.: RASP: efficient multidimensional range query on attack-resilient encrypted databases. In: CODASPY, pp. 249–260 (2011)
14. Wang, F., Yun, C., Goldwasser, S., Vaikuntanathan, V., Zaharia, M.: Splinter: practical private queries on public data. In: NSDI, pp. 299–313 (2017)
15. Chor, B., Gilboa, N., Naor, M.: Private information retrieval by keywords. IACR Cryptology ePrint Archive 1998, vol. 3 (1998)
16. Tillem, G., Candan, Ö.M., Savaş, E., Kaya, K.: Hiding access patterns in range queries using private information retrieval and ORAM. In: Clark, J., Meiklejohn, S., Ryan, P.Y.A., Wallach, D., Brenner, M., Rohloff, K. (eds.) FC 2016. LNCS, vol. 9604, pp. 253–270. Springer, Heidelberg (2016). https://doi.org/10.1007/978-3-662-53357-4_17

17. Groth, J., Kiayias, A., Lipmaa, H.: Multi-query computationally-private information retrieval with constant communication rate. In: Nguyen, P.Q., Pointcheval, D. (eds.) PKC 2010. LNCS, vol. 6056, pp. 107–123. Springer, Heidelberg (2010). https://doi.org/10.1007/978-3-642-13013-7_7
18. Boyle, E., Gilboa, N., Ishai, Y.: Function secret sharing. In: Oswald, E., Fischlin, M. (eds.) EUROCRYPT 2015. LNCS, vol. 9057, pp. 337–367. Springer, Heidelberg (2015). https://doi.org/10.1007/978-3-662-46803-6_12
19. Boyle, E., Gilboa, N., Ishai, Y.: Function secret sharing: improvements and extensions. In: ACM Conference on Computer and Communications Security, pp. 1292–1303 (2016)
20. Dingledine, R., Mathewson, N., Syverson, P., Paul, F.: Tor: the second-generation onion router. In: USENIX Security Symposium, pp. 303–320 (2004)
21. Swanson, C.M., Stinson, D.R.: Extended results on privacy against coalitions of users in user-private information retrieval protocols. Crypt. Commun. $7(4)$, 415–437 (2015). https://doi.org/10.1007/s12095-015-0125-x
22. LibFSS. https://github.com/frankw2/libfss

Blockchain II

2-hop Blockchain: Combining Proof-of-Work and Proof-of-Stake Securely

Tuyet Duong[1], Lei Fan[2], Jonathan Katz[3], Phuc Thai[1],
and Hong-Sheng Zhou[1(✉)]

[1] Virginia Commonwealth University, Richmond, USA
{duongtt3,thaipd,hszhou}@vcu.edu
[2] Shanghai Jiao Tong University, Shanghai, China
fanlei@sjtu.edu.cn
[3] George Mason University, Fairfax, USA
jkatz2@gmail.com

Abstract. Bitcoin-like blockchains use a proof-of-work (PoW) mechanism, where security holds if the majority of the computing power is under the control of honest players. However, this assumption has been seriously challenged recently, and Bitcoin-like systems fail if this assumption is violated. In this work we propose a novel *2-hop* blockchain protocol that combines PoW and proof-of-stake (PoS) mechanisms. Our analysis shows that the protocol is secure as long as the honest players control a majority of the *collective* resources (which consist of both computing power and stake). In particular, even if the adversary controls more than 50% of the computing power, security still holds if the honest parties hold sufficiently high stake in the system. As an added contribution, our protocol also remains secure against adaptive adversaries.

1 Introduction

Cryptocurrencies like Bitcoin [28] have been a phenomenal success. At the heart of Bitcoin is a global, distributed ledger, called a *blockchain*, that records transactions in successive time windows. The blockchain is maintained by a peer-to-peer network of *miners* via a so-called proof-of-work (PoW) mechanism: in each time window, cryptographic puzzles (also called proof-of-work puzzles [1,15]) are generated, and all miners are incentivized to solve those puzzles; the first miner who finds a puzzle solution is allowed to extend the blockchain with a block of transactions. The more computing power a miner invests, the better its chances of solving a puzzle first.

T. Duong—Work supported in part by a research gift from IOHK.

J. Katz—Portions of this work were done while at the University of Maryland, and were performed under financial assistance award 70NANB19H126 from U.S. Department of Commerce, National Institute of Standards and Technology.

P. Thai and H.-S. Zhou—Work supported in part by NSF award #1801470, and a research gift from Ergo Platform.

L. Chen et al. (Eds.): ESORICS 2020, LNCS 12309, pp. 697–712, 2020.
https://doi.org/10.1007/978-3-030-59013-0_34

Bitcoin is an *open* system; any player who invests a certain amount of computing resources is allowed to join the effort of maintaining the blockchain. This feature, along with a smart incentive strategy, have helped the system attract a huge amount of computing resources over the past several years.

The *Nakamoto consensus protocol* underlying Bitcoin has recently been proven secure in various models. In particular, Garay et al. [19] and Pass et al. [30] showed that, assuming the majority of mining power is controlled by honest miners, Nakamoto consensus satisfies several important security properties. On the other hand, if an adversary controls a majority of the computational power in the network, security of Bitcoin cannot be guaranteed.

While it is appealing to assume that the majority of computing power in a blockchain network is honest, this assumption has been seriously challenged in recent years. For example, in 2014 the mining pool GHash.io exceeded 50% of the computational power in the Bitcoin network [21]. In 2017, one mining pool controlled 50% of the mining power in the Zcash system.[1] Currently, many of the top Bitcoin mining pools are in China; at times, they have collectively controlled more than 60% of the mining power in the Bitcoin ecosystem.[2] Efforts have been made to address this crisis, with some work [27] trying to discourage the formation of mining pools. However, these ideas have not seen much adoption in practice, and it is anyway unclear whether they would prevent certain types of attacks (e.g., nation states who wish to disrupt a cryptocurrency).

In part to address these issues, other design paradigms for blockchains have been considered. The most prominent such designs are based on *proof-of-stake* (PoS) mechanisms, which require miners to own a certain amount of coins ("stake") in order to extend the blockchain; the probability that a particular miner is allowed to extend the blockchain in any iteration is proportional to the amount of stake it owns.

1.1 Our Results

We propose a *hybrid* blockchain protocol that uses a combination of PoW and PoS mechanisms. We prove that security of the blockchain holds as long as the honest parties control a majority of the collective resources in the system, where these collective resources consist of both computing power and stake. As an additional contribution, and in contrast to several other PoS protocols that have been proposed, we show that our protocol tolerates an *adaptive* adversary who can decide which parties to corrupt during the course of the protocol execution. Source code for our protocol is publicly available (https://bitbucket. org/twinscoinccs/twinscoin), and an experimental evaluation of the protocol has been done [10]. Our focus here is on definitions and proofs of security. In what follows, we give an overview of the underlying ideas.

Our main idea is to have two coupled blockchains, one (denoted $\mathcal{C}$) based a PoW mechanism and another (denoted $\tilde{\mathcal{C}}$) using a PoS-based approach; we

---

[1] See https://twitter.com/kyletorpey/status/910622595388715020.

[2] See https://www.buybitcoinworldwide.com/mining/pools.

refer to PoW-miners who extend the former and PoS-holders (or *stakeholders*) who extend the latter, but of course one entity may play both roles. These two blockchains are extended alternately, so that their respective heights are always within one block of each other. Roughly, the overall (logical) blockchain is extended by first having a PoW-miner extend $\mathcal{C}$ and then having a PoS-holder extend $\tilde{\mathcal{C}}$.

A pictorial illustration of our blockchain structure is given in Fig. 1. Rectangular blocks correspond to $\mathcal{C}$, while circular blocks correspond to $\tilde{\mathcal{C}}$. (Our 2-hop blockchain can be bootstrapped[3] from an already existing blockchain, denoted by grey blocks in the figure.) Intuitively, $\mathcal{C}$ serves as a (possibly biased) random beacon for choosing a stakeholder to extend $\tilde{\mathcal{C}}$. If Nakamoto consensus is a 1-hop protocol, then ours is a 2-hop*protocol.*

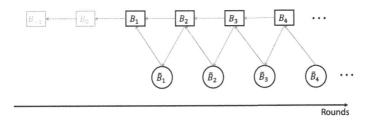

Fig. 1. 2-hop blockchain structure. Rectangular blocks denote the PoW chain, and circular blocks denote the PoS chain. Grey blocks (which need not be present) represent a pre-existing blockchain.

In more detail, say we have a PoW chain $\mathcal{C}$ consisting of blocks $B_1, \ldots, B_i$ and a PoS chain $\tilde{\mathcal{C}}$ consisting of blocks $\tilde{B}_1, \ldots, \tilde{B}_i$; when we refer to a *chain pair* we mean a pair of valid chains $\mathcal{C}, \tilde{\mathcal{C}}$ of the same height. A new *block pair*—consisting of a new block B_{i+1} on $\mathcal{C}$ and a new block $\tilde{B}_{i+1}$ on $\tilde{\mathcal{C}}$—is generated as follows:

1. A PoW-miner extends $\mathcal{C}$ in the usual way, but building on both $\mathcal{C}$ and $\tilde{\mathcal{C}}$. That is, a miner first computes $h = \mathsf{hash}(B_i, \tilde{B}_i)$, and then attempts to find a suitable nonce ω such that $\mathsf{H}(h, \omega) < \mathsf{T}$ for some target T. The new block on $\mathcal{C}$ takes the form $B_{i+1} = \langle h, \omega \rangle$.
2. Each PoS-holder holds two pairs of signing keys $(\mathsf{vk}, \mathsf{sk})$ and $(\mathsf{vk}', \mathsf{sk}')$, where the first is for a *unique* signature scheme and the second can be for an ordinary signature scheme. A PoS-holder can extend $\tilde{\mathcal{C}}$ if $\tilde{\mathsf{H}}(B_{i+1}, \tilde{\omega}, \mathsf{vk}) < \tilde{\mathsf{T}}$, where $\tilde{\omega} = \mathsf{Sign}_{\mathsf{sk}}(B_{i+1})$ and $\tilde{\mathsf{T}}$ is the current target. A new block takes the form $\tilde{B}_{i+1} = \langle (B_{i+1}, \tilde{\omega}, \mathsf{vk}), X, \sigma, \mathsf{vk}' \rangle$, where $X \in \{0,1\}^*$ is the payload of the block (also denoted as $\mathsf{payload}(\tilde{B}_{i+1})$); and $\sigma = \mathsf{Sign}'_{\mathsf{sk}'}((B_{i+1}, \tilde{\omega}, \mathsf{vk}), X)$.

While we defer a detailed discussion of the security of our protocol to Sect. 4, we observe some interesting properties of our protocol here:

---

[3] This also implies that our design could be used as a strategy for converting a PoW-based blockchain into a pure PoS one, via a sequence of hard forks.

- We can obtain adaptive security since the identity of the PoS-holder who can extend $\tilde{\mathcal{C}}$ is hidden before it publishes the new block; once the new PoS block is published and incorporated in the chain, it is too late for adversarial corruption to have any effect.
- Our protocol can resist a *nothing-at-stake* attack in which a malicious PoS-holder attempts to generate new blocks on multiple forks simultaneously. The reason is that in our 2-hop protocol the PoS chain builds on a PoW chain that, in general, will have fewer forks.
- Our protocol also resists *long-range attacks* in which an adversary tries to create a long chain, starting from the genesis block, that overtakes the main chain. This is because although creating a long PoS chain may be feasible, creating a long PoW chain is computationally infeasible.

1.2 Related Work

Bitcoin and the underlying PoW-based Nakamoto consensus protocol have been analyzed in both rational [16,17,32,33] and adversarial [19,22,23,30,34] settings. The idea of using proofs of *stake* in place of proofs of work was first introduced in an online forum [5], and several PoS-based protocols have been proposed and implemented in deployed cryptocurrencies [3,11,25,29,35]. These early proposals lack rigorous security analysis. Subsequent work [2,8,9,12,13,18,20,24,31], done concurrently with our own (an early version of this work [14] was posted online in 2016), has given formal proofs of security for PoS-based blockchain protocols. However, many proof-of-stake solutions [12,24,31] are not adaptively secure.

Hybrid PoW/PoS blockchains have been suggested by some previous work [4, 11,25] and cryptocurrencies (e.g., https://decred.org). However, none of these systems has a formal proof of security. In addition, they are easily seen to be insecure against an adaptive adversary.

1.3 Paper Organization

We present our model and definitions in Sect. 2, and the details of our protocol in Sect. 3. In Sect. 4, we provide the high-level idea of our security analysis; full proofs are deferred to the full version of our paper.

2 Preliminaries

2.1 System Model

In order to study the security of Bitcoin-like protocols, Garay et al. [19] and then Pass et al. [30] set up the first cryptographic models by following Canetti's formulation of the "real world" executions [6,7]. We further extend their models so that more blockchain protocols, e.g., 2-hop blockchains, are allowed. The underlying communication for blockchain protocols is the atomic unauthenticated broadcast in a semi-synchronous setting with an upper bound Δ network delay.

Protocol Players. We consider two types of players, PoW-miners and PoS-holders, who may generate two types of blocks, PoW blocks and PoS blocks; We can then define PoW-chain and PoS-chain, for PoW blocks and PoS blocks respectively. These two types of chains could be tied and grow together. In our model, without loss of generality, we assume all PoW-miners have the same amount of computing power and all PoS-holders have the same amount of stake. Note that this is an "idealized model". In the reality, each different honest PoW-miner or PoS-holder may have a different amount of computing power/stake; nevertheless, this idealized model does not sacrifice generality since one can imagine that real-world honest PoW-miners/PoS-holders are simply clusters of some arbitrary number of honest idealized-model PoW-miners/PoS-holders.

Protocol Execution. We consider the execution of the blockchain protocol $\Pi = (\Pi^w, \Pi^s)$ that is directed by an environment $\mathcal{Z}(1^\kappa)$ (where Π^w and Π^s denote the code run by PoW-miners and PoS-holders, and κ is a security parameter), which activates up to n PoW-miners and up to $\tilde{n}$ PoS-holders. For simplicity, in this paper, we consider the static computing power and stake setting (where the total amount of computing power and stakes invested to the protocol will not change over time). We also consider that, all players, i.e., n PoW-miners and $\tilde{n}$ PoS-holders, are activated at the beginning of the protocol execution by the environment. Note that the environment $\mathcal{Z}$ can "manage" protocol players through an adversary $\mathcal{A}$ who may adaptively corrupt honest parties.

Protocol execution typically consists of two phases, *initialization* phase and *blockchain-extension* phase, and the execution proceeds in *rounds*. In the initialization phase, each PoW-miner can join the protocol execution by investing certain amount of computing power. Similarly, each PoS-holder can join the execution by investing certain amount of stake. Note that, the state of the initialization phase, if needed, can be recorded in the genesis block of blockchain system.

The blockchain-extension phase consists of multiple rounds. In each round, $\mathcal{Z}$ provides inputs for all players and receives outputs from them; the players communicate with each other via the network. More concretely, in each round, each honest player receives an input from the environment $\mathcal{Z}$, and potentially receives incoming network messages (delivered by the adversary $\mathcal{A}$), and then updates its local state; then based on the stored information, the player carries out some (mining) operations; in the case that a new block is generated, the player sends out the new block which will be guaranteed to be delivered to all players in the beginning of the next round.

Let $\mathsf{EXEC}_{\Pi,\mathcal{A},\mathcal{Z}}$ be a random variable denoting the joint view of all parties in the above execution; note that this joint view fully determines the execution.

2.2 Security Properties

As in the original Bitcoin white paper [28], a proof-of-work blockchain is created and maintained by a set of players called PoW-miners. A PoW blockchain $\mathcal{C}$

consists of a sequence of concatenated PoW-blocks $B_0 \| B_1 \| B_2 \| \cdots \| B_\ell$, where $\ell \geq 0$, and B_0 denotes the genesis block. For each blockchain, we specify several notations such as head, length, and subchain: (I) BLOCKCHAIN HEAD, denoted $\mathsf{head}(\mathcal{C})$, refers to the topmost block B_ℓ in chain $\mathcal{C}$; (II) BLOCKCHAIN LENGTH, denoted $\mathsf{len}(\mathcal{C})$, is the number of blocks in blockchain $\mathcal{C}$ *after the genesis block*, and here $\mathsf{len}(\mathcal{C}) = \ell$; (III) SUBCHAIN, refers to a segment of a blockchain; we use $\mathcal{C}[1, \ell]$ to denote an entire blockchain, and use $\mathcal{C}[j, m]$, with $j \geq 1$ and $m \leq \ell$, to denote a subchain $B_j \| \cdots \| B_m$; in addition, we use $\mathcal{C}[i]$ to denote the i-th block B_i in blockchain $\mathcal{C}$; finally, if blockchain $\mathcal{C}$ is a prefix of another blockchain $\mathcal{C}'$, we write $\mathcal{C} \preceq \mathcal{C}'$. Similarly, we define a proof-of-stake (PoS) blockchain $\tilde{\mathcal{C}}$ by a sequence of concatenated PoS-blocks $\tilde{B}_0 \| \tilde{B}_1 \| \tilde{B}_2 \| \cdots \| \tilde{B}_{\tilde{\ell}}$ for $\tilde{\ell} > 0$ that is maintained by a set of PoS-holders; here $\tilde{B}_0$ denotes the genesis block.

Chain Growth, Common Prefix, and Chain Quality. Several important security properties have been considered for blockchain protocols. The *common prefix* and *chain quality* properties were originally formalized by Garay et al. [19], with the common prefix property later strengthened by Pass et al. [30]. The *chain growth* property was first formally defined by Kiayias et al. [22]. We provide corresponding definitions here, specialized to the case of a 2-hop blockchain protocol.

Definition 1 (Chain growth). *Consider 2-hop blockchain protocol Π. The chain growth property $\mathcal{Q}_{\mathrm{cg}}$ with parameter $g \in \mathbb{R}$, states that for any honest player with the local chain-pair $\langle \mathcal{C}, \tilde{\mathcal{C}} \rangle$ in round r and $\langle \mathcal{C}', \tilde{\mathcal{C}}' \rangle$ in round r' where $r' - r > 0$, in $\mathsf{EXEC}_{\Pi, \mathcal{A}, \mathcal{Z}}$. It holds that $\mathsf{len}(\mathcal{C}') - \mathsf{len}(\mathcal{C}) \geq g \cdot (r' - r)$ and $\mathsf{len}(\tilde{\mathcal{C}}') - \mathsf{len}(\tilde{\mathcal{C}}) \geq g \cdot (r' - r)$.*

Definition 2 (Common prefix). *Consider 2-hop blockchain protocol Π. The common prefix property $\mathcal{Q}_{\mathrm{cp}}$ with parameter $\kappa \in \mathbb{N}$ states that for any two honest players i in round r and j in round r' with the local chain-pairs $\langle \mathcal{C}_i, \tilde{\mathcal{C}}_i \rangle$ and $\langle \mathcal{C}_j, \tilde{\mathcal{C}}_j \rangle$, respectively, in $\mathsf{EXEC}_{\Pi, \mathcal{A}, \mathcal{Z}}$ where $r \leq r'$, it holds that $\mathcal{C}_i[\neg \kappa] \preceq \mathcal{C}_j$, and $\tilde{\mathcal{C}}_i[\neg \kappa] \preceq \tilde{\mathcal{C}}_j$.*

Definition 3 (Chain quality). *Consider 2-hop blockchain protocol Π. The chain quality property $\mathcal{Q}_{\mathrm{cq}}$ with parameters $\mu \in \mathbb{R}$ and $\ell \in \mathbb{N}$ states that for any honest player with the local chain-pair $\langle \mathcal{C}, \tilde{\mathcal{C}} \rangle$ in $\mathsf{EXEC}_{\Pi, \mathcal{A}, \mathcal{Z}}$, it holds that for large enough ℓ consecutive block-pairs of chain-pair the ratio of honest block-pairs (an honest block-pair is a pair of an honest PoW-block and an honest PoS-block) is at least μ.*

Note that each block-pair consists of a PoW block and a PoS block. When the payload is attached only to PoS blocks (resp., PoW blocks), we can define the property of chain quality based on the ratio of honest PoS blocks (resp., PoW blocks).

3 Construction

3.1 The Main Protocol

Our protocol uses standard cryptographic building blocks: As in the original Bitcoin design, we use hash functions H and hash, and a regular digital signature scheme $\Sigma' = (\mathsf{Gen}', \mathsf{Sign}', \mathsf{Verify}')$; In addition, we need a *unique* signature scheme $\Sigma = (\mathsf{Gen}, \mathsf{Sign}, \mathsf{Verify})$ and a third hash function $\tilde{H}$.

Initialization. In the initialization phase, PoW players join the system by investing certain amount of computing power (as in the original Bitcoin design). To enable PoS players to register to the system, each PoS player first generates two pairs of signing-verification keys based on the signature schemes Σ and Σ'. More concretely, for all $i \in [\tilde{n}]$, PoS player S_i computes $(\mathsf{sk}_i, \mathsf{vk}_i) \leftarrow \mathsf{Gen}(1^\kappa)$ and $(\mathsf{sk}'_i, \mathsf{vk}'_i) \leftarrow \mathsf{Gen}'(1^\kappa)$. Then based on the identity $\mathsf{vk}_i, \mathsf{vk}'_i$, the PoS player S_i can join the system via investing certain amount of stake. We note that, the registration information including all PoS players' identities $\{\mathsf{vk}_i, \mathsf{vk}'_i\}_{i \in [\tilde{n}]}$ will be recorded in the genesis block B_0.

Blockchain Extension. Our (logical) blockchain consists of a PoW-chain $\mathcal{C}$ and a PoS-chain $\tilde{\mathcal{C}}$. In order to extend the blockchain, for each block height, we will first extend PoW chain with one PoW-block, and then extend the PoS-chain with one PoS-block. Concretely, consider that we have a blockchain with height i; that is, PoW chain $\mathcal{C} = B_0 \| B_1 \| \ldots \| B_i$ and PoS chain $\tilde{\mathcal{C}} = B_0 \| \tilde{B}_1 \| \ldots \| \tilde{B}_i$. Next PoW block B_{i+1} and then PoS block $\tilde{B}_{i+1}$, will be generated, as follows.

In the first hop, PoW-miners attempt to extend $\mathcal{C}$ as usual, but building on both $\mathcal{C}$ and $\tilde{\mathcal{C}}$. That is, a miner first computes $h = \mathsf{hash}(B_i, \tilde{B}_i)$, and then attempts to find a suitable nonce ω such that $H(h, \omega) < T$ for some target T. The new block on $\mathcal{C}$ takes the form $B_{i+1} = \langle h, \omega \rangle$.

The protocol now moves to the second hop. Intuitively, $\mathcal{C}$ serves as a (possibly biased) random beacon for choosing a stakeholder to extend $\tilde{\mathcal{C}}$. Once the new PoW-block B_{i+1} is published in the system, a PoS-holder is allowed to extend $\tilde{\mathcal{C}}$ if $\tilde{H}(B_{i+1}, \tilde{\omega}, \mathsf{vk}) < \tilde{T}$, where $\tilde{\omega} = \mathsf{Sign}_{\mathsf{sk}}(B_{i+1})$ and $\tilde{T}$ is the current target. A new block takes the form $\tilde{B}_{i+1} = \langle (B_{i+1}, \tilde{\omega}, \mathsf{vk}), X, \sigma, \mathsf{vk}' \rangle$, where $X \in \{0,1\}^*$ is the payload of the block (also denoted as $\mathsf{payload}(\tilde{B}_{i+1})$); and $\sigma = \mathsf{Sign}'_{\mathsf{sk}'}((B_{i+1}, \tilde{\omega}, \mathsf{vk}), X)$.

At this moment, both PoW-chain $\mathcal{C}$ and PoS-chain $\tilde{\mathcal{C}}$ have been extended with one new block B_{i+1} and $\tilde{B}_{i+1}$, respectively, and the two-hop iterations continue. Please refer to Fig. 2 for the details of our main protocol. We note that all players collect blockchain information from the network, and wining players publish their generated blocks through the network; The protocol Π is parameterized by a content validation predicate $V(\cdot)$, which determines the proper structure of the information that is stored into the blockchain (as in [19, 30]).

Best Chain-Pair Strategy. In the above protocol execution, players including Protocol players, PoW-miners and PoS-holders, need to be aware, which chain-pair is the best one during the protocol execution. We describe a strategy to decide the best chain-pair via $\mathsf{BestValid}$ process; please see Fig. 3 for details.

PROTOCOL $\Pi = (\Pi^w, \Pi^s)$

The protocol $\Pi = (\Pi^w, \Pi^s)$ is executed by $(n + \tilde{n})$ players, including n PoW-miners and $\tilde{n}$ PoS-holders. Initially, each player holds local state $state_i := \{\langle \mathcal{C}_i, \tilde{\mathcal{C}}_i \rangle\}$ for $1 \le i \le n + \tilde{n}$, where $\mathcal{C}_i = \tilde{\mathcal{C}}_i = B_\emptyset$.

PoW-Miner Π^w by PoW-miner W_i, for $1 \le i \le n$, with local state $state_i$.
Upon receiving an input message from $\mathcal{Z}$, and/or receiving messages of the form (BROADCAST, $\langle \mathcal{C}, \tilde{\mathcal{C}} \rangle$) from the network, player W_i proceeds as follows:

1. *Select the best local chain-pair:*
   Set $\mathbb{C}$ to be the set of all chain-pairs collected from the network;
   Compute $\langle \mathcal{C}_{best}, \tilde{\mathcal{C}}_{best} \rangle := \mathsf{BestValid}(\mathbb{C} \cup \{\langle \mathcal{C}_i, \tilde{\mathcal{C}}_i \rangle\}, PoW\text{-}miner)$; // process
   BestValid() can be found in Fig. 3 below.
   Set $\mathcal{C}_i := \mathcal{C}_{best}$ and $\tilde{\mathcal{C}}_i := \tilde{\mathcal{C}}_{best}$.
2. *Attempt to extend PoW-chain:*
   - Compute $h := \mathsf{hash}(\mathsf{head}(\mathcal{C}_i), \mathsf{head}(\tilde{\mathcal{C}}_i))$;
   - Identify ω so that $\mathsf{H}(h, \omega) < \mathsf{T}$;
     If $\omega \ne \perp$, then set $B := \langle h, \omega \rangle$, $\mathcal{C}_i := \mathcal{C}_i \| B$, $state_i := state_i \cup \{\langle \mathcal{C}_i, \tilde{\mathcal{C}}_i \rangle\}$, and send (BROADCAST, $\langle \mathcal{C}_i, \tilde{\mathcal{C}}_i \rangle$) to the network;
   Return an output message to the environment $\mathcal{Z}$.

PoS-Holder Π^s by PoS-holder S_j, for $n + 1 \le j \le n + \tilde{n}$, with $state_j$.

Upon receiving an input message from $\mathcal{Z}$, and/or receiving messages of the form (MESSAGE, $\langle \mathcal{C}, \tilde{\mathcal{C}} \rangle$) from the network, player S_j proceeds as follows:

1. *Select the best local chain-pair:*
   Set $\mathbb{C}$ as the set of all chain-pairs collected from the network;
   Compute $\langle \mathcal{C}_{best}, \tilde{\mathcal{C}}_{best} \rangle := \mathsf{BestValid}(\mathbb{C} \cup \{\langle \mathcal{C}_j, \tilde{\mathcal{C}}_j \rangle\}, PoS\text{-}holder)$; // process
   BestValid() can be found in Fig. 3 below.
   Set $\mathcal{C}_j := \mathcal{C}_{best}$ and $\tilde{\mathcal{C}}_j := \tilde{\mathcal{C}}_{best}$.
2. *Attempt to extend PoS-chain:*
   - Set B as the new PoW-block in $\mathcal{C}_{best}$; Compute $\tilde{\omega} := \mathsf{Sign}_{sk}(B)$;
   - If $\tilde{\mathsf{H}}(B, \tilde{\omega}, \mathsf{vk}) < \tilde{\mathsf{T}}$, then compute $\sigma \leftarrow \mathsf{Sign}'_{sk'}((B, \tilde{\omega}, \mathsf{vk}), X)$, and set $\tilde{B} := \langle (B, \tilde{\omega}, \mathsf{vk}), X, \sigma, \mathsf{vk}' \rangle$; Set $\tilde{\mathcal{C}}_j := \tilde{\mathcal{C}}_j \| \tilde{B}$, and $state_j := state_j \cup \{\langle \mathcal{C}_j, \tilde{\mathcal{C}}_j \rangle\}$. and send (BROADCAST, $\langle \mathcal{C}_j, \tilde{\mathcal{C}}_j \rangle$) to the network.
   Return an output message to the environment $\mathcal{Z}$.

Fig. 2. Our main protocol $\Pi = (\Pi^w, \Pi^s)$.

The $\mathsf{BestValid}$ process is parameterized by a content validation predicate $V(\cdot)$ which determines the proper structure of the information that is stored into the blockchain as in [19], and takes as input a chain-pair set $\mathbb{C}'$. Intuitively, the process validates all chain-pair $\langle \mathcal{C}, \tilde{\mathcal{C}} \rangle$ in $\mathbb{C}'$, then finds the valid chain-pairs with the longest PoW-chain. It also ensures that, if *Type* = *PoW-miner*, every valid chain-pair should have its member chains $\mathcal{C}$ and $\tilde{\mathcal{C}}$ of the same length. On the other hand, if *Type* = *PoS-holder*, we allow the PoW-chain to be longer than the PoS-chain by one block since there may be a new PoW-block produced in the previous rounds. We emphasize that since each valid PoS-block is tied to a PoW-block, and each PoW-block or PoS-block is valid if their peers are valid. The strategy to deal with multiple chains with the same length is discussed in Remark 1 at the end of this section.

PROCESS BestValid

Upon receiving the input $(\mathbb{C}', \textit{Type})$, the process BestValid proceeds as follows:

For every chain-pair $\langle \mathcal{C}, \tilde{\mathcal{C}} \rangle \in \mathbb{C}'$,

- If $\mathsf{len}(\mathcal{C}) - 1 = \mathsf{len}(\tilde{\mathcal{C}})$, then
  - Set $\ell := \mathsf{len}(\mathcal{C})$; Parse $\mathcal{C}[\ell]$ into $\langle h_\ell, \omega_\ell \rangle$.
  - If $\mathsf{hash}(\mathcal{C}[\ell-1], \tilde{\mathcal{C}}[\ell-1]) \neq h_\ell$, remove this chain-pair from $\mathbb{C}'$;
  - If $\mathsf{H}(\mathcal{C}[\ell]) \geq \mathsf{T}$, remove this chain-pair from $\mathbb{C}'$.
- Else if $\big(\mathsf{len}(\mathcal{C}) = \mathsf{len}(\tilde{\mathcal{C}})$ and $V(\mathsf{payload}(\tilde{\mathcal{C}})) = 1\big)$, or $\big(\mathsf{len}(\mathcal{C}) - 1 = \mathsf{len}(\tilde{\mathcal{C}})$ and $\textit{Type} = \textit{PoS-holder}\big)$, then for i from $\mathsf{len}(\tilde{\mathcal{C}})$ to 1, proceed as follows:
  - *Verify PoW-block $\mathcal{C}[i]$:* Parse $\mathcal{C}[i]$ into $\langle h_i, \omega_i \rangle$;
    If $\mathsf{hash}(\mathcal{C}[i-1], \tilde{\mathcal{C}}[i-1]) \neq h_i$, or $\mathsf{H}(\mathcal{C}[i]) \geq \mathsf{T}$, set $b_1 := 0$; Else, set $b_1 := 1$;
  - *Verify PoS-block $\tilde{\mathcal{C}}[i]$:* Parse $\tilde{\mathcal{C}}[i]$ into $\langle B, \tilde{\omega}, \mathsf{vk}, X, \sigma, \mathsf{vk}' \rangle$;
    If $\mathsf{Verify}'_{\mathsf{vk}'}((B, \tilde{\omega}, \mathsf{vk}, X), \sigma) = 1$, set $b_2 := 1$; Else set $b_2 := 0$;
    If $\mathsf{Verify}_{\mathsf{vk}}(B, \tilde{\omega}) = 0$, or $\tilde{\mathsf{H}}(B, \tilde{\omega}, \mathsf{vk}) \geq \tilde{\mathsf{T}}$, or $B \neq \mathcal{C}[i]$, set $b_3 := 0$; Else, set $b_3 := 1$;
  - If $b_1 = 0$ or $b_2 = 0$, or $b_3 = 0$, remove this chain-pair from $\mathbb{C}'$.

Find the valid chain-pair $\langle \mathcal{C}_{\mathsf{best}}, \tilde{\mathcal{C}}_{\mathsf{best}} \rangle \in \mathbb{C}'$ with the longest PoW-chain. Then set $\langle \mathcal{C}_{\mathsf{best}}, \tilde{\mathcal{C}}_{\mathsf{best}} \rangle$ as the output.

Fig. 3. The chain set validation process BestValid. The process is parameterized by a content validation predicate $V(\cdot)$.

Remark 1 (Tie breaking). Our protocol primarily deals with length so it makes sense to adopt a simple tie-breaking strategy to choose the best chain-pair from two chain-pairs of equal length. While there is work that show the advantages of choosing a chain randomly (viz. [17]), we follow the simple strategy considered in [19]; in which the best chain-pair is the one with the PoW-chain that is lexicographically the smallest. If two chain-pairs have same length, and the PoW-chains are same, we compare the PoS-chains with the same tie breaking mechanism for PoW-chains.

Remark 2 (Attaching transaction payloads to the PoW-chain). In the 2-hop protocol description above, the transaction payloads are attached to the PoS-chain. We note that, this is just a design choice; alternatively, the payloads can be attached to the PoW-chain. In the full version, we will provide the details.

4   Security Analysis

For simplicity, we analyze security assuming a fixed set of participants. Denote the total number of PoW-miners by n, and the portion of malicious computing power by ρ. Let p be the probability that a player can generate a PoW-block in a round. Let $\alpha = (1 - \rho)np$ be the expected number of PoW-blocks that honest PoW-miners can find in a round. Let $\beta = \rho np$ be the expected number of PoW-blocks that malicious PoW-miners can find in a round. Thus $\frac{\alpha}{\beta} = \frac{1-\rho}{\rho}$. We assume $0 < \alpha \ll 1$, $0 < \beta \ll 1$ and $\alpha = \lambda\beta$ where $\lambda \in (0, \infty)$.

We then describe the important parameters in the second hop (i.e., proof-of-stake blockchain). Similarly, denote the total number of PoS-holders by $\tilde{n}$, and the portion of malicious stakes by $\tilde{\rho}$. Let $\tilde{p}$ be the probability that a PoW-block is mapped to a PoS-holder. We assume $\tilde{p}\tilde{n} \ll 1$. Let $\tilde{\alpha} = 1 - (1 - \tilde{p})^{(1-\tilde{\rho})\tilde{n}} \approx (1 - \tilde{\rho})\tilde{n}\tilde{p}$ be the probability that a PoW-block is mapped to at least one honest PoS-holder. Let $\tilde{\beta} = 1 - (1 - \tilde{p})^{\tilde{\rho}\tilde{n}} \approx \tilde{\rho}\tilde{n}\tilde{p}$ be the probability that a PoW-block is mapped to at least one malicious PoS-holder.

Now, we have a parameter $\hat{\alpha} = \alpha\tilde{\alpha}$ which is the probability that honest parties find a new PoW-block and is mapped to an honest PoS-holder in a round. We also have $\hat{\beta} = \beta\tilde{\beta}$, the expected number that malicious parties find new PoW-blocks and are mapped to malicious PoS-holders in a round. We say $\hat{\alpha}$ and $\hat{\beta}$ are **collective** resources for honest parties and malicious parties respectively. Note that $\hat{\gamma} = \frac{\hat{\alpha}}{1+2\Delta\hat{\alpha}}$ can be viewed as a "discounted" version of $\hat{\alpha}$ due to the fact that the messages sent by honest parties can be delayed by Δ rounds; $\hat{\gamma}$ corresponds to the "effective" honest collective resource.

As shown in the analysis of PoW protocol [19,30], due to the network delay, the block time (i.e., the time period between two consecutive blocks) has to be set very long; in other words, the probability to generate new blocks is very small. We note however in our 2-hop protocol, the block time of generating PoW-blocks can be much shorter. As long as the block time of generating new *block-pairs* is long, the security properties of our 2-hop protocol can be achieved.

Note that, the expected number of PoW-blocks that are generated in a round is $\alpha + \beta = pn$; the expected number of PoS-blocks that map to a PoW-block is $\tilde{\alpha} + \tilde{\beta} \approx \tilde{p}\tilde{n}$. In our analysis, we assume $(\alpha + \beta)(\tilde{\alpha} + \tilde{\beta})\Delta \ll 1$; that is, most of the time, no block-pair is generated. We are now ready to state our main theorems.

Theorem 1 (Chain growth). *Consider 2-hop blockchain protocol $\Pi = (\Pi^w, \Pi^s)$ in Sect. 3.1. For any honest player with the local chain-pair $\langle \mathcal{C}, \tilde{\mathcal{C}} \rangle$ in round r and $\langle \mathcal{C}', \tilde{\mathcal{C}}' \rangle$ in round $r' = r + t$ where $t > 0$. In $\mathsf{EXEC}_{\Pi, \mathcal{A}, \mathcal{Z}}$, the probability that*

$$\mathsf{len}(\mathcal{C}') - \mathsf{len}(\mathcal{C}) \geq g \cdot t, \qquad \mathsf{len}(\tilde{\mathcal{C}}') - \mathsf{len}(\tilde{\mathcal{C}}) \geq g \cdot t,$$

is at least $1 - e^{-\Omega(t)}$ *where* $g = (1 - \delta)\hat{\gamma}$, *for any* $\delta > 0$.

Theorem 2 (Chain quality). *We assume* $\hat{\gamma} = \hat{\lambda}(\alpha+\beta)\tilde{\beta}$ *and* $\hat{\lambda} > 1$. *Consider protocol* $\Pi = (\Pi^{\mathsf{w}}, \Pi^{\mathsf{s}})$ *in Sect. 3.1. For any honest player with the local chain-pair* $\langle \mathcal{C}, \tilde{\mathcal{C}} \rangle$. *In* $\mathsf{EXEC}_{\Pi,\mathcal{A},\mathcal{Z}}$, *the probability that for large enough* ℓ *consecutive block-pairs of chain-pair the ratio of honest block-pairs is no less than*

$$\mu = 1 - (1 + \delta)\frac{(\alpha + \beta)\tilde{\beta} + \beta\tilde{\alpha}}{\hat{\gamma} + \beta\tilde{\alpha}}$$

is at least $1 - e^{-\Omega(\ell)}$, *for any* $\delta > 0$.

Theorem 3 (Common prefix). *We assume* $\hat{\alpha} = \hat{\lambda}(\alpha + \beta)\tilde{\beta}$ *and* $\hat{\lambda} > 1$. *Consider protocol* $\Pi = (\Pi^{\mathsf{w}}, \Pi^{\mathsf{s}})$ *in Sect. 3.1. Let* κ *be the security parameter. For any two honest players* P_i *in round* r, *and* P_j *in round* r', *with the local best chain-pairs* $\langle \mathcal{C}_i, \tilde{\mathcal{C}}_i \rangle$, $\langle \mathcal{C}_j, \tilde{\mathcal{C}}_j \rangle$, *respectively, in* $\mathsf{EXEC}_{\Pi,\mathcal{A},\mathcal{Z}}$ *where* $r \leq r'$, *the probability that,*

$$\mathcal{C}_i[\neg\kappa] \preceq \mathcal{C}_j, \quad \mathcal{C}_j[\neg\kappa] \preceq \mathcal{C}_i, \quad \tilde{\mathcal{C}}_i[\neg\kappa] \preceq \tilde{\mathcal{C}}_j, \quad \tilde{\mathcal{C}}_j[\neg\kappa] \preceq \tilde{\mathcal{C}}_i,$$

is at least $1 - e^{-\Omega(\kappa)}$.

4.1 Proof Intuition

Due to space limitations, we defer the full security analysis to the full version of our paper. Here, we present the main ideas underlying the security analysis.

In our protocol, there are two types of players, PoW-miners and PoS-holders. Both PoW-miners and PoS-holders can be honest or malicious. In order to extend the pair of blockchains, a PoW-miner needs to generate a PoW-block first, and then the corresponding stakeholder will sign this block. We note that, our security analysis mainly focuses on PoS-chain, and the analysis for PoW-chain is followed from PoS-chain's. Consider that players may be honest or malicious, we have

- **Case 1:** An honest PoW-miner finds a new PoW-block which is mapped to an honest PoS-holder. The honest PoS-holder will generate the corresponding PoS-block faithfully.
- **Case 2:** A malicious PoW-miner finds a new PoW-block which is mapped to a malicious PoS-holder. The malicious PoS-holder may generate the corresponding PoS-block faithfully, or just discard it.
- **Case 3:** An honest PoW-miner finds a new PoW-block which is mapped to a malicious PoS-holder. Again, as in Case 2, the malicious PoS-holder may generate the corresponding PoS-block faithfully, or just discard it.
- **Case 4:** When a malicious PoW-miner finds a new PoW-block which is mapped to an honest PoS-holder. The malicious PoW-miner may publish the new PoW-block (so that the corresponding honest PoS-holder can generate the PoS-block), or withhold the PoW-block and discard it.

We note that, intuitively in Case 1, the malicious players cannot stop honest players from extending the chain-pairs; thus the chain growth property can be ensured. Now let's consider the total number of PoS-blocks from malicious players in Case 2 and in Case 3. If the number of PoS-blocks from honest players in Case 1 is larger than that from the malicious players in Case 2 and Case 3, we can also see that the common prefix property is ensured.

In Case 2 or Case 3, the malicious PoS-player may generate multiple PoS-blocks based on a single PoW-block. We remark here that this malicious strategy will bring no advantage to the attacker, since only *one* of the multiple PoS-blocks will be extended by honest PoW-miners.

As discussed above, $\hat{\alpha} = \alpha\tilde{\alpha}$ and $\hat{\beta} = \beta\tilde{\beta}$ are the collective probabilities of Case 1 and Case 2, respectively. We define them as the collective resources of the honest and malicious parties, respectively.

In our protocol, the malicious players are allowed to delay communication messages for at most Δ rounds. When the malicious players delay the communication messages, each honest player might not be able obtain its best chain-pair on time. As a consequence, honest miners may work on a wrong chain-pair during the delayed communication rounds. In our analysis, we thus use the *discounted version* of the computing/stake resource to calculate the probability that the honest players can generate a block in a round.

Chain Growth. The malicious players may delay all of the communication messages from the honest players up to Δ rounds. Consider that to generate a block-pair, two hops are needed; The adversary can delay at most 2Δ rounds for a PoS-block generation. We use $\hat{\gamma}$ to denote the discounted collective honest resources where $\hat{\gamma} = \frac{\hat{\alpha}}{1+2\Delta\hat{\alpha}}$.

In the formal proof, we introduce a hybrid execution, formalizing the worst case communication delay. In the hybrid execution, the malicious players will not contribute to the chain growth; furthermore, the adversary will delay all communication messages from the honest players with the goal of stopping the chain growth as much as possible. When Case 1 occurs, the longest chain-pair that can be observed by all honest players, will increase by 1 block-pair (one PoW-block and one PoS-block). Note that the probability that Case 1 occurs in a round is $\hat{\gamma}$. Also note that the probability that Case 1 occurs in our protocol execution, will not be smaller than that in the worst case hybrid execution. Thus the chain growth rate is guaranteed by $\hat{\gamma}$.

Chain Quality. Assume $\tilde{p}\tilde{n} \ll 1$. With high probability, at the same block height, there is at most one block-pair in Case 1 or Case 4. During any t consecutive rounds, the expected number of block-pairs generated in Case 1, is at least $\hat{\gamma}t$. Let θt denote the number of block-pairs generated in Case 4 during the t rounds, for some θ. Then we can have $0 \leq \theta \leq \beta\tilde{\alpha}$. The chain growth in the t round is $(\hat{\gamma} + \theta)t$. In addition, the expected number of block-pair that generated in Case 2 or Case 3 during t rounds, is at most $(\alpha + \beta)\tilde{\beta}t$. Therefore, the chain quality is at least $1 - \frac{(\alpha+\beta)\tilde{\beta}+\theta}{\hat{\gamma}+\theta} \geq 1 - \frac{(\alpha+\beta)\tilde{\beta}+\beta\tilde{\alpha}}{\hat{\gamma}+\beta\tilde{\alpha}}$.

Common Prefix. Assume $2(\alpha + \beta)(\tilde{\alpha} + \tilde{\beta})\Delta \ll 1$. We can compute that, the probability that no new block-pair is generated in a round, is $1 - 2(\alpha + \beta)(\tilde{\alpha} + \tilde{\beta})\Delta$. We can also compute that, the probability for honest players to generate *at least one* new block-pair in a round, is at least $\hat{\alpha}$. We can further argue that, the probability for honest players to generate *exactly one* new block-pair in a round, is $\hat{\alpha}(1 - \hat{\alpha})$, which approximates to $\hat{\alpha}$, given that we assume $\hat{\alpha} \ll 1$.

After the publication of one block-pair in the system, if in the upcoming 2Δ rounds, there is no block-pair published, then all honest players will have the same best chain-pair, and their views will be convergent. The malicious players may generate blocks to achieve their goal of stopping the honest players to develop convergent views of the best chain-pair. However, based on our assumption, the malicious players cannot generate enough number of block-pairs to achieve this goal.

On Adaptive Corruption. In our protocol, the adversary can corrupt any player adaptively at any time. We note that in the first hop the adversary cannot predict which PoW-player will be able to find a solution to the PoW puzzle before the solution is published. Thus, adaptively corrupting PoW miners will not bring the adversary any extra advantage. Then in the second hop, the solution to the PoS puzzle consists of the (unique) signature from a PoS-player. Again, the adversary cannot predict which PoS-player will be elected before the solution to the PoS puzzle is published. Similarly, the adaptive corruption strategy will not bring extra advantage.

A   Unique Signature Schemes

Unique signature schemes were introduced in [26], which consists of four algorithms, a randomized key generation algorithm KeyGen, a deterministic key verification algorithm KeyVer, a deterministic signing algorithm Sign, and a deterministic verification algorithm Verify. We expect for each verification key there exists only one signing key. We also expect for each pair of message and verification key, there exists only one signature. We have the following definition.

Definition 4. *We say* (KeyGen, KeyVer, Sign, Verify) *is a unique signature scheme, if it satisfies:*

Correctness of key generation: Honestly generated key pair can always be verified. More formally, it holds that

$$\Pr\left[(\mathrm{PK}, \mathrm{SK}) \leftarrow \mathsf{KeyGen}(1^\kappa) \; : \; \mathsf{KeyVer}(\mathrm{PK}, \mathrm{SK}) = 1 \right] \geq 1 - \mathsf{negl}(\kappa)$$

Uniqueness of signing key: There does not exist two different valid signing keys for a verification key. More formally, for all PPT *adversary* $\mathcal{A}$, *it holds that*

$$\Pr\left[\begin{array}{l} (\mathrm{PK}, \mathrm{SK}_1, \mathrm{SK}_2) \leftarrow \mathcal{A}(1^\kappa) \\ : \; \mathsf{KeyVer}(\mathrm{PK}, \mathrm{SK}_1) = 1 \wedge \mathsf{KeyVer}(\mathrm{PK}, \mathrm{SK}_1) = 1 \wedge \mathrm{SK}_1 \neq \mathrm{SK}_2 \end{array} \right] \leq \mathsf{negl}(\kappa)$$

Correctness of signature generation: For any message x, it holds that

$$\Pr \left[\begin{array}{l} (\text{PK}, \text{SK}) \leftarrow \text{KeyGen}(1^\kappa); \sigma := \text{Sign}(\text{SK}, x) \\ : \ \text{Verify}(\text{PK}, x, \sigma) = 1 \end{array} \right] \geq 1 - \text{negl}(\kappa)$$

Uniqueness of signature generation: For all PPT adversary $\mathcal{A}$,

$$\Pr \left[\begin{array}{l} (\text{PK}, x, \sigma_1, \sigma_2) \leftarrow \mathcal{A}(1^\kappa) \\ : \ \text{Verify}(\text{PK}, x, \sigma_1) = 1 \wedge \text{Verify}(\text{PK}, x, \sigma_2) = 1 \wedge \sigma_1 \neq \sigma_2 \end{array} \right] \leq \text{negl}(\kappa)$$

Unforgeability of signature generation: For all PPT adversary $\mathcal{A}$,

$$\Pr \left[\begin{array}{l} (\text{PK}, \text{SK}) \leftarrow \text{KeyGen}(1^\kappa); (x, \sigma) \leftarrow \mathcal{A}^{\text{Sign}(\text{SK}, \cdot)}(1^\kappa) \\ : \ \text{Verify}(\text{PK}, x, \sigma) = 1 \wedge (x, \sigma) \notin Q \end{array} \right] \leq \text{negl}(\kappa)$$

where Q is the history of queries that the adversary $\mathcal{A}$ made to signing oracle $\text{Sign}(\text{SK}, \cdot)$.

References

1. Back, A.: Hashcash–a denial of service counter-measure (2002). http://hashcash.org/papers/hashcash.pdf
2. Badertscher, C., Gazi, P., Kiayias, A., Russell, A., Zikas, V.: Ouroboros genesis: composable proof-of-stake blockchains with dynamic availability. In: Lie, D., Mannan, M., Backes, M., Wang, X. (eds.) ACM CCS 2018, pp. 913–930. ACM Press, October 2018
3. Bentov, I., Gabizon, A., Mizrahi, A.: Currencies without proof of work. In: Bitcoin Workshop (2016)
4. Bentov, I., Lee, C., Mizrahi, A., Rosenfeld, M.: Proof of activity: extending bitcoin's proof of work via proof of stake. ACM SIGMETRICS Perform. Eval. Rev. **42**, 34–37 (2014)
5. Bitcointalk: Proof of stake instead of proof of work (2011). Online post by Quantum Mechanic, https://bitcointalk.org/index.php?topic=27787.0
6. Canetti, R.: Security and composition of multiparty cryptographic protocols. J. Cryptol. **13**(1), 143–202 (2000). https://doi.org/10.1007/s001459910006
7. Canetti, R.: Universally composable security: a new paradigm for cryptographic protocols. Cryptology ePrint Archive, Report 2000/067 (2000). http://eprint.iacr.org/2000/067
8. Chen, J., Gorbunov, S., Micali, S., Vlachos, G.: Algorand agreement: super fast and partition resilient Byzantine agreement (2018). https://eprint.iacr.org/2018/377
9. Chen, J., Micali, S.: Algorand (2017). http://arxiv.org/abs/1607.01341
10. Chepurnoy, A., Duong, T., Fan, L., Zhou, H.-S.: Twinscoin: a cryptocurrency via proof-of-work and proof-of-stake. In: Proceedings of the 2nd ACM Workshop on Blockchains, Cryptocurrencies, and Contracts, pp. 1–13. ACM (2018)
11. CryptoManiac. Proof of stake (2014). NovaCoin wiki. https://github.com/novacoin-project/novacoin/wiki/Proof-of-stake/
12. Daian, P., Pass, R., Shi, E.: Snow White: robustly reconfigurable consensus and applications to provably secure proof of stake. In: Goldberg, I., Moore, T. (eds.) FC 2019. LNCS, vol. 11598, pp. 23–41. Springer, Cham (2019). https://doi.org/10.1007/978-3-030-32101-7_2

13. David, B., Gaži, P., Kiayias, A., Russell, A.: Ouroboros Praos: an adaptively-secure, semi-synchronous proof-of-stake blockchain. In: Nielsen, J.B., Rijmen, V. (eds.) EUROCRYPT 2018. LNCS, vol. 10821, pp. 66–98. Springer, Cham (2018). https://doi.org/10.1007/978-3-319-78375-8_3

14. Duong, T., Fan, L., Zhou, H.-S.: 2-hop blockchain: combining proof-of-work and proof-of-stake securely (2016). https://eprint.iacr.org/2016/716

15. Dwork, C., Naor, M.: Pricing via processing or combatting junk mail. In: Brickell, E.F. (ed.) CRYPTO 1992. LNCS, vol. 740, pp. 139–147. Springer, Heidelberg (1993). https://doi.org/10.1007/3-540-48071-4_10

16. Eyal, I.: The miner's dilemma. In: IEEE Symposium on Security and Privacy, pp. 89–103. IEEE Computer Society Press, May 2015

17. Eyal, I., Sirer, E.G.: Majority is not enough: bitcoin mining is vulnerable. In: Christin, N., Safavi-Naini, R. (eds.) FC 2014. LNCS, vol. 8437, pp. 436–454. Springer, Heidelberg (2014). https://doi.org/10.1007/978-3-662-45472-5_28

18. Fan, L., Zhou, H.-S.: A scalable proof-of-stake blockchain in the open setting (or, how to mimic Nakamoto's design via proof-of-stake), July 2017. https://eprint.iacr.org/2017/656/

19. Garay, J., Kiayias, A., Leonardos, N.: The bitcoin backbone protocol: analysis and applications. In: Oswald, E., Fischlin, M. (eds.) EUROCRYPT 2015. LNCS, vol. 9057, pp. 281–310. Springer, Heidelberg (2015). https://doi.org/10.1007/978-3-662-46803-6_10

20. Gilad, Y., Hemo, R., Micali, S., Vlachos, G., Zeldovich, N.: Algorand: scaling byzantine agreements for cryptocurrencies. In: Proceedings of the 26th Symposium on Operating Systems Principles, pp. 51–68. ACM (2017)

21. Goodin, D.: Bitcoin security guarantee shattered by anonymous miner with 51% network power (2014). http://arstechnica.com/

22. Kiayias, A., Panagiotakos, G.: Speed-security tradeoffs in blockchain protocols. Cryptology ePrint Archive, Report 2015/1019 (2015). http://eprint.iacr.org/2015/1019

23. Kiayias, A., Panagiotakos, G.: On trees, chains and fast transactions in the blockchain. In: Lange, T., Dunkelman, O. (eds.) LATINCRYPT 2017. LNCS, vol. 11368, pp. 327–351. Springer, Cham (2019). https://doi.org/10.1007/978-3-030-25283-0_18

24. Kiayias, A., Russell, A., David, B., Oliynykov, R.: Ouroboros: a provably secure proof-of-stake blockchain protocol. In: Katz, J., Shacham, H. (eds.) CRYPTO 2017. LNCS, vol. 10401, pp. 357–388. Springer, Cham (2017). https://doi.org/10.1007/978-3-319-63688-7_12

25. King, S., Nadal, S.: PPCoin: peer-to-peer crypto-currency with proof-of-stake (2012). https://peercoin.net/assets/paper/peercoin-paper.pdf

26. Lysyanskaya, A.: Unique signatures and verifiable random functions from the DH-DDH separation. In: Yung, M. (ed.) CRYPTO 2002. LNCS, vol. 2442, pp. 597–612. Springer, Heidelberg (2002). https://doi.org/10.1007/3-540-45708-9_38

27. Miller, A., Kosba, A.E., Katz, J., Shi, E.: Nonoutsourceable scratch-off puzzles to discourage bitcoin mining coalitions. In: Ray, I., Li, N., Kruegel, C. (eds.) ACM CCS 2015, pp. 680–691. ACM Press, October 2015

28. Nakamoto, S.: Bitcoin: a peer-to-peer electronic cash system (2008). https://bitcoin.org/bitcoin.pdf

29. NXT whitepaper (2014). https://www.dropbox.com/s/cbuwrorf672c0yy/NxtWhitepaper_v122_rev4.pdf

30. Pass, R., Seeman, L., Shelat, A.: Analysis of the blockchain protocol in asynchronous networks. In: Coron, J.-S., Nielsen, J.B. (eds.) EUROCRYPT 2017. LNCS, vol. 10211, pp. 643–673. Springer, Cham (2017). https://doi.org/10.1007/978-3-319-56614-6_22

31. Pass, R., Shi, E.: The sleepy model of consensus. In: Takagi, T., Peyrin, T. (eds.) ASIACRYPT 2017. LNCS, vol. 10625, pp. 380–409. Springer, Cham (2017). https://doi.org/10.1007/978-3-319-70697-9_14

32. Sapirshtein, A., Sompolinsky, Y., Zohar, A.: Optimal selfish mining strategies in bitcoin. In: Grossklags, J., Preneel, B. (eds.) FC 2016. LNCS, vol. 9603, pp. 515–532. Springer, Heidelberg (2017). https://doi.org/10.1007/978-3-662-54970-4_30

33. Schrijvers, O., Bonneau, J., Boneh, D., Roughgarden, T.: Incentive compatibility of bitcoin mining pool reward functions. In: Grossklags, J., Preneel, B. (eds.) FC 2016. LNCS, vol. 9603, pp. 477–498. Springer, Heidelberg (2017). https://doi.org/10.1007/978-3-662-54970-4_28

34. Sompolinsky, Y., Zohar, A.: Secure high-rate transaction processing in bitcoin. In: Böhme, R., Okamoto, T. (eds.) FC 2015. LNCS, vol. 8975, pp. 507–527. Springer, Heidelberg (2015). https://doi.org/10.1007/978-3-662-47854-7_32

35. Vasin, P.: Blackcoin's proof-of-stake protocol v. 2 (2014). http://blackcoin.co/blackcoin-pos-protocol-v2-whitepaper.pdf

Generic Superlight Client for Permissionless Blockchains

Yuan Lu[1]([✉]), Qiang Tang[1,2], and Guiling Wang[1]

[1] New Jersey Institute of Technology, Newark, NJ 07102, USA
{yl768,qiang,gwang}@njit.edu
[2] JDD-NJIT-ISCAS Joint Blockchain Lab, Newark, USA

Abstract. We initiate a systematic study on the light-client protocol of permissionless blockchains, in the setting where full nodes and light clients are rational. In the game-theoretic model, we design a superlight-client protocol to enable a light client to employ some relaying full nodes (e.g., two or one) to read the blockchain. The protocol is "generic", i.e., it can be deployed disregarding underlying consensuses, and it is also "superlight", i.e., the computational cost of the light client to predicate the (non)existence of a transaction in the blockchain becomes a small constant. Since our protocol resolves a fundamental challenge of broadening the usage of blockchain technology, it captures a wide variety of important use-cases such as multi-chain wallets, DApp browsers and more.

Keywords: Blockchain · Light client · Game-theoretic security

1 Introduction

The blockchain can be abstracted as a global ledger [22,38] that can be read and written by the users of higher level applications [16,17,54]. Nevertheless, the basic abstraction of *reading the ledger*[1] implicitly requires a so-called personal *full node* [8,25] to execute consensus and maintain a local blockchain replica.

However, with the rapid popularity of blockchain, an increasing number of users become merely caring about the high-level applications such as cryptocurrencies instead of maintaining personal full nodes [28]. Let alone many users are resource-starved, say browser extensions and smartphones [13,55,57] that have too limited resources to stay on-line and execute the underlying consensus.

Thus an urgent demand of blockchain's *lightweight clients* or superlight clients [10,12,33,36], rises up. Consider a quintessential scenario: Alice is the cashier of a pizza store; a customer Bob tells her ₿1,000 has been paid for some pizzas, via a bitcoin transaction with txid 0xa1075d..., and claims the transaction is already

---

[1] Writing in the blockchain is trivial, as one can gossip with some full nodes to diffuse its messages to the entire blockchain network (a.k.a., network diffuse functionality [4,22]). Then the blockchain's liveness ensures the inclusion of the messages [22].

© Springer Nature Switzerland AG 2020
L. Chen et al. (Eds.): ESORICS 2020, LNCS 12309, pp. 713–733, 2020.
https://doi.org/10.1007/978-3-030-59013-0_35

in the blockchain; then, Alice needs to check that, by activating a lite wallet app installed in her mobile phone. That is to say, Alice, and many typical blockchain users, need *stay off-line* to opt out of the consensus, and can still wake up any time to "read" the blockchain with high security and low computational cost.

1.1   Insufficiencies of Prior Art

The fundamental challenge of designing superlight clients stems from a fact: the records in the blockchain are de facto "authenticated" by the latest chain agreed across the whole blockchain network (a.k.a., the main-chain) [34,48,51]. So without a replica of main-chain at hand, the client has to rely on some other *full nodes* to forward the main-chain's records. That said, the protocol of blockchains' superlight clients must deal with the probably distrustful full nodes that might forward fake blockchain readings.

Some Ad-Hoc Attempts. A few proposals attempt to prevent the client being cheated, by relying on heavyweight assumptions. For example, a few proposals [14,19] assume a diverse list of known full nodes to serve as relays to forward blockchain readings. These relays are usually some "mining" pools and a few so-called blockchain "explorers", so the client can count on the honest-majority of these known relays to read the chain. But for many real-world permissionless blockchains, this assumption is too heavy to hold with high-confidence. Say Cardano [1], a top-10 blockchain by market capitalization in 2020, has very few "explorers" on the run; even worse, the naive idea of recruiting "mining" pools as relays is more elusive, as most of them would not participate without moderate incentives [28]. It becomes unclear how to identify an honest-majority set of known relays for each permissionless blockchain in the wild. As such, these ad-hoc solutions become unreliable for the elusive heavy assumptions.

Cryptographic Approaches. To design the light-client protocol against malicious relay full nodes, a few cryptographic approaches are proposed [10,33,48, 59].
– *Straight Use of SPV is Problematic.* The most straightforward way to instantiating the idea is to let the client keep track of the suffix of the main-chain, and then check the existence of transactions by verifying SPV proofs [48], but the naive approach causes at least one major issue: the client has to frequently be on-line to track the growth of main-chain. Otherwise, when the client wakes up from a deep sleep, it needs to at least verify the block headers of the main-chain linearly. Such bootstrapping can be costly, considering the main-chain is ever-growing, say the headers of Ethereum is growing at a pace of ∼1 GB per year. As a result, in many critical use-cases such as web browsers and/or mobile phones, the idea of straightly using SPV proofs becomes unrealistic.
– *PoW-Specific Results.* For PoW chains, some existing superlight clients such as FlyClient and NiPoPoW [10,33] circumvent the problem of SPV proofs. These ideas notice the main-chain is essentially "authenticated" by its *few suffix blocks*, and then develop some PoW-specific techniques to allow the *suffix blocks* be proven to a client at only sublinear cost. But they come with one major limit,

namely, need to verify PoWs to discover the correct suffix, and therefore cannot fit the promising class of proof-of-stake (PoS) consensuses [14, 24, 34].

– *Superlight Client for PoS is Still Unavailable.* For PoS chains, it is yet unclear how to realize an actual superlight client that can go off-line to completely opt out of consensus. The major issue is lacking an efficient way of proving the suffix of PoS chains to an off-line client, because the validity of the suffix blocks relies on the signatures of stakeholders, whose validities further depend on the recent stake distributions, which further are authenticated by the blockchain itself [12, 14, 24, 34]. Some recent efforts [23, 39, 44] allow the *always-online* clients to use minimal space to track the suffix of PoS chains, without maintaining the stake distributions. But for enabling off-line, there only exist few fast-bootstrapping proposals for *full nodes* [6, 41], which still require to download and verify a linear portion of the PoS chain, thus incurring substantial cost [15, 24].

Demands of "Consensus-Oblivious" Light Client. Most existing light-client protocols are highly specialized for particular consensuses (e.g., PoW). This not only prevents us adapting them to instantiate actual superlight clients for the PoS chains, but also hinders their easy deployment and user experience in many important use-cases in reality. A typical scenario is the multi-chain wallet that supports various cryptocurrencies atop different chains; each chain is even running a distinct consensus. Bearing the high-specialization of existing light-client protocols [10, 23, 33, 39, 44], the multi-chain wallet needs to instantiate different light-client protocols for distinct consensuses and ends up to contain many independent "sub-wallets", which not only is burdensome for the client users but also challenges the developers to correctly implement all sub-wallets. In contrast, with a generic protocol fitting all, we can simply tune some parameters at best.

Generic Solution in Another Different Setting. The cryptographic setting seems to be an inherent obstacle-ridden path to the generic light-client protocol, as it usually needs the full nodes to prove the main-chain's suffix validated by the consensus rules [10, 23, 33, 39]. Even if one puts forth a "consensus-oblivious" solution in this setting, it likely has to convert all those "suffix proofs" into a generic statement of verifiable computation (VC) [44], which is unclear how can be practical, considering VC itself is not fully practical yet for complicated statements [10] (see the full paper [42] for a thorough review on pertinent topics).

To meet the urgent demand of the generic light-client protocol, we explicitly deviate from the cryptographic setting and focus on the game-theoretic approach, in light of many successful studies such as rational multi-party computation [3, 7, 21, 26, 27, 29, 32, 37] and rational verifiable computation [16, 52, 56]. In the rational setting, we can expect a consensus-independent incentive mechanism to assist a simple light-client protocol, so all rational protocol participants (i.e., the relay nodes and the client) would follow the protocol for selfishness.

Following that, this paper would present: *a systematic treatment to the light-client problem of permissionless blockchains in the game-theoretic setting.*

1.2   Our Results

In the game theoretic setting the players are rational, we design a superlight protocol to enable a light client to recruit several relay full nodes (e.g., one[2] or two) to securely evaluate a general class of predicates about the blockchain.

Contributions. To summarize, our technical contributions are:

- Our light-client protocol can be bootstrapped in the rational setting, efficiently and generically. First, the protocol is superlight, in the sense that the client can go off-line and wake up any time to *evaluate* a general class of chain predicates at a tiny constant computationally cost; as long as the truthness or falseness of these chain predicates is reducible to few transactions' inclusion in the blockchain.
- Moreover, our generic protocol gets rid of the dependency on consensuses and can be deployed in nearly any permissionless blockchain (e.g., Turing-complete blockchains [11,58]) without even velvet forks [60], thus supporting the promising PoS type of consensuses.
- We conduct a systematic study to understand whether, or to what extent, the light-client protocol is secure in the rational setting (without trusted third-parties). We make non-trivial analyses of the incomplete-information extensive game induced by our light-client protocol and conduct a comprehensive study to understand how to design the incentives to achieve security in different scenarios, from the standard setting of non-cooperative full nodes to the pessimistic setting of colluding full nodes.
- Our protocol enables the rational client to *evaluate* non-existence of a given transaction besides the existence, i.e., the rational client can be convinced by the rational full nodes that a given transaction is *not* in the blockchain. That provides a simple way to performing non-existence "proof". In contrast, relevant studies in the cryptographic setting either give up non-existence proof [36,48] or have to heavily modify the blockchain's data structure [9,47].

Solution in a Nutshell. Assuming the light client and relay nodes are rational, we leverage the smart contract to facilitate a simple yet still useful incentive mechanism, so being honest becomes the best rational choice. From high-level, the light-client protocol proceeds simply as following:

- *Setup.* The client and relay node(s) place their initial deposits in an "arbiter" smart contract. An incentive mechanism can use these deposits to facilitate rewards/punishments and deter deviations from the light-client protocol.
- *Repeated queries.* After setup, the client can repeatedly query the relays to forward blockchain readings (up to k times). Each query proceeds as:
  1. *Request.* The client firstly specifies the details of the predicate to query in the arbiter contract, which can be done since writing in the contract is trivial for the network diffuse functionality (see footnote 1).

---

[2] Note that the case of one relay can model the pessimistic scenario that all recruited full nodes are colluding to form a single coalition.

2. *Response.* Once the relays see the specifications of the chain predicate in the arbiter contract, they are incentivized to evaluate the predicate and forward the ground truth to the client off-chain.
3. *Feedback.* Then the client decides an output, according to what it receives from the relays. Besides, the client shall report what it receives to the arbiter contract; otherwise, gets a fine.
4. *Payout.* Finally, the contract verifies whether the relays are honest, according to the feedback from the client, and then facilitates an incentive mechanism to reward (or punish) the relays. The incentive mechanisms leverage the deposits (placed by the client and relays) to ensure "following the protocol" to be a desired equilibrium, such that the rational relays and client would not deviate during any stage of the protocol.

Challenges and Techniques. The instantiation of the above idea is challenged by the limit of the "handicapped" arbiter contract. In particular, the arbiter contract cannot directly verify the non-existence of transactions, even if it can verify any transaction's existence [5,36]. Thus, for a chain predicate whose trueness (resp. falseness) is reducible to the existence (resp. non-existence) of some transactions, the arbiter contract can only verify its trueness but not its falseness. This allows the relays to adopt a malicious strategy: "always forward unverifiable bogus disregarding the actual ground truth", because doing so would not be caught by the contract and thus the relays are still paid.

To circumvent the limit of the arbiter contract, we squeeze the most of its "handicapped" verifiability to finely tune the incentive mechanism, such that "flooding fake unverifiable claims" become irrational. Following that, any deviations from the protocol are further deterred, from the standard setting of non-cooperative relays to the extremely hostile case of colluding relays:

- If two *non-cooperative relays* (e.g., two competing mining pools in practice) can be identified and recruited, we leverage the natural tension between these *two* selfish relays to "audit" each other. As such, fooling the client is deterred, because a selfish relay is incentivized to report the other's (unverifiable) bogus claim, by producing a proof attesting the opposite of the fake claim.
- In the extremely adversarial scenario where any two recruited relays can *form a coalition*, the setting becomes rather pessimistic, as the client is essentially requesting an unknown knowledge from a *single* party. Nevertheless, the incentive can still be slightly tuned to function as follows:
  1. The first tuning does *not* rely on any extra assumption. The adjustment is to let the arbiter contract assign a higher payoff to a proved claim while make a lower payoff to an unprovable claim. So the best strategy of the *only* relay is to forward the actual ground truth, as long as the malicious benefit attained by fooling the client is smaller than the maximal reward promised by the client.

     Though this result has limited applicabilities, for example, cannot handle valuable queries, it still captures a variety of meaningful real-world use-cases, in particular, many DApp browsers, where the relay is not rather interested in cheating the client.

2. The second tuning relies on another moderate rationality assumption, that is: at least one selfish *public* full node (in the entire blockchain network) can keep on monitoring the internal states of the arbiter contract at a tiny cost and *will not cooperate* with the recruited relay.

Thus whenever the recruited relay forwards an *unprovable* bogus claim to the client, our design incentivizes the *selfish* public full node to "audit" the relay by proving the opposite side is the actual ground truth, which deters the recruited relay from flooding unprovable bogus.

Application Scenarios. Our protocol supports a wide variety of applications, as it solves a fundamental issue preventing low-capacity users using blockchain:

- *Decentralized application browser.* The DApp browser is a natural application scenario. For example, a lightweight browser for CryptoKitties [13] can get rid of a trusted Web server. When surfing the DApp via a distrustful Web server, the users need to verify whether the content rendered by the server is correct, which can be done through our light-client protocol efficiently.
- *Mobile wallet for multiple cryptocurrencies.* Our protocol can be leveraged to implement a super-light mobile wallet to verify the (non)existence of cryptocurrency transactions. In particular, it can keep track of multiple coins atop different blockchains running over diverse types of consensuses.

2   Warm-Up: Game-Theoretic Security

The game-theoretic analysis of an interactive protocol starts by defining an extensive game [16,31,50] to model the strategies (i.e., probabilistic interactive Turing machines) of each party in the protocol. A utility function would assign every party a certain payoff, for each possible execution induced by the strategies of all parties. Then the security is argued by the properties of the extensive game, for example, its Nash equilibrium [29] or other refined equilibria [16,30,31,37,50].

Here we give a simple interactive "protocol" to exemplify the game-theoretic setting (c.f., our full paper [42] for rigor definitions of game-theory preliminaries). Consider the oversimplified "light-client protocol" that be described as the extensive game as shown in Fig. 1: *Alice is a cashier of a pizza store; her client asks a full node (i.e., relay) to check a transaction's (non)existence, and simply terminates to output what is forwarded by the relay.*

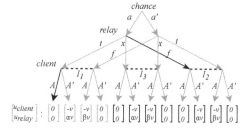

Fig. 1. The extensive game of an oversimplified light-client "protocol". The utility function is an example to clarify the *insecurity* of such a trivial idea.

Strategy, Action, History, and Information Set. Let the above *oversimplified* "protocol" proceed in synchronous round. In each round, the parties will execute its *strategy*, i.e., a probabilistic polynomial-time ITM in our context, to produce and feed a string to the protocol, a.k.a., take an *action*. During the course of the protocol, a sequence of actions would be made, and we say it is a *history* by the convention of game theory literature; moreover, when a party acts, it might have learned some (incomplete) information from earlier actions taken by other parties, so the notion of *information sets* are introduced to characterize what has and has not been learned by each party (see [42] for formal definitions). In greater detail, the *oversimplified* "light-client protocol" is interpreted as Fig. 1:

1. *Round 1 (chance acts).* A definitional virtual party called *chance* sets the ground truth, namely, it determines $True$ or $False$ to represent whether the transaction exists (denoted by a or a' respectively). To capture the uncertainty of the ground truth, the chance acts arbitrarily.
2. *Round 2 (relay acts).* Then, the relay is activated to forward $True$ or $False$ to the light client, which states whether the transaction exists or not. Note the strategy chosen by the relay is an ITM that can produce arbitrary strings in this round, we need to map the strings into the admissible actions, namely, t, f and x. For definiteness, we let the string of ground truth be interpreted as the action t, the string of the opposite of ground truth be interpreted as the action f, and all other strings (including abort) be interpreted as x.
3. *Round 3 (client acts).* Finally, the client outputs $True$ (denoted by A) or $False$ (denoted by A') to represent whether the transaction exists or not, according to the (incomplete) information acquired from the protocol. Note the client knows how the relay acts, but cannot directly infer the action of *chance*. So it faces three distinct information sets I_1, I_2 and I_3, which respectively represent the client receives $True$, $False$ and others in Round 2. The client cannot distinguish the histories inside each information set.

Utility Function. After the protocol terminates, its game reaches a so-called *terminal history*. A well-defined *utility function* specifies the economic outcome of each party, for each terminal history induced by the extensive game.

In practice, the utility function is determined by some economic factors of the parties and the protocol itself [16,29]. For example, the rationale behind the utility function in Fig. 1 can be understood as: (i) the relay is motivated to fool the client to believe the nonexistence of an existing transaction, because this literally "censors" Alice to harm her business by a loss of $\$v$, which also brings a malicious benefit $\$\alpha \cdot v$ to the relay; (ii) the relay also prefers to fool the client to believe the existence of a non-existing transaction, so the relay gets free pizzas valued by $\$\beta \cdot v$, which causes Alice lose $\$v$ (i.e., the amount supposed to be transacted to purchase pizzas), (iii) after all, the oversimplified protocol itself does not facilitate any punishment/reward, so will not affect the utility function.

Security via Equilibrium. Putting the game structure and the utility function together, we can argue the (in)security due to the equilibria in the game. In particular, we can adopt the strong notion of *sequential equilibrium* for extensive games [16,30,31,50] to demonstrate that the rational parties would not deviate, at each stage during the execution of the protocol. As a negative lesson, the oversimplified "light-client game" in Fig. 1 is *insecure*, as the relay can unilaterally deviate to fool the client for higher utility. In contrast, if the protocol is *secure* in game-theoretic settings, its game shall realize desired equilibrium, s.t., rational parties would not diverge for highest utilities.

3   Preliminaries

Blockchain Addressing. A blockchain (e.g., denoted by C) is a chain of block (headers). Each block commits a list of payload (e.g., transactions). Notationwise, we use Python bracket $C[t]$ to address the block (header) at the height t of the chain C, and $C[0]$ represents the genesis block. W.l.o.g., a block $C[t]$ is defined as a tuple of $(h_{t-1}, nonce, root)$, where h_{t-1} is the hash of the block $C[t-1]$, *nonce* is the valid PoX (e.g., the correct preimage in PoW), and root is Merkle tree root of payload. By $C[t].root$ it denotes the Merkle root of block $C[t]$.

Payload & Merkle Tree. Let $TX_t := \langle tx_1, tx_2, \cdots, tx_n \rangle$ denote a sequence of transactions that is the payload of the block $C[t]$. Recall TX_t is included by the block $C[t]$ through Merkle tree [48,58], which is an authenticated data structure scheme of three algorithms (BuildMT, GenMTP, VrfyMTP). BuildMT inputs $TX_t = \langle tx_1, \cdots, tx_n \rangle$ and outputs a Merkle tree MT with root. GenMTP takes the tree MT (built for TX_t) and a transaction $tx \in TX_t$ as input, and outputs a proof π_j for the inclusion of tx in TX_t at the position j. VrfyMTP inputs π_j, root and tx and outputs either 1 or 0. The Merkle tree scheme satisfies: (i) *Correctness.* $\Pr[\text{VrfyMTP}(MT.root, tx, \pi_i) = 1 \mid \pi_i \leftarrow \text{GenMTP}(MT, tx), MT \leftarrow \text{BuildMT}(TX)] = 1$; (ii) *Security.* for $\forall$ P.P.T. $\mathcal{A}$, $\Pr[\text{VrfyMTP}(MT.root, tx, \pi_i) = 1 \wedge tx \neq TX[i] \mid \pi_i \leftarrow \mathcal{A}(1^\lambda, MT, tx), MT \leftarrow \text{BuildMT}(TX)] \leq negl(\lambda)$. Note that by $nelg(\cdot)$ we denote a negligible function through the paper. The construction of the Merkle tree scheme is deferred to the full version [42].

Smart Contract. Essentially, a smart contract [11,58] can be abstracted as an ideal functionality with the access to a global ledger subroutine, so it can faithfully instruct the ledger to freeze "coins" and then correctly facilitate conditional payments [35,38]. This paper explicitly adopts the widely-used notations invented by Kosba *et al.* [38] to describe the smart contract, for example:

- The contract can access the global time clock T, which can be seen as an equivalent notion of the height of the latest blockchain.
- The contract can access a global dictionary ledger for conditional payments.
- We slightly enhance their notations to allow the contract to access a global dictionary blockhashes. Each item blockhashes$[t]$ is the hash of the block $C[t]$.[3] Note the local blockchain replicas of all full nodes would be consistent to blockhashes (within one clock) according to the global ledger model [35].

---

[3] Remark that the above modeling requires the block hashes can be read by smart contracts from the blockchain's internal states (e.g. available global variables) [20]. In Ethereum, this currently can be realized via the proposal of Andrew Miller [45] and will be incorporated due to the already-planned Ethereum enhancement EIP-210 [2].

- The contract would not send its internal states to the light client, which captures the client opts out of consensus. However, the client can send messages to the contract, due to the well abstracted network diffusion functionality.

4 Problem Formulation

This section rigorously defines the light-client problem in the rational model.

4.1 Defining the Readings from the Blockchain

The basic aim is to allow the resource-starved clients to evaluate the falseness or trueness about some statements over the blockchain [33]. This subsection would define these statements about blockchain as chain predicates.

Chain Predicate. We focus on a general class of chain predicates whose trueness can be induced by up to l transactions' inclusions in the chain, such as "whether a transaction tx is in the chain". Formally, the chain predicate is in the form of:

$$P^\ell(C[0:N]) = \begin{cases} False, \text{ otherwise} \\ True, \exists C' \subset C[0:N] \text{ s.t. } D^\ell(C') = True \end{cases}$$

where C' is a subset of the blockchain $C[0:N]$, and $D^\ell(\cdot)$ is a computable predicate taking C' as input and can be expressed as:

$$D^\ell(C') = \begin{cases} True, \exists \{tx_i\} \text{ that } |\{tx_i\}| \leq \ell : \\ \quad f(\{tx_i\}) = 1 \land \forall tx_i \in \{tx_i\}, \\ \quad\quad \exists C[t] \in C' \text{ and P.P.T. computable } \pi_i \text{ s.t.} \\ \quad\quad\quad \mathsf{VrfyMTP}(C[t].\mathsf{root}, H(tx_i), \pi_i) = 1 \\ False, \text{ otherwise} \end{cases}$$

where $f(\{tx_i\}) = 1$ captures that $\{tx_i\}$ satisfies a certain relationship, e.g., "the hash of each tx_i equals a specified identifier $txid_i$", or "each tx_i can pass the membership test of a given bloom filter", or "the overall inflow of $\{tx_i\}$ is greater than a given value". We let P_N^ℓ be short for $P^\ell(C[0:N])$.

Examples of Chain Predicate. The definition of chain predicate captures a wide range of blockchain "readings". For any predicate under this category, its trueness can be succinctly attested by up to ℓ transactions' inclusion in the chain. For $\ell = 1$, some concrete examples are:

- "The transaction tx is included in $C[0:N]$", the trueness of which can be attested by tx's inclusion in the chain $C[0:N]$.
- "tx is included in $C[0:N]$ and satisfies a given bloom filter $f(\cdot)$", which is reducible to tx's inclusion in the chain and the value of $f(tx)$.
- "A set of transactions $\{tx_j\}$ are included in $C[0:N]$", whose trueness can be attested by all tx_j's inclusions in the chain.

Limits of Chain Predicate. A chain predicate is a binary question, whose trueness is reducible to the inclusion of some transactions. The actual meaning of a chain predicate depends on how to concretely specify it. A "meaningful" chain predicate might need certain specifications from an external party outside the system. For example, the cashier of a pizza store can specify a transaction to evaluate its (non)existence, only if the customer tells the txid.

"Handicapped" Verifiability of Chain Predicate. We focus on the chain predicate in form of P_N^ℓ, namely, whose trueness is provable.[4] Such "handicapped" verifiability can be well abstracted through a tuple of two algorithms (evaluate, validateTrue) along with their properties:

- evaluate(P_N^ℓ) → σ or $\perp$: The algorithm takes the replica of the blockchain as auxiliary input and outputs σ or $\perp$, where σ is a proof for $P_N^\ell = True$, and $\perp$ represents its falseness; note the proof σ here includes: a set of transactions $\{tx_i\}$, a set of Merkle proofs $\{\pi_i\}$, and a set of blocks C';
- validateTrue(σ, P_N^ℓ) → 0 or 1: This algorithm takes blockhashes as auxiliary input and outputs 1 (accept) or 0 (reject) depending on whether σ is deemed to be a valid proof for $P_N^\ell = True$; note the validation parses σ as ($\{tx_i\}, \{\pi_i\}, C'$) and verifies: (i) C' is included by blockhashes[t] where $t \le N$; (ii) each tx_i is committed by a block in C' due to Merkle proof π_i; (iii) $f(\{tx_i\}) = 1$ where $f(\cdot)$ is the specification of the chain predicate.

The above algorithms satisfy: (i) *Correctness.* For any chain predicate P_N^ℓ, there is $\Pr[\text{validateTrue}(\text{evaluate}(P_N^\ell), P_N^\ell) = 1 \mid P_N^\ell = true] = 1$, and (ii) *Verifiability.* for any P.P.T. $\mathcal{A}$ and P_N^ℓ, there is $\Pr[\text{validateTrue}(\sigma \leftarrow \mathcal{A}(P^\ell), P_N^\ell) = 1 \mid P_N^\ell = false] \le negl(\lambda)$, where evaluate implicitly takes the blockchain replica as input, and validateTrue implicitly inputs blockhashes. In the remaining of the paper, evaluate can be seen as a black-box callable by any full nodes, and validateTrue is a subroutine that can be invoked by any smart contract.

4.2   System and Adversary Model

The system explicitly consists of a lightweight client, some relay(s) and an arbiter contract. The messages among them can deliver within a known delay ΔT. In details,

The Rational Lightweight Client. $\mathcal{LW}$ is abstracted as:

- It is **rational** and selfish; moreover, it is computationally bounded, i.e., it can only take an action computable in probabilistic polynomial-time;
- It opts out of consensus; to capture this, we assume:
  - The client can *send* messages to the contract due to the network diffusion functionality [22,38];

---

[4] Remark that in the full paper [42], we define another class of chain predicates whose falseness is provable instead of trueness, which can captured by our protocol as well, though we omit detailed discussions here for presentation simplicity.

– The client cannot receive messages from the contract except a short setup phase, which can be done in practice because the client user can temporarily boost a personal full node by fast-bootstrapping protocols.

The Rational Full Node. $\mathcal{R}_i$ is modeled as:

- It is **rational**. Also, the full node $\mathcal{R}_i$ might (or might not) cooperate with another full node $\mathcal{R}_j$. The **(non)-cooperation** of them is specified as:
  – The **cooperative** full nodes form a coalition to maximize the total utility, as they can share all information, coordinate all actions and transfer payoffs, etc. [49]; essentially, we follow the conventional notion to view the cooperative relays as **a single** party [7].
  – **Non-cooperative** full nodes maximize their own utilities independently in a selfish manner due to the standard non-cooperative game theory, which can be understood as that they are not allowed to choose some ITMs to communicate with each other [40];
- It can only take P.P.T. computable actions at any stage of the protocol;
- The full node runs the consensus, such that:
  – It stores the complete replica of the latest blockchain;
  – It can send/receive messages to/from the smart contract;
- It can send messages to the light client via an off-chain private channel.[5]

The Arbiter Contract. $\mathcal{G}_{ac}$ follows the standard abstraction of smart contracts [35,38], with a few slight extensions. First, it would not send any messages to the light client except during a short setup phase. Second, it can access a dictionary blockhashes [2,45], which contains the hashes of all blocks. The latter abstraction further allows the contract to invoke validateTrue to verify the proof attesting the trueness of any predicate P_N^ℓ, in case the predicate is actually true.

Economic Factors of Modeling. For the sake of completing our game-theoretic model, we clarify the economic parameters of the modeling as follows:

- v: The factor means the "value" attached to the chain predicate under query. If the client incorrectly evaluates the predicate, it loses v. For example, the cashier Alice is evaluating the (non)existence of a certain transaction; if Alice believes the existence of a non-existing transaction, she loses the amount to be transacted; if Alice believes the nonexistence of an existing transaction, her business is harmed by such censorship.
- $v_i(\mathsf{P}_N^\ell, \mathsf{C}) \to [0, v_i]$: This function characterizes the motivation of the relay $\mathcal{R}_i$ to cheat the light client. Namely, it represents the extra (malicious) utility that the relay $\mathcal{R}_i$ earns, if fooling the client to incorrectly evaluate the chain predicate. We consider $\sum_i v_i(\mathsf{P}_N^\ell, \mathsf{C}) \le v$, so the overall malicious utilities attained by fooling the client is up to the "value" attached to the query.

---

[5] Such assumption can be granted if considering the client and the relays can set up private communication channels on demand. In practice, this can be done because (i) the client can "broadcast" its network address via the blockchain [43], or (ii) there is a trusted name service that tracks the network addresses of the relays.

- In addition, all communications and P.P.T. computations can be done costlessly (unless otherwise specified).

Remark. We describe an advanced modeling of economic factors to capture the cost of maintaining a personal full node by the client user in the full version [42]. Here we ignore this factor by assuming the client cannot access any personal full node once the protocol is set up. This simplified modeling still makes sense to allow us argue security of our protocol, conditioned on the setup phase is done.

4.3   Security Goal

The aim of the light-client protocol $\Pi_{\mathcal{LW}}$ in the above game-theoretic model is to allow a rational light client employ some rational relaying full nodes (e.g., one or two) to correctly *evaluate* the chain predicates, and these recruited relay nodes are correctly paid as pre-specified. In details, we require:

- *Correctness.* If all parties are honest, we require: (i) the relay nodes are correctly paid; (ii) the light client correctly evaluates some chain predicates under the category of $P^\ell(\cdot)$, regarding the chain $C[0:T]$ (i.e. the chain at the time of evaluating). Both requirements shall hold with probability 1.
- *Security.* We adopt a strong game-theoretic security notion of *sequential equilibrium* [16,30,31] for incomplete-information extensive games. Consider an extensive-form game Γ that models the light-client protocol $\Pi_{\mathcal{LW}}$, and let $(\mathbf{Z_{bad}}, \mathbf{Z_{good}})$ as a partition of the terminal histories $\mathbf{Z}$ of the game Γ, where $\mathbf{Z_{good}}$ captures and only captures all protocol executions where no party deviates. Given a ϵ-*sequential equilibrium*[6] of Γ denoted by σ, the probability of reaching each terminal history $z \in \mathbf{Z}$ can be induced, which can be denoted by $\rho(\sigma, z)$.

  Our security goal requires: there is a ϵ-sequential equilibrium σ of Γ where ϵ is at most a negligible function $nelg(\lambda)$ in security parameter λ, such that under the ϵ-equilibrium σ, the game Γ terminates in $\mathbf{Z_{good}}$.

5   A Simple Light-Client Protocol

Here we present a simple light-client protocol, in which a client ($\mathcal{LW}$) employs two (or one) relays to evaluate the chain predicates P^ℓ_N (as defined in Sect. 4.1).

5.1   Arbiter Contract and High-Level of the Protocol

The light-client protocol centers around an arbiter smart contract $\mathcal{G}_{ac}$ as shown in Fig. 2. It begins with letting all parties place their initial deposits. Later, the client can ask the relays to forward some readings about the blockchain, and then feeds what it receives back to the contract. Once the contract hears the feedback from the client, it leverages the initial deposits to facilitate some proper incentive mechanism, thus preventing deviations by rewarding and/or punishing.

---

[6] Remark that due to the notion of ϵ-*sequential equilibrium*, the rational game players are not sensitive for any utility increments that are less than ϵ.

The arbiter contract $\mathcal{G}_{ac}$ for m relays ($m = 1$ or 2)

Init. Let state := INIT, deposits := {}, relays := {}, pubKeys := {}, ctr := 0, predicate := $\emptyset$, predicate.N := 0, T_{end} := 0

_____ Setup phase _____

Create. On receiving the message (create, $k, p, e, d_L, d_F, \Delta T$) from $\mathcal{LW}$:
- assert state = INIT and ledger[$\mathcal{LW}$] $\geq$ \$$k \cdot d_L$
- store k, p, e, r, d_L, d_F, and ΔT as internal states
- ledger[$\mathcal{LW}$] := ledger[$\mathcal{LW}$] $-$ \$$k \cdot d_L$
- ctr := k and state := CREATED
- send (deployed, $k, p, e, d_L, d_F, \Delta T$) to all

Join. On receiving (join, pk_i) from $\mathcal{R}_i$ for first time:
- assert state = CREATED and ledger[$\mathcal{R}_i$] $\geq$ \$$k \cdot d_F$
- ledger[$\mathcal{R}_i$] := ledger[$\mathcal{R}_i$] $-$ \$$k \cdot d_F$
- pubKeys := pubKeys $\cup$ ($\mathcal{R}_i, pk_i$)
- state := READY, if |pubKeys| $= m$

_____ Queries phase _____

Request. On receiving (request, P^ℓ) from $\mathcal{LW}$:
- assert state = READY and ledger[$\mathcal{LW}$] $\geq$ \$$(p + e)$
- ledger[$\mathcal{LW}$] := ledger[$\mathcal{LW}$] $-$ \$$(p + e)$
- predicate := P_T^ℓ //Note T is the current chain height
- T_{end} := $T + \Delta T$
- send (quering, ctr, predicate) to each full node registered in pubKeys
- state := QUERYING

Feedback. On receiving (feedback, responses) from $\mathcal{LW}$ for first time:
- assert state = QUERYING
- store responses for the current ctr

Timer. Upon $T \geq T_{end}$ and state := QUERYING:
- call Incentive(responses, predicate) subroutine
- let ctr := ctr $-$ 1
- if ctr > 0 then state := READY
- else state := EXPIRED

Fig. 2. The contract $\mathcal{G}_{ac}$ by pseudocode notations in [38]. The Incentive subroutine is decoupled from the protocol and will be presented separately in the later section.

For security in the rational setting, the incentive mechanism must be powerful enough to precisely punish misbehaviors (and reward honesty). Our main principle to realize such powerful incentive is letting the arbiter contract to learn as much as possible regarding how the protocol is actually executed off-chain, so it can precisely punish and then deter any deviations.

Nevertheless, the contract has "handicapped" abilities. So we have to carefully design the protocol to circumvent its limits, for the convenience of designing powerful incentive mechanisms to deter deviations later.

First, the contract $\mathcal{G}_{ac}$ does not know what the relay nodes forward to the light client off-chain. So the contract $\mathcal{G}_{ac}$ has to rely on the client to figure out what the relays did. At the first glance, the client might cheat the contract, by claiming that it receives nothing from the relays or even forging the relays' messages, in order to avoid paying. To deal with the issue, we require that: (i) the relays authenticate what they forward to the client by digital signatures, so the contract later can verify whether a message was originally sent from the relays, by checking the attached signatures; (ii) the contract requires the light client to deposit an amount of \$$e$ for each query, which is returned to the client, only if the client reports some forwarded blockchain readings signed by the relays.

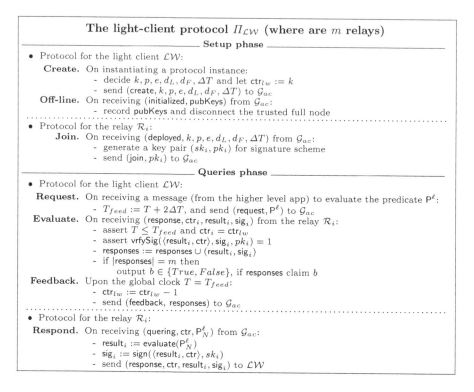

Fig. 3. The light-client protocol $\Pi_{\mathcal{LW}}$ among honest relay node(s) and the light client.

Second, the contract has a "handicapped" verifiability, which allows it to efficiently verify a claim of $\mathsf{P}_N^\ell = True$, if being give a succinct proof σ. To leverage the property, the protocol is designed to let the relays attach the corresponding proof σ when claiming the provable trueness. Again, this design is a simple yet still useful way to allow the contract "learn" more about the protocol execution, which later enables a powerful mechanism to precisely punish deviations.

5.2 The Light-Client Protocol

In the presence of the contract $\mathcal{G}_{ac}$, our light-client protocol can be formally described as Fig. 3. The protocol starts with a setup phase, during which the relay(s) and client make initial deposits. Then the client can work independently and request the relays to help it evaluate up to k chain predicates, repeatedly.

Setup Phase. As shown in Fig. 3, the user of a lightweight client $\mathcal{LW}$ connects to a trusted full node in the setup phase, and announces an "arbiter" smart contract $\mathcal{G}_{ac}$. After the contract $\mathcal{G}_{ac}$ is deployed, some relay full nodes (e.g. one or two) are recruited to join the protocol by depositing an amount of $\$k \cdot d_F$ in the contract. The public keys of the relay(s) are also recorded by contract $\mathcal{G}_{ac}$.

Once the setup phase is done, each relay full node places the initial deposits $\$k \cdot d_F$ and the light client deposit $\$k \cdot d_L$, which will be used to deter their deviations from the protocol. At the same time, $\mathcal{LW}$ records the public keys of the relay(s), and then disconnects the trusted full node to work independently.

In practice, the setup can be done by using many fast bootstrap methods [33,41,53], which allows the user to efficiently launch a personal trusted full node in the PC. So the light client (e.g. a smart-phone) can connect to the PC to sync. Remark that, besides the cryptographic security parameter λ, the protocol is specified with some other parameters:

- k: The protocol is expired, after the client requests the relay(s) to evaluate some chain predicates for k times.
- $k \cdot d_L$: This is the deposit placed by the client to initialize the protocol.
- $k \cdot d_F$: The initial deposit of a full node to join the protocol as a relay node.
- p: Later in each query, the client shall place this amount to cover the well-deserved payment of the relay(s).
- e: Later in each query, the client shall place this deposit e in addition to p.

Repeatable Query Phase. Once the setup is done, $\mathcal{LW}$ disconnects the trusted full node, and can ask the relay(s) to query some chain predicates repeatedly, as clarified in Fig. 3. It is immediate to see the *correctness* of the protocol: when all parties are honest, the relay(s) receive the payment pre-specified due to incentive mechanism in the contract, and the client always outputs the ground truth of chain predicate. However, the security would depend on the payoffs clauses facilitated by the incentive subroutine, which will be elaborated in later subsections as we intentionally decouple the protocol and the incentive design.

6   Adding Incentives for Security

Without a proper incentive subroutine, the simple light-client protocol is insecure to any extent, as the relays are always motivated to cheat the client. This section studies on how to squeeze most out of the "handicapped" abilities of the arbiter contract to design proper incentives to achieve desired equilibrium for security.

6.1   Basic incentive Mechanism and its Security

We firstly design the basic incentive subroutines that are only based the rationality of the light client and relays, and them analyze that these incentives make the "light-client game" secure to what extent.

Basic incentive for Two Relays. If two non-cooperative relays can be recruited, the incentive subroutine takes the feedback message from the client as input, and then facilitates the incentives following hereunder general principles:

- It firstly verifies whether the feedback sent from the client indeed encapsulates some responses that were originally sent from $\mathcal{R}_1$ and/or $\mathcal{R}_2$. If feedback contains two validly signed responses, return $\$e$ to the client; If feedback contain one validly signed response, return $\$e/2$ to the client.

- If a relay claims $\mathsf{P}_N^\ell = True$ with attaching an invalid proof σ, its deposit for this query (i.e. $\$d_F$) is confiscated and would not receive any payment.
- When a relay sends a response message containing $\perp$ to claim $\mathsf{P}_N^\ell = False$, there is no succinct proof attesting the claim. The incentive subroutine checks whether the other relay full node provides a proof attesting $\mathsf{P}_N^\ell = True$. If the other relay proves $\mathsf{P}_N^\ell = True$, the cheating relay loses its deposit this query (i.e. $\$d_F$) and would not receive any payment. For the other relay that falsifies the cheating claim of $\mathsf{P}_N^\ell = False$, the incentive subroutine assigns it some extra bonuses (e.g. doubled payment).
- After each query, if the contract does not notice a full node is misbehaving (i.e., no fake proof for truthness or fake claim of falseness), it would pay the node $\$p/2$ as the basic reward (for the honest full node). In addition, the contract returns a portion of the client's initial deposit (i.e. $\$d_L$). Moreover, the contract returns a portion of each relay's initial deposit (i.e. $\$d_F$), if the incentive subroutine does not observe the relay cheats during this query.

The rationale behind the above incentive clauses is straightforward. First, during any query, the rational light client will always report to the contract whatever the relays actually forward, since the failure of doing so always causes strictly less utility, no matter the strategy of the relay full nodes; Second, since the two relay full nodes are non-cooperative, they would be incentivized to audit each other, such that the attempt of cheating the client is deterred.

Basic incentive **for One Relay.** When any two recruited relays might collude, the situation turns to be pessimistic, as the light client is now requesting an unknown information from only a single distrustful coalition. To argue security in this rather pessimistic case, we consider only one relay in the protocol. To deal with the pessimistic case, we tune the incentive subroutine by incorporating the next major tuning (different from the incentive for two relays):

- If the relay claims $\mathsf{P}_N^\ell = False$, its deposit $\$d_F$ is returned but paid less than $\$p$, namely, $\$(p - r)$ where $\$r \in [0, p]$ is an incentive parameter.
- Other payoff rules follow those designed for two non-cooperative relays.

The ideas behind the above incentive clauses are letting the only relay node to "audit" itself, which means: the relay can expect a higher payment as long as it presents a verifaible claim instead of an unverifiable claim.

Analysis and Security Theorems of Basic incentive. To demonstrate the above delicately tuned incentive clauses are implementable, we describe them in the conventional pseudocode notations [38] in the full version [42]. In addition, due to page limit, we omit the detailed structure of the extensive games induced by the light-client protocol along with the utility functions induced by the incentive clauses, c.f., the full paper [42] for the detailed analysis about these extensive games. Here are the main security theorems (of the basic incentives):

Theorem 1. *If two non-cooperative relays are recruited, there exists a ϵ-sequential equilibrium in the extensive game of the light-client protocol, under*

which no rational party deviates from the protocol except with negligible proba-
bility, conditioned on $d_F + p/2 > v_i$ *and* $d_L > (p+e)$.

Theorem 1 states that: if there are two non-cooperative relays, the sufficient conditions of security are: (i) the initial deposit d_F of relay node is greater than its malicious benefit v_i that can be obtained by fooling the client; (ii) the initial deposit d_L of the client is greater than the payment p plus another small parameter e. The above conclusion hints us how to safely set up the light-client protocol to instantiate a cryptocurrency wallet in practice, that is: let the light client and the relays finely tune and specify their initial deposits, so the client can query the (non)existence of any transaction, as long as the transacted amount of the transaction is not greater than the initial deposit placed by the relay nodes.

Theorem 2. *If only one relay is recruited, there is a ϵ-sequential equilibrium in the light-client protocol's extensive game, under which no rational party deviates except with negligible probability, when* $d_F + p - r > v_i$, $r > v_i$, *and* $d_L > (p+e)$.

Theorem 2 reveals that: even in an extremely hostile scenario where only one single relay exists, deviations are still prevented when fooling the light client to believe the non-existence of an existing transaction does not yield better payoff .than honestly proving the existence. The statement presents a feasibility region of our protocol that at least captures many important DApps (e.g., decentralized messaging apps) in practice, namely: fooling the client is not very financially beneficial for the relay, and only brings a payoff v_i to the relay.

6.2   Augmented incentive and its Security

In the pessimistic scenario of only one recruited relay full node, we can introduce an extra rationality assumption that: at least one public full node (denoted by $\mathcal{PFN}$) can monitor the internal states of the arbiter contract at a tiny cost (say zero for the convenience of analysis) and does not cooperate with the only recruited relay. This extra rationality assumption can boost an incentive mechanism to deter the relay and client from deviating from the light-client protocol.

Augmented incentive for One Relay. The tuning of the incentive mechanism stems from the observation that: if there is *any* public full node that does not cooperate with the recruited relay (and monitor the internal states of the arbiter contract), it can stand out to audit a fake claim about $\mathsf{P}_N^\ell = False$ by producing a proof attesting $\mathsf{P}_N^\ell = True$. Thus, we slightly tune the incentive subroutine by adding merely few lines of pseudocode (see [42] for details), which can be summarized as:

- When the recruited relay node forwards a response that claims $\mathsf{P}_N^\ell = False$, the incentive subroutine shall wait few clock periods (e.g., one). During the waiting time, the public full node is allowed to send a proof attesting $\mathsf{P}_N^\ell = True$ to falsify a fake claim of $\mathsf{P}_N^\ell = False$; in this case, the initial deposit d_F of the cheating relay is confiscated and paid to the public full node.
- Other payoff rules are same to the basic incentive mechanism.

Analysis and Security Theorems of Augmented incentive. The formal instantiation of the above augmented incentive mechanism along with the detailed security analysis are deferred to the full version [42] due to page limit. The main security theorem about the augmented incentive mechanism is:

Theorem 3. *Given the augmented incentive mechanism, a ϵ-sequential equilibrium exists in the light-client protocol's extensive game, where no rational party deviates except with negligible probability when $d_F > v_i$, $d_L > (p+e)$ and a non-cooperative public full node that can "monitor" the arbiter contract costlessly.*

The economics behind Theorem 3 can be understood similarly as Theorem 1.

7 Discussions

Feasibility. We also shed light on the concrete implementation of the protocol in the full paper [42]. Our experiments atop Ethereum indicate that a non-optimized basic instantiation has been arguably practical. In particular, to query a transaction's (non)existence, the on-chain handling fee (which characterizes the on-chain feasibility and excludes the incentives to pay) is less than half US dollar at the time of writing (see [42] for details).

Future Outlook. As this is the first study that formally discusses the light clients of permissionless blockchains in game-theoretic settings, the area remains largely unexplored, and a few potential studies can be conducted for more realistic instantiations. For example, many crypto-economic protocols (e.g., PoS blockchains [14,24,34] and payment channels [18,46] already introduce locked deposits, and it becomes enticing to explore the composability of using the same collateral in the light-client protocol and other crypto-economic protocols, without scarifying the securities of all protocols.

Acknowledgment. We thank anonymous reviewers for valuable comments. Qiang is supported in part by JDDigits via the JDD-NJIT-ISCAS Joint Blockchain Lab and a Google Faculty Award.

References

1. Cardano. https://www.cardano.org/en/home/
2. Ethereum EIP-210. https://eips.ethereum.org/EIPS/eip-210
3. Abraham, I., Dolev, D., Gonen, R., Halpern, J.: Distributed computing meets game theory: robust mechanisms for rational secret sharing and multiparty computation. In: Proceedings of ACM PODC 2006, pp. 53–62 (2006)
4. Babaioff, M., Dobzinski, S., Oren, S., Zohar, A.: On bitcoin and red balloons. In: Proceedings of ACM EC 2012, pp. 56–73 (2012)
5. Back, A., et al.: Enabling blockchain innovations with pegged sidechains (2014). http://www.opensciencereview.com/papers/123/enablingblockchain-innovations-with-pegged-sidechains

6. Badertscher, C., Gaži, P., Kiayias, A., Russell, A., Zikas, V.: Ouroboros genesis: Composable proof-of-stake blockchains with dynamic availability. In: Proceedings of ACM CCS 2018, pp. 913–930 (2018)
7. Beimel, A., Groce, A., Katz, J., Orlov, I.: Fair computation with rational players (2011). https://eprint.iacr.org/2011/396
8. Bitcoin Core (2019). https://github.com/bitcoin/bitcoin
9. Boneh, D., Bünz, B., Fisch, B.: Batching techniques for accumulators with applications to IOPs and stateless blockchains. In: Boldyreva, A., Micciancio, D. (eds.) CRYPTO 2019. LNCS, vol. 11692, pp. 561–586. Springer, Cham (2019). https://doi.org/10.1007/978-3-030-26948-7_20
10. Bünznz, B., Kiffer, L., Luu, L., Zamani, M.: FlyClient: Super-light clients for cryptocurrencies. In: Proceedings of IEEE S&P 2020 (2020)
11. Buterin, V.: A next-generation smart contract and decentralized application platform (2014)
12. Buterin, V.: Light clients and proof of stake (2015). https://blog.ethereum.org/2015/01/10/light-clients-proof-stake/
13. CryptoKitties (2018). https://www.cryptokitties.co/
14. Daian, P., Pass, R., Shi, E.: Snow White: robustly reconfigurable consensus and applications to provably secure proof of stake. In: Goldberg, I., Moore, T. (eds.) FC 2019. LNCS, vol. 11598, pp. 23–41. Springer, Cham (2019). https://doi.org/10.1007/978-3-030-32101-7_2
15. David, B., Gaži, P., Kiayias, A., Russell, A.: Ouroboros Praos: an adaptively-secure, semi-synchronous proof-of-stake blockchain. In: Nielsen, J.B., Rijmen, V. (eds.) EUROCRYPT 2018. LNCS, vol. 10821, pp. 66–98. Springer, Cham (2018). https://doi.org/10.1007/978-3-319-78375-8_3
16. Dong, C., Wang, Y., Aldweesh, A., McCorry, P., van Moorsel, A.: Betrayal, distrust, and rationality: Smart counter-collusion contracts for verifiable cloud computing. In: Proceedings of ACM CCS 2017, pp. 211–227 (2017)
17. Dziembowski, S., Eckey, L., Faust, S.: FairsWap: how to fairly exchange digital goods. In: Proceedings of ACM CCS 2018, pp. 967–984 (2018)
18. Dziembowski, S., Eckey, L., Faust, S., Malinowski, D.: Perun: virtual payment hubs over cryptocurrencies. In: Proceedings of IEEE S&P 2019, pp. 327–344 (2019)
19. Electrum (2011). http://docs.electrum.org/en/latest/
20. Ethereum Foundation: Solidity Global Variables (2018). https://solidity.readthedocs.io/en/develop/units-and-global-variables.html
21. Fuchsbauer, G., Katz, J., Naccache, D.: Efficient rational secret sharing in standard communication networks. In: Micciancio, D. (ed.) TCC 2010. LNCS, vol. 5978, pp. 419–436. Springer, Heidelberg (2010). https://doi.org/10.1007/978-3-642-11799-2_25
22. Garay, J., Kiayias, A., Leonardos, N.: The bitcoin backbone protocol: analysis and applications. In: Oswald, E., Fischlin, M. (eds.) EUROCRYPT 2015. LNCS, vol. 9057, pp. 281–310. Springer, Heidelberg (2015). https://doi.org/10.1007/978-3-662-46803-6_10
23. Gaži, P., Kiayias, A., Zindros, D.: Proof-of-stake sidechains. In: Proceedings of IEEE S&P 2019 (2019)
24. Gilad, Y., Hemo, R., Micali, S., Vlachos, G., Zeldovich, N.: Algorand: scaling byzantine agreements for cryptocurrencies. In: Proceedings of the 26th Symposium on Operating Systems Principles, pp. 51–68 (2017)
25. Go Ethereum (2019). https://github.com/ethereum/go-ethereum

26. Gordon, S.D., Katz, J.: Rational secret sharing, revisited. In: De Prisco, R., Yung, M. (eds.) SCN 2006. LNCS, vol. 4116, pp. 229–241. Springer, Heidelberg (2006). https://doi.org/10.1007/11832072_16

27. Groce, A., Katz, J.: Fair computation with rational players. In: Pointcheval, D., Johansson, T. (eds.) EUROCRYPT 2012. LNCS, vol. 7237, pp. 81–98. Springer, Heidelberg (2012). https://doi.org/10.1007/978-3-642-29011-4_7

28. Gruber, D., Li, W., Karame, G.: Unifying lightweight blockchain client implementations. In: Workshop on Decentralized IoT Security and Standards (DISS) (2018)

29. Halpern, J., Teague, V.: Rational secret sharing and multiparty computation. In: Proceedings of ACM STOC 2004, pp. 623–632 (2004)

30. Halpern, J.Y., Pass, R.: Sequential equilibrium in computational games. ACM Trans. Econ. Comput. (TEAC) **7**(2), 1–19 (2019)

31. Halpern, J.Y., Pass, R., Seeman, L.: Computational extensive-form games. In: Proceedings of ACM EC 2016, pp. 681–698 (2016)

32. Izmalkov, S., Micali, S., Lepinski, M.: Rational secure computation and ideal mechanism design. In: Proceedings of IEEE FOCS 2005, pp. 585–594 (2005)

33. Kiayias, A., Miller, A., Zindros, D.: Non-interactive proofs of proof-of-work (2017). https://eprint.iacr.org/2017/963.pdf

34. Kiayias, A., Russell, A., David, B., Oliynykov, R.: Ouroboros: a provably secure proof-of-stake blockchain protocol. In: Katz, J., Shacham, H. (eds.) CRYPTO 2017. LNCS, vol. 10401, pp. 357–388. Springer, Cham (2017). https://doi.org/10.1007/978-3-319-63688-7_12

35. Kiayias, A., Zhou, H.-S., Zikas, V.: Fair and robust multi-party computation using a global transaction ledger. In: Fischlin, M., Coron, J.-S. (eds.) EUROCRYPT 2016. LNCS, vol. 9666, pp. 705–734. Springer, Heidelberg (2016). https://doi.org/10.1007/978-3-662-49896-5_25

36. Kiayias, A., Zindros, D.: Proof-of-work sidechains. In: Bracciali, A., Clark, J., Pintore, F., Rønne, P.B., Sala, M. (eds.) FC 2019. LNCS, vol. 11599, pp. 21–34. Springer, Cham (2020). https://doi.org/10.1007/978-3-030-43725-1_3

37. Kol, G., Naor, M.: Games for exchanging information. In: Proceedings of ACM STOC 2008, pp. 423–432 (2008)

38. Kosba, A., Miller, A., Shi, E., et al.: Hawk: the blockchain model of cryptography and privacy-preserving smart contracts. In: Proceedings of IEEE S&P 2016, pp. 839–858 (2016)

39. Kwon, J., Buchman, E.: Cosmos: a network of distributed ledgers (2017). https://github.com/cosmos/cosmos/blob/master/WHITEPAPER.md

40. Lepinksi, M., Micali, S., Shelat, A.: Collusion-free protocols. In: Proceedings of ACM STOC 2005, pp. 543–552 (2005)

41. Leung, D., Suhl, A., Gilad, Y., Zeldovich, N.: Vault: fast bootstrapping for cryptocurrencies. In: NDSS 2019 (2019)

42. Lu, Y., Tang, Q., Wang, G.: Generic superlight client for permissionless blockchains. arXiv preprint arXiv:2003.06552 (2020)

43. Luu, L., Narayanan, V., Zheng, C., Baweja, K., Gilbert, S., Saxena, P.: A secure sharding protocol for open blockchains. In: Proceedings of ACM CCS 2016, pp. 17–30 (2016)

44. Meckler1, I., Shapiro, E.: Coda: Decentralized cryptocurrency at scale. https://cdn.codaprotocol.com/v2/static/coda-whitepaper-05-10-2018-0.pdf

45. Miller, A.: Ethereum blockhash contract (2017). https://github.com/amiller/ethereum-blockhashes

46. Miller, A., Bentov, I., Kumaresan, R., McCorry, P.: Sprites and state channels: payment networks that go faster than lightning. In: Proceedings of FC (2019)

47. Miller, A.E., Hicks, M., Katz, J., Shi, E.: Authenticated data structures, generically. In: Proceedings of ACM POPL 2014, pp. 411–423 (2014)
48. Nakamoto, S.: Bitcoin: A peer-to-peer electronic cash system (2008)
49. Osborne, M., Rubinstein, A.: A Course in Game Theory (1994)
50. Park, S., Kwon, A., Fuchsbauer, G., Gaži, P., Alwen, J., Pietrzak, K.: SpaceMint: a cryptocurrency based on proofs of space. In: Proceedings of FC 2018, pp. 480–499 (2018)
51. Pass, R., Shi, E.: Rethinking large-scale consensus. In: 2017 IEEE 30th Computer Security Foundations Symposium (CSF), pp. 115–129. IEEE (2017)
52. Pham, V., Khouzani, M.H.R., Cid, C.: Optimal contracts for outsourced computation. In: Poovendran, R., Saad, W. (eds.) GameSec 2014. LNCS, vol. 8840, pp. 79–98. Springer, Cham (2014). https://doi.org/10.1007/978-3-319-12601-2_5
53. Poelstra, A.: Mimblewimble (2016). https://download.wpsoftware.net/bitcoin/wizardry/mimblewimble.pdf
54. Protocol Labs: Filecoin: A Decentralized Storage Network (2017). https://filecoin.io/filecoin.pdf
55. Steemit (2016). https://steemit.com/
56. Teutsch, J., Reitwießner, C.: A scalable verification solution for blockchains (2017). https://people.cs.uchicago.edu/~teutsch/papers/truebit.pdf
57. Tomescu, A., Devadas, S.: Catena: efficient non-equivocation via bitcoin. In: Proceedings of IEEE S&P 2017, pp. 393–409 (2017)
58. Wood, G.: Ethereum: A secure decentralised generalised transaction ledger (2014). https://ethereum.github.io/yellowpaper/paper.pdf
59. Xu, L., Chen, L., Gao, Z., Xu, S., Shi, W.: EPBC: efficient public blockchain client for lightweight users. In: Proceedings of the 1st Workshop on Scalable and Resilient Infrastructures for Distributed Ledgers, p. 1. ACM (2017)
60. Zamyatin, A., Stifter, N., Judmayer, A., Schindler, P., Weippl, E., Knottenbelt, W.J.: A wild velvet fork appears! inclusive blockchain protocol changes in practice. In: Proceedings of FC 2018, pp. 31–42 (2018)

LNBot: A Covert Hybrid Botnet on Bitcoin Lightning Network for Fun and Profit

Ahmet Kurt[1](✉), Enes Erdin[1], Mumin Cebe[2], Kemal Akkaya[1], and A. Selcuk Uluagac[1]

[1] Florida International University, Miami, FL 33174, USA
{akurt005,eerdi001,kakkaya,suluagac}@fiu.edu
[2] Computer Science Department, Marquette University, Milwaukee, USA
mumin.cebe@marquette.edu

Abstract. While various covert botnets were proposed in the past, they still lack complete anonymization for their servers/botmasters or suffer from slow communication between the botmaster and the bots. In this paper, we propose a new generation hybrid botnet that covertly and efficiently communicates over Bitcoin Lightning Network (LN), called LNBot. LN is a payment channel network operating on top of Bitcoin network for faster Bitcoin transactions with negligible fees. Exploiting various anonymity features of LN, we designed a scalable two-layer botnet which completely anonymize the identity of the botmaster. In the first layer, the botmaster sends commands anonymously to the C&C servers through LN transactions. Specifically, LNBot allows botmaster's commands to be sent in the form of surreptitious multihop LN payments, where the commands are encoded with ASCII or Huffman encoding to provide covert communications. In the second layer, C&C servers further relay those commands to the bots they control in their mini-botnets to launch any type of attacks to victim machines. We implemented a proof-of-concept on the actual LN and extensively analyzed the delay and cost performance of LNBot. Our analysis show that LNBot achieves better scalibility compared to the other similar blockchain botnets with negligible costs. Finally, we also provide and discuss a list of potential countermeasures to detect LNBot activities and minimize its impacts.

Keywords: Lightning Network · Botnet · Covert channel

1 Introduction

Botnets are networks of computing devices infected with malicious software that is under the control of an attacker, known as bot herder or *botmaster* [28]. The owner of the botnet controls the *bots* (i.e., devices that become part of the botnet) through command and control *(C&C) server(s)* which can communicate with the bots using a C&C channel and can launch various attacks through these

© Springer Nature Switzerland AG 2020
L. Chen et al. (Eds.): ESORICS 2020, LNCS 12309, pp. 734–755, 2020.
https://doi.org/10.1007/978-3-030-59013-0_36

bots, including, but not limited to, denial of service (DoS) attacks, information and identity theft, sending spam messages, and other activities. Naturally, a botmaster's goal is to make it difficult for law enforcement to detect and prevent malicious operations. Therefore, establishing a secure C&C infrastructure and hiding the C&C server identity play a key role in the long-lasting operation of botnets.

Numerous botnets have been proposed and deployed in the past [12,31]. Regardless of their communication infrastructure being centralized or peer-to-peer, existing botnet C&C channels and servers have the challenge of remaining hidden and being resistant against legal authorities' actions. Such problems motivate hackers to always explore more promising venues for finding new C&C channels with the ever-increasing number of communication options on the Internet. One such platform is the environment where cryptocurrencies, such as Bitcoin, is exchanged. As Bitcoin offers some degree of anonymity, exploiting it as a C&C communication channel has already been tried for creating new botnets [2,3]. While these Bitcoin-based botnets addressed the long transaction validation times, they still announce the commands publicly, where the botnet activity can be traced by any observer with the help of the Bitcoin addresses or nonce values of the transactions. By using Bitcoin for botnet communications, C&C leaves the history of malicious activities on the blockchain forever.

Nonetheless, the issues regarding the public announcement of commands and leaving traces in the blockchain are already being addressed in a newly developed Bitcoin payment channel network called Lightning Network (LN). LN enables off-line transactions (i.e., transactions which are not announced and thus not recorded on the blockchain) in order to speed up the transaction by eliminating the confirmation time and decreasing fees associated with that transaction. Additionally, users' identities are still kept anonymous since the transactions are not announced publicly. In this paper, we advocate using LN as an ideal C&C infrastructure for botnets with all the aforementioned features (i.e., faster transactions, decreased costs). Specifically, LN offers botmasters numerous advantages over existing techniques: First, LN provides very high anonymity since transactions on the off-chain channels are not recorded on the blockchain. Thus, a botmaster can covertly communicate with the C&C server(s). Second, the revelation of a server does not reveal other servers, and an observer cannot enumerate the size of the botnet. Most importantly, C&C communication over the LN cannot be censored.

Although LN is a fast-growing emerging payment network, it only has around 12K nodes which may not be ideal for large-scale botnets. Therefore, we propose a *two-layer hybrid* botnet to use LN as an infrastructure to maintain a network of C&C servers each of which can run its own botnet. The use of multiple C&C servers has been around for a while [21]. However, the communication with these servers was still assumed to be through the existing communication infrastructures which impairs the servers' anonymity. Therefore, further strengthening of anonymity is still needed.

Hence, this paper presents *LNBot*, which is the first botnet that utilizes LN infrastructure for its communications between the botmaster and C&C servers with a two-layer *hybrid architecture*. Specifically, at the first layer, a botmaster will maintain multiple C&C servers, which are nodes on the LN that have specialized software to control the bots under them. Essentially, each C&C server is controlling an independent isolated mini-botnet at the second layer. These mini-botnets are controlled using a specific C&C infrastructure that can rely on traditional means such as stenography, IRC channel, DNS, Tor, etc. Botmaster sends the commands to the C&C servers covertly through LN. This two-layer command and control topology not only enables scalability, but also minimizes the burden on each C&C server, which increases their anonymity.

To demonstrate the feasibility of the concept, we implemented the *LNBot* using real LN nodes in Bitcoin's Testnet which is the actual network for Bitcoin. Utilizing one-to-many architecture (i.e., botmaster sends commands to all C&C servers separately), we show that by encoding the commands in terms of payments sent over LN, one can successfully send commands to the C&C servers that are part of the LN. These C&C servers further relay those commands to the bots they control to launch any type of attack to victim machines.

Nevertheless, as sending the commands to every C&C server in the form of payment requires the botmaster to maintain high capacity LN channels (i.e., increased monetary cost) and pay forwarding fees to LN, we also propose mechanisms to further decrease these costs to the levels where they can be neglected. Specifically, when the attacks are executed, we circulate the received payments at C&C servers back to botmaster. Essentially, this means the botmaster will receive all of his/her money back except the fees charged by LN. To also minimize those fees, in addition to ASCII-based encoding, we propose a Huffman-based encoding mechanism which considers the frequency of characters that could potentially be used in constructing the attack commands. We demonstrate that for a network comprising 100 C&C servers, the total fixed fees for forming LNBot would be lower than $5.

Contrary to the traditional blockchain based communication schemes, LNBot covertly communicates with the C&C servers by utilizing the strong relationship anonymity of LN. This covert communication comes with a very little cost and latency overhead. Additionally, since LNBot does not require a custom C&C infrastructure, it is very practical to deploy it. All these features of LNBot makes it a botnet that needs to be taken seriously therefore we provide a list of countermeasures that may help detect LNBot activity and minimize damages from it.

The rest of the paper is organized as follows: In Sect. 2, we give some background information about LN. In Sect. 3, we describe the architecture and construction of our proposed LNBot. Section 4 is dedicated to proof-of-concept implementation in real world settings while Sect. 5 presents the evaluation results. In Sect. 6, possible countermeasures for LNBot is discussed. Related work is given in Sect. 7. Finally, we conclude the paper in Sect. 8.

2 Background

2.1 Lightning Network

The LN concept is introduced in [26]. It is a payment protocol operating on top of Bitcoin. Through this concept, an overlay payment network (i.e., LN) is started among the customers and vendors in 2017. The aim in creating the LN was to decrease the load on the Bitcoin network, facilitating transactions with affordable fees and reduced transaction validation times, and increasing the scalability of Bitcoin by establishing peer-to-peer connections. Despite the big fluctuations in the price of Bitcoin recently, the LN grew exponentially reaching 12,384 nodes and 36,378 channels in less than two years by the time of writing this paper [1]. In the following subsections, we briefly explain the components of LN.

2.2 Off-Chain Concept

The main idea behind LN is to utilize the *off-chain* concept [24] which enables near-instant Bitcoin transactions with negligible fees. This is accomplished through *bidirectional payment channels* which are created among two parties to exchange funds without committing the transactions to Bitcoin blockchain. The channel is opened by making a single on-chain transaction called *funding transaction*. The funding transaction determines the capacity of the channel. Whenever one of the parties wants to make a transaction, she basically conveys ownership of that amount of her money to her peer. So, after a transaction takes place the total capacity in the channel does not change but the directional capacities do. Therefore, the peers can make as many as transactions they want in any amount unless the amount they want to send does not exceed the directional capacity. The example shown in Fig. 1 illustrates the concept in more detail.

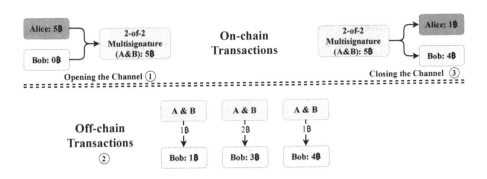

Fig. 1. Off-chain mechanism of LN

Per figure, ① Alice opens a channel to Bob by funding 5 Bitcoins to a multi-signature address and the multi-signature address is signed by both Alice and

Bob. ② Using this channel, Alice can send payments to Bob simply by transferring the ownership of her share in the multi-signature address until her fund in the address is exhausted. Note that these transactions are off-chain meaning they are not written to the Bitcoin blockchain which is a unique feature of LN and that feature is exploited in our botnet. Alice performs 3 transactions at different times with amounts of 1, 2 and 1 Bitcoin respectively. ③ Eventually, when the channel is closed, the remaining 1 Bitcoin in the multi-signature wallet is returned to Alice while the total transferred 4 Bitcoins are settled at Bob. Channel closing is another on-chain transaction that reports the final balances of Alice and Bob in the multi-signature address to the blockchain.

2.3   Multihop Payments

In LN, a node can make payments to another node even if it does not have a direct payment channel to that node. This is achieved by utilizing already established payment channels between other nodes and such a payment is called multi-hop payment since the payment is forwarded through a number of intermediary nodes until reaching the destination. This process is trustless meaning the sender does not need to trust the intermediary nodes along the route. Figure 2 depicts a multi-hop payment. As there is a direct payment channel between Alice and Charlie and between Charlie and Bob, Alice can initiate a transaction to Bob via Charlie. ① First, Bob sends an invoice to Alice which includes the hash (H) of a secret R (known as *pre-image*). ② Then, Alice prepares a payment locked with H, the answer of which is known by Bob. Hash-Locking is required for Alice to ensure that the payment is received by Bob. So, locked with H, Alice gives ownership of some of her money destined to Bob if and only if Charlie knows and discloses the answer to H. Likewise, ③ Charlie promises to give the ownership of some of his money which is locked by H to Bob if Bob knows the answer. As Bob receives a payment he naturally discloses the answer to Charlie and in return he gets the money from Charlie as promised. Now, as Charlie learned the answer, he discloses the answer to Alice and gets his money from Alice as promised. This mechanism is realized with the "Hash Time Lock Contracts" (HTLC). Through this mechanism of LN, as long as there is a path from source to destination requiring that the channels on the path have enough capacities, payments can be routed just like the Internet.

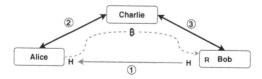

Fig. 2. Illustration of a multihop payment. R is the secret (i.e. *pre-hash*) generated by Bob, H is the hash of the secret. When the transaction is locked by H, yielding the secret R opens the lock. Namely, when asked, yielding R changes the ownership of the money in the channel

2.4 *Key Send* Payments

Key send in LN enables sending payments to a destination without needing to have an invoice first [22]. It utilizes *Sphinx* [9] which is a compact and secure cryptographic packet format to anonymously route a message from a sender to a receiver. This is a very useful feature to have in LN because it introduces new use cases where payers can send spontaneous payments without contacting the payee first. In this mode, the sender generates the pre-image for the payment instead of the receiver and embeds the pre-image into the sphinx packet within the outgoing HTLC. If an LN node accepts key send payments, then it only needs to advertise its public key to receive key send payments from other nodes. In LNBot, we utilize this feature to send payments from botmaster to C&C servers.

2.5 Source Routing and Onion Routed Payments

With the availability of multi-hop payments, a routing mechanism is needed to select the best route for sending a payment to its destination. LN utilizes *source routing* which gives the sender full control over the route for the transaction to follow within the network. Senders are able to specify: 1) the total number of hops on the path; 2) total cumulative fee they will pay to send the payment; and 3) total time-lock period for the HTLC [14]. Moreover, all payments in LN are *onion-routed payments* meaning that HTLCs are securely and privately routed within the network. Onion routing LN also prevents any nodes from easily censoring payments since they are not aware of the final destination of the payment. Additionally, by encoding payment routes within a Sphinx packet, following security and privacy features are achieved: the nodes on a routing path do not know: 1) the source and the destination of the payment; 2) their exact position within the route; and 3) the total number of hops in the route.

2.6 Motivation to Use LN for a Botnet

In this section, we justify why LN is suitable for a perfect botnet design.

- **No publicly advertised activity:** The drawback of using a cryptocurrency based communication infrastructure is that all of the activities are publicly stored in a persistent, transparent, append-only ledger. However, using the off-chain transaction mechanism, only the intermediary nodes in a multi-hop payment path know the transactions. Because, they are responsible to keep the state of their own channels just to prove the ownership of their share in case of a dispute. Namely, the activities taking place in a payment channel is locally stored by the nodes responsible for forwarding that transaction.
- **Covert messaging:** LN was proposed to ease the problems occurring in the Bitcoin network. Hence, all of the actions taking place in the network is regarded as financial transactions. In that sense, twisting this idea into using the channels for covertly forwarding commands will be indistinguishable from innocent, legitimate, and real financial transactions.

- **Relationship anonymity:** LN utilizes source-routing for payment forwarding. This feature enables the peers to enjoy a higher anonymity. Assume that, during a transaction let the next node successfully guess that the preceding node was the origin of the transaction. Ideally, there is no possibility for it to successfully guess the final destination for that transaction. This applies to any "curious" node in the network. Namely, without collusion it is impossible to know who communicates to whom, which is known as relationship anonymity feature.
- **Instantaneous communication:** Apart from being public, another drawback of using Bitcoin network is that a transaction is approved in 10 min the earliest. Moreover, for a transaction to be approved in the ledger for good, the peers have to wait for at least 60 min. By moving to the off-chain, a transaction simply becomes a network package traversing in the network through the intermediary nodes. In that sense, the communication latency in LN is nothing but the time for a packet to traverse on the Internet.
- **Minimal cost:** Bitcoin network charges fees for every transaction regardless of its amount. LN was also designed to transform these fees into negligible amounts. The fees charged by LN is comprised of the combination of a "base fee" and a "proportional fee" which are close to zero. In the lnd implementation of LN, default setting for the base fee is 1 millisatoshi[1]. The proportional fee is, as name suggests it is proportional with the amount being forwarded, 0.0001% of the payment.

3   LNBot Architecture

In this section, we describe the overall architecture of LNBot with its elements.

3.1   Overview

The overall architecture is shown in Fig. 3. As shown, the LN is used to maintain the C&C servers and their communication with the botmaster. Each C&C server runs a separate mini-botnet. Note that it is up to the botmaster how to populate these mini-botnets. Each C&C server can utilize a different botnet model (i.e., based on IRC, DNS, steganography, cryptocurrencies, etc).

The botmaster could set up the C&C servers by creating LN nodes at remote locations that are accessible to him/her. The botmaster knows the LN public keys of all C&C servers since s/he sets them up. These public keys are needed to communicate with them in the LN. Then s/he installs a special software on the C&C servers which are used to control the bots. In this way, it is enough for botmaster to release a malware into the wild for infecting user machines and upon infection, these machines connect to existing available C&C servers (i.e., they become bots). One possible way to achieve this would be to spread the malware via embedded advertisements on web pages frequently visited by

---

[1] A satoshi is defined to be 0.00000001 Bitcoin. In other words, 1 Bitcoin is 100 million satoshi.

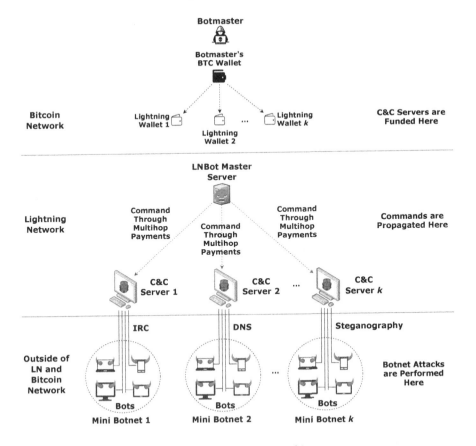

Fig. 3. Overview of LNBot architecture

intended victims. When a viewer clicks on the link, s/he is redirected to a website hosting malicious code that executes in the background and infects the victim's machine without his/her knowledge.

Upon infection, the bot establishes a communication with an available C&C server. The type of connection used depends on the communication method chosen by the C&C server the bot connects to. This can be picked among existing botnet C&C infrastructures such as IRC, DNS, steganography, cryptocurrencies or even the LN itself.

The botmaster's commands have to propagate to every C&C server, and then, ultimately to every single bot through the C&C servers. For this task, we propose one-to-many propagation where the botmaster sends commands to each C&C server separately. This approach is described in Sect. 3.5. The botmaster periodically issues commands to C&C servers by sending payments over LN. Thus, the commands have to be encoded into a series of LN payments. We implemented two encoding schemes to represent the commands as LN payments. These methods are detailed in Sect. 3.6.

With the availability of command propagation, the C&C servers could now listen to the incoming instructions from the botmaster. Next, we describe the details of setting up the C&C servers.

3.2   Setting up the C&C Servers

As mentioned earlier, the botmaster can set up the necessary number of C&C servers s/he would like to deploy. Depending on the objectives, the number of these servers and the number of bots they will control can be adjusted without any scalability concern. In Sect. 4, we explain how we set up real C&C servers running on LN on the real Bitcoin network.

Each C&C server is deployed as a *private* LN node which means that they do not advertise themselves within the LN. In this way, the other LN nodes do not know about the existence of the C&C servers and cannot open channels to them without knowing their public keys. However, without opening any channels on the network, C&C servers cannot get botmaster's payments on LN. Therefore, each C&C servers open a channel to at least k different random public LN nodes. To open the channels, they need some Bitcoin in their *lightning wallets*. This Bitcoin is provided to C&C servers by the botmaster before deploying them. The number k may be tuned depending on the size and topology of LN when LNBot will have deployed in the future.

3.3   Formation of Mini-Botnets

After C&C servers are set up, we need bots to establish connections to C&C servers. An infected machine (bot) connects to one of the C&C servers. As mentioned earlier, the details of bot recruitment and any malware implementation issues are beyond the objectives of this paper. It is up to the botmaster to decide which type of infrastructure the C&C servers will use to control the bots in their possession. This flexibility is enabled by our proposed two-layer hybrid architecture of LNBot. The reason for giving this flexibility is to enable scalability of LNBot through any type of mini-botnets without bothering for the compromise of any C&C servers. As it will be shown in Sect. 6, even if the C&C servers are compromised, this neither reveals the other C&C servers nor the botmaster.

3.4   Forming LNBot

Now that C&C servers are set up and mini-botnets are formed, the next step is to form the infrastructure to control these C&C servers covertly with minimal chances of getting detected. This is where LN comes into play. Botmaster has the public keys of all LN nodes running on C&C server machines. Since C&C servers have their LN channels ready, they can receive the commands from the botmaster. The botmaster uses an LN node called *LNBot Master Server* to initiate the commands to all the C&C servers through LN payments. Similar to the C&C servers, LNBot Master Server is also a private LN node and botmaster has flexibility on the setup of this node and may change it regularly. Without using any other custom infrastructure, the botmaster is able to control C&C servers through LN, consequently controlling all the bots on the botnet.

3.5   Command Propagation in LNBot

Once the LNBot is formed, the next step is to ensure communication from the botmaster to the C&C servers. We utilize a *one-to-many* architecture where the botmaster sends the commands to each C&C server separately. The botmaster uses *key send* method mentioned in Sect. 2.4 to send the payments. We designed a command sending protocol for botmaster-to-C&C server communication as shown in Algorithm 1.

Algorithm 1: Send Command

---

1   initialize *command*;
2   int *counter* = 0;
3   bool *isOnline* = checkIfC&CServerIsOnline();
4   if *isOnline* then
5   bool *result* = send(5 *satoshi*);
6   if *result*=*success* then
7   *counter* = 0;
8   for *character* in *command* do
9   bool *result* = send(*character*);
10   if *result*=*success* then continue;
11   else if *result*=*fail and counter* < *k* then
12   retry sending *character*;
13   *counter*++;
14   else reschedule(*command*, date, time);
15   end
16   *counter* = 0;
17   bool *result* = send(6 *satoshi*);
18   if *result*=*success* then
19   **Command has been successfully sent!**;
20   else if *result*=*fail and counter* < *k* then
21   retry sending 6 *satoshi*;
22   *counter*++;
23   else reschedule(*command*, date, time);
24   else if *result*=*fail and counter* < *k* then
25   retry sending 5 *satoshi*;
26   *counter*++;
27   else reschedule(*command*, date, time);
28   else
29   reschedule(*command*, date, time);
30   end

Before sending any payment, the botmaster first checks if the respective C&C server is online or not (LN nodes have to be online in order to send and receive payments). If the C&C server is not online, command sending is scheduled for a later time. Botmaster sends 5 satoshi as the special starting payment of a command before it sends the actual characters in the command one by one. Lastly, the botmaster sends 6 satoshi as the special ending payment to finish sending the command. Note that selection of 5 and 6 in this algorithm depends on the chosen encoding and could be changed based on the needs. If any of these separate payments fail, it is re-tried. If any of the payments fail for more than k times in a row, command transmission to the respective C&C server is canceled and scheduled for a later time. The details of encoding and decoding are explained next.

3.6   Encoding/Decoding Schemes

An important feature of LNBot is its ability to encode botmaster commands into a series of LN payments. We used two different encoding/decoding schemes for the purpose of determining the most efficient way of sending commands to C&C servers in terms of Bitcoin cost and time spent. We explain the details of each method below:

ASCII Encoding. American Standard Code for Information Interchange (ASCII) is a character encoding standard that represents English characters as numbers, assigned from 0 to 127. Numbers 0–31 and 127 are reserved for control characters. The remaining 95 codes from 32 to 126 represent printable characters. The decimal equivalent of ASCII characters can easily be looked up from an ASCII table.

Huffman Coding. When there is a need to losslessly compress the information being sent over a channel, due to its simple yet powerful approach, Huffman coding is one of the optimal options [13]. In usual communication systems, the communication is done in binary domain. However, in the communication scheme defined as in our approach, there is no strict need for binary communication. In the formation of the Huffman tree, n-ary number systems can be used. The advantage of $n-$ary numbering system over binary one is that the messages can be distributed among more compact symbols, hence the required number of transmissions per character will be reduced.

In order to come up with a codebook, a dictionary is needed. The frequencies, so-called probabilities of occurrences of the characters shape the size of the codebook. In its most frequently adapted style, users prefer to use bulky novels or texts in order to simulate a more inclusive dictionary.

3.7   Reimbursing the Botmaster

Another important feature of LNBot is the ability of the botmaster to get the invested funds back from C&C servers' lightning wallets to his/her Bitcoin wallet.

Depending on botmaster's command propagation activity, C&C servers' channels will fill up with funds received from the botmaster. Therefore, in our design, C&C servers are programmed to send the funds in their channels to an LN node called *collector*. Collector is set up by the botmaster as a private LN node which becomes active only when the C&C servers will send funds to it. Its LN public key is stored in C&C servers and thus they can send the funds to collector through LN using the collector's public key. In this way, the funds accumulate at the collector. The botmaster gets the funds accumulated at the collector when his/her channels starts running out of funds. Botmaster get the funds from collector by closing collector's channels so that the funds at these channels are settled at collector's lightning wallet. Then botmaster sends these funds through an on-chain Bitcoin transfer to his/her Bitcoin wallet.

4   Proof-of-Concept Implementation

In this section, we demonstrate that an actual implementation of the proposed LNBot is feasible by presenting a proof-of-concept. For development, we used lnd (version 0.9.0-beta) which is one of the implementations of LN developed by Lightning Labs [15]. LN nodes should interact with a Bitcoin network in order to run the underlying layer-1 protocols. There are two real environments where Bitcoin operations take place: *Bitcoin Mainnet* and *Bitcoin Testnet*. As the names suggest, Bitcoin *Mainnet* is the chain where Bitcoin transfers with a real monetary value take place. However, in Bitcoin *Testnet*, Bitcoins do not have a monetary value. They are only used for testing and development purposes. Nonetheless, they both provide the same infrastructure and LNBot will definitely run in the same manner on the *Mainnet* as it runs on the *Testnet*.

Thus, we used Bitcoin *Testnet* for our proof-of-concept development. We created 100 C&C servers and assessed certain performance characteristics for command propagation. We created a GitHub page explaining the steps to set up the C&C servers.[2] The steps include installation of *lnd* & *bitcoind*, configuring *lnd* and *bitcoind*, and extra configurations to hide the servers in the network by utilizing private channels. Nevertheless, to confirm that the channel opening costs and routing fees are exactly same in both Bitcoin *Mainnet* and *Testnet*, we also created 2 nodes on Bitcoin *Mainnet*. We funded one of the nodes with 0.01 Bitcoin (~$67), created channels and sent payments to the other node. We observed that the costs and fees are exactly matching to that of Bitcoin *Testnet*.

lnd has a feature called *autopilot* which opens channels in an automated manner based on certain initial parameters set in advance [17]. Our C&C servers on Bitcoin *Testnet* employ this functionality of *lnd* to open channels on LN. Using *autopilot*, we opened 3 channels per server. Note that this number of channels is picked based on our experimentation on Bitcoin *Testnet* on the success of payments. We wanted to prevent any failures in payments by tuning this parameter. As mentioned, these 3 channels are all private, created with *–private* argument,

---

[2] https://github.com/LightningNetworkBot/LNBot.

which do not broadcast themselves to the network. A private channel in LN is only known by the two peers of the channel.

lnd has an API for communicating with a local *lnd* instance through gRPC [16]. Using the API, we wrote a client that communicated with *lnd* in Python. Particularly, we wrote 2 Python scripts, one running on the C&C servers and the other on the botmaster machine. We typed the command we wanted to send to C&C servers in a terminal in the botmaster machine. The command was processed by the Python code and sent to the C&C servers as a series of payments.

5   Evaluation and Analysis of LNBot

In this section, we present a detailed cost and time overhead analysis of LNBot.

5.1   Cost Analysis of LNBot Formation

We first analyze the monetary cost of forming LNBot. As noted earlier, we opened 3 channels per server. The capacity of each channel is 20,000 satoshi which is the minimum allowable channel capacity in *lnd*. Therefore, a server needs 60,000 satoshi for opening these channels. While opening the channels, there is a small fee paid to Bitcoin miners since channel creations in LN are on-chain transactions. We showed that, opening a channel in LN can cost as low as 154 satoshi on both Bitcoin Testnet[3] and the Mainnet.[4]

So the total cost of opening 3 channels for a C&C server is 60,462 satoshi. While 462 satoshi is consumed as fees, the remaining 60,000 satoshi on the channels is not spent, rather it is just locked in the channels. The botmaster will get this 60,000 satoshi back after closing the channels. Therefore, funds locked in the channels are non-recurring investment cost for the formation of LNBot. Only real associated cost of forming LNBot is the channel opening fees.

Table 1 shows how the costs change when the number of C&C servers is increased. The increase in the cost is linear and for 100 C&C servers, the on-chain fees is only 0.000462 Bitcoin ($3 at current Bitcoin price of $6700).

5.2   Cost and Time Analysis of Command Propagation

To assess the command propagation overhead, we sent the following SYN flooding attack command to C&C servers from the botmaster (omitting start and end of command characters):

```
sudo hping3 -i u1 -S -p 80 -c 10 192.168.1.1
```

---

[3] Check LNB6's channel (1735152493945290752) opening transaction for instance: fc46c99233389d24c4fd9517cd503f08265c517a6f0570d806e7cc98b7f7963b.

[4] In a similar way, check one of our mainnet node's channel opening transaction: 1d81b6022ff1472939c4db730ca01b82d43b616e757d799aea17ee0db6427520.

Table 1. Channel opening fees for different number of C&C servers

Number of C&C servers	Channel opening fees
10	0.0000462 Bitcoin
25	0.0001155 Bitcoin
50	0.000231 Bitcoin
100	0.000462 Bitcoin

Table 3. Respective ASCII and Huffman encoding representation of 'sudo hping3 -i u1 -S -p 80 -c 10 192.168.1.1' command

Table 2. Obtained codebook for Huffman coding

's' 234	'n'233	'o'232	'h'231
'd'224	'g'223	'c'222	'9' 221
'6'214	'2'213	'3'212	'u' 211
'p'144	'i' 143	'8'142	'0' 141
'.' 24	'1'12	'-' 13	'E'4
'' 11	'S'3		

Command	ASCII encoding	Quaternary Huffman encoding
'sudo'	115, 117, 100, 111, 32	2, 3, 4, 2, 1, 1, 2, 2, 4, 2, 3, 2, 1, 1
'hping3'	104, 112, 105,	2, 3, 1, 1, 4, 4, 1, 4, 3, 2, 3, 3
	110, 103, 51, 32	2, 2, 3, 2, 1, 2, 1, 1
'-i '	45, 105, 32	1, 3, 1, 4, 3, 1, 1
'u1'	117, 49, 32	2, 1, 1, 1, 2, 1, 1
'-S '	45, 83, 32	1, 3, 3, 1, 1
'-p '	45, 112, 32	1, 3, 1, 4, 4, 1, 1
'80'	56, 48, 32	1, 4, 2, 1, 4, 1, 1, 1
'-c '	45, 99, 32	1, 3, 2, 2, 2, 1, 1
'10'	49, 48, 32	1, 2, 1, 4, 1, 1, 1
'192.168.1.1'	49, 57, 50, 46, 49	1, 2, 2, 2, 1, 2, 1, 3, 2, 4, 1, 2, 2
	54, 56, 46, 49, 46, 49	1, 4, 1, 4, 2, 2, 4, 1, 2, 2, 4, 1, 2
Total number of payments	44	108
Total cost	2813	215

We sent this command using both of the encoding methods we proposed earlier. For Huffman coding, we compared several different base number systems. The best result was obtained by using the Quaternary numeral system, the codebook of which is shown in Table 2.

Cost Analysis: The botmaster spent 2813 satoshi for sending the SYN flooding command using the ASCII encoding while this cost is only 215 satoshi with the Huffman coding. Table 3 gives details about the number of payments and how many satoshi have been sent in each payment. While in both cost cases the botmaster will be reimbursed at the very end, we would like to note that the lifetime of the channels is closely related with these costs. In case of the ASCII encoding, the initial funds will be spent faster and the botmaster needs to re-configure (or re-balance) the channels for continuous operation of the botnet. In case of the Huffman coding, this is not the case as the consumption of the channel funds is much slower. So, we can see that if channel lifetime is an important factor for the botmaster, the Huffman coding could be preferred. In other words, the Huffman coding gives the botmaster the ability to perform more attacks without creating high capacity channels.

However, the situation is reverse in case of routing fees. Table 4 shows how the routing fees change when the number of C&C servers is increased. The increase in the routing fees is linear for both the ASCII and Huffman coding. For 100 C&C servers, total routing fee paid is only 0.000176 Bitcoin (~$1 at current Bitcoin price of $6700) for ASCII while it is 0.000432 Bitcoin (~$3 at current Bitcoin price of $6700) for the Huffman coding. This indicates that despite its increased routing fees, the Huffman coding is still a viable option for longer operation of LNBot.

Table 4. Routing fees for different number of C&C servers

Number of C&C servers	Routing fees (ASCII)	Routing fees (Huffman)
10	0.0000176 Bitcoin	0.0000432 Bitcoin
25	0.000044 Bitcoin	0.000108 Bitcoin
50	0.000088 Bitcoin	0.000216 Bitcoin
100	0.000176 Bitcoin	0.000432 Bitcoin

Time Analysis: The propagation time of a command is calculated by multiplying the number of payments with the average delivery time of the payments. To estimate the average delivery time, we sent 90 *key send payments* with different amounts from botmaster to our C&C servers over LN at random times and measured the time it takes for payments to reach their destinations. The results are depicted in Fig. 4.

As shown, *key send payments* took 7 s on average to reach their destinations and the maximum delay was never exceeding 10 s. This delay varies since it depends on the path being used and the load of each intermediary node in the LN. We observed that the number of hops for the payments was 4, which helps to strengthen unlinkability of payments and destinations in case of any payment analysis in LN.

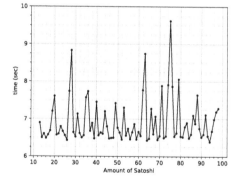

Fig. 4. Time for *key send payments* to reach their destinations with varying satoshi

Using an average of 7 s, the total propagation time for the ASCII-encoded payments is 7 × 44 = 308 s while it is 7 × 108 = 756 s for the Huffman coding. The Huffman coding reduces the cost of sending the command, but increases the communication delays which is not critical in performing the attack.

5.3   Comparison of LNBot with Other Similar Botnets

We also considered other existing botnets that utilize Bitcoin for their command and control. Using our SYN flooding attack command, we computed their cost and command propagation times to compare them with LNBot. We also included their scalability features. Table 5 shows these results.

Table 5. Time, cost and scalability comparison of LNBot with similar botnets

Botnet	Cost	Time	Scalability
Bitcoin testnet botnet [10]	51349 satoshi (Testnet)	~10 min	Low, thousands of bots
Zombiecoin 2.0 [3]	10000 satoshi	~10 s	Low, thousands of bots
LNBot	10 satoshi	~5 min	High, millions of bots

As seen, LNBot comes with minimal costs with a reasonable propagation time for attacks and can scale to millions of nodes with its two-layer architecture.

6   Security and Anonymity Analysis and Countermeasures

In this section, we discuss security properties of LNBot and possible counter-measures to detect its activities in order to minimize its impacts.

• *Taking LN down:* Obviously, the simplest way to eliminate LNBot's activities is taking down the LN as a whole once there is any suspicion about a botnet. However, this is very unlikely due to LN being a very resilient decentralized payment channel network. In addition, today many applications are running on LN and shutting down may cause a lot of financial loss for numerous stakeholders.

• *Compromising and shutting down a C&C Server:* In LNBot there are many C&C servers each of which is controlling a mini-botnet. Given the past experience with various traditional botnets, it is highly likely that these mini-botnets will be detected at some point in the future paving the way for also the detection of a C&C server. This will then result in the revelation of its location/IP address and eventually physical seizure of the machine by law enforcement. Nevertheless, the seizure of a C&C server will neither reveal the identity of the LNBot botmaster nor other C&C servers since a C&C server receives the commands through onion routed payments catered with Sphinx's secure packet format, which does not reveal the original sender of the message. Additionally, the communication between botmaster and C&C servers is 1-way meaning that botmaster can talk to C&C servers, but servers cannot talk back since the LN address of the botmaster is not known by them. This 1-way communication ensures that the identity of the botmaster will be kept secret at all times.

Note that since the C&C servers hold the LN public key of the collector, it will also be revealed when a C&C server is compromised. However, since the collector node's channels are all private, its IP address or location is not known by the C&C servers. Therefore, learning the LN public key of the collector node does not help locating the collector node physically. The only possibility is to continue monitoring a C&C server when it is compromised and as soon as it makes a payment (to collector), we can try to do a timing analysis on certain random nodes that are under our control to determine if one of them would be forwarding the same amount of money and happens to have a channel with the collector node. In that case, that node will know the IP address of the collector since they have a channel. While this possibility is very low, even if we are successful, the collector can always hide its IP address through certain mechanisms such as VPN or Tor. Eventually, we can see that taking down a single C&C server shuts down the botnet partially resulting in less damage to victims.

• *Payment flow timing analysis for detecting the botmaster:* As explained in Sect. 2.5, the intermediary nodes in a payment path do not know the origin of the payment; therefore they cannot distinguish between the botmaster and a regular forwarding node on the payment path unless the payment path just consists of 1-hop [6]. In our tests, we observed that our payments took 4 hops to reach C&C servers. Therefore, payment analysis for such multiple hops is a challenge. However, it can help increase our chances to detect the botmaster.

To further investigate this attack scenario, a topology of 8 nodes was created on Bitcoin Testnet as shown in Fig. 5. We assume that Node A, Node D and the C&C server are compromised and thus we monitored their payments. In this setup, a 100 satoshi payment was sent from the botmaster to the C&C server through hops Node A, Node B, and Node C and the payment was monitored at Node A. By monitoring the node, we got the payment forwarding information shown in Fig. 6.

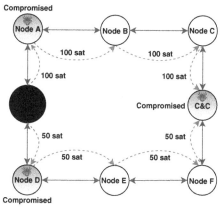

In the same way, another 50 satoshi payment was sent from the botmaster to the same C&C server following hops Node D, Node E, and Node F and the payment was monitored at Node D. Similar payment forwarding informa-

Fig. 5. The payments that are forwarded by Node A and Node D are monitored by an observer and the C&C server is compromised. Red arrows show the payment channels between the nodes and the green arrows show the flow of the payment

tion is obtained at node D. Here, particularly important information for us is the timestamp of the payment, and the *chan_id_in* and the *chan_id_out* arguments which represent the ID of the payment channels that carry the payment in and out from Node A. We can query these channel IDs to learn the public keys of the nodes at both ends of the channel by running *lncli getchaninfo chan_id*. Obtained LN public keys at Node A, in this case, belong to potential botmaster and Node B. In the same way, LN public keys of potential botmaster and Node E is obtained at Node D. After the payment is observed at Node A, payment with the same amount was observed at the C&C server. We now correlated these two payments (i.e., timing analysis) and suspected that the sender to Node A (or D) can be a potential botmaster. Obviously, there is no guarantee for this (e.g., imagine a different topology where real botmaster is 2 more hops away). We need to collect more data from many compromised nodes and continue this analysis for a long time. To increase the chances, well-connected LN nodes could be requested to cooperate in case of law enforcement investigation to share the timing of payments passing from them.

```
"forwarding_events": [
   {
      "timestamp": "1579043693",
      "chan_id_in": "1826219544504369152",
      "chan_id_out": "1826219544504434688",
      "amt_in": "101",
      "amt_out": "100",
      "fee": "1",
      "fee_msat": "1000",
      "amt_in_msat": "101000",
      "amt_out_msat": "100000"
   }]
```

Fig. 6. The payment forwarding information stored on Node A's local database in JSON format as the output of the command *lncli fwdinghistory*

• *Poisoning Attack:* Another effective way to counter the botmaster is through message poisoning. Basically, once a C&C server is compromised, its public keys will be known. Using these public keys one can send payments to C&C servers to corrupt the messages sent by the botmaster at the right time. There is currently no authentication mechanism that can be used by the botmaster without being exposed to prevent this issue. Recall that the commands are encoded in a series of payments and when a different payment is sent during a command transmission, it will corrupt the syntax and thus eventually there will not be any impact. The right time will be decided by listening to the payments and packets arriving at the C&C server. The disadvantage of this, however, is that one needs to pay for those payments. Nonetheless, this can be an effective way to continue engaging with the botmaster for detection purposes rather than just shutting down the C&C server while rendering any attack impossible.

• *Analysis of on-chain transactions:* Another countermeasure could be through analyzing the on-chain funding transfers of C&C servers (i.e., channel creation transactions stored on blockchain). For such forensic analysis, the Bitcoin addresses of the C&C servers should be known. As with many other real-life botnets, botmasters generally use Bitcoin mixers to hide the source of the Bitcoins. Usage of such mixers makes it very hard to follow the real source of the Bitcoins since the transactions are mixed between the users using the mixer service. Even though the chances of finding the identity of the botmaster through this analysis is low, it can provide some useful information to law enforcement.

7   Related Work

Botnets have been around for a long time and there have been even surveys classifying them [5,12]. While early botnets used IRC, later botnets focused on P2P C&C for resiliency. Furthermore, Tor has also been used for a botnet C&C but it is shown that botnet activity over Tor can be exposed due to the recognizable patterns in the C&C communication [8]. Our proposed LNBot falls under covert botnets which became popular much later. As an example, Nagaraja et al. proposed Stegobot, a covert botnet using social media networks as a command and control channel [19]. Some work has been done by Natarajan et al. to detect Stegobot [20]. Pantic et al. proposed a covert botnet command and control using Twitter [23]. Tsiatsikas et al. proposed SDP-Based Covert Channel for Botnet Communication [30]. Calhoun et al. presented a MAC layer covert channel based on WiFi [7].

Recent covert botnets started to utilize Blockchain although these are very few. For instance, Roffel et al. [27] came up with the idea of controlling a computer worm using the Bitcoin blockchain. [29] discusses how botnet resiliency can be enhanced using private blockchains. Pirozzi et al. presented the use of blockchain as a command and control center for a new generation botnet [25]. Similarly, ChainChannels [11] utilizes Bitcoin to disseminate C&C messages to the bots. These works are different from our architecture as they suffer from the issues of high latency and public announcement of commands. There are also Unblockable Chains [32], and BOTRACT [18], which are Ethereum-based botnet command and control infrastructures that suffer from anonymity issues since the commands are publicly recorded on the blockchain. Baden et al. [4] proposed a botnet C&C scheme utilizing Ethereum's Whisper messaging. However, it is still possible to blacklist the topics used by the botmaster. Additionally, there is not a proof of concept implementation of the proposed approach yet, therefore it is unknown if the botnet can successfully be deployed or not.

The closest work to ours are ZombieCoin [2] and Bitcoin Testnet botnet [10]. ZombieCoin uses Bitcoin transaction spreading mechanism as the C&C communication infrastructure. In this study, the botmaster announces the commands to the bots in terms of legitimate Bitcoin transactions on the Bitcoin network. Then, any legitimate Bitcoin nodes that receive these transactions check the correctness of the input address, the digital signature, and in&out Bitcoin amounts of the transaction. The bots extract the concealed commands from these transactions. However, this scheme has several drawbacks: First, the authors assumed that the bots identify related transactions from the botmaster's Bitcoin address, which Bitcoin miners can blacklist. Second, as in the case of other blockchain-based botnets, because all transactions are publicly announced, it leaves a public record about the botnet activity. To resolve this problem, in a further study they also proposed to employ subliminal channels [3] to cover the botmaster. However, subliminal channels require a lot of resources to calculate required signatures which is computationally expensive and not practical to use on a large scale.

Bitcoin Testnet botnet is a recently proposed botnet [10], where Bitcoin Testnet is utilized for controlling the botnet. Even though their C&C communication is encrypted, non-standard Bitcoin transactions used for communication exposes the botnet activity. Once the botnet is detected, the messages coming from the botmaster can be prevented from spreading, consequently stopping the botnet activity. Additionally, it is possible for Bitcoin developers to reset the current Bitcoin Testnet (i.e., Testnet3) and create a new Bitcoin testnet (e.g., Testnet4) to stop the botnet completely.

In contrast, our work is based on legitimate LN payments and does not require any additional computation to hide the commands. Also, these commands are not announced publicly. Moreover, LNBot offers very unique advantage for a botnet that does not contain any direct relation with C&C. This means even C&C itself is not aware of the botmaster due to LN's anonymous multi-hop structure. As a result, LNBot does not carry any mentioned disadvantages through its two-layer hybrid architecture and provides ultra scalability and high anonymity compared to others.

8   Conclusion

LN has been formed as a new payment network to address the drawbacks of Bitcoin transactions in terms of time and cost. In addition to relationship anonymity, LN significantly reduces fees by performing off-chain transactions. This provides a perfect opportunity for covert communications as no transactions are recorded in the blockchain. Therefore, in this paper, we proposed a new covert hybrid botnet by utilizing the LN payment network formed for Bitcoin operations. The idea was to control the C&C servers through messages that are sent in the form of payments through the LN. The proof-of-concept implementation of this architecture indicated that LNBot can be successfully created and commands for attacks can be sent to C&C servers through LN with negligible costs yet with very high anonymity. To minimize LNBot's impact, we offered several countermeasures that include the possibility of searching for the botmaster.

References

1. 1ml.com: Lightning network search and analysis engine (2019). https://1ml.com/
2. Ali, S.T., McCorry, P., Lee, P.H.-J., Hao, F.: ZombieCoin: powering next-generation botnets with bitcoin. In: Brenner, M., Christin, N., Johnson, B., Rohloff, K. (eds.) FC 2015. LNCS, vol. 8976, pp. 34–48. Springer, Heidelberg (2015). https://doi.org/10.1007/978-3-662-48051-9_3
3. Ali, S.T., McCorry, P., Lee, P.H.J., Hao, F.: Zombiecoin 2.0: managing next-generation botnets using bitcoin. Int. J. Inf. Secur. **17**(4), 411–422 (2018)
4. Baden, M., Torres, C.F., Pontiveros, B.B.F., State, R.: Whispering botnet command and control instructions. In: 2019 Crypto Valley Conference on Blockchain Technology (CVCBT), pp. 77–81. IEEE (2019)

5. Bailey, M., Cooke, E., Jahanian, F., Xu, Y., Karir, M.: A survey of botnet technology and defenses. In: Cybersecurity Applications & Technology Conference For Homeland Security, CATCH 2009, pp. 299–304. IEEE (2009)
6. Béres, F., Seres, I.A., Benczúr, A.A.: A cryptoeconomic traffic analysis of bitcoins lightning network. arXiv preprint arXiv:1911.09432 (2019)
7. Calhoun Jr, T.E., Cao, X., Li, Y., Beyah, R.: An 802.11 MAC layer covert channel. Wirel. Commun. Mob. Comput. **12**(5), 393–405 (2012)
8. Casenove, M., Miraglia, A.: Botnet over tor: the illusion of hiding. In: 2014 6th International Conference On Cyber Conflict (CyCon 2014), pp. 273–282. IEEE (2014)
9. Danezis, G., Goldberg, I.: Sphinx: a compact and provably secure mix format. In: 2009 30th IEEE Symposium on Security and Privacy, pp. 269–282. IEEE (2009)
10. Franzoni, F., Abellan, I., Daza, V.: Leveraging bitcoin testnet for bidirectional botnet command and control systems. In: Bonneau, J., Heninger, N. (eds.) FC 2020. LNCS, vol. 12059, pp. 3–19. Springer, Cham (2020). https://doi.org/10.1007/978-3-030-51280-4_1
11. Frkat, D., Annessi, R., Zseby, T.: Chainchannels: private botnet communication over public blockchains. In: IEEE ITHINGS-GREENCOM-CPSCOM-SMARTDATA 2018, pp. 1244–1252. IEEE (2018)
12. Grizzard, J.B., Sharma, V., Nunnery, C., Kang, B.B., Dagon, D.: Peer-to-peer botnets: overview and case study. In: HotBots 2007, p. 1 (2007)
13. Huffman, D.A.: A method for the construction of minimum-redundancy codes. Proc. IRE **40**(9), 1098–1101 (1952)
14. Learning Labs: Bolt #4: onion routing protocol (2019). https://github.com/lightningnetwork/lightning-rfc/blob/master/04-onion-routing.md
15. Learning Labs: Lightning network daemon (2019). https://lightning.engineering
16. Learning Labs: LND gRPC API reference (2019). https://api.lightning.community/
17. Learning Labs: Sample lnd.conf (2019). https://github.com/lightningnetwork/lnd/blob/master/sample-lnd.conf
18. Malaika, M.: Botract (2017). https://sector.ca/wp-content/uploads/presentations17/Majid-Malaika-Botract_SecTor.pdf
19. Nagaraja, S., Houmansadr, A., Piyawongwisal, P., Singh, V., Agarwal, P., Borisov, N.: Stegobot: a covert social network botnet. In: Filler, T., Pevný, T., Craver, S., Ker, A. (eds.) IH 2011. LNCS, vol. 6958, pp. 299–313. Springer, Heidelberg (2011). https://doi.org/10.1007/978-3-642-24178-9_21
20. Natarajan, V., Sheen, S., Anitha, R.: Multilevel analysis to detect covert social botnet in multimedia social networks. Comput. J. **58**(4), 679–687 (2015)
21. Ollmann, G.: Botnet communication topologies (2009). Accessed 30 Sept 2009
22. Osuntokun, O.: New draft sphinx send mode for spontaneous payments (2019). https://github.com/lightningnetwork/lnd/pull/2455
23. Pantic, N., Husain, M.I.: Covert botnet command and control using Twitter. In: Proceedings of the 31st Annual Computer Security Applications Conference, pp. 171–180. ACM (2015)
24. Pass, R., et al.: Micropayments for decentralized currencies. In: Proceedings of the 22nd ACM SIGSAC Conference on Computer and Communications Security, pp. 207–218. ACM (2015)
25. Pirozzi, A., Paganini, P.: Experts presented botchain, the first fully functional botnet built upon the bitcoin protocol (2018). https://securityaffairs.co/wordpress/77395/malware/botchain-botnet-bitcoin-protocol.html

26. Poon, J., Dryja, T.: The bitcoin lightning network: scalable off-chain instant payments (2015). https://lightning.network/lightning-network-paper.pdf
27. Roffel, D., Garrett, C.: A novel approach for computer worm control using decentralized data structures (2014)
28. Silva, S.S., Silva, R.M., Pinto, R.C., Salles, R.M.: Botnets: a survey. Comput. Netw. **57**(2), 378–403 (2013)
29. Sweeny, J.: Botnet resiliency via private blockchains (2017). https://www.sans.org/reading-room/whitepapers/covert/botnet-resiliency-private-blockchains-38050
30. Tsiatsikas, Z., Anagnostopoulos, M., Kambourakis, G., Lambrou, S., Geneiatakis, D.: Hidden in plain sight. SDP-based covert channel for botnet communication. In: Fischer-Hübner, S., Lambrinoudakis, C., Lopez, J. (eds.) TrustBus 2015. LNCS, vol. 9264, pp. 48–59. Springer, Cham (2015). https://doi.org/10.1007/978-3-319-22906-5_4
31. Wang, P., Wu, L., Aslam, B., Zou, C.C.: A systematic study on peer-to-peer botnets. In: 2009 Proceedings of 18th International Conference on Computer Communications and Networks, pp. 1–8. IEEE (2009)
32. Zohar, O.: Unblockable chains (2018). https://github.com/platdrag/UnblockableChains

Author Index

Printed in the United States
By Bookmasters